CORPORATE GOVERNANCE REGIMES

Corporate Governance Regimes

Convergence and Diversity

Edited by

JOSEPH A. McCAHERY
PIET MOERLAND
THEO RAAIJMAKERS
LUC RENNEBOOG

OXFORD
UNIVERSITY PRESS

OXFORD
UNIVERSITY PRESS

Great Clarendon Street, Oxford OX2 6DP

Oxford University Press is a department of the University of Oxford.
It furthers the University's objective of excellence in research, scholarship,
and education by publishing worldwide in

Oxford New York

Auckland Bangkok Buenos Aires Cape Town Chennai
Dar es Salaam Delhi Florence Hong Kong Istanbul Karachi Kolkata
Kuala Lumpur Madrid Melbourne Mexico City Mumbai Nairobi
São Paulo Shanghai Taipei Tokyo Toronto

Published in the United States
by Oxford University Press Inc., New York

First published 2002

British Library Cataloguing in Publication Data
Data available

Library of Congress Cataloging in Publication Data
Data available

ISBN 0–19–924787–0

1 3 5 7 9 10 8 6 4 2

Typeset by Newgen Imaging Systems (P) Ltd., Chennai, India
Printed in Great Britain
on acid-free paper by
Biddles Ltd., Guildford and King's Lynn

Preface

This volume of essays arose out of the November 1999 Law and Economics Conference at Tilburg University on Convergence and Diversity in Corporate Governance Regimes and Capital Markets, organized by the Faculties of Law and Economics and hosted by Royal Philips Electronics at the Evoluon Conference Center in Eindhoven. We are grateful to Royal Philips Electronics and Arthur Andersen for their generous support of our enquiry into comparative corporate governance and finance. We also received funding for this project from the Amsterdam Exchanges, Center for Company Law, Center for Economic Research, Globus, Leuven University, Schoordijk Institute, and Tias Business School. In addition, our efforts have been supported by the OECD (Paris).

The Conference brought together a large number of leading academic economists and lawyers from America, England, and Continental Europe to address questions, from a range of perspectives, about the forces inducing the convergence of corporate governance practices, the differences in national governance regimes and ownership patterns, the effectiveness of large blockholders in corporate governance, and the role of securities law in protecting minority stockholders. The interaction among the Conference participants was most helpful in producing considerable insights, which are reflected in many of the papers in this volume.

We decided to divide the papers into seven sections, corresponding to the themes of the underlying Conference: legal convergence, harmonization of corporate and securities law in the EU, concentration of ownership and control in Europe, economic performance and governance structures, the value of corporate control and corporate reorganization, the role of institutional investors in corporate governance, and executive compensation. The chapters in this collection should be of equal interest to lawyers and economists working in the fields of bankruptcy, corporate law, corporate finance, and securities law.

We should like to acknowledge the large number of people who have provided us with advice and invaluable forms of support as the Conference project has developed into this publication. We would particularly like to thank Lucian Bebchuk, Bill Bratton, Eric van Damme, Peter Essers, Henk de Jong, Colin Mayer, Phillipe Naert, Erik Vermeulen, and Reinout Vriesendorp. We are also grateful for the administrative support, in the form of a grant provided by the Center for Company Law. We are appreciative of the role Marjolijn Verhoeven played in organizing the conference, along with Grete Janssen, Inge Hoeppertz, and Eva Schupp.

We would like to thank all the contributors of papers, commentators, and chairs of sessions for their participation at the Conference. We are particularly grateful to the outstanding group of authors who have worked over many months to produce this collection.

We are extremely grateful to James J. Risser for his help in preparing this volume. We would like to thank Carmen Buijssen, Barbara Gabor, and Thomas Longmuir for able research assistance. Finally, we would like to extend our thanks to our editor at Oxford University Press, Andrew Schuller, for improving the manuscript.

Contents

List of Figures

List of Tables

List of Contributors

Thomas Andersson, is Adjunct Professor at the Stockholm School of Economics and Senior Advisor to the 'Swedish Institute for Growth Policy Studies' (ITPS) and the 'Swedish Agency for Innovation Systems' (VINNOVA). He further serves as the main Secretary of the Ministers' of Finance project on the new economy in the Nordic Ministerial Council. He was Deputy Director for Science, Technology and Industry at the OECD. From 1994 to 1996, he headed the Structural Policy Secretariat in the Swedish Ministry of Industry and Commerce, and represented Sweden in the European Commission's Meetings for Director Generals for Industry. Since 1993, he has been an Associate Professor at the Stockholm School of Economics and a Visiting Fellow at several international universities. He has published widely on topics such as industrial organization, environmental issues, and development.

Jonathan J. Bates is a Director of Institutional Design, a London-based research and information firm which specializes in corporate governance-related services for the international corporate, investment and regulatory communities. Previous positions include: Project Adviser in the Office of General Counsel of the European Bank for Reconstruction and Development, and Governance Adviser in the Company Secretary's Office of BP. His publication and research interests are founded in law and economics and focus on company law, securities regulation, corporate governance and transition economies, and theory of the firm. Jonathan graduated with a BA and an LLB (Hons) from the University of Auckland, and an LLM from King's College, University of London.

Lucian A. Bebchuk is the William J. Friedman and Alicia Townsend Friedman Professor of Law, Economics, and Finance at the Harvard University School of Law. He is also a Fellow of the American Academy of Arts and Sciences, a Research Associate of the National Bureau of Economic Research, and a frequent visitor to Tel-Aviv University. He has written extensively on a broad range of subjects at the intersection of law and economics, especially in the areas of corporate law and law and finance. Trained in both economics and law, Professor Bebchuk holds a BA in Mathematics and Economics from the University of Haifa, an LLB from the University of Tel-Aviv, an MA and PhD from the Harvard Economics Department, and an LLM and SJD from the Harvard Law School.

Ekkehart Boehmer is currently Senior Research Fellow at the New York Stock Exchange. He was a Heisenberg Research Fellow of the German Science Foundation (DFG) and held a visiting position at the University of Georgia. Previously, he was an economist at the US Securities and Exchange Commission and an Assistant Professor at Humboldt University and Louisiana State University. Ekkehart received an MA in Economics and a PhD in Finance, both from the University of Georgia. His research interests are in corporate finance, and especially in corporate governance and securities regulation.

William W. Bratton is Samuel Tyler Research Professor of Law at the George Washington University School of Law. Prior to joining the George Washington law faculty in 1999,

Professor Bratton was the Kaiser Professor of Law and Director of the Heyman Center on Corporate Governance at Cardozo Law School, and Professor of Law and Woodrow Wilson Scholar at Rutgers University School of Law, Newark. Professor Bratton has published articles on a variety of subjects in corporate law and law and economics. He is co-editor of the leading American textbook on corporate finance and an Oxford University Press collection on regulatory competition.

Wendy Carlin is Reader in Economics in the Department of Economics, University College, London. She spent the year 1994–5 as Senior Research Fellow at the Wissenschaftszentrum Berlin für Sozialforschung. She is Joint Managing Editor of Economics of Transition and is a Research Fellow of the Centre for Economic Policy Research and of the William Davidson Institute at the University of Michigan. Her research and teaching interests include the economics of transition (enterprise restructuring and performance); the role of financial institutions and corporate governance in economic performance; the post-war development of the German economy; and macroeconomics (open economy, imperfect competition models).

Brian R. Cheffins is the S. J. Berwin Professor of Corporate Law, Faculty of Law, University of Cambridge and Professorial Fellow, Trinity Hall. He holds a BA and an LLB from the University of Victoria (British Columbia) and an LLB from the University of Cambridge. Formerly, he was Professor at the Law Faculty, University of British Columbia. He was Visiting Scholar at the Centre for Socio-Legal Studies at Wolfson College, Oxford University and Visiting Professor at Duke Global Capital Markets Program. He is the author of *Company Law: Theory, Structure and Operation* (Oxford, 1997) and various articles on corporate law and corporate governance.

John C. Coffee Jr is the Adolf A. Berle Professor of Law at Columbia University Law School. He is a Fellow of the American Academy of Arts and Sciences, and served as a Reporter to the American Law Institute for its *Principles of Corporate Governance: Analysis and Recommendations.* He has been a member of Advisory Committees to the SEC, the New York Stock Exchange, and NASDAQ, and has co-authored leading casebooks on corporations and securities regulation. He has also taught at the Law Schools of Harvard, Stanford, Michigan, Virginia, and Georgetown Universities.

Martin J. Conyon is an Assistant Professor of Management at the Wharton School, University of Pennsylvania. Previously, he was a Professor at Warwick Business School (UK) and a Lecturer in Economics at the Queen's College, University of Oxford. His research interests are in corporate governance, boards of directors and executive compensation. He has acted as an adviser to many leading companies and policies on these issues.

Rafel Crespí is a Professor of Business and Economics at the Universitat Illes Balears (UIB). His research interests are in the field of corporate governance, mainly in empirical corporate finance, ownership structure and management. He holds a BSc and a PhD from the Universitat Autonoma of Barcelona (UAB). He has also taught at the Universitat Pompeu Fabra (UPF) and has been a visitor at the Centre for Economic Research (CentER), Tilburg University, and the Said Business School, Oxford University.

Isabelle Dherment-Ferere is Professor in Finance at the University of Toulon. She obtained her PhD and her DEA in Business Administration from the University of Aix-Marseille III and Toulouse Business School. She has published mainly on corporate governance, French control structures, directors' fiduciary duties, financial reporting, and banking.

Piet Duffhues is Professor of Finance at the Finance Department of Tilburg University and Director of Studies at the Tilburg Institute for Advanced Studies in Management (Tias Business School) both for the Financial Economics and Treasure Management Executive Programmes. He holds a PhD from Tilburg University. His research interests focus on corporate financial risk management, international capital budgeting theory, capital structure theory, and management options. His publications include books on corporate finance and on financial instruments. He has published numerous articles within the broad landscape of financial economics and is a co-editor of a book series on *Risk & Return and Financial Instruments.*

Mara Faccio is Assistant Professor of Finance at the Mendoza College of Business of the University of Notre Dame, Indiana. Formerly, she was Assistant Professor at the Catholic University of Milan. She received her MPhil in Accounting and Finance from the City University Business School in 1997, and her PhD from Universita Cattolica in 1999. She has published in the *American Economic Review* and in the *Journal of Corporate Finance.* Her current research interests are in international corporate finance, and cover different aspects of ownership and control structures, debt and dividend policies, and M&A.

Julian R. Franks is the City Corporation Professor of Finance at the London Business School. He was visiting Professor at the University of North Carolina (Chapel Hill), and the University of California (Berkeley and Los Angeles). He is a consultant to the UK government, regulator of telecommunications industry, and an advisor to various private companies. He is also a member of the joint DTI–Treasury working party reviewing the insolvency code and of the Company Law Review's working party examining corporate governance. He graduated with a BA (University of Sheffield) an MBA (Columbia University), and a PhD (London University). His publications are on takeovers, corporate restructuring, financial regulation, corporate bankruptcy, and ownership and control. He is an associate editor of several journals including the *Journal of Empirical Finance* and the *Journal of Corporate Finance.*

Carles Gispert is an Assistant Professor of Financial Economics at the Department of Business Economics of the Universitat Autonoma de Barcelona. He was a Visiting Research Fellow at the Center for Economic Research (CentER) and the Department of Finance of Tilburg University in the Netherlands. Carles graduated with a BSc and a PhD in Business Economics from the Universitat Autonoma de Barcelona. His current research focus is on corporate governance, ownership structures, managerial compensation, informativeness of earnings, capital structure, and equity duration.

Marc Goergen is a Lecturer in Finance at the Manchester School of Management, University of Manchester Institute of Science and Technology (UMIST). Previously, he was Assistant

Professor in Finance at the ISMA Centre of the University of Reading and the School of Accounting and Finance of the University of Manchester. He holds an MSc in Economics from the Free University of Brussels (ULB), an MBA in European Business from Solvay Business School (Brussels) and a DPhil in Economics from Keble College, University of Oxford. He is also a Fellow of the International Institute of Corporate Governance and Accountability of the Law School of the George Washington University. His areas of research include initial public offerings, investment models, and corporate governance.

Henry Hansmann is Sam Harris Professor of Law at the Yale Law School, and is also a member of the faculty at the Yale School of Management. Trained as both an economist and legal scholar, Professor Hansmann has focused his research primarily on the law and economics of enterprise organization. He has written extensively on nonprofit firms, cooperatives, mutual companies, employee-owned firms, condominiums, trusts, and public enterprise, as well as on conventional investor-owned business corporations.

Ulrich Hege is an Associate Professor in the Department of Finance at HEC School of Management in Paris. He is also associated with CEPR in London and CentER for Economic Research in Tilburg. Previously, he has held positions at Tilburg University and ESSEC Business School. A native of Germany, he received a degree in economics from Frankfurt University before moving to the United States of America and receiving a PhD from Princeton University. His work focuses on various topics in the theory of corporate finance, including bankruptcy, structural models of the dynamics of defaultable securities, venture capital, corporate governance, and joint ventures.

Klaus J. Hopt is Director of the Max Planck Institute for Foreign Private and Private International Law in Hamburg. Formerly, he was Professor at the Universities of Tuebingen, Bern, Munich, and at the European University Institute (Florence). He was a judge at the Court of Appeals in Stuttgart and a member of the Deputation of the Deutscher Juristentag. He held visitingships at Universities of Pennsylvania, Kyoto, Brussels, Geneva, Tokyo, Chicago, and New York, and at the Sorbonne and was awarded honorary doctorates by the ULB (Brussels), UCL (Louvain) and the Universite de Paris V Rene Descartes. He is the author of numerous books and articles on banking law, stock exchange regulation, comparative corporate governance, business law, and takeover regulation.

Rezaul Kabir is Associate Professor of Finance at Tilburg University and Guest Professor of Empirical Corporate Finance at University of Antwerp. He holds a PhD degree in Finance and Masters degrees in Economics and Business Administration from the Catholic University of Leuven. Rez's teaching and research interests include corporate finance, corporate governance, and strategic finance. He has written articles on a variety of issues including trading suspensions, stock market crash, insider trading, ownership structure, anti-takeover measures, equity issues, earnings announcements, and equity option listings.

Reinier Kraakman is Erza Ripley Thayer Professor of Law at the Harvard University School of Law. He was previously Professor of Law at Yale Law School and Visiting Professor of Law at both Georgetown University Law Center and New York University Law School. He received a JD degree from Harvard Law School and an AB degree from Harvard

College. He also completed three years as a graduate student in sociology (ABD) at Harvard. He was also a law clerk for Judge Henry J. Friendly of the US Court of Appeals for the Second Circuit. He has been an advisor on company law reform in Russia and Vietnam. Currently, he teaches corporate law, corporate finance, and conducts seminars devoted to theoretical issues in organizational law. He has written numerous professional articles on topics in corporate law, corporate governance, and liability strategies for controlling corporate behaviour.

M. Ameziane Lasfer is Professor of Finance at the City University Business School. He was Visiting Professor at HEC Paris and University Paris XII. He gained a Diploma in Accounting and Finance from the London School of Economics (LSE), MBA and PhD from the University of Bath, UK. His research interests include dividend policy, capital structure, investments in R&D, institutional trades, corporate restructuring, and corporate governance. Part of his research was sponsored by the National Association of Pension Funds (NAPF) and the Finance Lease Association (FLA). He published a number of papers in the *Journal of Finance, Journal of Banking and Finance, Journal of Corporate Finance, Financial Management,* and *European Financial Management.*

Davide Lombardo is an Economist at the International Monetary Fund. He graduated in Economics from Universita Bocconi of Milan, and from Stanford University with a PhD in economics. He has been the recipient of several scholarships and academic prizes. His main interests are in the areas of financial economics (especially corporate finance), public finance, law and economics, and international economics.

Maria Maher is a Senior Economist at the OECD and an Adjunct Associate Professor at the American University in Paris. At the OECD she has worked on corporate governance, regulatory reform, foreign direct investment, and sustainable development. She contributed to the OECD Principles for Corporate Governance. Formerly, she was a University Lecturer at Birkbeck College in London, a Research Officer at the Department of Applied Economics at Cambridge University, and a Fellow of Christs' College. She holds a PhD in Economics from Berkeley and her main research interests are industrial organization, theory of the firm, contract theory, financial structure, ownership, and governance issues.

Colin Mayer is Peter Moores Professor of Management Studies at the University of Oxford and Director of the Oxford Financial Research Centre. He has a professorial fellowship at Wadham College. He is currently the first Leo Goldschmidt Visiting Professor in Corporate Governance at the Solvay Business School, Universite Libre de Bruxelles. He researches in the fields of corporate finance, governance, regulation and taxation, and has worked on international comparisons of financial systems and corporate governance and their effects on the financing and control of corporate sectors. He also researches financial aspects of the regulation of utilities and the regulation of financial institutions. He has published numerous articles and several books on corporate finance, governance, regulation, and taxation.

Joseph A. McCahery is Professor of International Business Law at Tilburg University, Faculty of Law. He holds a visiting appointment at Leiden University, Faculty of Law. He was a law clerk for Judge Nathaniel Jones of the United States Court of Appeals for the Sixth Circuit. He received a PhD from Warwick University, where he taught prior to joining

Tilburg University. He has published widely on banking law, corporate law, corporate governance, regulation, securities markets, and taxation.

Pierre Mella-Barral is Assistant Professor of Finance at the London Business School and was previously a Lecturer at the London School of Economics. He has a PhD in Economics from Cambridge University. His main research interests are corporate finance and real options, and he has published in the *Journal of Finance*, the *Review of Financial Studies*, and the *Journal of Banking and Finance.*

Gerard Mertens is Professor of Accounting at the Erasmus University Rotterdam, and Director of the Research Institute for Corporate Finance of NIB Capital Bank. Previously, he was a Research Fellow of CentER and a Lecturer at the Accounting Departments of Tilburg University and the University of Maastricht. He obtained his PhD in financial accounting from the University of Maastricht and an MA in applied economics from the University of Nijmegen. His research interests are financial reporting, auditing, capital markets, and corporate governance.

Piet W. Moerland is Professor of Corporate Governance at Tilburg University where he teaches courses on mergers and acquisitions and corporate governance. Formerly, he was Professor at the University of Groningen and Policy Assistant at the central staff group of the Rabobank. Piet was also a member of the Dutch Corporate Governance Commission and is a policy adviser to the government. He also serves on the board of listed Dutch banks and companies. He graduated with a PhD in economics from Erasmus University Rotterdam and has published on Dutch taxation policy, mergers and acquisition, corporate defence mechanisms, privatization, employee remuneration, and international comparative corporate governance.

Kevin J. Murphy is Professor of Finance and Business Economics at the University of Southern California Marshall School of Business and is an expert on executive compensation. Prior to joining USC, he spent four years on the faculty of Harvard Business School and seven years on the faculty of the University of Rochester's Simon School of Business. He was also a visiting Scholar and Consultant at Towers Perrin. He received MA and PhD degrees in Economics from the University of Chicago, and a BA (summa cum laude) from UCLA. He is an Associate Editor of the *Journal of Financial Economics*, the *Journal of Accounting and Economics*, the *Journal of Corporate Finance, Managerial and Decision Economics*, and the *Economic Bulletin.*

Marco Pagano is Professor of Economics at the Universita di Salerno. Formerly, he was Professor at the University of Naples and at Bocconi University. He obtained a BA from Cambridge University and a PhD in Economics from MIT. He co-directs the Research Programme in Financial Economics of the Centre for Economic Policy Research, is a member of the Council of the European Economic Association and of the Italian Treasury's commission for privatizations. In 1997 he was awarded the BACOM European Prize for Economic and Financial Research. Most of his work is in financial economics, especially in the field of market microstructure, and more recently in banking and corporate finance. He has published in most top economics and finance journals.

Enrico Perotti holds the Chair in International Finance at the University of Amsterdam and is Director of the CIFRA research center, Fellow at the CEPR, at the Davidson Institute (Michigan) and at the Tinbergen Institute, and Board Member at the Russian European Center for Economic Policy (Moscow). Formerly, he taught at MIT, Boston University and the LSE. He was Visiting Professor at the IMF, the University of Michigan, LBS and the Central European University. He was a consultant to the IMF, World Bank, EC, NYSE, EBRD, and various Eastern European governments and financial institutions. He obtained his PhD in Finance from MIT and is an authority in international corporate finance and banking, financial reform in emerging economies and he has published in several top journals in finance and economics.

M. J. G. C. (Theo) Raaijmakers is Professor of Corporate Law at Tilburg University Faculty of Law, Former Legal Advisor to Royal Philips Electronics, Justice of the Court of Appeals (Arnhem, the Netherlands), and a Member of the Social Economic Council's Committee on Mergers. He is the author of a number of books including *Joint Ventures* (1976); *Herziening van de Fusiecode* (1994); and *Rechtspersonen-en Vennootschapsrecht* (2000). His areas of research include corporate law, securities law, partnership law, corporate finance, groups of companies, and corporate reorganizations.

Luc Renneboog is Associate Professor at the Department of Finance of Tilburg University and Research Fellow at the CentER for Economic Research (Tilburg). Previously, he held appointments at the Catholic University of Leuven and visiting appointments at Oxford University, London Business School, Venice University, and Centro Universitario de Estudios Financieros (Madrid). He graduated from the University of Leuven with degrees in management engineering (MSc) and in philosophy (BA), from the University of Chicago with an MBA in finance and from the London Business School with a PhD in financial economics. His research interests are corporate finance, corporate control, dividend policy, financial distress, and the economics of art.

Chris Robinson is Associate Professor at the Schulich School of Business of York University in Toronto, where he teaches corporate and personal finance, financial statement analysis, and environmental management. Chris graduated with a PhD and is a CA, CFP. He is also the founding Finance Editor of *Alternative Perspectives on Finance and Accounting* and an Associate Editor of *Financial Services Review* and *Financial Counseling and Planning*. His research interests include alternative and critical perspectives on finance and accounting, personal finance, corporate governance, dual class equity, dividend policy, the application of ecological philosophy to business and finance, and business and the environment.

Mark J. Roe is a Professor of Law at Harvard Law School. For the prior dozen years he was a Professor of Law at Columbia Law School where, for several years, he directed the Sloan Project on Corporate Governance. He is the author of *Strong Managers, Weak Owners: The Political Roots of American Corporate Finance* (Princeton University Press, 1994). The tentatively titled *Political Determinants of Corporate Governance*, a book related to the essay in this volume, is in progress for Oxford University Press, as the published form of his earlier Clarendon Lectures.

Roberta Romano is the Allen Duffy/Class of 1960 Professor of Law at Yale Law School. She is a Fellow of the American Academy of Arts and Sciences, a Research Associate of the National Bureau for Economic Research, and the author of *The Genius of American Corporate Law* (1993) and *The Advantage of Competitive Federalism for Securities Regulation* (2001). Her research has focused on state competition for corporate charters, the political economy of takeover regulation, shareholder litigation, institutional investor activism in corporate governance, and the regulation of financial instruments, and securities markets.

Peter Roosenboom is an Assistant Professor at Erasmus University Rotterdam. He was a PhD student at Tilburg University and the CentER for Economic Research. He holds an MA in Investment Theory from Tilburg University and has completed the Graduate Programme in Management at CentER. Peter is a member of the 'IPOS in Europe' initiative and a member of the programme committee of the 2000 International Conference on IPOs in Amsterdam. He has published a variety of papers on initial public offerings, entrepreneurial finance, venture capital, and corporate governance.

John Rumsey is Professor of Finance at Dalhousie University, Canada. He obtained a PhD from York University (Canada) and has held academic positions at the University of Toronto and at York University. His current research interests range from fixed income securities to Bayesian statistics.

Geof P. Stapledon is Associate Professor and Reader, and Deputy Director of the Centre for Corporate Law and Securities Regulation at the University of Melbourne. He is also Director of Institutional Analysis, a research and advisory firm specializing in corporate governance. He also holds Committee positions with the Australian Institute of Company Directors, and the Australian Accounting Research Foundation. He has degrees in Economics and Law from the University of Adelaide, and obtained his doctorate from the University of Oxford. Currently, he teaches corporate law, competition law and corporate governance, and is editor of the *Company and Securities Law Journal.*

Walter N. Torous is Professor of Finance at the Anderson School of Management at UCLA. He previously taught at the University of Michigan and at the London Business School. His PhD degree is in Economics from the University of Pennsylvania and he teaches classes in managerial finance, real estate finance, and empirical methods in finance. His research interests, in addition to the reorganization of financially distressed firms, include the pricing of financial instruments (options, futures, risky debt and mortgages), and statistical issues in finance.

Ernst-Ludwig von Thadden is Professor of Economics at the Deparement d'Econometrie et Economie Politique at the University of Lausanne. He obtained his PhD in Economics at the University of Bonn and his Habilitation at the University of Basel. He graduated with a BA in mathematics and economics at the University of Heidelberg and an MPhil at the London School of Economics. He is a Research Fellow at the Center for Economic Policy Research (London), former Resident Fellow of the Center for Advanced Study in the Behavioral Sciences in Stanford, and Director of the doctoral programme at the Universities of Lausanne and Geneva. Elu is board member of several academic journals and formal consultant to the World Bank and other international institutions. His research covers corporate finance, banking, international finance, political economy, and contract theory.

Alan White is a Professor of Finance in the Joseph L. Rotman School of Management at the University of Toronto. In addition to his work in corporate governance he is well known for his research in the area of derivative securities: their pricing and their use by financial institutions for risk management. Recently, this research has been focused on the pricing and hedging of credit risk. Other current research examines modelling the term structure of interest rates in a way that is consistent with observed market data.

Eddy Wymeersch is Professor of Commercial Law at the University of Ghent and Chairman of the Belgian Banking and Finance Commission. He is also consultant to EC Commission, World Bank and IFC; a member of the corporate governance commission of the Brussels Stock Exchange and Chairman of the Simpler Legislation for the Internal Market working party on the first and second directive. In addition, he is a member of the board of the National Bank of Belgium and the Belgian Corporate Governance Commission. He was Chairman of the Board of Brussels International Airport Company and adviser on governance issues to several Belgian companies. He has published extensively on securities regulation, company law, and comparative corporate governance.

1

Introduction: Recent Developments in Corporate Governance

JOSEPH A. McCAHERY AND LUC RENNEBOOG

1. PURPOSE AND AUDIENCE

Recently, policymakers have taken a keen interest in the economic function of corporate governance systems. The impact of globalization and the recent finance-driven troubles in East Asia and elsewhere have spurred this drive toward policies and institutions that address defects in corporate performance and propose comprehensive reforms said to foster higher firm productivity, more entrepreneurship, and better developed capital markets. In the corporate world today there is a lively debate about how to design an effective corporate governance system that promotes economic efficiency. Initially, policymakers and scholars answered this question by measuring the quality of governance in terms of an idealized set of legal rules. In this regard, a high quality corporate governance system would refer to a set of institutions and mechanisms that ensure: (1) management pursues the welfare of shareholders; (2) the corporate board is staffed primarily by non-executive directors; and (3) corporate law rules protect minority investors and minimize controlling shareholder diversions of private benefits of control (Fox and Heller 2000). This suggests that differences in legal rules will correspond closely to different levels of economic performance. Meanwhile, a new direction in research has opened up which embraces a broader perspective on corporate governance: competition and non-legal techniques are seen as important mechanisms for controlling incentive problems and maximizing the returns to investors (Zingales 1998; Allen and Gale 2000).

The focus on the link between corporate structures and economic growth has prompted considerable comparative empirical work on the institutional differences in ownership structures and legal rules (Carlin and Mayer, Chapter 14, this volume). Until recently, much of the work on comparative corporate governance assumed that the Berle and Means corporation, characterized by a separation of ownership and control, was the model traditionally associated with large enterprises. Contemporary research, however, shows that the Berle and Means model of the corporation is largely limited to Japan, the United States, and Britain (Becht and Mayer 2001). Broadly speaking, there are two systems of corporate ownership and control: market and control-based systems (Cheffins, Chapter 6, this volume). The new comparative research on corporate governance focused initially on the differences between the two dominant regimes (Berglöf 1997). The analytical approach attempts to incorporate the main aspects of the two corporate governance systems that offer competing approaches to deal with the fundamental agency problems of capitalism. The main corporate governance problem in most western countries is a trade-off between ownership and liquidity. Moreover, to a large extent, the trade-off between liquidity and control suggests that we focus also on another fundamental trade-off: between monitoring and management initiative (Coffee 1999). On the normative side, the continental European system of control focuses on the effect of shareholders on management whereas the market model places more emphasis on monitoring of management and incentives. The strengths and shortcomings of the market-oriented and control-oriented regimes are assessed in terms of their ability to protect shareholders against expropriation and limit managerial agency costs (Bratton and McCahery, Chapter 2, this volume).

Meantime, the debate about the comparative merits of governance regimes has focused on the crucial role of legal rules and institutions that are required to provide a country with a deep, broad, and liquid stock market (along with dispersed ownership). Creating a strong capital market is viewed as especially important for Europe's blockholding countries since it can facilitate economic growth by providing a more efficient way for companies to raise capital (Maher and Andersson, Chapter 17, this volume). It is notable that many continental European firms, which are controlled through extensive cross-ownership and holding structures, tend to have limited access to capital markets due to inadequate disclosure and must rely on internal financing or short-term bank loans (Edwards and Nibler 2001). As a consequence, a large section of European business has been forced, until recently, to suffer higher costs of capital which may account for their performance in relation to foreign firms.

To address this problem, proponents argue that rapid reforms are required in national governance structures to create an environment that would stimulate greater managerial reliance on external finance and a smooth transition to shareholder-oriented acts (Hansmann and Kraakman, Chapter 3, this volume). It has been suggested that European policymakers are changing their securities rules to realize the untapped potential for economic development that may lead to functional convergence (Coffee, Chapter 4, this volume). Yet, changing securities rules alone may not be sufficient to encourage a different pattern in ownership and governance of national institutions (Roe, Chapter 5, this volume). An open question is what explains the material differences in corporate governance systems. Roe (Chapter 5, this volume) argues that the differences in corporate governance regimes are the result of political and social choices about distribution and the resolution of conflict. Others argue that corporate governance systems are shaped by economic and political factors that can lead, in different countries, to either the elimination of systemic differences or resistance to domestic improvements (Bebchuk and Roe 1999). Consequently, path dependence makes structural convergence a highly unlikely prospect.

The aim of the collection then is to provide a framework for readers who are interested in thinking through the key legal and economic issues about the extent that corporate governance systems play a central role in the economic performance of the firm. The issues underlying these questions can also be understood in the context of a parallel debate about the convergence of corporate governance institutions and practices. This volume also explores claims respecting the relative competitive advantage of a governance system, the appropriate course of national level reform, and the circumstances under which the diverse systems of governance and securities regulation can be expected to converge systematically. These points raise the issue of whether nations undertaking reforms should develop corporate governance policies that mimic the legal rules and institutions of a dispersed ownership regime (Easterbrook and Fischel 1991; Whincop 2001). Or, conversely, should states avoid borrowing from other systems' best practices and pursue a course of internally designed governance reforms.

The thrust of these concerns can also be seen in terms of the debate about whether shareholder pressure is the most important mechanism influencing corporate decisions. This view of corporate governance has been challenged as too narrow (Allen and Gale 2000). Broadly speaking, the question about the institutional structure and mechanisms that are conducive to economic growth can be seen as a debate between those who claim that corporate law should seek only to maximize shareholder value and provide for optimal legal protection of investors and those who would argue that the effectiveness of market-oriented governance rules are mixed and that regulation should promote benefits for some of the other stakeholders (Deakin 2001). From a comparative perspective, it has been argued that there are other mechanisms that help solve the agency problems and enhance economic growth.

2. ISSUE COVERAGE

This volume is divided into seven parts. Part I, broadly speaking, provides not only a means for assessing the key features of market and control-based systems of governance but a standpoint for determining whether national governance systems are likely to converge to an optimal system of governance. Part II introduces the reader to the building blocks of European corporate law and the impact of the European Union (EU) and its harmonization of corporate and securities regulation. Part III examines the complex ownership structures that are found in Western Europe and investigates the consequences that large shareholdings may have for corporate governance. Part IV offers some preliminary analysis aimed at determining the relationship between legal and financial systems and corporate performance. Part V looks at the economic perspectives on the operation of the market for corporate control. After taking stock of the evidence on the effect of the market for corporate control, this section then analyses the key legal rules and institutions of the bankruptcy regimes in the USA and Britain. The authors in this section explore the effect of different legal rules on commercial activity, and introduce procedures that may avoid the practical difficulties associated with a structural bargaining regime. Part VI is devoted to the importance of institutional investors in corporate governance. In the light of their substantial role in corporate governance systems in the USA and Britain, the papers in this section focus on the debate on shareholder proposals, the reform of the voting procedures for institutional investors in Britain, and the performance of companies in which occupational pension funds hold large share stakes. The final section, Part VII, examines the executive compensation arrangements in the USA and Britain as well as in continental Europe (the Netherlands and Spain). These chapters supply a pool of current research on the motivational effect of performance-related remuneration and the substantial increases in top executive remuneration in the USA.

3. OVERVIEW

3.1. *Convergence in Corporate Law*

Is there a single optimal governance regime for the regulation of firms? Comparative corporate governance strives to provide empirical answers to the question about the productive advantage of governance systems. In this sense, economists and lawyers have sought to link the performance of companies to different patterns of distribution of shareholdings in a country and the quality of a country's corporate governance practices.

In the opening chapter, William Bratton and Joseph McCahery take up the main questions addressed by the literature on comparative corporate governance: whether national governance systems can be expected to converge in the near future, and whether the focal point of that convergence will be a new, hybrid governance system comprised of the best practices drawn from different systems. This chapter advances the view that neither global convergence that eliminates systemic difference nor the emergence of a hybrid best practice can safely be projected because each national government regime is an integrated system. Each system, rather than consisting of a loose collection of separable components, is tied together by a complex incentive structure. Interdependencies between each system's components and the incentives of its actors create significant barriers to cross-reference to and from other systems. The cross-reference hypothesis, in contrast, presupposes divisible corporate governance institutions—a world in which one system's components can be adapted for use in the other system.

Drawing on the key models of monitoring and blockholding, articulated in the incomplete contracts theory of the firm, Bratton and McCahery argue that different governance systems have incentive structures that entail different trade-offs—trade-offs between ownership concentration and liquidity, between monitoring and management initiative, and between private rent-seeking and activity benefiting shareholders as a group. The trade-offs delimit opportunities for productive cross reference. More particularly, blockholding systems, such as those in Europe, subsidize monitoring by permitting blockholders to reap private benefits through self-dealing and insider trading. Market systems, such as those in the USA and Britain, regulate such private rent-seeking toward the end of maintaining an institutional framework that supports diffuse share ownership and liquid trading markets. It follows that a legal framework conducive to blockholding may be ill equipped to foster dispersed equity ownership and liquid trading markets, and that a legal framework conducive to liquid trading markets may have properties that discourage blockholding. This gives rise to questions for law reform agendas on both sides of the Atlantic. In the USA, proponents ask for deregulation of controls on institutional investors, looking to encourage more blockholding and more effective monitoring. In Europe, proponents ask for stronger securities regulation, looking to encourage deeper trading markets. This suggests that each reform programme may lead to disappointing results because neither assures conforming adjustments to the pertinent actors' incentives. Alternatively, strict reforms that materially change prevailing incentive patterns could perversely destabilize workable (if imperfect) arrangements without assuring the appearance of more effective alternatives.

Henry Hansmann and Reinier Kraakman argue in Chapter 3 that powerful new forces—ideological and competitive—are pushing corporate structures toward convergence. What does it mean to say that there is convergence in corporate law? In analysing corporate law systems worldwide, this chapter shows that there is significant normative consensus among policymakers and academics on the fundamental issues of corporate governance. To the extent that the shareholder-oriented model of corporate governance is viewed as desirable, this consensus on the appropriate conduct of corporate law is also a consensus about the content of corporate law rules, which in turn should have a strong effect on the further development of corporate law.

While the shareholder-oriented model is the leading corporate governance regime, Hansmann and Kraakman acknowledge, nevertheless, that there are considerable obstacles to the evolution of efficient ownership structures, governance practices, and corporate law. Several scholars have begun to spell out with some precision the forces inhibiting the convergence of corporate structures (Bebchuk and Roe 1999; Milhaupt 1998). In some jurisdictions, large blockholders or powerful managers, with positional advantage inside the firm, will oppose effectively any corporate governance reforms that would force them to share the corporate earnings more equitably. Moreover, corporate structures will tend not to converge for path-dependent reasons. Despite the ability of these groups to influence corporate structure and governance, Hansmann and Kraakman argue that the prospects are decidedly less pessimistic if we resist the idea that the law will deter a controlling shareholder from adopting an efficient corporate law regime by making them share their private benefits and other gains with minority investors. Yet, there is a good likelihood that the law will allow the controlling shareholder to capture the gains associated with efficient restructuring in jurisdictions where incumbent structures support expropriation by insiders. On the whole, corporate practices are likely to converge more rapidly than convergence in legal rules. Shareholder pressure has forced legal changes in the direction of a single tier board, enhanced disclosure systems and accounting standards, and shareholder suits against directors and managers. A key point which Hansmann and Kraakman emphasize is that, while important steps toward convergence have taken place in many jurisdictions, convergence of legal rules does not always reflect efficiency.

In Chapter 4, John Coffee focuses on the debate over convergence in corporate governance, particularly the strong convergence thesis, which predicts that product and capital market competition will compel convergence, and the path dependence thesis that identifies powerful forces and interests impeding governance structures from converging. There is another position, however, that explains convergence of legal systems. Coffee argues that functional substitutes can provide a framework for convergence when formal convergence is blocked by legal, political, or institutional barriers. For example, he notes that firms whose home country has a weak securities market can seek a US or UK listing in order to access the benefits associated with the depth and liquidity of these trading markets. At the same time, European exchanges have, in order to increase their scale to compete globally, adopted tighter governance rules as a result of competitive pressures. The foregoing examples are but a small list of confirming examples that demonstrate the importance of functional substitutes.

In this essay, Coffee expands on the concept of functional convergence to show that self-regulation, as opposed to mandatory rules, may be a way to overcome the barriers to the emergence of a strong securities market. There are many studies that show that stock market development and liquidity are not likely to appear in a jurisdiction in which there are large concentrations of ownership. He stresses that while securities markets require strong legal protections for minority investors, the cause and effect relationship is backwards. He notes, having analysed the early development of the New York and London Stock Exchanges, that dispersed shareholders must arise initially before they can organize politically to gain legal protection. Coffee's central thesis is that legal change, which can be effectively constrained by interest groups, is often outpaced by economic change. Finally, Coffee casts doubt on Mark Roe's hypothesis that social democracy and strong securities markets are unlikely to coexist in Europe. According to Roe's thesis, continental European investors prefer concentrated ownership and limited transparency because it offers them protection against potential government expropriation of their corporate assets. The empirical accuracy of this claim has been challenged by Brian Cheffins (Chapter 6, this volume) who argues that England provides an example where a social democracy exists alongside a strong securities market. Coffee suggests, moreover, that the reason for the slow development of European securities markets is due to the dominance of the banks and their political allies that benefited from the persistence of a bank-dominated system of financing.

Mark Roe argues in Chapter 5 that there is evidence that in social democratic countries the norms and institutions supporting shareholder wealth maximization are relatively weak. He stresses that social democracies press managers to stabilize employment, to forgo some profit-maximizing risks with the firm, and to deplete existing capital rather than downsize the firm when markets are no longer aligned with a firm's production capacity. In practice, labour markets in continental Europe and Japan have tended to be protected, and the development of Anglo-American style instruments to discipline managers and reduce agency costs has been slow in taking root. Roe reasons that these labour market regularities and different corporate governance norms have an effect on the ownership structure of firms. Accordingly, the concentration of ownership is more common in large firms in continental Europe and Japan than it is in the USA. Roe notes a correlation between, on the one hand, closely-owned businesses and social democracies and, on the other hand, diffusely-owned firms and capitalist countries. Roe maintains that the origins of these differences may be due to a craving for stability, differences in fairness norms, and a difference in reconciliation of political and social conflicts. Evidence on the different political systems and economic performance does not emerge clearly from the empirical studies. Yet evidence on the positive effects of social democracy shows that it may enhance total social welfare, although with fewer public firms than less socially-responsive nations.

In terms of answering his critics, Roe acknowledges that there are other foundations, besides politics, for why nations develop strong securities markets and dispersed shareholding and others do not. Not only must nations achieve a requisite level of economic and technological development, but also the presence of legal rules and institutions are indeed necessary to the development of a securities market. Viewed in this light, it is unlikely that the political hypothesis can be undermined by monocausal counter-examples that focus on one salient political feature (e.g. pro-labour social democracy) in a nation. On the contrary, the counter-examples that have emerged, according to Roe, do not seem particularly challenging and, in turn, tend to reinforce the political theory.

Brian Cheffins provides a critique of the 'law matters' thesis in Chapter 6. The key assumption of the 'law matters' hypothesis is that a number of legal rules and regulatory institutions are required to provide a country with a deep, broad and liquid stock market, and dispersed share ownership. This work emphasizes the centrality of laws that provide investors with good information about the value of a company and protect them from the self-dealing transactions of the company's insiders. There is evidence that, to the extent that a country undertakes to initiate legal and institutional reforms along these dimensions, a country can expect to enhance the development of its stock market. For instance, support for the 'law matters' thesis can be derived from the work of Rafael La Porta and his collaborators (1998; 1999), which shows that legal factors are fundamental for the growth rates of firms in many jurisdictions. As a consequence, because so much evidence is emerging about the benefits of good corporate governance and disclosure for strong stock markets, countries worldwide attempt to ameliorate the deficiencies of their existing regimes by introducing governance arrangements designed to counter insider trading, share price manipulation, and other abuses.

The importance of the 'law matters' view is that it highlights the importance of showing the causal explanations of poor corporate governance and the implications these structures have for shareholders, corporate finances, and the economy. Nevertheless, Cheffins argues that the 'law matters' approach has yet to fulfil its promise. The critical thrust of the chapter is to attack the 'law matters' thesis by showing that a liquid and deep securities market can prosper without the assistance of strong legal rules that protect minority investors. Cheffins shows that there is a clear analytical link in the theory. The British experience appears to counter the suggestion that good legal protections are crucial for the development of a strong stock market. Apparently, investor protection was not a fundamental norm in UK law until recently. If there was no legal support for investors, then there must have been support from other institutions to ensure that investors would not be exposed unduly to moral hazard and other agency problems. There were two distinct and powerful reasons why British investors would have felt comfortable investing in securities between 1900 and 1979. First, in its capacity as regulator of share offerings, the London Stock Market played an active role in British corporate governance. Second, the presence of financial intermediaries in the market reduced the concealment of information prompting investors to have greater confidence in the authority of the disclosure statements of companies.

This raises a question whether or to what extent legal rules, designed to protect minority shareholders, can be substituted by a combination of market mechanisms and non-legal rules. The 'law matters' argument is effectively challenged for either of two reasons: (1) that private market mechanisms can be implemented successfully and that investors' interests are adequately served by the existence of these enforcement mechanisms; and (2) that quite apart from whether market mechanisms existed for the protection of minority investors, self-regulation can play an effective role as a substitute for legal institutions. Thus, there is no reason to assume that a specific set of principles and structures are necessary for the emergence of deep capital markets and dispersed ownership. In the end, however, it is an empirical question as to whether and to what extent various kinds of structures will tend to support the development of securities markets.

3.2. *Harmonization in European Law*

In Chapter 7, Klaus Hopt analyses the forces that are influencing change in the fields of corporate law across Europe, particularly in Germany and Britain. In particular, he discusses the German and European Commission (EC) law influences on the development of British corporate law and practice. He observes that, despite the differences in German and British company law, the standard of conduct for directors and the practical functioning of boards are similar in both countries. Hopt argues that an even more impressive example of convergence is takeover regulation. While he points out takeover regulation is mainly self-regulatory in Britain, the British approach has emerged as the standard for policymakers across Europe and at the EC. He shows how several principles of the City Takeover Code concerning information provision and disclosure, takeover procedures, corporate directors' conduct during the offer period, neutrality, and the mandatory bid rule, were incorporated into the now-defunct draft 13th Directive on Takeovers.

Hopt contends that, despite the overlap in some aspects of corporate law and practice, there remain fundamental differences between corporate governance mechanisms in continental Europe and in Britain. He stresses that German law varies considerably from the Anglo-American view that the aim of the corporation is the maximization of shareholder value. The wider and more open differences between British and German law as to stakeholder interest appear in the context of boardroom co-determination. In practice, labour co-determination works quite well in Germany and the Netherlands because it serves to better integrate and motive the labour force, and provides an effective technique for the board to make unpopular decisions about corporate restructuring. We can also distinguish the role played by large banks in Germany and Britain. In Germany, where there is concentrated ownership, universal banks are the source of considerable influence on corporate actions and consequently may limit the impact that equity markets have on managers. While recognizing the path-dependent differences in corporate governance systems, Hopt argues, nevertheless, that market forces are likely to prompt the harmonization of legal rules and practices across the different political and economic systems in Europe.

In Chapter 8, Theo Raaijmakers examines the structure and design of the draft 13th Directive on Takeovers in light of the Williams Act in the USA. He argues that the draft directive, which dates back to 1989, had as its main purpose: the obligation to make a mandatory bid for all the shares of a target company; equal treatment for all holders of securities; adequate information; prohibition of certain defensive tactics; and supervision of the bid at the member state level. In contrast with the 13th Directive—which was drafted as a company law directive—the Williams Act is part of federal securities law aimed primarily at regulating the procedural and disclosure process in the tender process. He observes that the function of the Williams Act is to create a level playing field. The rules tend to prevent creeping acquisitions, leaving aside corporate law issues on governance and internal affairs, as well as exit mechanisms and appraisal disputes. In contrast, the draft 13th Directive, which was designed initially to harmonize the securities law aspects of the bid process, has to a considerable degree commingled corporate law principles and securities law disclosure standards and is limited only to takeover bids. He praises the Williams Act for its neutrality and focus on the regulation of decent behaviour and proper disclosure. Raaijmakers argues that the challenge for EC lawmakers is to promulgate federal rules on public tender offers, which could serve to stimulate the development of European-wide takeover market. In light of the recent demise of the draft 13th Directive, one thing is clear: the EC will be forced to reconceputalize its approach to the regulation of cross-border takeovers.

In Chapter 9, Eddy Wymeersch analyses developments at the level of regulation and practice to ascertain whether corporate governance patterns are converging in Europe. He agues that there are a number of factors that have brought about change in corporate governance practices across the European Union. An increase in observable competition among business groups, a changed role in the business operations and philosophy of European states, and the renewed interest for equity investment have triggered the demand for changes in corporate law practices. Wymeersch argues that the competition between securities markets has also led to improved governance standards and listings standards. We have also witnessed the proliferation of codes of conduct at the national level in the wake of sluggish pace of reform at the European level. Some of the codes have directly impacted corporate governance practices. Particularly noteworthy is that many national codes share common features.

It is important to emphasize that there has been significant convergence in the law of takeovers across Europe. Indeed, the draft 13th Directive on Takeovers would have completed the process by imposing a mandatory bide rule, investor protection and eliminating post-bid takeover defences at the European level. Less visible, Wymeersch argues that European firms are explicitly taking important legal steps to align their firm-level corporate governance to a largely shareholder-oriented standard. Notwithstanding these developments, however, the barriers to convergence in European company law are formidable, due to the persistence of concentrated ownership structures, which serves to highlight the difficulty of changing legal rules.

3.3. *Concentration of Ownership and Control in Europe*

Marc Goergen and Luc Renneboog take up the question why the corporate landscapes in Germany and Britain are so different in terms of ownership and control in Chapter 10. They provide a partial answer to this question by focusing on the evolution of control in German and UK Initial Public Offerings (IPOs). They investigate whether differences in stock exchange listing regulation, in fiscal (inheritance) law, in securities regulation (e.g. the issuance of dual class shares) or in economic factors (like corporate growth, performance, risk) can explain why relatively more companies are widely held in the UK and why control transfers take place more frequently via mergers and acquisitions in the UK. Goergen and Renneboog empirically reject some of the legal theories (like differing inheritance regulation and listing requirements) that could explain the differences in ownership structures, but find that the mandatory takeover threshold of 30 per cent in the UK imposes in many cases an upper limit of control concentration. They also find an important impact on control of the nature of the controlling shareholder. Whereas the largest shareholder class, dominating two-thirds of the German companies with concentrated ownership are families, (domestic) companies control almost 30 per cent of the UK firms with concentrated ownership which went public six years prior.

When German and UK IPOs are risky and poorly performing, the probability of ending up with concentrated ultimate control increases. In such a case, the need for a strong shareholder with good monitoring abilities and a long-term investment horizon arises, which is brought about by mergers and acquisitions in the UK and by controlling block transfers in Germany. The probability that an IPO will evolve towards diffuse ownership increases if the founder does not own a substantial share stake at the moment of the public offering (which is more frequently the case in the UK than in Germany) and if the company experiences a high growth rate. In addition, specifically for German IPOs, the probability that the company's majority control is held by a new large shareholder augments when non-voting shares are issued at flotation and when the company experiences fast growth in turnover. The company's founders tend to maintain control in smaller, profitable companies with limited risk and limited growth. Finally, Goergen and Renneboog conclude that if one regards full takeovers in the UK as similar—in terms of control—to control changes resulting from controlling block sales (partial takeovers) in Germany, the overall picture of corporate ownership and control in the UK and Germany is less diverging than is usually ascertained.

In Chapter 11, Ekkehart Boehmer discusses data on the concentration of ownership and control of German firms. The average German firm is not only characterized by strong ownership concentration but the corporate sector also has controlling interests in itself. Boehmer focuses on the most powerful shareholders in Germany and illustrates that it is frequently difficult to ascertain which group exerts ultimate control over the shareholding firm itself. Turning to the financial services industry, Boehmer shows that the top five banks and top three insurance companies are closely related through direct ownership and voting control. Jointly, these eight firms control over 14 per cent of all listed firms. But Boehmer argues that this figure underestimates the true value under control of these shareholders. As it turns out, the large ownership links exist between the large shareholders that do not trigger legal reporting requirements.

In Chapter 12, Piet Moerland examines the corporate governance regime in the Netherlands, and evaluates the effectiveness of Structure Regime, which creates complete separation of ownership and control. The current Dutch company law was enacted in 1971. Moerland argues that the legislators, in response to a concern to increase management's accountability to a broader set of stakeholders, increased accountability to include the possibility of three boards: a supervisory board, the board of directors, and works council, each with a defined set of legal responsibilities. Moerland notes that the Stucture Regime has three variations, the most prevalent being the Full Structure Regime, legally required for Dutch companies with more than 100 employees, a legally installed works council and a book value of shareholders' equity in excess of 12 million dollars. The Full Structure Regime requires a supervisory board that takes the following powers from shareholders: establishment of annual accounts, the election of the board of directors, and the election of the supervisory board. Moreover, the supervisory board has authority over many of the main decisions made by the board of directors. Recently the Structure Regime has been seen as a weak basis for board legitimacy and oversight. There are few incentives for the supervisory board to monitor and advise the board of directors. Moerland argues that the Structure Regime ought to be designed to create higher accountability. Strengthening shareholder (voting) power would be useful to the Dutch system of supervision.

In Chapter 13, Isabelle Dherment-Ferere and Luc Renneboog argue that the standard agency approach to corporate governance relies on a combination of internal and external devices to help overcome the incentive problem between management and shareholders. There is some evidence that when the corporate governance mechanisms have been insufficient to limit the agency problem—and management has been insulated—markets will react positively to Chief Executive Officer (CEO) departures. Indeed, Dherment-Ferere and Renneboog confirm these studies by showing that forced CEO dismissals trigger small but positive abnormal returns in listed French companies. A more detailed analysis reveals that the increase in abnormal returns is much stronger when the performance-related forced CEO departure coincides with the nomination of an external manager. The cumulative abnormal return of an internal CEO promotion in a poorly performing firm drops by almost 1 per cent on the day of the announcement. Presumably, this is because the internal manager is held (partially) responsible for past poor performance. In companies with good past performance and CEO departure, there is a price decline reflecting the loss of human capital.

In terms of assessing the forces responsible for CEO turnover, they suggest that institutional investors, banks, financial holding companies and the government—even if they are controlling blockholders—do not appear to prompt CEO departures. On the positive side, Dherment-Ferere and Renneboog did find evidence that forced turnover is facilitated if corporations hold large equity blocks, if these corporations have a large number of non-executive directors on the board and if creditors have a board representative. Finally, founding families involved in the executive management of the firm seem somehow insulated against shareholder disciplining.

3.4. *Economic Performance and Governance Structures*

In Chapter 14, Wendy Carlin and Colin Mayer focus on the important question as to whether specific corporate governance regimes, defined as the interrelation among the structure of financial systems, corporate ownership, and corporate and securities law, influence the distribution of economic activity and economic performance. Corporate governance regimes matter as they determine the returns on investment demanded by suppliers of external finance. As a consequence, policymakers in many countries diagnose weaknesses in their existing legal regimes and propose new arrangements said to foster higher firm productivity, more entrepreneurship and better-developed capital markets. Carlin and Mayer's concern is the existence of a causal connection between productivity and given financial and corporate governance structures.

Carlin and Mayer report a significant relationship between market-based systems, the development of banking systems and legal protection of investors, and the growth of equity financed and skill-intensive industries. Market-oriented financial systems and those with dispersed ownership are expected to be associated with high risk R&D type activities. In some developing countries there is a positive relation between activity in bank-dependent sectors of the economy and the bank-oriented system of the country. Carlin and Mayer conclude that there is not necessarily a dominant financial and corporate system that is appropriate across jurisdictions, economies, or industries within an economy. There may be important trade-offs in matching systems with the industrial bases of countries and their stages of economic development and regulatory and legal policies. Financial and corporate systems need to be sensitive to these potential impacts on corporate activities. Davide Lombardo and Marco Pagano analyse how the law and its enforcement affects equilibrium equity market rates of return and the cost of capital (demand for external funds) in Chapter 15. Within a specific institutional setting and given a specific degree of international stock market segmentation, improvements in the legal system are expected to generate positive effects on equity returns, which vary across governance systems. In this chapter, Lombardo and Pagano attempt to clarify an important point about which the literature has been silent; microeconomic models of corporate finance have usually taken the opportunity cost of funds as exogenously given.

Lombardo and Pagano develop two reasons why better legal institutions influence equity rates of return and the demand for equity finance by companies. First, good laws and efficient courts curtail the private benefits of managers. Consequently, legal institutional improvement will increase the return paid to external shareholders as well as the availability of external equity finance. Second, better laws and more effective courts facilitate the contractibility of corporate relations with customers and suppliers and the enforceability of such contracts. As a result, companies are more profitable which hence raises their rate of return and the amount of external financing. Lombardo and Pagano analyse these reasons by developing two different experiments. In the first one, they reduce managerial private benefits by introducing legal limits to transactions with other companies that may dilute the income rights of minority shareholders (mergers, asset sales, etc.). In the second experiment, they reduce the legal and auditing costs that shareholders must bear to prevent managerial opportunism. Such cost reduction may for example result from the introduction of class action suits or voting by mail. The authors find that the size of these effects on the equilibrium rate of return is increasing in the degree of international segmentation of equity markets.

In Chapter 16, Enrico Perotti and Ernst-Ludwig von Thadden look at the effect of the diffusion of information in bank-dominated financing relationships, which have been found to be less transparent. In practice, bank financing may lead to a lower level of trading liquidity, which serves as a disincentive for the gathering of information by market investors. Perotti and von Thadden offer a new explanation to the quality of information gathering by banks. They acknowledge that when information may be disclosed to more than one person, it will have strategic effects in a context of imperfect competition. In this context, the authors argue that less transparent firms reveal less to competitors based on their competitive strength, which creates strategic advantages and disadvantages. They explain that when firms act on the basis of less information, their expectations are not of sufficiently fine grade. Badly run firms will not be affected but strong firms will be hurt since they will be forced to be more aggressive. Perotti and von Thadden argue that, given the lack of transparency, expected profits are lower and the volatility of profits and output are also lower. This argument supports the view that reduced volatility has the effect of increasing the return to investors who have a fixed claim on the firm. The explanation of Perotti and von Thadden is that lender-dominated firms will work hard to avoid transparency since this would reduce the value of lenders' claims. Evidence suggests that shareholder-dominated firms, however, will prefer price information since it has an effect on profitability.

In Chapter 17, Maria Maher and Thomas Andersson consider the relation between corporate governance and economic performance. They concentrate on the standard mechanisms employed in different systems to limit governance problems and examine the cross-country evidence to determine which corporate governance instruments show a clear effect on economic growth. Most studies reveal that there is no unambiguous relation between corporate governance systems and firm performance. Nevertheless, they point out that the role of corporate governance can have a positive effect on the development of equity markets, R&D, and innovative activity, and the development of an active small and medium sized business (SME) sector. They conclude by arguing that the identification of good corporate governance practices should be based on a particularized inquiry into the specific corporate and regulatory domain.

3.5. *The Value of Corporate Control and the Reorganization of the Firm*

Chris Robinson, John Rumsey, and Alan White investigate the value of a vote in the market for corporate control in Chapter 18. The authors build on earlier research that has shown that superior voting shares tend to be worth more than restricted or non-voting shares: the premium varies widely across countries and is, for example, about 5–10 per cent in the US and even 81 per cent in Italy. This premium results from the value of control but also from a takeover premium. Non-controlling voting shareholders may share in any premium paid in a takeover while the non-voting shareholders are unlikely to do so. Thus, the two classes of equity will differ in price by the present value of the expected takeover premium. In addition, the normative message embedded in the voting rights' studies has been to show that the level of shareholder protection is related inversely to the size of the premium over the market price per share paid for a majority voting block.

The authors find that the value of a vote ranges from 3.5 to 13 per cent for samples of firms listed on the Toronto Stock Exchange. The Canadian situation allows a unique experiment because half of the non-voting shareholders of the sample firms have a takeover protection (a so-called 'coat-tail'). If a takeover offer made to the non-voting shareholders differs from the offer made to the shareholders' controlling voting rights, the non-voting shares are convertible into voting shares. By investigating samples of Canadian firms with and without takeover protection (coat-tail), the authors conclude that the takeover premium explains to a large extent the premium paid for voting rights.

In Chapter 19, Julian Franks, Colin Mayer, and Luc Renneboog argue that although hostile takeovers may be significant in board restructuring, takeovers in the UK do not seem to focus on board restructuring in poorly performing companies. Therefore, the authors investigate the disciplinary role of large shareholders and of (new) shareholders who increase voting power. In other words, the role of ownership concentration and the role of the market for partial control (the market for equity blocks of less than 30 per cent) are analysed.

Franks, Mayer, and Renneboog document an interesting observation: there is a dynamic relation between ownership, control, and performance. Where poor performance is observed, sales of share stakes occur between different investors. Findings suggest that substantial changes in these share stakes occur in the absence of tender offers or mergers, and without a violation of the UK Takeover Code's mandatory offer rule (acquiring 30 per cent of the voting rights triggers a mandatory tender offer for all other outstanding shares). These trades in shares are associated with significant changes in boards of poorly performing companies. Consistent with the literature on free rider problems and large share stakes, concentrated ownership is associated with more active corporate governance than dispersed share ownership. However, the chapter also finds that the nature of the owner is of critical importance: corporate investors exercise more control than institutional investors and those with private benefits of control, such as directors, may impede the exercise of good governance. Managerial entrenchment is present most often in recent IPOs where director shareholdings are particularly high. There is not much evidence that the presence of non-executive directors and the separation of the role of chairman and chief executive exert a significant impact on corporate governance.

In Chapter 20, Julian Franks and Walter Torous provide a comprehensive overview of the legal insolvency regimes in the USA and UK, noting that the procedures can be classified according to the outcome that they are directed toward—liquidation or reorganization. While Chapter 7 settles the debts of the firm through liquidation, Chapter 11 provides a mechanism to reorganize a firm's debt. Having classified the respective regimes in terms of their form and function, Franks and Torous then proceed to analyse the appropriate goals of insolvency law. They note that there is substantial debate about the goals that a well-designed bankruptcy regime should pursue. Nevertheless, Franks and Torous argue that the aim of bankruptcy law should be to minimize premature and protracted liquidations, maintain pre-bankruptcy priorities, and limit the dead-weight costs of bankruptcy. In terms of evaluating the respective regimes, they emphasize that each system has its tradeoffs. For instance, the USA code encourages lengthy bargaining, has high direct and indirect costs, can lead to deviations from pre-bankruptcy priorities, and has a strong continuation bias. Conversely, the studies show that the UK insolvency procedures are designed to minimize costs, which can increase the size of repayment to the creditors. They conclude that UK law is not fully effective since minority creditors are not fully protected and weak companies often find it impossible to resolve their financial difficulties under the current insolvency regime.

Ulrich Hege and Pierre Mella-Barral explore the relationship between creditor structure and reorganization law in Chapter 21. The restructuring advantage of bank loans is contrasted with the cost advantage of going public. Specifically, they show how, due to incomplete information and hold-out incentives, the informal reorganization process will frequently fail for dispersed public debt. Typically, the introduction of Chapter 11-style renegotiation will benefit public debt firms and will be harmful for private debt firms. Hege and Mella-Barral argue that, in light of the recent US experience, the Chapter 11 reorganization procedure reduces the role of private debt in corporate borrowing. From an efficiency perspective, the fundamental features of US reorganization law are ambiguous. It is, however, argued that the three prominent shortcomings of Chapter 11 (its cost and delay, equity deviations and inefficient continuation) are shown to do little harm or to be even welfare improving as they increase the incentives for parties to renegotiate out-of-court and to choose private debt. Hege and Mella-Barral conclude that the cost of a low-cost reorganization procedure is likely to be positive in a market-based financial system.

In Chapter 22, Lucian Bebchuk introduces the idea of employing options in corporate bankruptcy, a proposal that he puts forward to reduce the severity of the creditor bargaining problems described in Chapter 11. Bebchuk's view is that corporate insolvency should be implemented through the distribution of appropriately designed options. He argues that the reorganization process under the existing bargain-based rules, is costly and time-consuming, contributing to the deterioration of the firm's asset value. Moreover, the bargaining-based approach often results in a division of value that derives from pre-bankruptcy priorities. The introduction of an options procedure, mandating the allocation of a fixed number of shares of the distressed firm's equity, would improve efficiency by supplying creditors with the incentives necessary to value the firm appropriately. The number of shares issued should be equal to the face value of equal proportion of all senior claims. As a consequence of exercising the options, it will be possible for the company to emerge from the bankruptcy process. This may in turn induce the company's shareholders to pursue an efficient course of action, namely maximizing firm value. The options procedure provides the key to the emergence of a reorganization approach that is ultimately welfare enhancing.

3.6. *The Role of Institutional Investor in Corporate Governance*

In Chapter 23, Roberta Romano critically assesses the impact of institutional investor activism in corporate governance activities in the USA. The shareholder participation movement has had modest success. Institutional investors have challenged the authority of managers of firms by making use of a federally-mandated privilege to have shareholder governance proposals included in the management's annual proxy statement and submitted to a vote. Since the 1980s, public pension funds and other institutions have submitted proposals to eliminate defensive tactics to takeovers, to adopt proxy voting, to enhance board independence, and to restrict executive compensation to many firms. More recently, unions are more involved than public pension funds in sponsoring proposals. As these discrete, issue-based interventions have become more important as means to exert pressure on management, economists have attempted to measure the impact of the proposals on the performance of targeted firms. Romano evaluates the corporate law and finance literature that shows that shareholder proposals have little impact on targeted firms' performance. These results are especially surprising because both activists and economists have been extremely positive about the role of shareholder activism in corporate governance.

Possibly, because the empirical findings were so different from the normative literature, some commentators have attempted to reconcile the diverse empirical studies. Yet others, such as Bernard Black, have been less reluctant to accept the normative implications of these studies. In contrast to his earlier view, Black doubts the significance of shareholder activism. A number of factors explain their limited impact: (1) precatory proposals are ignored by management; (2) institutional investors are poorly organized and do not understand well the issues they propose; (3) and the general level of activism is modest. Romano challenges Black's position, arguing that the precatory content of shareholder proposals does not explain the insignificant price effects. Moreover, she argues that institutional investors are often very knowledgeable and some may actually benefit from submitting worthless proposals. Although noting the level of shareholder activism tends to be low, she counters that it is the objective of their activism that is responsible for the absence of a positive price effect. This causation analysis provides an analytical framework to her main argument that most corporate governance structures, which are the subject of shareholder proposals, may not work to produce positive results. On the positive side, Romano recommends the adoption of a mechanism of internal control wherein institutional investors review their shareholder programme to determine which techniques are most effective. There is every reason to believe that these evaluations will yield more information and in turn improve the efficiency of a fund's activism. Moreover, Romano proposes a change in the Securities Exchange Commission (SEC) proxy rules that would require a proposal to obtain substantial voter support before receiving proxy expense reimbursement. Her proposal is attractive because it would shift incentives which could lead to changes in the shareholder proposal regime.

In Chapter 24, Geoff Stapledon and Jonathan Bates explain the difficulties that UK institutional investors face when voting their shares. The evidence shows that institutions hold more than 70 per cent of shares in UK listed companies. Even though UK institutions are not mandated to vote their shares, there is increasing interest among investors to vote their shares. Still, there are a number of factors that account for the difficulty of institutions exerting their voting rights. The main problem is that while institutions invest in shares, the share custodian's name is entered in the company register. This has led to a costly process whereby institutional voting instructions were routed to custodians. Stapledon and Bates offer a proposed revision of the law that involves a clear distinction between the operational (share-voting) and property incidents of shareholding. The reform promises to reduce the costs and simplify the process by eliminating the transfer of documentation and voting instructions from custodian to institutional investor.

Mara Faccio and Ameziane Lasfer examine the role of blockholders, and more specifically that of occupational pension funds, in corporate governance in Chapter 25. They report that, on the one hand, pension funds do not add value to the companies in which they hold large stakes, while on the other hand, these occupational pension funds, despite the relatively poor performance of the companies in which they invest, do not opt for an 'exit' strategy. Faccio and Lasfer show that pension funds are 'locked in': it is costly to monitor because their holdings tend to represent relatively small fractions of the total values of the funds' assets. Still, they cannot also sell their holdings for fear of selling at a discount or conveying information to the market. They may also refrain from intervening on account of using insider information.

3.7. *Executive Compensation*

In Chapter 26, Martin Conyon and Kevin Murphy assess the differences in CEO pay and stock incentives in the USA and the UK. Over the last decade there has been a dramatic surge in CEO compensation in the USA. For example, CEOs of the largest US corporations earned compensation in 1998 that was 419 times as high as their respective employees (Loewenstein 2000). Conyon and Murphy show that American CEOs receive 35 per cent higher cash compensation and 121 per cent more in total compensation, after controlling for firm size, sector and management position, than UK CEOs. Conyon and Murphy doubt that traditional principal–agent models can explain the differences in levels of managerial pay.

CEO compensation arrangements in the USA and UK contain many of the same elements: base salaries, share option grants, annual bonuses, long-term incentive plan share awards, and benefits. Still, the level and structure of compensation in the USA and UK are significantly different for the following reasons. First, Conyon and Murphy explain that the divergences in top wages in the UK and US are due to differences in corporate tax deductibility rules, which encourages option compensation in the USA while discouraging the practice in the UK. Second, they identify economic, political, and cultural factors that encourage large share option grants in the USA. The authors conclude that the differences in international pay practices would not be a real issue if managerial labour markets were isolated. But competition in a global marketplace may encourage executives to migrate to the higher paid labour markets.

In Chapter 27, Rafel Crespi, Carles Gispert, and Luc Renneboog examine the relationship between top executive cash-based compensation and corporate performance for the market-oriented and control-oriented systems of governance in Europe. Arguably, one might expect a stronger relationship between pay and corporate performance in market-oriented than in control-oriented regimes. Surprisingly (but in line with other UK research), they show that in UK companies with high control concentration, there was no signification pay-for-performance relation uncovered. The CEO's cash remuneration in the UK is strongly related to sales growth but not to the creation of shareholder value. Executive compensation in Spain (an example of a blockholder-oriented system) does not appear to depend solely on corporate sales growth but relies to a large extent on share price and accounting performance. Crespi, Gispert, and Renneboog show that executive directors of Spanish firms controlled by strong groups will benefit from large increases in cash remuneration provided that these executive directors generate significant shareholder value. However, this positive relation is only valid in so far as share returns exceed those of their industry peers. For Spanish firms without high control concentrations, modifications in managerial remuneration depend upon changes in accounting returns in prior years. Thus, in these companies, the lack of blockholders allows management more discretion to employ remuneration benchmarks that can be more easily adjusted to increase short-term profitability in order to maximize executive compensation. So, it seems that an efficient remuneration scheme is not a substitute to large shareholder monitoring, but large monitoring shareholders are needed to impose a compensation policy providing management with the right incentives to create value.

In Chapter 28, Piet Duffhues, Rezaul Kabir, Gerard Mertens, and Peter Roosenboom explain why stock-based compensation had been so limited in the Netherlands until the mid-1990s. Over the last few years, however, the recent rise of stock options in CEO compensation led to a sharp rise in criticism from political parties and interest groups. In response to the sharp debate about the appropriate use and level of stock option awards, policymakers and other reformers recommended increased disclosure standards on CEO compensation and employee stock options for listed firms. Against this background, Duffhues,

Kabir, Mertens, and Roosenboom examine the compensation practices of Dutch companies for the fiscal year 1998. Based on their sample of 168 industrial firms listed on the Amsterdam Exchanges, they show that executive board members and top executives hold 73 per cent of the total employee stock options. In terms of analysing the options and pay-for-performance link, they show that employee stock option grants strongly correspond to a firm's accounting performance. In addition, they find evidence that the introduction of stock option schemes leads to higher subsequent operating performance.

4. CONCLUSION

The debate on convergence and diversity in corporate governance regimes and capital markets has forced us to reconsider our assumptions on which legal rules and institutions promote efficiency and social welfare. The contributions to this book have offered insights on the different approaches to the problem of the role of boards of directors, the importance of capital markets in corporate governance, the position of institutional investors in corporate governance, the practice of executive compensation, the optimal design of bankruptcy law, and the problem of separation of ownership and control. The essays in this volume, which present new ideas from a number of disciplines, will contribute to the new research on comparative corporate governance.

References

Allen, F., and Gale, D. (2000). Corporate governance and competition. In X. Vives (ed.), *Corporate Governance, Theoretical and Empirical Perspectives.* Cambridge: Cambridge University Press.

Bebchuk, L., and Roe, M. (1999). A theory of path dependence in corporate law. *Stanford Law Review* 52: 127.

Becht, M., and Mayer, C. (2001). The control of corporate Europe. In F. Barca and M. Becht (ed.), *The Control of Corporate Europe.* Oxford: Oxford University Press.

Berglöf, E. (1997). Reforming corporate governance: redirecting the European agenda. *European Forum* 93: 92.

Coffee, J. C. (1999). The future as history: the prospects for global convergence in corporate governance and its implications. *Northwestern University Law Review* 93: 641.

Deakin, S. (2001). Regulatory competition versus harmonization in European company law. In D. Esty and D. Geradin (ed.), *Regulatory Competition and Economic Integration, Comparative Perspectives.* Oxford: Oxford University Press.

Easterbrook, F., and Fischel, D. (1991). *The Economic Foundations of Corporate Law.* Cambridge, MA: Harvard University Press.

Edwards, J., and Nibler, M. (2000). Corporate governance in Germany: the role of banks and ownership concentration. *European Forum* 239.

Fox, M., and Heller, M. (2000). Corporate governance lessons from Russian enterprise fiascoes. *New York University Law Review* 75: 1720.

La Porta, R., Lopez-de-Silanes, F., and Shleifer, A. (1998). Law and finance. *Journal of Political Economy* 106: 1113.

——— ——— ——— (1999). Corporate ownership around the world. *Journal of Finance* 54: 471.
Loewenstein, M. J. (2000). The Conundrum of Executive Compensation. *Wake Forest Law Review* 35: 1.
Milhaupt, C. J. (1998). Property rights in firms. *Virginia Law Review* 84: 1145.
Whincop, M. (2001). *An Economic and Jurisprudential Genealogy of Corporate Law*. Aldershot: Ashgate.
Zingales, L. (1998). Corporate governance. In P. Newman (ed.), *New Palgrave Dictionary of Economics and the Law*. London: Macmillan Reference Ltd.

PART I

LEGAL CONVERGENCE OF CORPORATE GOVERNANCE REGIMES

2

Comparative Corporate Governance and Barriers to Global Cross Reference

WILLIAM W. BRATTON AND JOSEPH A. McCAHERY

1. INTRODUCTION

In these globalizing times corporate law's leading question is whether one or another national corporate governance system possesses relative competitive advantage. The question arises in the wake of stepped-up competition in international product markets. Such competition is intense enough to make it plausible to project that the different national governance systems pursuant to which firms are managed and capitalized will become factors at the margin of competitive survival. If only the fittest governance practices can survive in the global market, it also becomes plausible to project that systemic differences will disappear as national governance systems converge upon those fittest practices. Related questions about relative competitive advantage and convergence to best practice come up in domestic policy discussions in many countries. Concerns about local firms' performance in international markets brings attention to alternative governance practices identified in international comparisons: If comparative advantage lies elsewhere, then domestic practice should be reformed to follow the international leader.

An extensive body of studies addresses these questions, identifying and evaluating national variations in management and financial practices, industrial organization, and corporate and securities laws. Unfortunately even as the descriptions have become thicker and more cogent, answers to the bottom-line questions respecting competitive advantage have become more elusive and convergence predictions have become more qualified. Working hypotheses have changed rapidly, more in response to external events than to developments in the discourse. American observers early in the 1990s looked to Japanese governance practices for guidance for the reform of their domestic market governance system, then viewed to be in the throes of a productivity crisis (Kester 1997: 227–8, 239–41; Porter 1997: 6–8). Now American observers comment on their system's robust ability to self-correct in the wake of external shocks (Boot and Macey 1998; Gilson 1998: 205–6) and wait for signs of market-style reform in Japan (Milhaupt 2001: 2108–19; West 2001). The change in view corresponds to the comings and goings of national economic distress: The USA started the 1990s in a severe recession that tested the resilience of its corporate institutions; Japan has experienced an intensifying economic and institutional crisis as the decade has progressed. Views about the likelihood of convergence also have changed. Although some observers still project convergence as an imminent possibility (Hansmann and Kraakman, Chapter 3, this volume; Kester 1996: 123–4), many now offer reasons why convergence should not be expected (Bebchuk and Roe 1999; Roe, Chapter 5, this volume).

Comparative governance has this tentative, reactive quality because no one has any direct, empirical answers to its basic questions. It follows that the principal assertions made in comparative discussions—claims respecting relative competitive advantage, the appropriate course of national level law reform, and the likelihood and shape of systemic convergence—cannot be falsified. They can be evaluated only indirectly, through appraisal of the theories of the firm and of competitive evolution that support them. Unsurprisingly, the comparative governance literature holds out alternative theoretical frameworks that support conflicting hypotheses.

The theoretical approach commanding widest acceptance looks at the prevailing national governance regimes and sees suboptimal performance caused by the operation of political forces over time. It thereby dismisses the possibility of evolutionary efficiency in its account of the status quo (Roe 1996: 643–62). But it nevertheless holds out a brighter future of productive cross reference between the two prevailing types of national systems: (a) 'Market' systems, obtaining mainly in English-speaking countries and characterized by widely-dispersed shareholding and thick, liquid trading markets; and (b) 'Blockholder' systems, obtaining with many variations in Europe, East Asia, and most other capitalist economies and characterized by control in insider coalitions or wealthy families and thin trading of non-controlling stakes (Becht and Mayer 2001; Roe 2001). The assertion is that each system can and should learn from the other—the failures of market governance systems can be ameliorated through interpolation of devices from blockholder systems and devices from market systems can ameliorate the failures of blockholder systems (Aoki 1990: 23–4; Roe 1994: 187–94). Restated as a convergence projection, this cross-reference hypothesis implies that global competition will cause the emergence of a hybrid best practice. It also suggests that we should assume in the meantime that the market and blockholder systems possess equal competitive fitness.

The leading opposition hypothesis proceeds in the neoclassical microeconomic mode to assert that market systems reflect the operation of efficient evolutionary processes (Miller 1997; Macey 1998*a*; Ramseyer 1998). Here, product market competition remains the causal mainspring but has a more powerful effect, supporting an assertion that the systemic differences identified as material in the cross-reference hypothesis are irrelevant. It follows that countries with market systems should avoid borrowing from blockholder systems and stick to internally-generated governance reform agendas. Convergence is a certainty from this perspective, but takes the particular form of worldwide hegemony for market institutions (Hansmann and Kraakman, Chapter 3, this volume).

This chapter advances a case for a third hypothesis. Under this view, we cannot safely project either global convergence that eliminates systemic differences or the emergence of a hybrid best practice. This is because each national governance system is a system to a significant extent. Different governance systems have incentive structures that entail different trade-offs—trade-offs between ownership concentration and liquidity, between monitoring and management initiative, and between private rent-seeking and activity benefiting shareholders as a group. The trade-offs delimit opportunities for productive cross reference. More particularly, blockholder systems subsidize monitoring by permitting blockholders to reap private benefits of control through self-dealing and insider trading. Market systems, in contrast, regulate such private rent-seeking toward the end of maintaining an institutional framework that supports diffuse share ownership and thick trading markets. It follows that a legal framework conducive to blockholding may be ill equipped to foster dispersed equity ownership and thick trading markets, and that a legal framework conducive to liquid trading markets may have properties that discourage blockholding.

This chapter, then, asserts that each system, rather than consisting of a loose collection of separable components, is tied together by a complex incentive structure. Interdependencies between each system's components and the incentives of its actors create significant barriers to cross reference to and from other systems. The cross-reference hypothesis, in contrast, presupposes divisible corporate institutions—a world in which one system's components can be adapted for use in the other system without significant frictions or perverse effects.

As it makes this case, the chapter draws on economic theory and the pertinent empirical studies to highlight assumptions and analytical infrastructure heretofore obscured in legal literature on comparative governance. This results in a taxonomy of comparative governance's leading assertions. Encapsulated as 'the corporate governance matrix', this framework imports transparency to the increasingly complicated subject matter, facilitating a more neutral appraisal of its conflicting positions.

Section 2 of the chapter recounts the results of the corporate governance comparison, describing the elements that distinguish market and blockholder systems. Section 3 looks at comparative corporate governance's theoretical infrastructure. Here, we compare and contrast the assumptions and assertions basic to both the cross-reference hypothesis and the neoclassical critique. We also draw on the economics of systemic convergence to show the thin theoretical foundation underlying strong convergence predictions. Comparative governance emerges as a debate over two closely-related points. Participants make basic choices between (a) the strong and weak convergence perspectives, and (b) alternative descriptions of governance institutions as either divisible and fitted for cross reference or indivisible and not so fitted. We plot these four positions on a matrix that shows four contrasting perspectives and go on to consider the taxonomy's implications for corporate governance debates. Section 4 lays foundations for a case against cross reference. Here, we show how existing comparative studies confirm the salience of barriers to cross reference—such as the shareholder free rider problem in market systems and the provision of private benefits of control in blockholder systems—without offering any cogent suggestions as to how they might be overcome. Section 5 concludes.

2. THE CORPORATE GOVERNANCE COMPARISON

This Section sets out the results of the governance comparison, describing the interrelated strengths and weaknesses of the market and blockholder systems and reporting on the findings of empirical studies. Bottom-line results turn out to be thin: We have no empirical basis for ascribing comparative advantage to either system, and most observers accordingly assume the systems to be equally competitively fit.

2.1. *Elements of Market Systems*

Market corporate governance systems are characterized by dispersed equity holding,[1] a portfolio orientation among equity holders, and a broad delegation to management of discretion to operate the business. Ownership and control are separated. This leads to two chronic productivity disadvantages.

The first disadvantage is the shareholder-management agency problem. Collective action problems prevent close monitoring of management performance by widely-dispersed shareholder owners holding small stakes. Imperfect performance incentives result for managers, who may rationally sacrifice shareholder value to pursue their own agendas. The classic case of this occurred with the American conglomerate firms of a generation ago: Managers built large empires by making investments that yielded uncompetitive returns and sacrificed shareholder value even as they caused the firm to grow (Porter 1997). Market systems provide three principal corrective mechanisms to address this management incentive problem and ameliorate the structural barrier to direct shareholder oversight. These are the hostile takeover, derivative lawsuits against management self-dealing,[2] and the inclusion of outside monitors on boards of directors (Berglöf 1998; Coffee 1999). The second productive disadvantage of the market system is a time-horizon cost that stems from the shareholders' tendency to rely on short-term performance numbers. This problem has been attributed to information asymmetries. Management has superior information respecting investment policy and the firm's prospects, but this information tends to be either soft or proprietary and therefore cannot credibly be communicated to actors in trading markets.[3] It has been said that management as a result is disinclined to make long-term capital investments necessary for international competitiveness. The problem becomes more severe as the takeover deterrent becomes more vigorous, causing managers to look for quick fixes to keep the shareholders satisfied (Porter 1997: 5–6). To restate this point in more general terms, market systems fail to provide clear-cut protections to managers who make firm-specific investments of human capital (Boot and Macey 1998: 219–24), a failure due in part to the system's reliance on takeovers, proxy fights, and boardroom coups to control agency costs (Roe 2001).

Market systems have countervailing advantages. Their shareholders can cheaply reduce their risk through diversification. Relative to shareholders in blockholder systems, they receive high rates of return. The systems' deep trading markets facilitate greater shareholder liquidity (Rajan and Zingales 1998*b*: 559). These capital markets also facilitate corporate finance, providing management with greater flexibility as to the type and sources of new capital than do markets in blockholder systems (Berglöf 1998: 113). More generally, they provide an environment relatively more conducive to management entrepreneurship, as reflected in increased investment in new technologies. Finally, although market system shareholders and their outside-director agents cannot access full information about firm operations, their very distance from operations yields a countervailing benefit. Distance makes them relatively immune to capture by the management interest and assures objective evaluation of the information they do receive (Boot and Macey 1998: 214–15). A practice of objective evaluation means relatively fewer barriers to disinvestment and related features of downside restructuring (Porter 1997: 11–12; Roe 1996: 650; Gilson 1998: 216–17).

2.2. *Elements of Blockholder Systems*

Blockholder systems are characterized by majority or near-majority holdings of stock held in the hands of one, two, or a small group of large investors.[4] In Europe, the largest block investors tend to be individuals or rich families, with nonfinancial firms and banks making a secondary appearance in some countries, particularly Germany and Sweden.[5] In the Japanese keiretsu system of blockholding, in contrast, individual and family holders are not prominent. There, blockholding means aggregations of smaller blocks than in Europe, held by (a) clusters of banks having lending relationships with the issuer firm, and (b) clusters of other nonfinancial companies in many cases in supplier or customer relationships[6] with the issuer. These corporate holders often belong to a formal keiretsu organization along with the issuer, ameliorating collective action problems.[7]

Blockholder systems, like market systems, leave management in charge of the business plan and operations.[8] But large-block investments imply a closer level of shareholder monitoring.[9] In addition, the coalescence of voting power in a small number of hands means earlier, cheaper intervention in the case of management failure (Aoki 1990: 14–17; Gilson and Roe 1993: 880). The systems' other primary benefit stems from the blockholders' ability to access information about operations. This lessened information asymmetry permits blockholders to invest more patiently (Porter 1997: 10–11). The longer shareholder time-horizon in turn frees management to invest for a long term and creates a more secure environment for firm-specific investments of human capital by the firm's managers.[10]

There are corresponding costs and limitations. Where the blockholders are firms, internal agency costs can constrain their effectiveness as monitors (Roe 1996: 649). Indeed, whatever the identity of the blockholder, its heightened oversight incentive does not appear in practice to be strong enough to prompt sharp oversight of management investment policy.[11] Although closer proximity lessens the information asymmetry problem, there is an accompanying increase in management influence and loss of critical objectivity (Boot and Macey 1998: 237–8). Freedom to make long-term investments thus often means pursuit of growth in market share at the cost of a suboptimal rate of return on equity investment.[12] Trading markets in blockholder control countries tend to be thinner than in market control countries (Van der Elst 2000), and firms in search of financing encounter a more restricted range of alternatives Saunders and Schmeits 2002: 11–18. Meanwhile, the blockholders themselves give up the benefits of diversification and, given thin trading markets, liquidity and the possibility of easy exit through sale (Berglöf 1998: 96). Finally, there is a shortage of loyalty. Blockholders, having sacrificed diversification and liquidity, extract a return in the form of private benefits yielded through self-dealing or insider trading (Bebchuk 1999). Legal regimes in blockholder states facilitate this quid pro quo with lax protection of minority shareholder rights and lax securities market regulation (La Porta *et al.* 1997*a, b*; 1998; 1999*a, b*). This in turn chills the development of robust trading markets.

2.3. *Empirical Studies, Comparative Advantage, and Equal Competitive Fitness*

Which of the two systems, market or blockholder, has comparative advantage? Most comparative governance discussants decline to answer this question, preferring a working hypothesis of equal competitive fitness. Caution dictates this position in part. Relative productivity advantage is at bottom an empirical question. Although there is an impressive and growing body of empirical studies comparing different aspects of national governance systems, the studies have not yet attempted to compare productivity.[13] Instead the studies use comparative data to try to establish causal connections between shareholder protection practices and other structural aspects of governance and finance. For example, one line of inquiry tests national systems against a multipart checklist designed to measure the level of investor protection (La Porta *et al.* 1998).

Items on the checklist include rules and practices respecting shareholder voting, legal protections against management self-dealing, creditors' rights, accounting rules, and enforcement practices. Application of the test shows that: (a) common law countries provide the strongest protection for investors; (b) France and similar civil law countries provide the weakest level of protection; and (c) Germany and similar civil law countries provide an intermediate level of protection.[14] The legal systems, thus differentiated, are then sorted again in accordance with data respecting capital markets. There results a strong positive correlation between the level of investor protection on the one hand, and the size and depth of the national securities market and the prevalence of dispersed shareholding on the other.[15] Weak investor protection, in contrast, corresponds with blockholding (La Porta *et al.* 1997*a*).[16] Other studies show analogous correspondences. The level of shareholder protection has been shown to relate directly to the size of the premium over the market price per share paid for a majority voting block, with higher premiums commanded in countries with weak protections (Zingales 1994; Nenova 2000). There also has been shown to be a direct connection between strong shareholder protections and the volume of initial public offerings. Conversely, relationships between Japanese firms and their main banks have been shown to result in reduced pain and easier financing during periods of financial distress (Hoshi *et al.* 1990; 1991; 1998).

What the studies tend to confirm, then, is the accuracy of the casual description of systemic differences, advantages, and disadvantages set out above. Subject to a couple of prominent exceptions, they do not purport to address the matter of comparative advantage among developed economies.[17] One exception is La Porta, Lopez-de-Silanes, and Shleifer's (1999*b*) finding of no significant relationship between per capita gross domestic product and the incidence of widely-held firms based on a study of twenty developed countries. An inference of equal competitive fitness arises. The second exception is a famous body of work by Kaplan (1994*a*, *b*) that looks at management replacement rates in the USA, Japan, and Germany. This finds no significant differences between the three countries and has been taken to imply equal competitive fitness. The respective systems' evolutionary survival in the context of national product markets is another fact that (albeit weakly) implies equal competitive fitness Windolf 1998: 713–14; Demirgue-Kunt and Maksimovic 1998: 2120–23; Rajan and Zingales 1995: 1422.

The informal comparison, recounted above, provides additional indirect support for the equal fitness hypothesis. Each system's weakness appears to be matched by a systemic strength on the other side, and vice versa, as the tables below illustrate. Table 2.1 shows, broadly, that stepped-up shareholder monitoring under the blockholder system comes at the cost of thick trading markets and associated benefits, and that thick trading markets exact a monitoring cost.

Table 2.1. *Monitoring versus markets*

	Market	Blockholder
Shareholder monitoring	Minus	Plus
Diversification	Plus	Minus
Liquidity	Plus	Minus
Shareholder legal rights	Plus	Minus
Thick trading markets	Plus	Minus

Table 2.2. *Investment policy/information asymmetry*

	Market	Blockholder
Short-term focus	Minus	Plus
Shareholder value focus	Plus	Minus
Long-term focus	Minus	Plus
Growth focus	Plus	Minus
Shareholder information level	Minus	Plus
Shareholder objectivity	Plus	Minus

Table 2.2 looks at management policy and shareholder information levels and highlights some points of tension in the comparison. Each system's investment minus is also its plus and each system's investment plus is also its minus.

Thus, the market system suffers from short termism because it sacrifices long-term projects to the demand for present shareholder value; meanwhile, the ability to deliver present shareholder value is the market system's plus. Conversely, the blockholder system suffers from an excessive growth focus because it does not concern itself with shareholder value; meanwhile, these suboptimal growth investments display the long-term time horizon said to be its plus. A similar plus-and-minus relationship prevails with shareholder information. Blockholding ameliorates information asymmetries, but the proximity that opens this access implies susceptibility to capture by the management interest and a loss of objectivity. Contrariwise, information asymmetries are more pronounced in market systems but shareholders (and director representatives) at a distance from managers evaluate firm performance with a clearer eye.

The literature explores the implications of the equal fitness hypothesis in two frameworks, one looking to global-level effects of competitive interaction among firms in international product markets, and the other looking to competitiveness in domestic contexts. Section 3 recounts and expands on these discussions.

3. FRAMEWORKS FOR COMPARING CORPORATE GOVERNANCE SYSTEMS—CONVERGENCE AND NONCONVERGENCE, CROSS REFERENCE AND INDIVISIBILITY

This Section proceeds as follows. Section 3.1 describes theoretical frameworks that facilitate projections of global convergence as to the terms of governance systems. Contrasting scenarios emerge. Some project a process of international cross reference that leads to a new hybrid system composed of elements drawn from both market and blockholder systems. Others assert the primacy of product market discipline and dismiss comparative governance policy inquiry as irrelevant, even as they assert evolutionary superiority for the market system and project its eventual emergence in global competition. Section 3.2 describes a contrasting analytical framework that projects persistent variation in national institutions even in a global economy. This approach, discussed in Section 3.3, is informed by social theory and second-best economics and rejects the technological determinism that informs projections of a unitary, global capitalism. It acknowledges the possibility of convergence, but at the same time emphasizes matters that make convergence unlikely, such as the embeddedness of national systems of production and political barriers to governance reform. Under this weak convergence perspective, comparative governance exercises have their primary bearing in domestic policy contexts. In Section 3.4, comparative governance emerges as a two-course menu. Participants make basic choices between (a) the strong and weak convergence perspectives, and (b) alternative descriptions of governance institutions as either divisible and fitted for cross reference or indivisible and not so fitted. In Section 3.5, we plot the four possible selections on a matrix that shows four contrasting perspectives. We then discuss the taxonomy's descriptive and normative implications.

3.1. *Comparative Analysis in a Global Framework: Strong Convergence and Irrelevance*

Many argue that the globalization of production, finance, and trade is causing national economies to converge as to performance and national economic institutions to converge as to form. Global competition, they say, will mean bigger markets calling for large and capital intensive but specialized producers, and necessitating cross-border collaboration among existing producing organizations (Boyer 1996: 47). These producers will access capital in financial markets uncoupled from national regulatory restraints (Milhaupt 1998: 1186–7). Innovative production technologies, like capital, will rapidly diffuse to firms worldwide. The same, they say, should follow for corporate governance institutions.

Many concrete examples of movement toward convergence of national governance systems can be cited to support this prediction, mostly resulting from cross-border investment and finance. For example, increasing numbers of firms from blockholder systems raise capital in securities markets in Britain and the USA and in consequence must conform to stricter accounting standards Licht 1998: 566. Some of these firms also have experienced pressure for American-style governance reform upon the acquisition of significant ownership stakes by American investment institutions (Bebchuk and Roe 1999). Conversely, American producers acquired by foreign firms have become subject to governance structures unique to blockholder systems (Baums 1999; Gordon 2000).

International cross reference also has become everyday practice in corporate policy debates. But here cross-border investment and finance did not provide the initial impetus. The first prominent round of discussions on comparative governance occurred in the USA in the early 1990s, prompted by a perception that shortcomings in domestic practice had contributed to American firms in several key sectors successfully to compete against foreign rivals (Porter 1997: 5–8).

Systemic shortcomings were alleged—the market system had operated in the USA in the 1980s to favour short-term increases in shareholder value and deter long-term investment in production processes. As a result, Japanese and German producers, who had invested more in search of growth, had a product market advantage. It was thought that America's short-term bias had arisen as perverse result of widespread hostile takeover activity in the 1980s. Ironically, by the early 1990s, new legal controls constrained takeovers, constraints that also deprived the governance system of a principal disciplinary device. It was thought that America therefore needed to look abroad for additional means of agency cost control if it was to reestablish a competitive position. It made sense to make reference to the systems whose firms were seen to be beating American firms in product markets—systems which had not evolved so as to rely on takeovers. Thus did European and Japanese practices of bank monitoring, cross holding, and blockholding present themselves as simultaneous correctives for both short-term investment bias and the takeover's decline.

Today's Europeans in effect return the favour, looking to the corporate governance institutions of the United States (and Britain) to improve the quality of boardroom operations and enhance the depth and liquidity of their trading markets (Lannoo 1999). Toward this end, the Italian government promulgated a package of securities and corporate government law reforms in 1998 (Macey 1998*b*: 692–3, Coffee 1999: 665–6). Japan has removed both process restrictions that inhibited shareholder derivative actions (West 1994) and legal restrictions on share issuance that prevented issuers from including stock options in management compensation arrangements (Milhaupt 1998: 1188–9). American-style shareholder activism also is spreading. French shareholders have been forming associations, initiating inquiries, and questioning entrenched practices (Pastre 1998: 86–8).

The list of confirming examples, although impressive, does not tell us much about the degree, character, and speed of the convergence being projected. Cross-border stock listing and merger and acquisition activity, for example, can continue to increase without entailing systemic convergence. The French or German company that avails itself of the New York or London equity market remains rooted in its blockholder system of origin even as it makes some governance concessions. Indeed, such a firm's very resort to a cross-border transaction to raise equity capital demonstrates the continuing salience of systemic differences. A convergence event does occur when the firm consents to a change in its governing rules. But this is convergence on a company-specific basis rather than at the level of a national system. Managers of multinational firms have for decades been making reference to international sources and engineering changes in internal governance processes that similarly imply convergence. In all of these cases, the firm's home governance system continues unchanged. Note that the convergence events such as these occur in the new global venue—in the world of transnational linkages generated by actors in a handful of international business centres that provide financial and corporate services on a global basis (Sassen 1998: 194–214). The vast majority of such linkages, to the extent that they entail legal obligations, rely on conventional national systems to guarantee contract and property rights and to create and define juridical corporations. Such global transactions and actors interact with and influence national systems but have not as yet fundamentally transformed them.

Other items on the list of confirming examples more directly signal possibilities for the convergence of national systems. Thickening trading markets and related law reform initiatives make the German and Italian blockholder systems more market-like; the USA's institutional investor movement seeks a more blockholder-like environment. Counter-anecdotes can be cited, however. The USA's institutional investor movement succeeded more in changing academic theory than in changing embedded market system practices Romano, Chapter 23, this volume. Europe-wide law reform in the form of EU directives related to insider-trading and disclosure of significant ownership stakes has been hobbled by slow implementation and indifferent compliance (Standen 1995; McCahery 1997; Coffee 1999: 669–71).

To catalogue anecdotes, then, is to collect evidence of both global convergence and persistent national differentials. The collected anecdotes provide little basis for projecting convergence's degree, character, and speed. To move beyond cataloguing and evaluate the anecdotes' meaning requires reference to a theoretical framework. To make that reference is to encounter three schools of thought, each supporting a different projection. The schools are: (a) A strong global perspective that posits a determinative causal link between corporate governance institutions and the competitive survival of firms in international product markets and stresses both the importance of governance reform and the possibility of successful systemic cross reference; (b) An irrelevance perspective that posits the same causal link but dismisses the importance of governance reform and the value of systemic cross reference; and (c) A weak convergence perspective that emphasizes impediments to the realization of at-the-margin competitive dynamics at the global level and questions the inevitability of institutional convergence. The strong convergence and irrelevance perspectives are discussed below. The weak convergence scenario and the closely related national framework of comparative corporate governance inquiry are discussed in Section 3.4.

3.2. *Strong Convergence and Productive Cross Reference*

Strong globalization scenarios depict national economic systems as firms competing in a frictionless world market that brings national institutions to the margin that determines competitive success or failure. Such a market does not in fact obtain in the real world, of course. But, citing growing international product competition, financial deregulation, and trade liberalization, many now hold this global, at-the-margin model to provide a plausible basis for making predictions about the future development of national economies (Ohmae 1991: 161–2). A series of projections follow. Under the law of a single price, each commodity should carry the same price throughout the world market and production costs should equalize worldwide. Given free trade and complete diffusion of technical knowledge, national productivity levels and growth rates also should converge, even assuming continued barriers to the movement of labour and capital (Boyer 1996: 30–1).

This model also projects that competition and emulation among producers will lead to homogenous institutional settings. Since coordination mechanisms, including corporate governance arrangements, figure into production costs, the viability of the best arrangements and innovations will be tested and proved in product and factor markets. Rational actors responding to price competition will seek to design or emulate optimal arrangements.[18] Actors and firms that fail to adopt these superior organizational technologies will in the short run lose money and in the long run disappear (Bebchuk and Roe 1999). Diffusion of knowledge respecting the best practices will follow as a practical matter from contacts among multinational managers, consultants, and lawyers, along with government actors and academics (Boyer 1996: 57). Accordingly, the only cognizable barrier to actual convergence to best practice comes from government controls (Ramseyer 1998: 544) like trade barriers and corporate governance mandates. More generally, to the extent that convergence proves to be slow or uncertain, it must be that government actors or rent-seeking interest groups are using resources generated outside of markets to sustain distinctive national institutions (Berger 1996: 1).

These predictions, if robust, imply a dividing point in the history of corporate governance systems. We come to a moment—whether in the immediate past, the present, or in the near future—at which intensifying competition in international product markets for the first time turns endowments derived from national systems into factors relevant to firms' competitive survival. Once this industrial divide is crossed, the identification of a material difference between two systems' governance practices gives rise to the possibility, first, of long-run relative competitive advantage for firms organized in one of the systems (and disadvantage for those in the other), and, secondly, of a need to reform the system not presently endowed with the better practice.[19] The exercise of comparison thus facilitates a just-in-time intervention that gives the firm or system with a comparative disadvantage a chance to self-correct at an early stage in the history of the global market.

Note also that once the divide is crossed, formerly irrelevant differences in governance practice start to bear on competitive fitness. To see this, continue to take a neoclassical, first-best view of the effects of product market competition, and assume further that governance institutions bear on product cost and that national product competition is keen, but that there is little or no international trade. It follows for any given nation that domestic firms following inferior governance practices have already disappeared or will do so forthwith. To the extent that all surviving firms within a given national system follow a common set of practices, the practices do not lie at the margin of competitive survival even if they are inferior to practices followed abroad. International product markets remain too thin to bring them to the margin. If we now change the facts and interpose expanding international product markets, there follows a projection of a second round of competitive testing in the global venue for the governance institutions of firms organized within each national system. National practices until now irrelevant to competitive fitness become relevant. No inference of competitive advantage in the new international environment arises from the fact of national-level survival. Identification of a point of difference between national systems can as easily imply future competitive disadvantage as advantage for a given set of national firms.

In a Coasean world, each competing firm would restructure itself and the necessary adjustments would occur on an informal, decentralized basis. In the real world, in contrast, law and political processes will matter for the adjustment of corporate governance institutions in the new global venue. Law influences shareholder protection, agency cost control, and the investment behaviour of financial intermediaries and blockholders, and thereby the form and relative effectiveness of governance arrangements of firms organized in a particular national framework. It follows that law reform can figure importantly in a given national system's adjustment process. Assuming no political barriers, it follows that convergence to best practice can be projected not only for firms' internal arrangements, but for national corporate law regimes (Bebchuk and Roe 1999: 2–3).

These strong convergence projections presuppose a high degree of technological determinism. In the world they posit all firms face the same optimizing problems and seize on the same solutions.[20] This adaptive dynamic in turn depends on the assumption of a pervasive high-powered incentives to innovate. This assumption, however, comes into tension with the equal competitive fitness hypothesis, discussed above. If they the systems are equally fit, it could follow that their differences, even their most prominent differences, are irrelevant to productivity.[21] Consider the fact that the market and blockholder systems share an inability to reduce the agency costs of management to zero even if they treated these costs differently. By hypothesis, then, each system could be reducing agency costs to roughly the same level at roughly the same cost. If all other systemic costs and benefits worked out roughly equally, then the differences among the systems would not impact on bottom-line results, at least until a change in the prevailing economic context caused the situation of cost equality to change. In this scenario, incentives to invest in innovative governance technologies arguably cannot be assumed: If nothing disturbs the equilibrium, corporate governance does not matter at the margin. It follows that the strong convergence proponent who subscribes to the equal competitive fitness view must articulate a plausible scenario that highlights a generative incentive to invest in governance reform.

The missing incentive lies encased in the prediction that competitive evolution will result in a new, hybrid system that adopts the best practices on an international menu (Aoki 1990: 23–4; Roe 1994: 187–94). Proponents predict that, given imperfections in both present systems, there will likely ensue a process of borrowing and modification of components of existing systems. Certain features of certain national systems will come to be seen as possessing problem-solving advantages and come in for widespread adoption. The incentive to adopt follows from the ordinary stress to reduce costs felt by actors under competitive pressure.

This is plausible enough, but one further operative assumption needs to be highlighted. For governance cross reference to hold out advantageous solutions in which business actors willingly invest, the existing systems must have divisible components. That is, a particular feature (or innovation) must be detachable from one system and adaptable to another (Kester 1996: 108–9). If the systems in fact are divisible, then the cross reference hypothesis emerges as robust. Policy discussion should indeed anticipate the hybrid's likely composition so as to identify barriers to its realization. Moreover, assuming intense global product competition and no other significant frictions, the systems should indeed converge in their broad outlines over time.[22]

3.3. *Irrelevance*

The connection just drawn between a strong convergence scenario and the cross-reference hypothesis has been controverted by an irrelevance contention following from neoclassical microeconomic assumptions.

Chicago School critics suggest that governance reform by cross reference at best would be a wasted effort and at worst could injure market systems (Miller 1997: 44–5). They posit a global marketplace just as (and perhaps more) competitive than that posited in the strong convergence story. Here, again product competition determines firm survival and any governance arrangement that hobbles a competitor with excess costs causes failure. But here it follows that firms not only must choose optimal governance arrangements in order to survive, but also that governance problems take care of themselves in the long run. In that long run, therefore, corporate governance policy enquiries are irrelevant.[23] Let us take a step away from the margin and introduce a small measure of room in which firms with different practices having positive cost implications can survive over an intermediate term. Here, the relevance of the comparative exercise depends on the observer's point of view. An observer with an investment or citizenship stake in one of the competing systems might be quite interested to know whether it possesses the relatively inferior or relatively superior practice. But if one changes perspectives and looks at the competing systems from a general efficiency point of view, then the comparison loses its urgency once again. From this point of view, any needed corrections are assured in the long run, along with the concrete identification of the superior practice. Only if all systems produce deadweight losses due to some shared perverse feature does this point of view counsel intervention at the planning level. In the meantime, the differences between governance systems highlighted in comparative discussions are immaterial. This is because blockholder systems' components and behavioural characteristics can be explained by reference to the same microeconomic model that explains the components and characteristics of market systems.[24] Convergence at a substantively significant level already has occurred in effect. Differences obviously exist, but these always can be accounted for as adjustments to legal barriers (Easterbrook 1997: 29; Ramseyer 1998: 538).

This two-sided irrelevance assertion is accompanied by the claim that the USA's market system is substantively sound and not in need of reform (Macey 1998*b*: 124–5). Proponents of cross reference, it is argued, overreacted when they claimed at the beginning of the 1990s that recent legal constraints on hostile takeovers created a need to look to blockholder systems for alternative arrangements to control agency costs. Subsequent events have shown that the market system has adjusted very well: Takeover activity again breaks volume records; new strategies for hostile tender offers have been developed; and institutional activism has become a governance constant (Boot and Macey 1998: 220–2; Easterbrook 1997: 24–5). In the alternative, it is admitted that the subset of hostile takeover activity has decreased in the 1990s, but it is argued that the decrease does not make much difference. A potential acquirer with a better governance strategy ends up taking over the target one way or the other. If regulation forecloses the option of a hostile takeover, then the acquirer will win over recalcitrant members of the defending board with side payments disguised as consulting agreements or as nonsubstantive high paying jobs. Hostile takeovers accordingly are not the only means to the end of bringing new governance strategies to the firms that need them. Friendly mergers and acquisitions can substitute for them, with the sole difference going to the pattern of distribution of merger gain (Ramseyer 1998: 540–1).

Some commentators in this vein go a step farther to argue that market systems occupy a higher evolutionary plateau and are intrinsically superior to the blockholder alternative (Miller 1997: 38–41; Easterbrook 1997: 26; Macey 1998*b*: 124–5). Nothing in economic theory makes this assertion untenable: It may be that the market system does have superior properties of competitive fitness and will achieve hegemony after a period of competitive struggle. On this view, present policy discussion in this system's home venues should be directed to the preservation and enhancement of its comparative advantage. It also must be noted, however, that nothing in economic theory guarantees the correctness of this evolutionary superiority claim either. The equal competitive fitness hypothesis could turn out to be more accurate. All such assertions lie at the level of hypothesis, pending the appearance of a decisive empirical literature or the occurrence of the long run.

A point of tension between the evolutionary superiority claim and the irrelevance claim also should be noted. If policy choices respecting systemic structure are absolutely irrelevant, then, by hypothesis, the Anglo-Saxon market system cannot meaningfully be deemed to be evolutionarily superior. The systemic superiority claim implies not only relevance for policymaking but an emphatic policy agenda. Under this, the market system needs protection from forces of interest group rent-seeking, protection that should be secured in advance of the promotion of structural change inspired by reference to the more primitive systems of Japan and Germany.

3.4. *Weak Convergence and Comparative Governance in a National Framework*

3.4.1. *Barriers to Convergence and the Weak Convergence Perspective*

A third body of theory controverts both strong convergence hypotheses described above, rejecting their technological determinism even while acknowledging the existence and importance of the emerging global markets (Kester 1996: 108–9). This alternative approach also rejects the idea that a single production technology always must emerge as the winner (OECD 1998). It instead posits that there may be more than one way to solve a given technical problem. Expanding on this point, it also suggests that there can be more than one type of capitalism: Not only may different national systems of production be functionally equivalent and equally fit, but national differences may persist indefinitely.

This perspective draws on social as well as economic theory to depict national systems as tightly bundled packages of specific resources, institutions, and legacies. It does not deny the possibility of convergence to best practice. But it asserts that when such convergence does occur, it does not follow from the operation of a self-implementing mechanism like the at-the-margin adjustment process described in strong convergence theory.[25] Convergence instead occurs within limits set by national contexts. Accordingly, its effects are uncertain and varied, depending on precise configurations of markets, technical competencies, property rights institutions, and related incentives. Nor can we safely assume that a universal best practice will emerge and be adopted universally. A materially different national system can survive in a competitive global market by finding a niche suited to its particular endowments (Boyer 1996: 31, 50).[26] Alternatively, a national system may be disabled from adopting a productive technical innovation because the necessary implementing reform lacks political feasibility when mooted in the context of a tightly-fitted set of national institutions. Given barriers such as these, significant, context-breaking steps toward convergence are most likely to be taken during the political crisis that follows an external economic shock (Berger 1996: 18–19, 21).

This picture of intermittent movement toward convergence can be restated in the terms of second-best microeconomics. Movement is intermittent because competition operates imperfectly, hobbled by asymmetric information, contracting frictions, sunk costs, increasing returns to scale, and public goods problems.[27] Instead of a unique, global equilibrium, then, we should expect unstable, punctuated equilibria. Convergence can indeed occur—but so can autonomous evolution, partial catch up followed by collapse, or catch up followed by forging ahead. Strong convergence predictions, meanwhile, can credibly be made only if special conditions obtain, including costless availability of requisite technology, total divisibility of production institutions, and independent availability on the part of each such divisible, systemic component (Boyer 1996: 55–8).

This weak convergence perspective is supported by a body of comparative studies of production practices. These antedate the comparative governance literature by a generation, looking at the shop floor rather than the boardroom. They show that during the post-war era different capitalist economies developed fundamentally different firm organizations that produce the same products.[28] The different organizational patterns are accounted for as the product of domestic interactions between political and social interests and economic strategies (Boyer 1996: 45–6). These studies anticipate and parallel the corporate literature, articulating a set of distinctions between market-based production institutions in English-speaking countries and societally and state-coordinated systems of Germany and Japan (Berger 1996: 4).

Additional support for the weak convergence view comes from the endogenous growth school of macroeconomic theory. This approach rejects earlier models of technologically-driven convergence of growth rates. It instead posits an endogenous model under which each country's equilibrium growth path depends on contextual factors such as past investments in research and development and education. On this view, rates of productivity growth will vary from country to country and movement toward convergence only be expected given a base of similar educational endowments and technical policies.[29] The basic chronology that emerges from this research supports the proposition that strong convergence cannot be assumed as an historical constant. Boyer (1996: 41) summarizes the research to show that there was significant divergence among countries until the end of the nineteenth century. At the beginning of the twentieth century there was some convergence, but this was disrupted in the 1930s. Significant reduction of productivity differences is a more recent phenomenon. From the 1950s to the present there has been convergence in productivity. On the other hand, in the post-1973 era many newly developing countries have fallen behind similarly-situated countries due to external shocks and other problems. Given similar economies, convergence respecting productivity growth rates in fact has been demonstrated empirically. But the rate is slow: Given strong similarities the underlying speed of convergence has been estimated at 2 per cent per year, meaning that it takes 25 years for similar economies to reduce an initial productivity gap by 50 per cent (Barro and Sala-I-Martin 1991; Blanchard 1991).

The weak convergence view influences much recent commentary on comparative governance. It now is accepted that large, successful firms do not operate at the razor-thin margin assumed in strong convergence scenarios. When a competitor's superior governance arrangements yield a product market advantage, the disadvantaged firms do not automatically go out of business. They can instead offset the disadvantage by cutting supply or other production costs, returning less to their equity investors, or, as a last resort, by securing state subsidies (Bebchuk and Roe 1999: 161–2). More broadly, national systems hold out real and persistent barriers that can prevent the emergence of a hybrid corporate governance system, even a hybrid holding out productivity advantages. Each of selective incentives,[30] cost barriers, interest group politics, and structural interconnections among systemic components can contribute. It follows that the only safe projection is weak convergence—hybrid innovation that supplements existing systems without threatening vested interests or requiring law reform (La Porta *et al.* 1999*b*: 513).

3.4.2. *Comparative Governance in a National Framework*

The weak convergence perspective has strong negative implications for comparative governance analysis in a global framework. If convergence due to the operation of global market mechanisms is not a significant possibility, then there remains very little 'globalized' corporate governance subject matter to discuss. But the weak convergence perspective does not thereby imply that comparative corporate governance exercises are irrelevant. They retain pertinence in national policy frameworks.

At the national level, the question is whether alternative mechanisms identified in an international comparison can help domestic firms solve governance problems. Any such benefit need only be potential—an experimental possibility—in order to provide a functional justification for the comparative exercise (Roe 1994: 187–209). Indeed, so long as different outside practices have cost implications, actors with a financial stake in a given national system should have an intrinsic interest in trying them. This is because the outside practices open an opportunity for domestic competitive advantage, provided they are productively superior and not culturally, technically, or geographically bound to the country of origin. This justification obtains even in the absence of international competition. In this scenario, competitive survival is exclusively a function of the operation of domestic markets. A new source of advantage always will be welcome, whatever its national origin.

The equal competitive fitness hypothesis holds out no negative implications for this domestic exercise. Even if neither the market nor the blockholder system has an overall advantage, it may remain possible to identify material productivity differences among the systems' individual components. The fact that the systems' respective strengths and weaknesses tend to cancel one another out suggests that a plus factor in one system may yield a productivity advantage if transplanted to firms in the other system. This possibility is strengthened to the extent that the systems result from accidents of political history (Roe 1996: 644–5). American observers dissatisfied with the amount and quality of shareholder monitoring in mature domestic firms thus can look to the stockholding patterns and monitoring activities of financial institutions in Japan and Germany to support law reform directed to development of home grown institutional monitors. Contrariwise, Europe, aware that firms in the USA and Britain have the advantage of a wider array of financing modes and sources due to deeper domestic securities markets, can look to governance reform to build investor confidence in domestic securities markets so as to promote their growth.

National-level comparison, then, is a cross-reference exercise in which firms and regulators experiment with new, imported techniques—the same exercise carried out in the global framework under the rubric of convergence to best practice. The source of the competitive imperative differs in the national framework, however. In the global story, the incentive lies at the international level and implicates a near-term threat of serious competitive disadvantage for a given nation's producers as a whole.[31] In the national story the incentive lies in the search for national-level advantage, with global advantage coming to bear as an additional but not essential factor. If, for example, institutional monitoring holds a productivity advantage for American firms, then American firms presumably will want to try it—and will have an incentive to work toward the removal of costly regulatory underbrush—toward the end of gaining a cost advantage over domestic competitors. If no productivity advantage proves out, no one should be the worse off since the experiment can be abandoned quickly.

The national and global frameworks overlap in one other respect. An extensive pattern of cross-referenced domestic governance experimentation could mean incidental steps in the direction of global convergence to a superior, hybrid governance system composed of the best components of existing systems (Aoki 1990: 22–4; Berglöf 1998: 115–17). But these converging convergence stories originate in materially different theoretical frameworks. In the national framework, convergence emerges as an incidental possibility. No deterministic vision of global economic evolution is asserted. The national framework thus proceeds on a more robust, less demanding base of assumptions than does the global. It implies no particular evolutionary projection. It requires no risky appraisals of systemic productivity. Yet, it makes important contributions to domestic policy discussions about governance and productivity in many different countries.

But the national framework still makes a strong assumption when it commends domestic experimentation by cross reference. As noted above, cross reference only works if the different systems have divisible components. To the extent that national systems resemble the tightly-fitted complexes of diverse elements depicted in the weak convergence view, then divisibility cannot safely be assumed. Indeed, the plus-is-minus character of the two systems depicted in Tables 2.1 and 2.2 also do not necessarily imply complementarities. They suggests the presence of internal dependencies. Each system may result from interconnected trade-offs that result in an overall balance among the interests of its various participants. The balance thus struck may not be so easily adjusted.

Questions accordingly arise as to the likely returns on investments in cross-referenced experimentation. If corporate governance institutions tend to be indivisible, returns may be nonexistent because frictions prevent experiments from being carried out in practice or because such experiments as are carried out fail to bring improvements. Alternatively, losses could result if experimentation occurs but unforeseen interconnections among components within a given system lead to perverse effects.

3.5. *The Comparative Governance Matrix*

Stripped to essentials, comparative corporate governance may be seen as a two-course menu that offers two choices as to each course. One first chooses a convergence model, strong or weak. This choice has determinative implications for the framework in which comparison then proceeds. Strong convergence models imply that global competitive forces dominate national level evolution. Weak convergence implies determinative influence for national social and political institutions, but holds open a door for the homogenizing influence of competitive forces, whether domestic or global. The second menu item is divisibility. Here, one decides whether it makes sense to view national governance systems as open to significant modification by cross reference to other systems' components. This choice determines the policy implications of the comparative exercise—whether it looks toward or looks away from the development of hybrid governance structures. The menu implies four basic points of view respecting comparative governance. Table 2.3 plots out the possibilities.

Box (1). Strong convergence and divisibility combine to imply a projection of a hybrid but unitary governance system worldwide. Scepticism respecting near-or intermediate term convergence possibilities makes this a minority point of view. Indeed, it is virtually absent from the legal literature.

Box (2). Strong convergence combined with indivisibility implies competitive struggle between entire systems with one system winning in the end. This is the position advanced by Chicago School participants in both legal and economic discussions. A caveat needs to be entered about the binary characterization of the Chicago position, however. Presumably, a Chicago School observer would not object if a reforming blockholder system adopted market system components piecemeal. Cross reference enters the Chicago story to this extent. But it does so only at an intermediate point in the time line. In the end the superior properties of the market system overwhelm the blockholder antecedent and no hybrid appears. Such a market system triumph is most easily imagined in a crisis context: Economic distress leads to political disruption, the blockholder system cracks under the strain, and there follows root and branch reform designed to foster market institutions. Thus seen, the Chicago School's strong evolutionary superiority claim implies a long run assertion of indivisibility. In the short run, however, cross reference is a possibility but a productive possibility only if it goes one way. Thus do this perspective's proponents insistently warn of the potential perverse effects for market systems of experiments in cross reference.

Box (3). An observer who chooses weak convergence and divisible institutions makes reference to other governance systems as a means to the end of effecting domestic improvements. This perspective sees value in cross reference even as it abandons breathless projections of near-term international convergence. It is manifested both in leading American discussions of Japanese and European institutional investors (Roe 1994: 169–209) and in European law reform initiatives directed to improving the depth of securities markets and

Table 2.3. *The comparative governance matrix*

	Divisible	Indivisible
Strong convergence	(1) Global cross reference	(2) Chicago School
Weak convergence	(3) National cross reference	(4) National embeddedness

in responsive economic discussions (Berglöf 1998: 115–17). During most of the 1990s, it prevailed as the international mainstream approach.

Box (4). The fourth and final perspective pairs weak convergence with indivisibility to emphasize barriers to both convergence and cross-referenced governance reform at the national level. This perspective is reflected in the present literature on convergence (Boyer 1996: 45–58), but has shown up only sporadically in legal comparative governance discussions (Mark 1995: 993–8; Fanto 1996: 180–91; Woolcock 1996: 181–2). It is, however, a possibility explored in the economic literature (Aoki 1990: 23–4; Berglöf 1998: 113–16).

Reconsider now the two questions posed at the start of this chapter in the context of the four perspectives in the matrix. The first question goes to possibilities for convergence. We have seen that it remains open, but that the weak convergence predictions appear to be safer on the state of the empirical studies. These predictions nevertheless remain subject to the usual caveat respecting external shocks. Strong convergence perspectives persist based on indirect empirical support and, more importantly, on descriptive assumptions derived from microeconomic theory: The closer the attachment to the neoclassical model, the stronger the convergence claim. Contrariwise, social theorists predisposed to see persistent structures amidst thick institutional descriptions have a tendency to dismiss strong convergence claims.

The second question, which concerns relative competitive fitness, now can be restated: Which of the four perspectives implies a strategy for governance policy best calculated to enhance the productivity of individual firms? Empirical evidence matters here as well. But, as we have seen, present results remain too thin to provide a basis for an educated guess. The only strong empirical result—that significant outsider investment in firms presupposes the rule of law—does not help us to distinguish among the systems in developed countries. There also is indirect but cogent empirical backing for the equal competitive fitness hypothesis. But this result does little to help us choose a strategy either. We have seen that equal competitive fitness synchronizes well both with the global cross-reference (Box (1)) and national cross-reference (Box (3)) perspectives. It is compatible with the national embeddedness view (Box (4)) for the same reasons. Equal competitive fitness becomes an issue only with the Chicago School view of market superiority (Box (2)). Its indirect empirical supports provide a basis for arguing against the market superiority view, but do not suffice to falsify it.

We have, in short, no conclusive means to assign equal fitness to both systems, to assign relative advantage to one system, or even to assign equal or relative advantage to an internal component of either system. Nor can we falsify the assertions basic to any of the perspectives in the matrix. Each of the four thus retains some vitality, leaving the literature as a whole in a speculative posture.

The very existence of such a broad, active menu of possibilities underscores the determinative role that theory plays in this discourse. Recall, by way of example, that the cross-reference hypothesis derives credibility from the assumption that cost savings accruing from improved governance lend an incentive to experiment to business actors. Yet, absent hard numbers it remains difficult to appraise the magnitude of the incentive posited. Indeed, if the actors are not operating at the margin, questions of the magnitude of the gain will be critical in practice: If only modest or speculative gains are projected, then business actors could turn out to be rationally indifferent to experiments in cross reference. The cross-reference hypothesis accordingly needs a cogent, albeit informal, description of the source and expected value of this gain. Such a specification can only be based on an economic theory of the firm.

More generally, differences identified in a governance comparison can only be made material and evaluated by reference to antecedent theories of the firm. It follows that better information about the theoretical alternatives on offer means better quality for the projections emerging.

4. COMPARATIVE RESULTS AND THE CASE FOR INDIVISIBILITY

The question as to the productivity advantages of different governance strategies ultimately devolves on the utility of cross reference: Can it improve bottom-line results for a given firm or system? Responses to this question turn on views as to divisibility. We have seen that positive projections of divisibility go together with positive predictions respecting cross reference in Boxes (1) and (3) of Table 2.3. Boxes (2) and (4) share suspicion about divisibility and cross reference, but for different reasons. The Chicago School holds incidents of blockholding to be intrinsically inferior; accordingly, cross reference should only proceed in one direction whatever its technical feasibility. The Box (4) view, in contrast, sees national systems as embedded and asks whether cross reference is technically feasible in the first place.

The comparative literature offers a long list of factors that can operate to embed governance institutions. Significantly, different projections tend to follow depending on the factor emphasized. For example, leading contributions to the legal literature emphasize past and present political sticking points and assert that but for them economic incentives would lead to cross referencing. The result is a straddle between Boxes (3) and (4) that puts the best gloss on the problematics of cross reference: But for the embedded acts of past legislatures and present public choice problems, a fitter hybrid would emerge.

This section explores an alternative view. On this view, economic factors by themselves make governance systems resistant to cross reference. The implication is that even the qualified case for cross reference put forward in the legal literature has been overstated. Negative implications follow for two leading law reform questions: (a) Whether productive monitoring by institutions and blockholders will result from the removal of regulations controlling the holding practices of American institutional investors; and (b) Whether equity trading markets on the European Continent will deepen as the result of enactment of regulation mandating transparency and barring insider trading.

The three sections that follow draw on the results of the informal comparison described in Section 2 to show how incentive structures built into the market and blockholder systems create sticking points for cross-referenced governance innovations.

4.1. *Comparative Corporate Governance and the Unsolved Free Rider Problem*

A question arises when Boxes (3) and (4) of Table 2.3 are contrasted with the pluses and minuses juxtaposed on Tables 2.1 and 2.2: Do the mirror-image relationships of the systems' respective strengths and weaknesses suggest divisibility or indivisibility? They have suggested divisibility to many observers. But there also arises an inference of interdependence among elements within a given system and thus indivisibility. Sticking points that have emerged in comparative governance exercises provide support for the latter reading.

The comparison's initial impetus came from within the USA, where observers were simultaneously dissatisfied with perverse effects displayed by the market system during the 1980s and concerned about antitakeover legislation's impact on the system's capacity for agency cost control. The solution to both problems was thought to lie in newly activist institutional shareholders. Institutions had come to hold larger proportionate stakes of publicly-traded shares. Larger stakes per institution meant higher expected returns from costs incurred in respect of monitoring individual firms in the institution's portfolio. Even if the proportionate stakes of individual institutions remained below the threshold point that would make significant investment in monitoring cost beneficial, it was thought that coalitions of institutions could pool their resources so as to reach the threshold point (Black 1990: 524–5, 585–9). But regulatory reform would have to come first, however, said the proponents: Politically-generated regulatory barriers were impeding the accumulation of large institutional holdings and deterring coalition formation (ibid.: 575)

The difficulty for this theory of agency cost control lay in a free rider problem. An institutional shareholder not participating in a coalition would get the same increased returns as a participating institution while saving the cost of monitoring. It accordingly was difficult to see how any given institution could have a financial incentive to take the lead in investing in monitoring and coalition building (Rock 1991: 474–5). At the same time, the financial benefits of cost-intensive relational investment remained underspecified. Underperforming companies appropriate for coalition intervention tended to be publicly identified in the ordinary course, and institutions already were informally (and cheaply) communicating their criticisms to their managers (Bratton and McCahery 1995).

The free rider problem and the gains specification problem had a disturbing implication in turn. Any institutional coalition building or block formation that actually occurred in practice carried a cognizable risk of perverse effects. The institutional monitor, rather than engaging in public-regarding monitoring and problem solving, rationally would look for compensation for its investment in information and intervention in the form of side payments from management. Since these by definition would not be shared with competing institutions in the shareholder group, they would solve the free rider problem as well as the returns specification problem (Bratton and McCahery 1995: 1905–6).

Comparative governance became the leading edge of corporate law scholarship in the United States when proponents of delegated institutional monitoring and related law reform looked abroad for material with which to rebut these objections. It was hoped that practices in Germany (Mayer 1998: 154) and Japan would show that free riding need not deter aggressive monitoring by investment institutions holding large equity stakes.

The domestic agenda strongly influenced the shape of the comparative inquiry. Roe's (1994: 171–94) leading study of Germany looks not at the blockholders who tend to control German firms but at the investment and monitoring practices of Germany's large banks. It finds significant bank shareholdings and governance input, but not the sort of institutional monitoring being envisioned for institutions in the USA (Gorton and Schmid 1996).

German bank monitors, as it turned out, do not take an activist role in effecting investment and divestment policies keyed to shareholder value. When they do monitor they tend to take a lender's point of view, intervening on the financial downside. Later studies question even this observation. It has been asserted, for example, that German banks do not actually take an active role in downside restructurings. More generally, studies give rise to serious questions as to whether German bank incentives lie on the side of shareholder value creation at all (Edwards and Fischer 1996; but cf. Edwards and Nibler 2000).

The comparison with Japan led to similarly awkward results. Like the German universal bank, the Japanese main bank engages in crisis monitoring from the lender's perspective and does not act like the idealized shareholder monitor (Milhaupt 2001). Insider trading rather than public-regarding monitoring is said to be the source of enhanced returns on the banks' equity holdings (Ramseyer 1993: 2013–14). Attention accordingly turned to a different Japanese phenomenon—cross-shareholding (and resulting monitoring) among nonfinancial firms in the keiretsu. But this did not fill the bill either.[32] These relationships came to be described as a means to the end of stabilizing incomplete long-term relational contracts among members of vertical production combines (Gilson and Roe 1993: 874–5). As such they had nothing to offer in the way of precedent for financial institutions in the United States of America, which hold significant stakes in companies in the absence of long-term buyer–seller relations.

The comparison, in sum, failed of its purpose of providing direct cross-referenced backing for United States law reform. Germany and Japan held out no institutional practices suited to fill the American system's monitoring gap.

4.2. *Can Relational Engagement Emerge in a System Open to Hostile Takeovers?*

Barriers to cross reference result in part from internal dependencies within the respective systems. This Section, by way of example, compares the patient, constructive engagement said to distinguish the relationship between blockholders and firm managers with the arm's length discipline of market system's hostile takeover. The question is whether both modes of monitoring can be incorporated in a single governance system. Just such a result has been a central aspiration of American corporate governance in the 1990s. American proponents of delegated monitoring envisioned such relational engagements among firms and institutional shareholders even as they joined the rest of the corporate law academy in disapproving state law constraints on hostile takeovers. The question whether the two objectives plausibly may be pursued simultaneously never came up in practice, because the states were no more ready to roll back their anti-takeover statutes than institutional investors were ready to make significant investments in monitoring. But it retains importance in the evaluation of the cross-reference hypothesis.

Minimal hostile takeover activity appears to be a precondition of relational engagement. If a hostile offeror holds out a significant premium over market price, institutional shareholders seeking good results for the year (and owing fiduciary duties to their clients) will have an overwhelming incentive to defect from any relational commitments and accept the offer. An active possibility of defection in turn chills the managers' ex ante incentive to cooperate with the institutional shareholder. Control in a blockholder, in contrast, disables the hostile tender offer as known in the United States. Indeed, stable Japanese cross-holdings have been accounted for as an antitakeover device (Roe 1994: 181).

This does not mean that blockholders cannot defect from a relational commitment to the firm's managers by selling out. Given an offer at a substantial premium, any holder, block or not, has a powerful incentive to defect from management's side. In a blockholder system, of course, such a control transfer would occur not through a tender offer made to the entire group of shareholders but through a private block sale. To see this possibility, hypothesize a firm with three large blocks, none of them large enough to enable unilateral exercise of control. An entrepreneur could unilaterally negotiate the purchase of each of the blocks, take control, and replace the managers (Ramseyer 1987: 21–6). Were such control transfers to become an everyday event in a given blockholder system, the quality of the 'relational engagement' between its managers and block shareholders presumably would deteriorate,[33] sacrificing some of the governance benefits of blockholding itself. It follows that disruptive control transfers are a constant theoretical possibility even in a blockholder system. Some stabilizing device would appear to be necessary. Side payments running from the firm to the blockholder nicely fill this bill (Pagano and Röell 1998: 191). The firm's managers in effect outbid the hypothetical offeror for the blockholder's loyalty, the bid (and the relational engagement) coming at the expense of small shareholders on the outside.

There arises a negative inference for the American case for delegated monitoring. If the institutional blockholder is disabled from collecting the payment, as it would be in the United States of America due to reputational (Black 1992: 851, 855) and legal constraints,[34] then a cross-reference scenario looking to institutional monitoring lacks a plausible incentive base (Bratton and McCahery 1995: 1921–4). More generally, it appears that you can have a system in which a vigorous corporate control market imports discipline or a system in which relational engagement imports discipline, but not both. On this reading, the comparative exercise backfires, not only failing to yield positive results for the USA domestic agenda, but yielding a strong negative implication for the case for delegated monitoring.

4.3. *Side Payments, Insider Trading, and the European Law Reform Agenda*

Relational engagement and side payments are closely linked, quite apart from the context of control transactions. As noted above, blockholders do not sacrifice liquidity and invest in monitoring without extracting returns. To get these, they exploit their positions through insider trading and self-dealing transactions. It follows that the principle of pro rata treatment for equity holders as a group can play no significant role in a blockholder system's legal and normative environment. The pro rata principle does, however, activate the investor protections identified in the economic literature as the mainstays of market systems—majority-to-minority fiduciary duties, one share one vote, and the insider trading ban. An inference of indivisibility arises.

In theory, of course, pro rata treatment is not a necessary element of an environment conducive to dispersed equity ownership. It has been argued that non-controlling holders of shares of block-controlled firms who are excluded from gain made available to inside holders in the form of side payments (and premiums in the case of block trades) have nothing to complain about so long as shared governance benefits stemming from the insiders' arrangements exceed the costs of side payments in the long run.[35] But the governance comparisons hold out a negative implication for this assertion as well. They show that conditions favourable to this Kaldor–Hicks neutral result cannot be assumed to obtain in the real world. The outside shareholders need substantive rights and process rules that provide a viable means to enforce the condition that the insider deals leave them at least as well off as before. Blockholding legal systems tend to fail to provide such minimal protections.[36]

The question as to the desirability of creating such a shareholder-protective legal regime presently is being debated in Europe's blockholder countries. The proponents look to corporate and securities law reform as the means to the end of deeper equity trading markets. Discussants in countries like Germany, France, and the Netherlands talk of direct controls on blockholders, such as self-dealing constraints to protect non-controlling, dispersed shareholders, voting caps and limits on the proportion of capital held by designated investors, and the one share, one vote rule.

Less thorough-going reforms have been recommended in reports promulgated by official committees formed in recent years in Europe to look into governance reform. The committee reports have been generated by business actors. Reflecting their source, they articulate best practice norms for voluntary adoption by firms. Interestingly, the reports appear to assume that transparency effected through disclosure and insider trading rules by itself will suffice to foster an environment conducive to dispersed shareholding. They do not confront the possibility that self-dealing transactions between blockholders and firms that do not involve purchases and sales of shares on securities exchanges could amount to an independent and significant barrier to dispersed shareholding.

Europe thus faces an intriguing choice implicating the connection between legal rules, corporate governance practice, and trading market depth. If the objective is deep national equity markets like those in London and New York, an analogy to the legal regimes of Britain and the USA suggests that stepped-up disclosure and insider trading rules amount to only half of the needed loaf of law reform. Both Britain and the USA (as elsewhere) add rules against self-dealing by managers and control shareholders, rules that contain insider opportunities to effect non pro rata distributions that reduce returns on outside equity contributions.

The problem is that meaningful reform following this lead could destabilize the incentives that sustain Europe's blockholder monitoring regime,[37] inadvertently causing the blocks to dissipate by cutting off the holders' sources of return. The move to deepen the market thus could imply a larger (and unintended) move to a market system. Conversely, limited reform that does not include self-dealing constraints may fail to deepen the markets significantly. The question as to divisiblity thus is joined, with the comparative governance literature offering no cogent advice respecting the likely outcome (Berglöf 1997: 114–16).

5. CONCLUSION

This chapter's analysis raises important questions for law reform agendas on both sides of the Atlantic. In the USA proponents ask for deregulation of controls on institutional investors, looking to encourage blockholding and more effective monitoring. In Europe proponents ask for stronger securities regulation, looking to encourage deeper trading markets. The suggestion is that each reform programme may lead to disappointing results because neither offers conforming adjustments to the pertinent actors' incentives. Alternatively, strict reforms that materially change prevailing incentive patterns could perversely destabilize workable (if imperfect) arrangements without assuring the appearance of more effective alternatives.

This analysis seconds the policy recommendations made in discussions in the USA by neoclassical critics of the cross-reference hypothesis. But it does not simultaneously endorse their theoretical presuppositions. This analysis works more comfortably in the capacious framework of reference employed by those articulating the cross-reference hypothesis. Both make second-best assumptions and both recognize the salience of political events. The difference lies in underlying theories of the firm. Proponents of cross reference assume that vast improvements in governance institutions would be within easy reach but for political barriers and historical path dependencies in the regulatory pattern. Our analysis challenges this diagnosis. Politics can indeed explain why a governance system has not evolved so as to be first best. But it cannot by itself show us how to improve that system. For that one needs an economic theory of the firm.[38] No economic theory yet articulated shows us how to splice blockholder components onto market systems so as to effect material improvement.

Notes

1. Dispersed debt holdings in the case of some large firms.
2. Different national systems emphasize different protections. The USA at present holds the derivative action for breach of fiduciary duty, where Britain holds out few incentives to plaintiffs but maintains a more robust takeover market. See Miller (1998: 52–3).
3. Roe (1996: 649) adds a third cost, an industrial organization cost stemming from American firms' tendency to resort to vertical integration as the solution for the commitment problems attending incomplete relational contracts with significant suppliers and customers. Full vertical integration implies the incentive problems attending and deadweight costs of bureaucratized management. In the Japanese keiretsu (and to a lesser extent in Germany), cross-holdings of shares between the vertically related firms ameliorate the commitment problem without carrying the costs of full vertical integration. See Gilson and Roe (1993: 882–3). Roe (1996: 649) suggests that in market systems, stronger financial intermediaries 'might have linked related suppliers and customers with partial cross-ownership, but without tight (and sometimes costly) vertical integration'. This pattern does not obtain in Japan, where significant nonfinancial cross-ownership invariably accompanies financial ownership. See Kester (1997: 231, table 1). Nor would it appear to be implicated in bank holding and voting patterns in Germany. See Roe (1994: 171–7).
4. In Germany, 64 per cent of large firms have a majority owner, in France 59 per cent. See Windolf (1998: 714). Jenkinson and Ljungvist (1997) provide a detailed report on blockholding patterns in Germany. Following Zwiebel (1995), this study assumes three types of firm: (1) firms with many small blocks but without a controlling block; (2) firms with one large block and many small blocks; and (3) firms with one very large block and no small blocks. Furthermore, there are five economically significant block sizes in Germany: (1) a 95 per cent controlling party can compulsorily acquire minorities shares; (2) a 75 per cent super-majority block; (3) a 50 per cent block that gives management control of the company; (4) a 25 per cent block that gives veto powers on corporate

charter amendments and supervisory board changes; and (5) a block less than 25 per cent that gives protection against other, larger blockholders. The study shows that just under three quarters of all German listed companies have a majority owner: 23.1 per cent have blocks in excess of 90 per cent of their equity capital; 18.4 per cent are super-majority controlled and 30.5 per cent have a simple majority owner. Only a quarter are not at least majority controlled by a blockholder. Taking a closer look at these 141 firms, they show that 86 of these firms have one or more blocking majority stakes, where of course two or three such stakes would amount to majority or super-majority control. The remaining 55 firms have no stakes in excess of 25 per cent. Thirty-seven of these firms have one or more disclosed non-blocking stakes while only 18 firms are widely held.

5. Berglöf (1998: 101, table 4). Financial advisors in France serve as proxies for financial advisors to controlling shareholders. They also figure into complex arrangements of cross-shareholdings among private French firms. See Fanto (1998: 107; 1996: 184–5).
6. But not necessarily. Kester (1997: 231 (table1), 234 (table 2)); Gerlach (1992).
7. The Japanese system also is distinguished for close ties between financial intermediaries and government regulators, see Milhaupt and Miller (1997) (describing regulatory cartel among government and private sector actors run according to informal norms and interlinked decision making institutions).
8. In France and Germany the family owners employ professional technocrats to do the managing and stay at arm's length. See Windolf (1998: 713).
9. The incomplete contracts models show this formally. See Bolton and von Thadden (1998). For empirical studies that support the assertion that ownership concentration improves the control of management and therefore can increase the value of the firm, see Hertzel and Smith (1993); Wruck (1989).
10. More generally, there tends to be a closer relationship between management and all of the stakeholders. When problems come up, the normal practice is for stakeholders to voice concern and for a change in management to take place rather than stakeholder exit. See Woolcock (1996: 183).
11. The result is satisficing (as opposed to optimizing) behaviour on the part of the managers, but satisfying relative to a higher frontier of production for a given level of inputs. See Kester (1996: 122–3).
12. Porter (1996: 12–13). This implies that equity investors in firms in blockholder systems settle for lower rates of return than do equity investors in firms organized in market systems. In the case of corporate investors, the explanation is that offsetting advantages lie in long-term business relationships with the issuer. See Kester (1997: 227).
13. It may be some time before we see such studies. State of the art work proceeds at a more general level. Compare Rajan and Zingales (1998*b*) (studying the connection between growth rates and financial market development and finding that industrial sectors relatively more in need of external finance develop more quickly in countries with well-developed financial markets), with Levine and Zervos (1998) (showing that each of stock market activity and banking development positively predict growth, capital accumulation and productivity improvements, but that stock market size is not robustly linked with growth). See generally, Carlin and Mayer (Chapter 14, this volume).
14. The study of La Porta *et al.* (1998) assumes that there are two broad traditions, civil and common law, and goes on to analyse the rights of investors in forty-nine countries that have publicly traded companies. It appears that relatively few countries have legal rules favouring outside shareholders: only 22 per cent mandate one share one vote; only 16 per cent allow cumulative voting; and only 22 per cent allow voting by mail. Creditors' rights presents a more difficult picture. To summarize simply, common law countries offer better legal protection for creditors. Correspondingly, the French civil law countries treat creditors and shareholders poorly.

15. The study confirms that common law countries have better access to equity finance than do civil law countries. The differences between England and France are particularly significant and strongly suggest that poor investor protection entails lower liquidity and smaller markets; (La Porta *et al.* 1997*a*: 1137). Strong antidirector rights (as well as one share one vote) also are linked to higher liquidity markets; ibid. at 1140. The level of legal enforcement and the origin of rules in common law are also correlated to valuation and depth of both equity and debt markets. Economic statistics, such as the total capitalization of equity held by outside shareholders, show that common law countries tend to have better stock markets; ibid. at 1146–8. The authors assert that these data confirm the view that the nature of legal rules and their efficient enforcement are positively related to the size and depth of a country's capital market.
16. The logic is straightforward: Given weak legal protection, only voting control will protect against expropriation by other equity investors (La Porta *et al.* 1999*b*). This study investigates the structure of the twenty largest corporations in twenty-seven different countries, along with smaller firms (in order to maintain consistency of size across jurisdictions). Its authors have chosen to bias large corporations because it is these firms which are most likely to possess dispersed ownership patterns. Their research shows that, based on a data set which included the ten largest publicly traded nonfinancial companies in the sample of countries tested and assuming a 20 per cent definition of control, that for large firms: (a) nearly 40 per cent worldwide are widely held; (b) 30 per cent are family controlled; (c) 18 per cent are stated controlled; and (d) the remaining fall into different categories of ownership. The Berle and Means image of the firm with separation of ownership and control dominates in Japan, Britain, and the United States of America, while in the rest of the world there are few firms that fit this description. In terms of firms with owners, the principal owner types, as noted, are families and the state. It follows that countries with poor shareholder protection have more concentrated shareholding (and vice versa). In summary, the study finds that dispersed shareholding is not universal. It also finds that bank-control is not common. Blockholding is more common, with blockholders employing control rights devices and other instruments to limit the power of minorities and typically participating in the management of the firm. For an extension, see La Porta *et al.* (1997*b*). This study starts with the proposition that trust is needed to support cooperation in large organizations and accepts an empirical measure of trust derived from a survey conducted worldwide. Trust is then connected to government effectiveness (measured by investor evaluations), civic participation (measured by participation rates) and firm size; ibid. at 334. Statistically significant results obtain, with higher trust countries having higher levels of cooperative success. The lowest levels of trust obtain in countries with high rates of membership in hierarchical religions; ibid. at 336.
17. Their main normative message lies with developing economies lacking either institutions of legal protection or blockholding. For a similar evaluation, see Shleifer and Vishny (1997).
18. Under post-war macroeconomic theory, given competitive markets and the availability in each country of the same technology, each country has the same growth rate (Boyer 1996: 34, 54).
19. These are not the only possibilities. The systems, although materially different, also could be equally competitively fit.
20. Carrying this point out to its logical conclusion, the implicit assertion is that there is a single optimal way of organizing production among a possible multiplicity of local optima, see Boyer (1996: 47).
21. One can reach the same insight by juxtaposing the two systems and then viewing both from the point of view of an observer in a Third World country. That observer sees commonalities for the most part. See Shleifer and Vishny (1997: 737–8).
22. It should be noted that the cross-reference hypothesis can be restated in a weaker form so as to allow for the persistence of national level colourations. See Berger (1996: 18–19).

23. This irrelevance point can be combined in a unitary description with the irrelevance point made above, in the text accompanying *supra* note 21, despite their different emphases. For a first step, juxtapose the two stories: The first focuses on a structural feature of a first-best world; the second follows from the fortuitous possibility that systemic differences may have equivalent cost implications. The juxtaposition highlights the point that neither irrelevance story eliminates the possibility that systemic differences can have important cost consequences for competing firms and national economies. A cost difference has the greatest impact for a firm at the margin, where any cost disadvantage impairs its survival. Ironically, the margin is base point for the first story's irrelevance claim, while under the second story it is the point of greatest relevance for governance difference. This is because what the first story makes irrelevant is less governance itself than governance policy talk. Talk matters least at the margin. There the uncompetitive firm runs out of room for manoeuvre, market practice identifies the most productive governance device, and no reference to theory is necessary.
24. Ramseyer illustrates this point with an historical explanation of the Japanese system couched solely in terms of rational, self-interested responses to the national economic and legal environment. Ramseyer (1998: 546–7, 555). The explanation falls short of completeness. Ramseyer admits he has no explanation for cross-shareholdings held by nonfinancial keiretsu members who do not stand in a vertical supplier–customer relationship with the issuer. Since the blocks of stock held by these firms are small on a percentage basis—less than 5 per cent of most keiretsu members—he dismisses the phenomenon as trivial or symbolic; ibid. at 557.
25. There is accordingly no tension between this description and the contemporary movement toward partial integration of national systems in Europe and North America. The conventional view of harmonization initiatives such as that of the European Union is that mutually designed institutional structures facilitate the development of competitive techniques in a more open marketplace. The European movement toward harmonization assumes partial divergence, in that some countries will be slower in adapting common standards due to their relative starting points.
26. This point derives from the observation of national product markets, where the same product can be sold for different prices and domestic firms develop niches, with different niches possibly calling for specific organizational forms.
27. Trade theory posits that free exchange causes factor incomes to converge without also asserting convergence as to the form of the institutional arrangements of trading nations. At the same time, international product competition can lead to several different equilibrium results, some of which do not include institutional convergence (Boyer 1996: 51–3).
28. For studies antedating the comparative corporate governance literature, see, for example, Dore (1973). For more recent contributions to this literature, see for example, Albert (1991).
29. It follows that underdeveloped countries can become trapped (Diamond 1990). Empirical tests of convergence hypotheses focus on per capita measures of gross national product. These applications of per capita gross national product measures have been applied so as to yield productivity levels from the late nineteenth century to the present. The best work models the convergence of income across regions, taking into account the effect of the interplay of net migration pattern and economic growth. See Barro and Sala-I-Martin (1991).
30. See Bebchuk and Roe (1999: 143–8) (noting possibility blockholding could persist after securities market reforms so long as not accompanied by effective reform of fiduciary law causing value of private benefits to blockholders to exceed proceeds on public sale of block, and possibility that dispersed shareholding could persist even though legal barriers to blockholding were removed due to resistance of managers seeking to retain positional advantage).
31. There is at least one practice in corporate law's past to which we can look as indirect source of historical support. This is the evolution of corporate codes and governance practices in the USA as it developed as a common market during the last 100 years. Famously, corporate law is

generated at the state level, with each of the fifty states having its own code and body of cases, and its generation is at the same time subject to a competitive constraint. The states compete for rents flowing from corporate charters. The historical result of a century of practice is convergence in the outline of the states' corporate codes. Any state that fails to conform to this basic outline loses incorporation business to the market leader, Delaware. Although each statute varies in its terms to some extent, the variation is not thought to create sufficient incidental costs as to justify a national level harmonization movement. But, at the same time, the normative implications of the system are hotly controverted. The argument is that the terms of US corporate law, although constrained by competition and convergent, remain subject to interest group influence. As a result, the state codes now constrain the field of operation of a mainstay of the American market control system–the hostile takeover. See Romano (1993: 52–84).

32. Roe (1994: 181) dismisses cross-holding shareholders in Japan as tending to play a protective function, insulating the managers in the groups from takeovers.
33. Significantly, Jenkinson and Ljungqvist (1997) show that German banks take an active role in cases of behind-the-scenes hostile stakebuilding.
34. The legal constraint is the basic duty of loyalty. See, for example, Del. Corp.L. section 144. But the duty leaves open room to siphon rents to insiders under the guise of contracting. For descriptions of the deals, see Rock (1994: 1004–6).
35. Ironically it is a prominent proponent of the market system superiority, Judge Frank Easterbrook, who has argued most forcefully for abandonment of the pro rata norm in American corporate law. See Easterbrook and Fischel (1982: 703–15). The argument, made in the context of the law of cash out mergers, may not carry over to the broader governance context, however. With merger gain, increased returns that presuppose a non-pro-rata rule are on the table in the present or near term. With the institutional investor context we deal with monitoring over a longer term. The small shareholder is being asked to abandon a range of claims for pro rata treatment on faith that returns in the long run are enhanced due to heightened institutional or blockholder attention. The problem is that in a non-pro-rata regime, the small holders make the give up without a guarantee as to a minimum rate of return. Once the ready yardstick of pro rata treatment is abandoned, nothing stops the blockholder from splitting the whole pie of enhanced value with management. Easterbrook also took up the case of the block trade at a premium. His analysis now is seen to be incomplete. See Bebchuk (1994: 957); Kahan (1993).
36. See Enriques (2000) which provides a detailed comparison of the fiduciary law of France, Germany, and Italy with that of Britain and the USA, and concludes that self-dealing regulation is 'less significant and less stringent' on the Continent. France has the most rigorous of the three continental regimes. But it tends to turn on shareholder ratification. In a world of blockholes and cross-holdings, shareholder ratification would appear to offer outside minority holders little practical protection. Enriques' survey of British fiduciary law provides a useful counterweight to the report in Miller (1998) which under-reports its provisions.
37. Indeed, these initiatives have a negative implication for blockholding because deeper equity markets presuppose larger proportions of widely-held equity.
38. Indeed, it needs to make reference to a theory of the firm to show that an evolved system is deficient in the first place.

References

Albert, M. (1991). *Capitalisme Contre Capitalisme.* Paris: Seuil.

Aoki, M. (1990). Toward an economic model of the Japanese firm. *Journal of Economic Literature* 28: 1.

Barro, R. J., and Sala-I-Martin, X. (1991). Convergence across states and regions. *Brookings Papers in Economic Activity* 1: 107.

Baums, T. (1999). Corporate contracting around defective regulations: The Daimler–Chrysler case. *Journal of Institutional and Theoretical Economics* 155: 119.

Bebchuk, L. A. (1994). Efficient and inefficient sales of corporate control. *Quarterly Journal of Economics* 109: 957.

—— (1999). A rent-protection theory of corporate ownership and control. Harvard Law School, Center for Law, Economics, and Business, Discussion Paper No. 260.

—— and Roe, M. J. (1999). A theory of path dependence in corporate governance. *Stanford Law Review* 52: 127.

Becht, M., and Mayer, C. (2001). The control of corporate Europe. In F. Barca and M. Becht (ed.), *The Control of Corporate Europe.* Oxford: Oxford University Press.

Berger, S. (1996). Introduction. In S. Berger and R. Dore (ed.), *National Diversity and Global Capitalism.* Ithaca: Cornell University Press, 1.

Berglöf, E. (1998). Reforming corporate governance: Redirecting the European agenda. *Economic Policy: A European Policy Forum* 51.

Black, B. S. (1990). Shareholder passivity re-examined. *Michigan Law Review* 89: 520.

—— (1992). Agents watching agents: The promise of institutional investor voice. *UCLA Law Review* 39: 811.

Blanchard, O. J. (1991). Comments and discussions. *Brookings Papers on Economic Activity* 1: 159.

Bolton, P., and von Thadden, E.-L. (1998), Liquidity and Control: a dynamic theory of corporate ownership structure. *Journal of Institutional and Theoretical Economics* 154:167.

Boot, A. W., and Macey, J. R. (1998). Objectivity, control and adaptability in corporate governance. In Columbia Sloan Project on Corporate Governance, *Corporate Governance Today* 223.

Boyer, R. (1996). The convergence hypothesis revisted: Globalization but still the century of nations? In S. Berger and R. Dore (ed.), *National Diversity and Global Capitalism.* Ithaca: Cornell University Press, 29.

Bratton, W. W., and McCahery, J. A. (1995). Regulatory competition, regulatory capture, and corporate self-regulation. *North Carolina Law Review* 73: 1861.

Coffee, J. C. Jr. (1999). The future as history: The prospects for global convergence in corporate governance and its implications. *Northwestern University Law Review* 93: 641.

Demirguc-Kunt, A., and Maksimovic, V. (1998). Law, finance, and firm growth. *Journal of Finance* 53: 2107.

Diamond, P. A. (1990). *Growth, Productivity, Unemployment: Essays to Celebrate Bob Solow's Birthday.* Cambridge, MA: MIT Press.

Dore, R. (1973). British Factory—Japanese Factory: *The Origins of National Diversity in Industrial Relations.* Berkeley: University of California Press.

Easterbrook, F. H. (1997). International corporate differences: Markets or law? *Journal of Applied Corporate Finance* 9: 23.

—— and Fischel, D. (1982). Corporate control transactions. *Yale Law Journal* 93: 698.

Edwards, J., and Fischer, K. (1994). *Banks, Finance and Investment in Germany.* Cambridge: Cambridge University Press.

—— and Nibler, M. (2000). Corporate governance in Germany: The role of banks and ownership concentration. *Economic Policy: A European Policy Forum* 237.

Enriques, L. (2000). The law on corporate directors' self-dealing: A comparative analysis. *International and Comparative Corporate Law Journal* 2: 297.

Ewing, J. *et al.* (1999). Enough spin-offs to make you dizzy. *Business Week International,* 10 May, 68.

Fanto, J. A. (1996), The absence of cross-cultural communication: SEC mandatory disclosure and foreign corporate governance. *Northwestern Journal of International Law and Business* 17: 119.

——(1998). The role of corporate law in the adaptation of French enterprise. *Columbia Business Law Review* 1998: 97.

Gerlach, M. I. (1992). Twilight of the Keiretsu? a critical assessment. *Journal of Japanese Studies* 18: 79.

Gilson, R. J. (1998). Reflections in a distant mirror: Japanese corporate governance through American eyes. *Columbia Business Law Review* 1998: 203.

—— and Roe, M. J. (1993). Understanding the Japanese Keiretsu: Overlap between corporate governance and industrial organization. *Yale Law Journal* 102: 871.

Gordon, J. N. (2000). Pathways to corporate convergence: Two steps on the road to shareholder capitalism in Germany: Deutsche Telekom and Daimler Chrysler. Columbia University, Center for Law and Economic Studies (available on SSRN id=208508).

Gorton, G., and Schmid, F. A. (1996). Universal banking and the performance of German firms. NBER, Working Paper No. 5453.

Hertzel, M., and Smith, R. (1993). Market discounts and shareholder gains for placing equity privately. *Journal of Finance* 48: 459.

Hoshi, T. (1990). The role of banks in reducing the costs of financial distress in Japan. *Journal of Financial Economics* 27: 67.

——(1991). Corporate structure liquidity and investment: Evidence from Japanese Industrial Groups. *Quarterly Journal of Economics* 106: 33.

——(1998). Japanese corporate governance as a system. In K. J. Hopt *et al.* (ed.), *Comparative Corporate Governance: The State of the Art and Emerging Research.* Oxford: Oxford University Press.

Jenkinson, T., and Ljungqvist, A. (1997). Hostile stakes and the role of banks in German corporate governance. Center for Economic Policy Research, Discussion Paper No. 1695.

Kahan, M. (1993). Sales of corporate control. *Journal of Law, Economics and Organization* 9: 368.

Kaplan, S. N. (1994*a*). Top executives, turnover, and firm performance in Germany. *Journal of Law, Economics and Organization* 10: 142.

——(1994*b*). Top executive rewards and firm performance: A comparison of Japan and the U.S. *Journal of Political Economy* 102: 510.

Kester, C. (1996). American and Japanese corporate governance: Convergence to best practice? In S. Berger and R. Dore (ed.), *National Diversity and Global Capitalism.* Ithaca: Cornell University Press, P. 107.

——(1997). Governance, contracting, and investment horizons: A look at Japan and Germany. In Chew (ed.), *Studies in International Corporate Finance and Governance System: A Comparison of the U.S., Japan and Europe.* New York: Oxford University Press, 227.

Lannoo, K. (1999). A European perspective on corporate governance. *Journal of Common Market Studies* 37: 269.

Levine, R., and Zervos, S. (1998). Stock markets, banks and economic growth. *American Economic Review* 88: 537.

Licht, A. (1998). Regulatory arbitrage for real: International securities regulation in a world of interacting securities markets. *Virginia Journal of International Law* 38: 563.

La Porta, R., Lopez-de-Silanes, F., and Shleifer, A. (1999*a*). Investor protection and corporate valuation. NBER, Working Paper No. 7403.

—— (1999*b*). Corporate ownership around the world. *Journal of Finance* 54: 471.

——and Vishny, R. (1997*a*). Legal determinants of external finance. *Journal of Finance* 52: 1131.

——(1997*b*). Trust in large organizations. *American Economic Review* 87: 333.

——(1998). Law and finance. *Journal of Political Economy* 106: 1113.

Macey, J. R. (1998*a*). Measuring the effectiveness of different corporate governance systems: Toward a more scientific approach. *Journal of Applied Corporate Finance* 10: 16.

Macey, J. R. (1998*b*). Italian corporate governance: One American's perspective. *Columbia Business Law Review* 1998: 121.

Mark, G. A. (1995). Realms of choice: Finance, capitalism and corporate governance. *Columbia Law Review* 95: 969.

Mayer, C. (1998). Financial systems and corporate governance: A review of international evidence. *Journal of Institutional and Theoretical Economics* 154: 143.

McCahery, J. A. (1997). Market regulation and particularistic interests: The dynamics of insider trading regulation in the US and Europe. In G. Underhill (ed.), *The New World Order in International Finance.* London: MacMillan.

Milhaupt, C. J. (1998). Property rights in firms. *Virginia Law Review* 84: 1145.

——(2001). Creative norm destruction: The evolution of nonlegal rules in Japanese corporate governance. *University of Pennsylvania Law Review* 149: 2083.

——and Miller, G. P. (1997). Cooperation, conflict, and convergence in Japanese finance: Evidence from the 'Jusen' problem. *Law and Policy of International Business* 29: 1.

Miller, G. P. (1998). Political structure and corporate governance: Some points of contrast between the United States and England. *Columbia Business Law Review* 1998: 51.

Miller, M. H. (1997). Is American corporate governance fatally flawed? In Chew (ed.), *Studies in International Corporate Finance and Governance Systems: A Comparison of the U.S., Japan, and Europe.* New York: Oxford University Press, 38.

Nenova, T. (2000). The value of corporate votes and control benefits: A cross-country analysis. Harvard University, Working Paper (available on SSRN at ID=237809).

OECD (1998). *Principles of Corporate Governance.* Paris: OECD.

Ohmae, K. (1990). *The Borderless World: Power and Strategy in the Interlinked Economy.* Cambridge, MA: Harvard University Business School Press.

Pagano, M., and Röell, A. (1998). The choice of stock ownership structure: Agency costs, monitoring, and the decision to go public. *Quarterly Journal of Economics* 113: 187.

Pastre, O. (1998). Corporate governance: The end of 'L'exception Francaise'? *Columbia Business Law Review* 1998: 79.

Porter, M. (1997). Capital choices: changing the way America invests in industry. In Chew (ed.), *Studies in International Corporate Finance and Governance Systems: A Comparison of the U.S., Japan, and Europe.* New York: Oxford University Press, 5.

Rajan R. G., and Zingales, L. (1995). What do we know about capital structure? Some evidence from international data. *Journal of Finance* 50: 1421.

—— (1998*a*). Which capitalism? Lessons from the East Asian crisis. *Journal of Applied Corporate Finance* 40.

—— (1998*b*). Financial dependence and growth. *American Economic Review* 88: 559.

Ramseyer, M. (1987). Takeovers in Japan: Opportunism, ideology, and corporate control. *UCLA Law Review* 35: 1.

—— (1993). Columbian Cartel Launches Bid for Japanese Firms. *Yale Law Journal* 102: 2005.

—— (1998). Are corporate governance systems converging: The A-contextual logic to the Japanese Keiretsu. In Columbia Sloan Project on Corporate Governance. *Corporate Governance Today.*

Rock, E. B. (1991). The logic and (uncertain) significance of institutional shareholder activism. *Georgetown Law Journal* 79: 445.

—— (1994). Controlling the dark side of relational investing. *Cardozo Law Review* 15: 957.

Roe, M. J. (1994). *Strong Managers, Weak Owners: The Political Roots of American Corporate Finance.* Princeton: Princeton University Press.

—— (1996). Chaos and evolution in law and economics. *Harvard Law Review* 109: 641.

—— (2001). The quality of corporate law argument and its limits. Columbia Law School, Working Paper No. 186 (available on SSRN at ID=260582).

Romano, R. (1993). *The Genius of American Corporate Law.* Washington, DC: American Enterprise Institute Press.

Sassen, S. (1998). *Globalization and its Discontents.* New York: Columbia University Press.

Saunders, A., and A. Schmeits (2002). *Topics in Corporate Finance, The Role of Bank Funding for the Corporate Sector.* Amsterdem: Amsterdem Center for Corporate Finance.

Shleifer, A., and Vishny, R. (1997). A survey of corporate governance. *Journal of Finance* 52: 737.

Standen, D. J. (1995). Insider trading reforms sweep across Germany: Bracing for cold winds of change. *Harvard International Law Journal* 36: 177.

Van der Elst, C. (2000). The equity markets, ownership structures and control: Towards an international harmonization? Ghent University, Financial Law Institute, Working Paper.

West, M. (2001). The puzzling divergence of corporate law: Evidence and explanations from Japan and the United States. *University of Pennsylvania Law Review* 150: 527.

—— (1994). The pricing of derivative actions in Japan and the United States. *Northwestern University Law Review* 88: 1436.

Windolf, P. (1998). The governance structure of large French corporations: A comparative perspective. In Columbia Sloan Project on Corporate Governance. *Corporate Governance Today* 705.

Woolcock, S. (1996). Competition among forms of corporate governance in the European community. In S. Berger and R. Dore (ed.), *National Diversity and Global Capitalism.* Ithaca: Cornell University Press, 179.

Wruck, K. (1989). Equity ownership, concentration and firm value: Evidence from private equity financings. *Journal of Financial Economics* 23: 3.

Zingales, L. (1994). The value of the voting right: A study of the Milan Stock Exchange experience. *Review of Financial Studies* 7: 125.

Zwiebel, J. (1995). Block investment and partial corporate control. *Review of Economic Studies* 62: 161.

3

Toward a Single Model of Corporate Law?

HENRY HANSMANN AND REINIER KRAAKMAN[1]

1. INTRODUCTION

The history of corporate law is an unfinished story of convergence in two parts. The more important part ended a hundred years ago, when the corporation displaced other entities as the principal legal form of large-scale enterprise in advanced jurisdictions. At the start of the nineteenth century, there were no general corporation statutes anywhere; by its end, the corporation was the dominant mode of organizing large firms throughout North America and Europe. Of course, jurisdictions differed, then as now, in the fine structure of their corporate laws as well as in their corporate governance practices, financing techniques, and reliance on capital markets. These differences persisted—and, in some cases, grew more pronounced—during much of the twentieth century. Over the past two decades, however, the centripetal tendencies at work in corporate governance have reversed, and the second part of the story has begun. Powerful new pressures are pushing corporate law into another phase of convergence. Chief among these pressures is a widespread acceptance of a shareholder-centred ideology of corporate law among international business, government, and legal elites. There is no longer any serious competitor to the view that corporate law should principally strive to increase long-term shareholder value. This emergent consensus has already profoundly affected corporate governance practices throughout the world; its influence increasingly conditions the reform of corporate law as well.

2. CONVERGENCE PAST: THE RISE OF THE CORPORATE FORM

We must begin with the recognition that the law of business corporations had already achieved a remarkable degree of worldwide convergence at the end of the nineteenth century. By that time, new large-scale enterprises in every major commercial jurisdiction had come to select the corporate form, and the core functional features of that form were essentially identical across these jurisdictions. Those features, which continue to define the form today, are (1) full legal personality, including well-defined authority to bind the firm to contracts and to bond those contracts with assets that are the property of the firm, as distinct from the firm's owners (Hansmann and Kraakman 2001*a*); (2) limited liability for owners and managers; (3) shared ownership by investors of capital; (4) delegated management under a board structure; and (5) transferable shares.

These core characteristics, both individually and in combination, offer important efficiencies in organizing the large firms that have come to dominate developed market economies. We explore those efficiencies in detail elsewhere (Hansmann 1996; Hansmann and Kraakman 2001*b*). What is important to note here is that, while those characteristics and their associated efficiencies are now commonly taken for granted, prior to the beginning of the nineteenth century there existed only a handful of specially chartered companies that combined all five of these characteristics. New York introduced the world's first general corporation statute in 1811. The joint stock company with tradeable shares was not made generally available for business activities in England until 1844, and limited liability was not added to the form until 1855 (Blumberg 1988: 9–20). By around 1900, however, every major commercial jurisdiction appears to have provided for at least one standard-form legal entity with the five characteristics listed above as the default rules, and this has remained the case ever since. Thus, there was already strong convergence a century ago on the basic elements of the law of business corporations. It is, in general, only in the more detailed structure of corporate law that jurisdictions have varied significantly since then.

The five basic characteristics of the corporate form provide, by their nature, for a firm that is strongly responsive to shareholder interests. They do not, however, necessarily dictate how the interests of other participants in the firm—such as employees, creditors, other suppliers, customers, or society at large—will be accommodated. Nor do they dictate the way in which conflicts of interest among shareholders themselves—and particularly between controlling and non-controlling shareholders—will be resolved. The issues have been foci of experimentation and debate throughout most of the last century. At the start of the twenty-first century it is coming to a close.

3. THE SHAREHOLDER-ORIENTED (OR 'STANDARD') MODEL

Recent years have brought strong evidence of an emerging consensus on the fundamental issues of corporate governance among the academic, business, and governmental elites in leading jurisdictions. The principal elements of this consensus are that ultimate control over the corporation should reside with the shareholder class; that corporate managers should be charged with managing the corporation in the interests of its shareholders; that other corporate constituencies, such as creditors, employees, suppliers, and customers, should have their interests protected by contractual and regulatory means rather than through participation in corporate governance; that non-controlling shareholders should receive strong protection from exploitation by controlling shareholders; and that the principal measure of the interests of the publicly traded corporation's shareholders is the market value of their shares in the firm. For simplicity, we shall refer to the view of the corporation comprised by these elements as the 'standard shareholder-oriented model' of the corporate form (or, for brevity, simply 'the standard model'). To the extent that corporate law bears on the implementation of this standard model—as to an important degree it does—this consensus on the appropriate conduct of corporate affairs is also a consensus as to the appropriate content of corporate law, and it is likely to have profound effects on the development of that law.

3.1. *In Whose Interest?*

As we argue in Section 4, the emerging consensus today on the shareholder-oriented model of corporate governance results in large measure from disenchantment with regimes that have assigned a privileged role to managers, employees, or the state in corporate affairs. This is not to say that there is agreement that corporations should be run in the interests of shareholders alone, much less that the law should sanction that result. All thoughtful people believe that corporate enterprise should be organized and operated to serve the interests of society as a whole, and that the interests of shareholders deserve no greater weight in this social calculus than do the interests of any other members of society. The point is simply that now, as a consequence of both logic and experience, there is convergence on a view that the best means to this end (that is, the pursuit of aggregate social welfare) is to make corporate managers strongly accountable to shareholder interests and, at least in direct terms, only to those interests. It follows that even the extreme proponents of the so-called 'concession theory' of the corporation can embrace the primacy of shareholder interests in good conscience.[2] Even if the legal power to form a corporation is regarded as a privilege conferred by the state for the benefit of all participants in the enterprise, these participants will enjoy the greatest benefits if the firm is governed in the interests of shareholders.

Of course, asserting the primacy of shareholder interests in corporate law does not imply that the interests of corporate stakeholders must or should go unprotected. It merely indicates that the most efficacious legal mechanisms for protecting the interests of non-shareholder constituencies—or at least all constituencies other than creditors—lie outside of corporate law. For workers, this includes the law of labour contracting, pension law, health and safety law, and anti-discrimination law. For consumers, it includes product safety regulation, warranty law, tort law governing product liability, antitrust law, and mandatory disclosure of product contents and characteristics. For the public at large, it includes environmental law and the law of nuisance and mass torts.

Creditors, to be sure, are to some degree an exception. There remains general agreement that corporate law should directly regulate some aspects of the relationship between a business corporation and its creditors. Conspicuous examples include rules governing veil piercing and limits on corporate distributions in the presence of inadequate capital. The reason for these rules, however, is that there are unique problems of creditor contracting that are integral to the corporate form, owing principally to the presence of limited liability as a structural characteristic of that form. These types of rules, however, are modest in scope. Outside of bankruptcy, they do not involve creditors in corporate governance, but rather are confined to limiting shareholders' ability to use the characteristics of the corporate form opportunistically to exploit creditors.

3.1.1. *Which Shareholders?*

The shareholder-oriented model does more than assert the primacy of shareholder interests, however. It asserts the interests of all shareholders, including minority shareholders. More particularly, it is a central tenet in the standard model that minority or non-controlling shareholders should receive strong protection from exploitation at the hands of controlling shareholders. In publicly-traded firms, this means that all shareholders should be assured an essentially equal claim on corporate earnings and assets.

There are two conspicuous reasons for this approach, both of which are rooted in efficiency concerns. One reason is that, absent credible protection for non-controlling shareholders, business corporations will have difficulty raising capital from the equity markets. The second reason is that the devices by which controlling shareholders divert to themselves a disproportionate share of corporate benefits commonly involve inefficient investment choices and management policies.

3.1.2. *The Import of Ownership Structure*

It is sometimes said that the shareholder-oriented model of corporate law is well suited only to those jurisdictions in which one finds large numbers of firms with widely dispersed share ownership, such as the United States of America and the United Kingdom. A different model is appropriate, it is said, for those jurisdictions in which ownership is more concentrated, such as the nations of continental Europe. This view, however, is unconvincing.

Closely-held corporations, like publicly-held corporations, operate most efficiently when the law helps assure that managers are primarily responsive to shareholder interests and that controlling shareholders do not opportunistically exploit non-controlling shareholders. Shareholder primacy does not logically privilege any particular ownership structure. Indeed, both concentrated and dispersed shareholdings have been celebrated, at different times and by different commentators, for their ability to advance shareholder interests in the face of serious agency problems. Thus, the shareholder model is distinct from the conventional opposition of a 'dispersed ownership' system of corporate governance to a 'concentrated ownership' system of governance (Coffee, Chapter 4, this volume). The only point of tangency between the two is the possibility that dispersed share ownership may, as a prerequisite, require shareholder-oriented corporate law—and, in particular, strong legal protection for minority shareholders.[3] But this connection, were it demonstrated, would merely highlight the value of shareholder-oriented law for widely-held firms; it would in no way imply that this law was without value for firms with concentrated ownership.

Still more to the point, differences in ownership structures of corporations among the major commercial jurisdictions are often exaggerated. Every jurisdiction includes a range of ownership structures. While both USA and UK have many large firms with dispersed ownership, both countries also contain a far larger number of corporations that are closely held.[4] Similarly, every major Continental European jurisdiction has at least a handful of firms with dispersed ownership (La Porta *et al.* 1999: 494–5), and the number of such firms is evidently growing. It follows that every jurisdiction should have a corporate law adequate to handle the full range of ownership structures.

Thus, just as the core features of the corporate form rapidly crystallized in the late nineteenth century, we are witnessing rapid convergence on the standard shareholder-oriented model of corporate governance at the beginning of the twenty-first century. This normative consensus will predictably result in substantial convergence in the law and practice of corporate governance as well.

4. FORCES OF IDEOLOGICAL CONVERGENCE

There are several principal factors driving consensus on the standard model: the failure of alternative models; the competitive pressures of global commerce; and the shift of interest group influence in favour of an emerging shareholder class. We consider these developments here in sequence.

4.1. *The Failure of Alternative Models*

The most basic debate and experimentation about corporate law during the twentieth century have centred on the ways in which that law should accommodate the interests of non-shareholder constituencies. In this regard, there are three principal alternatives to a shareholder-oriented model, which we term the manager-oriented, labour-oriented, and state-oriented models of corporate law respectively. Although each of these alternatives has, at various points and in various jurisdictions, achieved some success both in practice and in received opinion, all three have ultimately lost much of their normative appeal.

4.1.1. *The Manager-Oriented Model*

In the United States of America, there existed an important strain of normative thought from the 1930s through the 1960s that extolled the virtues of granting substantial discretion to the managers of large business corporations. Merrick Dodd and John Kenneth Galbraith, for example, were conspicuously identified with this position, and Adolph Berle came to it late in life.[5] At the core of this view was the belief that professional corporate managers could serve as disinterested technocratic fiduciaries who would guide business corporations to perform in ways that would serve the general public interest. The corporate social responsibility literature of the 1950s can be seen as an embodiment of these views.[6]

The normative appeal of this view arguably provided part of the rationale for the various legal developments in USA law in the 1950s and 1960s that tended to reinforce the discretionary authority of corporate managers, such as the Williams Act and amendments to the Securities Exchange Commission's (SEC) proxy rules. The collapse of the conglomerate movement in the 1970s and 1980s, however, largely destroyed the normative appeal of the managerial model. It is now the conventional wisdom that, when managers are given great discretion over corporate investment policies, they tend to serve disproportionately their own interests, however well-intentioned they may be. While managerial firms may be in some ways more efficiently responsive to non-shareholder interests than are firms that are more dedicated to serving their shareholders, the price paid in inefficiency of operations and excessive investment in low-value projects is now considered too great.

4.1.2. *The Labour-Oriented Model*

Large-scale enterprise clearly presents problems of labour contracting. Simple contracts and the basic doctrines of contract law are inadequate in themselves to govern the long-term relationships between workers and the firms that employ them—relationships that may be afflicted by, among other things, substantial transaction-specific investments and asymmetries of information.

Collective bargaining via organized unions has been one approach to those problems, an approach that lies outside corporate law, since it is not dependent on the organizational structure of the firms with which the employees bargain. Another approach, and one that importantly involves corporate law, has been to involve employees directly in corporate governance by, for example, providing for employee representation on the firm's board of directors. Although serious attention was given to employee participation in corporate governance in Germany as early as the Weimar Republic, unionism was the dominant approach everywhere until the Second World War. Then, after the War, serious experimentation with employee participation in corporate governance began in Europe. The results of this experimentation are most conspicuous in Germany where, under legislation initially adopted for the coal and steel industries in 1951 and extended by stages to the rest of German industry between 1952 and 1976, employees are entitled to elect half of the members of the (upper-tier) board of directors in all large German firms (Pistor 1999). This German form of 'codetermination' has been the most far-reaching experiment with employee participation. It is not unique, however. A number of other European countries have experimented in more modest ways, typically requiring between one and three labour representatives on the boards of large corporations. Moreover, the Dutch have adopted a wholly unique model for larger domestic companies that combines elements of the manager-, labour-, and state-oriented models. Under this Dutch 'structure' regime, supervisory boards are self-appointing, although both labour and shareholders retain their right to object to the board appointments. In the event of an objection, the commercial court decides.

Enthusiasm for employee participation crested in the 1970s with the radical expansion of codetermination in Germany and the drafting of the European Community's proposed Fifth Directive on Company Law,[7] under which German-style codetermination would be extended throughout Europe. Employee participation also attracted considerable attention in the USA during that period, as adversarial unionism began to lose its appeal as a means of dealing with problems of labour contracting and, in fact, began to disappear from the industrial scene. Since then, however, worker participation in corporate governance has steadily lost power as a normative ideal. Despite repeated watering-down, Europe's Fifth Directive has never become law, and it now seems highly unlikely that German-style codetermination will ever be adopted elsewhere.

The growing view today is that meaningful direct worker voting participation in corporate affairs tends to produce inefficient decisions, paralysis, or weak boards, and that these costs are likely to exceed any potential benefits that worker participation might bring. The problem, at root, seems to be one of governance. While direct employee participation in corporate decision-making may mitigate some of the inefficiencies that can beset labour contracting, the workforce in typical firms is too heterogeneous in its interests to form an effective governing body—and the problems are magnified greatly when employees must share governance with investors, as in codetermined firms.[8] In general, contractual devices, whatever their weaknesses, are (when supplemented by appropriate labour market regulation) evidently superior to voting and other collective choice mechanisms in resolving conflicts of interest among and between a corporation's investors and employees.[9]

Today, even inside Germany, few commentators argue for codetermination as a general model for corporate law in other jurisdictions. Rather, codetermination now tends to be defended in Germany as, at most, a workable adaptation to local interests and circumstances or, even more modestly, an experiment that, though of questionable value, would now be politically difficult to undo.[10]

4.1.3. *The State-Oriented Model*

Both before and after the Second World War, there was widespread support for a corporatist system in which the government would play a strong direct role in the affairs of large business firms to provide some assurance that private enterprise would serve the public interest. Technocratic governmental bureaucrats, the theory went, would help to avoid the deficiencies of the market through the direct exercise of influence in corporate affairs. This approach was most extensively realized in post-war France and Japan. In the USA, though there was little actual experimentation with this approach outside of the defence industries, the model attracted considerable intellectual attention. Perhaps the most influential exposition of the state-oriented model in the Anglo-American world was Andrew Shonfield's book, *Modern Capitalism* (1968: 84–5), with its admiring description of French and Japanese style 'indicative planning'. The strong performance of the Japanese economy, and subsequently of other state-guided Asian economies, lent substantial credibility to this model even through the 1980s.

The principal instruments of state control over corporate affairs in corporatist economies generally lie outside of corporate law. They include, for example, substantial discretion in the hands of government bureaucrats over the allocation of credit, foreign exchange, licences, and exemptions from anti-competition rules. Nevertheless, corporate law also plays a role by, for example, weakening shareholder control over corporate managers (to reduce pressures on managers that might operate counter to the preferences of the state) and employing state-administered criminal sanctions rather than shareholder-controlled civil lawsuits as the principal sanction for managerial malfeasance (to give the state strong authority over managers that could be exercised at the government's discretion).

The state-oriented model, however, has now also lost most of its attraction. One reason is the move away from state socialism in general as a popular intellectual and political model. Important landmarks on this path include the rise of Thatcherism in England in the 1970s, Mitterand's abandonment of state ownership in France in the 1980s, and the sudden collapse of communism nearly everywhere in the 1990s. The relatively poor performance of the Japanese corporate sector after 1989, together with the more recent collapse of other Asian economies that were organized on state corporatist lines, has now discredited this model even further. Today, few would assert that giving the state a strong direct hand in corporate affairs has much normative appeal.

4.1.4. *Stakeholder Models*

Over the past decade, the literature on corporate governance and corporate law has sometimes advocated 'stakeholder' models as a normatively attractive alternative to a shareholder-oriented view of the corporation. The stakeholders involved may be employees, creditors, customers, merchants in a firm's local community, or even broader interest groups such as beneficiaries of a well-preserved environment. These stakeholders, it is argued, will be vulnerable to exploitation by the firm and its shareholders if corporate managers are accountable only to the firm's shareholders; corporate law must therefore assure that managers are responsive to the interests of stakeholders as well as to the interests of shareholders. But if stakeholder theories address a single problem of protecting non-shareholder interests in the corporation, they posit at least two distinct solutions to this problem—what we will label, respectively, the 'trustee' model (Hansmann and Kraakman 2001) and the 'representative' model of stakeholder-oriented corporate governance.

(i) The trustee model

The trustee model charges a corporation's board of directors and senior managers to act on behalf of the entire enterprise by co-ordinating the contributions and returns of all of its stakeholders. In this model directors do not represent the shareholders that elect them but, rather, the enterprise as a whole as against the parochial interests of all stakeholders. As described by Margaret Blair and Lynn Stout (1999), two of its most sophisticated proponents, the theory that underlies the trustee model (as well as other stakeholder models) envisions the public corporation as a 'team' of stakeholders—shareholders, managers, employees, and perhaps creditors—each of whom must make firm-specific investments for the enterprise to function efficiently (see also Shleifer and Summers 1988; Gordon and Schmid 2000). Since such firm-specific investments expose all team members to the risk of opportunism from other members, all team members prefer a neutral party—an outsider without an interest in the firm—to co-ordinate contributions and allocate rewards among team members (Blair and Stout 1999: 253–4, 273–87). In the case of the public corporation, this outsider is said to be the board of directors, which in the USA typically includes a majority of independent directors who have little or no financial investment in the company.

For Blair and Stout, the trustee model is not only a normative ideal but also a positive depiction of what already exists under the principles of American corporate law.[11] Far from encouraging the single-minded focus on shareholder value that some Europeans fear, USA law, according to Blair and Stout, presses boards to mediate among the interests of all stakeholders. In particular, they point to features of USA law that protect board discretion at the expense of shareholder influence: the severe restrictions on the legal power of shareholders to take management decisions, the discretion apportioned to directors by the business judgement rule, the difficulties faced by shareholders who attempt to exercise their voting rights in a proxy contest, and the so-called 'constituency statutes' that expressly invite boards to consider the interests of non-shareholder constituencies when evaluating takeover proposals (ibid.: 287–319). Outside the USA, moreover, the trustee model remains a topic of active debate.[12]

(ii) The representative model

Nevertheless, as long as shareholders select directors under the trustee model, the board's power to arbitrate among conflicting stakeholder interests is limited.[13] By contrast, the representative model of stakeholder governance assigns rights to appoint directors directly to stakeholders rather than reserving them for shareholders alone. In this model, then, qualified non-shareholder constituencies appoint their own directors, who together elaborate policies that maximize the joint welfare of all stakeholders, subject to the bargaining leverage that each group brings to the boardroom table. The board, in this model, is the focal point for an unmediated 'coalition of stakeholder groups', which functions as 'an arena for co-operation with respect to the function of monitoring the management', as well as an arena for resolving 'conflicts with respect to the specific interests of different stakeholder groups' (Schmidt and Spindler 1999: 14).

(iii) Stakeholder models assessed

In our view, neither the trustee nor the representative model of stakeholder governance is likely to exert much influence on the development of corporate law today, even though both have strong partisans among legal academics. A principal reason is that they have been tried before. At bottom they are simply variants on the manager- and labour-oriented models of corporate governance of earlier decades, despite their novel rhetoric and economic justification.

The trustee model reformulates the manager-oriented model of the 1950s. Where that model depicted managers—and, in particular, chief executive officers—as professionals skilled at balancing the contributions and rewards of other stakeholders, the trustee model turns instead to corporate directors. Thus Blair and Stout see the autonomous power of USA boards as the legal foundation for a neutral trustee, a 'mediating hierarch', to superintend the set of long-term contracts among the factors of production (Blair and Stout 1999: 315–19). This move entails a certain loss of realism since CEOs are usually said to exercise far more power than boards in widely-held firms. Thus, the unusual legal autonomy of USA boards is better understood as an expression of the political power of managers rather than as a check on it. But even if boards do act as trustees distinct from managers, the trustee model does not improve on the old-fashioned manager-oriented model. While untethered directors can better serve the interests of some classes of stakeholders, such as a firm's existing employees and creditors, the director's own interests will often come to have disproportionate salience in their decision-making, with costs to other interest groups—such as shareholders, customers, and potential new employees and creditors—that outweigh any gains to the stakeholders who are benefited. Moreover, the courts are evidently incapable of formulating and enforcing fiduciary duties of sufficient refinement to assure that managers behave more efficiently and fairly.

Just as the trustee model recycles managerialism, representative stakeholder models repackage yesterday's labour-oriented model, which they sometimes extend to include non-labour constituencies. But the weaknesses of the labour-oriented regime remain, and in fact they grow more severe as the list of boardroom constituencies grow. The mandatory inclusion of any set of stakeholder representatives on the board is likely to impair corporate decision-making processes with costly consequences that outweigh any gains to the groups that obtain representation. Thus, the same forces that have been discrediting the older models are also undermining the stakeholder model as a viable alternative to the shareholder-oriented model.

4.2. *Competitive Pressure Toward Convergence*

The shareholder-oriented model has emerged as the normative consensus not just because of the failure of the alternatives, but because important economic forces have made the virtues of that model increasingly salient. There are, broadly speaking, three ways in which a model of corporate governance can come to be recognized as superior: by force of logic, by force of example, and by force of competition. The emerging consensus in favour of the standard model has, in recent years, been driven with increasing intensity by each of these forces. We examine them here in turn.

4.2.1. *The Force of Logic*

An important source of the success of the standard model is that, in recent years, scholars and other commentators in law, economics, and business have developed persuasive reasons, which we have already explored above, to believe that this model offers greater efficiencies than the principal alternatives. One of these reasons is that, in most circumstances, the interests of equity investors in the firm—the firm's residual claimants—cannot be adequately protected by contract. Rather, to protect their interests, they must be given the right to control the firm. A second reason is that, if the control rights granted to the firm's equity-holders are exclusive and strong, they will have powerful incentives to maximize the value of the firm. A third reason is that the interests of participants in the firm other than shareholders can generally be given substantial protection by contract and regulation, so that maximization of the firm's value by its shareholders complements the interests of those other participants rather than competing with them. A fourth reason is that, even where contractual and regulatory devices offer only imperfect protection for non-shareholder interests, adapting the firm's governance structure to make it directly responsible to those interests creates more difficulties than it solves.

This reasoning is today reflected in much of the current literature on corporate finance and the economics of the firm—a literature that is becoming increasingly international. The consequence is to highlight the economic case for the shareholder-oriented model of governance. In addition, the persuasive power of the standard model has been amplified through its acceptance by a worldwide network of corporate intermediaries, including international law firms, the big five accounting firms, and the principal investment banks and consulting firms—a network whose rapidly expanding scale and scope give it exceptional influence in diffusing the standard model of shareholder-centred corporate governance.

4.2.2. *The Force of Example*

The second source of the success of the standard model of corporate governance is the economic performance of jurisdictions in which it predominates. A simple comparison across countries adhering to different models—at least in very recent years—lends credence to the view that adherence to the standard model promotes better economic outcomes. The developed common law jurisdictions have performed well in comparison to the principal East Asian and continental European countries, which are less in alignment with the standard model. The main examples include, of course, the strong performance of the American economy in comparison with the weaker economic performance of the German, Japanese, and French economies.

One might surely object that the success of the shareholder-oriented model is quite recent and will perhaps prove to be ephemeral, and that the apparent normative consensus based on that success will be ephemeral as well. After all, only fifteen years ago, many thought that Japanese and German firms, which were clearly not organized on the shareholder-oriented model, were winning the competition, and that this was because they had adopted a superior form of corporate governance.[14] However, this is probably a mistaken interpretation of the nature of the economic competition in recent decades, and it is surely at odds with today's prevailing opinion. The competition of the 1960s, 1970s, and early 1980s was in fact among Japanese state-oriented corporations, German labour-oriented corporations, and American manager-oriented corporations. It was not until the late 1980s that one could speak of widespread international competition from shareholder-oriented firms.

4.2.3. *The Force of Competition*

The increasing internationalization of both product and financial markets has brought individual firms from jurisdictions adhering to different models into direct competition. It is now widely thought that firms organized and operated according to the shareholder-oriented model have had the upper hand in these more direct encounters as well.[15] Such firms can be expected to have important competitive advantages over firms adhering more closely to other models. These advantages include access to equity capital at lower cost (including, conspicuously, start-up capital), more aggressive development of new product markets (Frydman *et al.* 1998), stronger incentives to reorganize along lines that are managerially coherent, and more rapid abandonment of inefficient investments.

These competitive advantages do not always imply that firms governed by the standard model will displace those governed by an alternative model in the course of firm-to-firm competition, for two reasons. First, firms operating under the standard model may be no more efficient than other firms in many respects. For example, state-oriented Japanese and Korean companies have demonstrated great efficiency in the management and expansion of standardized production processes, while German and Dutch firms such as Daimler Benz and Philips (operating under labour- and management-oriented models, respectively) have been widely recognized for engineering prowess and technical innovation. Second, even when firms governed by the standard model are clearly more efficient than their non-standard competitors, the cost-conscious standard-model firms may be forced to abandon particular markets for precisely that reason. Less efficient firms organized under alternative models may over-invest in capacity or accept abnormally low returns on their investments in general, and thereby come to dominate a product market by underpricing their profit-maximizing competitors.

But if the competitive advantages of standard-model firms do not necessarily force the displacement of non-standard firms in established markets, these standard-model firms are likely, for the reasons offered above, to achieve a disproportionate share among start-up firms, in new product markets, and in industries that are in the process of rapid change.[16]

The ability of standard-model firms to expand rapidly in growth industries is magnified, moreover, by access to institutional investors and the international equity markets, which understandably prefer shareholder-oriented governance and are influential advocates of the standard model. Those equity investors, after all, are exclusively interested in maximizing the financial returns on their investments. Over time, then, the standard model is likely to win the competitive struggle on the margins, confining other governance models to older firms and mature product markets. As the pace of technological change continues to quicken, this competitive advantage should continue to increase.

4.2.4. *The Rise of the Shareholder Class*

In tandem with the competitive forces just described, a final source of ideological convergence on the standard model is a fundamental realignment of interest group structures in developed economies. At the centre of this realignment is the emergence of a public shareholder class as a broad and powerful interest group in both corporate and political affairs across jurisdictions. There are two elements to this realignment. The first is the rapid expansion of the ownership of equity securities within broad segments of society, creating a coherent interest group that presents an increasingly strong countervailing force to the organized interests of managers, employees, and the state. The second is the shift in power, within this expanding shareholder class, in favour of the interests of minority and noncontrolling shareholders over those of inside or controlling shareholders.

(i) The diffusion of equity ownership

Stock ownership is becoming more pervasive everywhere.[17] No longer is it confined to a small group of wealthy citizens. In the USA, this diffusion of share ownership has been underway since the beginning of the twentieth century. In recent years, however, it has accelerated substantially. Since the Second World War, an ever-increasing number of American workers have had their savings invested in corporate equities through pension funds. Over the same period, the mutual fund industry has also expanded rapidly, becoming the repository of an ever-increasing share of non-pension savings for the population at large (The Conference Board 1997). We have begun to see parallel developments in Europe and Japan, and to some extent elsewhere, as markets for equity securities have become more developed.[18]

The growing wealth of developed societies is a major factor underlying these changes. Even blue collar workers now often have sufficient personal savings to justify investment in equity securities. No longer do labour and capital constitute clearly distinct interest groups in society. Workers, through share ownership, increasingly share the economic interests of other equity-holders. Indeed, in the USA, union pension funds are today quite active in pressing the view that companies must be managed in the best interests of their shareholders (Schwab and Thomas 1998: 341).

(ii) The shift in balance toward public shareholders

As the example of the activist union pension funds suggests, diffusion of share ownership is only one aspect of the rise of the shareholder class. Another aspect is the new prominence of substantial institutions that have interests coincident with those of public shareholders and that are prepared to articulate and defend those interests. Institutional investors, such as pension funds and mutual funds—which are particularly prominent in the USA and are now rapidly growing elsewhere as well—are the most conspicuous examples of these institutions. Associations of minority investors in European countries provide another example. These institutions not only give effective voice to shareholder interests, but also promote, in particular, the interests of dispersed public shareholders rather than those of controlling shareholders or corporate insiders. The result is that ownership of equity among the public at large, while broader than ever, is at the same time gaining more effective voice in corporate affairs.

Moreover, the new activist shareholder-oriented institutions are today acting increasingly on an international scale. As a consequence, their influence now reaches well beyond their home jurisdictions (Steinmetz and Sesit 1999: A1, A8). We now have not only a common ideology supporting shareholder-oriented corporate law, but also an organized interest group to press that ideology—an interest group that is broad, diverse, and increasingly international in its membership.

In the USA, the principal effect of the expansion and empowerment of the shareholder class has been to shift interest group power to shareholders from managers. In Europe and Japan, the more important effect has been to shift power away from workers and the state and, increasingly, away from dominant shareholders.[19]

5. WEAK FORCES FOR CONVERGENCE

We have spoken here of a number of forces pressing toward international convergence on a relatively uniform standard model of corporate law. Those forces include the internal logic of efficiency, competition, interest group pressure, imitation, and the need for compatibility. We have largely ignored two other potential forces that might also press toward convergence: explicit efforts at cross-border harmonization and competition between jurisdictions for corporate charters.

5.1. *Harmonization*

The European Union has been the locus of the most intense efforts to date at self-conscious harmonization of corporate law across jurisdictions. That process, however, has proven a relatively weak force for convergence: where there exists substantial divergence in corporate law across member states, efforts at harmonization have generally borne little fruit. Moreover, harmonization proposals have often been characterized by an effort to impose throughout the EU regulatory measures of questionable efficiency, with the result that harmonization sometimes seems more an effort to avoid the standard model than to further it.

For these reasons, the other pressures toward convergence described above are likely to be much more important forces for convergence than are explicit efforts at harmonization. At most, we expect that, once the consensus for adoption of the standard model has become sufficiently strong, harmonization may serve as a convenient pretext for overriding the objections of entrenched national interest groups that resist reform of corporate law within individual states.

5.2. *Competition for Charters*

The USA experience suggests that cross-border competition for corporate charters can be a powerful force for convergence in corporate law and, in particular, for convergence on an efficient model (Romano 1993). It seems quite plausible, however, that the choice of law rules necessary for this form of competition will not be adopted in most jurisdictions until substantial convergence has already taken place. We expect that the most important steps toward convergence can and will be taken with relative rapidity before explicit cross-border competition for charters is permitted in most of the world, and that the latter process will ultimately be used, at most, as a means of working out the fine details of convergence and of ongoing minor experimentation and adjustment thereafter.

6. CONVERGENCE OF GOVERNANCE PRACTICES

Thus far we have attempted to explain the sources of ideological convergence on the standard model of corporate governance. Our principal argument is on this normative level: we make the claim that no important competitors to the standard model of corporate governance remain persuasive today. This claim is consistent with significant differences among jurisdictions in corporate practice and law over the short run; ideological convergence does not necessarily mean rapid convergence in practice. There are many potential obstacles to rapid institutional convergence, even when there is general consensus on what constitutes best practice. Nevertheless, we believe that the developing ideological consensus on the standard model will have important implications for the convergence of practice and law over the long run.

We expect that the reform of corporate governance practices will generally precede the reform of corporate law, for the simple reason that governance practice is largely a matter of private ordering that does not require legislative action. Recent events in most developed jurisdictions—and in many developing ones—bear out this prediction. Under the influence of the ideological and interest group changes discussed above, corporate governance reform has already become the watchword not only in North America but also in Europe and Japan. Corporate actors are themselves implementing structural changes to bring their firms closer to the standard model. In the USA, these changes include appointment of larger numbers of independent directors to boards of directors, reduction in overall board size, development of powerful board committees dominated by outsiders (such as audit committees, compensation committees, and nominating committees), closer links between management compensation and the value of the firm's equity securities, and strong communication between board members and institutional shareholders. In Europe and Japan, many of the same changes are taking place, though with a lag. Examples range from the OECD's promulgation of new principles of corporate governance, to recent decisions by Japanese companies to reduce board sizes and include non-executive directors (following the lead of Sony), to the rapid diffusion of stock option compensation plans for top managers in the UK and in the principal commercial jurisdictions of Continental Europe.

7. LEGAL CONVERGENCE

Not surprisingly, convergence proceeds more slowly in corporate law than in governance practice. Legal change requires legislative action. Nevertheless, we expect shareholder pressure (and the power of shareholder-oriented ideology) to force gradual legal changes, largely but not entirely in the direction of Anglo-American corporate and securities law. There are already important indications of evolutionary convergence in the realms of board structure, securities regulation, and accounting methodologies, and even in the regulation of takeovers.

7.1. *Board Structure*

With respect to board structure, convergence has been in the direction of a legal regime that strongly favours a single-tier board that is relatively small and that contains some insiders as well as a majority of outside directors. Mandatory two-tier board structures seem a thing of the past; the weaker and less responsive boards that they promote are justified principally as a complement to worker codetermination and thus share—indeed, constitute one of—the weaknesses of the latter institution. The declining fortunes of the two-tier board are reflected in the evolution of the European Union's Proposed Regulation on the Statute for a European Company. When originally drafted in 1970, that Regulation called for a mandatory two-tier board. In 1991, however, the Proposed Regulation was amended to permit member states to prescribe either a two-tier or a single-tier system. Meanwhile, on the practical side, France, which made provision for an optional two-tier board when the concept was more in vogue, has seen few of its corporations adopt the device (Aste 1999: 45).

At the same time, jurisdictions that traditionally favoured the opposite extreme of insider-dominated, single-tier boards have come to accept a significant complement of outside directors. In the USA, the New York Stock Exchange listing rules have long mandated that independent directors serve on the important audit committees of listed firms (NYSE 1998) and, more recently, state law doctrine has created a strong role for outside directors in approving transactions where interests might be conflicted.[20] In Japan, a similar evolution may be foreshadowed by the recent movement among Japanese companies, mentioned above, toward smaller boards and independent directors, and by the recent publication of a code of corporate governance principles advocating these reforms by a committee of leading Japanese managers.[21] The result is convergence from both ends toward the middle: while two-tier boards themselves seem to be on the way out, countries with single-tier board structures are incorporating, in their regimes, one of the strengths of the typical two-tier board regime, namely the substantial role it gives to independent (outside) directors.

7.2. *Disclosure and Capital Market Regulation*

Regulation of routine disclosure to shareholders, intended to aid in policing corporate managers, is also converging conspicuously. Without seeking to examine this complex field in detail here, we note that major jurisdictions outside of the USA are reinforcing their disclosure systems, while the USA has been retreating from some of the more inexplicably burdensome of its federal regulations, such as the highly restrictive proxy solicitation rules that until recently crippled communication among American institutional investors. Indeed, the subject matter of mandatory disclosure for public companies is startlingly similar across the major commercial jurisdictions today.[22] Moreover, disclosure practices on the European continent apparently track those of the USA and the UK even more closely than the law requires. American practices in particular set accepted international standards for disclosure, even when securities are issued outside the USA to non-USA investors (Jackson and Pan 2000).

Similarly, uniform accounting standards are rapidly crystallizing out of the Babel of national rules and practices into two well-defined sets of international standards: the Generally Accepted Accounting Principles (GAAP) accounting rules administered by the Financial Auditing Standards Board in the USA and the International Accounting Standards administered by the International Accounting Standards Committee in London. While important differences remain between the competing sets of international standards, these differences are far smaller than the variations among the national accounting methodologies that preceded GAAP and the new International Standards. The two international standards, moreover, are likely to converge further, if only because of the economic savings that would result from a single set of global accounting standards (MacDonald 1999).

7.3. *Shareholder Suits*

Suits initiated by shareholders against directors and managers are now being accommodated in countries that had previously rendered them ineffective. Germany recently reduced the ownership threshold that qualifies shareholders to demand legal action (to be brought by the supervisory board or special company representative) against managing directors, dropping that threshold from a 10 per cent equity stake to the lesser of a 5 per cent stake or a one million DM stake when there is suspicion of dishonesty or illegality (Baums 1999). Japan, in turn, has altered its rules on posting a bond to remove disincentives for litigation. At the same time, USA law is moving toward the centre from the other direction by beginning to rein in the country's strong incentives for potentially opportunistic litigation. At the federal level, there are recently-strengthened pleading requirements upon initiation of shareholder actions, new safe harbours for forward-looking company projections, and recent provision for lead shareholders to take control in class actions.[23] State law rules, meanwhile, are making it easier for a corporation to get a shareholder's suit dismissed.

7.4. *Takeovers*

Regulation of takeovers also seems headed for convergence. As it is, current differences in takeover regulation are more apparent than real. Hostile takeovers are rare outside the Anglo-American jurisdictions, principally owing to the more concentrated patterns of shareholdings outside those jurisdictions. As shareholding patterns become more homogeneous (as we expect they will), and as corporate culture everywhere becomes more accommodating of takeovers (as it seems destined to), takeovers will presumably become much more common in Europe, Japan, and elsewhere.[24]

Moreover, where operative legal constraints on takeovers in fact differ, they show signs of convergence. In particular, for several decades USA has been increasing its regulation of takeovers, placing additional constraints both on the ability of acquirers to act opportunistically and on the ability of incumbent managers to entrench themselves or engage in self-dealing. With the widespread diffusion of the 'poison pill' defence, and the accompanying limits that courts have placed on the use of that defence, partial hostile tender offers of a coercive character are a thing of the past—a result similar to that which European jurisdictions have accomplished with a 'mandatory bid rule' requiring acquirers of control to purchase all shares in their target companies at a single price.

To be sure, jurisdictions diverge in other aspects of takeover law where the points of convergence are still uncertain. For example, American directors enjoy far more latitude to defend against hostile takeovers than do directors in most European jurisdictions. Under current Delaware law, incumbent boards have authority to resist hostile offers, although they remain vulnerable to bids that are tied to proxy fights at shareholders' meetings. As the incidence of hostile takeovers increases in Europe, European jurisdictions may incline toward Delaware by permitting additional defensive tactics.[25] Alternatively, given the dangers of managerial entrenchment, Delaware may move toward European norms by limiting defensive tactics more severely. While we cannot predict where the equilibrium point will lie, it is a reasonable conjecture that the law on both sides of the Atlantic will ultimately converge on a single regime.

7.5. *Judicial Discretion*

There remains one very general aspect of corporate law on which one might feel that convergence will be slow to come: the degree of judicial discretion in resolving disputes among corporate actors ex post. Such discretion has long been much more conspicuous in the common law jurisdictions, and particularly in the USA, than in the civil law jurisdictions. Even here, though, there is good reason to believe that there will be strong convergence across systems over time. Civil law jurisdictions, whether in the form of court decision-making or arbitration, seem to be moving toward a more discretionary model.[26] The USA securities law is civilian in spirit and elaborated by detailed rules promulgated by the SEC. At the same time, there are signs of growing discomfort with the more extreme forms of unpredictable ex post decision-making that have sometimes been characteristic of, say, the Delaware courts. Scholars have begun to suspect the open-ended texture of Delaware case law (Macey and Miller 1987; Branson 1989; Kamar 1998), while the American Law Institute has offered a code-like systemization of the corporate law in the form of the Corporate Governance Project, which includes even the notoriously vague and open-ended USA case law that articulates the fiduciary duties of loyalty and care.

8. POTENTIAL OBSTACLES TO CONVERGENCE

To be sure, the movement toward the standard model threatens important interests, which can be expected to serve as a brake on change. We doubt, however, that these interests will be able to stave off for long the reforms called for by the growing ideological consensus focused on the standard model.

Lucian Bebchuk and Mark Roe (1999) make an opposing argument for strong path dependence in corporate law, which proceeds in three steps. First, they suggest that controlling shareholders divert to themselves a disproportionate share of corporate cash flows in jurisdictions with weak minority shareholder protections (most jurisdictions, perhaps). Second, because these controllers presently enjoy large private benefits of control, they have a strong incentive to oppose changes in ownership, governance, or the law. And third, Bebchuk and Roe argue that controlling shareholders can block what they do not like. Controlling shareholders can retain control by refusing to sell their shares; they can manipulate corporate governance though their power to select directors; and, in those societies in which closely-held firms dominate the economy, controlling shareholders have the political influence to block legal reforms that would otherwise reduce their private returns.

To us, however, this pessimistic view seems unwarranted—at least on the consensus assumption that the standard model of corporate law and practice increases firm value.

Consider first the case in which controlling shareholders are financially motivated and care only about maximizing profits. If these controllers can capture the gains of governance reform, they have an obvious interest in efficient governance structures and legal reforms that the standard model can provide. Moreover, it is plausible that they can capture the gains from reform in two ways: either (1) by selling out to buyers who can credibly signal their intention to operate under non-exploitative governance rules; or (2) by squeezing out minority shareholders and restructuring their firm themselves along these same efficient lines. To be sure, law reform might still deny controllers such gains. For example, it might bar controllers from cashing out minority shareholders or taking control premia, which would make it difficult to extract the gains from efficient restructuring. But if controllers have the political influence to block reform altogether, it is reasonable to suppose that they also have the influence to appropriate the returns from reform for themselves.

The more difficult case for convergence arises if controlling shareholders, although mired in inefficient corporate governance, nevertheless prefer reinvesting and presiding over their fading empires to maximizing their economic returns. In theory, such controllers might oppose legal or governance reforms indefinitely. We conjecture, however, that even these controllers cannot stand against the standard model of corporate governance over the long term. By hypothesis, their firms will be disadvantaged relative to the better governed foreign or domestic competition. Moreover, these firms are unlikely to attract new outside capital. Instead, foreign and domestic capital will flow to firms that adopt the shareholder protective measures of the standard model, even if these firms do so outside the domestic legal framework—for example, by subscribing to exchange listing rules that require disclosure and protect minority shareholders, by listing on Exchanges in other jurisdictions to bond their protective intentions (as some Israeli firms now do by listing on NASDAQ) (Coffee 1999), or by voluntarily adopting some of the governance practices that offer the protections of the standard model. Eventually, the result will be to partition off—and grandfather in—the older family-controlled or manager-dominated firms, whose costly governance practices will make them increasingly irrelevant to economic activity even within their local jurisdictions.

9. EFFICIENT NON-CONVERGENCE

Not all divergence among corporate law regimes reflects inefficiency. Efficient divergence can arise either through adaptation to local social structures or through fortuity. Neither logic nor competition is likely to create strong pressure for this form of divergence to disappear. Consequently, it could survive for a considerable period of time. Still, though the rate of change may be slower, there is good reason to believe that even the extent of efficient divergence, like the extent of inefficient divergence, will continue to decrease relatively quickly.

9.1. *Differences in Institutional Context*

Sometimes jurisdictions choose alternative forms of corporate law because those alternatives complement other national differences in, for example, forms of shareholdings, means for enforcing the law, or related bodies of law such as bankruptcy. A case in point is the new

Russian corporation statute, which deviates self-consciously from the type of statute that the standard model would call for in more developed economies. To take just one example, the Russian statute imposes cumulative voting on all corporations as a mandatory rule, in strong contrast with the corporate law of most developed countries. The reason for this approach was largely to assure some degree of shareholder influence and access to information in the context of the peculiar pattern of shareholdings that has become commonplace in Russia as a result of that country's unique process of mass privatization.[27]

Nevertheless, the efficient degree of divergence in corporate law appears much smaller than the divergence in the other institutions in which corporate activity is embedded. For example, efficient divergence in creditor protection devices is probably much narrower than observed differences in the sources and structure of corporate credit. Similarly, the efficient array of mechanisms for protecting shareholders from managerial opportunism appears much narrower than the observed variety across jurisdictions in patterns of shareholdings.

Moreover, the economic institutions and legal structures in which corporate law must operate are themselves becoming more uniform across jurisdictions. This is conspicuously true, for example, of patterns of shareholdings. All countries are beginning to face, or need to face, the same varied types of shareholders, from controlling blockholders to mutual funds to highly dispersed individual shareholders. Some of this is driven by the converging forces of internal economic development. Thus, privatization of enterprise, increases in personal wealth, and the need for start-up finance (which is aided by a public market that offers an exit for the initial private investors) all promote an increasing incidence of small shareholdings and a consequent need for strong protection for minority shareholders. The globalization of capital markets presses to the same end. Hence Russia, to return to our earlier example, will presumably evolve over time toward the patterns of shareholdings typical of developed economies, and it will ultimately feel the need to conform its shareholder voting rules more closely to the rules found in those economies.

9.2. *Harmless Mutations*

In various cases we anticipate that there will be little or no efficiency difference among multiple alternative corporate law rules. In these cases, the pressures for convergence are lessened, although not entirely eliminated (since we still expect global investors to exert pressure to standardize).[28] Accounting standards offer an example. As we noted earlier, there are currently two different accounting methodologies that have achieved prominence among developed nations: the American GAAP and the European-inspired International Accounting Standards. Because these two sets of standards evolved separately, they differ in many significant details. From the best current evidence, however, neither obviously dominates the other in terms of efficiency.

If the economies involved were entirely autarchic, both accounting standards might well survive indefinitely with no sacrifice in efficiency. The increasing globalization of the capital markets, however, imposes strong pressure not only for all countries to adopt one or the other of these regimes, but to select a single common accounting regime. Over time, then, the network efficiencies of a common standard form in global markets are likely to eliminate even this and other forms of fortuitous divergence in corporate law.

10. INEFFICIENT CONVERGENCE

Having just recognized that efficiency does not always dictate convergence in corporate law, we must also recognize that the reverse can be true as well: a high degree of convergence need not always reflect efficiency. The most likely sources of such inefficient convergence are flaws in markets or in political institutions that are widely shared by modern economies and that are reinforced rather than mitigated by cross-border competition.

10.1. *Third-party Costs: Corporate Torts*

Perhaps the most conspicuous example of inefficient convergence is the rule—already universal, with only minor variations from one jurisdiction to the next—that limits shareholder liability for corporate torts. This rule induces inefficient risk-taking and excessive levels of risky activities—inefficiencies that appear to outweigh by far any offsetting benefits, such as reduced costs of litigation or the smoother functioning of the securities markets. As we have argued elsewhere, a general rule of unlimited pro rata shareholder liability for corporate torts appears to offer far greater overall efficiencies (Hansmann and Kraakman 1991: 1882–3).

Why, then, has there been universal convergence on an inefficient rule? The obvious answer is that neither markets nor politics work well to represent the interests of the persons who bear the direct costs of the rule, namely tort victims. Since, by definition, torts involve injuries to third parties, the parties affected by the rule—corporations and their potential tort victims—cannot contract around the rule to capture and share the gains from its alteration. At the same time, owing to the highly stochastic nature of most corporate torts, tort victims—and particularly the very large class of potential tort victims—do not constitute an easily organized political interest group.[29] Moreover, even if a given jurisdiction were to adopt a rule of shareholder liability for corporate torts, difficulties in enforcement would arise from the ease with which shareholdings or incorporation can today be shifted to other jurisdictions that retain the rule of limited liability.

10.2. *Managerialism*

A second example of inefficient conversion, arguably, is the considerable freedom enjoyed by managers in almost all jurisdictions to protect their prerogatives in cases when they might conflict with those of shareholders, including particularly managers' ability to defend their positions against hostile takeover attempts. Again, political and market failures seem responsible. Dispersed public shareholders, who are the persons most likely to be disadvantaged by the power of entrenched managers, face potentially serious problems of collective action in making their voice felt. Managers, whose positions make them a powerful and influential interest group everywhere, can use their political influence to keep the costs of collective action high—for example, by making it hard for a hostile acquirer to purchase an effective control block of shares from current shareholders. Corporate law might therefore converge, not precisely to the shareholder-oriented standard model that represents the ideological consensus, but rather to a variant of that model that has a slight managerial tilt.

10.3. *How Big a Problem?*

The problem of inefficient convergence in corporate law appears to be a relatively limited one, however. Tort victims aside, the relations among virtually all actors directly affected by the corporation are heavily contractual, which tends to give those actors a common interest in establishing efficient law. Moreover, as our earlier discussion has emphasized, shareholders, managers, workers, and voluntary creditors either have or are acquiring a powerful interest in efficient corporate law. Indeed, limited liability in tort arguably should not be considered a rule of corporate law at all, but instead should be viewed as a rule of tort law. And even limited liability in tort may come to be abandoned as large-scale tort damage becomes more common and consequently of greater political concern. We already see some movement in this direction in USA environmental law, which pushes aside the corporate veil to a startling degree in particular circumstances.

11. CONCLUSION

The triumph of the shareholder-oriented model of the corporation over its principal competitors is now assured, even if it was problematic as recently as twenty-five years ago. Logic alone did not establish the superiority of this standard model or of the prescriptive rules that it implies, which establish a strong corporate management with duties to serve the interests of shareholders alone, as well as strong minority shareholder protections. Rather, the standard model earned its position as the dominant model of the large corporation the hard way, by out-competing during the post-Second World War period the three alternative models of corporate governance: the managerial model, the labour-oriented model, and the state-oriented model.

If the failure of the principal alternatives has established the ideological hegemony of the standard model, though perhaps this should not come as a complete surprise, the standard model has never been questioned for the vast majority of corporations. It dominates the law and governance of closely held corporations in every jurisdiction. Most German companies do not participate in the codetermination regime, and most Dutch companies are not regulated by the managerial 'structure' regime. Similarly, the standard model of shareholder primacy has always been the dominant legal model in the two jurisdictions where the choice of models might be expected to matter most: the USA and the UK. The choice of models matters in these jurisdictions because large companies often have highly fragmented ownership structures. In Continental Europe, where most large companies are controlled by large shareholders (La Porta *et al.* 1999), the interests of controlling shareholders traditionally dominate corporate policy no matter what the prevailing ideology of the corporate form.

We predict, therefore, that as equity markets evolve in Europe and throughout the developed world, the ideological and competitive attractions of the standard model will become indisputable, even among legal academics. And as the goal of shareholder primacy becomes second nature even to politicians, convergence in most aspects of the law and practice of corporate governance is sure to follow.

Notes

1. An earlier and different version of this essay, entitled 'The End of History for Corporate Law', was published in the proceedings of the Columbia Law School Conference on Convergence in Corporate Governance Systems, and in the *Georgetown Law Journal.*
2. In a hoary debate that cuts across jurisdictional boundaries, proponents of the view that corporations exist by virtue of a state 'concession' or privilege have also been associated with the view that corporations ought to be governed in the interests of society—or all corporate constituencies—rather than in the private interest of shareholders alone (Dodd 1932: 1148–50; Mahoney 2000). Conversely, proponents of the view that the corporation is at bottom a contract among investors have tended to advance the primacy of shareholder interests in corporate governance.

   In our view, the traditional debate between concession and contract theorists is simply confused. On the one hand, corporations—whether 'concessions' or contracts—should be regulated when it is in the public interest to do so. On the other hand, the standard model is, in effect, an assertion that social welfare is best served by encouraging corporate managers to pursue shareholder interests.
3. Raphael La Porta and his colleagues (La Porta *et al.* 1997; 1998; 1999) have pioneered this view in an influential series of articles.
4. Indeed, significant numbers of widely-held USA and UK firms are also controlled firms (La Porta *et al.* 1999: 494–5).
5. Dodd and Berle conducted a classic debate on the subject in the 1930s, in which Dodd pressed the social responsibility of corporate managers while Berle championed shareholder interests (Berle 1932; Dodd 1932: 1145). By the 1950s, Berle seemed to have come around to Dodd's celebration of managerial discretion as a positive virtue that permits managers to act in the interests of society as a whole (Berle 1959: 107–10). John Kenneth Galbraith (1967) takes a similar position.
6. Galbraith (1967) and Berle (1959). For an important collection of essays arguing both sides of the question of managerial responsibility to the broader interests of society, see Mason (1959).
7. Proposal for a Fifth Company Law Directive, 1983 O.J. (C240)2.
8. Pistor (1999) notes that participants in codetermination regimes see earlier employee involvement in decision-making and reduced labour-management conflict as the principal benefit of the system, and a deterioration of firm-level governance—including principally a marked decline in the ability of the supervisory board to monitor and control management—as the cost of the system.
9. (Hansmann 1993*a*: 589–606; Hansmann 1993*b*; Hansmann 1996: 89–119). On the weaknesses of German boards, see, for example, Roe (1998: 167). In one of the few quantitative studies of the effects of German codetermination, Gordon and Schmid (2000) find that it reduces shareholder value but hold out hope that there might be an offsetting increase in the protection of the firm-specific human capital of employees.
10. Some commentators, of course, continue to see codetermination as a core element of a unique Northern European form of corporate governance (Albert 1993). Even Albert (ibid.: 169–90) concedes, however, the growing ideological power of shareholder-oriented corporate governance.
11. Other academic commentators urge law reform to realize the trustee model (Mitchell 1992).
12. The trustee model has been considered most recently in the ongoing effort to reformulate the duties of directors under UK company law, and has apparently been rejected by the Steering Group in favour of an 'enlightened shareholder interest' model. Compare Company Law Reform

Steering group (March 1999: 39–46) (contrasting alternatives of a duty to follow enlightened shareholder interest with a 'pluralist' duty to all stakeholders to encourage firm-specific investment) with Company Law Reform Steering group (2000: 29–31) (proposing a duty based on shareholder primacy over pluralist duty). Legal formulations of directorial duty on the Continent, however, still generally avoid embracing the norm of shareholder primacy.

13. For this reason the Dutch 'structure regime', under which the supervisory boards of larger domestic companies are self-appointing, subject only to the possibility of objection by labour or shareholders, is the most radical existent form of a trustee regime.
14. To be fair, however, American commentators tended to praise corporate governance in Germany and Japan in the name of the shareholder model. Thus, it was the purported ability of German banks to monitor managers and correctly value long-term business projects that caught the eye of American commentators after the 1970s, not codetermination or the labour-oriented model of the firm (Jacobs 1991: 69–71).
15. Indirect evidence to this effect comes from international surveys such as a recent poll of top managers conducted by the *Financial Times* to determine the world's most respected companies. Four of the top five most respected companies were American and hence operated under the shareholder model (the fifth was Daimler-Chrysler, which is 'almost' American for these purposes). Similarly, twenty-nine of the top forty firms were either American or British (*Financial Times* Web Site, 17 December 1999).
16. In this regard it should be noted that small and medium-sized firms in every jurisdiction are organized under legal regimes consistent with the standard model. Thus, shareholders—and shareholders alone—select the members of supervisory boards in the vast majority of (smaller) German and Dutch firms. These jurisdictions impose alternative labour- or manager-oriented regimes only on a minority of comparatively large firms.
17. Stock market capitalization as a percentage of GDP has risen dramatically in virtually every major jurisdiction over the past twenty years. In most European countries, the increase has been by a factor of three or four (*The Economist*, 13 November 1999: 85–6). The Euro single currency is among the important factors driving the expansion and internationalization of the European capital markets.
18. Latin America offers a telling example. In 1981, Chile became the first country in the region to set up a system of private pension funds. By 1995, Argentina, Colombia, and Peru had done the same. By 1996, a total of $108 billion was under management in Latin American pension funds, which by then had come to play an important role in the development of the local equity markets. In 1997, it was estimated that total assets would grow to $200 billion by 2000 and to $600 billion by 2011 (*The Economist*, 9 December 1995: S15; Fidler 1997; *Latin Finance*, December 1998: 6).
19. Of particular interest are signs of change in the cross-ownership networks among major German and Japanese firms. New legislation proposed by the German government would eliminate the heavy (up to 60 per cent) capital gains taxes on corporate sales of stock, which is expected to result in widespread dissolution of block holdings (Simonian 1999: 1). In Japan, keiretsu structures are beginning to unwind as a result of bank mergers and competitive pressure to seek higher returns on capital (Abrahams and Tett 1999: 18).
20. See, for example, *Weinberger* v. *UOP, Inc.*, 457 A.2d 701 (Del. 1983).
21. Corporate Governance Principles: Final Report, Corporate Governance Committee of the Corporate Governance Forum of Japan (26 May 1998).
22. This can be seen, for example, by comparing the EU's Listing Particulars Directive with the SEC's Form S-1 for the registration of securities under the 1933 Act. If USA disclosure requirements remain more aggressive, one must remember that the EU Directives establish minimal

requirements that member states can and do supplement (Coffee 1999: 668–72). See generally Licht (1998) (discussing convergence in disclosure rules, accounting standards, and corporate governance).

23. See Private Securities Litigation Reform Act of 1995, 109 Sat. 737 (1995).
24. Already Europe has seen a remarkable wave of takeovers in 1999, culminating in the largest hostile takeover in history: Vodaphone's acquisition of Mannesmann. In addition, many established jurisdictions are adopting rules to regulate tender offers that bear a family resemblance to the Williams Act or to the rules of the London City Code. See, for example, Brazil's tender offer regulations, Securities Commission Ruling 69, 8 Sept. 1987, Arts. 1–4, and Italy's recently adopted reform of takeover regulation, Legislative Decree 58 of 24 February 1999 (the Financial Markets Act or so-called 'Draghi Reform').
25. Already there are signs of pressure in this direction. See Muelbert and Birke (2000: 3) (critiquing recent support for Delaware style defensive tactics by German industry and some academic commentators).
26. The Holzmüller decision of the German Federal Court, BGH 2, Zivilsenat, II ZR 174/80 (1982). (German case law extension of shareholder right to vote to all fundamental corporate transactions.)
27. Following Russian voucher privatization in 1993, managers and other employees typically held a majority of shares in large companies. Publicly-held shares were mostly widely dispersed, but there was often at least one substantial outside shareholder with sufficient holdings to exploit a cumulative voting rule to obtain board representation (Black and Kraakman 1996: 1922–3).
28. Gilson (2000) refers to processes in which facially different governance structures or legal rules develop to solve the same underlying functional problem as 'functional convergence'. On the assumption that formal law and governance practices are embedded in larger institutional contexts that change only slowly, Gilson conjectures that functional convergence is likely to outpace formal convergence. Such functional convergence, when it occurs, is what we term 'harmless mutation'. In contrast to Gilson, however, we believe that formal law and governance structures are less contextual and more malleable than is often assumed, once the norm of shareholder primacy is accepted. Functional convergence—rather than straightforward imitation—is thus less necessary than Gilson supposes. We also suspect that close substitutes among alternative governance structures and legal rules are less widespread than Gilson implies.
29. By way of contrast, the largely non-stochastic tort of environmental pollution has made an easier focus for political organizing in the USA and, as noted in the text below, has led to strong legislation that partially pierces the corporate veil for firms that pollute.

References

Abrahams, P., and Tett, G. (1999). The circle is broken. *Financial Times*, 9 November.

Albert, M. (1993). *Capitalism vs. Capitalism.* New York: Four Walls Eight Windows.

Aste, L. (1999). Reforming French corporate governance: A return to the two-tier board? *George Washington Journal of International Law and Economics* 32: 1.

Baums, T. (1999). Corporate governance in Germany: System and current developments. Universitat Osnabruck, Working Paper.

Bebchuk, L., and Roe, M. (1999). A theory of path dependence in corporate ownership and governance. *Stanford Law Review* 52: 127.

Berle, A. (1932). For whom corporate managers are trustees: A note. *Harvard Law Review* 45: 1365.

——(1959). *Power Without Property: A New Development in American Political Economy.* New York: Harcourt, Brace.

Black, B., and Kraakman, R. (1996). A self-enforcing model of corporate law. *Harvard Law Review* 109: 1911.

Blair, M., and Roe, M. (eds.) (1999). A team production theory of corporate law. *Virginia Law Review* 85: 247.

——and Roe, M. (eds.) (1999). *Employees and Corporate Governance.* Washington, D.C.: Brookings Institution Press.

Branson, D. (1989). The chancellor's foot in Delaware: Schnell and its progeny. *Journal of Corporate Law* 14: 515.

Blumberg, P. I. (1988). *The Law of Corporate Groups: Substantive Law.* Boston: Little, Brown.

Coffee, J. C. (1999). The future as history: The prospects for global convergence in corporate governance and its implications. *Northwestern University Law Review* 93: 641.

Company Law Reform Steering Group (1999). *Modern Company Law for a Competitive Economy: The Strategic Framework.* London: DTI.

——(2000). *Modern Company Law for a Competitive Economy: Developing the Framework.* London: DTI.

Commission of the European Communities (1983). Proposal for a Fifth Company Law Directive, O.J. (C240)2.

The Conference Board (1997). Institutional investment report: Patterns of institutional investment and control in the United States (Daly).

Corporate Governance Committee of the Corporate Governance Forum of Japan (1998). Corporate governance principles: Final report.

Dodd, E. M. (1932). For whom are corporate managers trustees? *Harvard Law Review* 45: 1145.

Economist (1995). Save amigo save. 9 December.

——(1999). School briefs: Stocks in trade. 13 November.

Fidler, S. (1997). Chile's crusader for the cause. *Financial Times,* 14 March.

Financial Times (1999). World's most respected companies. *Financial Times* Web Site, 17 December.

Frydman, R., Hessel, M., and Rapacyznski, A. (1998). Why ownership matters? Entrepreneurship and the restructuring of enterprises in Central Europe. Working Paper.

Galbraith, J. K. (1967). *The New Industrial State.* Boston: Houghton Mifflin.

Gilson, R. (2000). Globalizing corporate governance: Convergence of form or function. Columbia Law School, The Center for Law and Economics, Working Paper No. 174.

Gordon, G., and Schmid, F. (2000). Class struggle inside the firm: A study of German codetermination, NBER, Working Paper No. 7945.

Hansmann, H. (1993*a*). Worker participation and corporate governance. *University of Toronto Law Journal* 43: 589.

——(1993*b*). Probleme von Kollektivensteidungen und Theorie der Firma-Folgerungen für die Arbeitnehmermitbestimmung. In C. Ott and H.-B. Schäfer (ed.), *Ökonomische Analyse des Unternehmensrechts.* Heidelberg: Physica-Verlag.

——(1996). *The Ownership of Enterprise.* Cambridge, MA: The Belknap Press of Harvard University Press.

——and Kraakman, R. (1991). Toward unlimited shareholder liability for corporate torts. *Yale Law Journal* 100: 1879.

——(2001*a*). The essential role of organizational law. *Yale Law Journal* 110: 387.

——(2001*b*). What is corporate law? In Kraakman *et al.* (ed.) *The Anatomy of Corporate Law: A Comparative and Functional Approach.* (forthcoming).

——(2001*c*). Agency problems and legal strategies. In Kraakman *et al.* (ed.) *The Anatomy of Corporate Law: A Comparative and Functional Approach.* (forthcoming).

——(2001*d*). The basic governance structure. In Kraakman *et al.* (ed.) *The Anatomy of Corporate Law: A Comparative and Functional Approach* (forthcoming).

Jackson, H., and Pan, E. (September 2000). Regulatory competition in international securities markets: Evidence from Europe in 1999. Harvard Law School, Working Paper.

Jacobs, M. (1991). *Short-Term America: The Causes and Cures of Our Business Myopia.* Boston: Harvard Business School Press.

Kamar, E. (1998). A regulatory competition theory of indeterminancy in corporate law. *Columbia Law Review* 98: 1908.

La Porta, R., Lopez-de-Silanes, F., and Shleifer, A. (1999). Corporate ownership around the world. *Journal of Finance* 54: 471.

La Porta, R., Lopez-de-Silanes, F., Shleifer, A., and Vishny, R. (1997). Legal determinants of external finance. *Journal of Finance* 52: 1131.

————————(1998). Law and finance. *Journal of Political Economy* 106: 1113.

Latin Finance (1998). A private affair. December.

Licht, A. (1998). International diversity in securities regulation: Roadblocks on the way to convergence. *Cardozo Law Review* 20: 227.

MacDonald, E. (1999). U.S. accounting board faults global rules. *Wall Street Journal,* 18 October.

Macey, J., and Miller, G. (1987). Toward an interest-group theory of Delaware corporate law. *Tax Law Review* 65: 469.

Mahoney, P. (2000). Contract or concession? An essay on the history of corporate law. *Georgia Law Review* 34: 873.

Mason, E. (ed.) (1959). *The Corporation in Modern Society.* Cambridge, MA: Harvard University Press.

Mitchell, L. (1992). A theoretical and practical framework for enforcing corporate constituency statutes. *Texas Law Review* 70: 579.

Muelbert, P., and Birke, M. (2000). In defense of passivity—on the proper role of target management in response to a hostile tender offer, Working Paper.

New York Stock Exchange (1998). NYSE Listed Company Manual, Section 303.00. New York: New York Stock Exchange.

Ott, C., and Schäfer, H.-B. (eds.) (1993). *Ökonomische Analyse des Unternehmensrechts.* Heidelberg: Physica-Verlag.

Pistor, K. (1999). Co-determination in Germany: A socio-political model with governance externalities. In M. Blair and M. Roe (eds.) *Employees and Corporate Governance.* Washington, D.C.: Brookings Institution Press.

Rock, E. (1998). Mandatory disclosure as credible commitment: Going public, opting in, opting out, and globalization, Working Paper.

Roe, M. (1998). German securities markets and German codetermination. *Columbia Business Law Review* 1998: 167.

Romano, R. (1993). *The Genius of American Corporate Law.* Washington, D.C.: AEI Press.

Schmidt, R., and Spindler, G. (1999). Path dependence, corporate governance and complementarity—A comment on Bebchuk and Roe. The Johann Wolfgang Goethe-Universitat, Working Paper Series in Finance and Accounting No. 27.

Schwab, S., and Thomas, R. (1998). Realigning corporate governance: Shareholder activism by labor unions. In Estreicher (ed.) *Employee Representation in the Emerging Workplace: Alternatives/Supplements to Collective Bargaining.* Boston: Kluwer Law International.

Shleifer, A., and Summers, L. (1988). Breach of trust in hostile takeovers. In Auerbach (ed.) *Corporate Takeovers: Causes and Consequences.* Chicago: University of Chicago Press.

Shonfield, A. (1968). *Modern Capitalism: The Changing Balance of Public and Private Power.* London: Oxford University Press.

Simonian, H. (1999). Germany to abolish tax of disposal of cross-holding. *Financial Times,* 10 August, 14.

Steinmetz, G., and Sesit, M. (1999). Rising U.S. investment in European equities galvanizes old world. *Wall Street Journal,* 4 August.

4

Convergence and its Critics: What are the Preconditions to the Separation of Ownership and Control?

JOHN C. COFFEE, JR

1. INTRODUCTION

Contemporary assessments of corporate governance and structure today typically begin at the same point and then diverge. Each opens by noting that Berle and Means (1932) were myopic. When in 1932 they announced the separation of ownership and control, Berle and Means did not recognize that they were describing a largely Anglo-Saxon phenomenon, which did not characterize the corporate governance systems of most of the rest of the world. Next, the commentator typically points out that, like parallel universes, two rival systems of corporate governance exist today: (1) a dispersed ownership model, characterized by strong and liquid securities markets, high disclosure standards, high market transparency, and in which the market for corporate control is the ultimate disciplining mechanism; and (2) a concentrated ownership model, characterized by controlling blockholders, weak securities markets, low transparency, and disclosure standards and possibly a central monitoring role for large banks.[1]

Thus framed, the debate then usually turns to the prospective persistency of this binary division of the corporate universe. Here again, there are two standard positions. One obvious position—hereinafter called the 'Strong Convergence Thesis'—predicts that competition will force convergence. Thus, as markets globalize and corporations having very different governance systems are compelled to compete head-to-head, both in labour and capital markets, a Darwinian struggle becomes inevitable, out of which the most efficient form should emerge dominant.[2] The rival and newer position—hereinafter called the 'Path Dependency Thesis'—postulates instead that institutions evolve along path dependent trajectories, which are heavily shaped by initial starting points and pre-existing conditions (Bebchuk and Roe 1999; Licht 2000). In short, history matters, because it constrains the way in which institutions can change, and efficiency does not necessarily triumph.

This chapter is an abbreviated version of the author's article 'The Rise of Dispersed Ownership: The Role of Law and the State in the Separation of Ownership and Control'. Published by the *Yale Law Journal* vol. 111, no.1, October 2001.

These two polar positions do not, however, exhaust the field. In prior work, I have sought to distinguish 'functional convergence' from 'formal convergence' and argued that even when formal convergence (meaning convergence to common legal rules and practices) is blocked by political, legal or institutional barriers, functional convergence may yet arrive through a process of migration and substitution (Coffee 1999; Gilson 2001). Thus, for example, a corporation whose home country has weak securities markets may cross-list on a stronger, foreign securities market (e.g. in the USA or the UK) and thereby credibly bond its promise to shareholders to fully disclose material information. Many European firms appear to be migrating in this fashion today. Alternatively, the development of a pan-European securities market, possibly with listing and disclosure requirements more demanding than those of existing European markets, could conceivably provide the framework for the adoption of protections for minority shareholders that were essentially similar to those enjoyed today in common law countries. More importantly, the key idea here is that of functional substitutes that provide alternative means to the same end. In this piece, I will expand that concept to suggest that self-regulation is often the principal functional substitute to mandatory legal regulation and that we have historically observed its appearance, not as a lesser alternative to formal legal rules, but often as a precursor to such rules that arises precisely because the formal legal system cannot adopt or enforce adequate standards to support the business activity that self-regulation encourages.

The immediate relevance of this thesis stems from the possibility that self-regulation may be able to mitigate problems that otherwise seem to pose insurmountable obstacles to the appearance and growth of strong securities markets. Both on empirical and theoretical grounds, recent commentators have argued that liquid securities markets and dispersed ownership cannot develop in an environment characterized by concentrated ownership. Three basic arguments have been raised: first, the provocative new scholarship of La Porta, Lopez-de-Silanes, Shleifer, and Vishny ('LLS&V') has demonstrated that a strong, statistically significant association exists between liquid securities markets and certain specified legal protections for minority shareholders (La Porta *et al.* 1997; 1999; 2000). Although it may over-read the evidence to say that common law legal systems necessarily provide better or stronger legal protections for minority shareholders than do civil law systems, they certainly provide different legal protections, and dispersed ownership seems to have arisen only in their distinctive legal environment. Hence, if European securities markets are populated chiefly by insider-dominated firms and if insiders have little incentive to give additional protections to minority shareholders (which protections would come largely at the controlling shareholders' expense), then the conclusion seemingly follows that the existing structure of concentrated ownership should be stable (except to the extent that some firms migrate to US or UK markets or achieve dispersed ownership through cross-border mergers).

Second, Mark Roe (Chapter 5, this volume) has advanced the 'political' thesis that strong securities markets are inconsistent with the European political tradition of social democracy. In essence, he argues that concentrated ownership and low transparency are part of a defensive stance assumed by investors in these left-leaning countries, where the government characteristically favours employees over shareholders and might expropriate corporate assets (to a greater degree, anyway) if fuller transparency were required.

Third and finally, Lucian Bebchuk (Bebchuk 1999), also a proponent of the path dependency perspective, has advanced a persuasive 'rent protection' model of shareholder ownership, which posits that, when the private benefits of control are high, concentrated ownership will dominate dispersed ownership. The core concept in this model is that the entrepreneurs taking a firm public will not sell a majority of the firm's voting rights to dispersed shareholders in the public market, but will instead either retain control or sell a control block to a new incoming controlling shareholder, because dispersed shareholders cannot hold, or enjoy the benefits of, control and thus cannot pay an equivalent control premium. Some empirical evidence corroborates this theory, finding that in concentrated securities markets, Initial Public Offerings (IPOs) seldom distribute more than a minority of the firm's voting shares to the market, with the controlling blockholder generally retaining control and selling it only as a control block to an incoming control purchaser (Berglöf and von Thadden 1999; Holmen and Hogfeldt 2000).

This chapter will seek to reply to each of these arguments, not to refute them, but to suggest that the manner in which dispersed ownership has evolved in the past can repeat itself in the near future. Section 2 begins by surveying the latest evidence on convergence, which shows increasing signs of fission within the world of concentrated ownership. Despite the asserted barriers, securities markets are growing across Europe at an extraordinary rate, entrepreneurs in civil law countries are making use of IPOs at a rate equivalent to that in the common law world, and the market for corporate control has become truly international. Something is destabilizing the old equilibrium.

Section 3 will then examine the claim that securities markets require a strong legal foundation that protects the minority shareholder in order to become deep or liquid. It will argue that, although the association between minority protection and liquidity is real, the cause and effect sequence is backwards. Although 'law matters', legal developments tend to follow, rather than precede, economic change.[3] Specifically, Section 3.1.2 will examine the early development of the New York Stock Exchange (NYSE) and the London Stock Exchange (LSE). Although securities exchanges have existed since the seventeenth century, both these exchanges primarily traded debt securities up until the late nineteenth century. Then, in a relatively brief period (which overlapped, but was different for each nation) and at a time when the private benefits of control were unquestionably high, dispersed ownership arose—largely in the absence of strong minority protections, which came afterwards. Viewed in retrospect, this sequence makes obvious political sense: legal reforms are enacted at the behest of a motivated consistency that is protected (or at least perceives itself to be protected) by the reforms. Hence, the constituency (here, dispersed public shareholders) must first arise before they can become an effective lobbying force and an instrument of legal change.

This historical analysis still leaves open the question of how the separation of ownership and control arises. When and how can the public market in effect compensate the initial owners of the firm for surrendering their control rights by paying these holders a premium equal to, or greater than, that which another party seeking control would pay? In both the US and the UK, this question historically translated into a closely related question: when can the public market retain control and prevent its usurpation by persons who seek to seize control without paying a control premium? Section 2 and its subsections will suggest that private ordering can sometimes enable the public market to hold control in a manner that protects public shareholders from subsequent control seekers who wish to 'steal' the control premium without compensating them. When these conditions are realized, and possibly only then, dispersed ownership can arise and persist. Finally, Sections 2.4 and 2.5 will suggest that recent legal reforms in Europe, most notably the Thirteenth Company Law Directive, may have now satisfied these preconditions.

Based on this analysis, this chapter will suggest that the political thesis that social democracy and strong securities markets cannot co-exist rests on a doubtful foundation. Others have also challenged this very ambitious claim (Cheffins, Chapter 6, this volume), noting that the English example supplies a strong counter-example of social democracy co-existing with strong securities markets. This chapter will advance a more general objection: namely that financial institutions—including the much used example of German universal banks—do not naturally desire to perform the monitoring and oversight role accorded to them by the theorists of concentrated ownership. Only to the extent that such institutions are state controlled (directly or indirectly) and pressured to play such an activist role, or are locked into holding such illiquid blocks by restrictive tax legislation, do financial institutions accept the monitoring duties that the European system of concentrated ownership historically assigned them. Otherwise, as I have elsewhere argued (Coffee 1991), institutions prefer liquidity to control. Across Europe today, financial institutions appear on the verge of liberation—and seem delighted at the prospect of being able to liquidate their controlling blocks.

2. THE EVIDENCE ON CONVERGENCE

Some accounts of the ongoing transition in corporate governance and structure tend to refer dismissively to the evidence on convergence as 'anecdotal', implying that convergence may be only a transient or apparent trend. But the evidence is by now much stronger and involves quantitative as well as qualitative data. For the sake of convenience, the most salient evidence can be conveniently grouped under the following four categories. Although the transition is far from complete, the customary binary division of the corporate universe into separate worlds of diffuse ownership and concentrated ownership is now clearly out of date.

2.1. *Formal Legal Change*

This is the area where those adopting a 'path dependent' perspective have suggested that change would be the slowest and most marginal, because formal legal change generally requires legislative action and can be blocked by political interest groups or strongly motivated minorities, who may have little concern with overall efficiency. Still even here, significant change is evident.

The clearest evidence relates to the transition economies. Employing a methodology that uses cross-country formalized legal indicators to measure statistically the degree of legal change, Katharina Pistor (2000) constructed a data base covering twenty-four transition economies (i.e. most of the formerly socialist states in Europe and Eurasia) that tracked the development of shareholder and creditor rights from 1990 through 1994. She concluded that: '[d]espite substantial differences in the initial conditions across countries, there is a strong tendency towards convergence of formal legal rules as the result of extensive legal reforms' (ibid.: 2).

She notes, however, that 'law reform has been primarily responsive to economic change rather than initiating or leading it' (ibid.). As discussed below, this same pattern appears to be evident in the development of diffused securities markets in both the USA and the UK.

The direction of these changes has been uniformly in the 'Anglo-Saxon' direction: '[b]y 1998, legal changes had been introduced that raised the level of investor protection in most transition economies above the level of the civil law systems and brought them within close range of the average for common law countries....' (ibid.: 13). In overview, this transition seems to have largely involved the outright transplantation of common law legal rules for civil law rules, with the total package of legal reforms being usually designed by foreign legal advisors (often supplied by the USA). Still, because these reforms have been legislatively adopted, this wholesale transplantation seems to indicate that, at least under the pressures faced by transition economies, law makers have not felt obliged to maintain continuity with their traditional legal system. Radical legal change is sometimes possible.

A possible response to this evidence of sharp discontinuity in the law of transitional economies is that mass privatization programmes in these countries imposed a diffused, 'Anglo-Saxon' structure of share ownership on these countries and so required a corresponding movement to Anglo-Saxon (or common law) systems of corporate governance and securities regulation. From this perspective, one might argue that no similar rate of legal change should be predicted for those economies in which an insider-dominated system of concentrated ownership still prevails. In short, if form follows function (i.e. if legal rules are determined by the system of corporate governance that pre-exists those rules), then no similar rapid legal transition should necessarily be expected in the Continental economies in which concentrated ownership is still the norm.

Indeed, casual empiricism would suggest that no similar rate of rapid legal change is in progress in the larger European economies, at least regarding their corporate law rules. Still, one must remember that shifts in legal rules may follow and not precede shifts in the system of corporate governance and the structure of share ownership. As next discussed, significant, but subtler, shifts are discernible in these countries, both in the structure of share ownership, the growth of securities markets, and the emergence of new governance mechanisms, such as, most notably, the takeover.

2.2. *The Structure of Share Ownership*

Considerable evidence exists that the traditional system of concentrated ownership is weakening across Europe. Data compiled by the Conference Board shows a measurable decline in the stakes held in the twenty-five largest corporations by banks and non-financial corporations in Germany, France, and Japan (Brancato 2000: 1). Traditionally, these holders were the allies of the founding families and management that ran the largest European and Japanese companies. Yet, over just a one-year period between 30 September 1998 and 30 September 1999, these traditional stakeholders unwound their holdings to the degree shown in Table 4.1.

Of course, a one-year trend may be unrepresentative, and this data does not demonstrate that the shares so unwound necessarily moved into the hands of public investors. Yet there is also evidence of a substitution effect: that is, the shares are passing into the hands of more

Table 4.1. *Closely held ownership in 25 largest corporations*

Country	30 September 1998 (%)	30 September 1999 (%)
France	33.5	30.2
Germany	24.2	17.8
Japan	21.2	14.0

Source: Brancato 2000: 3.

activist owners. Thirty-five per cent of outstanding shares of the forty largest companies on the Paris Bourse are now held by American and British institutional investors (Tagliabue 2000). Over this same period, US institutional investors have dramatically increased their investments in foreign equity. The largest twenty-five US pension fund holders of international equity held $110.8 billion in foreign equities in 1996, $181.1 billion in 1998, and $265.6 billion in September, 1999—a nearly 150 per cent increase in only two years (ibid.: 3). With this heightened ownership comes, of course, a demand for additional voice.

More importantly, many expect that this rate of change will soon accelerate, at least in some of the largest and most traditional European economies. In Germany, high capital gains tax locked financial institutions into their elaborate web of cross-shareholdings, because any attempt to liquidate these blocks would have been punitively taxed (Simonian 2000: 14). Yet effective from 1 January 2002, the capital gains tax on such investments has been eliminated, and some of the largest German financial institutions have already announced plans to reduce the extent of their cross-shareholdings (ibid.). The apparent eagerness of German financial institutions to divest themselves of long-held blocks and to scale back non-core assets raises the always lurking question about how deeply the German system of concentrated ownership was truly entrenched. Professor Roe (Chapter 5) and others have suggested that concentrated ownership (and correspondingly weak securities markets) reflect a strong social and political commitment to a cluster of social values that he calls 'social democracy'. Yet, if a simple change in the corporate tax laws causes the system to collapse by the mutual consent of those locked into this system of cross-shareholdings, the simpler explanation for concentrated ownership may be that German tax laws either caused this system or, more likely, enforced its persistence well after competitive forces would otherwise have compelled its dismantling.[4]

2.3. *The Growth of European Stock Markets*

Continental stock markets have long been thin and illiquid. For some political theorists, this was actually a virtue of European corporate governance because it protected corporate managements from the 'tyranny' of a fickle stock market, preoccupied only with the short term, and instead permitted long term, 'statesman-like' business planning by corporations in conjunction with their principal banks. Whatever the historical validity of this story, it now seems increasingly dated.

A particularly useful recent study shows that the number of firms listing on European stock changes rose sharply at the end of the 1990s (see Table 4.2).

Table 4.2. *Evolution of the number of stock exchange listed companies*

Network-oriented	1990	1993	1996	1999	% growth (1990–9)
Belgium	182	159	136	140	−23.1
France (excluding Marche libre)	443	726	686	968	118.5
Germany	548	568	579	1,043	90.3
Italy	257	242	244	247	−3.9
Netherlands	222	239	217	233	5.0
Spain	429	464	357	718	67.4
Japan (Toyko)					
Market-oriented	1,627	1,667	1,756	1,838	13.0
UK	1,946	1,927	2,339	2,292	17.8
USA (Nasdaq)	3,876	4,310	5,167	4,829	24.6

Source: Van der Elst (2000).

Table 4.3. *Evolution of market capitalization as percentage of GDP (1990–9)*

Network-oriented	1975 (%)	1980 (%)	1990 (%)	1996 (%)	1999 (%)
Belgium	15	8	33	44	84.8
France	10	8	26	38	117.9
Germany	12	9	22	28	76.7
Italy	5	6	14	21	71.3
Netherlands	21	47	42	95	205.1
Spain	—	8	23	33	87
Switzerland					
Market-oriented	30	42	69	136	293.1
UK	37	38	87	142	247.5
USA	48	50	56	114	184.5

Source: Van der Elst (2000).

Although the pattern is far from uniform, the equity market grew rapidly in the late 1990s in France, Germany, and Spain. Elsewhere, the number of listed companies may have declined, possibly because of an international wave of mergers and acquisitions, which is itself a sign of convergence.

Beyond this growth in the number of listed companies, two other statistics reveal even more clearly the suddenly increased role of the equity markets in European economies, which transition again seems to date only from the latter half of the last decade. First, stock market capitalization as a percentage of Gross Domestic Product (GDP) skyrocketed in several European countries—indeed, to the point that it now equals or exceeds the same ratios in the USA or UK. The selected examples in Table 4.3 show how long-stable percentages veered suddenly upward at the end of the decade.

Of course, these percentages are subject to greater fluctuation in countries with small populations or modest GDPs (such as the Netherlands and Switzerland), and much of the market capitalization in these countries may remain in the hands of controlling owners. Nonetheless, the real point is the suddenness of the transition. Essentially, as the European market integrated in the mid-1990s, stock market values soared, both in absolute terms and as a percentage of GDP.

Second, while IPOs once characterized only the USA and the UK markets, they have become common across Europe. In 1999, Germany saw 168 IPOs, and France 75; for the decade, France led with 581 IPOs, Germany followed second with 380, and Spain a close third with 355 (ibid.: 9). The significance of this point bears emphasis, because systems of concentrated ownership were thought to lack the institutions necessary to bring new companies directly into the equity market. Instead, new firms were believed to be dependent on bank and debt financing, not equity finance. Yet by the end of the decade, several European countries were raising more equity through initial public offerings as a percentage of GDP than were either the USA or the UK.[5]

There is a double-edged significance to these findings. On the one hand, by the end of the last decade, the stock market was raising equity capital for European issuers at levels (and percentages of GDP) which were thought to characterize only market-oriented systems of corporate governance (i.e. the USA and UK). But, on the other hand, this sudden surge in the use of equity finance has occurred unaccompanied by any significant increase in the legal protections afforded to minority shareholders. In this sense, both the 'path dependence' theorists, who maintain that the stock market cannot grow in 'social democracies', and the economists (most notably, LLS&V), who maintain that the availability of equity finance depends on minority protections, appear to have been confounded. Neither the 'path dependency' claim nor the assertion that 'law matters' can draw unambiguous support from this evidence.

Institutionally, it is also clear that new market institutions and structures are appearing. A race has begun to create the first pan-European stock market. EASDAQ, which began trading as a pan-European exchange in November 1996, has been a modest success, but lists only some sixty-two issuers as of August 2000 (Karmin 2000: C-1; C-14). The German Neuer Markt, which has over 300 listings, appears to have overtaken it in the competition for high-tech listings, but still newer entrants have entered the competition including Tradepoint, an American planned ECN, which has linked up with the SWX Swiss Exchange.[6] The planned merger between the London and Frankfurt Stock Exchanges was disrupted by a hostile takeover bid by the Swedish stock exchange for the London exchange and may yet be further challenged by another rival bid made by the Paris, Amsterdam, and Brussels exchanges (*Wall Street Journal*, 5 September 2000). Whatever the outcome of this competition, the key point is that the dominant exchange in the near future will clearly be pan-European and supra national. To this extent again, path dependent theories may not apply well to supra national institutions.

2.4. *The Emergence of the Market for Corporate Control*

In market-centred economies, the market for corporate control is the ultimate disciplinary mechanism; and the hostile takeover, its final guillotine. In contrast, in concentrated ownership systems of corporate governance, the takeover has historically played only a minor role. But, once again, that pattern appears to be changing and rapidly. In 1986, 86 per cent of all takeovers involved at least one American party, but in 1999, this percentage fell to only 40 per cent (Stokes 2000: 2290). Over the same period the percentage of corporate takeovers involving at least one European party rose from 15 per cent to 43 per cent (and the percentage involving an Asian party rose from approximately 2 per cent to nearly 14 per cent) (ibid.). If one looks instead to the market value of these transactions, takeovers involving a European party grew from 11 per cent of the world total in 1985 to 47 per cent in 1999 (Black 2000: 4). Evidence of this sort has led some scholars to describe the last two years as amounting to the 'First International Merger Wave' (Stokes 2000: 2290).

What is driving this transition? One answer starts from the integration of European currencies into the Euro. One consequence of a single, unified currency has been the growth of a unified European corporate bond market, which tripled in size last year and has thereby ended the dependence of European acquirers on bank financing. Acquirers can now directly access the capital markets, offering debt, equity, or a package of both. To this extent, the growth of the takeover market has been concomitant with the declining role of the universal bank.

For the future, the uncertain fate of the Thirteenth Company Law Directive will probably serve as the clearest signal of how rapidly this transition will continue. Although initial approval by the European Union (EU) was obtained (*Financial Times*, 20 June 2000), the Thirteenth Directive has more recently encountered opposition. As proposed, it basically required all EU member states to legislate to bar anti-takeover defensive measures that were not approved by shareholders. Even if its terms are watered down, however, the legitimacy of the takeover as a mechanism of corporate governance seems to have been tacitly accepted. Indeed, the passivity of a German labour government in the face of a hostile takeover bid by a British acquirer (Vodafone) for a German target (Mannesmann) in 1999 already demonstrated this change in attitude (at least for Germany). Only in a few countries (most notably, the Netherlands and France) does real opposition seem to remain, and even then the objection is more to the foreign character of the bidder, not the use of the takeover device itself. Finally, a common international business culture has at least begun to develop around the use of the takeover. A wave of international mergers between law firms (chiefly between USA and British firms and British and German firms) has reportedly been driven by the perceived need to effect cross-border acquisitions.

2.5. *A Preliminary Evaluation*

Why now? The integration of Europe has been in progress for several decades, and the emergence of the transitional economies in the wake of the collapse of the Soviet Union is itself over a decade old. Why have stock markets suddenly surged, takeovers become accepted, and IPOs crested? Both a psychological and a political account seem necessary. Overused as the concept is, a paradigm shift seems in progress.

At the political level, one possible story is that regulators came to sense that economic growth depended on the encouragement of venture capital and high-tech start-up firms. Bank financing for such ventures is generally unavailable and also unattractive to the entrepreneurs. In this light, the success of the Neuer Markt (and other incubator stock markets) was necessary if Europe was not to fall rapidly behind the USA. From this perspective, policy planners saw at least some transition to a market centred economy as central to economic growth. Yet, even if this story sounds plausible, regulators have done relatively little to drive the foregoing transition.

Thus, the more plausible explanation is that economic changes have produced regulatory changes, rather than the reverse. The Thirteenth Company Law Directive (known popularly as the 'Takeovers Directive') may be a leading case in point; it has come in the wake of a de facto acceptance (at least throughout much of Europe) of the hostile takeover. Similarly, there is evidence that insider dealing prohibitions have recently been widely adopted around the world—in the wake of greater depth and diffusion in securities markets (Beny 1999). Mass privatization first deepened securities markets across Europe and thereby created a constituency that came to desire fairer rules.

Such a sequence seems predictable. Legal changes may have to await the appearance of a constituency to lobby for them. Mass privatization came overnight to the Czech Republic, and its securities market soon crashed, at least in part because of the absence of investor protections. Only then, several years later, were statutory reforms adopted to protect minority shareholders. Pistor (2000) has generalized that the same responsive reaction of law to economic change has characterized the adoption of common law reforms by transitional economies.

Thus, with the growth in European securities markets, a constituency for reform (or at least enhancement) of European securities regulation may soon coalesce. What would its objectives be? Once a truly pan-European securities market comes into existence, the next logical step would be the responsive creation of a European Securities Exchange Commission (SEC) to enforce a harmonized system of securities regulation. But such a step requires, first, the unequivocal emergence of a pan-European securities market that is supra national in character and, then, public dissatisfaction with its performance. The history of both the USA's and the UK's system of securities regulation, as next discussed, suggests that such a reform programme may only succeed once it is scandal-driven. Both the pan-European market and the requisite scandals have not arrived.

2.6. *The Status of the Insider-Dominated Firm*

While takeovers have come to Europe and securities markets have deepened and securities regulation may toughen, all this should not obscure the still unchanged status of the insider-dominated firm. Even if ownership concentration has broadened marginally, the average free float of German listed companies has been estimated at only 32 per cent, and 89 per cent of all listed companies have a single shareholder controlling more than 25 per cent of its equity (*Financial Times*, 30 June 2000: 4). Although many of these holders seem prepared to sell once the German capital gains tax is eliminated on 1 January 2002, the critical question becomes to whom they will sell: to a single purchaser of its controlling block or to the market generally through a secondary offering.

Those who believe that path dependent forces will limit corporate convergence and preclude the appearance of 'Anglo-Saxon' style dispersed ownership make the powerful argument that blockholders will continue to find it more profitable to sell control to a new controlling purchaser than to break up the controlling block through a secondary offering (Bebchuk 1999). Indeed, precisely this pattern of controlling blocks remaining intact after an initial public offering has long been observed in Scandinavia (Holmen and Hogfeldt 2000). But, as next discussed, that pattern can change and did so change in both the USA and the UK.

3. WHEN DOES SEPARATION OF OWNERSHIP AND CONTROL ARISE? A HISTORICAL PERSPECTIVE

Most of the participants in the recent debate over corporate convergence have implicitly agreed on one (and possibly only one) theme: deep, liquid securities markets arise only under special conditions. LLS&V (1997; 1998; 1999) have emphasized the legal backdrop: dispersed ownership is possible in their view only when the legal system provides adequate protection for minority shareholders. While stressing a path dependency perspective, Bebchuk (1999) has formulated a model that essentially states the reverse side of this coin: when the private benefits of control are high, dispersed share ownership will be a transient state, and controlling blockholders will eventually re-appear (Holmen and Hogfeldt 2000). In such an environment, leaving control 'up for grabs' would, he argues, only attract attempts by rivals to seize control and extract the private benefits of control. Hence, the firm's initial owner will not find it in his or her financial interest to sell a potentially controlling block of shares to the market, but will instead sell only to another incoming controlling blockholder.

These two positions do not conflict. Since the private benefits of control are likely to be highest when the law fails to accord minority shareholders 'adequate' legal protections, the positions of LLS&V and Bebchuk basically dovetail. Finally, Roe's view that the separation of ownership and control does not arise, except under certain political preconditions, also implies that the evolution of deep and liquid securities markets is an exceptional event. In common, all these theories suggest that liquid securities market should not naturally evolve—absent the prior satisfaction of special legal and/or political preconditions.

Yet, modern history seemingly supplies two counter-examples. Beginning in the last quarter of the nineteenth century and culminating no later than the 1930s, the largest private businesses in both the USA and UK were converted into publicly owned corporations.[7] In this process, control generally passed from families to the market.

More importantly, although both the timing and dynamics differed notably between these two countries, one common denominator was shared: neither country provided strong legal protections for minority shareholders during this period. Moreover, at least during the late nineteenth century in the USA, the private benefits of control appeared very high—indeed to the point that the exploitation of minority shareholders resembled that which has occurred in Russia and other transitional economies over the last decade. Finally, although one can reasonably debate the timing of this transition, dispersed ownership persisted and grew in both countries during periods in which the local political environment arguably satisfied Roe's definition of 'social democracy': namely the USA during the New Deal and UK during the labour governments of the 1940s and 1970s.

How then did these markets evolve? As next discussed, their experiences have less in common than their shared legal institutions or common cultural heritage might suggest. Instead, by very different means, both countries made it possible for corporate control to be held by the market—with the result that a company's initial owners could find it as profitable to sell control to the market as to an incoming controlling shareholder.

3.1. *The USA Experience*

The growth of public securities markets in the USA in the nineteenth century was driven by the enormous financing requirements of its railroads. The financial infrastructure that their insatiable demands for capital created was later utilized, with only modest adjustments, to serve the similar financial needs of the steel, auto, and telephone industries in the early twentieth century. As the greater geographic distances to be connected in the USA implied that the capital costs were necessarily higher than in Europe, financing the railroad industry in the USA necessarily required the infusion of foreign capital. An estimated 40 per cent of this capital came from Europe (Englebourg and Bushkoff 1996; Chandler 1990), most of it funnelled through London, which had already developed an expertise in international finance (Michie 1992: 109). This constantly increasing demand for capital and the reliance on foreign investors in turn produced two basic innovations that appeared in the late nineteenth century America in order to maximize the reputational capital underlying major stock issuance: (a) a corporate governance system in which investment bankers, originally protecting foreign investors, took seats on the issuer's board both to monitor management and to protect public investors from predatory raiders seeking to acquire control by stealth; and (b) the growth of self-regulation through stock exchange rules.

3.1.1. *The Role of Investment Bankers*

The financial infrastructure that arose in second half of the nineteenth century in the USA was designed to satisfy relatively sophisticated investors in countries that were at the time more financially developed. The first generation of the new American investment bankers were in essence bond salesmen to Europe: August Belmont was widely known as the Rothschild's agent in the USA, and even J. P. Morgan, himself, was the American representative of an Anglo-American investment bank founded by his father with British investment bankers (Carosso 1987; 1970: 9). These firms grew to dominance based on their ability to recruit foreign capital.[8]

As elsewhere, the financial institutions that arose in the USA were primarily engaged in the marketing of debt securities. Expanding into equity securities was essentially equivalent to an established merchant adding an additional product line; both the merchant and the investment banker carried its reputational capital with it into the new business. This extension into equity securities probably occurred earlier in the USA because of the highly leveraged status of US railroads. Inevitably, there are limits on the degree of leverage that any business firm can tolerate, and the greater capital needs of US railroads thus implied that public equity issuance were necessary. In consequence, public equity markets developed earlier in the USA than elsewhere, even though the overall American securities market was substantially smaller than the English market.

Formal corporate governance in these early railroad corporations did little to protect minority shareholders. Not only did control groups quickly form, but also in some cases the objective of these blockholders was primarily to manipulate the stock price of their corporation. The story of the epic battle for control of the Erie Railroad—the 'Scarlet Lady of Wall Street'—between Commodore Vanderbilt, on one side, and Jay Gould and Daniel Drew, the leading stock manipulators of the era, on the other, has been told many times,[9] but it deserves a further reconsideration in light of the recent debates over comparative corporate governance. At the high point of the 'Erie War' in the late 1860s, the Gould/Drew faction, which controlled the board, essentially prevented Commodore Vanderbilt from buying control of Erie in the open market by selling convertible bonds at heavily discounted prices to their allies, who would convert the bonds into stock in order to dilute Vanderbilt's voting power. Although not as elegant a takeover defence as the 'poison pill' of the late twentieth century, this tactic worked very effectively. Even though Vanderbilt secured judicial injunctions against this tactic (possibly by bribing judges), they were ignored by the Erie control group, who secured rival injunctions from the judges that they bribed. Ultimately, Gould bribed sufficient members of the New York State Legislature to obtain passage of legislation that legitimized his tactics.

What was the lesson here? Essentially, the Erie control battle illustrated the manner in which regulatory arbitrage, carried to the extreme, could nullify minority legal protections. In the absence of any federal regulatory authority, the contending sides could move from jurisdiction to jurisdiction, seducing courts and legislatures. To be sure, in less epic battles, the parties could not afford the transaction costs of massive corruption, but the real point is that investors were vulnerable less because of the substantive inadequacy of American corporate law itself than because of the lack of enforcement mechanisms and the prospect of corruption. In truth, substantive corporate law in the USA during this era was arguably favourable to the minority shareholder. Most state statutes restricted the issuance of 'watered' stock, the derivative suit had been recognized by the Supreme Court as a legal mechanism to protect minority shareholders, and the law of fiduciary duties generally required any corporate official who engaged in a self-dealing transaction with his firm to prove its 'intrinsic fairness'.[10] But, once the investor had committed his capital, he might discover that the corporation had migrated to another, more permissive jurisdiction or that its founders had amended its certificate of incorporation or caused the legislature to amend the law to give them greater freedom to exploit the public investor (Friedman 1985: 523–5). Or, a judge would simply be bribed to accept some pretext for clearly predatory misbehaviour. Due to these risks, some prominent underwriters (including Kuhn, Loeb) refused until the very end of the century to underwrite the common stock of industrial corporations (Carosso 1970: 43–4).

Given these legally primitive conditions plus the need to attract capital from foreign investors who clearly could not hope to stay abreast of current developments from across an ocean, investment bankers hoping to interest such investors in the equity securities of US corporations had to find some means by which these corporations and their entrepreneurs could credibly bond their promises. Foreign investors might buy debt and equity securities on the reputational capital of merchant bankers like J. P. Morgan, but this implied in turn that these agents had to develop a governance structure that enabled them to fulfil their representations to their clients that their investments were safe and sound.

One means to the end was developed by J. P. Morgan & Co.: namely, placing a partner of the firm on the client's board. Up until the First World War, the American investment banking industry was extremely concentrated, and any flotation of more than $10 million invariably was underwritten by one of six firms, of which the largest was J. P. Morgan & Co (Michie 1987: 226–7). Given their market power and the desires of distant investors for a 'hands on' representative protecting their interests, it became common in the USA (but much less so in the UK) for the investment banker to place one or more representatives on the issuer's board. During the last two decades of the nineteenth century, virtually every major US railroad developed close ties with one or more US investment banking firms, and the practice of partners from investment banks and officers of commercial banks going on the railroad's board became institutionalized.[11]

Recent research by financial economists suggests that these practices were both widespread and created value for investors. One survey of just the financial industry has found that during this period J. P. Morgan & Co. held twenty-three directorships in just thirteen banks; First National Bank, which worked closely with J. P. Morgan, held fourteen directorships in other banks, and National City Bank held thirty-two such positions in sixteen banks and trust companies (Ramirez 1995: 664–5). More importantly, Bradford De Long has assembled evidence suggesting that the presence of a J. P. Morgan & Co. representative on an issuer's board of directors added approximately 30 per cent to the value of the firm's common stock equity (De Long 1991).

But why? Financial economists have theorized that such a representative enabled bankers to monitor the firm's managers and investment projects, replacing those managers that were substandard and rejecting unpromising investment projects (ibid.). Perhaps this sometimes happened. Still, the problem with this simple 'agency cost' story is that investment bankers have generally not been viewed as activists in corporate governance, in part because any agent, including an investment banker, who intervenes aggressively in the principal's business risks losing the client. Perhaps also, these investment bankers on the boards of competing firms sometimes served as a mechanism for price collusion (as reformers in the Progressive Era clearly believed).

Still, an alternative, simpler and non-exclusive hypothesis merits consideration: the fundamental agency problem facing public investors in this era was not that their managers would expropriate wealth, but that incoming controlling shareholders would.[12] Hence, the presence of a major investment banking firm on the corporation's board offered mutual advantages both to the minority investors and to the corporate management by protecting both from the prospect of a stealth attack by a corporate raider seeking to acquire control without paying a control premium. That is, while the presence of the investment banker may have also reduced agency costs or prevented 'disastrous' price wars, the greater problem at the end of the nineteenth century was the instability of control and the relative inability of public investors to demand and receive a control premium for its transfer. Takeover raids occurred in the nineteenth century,[13] but lacked the visibility of the later tender offer wars of the late twentieth century, precisely because the control seeker did not need to publicly offer to purchase a majority of the issuer's shares at a premium, but instead could assemble a controlling block at low cost by buying in the open market secretly. Since the major investment banking firms were positioned close to the market, they were logically in a position to detect such a raid and to finance a counterbid or design appropriate defensive measures. More importantly, they also spoke for the foreign investors, who were likely to act collectively based on the advice of their American agent.

This explanation of the investment banker's role as a protector of the public shareholder from attempts by 'speculators' to steal a firm's control premium is not merely theoretical, but can be corroborated with actual examples. In the late 1880s, Kidder Peabody in conjunction with Barings, a British merchant bank, took control of the affairs of the Santa Fe railroad, which then was teetering on the brink of insolvency, placing three partners on its board. Kidder Peabody did not, however, hold a large equity stake itself, and so it devised a complicated voting trust strategy explicitly to defeat a perceived control threat from Jay Gould (Carosso 1970: 36–7).

Indeed, even the redoubtable J. P. Morgan first made his reputation as a railroad financier when as a young man in 1869 he co-ordinated the efforts of the Albany & Susquehanna Railroad to fight off the attempt of Jay Gould and Jim Fiasco to take control of that railroad in a battle popularly known as 'the Susquehanna War'. After each side obtained rival injunctions and a pitched battle between small armies hired by both sides proved inconclusive, Morgan resolved matters by negotiating a merger of the Albany & Susquehanna Railroad into the larger Delaware & Hudson, thereby putting the target beyond Gould's reach. Morgan then went on the board of the new entity. However, neither Morgan nor other investment bankers in similar battles during this era sought to take personal control of the corporations they defended. Their role was rather that of an agent protecting their investors. 'Board membership', as Ron Chernow (1990: 62) has generalized, 'became a warning flag to . . . [others] to stay away from a captive company.'

As a result, to the extent that public shareholders received protection from predatory raiders seeking to acquire control without paying a premium, public shareholders could afford to pay a higher premium for shares. Correspondingly, the firm's founders benefited from such a relationship because they now could in effect sell control to the market, rather than having to retain a control block until a majority purchaser appeared. Moreover, to the extent that the initial owners remained active in management, they also gained protection from a subsequent disruptive hostile takeover if the public shareholders could not protect their position.

From a comparative perspective, the most interesting aspect of this hypothesis is that it helps explain why control was not transferred to the market by similar means across Europe. First, financial institutions closely corresponding to the House of Morgan either did not exist outside the USA or simply did not wish to accept the risks inherent in underwriting equity securities. Partly, this was because J. P. Morgan & Co. and its very few peers were highly capitalized, specialized institutions that, from the 1890s on, focused on basically two activities: (1) underwriting very large issuance of securities, and (2) arranging mergers and acquisitions. The leading English merchants banks were unwilling (until later in the twentieth century) to engage in Morgan's high-risk underwriting activities, which typically involved buying the entire issue from the company and then reselling it to the market. Instead, English merchant banks largely left this rule to more marginal players, known as 'stock promoters', who also acted only as agents.[14] For reasons discussed later, English underwriters tended to be smaller in size and thus less able to take such risks. In addition, they did not develop in an equivalent environment in which their client industries had a constantly expanding need for capital that required ever larger flotation.

Second, investment bankers in the UK did not represent the same cohesive and substantial fraction of the public shareholders as did an American investment banker serving as agent for the foreign investors in US securities. Not only did foreign investors represent a smaller proportion of the UK equity market, but UK investment bankers, being smaller, would typically represent fewer domestic investors as well.

Finally, a third factor that played a role in both the growth of investment banking firms and the rapid appearance of dispersed ownership in the decades just before 1900 was the first great merger wave of 1895–1903. Historians believe that the merger wave of 1890–1905 was driven in large part by the passage of the Sherman Antitrust Act of 1890. That Act prohibited price-fixing and collusion among competitors, thereby outlawing the cartel-like structure that characterized many American industries. But if cartels of conspiring firms were forbidden, competitors could instead employ mergers to create monopolies—at least until this was later also prohibited. In any event, the Sherman Act triggered a wave of horizontal mergers among competitors that in the process also dilute existing blockholders and thereby created dispersed ownership. The classic example was the consolidation of some eight competing steel companies into a new firm, US Steel, in 1901; the transaction was engineered by J. P. Morgan and created the largest business corporation in the world. Such a firm was simply of a scale that was then beyond the ambitions of any potential raider, and hence its dispersed ownership was stable.

3.1.2. *The New York Stock Exchange as Guardian of the Public Investor*

Others have noted the active role played by the NYSE in American corporate governance, but its path-dependent history has escaped serious attention. Exchange activism was not the norm elsewhere, and the NYSE's active efforts contrast sharply with the passivity of the LSE or that of the European bourses generally. Much of the difference in behaviour relates to corresponding differences in their organizational structures. Between 1870 and 1905, the membership of the LSE rose from 1,406 to 5,567 (Michie 2000). In sharp contrast, the membership of the NYSE stayed constant. While admission to the LSE was 'cheap and easy' (ibid.), entry to the NYSE could only be gained by buying the seat of an existing member. The closed structure of the NYSE had several important consequences: First, seats on the NYSE had significant value, and this encouraged the growth of large, diversified financial services firms (such as J. P. Morgan & Co.), while the typical British brokerage firm remained small in size, with typically only six to seven partners. Second, larger firms both enjoyed greater reputational capital and had a greater interest in protecting their reputational capital. Third, the small size of the NYSE implied logistical constraints on the ability of its membership to trade all securities for which a public market might have been made; necessarily, the NYSE's decision to limit its membership fragmented the USA equity market, creating a high quality upper tier and a lower quality tier that traded elsewhere on an over-the-counter basis.

Further encouraging different institutional dynamics was another difference in the two exchanges' organizational rules: NYSE member firms could raise capital from 'special partners', and all partners in a firm were not required to be members of the exchange. In contrast, the LSE required all partners in a firm to be members of the exchange and further prohibited every member from engaging in any other business (Michie 1987: 256–7). The relative freedom enjoyed by NYSE firms in obtaining capital also explains their larger size—and their greater ability to engage in higher risk underwriting activities.

A final key difference was that throughout the late nineteenth century the NYSE had fixed brokerage commissions, while the LSE did not (at least until just before the First World War). Again, this difference reflected the cartel-like organization of the NYSE in comparison to the 'open market' character of the LSE. But because fixed commissions raise the cost of trading, this practice made the NYSE an unattractive venue in which to trade low volume stocks. Competitors could and did win the low volume business from the NYSE. In conjunction with the fact that the NYSE's small and fixed number of member firms could not logistically handle the trading in all firms that might wish to list on the NYSE, this circumstance led the NYSE to define its role narrowly and limit itself to a high volume, high quality business. In short, for economic reasons, the NYSE recognized by the mid-nineteenth century that it made sense for it to pursue a strategy of exclusivity (ibid.: 267). Accordingly, it would deliberately list and trade only large issuers whose high volume trading could support minimum commissions. Thus, as of 1900, the LSE listed 3,631 different issuers of securities, while the NYSE listed only 1,157 (ibid.: 264). But this was the NYSE's choice, and the product of its decision to reject most listing applications.

Another factor also reinforced the NYSE's preference for listing only large, high quality issuers: exchanges may be liable for the debts of a member firm that fails; at the least, its members will be exposed to significant losses upon the failure of a trading partner. Repeatedly, in the late nineteenth century, financial panics had caused NYSE member firms to fail and had imposed significant liabilities on the failed firm's trading partners. As the NYSE, being an essentially closed cartel, had far fewer members than the LSE, it also had more to fear from the failure of a member firm. Hence, to minimize the risk of member failure, the NYSE was far more conservative (and risk averse) about the securities that it would list. For example, it refused to list mining or petroleum companies during this period, because such securities were thought to be especially volatile (ibid.: 198, 273). The rationale here was less a paternalistic concern for the investor than a fear that in a financial panic a brokerage firm holding such securities could fail, resulting in losses borne by all NYSE members. In any event, the consequence was that to be listed on the NYSE, a company had to be at least five times larger than its counterpart on the LSE (ibid.: 272).

From these differences in the organizational structure of the NYSE and the LSE, very different policies toward self-regulation quickly emerged. From well before 1900, the NYSE saw itself as the guardian of the financial quality of the issuers listed on it. Perhaps, it imposed high listing standards for its own self-interested reasons, but it clearly did regularly reject issuer applications, either because the issuer lacked an adequate earnings track record, had insufficient assets, or was in an industry characterized by high risk. More importantly, under the NYSE's prodding, the standard of disclosure for public companies was significantly enhanced, and probably as a result, some financial historians date the advent of modern financial reporting from 1900, not from 1934 (Hawkins 1986: 166–7). In contrast, the LSE made no similar effort to police its securities market, at least until the period after the First World War (Michie 1999: 115).

To sum up, for a variety of 'path dependent' reasons, the NYSE organized itself as an exclusive, 'high quality' securities market which would list only securities that were suitable for the public investor—while the LSE did not. In the total absence of legal requirements, the NYSE imposed mandatory disclosure obligations on its listed firms. Correspondingly, the larger size of US brokerage firms, which again was originally attributable to differences in the organizational rules of the NYSE and the LSE, gave US brokers greater ability to underwrite securities and to pledge their reputational capital to their investor customers.

These twin developments—the development of a monitoring capacity by the NYSE and the bonding mechanisms first developed by US underwriters to attract foreign capital—constitute the twin pillars that supported the development of a liquid equity securities market in USA. Such a public market arose far quicker in the USA than in UK. For example, by 1907, one Wall Street firm already had 22,000 customers (Michie 1987: 22), indicating that it was providing services on a mass scale. Yet, the legal framework that today characterizes the USA securities markets did not arise until decades later.

3.2. *The British Experience*

In contrast to the high listing standards that the NYSE imposed by the late 1800s, the LSE's basic policy was to list any security that was expected to generate business (Michie 1996: 96). Only in 'rare cases where something adverse was known about the security or the circumstances surrounding its issuance', would a listing application be denied for reasons other than lack of trading interest (ibid.). Of course, this attitude reflected the natural attitude of an 'open' exchange with broad membership: more listings implied more business, and the failure of an occasional brokerage firm (which was characteristically smaller in size) did not constitute as serious a threat to the LSE as it did to the NYSE—in part because the LSE had a considerably deeper capital base (Michie 1987: 272). Finally, stock promoters, not the largest merchant banks, typically arranged stock issuance in the UK. These promoters often had unsavoury reputations and little reputational capital to pledge (Thomas 1978: 23; Kynaston 1999: 457–8; Armstrong 1990: 130–1).

Given the LSE's laissez-faire approach and, indeed, its caveat emptor attitude, it is thus not surprising that a public equity market developed more slowly in the UK than in the USA. But the deeper question is: how did it develop at all? In the absence of high listing standards or underwriting practices that placed the reputational capital of credible financial intermediaries behind most offerings, why would public investors place trust and confidence in such a market?

Several tentative hypotheses can be advanced. First, fewer efforts may have been expended on self-regulation in the UK because judicial corruption and regulatory arbitrage posed less of a threat. In this light, self-regulation is again an example of a functional substitute that arose at least in part to solve the problem of endemic judicial corruption in the USA during the late nineteenth century. Again, this is an illustration of 'functional convergence'. Second, there is some evidence that only wealthy private investors and financial institutions tended to invest in British equities (and chiefly in railroads) until at least the 1920s. Such investors might have relied on other agents or had other means by which to monitor. In any event, the democratization of the British market into a mass market seemingly lagged well behind the USA experience. Third, British substantive law did regulate securities offerings to a far greater degree than did US law and from an early point beginning in the 1890s. Thus, although US institutions moved more quickly to adopt self-regulatory standards, British mandatory law regulating disclosure was enacted well in advance of similar developments in the USA. Different paths were thus followed at different speeds to an approximately equivalent end point. If one looks at the aggregate effect of mandatory law plus self-regulation in both countries, the result by the middle of the twentieth century was arguably very similar. What one country did by legislation, the other did by self-regulation. One substituted for the other. That both could have arrived at the same point by different means is an example of what this author has elsewhere called 'functional convergence' (Coffee 1999: 649–50).

This claim that UK law did provide significant protections to minority investors will seem surprising to many, because the contrasts between US corporate law and British company law as of 1900 would all seem to favour the minority shareholders in the USA over their British counterpart. Basically, the UK shareholder had no appraisal right and only an ineffective derivative remedy, and the majority could ratify any conflict of interest transaction (Cheffins, Chapter 6, this volume). Worse yet, exculpatory provisions were permitted in the corporate charter that could cancel even the duty of loyalty (Davies 1997: 611–12).

Still, a focus limited to substantive corporate law can mislead. The one respect in which Britain did lead the USA was in its statutory regulation of disclosure to investors. A series of stock market scandals in the UK in the 1870s had led to two 'public inquiries' by Parliament, but had not produced legislation (Michie 1992: 2–3). Then, in 1890, at the very outset of the relevant transitional period for UK purposes, Parliament overruled a judicial decision that had narrowly construed the law of fraud by enacting legislation that permitted investors to recover damages if: (i) they suffered loss by reason of an untrue statement in a prospectus, and (ii) those responsible for its preparation could not prove that they had reasonable grounds to believe that the statement was true.[15] Not until 1933 was US law to reach a similarly pro-investor position when Congress enacted the Securities Act of 1933, whose Section 11 contains a similar standard for prospectuses that was in fact modelled after this 1890 statute. The Companies Act of 1900 supplemented this anti-fraud standard by specifying what the prospectus offering securities had to disclose.[16] In 1907, the first step toward a mandatory continuing disclosure system was taken with legislation that required publication of an annual balance sheet.[17] Legislation in 1908 addressed (albeit in a limited manner) abuses in the new issue market (Paish 2000: 24). Finally, in 1929, legislation obliged the issuer to provide an income statement and related data on current earnings.[18] Rudimentary as these requirements may seem today, they were enacted well ahead of corresponding legislation in the USA, although they were slightly behind practices at the NYSE. As a generalization then, the UK seems to have led the USA in the area of securities regulation, but lagged the USA in terms of minority protections in its substantive corporate law. Not until amendments to the Companies Act in 1948 were strong restrictions on self-dealing enacted.

The reluctance of the LSE to play any regulatory role in the protection of investors began to change after the First World War (Michie 1987: 115). In 1921, it adopted its first regulations governing the rights of members to deal in or quote a security (Paish 2000: 24–5), and during the between-the-wars period, the LSE's Share and Loan Department began to make enquiries before listing a company into the company's operations and the personnel connected with it. By the 1930s, the LSE's own disclosure requirements for listed companies were more extensive than those set forth in the UK's companies' legislation (Cheffins,

Chapter 6, this volume). Still, the LSE did not become a de facto regulator in partnership with the state until after the Second World War.

The willingness of the LSE to assume a greater regulatory role was to a considerable extent scandal-driven. Following a speculative boom in new issues in the 1920s, a major scandal shook the LSE in1929, when a flamboyant promoter, Charles Hatry, was found to have fraudulently sold counterfeit shares in established companies, intending to buy them back before dividends were declared (Michie 1987: 162–3). The Hatry scandal produced little, if any, legislation, but forced the LSE to accept some role as a guardian of issuer quality (ibid.: 268). The LSE became less willing to list what today would be called 'penny stocks' or development stage companies. By the 1950s, the LSE's listing rules had been tightened to require issuers to reveal all material information on an ongoing basis (Gower 1954: 437). Still, legislation establishing anything resembling a UK counterpart to the SEC did not come until the Financial Services Act of 1986.

If the LSE's efforts at self-regulation seem in general to have been more lax than those of the NYSE, there is a later chapter in this self-regulatory story in which the UK's efforts clearly outpaced those in the USA. Takeover bids first began to appear in the UK in the early 1950s, and by late 1959, the first voluntary code of conduct had been drawn up, largely at the request of the Bank of England, to regulate them (Johnson 1980: 19–20). While often ineffective, this voluntary code eventually evolved by the late 1960s into the City Takeover Code and its now well known Takeover Panel. In 1972, the Code was revised to require an acquirer to make a mandatory bid for all the target's shares once the acquirer crossed a specified threshold of stock ownership (generally 30 per cent) (ibid.: 91–2). The effect of this provision was to protect the right of the public shareholder to share in any control premium and to discourage stealth raids that sought to acquire control without the payment of such a premium. The UK's mandatory bid has, of course, now been incorporated into the Thirteenth Directive, but the more relevant point is that it encouraged dispersed ownership by effectively allowing the value of control to be held by public shareholders.

Thus, we come full circle: by a variety of means, including a substantial self-regulatory component, both the USA and the UK developed legal and institutional mechanisms that enabled dispersed ownership to persist. Generally, these mechanisms followed, rather than preceded, economic changes, but they did protect and permit the survival and growth of dispersed ownership. Finally, conspicuously absent from this process was politics. No political party in either country appears to have actively raised the issue of securities market reform (or opposed such reform) as a major issue.

3.3. *'Does Law Matter?' Reconsidered*

Opponents of the USA's mandatory disclosure system have long argued that SEC's disclosure requirements were unnecessary and costly because market mechanisms had already developed prior to 1933 to satisfy investors' real demand for information.[19] In the USA, there is at least some evidence consistent with this story, but in the UK, there is very little. The LSE did not recognize any obligation to protect investors or screen issuers until well after the First World War, and serious efforts probably did not begin until after the Second World War. Yet, securities markets developed in each country—in the USA, in the absence of legislative protections, and in the UK, in the absence of meaningful self-regulation or any significant private system for the pledging of reputational capital by financial intermediaries.

One possible way to read the USA and UK evidence is, of course, to reject the 'law matters' hypothesis. If one looks only at the USA experience, one could plausibly assert that private market mechanisms proved adequate and investor interests were well served without statutory protections. As next discussed, however, this thesis seems increasingly weak, more the product of an ideological antipathy to all regulation than an even-handed approach to the available evidence.

The alternative hypothesis is that law matters, but not in quite the way that the LLS&V (1999) model assumes. Self-regulation may best be viewed as a partial functional substitute for formal legal institutions. It arose in the US largely because of constraints on the judicial system (i.e. corruption plus the ability of the antagonists to pit one state's judges against another state's), even though substantive US corporate law was probably relatively protective of minority shareholders. This pattern is consistent with recent developments in transitional economies, where recent econometric studies have found the 'rule of law' and the 'effectiveness' of legal institutions to be more important variables in determining the depth of capital markets and the structure of share ownership than the specific legal rules on the books (Pistor *et al.* 2000).

Although securities markets may be able to arise in the absence of strong legal protections for minority shareholders because of such functional substitutes, they are generally unable to persist or expand in such an environment. Sooner or later, they predictably encounter crises and experience a loss of investor confidence. Conceivably, a strong system of self-regulation (as in the case of the City Takeover Code) may prove adequate to this challenge, but the line between self-regulation and indirect governmental regulation is often difficult to define. More typically, even when a strong private institutional structure exists (as it did in the case of the NYSE), there are still important deficiencies which require legislative intervention in order to provide adequate enforcement. Legislative action is thus likely to follow, rather than precede, the appearance of securities markets because a constituency of public investors must first arise before there will be pressures for legislative reform that intrudes upon the market. In addition, the legislature cannot anticipate problems that it has never seen (much as it cannot legislate with respect to the Internet before the Internet has first appeared).

This assertion that legislative action will generally be necessary because private ordering will encounter inevitable limitations leads one back to a long-standing academic debate over the impact of the passage of the federal securities laws (ibid.). George Stigler (1964: 120–1), the first and still the most vehement critic of the rationale for the federal securities laws, found that the variance in the relative price performance of new issues of securities declined by almost half after the passage of The Securities Act of 1933 (the 'Act'). Despite this dramatic change, Stigler interpreted this data to mean only that riskier new issues were being excluded as a result of the Act's passage. Subsequent economists have, however, interpreted this pronounced reduction in price dispersion to mean that greater pricing accuracy resulted (Friend and Herman 1964: 390–1; Fox 1999: 1369–80). Paralleling Stigler's work, George Benston focused on whether the new disclosure requirements mandated by the Act had any real impact. In particular, he focused on the new obligation imposed by the

Act to disclose sales data. While some firms already disclosed this data (but a substantial fraction did not), his research concluded that disclosure of sales data produced only a small, statistically insignificant decline in the riskiness of firms. Yet, as more recent economists have shown by reinterpreting Bentson's data (Fox 1999: 1385–91), there was an overall and significant decline of nearly one-third in the variance of the residuals of NYSE-listed firms (ibid. 1376–82). Thus, even if the impact of mandatory disclosure of sales data was uncertain, the total package of new disclosures produced immediate and observable results that are logically interpreted as an increase in pricing accuracy. Collectively, these studies support the conclusion that the federal securities laws increased pricing accuracy and the amount of meaningful information in the market.

At least as important as any enhancement in pricing accuracy effected by the mandatory disclosure system enacted by Congress was the system of enforcement and anti-fraud liability that came with the New Deal legislation. Severe constraints exist on both incentives and ability of a private body (such as a stock exchange) to enforce rules against its member firms and its listed companies. As we have seen earlier, the LSE did not make a serious effort until probably after the Second World War. While more activist as a self-regulator, the NYSE faced resistance from its listed companies when it sought to upgrade disclosure standards. For example, Merritt Fox (ibid.: 1376–84) has found that although the NYSE continually upgraded its listing requirements applicable to newly listed firms, it was unable (or unwilling) to apply these new rules to earlier listed firms (i.e. the great majority of the firms it traded). This is but one example of the enforcement shortfall that is inherent in a self-regulatory system. Such a shortfall is likely for several different reasons: (1) A private body has weak incentives to enforce rules against its own members and clients; (2) Enforcement is too costly for a private body to undertake on a thorough-going basis; and (3) Private bodies necessarily lack the investigative tools and punitive sanctions that the state has at its disposal. Each of these factors is evident in terms of the factors that led to the adoption of the federal securities laws in the 1930s.

When the US Congress enacted the federal securities laws in the early 1930s, it was dissatisfied not only with the level of disclosure in the securities market, but perhaps even more by the perceived pervasiveness of manipulative practices, including both the use of stock pools and short selling 'bear raids' that were intended to panic investors and artificially drive down stock prices.[20] Stock pools were temporary joint ventures formed by a group of traders who bought and sold a stock pursuant to a common plan to drive its price up or down through their collective action. Revisionist scholars have recently doubted their significance (ibid.: 1470–2), but the contemporaneous sources treat their existence as a well understood fact.[21] Historians have also noted that the market manipulation constituted the one context in which the NYSE seldom, if ever, enforced its own disciplinary rules (Banner 1997; Werner and Smith 1991: 32).

This limited enforcement effort should not be surprising. It is not simply a matter of weak incentives, but also difficulty of proof. Conspiracies by their nature do not reveal themselves to the observer. Only the public enforcer can threaten criminal penalties or truly punitive civil fines, and only public authorities have investigative tools, such as the grand jury, search warrants, and subpoena power, at their disposal. Absent a public regulatory body, victims may be left to enforce their rights through private litigation, and the high costs of enforcement may make it inadvisable for at least the public investor to seek to rely on such remedies.[22] As a practical matter, the creation of the SEC gave public investors a public guardian to champion their rights—in effect, a public subsidy for the prevention of fraud. This may be the most important way in which 'law matters'.

Even if one reaches the opposite conclusion and decides that the USA was over-regulated in the 1930s, while the UK's system of more limited self-regulation was closer to optimal, this conclusion does not truly challenge the 'law matters' hypothesis. Over-regulation of allegedly phantom culprits—such as the stock pool manipulator—could be justifiable, and even necessary, to the extent that it restored the trust and confidence of investors and so preserved dispersed ownership. The critical point is that serious efforts at self-regulation to protect minority investors seem to have characterized only common law countries. Thus, the LLS&V thesis would remain more right than wrong, even if it has arguably overemphasized some particular substantive corporate law provisions.

The foregoing account of the rise of dispersed ownership in the USA and the UK is also inconsistent with the leading counter-thesis to the LLS&V hypothesis: namely, that politics determines everything, and legal differences simply flow from deeply rooted political values. Put simply, politics played no more than a negligible role in the rise of dispersed ownership in either country. Although Roe (1994) has provocatively argued that politics constrained the development of powerful financial intermediaries in the USA, this hypothesis ignores that unconstrained institutional investors in the UK closely resemble their American counterparts, even though no regulatory inhibitions hobbled their growth (Black and Coffee 1994). Other things being equal, the simpler model is preferable to the more complex. Here, the simpler model is that financial institutions greatly value liquidity and so do not wish to hold large and illiquid equity stakes in business corporations (Banner 1997).

Even if an overtly political explanation cannot satisfactorily account for the development of dispersed ownership in the USA or the UK, can such a political story account for the persistence of concentrated ownership in Europe? Is, as Professor Roe suggests, the 'social democratic' character of European democracies the underlying cause of concentrated ownership? This claim rests on the behavioural premise that investors in such countries seek to avoid the culture of transparency that comes with the development of securities markets, because it would arguably subject them to even greater expropriation. The logical flaw in this reasoning is, however, that it ignores that 'social democracies' would have an incentive to enhance transparency if they believed that concentrated ownership were an important defence mechanism. Logically, on Roe's behavioural premise, left-leaning governments should favour the development of securities markets in order to gain greater control over the private sector. In principle, one should then observe across Europe private investors opposing the development of securities markets and the left favouring their growth. The reverse is probably closer to the truth (although no strong opposition to the growth of securities markets is apparent across Europe today and broad support seems to exist).

The better historical and political argument for the bank-centred system of corporate governance that dominated Europe until recently is that it maximized state control of the economy (Rajan and Zingales 2000). Particularly in times of war and social turmoil during the last century, those in power—whether socialistic or fascistic—preferred a bank centred system, because large banks were ultimately more subject to state control than were securities markets. That securities markets have developed slowly across Europe thus may well have a 'political' as well as a 'legal' explanation, but that political explanation is more that power seeking nationalists could use banks as their agents and that banks, once entrenched, had natural reasons to resist the rise of rivals for their business.

4. CONCLUSION

Two conclusions and one implication for the future emerge from a historical examination of the rise of dispersed ownership: first, the role of private institutional structures—most notably stock exchange rules and bonding mechanisms by which investment bankers pledged their reputational capital—probably was more important than mandatory legal rules in the early rise of dispersed ownership. The relative role accorded to self-regulation probably depended on the strength or weakness of the formal legal institutions in the particular country. Arguably, self-regulation played a greater role in the USA than in the UK, because judicial corruption and regulatory arbitrage were not significant problems in the UK. This conclusion does not refute the LLS&V hypothesis that 'law matters', but suggests that further enquiry is necessary as to why self-regulation developed and took deeper root in common law countries more than in civil law countries. Possibly, the more decentralized character of common law legal institutions facilitated the rise of both private and semi-private self-regulatory bodies in the USA and the UK, whereas in civil law systems the state retained a relative monopoly over law-making institutions. More broadly, the clearest generalization about the development of securities markets is that they have arisen only in societies (such as England and the Netherlands—one common law country and the other a civil law one) in which an autonomous private sector first evolved that was largely free from direct state supervision and control. Put simply, the role of the state has dominated the role of law in determining the financial structure of developed capitalist economies.

Second, the rise of dispersed ownership in both the USA and the UK was not accompanied by any significant degree of political self-consciousness. In the USA, the Progressive Era reform movement passed national legislation regulating drugs, foodstuffs, and railroads, but left the securities markets for a later day. In the UK, the legislative reforms that were adopted attracted little public attention or controversy. This is consistent with the broader pattern in which waves of securities regulation pass only in the period immediately following the burst of 'bubble' markets (Banner 1997). More generally, if dispersed ownership arose principally through private ordering, law may still 'matter' (although different legal institutions become central to the extent that they enabled or facilitated such private ordering), but politics matters much less. Indeed, politics seems relatively irrelevant because the rise of equity securities markets was relatively exogenous to ongoing political debates.

Political hostility to the rise of securities markets can be dimly discerned in Europe, but it dates back to the late nineteenth century and was most evident at that time in Germany,[23] a country that could not then be called by any stretch of the imagination a 'social democracy'. In this light, the reliance of German firms on bank finance seems to have been less a matter of choice than of legislative restrictions on the issuance of securities (ibid.: 287). But legislation restricting securities markets in Europe seems not to have been based on class conflict, but rather on the moralistic sense that trading on the stock market was 'little better than gambling' (ibid.: 286). The closer one looks, the more tenuous the connection becomes between the rise of the social welfare state and the suppression of securities markets. Rather than a defensive strategy by stockholders to resist governmental expropriation (as Roe proposes), concentrated ownership may have been more a system of implicit contracting by which 'social democracies' reached accommodations with the controlling shareholders of major firms and thus averted the need for direct confrontation and nationalization. Yet, precisely because social democracies might prefer to have controlling shareholders with whom they could negotiate, rather than an anonymous mass of dispersed shareholders, the new political environment in which nationalization is no longer a relevant threat means that shareholders are no longer constrained and can move to a dispersed ownership structure.

If private institutional structures played the pivotal role in the rise of dispersed ownership in the USA and the UK, what does this fact portend for European corporate governance? If, as just observed, politics has not been as central as the private institutional networks that enabled self-regulation and private bonding mechanisms to work, then the central implication for the future is that self-regulation might take hold in Europe and in the transitional economies, even though optimal legislation remains lacking. Indeed, to the extent that the 'rule of law' is only tenuously established in some transitional economies (as it was in the USA during the Robber Barron era), self-regulation may outperform legal rules, because it can more effectively enforce its commands. Today, the most dynamic forces on the European stage are not the various efforts to secure harmonized corporate and securities law, but rather the quieter changes that are currently underway in the markets, themselves, including: (a) the inexorable movement toward a pan-European stock exchange; (b) the increased activity of securities analysts with regard to European corporations with minority public ownership (Chang *et al.* 2000); (c) the accelerating convergence in international accounting standards (Land and Lang 2000); and (d) the current international wave of mergers and acquisitions. Even if legislation is ultimately needed to establish stronger minority protections, the USA and the UK experience suggest that if strong self-regulation can first bring about the appearance of deeper, more liquid securities markets, such legislation will predictably follow. Indeed, self-regulatory initiatives have begun to play a critical role in the development of European securities markets, particularly in countries where the prevailing legal rules seem weak.[24] Once these forces have created a stronger constituency for open and transparent markets, that constituency will demand and obtain the necessary legislative reform that fills in the inevitable gaps. If this occurs, the past would once again become prologue.

Notes

1. The seminal work of La Porta, Lopez-de-Silanes, Sheifler, and Vishny (hereinafter 'LLS&V') has established the existence of these rival systems, that they seem to have evolved along distinctive legal trajectories, and that correlate with significant differences in the legal protections provided to minority shareholders. See La Porta, Lopez-de-Silanes, and Sheifler (1999).
2. For representative statements of this position, see Hansmann and Kraakman (Chapter 3, this volume); see also Easterbrook and Fischel (1991: 4–15).
3. Stuart Banner (1997) has made the interesting argument that, over the last three hundred years, most major waves of securities regulation have followed a sustained price collapse on the securities

market. It is not surprising that 'bubbles' produce victims and hence a political demand for reform. But perhaps the deeper meaning of this finding is that the reform of securities regulation has not been associated with any broader political movement. Thus, this evidence is in tension with Roe's claim that there are 'political preconditions' to the growth of securities markets. See Roe (Chapter 5, this volume).

4. German scholars have also suggested that the German tax system may be the better explanation for at least the contemporary system of concentrated ownership in Germany. See Kubler (1999: 214).
5. Van der Elst (2000: 10) finds that both the Netherlands and Spain raised significantly more equity capital in IPOs as a percentage of GDP than did the USA or the UK. Nor is this simply an artefact of small GDP size, as in 1999 Germany raised equity capital equal to 1.02 per cent of its GDP through IPOs, while the UK raised only 0.6 per cent and the USA 1.23 per cent.
6. More importantly, some 500 fledgling firms are now listed on one or more of these new markets for start up firms (ibid.)
7. There is some dispute about when the separation of ownership and control truly arrived in the UK. Cheffins (Chapter 6, this volume) reviews the alternative views, one of which dates the transition as of the 1920s and the other as of mid-century. For present purposes, the arrival of broad public ownership, which came earlier, is the immediate focus.
8. For example, it is noteworthy that, as late as the First World War, 18 per cent of the stock of US Steel, a firm founded by J. P. Morgan & Co., was still owned by foreign investors. See Michie (1987: 56). It seems likely that higher percentages of stock in the largest American corporations would have been held by foreign investors as of the end of the nineteenth century and that their investment decisions would have been co-ordinated, or at least strongly influenced, by their American investment bankers.
9. For standard accounts, see Grodinsky (1957); Gordon (1988). For a recent and highly relevant review of Gould's manipulative schemes from a corporate law perspective, see Rock (1999).
10. Later, many of these rules were relaxed. For a review of American corporate law at this late nineteenth-century stage, see Friedman (1985: 511–25). Harold Marsh (1996) has also surveyed the status of the officer and director's fiduciary duty to the corporation during this era and concluded that strong prophylactic rules against self-dealing existed.
11. See Carosso (1970: 32–3). It should be noted that one firm (Kuhn Loeb & Co.) characteristically did not place its representatives on the issuer's board. It was seemingly the exception that proved the rule, but it may have limited its clientele to firms that found other means by which to bond their commitments to investors.
12. A single-minded focus on managerial expropriation is probably a legacy of Berle and Means' continuing influence. More recent scholars have argued, however, that investors are more exposed to expropriation by controlling shareholders. See Sheifler and Vishny (1997: 737).
13. See Werner and Smith (1991). Jay Gould in particular was noted for conducting proxy fights after buying a substantial block of stock. Often, these contests produced a greenmail payment to him, or he would short the stock before announcing the end of his proxy contest. See Klein (1986: 197–205; 277–80).
14. See Chernow, (1990: 32).
15. According to some authorities, British merchant banks did not become interested or heavily involved in underwriting domestic new issues until the 1920s. See Kynaston (1999: 135–6).
16. See Directors' Liability Act 1890, 53 & 54 Vict. Ch. 64 (UK) (overruling *Derry* v. *Peak*, 14 App. Cas. 337 (H.L. 1889)).
17. Companies Act 1900, 63 & 64 Vict., ch. 48, § 10(1) (UK).
18. Companies Act 1907, 7 Edw., ch. 50, §§ 19, 21 (UK).
19. Companies Act 1929, § 123.

20. Many commentators have revisited this debate, which goes back to the work of Stigler and Benston in the 1960s. See Stigler (1964); Benston (1973). But see Friend and Herman (1964) (arguing that Stigler's data demonstrates the positive impact of the federal securities laws); see also Simon (1989: 311–13).
21. See Mahoney (1997: 1464–5). Although Mahoney challenges the accuracy of this perception, the more important point is such perceptions are likely to persist, thereby eroding investor trust and confidence in an entirely private system of self-regulation.
22. Although Mahoney disparages the congressional findings that stock pools manipulated securities prices, he ignores the similar findings by economists in the 1930s who contemporaneously studied the operations of pools. See Twentieth Century Fund (1934) (surveying actual techniques used by stock pools in the 1930s).
23. This is particularly true in the UK where small investors may be deterred by the UK's 'loser pays' rule under which the losing side must pay the litigation expenses of the winning side. In the USA, private enforcement constitutes a greater deterrent threat, principally because of the availability of the class action, which did not develop, however, until the late 1960s.
24. Coffee (1991) has argued this thesis at considerable length elsewhere, and will not belabour it further here. Suffice it to say that banks, as institutions with short-term liabilities to depositors, have a major problem with making illiquid long-term investments.
25. See Banner, *supra* note 10.
26. See Michie (2000: 286–870) (finding that 'German companies were denied the ease of access to finance via security issues that their British counterparts enjoyed').
27. The clearest example is the Neuer Markt, the rapidly growing German stock market for start-up companies, which prides itself on being both the 'most regulated market' and the fastest growing. In just over three years, it has grown from 2 to 302 listed companies with a collective market capitalization of $172 billion. See Fuhrmans (2000: at C1). The Neuer Markt has substantially higher listing and disclosure standards than does the Deutsche Borse, its parent. Moreover, German corporate law ranks relatively low on the LLS&V scale of minority protection. The Neuer Markt thus stands as a modern example of what the NYSE did in the late nineteenth century: establish itself as a higher quality market through self-regulatory standards that were more stringent than those established by prevailing law. As it succeeds, such a market pledges its reputational capital to investors that it will continue to uphold these standards.

References

Armstrong, J. (1990). The rise and fall of the company promoter and the financing of British industry. In Van Helten and Cassis (ed.).

Banner, S. (1997). What causes new securities regulation?: 300 years of evidence. *Washington University Law Quarterly* 75: 849.

——(1998). The origin of the New York Stock Exchange, 1791–1860. *Journal of Legal Studies* 27: 113.

Bebchuk, L. (1999). A rent protection theory of corporate ownership and control. NBER, Working Paper No. 7203.

——and Roe, M. (1999). A theory of path dependence in corporate ownership and governance. *Stanford Law Review* 52: 127.

Benston, G. (1973). Required disclosure and the stock market: An evaluation of the Securities Exchange Act of 1934. *American Economic Review* 63: 132.

Beny, L. (1999). A comparative investigation of agency and market theories of insider trading. Harvard Law School, Discussion Paper No. 264.

Berglöf, E., and von Thadden, E.-L. (1999). The changing corporate governance paradigm: Implications for transition and developing countries. In *Annual World Bank Conference on Development Economics*, 135.

Berle, A., and Means, G. (1932). *The Modern Corporation and Private Property*. New York: Harcourt, Brace & World, Inc.

Black, B. S. (2000). The first international merger wave (and the fifth and last USA wave). *University of Miami Law Review* 54: 799.

—— and Coffee, J. (1994). Hail Brittania?: Institutional investor behavior under limited regulation. *Michigan Law Review* 92: 1997.

Brancato, J. (2000). Corporations outside USA become more subject to investor demands. *Corporate Governance Advisor*, July/August, 1.

Carosso, V. (1970). *Investment Banking in America*. Cambridge, MA: Harvard University Press.

Carosso, V. (1987). *The Morgans: Private International Bankers, 1854–1913*. Cambridge, MA: Harvard University Press.

Chandler, A. D. (1990). *Scale and Scope*. Cambridge, MA: Harvard University Press.

Chang, J., Khanna, T., and Palepu K. G. (2000). Analysts activity around the world. Harvard Business School, Working Paper.

Cheffins, B. R. (2000). Does law matter?: The separation of ownership and control in the United Kingdom. ESRC Center for Business Research, University of Cambridge Working Paper No. 172.

Chernow, R. (1990). *The House of Morgan: An American Banking Dynasty and the Rise of Modern Finance*. New York: Atlantic Monthly Press.

Coffee, J. C. (1991). Liquidity versus control: The institutional investor as corporate monitor. *Columbia Law Review* 1991: 1227.

—— (1999). The future as history: The prospects for global convergence in corporate governance and its significance. *Northwestern University Law Review* 93: 641.

Companies Act 1900 (63 & 64 Vict. c. 48) § 10(1) (UK).

Companies Act 1907 (7 Edw. c. 50) §§ 19, 21 (UK).

Companies Act 1929 (19 & 20 Geo. 5, c. 23) § 123 (UK).

Davies, P. L. (1997). *Gower's Principles of Modern Company Law*. London: Sweet & Maxwell.

De Long, J. B. (1991). Did J. P. Morgan's men add value? An economist's perspective on financial capitalism. In Temin (ed.), *Inside the Business Enterprise: Historical Perspectives on the Use of Information*. Chicago: University of Chicago Press.

Directors' Liability Act 1890 (53 & 54 Vict. c. 64) (UK).

Easterbrook, F., and Fischel, D. (1991). *The Economic Structure of Corporate Law*. Cambridge, MA: Harvard University Press.

Englebourg, S., and Bushkoff, L. (1996). *The Man who Found the Money: John Stewart Kennedy and the Financing of the Western Railroads*. East Lansing: Michigan State University Press.

Financial Times (2000). AEU passes takeover Directive. 20 June, 20, 28.

—— (2000). *Financial Times* survey—international mergers and acquisitions: The weak will become prey. 30 June, 4.

Fox, M. (1999). Retaining mandatory disclosure: Why issuer choice is not investor empowerment. *Virginia Law Review* 85: 1335.

Friedman, L. M. (1985). *A History of American Law* New York: Simon & Schuster.

Friend, L., and Herman, E. (1964). The S.E.C.: Through a glass darkly. *Journal of Business* 37: 382.

Fuhrmans (2000). Playing by the rules: How Neuer Markt gets respect. *Wall Street Journal*, 21 August, 21, C1.

Gilson, R. (2001). Globalizing corporate governance: Convergence of form or function. *American Journal of Comaprative Law*, Spring, 329.

Gordon, J. S. (1988). *The Scarlet Woman of Wall Street.* New York: Wiedenfeld and Nicolson.

Gower, L. C. B. (1954). *Principles of Modern Company Law.* London: Sweet & Maxwell.

Grodinsky, J. (1957). *Jay Gould, His Business Career 1867–1892.* Philadelphia: University of Pennsylvania Press.

Hawkins D. (1986). The development of modern financial reporting practices among American manufacturing corporations. In R. Tedlow and R. John Jr. (ed.), *Managing Big Business.* Cambridge, MA: Havard University Business Press.

Holmen, M., and Hogfeldt, P. (2000). A Law and Finance Analysis of Initial Public Offerings, Stockholm School of Economics Working Paper (available on SSRN at ID=236042).

Johnson, A. (1980). *The City Take-over Code.* New York: Oxford University Press.

Karmin, C. (2000). World stock markets: Europe's Easdaq finds that success doesn't come easy. *Wall Street Journal,* 14 August, C-1.

Klein, M. (1986). *The Life and Legend of Jay Gould.* Baltimore: Johns Hopkins University Press.

Kubler, M. (1999). Comment: On Mark J. Roe, German codetermination and the German securities market. *Columbia Journal of European Law* 5: 213.

Kynaston, D. (1999). *The City of London: Illusions of Gold,* Volume IV: *Illusions of Gold 1912–1925.* Oxford: Oxford University Press.

Land, J., and Lang, M. H. (2000). Empirical evidence on the evolution of global accounting. Working Paper (available on SSRN).

La Porta R., Lopez-de-Silanes, F., and Sheifler, A. (1999). Corporate ownership around the world. *Journal of Finance* 54: 471.

———————— and Vishny (1997). Legal Determinants of External Finance. *Journal of Finance* 52: 1131.

—————————— (1998). Law and finance. *Journal of Political Economy* 106: 1113.

—————————— (2000). Investors protection and corporate governance. Harvard University Working Paper.

Licht, A. (2000). The mother of all path dependencies: Toward a cross-cultural theory of corporate governance systems. *Delaware Journal of Corporate Law* 26: 147.

Mahoney, P. (1997). The exchange as regulator. *Virginia Law Review* 83: 1453.

Marsh, H. (1966). Are Directors Trustees? *Business Law* 22: 35.

Michie, R. (1987). *The London and New York Stock Exchanges, 1850–1914.* London: MacMillan Academic and Professional.

——(1992). *The City of London, Change and Continuity, 1850–1990.* London: MacMillan Academic and Professional.

——(1999). *The London Stock Exchange: A History.* Oxford: Oxford University Press.

——(2000). Different in name only?: The London Stock Exchange and foreign bourses, 1850–1914. In R. Michie (ed.), *The Development of London as a Financial Centre,* Volume IV. Cheltenham: Edward Elgar.

Paish, F. W. (2000). The London new issue market. In R. Michie (ed.), *The Development of London as a Financial Centre,* Volume IV. Cheltenham: Edward Elgar.

Pistor, K. (2000). Patterns of legal change: Shareholder and creditor rights in transition economies. EBRD, Working Paper No. 49.

——, Raiser, M., and Gelfer, S. (2000). Law and finance in transition economies. EBRD, Working Paper.

Rajan, R., and Zingales, L. (2000). The great reversals: The politics of financial development in the 20th century. University of Chicago, Working Paper.

Ramirez (1995). Did J. P. Morgan's men add liquidity?: Corporate investment, cash flow, and financial structure at the turn of the twentieth century. *Journal of Finance* 50: 661.

Rock, E. (1999). Encountering the Scarlet Woman of Wall Street: Speculative comments at the end of the century. University of Pennsylvania Law School, Institutes for Law and Economics, Working Paper No. 276.

Roe, M. (1994). *Strong Managers, Weak Owners: The Political Roots of American Corporate Finance.* Princeton: Princeton University Press.

Sheifler, A., and Vishny (1997). A survey of corporate governance. *Journal of Finance* 52: 737.

Simon, H. (1989). The effect of the 1933 Securities Act on investor information and the performance of new issues. *American Economic Review* 79: 295.

Simonian, H. (2000). Germany unbound: Measures to redeem the country's restrictive tax burden have delighted many businesses. *Financial Times*, 10 August 10, 14.

Stigler, G. (1964). Public regulation of the securities markets. *Journal of Business* 37: 117.

Stokes, M. (2000). The M&A game's global field. *National Journal*, 15 July, 2290.

Tagliabue, J. (2000). Resisting those ugly Americans. *New York Times*, 9 January, Sec. 3, 1.

Thomas, W. A. (1978). *The Finance of British Industry*. London: Methuen.

Twentieth Century Fund (1934). *Stock Market Control*. New York: Twentieth Century Fund.

Van der Elst, C. (2000). The equity markets, ownership structures and control: Towards an international harmonization? Ghent University, Financial Law Institute, Working Paper.

Wall Street Journal (2000). Euronet and Reuters are said to consider their own LSE bids. 5 September, A-25.

Werner, W. and Smith, S. (1991), WALL STREET. New York: Columbia University Press.

5

Political Foundations for Separating Ownership from Control

MARK J. ROE[1]

1. INTRODUCTION: WHY DO ONLY SOME NATIONS HAVE PUBLIC FIRMS?

The public firm, with dispersed stockholders in deep liquid securities markets, dominates business in the United States of America. Despite its pervasiveness, it has well-known infirmities, namely in the fragile ties that bind managers to shareholders. If shareholders strongly fear managers' disloyalty or incompetence, they will invest warily; if sufficiently fearful, they will not invest at all, and other ownership structures will prevail. But the core problems of binding managers to shareholders in the USA have shrunk to acceptable levels; investors are not so afraid of managers that they refuse to invest. Indeed, these problems have been handled so well that we fail to recognize the political prerequisites to resolving them and tying American managers to dispersed stockholders.

I argue here that the core problems of the public firm cannot be resolved readily, or at all, in a strong social democracy. Social democracies press managers to 'defect' from loyalty to shareholders and make it harder to align managers with shareholders. When we see how social democracies weaken shareholders' ties to managers, we shall thereby discover a key political prerequisite to the rise and persistence of the public firm in the USA, namely the absence of a social democracy and its concomitant powerful pressures on the business firm.

In contrast to the American-style public firm, the family firm, or the public firm with concentrated ownership, dominates business in France, Germany, Italy, and Scandinavia. A main bank system with significant bank stockholdings was historically important in Japan, and may still have some strength left to it. How do we explain this difference, between the USA and most of the rest of the developed world, and its persistence?

Diffusely-owned public firms must make managers loyal to shareholders. Agency costs arise from managers having agendas that differ from shareholders' agendas. Diffuse shareholders want the firm to maximize profits; unconstrained managers often prefer to maximize the firm's size, prefer not to take severe risks with the firm even if the risks would maximize profits, and often prefer to defer hard, disruptive actions. When blockholders and private ownership persist, they may persist because they serve a function for shareholders. Blockholders and private owners have the means and the motivation to monitor managers, a motivation and an authority that dispersed shareholders in the Berle–Means Corporation often lack. Hence, blockholding may have persisted on the European continent because managerial agency costs were potentially higher there and stockholders lack good alternative means of keeping managers loyal.

Most corporate governance analyses ignore employees, and when we put them back into the governance inquiry, we get a richer understanding of how a society organizes its corporate institutions: social democracies and the American-style public firm mix badly because public firm agency costs in social democracies are higher and the mechanisms that would control the agency costs are harder to implement.

A tension always exists between current employees and invested capital, and a great deal of American corporate governance mitigates this tension. It does so by inducing managers to act in shareholders' interests, and, oftentimes, against the immediate interests of employees with jobs in place. When economic realities change, employees could be laid off. When technologies change, managers must alter the firm's structure and day-to-day working environment in ways that make incumbent employees and often the managers themselves unhappy. Employees' and managers' jobs must be restructured or put at risk. Work, if the excitement of change is unattractive, becomes disruptive, difficult, and risky; workers and managers may resist change. Managers, for their own reasons, not only frequently delay these restructurings, but also have a long-known propensity to expand the firm's ongoing operations, even at the cost of shareholder profits; their expanding the firm down a known path usually favours themselves and current employees, but it often fails to maximize shareholder profits.

In social democracies—nations committed to private property, whose governments play a large role in the economy, emphasize distributional considerations, and favour employees over capital-owners when the two conflict—public policy emphasizes managers' natural agenda and demeans shareholders' natural agenda (cf. Przeworski 1993: 832–7; Stimson 1998: 395). The pressure on the firm for low-risk expansion is high, the pressure to avoid risky organizational change is substantial, and the tools that would induce managers to work in favour of invested capital—high incentive compensation, hostile takeovers, transparent accounting, acculturation to shareholder wealth maximization norms—are weak. Unconstrained managers may well go along, but shareholders would prefer to go slow in, say, expanding the firm, because expansion is harder to reverse later on than it would be in another political environment. Life may well be better for more people, but the internal structure of public firms must necessarily be weaker for shareholders.

Hence, managerial agency costs are higher in social democracies than elsewhere, and we have just found a deeper, richer social and political explanation not only for the history of family ownership in France, Germany, Italy, and Scandinavia, and possibly for the Japanese main banks, but also for the rise of the public firm in the USA. Social democracies do not strongly control public firm agency costs well, because they do not want unbridled shareholder wealth maximization, and, hence, by weakening shareholder wealth maximization institutions, they widen the gap. When the gap is wide enough, the large American-style public firm is rendered unstable without subsidy, making it incompatible with social democracy. Social democracies may improve aggregate welfare, but they do so with fewer public firms.

A road map for this chapter: In Section 2, I first set out the structural contrast in ownership around the world and next show how social democracy both (a) wedges open the gap between managers and shareholders and (b) raises the costs of closing the gap. In Section 3, I show some fundamental correlations: if we array the world's richest nations along a left–right spectrum, this spectrum correlates powerfully with ownership concentration. I also briefly discuss the reasons for American exceptionalism. In Section 4, I discuss stronger tests and provide alternative formulations of the thesis. In Section 5, I describe some reservations. In Section 6, I explicitly draw out the implications for understanding the American public firm. Finally, I conclude.

2. SOCIAL DEMOCRACIES' PRESSURES ON THE PUBLIC FIRM

Some nations' large firms are diffusely-held, while others are closely-held, because many never go public, and big blockholders persist even in those that do. In Germany, in the 1990s, nearly every large firm has a large blockholder, usually from a family, but for some firms from a bank, an insurance company, or another corporation (Franks and Mayer 2000). In France, the family or entrepreneurially-controlled sector was large, growing, and highly competitive (Windolf 1998). In Italy, family firms persist and few firms are truly public (Ruggiero 1998: 82). In Japan, the largest firms have had four or five banks and insurers that each own about 5 per cent of each firm's stock. Most such differences thus far persist, despite converging living standards and business technology.

No single factor can fully explain every difference and I discuss the conventional explanations elsewhere (Roe 2001*a*, 2002). I do not wish to displace the other explanations completely, but rather to make a large space for the unrecognized political explanation and show why it is as, or more, important for the world's richer nations as any current explanation.

2.1. *Agency Costs and the Public Firm*

The US has a rich literature on agency costs, of the disjunction between managers' goals and shareholders' goals. Shareholders, particularly diversified shareholders who are distant from the corporation, want their firm's profits maximized. Managers historically preferred to expand their firms, as expansion yielded them more power, prestige, and pay. Managers, with their own human capital tied up in the firm, often wanted to avoid many profit-maximizing risks; shareholders, who can diversify better than managers, have usually preferred their firms to maximize expected value, without respect to risk. Managers often used up capital in place rather than restructure a firm, because restructuring can be painful. And in simple terms managers may not have wanted to work as hard and as long as shareholders would prefer.

Corporate governance is traditionally seen in the USA as a principal–agent problem. Principals cannot get agents to perform perfectly. The principals often are less well informed than their agents about the tasks to be performed and, afterwards, about how well the agents performed them. The principals usually are more time-constrained than the agents in the activity involved. Stockholders as principals cannot automatically get their agents, the firm's managers, to pursue stockholders' interests. In the USA, the public firm principal–agent problem is layered over a free-rider problem because the stockholders are fragmented and distant from the firm, with each unwilling to invest heavily in monitoring their managerial agents and in making those agents toe the line to perform for shareholders. This much is not new.

That is, when stockholding is diffuse, these agency cost problems for shareholders' increase, because diffuse, free-riding shareholders lack the motivation to monitor managers. Moreover, their small holdings deny them the means to monitor effectively—managers have little reason to pay attention to a small shareholder acting alone—and deny them the information base they would need to be effective. Yet, despite these problems, the USA has many public firms, whose shares are diffusely-owned. Part of the reason this is so is well known: diffuse ownership yields risk-bearing advantages that partly offset the agency cost disadvantages of large firms. Part of the reason is that professional managers despite their debilities are often better at their job than the second or third generation of family managers (Chandler 1977; Demsetz 1983).

And part of the reason that the USA has so many public firms is that it developed tools to constrain managerial agency costs. These institutions have been the independent and active board, incentive compensation, hostile takeovers and proxy contests, securities markets signalling from securities analysts, competitive capital and product markets, and socialization in business schools and on-the-job to a shareholder wealth maximization norm. I hardly argue that these devices perfectly align managers with stockholders; but since the USA has so many Berle–Means firms with diffuse ownership: (i) we will see more agency cost failures in the USA in the aggregate, and (ii) corporate law academics and finance economists, because they correctly focus their attention on improving or understanding the core American corporate governance institutions, are susceptible to incorrectly believing that the USA controls agency costs badly, when the prevalence in the USA of the Berle–Means firm more likely shows an institution whose costs even if not trivial and even if still susceptible of improvement are sufficiently contained to be viable for all of its key players.

2.2. *Social Democracies and Agency Costs: Raising the Stakes*

Social democracies raise agency costs for shareholders in the public firm, and, to the extent they do so, shareholders' natural reaction would then be to find an alternative organizational form. German codetermination—by which labour gets one-half of the supervisory board of Germany's largest firms—is an explicit manifestation of social democracy, one that well illustrates the effects on corporate organization of social democracy. We first look at social democracy's effects through codetermination, seeing the dilemma a family-owned firm faces when considering whether to take their firm public, and then we generalize to look at social democracy's effects on agency costs and ownership structure without codetermination. The formal social democratic institution of codetermination is not needed for social democracy to affect the public firm's internal workings, but the formal institution boldly illustrates the political effects.

2.2.1. *Social Democracy's Effects through Codetermination*

Germany has had a long ideological and political encounter with codetermination. It first arose after the First World War when revolutionary leaders established workers' councils (counterparts to the better-known soviets arising elsewhere), which evolved into employee representation on the supervisory council of the larger firms. After the Second World War, labour leaders sought to be represented on the boards, partly to convince the Allies not to dismantle Germany's coal and steel industry, by asserting that they, labour, would constrain the wartime industrialists via positions on the firms' supervisory boards. From this 'deal' came full-parity codetermination of labour and shareholders in the coal and steel industry. Codetermination also had its capitalist promoters, who sought a 'middle way' between the raw capitalism of the marketplace and the extreme socialism of state-ownership. Later political events expanded this codetermination, to one-third of the supervisory board of most other industrial firms, and in 1976 to one-half of the board of Germany's larger firms.

Consider how codetermination affects agency costs, and thereby affects German corporate ownership structure and securities markets, by seeing how a successful family firm, thinking about an initial public offering (IPO) and withdrawing from managing and owning the company, might react to codetermination. Their supervisory board has never been strong. It has met for the statutory minimum of (until recently) twice annually. The meetings are formal, without serious give and take. The accounting reports that the board gets are not very good, the board gets them at the very beginning of a semi-annual meeting, and then the reports are whisked away from them at its end. The board is not a serious monitoring mechanism inside the firm. This is the typical traditional picture painted of the German boardroom.[2]

Board-level monitoring has not thus far been critical to the firm for two reasons. First, many family owners are also the firm's managers; hence, the disjunction between ownership and management is weaker than in the public firm, and agency costs lower. Second, even if the family does not manage the firm directly but hires professional managers, the family members meet monthly with managers to review results and performance. In effect, the monitoring role of the active board is fulfilled apart from the supervisory board, whose meetings are stale, formal, and ineffective.

The family may have considered moving more of the monitoring into the boardroom, partly to get ready for a public offering, partly to formalize the informal monthly meetings with managers. But they concluded not to move it inside the boardroom, because they preferred not to give more information and authority to the labour members of the supervisory board.

The family, as we have hypothesized, is hoping to leave the firm. They want to sell their stock and diversify their investments. The firm has been returning $50 million in earnings to them annually, and they accord a capitalization rate of 10 to those earnings, valuing the firm at $500 million.

The underwriters with whom they speak confirm that the firm would be worth $500 million if the average annual earnings of $50 million were expected to persist. But the underwriters, thinking about selling the stock to the potential diffuse public stockholders, indicate that they fear the earnings will not persist if the board remains weak, meeting only twice annually and receiving such poor information. Eventually, there will be an external crisis in the firm's markets or an internal one in the firm's organization, and a weak, poorly informed board is likely to respond more slowly and less effectively than a stronger one. Eventually, current managers will retire or be unable to manage the firm well, and a weak board will resolve a succession crisis less effectively than a strong one. Thus far, the underwriters say, the family has fulfilled the role that a strong board would play. But if the family leaves, the firm will at times be rudderless.

The underwriters put a value on the weak board if the firm lacks direction from the family owners, saying that over time, they would expect that earnings would be $40 million, not $50 million, if the board were weak and ineffective. They accord those earnings the same capitalization rate of 10, valuing the firm at $400 million, not $500 million.

The family and underwriters then consider charging up the board: they consider changing the by-laws to have the board meet monthly; they consider improving the information flow to the board; they consider adopting transparent, understandable accounting, with statements going to the board well before the meetings; they consider instilling in the board an ethic of involvement; and they consider building aggressive audit, executive, and compensation committees. These improvements to the board, the family tells the underwriters, will reduce the monitoring and weak board problems, the expected earnings should then be re-pegged to $50 million, and the firm should be valued at the original $500 million in the IPO, not $400 million.

The underwriters respond that, yes, the board will be better. But, they ask, in whose interest will the board run the firm? With the supervisory board codetermined, the charged-up board will tilt more to labour when labour and shareholders' interests conflict than would a purely shareholder-dominated board. Managers will be monitored more, but they will not necessarily be monitored in shareholders' interests. The enhanced board will create value, but some of that value will go to labour not stockholders. The underwriters conclude that the firm will indeed be worth $500 million, but $100 million of that value will go to labour. These numbers are not out-of-line with the current empirical work on the effect of the 1976 co-determination law, the one that expanded labour's representation from one-third of the supervisory boards of large firms to one-half. The data available show a ten to twenty per cent effect on shareholder value.[3]

The family wants to keep that $100 million. They can re-visit whether they should sell out completely. They may decide to keep the firm private and re-examine whether they can find an heir who will run it. Or they may hire professional managers to run the firm, if they have not done so already. Or they may sell the firm, but sell it not to diffuse stockholders who will discount the price because they would fear agency costs, but to another dominant owner, who need not discount the price because he or she can overcome those costs. Such block sales are common in Germany (Franks and Mayer 2000). To keep that $100 million difference, the family does not launch an IPO; hence there is one less public firm in Germany and one less family interested in seeing Germany developing a strong securities market.

And thus German social democracy, institutionalized in corporate governance via codetermination, induces this firm to stay private, so as to avoid the costs to shareholders of enhanced labour voice inside the firm. Social democracy in the form of supervisory board codetermination, hence, mixes badly with the public firm.

2.2.2. *Social Democracy's Effects without Codetermination*

Social democracy's pressure on the public firm persists even if we remove the formal institution of German supervisory board codetermination.

(i) General effects: Favouring employees over shareholders—Recall the basic agency costs to shareholders: unconstrained managers, unlike shareholders, prefer to expand their firms for more satisfaction, power, prestige, and pay. Managers want to avoid many profit-maximizing risks that would risk their careers. Managers prefer to use up capital in place rather than to restructure a firm, because restructuring is painful. And managers may be more willing to tolerate slack than would shareholders.

These managerial tendencies fit well with employees' goals, and a second basic corporate governance problem—for employees and capital-providers—is the persistent tension between invested capital and current employees, a tension muted in the USA, but not muted everywhere. Employees also are averse to risks to the firm, as their human capital is tied up in the firm and they are not fully diversified. Employees also prefer that the firm expand, not downsize, because expanding often yields them promotion opportunities while downsizing risks leaving them unemployed.[4]

On a simple level, employees prefer higher wages, shareholders prefer lower wages (at the same level of productivity). As wages are not precisely determined, managers hold some discretion in setting wages (Reynolds 1951; Lester 1952); weakly monitored managers will not fight as strongly for shareholders as strongly monitored managers (Acemoglu and Newman 1997). Even in the USA, slight differences in shareholder control of managers affect wage rates, with less-monitored managers, in states where anti-takeover laws are strong, conceding higher salaries to employees than where the laws are weak (Bertrand and Mullainathan 1999). On a more complex level, American managers of firms in declining industries tended in the 1980s to use up their equity capital before shrinking their firms unless corporate governance controls induced them not to use up equity first (Jensen 1986); this is the strategy that incumbent employees would prefer.

(ii) Direct effects: Softening change and raising agency costs—Social democracies favour incumbent employees. They act directly by insisting that firms not lay off employees; managers not tied tightly to shareholders will resist such efforts only weakly (because they do not pay for going along, but take a great deal of heat for resisting the government). Such governments will also seek to stabilize employment in firms with dominant stockholders, but dominant stockholders, with their own money on the line, can oftentimes resist the government's actions more vigorously.

(iii) Indirect effects: Rigid labour markets as raising agency costs—Even when social democratic employment policies affect diffusely-held and closely-held firms equally, these policies ought to affect ownership structure. Social democratic policies often make it hard to lay off workers, even during economic adversity.[5] True, when the firm faces adversity and seeks to downsize, each ownership structure faces the same constraints. Hence, one might (mistakenly) conclude that social democracies would not affect the choice between ownership structures. But dominant stockholders would be more averse to expanding *ex ante* when labour markets are rigid than if employment rules were looser. Unconstrained managers often prefer to expand their firm, as is quite well developed in the managerial literature. Since they gain from expansion, but do not always pay the price if expansion turns out to be unprofitable, they may well (unless constrained) expand, their firms may deteriorate more, and in anticipation of this risk, stock has diffused into public markets less in social democracies than in more conservative nations, because in such a nation the stock would have been worth less to diffuse stockholders than to close owners.

Government policies wedge open the gap between shareholders and employees, by creating laws and a social climate that make it harder for managers to downsize when technology demands downsizing or harder for managers to take risks with the enterprise when markets warrant it (from a shareholder perspective). They give employees more rights to resist change.[6] They construct nation-wide bargaining platforms that favour employees, platforms in which 'coalition costs' among shareholders are lower, and hence shareholders ought to be more successful, by acting cohesively. They see managers and employees as allied, and opposed to distant institutional shareholders,[7] who, because they merely seek financial gain, must be constrained.[8] Managers, already disposed for their own reasons to expand unnecessarily, to go slow when re-vamping the firm, to avoid risk, and to refuse to downsize, feel pressured to slow down further and face social opprobrium if they move too quickly. Managers who excessively expanded their enterprises in a strong social democracy would especially burden their shareholders, as reversing a mistaken expansion is hard to accomplish in a social democracy.

Strong social democracies raise the pressures on managers to abandon their shareholders and side with employees to do what managers want to do all along: expand, avoid risk, and avoid rapid change. Social democracies, in short, raise managerial agency costs.

2.3. *Social Democracies and Agency Costs: Shareholders' Control of Managers*

Moreover, social democracies hinder, or break, the mechanisms that could control agency costs. When the gap separating managers from shareholders is small, some of the tools may not be worth their cost. Nations with lower agency costs may not need all of them. But as agency costs rise—as the gap between managers and shareholders widens—or as intense competition makes even a moderate gap harder to tolerate, the demand for gap-closing tools will rise. Social democracies not only widen the gap as we saw in the prior section, but make the gap-closing tools—shareholder wealth maximization norms, transparent accounting, incentive compensation, and hostile takeovers and proxy fights—harder to employ.[9]

That is, in the USA, much corporate governance has the effect, and often the intention, of breaking managers' preference for continuance, excessive risk reduction, and over-expansion, the goals employees also prefer. When these governance devices succeed, they align managers more closely with shareholders than they would otherwise be aligned. They reduce the overlap between managers' goals and employees' goals, and enhance the overlap between managers' goals and distant stockholders' goals. Managers become stockholders themselves and get stock options that are valuable if their firm's stock price rises. Managers see their results 'posted' daily in liquid stock markets. Managers are monitored by outside directors, whose lawyers tell them that they, the directors, work primarily for shareholders.[10] Managers and directors are socialized in business school and at work to believe that shareholder wealth maximization is a valid norm, one that they should pursue. These tools are usually weaker, and sometimes denigrated, in a social democracy (Roe 2001*a*, 2002).

Consider, for example, a soft control: a belief in shareholder wealth maximization. This norm, widespread in American business circles, surely affects what managers think about their tasks.[11] But it is not self-evident outside of American business circles that business be organized around a shareholder wealth maximization norm, a norm that does not inherently and directly derive from even a utilitarian norm: why shareholders' wealth, when shareholders make up such a small and already-favoured part of society?[12] One answer is that this is the distributional 'price' for getting good capital allocation. Another is that shareholder wealth roughly proxies for total wealth and no other norm is, right now, plausible to implement in diffusely-owned firms: managers need, in this analysis, a measurable guide and total wealth maximization is too hard to measure and implement. But this 'proxy' justification is theoretically contestable and widely disbelieved in social democracies. Managers there see more newscasts, read more articles, and have more conversations disparaging shareholder wealth maximization than their counterparts see, read, and have in a non-social democracy. Political leaders sympathize with employees more there than elsewhere. American labour has tolerated a corporate focus on profitability more willingly than has labour abroad.

Social atmosphere is important when managers have discretion, as they must have; the social pressures they feel affects how they exercise that discretion. Weakly monitored public firm managers in social democracies find it psychologically hard to work primarily for shareholders. They believe themselves to be somewhat evil, or at least not wholly good, if they maximize shareholder value and tighten up the workplace.[13] Hence, they do so only reluctantly, and sometimes not at all.

Incentives and techniques that would otherwise control and align managers with public shareholders are weaker and used only sporadically. Labour market rigidities are more costly to shareholders of diffusely-owned firms than closely-owned firms. The Berle–Means firm's higher relative cost to shareholders in social democracies reduces its incidence, and shareholders would seek another means of control, namely, direct control via block ownership.

3. THE DATA

3.1. *A Regressing Ownership Concentration on Politics*

We now have a simple, powerful theory, that social democracies open up a gap between managers and distant stockholders, and that they impede firms from developing the tools that would close up that gap. What correlations should flow from the theory, and do the data confirm or contradict the predictions? We could compare political orientation with ownership structure, expecting that left nations would correlate with lower diffuse ownership and right nations with higher diffuse ownership.

So they do. Table 5.1 lists nations' politics from most left to most right, based on a poll of political scientists around the world.[14] Table 5.2 lists the nations' incidence of block

Table 5.1. *Political placement of richest nations' governments in 1980s*

Sweden	2.22	Belgium	3.16
Austria	2.37	Denmark	3.40
Australia	2.50	Switzerland	3.43
Norway	2.63	Canada	3.67
Finland	2.68	Germany	3.82
Italy	2.76	United States	3.92
France	2.83	Japan	4.00
Netherlands	3.14	United Kingdom	4.00

Table 5.2. *Percentage of widely-held firms among twenty largest public firms*

Austria	0.05	Germany	0.50
Belgium	0.05	Canada	0.60
Italy	0.20	Switzerland	0.60
Norway	0.25	France	0.60
Sweden	0.25	Australia	0.65
Netherlands	0.30	United States	0.80
Finland	0.35	Japan	0.90
Denmark	0.40	United Kingdom	1.00

Table 5.3. *Regressing diffusion on politics*

	Regression coefficient (*t*-statistic)	**Adjusted *R*-squared**
Index of diffusion versus 1980–91 political index (Table 5.2 versus Table 5.1)	0.33 (3.66*)	0.45
Index of diffusion versus four decade political index (four decade index available from author)	0.45 (5.23**)	0.63

* Significant at 0.005 level.
** Significant at 0.0005 level.

ownership in their larger firms; those with the highest score have the fewest firms with concentrated ownership and, hence, their largest firms have the most diffuse ownership.[15] Table 5.3 shows the correlations' statistical significance, which is high.

3.2. *Discussion of Data*

Again, these results are statistically significant; the *R*-squared value suggests that political orientation explains quite a bit of the variation.[16] The reader need not be reminded that correlation need not imply causation; the facts here though comport with the theory that social democracies drive a wedge between shareholders and managers, and thereby raise agency costs.

One should be cautious in interpreting these statistical results. True, they are strikingly strong in that the indices are only partly tuned to the political hypothesis I have set out here. But first, the ownership index does not include privately-held firms that have never gone public.

European accounts say these are many, but systematic, comparable data for these nations is unavailable. (It is not surprising, based on the political thesis here, that such financial data for the strongest social democracies is not easy to uncover; some owners keep their firms private to keep their profile low.) The twenty largest USA firms are nearly all public firms; the twenty largest firms in each European country may include several fully private firms. If so, better data here should strengthen the political hypothesis.[17]

Second, the ownership index uses each nation's twenty largest firms. Perhaps there is a size beyond which only public firms can exist, because, for example, private parties lack the wealth to take on a major ownership interest. If only the USA's economy has historically been big enough to generate twenty of these very big firms, then size not politics might be the underlying determinant. But one can correct for size, by using the twenty largest firms in each economy worth just over $500 million. Elsewhere, I do so and find that the powerful political correlation persists (Roe 2001*a*, 2002). Size is not the primary determinant.

Third, the political indices are based on the averaging of a poll of political scientists who rated political parties from left to right on a numerical scale (Castles and Mair 1984); characteristics beyond economic issues, such as nuclear disarmament, race, and other non-economic issues surely figured into the judgement. These characteristics only roughly correlate with the economic left–right scale that would be the best foundation for this study. For example, the French conservative parties were consistently rated as more conservative than the American Democratic Party (ibid.: 78, 83), although on economic issues I see them as to the left of the Democratic Party. Despite the 'noise', politics correlates with ownership concentration.

We can reduce this third problem by looking at another measure of the strength of a nation's social democracy, the extent it compresses incomes and reduces inequality. A standard measure of income inequality, the Gini coefficient, can relate the richest nations' relative tolerance for inequality and, hence, the relative strength of social democracy. Elsewhere I report correlations between income inequality to diffuse ownership: nations that refuse to tolerate much inequality have fewer diffusely-owned public firms and much more concentrated ownership (Roe 2001*a*, 2002). A second rough measure of social democracy could be government spending as a percentage of gross domestic product; this also yields a statistically strong correlation. Another would measure the extent to which a nation protects employees with jobs against dismissal; if the theory here is right, stronger protection should predict weaker diffusion, as it does.

And on the ownership side, one would want an alternative to the concentration indices prevailing in the finance literature, because these indices include government ownership blocks (a social democratic factor to be sure, but not one that is the focus of this chapter) and do not include privately-held firms that never have gone public. An alternative index measures the size of each nation's stock market in proportion to the size of its economy, data that the OECD puts together. I substituted this for the concentration index, re-ran the regressions, and the statistical strength persisted, as I show elsewhere (ibid.). We thus have several measures of concentration and several proxies for social democracy; all the correlations between social democracy and ownership concentration and weak securities markets were strong.

But while the correlations are strong, a sample of the world's sixteen richest nations is not big enough to readily test out the comparative power of other explanations. But we cannot extend the sample, because the poorer nations are not economically 'ripe' for large public firms. So, the nature of legal systems (common law versus civil law) has been advanced as helping to explain ownership concentration, with French and German systems protecting

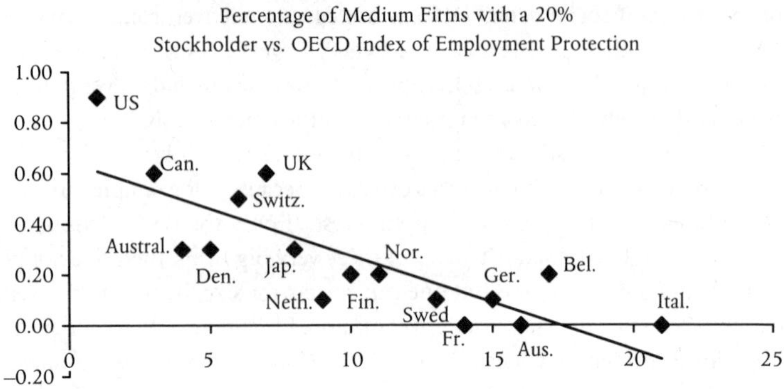

Figure 5.1. *Depth of a nation's stock market and its Gini coefficient*

minority stockholders badly (La Porta *et al.* 1999). We would want to test out the comparative explanatory power of politics and law, by, say, finding those nations that protect minority stockholders well, but are strong social democracies, and then see the density of public firms there. If such nations regularly had diffuse ownership, the legal theory would seem stronger; but if they had concentrated ownership, the political explanation would seem to trump the law-based one. Sweden fits this category: good law, strong social democracy, and few public firms. If this result were generalized, it would support the political thesis over a legal thesis.[18] The theory is not that corporate law is unimportant: transition economies that fail to produce satisfactory legal institutions, may never get public firms, regardless of whether social democratic policies are strong; rather the argument here is that in Europe and the wealthy west, legal differences are joined, and perhaps overshadowed by, political differences.

I ran pair-wise comparisons of politics against each of relative wealth, size of the economy, and an index of legal protection of minority stockholders. The pair-wise comparisons indicate that politics has a strong rapport with ownership concentration when compared to wealth and size of the economy. The legal index is the only one that survives as a plausible determinant, although even then the political determinants are still stronger. These results do not mean that per capita wealth and size of the economy are irrelevant as prerequisites to public firms and securities markets; rather, the argument here is again that at the economic levels prevailing in Europe and the wealthy west, disparities in wealth and economic size among these nations do not explain the relative strength of securities markets, but that political differences among them do seem to.

Thus, the correlations here make for, in a lawyer's rhetoric, a prima facie case that political placement affects structure, but does not give us a clear sense how heavily to weight the political explanation against the prevailing more standard ones. Hence, the discussion of competing theories needs also to be qualitative, not quantitative, and I offer that discussion next, by looking behind the numbers at several of the nations, such as France, Germany, Italy, Sweden, the UK, and the USA. Such a qualitative, nation-by-nation look tends to buttress the political theory.

3.3. *Qualitative Discussion of Selected Nations*

3.3.1. *France*

France displays a medium number of 'widely-held' firms, although commentators see it as an exemplar of family- and state-ownership (Charkham 1994: 125; Fanto 1995; Windolf 1998). This result arises because French government policy sought to structure major French firms with a 'hard core'—in French, *noyau dur*—of national ownership, but typically did not seek to have 20 per cent of the stock (the cutoff for blocks in Table 5.2) owned by a single French firm. A 10 per cent cutoff drops France's proportion of widely-held firms dramatically, down to only one in three, while it hardly changes that for the USA, Britain, and others (La Porta *et al.* 1999: 493, table II, panel B). And when one controls for size by comparing only 'medium-sized' firms—those with a market capitalization of at least $500 million—France has no widely-held firms, while 90 per cent of the similarly-sized American firms (and 60 per cent of the British) are widely-held.[19] Moreover, the recent privatizations in France led workers, on average, to own 8 per cent of those firms' stock and have three of their board seats (Goyer 1999: 41). Regressing both the 'size-corrected' data and the '10%-cutoff' data yields persisting correlations.

Qualitative French business histories are consistent with the social democracy thesis. Consider Charles Kindleberger's (1964: 115) perhaps hyperbolic description in a standard work of European economic history: '[The French family firm] is said to have sinned against economic efficiency... by failing... to extend into new markets.... Public sale of stock was avoided.... Recruiting was undertaken from within the family, except for faithful retainers who assisted the firm against the revolutionary working force'.

Profitable French firms that seek to downsize have been excoriated in the press by political leaders, with political threats deny them discretionary government benefits if they persisted.[20] Employee stock ownership is promoted as a means to resist takeovers,[21] presumably and especially those that would lead to lay-off and downsizing. Reports to the French Prime Minister extol employee stock ownership not for the perhaps denigrated Anglo-Saxon reasons of promoting employee loyalty and motivation, but to shift the balance of power inside the firm away from owners and to employees.[22] Modern French managers have been socialized in two elite schools—two small state schools, l'Ecole Nationale d'Administration and l'Ecole Polytechnique, account for half of the managers and directors of France's leading firms (Bauer 1997)—to think more of national progress than of shareholder profit maximization.[23]

One might believe that the 'real' reason for low separation in France is its statist, dirigiste political orientation. If the bureaucrats disrupt the stock market, then innovations that make such markets work will be undermined and investors will go elsewhere.[24] The difficulty with this view is that a statist but conservative government could *promote* the stock market. Indeed, before the First World War, the current data show[25] French stock markets developing nicely, better by some measures than the American markets. France was statist and dirigiste back then, but it was much more conservative. A statist but conservative regime can copy another nation's legal and political institutions, save on the expense of innovation, and promote stock markets. It might be late, but it will not suppress the securities markets. The question is not whether the nation is statist, but whether it is inclined to be friendly to stock markets. When France was friendly, stock markets flourished. When it was not, they did not.

By mid-20th-century (after the French economy was essentially re-set to ground zero during the Second World War), France was still statist but it was no longer reliably conservative. Left-oriented parties were popular, won elections, and induced the whole political spectrum to move leftwards, a move that has only halted and reversed quite recently. Before the spectrum started to shift back, it was true that French policy tended to undermine, or not support stock markets, but the cause was not pure dirigisme. It was due to the politicians (and those who elected them) having little sympathy with capitalism, stock markets, and securities institutions. Those who point to the French governments' hostility or indifference here are (merely?) pointing to one of the mechanisms by which social democracy undermined stock markets and the separation of ownership from control.[26]

3.3.2. *Germany*

Germany's formal board structure strongly illustrates the 'social democracy' effect, as we saw in Section 2. German boards for large firms must have half of the directors from labour. This codetermination affects boardrooms. Meetings are infrequent, the information background is weak, and the meetings are quite formal; codetermination makes it hard for shareholders and managers to charge up the boardrooms with frequent, substantive, well-informed meetings, because to do so would enhance labour's voice and authority inside the firm. Managers and shareholders prefer not to further empower labour, so they weaken (or fail to strengthen) the boardroom.

Shareholders control managers otherwise. Dominant blockholders meet managers informally outside of the boardroom. Were ownership diffuse, shareholders would lose this means of monitoring managers, and shareholder value would presumably decline. With the board codetermined, shareholders could find the alternative of a more powerful boardroom unattractive: if they charged up the boardroom to better monitor managers, they would make labour more powerful. The trade-off for shareholders—better monitoring of managers versus more powerful labour influence—might be tough to make; shareholding might therefore remain concentrated so that shareholders can avoid making the trade-off (Roe 2001*b*).

This trade-off helps to explain the resistance in Germany to changing corporate and securities laws, accounting practice, and other institutions to better support diffuse ownership. Germany has had little problem in writing and passing good laws in other areas, or in building effective bureaucracies. True, public choice pressures could explain the result—banks prefer not to see good securities markets develop and family owners want their perquisites to persist. But public choice resistance can sometimes be overcome, and it is plausible that when it is not, it is because countervailing pressures for reform do not come from shareholders, managers, and policy-makers. The countervailing pressures might not come because these players cannot profit from going public in Germany's social democracy, with Germany's boardroom structure.

3.3.3. *Italy*

Italy has many small family-owned firms and few public firms. A simple legal theory, one based solely on poor minority stockholder protection, is plausible for Italy, which is reputed to have a slow and inefficient court system (Zingales 1994). Indeed, the direction in the statistics supports the idea that a factor beyond politics is at play in Italy: its firms are even less diffusely owned than political placement would predict. Weak corporate law though may be only part of the story even in Italy. Players dissatisfied with basic corporate law have not been unable to use contract to give themselves the private law rules that they want.[27] Economic-based social conflict has been historically high, labour-influenced political parties powerful, and a communist party that for several decades was supported by a quarter of the Italian electorate. Italian Christian Democratic governments fostered small closely-held businesses, because they thought employees would identify with owners in small firms, but oppose them, especially distant owners, in large firms. Large firms provoked more social tension than smaller closely-held ones (Weiss 1988: 127–37).

3.3.4. *Japan*

Japan does not fit as a traditional social democracy, but post-Second World War Japanese social history might be consistent with the thesis. As is well known to Japanese economic historians, the Japanese main bank system was not a traditional element of Japanese corporate structure, but one that developed strongly after the Second World War.

Labour history in Japan also suggests the importance of post-Second World War developments. Lifetime employment was not a key Japanese labour institution before the war. Rather, it developed after the war, partly in response to vicious labour conflict, as managers and other leaders sought to bring enough peace to Japanese factories to allow production to go forward. At roughly the same time, the main bank system, by which banks owned noticeable blocks of stock of large industrial firms and had a say in their governance, expanded.

The labour institution did not have to induce the ownership institution for the political theory here to be confirmed. All that is needed is for the two to be stable complements once each arose, even if one did not induce the other. Some leading commentators on the Japanese firm say that they indeed do operate as complements (Aoki 1997*b*).

3.3.5. *Sweden*

The world's first democratically elected socialist government took power in Sweden in 1920 (Przeworski 1993: 835). It has been for quite some time the paradigm of the social welfare state, with cradle-to-grave social coverage.

Sweden presents variants of the political theory here. First, Sweden is reputed to have a good corporate law that protects minority stockholders. That is, a leading explanation for why concentrated ownership persists is that if minority stockholder protection is poor, outsiders will buy stock only reluctantly, or only at a steep discount. Their reluctance translates into heavy ownership concentration and few public firms. But by conventional measures Swedish institutions protect minority stockholders well: Not only are there no anecdotes of insider blockholders diverting value to themselves (Agnblad *et al.* 2000), but the premium for voting stock, a measure of the value of control (and the opportunity to divert value into the controllers' pockets) is low, approaching that prevailing in the USA, at about

7 per cent.[28] Outsiders could buy without gross fear of expropriation from insiders; and insiders could sell and diversify without taking a gross discount. Yet they do not.[29]

Second, closely related to the legal theory is a theory based on trust. In mistrustful cultures, outsiders will greatly fear the depredations of insiders. But if trust is high and insiders will no more steal from outside stockholders than would citizens steal an unlocked bicycle, outsiders will entrust their investments to insiders. Sweden is a high trust society. Yet, ownership remains concentrated, despite the high level of trust. Outsiders feel protected, but public securities markets are poorly developed.

Third, Swedish ownership has a high disjunction between cash flow rights and control rights. That is, the controlling family, often the Wallenberg family, has, say, 51 per cent of the company's votes, but gets a smaller fraction of the company's profits. It does so by building ownership pyramids (by which it owns 51 per cent of the 'top' holding company, which in turn owns 51 per cent of an intermediate company, which in turn owns 51 per cent of other intermediate companies, until finally a lower-level company owns 51 per cent of the operating company) or by using dual-class common stock (in which one class of stock gets ten votes per share and another one vote per share).

Complex and intricate theories have arisen to explain the use of pyramids, dual-class structures, and non-voting stock. The most sophisticated rely on the owner seeking to protect the rents it gets from controlling the firm. That is, the controller is reluctant to leave control 'up for grabs' because if the controller dips below 51 per cent control of the operating company, an outsider could grab a majority and then reap the benefits of control (Bebchuk 1998; 1999; Bebchuk *et al.* 1999; La Porta *et al.* 1999). The theory is plausible. However, in its current stark form, it cannot explain the Swedish situation well, or at all, because Sweden is said to protect minority stockholders well. Hence, in Sweden, little of value would be left up for grabs by controlling shareholders who exited and diversified.

Adding employees and social democratic pressures back into the Swedish equation lets us explain the Swedish ownership concentration. Social democracy affects ownership in two ways here. One, the concentrated owner has stronger incentives than the Berle–Means managers do to avoid giving up too much in shareholder value to social pressures. Although an owner whose 51 per cent in control rights corresponded to equal cash flow rights would have even greater incentives to retain shareholder value, the issue here is one of relative strength. The pyramid, dual-class, or non-voting structure is less than ideal in providing incentives, but it still motivates a focused owner to deflect some social pressures: (a) A lot of the controller's wealth is still on the line, and (b) the structure preserves the controller's authority even while cash flow rights decline.

Moreover, if the concentrated owner is progressive, has a social conscience, and is not a thirsty shareholder-wealth-maximizer, then the political authorities and voters may prefer the incumbent to someone else who might grab control. That is, the authorities may prefer to avoid government ownership for its well-known inefficiencies, but not want the crass, cold market as the alternative. If the Swedish incumbents, such as the Wallenbergs, are 'soft' players, who co-operate with a social democratic ethos, then it may well be the social democratic forces that want to stop control from going 'up for grabs'. If control were 'up for grabs', an American-style shareholder-wealth-maximizer might grab control, tighten the workplace, and undermine the social democratic programme.[30]

Rents are to be protected, but they are not the ordinary owner's rents from control (because the evidence is that value diversions in Sweden are low), but the political rents that a social democracy produces for the firm's employees and political players.

Two, social democracies level wealth and income. While they raise the 'incentive' to focus control, they constrict the 'supply' of rich people with the wealth to own very large industrial companies. When technology and scale economies demand very large industrial firms, and when social democratic pressures demand focused ownership but reduce the number of wealthy people, then tools to yield control without vast wealth will be demanded. Pyramids, dual-class structures, and non-voting stock are the typical such tools. Sweden, like several of the other social democracies, has them.

3.3.6. *United Kingdom*

The UK would seem the hardest case for the political theory here, in that by reputation Britain has had a deep securities market for quite some time, but has been on both sides of the fence politically, having been a strong social democracy for a good part of the twentieth century, and having been one of the planet's economically most conservative nations since 1979.

But the UK also seems to fit badly with a law-driven theory. A competing theory to the political theory is that the law protecting minority stockholders is the key to creating diffuse ownership, with family-founders turning their firms over to professional managers by selling out into the stock market. British common law judges are said to have protected minority stockholders well. Yet, leading business historians such as Alfred Chandler say flatly that the largest British firms were family-dominated as late as the Second World War, and that family influence and control persisted well after then as well.[31] Chandler blames family control for Britain's industrial decline in the mid-twentieth century (see also Elbaum and Lazonick 1986; Davenport-Hines and Jones 1988; Kirby 1989: 931, 936).

This persistent family ownership during Britain's social democratic era seems consistent with the political theory, but not with a legal theory: if law protected the minority stockholders, why did not the families sell out and diversify quickly (as some eventually started to do in the 1970s and many did in the conservative 1980s (Brennan and Franks 1997: 407 table 7))? Many of these families were still block-owners in the 1970s. (The 'managerial revolution heralded by Berle and Means in 1932 has probably not yet happened [here]....: over 55 per cent of the largest 250 UK industrial companies [are] under owner control' said one authority in 1980, and, not anticipating the results in the subsequent two decades, concluded: 'most [British] firms are unlikely ever to become controlled by their own professional managers' (Francis 1980: 29).) But within several years, by the mid-1980s, many of these families were in fact gone from the largest British firms (Scott 1990: 366–7); Britain's revolution from the right in 1979 made, on the theory presented here, the fully public, diffusely-owned firm a more viable entity.

Yet Britain by many measures had deeper securities markets and more public firms than much of the rest of the world earlier in the twentieth century, although families held on to blocks and managerial positions until quite late in the century. To explain this pattern, a synthesis of the minority-protection theory and the political theory works well. That is, British institutions protected minority stockholders, so that family owners could sell much stock even in the early twentieth century without too severe a discount. Yet, during that time, class conflict was often severe (Kirk 1998: 166). The potential for high agency costs in the managerial firm was there and, hence, the family owners had reason to retain concentrated ownership. This hybrid theory seems to explain the British facts: (a) a long history of firms going public; (b) family retention of control in many public firms until well after the Second World War (when good law arguably protected the minority stockholders and politics made concentration desirable for shareholders); and (c) a sell-off by the family owners in the late 1970s and in the 1980s (when Britain's lurch to the economic right made diffuse ownership more stable).[32]

This political interaction with ownership structure helps to explain Chandler's conundrum: if the British families held onto control (as Chandler reports), and ran many firms into the ground (as he argues), why did they not sell out when they got bored with running their firms? Many offer cultural reasons to explain the result. But perhaps more was at work. Family owners may have run their firms badly, but when class conflict was rife, perhaps the alternative to family control was worse for owners.

Timing and path dependence are important in understanding Britain: Britain's social democracy arose well after its basic securities markets were well-developed. Had investors and companies tried to develop stock markets for the first time in, say, the 1950s, they would have had a much rougher time than they did earlier in the century. But when Britain lurched to the left, stock markets already were in place, and the institutions had more than a little staying power.[33] British political authorities could implement their goals by nationalizing target industrial firms: they did not need to undermine all stock market institutions (although they might not have supported them were they first emerging then). I suspect that one would find that neither stock markets nor ownership grew much during this political period; they treaded water and survived, and then only because other changes were higher on the political authorities' agenda.

Path dependence can mean that an institution could persist even if the environment would not call it forth at the time.[34] British securities markets and their initial, modest steps toward separation arose when Britain was conservative and laissez-faire. Later, when British politics alternated between social democracy and mainstream conservatism (and then stepped toward strong conservatism in 1979), the institutions in place persisted, but did not seem to grow. The City's institutions presented an interest group that could resist some change. They also were a source of revenue (from trading in international securities) that even social democratic governments might not have wanted to demolish. Moreover, even here one would not want to dismiss the possibility of there having been moderate social democratic effects. The City had reason to fear nationalization during Britain's social democratic era, and this social democratic fear accounts for some of their passivity in corporate governance: if they took the lead in rationalizing an industry, and the disruption engendered salience and opposition, nationalization (the result for French financial institutions) would have been more likely. This they understood. And, hence, better to be quiet.

3.3.7. *United States of America*

Why has the USA had fewer social conflicts of the type that would debilitate the public firm? The reasons why it has had less conflict, and hence more diffuse ownership, correspond to the reasons why a strong socialist movement did not arise in the USA.

Mobility, both geographic and economic, has been high, or at least the average person has believed it high (Turner 1920). Dissatisfied people have blamed their local circumstances (which they thought they could change, by heading out West or by getting another job) more than their class position. Hence, class conflict was less likely. And incipient conflicts were violently suppressed (Commons 1997*a*, 1997*b*).

The USA has also had a long and deep anti-government bias, so citizens have not looked as longingly to the government to resolve problems as Europeans did. Economic conflict was not absent in the USA, but manifested itself differently than in Europe, often leading politicians to break up concentrations of economic power, a result that further propelled the public firm, because there were fewer financial institutions that could build up large American firms at the end of the nineteenth century than there otherwise would have been (Roe 1994).

In the nineteenth century, America systematically destroyed strong financial institutions: American voters historically tended to be intolerant of big government and of big private finance. This fragmenting of finance may also have later diluted other social conflict, by removing the visible targets of a strong social democracy movement; and, with the visible targets gone, norms like shareholder-wealth-maximization flourished more easily than they otherwise would have. (Similarly, destroying family control in continental Europe could reduce subsequent social conflict sufficiently so that managerial agency cost control institutions could emerge in the newly created public firms.) Political packages might be complementary: American politics can tolerate pro-shareholder institutions, if the typical shareholder is CalPERS, not J. P. Morgan. European politics can tolerate large, influential stockholders, banks and families, as long as it also stabilizes employment and circumscribes the range of actions of the stockholders, bankers, and the family owners.

Moreover, ethnic conflict in the USA has been deep, at times vicious. For some of the social conflicts that would affect the Berle–Means firm to express itself in the political arena, employees would have had to act together or politicians would have had to appeal to all employees to elect them to enact a common programme (Commons 1997*a*: 118–19; 1997*b*). But if ethnic divisions—principally based on race—made it historically hard for American politicians to make an economic appeal across racial lines, then the kinds of conflicts that increased agency costs in public firms on the European continent became rarer in the USA.

3.3.8. *Extending the Sample?*

One could extend the 'sample' to include more nations outside of western Europe, developed Asia, and North America, adding, say, Thailand, Malaysia, Nigeria, and Argentina. But extension would reveal little, because too many of these nations have not yet arrived economically at the point where their economies demand many large firms. And some lack the basic institutions needed for a very advanced economy, such as a capacity to enforce contract effectively. More telling is to look at those nations that have already developed many of the needed institutions, and have a high demand for large economic units, but for which politics in some of them makes some institutions function poorly or not worth building.

4. ALTERNATIVE FORMULATIONS OF THE THESIS

4.1. *Political Change and Time-Series Data*

As politics changes, ownership structure could also change. Thus, one could try to measure political change and see if ownership changes. But this kind of longitudinal study is not technically possible right now—the multi-nation historical ownership data are either unavailable or unreliable (Becht and Röell 1998). Moreover, there are surely lags, of uncertain length, in economic reaction to political change. And, most importantly, one would need to hold the other conditions constant. Economic, technological, and institutional conditions have changed greatly during the past decades. Economies used to be less competitive—American industry tended toward oligopoly, European firms were small and largely confined to their national economy, and globalization was an idea then for the future. Weaker competition produced more organizational slack, some of which was 'spent' in looser ownership and organizational arrangements (Roe 1996*a*: 102–27; 2001*b*). It will be hard, or impossible, to do a time-series test that holds these other conditions constant, and measures only politics' effects on ownership structure.

But in gross, recent shifts in Europe are consistent with the social democracy thesis. Economic policy has moved rightward in recent decades in Europe. One cannot simply measure 'social democracy' by the names of the political parties in power, as their programmes have changed, with social democratic parties becoming less interventionist and less hostile to shareholders. This could lead to other predictions: As economic politics has moved rightward, diffuse ownership has become more feasible in Europe. As it becomes more feasible, the demand from policy-makers and investors could increase (as it has) for institutions that better support diffuse ownership.

Britain illustrates this nicely. All the basic institutions for diffuse ownership, save one, namely a non-social democratic economic consensus, were in place in Britain from the nineteenth century onwards. But right after the Second World War, Britain's large firm ownership structure was said to be closer to continental family ownership structures than to American structures, with family-owners as players in many, or most, big firms.[35] But Britain's economic policy moved rightward during the ensuing decades; not only did Margaret Thatcher's 'revolution' overturn British socialism after Heath's government had softened it, but Tony Blair's British Labour Party of the 1990s, is less of a socialist party than was the party of his predecessors.[36] In the 1980s, Britain's securities markets increased massively, much more than they did in the USA,[37] which had at that time an equally conservative government, but one that did not break with the American past as strongly as did the British government of the time.

4.2. *Political Change and Alternative Formulations of the Thesis*

I have thus far looked on the political players as public-regarding actors with sincerely held views seeking to build the good society, and in social democracies that vision differs from the one prevailing in the USA. Those holding these ideologies might seek to maximize social well-being, but in doing so they reduce the incidence of public firms, securities markets, and diffuse ownership. One can, however, look more crudely at the phenomena.

4.2.1. *Social Democracy as Rent-Seeking*

Interest groups seek laws and structures that benefit themselves. So, one could see social democracies as labour's crude but successful rent-seeking. (Or see conservative nations as financial interests' crude but successful rent-seeking.) Ideology may help or retard success of one group or another, but in this public choice view it is raw self-seeking that is at stake. Labour wins in the name of stability in some nations; shareholders win in the name of fluid capital markets in other nations. Concerted arrangements via tripartite bargaining characterize some nations, as the three players—labour, owners, and the government—negotiate corporatist deals. This is not exactly social democracy, but it is government (often) taking labour's side in negotiations inside the firm.

4.2.2. *Social Democracy as Simple Micro-Economic Foundations*

We could begin without using social democracy, by viewing the firm as having three inputs: capital, management, and labour. We could begin the abstraction with labour institutions determined first, with capital and management variable. If labour markets are rigid, with employees 'owning' their jobs, then management and capital structures will evolve differently there than in economies with fluid labour markets, where employees have few 'property' rights in their jobs.

4.2.3. *Concentrated Ownership as Facilitating Social Democratic Politic*

I have thus far relentlessly viewed politics as independent of business structure, with social democracy inducing, or strengthening, concentrated ownership structures. But causation may run the other way, at least at times.

German codetermination again provides a concrete example. Earlier in the last century, the visible power of Germany's large banks, people's envy and resentment of rich industrialists, and the disorientation and anomie induced by Germany's rapid transformation from an agricultural nation to an industrial one helped call forth codetermination to tame the bankers and industrialists, and to give the workers voice in the strange new industrial enterprises. Corporate structure may have induced politics then, as much as it was induced by politics. Not all productive arrangements are equally stable politically; some induce political opposition, some a democratic polity finds more acceptable (Roe 1998*a*, 1998*b*). Social democracy and concentrated ownership mutually reinforce one another.

4.2.4. *Rent-Seeking in Small National Economies*

Business structure may induce social democratic politics in another way. Many of the strongest social democracies have been small nations, in which product markets have been less competitive, because only a few firms can reach efficient economies of scale. Weaker competition produces rents—profits above those needed by capital to invest—and these rents can be captured not just by the capital-owners but shared with managers and employees. There is thus more 'give' and more of a possibility of successful rent-seeking through government and social action when there are supra-competitive profits. These rents may also strengthen social democracy by increasing envy and perceived unfairness. And they may provide more to fight over. Rent-seeking employees may win more often in small economies, especially those whose oligopolistic firms are not fully exposed to world markets (Roe 2001*b*).

When product market competition is fierce, rents are reduced and excess profits competed away. One reason for American exceptionalism is that the American economy has been more competitive, making rents in the USA smaller and more fragile (i.e. more easily lost as they will be competed away and therefore less worth seeking).[38] In the smaller national economies, rent-seeking below the surface and social democratic ideologies above it could have produced concentrated economies unable to strongly support diffuse stockholders. The parallel here between corporate results and James Madison's famous analysis in the Federalist No. 10 is obvious.

As the small economies integrate into free-trade zones, the potential for local rent-seeking will diminish, enhanced product market competition will make traditional social democratic corporate governance harder to maintain, and the demand for securities institutions will rise (Bebchuk and Roe 1999). Governments whose firms face intense competition that renders them unable to implement a social democratic programme through firms or labour markets may either abandon their goals or implement them via social insurance that leaves firms out of the picture.

4.2.5. *Craving Stability*

Social democracy may not fully capture the ideological metric here. Some nations may crave stability more than do others. Histories of war, devastation, social instability, market collapse, or starvation can drive this craving. If voters crave stability, they may insist on rules and a business atmosphere that makes change harder than it would otherwise be. The core cause though may then not be social democratic ideology, or employee rent-seeking, but a society seeking stability (Polanyi 1944).

Indeed, before the First World War's start to Europe's self-destruction and economic instability, securities markets were stronger on the continent than they are today, and not that much weaker than they were in the USA (Rajan and Zingales 1999: 76; Miwa and Ramseyer 2000).[39] Politics was more conservative, and social democratic movements were on the political fringe.

4.2.6. *Managers' Utility Functions*

Another way to look at this issue could be through managers' utility functions. Human nature does not demand that managers maximize, say, firm size or profitability. In cultures that emphasize other values, and inculcate them through schooling and other means, managers may maximize something else, and that something else may make them less able, or less willing, to do shareholders' bidding.

4.3. *Technological Change*

As technology evolves, the underlying organizational forms may evolve as well. Movement away from heavy smokestack manufacturing toward rapidly moving service industries could affect corporate governance in two ways. First, the new industries may be less susceptible to the social and economic conflicts that raise agency costs. Second, further empowering employees in service industries may be efficient from capital's perspective.

Even if agency problems arise due to continuing conflict there, these agency problems may not be as costly to invested capital because the ratio of invested capital to human capital is often less in the new service and high-tech industries than in the old heavy manufacturing industries. Stock options for managers and employees are common in high-tech firms, where commitment and human capital are important. When technology renders the old-style smokestack factory less important, social conflict cannot lead to it being expropriated. More simply, when a firm is expanding, fewer conflicts irritate the relationship between social democracy and the public firm.

5. RESERVATIONS AND REFINEMENTS

I hardly mean here that we have discovered the single cause that explains why some nations get deep securities markets and strong ownership separation and other nations do not. There are other foundations, both economic and institutional, and they too can affect the results. A nation must be at a level technologically and economically to demand very large enterprises and wide capital-gathering. It must have basic legal institutions that enforce contracts and corporate obligations (or substitutes for these institutions). I only mean here to add politics as a key foundation, one that is missing from the current literature, which I do not intend to challenge but to extend.

So, one could find some non-social democracies that are poor and not yet technologically ready for a variety of reasons for large public firms and ownership separation. (Those kinds of firms just will not add value.) This observation would be important for many purposes, but it would not contradict the thesis here, since there are several preconditions, political, economic, and institutional. Similarly, one might find a rich, non-social democracy but one whose institutional structure—say, via weak corporate or contract law enforcement—does not yield strong securities markets and ownership separation. For the same reason, this would not contradict the political theory.

Moreover, I have focused in this chapter on one feature: the strength of pro-labour social democracy in a nation. It is an important political feature in the modern West, but it is not the only political feature. Thus, other political institutions can affect the corporation: if a nation is populist and uncomfortable with strong financial institutions, then we should see fewer strong financial institutions (and, hence, one big block player would have been removed from the scene).

Or, if a nation has an extremely strong levelling culture, then we might see fortunes taxed away after a single generation or conceivably even taxed away during the first generation (by a high and effective income tax and wealth tax); this could have corporate ownership implications as well. (Presumably it would propel means to maintain control via pyramids and dual class stock that require little invested capital to maintain control.) One might point out these features as alternative or additional political influences. They do not undermine a political theory, but enrich it.

Counter-examples would be important in undermining a monocausal theory. But they do not directly undermine a theory that promotes a contributing, even a strongly contributing, cause. This is why one must look to general trends, with tools such as regression analysis, however crude that may be. Moreover, the strongest counter-examples in the literature do not even seem to be strong counter-examples. That is, as I have previously noted, Britain has had good securities markets, but has been on both sides of the fence politically. But it is telling that Britain's social democratic era came after the laissez-faire era in which its securities markets first developed. Britain's securities markets and strong ownership separation did not occur first and during Britain's social democratic era. It occurred before. Strong securities markets survived the social democratization era, but may well have not arisen during it.

Moreover, ownership separation seems, according to Chandler (1990) and others, to have gone much more slowly in Britain than in the USA. Families may well have hung on longer there than in the USA because when they were ready to sell and turn the firm over to professional managers, the political environment was not conducive.

France is also said to be a counter-example, in that it is said that French statism undermined its securities markets. It is true that France was statist and hostile or indifferent to securities markets. It is also true that French securities markets have been weaker relative to similarly wealthy nations during the modern post-Second World War era. But France also was not a conservative nation during this era. Commentators who point out that the modern French government was either indifferent to, or hostile to the development of the French stock market may only be telling us one of the manifestations of French social democracy, that is, a hostility to capital and its supporting institutions.

In an earlier era, before the First World War, France—statist then as well, having licensed stock brokers in a way that made them state agents—nevertheless had a powerful stock market that rivalled that of London and surpassed that of New York in many dimensions. How could it have done so if statism was the key relevant variable? It could not have. But statism alone was not the relevant variable. Rather, it is that the government then was not social democratic and tolerated stock markets and capital institutions development.

6. POLITICAL PRECONDITIONS IN THE UNITED STATES OF AMERICA

While I have thus far primarily analysed the political realities around the world, I need not remind the reader that this chapter is as much about the USA as it is about the rest of the world. The American Berle–Means firm is usually seen by American analysts as an economic institution that evolved because of the technological and financial problems of large size, learned how to feed its concomitant voracious demand for capital, and developed means to control the loosely-supervised managerial agents at the top of the firm.

But substantial political prerequisites existed to the rise, evolution, and business domination of the large public firm. Economic-based social conflict in the USA was lower than it was elsewhere. With conflict lower, shareholders could remove themselves from overseeing the firm day-to-day without fearing that managers would be 'captured' by social democratic pressures. In time, ways to tie managers to shareholders arose, and they could not easily have arisen were the US more of a social democracy.

7. CONCLUSION: LABOUR POLICY, SHAREHOLDER VALUE, AND SEPARATING OWNERSHIP FROM CONTROL

The American-style public corporation is a fragile contraption, filled with contradictions, one easy to destabilize and destroy. It dominates American business, due to its ability to agglomerate capital and efficiently spread private risk, but needs multiple preconditions to arise, survive, and prosper. One powerful precondition is the institutional ability to control agency costs, an ability that a social democracy reduces, or destroys.

True, the benefits with which the public firm is associated—innovation, competition, and high tech, for example—might be obtained without Berle–Means firms. The American-centred view that the public firm is the pinnacle of business organization may be incorrect. Innovation, competition, and efficient production can be reached in different organizations. Nations that deny themselves one organizational form do not condemn themselves to economic backwardness, but leave themselves without one tool in the organizational toolkit. (And, similarly, nations that overly fragment institutional shareholding and financial voice inside the corporate boardroom deny themselves a different tool.)

Moreover, this is hardly a reason to condemn social democracies. What gets lost in shareholder tools may be gained on the shop floor; net efficiency effects may be zero. And the solidarity and equality in these nations may make more citizens happier, and those societies may in the long run be more stable and productive. Many European players, even managerial players, believe this to be so (Albert 1991). Citizens in nations with a yearning for stability, perhaps one created by gloomy destructive histories, may get special value from the stability of a social democracy.

But productivity effects and the overall value of a social democracy are not the principal lines of thought here. The key point here is that a nation's creating many public firms and deep securities markets in social democracies is more than just a technical problem of it creating the right legal institutions, but a problem that goes to the core of the social and political organization of that society. As such, reformers will find technical solutions frustrating or impossible to implement; and even if implemented, the technical reforms will have little effect unless and until the underlying political reality changes. One may see little demand for the institutions that support securities markets until a social democracy has softened enough to lay the political foundation for making public firms viable.

Capital markets and institutions, managerial markets and institutions, and labour markets and institutions interrelate. Some types fit well together, complementing one another, and some do not. Politics can determine one type of the three and thereby indirectly determine the other two, because sometimes only a restricted set of the others will fit the one that politics determined. America's historical antipathy to private institutional power over-emphasized one kind of capital market, and thereby affected the managerial institutions of the public firm (Roe 1994: 283–7). Foreign politics affected labour institutions and these in turn affected managerial institutions and capital structure. Had American labour institutions differed—had the USA been more of a social democracy—the public firm would have had rougher going in the USA and may have been a minor, not a major American business institution.

This result is not merely technical, and, hence, any change will not be purely technical either. The result maps back to a society's political condition: Social democracies raise the agency costs to shareholders in the Berle–Means public firm. They exacerbate managerial tendencies to expand unprofitably, to avoid risk, and to avoid biting the bullet and forcing organizational change when markets and technologies have shifted. In each case incumbent employees tend to prefer that these changes not go forward, incumbent employees have a strong political voice in social democracies, and managers have a rougher time bringing about organizational change in the social democracies. Oftentimes they do not want to bring about these organizational changes anyway.

Aligning managers with shareholders is harder in social democracies than elsewhere: owners dislike transparent accounting, which would give employees more information than many owners would be happy with their employees having, but transparent accounting is necessary for distant securities holders. Hence, the demand for accounting transparency has been weaker in the social democracies and, as long as accounting was opaque, close owners (who can privately extract information from the firm and its managers) persisted. Shareholder wealth maximization norms have been weaker in the social democracies. The strong control mechanisms of the hostile takeover and publicly known incentive compensation have been harder or impossible to implement in the social democracies.

The political theory here is that social democracies wedge open the gap between shareholders and managers in public firms, by raising agency costs higher and reducing the efficacy of the techniques that would control them. This wedge has been small in the USA, and we have thereby uncovered the critical precondition to ownership separating from control and, hence, to the rise and persistence of the dominant form of business organization in the USA, namely the historical absence of a strong social democracy.

Notes

1. A deeper presentation of the argument in this chapter and supporting data, is in Roe (2001*a*, 2002).
2. See Pistor (1999); Edwards and Fischer (1994); von Schimmelmann (1997); cf. Semler (1998) (some boards get good supporting information, some do not); Schilling (1994) (reporting German survey of business leaders who conclude supervisory board is weak and that, as a result of codetermination, it avoids controversial topics). Recent pressures, and then some legal changes, have pushed the supervisory boards to meet three or four times a year. See André (1996); cf. Vafeas (1999) (more frequent meetings improve corporate performance).
3. FitzRoy and Kraft (1993); Schmid and Seger (1998); but see Baums and Frick (1999) (finding no impact); Frick, Speckbacker, and Wentges (1998-V) (critiquing studies showing codetermination as negatively affecting stock price).
4. And institutional creditors, who loom larger in European firms than in their American counterparts, prefer to avoid risk and to maintain stability. Incompletely diversified family stockholders, the last key player in large continental European firms, also prefer stability more strongly than diversified American public firm stockholders. The key risk-avoiding pieces all fit together in continental Europe. The fit here may not be accidental. European history may have created a craving for stability to overcome an unstable past. Corporate institutions that facilitate that stability survived. An American analyst (such as myself) sees the lack of a key corporate structure as a failing, but social democracy may not only have satisfied a European demand for stability but the sense of solidarity it has yielded its participants may have increased social welfare.

5. See *Le Monde* (1999: 16), quoting the leader of the governing French party: 'It's unacceptable that a large firm can decide to reduce employment simply to enhance shareholder profits.'
6. Cf. Lepartmentier, *Le Monde* (1998: 17) (Gerhard Schröder, when minister of Lower Saxony—he is now the German Prime Minister—had a steel mill nationalized rather than see it taken over by a foreign firm because he did not want a restructuring that would affect the German employees); Faujas, *Le Monde* (1999: IV) ('60 per cent [of the French] feel that government regulation and taxes handicap French firms, but [they applaud this result] as 51 per cent also say the State must more severely control firms to prevent them from degrading social conditions'); (ibid.) (a majority in each of Germany, Italy, and France believe 'the firms' interests and the people's interest are not the same,' while in Britain a majority thought the contrary).
7. From a book well known in European business circles: 'is the firm a simple piece of merchandise? Or is it a community in which the stockholders' power is balanced by managerial power, which is in turn co-opted by the employees?' Albert (1991: 19) (translated from the French) (emphasis added); cf. Charny (1999) (distinguishing labour/corporate governance regimes, as 'hard', 'soft', and 'mixed').
8. Lemaître *Le Monde*, (1999: 15).
9. The USA historically lacked some but not all of these tools, but its gaps were smaller than elsewhere because American firms felt only weak social democratic pressures. In recent decades, intensified competition and technological change have called forth stronger tools than American shareholders previously needed. And, when American industries were less competitive, large firm oligopolies lost something from managerial agency costs, but gained oligopoly profits to spread around to shareholders, managers, and employees. (See Roe 1996*a*: 102, 105, 111–13; cf. Jagannathan and Srinivasan 1999.)
10. In one well-known merger, directors asked their attorney, a leading merger adviser, to what extent they could consider other constituencies when evaluating offers. 'A buck a share', the adviser is said to have replied.
11. See, for example, the famous essay by Milton Friedman (1970: 33). Although aggressive when it appeared, in the USA, Friedman's perspective is now mainstream in business circles and not unthinkable then (as it may be in some social democracies now). Cf. Graham (1997: 119) (cultural primacy of profit in Margaret Thatcher's Britain); Porter (1999: 42) ('In Western Europe the inability to place profitability as the central goal is the greatest constraint to economic development.').
12. Cf. Kuttner (1996: 28) (wealthiest 20 per cent own 98 per cent of American stocks).
13. This anti-shareholder sentiment is hardly absent in the USA. It ebbs and flows, stronger during the years of Ralph Nader's 1970s Campaign GM, say, and weaker during the Reagan 1980s, but surely it is much weaker in the USA than in continental Europe.
14. The political data is from Cusack (1997: 383–4), which arrays a survey from Castles and Mair (1984).
15. The ownership data and judgement are from La Porta, Lopez-de-Silanes, and Shleifer (1999: 492), who sought to show something else: that failure to protect minority stockholders is the primary determinant of a nation's inability to get diffusely-held firms.
16. The four-decade political average correlates more strongly with ownership structure. It ought though to be weaker since it matches a forty-year political index with a single moment's concentration ratios. Perhaps a better longitudinal look would correlate concentration in each decade with the political index in each decade. On the other hand, political coalitions come and go; corporate structures are the result of long-term expectations of governmental orientation.
17. The financial researchers building the concentration index classified government-owned blocks as if they were privately-owned blocks. But publicly-owned blocks do not at first reflect owners

deciding that concentration will promote shareholder wealth better than would dispersion. Still, governments often take blocks if social pressures deter private players from investing, and the firm can continue, or arise, only if the government invests. Thus linkage is plausible. Government blocks for purposes of a competing theory that poor legal protection of minority shareholders induces blockholding is questionable, as governmental motives in keeping blocks are unlikely to link directly to minority shareholder protection, although it is true that the government might invest if capital markets do not fund very large firms.

18. Data suggests that Denmark, Germany, Norway, and Sweden have good minority shareholder protection but weak ownership diffusion. They have all been social democratic nations (Roe 2001*a*, 2002).
19. La Porta *et al.* (1999: table VII) (table III, panel A, 20 per cent cutoff, first ten firms with a market capitalization exceeding $500 million).
20. "Michelin", *Le Monde* (1999); Owen (2000) (the Prime Minister's 'remarks were seen as a warning that there were limits to the extent to which big French companies should adopt aggressive Anglo-American style profits-oriented tactics').
21. Mauduit, (2000: 6).
22. Ministère de l'Economie, des Finances et de l'Industrie, (2000: 2, Pt. II at 8–10, 15).
23. Cf. Hollande (1999) (leader of France's governing socialist party says that 'although our goal is not to socialize the means of production, one can neither leave the private sector without rules... nor allow stockholders alone to decide, without any input from employees, what to do solely due to shareholders' purely financial interests').
24. John Coffee (see Chapter 4, this volume) has so argued.
25. See, for example, Rahhuram G. Rajan and Luigi Zingales (1999).
26. Again, John Coffee (see Chapter 4, this volume) has made this kind of argument. As I note in the text, he may be identifying one of the modern political mechanisms by which the French social democracy has undermined French stock markets, not, as he suggests, posing a counter-example to a political theory.
27. Minority stockholders in Mediaset, Silvio Berlusconi's principal corporate vehicle—Berlusconi is the Prime Minister and has a wheeler-dealer reputation—insisted on a corporate charter term: super-majority board approval for any related-party transaction. They expected board representation and, hence, veto power. Board approval for such transactions is not required under Italian corporate law, but contract could fill the gap. I discuss contract and corporate law in Roe (2000*c*, 2002).
28. See Zingales (1994: 146–7) (discussing and citing sources on the value of the voting right in Sweden); cf. Bergström and Rydqvist (1990*a*: 267) ('data do not support the argument that dual classes are used [in Sweden] for wealth expropriation by holding control with little equity'); Bergström and Rydqvist (1990*b*: 237) ('the value of control does not derive from the possibility to expropriate the fringe of minority shareholders... [but] has to be motivated by some other economic motives') (emphasis supplied); Holmén and Högfeldt (1999: 39) ('Outside shareholders do not refrain f[ro]m investing on the Stockholm Stock Exchange since 55 per cent of the Swedish population own shares... and 33 per cent of outstanding shares are owned by foreign investors.... [T]he ratio of the stock market capitalisation held by minority shareholders in relation to GDP... is 0.51 for Sweden compared to 0.58 for the U.S.... Thus, it is not likely that weak investor protection has hampered financial market development in Sweden...') (emphasis supplied).
29. German results are similar. When a block is sold, the sales premium reflects the benefit to the blockholder of diverting value from the outside stockholders. But the premium is only 10 per cent, about that of control premium in the USA, and not much different than the 7 per cent voting

premium in dual class companies (Franks and Mayer, 2000). Blockholders seem not to be diverting much more value from minority stockholders in Germany than in the USA.

30. Cf. Latour and Steinmetz (1998: A1) (Wallenbergs resist outside shareholders' wealth maximization goals as 'not [necessarily] serving society's best interests').
31. Chandler (1990: 242); Chandler and Daems (1980: 6) ('Until World War II, the British economy was for the most part an example of family capitalism'); Hannah (1980: 53) ('The separation of ownership and control... had not progressed far enough to displace founding or family directors from company boards[;]... 119 [out of the 200 largest firms in Britain], or 59.5 per cent, [had founding or family directors] in 1948'); cf. Hannah (1979: 396) ('In the period before 1914... it seems that the United States and Germany led the industrial world in introducing large-scale corporate organisation, whereas Britain retained a stronger inherited structure of family enterprise....').
32. On another note, I earlier argued that America's populist financial politics precluded a hand-off early in the twentieth century from the family owners to financial institutions who might have taken larger blocks of stock, were they permitted to do so. Some have posed Britain's history as a counter-example. Britain's financial institutions did not take the blocks, but neither did the families sell out until very late in the twentieth century. In the USA though at the beginning of the twentieth century, the drive to build enterprises in the much larger American economy induced a demand for size and a demand for a new ownership norm (apart from family ownership). Britain did not have this impulse, because it was smaller.
33. Brian Cheffins (Chapter 6, this volume) and John Coffee (Chapter 4, this volume) believe that this British example fully undermines the social democracy thesis. But they exaggerate its importance. Had strong British securities markets first arisen *at the time of social democracy, instead of well before* then the example—the best they have—would be more telling. Or, for it to be useful, they need to show that British securities markets and ownership separation were proceeding at the same rate as before Britain became social democratic, and after it became social democratic. This they do not do. The data is not readily available, so they should hardly be faulted here for not spending two years of research uncovering the data, but the secondary indications (size of security market—it was growing—and Chandler's and other qualitative observations of persistent family domination even of public companies) both point in the opposite direction from the one they need. Securities development and separation were slow, or perhaps non-existent, during that era.
34. See Roe (1996*b*: 641); Bebchuk and Roe (1999: 127).
35. Even today, Britain's ownership structure is more concentrated than the American. On average, the largest British firms do have a blockholder with just under 10 per cent of the firm's stock, just below the cutoffs for the concentration data used here and in the underlying database from La Porta *et al.* (1999: 495). Becht and Röell (1998: 11) (showing that 9.9 per cent is the median of British big firms' biggest stockholder). These blocks are today typically held by financial institutions.
36. Cf. (Dahrendorf 1999: 13); (Sullivan 1999: 54) ('Blair... had long since lost faith in the sclerotic European social-democratic model... [H]e made some Clintonite changes:... all were worthy ameliorations of Thatcherism—but no reversal'); (Hoge 1999: A6) ('Blair says he... will free Britain from the grip of class consciousness,... liberate British business from restrictions that discourage enterprise and punish risk-taking, [and] reduce the poor's dependency on the state...').
37. OECD (1998: 18). In 1985, the British domestic stock market, as a percentage of gross domestic product, more than doubled from that of 1975. In contrast, the American percentage rose only modestly.

Market capitalization of listed domestic equity issues as per cent of GDP

	1975	1980	1985	1990
United Kingdom	337	338	777	887
United States of America (NYSE, Amex, and NASDAQ)	448	550	557	556

Privatization complicates but does not contradict the social democracy thesis, accounting for some but not all of the 1985 increase; the top 250 firms included thirteen government corporations in 1976 and still had eleven in 1988. Scott (1990: 366–7) (showing a 'decline of family control' from 1976 to 1988). Note that firms had been nationalized either because markets demanded a downsizing that political actors would not permit or because of ideologies of state ownership. When these social democratic, or socialist, sentiments declined, the government began to privatize these firms.

38. Even modest rents create indeterminacy in corporate ownership and governance. Rents allow different players to get value out of the firm, and different players may win by chance in some political environments and lose in others. When competition in the American economy was weaker, and oligopoly stronger, mild pressures to soften the workplace and make managers socially responsible to employee constituencies may have been more effective than they would be today (Roe 1996*a*).
39. See Rajan and Zingales (1999: 76) (stating the total securities issuance as a percentage of GNP was higher in France in 1913 than in the USA, and only slightly lower in Germany). In the 1900–13 period, French and Japanese firms sold more stock in their nations than American firms did in the USA. Cf. Miwa and Ramseyer (2000).

References

Acemoglu, D., and Newman, A. (1997). The labor market and corporate structure. MIT Department of Economics, Working Paper No. 97–8.

Agnblad, J., Berglöf, E., Högfeldt, P., and Svancar, H. (2000). Ownership and control in Sweden—strong owners, weak minorities, and social control. Working Paper.

Albert, M. (1991). *Capitalisme contre Capitalisme.* Paris: Seuil.

André, T. J. Jr. (1996). Some reflections on German corporate governance: A glimpse at German supervisory boards. *Tulane Law Review* 70: 1819.

Aoki, M. (ed.) (1997*a*). *The Role of Government in East Asian Economic Development.* New York: Oxford University Press.

—— (1997*b*). Unintended fit. In M. Aoki (ed.), *The Role of Government in East Asian Economic Development.* New York: Oxford University Press.

Bauer, M. (1997). Administrateurs et Dirigeants du CAC 40. Report of CNRS Observatoire des Dirigeants.

Baums, T., and Frick, B. (1999). The market value of the codetermined firm. In Blair and Roe (ed.), Employees and Corporate Governance. Washington, DC: Brookings.

Bebchuk, L. A. (1998). A theory of the choice between concentrated and dispersed ownership of corporate shares and votes. Harvard Law and Economics, Working Paper.

—— (1999). A rent protection theory of corporate ownership and control. Harvard Law School, Center for Law, Economics, and Business, Discussion Paper No. 260.

—— and Roe, M. J. (1999). A theory of path dependence in corporate ownership and governance. *Stanford Law Review* 52: 127.

—— Kraakman, R., and Triantis, G. (1999). Stock pyramids, cross-ownership, and dual class equity: The creation and agency costs in separating control from cash flow rights. NBER, Working Paper No. 6951.

Becht, M., and Röell, A. (1998). Blockholdings in Europe: An international comparison. European Corporate Governance Network, Overview Paper.

Bergström, C., and Rydqvist, K. (1990*a*). Ownership of equity in dual-class firms. *Journal of Banking and Finance* 14: 255.

—— (1990*b*). The determinants of corporate ownership—An empirical study on Swedish data. *Journal of Banking and Finance* 14: 237.

Bertrand, M., and Mullainathan, S. (1999). Is there discretion in wage setting? A test using takeover legislation. *RAND Journal of Economics* 30: 535.

Brennan, M. J., and Franks, J. (1997). Underpricing, ownership and control in initial public offerings of equity securities in the UK. *Journal of Financial Economics* 45: 391.

Castles F. G., and Mair, P. (1984). Left–right political scales: Some 'Expert' judgments. *European Journal of Political Science* 12: 73.

Chandler, A. P. (1977). *The Visible Hand: The Managerial Revolution in American Business.* Cambridge, MA: Harvard University Press.

—— (1990). *Scale and Scope.* Cambridge, MA: Harvard University Press.

—— and Daems, H. (eds.) (1980). *Managerial Hierarchies—Comparative Perspectives on the Rise of the Modern Industrial Enterpise.* Cambridge, MA: Harvard University Press.

Chandler, A. D. Jr., and Daems, H. (1980). Introduction. In A. D. Chandler, Jr. and H. Daems (ed.).

Charkham, J. P. (1994). *Keeping Good Company: A Study of Corporate Governance in Five Countries.*

Charny, D. (1999). Workers and corporate governance: The role of political culture. In M. Blair and M. Roe (ed.), *Employees and Corporate Governance,* Washington, DC: Brookings.

Commons, J. R. (1997*a*). History of labor in the United States—1896–1932 (1935). reprinted in M. Rutherford and W. J. Samuels (ed.), *III Classics in Institutional Economics.*

—— (1997*b*). Is class conflict in America growing and is it inevitable? *American Journal of Sociology* 13: 756, reprinted in M. Rutherford and W. J. Samuels (ed.), *III Classics in Institutional Economics.*

Cusack, T. R. (1997). Partisan politics and public finance: Changes in public spending in the industrialized democracies, 1955–1989. *Public Choice* 91: 375.

Dahrendorf, R. (1999). The third way and liberty. *Foreign Affairs* September/October, 13.

Davenport-Hines and Jones, G. (ed.) (1988). *Enterprise, Management and Innovation in British Business, 1914–1980.*

Demsetz, H. (1983). The structure of ownership and the theory of the firm. *Journal of Law and Economics* 26: 375.

Edwards, J., and Fischer, K. (1994). *Banks, Finance and Investment in Germany.* Cambridge: Cambridge University Press.

Elbaum, B., and Lazonick, W. (ed.) (1987). *The Decline of the British Economy.* Cambridge: Cambridge University Press.

Fanto, J. A. (1995). The transformation of French corporate governance and United States institutional investors. *Brooklyn Journal of International Law* 21: 1.

Faujas, A. (1999). Français, Allemands et Italiens n' Attendent Rien de Bon des Entreprises, *Le Monde Economie,* 1 June, IV.

FitzRoy, F. R., and Kraft, K. (1993). Economic effects of codetermination. *Scandinavian Journal of Economics* 95: 365.

Francis, A. (1980). Families, firms and financial capital: The development of UK industrial firms with particular reference to their ownership and control. *British Journal of Sociology* 14: 29.

Franks, J., and Mayer, C. (2000). Ownership and control of german corporations. Oxford University, Working Paper.

Frick, B., Speckbacker, G., and Wentges, P. (1998), Arbeitnehmermitbestimmung und moderne Theories der Unternehmung. *Zeitschrift für Betriebswirtschaft*, p. 745.

Friedman, M. (1970). The social responsibility of business is to increase its profits. *New York Times Magazine*, 13 September, 33.

Goyer, M. (1999). The transformation of corporate governance in France and Germany. Working Paper, 41.

Graham, A. (1997). The UK 1979–95: Myths and realities of conservative capitalism. In C. Crouch and W. Streeck (ed.), *The Political Economy of Modern Capitalism: Mapping Convergence and Diversity*. London: Sage.

Hannah, L. (1980). Visible and Invisible Hands in Great Britain. In A. Chandler & H. Daems (eds.), *Managerial Hierarchies—Comparative Perspectives on the Rise of the Modern Industrial Enterprise*. Cambridge, Mass.: Harvard University Press.

Hoge, W. (1999). Tony Blair rides triumphant, either as a visionary or as a good promoter. *New York Times*, 2 February, A6.

Holmén, M., and Högfeldt, P. (1999). Corporate Control and Security Design in Initial Public Offerings, working paper, p. 38.

Hollande, F. (1999). Pour une extension des stock-options à l'ensemble du personnel. *Le Monde*, 7 October, 6.

Jagannathan, R., and Srinivasan, S. B. (1999). Does product market competition reduce agency costs? University of Minnesota, Working Paper.

Jensen, M. C. (1986). Agency costs of free cash flow, corporate finance and takeovers. *American Economic Review* 76: 659.

Kindleberger, C. P. (1964). *Economic Growth in France and Britain*. Cambridge, MA: Harvard University Press.

Kirby, M. W. (1989). Institutional rigidities and Britain's industrial decline. *Business History Review* 63: 930.

Kirk, N. (1998). Change, Continuity and Class: Labour in British Society.

Krieger, J. *et al.* (eds.) (1993). *The Oxford Companion to Politics of the World*. Oxford: Oxford University Press.

Kuttner, R. (1996). Soaring stocks: Are only the rich getting richer? *Business Week*, 22 April, 28.

La Porta, R., Lopez-de-Silanes, F., and Shleifer, A. (1999). Corporate ownership around the world. *Journal of Finance* 54: 471.

Latour, A., and Steinmetz, G. (1998). Swedish giant: Barnevik set about task of preserving Wallenberg empire. *Wall Street Journal* 18 May, A1.

Lemaître, F. (1999). Le succès de l'actionnariat salarié bouleverse le capitalisme français. *Le Monde* 2 March, 15.

Le Monde (1999). Des réactions politiques et syndicales sévères. 11 September, 16.

Leparmentier, A. (1998). L'Allemagne industrielle de nouveau conquérante. *Le Monde*, 28 November, 1.

Lester, R. (1952). A range theory of wage differentials. *Industrial and Labor Relations Review* 5: 483.

Mauduit, L. (2000). M. Jospin ouvre avec précaution le dossier de l'épargne salariale. *Le Monde*, 29 January, 6.

"Michelin" (1999). *Le Monde*, 23 September.

Ministère de l'Economie, des Finances et de l'Industrie (2000). Rapport au Premier Ministre sur l'Epargne Salariale. (Part II), 8.

Miwa, Y., and Ramseyer, J. M. (2000). Corporate governance in transitional economies: Lessons from the pre-war Japanese cotton textile industry. *Journal of Legal Studies* 29: 171.
OECD (1998). *Financial Market Trends*, p. 18.
Owen, D. (2000). Provision put brakes on Michelin. *Financial Times*, 15 March, 20.
Pistor, K. (1999). Codetermination: A sociopolitical model with governance externalities. In B. Blair and M. Roe (ed.), *Employees and Corporate Governance.* Washington, DC: Brookings.
Polanyi, K. (1944). *The Great Transformation.* Boston: Beacon Press.
Porter, M. E. (1999). The microeconomic foundations of economic development'. In *World Economic Forum*, The Global Competitiveness Report, 38.
Przeworski, A. (1993). Socialism and social democracy. In J. Krieger *et al.* (ed.), *The Oxford Companion to Politics of the World.* Oxford: Oxford University Press.
Rajan, R. A., and Zingales, L. (1999). The politics of financial development. University of Chicago, Working Paper, 76.
Reynolds, L. (1951). *The Structure of Labor Markets: Wages and Labor Mobility in Theory and Practice.*
Roe, M. J. (1994). *Strong Managers, Weak Owners: The Political Roots of American Corporate Finance.* Princeton: Princeton University Press.
—— (1996*a*). From antitrust to corporate governance: The corporation and the law: 1959–1994. In C. Kaysen, (ed.), *The American Corporation Today.*
—— (1996*b*). Chaos and Evolution in Law and Economics. *Harvard Law Review.* 109: 641.
—— (1998*a*). German codetermination and German securities markets. *Columbia Business Law Review* 1998: 167.
—— (1998*b*). Backlash. *Columbia Law Review* 98: 217.
—— (2000*a*), Political foundations for separating ownership from corporate control. Stanford Law Review 53: 539.
—— (2001*b*). Rents and their corporate consequences. Stanford Law Review 53: 1463.
—— (2001*c*). Corporate Law's Limits. Working Paper.
—— (2002). Political Determinants of Corporate Governance. Oxford: Oxford University Press (forthcoming).
Ruggiero, E. (1998). Italy. In the legal basis of corporate governance. In A. R. Pinto and G. Visentini (ed.), *Publicly Held Corporations: A Comparative Approach.* The Hague: Kluwer Law International.
Schilling, F. (1994). Die Aufsichtsrat ist für die Katz, *Frankfurter Allgemeine Zeitung* 27 August.
Schimmelmann, W. Von (1997). Unternehmenskontrolle in Deutschland. In B. Gahlen, H. Hesse, and H. J. Ramser (ed.), *Finanzmärkte*, 7.
Schmid, F. A., and Seger, F. (1998). Arbeitnehmer mitbestimmung, Allokation von Entscheidungsrechten und Shareholder Value. *Zeitschrift für Betriebswirtschaft* 5: 453.
Scott, J. (1990). Corporate control and corporate rule: Britain in an international perspective. *British Journal of Sociology* 41: 351.
Semler, J. (1998). The practice of the German aufsichtsrat. In K. J. Hopt, H. Kanda, M. J. Roe, E. Wyeersch, and S. Prigge (ed.), *Comparative Corporate Governance: The State of the Art and Emerging Research.* Oxford: Oxford University Press.
Stimson, S. C. (1998). Social democracy. In J. Eatwell *et al.* (ed.), *The New Palgrave Dictionary of Economics*, Vol. 4, p. 395.
Sullivan, A. (1999). The end of Britain. *New York Times Magazine* (21 February), 39.
Turner, F. J. (1920). *The Frontier in American History.*
Vafeas, N. (1999). Board meeting frequency and firm performance. *Journal of Financial Economics* 53: 113.

Weiss, L. (1988). *Creating Capitalism: The State and Small Business Since 1945*. p. 104.
Windolf, P. (1998). The governance structure of large French corporations. In Columbia Law School Sloan Program, Corporate Governance Today.
Zingales, L. (1994). The value of the voting right: A study of the Milan stock exchange experience. *Review Financial Studies* 7: 125.

6

Putting Britain on the Roe Map: The Emergence of the Berle–Means Corporation in the United Kingdom

BRIAN R. CHEFFINS

1. INTRODUCTION

Almost all of America's largest business enterprises have their shares traded on the stock market, which means publicly quoted corporations play a dominant role in the country's economy (Moerland 1995: 19). Such firms are typically run by professionally trained managers and owned by widely dispersed shareholders who buy and sell stock freely in well-developed securities markets. A central feature of American corporate governance therefore is the separation of ownership and control (Gilson 1996: 330). Various leading corporate law scholars have sought over the past few years to explain why capitalism in the USA has evolved in accordance with the foregoing pattern (e.g. Gilson 1996; Easterbrook 1997; Coffee 1999). Work done by Mark Roe, a law professor at Harvard, has helped to trigger this research activity.

The orthodox explanation for the corporate governance framework which prevails in the United States is economic in orientation. Essentially, the advantages arising from economies of scale and specialization of functions meant that a separation of ownership and control in large business enterprises was economically inevitable in a market system. Roe, in a wide range of published work (e.g. 1990; 1994*a*,*b*; 1997; Chapter 5, this volume), has constructed a forceful and provocative challenge to this thesis. He has argued that the American system of ownership and control was politically and historically contingent instead of simply being the product of market forces.[1]

Roe's work on the separation of ownership and control has proved to be highly topical. By the mid-1990s it was fashionable to set off the approach to free enterprise prevailing in Germany and Japan against its American equivalent in a sort of capitalist beauty contest (Cheffins 1998*b*: 73). Roe's politically oriented explanation of the separation of ownership and control was directly relevant to this debate because it cast doubt on the superiority of the American approach to corporate governance. If one thinks of the USA's version of the public corporation as the evolutionary pinnacle, other systems with different institutional characteristics can be safely ignored: 'neither laggards nor neanderthals (compel) significant academic attention' (Gilson 1996: 332). On the other hand, if the American corporate governance regime evolved as a result of historical accident rather than fundamental economic logic, this implies that a different ownership and control framework should be fully capable of delivering similar or even superior results.

This chapter builds upon Roe's analysis of the public corporation by discussing developments in the UK. Even though Roe himself has only referred to Britain briefly in his own work (e.g. 1994*b*: 4–5, 201–2; Chapter 5, this volume), ascertaining how matters developed in the UK can potentially provide unique insights concerning events in America. This is because with respect to corporate governance, the USA has more in common with Britain than it does with other major industrial nations.[2] As we will see, one unfortunately cannot rely on the British experience to draw firm conclusions concerning Roe's work. This, in large part, is because the historical record is ambiguous. Still, on balance, developments in the UK serve to cast doubt on his thesis that the paradigm American corporation, with its strong managers and widely dispersed shareholders, is primarily a 'path-dependent' political artefact.

The chapter proceeds as follows. We will begin with an overview of corporate governance arrangements in the United States. Next, we will consider the orthodox explanation for the dominance of the widely held public company and Roe's challenge to this line of thinking. The links which exist between the British and American systems of corporate governance will then be identified. After this, relevant historical developments in the UK will be outlined. Finally, we will see that the explanations which Roe has offered for the emergence of America's version of corporate governance—the presence of a deeply ingrained popular mistrust of concentrated economic power and the absence of a tradition of 'social democracy'—do not seem convincing in a British context.

2. AN OVERVIEW OF THE AMERICAN SYSTEM OF CORPORATE GOVERNANCE

The ownership and control arrangements which exist in the USA have been characterized as an 'outsider' or arm's-length system (Berglöf 1997: 152, 157–64; Goergen 1998: 1–2). The outsider typology is apt because share ownership is highly diffused instead of being concentrated in the hands of families, banks or other firms. The fact that corporations which have distributed shares to the public play a dominant role in the American economy helps to ensure that this situation exists. Statistical evidence illustrates how important public companies are in the United States. As of 1996, the country had thirty publicly quoted companies per one million people whereas Japan had eighteen, France had eight, Germany had five, and Italy had four (La Porta *et al.* 1997: 1137–8). Moreover, according to data compiled that same year, the market capitalization of stock markets in the United States (the total market value of all of the shares of all corporations listed for trading) was over 110 per cent of the country's Gross Domestic Product (GDP). In other major European countries, the equivalent figure was 35 per cent or less, and in Japan it was 66 per cent (see *Economist* 1996; La Porta *et al.* 1997: 1137–8; Wymeersch 1998: 1061).

Characterizing the American system of corporate governance in outsider terms is also appropriate because the country's major publicly quoted corporations rarely have a shareholder who owns enough equity to have any sort of "inside" influence. Instead, large shareholdings, and especially majority ownership, are uncommon (Shleifer and Vishny 1997: 754; La Porta *et al.* 1999: 491–7). This pattern exists despite the fact that major institutional investors (pension funds, insurance companies, mutual funds and the like) own approximately 50 per cent of the equity in American public corporations (Rao and Lee-Sing 1995: 50; Waters 1998). Such institutions generally have a highly diversified investment portfolio and tend not to acquire large blocks of shares in any one corporation. Hence, in a typical big American firm the twenty largest institutional shareholders will only own one-third of the equity (Lowenstein 1991: 210).

With respect to corporate governance in the United States, the term arm's-length signifies that shareholders maintain their distance and give executives a free hand to manage. This approach prevails because in the ordinary course investors are more concerned with the overall performance of the portfolio of shares they own than they are with developments affecting any one particular company. Admittedly, US American stockholders are not always apathetic towards the functioning of individual corporations. Indeed, there has been a well-chronicled increase in institutional activism in the past decade (Smith 1996: 1104–5). Still, such intervention has generally been restricted to crisis situations (ibid.: 1105–6) and public pension funds (those which invest on behalf of government employees) have pursued an activist agenda with much more enthusiasm than other institutional investors (Coffee 1994: 849–50; Cheffins 1998*a*: 54–5). Thus, overall, it is fair to say that shareholders in American public companies are rarely poised to intervene and take a hand in running the business.

3. EXPLAINING THE EMERGENCE OF THE SEPARATION OF OWNERSHIP AND CONTROL IN USA: MARK ROE'S CONTRIBUTION

In *The Modern Corporation and Private Property*, 'the most important study ever written about the ownership and governance of the American business corporation' (Mark 1995: 973), Adolf Berle and Gardiner Means drew attention to the pattern of corporate governance which is now common in publicly quoted corporations in the United States (Berle and Means 1932). The authors asserted that, while the law treated stockholders as a company's owners, those who invested in public corporations usually did not act in the manner one would expect of an owner. Instead, widely dispersed shareholders, each lacking a sufficient financial incentive to intervene directly, left it to professionally trained executives to deal with matters of importance. The upshot was that there was a separation of ownership and control.

An inference which could be drawn from Berle and Means' work was that executives in American public companies had a licence to exercise substantial power without being held fully and properly accountable for their actions. Concerns about this led various observers to recommend tighter regulation to ensure that individuals running companies would act in an honest and responsible manner (e.g. Gilbert 1956; Ruder 1965; Cary 1974). Such reformist thinking was not universally accepted, however (Mark 1995: 973–6). Corporate law academics writing from a law and economics perspective acknowledged that executives in a public company might be tempted to act in a self-serving manner and could thereby impose agency costs on investors (e.g. Easterbrook and Fischel 1991: 9–11, 14–15, 91–2, 217–18). These analysts did not accept, however, that thoroughgoing regulatory intervention was justified. This was because product markets, managerial labour markets, capital markets and the market for corporate control were doing a great deal to discipline executives and ensure managerial accountability (e.g. Butler 1989: 110–20).

While those writing from an economic perspective disagreed with the reformist school on the regulatory implications of a separation of ownership and control, typically all concerned implicitly agreed on an important point: fragmented share ownership was inevitable in major business enterprises.[3] Technology dictated that dominant firms must be large and the capital needs of big companies were so great that a handful of wealthy individuals could not provide proper financial backing. Also, a separation of ownership and control was beneficial since executives could be hired solely on the basis of their managerial credentials. This could occur because managerial recruits would not be expected to make any sort of financial contribution to the firm hiring them or to have any sort of connection with key shareholders (e.g. as a member of a family owning a substantial block of equity).

Admittedly, the 'Berle–Means corporation' was not perfect. Instead, it had some detrimental features, such as weakened managerial incentives and diminished coordination between executives and shareholders. Nevertheless, the advantages arising from economies of scale and the use of professionalized management were large enough to offset these drawbacks. Therefore, the American version of the public corporation was the logical winner of a Darwinian struggle between different forms of corporate structure.

Mark Roe has sought to discredit this Darwinian story by arguing that the American system of ownership and control was politically and historically contingent (e.g. Roe 1990; 1994*b*; 1997). A key theme in his writing is that the Berle–Means corporation was, at least in part, a product of a deeply ingrained popular mistrust of concentrated financial power. Roe has argued that at several points in the twentieth century, large financial institutions were poised to take substantial block positions in American business firms and adopt an activist approach to corporate governance. On these occasions, however, politicians intervened, forced corporate ownership to remain fragmented and deterred big financial institutions from taking a close interest in the activities of corporate executives. The Berle–Means corporation, then, was not a necessity. It was an adaptation that arose to fit the kind of financial system US history produced.

Roe has also drawn attention to an additional political contingency that allegedly has had an influence on corporate governance patterns. He says there is a statistical correlation between a country's position on the ideological spectrum and its corporate ownership structure (Roe, Chapter 5, this volume). According to his findings, 'left-wing' social democracies have fewer publicly quoted firms and significantly higher levels of ownership concentration than 'right-wing' countries where there is little or no tradition of social democracy. Roe's explanation for this pattern is that social democracies favour employees over investors. The protection left-wing countries provide to workers allegedly exacerbates the agency cost 'gap' between managers and shareholders, thereby increasing substantially the disadvantages associated with the Berle–Means corporation. The ownership format characteristic of this type of firm is therefore less likely to emerge in a social democracy than it is in a country without a strong socialist tradition, such as the United States (Roe 2000: 15–22, 36–7).

Roe, by drawing attention to political and historical factors, has no doubt made a highly original contribution to the literature on the public company (Mark 1995: 969). Is it true, however, that the dominance of the Berle–Means corporation can best be explained in political and ideological terms? A helpful way to analyse this question is to examine what happened in the UK (Black and Coffee 1994: 2001). This is because, as the next section of this chapter will show, Britain has a system of corporate governance which is uniquely similar to that which exists in the USA.

What lessons can be derived by considering the British experience with the widely held public company? If Mark Roe is correct and the dominance of the Berle–Means corporation in the United States was a politically and historically contingent outcome, one would expect to find that the social, economic, and ideological context was much the same in Britain as it was in America. On the other hand, if the British system of corporate governance evolved in a different institutional environment, it would seem to follow that factors other than the ones Roe has identified account primarily for the emergence of a separation of ownership and control. Ultimately, we will see that the latter version of events seems to be more accurate.

4. THE UNIQUE LINKS BETWEEN THE SYSTEMS OF CORPORATE GOVERNANCE IN THE UK AND THE USA

An important corporate governance link between the US and the UK is that the two countries share an 'outsider/arm's-length' system of ownership and control (Stapledon 1996: 3–4; Berglöf 1997*a*: 158–9, 163; Mayer 1997: 298–9). In Britain, as in the US, the 'outsider' terminology is appropriate because share ownership is widely dispersed. Since most of the UK's largest corporations are quoted on the stock market, the British economy, like its American counterpart, is dominated by companies which have carried out public offerings of shares (Moerland 1995: 19; Franks and Mayer 1997: 283). Indeed, the country has more public companies per one million people than does the USA (36 versus 30, according to 1996 figures) (La Porta *et al.* 1997: 1137). Furthermore, while as of 1996 the market capitalization of American stock markets was approximately 110 per cent of the country's GDP, in Britain the proportion exceeded 135 per cent (Wymeersch 1998: 1057, 1061).

As is the case in the United States, the fact that it is uncommon for British public companies to have a dominant shareholder confirms that the 'outsider' typology is apt. Less than one-fifth of Britain's publicly quoted firms have an owner who controls more than 25 per cent of the shares (Berglöf 1997*b*: 101; Davies 1997*b*: 48; Wymeersch 1998: 1170–2). Part of the reason for this pattern is that families rarely own a dominant percentage of shares in large UK companies (La Porta *et al.* 1999: 501, table V). Also, while the proportion of the equity market owned by institutional investors is higher in the UK than it is in the US,[4] only the very largest institutional investors control ever more than 5 per cent of the equity in individual British companies (Stapledon 1996: 106–17; Cheffins 1997: 634).

The 'arm's-length' label is suitable for the UK because the country's shareholders act in the same manner as their USA counterparts and generally take a 'hands-off' approach with companies they own. Take the example of British institutional investors. Traditionally, they prefer to leave it to management to run companies and often respond to poor corporate performance by selling their stake rather than by intervening in order to try to rectify matters (Cheffins 1997: 63–4). Admittedly, the fund managers who make decisions on behalf of institutional investors do not ignore completely developments at individual companies.

Still, when they do act, they usually do so on a quiet, 'behind the scenes' basis and only become deeply involved in a company's affairs when the incumbent management team has been fully discredited (Stapledon 1996: 101–6, 121–4; Cheffins 1997: 64, 616–17, 620).

Other major industrial countries do not share the system of ownership and control that exists in the US and the UK. In these other jurisdictions, 'core' shareholders and/or dominant creditors monitor corporate activities closely and are well situated to exercise considerable influence over management. The prevailing approach to corporate governance therefore is 'insider' or 'control-oriented' (Berglöf 1997*a*: 157–64; Hoshi 1998: 851–66).[5] This pattern exists in part because of the role that banks play. In the USA and the UK, there is little interdependence between banks and larger industrial or commercial firms (Charkham 1994: 196–7, 297–300). In continental Europe and Japan, on the other hand, banks exercise considerable authority (Charkham 1994: 35–43, 97–106; Macey and Miller 1997: 61–3; Scott 1997: 142–52; Prigge 1998: 1014–24). This is due to the many corporate governance related functions they occupy (e.g. as advisers, as lenders, as owners of shares on their own behalf and as proxies for other shareholders).

In Japan and continental Europe, the prevailing corporate governance pattern is also 'insider/control-oriented' because publicly traded companies play a comparatively minor role in the economy. Japan, France, Germany, and Italy have considerably fewer public companies per one million people than do the USA and the UK (La Porta *et al.* 1997: 1137–8). Similarly, the market capitalization of the stock markets in these four countries constitutes a significantly smaller percentage of GDP (Le Défi Américan 1996; Wymeersch 1998: 1061).

A further reason why the system of ownership and control in Japan and continental Europe is 'insider/control-oriented' is that, with those companies which have publicly quoted equity, one shareholder or a closely allied set of investors will often be suitably positioned to exercise a dominant influence. European public companies are frequently a member of a corporate group established by way of an elaborate cross-shareholding scheme and this sort of arrangement is commonly designed to ensure that control ultimately rests in the hands of one party or a tightly affiliated group, such as a family (Moerland 1995: 20–1; Wymeersch 1998: 1152–79; Adams 1999).[6] In Japan, a public company will often be part of a dense network of reciprocal shareholdings, with a stable coalition of major creditors, key customers/suppliers and firms in the same business group owning a majority of the company's shares (Hoshi 1998: 860–1).[7]

In addition to sharing an 'outsider/arm's-length' system of ownership and control, Britain and America both have what has been referred to as a 'shareholder economy' (Bolkestein 1999; Cunningham 1999: 1136–9). Under this 'Anglo-American' form of capitalism, private enterprise is about maximizing profits for those who invest and shareholders occupy the central position with respect to companies (Bolkestein 1999). Those who own equity dominate because they elect the directors and because the law has traditionally defined the interests of the company as the interests of the shareholders (Parkinson 1993: 77; Scott 1997: 56–7; *Dodge* v. *Ford Motor Co.*, 170 N.W. 668 (Mich. 1919).[8]

Britain and the United States are not the only jurisdictions that adhere to the shareholder-oriented 'Anglo-American' model of capitalism. Other examples include Canada, New Zealand, and Australia (Scott 1997: 3–4, 56–7). These three countries differ, however, from their two 'Anglo-American' counterparts in an important way. As mentioned, in the US and Britain larger public companies generally do not have an investor who owns enough shares to exercise a dominant influence. Concentrated ownership, on the other hand, is prevalent in Canada, Australia, and New Zealand (Daniels and MacIntosh, 1991: 884; Ramsay and Blair 1993: 165–8; Morck 1996: 69; Fox and Walker 1997: 128–9).

In contrast to jurisdictions where the 'Anglo-American' model of capitalism prevails, continental European countries and Japan have what can be characterized as a 'stakeholder economy' (Kaplan 1997: 86–7; Bolkestein 1999; Roe 2000: 30–1). This sort of market regime is characterized by a comparatively high degree of state intervention and by a consensus-minded approach to potentially contentious issues. Moreover, the maximization of profits for investors is not an overriding priority (Hopt 1994: 208; Miller 1997: 38).[9] Instead, there is a desire to strike a balance between various constituencies linked with companies and the main concern is said to be sustainable, stable, and continuous economic growth.

Consistent with the 'stakeholder' model, in various continental European countries formal mechanisms exist which ensure that employee representatives are kept informed about key developments and encourage those affected by corporate activity to resolve disagreements on the basis of consensus (Wymeersch 1998: 1142–50; Cunningham 1999: 1141–2). Arrangements are less structured in Japan. Still, the country's executives seek to involve employees where possible, particularly with respect to production and technical issues and major corporate decisions arising during times of crisis (Hoshi 1998: 861–2; Cheffins 1998*b*: 61).

A final point. One should not assume that the systems of ownership and control which exist in the US and the UK are identical. Instead, there are significant differences. For instance, though institutional investors play an important role in both countries, the British equities market is more institutionally dominated than its American counterpart (Black and Coffee 1994: 2002). Also, shareholder concentration is higher in Britain. Whereas in the United States a company's twenty largest institutional investors will typically own about one-third of the equity in a corporation (Lowenstein 1991: 210), in the UK a similar number of institutions can be expected to own a majority of the shares (Black and Coffee 1994: 2002). Still, while corporate governance arrangements are not identical in the two countries, the foregoing discussion illustrates that the US has more in common with the UK than it does with other major industrial nations. Studying historical developments in Britain should therefore provide a unique opportunity to evaluate Mark Roe's theories concerning the Berle–Means corporation.

5. THE EMERGENCE OF THE BERLE–MEANS CORPORATION IN THE UK: THE HISTORICAL EVIDENCE

5.1. *The Move Towards the Stock Market by UK Companies*

Now that we have established why examining developments in Britain is likely to be a helpful exercise, we can turn to the historical evidence. By 1890, the UK had almost completed its transformation from an agrarian commercial economy to an industrial one.

Also, a steady migration of people to urban areas served to create a highly concentrated consumer market. As a result, Britain had become the world's first industrial nation and its first consumer society (Chandler 1990: 251).

Though the UK was well-established as an industrial power as the nineteenth century was coming to a close, the country did not yet have a sophisticated corporate economy. The Joint Stock Companies Act enacted in 1856 (19 and 20 Vict. *c*.47) established the legislative framework for the modern style limited liability company (Davies 1997*a*: 44–5). Still, as late as the 1880s, only five to ten per cent of the country's larger business enterprises had in fact incorporated (Hannah 1976: 19). Moreover, at this juncture there were barely sixty domestic commercial and industrial companies with shares quoted on London's Stock Exchange, accounting for hardly one per cent of all quoted securities (Prais 1976: 90). London was the largest and most sophisticated capital market in the world but it was a market dealing primarily in government debt and, to a lesser extent, railway bonds (Cassis 1990: 1–3, 6–7; Michie 1990: 96–9; Kennedy 1994: 125, 127–30).

As we have seen, most large British business enterprises are now publicly quoted and the Berle–Means corporation constitutes the paradigm. How did all of this come about? The move British firms made towards the stock market can be traced fairly easily. It began in earnest in the final few years of the nineteenth century and by 1907 almost 600 industrial and commercial companies were quoted on London's Stock Exchange (Hannah 1976: 20; Armstrong 1990: 118–23). Apart from disruptions imposed by war, the number approximately doubled in each decade thereafter until a peak of about 3,500 companies was reached in 1951 (Prais 1976: 90).[10] Publicly traded firms, in turn, became a dominant force in the economy. By the middle of the twentieth century they accounted for over 70 per cent of the profits generated by the British corporate sector (Hannah 1974: 65).

The move towards the stock market served to transform UK capital markets. In the years immediately prior to the beginning of the First World War in 1914, British companies accounted for approximately one-third of the funds raised on London's Stock Exchange. By the mid-1930s, well over 50 per cent of the 'new issue' market was concerned with the finance of domestic firms and the percentage exceeded 90 per cent in the years following the Second World War (Thomas 1978: 24, 145).[11] Not surprisingly, a committee investigating the monetary system acknowledged in 1959 that 'the new issue market is an effective and important mechanism for the raising of long-term capital by public companies' (quoted in Michie 1992: 127). Ultimately, by 1972, company securities accounted for four-fifths of the value of all securities quoted on the London Stock Exchange (Prais 1976: 90).

A number of lines of development helped to transform the London Stock Exchange from a market for government and railway debt to one where the primary focus was domestic corporate securities. One was that there was a marked decline in British lending to foreign borrowers (*Economist* 1937; Grant 1967: 154, 177; Thomas 1978: 24). Another was that wealthy investors increasingly began to shift their assets away from traditional standbys, such as government securities and land, so as to capture the potentially more lucrative returns offered by corporate equity (Armstrong 1990: 119–23). A third was that the families which owned successful private firms became interested in creating an 'exit option' and treated a move to the stock market as an opportunity to liquidate at least part of their investment (Hannah 1976: 57–8; Armstrong 1990: 118–19; Michie 1992: 115–16).

A final reason that the London Stock Exchange evolved into a market for domestic corporate securities was a demand for capital. Many of the country's larger business enterprises required funding to carry out expansion plans and acquisition activity and alternative mechanisms were not adequate for their needs (Thomas 1978: 24–5; Armstrong 1990: 119).[12] One reason suitable finance was unavailable was that it was not a major function of the banking system to provide working capital for industry, whether in the form of long-term loans or direct ownership of securities (Grant 1967: 172–5, 184–9; Thomas 1978: 24–5, 53, 189–90; Capie and Collins 1992: 50–9). Moreover, sources of private local finance that had been available prior to the First World War proved to be largely depleted thereafter (Best and Humphries 1986: 225–6; Michie 1990: 102–5, 110; Collins 1991: 34, 82–3).

5.2. *The Emergence of a Separation of Ownership and Control in UK Public Companies*

While the move towards the stock market by British companies can be described in a relatively straightforward manner, ascertaining when the Berle–Means corporation became predominant is a more challenging exercise. It might have been thought that a separation of ownership and control would have evolved as soon as it became common for UK firms to have publicly quoted shares. This, however, was not so. Though a move towards the stock market had begun by the end of the nineteenth century and went into full swing in the decades which followed, the professionalization of management associated with the Berle–Means corporation was slower to develop. The complicating factor was the continuation of family involvement. With many British public companies that joined the stock market, the entrepreneurs who founded the firms and their heirs retained a sizeable percentage of the shares and continued to play a prominent role in the making of middle and top-management decisions. A commitment to personal ways of management was therefore perpetuated (Chandler 1990: 240).

As we will see in a moment, those who have studied the evolution of the British business enterprise disagree on just how important family control was over time. Nevertheless, there can be little doubt that in the years prior to 1914 family dominance was very much the prevalent pattern (Chandler 1976: 32–40; Hannah 1976: 24). It was common practice for company 'promoters', as the intermediaries who organized conversions of private firms to publicly quoted companies, to encourage existing owners to retain a major interest. Also, even those firms which were well-established as public companies were often built around old family enterprises, which meant that the directors and senior executives were recruited principally from among the founding families. In sum, owners managed and managers owned (Chandler 1976: 40).

In the decades following the end of the First World War, existing patterns began to change and family control became less pervasive. It is not precisely clear, however, when matters had progressed sufficiently so it could be said that the Berle–Means corporation was dominant in the UK.[13] There is some evidence which suggests that the period prior to 1950 was pivotal. Contemporaries, for example, were aware of a trend towards increasingly dispersed share ownership. In 1929, the *Economist* newspaper investigated documents various well-known companies had filed with the UK companies registry and said the research 'suggested that the proprietors of British companies were, as a rule, a scattered body of small holders' (*Economist* 1929: 691). Eight years later, the same journal published an article entitled 'The Changing Capital Market' in which it was said:

> From choice or necessity, industrialists now deem it worth their while, in the periods when the market is active, to turn family businesses into public companies with widely diffused shareholdings. The public, for its own part, is prepared to buy and hold equities in undertakings about which shareholders know comparatively little and in whose management they cannot hope to have any decisive influence.... [I]t remains to be seen what will be the ultimate effect of the widening divorce between ownership and management in the case of medium-sized businesses.
>
> (*Economist* 1937: 1508)

Though the decline in owner control in the UK was sufficiently noteworthy to attract the attention of financial journalists, only one academic researcher gave serious attention to the issue during the period from the 1930s to the 1950s (Scott 1997: 79). This was P. Sargant Florence, an economist (1961; 1972: 213–41). He examined share ownership patterns in Britain's larger industrial and commercial companies at two different points in time, 1936 and 1951.

According to Florence, as of 1936, sixty-six companies were 'very large', meaning they had over £3 million of issued share capital (1961: 36). With these firms, in nine there was a majority shareholder and in thirteen the largest single vote-owner held 20–50 per cent of the total vote (ibid.: 70–1). By 1951, share ownership was more widely dispersed. Though more companies qualified as very large than was the case in 1936 (ninety-two), a smaller number had a majority shareholder (six) or a largest single shareholder with 20–50 per cent of the total vote (ten) (ibid.: 71). Moreover, the median percentage of votes held by the largest twenty shareholders in very large companies fell from 30 per cent in 1936 to 22 per cent in 1951 (ibid.: 72). Florence concluded on the basis of his evidence that a 'managerial evolution, if not revolution' was taking place and said that a trend towards a divorce between control and ownership 'was clear for very large companies' (ibid.: 186–7).

Analysis done subsequently by Leslie Hannah, a British business history expert, lends support to the idea that the foundations of American-style managerial capitalism were firmly established in the UK by the middle of the twentieth century. One point he makes is that British companies were being organized along increasingly sophisticated and complex lines prior to 1950 (1976*b*: 90–1, 123–4; 1980: 41–2, 60). Most notably, a substantial merger wave occurring during the 1920s and early 1930s served to increase the size of British companies, the number of multiunit enterprises and probably the degree of vertical integration (Hannah 1980: 60; Cassis 1997: 35–46). Indeed, prior to the Second World War, Britain was the European country where big business had reached its highest development (Cassis 1995: 216–17; 1997: 5, 33–4, 46, 231).

Hannah has also drawn attention to takeover bids to demonstrate that managerial enterprise had effectively displaced family control in Britain by the middle of the twentieth century (1974: 67–8; 1976*b*: 130–1, 149–50). He says that during the 1920s and 1930s it was generally not feasible for a bidder to by-pass the directors and appeal directly to the shareholders. This, in part, was because family domination of companies was commonplace.

Under such circumstances, family members had a de facto veto over any proposed bid for control. By the 1950s, however, the divorce of ownership and management had proceeded sufficiently to ensure that a wide range of quoted companies were vulnerable to takeover offers where the directors would otherwise have preferred not to enter into merger negotiations.

Hannah concedes that the transformation of British business had not progressed far enough by the middle of the twentieth century to displace founding or family directors from company boards. According to his own figures, 140 of the largest 200 British firms had family board members in 1930, as did 119 in 1948 (1980: 53). He argues, however, that the persistence of family names on the board did not mean that families exercised a dominant role in direction and management (ibid.: 53; 1991: 302; Cassis 1997: 158). Instead, family members were often present merely to represent their interests as minority shareholders. Others had seats on the board as the price of a merger agreement where their own firms had been absorbed. In such cases, according to Hannah, family influence was dwindling as the power of professional managers was growing.[14]

Despite what Florence and Hannah have said, it is in fact not clear whether a separation of ownership and control was well-established in the UK by the middle of the twentieth century. Empirical studies dealing with share ownership patterns in British companies during the mid-1970s illustrate this (Nyman and Silberston 1978; Scott and Griffe 1984: ch. 4; Scott 1985: 77–8). According to this research, of Britain's 200 or so largest firms, nearly half had an individual, institution or cohesive group which owned a stake of 10 per cent or more. Such evidence was sufficient to convince some that 'the managerial revolution heralded by Berle and Means in 1932 has probably not yet happened' (Francis 1980: 1).

Alfred Chandler, an eminent American business historian,[15] has also cast doubt on the extent to which the Berle–Means corporation was the paradigm in Britain by 1950. Chandler, who has written widely on both the United States and Britain, says that during the first half of the twentieth century the nature of industrial capitalism was considerably different in the two countries (1976; 1980*a*; 1991: ch. 7). In larger American companies, professionally trained, salaried executives made the key decisions and administered their firms through extensive impersonal hierarchies. In Britain, in contrast, a commitment to personal ways of management prevailed.

Chandler admits that large UK firms were hiring salaried managers on a regular basis by the middle of the twentieth century. Also, whenever family-owned firms moved to the stock market, the influence of the family was inevitably diminished to some degree. Still, Chandler maintains that administrative hierarchies in larger British companies remained, for the most part, primitive and unsophisticated. Moreover, many family owners successfully resisted losing personal control over the enterprises they had either created or inherited.[16] They were able to do this because selection to senior executive positions depended as much on private ties as on managerial competence.

Chandler argues that the prolonged survival of family domination in major British companies had seriously detrimental consequences for the country. Throughout much of the twentieth century, the UK's economic performance suffered in comparison to its main national rivals (Hall 1986: 266; Kennedy 1994: 6–10; Sanderson 1997). Chandler claims that the persistence of family involvement in corporate boardrooms contributed to Britain's relative decline. He asserts that the belated introduction of professionalized management made industrial capitalism in Britain less dynamic than it was in other major industrial countries, such as the US and Germany. Such 'managerial failure' in turn hindered Britain's economic progress and helped to ensure that the UK became a laggard (1980*a*: 410; 1990: 293–4, 591–2).

If the foundations of American-style managerial capitalism were not well-established in the UK by the middle of the twentieth century, when did the Berle–Means corporation emerge decisively as the paradigm? Chandler points to the 1970s, saying that during this decade managerial enterprise rapidly replaced personal and entrepreneurial capitalism (1976: 46, 49; Fitzgerald 1995: 48). To support this assertion, he cites hiring practices (1976: 46). By the 1970s, only a small percentage of directors had family connections with important shareholders, which suggests top executives were being selected primarily on the basis of their managerial qualifications (Perkin 1989: 301). Chandler also draws attention to the fact that UK companies were adopting on a wide scale the sort of complex hierarchical managerial structures which had been common in the USA for a considerable period of time (1976: 45–6, 49). The move towards an American format was not simply coincidental. By the early 1970s no less than twenty-two of Britain's hundred largest firms had employed American managerial consultants McKinsey and Company to provide guidance on corporate restructuring (Chandler 1976: 46; Perkin 1989: 300).

Research carried out by sociologist John Scott indicates that a shift towards greater 'outsider' ownership accompanied the transformation of managerial arrangements which was taking place. Following up on work he carried out covering the year 1976, he examined ownership patterns in the UK's 200 largest industrial companies and fifty largest financial businesses as of 1988 (Scott 1990; 1997: 83–4; on the 1976 material, see Scott and Griffe 1984; Scott 1985). According to Scott's 1988 data, of the 173 firms which were not state-owned, wholly owned subsidiaries or owned by depositors and policy holders (e.g. building societies and insurance companies), just over one in three had a shareholder owning more than 10 per cent of the equity (Scott 1990: 362, derived from table I).[17] In 1976, the equivalent ratio was almost one out of two (Scott 1985: 77, derived from table 15). Scott attributed this shift primarily to the decline of family control in UK companies (1990: 366–7; 1997: 89–90). The upshot is that while the key elements of American-style managerial capitalism may not have been well-established by the middle of the twentieth century in Britain, they were by the 1980s.

6. MARK ROE AND THE SEPARATION OF OWNERSHIP AND CONTROL IN THE UK

6.1. *Widely Dispersed Share Ownership and the Regulation of Financial Institutions*

Since we have examined in a chronological manner how the Berle–Means corporation came to play a prominent role in the UK, we can now assess whether Mark Roe's explanations for the dominance of this type of firm in the USA are persuasive in a different national context. As we have seen, a key theme in his writing is that the Berle–Means corporation was, at least in part, a product of a deeply ingrained popular mistrust of concentrated financial power. Roe has argued that American politicians, mindful of such mistrust, passed laws which deterred big financial institutions from taking a close interest in the activities of corporate executives. Such legislation in turn ensured that widely dispersed share ownership became the predominant pattern.

Given what Roe has said, one would expect to discover that in a jurisdiction where the government has taken a 'hands-off' approach towards firms offering financial services, the outcome would be different. If large financial institutions were not precluded by regulation from playing a full and active role in the governance of industrial and commercial enterprises, then substantial interdependence would presumably develop. This, however, was not the outcome in the UK.[18] The point can be illustrated most vividly by examining the activities of British banks.

Commercial deposit-taking or 'clearing' banks in Britain traditionally have not been closely involved in the process of supplying working capital to major industrial enterprises (Grant 1967: 172–5, 184–9; Thomas 1978: 24–5, 53, 189–90; Capie and Collins 1992: 50–9, 67). Their American counterparts have similarly shied away from developing close links with industry. Roe says that in the USA government regulations dictated this outcome (1994*b*: chs. 5 and 7). The situation was different, however, in the UK. For instance, though federal laws affecting American banks put a fault line between banking and industry, British banks were permitted to own shares in their customers so long as they were authorized by their corporate constitution to do so (Jacobs 1923: 579). Moreover, during the 1920s and 1930s, the Bank of England (acting as a de facto central bank) was cajoling clearing banks to help industrial firms which were struggling to succeed in a difficult economic environment (Best and Humphries 1986: 233–4; Capie and Collins 1992: 45, 55).[19]

If government policies did not deter banks from taking a close interest in the affairs of British companies, what caused them to shy away from such involvement? Financial resources were not a serious constraint. As a result of mergers and acquisitions, by 1920 a handful of London-based banks accounted for the vast majority of deposits and were considerably larger than their counterparts in other European countries (Collins 1991: 26–7, 37; Cassis 1997: 35). Such consolidation of financial resources meant that the theoretical potential existed for the banking community to develop close relations with companies seeking financial backing (Capie and Collins 1992: 35, 42).[20]

The key reason why UK banking institutions shied away from taking on responsibility for the operation and development of British companies was business policy (Collins 1991: 36, 41, 49, 69–71; Kynaston 1995: 455). Contemporary bankers were deeply concerned about the need to maintain public confidence in their ability to pay cash on demand, which served to create a strong bias in favour of liquidity. Influenced by such conservatism, banks carrying out corporate lending required that there be provision for repayment on a prompt basis. Furthermore, owning shares in companies was dismissed as an option on grounds of poor marketability and high risk. Establishing a substantial degree of interdependence with industry was therefore generally not considered a legitimate function of deposit banks.[21]

Banks were not the only British financial institutions which could have become closely involved with the ownership and control of UK companies but opted not to because of financial conservatism. Insurance companies constitute another example. They are currently important investors in British equities, having owned since the early 1980s approximately 20 per cent of the market (Black and Coffee 1994: 2008, 2010). Prior to the Second World War, however, insurance companies invested only a small fraction of their assets in UK equities (Grant 1967: 189–91; Supple 1970: 332, 347, 443, 527; Prais 1976: 117). Legal restrictions did not dictate this outcome since insurers were free to buy shares for investment purposes if they saw fit to do so (Roe 1994*b*: 201).[22] Instead, as with banks, insurance companies were reluctant to proceed because they were guided by a strong sense of prudence and caution (Supple 1970: 311; Kennedy 1994: 131–2). The upshot is that, while Roe has suggested that government regulation of financial institutions can affect the extent to which the Berle–Means corporation becomes dominant, in the UK politics was not pivotal.

6.2. *Social Democracy*

Developments in Britain cast doubt on another aspect of Roe's politically oriented analysis. Again, he has argued public companies with widely dispersed share ownership are less likely to play a key role in 'left-wing' social democracies than they are in 'right-wing' countries (Roe 2000). Roe has considered briefly in his work whether developments in the UK provide support for this thesis and he says they do (ibid.: 573–8). He accepts, without referring to any of the historical evidence to the contrary, Chandler's argument that American-style managerial capitalism only became predominant in Britain well after the middle of the twentieth century. He then proceeds to offer a political explanation for what happened. Roe says that the UK had all the basic institutions required for diffuse share ownership from the nineteenth century onwards, save one: a non-social democratic consensus (ibid.: 575–6). The final piece of the puzzle fell into place when Margaret Thatcher's right-wing Conservative administration came to power in 1979. After this, UK securities markets flourished and the transition to Berle–Means dominance became complete.

In order for Roe's version of events to be correct, it would seem that Britain must have had governments with a social democratic orientation prior to 1979. Otherwise, all of the elements required for the dominance of the Berle–Means corporation would have in fact been in place at some earlier point. Even a cursory examination of British history suggests that there is something amiss with this story.

Roe defines a social democracy as a nation whose government is deeply concerned about distributional issues, favours employees over investors and plays a large role in the economy (ibid.: 543). It is unlikely that the UK satisfied these criteria in the opening half of the twentieth century. The two quotes which follow illustrate this. Peter Hall, an historian from Harvard, said the following in an article published in 1986:

> . . . Britain had one of the most unconstrained market economies in the world. She was the first European nation to develop a self-regulating market system, and her markets have been free from state intervention to a degree that has no continental parallel. From the repeal of the Corn Laws in 1846 to the tariff measures of 1930s, Britain remained the principal defender of free trade in the international system. Her governments stayed with this policy throughout the Great Depression of 1876–90 when most other countries enacted substantial trade barriers; and during the 1930s, when

many countries employed public works programmes to secure reflation, Britain relied on the market system to revive the economy.

(1986: 268, references omitted)[23]

In 1956, Otto Kahn-Freund, Britain's pre-eminent academic labour lawyer of the time, characterized the nation's system of industrial-relations as follows:

There is, perhaps, no major country in the world in which the law has played a less significant role in the shaping of [labour–management] relations than in Great Britain and in which today the law and the legal profession have less to do with labour relations.

(1956: 44)[24]

Since the UK was in fact probably not a social democracy in the first few decades of the twentieth century, Roe's analysis of the British situation requires modification. There are two possible ways to do this. One is to focus on the historical evidence. Again, Roe accepts Chandler's argument that the key elements of American-style managerial capitalism were not in place in the UK by 1950. As we have seen, a plausible argument can be made that the Berle–Means corporation was in fact well-established in Britain by this time. Assuming this to be so, Roe would have made an error by relying on Chandler. On the other hand, his social democracy thesis would be vindicated: the move towards a separation of ownership and control in Britain would have occurred in a 'right-wing' political environment.

A second way of looking at events occurring prior to 1950 casts Roe's views concerning social democracy in a less favourable light. Assume that Chandler was correct and managerial capitalism was not well-established in Britain until after the middle of the twentieth century. Since the political conditions apparently were hospitable to the emergence of the Berle–Means corporation prior to this time, it would seem that ideological factors had little meaningful influence on events. The British evidence, then, would not substantiate Roe's social democracy explanation for the presence or absence of a separation of ownership and control.

While the UK was probably not a social democracy in the first half of the twentieth century, a plausible case can be made that the country took important strides in this direction between the end of the Second World War and Margaret Thatcher's rise to power in 1979. Again, according to Roe, a government which qualifies as a social democracy will be favourably disposed towards a redistribution of wealth in favour of the less well-off. The approach taken towards the taxation of income indicates that the UK met this test in the decades after the Second World War. During the 1960s and 1970s the top of rate of tax was usually 70 per cent or more and at certain points reached more than 90 per cent (Michie 1992: 123; Cheffins 1997: 704).[25]

With respect to employee relations, Roe's view is that a government which qualifies as a social democracy will favour workers over investors. The Labour Party took this approach when it was in office from 1964 to 1970 and 1974 to 1979. During these years, the British Parliament enacted various statutory measures designed to protect employees. These included laws which bolstered the bargaining power of unions, required employers to provide workers with notice prior to dismissal (or pay in lieu of notice) and allowed staff to claim lump-sum payments in the event of redundancy (i.e. dismissal where the employer ceased to have a business reason for the jobs in question) (Davies and Freedland 1993: 144–6, 385–6,

414–15). Moreover, a committee appointed by the Labour government recommended in 1975 that unions be given representation on company boards (Bullock Report 1977), but the party's defeat in the 1979 general election intervened before any legislation could be brought forward.

According to Roe, an additional trait of a social democracy is that the government plays an important role in the economy. In Britain, there was a dramatic expansion of state activity in this field between the end of the Second World War and Margaret Thatcher's election victory in 1979. Public expenditure as a share of GNP rose from 32 per cent in 1950 to 45 per cent in 1980 (Hall 1986: 267). An aggressive nationalization policy carried out by a Labour government between 1945 and 1951 meant that state-owned enterprises accounted for approximately 10 per cent of Britain's GNP for the next three decades (Thomas 1978: 276–7; Hannah 1994: 171, 174, 182). Throughout the 1960s and 1970s, Labour and Conservative administrations both sought to enlist the cooperation of employers and unions as participants in government sponsored schemes designed to suppress wage costs and reduce industrial conflict (Krieger 1987: 39–40; Davies and Freedland 1993: 141, 164–77, 349, 365–6). The Labour government of 1964 to 1970, inspired by developments in France, experimented with detailed economic planning (Hall 1986: 276; Davies and Freedland 1993: 141–3, 268). Moreover, Labour, when it was elected to power in 1974, was intent on moving progressively towards a socialist relationship between the state and the market but its ability to follow up was compromised considerably by an economic crisis prompted by a dramatic rise in oil prices (Cox and Sanderson 1997*a*: 28–30).

If Britain was in fact a social democracy between the end of the Second World War and 1979, this causes some problems for Roe's analysis of events in the UK. Roe again accepts Chandler's view that USA-style managerial capitalism was not well established in Britain prior to the middle of the twentieth century. Chandler has conceded, though, that by the 1970s managerial enterprise was rapidly replacing the personal and entrepreneurial version of corporate governance that had formerly been predominant (1976: 46, 49).[26] Assuming this is correct, it would mean that the Berle–Means corporation was achieving predominant status during a period when left-wing ideology was influential in the UK. An historical pattern of this nature directly contradicts Roe's social democracy thesis.

After Margaret Thatcher's right-wing Conservative administration came to power, many of the policies which arguably had made Britain a social democracy were dismantled (Cox and Sanderson 1997: 32–41; Great Debate 1996). The growth of public expenditure as a share of GNP was halted and even reversed slightly. Privatization took place in a variety of important nationalized industries (e.g. telecoms, airways, electricity, water, and gas). The top marginal income tax rate was cut significantly (by the end of the 1980s it was 40 per cent). Successive rounds of industrial-relations laws weakened substantially the legal protections offered to unions, which helped to foster a dramatic reduction in their power and influence.

Events occurring after 1979 in the UK can be interpreted in a manner which lends support to Roe's thesis that the Berle–Means corporation is more likely to thrive in a 'right-wing' country than a 'left-wing' social democracy. As we have seen, a shift towards more widely dispersed share ownership occurred between 1976 and 1988. Also, as a percentage of GDP, the market capitalization of the UK stock market doubled between 1975 and 1985

(Roe 2000: 39, n. 88). It therefore is fair to say, consistent with what Roe has argued, that features associated with Britain's outsider/arm's-length system of corporate governance became more pronounced after Margaret Thatcher came to power. Still, since events occurring prior to 1979 do not demonstrate any sort of strong link between the presence or absence of social democracy and the emergence of the features associated with the Berle–Means corporation, overall the evidence from the UK tends to refute rather than support what Roe has had to say.

7. CONCLUSION

Mark Roe, by arguing that dominance of the Berle–Means corporation in the United States was a politically and historically contingent outcome, has had a pivotal influence on corporate law scholarship. Before he began writing about the origins of the widely held public company, interested observers implicitly agreed that fragmented ownership was economically inevitable in major business enterprises. As a result of Roe's intellectual contribution, this proposition can no longer be taken for granted. Indeed, his work has motivated various leading corporate law academics to offer explanations why the central feature of American corporate governance is a separation of ownership and control.

Britain's system of corporate governance is uniquely similar to that which exists in the USA. As a result, examining events in Britain should provide insights for those seeking to account for the dominance of the widely held company in America. When one is assessing the lessons to be derived from developments in the UK, allowances need to be made for historical uncertainties. Most notably, it is not entirely clear whether a separation of ownership and control was well-established by the middle of the twentieth century. Regardless, it is fair to say that developments in Britain do not appear to do very much to validate Mark Roe's politically oriented analysis of corporate governance. Business policy, not populist sentiment, caused banks and insurance companies to shy away from seeking close involvement with British public companies. There also does not seem to be much correlation between the fluctuating fortunes of social democracy in the UK and the emergence of Britain's 'outsider/arm's-length' system of corporate governance.

Since Roe's political/path dependency analysis does not provide a fully satisfactory explanation for the emergence of the Berle–Means corporation in the UK, this leads one to wonder whether another theory offers greater promise. One possibility is that developments in Britain can be characterized in a manner consistent with a story of Darwinian corporate struggle. As we have seen, until Mark Roe described the Berle–Means corporation as a path-dependent artefact, the accepted orthodoxy was that the publicly quoted corporation with widely held shares and professional management represented the evolutionary pinnacle.

The description of British business history provided by business historian Alfred Chandler correlates with this Darwinian story. As we have seen, he argues that managerial enterprise was not well-established in Britain until after the Second World War. This failure to develop organizational capabilities comparable to foreign competitors allegedly was a fatal mistake (Chandler 1980*a*: 410; 1990: 293–4, 591–2). Profitable opportunities were lost, British industry fell behind and the country's overall economic performance was chronically poor as compared to other major industrial nations throughout much of the twentieth century. The

Berle–Means corporation ultimately did become dominant in the UK. Still, delay meant that market forces imposed a harsh and inevitable penalty.

An additional hypothesis can potentially be relied on to account for the 'outsider/arm's-length' system of corporate governance which currently prevails in the UK. This is that the law matters. Britain (Scotland excepted) can be categorized as a 'common law' jurisdiction since it continues to follow judicially oriented English legal traditions.[27] As compared with 'civil law' jurisdictions (those following a scholar- and legislator-made tradition dating back to Roman law), common law countries are significantly more protective of minority shareholders (La Porta *et al.* 1998: 1117–34). Common law countries also have larger and more broadly based capital markets than civil law jurisdictions and a significantly higher fraction of widely held firms (La Porta 1997: 1137, 1142–6). An inference one can draw from these trends is that patterns of ownership and control are a consequence of the legal protection offered to minority shareholders (Coffee 1999: 643–4, 647–9, 657–60, 697–9, 704–7; La Porta *et al.* 1999: 496–8, 511–13). Perhaps, then, attributes of the legal regime governing UK companies explain why the Berle–Means firm ultimately became dominant.

Though the Darwinian account of industrial capitalism and the 'law matters' story may offer insights which are relevant in the British context, neither version of events should simply be accepted at face value. For instance, among British business historians, Alfred Chandler's analysis of managerial failure in the UK has been the subject of scepticism and criticism (Fitzgerald 1995: 32). Also, with respect to protection of minority shareholders, UK company law has not necessarily been particularly forthcoming. Leonard Sealy, a leading British company law academic, said in a series of lectures published in 1984:

> ...the courts have made it very difficult, and in many cases impossible, for shareholders with grievances—sometimes, shareholders who are the victims of very real injustices—to obtain a legal remedy.
>
> (1984: 53)

The upshot is that at present it is not possible to account in a fully satisfactory manner for the rise of Berle–Means corporation in the UK. Since from a corporate governance perspective the USA has more in common with Britain than it does with other major industrial nations, further investigation of the topic should be of interest to those who study corporate behaviour in both jurisdictions.

POSTSCRIPT

Mark Roe's contribution to this volume is based on a draft paper he circulated via the Social Science Research Network (SSRN) in 1999 (Roe 1999).[28] In Roe's 1999 draft, his analysis of the UK was very brief and he observed that Britain illustrated well his social democracy thesis (Roe 1999: 29–30). In the chapter published in this volume, Roe's treatment is quite different. He examines the British situation in some detail and concedes that '(t)he United Kingdom would seem the hardest case for political theory here...'(Chapter 5, this volume).

To address the difficulties Britain potentially poses for his social democracy hypothesis, Roe essentially offers a 'deep freeze' version of events. According to him, Britain had strong securities markets prior to the Second World War but social democracy then intervened. The existing institutional structure had 'staying power' but left-wing ideology meant that until 1979 '(s)ecurities development and separation were slow, or perhaps non-existent' (Chapter 5, this volume, n. 33). Frantic Thatcher-driven ownership dispersion then followed.

It is very much open to question whether corporate Britain experienced between 1945 and 1979 the social democratic 'deep freeze' that Roe hypothesizes. Instead, contrary to what he suggests (ibid.), there is plenty of secondary evidence which suggests that important changes were taking place. For instance, as is discussed earlier in this chapter, ownership dispersion evolved sufficiently during the 1950s and 1960s to create suitable conditions for hostile takeover bids. Moreover, according to a historical survey of British industrial entrepreneurship and management published in 1978, '(i)n the post-1945 period there has been considerable discussion of the democratisation of company holdings (and) ... this increasing democratisation has clearly involved increasing separation of ownership and control' (Payne 1978: 221). A distinguished business historian subsequently offered a similar verdict, saying:

> In the postwar world the structure of British business changed radically. Family firms and family directors progressively disappeared off the corporate scene. By 1970 it would make little sense to talk of British personal capitalism.
>
> (Jones 1997: 118)

Ironically, certain left-wing policies adopted between 1945 to 1979 may have helped to foster the move away from traditional ownership structures (Cheffins 2001: 106). For example, after Labour increased death duties in 1949, large shareholders in family-owned companies often felt obliged to sell some of their shares to meet tax obligations. Such pressures probably encouraged families to go public, thus accelerating the dispersion of share ownership.

As Roe (Chapter 5, this volume, n. 33) observes, statistical data is not readily available that indicates whether Britain's pattern of ownership and control changed substantially between 1945 and 1979. Moreover, as he notes, I have not spent the time seeking to uncover the relevant primary evidence. Nevertheless, subsequent to the 1999 conference for which I drafted this chapter, I have followed up on various points I raise in the main text.

For instance, the analysis of financial institutions in my chapter focuses on UK banks. Elsewhere, I have extended my analysis to encompass the financial institutions that currently own equity in UK publicly quoted companies (pension funds, insurance companies, unit trusts, and investment trusts) (Cheffins 2001*b*: 103–4). The general lesson seems the same for banks: laws governing financial institutions did not have a pivotal influence on the UK's system of ownership and control. Again, in other words, the British experience is inconsistent with Roe's thesis that financial services regulation helps to dictate whether the Berle–Means corporation will become pre-eminent.

In another respect, additional work I have carried out lends support to Roe's analysis of the situation in Britain. I speculate in the conclusion to my chapter in this volume that the experience in the UK is inconsistent with the thesis that patterns of ownership and control are a consequent of the legal protection offered to minority shareholders. Roe agrees, saying that 'the UK also seems to fit badly with a law-driven theory' (Chapter 5, this volume). In another paper, I have considered the UK experience in detail and argued that British corporate law did not do a great deal to offer a 'protective environment' for minority shareholders (Cheffins 2001*a*). Jack Coffee, in his chapter in this volume, largely concurs with this assessment (Chapter 4, this volume). Correspondingly, the law seemingly did not provide the foundation for the dominance of the Berle–Means corporation in Britain.

The fact that Roe specifically addresses the UK experience in his chapter in this volume and Coffee does likewise illustrates that there is intellectual curiosity concerning developments in Britain. This bears out a point that I make in the conclusion to my chapter, which is that UK history can potentially offer lessons for those who study corporate behaviour. The conflicting interpretations advanced in the papers published in this volume suggests inferences currently need to be drawn with caution. It remains to be seen whether further investigation of the British experience will resolve open issues and yield clear lessons concerning the status of the Berle–Means corporation in the UK (and elsewhere).

Notes

1. Others have made the same point (e.g. Grundfest 1990), but Roe's work has been the dominant influence in the field (Coffee 1999: 643, n. 4).
2. This does not mean that the USA and the UK are identical. Some important differences that exist are discussed *infra*. For discussion of the difficulties associated with 'lumping or splitting' countries for analytical purposes, see Cassis 1997: 236–7.
3. On the prevailing orthodoxy, see Roe 1994*b*: ch. 1; Mark 1995: 973–4; Gilson 1996: 330–1.
4. Institutional ownership exceeds 60 per cent in Britain (Monks and Minow 1995: 303; Hampel Report 1998: para. 5.1).
5. There is some evidence which suggests, however, that a shift towards the Anglo-American corporate governance pattern may be taking place (e.g. Coffee 1999: 663–7, 671–2).
6. On family control in public companies in Europe, see Berglöf (1997*b*: 99–101) and Thomsen and Pedersen (1996: 150–2). In Japan, for historical reasons, family ownership of large business enterprises is rare (Scott 1997: 187–8).
7. There is anecdotal evidence which suggests that the cross-ownership networks that prevail in Japan are beginning to fall apart (e.g. *Economist* 1999).
8. For critical evaluations of the received wisdom on the 'shareholder primacy norm', see Grantham 1998; Smith 1998.
9. For a contrary view on the situation in Japan, see Kaplan and Ramseyer, 1996.
10. The number fell subsequently as a result of merger activity (Prais 1976: 90).
11. Some of the funds raised would have taken the form of debt rather than equity.
12. Michie (1992: 101, 125–7) and Cassis (1997: 181, 183) make the same point but note that retained income remained the principal source of industrial finance throughout for most companies.
13. Part of the problem is insufficient evidence (Hannah 1980: 52; Chandler 1990: 628; Scott 1997: 79–80).
14. Hannah concedes, however, that managerial hierarchies in British firms were not as deep, well-trained or professional as those in the US (1991: 301).
15. On the importance of Chandler's contribution to modern business history, see Hannah 1991: 297; Supple 1991: 500–4, 507, 513; Bruland 1998*a*: 11–12.

16. Contemporaries remarked upon the reluctance of family owners to give up control (Hannah 1976: 128–9).
17. According to Scott, all of the firms that did not have a shareholder owning more than 10 per cent of the shares were controlled by a 'constellation of interests'. He says such a 'constellation' exists when the largest twenty shareholders hold more than 10 per cent of the equity (1990: 362).
18. Roe has recognized this point and addresses it briefly in 1994*b*: 201.
19. The Bank of England was nationalized in 1946 and then took on officially the central bank role. For a different appraisal of the Bank of England's attitude towards bank involvement in corporate finance, see Roe 1994*b*: 201.
20. For a contrasting view on the status of UK banks at the relevant time, see Black and Coffee 1994: 2066.
21. The general stance apparently is little different today (Charkham 1994: 299–300; Hutton 1995: 149), though Bank of England policies also influence the approach banks take towards industrial finance (Prowse 1995: 11–12).
22. For additional background on regulation of the financial status of insurance companies in the early decades of the twentieth century, see Assurance Companies Act 1909, 9 Edw. 7, c. 49, discussed by Bateman 1923: 5–12; Welford 1932: 18–22.
23. See also Kennedy 1994: 3 ('Victorian Britain came perhaps as close as any society has ever done to approaching the ideal of economic laissez-faire.').
24. See further Davies and Freedland 1993: ch. 2, who essentially quote Kahn-Freund and endorse his characterization of the situation.
25. The trend towards higher marginal tax rates was established in earlier decades but became more pronounced during and after the Second World War (Michie 1992: 120, 123; McKibbin 1998: 38, 41).
26. Roe, despite relying on Chandler's work to support his analysis of developments in the UK, does not acknowledge that important changes may have been taking place in the 1970s (2000: 574).
27. Scotland is a follower of the civil law tradition, but UK companies legislation applies there (Davies 1997*a*: 8, n. 26).
28. Roe (1999) is no longer available on SSRN. According to SSRN archive (http://papers.ssrn.com/so13/DisplayAbstractsSearch.cfm) the paper upon which Roe's chapter in this volume is based was posted in June 1999. The paper currently available for download, however, is a revised version, dated January 2000 (Roe 2000). The Roe (1999) paper is not cited in the main body of my chapter because I revised my paper in February 2000 and substituted references to Roe (2000). I submitted the revised paper to the editors for publication and, save for the postscript, my chapter has not been updated since. It is for this reason that the sources have a somewhat dated quality.

References

Adams, M. (1999). Cross holdings in Germany. *Journal of Institutional and Theoretical Economics* 155: 80.

Armstrong, J. (1990). The rise and fall of the company promoter and the financing of British industry. In J.-J. van Helten and Y. Cassis (ed.), *Capitalism in a Mature Economy: Financial Institutions, Capital Exports and British Industry, 1870–1939*. Aldershot: Edward Elgar.

Bateman, R. A. (1923). *Bunyon's Law of Fire Insurance*, 7th edn. London: C. & E. Layton.

Berglöf, E. (1997*a*). A note on the typology of financial systems. In K. J. Hopt and E. Wymeersch (ed.), *Comparative Corporate Governance: Essays and Materials*. Berlin: Walter de Gruyter.

—— (1997*b*). Reforming corporate governance: Redirecting the European agenda. *Economic Policy* 24: 93.

Berle, A. and Means, G. (1932). *The Modern Corporation and Private Property*. New York: Macmillan.

Best, M. H., and Humphries, J. (1986). The City and industrial decline. In B. Elbaum and W. Lazonick (ed.), *The Decline of the British Economy*. Oxford: Clarendon Press.

Black, B. S., and Coffee, J. C. (1994). Hail Britannia?: Institutional investor behavior under limited regulation. *Michigan Law Review* 92: 1997.

Bolkestein, F. (1999). The high road that leads out of the low countries. *Economist* (UK edition). 22 May, 115.

Bruland, K. (1998). Introduction. In K. Bruland and P. O'Brien (ed.), (1998). *From Family Firms to Corporate Capitalism: Essays in Business and Industrial History in Honour of Peter Mathias*. Oxford: Clarendon Press.

Bullock Report (1977). Report of the committee of inquiry on industrial democracy (Lord Bullock, chair), Cmnd. Paper 6706. London: HMSO.

Butler, H. N. (1989). The contractual theory of the corporation. *George Mason University Law Review* 11: 99.

Capie, F., and Collins, M. (1992). *Have the Banks Failed British Industry? An Historical Survey of Bank/Industry Relations in Britain, 1870–1990*. London: Institute of Economic Affairs.

Cary, W. L. (1974). Federalism and corporate law: Reflections upon Delaware. *Yale Law Journal* 83: 663.

Cassis, Y. (1990). British finance: Success and controversy. In J.-J. van Helten and Y. Cassis (ed.), *Capitalism in a Mature Economy: Financial Institutions, Capital Exports and British Industry, 1870–1939*. Aldershot: Edward Elgar.

——(1995). Big business in Britain and France, 1890–1990. In Y. Cassis *et al.* (ed.) (1995), *Management and Business in Britain and France: The Age of the Corporate Economy*. Oxford: Clarendon Press, p. 214.

——(1997). *Big Business: The European Experience in the Twentieth Century*. Oxford: Oxford University Press.

Chandler, A. D. (1976). The development of modern management structure in the US and the UK. In L. Hannah (ed.), *Management Strategy and Business Development: An Historical and Comparative Study*. London: Macmillan, p. 24.

——(1980). The growth of the transnational industrial firm in the United States and the United Kingdom: A comparative analysis. *Economic History Review* 33: 396.

——(1990). *Scale and Scope: The Dynamics of Industrial Capitalism*. Cambridge, MA: Changing Capital (1937). The Changing Capital Market. *Economist*, 507. Belknap Press.

Charkham, J. (1994). *Keeping Good Company: A Study of Corporate Governance in Five Countries*. Oxford: Clarendon Press.

Cheffins, B. R. (1997). *Company Law: Theory, Structure and Operation*. Oxford: Clarendon Press.

——(1998*a*). Michaud v. National Bank of Canada and Canadian Corporate Governance: A 'Victory' for Shareholder Rights? *Canadian Business Law Journal* 30: 20.

——(1998*b*). Trust, loyalty and cooperation in the business community: Is regulation required? B. A. K. Rider (ed.) (1998), *The Realm of Company Law: A Collection of Papers in Honour of Professor Leonard Sealy*. London: Kluwer Law International.

——(2001*a*). Does law matter? The separation of ownership and control. *Journal of Legal Studies* 30: 459.

——(2001*b*). History and the global governance revolution. *Business History* 43: 87.

Coffee, J. C. (1994). The SEC and the institutional investor: A half-time report. *Cardozo Law Review* 15: 837.

——(1999). The future as history: Prospects for global convergence in corporate governance and its implications. *Northwestern University Law Review* 93: 641.

Collins, M. (1991). *Banks and Industrial Finance in Britain 1800–1939*. London: Macmillan Education.
Cox, A., and Sanderson, J. (1997). The political economy of Britain since 1939. In A. Cox *et al.* (ed.), *The Political Economy of Modern Britain*. Cheltenham, UK: Edward Elgar.
Cunningham, L. A. (1999). Commonalties and prescriptions in the vertical dimension of global corporate governance. *Cornell Law Review* 84: 1133.
Daniels, R. J., and MacIntosh J. G. (1991). Toward a Distinctive Corporate Law Regime. *Osgoode Hall Law Journal* 29: 863.
Davies, P. L., and Freedland, M. (1993). *Labour Legislation and Public Policy: A Contemporary History*. Oxford: Clarendon.
Davies, P. L. (1997*a*). *Gower's Principles of Modern Company Law*, 6th edn. London: Sweet & Maxwell.
——(1997*b*). Institutional investors as corporate monitors in the UK. In K. J. Hopt and E. Wymeersch (ed.) (1997), *Comparative Corporate Governance: Essays and Materials*. Berlin: Walter de Gruyter.
Easterbrook, F. H., and Fischel, D. R. (1991). *The Economic Structure of Corporate Law*. Cambridge, MA: Harvard University Press.
——(1997). International corporate differences: Markets or law? *Journal of Applied Corporate Finance* 9: 23.
Economist (1929). Shareholders and control. 30 March, 691.
——(1996). The great debate: A survey of Britain's new politics. 21 September, 1.
——(USA edition) (1996). LeDéfi Américan, again. 13 July, 21.
——(1999). Mindset. 23 Oct., 117.
Fitzgerald, R. (1995). Ownership, organization, and management: British business and the branded consumer goods industries. In Y. Cassis *et al.* (ed.), *Management and Business in Britain and France: The Age of the Corporate Economy*. Oxford: Clarendon Press.
Florence, P. S. (1961). *Ownership, Control and Success of Large Companies: An Analysis of English Industrial Structure and Policy 1936–1951*. London: Sweet & Maxwell.
——(1972). *The Logic of British and American Industry: A Realistic Analysis of Economic Structure and Government*. London: Routledge & Kegan Paul.
Fox, M. A., and Walker, G. R. (1997). Sharemarket ownership, control and regulatory choice. *Australian Journal of Corporate Law* 8: 127.
Francis, A. (1980). Families, firms and finance capital: The development of UK industrial firms with particular reference to their ownership and control. *British Journal of Sociology* 14: 1.
Franks, J., and Mayer, C. (1997). Corporate ownership and control in the UK, Germany, and France. In D. H. Chew (ed.), *Studies in International Corporate Finance and Governance Systems: A Comparison of the US, Japan, and Europe*. New York: Oxford University Press.
Gilbert, L. D. (1956). *Dividends and Democracy*. Larchmont, NY: American Research Council.
Gilson, R. J. (1996). Corporate governance and economic efficiency: When do institutions matter? *Washington University Law Quarterly* 74: 327.
Goergen, M. (1998). *Corporate Governance and Financial Performance: A Study of German and UK Initial Public Offerings*. Cheltenham, UK: Edward Elgar.
Grant, A. T. K. (1967). *A Study of the Capital Market in Britain from 1919–1936*, 2nd edn. London: Cass.
Grantham, R. (1998). The doctrinal basis of the rights of company shareholders. *Cambridge Law Journal* 57: 554.
Grundfest, J. A. (1990). Subordination of American capital. *Journal of Financial Economics* 27: 89.
Hall, P. A., (1986). The state and economic decline. In B. Elbaum and W. Lazonick (ed.), *The Decline of the British Economy*. Oxford: Clarendon Press.
Hampel Report (1998). Report of the committee on corporate governance (chaired by Sir Ronald Hampel). London: Gee Press.

Hannah, L. (1974). Takeover bids in Britain before 1950: An exercise in business 'Pre-History'. *Business History* 16: 65.

——(1976). *The Rise of the Corporate Economy*, 2nd edn. London: Methuen.

Hannah, L. (1980). Visible and invisible hands in Great Britain. In A. D. Chandler and H. Daems (ed.), *Managerial Hierarchies: Comparative Perspectives on the Rise of the Modern Industrial Enterprise.* Cambridge, MA: Harvard University Press.

——(1991). Scale and scope: Towards a European visible hand? *Business History* 33: 297.

——(1994). The economic consequences of the state ownership of industry. In R. Floud and D. McCloskey (ed.), *The Economic History of Britain since 1700*, Volume 3: *1939–1992*, 2nd edn. Cambridge: Cambridge University Press.

Hopt, K. J. (1994). Labor representation on corporate boards: Impacts and problems for corporate governance and economic integration in Europe. *International Review of Law and Economics* 14: 203.

Hoshi, T. (1998). Japanese corporate governance as a system. In K. J. Hopt *et al.* (ed.), *Comparative Corporate Governance: The State of the Art and Emerging Research.* Oxford: Clarendon Press.

Hutton, W. (1995). *The State We're In.* London: Johnathan Cape.

Jacobs, H. (1923). *Grant on the Law Relating to Bankers and Banking Companies.* London: Butterworths.

Jones, G. (1997). Big business, management, and competitiveness in twentieth-century Britain. In A. D. Chandler *et al.* (ed.), *Big Business and the Wealth of Nations.* Cambridge, MA: Belknap Press.

Kahn-Freund, O. (1956). Legal framework. In A. Flanders and H. Clegg (ed.), *The System of Industrial Relations in Britain.* Oxford: Blackwell.

Kaplan, S. N. (1997). Corporate governance and corporate performance: A comparison of Japan, Germany, and the US. *Journal of Applied Corporate Finance* 9: 86.

Kaplan, S. N., and Ramseyer, M. J. (1996). Those Japanese firms with their disdain for shareholders: Another fable for the academy. *Washington University Law Quarterly* 74: 403.

Kennedy, W. P. (1994). *Industrial Structure, Capital Markets and the Origins of British Economic Decline.* Cambridge: Cambridge University Press.

Kynaston, D. (1995). *The City of London*, Volume II: *Golden Years 1890–1914.* Oxford: Oxford University Press.

Krieger, J. (1987). The United Kingdom: Symbiosis or Division. In G. C. Lodge and E. F. Vogel (ed.), *Ideology and National Competitiveness: An Analysis of Nine Countries.* Boston: Harvard Business School Press.

La Porta, R. *et al.* (1997). Legal determinants of external finance. *Journal of Finance* 52: 1131.

——(1998). Law and finance. *Journal of Political Economy* 106: 1113.

——(1999). Corporate ownership around the world. *Journal of Finance* 54: 491.

Lowenstein, L. (1991). *Sense and Nonsense in Corporate Finance.* Reading, MA: Addison-Wesley.

Macey, J. R., and Miller, G. P. (1997). Universal banks are not the answer to America's corporate governance 'problem': A look at Germany, Japan, and the US. *Journal of Applied Corporate Finance* 9: 57.

Mark, G. A. (1995). Realms of choice: Finance capitalism and corporate governance. *Columbia Law Review* 95: 969.

Mayer, C. (1997). The City and corporate performance: condemned or exonerated?. *Cambridge Journal of Economics* 21: 291.

McKibbin, R. (1998). *Classes and Culture: England 1918–1951.* Oxford: Oxford University Press.

Michie, R. C. (1990). The Stock Exchange and the British economy, 1870–1939. In J.-J. van Helten and Y. Cassis (ed.), *Capitalism in a Mature Economy: Financial Institutions, Capital Exports and British Industry, 1870–1939.* Aldershot: Edward Elgar.

——(1992). *The City of London: Continuity and Change, 1850–1990.* London: Macmillan Academic and Professional.

Miller, M. H. (1994). Is American corporate governance fatally flawed?. In D. H. Chew (ed.) (1997), *Studies in International Corporate Finance and Governance Systems: A Comparison of the US, Japan, and Europe.* New York: Oxford University Press.

Moerland, P. W. (1995). Alternative disciplinary mechanisms in different corporate systems. *Journal of Economic Behavior and Organization* 26: 17.

Monks, R. A. G., and Minow, N. (1995). *Corporate Governance.* Cambridge, MA: Blackwell.

Morck, R. K. (1996). On the economics of concentrated ownership. *Canadian Business Law Journal* 26: 63.

Nyman, S., and Silberston, A. (1978). The ownership and control of industry. Oxford Economic Papers, NS 30: 74.

Parkinson, J. E. (1993). *Corporate Power and Responsibility: Issues in the Theory of Company Law.* Oxford: Oxford University Press.

Perkin, H. (1989). *The Rise of Professional Society: England Since 1880.* London: Routledge.

Prais, S. J. (1976). *The Evolution of Giant Firms in Britain: A Study of the Growth of Concentration in Manufacturing Industry in Britain 1909–70.* Cambridge: Cambridge University Press.

Prigge, S. (1998). A survey of German corporate governance. In K. J. Hopt *et al.* (ed.), *Comparative Corporate Governance: The State of the Art and Emerging Research.* Oxford: Clarendon Press.

Prowse, S. (1995). Corporate governance in an international perspective: A survey of corporate control mechanisms among large firms in the US, UK, Japan and Germany. *Financial Markets, Institutions and Instruments* 4: 1.

Ramsay, I. M., and Blair, M. (1993). Ownership concentration, institutional investment and corporate governance: An empirical investigation of 100 Australian companies. *Melbourne University Law Review* 19: 153.

Rao, P. S., and Lee-Sing, C. R. (1995). Governance structure, corporate decision-making and firm performance in North America. In R. J. Daniels and R. Morck (ed.), *Corporate Decision-making in Canada.* Calgary: University of Calgary Press.

Roe, M. J. (1990). Political and legal restraints on ownership and control of public companies. *Journal of Financial Economics* 27: 7.

——(1994*a*). German 'populism' and the large public corporation. *International Review of Law and Economics* 14: 187.

——(1994*b*). *Strong Managers, Weak Owners: The Political Roots of American Corporate Finance.* Princeton, NJ: Princeton University Press.

——(1997). The political roots of American corporate finance. *Journal of Applied Corporate Finance* 9(4): 8.

——(1999). Political preconditions to separating ownership from corporate control. The incompatibility of the American public firm with social democracy (unpublished working paper).

——(2000). Political preconditions to separating ownership from corporate control.

Ruder, D. S. (1965). Public obligations of private corporations. *University of Pennsylvania Law Review* 114: 209.

Sanderson, J. (1997). Britain in decline? A statistical survey of Britain's relative economic performance since 1950. In A. Cox *et al.* (ed.), *The Political Economy of Modern Britain.* Cheltenham, UK: Edward Elgar.

Scott, J., and Griffe, C. (1984). *Directors of Industry: The British Corporate Network 1904–76.* Cambridge: Polity Press.

Scott, J., (1985). *Corporations, Classes and Capitalism,* 2nd edn. London: Hutchinson.

——(1990). Corporate control and corporate rule: Britain in an international perspective. *British Journal of Sociology* 41: 351.

——(1997). *Corporate Business and Capitalist Classes.* Oxford: Oxford University Press.

Sealy, L. S. (1984). *Company Law and Commercial Reality.* London: Sweet & Maxwell.

Shleifer, A., and Vishny, R. W. (1997). A survey of corporate governance. *Journal of Finance* 52: 737.

Smith, D. G. (1996). Corporate governance and managerial incompetence: Lessons from Kmart. *North Carolina Law Review* 74: 1037.

——(1998). The shareholder primacy norm. *Journal of Corporate Law* 23: 277.

Stapledon, G. P. (1996). *Institutional Shareholders and Corporate Governance.* Oxford: Clarendon Press.

Supple, B. (1970). *The Royal Exchange Assurance: A History of British Insurance 1720–1970.* Cambridge: Cambridge University Press.

——(1991). Scale and scope: Alfred Chandler and the dynamics of industrial capitalism. *Economic History Review* 44: 500.

Thomas, W. A. (1978). *The Finance of British Industry.* London: Methuen.

Thomsen, S. and Pedersen, T. (1996). Nationality and ownership structures: The 100 largest companies in six European nations. *Management International Review* 36: 149.

Waters, R. (1998). Large investors' power wanes. *Financial Times,* 12 June, 25.

Welford, A. W. B. (1932). *The Law Relating to Accident Insurance,* 2nd edn. London: Butterworth.

Wymeersch, E. (1998). A status report on corporate governance rules and practices in some continental European states. In K. J. Hopt *et al.* (ed.), *Comparative Corporate Governance: The State of the Art and Emerging Research.* Oxford: Clarendon Press.

PART II

HARMONIZATION AND DIVERSITY OF GOVERNANCE PRINCIPLES IN EUROPE

7

Common Principles of Corporate Governance in Europe?

KLAUS J. HOPT

1. INTRODUCTION: THE CONVERGENCE OF THE COMMON LAW AND THE CIVIL LAW IN THE FIELD OF CORPORATE AND CAPITAL MARKET LAW

The convergence of the common law and the civil law is an old dream—or nightmare—an outlook that depends less on which side of the Channel or the ocean the idea is held, and more on how international the outlook of the academic or practitioner is. Academics who have studied abroad or are even comparativists[1] look at this differently than those who are firmly and exclusively embedded in their own national law and its legal subtleties. The same is true for the practitioners both in the legal profession and the enterprises, though a growing number of them are exposed professionally to European law and to international legal issues.[2] Sometimes one has the impression of witnessing a battle in which the adversaries are labelled as 'ahistoric' and 'unpatriotic' or else 'backward-minded' or 'outright provincial'. This is by no means just a difference of opinion; though it is seldom admitted, there are turfs to defend for which professional investment, knowledge, and language skill (or lack of it) count.

While a commercial or corporate lawyer may find this amusing, he or she is more interested in facts, and these facts differ considerably depending on the legal field one looks at. This is obvious for fields like family or inheritance law, which remain national domains untouched by European harmonization. But also in the law of goods, tangible—and even more so intangible—concepts of common law and civil law are very different. As an example, consider credit securities and compare the British floating charge and the German 'Sicherungsübereignung'.[3] Still, international legal practice finds its way. In other fields, famous inimical brethren are, for example, 'Trust und Treuhand', the title of a well-known book by my colleague, Kötz, at the Max Planck Institute.[4] Yet as irreconcilable as both concepts seem to appear, there are parallel problems and developments.[5] In the field of corporate and capital law, things move quicker due to market forces and economic actors who are

An earlier English version can be found in: B. S. Markesinis (ed.) (2000), *The Clifford Chance Millenium Lectures. The Coming Together of the Common Law and the Civil Law*. Oxford: Hart, p. 105.

facing competition on a transnational level, but also because of political factors which further harmonization. This is also true for corporate governance, where there are strong trends towards the coming together of Anglo-Saxon and Continental law. These trends are not so much due to the European Union (EU) and its harmonization efforts, although some of the convergence can be attributed to this (*infra* Section 4). What proves to be more important, thoroughgoing, and probably irreversible is market-driven approximation (*infra* Section 2). As important as market forces are, though, there are still other forces such as tradition, history, and culture which have shaped and still determine the law. Modern theory calls this path dependency[6] (*infra* Section 3).

What is corporate governance? Although the concept is not yet very old, it is being discussed worldwide and with great controversy, and has already led to the production of a vast body of legal and interdisciplinary literature. Corporate governance relates to the internal organization and power structure of the firm; the functioning of the board of directors in the one-tier and the two-tier system; the ownership structure of the firm; and the interrelationships among management board, shareholders, and other stakeholders, in particular the company's workforce and its creditors.[7] Internal corporate governance, or insider control system, is commonly distinguished from external or outsider control system. The former concerns the forces working inside the corporation. The latter are external actors and the market forces, in particular the market on corporate control (takeovers), capital and labour markets, and, in Germany, the banks. Somewhere between inside and outside are disclosure and auditing, which hold this position because they take place inside the corporation but are effective on and addressed to the market. This chapter shows that, while corporate governance is a different mix of legal and other norms and institutions in various countries, common principles of corporate governance in Europe do appear.

While it would be challenging to develop this in a strictly comparative way,[8] this chapter focuses on German and EU law and the influences of British law and corporate governance on them, rather than on the influences of the former on British law, which may be better perceived from the inside. In a way, therefore, this chapter should be considered as a kind of comparatist advance payment in the hope that a similar inquiry will soon be made in the reverse direction.

2. MARKET-DRIVEN APPROXIMATION OF CORPORATE GOVERNANCE IN ANGLO-SAXON AND CONTINENTAL COUNTRIES, PARTICULARLY GERMANY

2.1. *Internal Corporate Governance: One-Tier and Two-Tier Boards*

a) The core of internal corporate governance is the board. Traditional wisdom is that there are two fundamentally different board systems, the one-tier and the two-tier board. The Anglo-Saxon and many other—in particular Southern European—countries have a one-tier board; Germany and some other Continental European countries (German-speaking as well as Northern European countries) have a two-tier board through which the tasks of management and supervision are split up by mandatory law and entrusted to two separate organs, the management board (Vorstand) and the supervisory board (Aufsichtsrat). The latter is elected by the shareholders and elects and dismisses the former.[9]

Much of the literature seems to be devoted to showing the advantage of one system over the other. Not so surprisingly, each evaluator's own system is usually found to be the one that is better, more logical, and certainly not to be given up. This shows also in practice. In Britain, the Hampel Report poll found that there is 'overwhelming support in the UK for the unitary board, and virtually none for the two tier board'.[10] On the other hand, the one-tier board model is 'rejected by the majority of German business leaders as well as German academics'.[11]

b) Upon closer inspection, the seemingly fundamental difference appears less marked. First, the two-tier model is mandated by German law only for stock corporations. Other companies, including the limited liability company (GmbH), are free to have a one-tier or a two-tier board, and—apart from labour codetermination, which is also mandatory in the GmbH and is considered to be tolerable for enterprises only under the two-tier system—nearly all GmbHs have just a management board under the direction of the general assembly of the associates. Reality counts: there are around 9,279 stock corporations (AG and KGaA, as of August 2000) versus more than one million limited liability companies.

What is even more important is that in both German and Anglo-Saxon practice, the homogeneity of the board is split up. In the latter there is a clear movement towards independent outside directors who are part of the one-tier board but have special functions. In critical cases, management and control are divided.[12] Furthermore, the Cadbury Report has already recommended against having the same person as CEO and as chairman of the board.[13]

In addition, there is a certain approximation of the practical functioning of the one-tier and the two-tier board. In both countries there have been recent board reforms, though enacted in each country's different style. British board reform[14] has come about by the code movement, which finally led to the supercode of the stock exchange and is thereby binding on listed companies. German board reform has taken the form of a law.[15] Candidates for reform were, *inter alia*, more division between management and supervision, more transparency and reporting, installation or improvement of the company's system of internal control, more and better committee work, more outside advice, and more concentration on the job (limits to the number of board seats held by the same person in other companies). A reform that was not possible in Germany was the deregulation of the mandatory size of the board, which in large codetermined enterprises is 20 (in the coal and steel industry 21). This was due to the influence of the trade unions and the Federal Ministry of Labour, which held up the reform for more than half a year and finally had their way, although the Federal Ministry of Justice, which had prepared the draft law, and legal experts, comparativists, and business representatives all agreed that this would have been an important improvement to a better working body of supervision. Here and in other financial matters the Swiss are much more flexible and quicker to learn.[16]

The standards of conduct for the directors are also broadly similar. In particular, in German law like in American and English law the duty of care is determined by an evolving business judgement rule. As to the duty of loyalty, which was traditionally less developed in German corporate law, the courts and legal authors have become aware of the problem and are quickly elevating the requirements to international standards. Enforcement presents an acute difference not between English and German law, but between American and European law. While there is a clear tendency in German law towards more liability cases of directors both under stricter procedural law (minority rights to sue) and enforcement practice,[17] the number of cases and the amounts of claims and settlements are inordinately higher in the USA. In Germany and probably also in the UK it is common opinion that this is legally and socially undesirable and to be avoided.[18]

c) Problems and different outlooks on how to solve them remain. In particular, it is an open question how far the independence requirement for non-executive directors should go, or else how to find the right line between independence and expertise of the outside board members. In the German supervisory board, there is of course mandatory independence of management for all—not just for some—of the supervisory board members. This goes beyond the British requirements. On the other hand, the Cadbury Code of Best Practice already recommended that a majority of the non-executive directors should not only be independent of management but also 'free from any business or other relationship which could materially interfere with the exercise of their independent judgement, apart from their fees and shareholding'.[19] This is of course not the case for the typical German supervisory board member (of the shareholder side) who is appointed to the board precisely because of the banking, business, or other relationship he or his employer has with the corporation.[20] This leads to a further more fundamental distinction. In Germany, a widespread practice has developed not only of personal links between enterprises and their boards, but also of share crossholdings. Despite a number of restrictions, such as voting in case of reciprocal shareholdings, German law has not yet come to grips with this networking. Reform proposals are on the table, but they remain controversial. They reach from outright prohibitions,[21] in particular for banks, to smoother arrangements which would make use of legislative and judge-made rules on conflicts of interest. Some consider this to be the sensitive centre of the German internal corporate governance problem. It is revealing that the American institutional investor CalPERS in its 'Principles for Good Governance in Germany' considers this to be an important drawback.[22]

2.2. *External Corporate Governance: The Market for Corporate Control*

a) An even more impressive example of the coming together of British and Continental European law is takeover regulation. This is not at all self-evident. As already mentioned above in the context of board reform, there are very different traditions of self-regulation in Great Britain and in other countries, particularly Germany. In Britain, takeover regulation is mainly self-regulatory by the Panel with its City Code on Takeovers and Mergers. After initial difficulties with this kind of self-regulation in the 1950s and 1960s, the City Code of 1968 and the obligatory bid requirement of 1972 with revisions of 1974 and 1976 proved to be a tool which the Panel was able to administer in a highly successful way. At least this is the impression abroad.[23]

In contrast, German experiences with this kind of self-regulation proved to be disappointing. The German Insider Trading Guidelines of 1970, which were administered by Insider Trading Inquiry Commissions at the various German stock exchanges, were severely criticized from the very beginning as being toothless and secretive and in the end aimed more at preventing legislation than honestly solving the problem. Under the impression of clear competitive disadvantages for the German stock exchanges and under the pressure of the European Insider Trading Directive of 1989, the Guidelines were replaced by a law.[24]

The German Takeover Code of 1995, as revised in 1997 and administered by the Takeover Commission in Frankfurt, is more successful, but not successful enough. In February 1999, the Stock Exchange Experts Commission at the Federal Ministry of Finance, which was the father of this self-regulation, concluded that the Takeover Code had proven its worth in its practical application, but that the goal of its all-encompassing recognition by the German industry had not been achieved.[25] Therefore, a takeover law is now generally deemed to be unavoidable, quite apart from the fate of the Thirteenth European Directive. It remains to be seen whether, as in the case of insider dealing regulation, this takeover law will replace self-regulation completely or will leave self-regulation working 'in the shadow of the law', which in my opinion would have the advantages of flexibility and practical experience.[26]

b) In the substance of takeover regulation, the British model proved very attractive indeed. It is safe to say that it has developed into the standard all over the Continent. Modern takeover regulations, for example, in Spain, Portugal, Italy, Switzerland, Austria, Denmark, Sweden, Norway, and Finland are very much influenced by the British example.[27] So is the draft Thirteenth European Directive on takeovers. While this is true for many principles of takeover regulation, such as information and disclosure, takeover procedure, conduct during the offer, partial offers, and competing offers, two more controversial points shall be stressed, namely the neutrality of the board and the mandatory bid. Both are dealt with in American law very differently from the British example and the Continental European laws which follow the latter.[28]

The neutrality principle says in the words of Rule 21 of the British Code that '(D)uring the course of an offer, or even before the date of the offer if the board of the offeree company has reason to believe that a bona fide offer might be imminent, the board must not, except in pursuance of a contract entered into earlier, without the approval of the shareholders in general meeting' engage in frustrating action such as issuing shares, selling, disposing or acquiring assets of a material amount or 'enter(ing) into contracts otherwise than in the ordinary course of business'. This neutrality principle has been taken up by nearly all Continental European countries which have enacted laws or codes on takeovers. In Germany this took some time. In 1993, the issue was still the subject of controversial debate during a meeting of the leading German general counsels and law professors. The majority still thought that it was up to the management board to take all measures necessary in case of a hostile takeover in order to keep harm away from the company. The concepts of full competence for management (section 76 of the German Stock Corporation Act)[29] and of shareholder sovereignty stood against each other. Finally, however, the view of the management board as trustee for the shareholders and of section 76 as but an emanation of general civil law rules on the mandate with its principle of sovereignty of the mandator carried the way. In 1995, the new German Takeover Code expressly adopted the neutrality principle, and it is virtually a certainty that the future German Takeover Law will do the same.[30] This is not to say that in Europe the problem of defences against hostile takeovers has been solved, Gucci would not have been successful to fight off the recent hostile bid if it had not chosen to incorporate in the Netherlands. There will be more work to do for the EU.[31]

The mandatory bid is a feat of British self-regulatory takeover law. The essence of the mandatory bid is a right for all shareholders to sell their shares to the bidder against full consideration. They thereby are able to leave the corporation before the possible dangers resulting from the control of the bidder are felt, and they need not rely on group law provisions which may or may not protect them later on when the bidder has taken and exercised control in his own interest or in the interest of the group of companies which he is running. I shall come back to this issue later on when we deal with group law. Here it suffices to say that the mandatory bid requirement has swept all over Continental European takeover laws and codes. Despite the fact that Germany has a far-reaching group law, the German Takeover Code of 1995 has at its core a mandatory bid requirement, and such a rule will certainly also be part of the coming German Takeover Law. Even Sweden, where the mandatory bid was still rejected by the Swedish Company Law Committee in 1995 with remarkable economic and country-specific arguments,[32] adopted the mandatory bid rule in 1999.[33] The reason for this, however, seems to have been not so much care for the minority shareholders at large, but rather the more subtle thought of the leading industrialist family in Sweden which, in a world of globalization and threats of hostile takeovers by foreigners, might feel better off with a mandatory bid rule: such a rule makes bids more difficult because the bidder has to come up with more capital, but if he does, even large minority shareholders can walk away under better conditions. This may also have been the reason why some major Swedish stock corporations like for example Nokia have inserted a mandatory bid rule in their articles of incorporation even before the 1999 recommendations.

c) Apparently there is again a great difference between European law, including British law, and American law. Apart from a number of states which have adopted the so-called control share acquisition statutes,[34] American corporate law (which is state law) allows the board of directors to fight off hostile takeovers. Similarly, there is no general requirement of a mandatory bid to all shareholders of the target. At first glance this is surprising because American corporate and securities law has long been very far-reaching with much influence on other countries. The very movement of shareholder value originated in the USA and swept from there over Europe. Yet things are more complicated[34a]. It is true that the American board has a crucial role in taking stands in case of a hostile takeover bid. But it is vital to see that the board can act only as a fiduciary of the shareholders. These strong fiduciary duties are upheld by the American court[35] under a procedural law which, as mentioned before, is extremely plaintiff-friendly. If one takes into account this pivotal role of American procedural law and courts, then it is clear that American takeover rules would have a very different effect in European states. What appears to be a great difference in law may be much less different in fact.

Similar problems exist with the mandatory bid, which is not common in the USA. But if one looks at the takeover practice it is said that maybe 95 per cent of all bids are for all shares and today most USA bidders agree on a non-premium bid. As to remaining differences it must not be forgotten that in a country with many more public corporations (i.e. corporations without controlling or even major stockholders) and with very developed securities markets, the shareholders are much less likely to be locked into a stock corporation in which the bidder takes over control. In Continental Europe, in contrast, where stock ownership is much more concentrated and securities markets are more narrow and less deep, the minority shareholders are better protected by a mandatory exit right opened up by a mandatory bid. The corresponding effect, of course, as stated before, is that the hurdle a bidder must take is higher and the chances for the old, possibly inefficient, management to remain in office are better. But there is a natural trade-off between two principal/agent problems: the one between the shareholders and the board—this is the emphasis of American law and American economic and legal theory—and between the minority shareholders and the bidder, that is, the possible future majority shareholder.

2.3. *Corporate Governance between Inside and Outside: Disclosure, Auditing, and Intermediation*

a) Disclosure is a regulatory instrument which is nowadays used nearly everywhere in commercial and corporate law and, in particular, in corporate governance. Of course there is a host of detailed disclosure regulation that differs from one country to another. It suffices to say that even the Fourth European Directive, which has striven to harmonize the law of accounting and balance sheets of the corporation, contains no less than forty options for the Member States. This is quite apart from all the hidden regulatory and interpretative differences, and from all those points which openly have not been harmonized at all.[36] In particular, the true and fair view principle, which is the overriding principle of British balance sheet law, though embodied as a general principle into the Fourth Directive, has been 'uncoupled' in the transformation laws of some Member States such as Germany.[37]

Furthermore, there are deep-rooted patterns of behaviour that are not easy to change. Many German corporations still have the practice of trying to stick to the same dividends each year in the short-sighted belief that this is needed to maintain continuity and keep confidence. This, of course, is incompatible with the shareholder value concept. Hidden reserves continue to play a prominent role in the balance sheets of German banks and insurance companies, and it is a fact for all enterprises that as far as the Fourth Directive allows, German balance sheet law is creditor-friendly, not shareholder-friendly. This is the greatest difference as compared with American law and the USA GAAP.

Yet what is really remarkable is not so much these traditional differences, but the extent to which globalization, and more specifically the attractions of the American capital markets and the access to them via the New York Stock Exchange (NYSE), have brought about changes. The large German enterprises aiming in this direction had first tried jointly to obtain alleviations from the USA GAAP when getting listed at the NYSE. But these efforts failed thunderously when Daimler-Benz unilaterally left this coalition and, in order to be the first German enterprise to be listed at the NYSE, gave in completely to the American demands.[38] Other major German corporations had no other choice but to follow this path, albeit with a scowl at Daimler-Benz. The consequence was the need to prepare two different balance sheets, one complying with German (and harmonized European) accounting law, one with American GAAP. This was time-consuming, expensive, and potentially misleading for German investors. Accordingly, industry leaders exercised pressure on German legislators to achieve freedom of choice between the traditional German standards and 'internationally recognized balance sheet principles', at least when preparing group accounts. This was headed in particular to the option of using International Accounting Standards (IAS). German legislators gave in in 1998 in order to facilitate capital raising by German enterprises, but they limited this option until 2004 in the hope that by then there would be a breakthrough in the international harmonization of balance sheet law.[39] Meanwhile, the EU is working hard not to be left behind. While it has been made clear that departures from the Seventh Directive will not be acceptable,[40] the Commission announced a new strategy concerning international accounting harmonization[41] and has begun the process of reforming the European accounting law.[42] In the meantime, the accounting profession and its national and international bodies, together with accounting economists and lawyers, are in the middle of comparing USA GAAP, IAS, and national accounting standards in view of reaching harmonization from the bottom up and a German Accounting Standards Committee has begun its work similarly to the IAS Committee.[43]

b) It has been said that accounting and balance sheets are only as good as their certification. While this may be an exaggeration, it is certainly true that in the market, and particularly in the international market, certification by auditors is a must. The Fourth and Eighth European Directives have already achieved some harmonization as to auditing and auditors. But the legal requirements for auditors in the EU are still very different. This is true also as to the independence of the auditor, a point on which the Eighth Directive has not brought much clarity and progress. In its 1996 Green Book on 'The Role, the Position and the Liability of the Statutory Auditor within the European Union', the Commission came up with new ideas.[44] It is significant to see that in this paper, the Commission relied, *inter alia*, on the Cadbury Report and on other reports and codes concerning corporate governance.

In the meantime, some Member States have taken the lead and have started to integrate the auditors into their corporate governance system much more intensively. It is clear that these reforms were driven by the desire to keep up with international competition. In Germany, for example, the aforementioned board reform of 1997 extended the role of the statutory auditor considerably by making him a corporate governance partner of the supervisory board.[45] While he still is elected by the general assembly of shareholders, it is no longer the management board but the supervisory board which concludes the contract with the auditor and to whom he reports, and the auditor is required to attend the meetings of the supervisory board or of its financial audit committees held to approve the annual accounts.[46] The tasks of the auditors encompass now, *inter alia*:[47]

(1) auditing the report of the management board on the risk of future business development which is to be contained in the management report (Lagebericht), and
(2) organizing the audit in such a way that errors and violations against law, company statute, and by-laws which may have material effects on the true and fair view of the assets, finance, and profit situation of the corporation will be discovered.

This goes together with a clearer formulation of the auditing report and more nuanced formulas for the certification of the financial statements, with stiffer requirements of independence (namely incompatibility if the auditor has received more than 30 per cent of his income in the last five years from a specific company) and with a (modest) modernization of professional liability.

Among the reform proposals which German legislators did not dare to touch are the merits of a rotation requirement for auditing firms (not just of individual members of the firm)[48] and of liability of the auditor towards third parties.[49] Both are extremely controversial both in economic and in legal evaluation. It remains to be seen whether the trust placed into the auditing profession by the legislator will prove to be well-founded. The misperfomance of leading auditing firms in the scandalous case of the Bayerische Hypotheken- und Wechselbank in 1998 and the thunderous failure of the building enterprise Holzmann (in which the Deutsche Bank held a major participation) in November 1999 may dampen the hopes—or induce the profession to do some rethinking.

c) Let me finish this section on market-driven approximation of corporate governance in Anglo-Saxon and Continental countries with a few words on intermediation. Intermediation is usually seen as the function of going in between two partners in the market who otherwise would have difficulties in coming together. Yet intermediation also has another function, namely improving information, helping with advice, and even protecting the one side from the other by the professional or legal standards of the intermediator. While there is a clear trend in financial transactions to cut back in bank intermediation business (disintermediation and securitization), there seems to be the inverse trend as to the second function. This is also true in corporate governance. One example which has just been mentioned are the auditors who are entrusted by law with the task of helping the board in its supervisory tasks. Another example is the financial intermediaries, such as banks, which are getting more and more burdened with duties to inform, to warn, and to give advice[50]—a development which may also be seen in the light of a contribution to improve corporate governance from the transaction or market side.

I shall mention here another example, namely the rules on independent advice to be taken during a takeover bid. Rule 3 of the British City Code requires the board of the offeree company to obtain competent independent advice on any offer and the substance of such advice must be made known to the shareholders. Similarly, the board of an offeror must obtain competent independent advice on any offer when the offer being made is a reverse takeover or when the directors are faced with a conflict of interest; again the substance of such advice must be made known to its shareholders. The first draft of the Thirteenth Directive contained a similar requirement—but only for the board of the target—namely obtaining a report by an independent expert in cases in which the offered consideration comprises non-listed securities. This was dropped in later drafts during the process of slimming down the Thirteenth Directive in order to reach a compromise limited to the essentials of takeover regulation. Yet even without a European law provision, it seems fair to say that such a duty to obtain competent independent advice may already result from general legal principles on the duty of care and the duty of loyalty of the board members. The Cadbury Code of Best Practice holds in No. 1.5 that there should be an agreed procedure for directors in the furtherance of their duties to take independent professional advice if necessary, at the company's expense. This may very well be the direction in which the corporate law of Germany and some other Member States will develop even beyond mere takeover situations.

3. PATH-DEPENDENT DIFFERENCES IN CORPORATE GOVERNANCE BETWEEN GREAT BRITAIN AND GERMANY

Many differences, some fundamental, still remain between the corporate governance of Anglo-Saxon and Continental European countries. Without going into much detail, I should like to take three examples. Each of these examples not only presents many legal problems, but it is embedded in the particular country's tradition, history, and culture, thus making it more difficult to describe and explain. For this reason, in Part II the outlook shall be narrowed down to path-dependent differences in corporate governance between Great Britain and Germany.

3.1. *Labour Codetermination versus Shareholder Value?*

a) The most obvious difference in internal corporate governance between Great Britain and Germany is labour codetermination on German corporate boards. Is this opposed to the British (and American) idea of shareholder value? The answer should start with a glimpse at the old, detailed German discussion of the aims of the stock corporation and the duties of the management board towards shareholders as well as other stakeholders. This discussion has been carried on in Germany as well as in Great Britain.[51] The traditional German view, which is clearly the majority view, holds that the aims of the corporation include the interest of the shareholders (e.g. voting rights, dividend rules, minority rights, shareholder suits, etc.), the interest of the creditors (e.g. minimum capital and relating rules), and, as a separate category of the latter, the interest of the employees of the corporation. Unlike under the Stock Corporation Act of 1937,[52] the public interest, that is, interest of the people and the state, is no longer part of the aims of the corporation. Yet this discussion need not be restated here in detail, for despite its theoretical pomp, its practical relevance is small. Not only is it restricted to stock corporations (while the limited liability company is clearly steered by the partners themselves who can give detailed instructions to their manager), but the medium-term interest of the shareholders together with the business judgement rule cover nearly all activities of the board in favour of the employees, and even many public activities of the corporate good citizen, such as donations, the creation of a foundation, and environmental measures. It is true that this stakeholder interest provision holds a clear danger that, under the cover of stakeholder interest, the management board could pursue its own interest, for example, in the course of a hostile takeover. Yet this is a well-known problem that we know also from the stakeholder statutes of a number of American states. Of course, as in many other states, the concept of shareholder value has also been more recently discussed in Germany.[53] But this discussion has also been carried on at a rather theoretical level, and it has not changed the above-mentioned view on the aims of the corporation and the rights and duties of the board under the current law.

b) On the contrary, eminent practical differences between British and German law as to stakeholder interest appear under boardroom codetermination. The content and the consequences of this form of labour codetermination have been described elsewhere.[54] Therefore, a few words suffice. First of all, this boardroom codetermination, which comprises all kind of decisions of the supervisory board, must be clearly distinguished from the codetermination of the works council at the plant level under the Works Council Statute of 1988, which extends only to conditions of labour. Second, there are three different systems of boardroom codetermination with the following characteristics: (1) full-parity codetermination: only coal and steel, only stock corporations, and limited liability companies, more than 1,000 employees, boards up to twenty-one members; (2) quasi-parity codetermination under the Codetermination Law of 1976: stock corporations, limited liability companies, and some other company forms, more than 2,000 employees, boards up to twenty members;

and (3) the general one-third labour codetermination: stock corporations, limited liability companies, and other company forms, more than 500 employees, board up to twenty-one members. To all these forms there exist various exemptions, *inter alia*, for partnerships and for media-, church-, union-, and politics-related companies.

German business seems to have accommodated quite well to labour codetermination. Of course, as always, there are advantages and disadvantages. Counted among the advantages are better integration and motivation of the workforce and their leaders and better and quicker execution of decisions that have been approved by the codetermined supervisory board. In particular, it is said that in difficult times, having labour representatives as members of the board helps to make unpopular but unavoidable decisions, including layoffs and rescue operations. It is reported from some Eastern German enterprises that labour codetermination helped considerably in coping with the enormous difficulties of adaptation. Disadvantages are, *inter alia*, a marked slow-down of the decision-making process, a generally observed factionalization of the board into the shareholder and the labour side, undeniable problems for board secrecy, and, as a result, hesitation of the management board to inform the normal members of the supervisory board on sensitive issues at an early stage. The conclusion of the merger between the management board of Daimler-Benz and the Chrysler board is a good example: the supervisory board of Daimler-Benz, whose consent was needed under the law, was informed only when the deal was fully negotiated. Yet Daimler-Chrysler is also an example of a transnational merger in which the German labour codetermination system was fully maintained and (at least verbally) has been praised by Schremp as an asset for the merged corporation. On the other side, there is the example of the Hoechst/Rhône-Poulenc merger in which it was decided to have the holding in Strasbourg/France, resulting in not having labour codetermination at the holding level. The merger report contains a brief provision according to which the management board of Hoechst will endeavour to get the consent of the management board of Aventis for creating a committee that contains representatives of both the management board of Aventis and Hoechst as well as representatives of labour. This committee shall inquire into whether codetermination of labour in the board of Aventis on a voluntary basis will be feasible.

c) On the whole, it is fair to say that outside Germany and the Netherlands, transnational enterprises shy away from (voluntary) boardroom codetermination. This is why the Dutch law, when introducing its far-reaching labour codetermination system in 1973, made sure to grant certain exemptions to Dutch transnational enterprises.[55] German experience also shows that normal employee representatives and union members on the board do show a rather different outlook and behaviour in the codetermined supervisory boards. Nevertheless, labour codetermination works quite well in Germany because in principle the trade unions are upholding the system. Indeed, labour codetermination was introduced after the First World War and extended after the Second World War when it was vital for capital and labour to work together in reconstructing the destroyed country. This is a very good example of path dependency, and may be fundamentally different in a number of other countries that have trade unions which still live and act in the old Communist tradition. In any case, labour codetermination has for many decades now been the major stumbling block for European company law and has held up the Statute of a European Stock Corporation and the Fifth, Eleventh, and Fourteenth Directives. As recently as 1999, Spain vetoed the enactment of a long- and well-prepared European compromise on the European Stock Corporation, allegedly because of the minimum labour codetermination rules in the draft which is still considered to be too harmful for the Spanish business and labour environment.

3.2. *Universal Banks Versus Capital Markets?*

a) Another far-reaching difference between Great Britain and Germany is the different role played by universal banks and capital markets. It is well known that in Germany the capital markets developed much slower than in Great Britain. This has important consequences on corporate governance since the disciplining forces of the capital market and, as mentioned above, particularly those of the market of corporate control, are less effective than in Great Britain. Part of the financing functions that elsewhere are exercised by the capital markets are exercised in Germany by the universal banks. The universal banking system in Germany is characterized by letting banks combine both the credit business and the investment business. There is no legally mandated separation between both kinds of banks and banking business such as that which exists most obviously in the USA under the Glass–Steagall system, a system that has been under attack in the USA for decades but has prevailed until autumn 1999 when the long-expected reform was finally embarked upon. In Germany, there has been much ado about the 'power of the German universal banks'. This fear is already old and from time to time has led to public attempts to curb this bank power in one way or another. In the international corporate governance discussion, the influence of the banks is also considered to be characteristic of German corporate governance. German universal banks, it is said, stabilize management to the detriment of the shareholders and are one of the reasons why the German capital markets have developed more slowly than in other countries, in particular the USA and Great Britain.[56]

b) There is some truth in this, though also some exaggeration. This has been discussed in more detail elsewhere.[57] It suffices here to say that German universal banks do indeed have four important sources of influence on the corporations which in conjunction give them more leverage than banks and financial institutions in Great Britain and many other countries. Apart from the credit business links that allow the credit-giving bank deep insights into the credit-taking corporation, there is an old and intensive pattern of German universal banks holding major participations in key industrial enterprises. In 1994, the ten largest private banks held a total of 135 participations with over 5 per cent of the shares of the respective corporations. Thirty of these participations were in listed companies. Furthermore, the German universal banks hold many directorships in large German corporations. According to a poll of the German Association of Private Banks of 1993, 89 of the largest 100 enterprises had a supervisory board. The total amount of seats in these boards were 1,561. Representatives of the private banks held 99, and representatives of other credit institutes (including savings banks) and of insurance companies held another 53. Labour held 760 seats under boardroom codetermination. The shareholder side alone is composed of 152 representatives of financial and insurance companies, 427 representatives of industry and other business enterprises, and 155 other directors such as lawyers, public notaries, representatives of shareholder associations, and so forth. Finally, the so-called depository voting right must be mentioned. It is common practice of shareholders in Germany to let the bank which holds their shares in custody vote these shares in the general assembly. Under corporate law this can be done only under rather severe restrictions. For example, the banks must ask the client for a specific mandate to represent him and for instructions on how to vote. The bank must state clearly how it will vote if it does not get such instructions. And the law makes clear that the bank must act only in the interest of the client, otherwise it makes itself liable for damages. Still, the fact is that the banks usually receive these mandates without specific instructions, and they usually vote for the proposals made by the management. These four factors of influence combined do indeed give the banks influence and may dampen corporate governance of the shareholders more than in countries in which the forces of the capital markets play a more important role.

c) To state the fact that German universal banks have such an influence is one matter. To evaluate the impact of this influence both on the single enterprises and on corporate governance in Germany as a whole is of course much more difficult. It is astonishing how quick some of the (German and foreign) observers are in presenting theories and making judgement on possible reforms. At a minimum, more clarity about the economic facts is needed. The studies of Edwards and Fisher[58] and the most recent and comprehensive report by Prigge[59] may be recommended as excellent sources. So is the study of Mülbert as to whether reforms limiting the influences of credit institutions on stock corporations are to be recommended to legislators.[60]

In the Board Reform Act of 1998, legislators put the emphasis on the board and the auditors and—apart from more transparency and a few incompatibility rules—refrained from fundamental reforms concerning the universal banks and their influence on the stock corporations. This was, of course, controversial and against the proposals of the then opposition which now is in power. Yet, the proposals made in the reform discussion are in part very problematic, such as, for example, excluding banks from proxy voting and instead hoping that auditors and other commercial trustees take their place; or limiting shareholdings of banks to 5 per cent of the shares of any corporation; or cutting back by law the number of seats the banks hold in supervisory boards while leaving the seats held by labour untouched, etc. It remains to be seen whether the new government coalition will come back to the plans it made while it was still the opposition, though this is doubtful because many other, clearly, much more important structural reforms are overdue in Germany.

This does not mean that the universal banks as they are now in Germany will remain untouched. But this is not the task of the legislators, for they should refrain from interference with the market, particularly if they are not sure about the consequences of their interference on the system as a whole. After all, the universal banking system is not forcing the banks to be universal banks, but rather letting them if they feel that this is more successful at the market than offering specialist banking services. In this perspective, the universal banking system is the banking system which is most free, deregulated, and market conformed. Yet international and global competition do exercise market pressures on the German universal banks. Investment banks, in particular from the USA, have entered the market and proven that their banking business is much more profitable than the traditional credit business. The Deutsche Bank and other major players have already tried to react by reorganization and national and international mergers. Whether this will be successful is another difficult question. The situation is also changing in other respects. The German capital markets and the stock exchanges are growing quickly and undergoing fundamental, internationally driven changes which by themselves are eroding traditional credit banking business. The process of securitization is in full swing and blurs the traditional distinction between bank-based and market-based countries viz. systems. Also in Germany the market for bond issues by enterprises is growing fast and the traditional housebank relationships are quickly eroding and has been called a mere myth.[61] And one last remark: It has been said that German universal banks are opposed to hostile takeovers and will impede their rise in Germany. In my opinion this is wrong. The pressures of the market and of an international clientele combined with high profit margins will also convince the German universal banks in the near future that this type of business is attractive. The (unsuccessful) bid of Krupp for Thyssen and the role of the German banks in this affair in 1997 has already marked the change of the trend. The successful hostile takeover of Mannesmann by Vodafone in 2000 was the point of no return.

3.3. *Groups of Companies Law Versus Exit, Fiduciary Principles, and Veil-Piercing?*

a) The third example for deep-rooted, path dependence-driven differences between Great Britain and Germany is the law of groups of companies. This particularity of German corporate law has already been presented to an English-speaking audience several times[62] and has been the object of early and quite unsuccessful harmonization endeavours of the European Commission in its predraft of a Ninth Directive. It should be enough to mention three characteristic elements of the German law of groups of companies as distinguished from British law. For many other differences, reference is made to the host of books and articles about the subject.[63] The first is that the control concept is substantive instead of formal. This means that under German group law, provisions apply already if it is a de facto control by the parent. It is not necessary for the parent to hold more than 50 per cent of the shares or voting rights in the subsidiary. This, of course, goes very far and extends the reach of group law considerably. Second, there is a fundamental distinction between the so-called contractual and merely factual groups of companies. In contractual groups, the creditors of the subsidiary are protected by the legal obligation of the parent towards the subsidiary to make good the losses at the end of the year. Outside shareholders of the subsidiary have a right to periodic compensation payments and must be offered the opportunity of selling their shares to the parent as against equitable indemnity. As a quid pro quo for entering into such an enterprise contract, the parent is permitted by law to instruct the subsidiary to act not in its own interest, but in the interest of the group as a whole. Third, there are several provisions which try to protect minority shareholders and creditors also in a de facto group. In particular, the controlling enterprise may not use its influence to induce the subsidiary to enter into transactions disadvantageous to it or to take or refrain from taking measures to its disadvantage unless compensation is granted for such disadvantage, usually within the same fiscal year. If compensation is not granted, the controlling enterprise and its board are liable to the subsidiary unless they have acted in a diligent and prudent way.

On the other side, German law of groups does not trust instruments which British law uses, *inter alia*, to cope with group situations, such as, for example, exit rights, fiduciary principles, and piercing of the corporate veil both before and after insolvency. As to exit rights, it has been stated above that there is no general early exit right by the requirement of a mandatory bid procedure. Rather, there are some special cases in which special exit rights are granted to the minority shareholders in the group, for example, when a contractual group is formed (sections 305 and 306 of the Stock Corporations Act) or in case of statutory mergers (sections 29 and 34 of the Fundamental Changes Act, Umwandlungsgesetz). Fiduciary principles are less needed in German group law because of the above-mentioned statutory provisions, but are developed by the courts for groups of limited liability companies. Finally, the doctrine of piercing the corporate veil is known in civil law, but it is seldom used for groups of companies out of fear of disavowing the overriding principle of separate entity.

b) The distrust of the just-mentioned general civil law instruments in group situations and instead the formation of a specific law of corporate groups in Germany is a particular path German law has taken as a result of the fundamental stock corporation law reform in 1965. It was the result of a very controversial legislative debate in which academia had a fair deal of influence. The fact that the German Cartel Act had just been enacted some years before and that the state of the law under the old stock corporation act of 1937 was very unsatisfactory added to this. In particular, the courts were not able to develop principles of group law that could have been considered able to deal with the major group problems. Be this as it may, what counts today is that since 1965 there is a huge amount of legal doctrine and many cases applying principles developed from this. This jurisprudence and case law, in addition to the detailed group law provisions in the Act of 1965, have a strong momentum of their own. Therefore, a change within German group law cannot be expected.

c) I do not think that this will change by harmonization measures of the EU. Certainly, there will be no change through exporting German group law concepts to the other Member States of the EU by way of harmonization. The Ninth Directive must be considered dead. There is more chance of importing certain concepts concerning groups from other countries and to try to reach a certain harmonization in this way. The Forum Europaeum Group Law has just tried to make proposals for such a European Law of Groups. These proposals have been presented to the English audience both orally and in writing.[64] The first reaction to them when they were presented on an international conference sponsored by the German Ministry of Justice at Bonn in April 1999 was positive and apt to create hopes for some further progress on this way.[65]

4. LEGAL HARMONIZATION OF CORPORATE GOVERNANCE IN THE EUROPEAN UNION?

4.1. *The Present State*

a) Corporate governance appeared only fairly recently on the agenda of possible harmonization of the European Commission. In the most recent German book on 'European Corporate Law' of 1999,[66] not even a hint at corporate governance can be found, and this is not to be criticized, but rather an accurate reflection of the state of European company law harmonization. It was only at the 'Conference on Company Law and the Single Market', held in Brussels on 3 December 1998, under the auspices of the European Commission, that Paul Davies was asked to present his views about 'Issues in Corporate Governance'.[67] This relatively late start is not too surprising. The European Commission has experienced political and other difficulties with company law harmonization for some time. Major projects such as the Statute of the European Stock Corporation and the draft directives of the Fifth, Eleventh, Thirteenth, and Fourteenth Directives were held up, some of them for decades, because the Member States (in particular Germany, which was not prepared to make compromises on labour codetermination) could not agree on a common regulatory core. Member States predicted crisis or even the end of European company law harmonization. This was exactly what some political players—but also many academics, most of them economists—wanted, for federalist reasons or for reasons of economic theory. Politically and legally, the subsidiarity principle embedded in the European Community Treaty (formerly Article 3(b), now in the consolidated version under the Amsterdam Treaty Article 5) served as the bastion. For academics it was the concept of competition of legislators which counted. In this unfavourable climate, the European Commission had to look for new beginnings and ideas, and corporate governance became one of the possibilities for exploration.

b) In his paper to the Commission, Davies explains why corporate governance, that is, in particular the accountability of those in control of companies to the shareholders (and possibly certain stakeholders), has recently received so much attention in many Member States. He mentions, *inter alia*, the blurring of the public and private sectors, the growth of old age/pension funds and other institutional investors, but most importantly globalization and competition. The latter are bound to lead to the question of comparative corporate governance, which has already become a separate field of international research.[68]

c) To be sure, there already exists a certain body of European law touching corporate governance, part of which is already in force and part of which has been proposed by the European Commission and is still in the draft stage. As to internal corporate governance, much of the company law harmonization must be mentioned, even though key parts as far as corporate governance is concerned are not yet in force, such as the Fifth Directive on company structure. This deals, *inter alia*, with the board and shareholder rights in the general assembly and the decision on and the auditing of the annual accounts; the Statute of the European Stock Corporation and its corresponding provisions on the shareholders and the board; and the Eleventh and Fourteenth Directives, etc. As to external corporate governance—that is, harmonization of the corporate control and securities markets—the record looks better, even though the key piece on takeover regulation, namely the Thirteenth Directive, has still not yet been finally enacted because the Common Standpoint of the Council has not been accepted by the European Parliament.[69] Stock exchange harmonization in particular has come a long way. A short mention must be made also of the area in which the Commission was particularly successful, namely bank supervision. Insofar as well-led, risk-conscious banks contribute to corporate governance, the harmonization of bank supervision, including consolidated bank supervision, must not be forgotten, even though its focus is, of course, elsewhere, namely on risk. It is true, however, that the credit for this regulation belongs not only to the European Commission, but to a high (and maybe even higher) degree to the Bank of International Settlements and its Basel Committee.

4.2. *Further Plans of the European Commission as to Corporate Governance*

a) This is not the place to describe the further plans of the European Commission concerning the just-mentioned well-known proposals for a European company law. I have done this and evaluated the prospects of it elsewhere.[70] What is interesting is whether the Commission will pursue its ideas of specifically harmonizing some corporate governance measures. The Commission had already mentioned corporate governance as one of its concerns in its Action Framework of October 1998, which was the basis for the above-mentioned Brussels Conference of December 1998. In the meantime, the Commission also included corporate governance as a topic in its finalized Action Programme of 11 May 1999.[71] Under the heading of 'General Conditions for an Efficient EU Financial Market', the Commission mentions: (1) structure of the corporation, and (2) tax provisions. The Commission says there that differences in the structure of corporations may lead to unnecessary uncertainties for the investors and might create impediments for the development of the EU financial market. It gives as an example the practical rules for the exercise of voting rights by the shareholders in the different Member States. Another concern of the Commission is that current national codes on corporate structure and governance might create legal or administrative impediments for the development of uniform EU financial markets. The Commission therefore intends to commission an inquiry into the content of such codes and their possible impeding effects on the internal market.

It is hardly deniable that this action programme remains rather vague as to corporate governance, and that the two projects on the agenda of the Commission relating to it are piecemeal. But this is hardly surprising. The fact is that corporate governance is a very difficult task which does not promise to give quick and palpable results of the kind the Commission needs in the political process.

b) If one looks critically at the prospects of legal harmonization of corporate governance in the EU, one must start with the premise that all legislative activism in this field is wrong. The legal principle of subsidiarity as embedded in the European Community Treaty, as well as the economic concept of competition—also among legislators—put the burden of proof on those who plead for European harmonization. Therefore, it must not only be shown that a particular legislative interference with unregulated corporate governance is legitimate—for example, because of market failure, or external effects, or the necessary implementation of the political decision of bringing about the internal market. Very often the answer and the right way will not be regulation, but rather non-regulation, or even deregulation. But it is further necessary to prove that this kind of legislation, in order to be successful, needs to be undertaken by the European Commission at the European level and not just at the level of the Member States.

This in turn would require scientific, comparative, and in certain cases interdisciplinary preparation of major legislative projects by the European Commission or the European Parliament just as it is done in many Member States, for example, in the preparation of the German insolvency law reform or more recently of the German Stock Exchange law reform.[72]

c) If these principles are observed and the legislative work is well prepared, what would be possible candidates for corporate governance reforms, and how should this legislative task be divided between the Member States and the European legislators? There is of course no short answer to either of these questions. For answering the latter, it is necessary in principle to search for those parts of corporate governance which need to be unified in an internal market. These are typically those provisions which will help to cut down impediments for open markets and lead to more competition, and by this to better corporate governance. It is evident that both the Eleventh and Fourteenth Directives point in this direction. But are there more concrete examples for candidates for a body of European corporate governance law?

Davies mentions with all due restraint:

(1) principal–agent and minority protection;
(2) voice and exit, with more weight on the first in some countries, and in others more on the second;
(3) accountability (and dismissal) of directors;
(4) buy-out and possibly squeeze-out rights; and
(5) disclosure.

All these can be very well debated, but they would need to be scrutinized at more depth as to whether different national legal rules relating to them will be impediments for the internal market.

In this respect, it does not make a decisive difference whether the impediments result from the law or from private codes, be they stock-exchange-made or other codes on corporate governance. For example, if a national stock exchange admits a foreign corporation to be listed only if it has a one-tier board, this would be an impediment for the internal market. Insofar the European Commission is right in commissioning an inquiry as to whether the codes movement in the different Member States may contain rules which function as such impediments. This is not to say that the stock exchanges should not take the lead in furthering corporate governance. The Combined Code of the London Stock Exchange—'Principles of Good Governance and Code of Best Practice' as of 25 June 1998, an appendix to the listing rules[73]—is an example to be imitated by German and other national stock exchanges.[74] Depending on the circumstances and on different national traditions, such self-regulatory efforts may have better chances for success in practice than legislation.

A further suggestion could be to mandate free choice for the corporations between a one- and two-tier system as already exists in France. It is true that only a small percentage of French corporations opts for the two-tier board, namely around 3,000 out of 158,000 companies. But among these there are some very successful and international enterprises.[75] It is particularly interesting to see in this context, how in transnational mergers the enterprises try to create appropriate board structures.[76]

Disclosure also plays a key role in the international context and for investors and shareholders who want to invest in foreign corporations and securities. Therefore, the core of disclosure regulation is rightly European. This does not preclude individual Member States as well as single enterprises from going further in disclosure and thereby trying to outcompete their competitors. On the other hand, the use of disclosure requirements as a means to systematically keep out foreign competitors, be it by mandating too high disclosure standards or, worse, too specific disclosure formats, must be avoided. An unresolved question in this context is whether it is warranted to restrict harmonization of disclosure to listed companies.

This seems to be practical and less demanding, but checks should be made as to whether it may have distortive effects on competition.

As to external corporate governance, possible candidates for European harmonization efforts could be, *inter alia*, keeping the securities markets open to foreign enterprises and their securities; setting core rules for the development of an open market for corporate control; cutting down defensive measures if they are used systematically to keep out foreigners; and looking into structural and institutional conditions which function as a defence against takeovers.[77]

Corporate governance of institutional investors, in particular of banks and insurance companies, is another possible point for the agenda. Good corporate governance of the banks themselves is not only in the interest of the bank's shareholders, but indirectly contributes also to more competition and to the better functioning of the financial and economic system. Common principles of corporate governance in Europe for banking and insurance business may be even quicker to come about than elsewhere because market forces are particularly strong and joint efforts of the regulators could help. It may even be that developments in these fields will stimulate corporate governance more generally as is the case for internal risk management systems which since 1998 are mandatory for all German corporations, not only banks.

5. SUMMARY AND CONCLUSION: SOVEREIGNTY AND GLOBALIZATION AT THE BEGINNING OF THE NEW MILLENNIUM

This leads back to the opening question: Are there common principles of corporate governance in Europe? My answer is yes and no, but more yes. As shown in the first part of the chapter, there has already been and will be more convergence of the Anglo-Saxon and Continental European countries in the field of corporate and capital market law, and specifically in corporate governance.

Most of this convergence will be market-driven. The forces of globalization and international competition are enormous, and have led or are leading to harmonization of legal and economic practice even under very different legal systems and rules. The examples of the practical approximation of the one-tier and two-tier board system, the development of the market for corporate control in countries in which hostile takeovers were virtually unknown, and the increased importance of disclosure, auditing, and intermediation in the different countries illustrate this development.

On the other hand, there remain path-dependent differences in corporate governance that are deeply embedded in the country's tradition, history, and culture, and will therefore not change or change only very slowly and in an unpredictable way. The examples given for German corporate governance are labour codetermination, the universal banking system, and the existence of a special law of groups of companies. They stand for particular political arrangements, historically grown economic systems, and particular legal doctrines that are upheld by an influential academia and active courts. Any changes to these are bound to affect vested rights and interests. But even here market forces can be expected to be stronger, at least in the long run.

Legal harmonization of corporate governance could be a way by which common principles of corporate governance could be furthered in Europe. Indeed, there is already an important body of European company and capital markets law which affects corporate governance. Yet the action programme of the European Commission as to corporate governance more specifically remains rather vague. This is not surprising given the complexity of internal and external corporate governance, that is, corporate governance between the board and the markets. But there is more: even if a particular interference of the legislature with unregulated corporate governance turns out to be legitimate—for example, because of market failure or external effects or the necessary implementation of a political decision of bringing about the internal market—it is by no means sure that this kind of legislation must be done by the European Commission at the European level. The legal principle of subsidiarity and the economic concept of competition, also among the legislators, put the burden of proof on those who plead for European harmonization.

The conclusion goes beyond corporate governance and corporate and capital market law. The traditional idea that each sovereign state is free to choose which law should reign in the land is no longer true in a world of international competition and of globalization.[78] As far as we can see, at the beginning of the new millennium the market forces will have their way across borders and legal systems. It remains a task for transnational political and legal cooperation to see that the necessary rule of law is not lost.

Notes

1. See Markesinis (1995). A great many of the German commercial and business lawyers have studied in the USA. Whole fields of law, such as corporate law, antitrust, securities regulation, banking and telecommunications, show the influence of this trend. It would be interesting to look into this fertilization in a more systemic way, see also the critical piece by Stiefel and Maxeiner (1997).
2. An indicator is the merger movement in the legal profession which goes across national borders and beyond mere strategic alliances to outright international mergers, most recently between large British and German law firms. This will not only change the professional scene, but will have a deep impact also on procedural and substantive law. This impact is already felt in areas like mergers and financial transactions, which are the domain of international practice and standards. It suffices to look at the German words of trade, which are English—for example, share deal, asset deal, due diligence, Chinese walls, compliance letter, letter of intent, asset-backed securities, insider dealing, etc. Anglo-American contract practices used for German contracts are described by Döser (2000). With regard to corporate governance, see Hertig (2000*b*: 270) and cf. André (1998). As to export in the reverse direction, see Markesinis (1999). As to Switzerland, see the remarkable influence of American law as described by Böckli (1995*a*: 222); "invasion des idées anglo-saxonnes." Cf. also the same (1995*b*: 9) and Wiegand (1991, 1996). Useless polemics can be found in Honsell (1999). For the global perspective ("the West and the Rest"), see Huntington (1993) and the broad debate that followed.
3. See von Wilmowsky (1996), Röver (1999), Dalhuisen (1994: 361), and Drobnig (1999: 9).
4. Kötz (1963) and cf. Helmholz and Zimmermann (1998).
5. Grundmann (1998: 492).
6. Roe (1996), Bebchuk and Roe (1999), and Teubner (1998).
7. Hopt *et al.* (1998: v), and the selected bibliography (idem 1201–1210), and see also Keasey *et al.* (1997, 1999).

8. See, for example, Wymeersch (1999).
9. Sections 76 *et seq.*, 95 *et seq.* of the German Stock Corporation Act (1965) and see also Hopt (1997*b*). See most recently Grundmann and Mülbert, Lutter and Davies (all 2000) and Leyens (2003).
10. Committee on Corporate Governance (1998), Summary No. 10.
11. Theisen (1998).
12. Windbichler (1985).
13. Cadbury Report (London) 1992, 4.9; Code of Best Practice No. 1.2.
14. Cheffins (1997: 602 *et seq*).
15. See the so-called Law on Control and Transparency in the Corporate Sector (KonTraG) of 27.4.1998, BGB1 I 786. A short summary of the reforms can be found in OECD (1998: 21 *et seq*).
16. "The traditional large and unwieldly Swiss Board of Directors is being phased out." See Böckli (1996: 158).
17. A recent study has counted 30 D&C insurance cases (corporation v. management) from 1886–1995, and 166 insurance cases (third party v. management); 1976–1985, 113 cases; 1986–1995, 206 cases; see Ihlas (1997: 317 *et seq*). The most recent and comprehensive commentary on director's liability can be found in Hopt (1999*b*).
18. See the study on procedural law reform by the Max Planck Institute for Foreign Private and Private International Law that was commissioned by the Federal Ministry of Justice. The study is published in a more detailed book form: Basedow *et al.* (1999), see also Miller (1998). For a less sceptical view, see Hertig (2000*b*: 280).
19. Code of Best Practice No. 2.2.
20. See Korn/Ferry International (1996) and see also Prigge (1998: 955 *et seq*).
21. For instance, Italy prohibited in 1974 cross-shareholdings over 2 per cent. Recently, the Government introduced a provision that if a takeover bid is made, this limit is not applicable. Interestingly, cross-shareholdings seem to have faded away in France.
22. See CalPERS (1999: II 7 B). CalPERS also advocates "a substantial number of independent directors" (idem: II 6 A).
23. There are several well-researched theses in Germany on the British model. See Lüttmann (1992) Herkenroth (1994), and Krause (1995).
24. This development is described by Hopt (1993*b*).
25. Börsensachverständigenkommission beim Bundesministerium der Finanzen (1999). More generally on the German experience with self-regulation, see Hopt (1998*b*).
26. Hopt (1997*a*: 407 *et seq*).
27. For comparative law, see Hopt and Wymeersch (1992), Kozyris (1996), Wymeersch *et al.* (1996), and Wymeersch *et al.* (1997).
28. With regard to American takeover law, see Gilson (1986), Auerbach (1988), Romano (1997), and Lüttmann (1992: 83).
29. See section 76 subsection 1 of the Aktiengesetz (1965) which states that 'The managing board is charged with the personal responsibility of directing the company.' In contrast, see section 70 subsection 1 of the Aktiengesetz (1937), infra note 52.
30. See Hopt (1993*a*) with further references, and same (2002). Article 19 of the German Takeover Code states that: 'Following publication of a public tender offer... the executive or managing body of a target company, including the executive or managing bodies of the related companies of the target company, may not take any measures that run counter to the interest of the holders of securities in taking advantage of the tender offer.' A prohibition of frustrating actions is contained in Art. 9 of the common standpoint of the European Council (2000) and in section 33 of the draft

of the German Takeover Act (2001). But is considerably watered down in the final Act (2001/2002). This causes great concern.

31. See Section 4.2 (at the end).
32. See Skog (1995).
33. NBK (1999).
34. For details, see Lüttmann (1992: 90 *et seq*).
34a. Cf. most recently High Level Group of Company Law Experts (2002: 39 *et seq*).
35. Cf. Sullivan and Conlon (1997) and Miller (1998: 54).
36. Ernst and Whinney (1979) and Albach and Klein (1998).
37. Schön (1997), see also the critique by van Hulle (1994) (charged with corporate law and accounting at DG XV of the European Commission), and same (1995: 318).
38. See the report by Bruns (1997).
39. Kapitalaufnahmeerleichterungsgesetz—KapAEG of 20.4.1998, Federal Gazette 1998 I 707. Section 292 a subsection 2 No 2 b makes it clear that the balance sheet must comply with the 7th European Directive.
40. No. 61 of the Mitteilung der Kommission zu Auslegungsfragen im Hinblick auf bestimmte Artikel der Vierten und der Siebenten Richtlinie des Rates auf dem Gebiet der Rechnungslegung, O.J.E.C. 20.1.1998 C 16/5.
41. Mitteilung der Kommission, Harmonisierung auf den Gebiet den Rechnungs legung: Einc nene strategie im hinblick auf die internationale Harmonisierung, 14.11.1995, ROM (95) 508 endg., and see the comments by van Hulle (1997), and same (2000).
42. See, for example, European Commission (1998*a*). See also the communication of the European Commission on the accounting strategy and the future action, European Commisson (2000).
43. See Schön (1997: 154), Born (1997), Ballwieser (1998), and Ebke (1999).
44. European Commission (1996), Hommelhoff (1998*c*).
45. Cf. Hommelhoff (1998*b*: 2625), and Mattheus (1999).
46. Section 111 subsection 2 of the Stock Corporation Act, section 321 subsection 5 of the Commercial Code, section 171 subsection 1 of the Stock Corporation Act.
47. See sections 289, 317, 321, 322, 319, subsection 2 No. 8 and 323 of the Commercial Code.
48. See section 319 subsection 3 No. 6 of the Commercial Code: rotation of the individual auditor after having audited six annual reports during the last 10 years. For a similar proposal made by the Cadbury Report, 5. 12: no compulsory rotation of audit firms, but periodic change of audit partners in the case of listed companies.
49. For example, Ekkenga (1996), Contra: Ebke and Struckmeier (1994). With regard to the similar controversy in Great Britain, see Cadbury Report, 5.31 *et seq.* and Appendix 6 on *Caparo Industries plc* v. *Dickman and others* (1990).
50. See the critical comment made by Haire (1999).
51. Cf. Lord Wedderburn of Charlton (1985) and Deakin and Hughes (1997).
52. Section 70 subsection 1 of the Stock Corporation Act of 1937 stated that: 'The management board is charged with the personal responsibility of directing the corporation in such a way as required by the welfare of the enterprise and its workforce and the common benefit of the people and the Reich.' Despite this wording, which was the language of the Third Reich, the content of the provision was not Nazi, but rather corresponded to a much longer tradition. See Riechers (1996 p. 166 *et seq.*, 191). For example, see the explanations of the 1930 Draft for a reform of the Stock Corporation Act which provide that: 'shareholders have to acknowledge that the modern stock corporation is not only for the individual pursuit of profit but it also has to serve to varying degrees the general interests of the people' (Riechers 1996: 102). As to the Stock Corporation Act of 1997, see Mann (1937) and see also Spindler (1993).

53. For example, see Mülbert (1997), von Colbe (1997), Schmidt and Spindler (1997), Wagner (1997), Bühner and Tuschke (1997), Hachmeister (1997), Kübler (1998), and Drukarczyk (1999).
54. See Hopt (1994*a*; 1994*b*), Raiser (1997), Roe (1998), Bainbridge (1998), Bertelsmann-Stiftung and Hans-Böckler-Stiftung (1998), Gerum (1998), Kübler (1999), Oetker (1999), and Endres (1999: 454 *et seq.*) (former member of the board of Deutsche Bank).
55. Hopt (1982: 233 *et seq.*) and Dorresteijn (1994: 209).
56. Most recently on this point: Charny (1998) with further references.
57. Mülbert (1998), Hopt (1996), Westermann (1996), Hommelhoff (1998*a*), Kohler (1999: 225), Hertig (2000*b*). A rather different bank-bashing view is articulated by Wenger and Kaserer (1998). The most recent policy study was conducted by Hoffmann (1999).
58. See Edwards and Fisher (1994).
59. Prigge (1998).
60. See Mülbert (1996).
61. Gerke bank and stock exchange economist (1999).
62. See, for example, Wiedemann (1982) and Hopt (1991).
63. See the well-documented book of Emmerich, Sonnenschein and Habersack (2001).
64. Forum Europaeum Konzernrecht (Forum Europaeum Corporate Group Law) (2000: 165–264), Hopt (2000*b*), and same (2000*c*).
65. Blaurock (2000), Windbichler (2000), and Lübking (2000).
66. See Habersack (1999), Schwarz (2000: comment 1461), who mentions corporate governance only at the end and very briefly. A more general inquiry is the one by Franzen (1999).
67. See Davies (1998). Here, it is referred to the written version which is more detailed. A shorter, oral version is printed in European Commission (1998*b*). See also Berglöf (1997) and Lannoo (1999).
68. See Hopt *et al.* (1998) with many further references.
69. See Common Standpoint of the European Council as to the 13th Directive as of 19 June 2000; on this and on the amendments proposed by the European Parliament. Hopt (2001*b*).
70. See Hopt (1998, 1999), Habersack (1999), Magnier (1999) and Schwarz (2000).
71. See Kommission der Europäischen Gemeinschaften (1999), Mogg (1999), Hertig (2000*a*), and Hopt (2000*a*: 322 *et seq.*).
72. See the study on stock exchange reform by the Max Planck Institute for Foreign Private and Private International Law in Hamburg which was commissioned by the Federal Ministry of Finance. The study is published in book form in Hopt *et al.* (1997). For a comment, see Hellwig (1999).
73. Pettet (1998).
74. See CalPERS (1999), see also OECD (1999). With regard to the international convergence of many of the codes of best practice, see Van den Berghe and De Ridder (1999). See also, the interesting study by Harrison (2000).
75. Twenty per cent of the companies forming the French index CAC 40 have opted for the two-tier board. See Cozian *et al.*, (1999: 780).
76. Schmidt (1999). See Maeijer and Geens (1990); see also the contributions by Hopt, K. J., Davies, P., Schaafsma, J. R., Simont, L., and Maier-Reimer, G. (1992), in K. J. Hopt and E. Wymeersch (ed.), *European Takeovers*, Chs. 6–8.
78. The Chairman of the Board of Daimler Chrylser, J. E. Schrempp, at the Übersee-Club Hamburg on May 7, 1999 (Reden zum 50. Übersee-Tag, Hamburg p. 68 at 74): 'Nationale Regierungen und ihre Organe können nur noch begrenzt beeinflussen und steuern.... (Es) werden im globalen Dorf schonungslos die Fehler staatlicher Reglementierungen offengelegt.

Industrienationen können nicht von den Vorteilen der Weltwirtschaft profitieren und fleichhzeitig auf die notwendigen inneren Reformen verzichten.' As to the economic theory, see Kerber (2000*a*,*b*).

References

Aktiengesetz (1937).

Albach, H., and Klein G. (ed.) (1988). *Harmonisierung der Rechnungslegung in Europa.* Wiesbaden: Gabler.

André, T. S. (1998). Cultural Hegemony: The Exportation of Anglo-Saxon Corporate Governance Ideologies to Germany. *Tulane Law Review* 73: 69.

Auerbach, A. J. (ed.) (1988). *Corporate Takeovers: Causes and Consequences.* Chicago: University of Chicago Press.

Bainbridge, S. M. (1998). Privately ordered participatory management: An organizational failures analysis. *Delaware Journal of Corporate Law* 23: 979.

Ballwieser (ed.) (2000). *US-amerikanische Rechnungslegung,* 4th edn. Stuttgart: Schäffer-Poeschel.

Basedow, J., Hopt, K. J., Kötz, H., and Baetge, D. (ed.) (1999). *Die Bündelung gleichgerichteter Interessen im Prozeß—Verbandsklage und Gruppenklage.* Tuebingen: Mohr Siebeck.

Bebchuk, L. A., and Roe, M. J. (1999). A Theory of Path Dependence in Corporate Ownership and Governance. *Stanford Law Review* 52: 127.

Berglöf, E. (1997). Reforming Corporate Governance: Redirecting the European Agenda. *Economic Policy* 24: 93.

Bertelsmann-Stiftung and Hans-Böckler-Stiftung (ed.) (1998). *Mitbestimmung und neue Unternehmenskulturen—Bilanz und Perspektiven.* Gütersloh: Bericht der Kommission Mitbestimmung.

Blaurock, U. (2000). Bemerkungen zu einem Europäischen Recht der Unternehmensgruppe. Heidelberg: *Festschrift für O. Sandrock,* p. 79.

Böckli, P. (1995*a*). Droit des marchés de capitaux—La vis se resserre. *SZW,* 219.

—— (1995*b*). Osmosis of Anglo-Saxon Concepts in Swiss Business Law. In N. D. Vogt (ed.), *The International Practice of Law: Liber Amicorum for Thomas Bär and Robert Karrer.* Basel/The Hague: Kluwer p. 9.

—— (1996). Corporate Governance: The 'Cadbury Report' and the Swiss Board Concept of 1991. *SZW,* 149.

Born (1997). *Rechnungslegung international.* Stuttgart: Schäffer-Poeschel.

Börsensachverständigenkommission beim Bundesministerium der Finanzen (1999). Standpunkte zur künftigen Regelung von unternehurunshburnahmen. Bonn.

Bruns, H. G. (1997). (Daimler-Benz), Der Gang an die New York Stock Exchange: Das Beispiel der Daimler-Benz AG. *Wirtschaftsprüferkammer-Mitteilungen* (*WPK-Mitt.*), (Sonderheft Juni), 31.

Bühner, R., and Tuschke, A. (1997). Zur Kritik am Shareholder Value—eine ökonomische Analyse. *BFuP* 49: 499.

CalPERS (1999). International Corporate Governance, Germany Market Principles.

Caparo Industries plc v. *Dickman and others* (1990). 1 *All ER* 568.

Charny, D. (1998). The German Corporate Governance System. *Columbia Business Law Review* 1: 145.

Cheffins, B. (1997). *Company Law: Theory, Structure, and Operation.* Oxford: Oxford University Press.

Committee on the Financial Aspects of Corporate Governance ('Cadbury Committee') (1992).

—— (1993). Report of the Committee on the Financial Aspects of Corporate Governance. London: GCC & Co.

—— (1993). Report of the Committee on the Financial Aspects of Corporate Governance: The code of Best Practice. London: Gee & Co.

Committee on Corporate Governance (1998). Hampel Report (Final Report). London: Gee & Co.

Cozian, M., Viandier, A., and Deboissy, F. (1999). *Droit des sociétés*, 12th edn. Paris: Litec.

Dalhuisen, J. H. (1994). Security in Movable and Intangible Property, Finance Sales, Future Interests and Trust. In A. S. Hartkamp *et al.* (ed.), *Towards a European Civil Code.* Nijmegen *et al.*: Ars Aequi Libri p. 361.

Davies, P. (1998). Issues in Corporate Goverance. Paper prepared for the Brussels conference. 3.12.1998 Brussels: Commission of the European Communities.

—— (2000). Board Structure in the UK and Germany: Covergence or Continuing Divergence? *International and Comparative Corporate Law Journal* 2: 435.

Deakin, S., and Hughes, A. (ed.) (1997). *Enterprise and Community: New Directions in Corporate Governance.* Cambridge: Cambridge University Press.

Dorresteijn, A. (1994). Corporate Governance Issues in the Netherlands, the Legal Structure for Large Companies. In E. Wymeersch (ed.), *Further Perspectives in Financial Integration in Europe.* Berlin/New York: de Gruyter.

Döser, W. H. (2000). Anglo-amerikanische Vertrags strukturen in deutschen Vertriebs- Lizenz- und sonstigen Vertikalverträgen. *NJW*, 1451.

Drobnig, U. (1999). Mobiliarsicherheiten—Vielfalt oder Einheit? Ein Vergleichender Generalbericht. In K. Kreuzer (ed.), *Mobiliarsicherheiten—Vielfalt oder Einheit?* Baden-Baden: Nomos.

Drukarczyk, J. (1999). Shareholder Value, Conference held at the European Business School, Schloß Reichartshausen, 13.04.1999.

Ebke, W. F. (1999). Der Deutsche Standardisierungsrat und das Deutsche Rechnungslegungs Standards Committee ... *ZIP* 1193.

—— and Struckmeier, D. (1994). The Civil Liability of Corporate Auditors: An International Perspective. In International Bar Association, *Capital Markets Forum.* London.

Edwards, J., and Fisher, K. (1994). *Banks, Finance and Investment in Germany.* Cambridge: Cambridge University Press.

Ekkenga, J. (1996). Die Fahrlässigkeitshaftung des Jahresabschlußprüfers für Insolvenzschäden Dritter, WM Sonderbeilage 3.

Emmerich, V., Sonnenschein, J., and Habersack, M. (2001). *Konzernrecht*, 7th edn. Munich: Beck.

Endres, M. (1999). Organisation der Unternehmensleitung aus der Sicht der Praxis. *ZHR* 163: 441.

Ernst and Whinney (1979). *The Fourth Directive, Its Effect on the Annual Accounts of Companies in the European Economic Community.* London: Ernst & Whinney.

European Commission (1996). Green Book, 2.10.1996, O.J.E.C. 28.10.1996 C 321/01.

—— (1998*a*). DG XV Proposal for Amending Directive 78/660/EEC on Annual Accounts as Regards the Use of the Fair Value Method. Brussels: Commission of the European Communities.

—— (1998*b*). *Acts of the Conference on Company Law and the Single Market.* Office of Official Publications of the European Communities: Luxemburg.

—— (2000). European Commission on the accounting strategy and the future action. 13.6.2000, COM 359. Brussels: Commission of the European Communities.

European Council (2000). Common Standpoint of the European Council as to the 13th Directive. 19 June, Brussels: Commission of the European Communities.

Forum Europaeum Konzernrecht (Forum Europaeum Corporate Group Law) (2000). Corporate group law for Europe. *European Business Organization Law Review* 1: 165.

Franzen, M. (1999). *Privatrechtsangleichung durch die Europäische Gemeinschaft.* Berlin: de Gruyter.

Gerke, W. (1999). Interview with W. Gerke by the *Frankfurter Allgemeine Zeitung*, No. 159, 13 July, 27.

German Stock Corporation Act (1965).

German Takeover Act (2001). Draft, July.

German Takeover Act (2001), in force since 1.1.2002.

Gerum, E. (1998). *Mitbestimmung und Corporate Governance.* Gütersloh: Bertelsmann Stiftung.

Gilson, R. (1986). *The Law and Finance of Corporate Acquisitions.* New York: Foundation Press.

Grundmann, S. (1998). The Evolution of Trust and Treuhand in the 20th Century. In R. Helmholz and R. Zimmermann (ed.), *Itinera Fiduciae, Trust and Treuhand in Historical Perspective.* Berlin, Duncker and Humblot, p. 469.

Habersack, M. (1999). *Europäisches Gesellschaftsrecht.* Munich: Beck.

Hachmeister, D. (1997). Shareholder Value. *Die Betriebswirtschaft* 57: 823.

Haire, M. Breen (1999). The Fiduciary Responsibilities of Investment Bankers in Change-of-Control Transactions: In re Daisy Systems Corp. *New York Univesity Law Review* 74: 277.

Harrison, C. S. (2000). Global Corporate Governance: An Empirical Study of International Corporate Governance Guidelines. Working Paper.

Hellwig, H.-J. (1999). Möglichkeiten einer Börsenreform zur Stärkung des deutschen Kapitalmarkts. *ZGR* 781.

Helmholz, R., and Zimmermann, R. (ed.) (1998). *Itinera Fiduciae, Trust and Treuhand in Historical Perspective.* Berlin: Duncker & Humblot.

Herkenroth, K. E. (1994). *Konzernierungsprozesse im Schnittfeld von Konzernrecht und Übernahmerecht.* Berlin: Duncker & Humblot.

Hertig, G. (2000*a*). Regulatory Competition for EU Financial Services. *Journal of International Economic Law* 349.

—— (2000*b*). Western Europe's Corporate Governance Dilemma. In T. Baums, K. J. Hopt, and N. Horn (ed.), *Corporations, Capital Markets and Business in the Law: Liber Amicorum for Richard M. Buxbaum.* London/The Hague *et al.*: Kluwer Law International, p. 267.

High Level Group of Company Law Experts (2002). *Report on Issues Related to Takeover Bids.* European Commission. Brussels, 10, January 2002.

Hoffmann, J. (1999). *Systeme der Stimmrechtsvertretung in der Publikumsgesellschaft.* Baden-Baden: Nomos.

Hommelhoff, P. (1998*a*). Der Einfluß der Banken in der Aktiengesellschaft. In *Festschrift für W. Zöllner.* Cologne: Heymanns, p. 235.

—— (1998*b*). Die neue Position des Abschlußprüfers im Kraftfeld der aktienrechtlichen Organisationsverfassung, (Teil I, II), *BB,* 2567.

—— (1998*c*). Europäisches Bilanzrecht im Aufbruch. *RabelsZ* 62: 381.

Honsell, H. (1999). Amerikanische Rechtskultur. *Festschrift für Zäch.* Zurich: Schulthess, p. 39.

Hopt, K. J. (1982). Grundprobleme der Mitbestimmung in Europa. *ZfA* 207.

—— (1991). Legal Elements and Policy Decisions in Regulating Groups of Companies. In C. M. Schmitthoff and F. Wooldridge (ed.), *Groups of Companies.* London: Sweet & Maxwell, p. 81.

—— (1993*a*). Aktionärskreis und Vorstandsneutralität. *ZGR* 534.

—— (1993*b*). Auf dem Weg zum deutschen Insidergesetz—Die Vorüberlegungen vom Herbst 1992—*Festschrift für Beusch.* Berlin: de Gruyter, p. 393.

—— (1994*a*). Arbeitnehmervertretung im Aufsichtsrat—Auswirkungen der Mitbestimmung auf corporate governance und wirtschaftliche Integration in Europa. In *Festschrift für U. Everling.* Baden-Baden: Nomos, p. 235.

—— (1994*b*). Labor Representation on Corporate Boards: Impacts and Problems for Corporate Governance and Economic Integration in Europe. *International Review of Law and Economics* 14: 203.

—— (1996). Corporate Governance und deutsche Universalbanken. In D. Feddersen, P. Hommelhoff, and U. H. Schneider (ed.), *Corporate Governance.* Cologne: Otto Schmidt, p. 243.

—— (1997*a*). Europäisches und deutsches Übernahmerecht. *ZHR* 161: 368.

—— (1997*b*). The German two-tier board (Aufsichtsrat), a German view on corporate governance. In K. J. Hopt and E. Wymeersch (ed.), *Comparative Corporate Governance, Essays and Materials.* Berlin/New York: de Gruyter, p. 3.

—— (1998*a*). Europäisches Gesellschaftsrecht—Krise und neue Anläufe. *ZIP* 1998: 96.

—— (1998*b*) (ed.) Self-regulation in banking and finance: Practice and theory in Germany. In *La Déontologie bancaire et financière, The Ethical Standards in Banking and Finance.* Brussels: Bruylant, p. 53.

—— (1999*a*). Company law in the European Union: Harmonisation and/or subsidiarity? *International and Comparative Corporate Law Journal* 1: 41.

—— (1999*b*). §93 Aktiengesetz. In K. J. Hopt and H. Wiedemann (ed.), *Großkommentar zum Aktiengesetz.* 4th ed. Berlin *et al.*

—— (2000*a*). Europäisches Kapitalmarktrecht—Rückblick und Ausblick. In S. Grundmann (ed.), *Systembildung und Systemlücken in Kerngebieten des Europäischen Privatrechts.* Tübingen: Mohr Siebeck, p. 307.

—— (2000*b*). Europäisches Konzernrecht—Zu den Vorschlägen und Thesen des Forum Europaeum Konzernrecht. In T. Baums, K. J. Hopt, and N. Horn (ed.), *Corporations, Capital Markets and Business in the Law: Liber Amicorum for Richard M. Buxbaum.* London/The Hague: Kluwer Law International, p. 299.

—— (2000*c*). Towards a corporate group law for Europe. Annual Lecture of the Centre of European Law at King's College London, 11 October.

—— (2001*a*). Das System der Unternehmenüberwachung in Duetschland. In Institut der Wirtschaftsprüfer (ed.), *Kapitalmarktorientierte Untermekmensüberwachung.* Düsseldorf: IDW-Verlag, p. 27.

—— (2001*b*). Auf dem Weg zum deutschen Übernahmegesetz—Gemeinsamer Standpunkt des Rates zur 13. Richtlinie und Diskussionsentwurf des Übernahmegesetzes. In *Festschrift für H.-G. Koppensteiner.* Wien, p. 61.

—— (2001*c*). Konzernrecht in Europa-Zur Diskussion um die Vonchläge des Forum European Konzernrecht. In J. Basedow, U. Drobnig, R. Ellger, K. J. Hopt *et al.* (ed.). *Aufbruch nach Europa, 75 Jahre Max Planck Institut für Privatrechts.* Tübingen: Mohr Siebeck, p. 17.

—— (2002*a*). The duties of the directors of the target company in hostile takeovers—German and European perspectives. In G. Ferrarini, K. J. Hopt, and E. Wymeersch (ed.), *Capital Markets in the Age of the Euro.* London: Kluwer.

—— and Wiedemann, H. (ed.) (1999). *Großkommentar Aktiengesetz,* 4th edn. Berlin/New York, p. 93.

—— and Wymeersch, E. (ed.) (1992). *European Takeovers: Law and Practice.* London: Butterworths.

—— Kanda, H., Roe, M. J., Wymeersch, E., and Prigge, S. (ed.) (1998). *Comparative Corporate Governance: The State of the Art and Emerging Research.* Oxford: Oxford University Press.

—— Rudolph, B., and Baum, H. (ed.) (1997). *Börsenreform—Eine ökonomische, rechtsvergleichende und rechtspolitische Untersuchung,* Stuttgart.

Huntington, S. P. (1993). The Clash of Civilizations? *Foreign Affairs* (Summer), p. 22.

Ihlas, H. (1997). *Organhaftung und Haftpflichtversicherung.* Berlin, p. 317.

Keasey, K., Thompson, S., and Wright, M. (ed.) (1997). *Corporate Governance: Economic and Financial Issues.* Oxford: Oxford University Press.

—— (1999). *Corporate Governance.* Cheltenham/UK: Edward Elgar (4 volumes) (reprints).

Kerber, W. (2000*a*). Interjurisdictional Competition Within the European Union. *Fordham International Law Journal* 23: 217.

—— (2000*b*). Rechtseinheitlichkeit und Rechtsvielfalt aus ökonomischer Sicht. In S. Grundmann (ed.), *Systembildung und Systemlücken in Kerngebieten des Europäischen Privatrechts.* Tübingen: Mohr Siebeck, p. 67.

Kohler, K. (1999). Zur Neuregelung des Vollmachtstimmrechts insbesondere bei Eigenbesitz von Banken. In F. Kübler, J. Scherer, and J. Treeck (ed.), *The International Lawyer, Freundesgabe für W. H. Döser.* Baden-Baden: Nomos, p. 225.

Kommission der Europäischen Gemeinschaften (1999). Umsetzung des Finanzmarktrahmens: Aktionsplan, Mitteilung vom 11.5.1999. KOM 1999: 232, reprinted in *ZBB* 1999: 254.

Korn/Ferry International (1996). *Board Meeting in Session, European Board of Directors' Study*, London.

Kötz, H. (1963). *Trust und Treuhand. Eine rechtsvergleichende Darstellung des anglo-amerikanischen trust und funktionsverwandter Institute des deutschen Rechts.* Göttingen: Vandenhoeck & Ruprecht.

Kozyris, P. J. (ed.) (1996). *Corporate Takeovers through the Public Markets.* The Hague: Kluwer.

Krause, H. (1995). *Das obligatorische Übernahmeangebot.* Baden-Baden: Nomos.

Kübler, F. (1998). Shareholder value: Eine Herausforderung für das Deutsche Recht? In *Festschrift für Zöllner.* Cologne: Heymanns, p. 321.

—— (1999). Aufsichtsratsmitbestimmung im Gegenwind der Globalisierung. In F. Kübler, J. Scherer and J. Treeck (ed.), *The International Lawyer, Freundesgabe für W. H. Döser.* Baden-Baden: Nomos, p. 237.

Lannoo, K. (1999). A European Perspective on Corporate Governance. *Journal of Common Market Studies* 37: 269.

Leyens, P. C. (2003). Aufsichtsrat und Board: ein-oderzweisterfiges Verwaltungs system?-Zum Stand der rechts vergleinchenden Corporate Governance-Debatte. *Rabelsz* (forthcoming).

Lübking, J. (2000). *Ein einheitliches Konzernrecht für Europa.* Baden-Baden: Nomos.

Lüttmann, R. (1992). *Kontrollwechsel in Kapitalgesellschaften.* Baden-Baden: Nomos.

Lutter, M. (2000). Comparative Corporate Governance: A German Perspective. *International and Comparative Corporate Law Journal*, 2: 423.

Maeijer, J. M. M., and Geens, K. (ed.) (1990). *Defensive Measures against Hostile Takeovers in the Common Market.* Dordrecht: Kluwer.

Magnier, V. (1999). *Rapprochement des droits dans l'Union européenne et viabilité d'un droit commun des sociétés.* Paris.

Mann, F. A. (1937). The New German Company Law and Its Background. *Journal of Comparative Legislation and International Law* 19: 220.

Markesinis, B. S. (1995). The comparatist (or a Plea for a Broader Legal Education). *Yearbook of European Law* 15: 261.

—— (1999). Homage an das deutsche Recht. *European Review of Private Law* 7: 429.

Mattheus, D. (1999). Die gewandelte Rolle des Wirtschaftsprüfers als Partner des Aufsichtsrats nach dem KonTraG. *ZGR* 1999: 682.

Miller, G. (1998). Political structure and corporate governance: Some points of contrast between the United States and England. *Columbia Business Law Review* 1998: 51.

Mitteilung der Kommission (1995). Harmonisierung auf dem Gebiet der Rechnungslegung: Eine neue Strategie im Hinblick auf die internationale Harmonisierung. *KOM* 95: 508.

Mogg, J. (1999). Looking Ahead to the Next Century: EU Priorities for Financial Services. *Revue Européene de droit bancaire et financier/European Banking and Financial Law Journal Euredia*, 9.

Mülbert, P. O. (1996). *Empfehlen sich gesetzliche Regelungen zur Einschränkung des Einflusses der Kreditinstitute auf Aktiengesellschaften?* Gutachten E für den 61, Deutschen Juristentag Karlsruhe.

—— (1997). Shareholder value aus rechtlicher Sicht. *ZGR* 1997: 129.

—— (1998). Bank Equity Holdings in Non-Financial Firms and Corporate Governance: The Case of the German Universal Banks. In K. J. Hopt, H. Kanda, M. J. Roe, E. Wymeersch, and S. Prigge (ed.), *Comparative Corporate Governance: The State of the Art and Emerging Research.* Oxford: Oxford University Press, p. 445.

NBK (1999). The 1999 Swedish Takeover Recommendations: NBK Recommendations Concerning Public Offers for the Acquisitions and Transfers of Shares etc., Stockholm.

OECD (1998). *Financial Markets Trends*, November, Paris: OECD.

—— (1999). *Principles of Corporate Governance.* Paris: OECD.

Oetker, H. (1999). Mitbestimmungsgesetze. In K. J. Hopt and H. Wiedemann (ed.), *Großkommentar zum Aktiengesetz*. 4th ed. Berlin/New York: de Gruyter.

Pettet, B. (1998). The combined code: A Firm Place for Self-Regulation in Corporate Governance. *Journal of International Business Law* 1998: 394.

Prigge, S. (1998). A Survey of German Corporate Governance. In K. J. Hopt, H. Kanda, M. J. Roe, E. Wymeersch, and S Prigge (ed.), *Comparative Corporate Governance: The State of the Art and Emerging Research*. Oxford: Oxford University Press, p. 943.

Raiser, T. (1997). Bewährung des Mitbestimmungsgesetzes nach zwanzig Jahren? In *Freundesgabe für F. Kübler*, Heidelberg, p. 477.

Riechers, A. (1996). *Das Unternehmen 'an sich'*. Tübingen: Mohr Siebeck, p. 166.

Roe, M. J. (1996). Chaos and Evolution in Law and Economics. *Harvard Law Review* 109: 641.

—— (1998). German Codetermination and German Securities Markets. *Columbia Business Law Review* 1: 167.

Romano, R. (1997). A Guide to Takeovers: Theory, Evidence and Regulation. In K. J. Hopt and E. Wymeersch (ed.), *Comparative Corporate Governance, Essays and Materials*. Berlin/New York: de Gruyter, p. 3.

Röver (1999), *Vergleichende Prinzipien dinglicher Sicherheiten*. München: Beck.

Schmidt, R. (1999). Cross-border Mergers and Corporate Governance—An Empirical Analysis from 1988 to 1999. Universität Halle-Wittenberg, Betriebswirtschaftliche Diskussionsbeiträge No. 36/99.

Schmidt, R. H., and Spindler, G. (1997). Shareholder-Value zwischen Ökonomie und Recht, *Freundesgabe für F. Kübler*. Heidelberg: C. F. Müller, p. 515.

Schön, W. (1997). Entwicklung und Perspektiven des Handelsbilanzrechts. *ZHR* 161: 133.

Schwarz, G. C. (2000). *Europäisches Gesellschaftsrecht*. Baden-Baden: Nomos.

Skog, R. (1995). *Does Sweden Need a Mandatory Bid Rule? A Critical Analysis*. Stockholm: Jurist för Caget.

Spindler, G. (1993). *Recht und Konzern, Interdependenzen der Rechts- und Unternehmensentwicklung in Deutschland und den USA zwischen 1870 und 1933*, Tübingen.

Stiefel, E., and Maxeiner, J. R. (1997). Why are U.S. Lawyers not Learning from Comparative Law? In N. D. Vogt (ed), *The International Practice of Law. Liber Amicorum for Thomas Bär and Robert Karrer*, Basel/The Hague: Kluwer p. 213.

Sullivan, D. P., and Conlon, D. E. (1997). Crisis and transition in corporate governance paradigms: The role of the chancery court of Delaware. *Law and Society Review* 31: 713.

Teubner (1998). Rechtsirritationen: Der Transfer von Rechtsnormen in rechtssoziologischer Sicht. In *Festschrift für E. Blankenburg*. Baden-Baden: Nomos, p. 233.

Theisen, M. R. (1998). Empirical Evidence and Economic Comments on Board Structure in Germany. In K. J. Hopt, H. Kanda, M. J. Roe, E. Wymeersch, and S. Prigge (ed.), *Comparative Corporate Governance: The State of the Art and Emerging Research*. Oxford: Oxford University Press, p. 259.

Übersee-Tag (1999). J. E. Schrempp in a speech at the Übersee-Club Hamburg on 7 May, (Reden zum 50. Übersee Tag) (Hamburg), p. 68.

Van den Berghe, L., and De Ridder, L. (1999). *International Standardisation of Good Corporate Governance: Best Practices for the Board of Directors*. Boston: Kluwer Academic.

van Hulle, K. (1994). Das Europäische Bilanzrecht—Entwicklungen und Herausforderungen. *Schriftenreihe des Zentrums für Europäisches Wirtschaftsrecht der Universität Bonn*, No. 34, 5.

—— (1995). 'True and Fair View' im Sinne der 4. Richtlinic. In *Festschrift für W. D. Budde*. München, p. 313.

—— (1997). International harmonisation of accounting principles: A European perspective. *Wirtschaftsprüferkammer-Mitteilungen* (WPK-Mitt), (Special Issue, June), p. 44.

—— (2000), Die Reform des europäischen Bilanzrechts: Stand, Ziele und Perspektiven. *ZGR* 537.

von Colbe, W. B. (1997). Was ist und was bedeutet Shareholder Value aus betriebswirtschaftlicher Sicht. *ZGR* 271.

von Wilmowsky, P. (1996). *Europäisches Kreditsicherungsrecht.* Tübingen: Mohr Siebeck.

Wagner, F. W. (1997). Shareholder Value: Eine neue Runde im Konflikt zwischen Kapitalmarkt und Unternehmensinteresse. *BFuP* 49: 473.

Wedderburn of Charlton, Lord (1985). The Legal Development of Corporate Responsibility, For Whom Will Corporate Managers be Trustees? In K. J. Hopt and G. Teubner (ed.), *Corporate Governance and Directors' Liabilities.* New York/Berlin: de Gruyter.

Wenger, E., and Kaserer, C. (1998). German Banks and Corporate Governance: A Critical View. In K. J. Hopt, H. Kanda, M. J. Roe, E. Wymeersch, and S. Prigge (ed.), *Comparative Corporate Governance: The State of the Art and Emerging Research.* Oxford: Oxford University Press, p. 499.

Westermann, H. P. (1996). Vollmachtsstimmrecht und Streubesitzaktionäre in der Hauptversammlung deutscher Aktiengesellschaften. In D. Feddersen, P. Hommelhoff, and U. H. Schneider (ed.) (1996), *Corporate Governance.* Cologne: Otto Schmidt, p. 264.

Wiedemann, H. (1982). The German experience with the law of affiliated enterprises. In K. J. Hopt (ed.), *Groups of Companies in European Laws.* Berlin/New York: de Gruyter, p. 21.

Wiegand, W. (1991). The Reception of American Law in Europe. *American Journal of Comparative Law* 39: 229.

—— (1996). Americanization of Law: Reception or Convergence? In L. Friedman and H. N. Scheiber (ed.), *Legal Culture and the Legal Profession.* Boulder/Oxford: Hart, p. 137.

Windbichler, C. (1985). Zur Trennung von Geschäftsführung und Kontrolle bei amerikanischen Großgesellschaften. *ZGR*, 50.

—— (2000). 'Corporate Group Law for Europe', Comments on the Forum Europaeum's Principles and Proposals for a European Corporate Group Law. *European Business Organization Law Review* 1: 265.

Wymeersch, E. (1999). A Status Report on Corporate Governance Rules and Practices in Some Continental European States. In K. Keasey, S. Thompson, and M. Wright (ed.), *Corporate Governance: Economic and Financial Issues.* Oxford: Oxford University Press, p. 1045.

—— *et al.* (1996). The Proposal for a 13th Company Law Directive on Takeovers: A Multi-jurisdiction Survey. *European Financial Services Law* 3: 301.

—— (1997). The Proposal for a 13th Company Law Directive on Takeovers: A Multi-jurisdiction Survey. *European Financial Services Law* 4: 2.

8

Takeover Regulation in Europe and America: The Need for Functional Convergence

THEO RAAIJMAKERS

1. INTRODUCTION

How should European Community (EC) policymakers respond to the growth in cross-border takeovers across Europe? Does the increase in cross-border mergers give rise to regulatory concern? To what extent will policymakers develop a regulatory approach that establishes procedures that enhance takeover bids while taking into account shareholder interests? And to what extent has the growing market for cross-border takeovers increased pressure on regulators to emulate the USA rules of disclosure and substantive regulation of tender offers?

Mergers and acquisitions continue to be an important mechanism for the growth of firms in the USA and across the European Union (EU). Besides the desire to restructure firms, there are other more powerful reasons that may explain the interest of lawmakers in creating legal rules and institutions to regulate a full legal merger or takeover. The perceived need to compete globally is satisfied through cross-border mergers, which allow companies to build up optimal scale. Consequently, European firms have stepped up the pace in their pursuit of cross-border arrangements. By the end of the first quarter of 1999, merger activity involving European companies had reached \$345 billion, up from \$145 billion in the same period of the prior year. A variety of factors cause firms to invest and divest and change their portfolio. Important as these pressures are on corporate mobility, there remains a great deal of uncertainty about the legal rules for facilitating mergers. It is well accepted that the differences in national legal structures, as well as valuation and accounting systems, create more than a few difficulties in producing takeover regulation that will increase the probability of a bid occurring.

The regulation of the proper role for bidders in the context of takeovers varies from legal system to legal system. For instance, congressional policymakers in the USA, appreciative of the role of tender offers in a complex market, passed the Williams Act[1] that amended the Securities Exchange Act of 1934. In the EU, member states possess a variety of legal rules, ranging from securities and civil law regulation to self-regulatory codes, targeted to the regulation of a tender offer. As part of the EU's Financial Services Action plan, the European Commission (Commission) has sought, through the introduction of a revised 13th Company Law Directive on Takeover Bids, to provide a pan-European framework for takeovers composed of some core principles and requirements to be implemented by the member states in order to coordinate procedures for takeovers.

Against the background of the transformations taking place in the EU, this chapter offers a perspective for analysing the European law of takeover regulation. In light of the recent advances in the study of comparative corporate governance, this chapter will consider whether and to what extent legal convergence of USA and EC law is imminent. In Section 2, we begin by introducing the legislative history of the 13th Directive. We then describe the main elements of the 13th Directive contrasting them to the core elements of the Williams Act. Discussion of the respective regimes will extend to examining the nature and scope of the rules for the commencement of a tender offer, focusing on the major differences that exist in upfront disclosure rules. Section 3 examines the respective rules for the commencement of a tender offer. Also, the current EC reforms are discussed in light of the USA rules on acceptance, withdrawal rights, and best price. Section 4 describes the role of the target firm, particularly with respect to takeover defences. We begin by analysing the EC's position to the use of defensive devices to defeat hostile takeovers. The key provisions of the 13th Directive dealing with defensive devices are analysed in terms of the key practical and theoretical aspects of the regulation. The new EC legislation is contrasted with Delaware law on anti-takeover devices. Section 5 argues that European market practices are well advanced and, consequently in light of the EC's programme for the integration of financial markets, the member states must proceed rapidly to create a body of procedural and substantive disclosure rules located within the EC's system of securities regulation. A complementary framework of supervision and rulemaking is required also as a precondition to the further deepening of financial integration in Europe.

2. COMPARING THE WILLIAMS ACT AND THE 13TH DIRECTIVE

2.1. *Historical Background*

During the 1960s, the securities markets witnessed a substantial increase in tender offers, that is, publicly announced offers to purchase the shares of a target company as a means of effecting corporate mergers. In the USA the tender offer was used to replace or supplement the then more conventional statutory merger route and the use of proxy contests. The increased use of tender offers was partly due to the fact that target corporations subject to the Exchange Act's reporting requirements were required to hold a shareholder vote and to comply with the Act's proxy rules when participating in a statutory merger. Proxy contests at the time were subject to federal disclosure rules. In the competitive atmosphere in which tender offers were being made, a new phenomenon emerged, that is, that of the contested takeover. Banks had thus far not been willing to assist in such transactions, but this changed in the early to mid-1980s when Drexel Burnham and Michael Milken issued junk bonds to finance takeovers (Holmstrom and Kaplan 2001). The lack of adequate disclosure rules in cash tender offers, which made it relatively difficult for investors to make a rational decision based on all relevant information, was one of the main elements causing the debate on changes to the federal securities law (Clarke 1986: 546).

The debate led to the Williams Act (1968), which contained changes made to Sections 13(d) and 14(d)–(f) of the Exchange Act. The Williams Act does not distinguish between friendly and contested takeovers, but aims at striking a balance in a 'market approach' in which the function of federal regulation was to let the investor, on a fully informed basis, decide for himself, after allowing both the offeror and incumbent management to fully present their arguments (Hazen, 1996: 684). It therefore not only prescribes disclosure of the acquirer's intent and forces the target firm to respond promptly, but also requires the disclosure of any intent to make a tender offer for a corporation's shares. The Williams Act is neutral in the sense that its primary aim is to ensure proper disclosure in the process of a tender offer. It focuses on creeping, open-market and privately negotiated acquisitions of securities subject to the Exchange Act's registration and reporting requirements.[2] By requiring disclosure of any acquisition involving 5 per cent of the target's public securities, it prevents creeping or overnight acquisitions, because the public and the target will be alerted to a possible takeover attempt. It does not interfere with anti-takeover statutes (to the extent that these respect the federal regulatory aims) or the target's devices adopted under its own jurisdiction.

The 13th Directive, as part of the EU's programme on harmonizing corporate law in the EU, has a long history (Hopt 1997: 372). In the early 1970s the EC commissioned Professor Pennington to advise on the need for a European Directive on takeovers and other offers. His report was published in 1974 (Pennington 1974). The background and economic developments were more or less similar to those leading to the Williams Act. The creation of the EEC by the Treaty of Rome (1958) gave rise to increasing concentration through a series of mergers within Europe. Regulation, however, was almost non-existent. The UK introduced its self-regulatory City Code on Takeovers and Mergers in 1968, followed by the Netherlands with a self-regulatory 'Code' from the Social and Economic Council (1970, amended in 1975) (Wouters 1993: 270; Wymeersch 1996: 311, 313). Germany published a takeover code in 1995 which was subsequently revised in 1997. Belgium, upon the takeover battle of Carlo De Benedetti against the Société Generale, introduced takeover regulations in 1989 (Wymeersch 1996: 313). France opted for partly self-regulatory and mandatory provisions in 1989.

It took until 1989 before the EC published its first official draft,[3] followed shortly thereafter by its revised draft of 1990.[4] The 1990 draft was primarily aimed at harmonizing 'traffic rules' and proper disclosure rules rather than at interfering in the bid process between offeror and target as such, albeit that it—in contrast to the Williams Act—prevented the target's incumbent management from taking any defensive action after announcement of the offer other than agreed upon by its general meeting of shareholders. It contained detailed provisions on the scope of the directive (national and foreign listed corporations), the tasks and powers of national supervising authorities, disclosure items of the offering document, the takeover announcement, possible review, and other issues. In that sense its approach (including with respect to disclosure) was similar to that of the 'neutral' Williams Act.

In its 1996 draft, the EC took a rather different route by choosing a framework that focused on minimum protective rules for 'outside' (i.e. minority) shareholders, leaving much room for national legislators in the implementation process. As an alternative to the protection provided for by national corporate law systems—particularly on the German Law on Corporate Groups, it followed the UK City Code's provisions[5] by introducing a mandatory offer upon de facto acquisition or the intention to acquire control through a public offer. In 1999, the EU Council of Ministers adopted the 13th Directive with substantial changes. Its scope was narrowed to takeover offers, and the mandatory offer became the focus point of protecting investors in the event of an intended or de facto change of control. A dispute between the UK and Spain on the status of Gibraltar caused its official publication to be delayed until recently.

Since the Williams Act's process of tender offers starts with disclosure rules on acquisitions and the offeror's data (including his intention to make an acquisition) to prevent creeping acquisitions, it should be noted that, before and separately from the 13th Directive, the EU adopted the Major Holdings Directive, which was implemented in member states' legislation (1998 O.J. L348/62). The aim of this directive was to improve market transparency for a corporation's major investors, not to disclose the 'intent' of an acquirer, which was dealt with as a separate subject (Edwards 1999: 292).

2.2. *The Nature, Scope and Effectiveness of the Williams Act and the 13th Directive in Federal Law and State Law*

The Williams Act was enacted by the USA Congress as part of an amendment to the Exchange Act (1934). The Williams Act and the rules and regulations of the Securities Exchange Commission (SEC) promulgated under it thus constitute federal mandatory law, actionable before the federal courts. In contrast, the 13th Directive contains minimum rules and only provides some general principles which the member states are left to implement in their own state law, albeit with the complexity of 'translational' differences. The rules of the Directive will become national law for the member states, and will consequently not be actionable under any general 'federal' principles. The general rules are adopted in summary form only, leaving much room for the member states to 'translate' them into their own national corporate and securities law (so far based on rather different traditions and civil and commercial law concepts). Their enforcement will also be subject to state law rather than any 'federal' law.

EC efforts towards harmonization of securities regulation have dealt with reforms of national law, for example, the regulation of insider trading, disclosure and registration. Less comprehensive than USA securities regulation, the EC directives are designed to enhance the further integration of securities markets in member states. At the same time, efforts to harmonize national corporate law have not been terribly successful. In light of this, we project that there may be concerns arising from the proposed takeover directive's interpretation and implementation which may have to be solved by the European Court of Justice.

Section 14(e) of the USA Exchange Act prohibits fraud, deceit and material misrepresentation or omissions in connection with and throughout any tender offer or request or invitation for tenders, or any solicitation of security holders in opposition or in favour of any such offer, request or invitation. It constitutes actionable rights. Article 10b of the 13th Directive only requires member states to determine sanctions against infringement of the measures taken pursuant to the Directive, which is assumed to be sufficient to promote compliance with those measures. The UK has emphasized discouraging 'tactical litigation'.

2.3. *Flexibility to Adapt Rules to New Developments*

Just like military and diplomatic means of acquiring control over nations, from time to time and under different circumstances throughout corporate history, people have been able to develop new strategies, techniques and weapons to acquire corporate control. The rules are by no means universal, and it is important that rulemaking authorities are able to respond adequately to new developments.

The SEC has rulemaking and enforcement authority and has promulgated further rules and regulations under Sections 13(d), 14(e) and 14(f) of the 1934 Act. The Commission can thus, on its own authority, respond quickly to market developments by issuing releases for discussion and subsequent rulemaking. In contrast, the disadvantage of EU Directives—also in respect of market regulation—is that these create 'petrified' law, since the process of changing the law is as difficult and time-consuming as creating it. The 13th Directive has been drafted as a 'framework' directive, and this is also true for its substantive rules and principles. Article 10a only provides for a Contact Committee to facilitate harmonized application of the Directive and advise the EC 'if necessary' on additions or amendments to the Directive.

2.4. *Securities and Corporate Law*

The Williams Act is part of federal securities law aiming primarily at procedural and disclosure rules in the tender process. Although it has, of course, an impact on the rules of the game (e.g. preventing creeping acquisitions), it leaves aside corporate law subjects on governance and internal affairs, as well as on exit mechanisms and appraisal disputes. It is worth pointing out that the Williams Act was promulgated to create a level playing field for offeror and target and safeguarding the right of the market to information. Federalization of USA corporate law never succeeded, although the 'harmonizing' effect of the Model Acts (such as the (Revised) Model Business Corporation Act) and the Delaware corporate law (Romano 1995) should not be underestimated. Moreover, the Exchange Act, as part of USA securities law, contains specific rules on closely related subjects, such as the disclosure of substantial acquisitions (to prevent creeping acquisitions) and the proxy regulation in the framework of a control battle. USA corporate law thus allows for an integrated approach to such related subjects in the tender process. Although the draft 5th EU Directive provides for some rules on proxy solicitation, this draft was blocked on the element of employee participation in the governance of large firms (Dine 1983; Wouters 2000: 261).

The 13th Directive, although primarily aimed at harmonizing securities law aspects of the tender process, was framed as a company law directive (based on Article 44 of the Treaty). Consequently, the Directive does not avoid commingling, for instance, corporate law principles and rules on exit rights of 'outside' securities holders with the disclosure standards and general principles of market regulation to be observed in the tender process.

It provides very general rules on disclosure in the tender process on the one hand, and just as general principles on 'outsider' protection on the other hand. As it focuses on 'takeover bids', the Directive does not deal with proxy rules, particularly when used in a contested takeover attempt.[6] However, it does provide for a mandatory bid upon acquiring 'control', a term whose definition is left to the member states (Edwards 1999: 117–98).

While the Williams Act deals with both acquisitions of control through open market purchases and with acquisitions through tender offers, the 13th Directive does not integrate the rules for acquisitions in the open market, particularly with respect to the disclosure of acquisition of holdings. Such rules are the subject of a separate Large Holdings Directive. Moreover, while Section 14(a) of the USA Exchange Act (and the SEC Rules thereunder) regulates the solicitation of proxies including those to be observed in a proxy contest, EU law does not cover the subject at all.[7] An important difference, directly related to the course of events in an (attempted) takeover scenario, is that under Section 13(d) of the USA Exchange Act, the acquirer, unless he is a professional investor, has to fully disclose his or her intents on further steps and acquisitions. Obviously, such information is of crucial importance in a control battle, since it allows the market (investors, analysts, and press) to estimate the resulting influence on the share price.

2.5. *Scope*

The scope of the Williams Act includes all tender offers, a term that is not defined in the Act itself. Remarkably, the Williams Act and the regulations based on it do not only regulate partial bids, but also tender offers for the corporation's own securities, be it in a 'going private' transaction (de-listing or termination of public trading) or in the framework of a 'share buy back' programme (Johnson and Millon 1989).

The 13th EU Directive (unlike its earlier drafts of 1989 and 1990) is limited to takeover bids and no longer applies to 'other bids'. Takeover bids are defined as 'a public offer (other than by the offeree company itself) made to the holders of the securities of a company to acquire all or part of such securities'. Allowing partial bids, the Directive's language is ambiguous with respect to the question of whether a two-step front-loaded merger is allowed. According to Article 2(a), a bid 'must follow or have as its objective the acquisition of control'. The term 'must follow' apparently refers to the mandatory bid after or upon acquisition of control (by other means, for example, a privately negotiated acquisition). Equal treatment is mandatory. Consequently, any offer being made should be made to all holders of securities. If the interpretation is correct that any 'scope offer' should be 'to acquire control', the offeror is obliged to make an offer for all outstanding shares, but may make acceptance conditional on a certain percentage (conferring control or majority)[8] of the shares being tendered. Insofar as partial offers are not aimed at acquisition of control, such offers are not takeover offers and are therefore excluded from the Directive's scope.

2.6. *'Constituency' Elements*

While the Williams Act focuses exclusively on the capital market, the 13th Directive reflects a constituency approach in that it requires the board of the target firm to act in the interests of all the company, including the employees when responding to a bid (Deakin 2001: 215). In the context of the debate about stakeholder protection, it should be pointed out that the current draft of the 13th Directive requires bidders to state their intentions with regard to future treatment of employees. This reflects the idea that apart from investors, the target company itself, as well as its employees (human capital) have a direct interest in control transactions. In a considerable number of northern and central European jurisdictions, the employee's interest in the company is reflected in the organic structure of the company's charter itself. Their representatives or members appointed with their support in the Supervisory Board may therefore be directly involved in the decision-making process of the target company. In addition, works councils or similar bodies representing employees' interests may have rights of information and consultation. To that end, these bodies are entitled to the public information available about the offer. Further procedures will follow the rules of the target company's jurisdiction.

The Williams Act does not provide for similar rules, but the subject is very much related to the scope of the business judgement rule and 'state constituency statutes', the (same or similar) question being whether and to what extent the Board may take into account other interests than those of shareholders. Furthermore, the USA discussion on Team Production reveals that in the USA, too, attention is dedicated to the analysis of the firm's human capital (Blair and Stout 1999).

2.7. *Neutrality re: Anti-Takeover Devices and Statutes*

There is a remarkable difference between the Williams Act and the 13th Directive in that, at federal level, the former is effectively neutral with respect to the target taking any defensive measures, since disputes related to such measures may be litigated under the target's state jurisdiction (corporate law). Whether the validity of anti-takeover statutes may impose an unconstitutional burden on interstate commerce is another question. As we will see below, an extensive arsenal of both statutory and other anti-takeover mechanisms is available under USA law and practice, which consequently is not dealt with by the Williams Act.

In contrast, Article 8 of the 13th Directive causes member states to enact rules that will block the target in taking any defensive measures after the offeror has announced his intent to make a control offer. In effect, the provision is designed to prohibit the use of technical barriers to fend off an unwanted, hostile bid (Gilson 1992: 184). The limitations on defensive measures are akin to the General Principle 7 of the City Code which restricts companies from freely adopting measures that could frustrate a bid (Wouters 1993: 291). Recently, the European Commission announced that it will bring cases against some member states to test their protected control arrangements (e.g. 'golden shares') for some public utilities firms.

2.8. *The general principles of the Williams Act and the 13th Directive*

The federal nature of the Williams Act and the Commission's rules and regulations promulgated under the Act provide for direct regulation of the tender process. In order to provide more detailed rules, the SEC promulgated Rules 13d and 14e in addition to the provisions of Sections 13(d) and 14(e) of the Exchange Act.

By contrast, in view of its harmonization character, the 13th EU Directive (Article 5) only requires member states to observe some general principles in drafting their own regulation:

(1) all holders of securities of an offeree company of the same class shall be given equal treatment; in particular, if a person acquires control of the company, the holders of securities shall be protected;
(2) holders of securities of an offeree company shall have sufficient time and information to enable them to reach a properly informed decision on the bid;
(3) the board of an offeree company shall act in the interests of the company as a whole and shall not deny the holders of securities the opportunity to decide on the merits of the offer;
(4) false markets shall not be created in the securities of the offeree company, the offeror company, or any other company concerned by the bid in such a way that the rise or fall in the prices of the securities become artificial and the normal functioning of the markets is distorted;
(5) an offeror shall announce a bid only after ensuring that it can fulfil in full any cash consideration if so offered and after having taken all reasonable measures to secure the implementation of any other type of consideration;
(6) offeree companies shall not be hindered in the conduct of their affairs for longer than is reasonable by a bid for their securities.

In my opinion, the Directive's approach leaves far too much room for 'translation' in the domestic laws of the member states, particularly in light of the fact that the subject finds itself on the crossroads of corporate and securities law. The internationalization of both the financial markets, stock exchanges, trade systems as well as the complete securities and services industries, requires clear rules. As will be explained below, the present Directive by no means provides such EU-wide clarity and consistency. The mere comparison between UK rules and German rules clearly shows this.

3. MARKET TRANSPARENCY, CREEPING ACQUISITIONS AND COMMENCEMENT RULES

Cash tender offers may be made in the middle of the night and completely surprise the target.[9] Similarly, in a creeping acquisition, someone can slowly increase his ownership until he reaches the level of voting power that allows him to control the target. As stated above, the Williams Act, through adequate disclosure rules, was intended both to prevent creeping acquisitions and to regulate tender offers. The 13th EU Directive does not link disclosure rules to the control transactions and does not require the disclosure of the acquirer's intentions. The EU Large Holdings Directive does not require such information either. Since both Directives only make minimum requirements, the member states are not precluded from enacting stricter rules (Article 3(2) of the 13th Directive). However, this may cause substantially different regulation among the member states on this key issue.

Both the Williams Act and the EU Large Holdings Directive require disclosure of ownership of holdings upon crossing certain thresholds. For instance, Section 13(d) of the

Exchange Act requires any person acquiring, directly or indirectly, a 5 per cent beneficial ownership interest in any class of securities subject to the reporting requirements of the Exchange Act to file a statement with the SEC within ten days of reaching the threshold, thus leaving—and this is an important element of the Williams Act—a ten-day window for undisclosed additional acquisitions.[10] Both the Williams Act and the EU Large Holdings Directive therefore effectively prevent, albeit in a different way, creeping acquisitions, since both instruments result in market transparency through informing the public and alerting the target on a possible takeover attempt. There is, however, an important difference. Where disclosure under the Williams Act per se causes its tender rules to commence, disclosure under the EU Large Holdings Directive does not have such a per se effect. This difference is illustrated by the USA ten-day rule,[11] which allows for a window to increase undisclosed ownership of the target's shares during that period, and by comparing it with the neutral rule of the EU Large Holdings Directive, which has no direct bearing on any commencement rule of or under the 13th Directive. Evidently, member states are not precluded from integrating both regulations, but—again—this is not indicated by the EU Directives itself. It creates an important difference between the USA and EU rules of the game: the Williams Act integrates the pre-tender disclosure on holdings into the tender process regulation, while the EU Directives do not.

Upon closer analysis, we see that neither the 13th Directive nor the Large Holdings Directive require disclosure of the acquirer's intention. Section 13(d) of the Williams Act, however, requires disclosure of facts about the identity and background of the acquirer, the source of funds used in the acquisition, the number and percentage of shares held, but also his intentions. If the acquirer intends to acquire control of the target, he must disclose 'any plans or proposals which such person may have to liquidate such issuer, to sell its assets or to merge it with other persons, or to make any other major change in its business or corporate structure'. Schedule 13D is more detailed. In addition to providing certain exemptions for acquisitions by qualified institutional investors in the ordinary course of their investment business,[12] it requires disclosure of details on the acquirer's identity (including whether he has been convicted of a criminal offence or been a party to an SEC proceeding), on the source and amount of funds or other consideration used for the acquisition, and on any arrangements between the acquirer and the target with respect to the latter's securities.

Under both EU Directives it remains possible to acquire a percentage and even a certain degree of 'control' without any commencement of tender rules, although both acquirer and target are required under listing and other market rules to disclose intent and response thereto, respectively. This causes an important difference between the market regulation in the USA and the EU, since the mere acquisition of a block cannot always be properly interpreted without reliable disclosure of the acquirer's intentions. The degree of market transparency in the initial stage is clearly different. In the EU, this period may be characterized by mere speculation, although the offeror and the offeree company may be subject to obligations under applicable listing requirements or trading rules to disclose their intents vis-à-vis their 'own constituency', that is, their own public shareholders. While applicable EU law is victimized by its dispersed nature, under USA regulation, this element is integrated into the general framework of the 1934 Exchange Act.

In this respect, it is important to point out that the lack of adequate disclosure under the Exchange Act may be remedied under Section 14(e) of the Act concerning the disclosure of false or misleading statements (Hazen 1996). Any significant changes in the information that has initially been filed should be disclosed through subsequent amendments. This rule puts the acquirer in a delicate position, because he should not understate nor overstate his intentions, to prevent being sued under Section 14(e) for having misled the market in contravention of the Act's disclosure philosophy. In this respect, the impact of the general disclosure obligations of Section 14(e) of the Exchange Act should be noted. These prohibit material misstatements, omissions and fraudulent practices regardless of whether the target company is subject to the Exchange Act's reporting requirements. It is a delicate question whether and when any preliminary merger discussions and negotiations have crossed the materiality threshold. This remains essentially a question of fact. And whether a fact is material will depend upon whether a reasonable investor would consider it significant for making his investment decision. In the real world, the problem focuses on how to respond to questions concerning rumoured takeovers. Here we touch upon the crossroads of general disclosure rules for listed companies and companies whose shares are otherwise publicly traded. Soft information may be allowed but material misstatements are not (Hazen 1996: 633–4).

In the EU, the question of whether public shareholders have an actionable right is diffuse and depends on the securities and corporate law regulations of the member states. The element of initial disclosure is evidently directly related to the commencement rules of both the Williams Act and the 13th Directive. When and from which moment on will public shareholders of the offeree company be protected under their rules?

Obviously, the disclosure of acquisitions and of intent and the commencement of procedural and disclosure rules are closely linked. The 13th Directive, however, is not very well suited to resolve the many questions that arise in this connection. It is left to the member states to fill the gap, but the choices they make may be substantially different. Consequently, the European Court of Justice will have a hard job interpreting the gist of the Directive in 'prejudicial' proceedings under Article 177 of the Treaty.

3.1. *Tender Offers*

Tender offer rules, providing mandatory rules aimed at a fair and orderly market, market transparency and (equal) protection of investors, should become applicable if and as soon as there is 'a public offer'. These rules should not be circumvented and also be enforceable by a supervising authority and/or directly interested parties. When do these rules start to be applicable, what is the trigger for their commencement, and what is a public tender offer exactly? Obviously, commencement and the definition of tender offer are very closely related.

The Williams Act does not actually define 'tender offer', but it determines the commencement of the rules on tender offers (irrespective of whether these are friendly or hostile), the applicability of the filing requirements of Section 14(d), the general antifraud rules of Section 14(e) and also the disclosure requirements of Section 14(f). The term covers more than traditional takeover attempts and involves public solicitation and, under certain circumstances, may include privately negotiated and open market purchases. The SEC suggested testing the offer on eight factors, that is, (a) active and widespread solicitation of public shareholders; (b) solicitation for a substantial percentage of the target's shares; (c) whether the offer is made at a premium over prevailing market prices; (d) whether the terms of the offer are firm rather than negotiable; (e) whether the offer is conditioned on the tender of a fixed minimum number of shares; (f) whether the offer is open for a limited period of time; (g) whether offerees are subject to pressure to sell their shares; and (h) existence of public announcements of a purchasing programme that precede or accompany a rapid accumulation of shares.

Note that the disclosure rules of Section 13(d) are triggered upon acquisition of more than 5 per cent (with a ten-day window), but that the filing requirements of Section 14(d) begin with the commencement of the offer. Consequently, in the latter case, full disclosure should be made simultaneously with the first of a series of open market purchases. Privately negotiated purchases may constitute a 'tender offer' if they 'result in interfering with a shareholder's unhurried investment decision' and 'fair treatment of investors that defeat the protections of the Williams Act' (Hazen 1996: 623). Generally, secrecy and high pressure in 'midnight specials' and 'bear hugs' should be prevented to avoid the applicability of the Williams Act.

As noted before, instead of 'tender offer', the 13th Directive uses the term 'takeover bid'. According to Article 2(a), the term means a public offer (other than by the offeree company itself) made to holders of the securities of a company to acquire all or part of such securities. A takeover bid may be either mandatory or voluntary, and must follow or have as its objective the acquisition of control. The language used in the Directive is not very clear and to some extent even contradictory. For example, the last sentence seems to limit the term to those tender offers that aim at or result in 'the acquisition of control', while the first sentence seems to allow a partial bid. In combination, one is tempted to read the text as referring to partial bids only if these 'follow or have as its objective the acquisition of control'. It is worth pointing out that Article 5 requires that any bidder attempting to take control of a target corporation cannot acquire a controlling right without making an offer to purchase all the target's shares.[13] May we then conclude that no tender offers other than those intended to acquire control are subject to the 13th Directive? The language remains ambiguous. The key question is: If A wants to acquire control of B, what is he allowed to do apart from making a fully fledged offer? Apparently, a creeping acquisition is not forbidden, disclosure of intent is not required, and privately negotiated acquisitions are not forbidden either. Only if someone crosses the Article 5 threshold should he make a public offer.

3.2. *Commencement*

In addition to Section 13(d) and other disclosure items referred to above, Rule 14d-2 explicitly constitutes a tender offer to commence at 12.01 a.m. of the earliest date of the following events: (a) first publication of a long-form tender offer; (b) first publication of a summary advertisement; or (c) first public announcement of a tender offer (unless the offer is publicly withdrawn within five days). As from commencement, Rule 10b-13 prohibits a tender offeror from purchasing the target's securities other than through the tender offer.

Article 6(1) of the 13th Directive provides that member states shall ensure that rules are in force 'requiring that the decision to make a [takeover] bid is made public without delay and that the supervisory authority is informed of the bid'. Member states may require their supervisory authority to be informed 'before this decision is made public', which evidently refers to the decision to make a bid. It does not constitute a bid that can be accepted by the public shareholders to whom the information is disseminated. Such acceptance is only possible upon the offer document having been published, indicating the terms of the offer (price, acceptance period and conditions to closing). This means that whereas the Williams Act's commencement rules are triggered by public 'events', the rules of the 13th Directive are, by contrast, triggered by a 'decision to make a bid', which is an internal corporate decision, leaving open questions of corporate action to be taken (e.g. approval of Supervisory Board or non-executive board members).

The 13th Directive seems to result in mandatory commencement rules that only apply when the offeror acquires or surpasses a 'specified percentage of voting rights in that company (i.e. the target), conferring on him the control of that company'. In that case, using corporate law language, the Directive requires that 'minority shareholders'[14] should be protected by a mandatory offer directed to all holders for all shares ('at an equitable price'). Whereas the Williams Act allows acquisitions of blocks that do not yet confer control, but are acquired with the intention to build up towards control (albeit with Section 14(d) filing requirements beginning with the commencement of the offer), the 13th Directive apparently aims at an either/or approach: if it is the offeror's intention to acquire control—see Article 2(a) of the 13th Directive in fine—he should make a public offer to all holders for all shares. Conversely, the Williams Act limits subsequent acquisitions.

The key issue here is whether and how consolidation of the offer is possible and regulated. The Williams Act was not successful in preventing shareholders becoming confronted with partial or two-tier bids. While the Williams Act does not proscribe partial bids, the SEC has issued regulations designed to ensure that all shareholders receive equal treatment as to price (Wouters 1993: 287 n. 70). Similarly, the 13th Directive was drafted to prevent such a two-step merger in view of the mandatory offer to be made upon the acquisition (or intended acquisition) of control, which in itself provides for a consolidation mechanism. Still the 13th Directive allows for acquiring creepingly shares up to the threshold for a mandatory bid to be made.

3.3. *Disclosure Items in the Offer Document and Procedures*

Having discussed the initial disclosure requirements, it should be noted that the Williams Act requires disclosure of the acquirer's intention already upon crossing the threshold of Rule 13d. With respect to the offer document itself, member states, under the 13th Directive, must ensure that rules are in force requiring the offeror to draw up and make public in good time an offer document containing the information necessary to enable the holders of securities of the offeree company to reach a properly informed decision on the bid (Article 6(2)). The document must be communicated to the member state's supervisory authority before it is made public. The Directive does not explicitly state that the supervisory authority can or will review the document before its publication, but apparently member states may so provide, since the text explicitly allows for this.[15] Note that under the Williams Act the offer document is to be 'approved' by the SEC. According to Article 7 of the 13th Directive, disclosure of the offer document shall be made in such a way 'as to ensure market transparency and integrity for the securities of the offeree company, of the offeror or of any other company affected by the bid, and which particularly avoid the publication or dissemination of false or misleading information'.

Unlike its more detailed 1990 draft, the 13th Directive (Article 6) provides only general indications of what the offer document should contain: terms of the bid, the identity of the offeror, securities for which the bid is made, the consideration offered (and, in the case of a mandatory bid, basis of valuation), the maximum and minimum percentages that the offeror undertakes to acquire, details on existing holdings and 'related' persons, all conditions to which the offer is subject, the offeror's intentions with regard to the future business and undertakings of the offeree company, its employees and its management, including any material change in the conditions of employment, period of acceptance of the bid, information on the securities offered in an exchange offer, information on the financing of the bid, identity of persons and entities acting in concert with the offeror. In comparison, the Williams Act, and more specifically Rule 14(e), requires detailed information on substantive terms of the tender itself. Given the general rules on the items to be discussed in the offer document, it should be noted that the implementation of more detailed rules under the USA Exchange Act is assigned to the SEC, which did indeed promulgate such detailed rules in Rule 14(e), while under the 13th EU Directive this is left to the member states (thus causing a possible material variety of different rules). For these reasons I believe that the EU takeover rules should be regulated by a European Regulation rather than by a Company Law Directive.

3.4. *The Requirement to Disclose Rules During the Tender Offer Process*

As stated above, tender offer rules aim for adequate disclosure being made by the offeror (and the target corporation's response) concerning 'preceding' acquisitions and, upon commencement, concerning all relevant data of the offeror. This should allow investors to make a well-considered and duly informed decision whether or not to accept the offer.

Section 14(e) of the Exchange Act provides that the principle of fair disclosure should be adhered to throughout the bidding process. Hence it requires current information to be updated and disclosed if the materiality test is met. Non-observance may cause the information to become misleading and is therefore actionable in different ways. Furthermore, in accordance with Rule 14e-3 in the sense of Section 14(e) it is unlawful for anyone to purchase or sell any securities of the offeree company on the basis of inside knowledge rather than publicly available information.

The 13th Directive does not direct the member states to legislate or regulate for such rules, at least not explicitly. Again, the Directive contains only minimum requirements, leaving the member states free to enact the provisions. Article 6(4) requires member states to ensure that parties provide the supervisory authority with all information in their possession concerning the bid 'which is necessary for the supervisory authority to discharge its functions'. This only relates to the position of the supervisory authorities.

The position of investors is covered in an indirect way by Article 7(2): 'the member states shall ensure that rules are in force which provide for the disclosure of all information or documents required in such a manner as to ensure that they are both readily and promptly available to the holders of securities at least in those member states where the securities of the offeree company are admitted to trading on a regulated market and to the representatives of employees of the offeree company or, where there are no such representatives, to the employees themselves.' In addition, Article 10b of the 13th Directive provides: 'Each member state shall determine the sanctions to be applied for infringement of the measures taken pursuant to this Directive. The sanctions shall be sufficient to promote compliance with these measures.' This element of tender offers and takeover bids also seems to be so essential that it should not be left to differences.

3.5. *Acceptance, Withdrawal Rights, Proration and Best Price Rules*

Article 6a of the 13th Directive only generally requires member states to ensure that the period of acceptance to be disclosed in the offer document shall not be less than two weeks and no longer than ten weeks. This period may be extended on condition that the offeror gives at least two weeks' prior notice of its intention to close the bid. In contrast to the Williams Act, the Directive does not contain any rules on withdrawal rights. Section 14(d)(5) of the Williams Act provides that all securities deposited pursuant to a tender offer may be withdrawn by or on behalf of the depositor at any time until the expiration of seven days after the first publication of the formal tender offer (or request or invitation) and at any time after sixty days from the date of the original tender offer or request or invitation, unless a different rule is provided for by the SEC. Rule 14d-7 provides that withdrawal rights may be exercised throughout the period that the tender offer remains open, which must be at least twenty business days. The 13th Directive does not contain any explicit rules on withdrawal rights. Under Article 6a(2), the member states may allow extension of the period for acceptance for specific, appropriate cases.

Furthermore, Section 14(d)(6) of the 1933 Act provides that if a greater number of shares is deposited, a person tendering for less than all the outstanding shares is bound to take up the securities 'as nearly as may be pro rata, disregarding fractions, according to the number of securities deposited by each depositor'. The 13th Directive does not explicitly provide for such proration, albeit that under its general principles of equal treatment of securities holders in the offeree company (Article 3(1a)), such pro rata rule seems to be indicated.

As noted earlier, the SEC has promulgated best price requirements for a single transaction. Rule 14d-10, addressing equal treatment of security holders, prevents a bidder from making a tender offer unless (a) the tender offer is open to all security holders of the class of securities subject to the tender offer,[16] and (b) the consideration paid to any security holder pursuant to the tender offer is the highest consideration paid to any other security holder during such tender offer.[17] These latter words clearly indicate (a) that the best price formula is limited to the period during which the offer is outstanding and (b) that, consequently, two-tiered offers (including front-loaded two-step mergers) consummated in two distinct steps are not covered by this best price rule of Rule 14d-10.[18]

Article 3 of the 13th Directive only requires the member states to observe the general principles of equal treatment in their national rules. It should be noted, however, that the regulation of member states may provide otherwise and adopt best price rules that de facto constitute an anti-takeover device, for example, by extending such a rule to the highest price being paid during a certain period of time before the offer.[19]

3.6. *Lapse, Revision, Disclosure of Results of the Bid, Irrevocability and Conditions Permitted*

Without any further guidance, Article 9 of the 13th Directive requires the member states again rather generally to ensure that rules are in force which govern the conduct of bids, at least for the following items: (a) lapse of the bid; (b) revision of the bid; (c) competing bids; (d) disclosure of the results of bids; and (e) irrevocability of the bid and conditions permitted. With respect to revision of the consideration offered, Section 14(d)(7) of the Exchange Act provides that any variation to a tender offer before its expiration should result in the best price being paid to the offerees.

3.7. *The Mandatory Bid, Protection of Minority Shareholders and Consolidation*

Under the Williams Act, a merger may take place through a 'front-loaded two-step merger': at the first step, an offeror may acquire a controlling interest and subsequently freeze out any remaining minority under applicable corporate state law of the target. The rules concerning 'all holders' and 'best price' warrant equal treatment. The second step usually takes place through the use of consolidation mechanisms available under the jurisdiction of the target.

Article 5 of the 13th Directive takes a different route. If a person, as a result of his own acquisition or the acquisition by persons acting in concert with him, holds securities of a company (added to any existing holdings and the holdings of persons acting in concert with him) so that he, directly or indirectly, has a specified percentage of voting rights of the target company, conferring on him the control of that company, member states will ensure that such a person is obliged to make a bid as a means to protect the minority shareholders of that company. This bid shall be addressed to all holders of securities for all their holdings at an equitable price. If non-liquid (listed) securities are offered in exchange, the bid should offer a cash alternative. This mandatory bid leaves open the question as to whether and how consolidation of the offer may take place if not all holders accept. That, also under the law of the member states, will remain a question of the target's national corporate law. Moreover, much will depend on the definition of each member state's law of what exactly constitutes 'control'. In that respect, another question is whether through the mechanism of proxy voting 'control' can be required if the contesting shareholder(s) do not have a majority of the voting securities. Does Article 5 of the 13th Directive allow such control to be included?

The basic philosophy behind the mandatory bid seems to be the protection of investors when a transaction results in a change of control. This is a subject at the crossroads of market regulation and corporate law, and more specifically, the law on groups of companies. This 'mixed character' can be illustrated by comparing German, UK, and Netherlands law.

In the German 'Aktiengesetz', an 'Aktiengesellschaft' (formal public corporation, also known as AG) can only be brought under full control of another firm by means of an 'Unternehmensvertrag' (corporate contract between the AG and the firm wishing to establish control, thus creating a special group relationship) that has to be agreed upon by the general meetings of shareholders of both firms. The controlling firm may have corporate voting power, but this is not necessarily the case. It may also only have a minority of the target's shares. Other shareholders stand outside the special group relationship thus created (or already existing in an informal way).[20] They are therefore dealt with as 'outside' shareholders (aussenstehende Aktionäre), which, incidentally, are not necessarily minority shareholders. The entering into such an Unternehmensvertrag entitles the parent to full and unrestricted control, resulting in the outside shareholders becoming in effect holders of 'non-voting shares'.[21] Consequently, the contract provides for special protection of these outside shareholders: they are entitled to either (a) a dividend guarantee or (b) a cash-out. One can regard these rules as constituting a specific regime for acquiring control in an AG. We should, however, keep in mind that there is a broader background to these provisions. The statutory structure of the German AG is in fact the enactment of the Berle and Means model of a public corporation, in which ownership is separated from control.[22] This is evidenced by, amongst other things, the very limited powers of the AGM and control being effectively vested in the Board of Management under supervision of a Supervisory Board.[23] These provisions prevent even a majority (or sole) shareholder from taking full control. Furthermore, the Aktiengesetz establishes very severe rules on capital protection as a means of protecting the interests of its creditors, while at the same time underscoring the limited liability of its shareholders. Full control with power to instruct the subsidiary AG in this framework has to be legitimized by the specific provisions just mentioned.[24]

The German example illustrates the difficult concept of 'control'. In Germany it stands for the power to give binding instructions to the management of the subsidiary even if these are 'harmful' to the subsidiary's 'own interest'. More generally, 'control' starts when another person is able to appoint and dismiss (the majority or all) members of the board and/or to effectively direct the corporation's charter and bylaws to be changed or the corporation to be reorganized in another way.

Comparing the German corporate concept with the UK concept of shareholders' supremacy, the intermediate Netherlands concept of organized corporate oligarchic structures, and the often family-held public corporations in Italy, France and Belgium, we see remarkable differences in the way the concept of control is interpreted, not only from a theoretical and conceptual point of view, but also in practical terms. In the UK, the City Code obliges a person acquiring 30 per cent or more of the shares in a publicly traded company to make a mandatory offer for the remaining outstanding shares. If in such an offer not all shares are acquired, the offeror may petition the remaining shares by judicial decree to be attributed to him against the consideration that was promised in the offer. Conversely, the remaining minority shareholders may petition that their shares be taken up by the offeror. In the concept of the City Code, 'control' does not play an explicit role: the mere acquisition of 30 per cent or more forces the acquirer to tender for the rest of the shares. Conceptually, this is a matter of market regulation rather than—as in the German Aktiengesetz—of corporate law. Similarly, the Belgian Royal Decree (1989) obliges a person 'acquiring control' to tender for the remaining shares, the best price rule being extended to the highest price paid in the preceding twelve months. The concept is meant to discourage persons from acquiring control against a premium.

The result of the City Code and the Belgian regime is that a premium can be paid as long as the bidder does not cross the boundary of control. The USA framework does result in early disclosure of acquisition (and intent) of holdings, triggering commencement. Under Netherlands law, there is no general concept of control. For accounting purposes, a concept is used (inspired by the 7th EU Directive on the single and consolidated annual accounts) that is essentially based on decisive control of the subsidiary.[25]

Returning to Article 5 of the 13th Directive, we notice a remarkable difference with the Williams Act. Under this article, a person may well pass the 10 per cent threshold of the Williams Act and acquire additional shares, even with a 'premium', up to the level of 'control'. Since he crosses that threshold, he is obliged to make an offer for the remaining shares 'at an equitable price'. On the other hand, if he intends to acquire control, the somewhat vague description of Article 2(a) of the Directive may be interpreted as forcing member states to provide for a Williams Act translation, resulting in triggering commencement at that earlier point in time. The missing link is again the integration of the 13th Directive with the Large Holdings Directive.

Apart from this important difference, even a very brief comparison of some prevailing systems in the EU illustrates that very different control concepts exist alongside each other, both in terms of percentages and concepts, and with respect to their corporate or market-orientation. The 13th Directive does not provide clear guidance as to how its provisions on the mandatory offer should be implemented in national law. If member states provide for a certain percentage of the voting securities, should an exemption be made when such a percentage does not effectively result in control for the acquirer? The Williams Act, on the other hand, simply refrains from such fluid concepts.

Corporate and financial market concepts are apparently commingled in the framework of the 13th Directive, and substantial differences in the resulting national systems are therefore expected to emerge. That may take place even to the extent that the substance of the 13th Directive is endangered. If, for example, the best price rule would be extended as to include the best price paid (in a certain period) before the commencement of the tender offer rules, the result may be that the system in fact works as a quasi anti-takeover rule. Under Netherlands law, one may pay a premium for a block of shares before the public offer, but subsequent consolidation of the offer is hampered by the rule that within three years of the consummation of the offer, the offeror is not allowed to pay a higher price for further acquisitions, unless explicitly allowed by the supervisory authority, upon acquisition in normal trade and in the course of a consolidation transaction (so far only allowed if the offeror acquires more than 95 per cent of the target's shares).[26]

4. POSITION OF THE TARGET COMPANY—ANTI-TAKEOVER DEFENCES

4.1. *Obligations of the Offeree Company*

Both the Williams Act and the 13th Directive address the obligations of the offeree company with respect to its response to the offer, and require in that respect proper disclosure of the company's response to the offer or the announcement of the offer. Rule 14e-2 requires the target company's management to respond to the offer within ten days from the first date upon which the tender offer is published. It may (a) recommend acceptance or rejection of the offer; (b) express no opinion and remain neutral towards the bidder's offer; or (c) make a statement that it is unable to take a position with respect to the offer. Any such statement is subject to all the rules concerning materiality, as well as the potential civil and criminal liabilities for material misstatements (Hazen, 1996: 637). According to Rule 14e-2 (3b), any material change in the required disclosure has to be published promptly or be communicated to security holders.

Article 8(1b) of the 13th Directive requires member states to ensure that rules are in force that require the board of the offeree company to draw up and make public 'a document setting out its opinion on the bid, together with the reasons on which it is based including its views on the effects of the implementation on all the interests of the company, including employment'. The Directive does not prescribe this to be accomplished in a certain (short) period of time. It should also be recalled that, according to Article 10b, member states shall determine the sanctions to be applied against infringement of the national rules implemented under the scope of the Directive, which should be sufficient to promote compliance with those measures. Although the gist of both the Williams Act and the 13th Directive in this respect is not very different, the sanctions may be substantially different.

4.2. *Anti-Takeover Tactics: The USA Perspective*

Despite several attempts to bring about changes, the Williams Act takes a neutral stand on, and does not interfere with, any defensive action being taken by the target company (Hazen 1996: 608). However, the Act's disclosure requirements referred to above are designed to make sure that whatever defensive tactics may be taken are open and above board. Note that the validity of state law anti-takeover legislation can be challenged under the Supremacy Clause and the Commerce Clause of the USA Constitution.

A great variety of defensive tactics have been developed, both by states through anti-takeover statutes and by target companies themselves, allowing corporations under the state's jurisdiction to resist takeover attempts (Bebchuk and Ferrell 2001). For instance, Delaware allows firms in anticipation of a hostile bid to adopt a device subject only to the standards of the business judgement rule. Paragraph 6.01 of the ALI Principles of Corporate Governance, building upon Rule 14e-2 and reflecting in substance the present law in most USA jurisdictions, allows the target company's board in the exercise of its business judgement (also upon and after the announcement of an unsolicited offer) to approve, reject or decline a proposal to engage in a transaction in control. A transaction in control to which the company is a party requires approval by the shareholders. The board (under para. 6.02) can take an action that has the foreseeable effect of blocking an unsolicited offer, but only if this is a reasonable response to the offer.

In considering the reasonableness of its response, the board may take into account all factors relevant to the best interests of the company and its shareholders, including questions of legality and whether the offer, if successful, would threaten the company's essential economic prospects and, in addition, whether it has regard for interests of groups (other than the shareholders) with respect to which the company has a legitimate concern if to do so would not significantly disfavour the long-term interests of shareholders. A person challenging the board's action(s) has the burden of proof. An action that does not meet the standards of a reasonable response to the offer may be enjoined or set aside, but directors authorizing such an action are not subject to liability for damages if their conduct meets the standards of the business judgement rule.

The business judgement rule (as described in paragraph 4.01 of the ALI Principles) can be summarized as follows. Directors have a duty to the company to perform their jobs in good faith, in a manner that they reasonably believe to be in the best interests of the company, and with the care that an ordinarily prudent person would reasonably be expected to exercise in a similar position and under similar circumstances. Directors should make inquiries to the extent that they reasonably believe to be necessary when the circumstances would alert a reasonable director to the need for that. In performing their duties, they may rely on materials and persons. Directors making a business judgement in good faith fulfil their duties if they (a) are not interested in the subject matter of the business judgement; (b) are informed with respect to the subject of the business judgement to the extent that they reasonably believe to be appropriate under the circumstances; or (c) rationally believe that the business judgement is in the best interest of the company. These principles reflect the state of the art in most jurisdictions and, primarily, that of the State of Delaware, under which most NYSE companies are incorporated.

4.3. *Anti-Takeover Tactics: Differences Between 13th Directive and Williams Act*

In a transatlantic and even global perspective, the approach taken by the EU in the 13th Directive is remarkable. In at least two respects, the Directive is not 'neutral' in the same sense as the Williams Act, which is primarily aimed at rules on decent behaviour and proper disclosure.

Paragraph 8 of the Directive requires member states to regulate that the target's board 'at the latest after receiving the information [on an unsolicited bid] and until the bid is made public or the bid lapses, (...) should abstain from completing any action other than seeking alternative bids which may result in the frustration of the offer, and notably from the issuing of shares which may result in a lasting impediment to the offer or to obtain control over the offeree company, unless it has the prior authorisation of the general meeting of shareholders given for this purpose, during the period of acceptance of the bid'.

In a transatlantic perspective, this provision far from converges the rules of the game, since member states are hampered in their jurisdictional freedom to regulate the country's corporate and business law[27] to include anti-takeover statutes (irrespective of the business scope of firms to be included and the (exempted) competitive nature thereof) or legislation that has the foreseeable effect of constraining the acquisition of effective control (such as prior permission from the government or the acquisition of cooperation of employees' representatives). Similarly, the position of individual firms will be hampered. If the Directive comes into force, one may expect that both member states and individual firms will seek for *ex ante* structural protection against unsolicited tender offers to avoid the apparent problems Article 8 of the Directive will cause.

The lack of a well-established business judgement rule will play an important role in litigation on the behaviour of the incumbent management. Uncertainty will arise with respect to the interpretation of 'constituency statutes' within the EU, as is reflected in Section 309 of the UK Companies Act and Article 2:140 of the Netherlands Civil Code.

Another consideration needs to be made with respect to the effects in the real world that the Directive presumably would have over time. Unlike the USA, Europe does not have—and in more than one respect—one common securities market. Despite the recent concentration, resulting in Euronext, for instance, and the creation of EASDAQ, Europe still does not have a single major market place such as the NYSE and the NASDAQ. Listing rules, trading systems and applicable securities laws are still governed by the jurisdiction of the member states. But in the discussion of the possible effects in the real world, the non-existence of one common market structure is even more important. There are still major differences within the EU with respect to market structures, including liquidity, degrees of dispersion of shares, the existence of block holders, concentrated investment by pension funds and institutional investors. These differences will cause the implementation of the 13th Directive to result in just as many major differences in its practical implications and results. These will fuel (and will remain to be fuelled by) differences in corporate, securities and applicable civil and commercial law.[28] In addition, there are the differences discussed earlier, that is, those that may derive from institutional provisions in corporate law (causing problems in establishing degrees of control), as well as different provisions with respect to the consolidation of an offer upon its successful consummation.

Finally, an important difference between the USA and the EU remains that proxy solicitation and therefore also proxy fights are not well developed in Europe, if they exist at all. It is too easy to suppose that a common set of rules will emerge just from market integration. The extensive rules of the Securities Exchange Act and the SEC Rules and regulations promulgated thereunder are evidence of the complicated 'market' character that surpasses the complexity of agency rules in general.

5. TOWARDS FEDERALIZATION AND TRANSATLANTIC CONVERGENCE OF EU TENDER OFFER RULES?

In my view, there is an urgent need for homogenous and federal EU rules on the market regulation of public tender offers. The 13th Directive is just not offering such rules. Its 'framework for harmonization' approach is not fit for the purpose of an integrated solution. The implementation of its general principles and even of its mandatory offer provisions may lead to seriously different substantive and procedural national rules, not the least in view of its mixed character of securities and corporate law. I believe that, without any delay, the EU should start discussions on federalization of homogenous and federal rules on public tender offers and contribute its own jurisdictional part to the development of a global market system by not losing precious time reinventing a wheel that has already been invented, developed and tested in the USA market. Here, there ought to be no problem of diverging national rules, since the subject is really part of international market regulation, not unlike commercial laws in the old days (Wouters 2000).

The 13th Directive already provides for cooperation between national supervisory authorities with a view to building consistency in the application of the rules and advising on changes to be made. In my view, this does not in itself take away the 'petrifaction' of the

EU Directive as such. An indispensable condition for an integrated EU financial market is that the rules of the game are supervised (but also, as soon as is necessary, changed) by a body with teeth: a European Securities and Exchange Commission. In addition to the already existing ECB, it should take part in EU-wide supervision over the integrity of its financial markets. Since democratic values are only slowly developing in the EU, the European SEC should also be given regulatory power, the use of which should be made subject to proper consultation mechanisms, for example, in the form of 'exposure drafts', green papers or otherwise.

Given the above summary comparison of the Williams Act and the 13th Directive, the question may be raised whether and to what extent we may expect the two systems of tender regulation to converge. A preliminary question is whether and to what extent any such convergence is desirable and feasible. With respect to that latter question, I have no doubt that convergence, at least with respect to the part of securities laws that we are dealing with here, is indeed desirable. In our globalizing economies (as a result of the integration of securities markets and the securities and services industries, as well as transatlantic investments and acquisitions in both directions), securities markets have indeed developed as an almost 'supra-national' area of business activities. An international and transatlantic market for corporate control has been developing over the past few decades in a way that seems to have no precedent in history. Nevertheless, different systems of general securities regulation and national corporate, civil and commercial laws still exist alongside each other. Of course, it is unrealistic to think that full unification of the systems across the Atlantic would be feasible, and there is no urgent need for that either. However, we cannot ignore the fact that in the global M&A industry, both acquirers and targets are at both sides of the Atlantic. A certain degree of convergence of the rules of the game therefore seems justifiable. This is particularly true for the regulatory elements of the financial market, and more specifically securities regulation. There is no need to discuss a Lex Mercatoria to arrive at the conclusion that this is indeed a matter of international 'commercial law'.

We can draw several conclusions from our comparison between the Williams Act and the 13th Directive. First, the comparison reveals that the USA has managed to succeed in providing one common set of federal rules, whereas the 13th Directive has not. In the EU, too many important questions are left to the member states, which inhibits the creation of one common set of relatively simple and neutral rules. Not only does each member state have to implement the Directive into its securities, civil and commercial law, governmental supervision and enforcement of these rules is also left to separate national authorities. Growing cooperation between these authorities may be welcomed, but is by no means a guarantee that the basic rules of the game will become the same throughout the EU.

Also, it is unclear whether firms should be treated as commodities. The basic issue is whether a corporation as a 'person' can be 'enslaved' against its will. In the twentieth century we became accustomed to no longer regard legal persons as 'fictions' (which Von Savigny did), but as 'real persons'. People and tools organized as a firm are now able to commit tort and be the subject of constitutional and treaty rights, something which had previously been attributed to natural persons only; they can also commit felonies and misdemeanours and be liable under penal law. The corporate governance debate revealed more than one good reason to revise the 'institutional' approach to the public corporation, specifically the disciplinary mechanisms being developed (or rather reinvented) to deal with moral hazard and self-dealing on the part of incumbent management teams. But all this did not take away the concept of firms being 'persons' under their constituent jurisdiction in their own right. It has been the subject of numerous studies and research. Still, 'personhood' is in the realm of national legislators, and the meaning of the term is very much a subject of a far broader societal and environmental impetus. Most of the Northern European member states for long have some form of employee participation to be formalized into their corporate law, that is, 'internalized' into the dissemination of corporate powers and the decision-making process. Similarly, many USA states provide statutes for broad 'constituent' corporate objectives in their corporate law and allow their well-established business judgement rule to provide a target board with large discretionary power to resist an unsolicited tender offer. That is the other side of the coin.

The second conclusion we may draw from our comparison is that the Williams Act clearly does not interfere with the power of a firm to resist an unsolicited tender offer under its corporate charter, whereas the 13th Directive gives the supervising authority the power to restrain a target trying to defend itself after the announcement of a tender offer. In light of existing legislative differences between the member states and differences in market structure, the Directive presumably will not lead to convergence of practice.

In practice, much flexibility is observed, including when one is confronted with new regulations. The creative power of the securities industry, as well as the managers of the potential targets, will prompt the development of new techniques to frustrate hostile bids. Here, another and again a difficult question arises. Can we foresee the influence of the implementation of the 13th Directive (in different ways for separate member countries) with respect to (a) transatlantic deals; (b) the development of a level playing field within the EU; and (c) the development of mechanisms used in the M&A industry?

The third observation is that in practice, new answers to ever-changing circumstances will continue to be developed. Many questions will arise again and again, and research on such changing questions and solutions should continue, both in the EU and the USA. For example, are creeping acquisitions preceding a full offer always 'bad'? What stance should be taken as to the possibility of block trades and the premium to be paid for blocks? What effects are to be expected in real life (and different markets) from the introduction of mandatory bids? What will it mean in terms of allocation of market resources and powers over (parts of) industry?

A fourth observation concerns the further development of the law with respect to the powers and duties of target corporations. The EU does not have a single standard on the accountability of a target's board comparable to the well-established USA business judgement rule (and related standards regarding indemnification of board members). Nevertheless, there seems to be a certain degree of convergence between the fiduciary duties in US (Delaware) case law, since the broader interest of the target as such plays a dominant role in contesting an unsolicited public offer, allowing the board to balance the different interests of stakeholders. The EU and its member states should not spend precious time on very time-consuming debates with various interest groups (securities industry, stock exchanges, industry, trade unions, etc.) about dismantling the multitude of statutory[29] or by-law provisions that had the effect (intended or consequential) of constraining control transactions in any way. Here, too, professionalism and sophistication seem to be key to the development of the law, as evidenced by the example of Delaware law. Why do we not in the EU take the initiative to draft European Corporate Governance Principles, building on the principles as developed by the OECD and the American Law Institute? This would also be helpful for developing mechanisms on post-bid consolidations, the prevention of insider trading during a public offer and a proper mechanism for proxy solicitation. In this context, we should remind ourselves that the Williams Act was enacted partly as a reaction to the circumvention of the disclosure rules for proxy solicitation (and fights). The issue is therefore related to the more general question of whether a control transaction is subject to shareholder vote.

Finally, Europe is currently in the middle of a concentration of stock exchanges, with no combination being ruled out. This will undoubtedly fuel the issues discussed in this chapter in the broader context of harmonizing listing and trading rules. The securities industry thus may take the lead with a 'first mover' effect, possibly evolving in such regulatory competition. The EU should, however, stay in control of the process as far as market integrity is concerned.

POSTSCRIPT

This article was finished before publication of the 2001 text of the draft 13th Directive and does not take into account changes made in the draft. The 2001 draft meanwhile has been rejected by the European Parliament. The European commission thereupon assigned a High Level Expert Group, chaired by Professor Jaap Winter, to advise on means to achieve a level playing field in the European market for corporate control, the determination of a equitable price in mandatory bids and mechanisms to squeeze out minorities after change of control. Their advise was published in January 2002. There is reason to believe that the comparative analysis of the basic structure of the Williams Act and the draft 13th Directive is still highly relevant to the ongoing regulatory debate.

ACKNOWLEDGEMENT

The author wishes to thank Professor Dr Christel Grundmann-Van de Krol, Professor Dr Joseph A. McCahery, and Prof Dr Cor. AE. Uniken Venema, for their comments on an earlier version of this chapter.

Notes

1. 15 U.S.C. §§ 78m(d)–(f) (1998).
2. An offeree company in the 13th Directive is defined as 'a company whose securities are the subject of a bid', not necessarily a public corporation whose securities are listed and/or publicly traded and, in the latter case, subject to securities law disclosure and reporting requirements.
3. For the original proposal see, Proposal for a Thirteenth Council Directive on Company Law Concerning Takeover and Other General Bids, O.J. 1989, c 64/8 and Bull. EC, Suppl. 3/89.
4. See O.J. 1990, C 240/7.

5. See Rule 9 of the City Code. Some other member states had also introduced such mandatory bid rules: for example, Art. 32 of the Belgian Royal Decree (1989).
6. The question of whether a change in the board following a proxy fight constitutes a shift in control as meant in Art. 5 of the Directive is not answered explicitly by the Directive itself, but is left open to the member states in defining 'control'.
7. Since the member states provide their own definition of 'control', this may include acquisition of control by means of a proxy fight.
8. It is unclear whether a majority of the voting securities really confers control. See the example of the German Aktiengesetz given below.
9. Of course, exchange offers usually require a shareholder vote of the offeror to authorize his 'issuing' of shares in exchange for the target's shares tendered by its shareholders.
10. This window has often been criticized, but recommendations to close it, for instance, by requiring advance filing of an intent to acquire more than 5 per cent, have so far not led to changes in the Exchange Act or Schedule 13D.
11. Attempts to close that window or even to subject such acquisition to advance filing failed Hazen (1996: 621). State laws also attempted to close that window.
12. Amongst other things, institutional investment managers must fill in on Form 13F the degree of voting control exercised by them. Disclosure of investment strategies may be exempted.
13. Furthermore, it should be noted that a tender offer for a public company's own shares is explicitly excluded, thus not providing minimum protective standards for holders of securities in such a transaction (going private, buy back programmes).
14. The term 'minority' shareholders is incorrect since member states may define control to be changed upon acquisition of effective working control or through other means not based on majority control.
15. 'Where the offer document is subject to the prior approval by the supervisory authority and once it has been approved, it shall be recognized, subject to any translation, in the other Member States [...]' (Art. 6(2) of the 13th Directive).
16. The question has arisen whether an 'opponent' in a control contest may be excluded from the offer. See Hazen (1996: 631).
17. Cf. Section 14(d)(7) of the Exchange Act.
18. Cf. the different approach of the 'best price rule' in Art. 32 of the Belgian Royal Decree.
19. Cf. Section 14(d)(7) of the Exchange Act.
20. In which case the 'parent' firm is subject to certain limitations in exercising its 'control'. See paragraphs 308–311 of the Aktiengesetz.
21. This expression is not entirely correct in that they remain entitled to vote, although their votes can no longer result in the company taking a direction other than following from its parent's lawful instructions.
22. It is interesting that Berle and Means (1932) themselves referred to Rathenau's analysis of the modern corporation in Germany to be regarded as an 'institution' in his article 'Von kommenden Dingen' (1918).
23. See para. 119 and 76 of the Aktiengesetz, respectively. Moreover it should be noted that under the German Codetermination Act (1976) the members of the Supervisory Board of firms with more than 2,000 employees are appointed half by the shareholders and for the other half by workers' representatives (incl. trade unions).
24. Note that additional rules protect the creditors of subsidiaries.
25. Remarkably, in a contested takeover, the acquirer may petition the remaining obstacles for (full) control to be removed by judicial decree. This may be interpreted as the acquisition of control being delayed and conditioned upon such a decree.

26. See, Art. 12 Fusiegedragsregels Commentaar (FC) (Decree on Public Offers).
27. Including competition laws and the supervision of certain branches of industry, such as banking, savings, insurance and pensions or public utilities.
28. We have already mentioned various elements. One may think of questions related to civil liability for non-observance of disclosure rules, but also of questions related to business judgements made during the offer.
29. Including competition rules and standards for certain parts of the industry, such as banking, insurance, and public utilities.

References

Bebchuk, L. A., and Ferrell, A. (2001). Federalism and takeovers: The race to protect managers from takeovers. In D. Esty and D. Geradin (ed.), *Regulatory Competition and Economic Integration.* Oxford: Oxford University Press.

Berle, A. A., and Means, G. A. (1932). *The Modern Corporation and Private Property.* New York: Harcourt, Brace & World.

Blair, M. M., and Stout, L. A. (1999). Team production in business organizations: An introduction. *Journal of Corporation Law* 24: 243.

Clarke, R. C. (1986). *Corporate Law.* Boston: Little, Brown & Company.

Deankin, S. (2001). Regulatory competition versus harmonization in European company law. In D. Esty and D. Geradin (ed.), *Regulatory Competition and Economic Integration.* Oxford: Oxford University Press.

Dine, J. (1983). The fifth draft directive—a false dawn?. *European Law Review* 8: 83.

Edwards, V. (1999). *EC Company Law.* Oxford: Oxford University Press.

Gilson, R. (1992). The political ecology of takeovers: Thoughts on harmonizing the European corporate governance environment. *Fordham Law Review* 61: 161.

Hazen, T. L. (1996). *Securities Regulation.* Minneapolis: West Publishing Co.

Holmstrom, B., and Kaplan, S. N. (2001). Corporate governance and merger activity in the U.S.: Making sense of the 1980s and 1990s (available on SSRN at ID=261112).

Hopt, K. J. (1997). Europäisches und deutsches Übernahmerecht. *Zeitschrift für das gesamte Handelsrecht und Wirtschaftsrecht* 161: 368.

Johnson, L., and Millon, D. (1989). Misreading the Williams Act. *Michigan Law Review* 87: 1862.

Pennington, J. (1974). *Report on Takeovers and Other Bids* (Brussels).

Romano, R. (1995). *The Genius of American Corporate Law.* Washington, D.C.: American Enterprise Institute Press.

Wouters, J. (1993). Towards a level playing field for takeovers in the European community? An analysis of the proposed Thirteenth Directive in light of the American experience. *Common Market Law Review* 30: 267.

——(2000). European Company Law: Quo Vadis? *Common Market Law Review* 37: 257.

Wymeersch, E. (1996). The regulation of takeover bids in a comparative perspective. In R. Buxbaum, G. Hertig, A. Hirsch, and K. Hopt (ed.), *European Economic and Business Law.* Berlin/New York: de Gruyter.

9

Convergence or Divergence in Corporate Governance Patterns in Western Europe?

EDDY WYMEERSCH

1. INTRODUCTION

Are there signs that corporate governance patterns are converging? What factors indicate convergence or divergence? What are the forces underpinning this evolution? In which direction are the new patterns evolving? These are but a few of the fundamental questions that require answers. Before commencing this essentially descriptive analysis, a few provisos are required. There have been previous attempts to measure convergence of governance patterns, but no convincing yardstick has emerged. The subject should therefore be put in perspective: do governance structures matter? This question has received many different answers (Baysinger and Butler 1985; Lin 1996: 98; Bhagat and Black 1998: 81; Black 1998). Convergence as such is not important. In the long run, economic structure and efficiency may be unrelated to governance convergence. Indeed the lessons from the early 1990s show, scholars may be very mistaken about the effect of corporate governance on economic efficiency, which is determined more by the business cycle, monetary policies, and fundamental changes in technology than by governance mechanisms.

Corporate governance patterns are for the most part viewed as homogeneous. Yet, more detailed analysis reveals that this is far from true: dispersed ownership is found in numerous European companies, especially the largest ones, while concentrated ownership exists in a number of UK and USA companies. Within a given system, all possible shades are met.

Governance systems are constantly evolving, both at the level of regulation and in practice. The purpose of this chapter is to draw attention to some evolutionary forms, which, from a European perspective, appear significant. Competition between systems (and between regulations) is clearly taking place. It seems that most systems are adapting to competition by promulgating similar pieces of legislation, it seems, but formidable forces of resistance remain in place. Based on these considerations, a new governance system is now under construction. Whether this will lead to more convergence, and at what level, is an open question.

2. CORPORATE GOVERNANCE PATTERNS AT THE END OF THE 1980s

In the late 1980s, when international interest in the subject of corporate governance grew, commentators distinguished between two or three patterns of corporate governance visible in Western Europe. Several studies indicated that due to differences in tradition and legislation, almost every one of the European states had its own pattern. Within each state, there were several subsystems, while each company had more or less its own corporate governance culture.

Beginning with the French writer Michel Albert (1993), it became common to distinguish two main patterns: the Rhineland model,, followed in Germany and the Netherlands—but also in France, Belgium and other states of Latin European tradition—versus the Anglo-Saxon model. In fact, the situation is much more complex: anyone familiar with the Dutch and the German model will point to fundamental differences between the adversarial pattern underlying the German structure and the more co-operative ideas characterizing the Dutch one. Similar, but less striking differences exist between the systems of Latin European tradition.

Looking only at stock exchange listed companies, we would find a wide range of differences between the listed companies in each individual state. From the angle of their ownership structure, one would find in each state the same range of control situations: most companies continue to be dominated by one owner or are based on family ownership; frequently found are group structures, in which conglomerate holding companies play a dominant part, and finally but less frequently found, there are some widely owned companies, with no major shareholder (e.g. 25 per cent). A vast majority of listed companies, therefore, are in fact subsidiaries of other companies, and often are part of conglomerate groups. But some overall differences appear: the striking difference between the more open UK ownership structure, and the evidently lower degree of dispersion of ownership in Germany, Belgium, and Italy. These differences are illustrated by the figures in Tables 9.1 and 9.2 which may be somewhat outdated, but still reflect the overall picture in Europe.

Table 9.1. *The difference between UK ownership structure and the low degree of dispersion of ownership in other countries*[1]

	D	B	I	CH	SW	N	F	UK
Over 50%	68	68	66	55	45	44	37	7
25–50%	21	26	19	17	39	20	32	12
Under 25%	11	6	15	28	16	36	31	81
Date	1995	1997	1995	1995	1985	1996	1995	1994

Table 9.2. *The difference between UK and US ownership structures and the low degree of dispersion of ownership in other countries*

	B	I	F	D	S	N	UK	US
Over 50%	62.1	62	57.5	48.5	27.3	19.5	12.5	10.3
25–50%	25.7	17.9	21.9	26.6	28.9	22.6	20.1	20.7
10–25%	6.4	14.5	13.1	17.7	33.1	34.0	42.5	39.1
Under 10%	5.7	5.6	7.5	7.2	10.7	23.9	25.0	29.9
Date	1999	1999	1999	1999	1999	1998	1994	1996

Governance patterns change over time. More recent, but also more refined research[2] makes it appear that there has been some change in the ownership pattern. Differences in ownership will be reflected in the board: not so much in its structure, as this is largely dictated by the legal system, but in its composition, which is often exclusively a function of the influence of the shareholders. Usually, directors are appointed by the shareholders that own or control the majority of the shares at the general meeting by which the director is selected. In practice, most directors are appointed by this controlling shareholder, which is not necessarily a majority shareholder. If one reviews changes in governance, these will not affect all companies throughout the range. Companies with dispersed ownership are clearly the most affected by the trend to better governance, while the message is only slowly being perceived by family owned companies. The movement is still slower—but the need not less great—for unlisted companies, and for state owned entities.

3. FACTORS OF CHANGE

3.1. *What Factors can be Identified as having brought about the Broad Interest for Governance Matters?*

Looking retrospectively at the 1990s, a broad range of factors can be identified as having started the movement for better governance; fundamental economic changes should be considered as decisive. Among these one could mention the creation of a single internal market in Europe and its new, more competitive environment, the lower interest rates throughout the second half of the 1990s, the increasingly perceived need for old age provisions, and more generally, the renewed interest for equity investment. But of course, many other elements triggered these developments: A few very conspicuous scandals (Metallgesellschaft, Schneider, Maxwell, Poly Peck, but also Crédit Lyonnais) called attention to weaknesses in the existing governance structure. Psychology always played its role: in the early 1990s, the German–Japanese scheme was considered superior, while the USA–UK model was admired throughout the boom period of the second half of the same period.

3.1.1. *Restructuring of Europe's Business Firms*

The formation of the internal market has led to a vast extension of the geographical area which large business firms aim to cover. This evolution led to successive waves of mergers, acquisitions, takeovers and reorganizations, which continue to go on. More recently, one sees transnational groups being formed, linking companies originating in totally different cultural and legal environments: Daimler-Chrysler is the most prominent example, in which one overall firm resulted. Aventis, formed out of Hoechst AG and Rhône-Poulenc SA offers a comparable example. Several new bi-national horizontal groups were formed: these are presented as 'mergers between equals': Reed-Elsevier, Fortis (Belgium and Holland), Dexia (French Crédit local de France and Belgian Gemeentekrediet) and very recently KPN and Spanish Telefonicà. Simultaneously, mergers at the national level were frequent: Thyssen-Krupp, Bayerische Hypo-Bank and Bayerische Vereinsbank, Veba and VIAG to name but a few. New governance issues emerge and are solved more in conformity with securities market objectives in mind.[3]

An equally powerful factor has been the change in the business philosophy of the European states. From running businesses, several EU-states have reduced their task to the surveillance of business activities, the firms being transferred into private hands. Where still present, new ways of ensuring the public interest have been devised: in some this was imposed within the framework of a management contract, in others by techniques like the 'golden share'. Privatizations by listing securities on the markets have been numerous and will continue to stimulate the interest of the markets. In formerly or partly state-owned companies, new issues of governance emerge, especially dealing with the relationship between the government and the state controlled company, such as conflicts with the government's tax policy, with its employment objectives or burdening its social security budget, and so on. When the state holds a significant stake in a business firm, and wants to exercise some influence, traditional governance techniques may offer solutions to these conflict of interests, without subjecting the entire firm to government oversight.

The successive takeover waves, involving most of the time the largest—because their shares were widely owned—firms, have considerably stirred interest in the issue of change of control. In contrast with the USA, Europe will extend to all Member States the rule that exists already in a majority of states, whereby the acquisition of control leads to the obligation to bid for all the remaining shares. This rule, albeit controversial,[4] is considered necessary to protect investors against the predatory conduct of the bidder. In practice, it mainly served to avoid the seller pocketing 100 per cent of the control premium, or allowing side payments to take place. Whether the rule is economically efficient has never been investigated: populist investor protection has gained from economic analysis.[5]

3.1.2. *Renewed Interest for Equity Investment*

The 1990s are characterized by a renewed and strong interest in equity investment. Even in states like Germany where investors traditionally preferred debt instruments, equity investment has become popular. Once more, several factors have contributed to this development:

(1) the abundance of private savings in many European states;
(2) the fall of interest rates, inciting investors to diversify to equity and taking up less debt instruments;
(3) more fundamentally: the almost continuous stock market rise, leading to increased interest for equity investment;
(4) the higher returns on shares, especially due to the rising markets;
(5) the increasing offer of newly issued securities and new listings, with potentially very high returns in the case of some IPOs;
(6) more listings of unseasoned stocks, development of more submarkets offering investments in innovative business sectors (EASDAQ, Neuer Markt);
(7) the increased complexity of investment techniques, leading investors to investment funds;
(8) large offer of investment funds: formation of numerous investment funds in Luxembourg and Ireland, the two main tax efficient regimes;[6]
(9) pension funds are more favoured, and are increasingly seen as an alternative to state funded pensions; and

(10) improved accessibility of markets by electronic linkages, leading to increased concentration in main markets. Hence smaller operators try to excel in presenting shares in companies that do abide by better governance rules ('corporate governance as a marketing device').

3.1.3. *Competition between Markets and their Regulators*

Europe still has numerous regulated equity markets, at least one per Member State. Each of these is relatively small. Traditionally, competition was limited: securities were listed on the home market of the company, for the larger ones with some secondary listings in other markets. These secondary listings[7] have no real significance: the home market dominates most of the time. In the early 1990s London was considered a threat to the continental markets, inciting the latter to reorganize and become more competitive. Hence, a greater awareness of the competitive forces, and of the need to attract investors. One of the instruments has been to support[8] or even enact better governance rules[8b]. This also answers demands from part of the local investment community, trying to attract investors by urging local issuers to adhere to widely accepted governance standards.

In the last years of the 1990s, securities markets have been competing against each other, whether as organizations ('market for markets'), compete more visibly as far as their products are concerned. All offer a whole range of products, including derivatives, although turnover in the latter remained small.

1. Increasingly, investors have left portfolio selection along national lines for selection by the business sector. This line of portfolio selection has been more prominently pursued since the introduction of the Euro, but is also a function of the greater convergence of the economies in the Euro-zone. Currently, quotations take place in Euro, undermining the meaning of dual listings. Although still used, national market indices are being replaced by an overall European index, the Stoxx, referring to 400 selected blue chips listed in all of the European states.
2. More recently, a long overdue development towards integration of the markets has become visible: the exchanges are negotiating whether to fully integrate, or to form a common trading platform. However, evolutions are far from clear: the original Frankfurt–London deal has not materialized. Negotiations for a common trading platform between eight exchanges seem to have faltered. Three exchanges (Paris, Amsterdam, and Brussels) have announced a merger, based on a common trading platform (Euronext). Simultaneously, clearing and settlement organizations are being merged: Clearstream regroups DKV and Cedel, while Euroclear has announced plans to absorb French, Belgian, and probably also Dutch settlements systems. The new structure of the securities markets in Europe will not be stabilized for another year.
3. Whether these developments will create a fully integrated, electronic market, remains to be seen. A two-tier market structure seems more likely, with an upper market, where a 300 to 400 large European stock is being traded, and regional markets, with local securities.
4. In the meantime, competition is increasing with several new initiatives being taken, often referred to PTS or ECN[9] but covering a wide range of trading systems, some

internalizing trading facilities within one firm, others offering substitutes for trading on the open market. The legal position of these systems is still far from clear. Segmentation and therefore overall inefficiency is a clear danger.

In the likely hypothesis that further integration at the level of market organizers is to be achieved, it seems logical that more attention will be paid to the creation of a single set of corporate governance principles, in which case the differences between the German–Dutch and the other patterns will have to be overcome. Therefore, one will not be astonished that the European Commission is planning to take an initiative in this field.

5. These developments lead to increased competition, not only in the markets in general but also on governance standards, and a sharper awareness of governance practices in terms of attracting investors. With some overstatement, one could say that policing governance rules and practices is considered by some exchanges, especially the smaller ones, as being part of the product range they offer the investing public. Hence their motivation for enacting codes, and monitoring their implementation. A market for 'corporate governance' can be said to have sprung up, of special importance to service providers and consultants.

3.1.4. *Miscellaneous Factors*

The interest for governance matters is in part also led by many other factors. Only some can be mentioned. The occurrence of some high profile scandals have triggered the interest for the way companies are managed and monitored, and revealed some obvious weaknesses in monitoring and prudential surveillance. In the UK, the drive for better governance was triggered by cases like BCCI, Maxwell, and Poly Peck, but also by developments in the recently privatized public utilities. In Germany, Metallgesellschaft, Schneider, and recently Holzmann attracted international interest as they illustrated the relationship with the banks. In France, Crédit Lyonnais could be cited as an 'example', although governance initiatives did not stem from there.

Over the last decade, a debate raged in Europe about the rules relating to takeover bids provoked by the European Commission's attempts to introduce a harmonization directive that finally occurred in June 1999. The debate surrounding this directive exceeded the boundaries of takeovers, and involved issues such as the role of the board in case of a takeover,[10] or de facto protection yielded by co-determination, as well as other issues. In November 2000, it seems that the final objections against the directive have been lifted although the European Parliament has threatened to alter fundamentally the legislation.

Better practices have resulted, first in the upper tier—the listed companies—but now seeping down to the wide range of firms and legal entities, including not-for-profit organizations, where tremendous needs for better governance can be identified, and to government owned bodies as well. May we hope that universities and even faculties will one day be hit by the better governance wave?

Institutional investors are becoming increasingly activist in governance terms: This development will be supported by the prudential requirement to separate fund management from the bank which is patronizing the fund, thereby introducing governance mechanisms in the investment fund industry. Although the blocks owned by institutional investors are relatively significant, their role in governance terms is not comparable to that of the holders of large or even controlling blocks that are still often met in European companies, the latter acting in a very long-term perspective, with more directly identifiable private benefits in mind. Furthermore, organizations specializing in shareholders' representation and defence and practising lawyers supporting minority investors have become more vocal, and more active in the courts.

Some influence can be attributed to scientific research and writing in general. Starting from the 1990s one could detect a certain fashion in research and applied research, calling attention to the American developments and initiating studies along the same lines in Western Europe. However, due to lack of data, the available information in Europe, especially in some of the individual states, continues to lag behind the information available in the USA, Japan, or even Germany.[11]

Interestingly enough, the governments and legislators were most of the time wise enough to abstain from moulding governance rules and practices in hard laws. Some attempts were made in Belgium and in France, but these remained unsuccessful. In Italy, some governance rules were introduced in the Test Unico especially with respect to the supervisory board or 'collegio sindacale'.[12] But the overall thrust remains on 'soft law'. Recently however, marginal changes in the governance rules are being considered both in France[13] and in Belgium.[14]

4. SIGNS OF CONVERGENCE

Whether there has been convergence in governance patterns is controversial.[15] This first raises the question about the meaning of this convergence: One could identify it as evolution to more objective decision making that takes into account the interests of the shareholders and investors. Although it seems unreasonable to expect companies to converge across the board, there are signs pointing towards greater awareness of the issue of objective and more efficient governance rules and practices in most European states, changes that are flowing from a greater sensitivity to market developments and less reliance on support from large investors. Convergence in governance patterns could be measured by numerous criteria. In-depth analysis would probably reveal that changes have been slow and followed divergent paths. Many will be described as cosmetic. However, cosmetic changes have an impact on real life. Therefore, it seems easier, and not necessarily false to try to identify changes from external parameters, such as changes in regulation, or the enactment of corporate governance codes and their implementation.

4.1. *The Corporate Governance Codes and Reform Proposals*

One may think that to deal with the codes of conduct as elements of convergence is a rather superficial approach to the subject of convergence. This is not the case: these codes have had an in-depth influence, both as anchor points for the governance discussion—the term 'governance' is still puzzling to many Europeans—but also as models for a structured discussion, and reference for good practice.[16]

The Cadbury 'Code of best practice' has influenced the corporate governance thinking, rules and practices, triggering developments, debates and regulation in many parts of

Europe. These influences differ considerably from state to state: in some states it has led to a reflection on actual practices and the need to recommend reform, in others it has resulted in the adoption of instruments similar to the Cadbury code. Independent developments were predominant in other states, although there too, the Cadbury rules have inspired changes in the law, or actual business practice. These influences are often of a diffuse nature. A short overview may clarify this proposition.

The Belgian recommendations are directly inspired by the Cadbury Code, and even duplicate a certain number of its statements. The French Reports on corporate governance, known as the Viénot reports, especially the most recent one of July 1999—while referring to the Cadbury and even the Hampel reports—formulate a series of recommendations that, although in a somewhat different approach, go a long way in the direction of the UK documents. The Italian document,[17] dated September 1999, follows more or less the same pattern.

Due to differences in the legal structure of their companies, the reform proposals have been framed differently in Germany and in the Netherlands. In Germany, changes were introduced in the law, the so-called KonTraGesetz. These changes have a significant effect on anti-takeover protections. In early 2000, a code of conduct was published.[18] The Dutch Report criticized the functioning of the dual board in the Netherlands, and recommended a wide range of changes in actual practice. It also contained a call for more influence from the shareholders. The latter topic continues to figure at the centre of the Dutch governance debate: changes of the law with respect to anti-takeover devices have been under consideration,[19] but will probably have to be revised under the effect of the Thirteenth Company Law Directive on takeovers.[20]

4.2. *New Forthcoming Legislation*

The increasingly popular soft law approach to corporate governance has not prevented legislators from pursuing traditional governance reforms, especially in regard to facilitating better governance practices.

The UK government has recently launched a major reflection on its Company Law, dealing with all aspects of company law. Two sub-items deal with corporate governance: one with the role of the board of directors including the delicate issue of the fiduciary duties, while the other deals with the functioning of the general meeting. The French government tabled a bill in parliament, allowing companies to do away with the system of the président-directeur-général who concentrated in his hands all effective, and not only executive power in the company.[21] The Belgian government announced that new rules would allow companies to introduce more effective management, in a scheme that comes close to a two-tier board structure. Also, the rules on conflicts of interest, especially in the relation between a Belgian listed company and its controlling shareholders will be reinforced. The German government has introduced a bill dealing with registered shares and shareholder voting.[22] The Dutch government has ordered several studies to be made questioning whether the specifically Dutch co-determination system still serves its original purpose. Some of these studies have indicated that many companies voluntarily adhere to the Dutch co-determination system, probably to avoid a takeover. The Social-Economic Council has been invited to reflect on these findings.

More generally, all Member States are preparing to adapt their legislation to the Thirteenth Company Law Directive on takeover bids. This may require a major overhaul of legal thinking in several states, especially in Germany and in the Netherlands. As mentioned earlier, the European Commission has developed a new strategic programme which has been recently published. Corporate governance will be on the table, although at present commission officials indicate their preference for non-regulatory intervention. The functioning of the general meeting, especially in the light of the increasing need for cross-border voting mechanisms will probably be part of the Commission's proposals.

4.3. *Common Elements in the Governance Codes*

In order to illustrate some areas in which convergence has been visible, one may review some of the salient features of the Corporate Governance recommendations. Only a few of these items can be touched upon here. They should be considered as illustrations for the drive towards convergence that these codes have initiated.

4.3.1 *Independent Directors*

The appointment of independent directors counts among the most conspicuous instruments advocated in most systems. In both the German and the Dutch systems, there is no need for independent directors given the two-tier systems in which directors are either representatives of certain constituent interests, or are more or less neutral vis-à-vis these interests. Independent directors are heavily relied on in Belgian, Italian, and French practice. In Switzerland larger companies follow the same trend. As to what constitutes independence, there is a common core of thinking, focusing on the duty of the director to take into account the sole interest of the company. Therefore, looking at the specific situation in continental companies, codes especially take into account relations with dominant shareholders and group structures. Specific differences in approach appear.

The French recommendation defines independence vis-à-vis the management of the company and its main shareholders: it is 'the director who has no link whatsoever with the company, or the group to which it belongs that is likely to influence his independence of judgement'.[23] The Italian approach is less restrictive, as it limits the evaluation to business relationships and ownership of shares.

A more elaborate definition is given in the Belgian document:[24]

- the director is not a member of the executive management or of the board of associated companies (subsidiaries etc.) and has not held any such appointment for the past year;
- he has no family ties with any of the executive directors, which might interfere with the exercise of his independent judgement
- he is not a member of the executive management board or board of directors of one of the dominant shareholders and has not been selected on the nomination of and has no business financial or other relationship with the latter
- he is not a supplier of goods or services of a nature which might interfere with the exercise of his independent judgement, and nor is he a member of the firm of which the company advisor or consultant is part; and

- he has no other relationship with the company which in the opinion of the board of directors, is of a nature which might interfere with the exercise of his judgement; no such influence is deemed to exist to arise from the remuneration he receives of or from his restricted shareholding in the company.

From these examples we may draw the conclusion that if technically there are still differences in definitions used, in substance there is a common understanding as to the core governance issue, that is, that there should be countervailing powers on the board, and that not everything should be decided whether by the controlling shareholder, or by the chairman of the board, the French Président-directeur-général. Whether these guarantees are sufficient is another debate.

Further steps become visible: the presence of independent directors is not merely a matter of good governance, but is becoming a legal tool in curbing the influence of the major shareholder. This evolution is apparent from developments in Belgium, where the dominance of controlling groups has traditionally been very strong. Two significant items can be mentioned: on the one hand, the companies act was adapted to impose at least three independent directors to give their opinion to the board as far as transactions between a listed subsidiary and its controlling shareholder are concerned.[25] More recently, a court decision considered 'irregular' the opinion given by a board of directors of the target company as to whether the bid was in the interest of the company, its shareholders, creditors and employees,[26] by taking into account that the so-called independent directors, although independent in the sense of the articles of association, had been involved in framing the bid on behalf of the bidder, also the parent company of the target. However, the judge did not declare the opinion void, but merely imposed additional disclosure.[27] The 'juridification' of these 'soft law' rules is clearly under way.

4.3.2 *The Separation of the Functions of Chairman and CEO*

In the two-tier structure, this issue is not relevant: each board has its own chairman, and no member can take part in both bodies. In the other systems, the subject is still controversial.

The Hampel report endorsed the Cadbury report's recommendation and reasoning: the roles of chairman and chief executive officer should in principle be separate. If not, the onus is on the company to explain and justify.[28] A similar recommendation was made in the Belgian code. In practice, more and more companies have separated the two functions. The French second Viénot report recently declared itself in favour of the separation: this was not evident, as traditionally the French law imposes a pattern whereby the Président-directeur-général concentrates all powers in his hand. Unless adhering to the two-tier structure, companies could not separate the two functions. Recently, a proposal to change the law was tabled.[29]

The Italian attitude is equally flexible: although in principle, the Committee found that each body has its own tasks, it is not infrequent for the same person to hold the two positions, or that some management powers are delegated to the chairman.[30] One could conclude that on this issue, some convergence can be noticed, but developments have been slower.

4.3.3. *The Board's committees*

Much attention has been given to 'comitology', and here again practice has adapted very much to the recommendations. Most large companies today would have audit committees, while the other traditional committees (most frequently: nomination and remuneration committees) can often be found.

4.3.4. *The functioning of the general meeting*

A subject to which increasing interest is being paid is that of the functioning of the general meeting. The Hampel report contains a chapter on the 'Shareholders and the AGM', a subject which also retained ample attention in the UK *Company Law Review.* Due to the presence of dominant shareholders, the general meeting of continental-European companies was generally a rubber-stamp of decisions taken elsewhere. Renewed interest in the functioning of the meeting, in terms of disclosure, more effective exercise of voting rights,[31] proxy solicitation,[32] remote access to meetings and so on becomes visible, linked to the increasing facilities offered by electronic communication. Some recent codes of conduct contain references to this topic.[33] The interest in shareholder rights has been more recent, and developments are still somewhat timid.

4.4. *The Ownership Structure*

The ownership structure seems the single most significant variable factor in explaining differences in governance structures. To what extent convergence has already taken place or can still be expected will be heavily influenced by changes in the ownership patterns, essentially to what extent systems are migrating from concentrated to dispersed ownership, or vice versa.

It is a well-known fact that in most continental-European systems, share ownership is fairly concentrated: there are a limited number of companies that have their shares widely dispersed in a sense which is comparable to their USA or UK counterparts. In recent years however, their number has significantly increased pointing to a more open ownership, without excluding in some cases a tendency towards additional concentration.

The following indications can be mentioned:

(1) the number of companies with no controlling shareholder has increased. This evolution seems mainly due to the listing of large, previously publicly owned firms that have been privatized. The Telecom and other public utilities companies are examples;
(2) many new entrants have been noticed. However, most of these have been listed with one or a few shareholders continuing to hold control. Here the traditional patterns seem not to have changed, but these may be attributed to transitory situations;[34]
(3) at least in some states, the concentration wave has led to several listed subsidiaries being fully taken over to form larger groups.[35] These resulted in public takeover bids, often for all the outstanding shares, mostly by way of an exchange bid. Differently from before, concentration did not take place by acquiring a controlling stake without more, but by bidding for 100 per cent of the outstanding shares, leading to full integration of the target in the bidder. This movement has also led to deeper markets in the parent's shares, and the relative dilution of blocks holdings in the bidder;

(4) due to the increasing threat of takeovers—as will be shown later, anti-takeover devices have become less effective—there is evidence of stronger ownership concentration, and then often above the 50 per cent threshold; and
(5) in some states there has been an increased interest from institutional investors (e.g. in France, from foreign institutionals). In other states, rather mixed views emerge.[36] With a few noticeable exceptions, institutional holdings rarely exceed the 5 per cent threshold. In terms of governance activism, these cannot be considered a critical mass. Also due to the absence of effective legal instruments, the degree of activism by institutionals has remained rather low.

4.5. *Takeover Bids and the Thirteenth Directive*

One of the fields in which convergence has been rather conspicuous is that of takeovers. There have been numerous takeovers all over Europe, while even in Germany and the Netherlands, the markets have become aware of the phenomenon. Many takeovers still take place with the consent of the controlling shareholder, and are less involving the board or the management. Traditionally, the deal starts with the transfer of a control block, upon which the acquirer accepts to bid for all the remaining shares. Contested bids have become more numerous, leading to new debates about defensive mechanisms.

The future Thirteenth Directive will have a significant effect on convergence by imposing in all states the mandatory bid rule, whether at a one-third threshold, as is the case in most states, or at a higher level (40 per cent or 50+ per cent). The rule is important as an investor protection instrument in case of change of control: in fact it is considered the minority protection instrument par excellence. It should also be seen as a protection in case of inclusion of a company in a group context, and constitutes one of the principal alternatives to a law on groups of companies.[37]

To what extent companies will continue to be able to use anti-takeover instruments has been the subject of intensive discussion at the European level: the adopted—but not yet promulgated—Thirteenth Company Law Directive has taken a clear stand on the matter. The board should not undertake nor complete any action that would frustrate the bid. The precise wording of the relevant section of the directive reads as follows:

> the board of the offeree company should abstain from completing any action other than seeking alternative bids which may result in the frustration of the offer, ... unless it has prior authorization of the general meeting given for this purpose, during the period of acceptance of the bid.

The second paragraph of Article 8 contains a further refinement of the rule:

> Member states may allow the board of the offeree company to increase the share capital during the period for acceptance of the bid on the condition that prior authorization has been received from the general meeting of shareholders not earlier than 18 months before the beginning of the period of acceptance of the bid, with full recognition of the rights of pre-emption of all shareholders.

The interpretation of this provision will certainly lead to interesting legal questions.[38] In Belgium, and in some other states[39] the opinion is that it will prevent most of the traditional anti-takeover techniques such as

(1) issue of additional shares to one party, often a controlling shareholder;
(2) repurchase of previously issued shares;
(3) issue of shares pursuant to previously placed warrants or other instruments giving rights to shares;
(4) probably also: issuance of shares due to conversion rights attached to convertible bonds;
(5) accept offers to transfer substantial assets of the company to third parties.

The directive leaves untouched a great number of pre-bid anti-takeover defences. These aim at protecting the company even in the absence of an actual bid, and therefore have a continuous, often structural effect on the company's governance.

A few examples can be mentioned

(1) multiple voting rights, very popular in France where the law itself provided for dual voting rights for faithful shareholders that have been registered as shareholder for at least two years. In some states voting rights are attributed with a multiple of 100, or even 1,000;
(2) securities with conditional rights, to be exercised only in case of unfriendly takeover provided no intervention of the board is required;
(3) presentation rights, whereby board members will be appointed only upon presentation of the holders of certain shares;
(4) voting trust like mechanisms: the shares are deposited with a party—often a foundation, directed by affiliates to the board—in exchange for certificates with the same financial privileges, but without voting rights; and
(5) several layers of holding companies, with controlling interests at each layer, leading to ultimate control with small financial contribution to the portfolio company.

The possible effects of this change of policy are difficult to predict. The likely outcome of the introduction of pre-bid defences is a negative influence on the market valuation of the shares, at least for those companies that previously were potential targets of takeovers. Institutional investors will loudly protest, and may even take legal action. In the Netherlands, several companies have voluntarily given up their strong defences. In France, there have been talks about abolishing double voting rights. In each case, the objective has been to act more clearly in conformity with market interest.

5. SHAREHOLDER VALUE AND THE ENTERPRISE INTEREST

On a more theoretical point, one could also analyse whether there have been signs of convergence in the philosophy underlying the private business firm. On this topic, there continues to be wide differences of opinion as to whether the ultimate aim of the company is the welfare of the shareholders, and of the shareholders only, or rather would include the interests of all stakeholders. The relatively recent discussion about the role of the stakeholders in the UK has activated the debate in some segments of the public opinion on the continent as well, although the companies themselves, often looking at the reactions of the markets, would rather prefer to limit their role to the creation of wealth for their shareholders.

There are several instruments for measuring a possible change of mind: annual reports, the address of the chairman at the general meeting, the official codes of conduct, and so on. The official documents on corporate governance being the most easily accessible, the following short overview can be given.

—*The Hampel Report* It acknowledged wider accountability but reminded that the boards' first responsibility consists of 'enhancing the prosperity of the business over time'.[40] Good governance ensures that constituencies (stakeholders) with a relevant interest are fully taken into account.

—*The Italian Code* This code emphasizes 'the maximization of shareholder value as the primary objective of good Corporate governance, with on the longer term beneficial effects for other stakeholders such as customers, creditors, consumers' suppliers, employees, local communities and the environment'.[41]

—*The French Report* The French report obviously considered its tasks in a more technical sense, and did not refer to the role of the company and its attitude vis-à-vis the stakeholders.

—*Dutch Peters Report* It sees the role of the company as 'primarily to sustain the firm's continuity. Therefore the board should pursue a reasonable balance between the interests of the purveyors of risk bearing capital, and the other interests affected by the company and its enterprise.'

—*The Belgian Report* It did not pay any special attention to this issue: the directors are considered to act for the company.

—*The Spanish Olivencia* This report is mainly dealing with the relationship between the board and the shareholders, and does no pay any specific attention to the stakeholders.

In general one could conclude that at least officially there is more interest for the position of the shareholders. The promotion of the interest of the company is seen as including responsibility vis-à-vis the other constituencies, but these interests are not part of its ultimate goal. Employee participation is opening new perspectives, as investment in the company shares may blur the distinction of share- and stakeholders. In the longer term, and on the essential matters—takeovers, for example—the company is to be run in the interest of the shareholders, with shareholder value as the central touchstone, while due respect is to be paid to the mostly contractual rights of the other stockholders.

Whether that also means that the shareholders would be better protected remains open: technical remedies and their use in European companies are still underperforming. Dominant shareholders continue to exercise a central role in European business firms. This leads to underlining the importance of the rules on groups of companies and their accompanying obligation to launch a mandatory bid in case of a change of control. Minority protection is increasingly flowing from securities market rules, rather than from traditional company law.

6. CONCLUSION

There is little doubt that the debate on corporate governance, which has been very active these last five years, has contributed to render business leaders, politicians, academics and the public opinion at large more conscious about the phenomenon and its objective of better management. In the meantime, due to their function as models, the codes of conduct have influenced actual practices and conduct. Whether these developments also mean that more fundamental changes have occurred, and that the patterns of the business firms have come closer to each other, remains doubtful. The main difference continues to be the preponderant role of the major shareholder: he may have left more leeway to the board under the governance rules, but the ultimate decisions will remain in his hands. Convergence is a process of manifold developments, where progress was made in some fields, not necessarily in others.[42] This analysis leads to one of the central questions of the governance debate, viz. which is the best pattern, the one with dispersed share ownership, without substantial external control, or the one with external monitoring by a major shareholder? Here the comparative study of governance techniques may offer interesting insights for an in-between answer: external control on a relatively independent board of directors. After all, is that not the model of the Dutch business firm, and a clue to its success?

Notes

1. Source: Wymeersch (1994).
2. Wymeersch (1994: 83) and Van der Elst (2000).
3. By way of illustration, see the voluntary arrangement in Aventis with respect to co-determination.
4. See Wymeersch (1992: 351). But the rule is a powerful alternative solution to the issues of groups of companies, prevalent in European listed companies: see for a further discussion of this topic: 'Forum Europaeum, Konzenrecht für Europa', *ZGR* 1998, 725 e.s. and K.J. Hopt, n. 19.
5. For the latter: see Bebchuk (1994: 957)
6. Although cross–border placement of investment funds remains of marginal significance: see Kahan (1993: 368).
7. Mutual recognition would have supported this multiple listing policy. The share flow back is, however, a universal phenomenon, and lies at the basis of the Daimler-Chrysler decision to form one company, with one type of shares.
8. So in the Netherlands (mixed commission), but not in France where the rules were laid down by a committee composed of representatives of the employers.

8b. The Belgian, Italian, and Spanish exchanges themselves patronized the formulation of the governance rules.

9. Proprietary trading system or electronic communication network. See eg. "Les marche's *électroniques privés en Europe menacent l' existence des bourses classiques" Le Monde, 16 September 1999.*
10. On the so-called neutrality rule, see Hopt (1993: 534).
11. See for some leading studies: Baums (1996), Edwards and Fischer (1994).
12. See for an extensive comment, Marchetti and Bianchi (1999).
13. French bill Nr. 2250 of 15 March 2000, on 'nouvelles régulations économiques', available in April 2000 on (http://www.assemblee-nationale.fr/2/projets/pl2250.html).
14. See *Project de loi der 23 avil 2000 modifiant le code des sociétés et le loi du 2 mars 1983 relative à la publicité des participations importantes dans les sociétés cotíes en bourse et ríglementant les offres publiques d'acquisition, Doc 1211/001.*
15. See among the important recent publications: Gordon and Roe (2000); Hopt (2000); Coffee (1999: 641); Bratton and McCahery (1999: 213); Hansmann and Kraakman (2000); Balling, Hennessy, and O'Brien (1997).
16. For a comparative study, see Van den Berghe and De Ridder (1999: 237).
17. Of the 'Committee for the Corporate governance of Listed Companies' of the Borsa Italiana s.p.a.

18. See Grundsatzkommission Corporate Governance (German panel on corporate governance). Corporate Governance-Grundsätze ('code of best practice') für börsennotierten Gesellschaften. Corporate Governance rules for quoted German companies, January 2000, published in *Der Betrieb*, 2000, 238.
19. See Buijs and Wouters (1998).
20. See further for the text of Art. 8 of the directive.
21. See *infra* p. 240.
22. Namensaktiengesetz-NaStraG, 15 November 1999, available on the website of the Bundesministerium der Justiz.
23. See Viénot report 1999, I. 22.
24. A similar definition was used in the proposals submitted by the Commission De Grauwe.
25. Article 60 bis Belgian companies act. The government recently proposed to strengthen this provision, by reinforcing the position of these independent directors.
26. On the basis of Art. 15, RD 8 November 1989.
27. Pres. Trib. Comm. Brussels, 26 October 1999 (Tractebel), Rev. Banque (Belgium), 1999, 478.
28. Hampel report, 2.17.
29. See 20 March 2000 proposal, mentioned *supra* n. 16.
30. Italian Report, 1999, § 4.3 and comments.
31. See Baums and Wymeersch (ed.) (1999).
32. See Winter (1998: 81); Winter (2000).
33. To be mentioned: the recommendations of the French AFG-ASFFI's Commission on cg, 19 June, 1998. The Italian Report, §12. The Dutch Peters report contained interesting elements with respect to shareholder rights.
34. See, about the phenomenon: Mayer (2000).
35. 'going private', mainly by becoming subsidiaries. The cases of large MBO have been substantially less.
36. Insurance companies in Germany held 7.6 per cent in 1988, and 13.7 per cent of overall market capitalization in 1998 (DAI Report 1999). In the UK, there was a slight increase, but a substantial change among the different institutions: pension funds have lost market shares (−8.5 per cent) while trusts (+3.1 per cent) and insurance companies have increased (+4.9 per cent) (1989–97).
37. See for the proposals along these lines: Forum Europaeum, Konzernrecht für Europa, *ZGR* 1998, 725 e.s.; also in French in *Rev. Sociétés*, 1999, 43 e.s.; Hopt (2000: 299).
38. For a first analysis, see E. Wymeersch, 'Les défenses anti-opa après la treizième directive, commentaires sur l'article 8 de la future directive', in FS Jean Stoufflet, to be published.
39. For example, in the Netherlands, Timmerman (1999: 280).
40. Section 1.1. of the Hampel Report.
41. See § 4 of the introductory section.
42. The indivisibility view is strongly argued by Bratton and McCahery (1999: 213). In practice, although there are clearly interrelations between some subfields, overall convergence can only be the result of numerous processes that point in the same direction. Where the critical point is situated is a matter of debate, and perhaps also of taste.

References

Albert, M. (1993). *Capitalisme Contre Capitalisme*. Paris: Editions du Seuil.

Balling, M., Hennessy, E., and O'Brien, R. (1997). Corporate Governance, financial markets and global convergence. Société Universitaire Européenne de Recherches Financières.

Baums, T. (1996). Corporate Governance Systems in Europe—Differences and Tendencies of Convergence. Universität Osnabrück Law School Working Paper.

——and Wymeersch, E. (ed.) (1999). *Shareholder Voting Rights and Practices in Europe and the United States.* The Hague: Kluwer Law International.

Baysinger, B., and Butler, H. (1985). Corporate governance and the board of directors: Performance effects of changes in board composition. *Journal of Law, Economics, and Organization* 1: 225.

Bebchuk, L. (1994). Efficient and inefficient sales of corporate control. *The Quarterly Journal of Economics* 109: 957.

Bhagat, S., and Black, B. (1998). The relationship between board composition and board performance. In K. J. Hopt, H. Kanda, M. Roe, and E. Wymeersch (ed.) *Comparative Corporate Governance: The State of the Art and Emerging Research.* Oxford: Clarendon Press.

Black, B. (1998). Shareholder activism and corporate governance in the United States. In P. Newman (ed.) *The New Palgrave Dictionary of Economics and the Law.* London: Macmillan.

Bratton, W., and McCahery, J. (1999). Comparative corporate governance and the theory of the firm: the case against global cross-reference. *Columbia Journal of Transnational Law* 38: 213.

Buijs, D. C., and Wouters, J. (1998). Wetsvoorstel Beschermingsconstructies. *Vereniging Handelsrecht.*

Coffee, J. C. (1999). The future as history: the prospects for global convergence in corporate governance and its implications. *Northwestern University Law Review* 93: 641.

Edwards, J., and Fischer, K. (1994). *Banks, Finance and Investment in Germany.* Cambridge: Cambridge University Press.

Forum Europaeum (1998). Konzernrecht fur Europa. *Zeitschrift fur Unternehments und Gesellschaftsrecht* 725.

Gordon, J., and Roe. M. J. (ed.). *Are Corporate Governance Systems Converging?* Chicago: University of Chicago Press (forthcoming).

Grundsatzkommission Corporate Governance (German panel on corporate governance) (2000). Corporate Governance-Grundsätze ('code of best practice') für börsennotierten Gesellschaften. Corporate Governance rules for quoted German companies, *Der Betrieb,* January at 238.

Hansmann, H., and Kraakman, R. (2000). The end of history for corporate law. Yale Law School Law and Economics Working Paper Number 235, January.

Hopt, K. J. (1993). Aktionärskreis und Vorstandsneutralität. *Zeitschrift für Unternehmens- und Gesellschaftsrecht* 534.

——(2000). Europäisches Konzernrecht: Zu den Verschlägen und Thesen des Forum Europaeum Konzernrecht. In T. Baums, K. Hopt, and N. Horn (ed.) *Developments in Economic Law—Festschrift in Honour of Professor Buxbaum* Kluwer L. Int (2000).

Kahan, M. (1993). Sales of corporate control. *Journal of Law, Economics and Organization* 9: 368.

Le Monde (1999). Les marchés privés électroniques en Europe menacent l'existence des bourses classiques. 16 September.

Lin, L. (1996). The effectiveness of outside directors as a corporate governance mechanism: theories and evidence. *Northwestern University Law Review* 90: 898.

Marchetti, P., and Bianchi, L. (ed.) (1999). *La disciplina delle società quotate nel Testo Unico della Finanza D. Lgs.* 3 volumes, 24 febbraio, N.58.

Mayer, C. (2000). Ownership matters. Lecture delivered for the L. Goldschmidt Chair.

Timmerman, L. (1999). Een gunstiger klimaat voor zeggenschap van aandeelhouders van Nederlandse beursvennootschappen. *R. M. Themis* 280.

Van den Bergh, L., and De Ridder, L. (1999). International Standardisation of Good Corporate Governance, Best Practices for the board of Directors, p. 237.

Van der Elst, C. (2000). The equity market, ownership structures and control: towards an international harmonisation? University of Ghent Financial Law Institute Working Paper.

Winter, J. W. (1998). Stemmen op afstand via het Communicatiekanaal Aandeelhouders. In *Corporate Governance voor juristen.* Groningen: Universiteit Groningen Press.

——(2000). *Grensoverschrijdend stemmen.* Kluwer: Deventer.

Wymeersch, E. (1992). Mandatory takeover bids: a critical view. In K. Hopt and E. Wymeersch (ed.), *European Takeovers: Law and Practice.* London: Butterworths.

——(1994). Elements of comparative corporate governance in Western Europe. In M. Isaksson and R. Skog (ed.), *Aspects of Corporate Governance.* Stockholm: Juristforlaget.

——(1998). A status report on corporate governance. Rules and practices in some continental European states. In K. Hopt, H. Kanda, M. Roe, and E. Wymeersch (ed.) *Comparative Corporate Governance: The State of the Art and Emerging Research.* Oxford: Clarendon Press.

——Les défenses anti-opa après la treizième directive, commentaires sur l'article 8 de la future directive. In *Mélanges offerts à Jean Stoufflet* (forthcoming).

PART III

CONCENTRATION OF OWNERSHIP AND CONTROL IN EUROPE

10

Prediction of Control Concentration in German and UK Initial Public Offerings

MARC GOERGEN AND LUC RENNEBOOG

1. INTRODUCTION

At first glance, the corporate-governance systems of the UK and Germany could not be more different. The German blockholder system is characterized by a small number of quoted firms and poor liquidity. Most firms have complex concentrated shareholding structures. Weak managers are believed to be disciplined by large shareholders rather than by the market for corporate control and there are potential agency conflicts between controlling and minority shareholders. The Anglo-American market-oriented or outsider system has, in contrast, a large number of listed companies with mostly dispersed ownership. The high dispersion increases the potential lack of monitoring and poor corporate performance is disciplined by hostile takeovers. Not only are the capital markets different under both governance mechanisms, but there is also a wide divergence between the legal systems in both countries: a codified system versus a case-based system. In the light of high product market competition, the joint existence of two distinct corporate-control mechanisms—the market-oriented and the blockholder systems—is puzzling. No economic theory—be it principal–agent theory, incomplete contracting or transaction-cost theory—can justify the coexistence of different ownership and control systems.

Some scholars, such as La Porta *et al.* (1997, 1998, 1999), expect the market-oriented system to emerge eventually as the superior corporate-governance model through an evolutionary process. Consequently, they expect that the blockholder system will gradually develop more liquid capital markets, emulate Anglo-American style financial regulation, stimulate better shareholder-rights enforceability in courts and dismantle complex shareholding cascades. In the Anglo-American system, there seems to be no need to build up large equity stakes yielding control and facilitating monitoring because the common law system is providing superior protection of shareholders and creditors. Furthermore, it is argued that increased monitoring by institutional investors will solve the potential agency costs due to high managerial discretion (Black 1990; Gilson and Kraakman 1991).

Conversely, others such as Roe (1996) argue that reform is unlikely given the resilience of legal and institutional elements of corporate-governance systems. Bebchuk (1998), for instance, argues that concentrated ownership—and hence uncontestable corporate control—prevails in continental Europe because the lax corporate-governance regulation allows large shareholders to reap substantial private benefits of control. As long as continental European regulation is not altered, large-shareholder concentration will resist change.

This chapter does not attempt to advance arguments about the superiority of one corporate-governance system over another.[1] Instead, we ask (i) why the German and UK corporate landscapes are so different in terms of the number of quoted companies; (ii) how ownership evolves after initial public offerings in both countries; and (iii) whether the state of ownership and control concentration in the years following the Initial Public Offering (IPO) is predictable from corporate characteristics such as risk, profitability, growth, size, the founding family's involvement, and the issuance of non-voting rights.

A possible answer to the first question may be that the listing requirements between Germany and the UK differ. However, Goergen (1998) shows that stock exchange listing regulations are very similar in Germany and the UK, and cannot possibly be responsible for the difference in the number of IPOs in the two countries. The requirements are very similar in terms of minimum size, minimum ownership dispersion, and trading history. Conversely, the answer to the same question may be the existence of differences in inheritance tax: succession problems are an important reason for IPOs. High inheritance taxes may encourage owners to increase the liquidity of their wealth locked up in a corporation by seeking a stock exchange listing (Hay and Morris 1984). Indeed, higher inheritance tax in the UK than in Germany could partially explain the higher proportion of corporate listings in the UK. However, during the 1980s and 1990s the levels of inheritance tax in Germany have exceeded those in the UK (Goergen 1998). A possible explanation is based on the historical evolution of systems. Path-dependence theory (Bebchuk and Roe 1998) emphasizes that differences in the evolution of corporate legislation, regulation, and structures produced actual discrepancies between governance systems. It is argued that current ownership structures depend on initial economic structures (structure-driven path dependence) and on the financial and corporate regulation (rule-driven path dependence) which in turn is influenced by the initial corporate structure. Both structure-driven and rule-driven mechanisms tend to lead to persistence in ownership and control structures for reasons of efficiency because initial ownership patterns influence which type of corporate regulation would be efficient. Another reason for persistence, which is the second component of the path-dependence theory, is rent-seeking by specific classes of agents who would impede changes even if the change would be efficient (ibid.).

This theory offers a plausible macroeconomic view of the persistence of corporate structures, but does not explain the microeconomic process of the change from concentrated control at the time of the IPO towards majority control in Germany and towards diffuse control in the UK, respectively. The remainder of the chapter will address this issue. In Section 2 we provide some stylized facts about the ownership evolution in German and UK IPOs. Section 3 describes the data sources and methodology. Section 4 focuses on the control structure of IPOs that were targets of full or partial takeovers. Section 5 discusses the results from the binominal and multinominal models that attempt to predict the state of control towards which IPOs evolve six years after going public. Section 6 concludes the chapter.

2. THE DETERMINANTS OF CONTROL CONCENTRATION

This section investigates the determinants of control (and ownership) concentration. In order to use a common basis for study of the evolution of control and ownership in the two countries, size- and industry-matched samples of recent IPOs are constructed. A first determinant is firm size as Demsetz and Lehn (1985) argue that wealth limitations restrict the existence of substantial share stakes in large corporations. Therefore, we expect that the larger the firm, the higher the probability that the firm will become widely held. This in turn may increase the probability of a takeover.

We turn next to examine the relation between control patterns and IPOs. Interestingly, if the founder or his heirs are still involved in the company in terms of managerial responsibility and voting rights at the flotation, there is a high probability that they will still be among the major shareholders six years after the IPO. Founder commitment at the time of the IPO is included in the model as a proxy for the private benefits he or she extracts from controlling the firm. Likewise, Morck *et al.* (1988) explain that the founder of a firm may provide essential leadership skills, especially in younger firms. In contrast, Zingales (1995) and Mello and Parsons (1996) suggest that the presence of the founder should not negatively influence the probability of a full or partial takeover. The founders/initial shareholders should take a firm public stand in two discrete steps to maximize the proceeds. In a first step, they should sell cash flow rights to a large number of investors in order to retain control.[2] In a second step, the original owner should sell control to a new controlling shareholder.

Bolton and von Thadden (1998) model the evolution to the optimal level of control and ownership concentration and find that high-risk firms will end up being widely held. Their proposition has been supported by several empirical studies (e.g. Demsetz and Lehn 1985; Leech and Leahy 1991). Based on these studies we propose, therefore, that stable returns facilitate control retention by individual investors or families and that the probability that the firm's original owners will diversify their shareholding increases with the volatility of returns. Furthermore, rapidly growing firms may have to resort to attracting more outside equity than firms operating in mature industries. Thus, the higher the growth rate, the higher will be the probability that the firm will either be taken over or become widely held (Crespi 1998).

The initial owners, by selling non-voting shares to the general public, can diversify their cash flow rights in the firm without relinquishing control. Although non-voting shares are in principle admitted by the London Stock Exchange (LSE), issues of non-voting shares have been actively discouraged by the authorities (Brennan and Franks 1997). Goergen and Renneboog (2001) report that the few listed UK companies that had issued non-voting shares converted them into voting shares under the pressure of the LSE and institutional investors during the early 1990s. In Germany, in contrast, non-voting shares are frequently issued with the IPO. In line with DeAngelo and DeAngelo (1985) for the USA, we find that in German IPOs, voting shares are normally held by the initial owners whereas non-voting shares are issued in the IPO. Goergen (1999), who investigates ownership of all the German firms going public, finds that generally only IPOs floated by families issue non-voting shares. Immediately after the IPO, the family shareholder owns on average 57 per cent of the voting rights, but only 47 per cent of total equity (voting plus non-voting shares). For other categories of shareholder there is no violation of the one vote-one share rule.

Profitable firms generating sufficient cash flows allow the initial shareholders to retain control for a longer time than poorly performing firms. Poor performance may reflect not only weak management but also poor corporate monitoring, which may activate the market for corporate control. In the UK, this market for corporate control consists in full takeovers, whereas in Germany it seems to operate via partial takeovers or a change in the major shareholder. We expect poor performance to lead to changes in control.[3]

3. DATA SOURCES, VARIABLE DESCRIPTION, AND METHODOLOGY

3.1. *Sample Description and Data Sources*

This section will discuss the data sources and methodology employed in this chapter. From 1981 to 1988, a total of ninety-six German firms went public, fifty-one of which were listed on the Official Market and forty-five chose a listing on the Regulated Market (the second-tier market). About 83 per cent (eighty firms) were closely held by individuals just prior to the IPO. Control and ownership concentration of sixty-one of these eighty German firms could be traced reliably over time.[4] During the same period, the number of UK firms going public was substantially higher with 764 firms, of which 284 were floated on the Official Market and 480 on the Unlisted Securities Market (USM), that is, the second-tier market. This study concentrates only on domestic IPOs listed on the official and secondary markets, as data for lower market tiers[5] are normally not available. Furthermore, in order to increase direct comparability, only those German and UK IPOs in which the largest shareholder (in terms of voting equity prior to the IPO) is an individual or a group of persons (e.g. a family or unrelated associates) are selected.

There are marked differences between the sample of German and UK IPOs in terms of age, corporate size, industry and riskiness. On average, the German firms were founded fifty-one years prior to the flotation whereas UK firms were set up only fourteen years before the initial public offering. Moreover, the German companies were only twice as large as the UK IPOs with respective market capitalizations at the closing of the first day of listing of £113 and £56 million.[6]

The distribution of German and UK IPOs across industries also reveals significant differences.[7] Although the industry with the highest proportion of IPOs is the same for both countries (electricals, electronics, and office equipment), there are proportionally more German IPOs in mature industries (such as mechanical engineering with 15.5 per cent of the total number of IPOs and motor components with 5.2 per cent). UK IPOs are better represented in cyclical service industries with 29 per cent of the sample: service agencies with 9.0 per cent, property with 6.0 per cent, leisure with 5.7 per cent, chain stores with 3.6 per cent and construction with 4.9 per cent. Within each industry, UK IPOs are also usually smaller than German IPOs.

Information on the identity of initial shareholders and on pre- and post-IPO holdings was obtained from the IPO prospectuses. For the years subsequent to the IPO substantial share stakes were traced in annual reports as well as in the LSE Yearbooks for the UK and in the Saling Aktienführer for Germany. Both the direct and the ultimate equity (and control) stakes were collected. To identify the ultimate shareholder and his control stake, the ownership pyramids were reconstructed. The ultimate level of control was reached when the ultimate shareholder is either an individual or a family, or a widely held company or (financial) institution. Ultimate control is only relevant for German companies; UK regulation has kept ownership structures simple and has avoided ownership pyramids or cascades.

Share prices were collected from the Karlsruher Kapitalmarktdatenbank (KKMDB) and the London Share Price Database (LSPD). IPO characteristics (age and industry) and the closing market capitalization for the first day of listing were obtained from the Deutsche Börse AG and the LSE. Accounting information was collected from the IPO prospectuses, company reports, the Extel Financial Company Research and Global Vantage CD-ROMs for both countries, and from Datastream and the Extel Microfiches for the UK.

3.2. *Methodology*

The German IPOs are matched by size with UK IPOs to obtain a size-matched sample consisting of fifty-four German firms and fifty-four UK firms. Industry-matching yields a second matched sample with fifty-eight IPOs from each country.[8]

For the size- and industry-matched samples, the following cross-sectional multinomial model is estimated:[9]

$$U_{ij}=\beta' z_{ij}+\varepsilon_{ij} \quad \text{for } j=1,2,\ldots,J$$

$$\Pr(Y=0)=\frac{1}{1+\sum_{k=1}^{J} e^{\beta_k' x_k}}$$

$$\Pr(Y=j)=\frac{e^{\beta_j' x_j}}{1+\sum_{k=1}^{J} e^{\beta_k' x_k}}$$

We distinguish between four states of control six years after the flotation: firm i is (i) controlled by the original owners (SC); (ii) widely held (WH); (iii) taken over by a closely held bidder (TC) who is ultimately controlled by an individual or family; or (iv) taken over by a widely held bidder (TW). Six years after the flotation, two-thirds of the German size-matched sample were still controlled by the initial owner. This proportion is three times higher than for the UK sample (see Fig. 10.1). However, the number of (full and partial) takeovers is similar: nineteen and twenty-three German and UK firms, respectively.

As both German and UK IPOs are included in the model, a dummy variable COUNTRY is used, which equals 1 for a German company and 0 otherwise. The coefficient on this dummy registers a possible difference in the intercept between German and UK IPOs. Firm size (SIZE) is the natural logarithm of the market capitalization at the closing price on the first day of trading and converted into 1985 pounds sterling. Founder involvement is captured by the dummy variable FOUNDER, which equals 1 if the founder or his heirs hold an equity stake in the firm immediately prior to the IPO, and equals zero otherwise. The level of a firm's riskiness (RISK) is measured by the standard deviation of monthly stock returns over a five-year period subsequent to the IPO. The growth rate (GROWTH) is defined as the average annual growth rate of total assets over the first five years after the flotation. Non-voting shares (NON-VOTING) is a dummy variable capturing the issue of non-voting

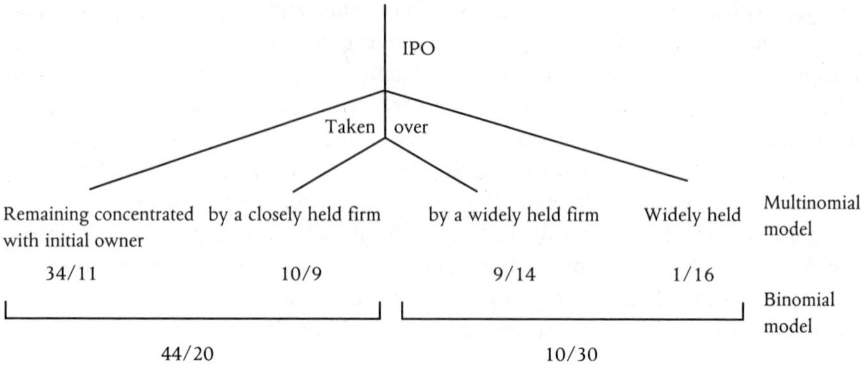

Figure 10.1. *Ultimate shareholder six years after the IPO for the size-matched sample: The numbers underneath the states of control show, respectively, the number of German (at the left) and of UK (at the right) companies. The closely held firm which acquires an IPO is controlled by an individual or a family. If a takeover takes place where the bidder is closely held by another company which is widely held, this takeover is classified as a takeover by a widely held firm. The two UK firms that went private and the two UK firms that went bankrupt are excluded*

shares at the time of going public (dummy equals 1). We note that twenty-three German firms issued non-voting shares in the size- and industry-matched samples, respectively. The profit rate (PROFIT) is defined as the annual cash flow standardized by book value of total assets.[10]

In order to determine whether there is a country-specific effect for each of the variables described above, an interactive term consisting of the product of each of the above variables with the COUNTRY dummy was included in the model. The interactive terms pick up the differential effect (i.e. they are the differential slope coefficients) for the German firms.

We also estimate a binomial logit regression with only two states of control (Fig. 10.1): (i) the firm is concentrated in the hands of the original owner or a new owner, and (ii) the firm is widely held, that is, does not have a large shareholder at the direct ownership level (ownership tier 1) or the large shareholder at tier one is ultimately widely held. This means that this model only distinguishes between two possible states of ownership and control concentration (high concentration versus diffuse ownership) without discerning how this state was reached. For example, in the case of strong control, no distinction is made between strong control by the initial shareholders or by a new controlling shareholder. In other words, we use the binomial model to predict ownership states independent of the path along which the control state was reached in the first five years subsequent to the IPO.

4. CONTROL EVOLUTION SUBSEQUENT TO THE FLOTATION: STYLIZED FACTS

4.1. *Initial-Shareholder Control Dilution*

In the UK, companies listed on the LSE tend to issue voting shares only which implies that ownership and control can be used interchangeably. In contrast, non-voting shares are

Table 10.1. *Proportion of voting rights held by original shareholders in recent German and UK IPOs*

Time after IPO	German firms		UK firms	
	Proportion held (%)	Sample size	Proportion held (%)***	Sample size
Immediately after the IPO	76.40	54	62.6	54
1 year	73.60	54	51.3	54
2 years	69.10	54	47.0	54
3 years	63.80	54	38.7	52
4 years	59.00	54	30.3	52
5 years	51.20	54	25.5	52
6 years	45.30	54	24.2	48

The German IPOs are matched by size with UK IPOs. (1) If a company is taken over and delisted, it is classified as a case of 100 per cent control by new shareholders as of the year of the takeover. If a company is made private by its original shareholders, it will be recorded as a company owned 100 per cent by its original shareholders. (2) The differences in means for each year are significantly different from zero at the 1 per cent level. ***indicates that the average stake held by original shareholders in UK firms is statistically different from the stake in German firms at the 1 per cent significance level.

Sources: IPO prospectuses, Saling Aktienführer, company reports, London Stock Exchange and Extel.

common for German corporations and about 38 per cent of our sample of German IPOs issued non-voting shares. Throughout the chapter, we focus on control (and hence on voting shares only) to distinguish between the four states of control of listed companies.

Table 10.1 records the voting power held by the initial shareholders over the six-year period after the IPO for the sample matched by size. Initial shareholder control is diluted much more rapidly in the UK than in Germany. The original shareholders of British IPOs lose majority control on average merely two years subsequent to the flotation whereas their German counterparts retain majority control up to five years. Although control dilution of the original shareholders is slower in German IPOs, as much as 55 per cent of the company's voting equity has changed hands at the end of the six-year period. The differences in initial shareholder concentration in German and UK IPOs are statistically significant at the 1 per cent level for each of the six years following the flotation.

4.2. *Direct Control Concentration Six Years After Going Public*

Panel A of Table 10.2 reports direct control concentration at the end of the six-year period subsequent to flotation. We distinguish among four different types of share concentration: (a) 100 per cent control concentration following a takeover with subsequent delisting; (b) a change of the major shareholder (the major shareholder being the largest shareholder holding at least 25 per cent of the voting equity); (c) diffuse control (no single shareholder owns more than 25 per cent of the voting rights); and (d) initial shareholder control.[11]

Panel A shows that full takeovers are uncommon in Germany with only one case in our sample.[12] In contrast, in the UK 35 per cent of our sample companies were acquired in a full takeover within six years after the flotation and hence delisted. The German market for

Table 10.2. *State of control of recent IPOs six years after flotation at the first tier*

	Size sample		Industry sample	
	Germany	UK	Germany	UK
Panel A: Number of firms by state of control				
Full takeover	1	19	1	18
Control change	18	5	20	4
Widely held	1	17	1	16
Still controlled by initial shareholders	34	13	36	20
Total	54	54	58	58
Panel B: Average number of years before reaching the new state of control				
Full takeover	6.0	3.7	6.0	3.5
Control change	4.4	3.0	4.3	3.5
Widely held	—	1.8	—	1.7

The disclosed state is the one six years after the IPO or the one of the last year of listing, if the firm was delisted before the sixth year after the flotation. A full takeover is a takeover of the entire equity of the firm, followed by the delisting of the firm. A control change is a change of the major shareholder, the major shareholder being the largest shareholder holding at least 25 per cent of the voting equity. A firm is widely held, if no single shareholder owns more than 25 per cent of the voting rights. A firm is still controlled by an initial shareholder, if the initial shareholder is the largest shareholder and holds more than 25 per cent of the votes.

Sources: McCarthy microfiches, Saling Aktienführer, *Financial Times*, company reports.

corporate control depends largely on changes of control, which are in fact partial takeovers.[13] Such partial takeovers are infrequent in the UK because of the legal requirement to make a tender offer for the entire equity of the firm as soon as an investor acquires more than 30 per cent of a firm's equity.[14] Thus, a shareholder in a UK company will end up with 100 per cent control or will deliberately remain underneath the 30 per cent threshold (Goergen and Renneboog 2001).

In terms of control change, partial takeovers in Germany and full takeovers in the UK are similar (Goergen 1998).[15] Therefore, Table 10.2 shows that, after amalgamating all control changes (both full and partial) takeovers, the percentage of German and UK IPOs (36 and 38 per cent) is almost equal. However, the distribution of control concentration across the remaining German and UK firms is still substantially different, as 64 per cent of the German firms remain in the hands of the initial owners whereas this is the case for only 24 per cent of the UK firms. Only one German company does not have a shareholder with a share stake of at least 25 per cent versus 17 widely held firms in the UK. Panel B of Table 10.2 shows that control changes in recent UK IPOs take place from three to four years after the flotation whereas in German IPOs they happen after four to six years.

Not only does control concentration in Germany and the UK differ, but there are also discrepancies in the nature of control. Table 10.3 shows the identity of the major shareholder at the first tier (or direct shareholder level) six years after the flotation in the

Table 10.3. *Voting rights in excess of 25 per cent in German and UK firms six years after the flotation*

	Germany (%)	UK (%)
Companies without a large shareholder	1.85	33.33
Companies with a large shareholder	98.15	66.67
Another domestic company	7.41	29.63
A foreign company	22.22	5.56
An insurance company	1.85	0.00
A trust/an institutional investor	0.00	3.70
A family group	66.67	27.78
A bank	0.00	0.00
Total	100.00	100.00

The table is based on a sample of German and UK IPOs matched by market capitalization. The sample is unbalanced, that is, if a firm is delisted prior to its sixth year after going public, the largest shareholder as in the last year prior to the delisting is reported.

Sources: Company reports, Saling for Germany and London Stock Exchange, and Extel for the UK.

size-matched sample.[16] An individual or a family is the largest shareholder class in 28 per cent of the UK IPOs, whereas this class of shareholders controls two-thirds of the German IPOs. In about one-third of both the German and UK IPOs, the major shareholder (at the first tier) is another domestic or foreign company, with the foreign firms being better represented in Germany.

4.3. *Ultimate Control*

While in a full takeover the entire equity is acquired and the acquired company is delisted, this does not necessarily imply transition to complete concentration. For example, if a UK company is taken over by a widely held company, it is the management of the bidder that acquires control rather than a large shareholder. Similarly, a change in the controlling shareholder of a German company may also lead to control dilution on the ultimate level if the new controlling shareholder is a widely held company. Table 10.4 focuses on the two types of takeovers (full and partial ones) and investigates whether or not the bidder's control structure is (ultimately) dispersed. The control structure of the bidder or the new controlling shareholder is therefore analysed through different ownership tiers. The largest shareholders on consecutive levels in the control cascade—control cascades are rare in the UK but common in Germany (Becht and Boehmer 2001)—were identified if these shareholders held control and formed an uninterrupted control chain.[17]

In 52 per cent of the German takeover targets in the size-matched sample, an individual or family was the ultimate shareholder. The remaining German companies were ultimately widely held, because the controlling shareholder at the top of the cascade was a company with diffuse control. Out of the twenty-four UK companies which were fully or partially taken over, fourteen had a dispersed share structure. Taking into account the ultimate control

Table 10.4. *Ultimate shareholder in targets of full and partial takeovers*

	Targets full takeover		Control change (excluding takeover)		All full takeovers and control changes	
	Germany	UK	Germany	UK	Germany	UK
Panel A: Size-matched sample						
Widely held	1	14	8	—	9	14
Closely held	—	5	10	5	10	9
Panel B: Industry-matched sample						
Widely held	—	13	10	—	10	13
Closely held	—	5	10	3	10	8

A firm is classed as widely held, if its ultimate largest shareholder is widely held, that is, not controlled by a person or family holding more than 25 per cent of the votes. A firm is classed as closely held, if the ultimate largest shareholder is a person or a family.

Sources: McCarthy microfiches, Saling Aktienführer, *Financial Times*, company reports.

structure is important because the potential agency problems in widely held (and hence management-controlled) firms are different from those in closely held firms (Shleifer and Vishny 1997; Bratton and McCahery 1999). Renneboog (2000) concludes that, for companies quoted on the Brussels stock exchange, it is this ultimate shareholder at the top of the cascade who takes managerial disciplining decisions.

Therefore, the full and partial takeovers are subdivided into control changes (takeovers) with ultimately dispersed voting rights and those with concentrated voting rights at the ultimate shareholder level. This brings the number of distinct states of control to four: a recent IPO (i) evolves gradually towards diffuse control, (ii) becomes widely held via a full or partial takeover, (iii) undergoes a control change (via a full or partial takeover) resulting in substantial shareholder control or (iv) remains controlled by the initial shareholders. In Section 4.4, the state of control is correlated with firm characteristics for both countries.

4.4. *Control State Prediction*

Multinomial logit models are estimated to predict the evolution of the state of control six years subsequent to the flotation of the sample of German and UK IPOs. In both models, the degree of control is classified based on both direct and indirect (ultimate) control.[18] Hence, the results reported in this section are the ones obtained from using the ultimate-shareholder data from the size-matched sample. The multinomial model allows for four different states six years after the IPO: original shareholder control (SC), diffuse control (WH), takeover by a closely held bidder (TC) or takeover by a widely held bidder (TW). As mentioned above, we do not distinguish between a full takeover (common in the UK) and a partial takeover, which comprises a change in the major shareholder (common in Germany).

The model presented in Table 10.5 includes a differential intercept and interactive slope coefficients, which pick up possible differential effects for the German IPOs. The model predicts the correct state of control for 80 per cent of the firms. Interestingly, firm size does

Table 10.5. *Prediction of the state of control*

	Log (P_{WH}/P_{SC})	Log (P_{TC}/P_{SC})	Log (P_{TW}/P_{SC})
Constant	0.294 (0.950)	−34.007 (1.000)	−92.916 (1.000)
Country	−33.940 (1.000)	31.427 (1.000)	17.605 (1.000)
Size	0.848 (0.423)	−2.479 (0.162)	0.984 (0.400)
Size * country	1.434 (1.000)	3.988 (0.078)	4.859 (0.048)
Founder	−8.018 (0.082)	34.442 (1.000)	26.777 (1.000)
Founder * country	2.736 (1.000)	−36.937 (1.000)	−15.785 (1.000)
Risk	−7.583 (0.696)	79.780 (0.061)	−36.246 (0.268)
Risk * country	−73.887 (1.000)	−118.425 (0.108)	−310.422 (0.021)
Growth	14.008 (0.064)	−1.667 (0.754)	25.202 (0.012)
Growth * country	−9.901 (1.000)	21.674 (0.040)	−24.990 (0.130)
Non-voting	−4.220 (1.000)	−3.062 (0.091)	−17.350 (0.012)
Profit	−8.873 (0.422)	−42.280 (0.065)	30.240 (0.032)
Profit * country	10.258 (1.000)	32.133 (0.125)	74.057 (0.059)
Chi-squared (d.f., *p*-value)	138 (63, 0.000)		
Percentage of correct predictions	79.76		
Observations	84		

(1) P_{SC} is the probability of being still controlled by the original owner, P_{WH} is the probability of being widely held, P_{TC} is the probability of being taken over by a closely held firm and P_{TW} is the probability of being taken over by a widely held firm.
(2) The *p*-values are in parentheses.
(3) Each model contains time dummies and industry dummies.

not influence the odds of evolving towards a diffuse shareholding structure or towards concentrated control. However, the differential SIZE-coefficient (of the interaction term with COUNTRY) is significant for the two types of takeovers suggesting that substantial control changes are more likely in large German companies.[19]

If the founder or his heirs are still shareholders (FOUNDER = 1) at the time of the IPO, the probability that the firm will evolve towards low control concentration over the six years subsequent to the IPO decreases. However, founder involvement at the flotation does not seem to influence the probability of being taken over, which provides support for the predictions of the models of Zingales (1995) and Mello and Parsons (1996). This result is consistent also with the empirical findings for the USA (Chung and Pruitt 1996).

Companies with a high risk-profile are expected to evolve towards a state of dispersed ownership of voting shares for reasons of risk sharing. However, Table 10.5 reveals that high volatility significantly increases the probability of a takeover by an individual/family or by a company which is in turn controlled by a large shareholder. Likewise, the negative signs hint (although without statistical significance) that high risk does not lead to dispersed corporate control. There is also evidence that high risk decreases the odds for German IPOs to be taken over by a bidder that is ultimately widely held. This contradicts the predictions of Bolton and von Thadden's (1998) model.

High growth rates (GROWTH) could lead to control dilution resulting from the limited availability of internally generated funds and the implied need to attract external capital to finance investment opportunities.[20] Table 10.5 confirms this hypothesis: both diffuse control or a takeover by a widely held company are the more likely 'equilibrium' states six years subsequent to a flotation for growth companies. Fast growing German IPOs face also higher odds of a partial takeover by a closely held bidder relative to the probability of remaining controlled by the pre-IPO shareholders. For German firms, non-voting shares are shown to be an impediment to takeovers as dual class shares enable owners to keep control and simultaneously to diversify their cash flow rights.

Table 10.5 supports the proposition by Burkart *et al.* (1997) that claims that different states of the world require specific control structures. In some states of the world (such as the one with low profitability), a large stable shareholder with a long-term perspective is needed, while in other cases a dispersed share structure allows sufficient managerial discretion. We find that a low profit rate augments the probability of a recent IPO being acquired by a concentrated bidder. Incumbent shareholders may sell out to a concentrated bidder, if they are not able to provide sufficient monitoring to improve their firm's performance. Indeed, poor performance not only results from poor managerial performance, but also from a breakdown of corporate control. Even more striking is the fact that the higher the profit rate, the higher the odds that the firm will be taken over by a widely held bidder. The fact that widely held companies prefer profitable takeover targets can be explained in an agency-cost setting: managers of widely held firms may find it easier to boost financial performance by taking over profitable corporations rather than to improve the financial results of their current business.[21] Alternatively, widely held bidders may not be able to provide the level of monitoring, which would be required to turn around a badly performing target firm. Finally, the differential slope coefficient is positive and significantly different from zero, suggesting that this effect is even more pronounced for the German IPOs.

From the results of the multinomial model, we can conclude that there are substantial differences between takeovers with concentrated (ultimate) control and acquisitions by widely held companies. The probability of a control change with concentrated ultimate control increases when the IPO is risky and poorly performing. Furthermore, in the case of German IPOs, the odds of being taken over by a closely held bidder increase if the company is large, has not issued any non-voting shares and experiences a high growth rate. The probability of an acquisition by a bidder with a diffuse share structure, increases for profitable IPOs, and even more so for German IPOs which are large, not risky and without non-voting equity. Founder involvement at the time of going public augments the probability that the firm remains controlled by the initial owners.[22]

As the coefficient on the dummy COUNTRY is not significantly different from zero, there are no country effects apart from the ones already captured by the interaction terms.

5. CONCLUSION

This chapter provides a partial answer to the question why the corporate landscapes of listed companies are so different in Germany and the UK in terms of control. For this purpose, ownership and control evolution in recent German and UK IPOs is investigated.

Initial shareholders in the average German company lose absolute majority control six years subsequent to the public offering, whereas initial owners in UK companies decrease their holding to less than 50 per cent merely two years after going public. Acquisitions are frequent in the UK with 35 per cent being taken over versus only one German sample company. Partial takeovers are common in German firms: in one-third of the sample a large controlling shareholder acquires control from another controlling shareholder. Contrary to the UK where 31 per cent of IPOs become widely held, the initial shareholders retain absolute control in a majority (63 per cent) of German IPOs even six years after the flotation.

The nature of the controlling shareholder differs between the average German and UK firm: the largest shareholder class, dominating two-thirds of the German companies with concentrated ownership are families, whereas (domestic) companies control almost 30 per cent of the UK firms with concentrated ownership which went public six years prior.

We also analysed changes in control based on ultimate ownership structures and distinguished between two types of takeovers: acquisitions by a (ultimately) widely held company and acquisitions by individuals or families. In the UK, the acquisition of a controlling block of 30 per cent of the voting equity results in the obligation to tender for all other shares; a requirement which does not exist in Germany. Consequently, we argue that if we regard the full takeovers in the UK as similar—in terms of control—to changes in control due to the selling of a controlling block to a new large shareholder (a partial takeover) in Germany, the overall picture of corporate ownership and control is less diverging than usually ascertained.

In order to predict the state of ownership and control six years subsequent to going public, a multinomial logit model is used with four possible states of control: the company is (i) still controlled by the shareholders who controlled the company prior to the flotation; (ii) acquired by a closely held shareholder (i.e. an individual or family); (iii) acquired by a shareholder with diffuse control; and (iv) widely held. The model has a high predictive power with about 80 per cent of correct predictions. The probability that an IPO will evolve towards diffuse control increases if the founder does not own a substantial share stake at the moment of the public offering and if the company experiences a high growth rate. When German and UK IPOs are risky and poorly performing, their odds of ending up with concentrated ultimate control increased. In such a case, the need for a strong shareholder with good monitoring abilities and a long-term investment horizon arises. In addition, specifically for German IPOs, the probability that the company's majority control is held by a new large shareholder augments when non-voting shares are issued at flotation and when the company grows fast. Profitable, non-risky, large companies tend to be widely held six years after being listed. The company's founders tend to maintain control in smaller, profitable companies with limited risk and limited growth.

Notes

1. For a comparative evaluation see Bratton and McCahery (1999). Empirical differences between the market-oriented system and the blockholder system have been documented in the following: Roe (1994); Moerland (1995); Shleifer and Vishny (1997); Renneboog (1998, 1999); and Barca and Becht (2001).

2. Brennan and Franks (1997) show that control retention is an important reason for underpricing: share rationing schemes enable original shareholders to disperse shares to atomistic subscribers.
3. The use of performance as an explanatory variable raises the question of the direction of causality between ownership and profit. Goergen (1998) shows that the early literature (see, for example, Morck *et al.* (1988); Wruck (1989); and McConnell and Servaes (1990)) suggests that financial performance is influenced by ownership, but only finds a weak relation between profit and exogenous ownership. Recent studies (Agrawal and Knoeber (1996); Denis and Denis (1994); and Himmelberg *et al.* (1999)) do not make this strong exogeneity assumption but do not find that ownership conditions financial performance.
4. For most of the other IPOs, the identity of the shareholders was available, but not the exact size of their holdings.
5. Lower tier markets are the Unregulated Unofficial Market, and the OTC for Germany; and the Third Market, and OTC for the UK.
6. Market capitalization is adjusted for UK inflation by the annual GDP deflator (base year 1985) of the IMF. Several German firms in our sample have dual class shares of which one class is not listed. The market capitalization for these firms was computed by multiplying the total number of shares by the market price of the listed class of shares.
7. Industry classification is based on the two-digit UK SE Groups, the industrial classification retained by the LSE to compile its quarterly lists of new issues. The groups are covered by the F.T. Actuaries Investment Index Classification with the amalgamation of certain related groups. For each German firm, the industry description at the time of the IPO in the Saling Aktienführer was recorded. Subsequently, German firms were reclassified into the two-digit UK SE Groups. We have merged specific groups that only had a small number of IPOs: for example, groups 27 (Misc. Mechanical Engineering) and 28 (Machine and Other Tools) were merged. Groups 19 (Electricals), 35 (Electronics) and 69 (Office Equipment) were also merged since groups 35 and 69 did not exist at the beginning of the 1980s and computer and software manufacturers were first assigned to group 19, then to group 69 and only later to group 35.
8. The average difference in size between the German IPO and its UK match is 2.7 per cent. The median is 0.5 per cent and the standard-deviation amounts to 4.7 per cent. For seven German firms, a close match, defined as a match within a ±25 per cent difference in size, could not be found; neither was it possible to find a UK industry match for three German IPOs. The two German samples have fifty-two firms in common. The German size-matched sample includes two companies not included in the industry-matched sample, because there were no UK IPOs in these specific industries in the studied time period. The German industry-matched sample comprises six firms not included in the size-matched sample. It may be argued that another matching based on the age of firms should have been performed. However, a reasonable match (plus or minus two years of difference) could only be found for about nineteen German firms. Similarly, we tried to match firms simultaneously by size and industry. However, again for more than three-quarters of the firms a satisfactory match within the 25 per cent standard-deviation range could not be found.
9. More specifically, U_{ij} is the state of control j in company i.

$$
\begin{aligned}
\text{STATE}_{ij} = {} & \alpha + \beta_1\,\text{COUNTRY}_i + \beta_2\,\text{SIZE}_i + \beta_3\,\text{FOUNDER}_i + \beta_4\,\text{RISK}_i + \beta_5\,\text{GROWTH}_i \\
& + \beta_6\,\text{NON-VOT}_i + \beta_7\,\text{PROFIT}_i + \beta_8\,\text{COUNTRY}_i{*}\text{SIZE}_i + \beta_9\,\text{COUNTRY}_i \\
& {*}\,\text{FOUNDER}_i + \beta_{10}\,\text{COUNTRY}_i{*}\text{RISK}_i + \beta_{11}\,\text{COUNTRY}_i{*}\text{GROWTH}_i + \beta_{12} \\
& \text{COUNTRY}_i\,{*}\text{PROFIT}_i \\
& + \text{time dummies} + \text{industry dummies} + \varepsilon_{ij}.
\end{aligned}
$$

10. The annual cash flow is measured as the profit gross of depreciation, interest, taxes and changes in tax, pension, and special provisions. For firms that changed their control state during the year of the IPO (year 0), the profit rate was not included in the model, as for these firms the profit rate measures the profitability after the change (*ex post* measure) rather than before the change. This is equivalent to multiplying the profit variable by a dummy variable, which is zero if the firm changed its state during the year of the IPO and one otherwise.
11. Whereas Table 10.2 considers only direct holdings, Table 10.4 takes both direct and indirect shareholdings into account.
12. Franks and Mayer (1998) report that hostile takeovers have been a rare phenomenon in Germany. Since WWII there have only been three attempts.
13. We therefore define a partial takeover as a control change involving at least 25 per cent of the equity. The threshold of 25 per cent was chosen as it gives an investor a veto right at the AGM.
14. The Takeover Panel may grant an exception to this rule, which makes a tender offer mandatory to a party which reaches the 30 per cent threshold of equity (or voting rights), in the case where a shareholder takes a large stake in a financially distressed company.
15. Corporate performance in Germany and UK prior to partial takeovers and complete acquisitions is similar.
16. The results for the industry-matched sample are similar and are available upon request.
17. A large shareholder controls a company on a lower tier if he holds the largest stake exceeding 25 per cent of the voting equity.
18. The predictive power of these models with control based on direct shareholding was lower than the one based on direct and ultimate control, which is in line with the findings by Renneboog (2000) and Goergen and Renneboog (2000). Statistical significance for the direct ownership models was always worse for the case of the size-matched sample, and worse or similar for the industry-matched sample.
19. In order to avoid multicollinearity, the variable AGE (corporate age at the time of the IPO) was excluded from the model.
20. All results in this section—apart from the conclusions concerning corporate growth—are also valid for the industry-matched sample. These results are not reported in the chapter but are available upon request. The only difference in results is that the GROWTH coefficient is not significantly different from 0 at the 10 per cent level for the industry sample. This is probably due to the fact that firms matched by industry have more comparable growth rates than those matched by size; see also Goergen (1999).
21. This finding is confirmed by a study on hostile takeovers in the UK by Franks and Mayer (1996).
22. As it is possible that only the degree of control matters and not how this 'optimal' control state is reached, a model with only two control states (concentrated versus dispersed control) may yield stronger predictions. In this case, it is assumed that an IPO reaches an equilibrium state of control six years after the flotation or earlier. This maybe a fair assumption as Table 10.2 shows that most changes in control take place before the sixth year following the IPO. If a firm's optimal control structure is concentrated, it should either stay concentrated and held by the initial shareholder or its control should be directly transferred to a new shareholder. Alternatively, if the optimal state of control is dispersed, the voting shares should be held by a large number of small investors or a company with dispersed shareholders. The results from such a binomial logit model (not shown) demonstrate that the predictive power of the two-state model is marginally better than the one of the four-state model. The binomial model predicts the correct state for 83 per cent of the IPO firms. Although this is an improvement in terms of predictive power and suggests that the path along which the equilibrium state of control for recent IPOs does not matter, some information has been lost in the aggregation process. In addition, the binomial logit

model corroborates the results of the multi-state model: the probability that control becomes dispersed in recent IPOs increases for larger, profitable, high growth companies, and with no founder ownership immediately before the flotation. German IPOs tend towards more diffuse control in the case of low risk, when the company has not issued non-voting equity and when the founder held a stake in the firm at the time of going public.

References

Agrawal, A., and Knoeber, C. (1996). Firm performance and mechanisms to control agency problems between managers and shareholders. *Journal of Financial and Quantitative Analysis* 31: 377.

Barca, F., and Becht, M. (2001). *The Control of Corporate Europe.* Oxford: Oxford Universtiy Press.

Bebchuk, L. (1998). A theory of the choice between concentrated and dispersed ownership of corporate shares and votes. Harvard Law School, Working Paper.

—— and Roe, M. (1998). A theory of path dependence in corporate governance and ownership. *Stanford Law Review* 53: 127.

Becht, M., and Boehmer, E. (2001). Ownership and control in Germany. In F. Barca and M. Becht (ed.), *The Control of Corporate Europe.* Oxford: Oxford University Press: 128.

Black, B. (1990). Shareholder passivity re-examined. *Michigan Law Review* 89: 575.

Bolton, P., and von Thadden, E.-L. (1998). Liquidity and control: A dynamic theory of corporate ownership structure. *Journal of Institutional and Theoretical Economics* 154: 177.

Bratton, W., and McCahery, J. (1999). Comparative corporate governance and the theory of the firm: The case against global cross reference. *Columbia Journal of Transnational Law* 38: 213.

Brennan, M., and Franks, J. (1997). Underpricing, ownership and control in initial public offerings of equity securities in the UK. *Journal of Financial Economics* 45: 391.

Burkart, M., Gromb, D., and Panunzi, F. (1997). Large shareholders, monitoring and the value of the firm. *Quarterly Journal of Economics* 112: 693.

Chung, K., and Pruitt, S. (1996). Executive ownership, corporate value, and executive compensation: A unifying framework. *Journal of Banking and Finance* 20: 1135.

Crespi, R. (1998). Determinantes de la estructura de propiedad: Una aproximacion al caso espanol con datos de panel. *Moneda-y-Credito* 206: 167.

DeAngelo, H., and DeAngelo, L. (1985). Managerial ownership of voting rights—a study of public corporations with dual classes of common stock. *Journal of Financial Economics* 14: 33.

Demsetz, H., and Lehn, K. (1985). The structure of corporate ownership: Causes and consequences. *Journal of Political Economy* 93: 1155.

Denis, D. J., and Denis, D. K. (1994). Majority owner-managers and organizational efficiency. *Journal of Corporate Finance* 1: 91.

Franks, J., and Mayer, C. (1996). Hostile takeovers in the UK and the correction of managerial failure. *Journal of Financial Economics* 40: 163.

—— (1998). Bank control, take-overs and corporate-governance in Germany. *Journal of Banking and Finance* 22: 1385.

Gilson, R., and Kraakman, R. (1991). Reinventing the outside director: An agenda for institutional investors. *Stanford Law Review* 43: 863.

Goergen, M. (1998). *Corporate Governance and Financial Performance: A Study of German and UK Initial Public Offerings.* Cheltenham: Edward Elgar.

—— (1999). Insider retention and long-run performance in German and UK IPOs. UMIST School of Management, Working Paper.

—— —— (2000). Insider control by large investor groups and managerial disciplining in listed Belgian companies. *Managerial Finance* 26: 22.

——and Renneboog, L. (2001). Strong managers and passive institutional investors in the UK. In F. Barca and M. Becht (ed.), *The Control of Corporate Europe.* Oxford: Oxford University Press: 259.

Hay, D., and Morris, D. (1984). *Unquoted Companies: Their Contribution to the United Kingdom Economy.* London: Macmillan.

Himmelberg, C., Hubbard, R. G., and Palia, D. (1999). Understanding the determinants of managerial ownership and the link between ownership and performance. *Journal of Financial Economics* 53: 353.

La Porta, R., Lopez-de-Silanes, F., Shleifer, A., and Vishny, R. (1997). Legal determinants of external finance. *Journal of Finance* 52: 1131.

————————(1998). Law and finance. *Journal of Political Economy* 106: 1113.

————————(1999). Ownership around the world. *Journal of Finance* 54: 471.

Leech, D., and Leahy, J. (1991). Ownership structure, control type classifications and the performance of large British companies. *Economic Journal* 101: 1418.

McConnell, J., and Servaes, H. (1990). Additional evidence on equity ownership and corporate value. *Journal of Financial Economics* 27: 595.

Mello, A., and Parsons, J. (1996). Going public and the ownership structure of the firm. University of Wisconsin, Working Paper No. 5-96-1.

Moerland, P. (1995). Corporate ownership and control structures: An international comparison. *Review of Industrial Organization* 10: 443.

Morck, R., Shleifer, A., and Vishny, R. (1988). Management ownership and market valuation. An empirical analysis. *Journal of Financial Economics* 20: 293.

Renneboog, L. (1998). Corporate governance systems: The role of ownership, external finance and regulation (Part I). *Corporate Governance* 1: 37.

——(1999). Corporate governance systems: The role of ownership, external finance and regulation (Part II). *Corporate Governance* 2: 4.

——(2000). Ownership, managerial control and the disciplining of poorly performing companies listed on the Brussels stock exchange. *Journal of Banking and Finance* 24: 1959.

Roe, M. (1994). *Strong Managers, Weak Owners: The Political Roots of American Corporate Finance.* Princeton: Princeton University Press.

——(1996). Chaos and evolution in law and economics. *Harvard Law Review* 109: 643.

Shleifer, A., and Vishny, R. W. (1997). A survey of corporate-governance. *Journal of Finance* 52: 737.

Wruck, K. (1989). Equity ownership concentration and firm value. *Journal of Finance* 23: 567.

Zingales, L. (1995). Insider ownership and the decision to go public. *Review of Economic Studies* 62: 425.

11

Who Controls German Corporations?

EKKEHART BOEHMER

1. INTRODUCTION

It is well known that German corporations are characterized by highly concentrated ownership and that banks and other financial institutions play an important role. Large shareholders dominate most listed corporations and financial institutions exert control via direct ownership, interlocking directorships, and proxy votes. In addition, retail investors typically delegate their voting rights to their financial institutions. As a consequence, banks control a large fraction of voting rights associated with widely held shares.[1] Detailed knowledge of who controls German corporations is essential to evaluate the German system of corporate governance, which continues to attract academic and political interest. Before 1995, publicly available information on blockholdings was limited, because there were no ongoing reporting requirements. Only the 1995 Wertpapierhandelsgetz (WpHG) made the immediate disclosure of large voting blocks mandatory for firms trading in official markets. I use these filings in the empirical description below.[2]

In Germany's system of powerful large shareholders, blockholder actions have a potentially large impact on firm performance and hence on the returns to small shareholders. A large shareholder may be able to divert resources from the partially owned firm to other entities that he owns. To investigate whether it is in the interest of blockholders to increase the value of the firm or to divert resources, it is important to know their identity. This first step allows an assessment of blockholder incentives and supervision. Despite the importance of these issues, in-depth empirical descriptions of corporate governance in Germany are rare.[3] To fill this gap, this paper uses a cross-sectional data set of blockholdings of voting rights in German corporations. It provides a detailed account of the relative importance of different blockholder types. Additionally, I examine the identity and power of Germany's largest shareholders. To estimate control, I measure the size of ultimate voting control and provide an empirical description of the largest blockholders.

The remainder of this chapter is organized as follows. In Section 2, I describe the data used to analyse voting power. Section 3 presents the results from the perspective of individual shareholders. It describes the distribution of control across shareholders and analyses the power of different shareholder types. In Section 4, I analyse the economic importance and identity of Germany's most powerful shareholders. Section 5 discusses the incentives of blockholders and the consequences of large voting blocks for shareholder wealth and provides some concluding remarks.

2. DATA AND SAMPLE CONSTRUCTION

The analysis is based on data from BAWe (1996), the first-ever official cross-sectional 'snapshot' of the distribution of voting blocks in Germany on 30 September 1996. It contains the cumulative result of all notifications up to this date according to §§ 21, 22, and 41 WpHG since 1 January 1995. By year-end 1996, 436 firms trade in the official market segments in Germany. All of these firms should have declared any blockholders controlling 5 per cent or more by early 1996. The BAWe (1996) report, however, includes only 402 German companies. Therefore, thirty-four companies or 7.6 per cent of all officially listed firms had not received any notifications or had failed to report them since the WpHG came into force. To obtain a more complete data set, I investigate the missing firms.

First, Deutsche Telekom went public in October 1996 and was not traded in September. An additional seventeen firms were included in later versions of the BAWe report, even though their filings had in several cases been made before September 1996. For an additional eleven firms, I find ownership information in Hoppenstedt's Konzernstruktur-Datenbank (KSD).[4] For six firms (Bremer Vulkan, Georg, Arn., Marschollek Lautenschl. und Partner AG, Terrex Handels-AG, Traub AG, and Würzburger Hofbräu AG) I was not able to find any reliable information and excluded them from the analysis below. Thus, the final sample includes 430 firms and consists of the original 402 from BAWe (1996), seventeen from BAWe (1997), and eleven from KSD. For all firms I cross-checked KSD and BAWe data to eliminate errors and to confirm reported figures. I also discarded all stakes below 5 per cent that are included in BAWe (1996) but are not attributed to some other controlling party. These filings are not required by law and are most likely erroneous notifications and/or data entries.

The BAWe has taken the data from the WpHG notifications and tabulated them. The BAWe publishes the aggregate of direct and attributed voting rights that the notifying company controls. In addition, it reports the fraction of total votes that are indirectly controlled and hence attributed to the shareholder. From these figures, I calculate voting blocks in the reporting listed firm following Becht and Boehmer (1997). Since the direct and attributed shares cannot simply be summed up to avoid double counting, I trace all direct stakes to their ultimate reporting owner in order to determine manually total block ownership. This process requires knowledge of the ownership and control relations between the reporting shareholders. Since the BAWe does not publish this information, it is taken from various editions of KSD, Hoppenstedt's *Handbuch der Aktiengesellschaften*, and *Wer gehört zu wem?*, a triennial publication by Commerzbank.

The difficulty of appropriately assigning voting blocks is best illustrated using an example. Suppose that shareholder A owns 10 per cent directly and 5 per cent indirectly, and shareholder B owns 5 per cent directly. Then the information that can be inferred from the BAWe publication is as shown in Table 11.1.

It is not immediately obvious whether 10 or 15 per cent of the investigated firm are held by reporting shareholders. If B is controlled by A, then the only voting block of 15 per cent would be assigned to A and represents the total fraction of votes controlled by large shareholders. If A and B are unrelated, one voting block of 15 per cent would be assigned to A, and another one of 5 per cent to B, and a total of 20 per cent is controlled by large

Table 11.1. *Reporting opaqueness of direct and indirect ownership*

Shareholder	Direct holdings (%)	Attributed holdings (%)
A	10	5
B	5	

shareholders.[5] Thus, the relation between B and A determines the number of voting blocks that are assigned in the process and the inferred concentration of control. This example also illustrates the substantial information content that is lost in the BAWe publications by not reporting the attribution reason (which, in the first example, could state that the 5 per cent attributed to A are directly held by its subsidiary B).[6]

Throughout this chapter, I use the market value of equity as a measure of firm size. Market value is measured at year-end 1995 and are calculated on the basis of outstanding equity by the end of December 1995. The sample firms have up to three classes of shares outstanding (ordinary shares, preference shares without voting rights, and registered shares with or without transfer restrictions and other special rights). All firms have at least one class listed in the official Frankfurt market, triggering mandatory reporting to the BAWe. To calculate the value of non-traded shares, I make the following assumptions: (1) ordinary shares trade at a premium of 20 per cent relative to preference shares, and (2) registered shares trade at the same price as ordinary shares. The premium of around 20 per cent for voting shares is supported by several studies and own calculations. The second assumption cannot be supported empirically, because registered shares and another class are rarely listed simultaneously for the same firm. The average (median) market value is DM 2.4 (0.3) billion across all sample firms, DM 4.2 (1.7) billion for banks, DM 6.3 (1.1) billion for insurance companies, and DM 2.0 (0.3) billion for industrial firms.

3. THE CONCENTRATION OF VOTING CONTROL

The objective of this and the following section is to describe the concentration of voting control over listed firms in Germany. To analyse the identity of blockholders, concentration is measured across shareholders and not across firms. All results in this paragraph are based on aggregation across the 514 blockholders who control 755 voting blocks in excess of 5 per cent. About 85.0 per cent of all large shareholders control just a single stake. The remaining parties control up to twenty-five voting blocks. This distribution indicates that a few investors may have substantial impact on several firms.

Panel A of Table 11.2 presents means and medians of size-weighted stakes. The table shows the mean and median market value of ultimate voting blocks, and also presents the number of different shareholders (the denominator in the means calculations). The right-most column shows the percentage of the aggregate market value controlled by voting blocks. For the whole sample, notifying shareholders control on average a market value of DM 950 million. The remaining rows present the corresponding figures for different types of shareholders. The German government (largely due to its stake in Deutsche Telekom), foreign governments, banks, and insurance firms control the largest blocks, although foreign governments' share of aggregate market value is only 0.8 per cent. All blockholders jointly control 47 per cent of the market value of officially listed firms.

Table 11.2. *Market value of ultimate voting blocks held by different shareholder types*

A. Summary statistics on the market value of voting blocks

Sample (number of blocks)	Mean (DM million)	Median (DM million)	Number of different blockholders	% of total market value of listed firms with voting blocks
All shareholders (755)	950	93	510	47.3
Foreign investors (3)	3,895	3,895	2	0.8
Banks (116)	2,795	330	30	8.2
Industrial firms (185)	731	135	133	9.5
Families or worker pools (22)	644	110	21	1.3
Government (23)	4,339	639	19	8.0
Holding companies (59)	917	329	48	4.3
Investment firms (41)	431	133	38	1.6
Bank-controlled investment firms (11)	1,021	685	6	0.6
Individuals (207)	247	33	179	4.3
Foundations (17)	761	376	11	0.8
Insurance companies (71)	3,499	164	23	7.9

B. Total market value by sector (DM million)

	Bank	Insurance company	Industrial company	Total
All shareholders	39,972	105,539	338,966	484,477
Foreign investors	0	0	7,790	7,790
Banks	15,720	41,339	26,789	83,848
Industrial firms	1,086	2,817	93,510	97,280
Families or worker pools	0	0	13,381	13,515
Government	4,962	457	77,025	82,445
Holding companies	4,604	8,491	30,918	44,013
Investment firms	493	1,399	14,495	16,386
Bank-controlled investment firms	1,841	687	3,601	6,129
Individuals	245	213	43,762	44,220
Foundations	272	0	8,099	8,370
Insurance companies	10,750	50,137	19,596	80,482

The sample consists of all 430 firms and 755 ultimate voting blocks reported to the BAWe by September 1996. Market value refers to the market value of all equity. Holding companies (investment firms) are defined as firms whose main purpose is to fully own and operate (hold stakes in) independent companies. Bank-controlled investment firms include investment firms that are primarily controlled by banks and insurance companies. This subsample is only a subset of bank-controlled investment firms, because ownership and control data are only available for some of the mostly unlisted holdings and investment firms.

To provide further illustration of the relative importance of various shareholders, I calculate the aggregate market value controlled by the various shareholder types. Panel B reports blockholder-controlled market value separately for banks, insurance companies, and industrial firms. Each cell contains the aggregate market value controlled voting blocks. The table shows that banks, the government, and insurance companies command ninety-eight voting blocks, controlling DM 247 billion. In contrast, industrial companies and individuals own 319 voting blocks, but control only DM 142 billion in market value. Therefore, holdings of banks, the government, and insurance firms are more concentrated and more strategically placed in that they command the assets having the largest value. This observation holds for all types of listed companies, although to a lesser extent for listed industrial firms and a larger extent for listed banks and insurance companies (see panel B). Several different studies have attempted to assess costs and benefits of large blocks held by different shareholder types in Germany. Unfortunately, they disagree with respect to whether these blocks are beneficial or not.[7]

Becht and Boehmer (1997) show that current reporting practice does not provide full transparency of control. They discuss several listed firms where the control structures remain opaque despite the disclosure regulations enacted by the WpHG. Among the reasons are substantially limited reporting requirements for banks and investment funds, and the failure of the WpHG to generally require attribution of control to individuals controlling less than the majority of votes in holding/investment firms. For example, suppose a holding company that has two 50 per cent owners holds a stake in a listed firm. Then the holding company has to file its stake with the BAWe, but neither of its 50 per cent owners has to file. I show above that holding companies, investment firms, and foundations control about 13 per cent of listed equity. Their owners remain anonymous, since attribution of voting rights stops at that level. The same argument holds also for all industrial firms, banks, and insurance companies that control voting blocks and are not listed in the official market: the BAWe filings do not reveal who exerts ultimate control over these large blockholders. The identities of ultimately controlling individuals are only known for the shareholder categories 'individuals' and 'family and worker pools', who jointly hold 15 per cent of all voting rights but only 5.6 per cent of the market value of listed equity.

Moreover, the cross-ownership between shareholders reporting to the BAWe is generally not revealed, and neither is control due to proxy voting by banks and investment firms. Given the highly concentrated ownership structure in Germany, this appears to be a tremendous obstacle to transparent control structures. As a consequence, the data presented above should be viewed as a lower bound to the concentration of control and to the control attributed to the various shareholder types.

4. THE ECONOMIC IMPORTANCE AND IDENTITY OF THE LARGEST SHAREHOLDERS IN GERMANY

Blockholders may have incentives to maximize their personal (or corporate) wealth; this does not automatically involve maximizing the market value of the firm they share with outside shareholders. For example, if they can divert resources from their firms of which the equity is partially held by other outside shareholders to other wholly owned firms, these blockholders may be tempted to expropriate other shareholders' rights. Investigating the identity of large shareholders may help to shed some light on this question. In the following, I provide descriptive statistics on the overall top ten shareholders and the top five of each major shareholder category. Shareholders are ranked by the market value of all the voting blocks they report to the BAWe. Only blockholdings greater than DM 300 million are listed. For the ten largest shareholders, the first two columns in Table 11.3 list their primary voting interests (in excess of DM 300 million) and also their own blockholders. The remaining two columns report the market value of controlled voting blocks and their value as a percentage of the aggregate market value of all 430 sample firms, respectively.

The economic power of blockholders is illustrated in absolute and percentage terms. Rank 1 is held by a government agency through its control over Deutsche Telekom. Since this stake is transitory and will be sold over time as the privatization proceeds, it is more interesting to examine the next largest shareholders.[8] Ranks 2 and 4 are held by insurance firms (Allianz and Münchner Rück) and ranks 3, 5, and 6 are held by banks (Deutsche Bank, Dresdner Bank, and Bayerische Vereinsbank). An individual is on rank 7, and ranks 8, 9, and 10 are held by industrial firms (RWE, VIAG, and Kuwait Petroleum). Jointly these ten blockholders control voting blocks worth DM 227 billion, corresponding to 22 per cent of listed market value.

In fact, the actual market value under control of the top ten is much larger considering cross-holdings among the largest shareholders. Even though the individual stakes are typically minority blocks, a business group as a whole may have majority control. This argument is illustrated by using the top five private shareholders (ranks two through six), whom alone control 13 per cent of aggregate market value. Comparing this figure to the 47 per cent controlled by all reporting blockholders jointly indicates their economic importance and shows how top-heavy the size-weighted distribution of control is. The blockholder column shows that these five firms are interconnected via substantial ownership interests.

Table 11.4 reports the major ownership (as opposed to voting) interests among the top five private shareholders. Whereas Allianz, Münchner Rück, and Dresdner Bank are majority-controlled by those five major shareholders, Deutsche Bank and Bayerische Vereinsbank are widely held except for stakes of 6.53 and 10.61 per cent, respectively, held by the circle of five shareholders. Deutsche Bank and Bayerische Vereinsbank, in turn, control sizeable stakes in Allianz, Münchner Rück, and Dresdner Bank. The presented figures still substantially underestimate true interconnections since proxy votes are not considered in the table. Furthermore, several additional cross-holdings exist that involve lower-tier holding companies jointly owned by some of the top five. Holding companies frequently hold stakes in other related firms, which in turn may control voting rights in the top five. These additional control rights are not included in Table 11.4. Finally, the top shareholders frequently share stakes in the same target firms, which also tends to understate the mutual control exerted by the top five in each other.

Therefore, the value controlled by the top five is much larger than indicated in Table 11.3. The reason is that, due to interconnections between the five, they jointly have majority control over several firms as shown for Allianz, Münchner Rück, and Dresdner Bank in Table 11.4. To calculate the true value controlled, the value of dispersed shares in these

Table 11.3. *Ultimate voting blocks held by the ten shareholders controlling the greatest market value*

Rank	Shareholders (number of voting blocks included in calculations)	Main targets controlled by the shareholder (voting blocks in listed firms exceeding DM 300 million market value, sorted by decreasing market value)	Blockholders controlling stakes in the shareholder	Total and median market value of controlled voting blocks in Mn. DM	Voting blocks as % of market value of all 430 listed firms
1	Bundesanstalt für Post und Telekommunikation (1)	Deutsche Telekom	None, government	49,431 49,431	4.82
2	Allianz (25)	Münchner Rück, VEBA, Dresdner Bank, BASF, Bayr. Hypo, RWE, BDF Beiersdorf, Bayer, Deutsche Bank, Linde, Schering, BHF-Bank, Lahmeyer, Rheinelektra, AMB	Münchner Rück 26%, Bayer. Vereinsbank 10%, Deutsche Bank 10%, Dresdner Bank 10%, Bayer. Hypobank 5%	45,820 1,833	4.47
3	Deutsche Bank (27)	Daimler-Benz, Allianz, Münchner Rück, Frankfurter Hypo, Südzucker, Linde, Bayerische Vereinsbank, Metallgesellschaft, Heidelberger Zement, Karstadt, Ph. Holzmann, AMB	Allianz 5%	31,688 1,174	3.09
4	Münchner Rück (14)	Allianz, Bayerische Hypo, Victoria, AMB, Hermes Kreditversicherung	Allianz 25%, Bayer. Vereinsbank 10%, Deutsche Bank 10%, Dresdner Bank 10%, DIA VV 6%	22,085 1,578	2.15

5	Dresdner Bank (14)	Allianz, Münchner Rück, Deutsche Hypo, OLB, Heidelberger Zement, AMB, Hamburghyp, Bilfinger & Berger, Metallgesellschaft	Allianz 22%, Nona VV 10%, Vermo VV 11%	19,595 1,400	1.91
6	Bayerische Vereinsbank (9)	Allianz, Münchner Rück, Vereins- und Westbank, BHB, Nürnberger Hypo, Süddeutsche Bodencreditbank	Viag 7%, Bayernwerk 7%, Deutsche Bank 5%	14,839 1,649	1.45
7	Dietmar Hopp (1)	SAP	none	13,387 13,387	1.31
8	RWE (10)	RWE-DEA, Rheinelektra, Lahmeyer, LEW, Ph. Holzmann, MKW, Rhenag	RW Holding 12%, City of Essen 8%, Allianz 8%	11,598 1,160	1.13
9	VIAG (14)	Contigas, OBAG, SKW Trostberg, Bayerische Vereinsbank, EVO, VEW, BEWAG, Schmalbach-Lubeca, Grosskraftwerk Franken, Gerresheimer Glas, ÜWU	State of Bavaria 25%, VI Industriebet. 11%, HI VV 10% (VI and HI are majority controlled by Viag itself)	10,207 729	1.00
10	Kuwait Petro (1)	Hoechst	unknown	8,204 8,204	0.08
	Total (116)			226,853	22.13

The sample consists of all 430 firms whose shareholders reported voting control to the BAWe by September 1996. Each cell reports the sum and the mean of each variable. Market value refers to the market value of all equity. Data on blockholders come from BAWe (1996) and are supplemented by data from KSD.

Table 11.4. *Minimum ownership relations between the top five private shareholders*

Target	Shareholder						
	Allianz (%)	Deutsche Bank (%)	Münchner Rück (%)	Dresdner Bank (%)	Bayerische Vereinsbank (%)	Other firms controlled by top five (%)	Stakes controlled by the other four (%)
Allianz		10.00	25.00	10.00	10.00	5.00	60.00
Deutsche Bank	5.03		1.50				6.53
Münchner Rück	25.00	9.90		9.90	9.90	5.00	59.70
Dresdner Bank	10.18	10.00	2.30			31.36	53.84
Bayerische Vereinsbank		5.21	5.40				10.61

The table contains ultimate cross-ownership among the top five shareholders in officially listed German corporations. The voting blocks come from BAWe filings and are supplemented by information from Hoppenstedt's Konzernstruktur Datenbank. True control exceeds the figures reported in the table, because only direct stakes held by firms that are majority-controlled by the top five are considered. Several additional links exist among the five through firms in which they hold only minority stakes. For example, VIAG owns a 7.2 per cent stake in Bayerische Vereinsbank. Major stakes in VIAG include 5.9 per cent. Another example is VERMO Vermögensverwaltung, in which RWE and Bayer own minority stakes, and Allianz and Münchner Rück in turn own minority stakes in Bayer and RWE, respectively. These minority links are not included in the figures presented in the table. The 5 per cent Allianz stake is held by Bayerische Hypotheken- und Wechselbank, in which 40 per cent are held by Bayerische Vereinsbank, 5.8 per cent by Münchner Rück, 10.22 per cent by Allianz, and 10.93 per cent by Quinta Vermögensverwaltung, a holding controlled by Allianz and Münchner Rück. The 5 per cent Münchner Rück stake is held by the Bayerische Hypotheken- und Wechselbank, in which 40 per cent are held by Bayerische Vereinsbank, 5.8 per cent by Münchner Rück, 10.22 per cent by Allianz, and 10.93 per cent by Quinta Vermögensverwaltung, a holding controlled by Allianz and Münchner Rück. The 10 per cent Dresdner Bank stake is held by Deutscher Herold, an insurance subsidiary of Deutsche Bank. Of the 31.36 per cent Dresdner Bank stake, 10.6 per cent are held by FGF and 10.58 per cent by Vermo Vermögensverwaltung, two holdings controlled jointly by the top five. The remaining 10.18 per cent are held by Nona Vermögensverwaltung, which is controlled by Allianz and Münchner Rück.

firms could be added to the value of the actual blocks, which could almost double the 13 per cent estimated above, assuming that a majority stake effectively confers full control to the blockholder. Considering in addition controlled stakes in unlisted firms and, in turn, their holdings in listed corporations could increase this estimate even further.

It is difficult to conduct this estimation rigorously for all firms, because the links between shareholders are generally not known. In the example above, the top five have no single majority stake in each other. Therefore, the WpHG does not require that votes controlled by, say, Allianz, are attributed to Deutsche Bank or another group member. For better transparency, the votes would need to be attributed to the top five jointly and be reported in addition to the individual figures.

The top five banks, presented in Table 11.5, control DM 74 billion or 7.22 per cent of all listed market value in Germany via reported voting blocks. This share does not include control via proxy votes or 'dormant' control via shares held for trading purposes. Banks must not vote trading-book shares but can potentially build up a significant holding without reporting ownership. Such a block could command a significant control premium if sold to a third party or could be declared a voting block by reporting it to the BAWe at any point in time. To the

Table 11.5. *Ultimate voting blocks held by the five banks controlling the greatest market value*

Shareholders (number of direct stakes, voting blocks included in calculations)	Main targets controlled (voting blocks in listed firms exceeding DM 300 million market value, sorted by decreasing market value)	Blockholders	Market value of controlled voting blocks in Mn. DM	Voting blocks as % of market value of all 430 listed firms
Deutsche Bank (24, 27)	Daimler-Benz, Allianz, Münchner Rück, Frankfurter Hypo, Südzucker, Linde, Bayerische Vereinsbank, Metallgesellschaft, Heidelberger Zement, Karstadt, Ph. Holzmann, AMB	Allianz 5%	31,688	3.09
Dresdner Bank (11, 14)	Allianz, Münchner Rück, Deutsche Hypo, OLB, Heidelberger Zement, AMB, Hamburghyp, Bilfinger & Berger, Metallgesellschaft	Allianz 22%, Nona VV 10%, Vermo VV 11%	19,595	1.91
Bayerische Vereinsbank (9, 9)	Allianz, Münchner Rück, Vereins- und Westbank, BHB, Nürnberger Hypo, Süddeutsche Bodencreditbank	Viag 7%, Bayernwerk 7%, Deutsche Bank 5%	14,839	1.44
Commerzbank (8, 8)	Rheinhyp, Linde, Karstadt	none	3,975	0.39
Bayerische Hypo (6, 6)	Allianz, Württemberger Hypo	Allianz 23%, Münchner Rück 6%,	3,905	0.38
Total (58, 64)			74,001	7.22

The sample consists of all 430 firms whose shareholders reported voting control to the BAWe by September 1996. Each cell reports the sum and the mean of each variable. Market value refers to the market value of all equity. Data on blockholders come from BAWe (1996) and are supplemented by data from KSD.

extent that such a holding becomes pivotal in a takeover contest it could also represent substantial voting power without the explicit ability to exercise voting rights.

Holdings of the remaining thirty-nine banks are negligible relative to those of the top five. I find that all reporting banks jointly control 8.2 per cent of aggregate market value. Therefore 88 per cent of the aggregate value controlled by banks is concentrated in the top five institutions, and the remaining thirty-nine share the rest. These five banks are subject to few external controls. First, they share blockholders and other ownership links as illustrated in Table 11.4. Second, Baums and Fraune (1995) show that at their respective 1992 AGMs, these five banks controlled a majority of each others voting rights. Therefore, these five companies most likely represent the single most powerful (informal) voting pool in Germany, even without considering the additional influence through the affiliated insurance companies.

The five largest industrial shareholders (Table 11.6) control DM 41 billion or 4 per cent of the market capitalization. The top two firms which control about half of that, are utility companies controlling stakes in several regional utilities in addition to other holdings. The other three firms are foreign corporations holding only one voting block.

The top five families and voting pools (Table 11.7) control DM 12 billion or 1.2 per cent of market capitalization. This group includes reported control rights that derive from formal and explicit arrangements among a limited number of individuals.

The top five governmental shareholders (Table 11.8) control DM 69 billion or 6.7 per cent of the market. The classification is somewhat arbitrary, since it is not clear how control is exerted in practice. For example, the federal government of Germany controls

Table 11.6. *Ultimate voting blocks held by the five industrial firms controlling the greatest market value*

Shareholders (number of direct stakes, voting blocks included in calculations)	Main targets controlled (voting blocks in listed firms exceeding DM 300 million market value, sorted by decreasing market value)	Blockholders	Market value of controlled voting blocks in Mn. DM	Voting blocks as % of market value of all 430 listed firms
RWE (4, 10)	RWE-DEA, Rheinelektra, Lahmeyer, LEW, Ph Holzmann, MKW, Rhenag	RW Holding 12%, City of Essen 8%, Allianz 8%	11,598	1.13
VIAG (2, 14)	Contigas, OBAG, SKW Trostberg, Bayerische Vereinsbank, EVO, VEW, BEWAG, Schmalbach-Lubeca, Grosskraftwerk Franken, Gerresheimer Glas, ÜWU	State of Bavaria 25%, VI Industriebet. 11%, HI VV 10% (VI and HI are majority controlled by Viag itself)	10,207	1.00
Kuwait Petroleum (0, 1)	Hoechst	unknown	8,204	0.80
Ford Motor Co (1, 1)	Ford-Werke	unknown	6,111	0.60
Stora AB (0, 1)	FPB Holding	unknown	4,478	0.44
Total (7, 27)			40,598	3.96

The sample consists of all 430 firms whose shareholders reported voting control to the BAWe by September 1996. Each cell reports the sum and the mean of each variable. Market value refers to the market value of all equity. Data on blockholders come from BAWe (1996) and are supplemented by data from KSD.

Table 11.7. *Ultimate voting blocks held by the five family or worker pools controlling the greatest market value*

Shareholders (number of direct stakes, voting blocks included in calculations)	Main targets controlled (voting blocks in listed firms exceeding DM 300 million market value, sorted by decreasing market value)	Blockholders	Market value of controlled voting blocks in Mn. DM	Voting blocks as % of market value of all 430 listed firms
Aktienbindungsvertrag Henkel, 48 members (1, 1)	Henkel	none	4,948	0.48
Südd. Zuckerrübenverw. Cooperative (1, 1)	Südzucker	none	3,275	0.32
Merck Family (0, 1)	Merck	none	2,620	0.26
Porsche Voting Pool (0, 1)	Porsche	none	987	0.10
Association of family shareholder Dyckerhoff, 295 members (1, 1)	Dyckerhoff	none	553	0.05
Total (3, 5)			12,382	1.21

The sample consists of all 430 firms whose shareholders reported voting control to the BAWe by September 1996. Each cell reports the sum and the mean of each variable. Market value refers to the market value of all equity. Data on blockholders come from BAWe (1996) and are supplemented by data from KSD.

Table 11.8. *Ultimate voting blocks held by the five government agencies controlling the greatest market value*

Shareholders (number of direct stakes, voting blocks included in calculations)	Main targets controlled (voting blocks in listed firms exceeding DM 300 million market value, sorted by decreasing market value)	Blockholders	Market value of controlled voting blocks in Mn. DM	Voting blocks as % of market value of all 430 listed firms
Bundesanstalt für Post und Telekommunikation (1, 1)	Deutsche Telekom	none	49,431	4.82
State of Berlin (2, 3)	Bankgesellschaft Berlin, BEWAG, bhh	none	6,997	0.68
Kommunal Energie-Beteiligungsges. mbH (1, 1)	VEW	none	4,698	0.46
State of Lower Saxony (1, 1)	Volkswagen	none	3,909	0.38
State of Bavaria (1, 1)	VIAG	none	3,754	0.37
Total (6, 7)			68,788	6.71

The sample consists of all 430 firms whose shareholders reported voting control to the BAWe by September 1996. Each cell reports the sum and the mean of each variable. Market value refers to the market value of all equity. Data on blockholders come from BAWe (1996) and are supplemented by data from KSD.

more stakes than reported in the table. It is not clear, however, to what extent nominally independent government agencies depend on decisions made at the federal level (implying that all government entities should be treated as a single shareholder) and to what extent they are able to make independent decisions.

By construction, all holding and investment companies (Table 11.9) are firms within a business group that are used to control voting blocks in listed corporations. Thus, most holding companies vote only one block (with the exception of Metro Holding) and jointly control DM 18 billion or 1.8 per cent of market capitalization. Owners of the holding companies are often unknown, because only officially listed firms must report their control structure to the BAWe. The ones I could identify from other sources are listed in the blockholder column.

The top five individuals (Table 11.10) control DM 26.1 billion or 2.5 per cent of market capitalization. It also illustrates that various members of the same family need not report their joint holdings, even if an informal voting contract existed.

The top five foundations (Table 11.11) control DM 6.6 billion or 0.6 per cent of market capitalization. It also illustrates that some foundations serve as group layers above the main

Table 11.9. *Ultimate voting blocks held by the five holding companies and investment firms controlling the greatest market value*

Shareholders (number of direct stakes, voting blocks included in calculations)	Main targets controlled (voting blocks in listed firms exceeding DM 300 million market value, sorted by decreasing market value)	Blockholders	Market value of controlled voting blocks in Mn. DM	Voting blocks as % of market value of all 430 listed firms
Vereinte Holding AG (1, 1)	Vereinte Versicherung	Allianz 100%	4,493	0.44
RW Holding AG (1, 1)	RWE	Municipalities 32%, rest unknown	3,829	0.37
DIA Verm. Verw. (1, 1)	Münchner Rück	unknown	3,682	0.36
FGC mbH (1, 1)	Hoechst	Dresdner Bank 20%, Gerling 10%, Münchn. Rück 30%	3,415	0.33
Metro Holding AG (0, 5)	Praktiker, Horten, Massa, Kaufhalle	Three families (Schmidt-Ruthenbeck, Beisheim Stiftung, Haniel) 33.3% each	3,290	0.32
Total (4, 9)			18,709	1.82

The sample consists of all 430 firms whose shareholders reporting voting control to the BAWe by September 1996. Each cell reports the sum and the mean of each variable. Market value refers to the market value of all equity. Data on blockholders come from BAWe (1996) and are supplemented by data from KSD.

Table 11.10. *Ultimate voting blocks held by the five individuals controlling the greatest market value*

Shareholders (number of direct stakes, voting blocks included in calculations)	Main targets controlled (voting blocks in listed firms exceeding DM 300 million market value, sorted by decreasing market value)	Blockholders	Market value of controlled voting blocks in Mn. DM	Voting blocks as % of market value of all 430 listed firms
Hopp, D. (1, 1)	SAP	none	13,387	1.31
Klatten, S. (2, 2)	Altana, BMW	none	4,327	0.45
Quandt, J. (1, 1)	BMW	none	3,069	0.30
Quandt, S. (1, 2)	BMW	none	2,966	0.29
Schwarz-Schütte, P. (1, 1)	Schwarz Pharma	none	2,018	0.20
Total (6, 7)			26,067	2.54

The sample consists of all 430 firms whose shareholders reported voting control to the BAWe by September 1996. Each cell reports the sum and the mean of each variable. Market value refers to the market value of all equity. Data on blockholders come from BAWe (1996) and are supplemented by data from KSD.

Table 11.11. *Ultimate voting blocks held by the five foundations controlling the greatest market value*

Shareholders (number of direct stakes, voting blocks included in calculations)	Main targets controlled (voting blocks in listed firms exceeding DM 300 million market value, sorted by decreasing market value)	Blockholders	Market value of controlled voting blocks in Mn. DM	Voting blocks as % of market value of all 430 listed corporations
A. Krupp Stiftung (1, 1)	Krupp	unknown	2,579	0.25
Bayer. Braustiftung J. Schörghuber & Co. Holding KG (2, 4)	Paulaner-Salvator, Hacker-Pschorr	unknown	1,424	0.14
Hertie Stiftung (1, 1)	Karstadt	unknown	1,363	0.13
F. Thyssen Stiftung (1, 1)	Thyssen	unknown	728	0.07
Schickedanz Holding-Stiftung & Co. KG (3, 4)	(none greater DM 150 million)	unknown	504	0.05
Total (8, 11)			6,599	0.64

The sample consists of all 430 firms whose shareholders reported voting control to the BAWe by September 1996. Each cell reports the sum and the mean of each variable. Market value refers to the market value of all equity. Data on blockholders come from BAWe (1996) and are supplemented by data from KSD.

group corporation, while others serve as holding companies. Since foundations have no owner, it is generally difficult to identify who controls their decisions and those related to their voting blocks.

Finally, the top five insurance companies (Table 11.12) control DM 76.2 billion or 7.4 per cent of market capitalization. German banks control substantial stakes in the top three, while the remaining two are majority owned by foreign insurance firms.

Table 11.12. *Ultimate voting blocks held by the five insurance firms controlling the greatest market value*

Shareholders (number of direct stakes, voting blocks included in calculations)	Main targets controlled (voting blocks in listed firms exceeding DM 300 million market value, sorted by decreasing market value)	Blockholders	Market value of controlled voting blocks in Mn.Dm	Voting blocks as % of market value of all 430 listed corporations
Allianz (18, 25)	Münchner Rück, VEBA, Dresdner Bank, BASF, Bayr. Hypo, RWE, BDF Beiersdorf, Bayer, Deutsche Bank, Linde, Schering, BHF-Bank, Lahmeyer, Rheinelektra, AMB	Münchner Rück 26%, Bayer. Vereinsbank 10%, Deutsche Bank 10%, Dresdner Bank 10%, Bayer. Hypobank 5%	45,820	4.47
Münchner Rück (12, 14)	Allianz, Bayerische Hypo, Victoria, AMB, Hermes Kreditversicherung	Allianz 25%, Bayer. Vereinsbank 10%, Deutsche Bank 10%, Dresdner Bank 10%, DIA VV 6%	22,085	2.15
AMB (5, 6)	Volksfürsorge, Thuringia Versicherung, AM Leben, AM Vers, Aachener Rück	AGF 27%, Dresdner Bank 15%, Münchner Rück 9%, Deutsche Bank 5%, Allianz 5%	4,824	0.47
CKAG (1, 1)	Nordstern Allg. Vers.	Compagnie UAP 75%	1,865	0.18
General Re (0, 1)	Köln. Rück	U.S. Health and Life Insurance Co. 66%, rest unknown	1,608	0.16
Total (36, 46)			76,202	7.43

The sample consists of all 430 firms whose shareholders reported voting control to the BAWe by September 1996. Each cell reports the sum and the mean of each variable. Financial-statement data are based on the broadest available annual report in the sequence world report, mother report, group report, and individual-company report. Sales are 1/10 of total assets for banks, total premium receipts for insurance firms, and actual sales for other firms. Cash flow is defined as profit after taxes plus depreciation. Market value refers to the market value of all equity. Holdings (investment firms) are defined as firms whose main purpose is to fully own and operate (hold stakes in) independent companies.

5. CONCLUSION

I have analysed the most powerful shareholders in Germany to illustrate the concentration of control over listed corporations. The German stock market is dominated by large shareholders that control about 47 per cent of the market value of all firms listed in Germany's official markets. If a large voting block effectively controls a higher percentage than its nominal stake via, for example, undisclosed indirect shareholdings, this figure may even be substantially larger. For example, a 60 per cent voting block may represent a much higher percentage of voting rights present at the AGM.

About two-thirds of the 47 per cent is controlled by banks, industrial firms, holdings, and insurance companies. I show that it is unclear, largely due to current legislation, who exerts ultimate control for these blockholders. For the remaining blockholders, only blocks controlled by voting pools and individuals can be traced back to the highest level of ownership. In the aggregate, both groups control only 5.6 per cent of all reported blocks. The German government controls 8 per cent, but it is not clear who ultimately is responsible for the consequences of decisions. Not knowing who ultimately controls the blockholders may pose significant problems.

As noted by Shleifer and Vishny (1997), the presence of blockholdings does not generically imply shareholder wealth maximization. Large blockholders have incentives to maximize the value of their shares. Whether this involves maximizing firm value depends on the degree to which they can extract transfers from small shareholders. First, the typical German business group includes several firms with outside equity and several without. Thus, it may be beneficial for large shareholders to transfer resources from subsidiaries with outside equity to other group units. Second, German law effectively allows sizeable transfers to blockholders once a coalition owns at least 75 per cent of the votes. Specifically, a 75 per cent majority may legally make a binding tender offer to minority shareholders below market value.[9] Wenger *et al.* (1996) analyse such offers to minority shareholders and find that in thirty-nine of fifty-three cases the offer is below the market value on the day before, and in thirty-two cases below the market value three months earlier. For the former thirty-nine cases, the market value on average exceeds the compensation to minority shareholders by 74 per cent. Additionally, blockholders may use cross-holdings and pyramidal groups to transfer resources from subsidiaries with outside shareholders to units without.[10] Therefore, a priori, it is not clear that it is easier for blockholders to increase the value of their stake by acting on behalf of all shareholders.

A similar argument holds for voting blocks controlled by the financial sector. The top five banks and the top three insurance companies are closely related through direct ownership and voting control. Jointly, these eight firms report control over 14 per cent of all listed firms, or a market value of DM 147 billion considering only reported voting blocks. It was shown this figure substantially underestimates the true value under control of these blockholders. The reason is that large ownership links exist between the large shareholders that do not trigger legal reporting requirements. Therefore, joint majority control by business groups cannot be inferred from published data. Due to their information advantage, banks are potentially very effective monitors, but will generally have little incentive to act on behalf of other shareholders. First, due to proxy votes and board memberships their control rights substantially exceed their interest in equity cash-flow. Second, for the typical firm, the amount of debt held by banks exceeds the amount of equity held in the same firm by a factor greater than ten and probably substantially larger.[11] Therefore, such a bank would optimally use its votes to maximize the value of debt and not that of equity.[12] Thus, the effectiveness of banks as actively monitoring shareholder representatives is ultimately an empirical question.

This exploratory study raises intriguing questions for future research and has important economic and policy implications. For example, the potentially adverse effects of insufficient transparency are amplified by the ability of large blockholders to extract value from smaller shareholders. An investor in a typical German corporation faces a majority of voting rights controlled by large shareholders. To the extent that expropriation is possible, he will discount the value of shares to reflect his weak bargaining position. Improved disclosure of control would likely reduce uncertainty with respect to expropriation. This, in turn, would have the desirable effect of reducing the cost of capital for German corporations and therefore their market value. To determine the cross-sectional value of transparency is an important question for future empirical research.

Notes

1. Edwards and Fischer (1994) wrote a comprehensive analysis of financial institutions' involvement in the corporate sector. See Koendgen (1994) for a discussion of banks' fiduciary duties in this regard, and Baums and Fraune (1995) for some empirical evidence on the resulting voting power.
2. Proxy votes exercised by banks are public, even before 1995, but these data do not lend themselves to empirical research. They are contained in the minutes of the annual shareholder meeting and filed with local courts. While these records are publicly accessible, no centralized source exists and documents are often missing and incomplete.
3. See Boehmer (2001) for a critical discussion of empirical studies on German corporate governance.
4. KSD contains mostly ownership information, but not always voting information as used in this analysis. The eleven firms I found on KSD are the following: Amira Verwaltungs AG, Commerzbank AG, Custodia Holding, Garant Schuh AG, IWKA Industrie-Werke Karlsruhe Augsburg AG, Leica Camera, Mannesmann AG, Merck, MLF Holding AG, Quante AG, Westag & Getalit AG. Out of those, Amira, Custodia, Leica, Merck, Quante, and Westag have substantial blockholdings (greater than 5 per cent) that were not reported to the BAWe by May 1998.
5. Such a situation could arise, for example, if the votes controlled indirectly by A belong to shareholders that individually fall below the reporting threshold of 5 per cent.
6. Such difficulties also occur in the sample. For example, the sum of voting blocks of Jute-Spinnerei und Weberei Bremen is 100.03 per cent if we use the standard procedure. K. H. Rehkopf controls 50.134 per cent without holding a direct stake and the BAWe report further shows two direct stakes of 49.9 and 50.084 per cent. Thus, if the filings are correct, it must be the case that Rehkopf controls part of both direct stakes. Unfortunately, this information cannot be inferred from the BAWe data. The resulting error is, however, very small and we assign one block of 50.134 per cent and one of 49.866 per cent.

7. Empirical results vary substantially with sample selection and period, and across different methodologies. See Boehmer (2001) for a brief survey.
8. Between 1996 and 1999 the German government has reduced its holdings from 75 per cent to 63 per cent of Telekom. The figure reported in Table 11.8, which represents only part of the government holdings of Telekom, has declined by about one-fifth during the same period.
9. Sections 304, 320b AktG. See also Bebchuk and Kahan (1999) for a more general analysis of problems associated with freeze-outs.
10. Several such cases are discussed by Wenger and Kaserer (1996).
11. No publicly available figures provide information on the precise composition of banks' interest in equity and debt to German listed corporations. Economy-wide, Edwards and Fischer (1994) estimate that bank-supplied equity to non-banks is about 3 per cent of bank-supplied loans to the same firms. Alternatively, a back-of-the-envelope calculation proceeds as follows. In 1996, the DAI reports that the equity-to-capital ratio of listed corporations is 39 per cent (DAI Fact Book 1996). Own calculations reveal that banks own about 8 per cent of these firms' equity. Since German firms very rarely use public bonds, it is safe to assume that most long-term debt consists of bank loans. Thus, the portfolio of a typical bank can be described as a function of the ratio of bank loans to total corporate liabilities. For example, if all corporate debt were from banks, the banks finance $8\% \times 39 = 3.12\%$ of listed firms' total assets in the form of equity shares, and 61 per cent in the form of loans. Using the cautious assumption that corporate liabilities consist of only one-third of bank loans, banks still finance about 20 per cent of the corporations' total assets using loans. Therefore, for the typical bank, the value of its loan portfolio to a typical listed corporation exceeds the equity interest in the same firm by a factor between 7 and 20.
12. For the USA, Payne *et al.* (1996) document evidence consistent with the view that banks use their voting rights in the interest of management (as opposed to that of shareholders) when banks have debt or fee-related income associated with the firm.

References

BAWe, (1996). Bedeutende Stimmrechtsanteile an amtlich notierten Aktiengesellschaften zum (and other annual issues), 30 September (Frankfurt am Main: BAWe).

Baums, T., and Fraune, C. (1995). Institutionelle anleger und publikumsgesellschaft: Eine empirische untersuchung. *Die Aktiengesellschaft*, 40: 97.

Bebchuk, L. A., and Kahan, M. (1999). The 'lemons effect' in corporate freeze-outs. Harvard Law School, Discussion Paper No. 248.

Becht, M., and Boehmer, E. (1997). Transparency of ownership and control in Germany. Humboldt-University Berlin, Working Paper, and Preliminary Report to the European Commission.

Boehmer, E. (2001). Ownership and performance in Germany: Institutional background and empirical evidence. in K. gugler (ed.), Corporate governance and economic performance, Oxford University Press (2001).

DAI (1996). Factbook, DAI: Frankfurt.

Edwards, J., and Fischer, K. (1994). *Banks, Finance, and Investment in Germany.* Cambridge: Cambridge University Press.

Koendgen, J. (1994). Duties of Banks in Voting their Clients' Stock. In T. Baums, R. M. Buxbaum, and K. J. Hopt (ed.), Institutional investors and corporate governance. Berlin: Gzuytez.

Payne, T. H., Millar, J. A., and Glezen, G. W. (1996), Fiduciary responsibility and bank–firm relationships: An analysis of shareholder voting by banks. *Journal of Corporate Finance* 3: 75.
Shleifer, A., and Vishny, R. (1997). A survey of corporate governance. *Journal of Finance* 52: 737.
Wenger, E., and Kaserer, C. (1996). The German system of corporate governance in Germany—a model which should not be imitated. Universität Würzburg, Working Paper.
——Hecker, R., and Knoesel, J. (1996). Abfindungsregeln und minderheitenschutz bei börsennotierten kapitalgesellschaften. University of Würzburg, Working Paper.

12

Complete Separation of Ownership and Control: The Structure-Regime and Other Defensive Mechanisms in the Netherlands

PIETER W. MOERLAND

1. INTRODUCTION

The Dutch system of corporate supervision is currently in the throes of reform. The unique Dutch 'structure-regime', which separates ownership and control, has been legally prescribed for 'large' companies since 1971. In this system, supervisory boards are granted considerable power, which is usually the prerogative of the shareholders at the annual meeting. The co-optation system grants also the supervisory board the right to appoint and dismiss its own members. An important policy debate was sparked by the report of the Dutch Corporate Governance committee (1997)[1] (hereinafter the Peters Committee) which questioned the need and role of the structure-regime and other aspects of the Dutch corporate governance system. In particular, the structure-regime, which creates a complete immunization against hostile takeovers, is questionable since immunity reinforces incumbent management entrenchment against hostile takeovers, but also limits effective shareholder monitoring and control of the firm. The Social and Economic Council has recently suggested further reforms which the government has accepted and legislative action is forthcoming. Against this background, the aim of this chapter is to examine the respective trade-offs of the structure-regime in relation to other corporate governance mechanisms.

This chapter has five sections. Section 2 offers an introduction to the Dutch system of corporate supervision, particularly the structure-regime. Attention will be given to sketching its historical background and the main attributes of the regime. Furthermore, the section will evaluate the recent information collected by the so-called Monitoring Committee to clarify the relationship between the structure-regime and other aspects of the system of corporate governance. Section 3 focuses on the importance of board independence. Section 4 canvasses the empirical studies on board effectiveness, so as to evaluate the effect of the structure regime on the performance of Dutch companies. Section 5 concludes by assessing critically the merits and drawbacks of the Dutch structure-regime.

2. THE DUTCH SYSTEM OF CORPORATE SUPERVISION

Unlike the Anglo-American system, the board structure in the Netherlands is characterized by a formal separation of executive and supervisory responsibilities. The two-tier board structure consists of a supervisory board ('Raad van Commissarissen') which comprises only independent non-executive directors and a managing board ('Raad van Bestuur'). The boards are formal legal organs of the company that are directly responsible to the general meeting of shareholders.

In the Netherlands, two distinct regimes of corporate supervision have been enacted: the 'structure'-regime and the 'normal' regime.[2] The introduction of the structure-regime into Dutch corporate law in the early 1970s was the result of a debate during the 1960s about further modelling the post-war economic consensus.[3] Participation by employees in firm decision-making was broadly advocated and eventually formalized in specific legal terms. Share-ownership had become more widely dispersed among many small, anonymous shareholders of bearer shares, which was accompanied by a relatively high degree of absenteeism at the annual meetings (Kabir *et al.* 1997). It was the view that the managing board was experiencing only modest monitoring from the general meeting of shareholders and that a powerful supervisory board should fill that gap. The structure law, as noted above, was adopted in 1971.

The structure-regime is mandatory for 'large' corporations that meet the following three conditions during a three-year period: outstanding capital (issued capital and reserves) amounts to at least DFL 25 million according to the balance sheet; a works council is installed—a requirement for every company with thirty-five employees or more; and at least 100 employees are employed in the Netherlands by the company and its dependent companies. The structure-regime obliges the company to establish a supervisory board whose members are appointed (by the board) by way of co-optation. However, the general meeting of shareholders and the works council are allowed to object to candidates if they believe a candidate is not qualified or if they judge the composition of the board to be inappropriate. Moreover, the general meeting of shareholders, the works council and the managing board are allowed to recommend candidates for appointment to the supervisory board. However, their recommendations are not binding. Unlike the American system, the board is legally obliged to protect the interests of the company as a whole and not just those of the shareholders. A recent estimate indicates that there are some 400 publicly listed and privately owned companies currently operating under the structure-regime. Within this total group, about 100 firms have their shares of equity (or certificates) listed on the Amsterdam Exchanges (AEX). This number roughly corresponds to about 60 per cent of all domestic publicly listed companies (investment funds not included).

The supervisory board of the corporations with structure-regime is legally endowed with a number of responsibilities which, under the normal regime, are allotted to the general meeting of shareholders. These responsibilities include the right to appoint and dismiss members of the managing board and to adopt the annual accounts. Furthermore, a number of major managerial decisions are subject to approval by the supervisory board (i.e. investment plans, company restructuring, etc.) (Maeijer and Geens 1990).

Certain types of companies that meet the criteria for the 'large' company may request dispensation from the application of the structure-regime. Dispensation is granted to international concerns that have their principal residence in the Netherlands, function merely as a management company, and employ the majority of its employees outside the Netherlands. Its Dutch subsidiaries, which meet the criteria for the 'large' company, are then subject to a milder regime, which implies that they must have a supervisory board. However, under this mild regime, the supervisory board is not given the right to appoint and dismiss members of the managing board or to adopt the annual accounts. The members of the managing board are then appointed by the shareholders. In contrast, if a parent company with its principal seat in the Netherlands is fully or partly subject to the structure-regime, its subsidiary is exempted from the regime. Companies that do not meet the above-mentioned criteria for the 'large' company are legally allowed to voluntarily opt for the structure-regime by including this in their articles of association. This is, however, only possible if they have a works council.

One important implication of the structure-regime is that an unwanted large shareholder—or even a majority shareholder—cannot easily obtain control of the company's key positions, as the members of the supervisory board and the members of the managing board are appointed and dismissed by the supervisory board. This means that the structure-regime, especially if voluntarily chosen, may be used as a defensive mechanism against hostile takeovers and proxy contests.

In a recent study, the degree of compliance with the recommendations of the Peters Committee was analysed for 159 domestic listed firms (excluding investment funds).[4] In the monitoring process, which took place in 1998, information was also collected on the occurrence of the structure-regime and a number of other defensive mechanisms (priority shares, certificates, voting rights restrictions, and preferred shares). From the 159 companies, 97 (or 61%) had adopted the structure-regime: 72 firms (45%) on a compulsory basis (66 (42%) full regime, 6 (4%) mild regime) and 25 firms (16%) on a voluntary basis. Certificates disconnect the voting rights from the cash flow rights. Whereas voting rights are held by a trustee office, the shareholders only own the cash flow rights. Protective preferred shares could be issued in case of specific events, such as hostile takeovers, in order to dilute the bidder's stake. Priority shares are shares which entitle the holder to certain privileges such as special voting rights which include the right to present a binding nomination for the appointment of members of the supervisory board and members of the managing board, the right to approve the issue of common shares, and the right to propose and approve any amendment to the company's charter.[5] For the sample of 159 firms, 41 companies (26%) had adopted priority shares, 56 firms (35%) had issued certificates, 88 firms (55%) had issued protective preferred shares. Only a few firms still had voting right restrictions in their articles of association.

Thirty-one companies (19% of the sample) had a majority shareholder and 67 firms (42%) had a shareholder with a stake exceeding 25%. The voluntary structure-regime is chosen less frequently by companies with relatively concentrated share-ownership than by widely held companies. This is because in companies with high ownership (and control) concentration, a choice for the structure-regime would entail that the large shareholders are voluntarily relinquishing control. The study confirms this hypothesis. As majority ownership effectively provides a natural defence against takeovers, the voluntary adoption of the structured regime in widely held companies can be considered as an alternative mode of defence against hostile takeover attempts. The data also yield a negative relationship between the occurrence of the other defensive mechanisms (priority shares, certificates, voting right restrictions, and preferred shares) and the degree of concentration of share-ownership. The statistics show clearly that ownership concentration and defensive mechanisms are being utilized as substitutes by Dutch listed firms.

The use of defence mechanisms may entrench management of Dutch corporations, especially in case of the breakdown in control by the supervisory board. That is the reason that both the AEXs and the Peters Committee have discouraged listed corporations from making use of the abundance of defensive mechanisms available in Dutch corporate law. Furthermore, the Dutch Association of Shareholders (Vereniging van Effectenbezitters) also objects to too restrictive defence walls. Also, the recent approval of the thirteenth EU directive on mandated public offers may have the effect of rescinding the legal use of a number of currently applied defensive weapons.

3. THE ROLE OF THE SUPERVISORY BOARD

The board of directors is usually organized as a one-tier or a two-tier structure. In the first case, managers as well as non-executive directors are included in a unitary board of directors, all having equal responsibilities and liabilities. Two-tier structures allow for a formal separation of management and governance: they provide a division between the control function (via a supervisory board) and the executive part of the board (the managing board). In most countries, such as the USA, the UK, the Southern European countries, France and Belgium, the one-tier structure applies.[6] In Germany and the Netherlands, a two-tier structure of corporate supervision is used.

The importance of independent non-executive board members has been acknowledged and strongly advocated since the early 1990s. Corporate (supervisory) boards are charged with overseeing and rewarding managers in order to protect and promote the interests of shareholders, at least in the Anglo-American context (Moerland 1995). The board has the legal authority to ratify and monitor managerial decisions, evaluate the performance of top managers, and reward or penalize performance (Byrd and Hickman 1992; John and Senbet 1998). Non-executive directors (have to) play prominent roles in evaluating the managers' initiatives by their expertise, objectivity, and independence. The importance of board independence has made American investors wary of non-executive (outside) directors with ties to management through family relations, consulting contracts, or interlocking directorships (Russell Reynolds Associates 1997).

The British Cadbury Committee (1992) emphasized board independence as a vital element of best practice in corporate governance. It formulated its pertinent recommendations as follows: 'Non-executive directors should bring an independent judgement to bear on issues of strategy, performance, resources, including key appointments, and standards of conduct.' The Committee further stated that: 'The majority should be independent of management and free from any business or other relationship which could materially interfere with the exercise of their independent judgement, apart from their fees and shareholding.' It is worth noting that the OECD (1999) advocates board independence in its principles on corporate governance: 'Board independence usually requires that a sufficient number of board members not be employed by the company and not be closely related to the company or its management through significant economic, family or other ties. Independent board members can contribute significantly to the decision making of the board. They can bring an objective view to the evaluation of the performance of the board and management. In addition, they can play an important role in areas where the interests of management, the company and shareholders may diverge....'

While there are two board structures, the main policy question concerns which structure is said to create the most advantages for shareholders within the context of the need for a more independent board. In principle, a two-tier board is to be preferred because the supervisory boards comprise only non-executive directors, have a non-executive chairman, set their own agenda.[7] The responsibilities and liabilities of the supervisory board are clearly distinct from those of the management board. In the annual general meeting, supervisory board members are separately discharged. In contrast, it is possible that the degree of independence in unitary boards is compromised if executive directors dominate the board. Hence, board independence is expected to be a function of the proportion of board seats occupied by non-executive directors, of current or former ties with the firm (e.g. in the form of consulting contracts or a relation derived from previous employment) and of the separation of the functions of chairman and chief executive officer (CEO). The degree of independence in Anglo-American boards has increased considerably over the past decades. Many publicly listed companies have strong independent boards in the USA. A survey of 100 of the largest American public corporations reports that half of the firms had only one or two inside directors (Bhagat and Black 2000). The study of Van den Muyzenberg and Schukken (1998) reveals that almost all British public corporations have chosen to have their boards chaired by a non-executive director. In addition, many Anglo-American boards installed special committees—such as nominating committees, audit committees, and compensation committees—which are comprised only of non-executive directors. The differences in degrees of independence between one-tier and two-tier boards have become more shaded.

Board independence was also a central concern in the 1997 report of the Peters Committee. Nine of the forty recommendations for good corporate governance, explicitly or implicitly, focus on board independence. In the Dutch setting, two different types of (supervisory) board member independence are distinguished: supervisory board members should be able to operate independently of one another and of the managerial board; and supervisory board members should perform their duties independently of any subsidiary interests of specific stakeholders associated with the company. The former type of independence relates to the interaction between the supervisory and the managerial board; and corresponds to the form of independence advocated by the Cadbury Committee and the OECD. The latter type of independence relates to the interaction between the supervisory board and the firm's stakeholders, such as employees, debtors, and shareholders. Members of Dutch supervisory boards are bound to perform their duties without the mandate of those who nominated them. As mentioned earlier, they are required to protect the interest of the company as a whole. Consequently, the Dutch concept of corporate governance reflects a stakeholder bias rather than a shareholder approach.[8]

The Dutch stakeholder approach is unique as most other Continental European countries as well as Anglo-American countries adhere to the norm of shareholder wealth-maximization.

Directors in the USA and UK have to fulfil their fiduciary duty to serve the shareholders' interests. The fact that part of the remuneration depends on share price performance (e.g. shares or stock options) tends to reinforce that orientation. In Southern European countries, France and Belgium, particularly shareholders' interests also prevail because share-ownership is concentrated in the hands of one or more large shareholders (quite often majority shareholders), who are directly or indirectly represented on the firm's board (Barca and Becht 2001). The nearest model to the Dutch system is the German supervisory board approach in which both shareholders' and employees' interests are represented on the board. In this regime the shareholders and employees each occupy 50 per cent of the board seats.

4. ON THE EFFECTIVENESS OF THE SUPERVISORY BOARD

Several studies, albeit mainly for the USA and UK, have examined whether board composition influences corporate performance and whether non-executive directors are involved in disciplining poor performance. The results are mixed. For instance, Bhagat and Black (2000) conclude that board independence in the US does not have any impact on corporate performance. However, in terms of managerial disciplining, Weisbach (1988) finds that US boards, with a high proportion of independent non-executive directors, are more likely to remove the CEO than boards dominated by management. In contrast, Franks *et al.* (2001) found that UK non-executive directors seem to support the incumbent management even in the wake of poor corporate performance. In France and Belgium, non-executive directors appear to be monitored actively by management. Still, given that most non-executive directors are appointed by large shareholders, non-executive monitoring tends to reflect the level of shareholder involvement.

Recently, Renneboog (2000) has studied the relevance of a variety of disciplinary devices for Belgian listed firms. This work shows that the role of the non-executive directors is important in the disciplining process: a high proportion of non-executive directors leads to increased executive board turnover. For French listed companies, Dherment-Ferere and Renneboog (Chapter 13, this volume) are able to identify the interests that the directors' represent: shareholders, creditors, or the founding family. A high proportion of shareholder representatives on the board leads to increased executive board turnover when performance is poor. No such relation is disclosed when the board has creditor representatives but when (executive) directors are members of the founding family, they succeed in impeding board restructuring.

A recent empirical study, commissioned by the Dutch Ministry of Finance (2000), contrasts the effect of board supervision without shareholder involvement (structure-regime) and the effect of ownership concentration (no structure-regime) while controlling for other corporate governance devices on firm performance in the Netherlands over the period 1993–7.[9] Apart from the size and composition of the supervisory board, the study includes ownership concentration and identity of shareholders, defensive mechanisms and a dummy variable for the structure-regime. Of the sample of Dutch listed non-financial firms, 56 per cent of companies had taken the structure-regime and 44 per cent had not. Three measures of performance are used: market return, accounting return and Tobin's Q. The regressions take potential linkages between various corporate governance characteristics into account and control for firm size and leverage. The results show that the firms' market returns are affected by concentration of share ownership (positive effect), the size of the supervisory board (negative effect),[10] certificates (negative effect), and the structure-regime (negative effect). Structure companies show a lower return than companies without structure-regime for all measures of performance. The positive effect of ownership concentration suggests that it is large shareholders that generally monitor the firm's management. The negative impact connected with certificates, which takes the voting rights away from the shareholders, points towards underperformance due to a lack of investor control. Furthermore, companies with structure-regime seem to underperform in comparison to firms without the structure-regime. This suggests that companies that just rely on the discipline of the supervisory board and are isolated from market forces suffer from underperformance which may follow from lack of accountability.

De Jong *et al.* (2000) also investigate the influence of the structure-regime and other anti-takeover mechanisms on corporate performance in Dutch corporations. They confirm that the structure-regime negatively influences performance (measured by Tobin's Q), but this effect is less prominent for the Dutch multinationals who voluntarily adopt the structure-regime. In companies with structure-regime, a high number of interlocked directors negatively influences firm value. The negative effects of the structure-regime are mitigated by remuneration packages offered to the management and supervisory board. The presence of strong shareholders in companies without structure-regime increases corporate value but institutional investors do not contribute value that is expected given their passive attitude towards governance. Contrary to the usual monitoring hypothesis related to the debt market, Dutch banks seem to constrain firm behaviour that leads to a reduction in corporate value.

5. CONCLUSION: MERITS AND DRAWBACKS OF STRUCTURE-REGIME

The Dutch structure-regime has been criticized for a number of reasons. A serious criticism levelled against the co-optation system involves a concern as to how the supervisory board appoints (and dismisses) its own members. That system is felt to provide a weak basis for board legitimacy. To whom are supervisory board members themselves accountable? Who can dismiss them if they function poorly? For orderly checks and balances in the field of corporate governance, people endowed with distinct power should be closely monitored. While the supervisory board is required to monitor and advise the managerial board, the supervisory board is insulated from monitoring. The system of co-optation is thought to give rise to an 'old boys' network', as the recruitment of new members typically occurs within a network of people who know each other. That practice might undermine their mutual independence and, by interlocking directorships, also the independence from management. Some commentators refer to inherent tendencies to aim at harmony and consent and avoid nurturing critical attitudes (Boot 1994).

Under the structure-regime the supervisory board may have too many powerful rights, which usually belong to the general meeting of shareholders. A much-disputed issue in this respect concerns the setting of stock option plans for managers. Finally, the structure-regime may turn out to be a thinly-veiled anti-takeover defensive mechanism, which may explain why some firms voluntarily contract into the structure-regime. In response, the Peters Committee has proposed that voluntary application for the structure-regime should be denied if there is no evident justification for it.

In contrast to these alleged drawbacks of the structure-regime, some commentators emphasize the beneficial nature of the system. For instance the system of co-optation makes it possible to recruit supervisory board members on the basis of expected monitoring and advisory qualities, rather than on the basis of representation. The fact that members of the supervisory board do not represent specific categories of shareholders gives these directors the freedom to make corporate decisions in the interest of the company as a whole. This could result in an equitable balancing of all stakeholders' interests. Interlocked directors may have a good overview of corporate activity in other firms and industries.

The structure-regime is a unique system of corporate supervision. Its introduction into Dutch corporate law in the early 1970s was the result of modelling consensus-economics. The combination of a desire for more employee participation, increasing shareholder absenteeism, and concern about poorly controlled managing boards culminated in the structure law. Presently, the system of co-optation is under pressure, supervisory boards appear to lack sufficient legitimacy, employees are demanding board representation and shareholders are beginning to claim larger influence over the system. Moreover, it is questionable whether the voluntary adoption of the structure-regime should be continued as it may be selected only for use as an anti-takeover mechanism. In general, the structure-regime is alleged to potentially suffer from insufficient accountability to shareholders and other stakeholders. Despite the undeniable merits of the typical Dutch system of corporate supervision, this may be a propitious occasion to consider the reformulation of the Dutch structure-regime.

Notes

1. This report, entitled 'Corporate Governance in the Netherlands' contains forty recommendations for sound management, effective supervision, and accountability. The Peters Committee primarily focused on the firm's relations with its shareholders under 'peace-time' conditions. The previous long-lasting debate on anti-takeover defensive mechanisms is often referred to as a 'war-time' debate because of the context of hostile bidders and defensive weapons. In contrast, 'peace-time' refers to normal conditions in the absence of such events.
2. Under the normal regime, the establishment of a supervisory board is optional. In that case, the members of the supervisory board are appointed by the general meeting of shareholders.
3. In 1969, the Social and Economic Council advised adopting a system of 'controlled' co-optation and the supervisory boards ought to be 'appropriately composed', reflecting the viewpoints of all relevant stakeholders. Furthermore, independence of supervisory boards should be pursued.
4. Unpublished report written by Center-Applied Research of Tilburg University, mandated by the Monitoring-committee.
5. A binding recommendation by the holders of priority shares can be undone by a two-third majority in the general meeting of shareholders, representing more than 50 per cent of the issued share capital.
6. In France, firms are allowed to opt for a one-tier structure or a two-tier structure. However, in practice, the one-tier structure prevails.

7. In contrast, the degree of independence of supervisory boards in the two-tier system may, in practice, be hampered by interlocking directorships, former memberships of the firm's managerial board, and the fact that the supervisory boards commonly hold their meetings together with the managerial board. The Peters Committee recommends that no more than one former member of the managerial board serve on the supervisory board (fourth recommendation).
8. Dutch Civil Code, Book 2, sections 140,2 and 250,2.
9. This study, executed by Center-Applied Research of Tilburg University, is entitled: 'Zeggenschapsverhoudingen en financiële prestaties van beursvennootschappen' (translated: Corporate governance characteristics and financial performance of listed corporations). The set-up of this study is in line with Agrawal and Knoeber (1996) and Rediker and Seth (1995) who include alternative governance mechanisms.
10. The average size of supervisory boards was 5.3 persons. Larger board size tends to be accompanied by lower firm performance. Yermack (1996) also reported a negative correlation between board size and firm performance. However, Bhagat and Black (2000) state that Yermack's results are not robust in the choice of performance measure.

References

Agrawal, A., and Knoeber, C. R. (1996). Firm performance and mechanisms to control agency problems between managers and shareholders. *Journal of Financial and Quantitative Analysis* 31: 377.

Barca, F., and Becht, M. (eds.) (2001). *Ownership and Control: A European Perspective.* Oxford: Oxford University Press.

Bhagat, S., and Black, B. (2000). Board independence and long term firm performance. Working paper, Columbia Law School and Stanford Law School.

Boot, A. W. A. (1994). *De financiering van het bedrijfsleven; tussen structuurregime en financiële sector.* Amsterdam: Amsterdam University Press.

Byrd, J. W., and Hickman, K. A. (1992). Do outside directors monitor managers: Evidence from tender offer bids. *Journal of Financial Economics* 32: 195.

Cadbury, A. (1992). *Financial Aspects of Corporate Governance* (Cadbury Report). London: Burgess Science Press.

De Jong, A., De Jong, D., Mertens, G., and Wasley, C. (2000). The role of self-regulation in corporate governance: Evidence from the Netherlands. Tilburg University Center, Discussion Paper.

Dutch Corporate Governance Committee (1997). *Corporate Governance in the Netherlands: Forty Recommendations.* Amsterdam: Dutch Corporate Governance Committee.

Dutch Ministry of Finance (2000). Zeggenschapsverhoudingen en financiële prestaties van beursvennootschappen. Tilburg University, Center-Applied Research Report.

Franks, J. R., Mayer. C., and Renneboog, L. (2001). Who disciplines management in poorly performing Companies? *Journal of Financial Intermediation.* 10: 209.

John, K., and Senbet, L. (1998). Corporate governance and board effectiveness. *Journal of Banking and Finance* 22: 371.

Kabir, R., Cantrijn, D., and Jeunink, A. (1997). Takeover defenses, ownership structure and stock returns in the Netherlands: An empirical analysis. *Strategic Management Journal* 18: 97.

Maeijer, J. M. M., and Geens, K. (eds.) (1990). *Defensive Measures against Hostile Takeovers in the Common Market.* Dordrecht: Martinus Nijhoff Publishers.

Moerland, P. W. (1995). Alternative disciplinary mechanisms in different corporate systems. *Journal of Economic Behavior and Organization* 26: 17.

Muyzenberg, L. v.d., and Schukken, F. (1998). Corporate boards: Structure, governance and performance; an international comparison, USA, Britain, France, Germany, the Netherlands and Sweden. University of Utrecht, Working Paper.

OECD (1999). OECD principles on corporate governance. Report by Directorate for Financial, Fiscal and Enterprise Affairs. Paris: OECD.

Rediker, K. J., and Seth, A. (1995). Boards of directors and substitution effects of alternative governance mechanisms. *Strategic Management Journal* 16: 85.

Renneboog, L. (2000). Ownership, managerial control and the governance of companies listed on the Brussels Stock Exchange. *Journal of Banking and Finance* 24: 1959.

Russell Reynolds Associates (1997). *Setting New Standards for Corporate Governance: U.S. Survey of Institutional Investors.* New York: RRA.

Weisbach, M. (1988). Outside directors and CEO turnover. *Journal of Financial Economics* 20: 431.

Yermack, D. (1996). Higher market valuation of companies with a small board of directors. *Journal of Financial Economics* 40:185.

13

Share Price Reactions to CEO Resignations and Large Shareholder Monitoring in Listed French Companies

ISABELLE DHERMENT-FERERE AND LUC RENNEBOOG

1. INTRODUCTION

Managerial quality is maintained by the intervention of internal and external corporate governance mechanisms. Yet, when insufficient monitoring or when managerial entrenchment has insulated management, markets will tend to react favourably to the CEO departures. In this chapter, we investigate whether forced CEO dismissal triggers positive abnormal returns in listed French companies. Voluntary CEO departures or unexpected deaths of CEOs may entail a loss of human capital to the firm. We analyse whether negative abnormal returns are generated in these cases. However, these market reactions may be dimmed or intensified depending on the qualities of the CEO's successor and corporate characteristics.

This study not only analyses price reactions after the change in top management, but also investigates whether or not specific corporate governance mechanisms are involved in bringing about CEO departures. We investigate the role of holding companies (the dominating large shareholders), industrial companies, families, institutions, and the government in exerting corporate control. In the remainder of this section we formulate the propositions and embed them in the literature.

1.1. *Board Restructuring and the Equity Market*

1.1.1. *Market Reactions to Forced Managerial Resignations*

Jensen and Meckling's (1976) agency theory highlighted that managers may seek maximization of their own utility curve at the detriment of corporate value. Remuneration contracts may reduce conflicts of interest if performance-related contracts can focus managers' attention on the corporate value drivers. However, in contrast to Anglo-American countries, remuneration contracts fashioned in terms of pay-for-performance, are not yet as widespread in Continental Europe. Hence, as performance-related contracts are rare, bad corporate performance often leaves the shareholders no alternative but to substitute incumbent management. Forced managerial turnover is expected to lead to significant share price increases (*proposition 1*), even though the following costs have been incorporated: the search and hiring costs of new management (Walsh and Seward 1990), the costs of breaking the contract with the fired manager (Knoeber 1986), and the loss of company-specific human capital.

The first event studies investigating the price impact of forced managerial turnover in the USA (Furtado and Rozeff 1987) reveal a positive but not statistically significant price increase. Worrell *et al.* (1993) confirm a price increase of 2.3 per cent but their results are statistically significant at the 1 per cent level provided that the managerial resignation announcement includes the nomination of a successor.[1] The degree of price reaction also depends on the presence of internal monitoring mechanisms in the study by Weisbach (1988): there is no wealth impact if the managerial resignation takes place in a company where the board is dominated by executive directors. However, top management substitution leads to a significantly positive price increase when the majority of the board consists of external independent directors. Denis and Denis (1995) study sixty-nine forced resignations and find that the dismissal of underperforming management is greeted with relief by the market. There is a positive market reaction of 2.25 per cent on the announcement day for companies that experienced a fall in performance over a three-year period prior to the managerial change.

However, the findings on forced managerial resignations are not unambiguous. Warner *et al.* (1988) uncover significantly negative cumulative abnormal returns of −4.3 per cent subsequent to forced turnover (in the period of 5–30 days following the dismissal). This negative market reaction is explained by an information effect which masks the real impact of forced turnover on shareholder wealth: forced turnover may signal poor current and future performance which had not yet been uncovered nor anticipated by the market. Mahajan and Lummer (1993) confirm a (weakly) significant negative cumulative abnormal return measured over a two-day period (the day before and the day of the announcement) for USA companies. Whereas the studies described above are about USA companies, Pige (1994) does not discover any such relations for a small sample of French companies.

1.1.2. *Market Reactions to the Death of the CEO*

Making abstraction of corporate performance, one would expect that the unanticipated death of the CEO would trigger a negative price reaction (*proposition 2*) since the company faces a loss in human capital, which may have been company-specific. Johnson *et al.* (1985) do not detect any significant share price reaction around the announcement date, but discover increased volatility of abnormal returns subsequent to the announcement period. Worrell *et al.* (1993) reveal that the market reacts more negatively when the death of a CEO occurs suddenly compared to the cases in which the CEO dies after an illness, which provides some support for the informational efficiency of equity markets. Etebari *et al.* (1987) confirm the negative relation between CEO death and cumulative abnormal returns, but they find—after splitting the sample of deaths according to the cause of death (heart attacks, accidents, and suicides)—that accidents trigger significant positive market reactions of 8.25 per cent over a six-week window (symmetrically around the event day). This finding may result from the fact that CEOs may be entrenched—perhaps due to a long tenure with positive track record or due to a substantial ownership stake—and are difficult to dismiss even in the wake of poor performance.

1.1.3. *Market Reactions to Non-Conflictual Resignations and Retirements by Top Managers*
As retirements at the normal retirement age can usually be well anticipated, there is no reason that the announcement of a retirement would cause a price reaction (*proposition 3*). On the other hand, a non-conflictual resignation prior to retirement age may create a negative price reaction if the company loses valuable company-specific human capital (*proposition 4*). The wealth effects of non-conflictual resignations were investigated in French and USA companies by Hubler and Schmidt (1996) and Mahajan and Lummer (1993), respectively. Both studies reveal that the announcement of an executive director leaving the company on a non-conflictual basis coincides with a negative cumulative abnormal return (significant in the former, not significant in the latter). Still, the Mahajan and Lummer study shows that there is a (significant) positive share price change when a CEO steps down but remains on the board as a director or when an executive director relinquishes his or her function but maintains a managerial role within the firm.

The findings on market reactions to age-related retirements are in line with the expectations: Weisbach (1988), and Mahajan and Lummer (1993) show that there are no price reactions. Exceptional are the results of Denis and Denis (1995) who uncover a small but positive significant abnormal return of 0.6 per cent. Presumably, the market reacts with relief as, in the USA, some directors stay on the board beyond the retirement age of 65.

1.2. *The Choice of a Successor*

Most event studies test hypotheses based on the reasons why top management is substituted but do not consider the price impact related to the qualities of newly hired or promoted management. For example, the market may react differently depending on whether or not an internal candidate is nominated as CEO. Promoting internal candidates may hold two advantages: they may have (i) better company-specific process and technological knowledge, clearer insights in products, markets and competition, and a closer relation with clients, and (ii) strong existing social networks via which they acquire specific internal information. However, if a radical break with an existing strategy is essential, an external successor may be preferred as he or she may bring about change and revived creativity. The choice of a new CEO may also depend on corporate characteristics such as performance, corporate size, and the degree of diversity of corporate activities. These characteristics may dim or amplify the price reactions to the different types of CEO departures described above. Persistent poor corporate performance leads to higher CEO dismissal (Franks *et al.* 2001). As the CEO and his management team is responsible for poor performance, external succession—especially following forced turnover—is expected to trigger a positive market price reaction whereas internal promotion following poor performance may not be regarded favourably by the market (*proposition 5a*). In well-performing companies, internal succession (after non-conflictual turnover) is less costly than external CEO succession. This implies that the expected negative price reaction after internal succession may be less substantial than after external succession (*proposition 5b*).

For large companies, it may be relatively less costly to nominate an internal successor than for small companies because large companies usually have a pool of potential successors. Hence, in the absence of poor performance, internal succession (after non-conflictual turnover) may cause less strongly negative reactions in larger companies than in smaller ones (*proposition 6a*) (Furtado and Rozeff 1987). If the need for new managerial skills is essential, external succession will cause a larger positive market reaction in smaller companies as it is easier to refocus the strategy of such firms (*proposition 6b*). The market reaction to a new top manager's appointment may also depend upon the industry in which a company operates. If the company is diversified and operates in several unrelated industries, the value of the human capital of a new top manager can be assessed with less precision than in undiversified companies. Hence, external succession may trigger a stronger price reaction[2] in a diversified company compared to undiversified firms (*proposition* 7), because a new external manager may bring about higher value added in diversified firms (Parrino 1997).

1.3. *Corporate Governance Mechanisms*

As the CEO is ultimately responsible for the corporate performance, disciplinary actions are to be expected as a result of poor share price and accounting returns if an efficient corporate governance policy is exerted. Both the share price return and accounting performance portray a myopic view of the true value of managerial skills reflected by corporate performance. The relation between executive director or CEO resignations and share price performance may be weaker because share prices already incorporate market expectations regarding managerial replacement. On the other hand, accounting data can be manipulated (temporarily) by the choice of accounting policies (Teoh *et al.* 1998). Therefore, the impact of both share price returns, and levels of and changes in operating and net accounting earnings on turnover are to be analysed.

A balanced board including both executives and non-executives reduces the agency costs and potential conflicts among decision-makers and residual risk bearers. Non-executives are not only legally bound to monitor given their fiduciary duty, but they also often represent the large shareholders in an equity market with strong ownership concentration such as in France (Becht and Mayer 2001). Furthermore, non-executives have incentives to develop a reputation as monitors as they face an external labour market which provides some form of disciplining for passive leadership. Separating the roles of CEO and non-executive chairman is also considered to be a strengthening factor of the board's monitoring ability since a non-executive chairman ensures more independence from management. Such recommendations have been included over the past few years into several 'codes of best practice' such as the Cadbury Report of 1992 in the UK, the Dutch Peters Committee code of 1996, and the Belgian Commission of Banking and Finance code of 1998 (Goergen and Renneboog 2001). In contrast, French corporate law states that the chairman of the board of directors needs to assume the task of general management (*'doit assumer la direction générale de la société'*), but also that two managing directors can help him in this task. In 83 per cent of listed public limited corporations (*sociétés anonymes, SAs*), the functions of chairman of the board and of the CEO are combined by one person (Dherment 1998).[3] The first French proposal of a corporate governance code by the Viénot Commission in 1995 did not follow the international consensus of appointing non-executive chairmen. This may be explained by the fact that the Viénot committee was composed of Chairmen/CEOs of listed corporations. The second Viénot report of July 1999 tones down its earlier conviction and suggests the option to introduce unitary or dual control.[4]

The incentives to monitor and correct managerial failure depend on whether the amount of equity held by a shareholder (group) is large enough to internalize the costs of corporate control (Grossman and Hart 1980). Moreover, specific classes of owners may value control differently. This is reflected in the differences in control premium by category of owner because the additional compensation and perquisites that the controlling security holders can accord themselves may differ across categories of shareholders. (Financial) holding companies are prevalent in France and their private benefits and reasons for control accumulation are manifold: capturing tax reductions by facilitating intercompany transfers and reducing transaction costs by offering economies of scale or by supplying internal sources of funds (Banerjee *et al.* 1997). Likewise, corporate shareholders may hold substantial share stakes in companies of a supplier or customer in order to influence and/or capitalize on their strategic decisions (Johnson *et al.* 2000). Financial institutions are often controlled by a holding company that also holds equity in the target firms. Consequently, the interests of a financial institution as a creditor and as an equity holder may diverge, such that in order to avoid conflicts of interest, this category of shareholder is not expected to actively monitor (Renneboog 2000). Therefore, a positive relation is expected between turnover and the equity stake held by holding companies, industrial and commercial firms, individuals and families and no relation between turnover and institutional ownership concentration (*proposition 8*).

Contrary to Anglo-American countries, ownership structures in France are usually complex and pyramidal, and are constructed for reasons of control leverage (Wymeersch 1994). Therefore, decisions about disciplining management may not be taken by direct investors but rather by the ultimate shareholders who control the share stakes directly or through multiple tiers of ownership. Similarly, monitoring of Belgian listed firms is not performed by intermediate holding companies which are investment vehicles of controlling industrial companies or individuals and families, but by these industrial companies and families themselves (Goergen and Renneboog 2000) (*proposition 9*). When performance is poor, this may not only be the result of bad management but also of a breakdown in corporate control. Consequently, a (partial) corporate control market may arise as shareholders with little monitoring ability sell substantial share stakes to monitors aiming to improve poor corporate performance. Bolton and von Thadden (1998) point out that equity concentration embeds state-contingent control. If the new shareholders replace low quality monitors, stronger disciplining of the incumbent management may be expected (see Burkart *et al.* 1997).

When high leverage increases the probability of bankruptcy, close creditor monitoring may be expected. Thus, setting a high capital gearing amounts to the creation of a bonding mechanism for management (Aghion and Bolton 1992) and high turnover is expected to be positively related to high gearing (*proposition 10*). Denis and Denis (1993) show that creditor monitoring (measured by high leverage) combined with managerial ownership improves shareholder returns.

In the remainder of this study, we investigate how the resignation of top managers in French companies is received by the market. To summarize, we expect: (i) an immediate positive price increase at the announcement of forced dismissals; (ii) a negative price change coinciding with non-conflictual resignations and with CEO departures due to illness or decease; and (iii) no market reaction at age-related retirements. CEO departure usually coincides with the nomination of a new CEO and the choice between internal and external succession may depend on corporate characteristics such as corporate size, sector homogeneity, and past corporate performance. We investigate whether these characteristics have a bearing on relations (i) to (iii). In Section 2, the sample selection is described and the data sources and variables are disclosed. Section 3 describes the methodology. Section 4 discusses the results of the event studies and of the analysis of the determinants of top management turnover. Section 5 concludes.

2. SAMPLE SELECTION AND DESCRIPTION OF DATA SOURCES AND OF VARIABLES

The sample consists of 235 companies which experienced a change of their CEO (Président Directeur Général) during at least one of the years in the period 1988–92, and were listed on the First Market, the Paris Stock Exchange.[5] Over the five-year period, 325 changes of CEO were recorded for the 235 listed companies. Incomplete data on share prices and undisclosed reasons for turnover reduced the number of companies to 207 (and to 277 CEO changes).

Information about the board of directors and the resignation of directors was collected from several sources. The database of the *Banque de France* (BdF) contains for each director of a listed company, the name, date of birth, dates of nomination to and resignation from the board. The information concerning changes in the positions of CEO was verified with data from *l'Annuaire des Sociétés Cotées Desfossés* (Dafsa-Desfossés). In order to collect announcement dates, a press search was performed using the newspaper *Les Echos*, the most important economic French journal. *Les Echos* contains a special section with new nominations of managers and directors. The findings were double checked with information from *La Tribune Desfossés*. In this press search, the following information was collected: the reasons given for the CEO departure, the controlling mechanism that intervened to remove a top manager, and the number of directors departing along with the CEO. In addition to the announcement date of the resignation, other market sensitive information released close to the same date was also collected to disentangle the pure informational effect of the resignation.

Distinguishing between forced and non-conflictual resignations is difficult as euphemistic terms are often used to mask the dismissal or as no reasons are given. We consider as forced resignations, those cases where the CEO departure resulted from the non-renewal of the CEO's mandate as a director and from the formal CEO dismissal as reported in the database of the BdF. This information was supplemented with data from *Les Echos*: although some resignations are classified as voluntary in the BdF-database, they were considered as forced if a press article alluded to a conflict (e.g. departure following a change in control, conflict with shareholders or the board of directors or another member of the management team, difference in strategic views, etc.). The sample of non-conflictual resignations includes departures where the CEO has taken the initiative and for which there are no press articles suggesting a conflict. This category of non-conflictual resignations also includes departures due to illness or disease. Hence, we are relatively certain that the subsample of forced turnover consists of turnover due to conflicts. However, the sample with non-conflictual turnover which consists of voluntary resignations, may also contain some case of forced turnover due to poor or uninformative disclosure of the reasons for CEO departure. A third category of CEO departures consists of age-related retirements. Data on new corporate destinations of departing directors and on the professional origins of nominated directors were collected from the guide *Who's Who*. This source allows us to distinguish between internal and external promotions to the board. We consider an external nomination to have taken place when an outsider was nominated to the board less than one year prior to his or her promotion to CEO.

In the annual reports of 207 French companies over the period 1988–92, 277 CEO resignations were identified. In 38 per cent of these CEO departures, part of the management team left the firm along with the CEO. Table 13.1 shows that the BdF database reports 242 CEO changes whereas the financial press (the financial paper *Les Echos*) only reports 128 cases. Seventeen per cent of the CEO turnover was age-related retirement and 7 per cent of the resignations were caused by death or illness. Conflicts with the board of directors, the shareholders or other members of the management committee resulted in forced turnover in 10 per cent of all the CEO departures; whereas in 20 per cent there was no sign of conflict with 13 per cent of the CEOs invoking personal reasons and 7 per cent leaving to pursue other professional opportunities. Still, such voluntary resignations may have been the consequence of undisclosed managerial disciplining. Table 13.1 also exhibits the differences in classifying the reasons of resignation between the BdF and the financial press. In 45 per cent of the CEO departures mentioned in the financial press, no reason for departure was given and the cases classified as 'dismissals' in the BdF database appeared to be a category in which departures for a variety of reasons were amalgamated. Consequently, only ninety-two CEO departures could be classified with almost complete certainty into one of the following categories (Table 13.1): forced turnover (37 cases), non-conflictual resignations (34 cases), and age-related retirements (21 cases). It is these 92 cases which will be used in the event study analysis of Sections 3.1 and 3.2, and the share price reaction model of Section 3.3. In the CEO disciplining logit model of Section 4, all data are included; if no reason is provided in the financial press or BdF database the turnover is assumed to be conflictual.

Company characteristics such as industrial sector, ownership structure, capital structure, market capitalization, number of employees, and accounting data, were collected from the DAFSA fiches (1987–93). Share price and dividend pay-out data were collected from the database FININFO which contains the daily closing prices for the French market indices CAC40 and SBF, for the sector indices and for all listed companies for the period 1988–92. The interest rate on short-term government bonds is used as a proxy for the risk-free rate and collected from the Statistiques Annuelles de la Société des Bourses Françaises (SBF). Corporate size was measured by market capitalization, total sales, total assets, and total number of employees.[6] The following performance measures prior to the board turnover

Table 13.1. *Reasons for CEOs' resignations and their destinations*

Panel A: Number of CEO resignations

	%	Number
Companies with CEO change		207
Changes of CEO		277
Only CEO leaves	62	172
CEO and part of management leaves	38	105

Panel B: Reasons for resignation

	Mentioned in financial press		Mentioned in BdF-database	
	%	No. of cases	%	No. of cases
Age-related retirement	17	21	3	8
Death	4	5	3	6
Illness	3	4	—	—
Personal reasons	13	17	—	—
Non-renewal of contract	—	—	7	17
Dismissal	—	—	72	175
Change in the company's statutes	1	1	4	10
Other professional opportunity	7	9	—	—
Conflict with shareholders or board	10	13	1	3
Merger	—	—	1	2
No reason given	45	58	9	21
Total	100	128	100	242

Panel C: Forced versus other turnover

	%	No. of cases	Age	Tenure
Forced departures	40	37	60	4.5
Non-conflictual resignations	37	34	59	8
Age-related retirements	23	21	66	7
Total	100	92	61	6.5

Panel D: CEOs' destination after resignation

	%	No. of cases
Remains in same company	49	61
Joins firm of same corporate group	12	15
Moves to other (non-related) firm	39	48
Total	100	124
Resigning CEO becomes		
CEO of another company	34	96
Honorary chairman in old company	31	87

This table details CEO departures in French listed firms and distinguishes among the reasons of resignation. Departures are considered as forced resignations: (a) if the financial press alludes to a conflict with shareholders, or the board of directors (13 cases), (b) if the press does not specify the reason but the database of the Banque de France mentions the non-renewal of contracts (13 cases), (c) if the financial press mentions 'personal reasons' but the Banque de France specifies a case of non-renewal of the contract (11 cases). Departure is considered non-conflictual: (a) if the financial press or the Banque de France report a death (6 cases), (b) if the press indicates that the CEO left for reasons of illness (4 cases), (c) if there was another professional opportunity (9 cases), (d) if the CEO invoked personal reasons, excluding the non-renewal of contracts (15 cases). The departure is accepted as a retirement if the CEO reaches the age limit or retirement age.

were chosen: ROE (on market and book value basis), market adjusted returns, Marris ratio, Treynor ratio, Tobin's Q for the year of turnover and one and two years prior. In addition, these performance variables were adjusted by taking the deviation from the industry averages.

Companies are considered to be sector-homogeneous when their markets, technologies and structures are similar. To determine sector-homogeneity, the average of the partial correlation coefficients between the returns of companies and that of their industrial sector is calculated by means of a multiple regression with corporate return as the dependent variable and with the returns of the market index and of the industrial sectors as independent variables. The partial correlation coefficient (C^P) measures the percentage of the return variation of the company explained by variation in sector returns: $C^P = (\beta/\mathrm{SE})/[(\beta/\mathrm{SE})^2 + (n-k-1)]^{1/2}$ with β representing the correlation of the corporate return with the industry return, SE the standard error of the estimated β, n the number of observations, and k the number of independent variables.

3. METHODOLOGY

3.1. *Abnormal Return Calculation and Event Studies*

In order to measure the abnormal return of share i at day t, the market and risk adjusted return is calculated which assumes that a version of the CAPM generates expected returns. For example, the Treynor–Sharpe–Lintner model, $E(R_{i,t}) = E(R_{F,t}) + \beta_i[E(R_{m,t}) - E(R_{F,t})]$, generates a return for every share i with $R_{F,t}$ being the return of a risk free asset and $R_{m,t}$ being the return of the market portfolio. The abnormal return $\mathrm{AR}_{i,t}$ is the difference between the (logarithmic) nominal return and the expected return, $R_{i,t} - E(R_{i,t})$. Betas (β) were estimated with daily returns over a period of 260 to 60 days prior to the announcement day 0. As the companies in our sample are liquid companies listed on the 'first market', a correction for thin trading was deemed not necessary.

To test whether the equally weighted arithmetic average of the abnormal returns ($\overline{\mathrm{AR}}_t$) is statistically different from zero, the following test-statistics are used. N stands for the number of events, S stands for the standard deviation of the cross-sectional average abnormal returns, $(T-\tau)$ is the number of (trading) days over which the standard deviation of the cross-sectional mean abnormal returns are calculated. If the abnormal returns have an independent and identical distribution, the test-statistic has a Student t-distribution

$$t\text{-stat} = \overline{\mathrm{AR}}_t \,/\, S(\overline{\mathrm{AR}}_t)$$

with

$$(\overline{\mathrm{AR}}_t) = \frac{1}{N_t} \sum_{i=1}^{N_t} (\mathrm{AR}_{i,t})$$

$$S(\overline{\mathrm{AR}}_t) = \sqrt{\sum_{t=\tau}^{t=T} (\overline{\mathrm{AR}}_t - \overline{\overline{\mathrm{AR}}})^2 / N(N-1)}$$

$$\overline{\overline{\mathrm{AR}}} = \frac{1}{(T-\tau)} \sum_{t=\tau}^{t=T} \overline{\mathrm{AR}}_t$$

Subsequently, the cumulative abnormal return (CAR) can be calculated which cumulates systematic deviations from the expected return over time. For example, the CAR over a

$(T-\tau)$ day time window following an event can be computed as follows (see e.g. Ritter 1991):

$$\text{CAR}_{\tau,T} = \sum_{t=\tau}^{t=T} \overline{\text{AR}_t}.$$

Daily returns deviate more from the normal distribution than monthly returns. However, if the abnormal returns in the cross section of shares are from independent and identically distributed samples from a distribution with finite variance, the central limit theorem shows that the distribution of abnormal returns converges towards a normal distribution when the number of shares increases. Brown and Warner (1980) show that, for small samples of 5 or 10 shares, the distribution of abnormal returns deviates from the normal distribution, but the non-normality of daily returns does not have a significant impact on the event study methodology.

3.2. *Price Reaction Regression Models*

In order to explain the market price reaction at the announcement, the voluntary or forced CEO turnover (measured by a 2-day abnormal return around the announcement day), the regression model presented in Table 13.2, is estimated. The cases of turnover for which no unambiguous reason could be determined were excluded. The explanatory variables are corporate performance, size, sector homogeneity of the firm, a dummy variable indicating internal succession (a CEO promoted from the pool of managers of the firm) or external succession (CEO is recruited externally), and a dummy variable reflecting the type of resignation (forced versus voluntary departure). Table 13.2 (panel B) also shows the reduced regression models for the specific combinations of forced/voluntary turnover with internal/external succession. For example, the degree to which the price reaction depends on past corporate performance and on the fact that the CEO was forced to resign while an external candidate was nominated, can be computed by summing up the parameter estimates β_{i2}, β_{i6}, and β_{i8}. The coefficient β_{i2} by itself reflects the relation between the market price reaction and past performance when the CEO leaves voluntarily and is succeeded by an internal CEO.

Table 13.2. *Share price reaction model*

Panel A: Explanation of price reactions following CEO substitution

Dependent variable	Independent variable	Expected sign	Proposition
(Price reaction)$_i$ =	$\alpha_i + \beta_{i1}$ corporate size	+	6
	$+ \beta_{i2}$ corporate performance	−	1
	$+ \beta_{i3}$ sector homogeneity of the firm	+	7
	$+ \beta_{i4}$ successor's origin (1 = external)	+	5a
	$+ \beta_{i5}$ type of resignation (1 = forced)	+	4
	$+ \beta_{i6}$ corporate performance $*$ type of resignation	−	1
	$+ \beta_{i7}$ size $*$ successor's origin	+	6
	$+ \beta_{i8}$ corporate performance $*$ successor's origin	−	5b
	$+ \beta_{i9}$ sector homogeneity $*$ successor's origin		
	$+ \varepsilon_i$	+	7

Table 13.2. (*Cont.*)

Panel B: Reduced versions of the general regression model

Forced departure	Successor's origin	Reduced regression models
Yes	Internal	$(\text{Price reaction})_i = (\alpha_i + \beta_{i5}) + \beta_{i1} * \text{Size} + (\beta_{i2} + \beta_{i6}) * \text{Performance} + \beta_{i3} * \text{Homogeneity} + \varepsilon_I$
Yes	External	$(\text{Price reaction})_i = (\alpha_i + \beta_{i4} + \beta_{i5}) + (\beta_{i1} + \beta_{i7}) * \text{Size} + (\beta_{i2} + \beta_{i6} + \beta_{i8}) * \text{Performance} + (\beta_{i3} + \beta_{i9}) * \text{Homogeneity} + \varepsilon_I$
No	Internal	$(\text{Price reaction})_i = \alpha_i + \beta_{i1} * \text{Size} + \beta_{i2} * \text{Performance} + \beta_{i3} * \text{Homogeneity} + \varepsilon_I$
No	External	$(\text{Price reaction})_i = (\alpha_1 + \beta_{i4}) + (\beta_{i1} + \beta_{i7}) * \text{Size} + (\beta_{i2} + \beta_{i8}) * \text{Performance} + (\beta_{i3} + \beta_{i9}) * \text{Homogeneity} + \varepsilon_I$

4. DISCIPLINING TOP MANAGEMENT

Logit regressions with panel data over the period 1988–92 whereby every year represents an individual observation are estimated to determine whether or not conflictual CEO turnover (dummy = 1) is initiated by concentrated ownership or another monitoring mechanism. Industry and time specific fixed effects models are estimated with the executive board turnover as an independent variable. With regard to ownership concentration, a distinction is made among holding companies, institutions, industrial companies, government controlled investment agencies, and individuals and families. Variables capturing past corporate performance, the degree of leverage and board characteristics such as board size, the percentage of non-executives, the separation of CEO and chairman, the percentage of directors representing shareholders, debtholders, and founders are also included. The robustness of the models is tested by including corporate dummies and by including taking innovations to remove firm-specific effects. In order to address the endogeneity problems, lagged data for ownership, performance, and debt policy were included in the models.

The relation between board restructuring, performance, ownership, leverage, board structure is examined in the following model:

$$
\begin{aligned}
&\text{Board restructuring}_{i,t,k}\\
&= \alpha_{i,t} + \sum_{k=1}^{2} \beta_{i,k} * \text{PERF}_{i,t-k} \quad \text{(Performance (lagged))}\\
&+ \sum_{l=1}^{9} \gamma_{i,l} * \text{CONC}_{i,l,t-1} + \sum_{l=1}^{8} \delta_{i,l} * \text{CONC}_{i,l,t-1} * \text{PERF}_{i,l,t-1} \text{(Ownership/interaction)}\\
&+ \phi_1 * \text{DEBT}_{i,t-1} + \eta_{i,l} * \text{DEBT}_{i,t-1} * \text{PERF}_{i,t-1} \quad \text{(Debt policy/interaction)}\\
&+ \sum_{n=1}^{5} \varphi_{i,n,l} * \text{BOARD}_{i,n,t} + \sum_{n=1}^{5} \lambda_{i,l} * \text{BOARD}_{i,n,t} * \text{PERF}_{i,n,t-1}\\
&\quad \text{(Board composition/interaction)}\\
&+ \xi_{i,t} * \text{Leg. form} + \zeta_{i,t} * \text{Stock Exch.} \quad \text{(Legal form, type of market)}\\
&+ \kappa_{i,t} * \text{SIZE}_{i,t} + \sum_{p=1}^{8} \iota_{i,p} * \text{industry} + \sum_{q=1}^{4} \tau_{i,q} * \text{year} + \varepsilon_{i,t} \text{ (Size, industry, time dummies)}
\end{aligned}
$$

where i = company, t = year, k = type of board restructuring, l = classes of owner, n = number of board composition variables, p = number of industries, q = number of years.

1. Board restructuring: a dummy variable = 1 when the CEO is forced to resign, and = 0 if there is no CEO departure or if the CEO's departure is voluntary.
2. PERF = performance variable measured by lagged (1) market adjusted returns, (2) level of ROE (earnings defined as earnings after tax), (3) changes in ROE, (4) level of ROA (earnings defined as operating earnings), (5) changes in ROA, (6) level of Tobin's Q (market value of assets / book value of net assets), (7) changes in Tobin's Q.
3. CONC = ownership concentration (in %) by class of owner: (i) holding companies; (ii) banks; (iii) institutional investors (pension funds, investment funds, funds managed by insurance companies); (iv) industrial and commercial companies; (v) families and individual investors, not related to a director; (vi) federal or regional authorities; (vii) executive directors and families; (viii) non-executive directors and families; and (ix) employees. Both the percentages of ownership by category of owner and the percentage held by the largest shareholder are included (in separate regressions). Both direct shareholdings by category of owner are included as are the direct shareholdings reclassified into the categories of owner based on the category of the ultimate (reference) shareholder (in separate regressions).
4. DEBT = debt/total assets.
5. BOARD = board composition (% of non-executive directors), separation of the functions of CEO and chairman (1 = no separation), percentage of directors representing the founding family, percentage of directors representing the debtholders, percentage of directors representing the shareholders.
6. SIZE = logarithm of total assets or of total employees.
7. Leg. form. = Legal Form : Dummy is 0 if company is a *Société Anonyme*, is 1 if company is a Société Anonyme à Directoire, is 2 if company is a *Société à Commandite par Actions.*
8. Stock Exch. = Type of stock exchange: Dummy = 0 if share is listed on the *reglement mensuel* (most liquid market) and 0 if listed on the cash market (CPT).

4.1. *Market Reactions to Changes in Top Management*

4.1.1. *Share Price Movements at Announcement of CEO Resignations: Event Study Results*

Of all the CEOs who relinquished their functions, the destination of 124 could be traced: forty-eight moved to another firm, whereas sixty-one remained employed by the same company or became non-executive directors, and fifteen joined a firm belonging to the same corporate group. Ninety-eight per cent of the announcements of CEO departures included the nomination of a successor. Contrary to the recommendations of good corporate governance in most countries, the functions of CEO and Chairman of the board are not separated in 84 per cent of our sample.

Table 13.3 shows the market price reactions (cumulative abnormal returns) surrounding the announcement of ninety-two CEO resignations which could be unambiguously classified into the following categories—voluntary resignation, forced turnover and age-related retirement. Panel A reveals that non-conflictual CEO departures, including voluntary resignations as well as deaths and illness-related resignations, do not trigger any significant market price reaction. Thus, there is no evidence that propositions 2 and 4, which state that the loss of the human capital coincides with the non-conflictual CEO departure (including

Table 13.3. *Market price reactions and the announcement of CEO resignations*

Event Window (Days)	Observations	CAARs	Student *t*-stat	*p*-value
Panel A: Announcement of non-conflictual resignation				
0	34	0.003	0.388	0.704
−1 to 0		0.005	0.405	0.692
−2 to 2		−0.009	−0.395	0.700
−5 to 5		0.000	−0.001	1.000
−10 to 10		0.011	−0.537	0.600
−60 to −1		−0.054	−0.978	0.378
−60 to 30		−0.061	−0.974	0.359
Panel B: Announcement of forced resignation				
0	37	0.005	0.782	0.454
−1 to 0		0.004	0.455	0.660
−2 to 2		0.060	0.313	0.761
−5 to 5		0.016	1.001	0.343
−10 to 10		0.046	2.953	0.016**
−60 to −1		0.057	1.355	0.213
−60 to 30		0.079	1.261	0.243
Panel C: Announcement of retirement				
0	21	0.000	0.102	0.921
−1 to 0		0.000	−0.043	0.966
−2 to 2		−0.003	−0.604	0.557
−5 to 5		−0.016	−2.392	0.034**
−10 to 10		0.002	0.070	0.946
−60 to −1		0.010	0.267	0.795
−60 to 30		0.046	0.848	0.418

	Difference in means	Student *t*-stat (equal σ^2)	Student *t*-stat (unequal σ^2)	*p*-value
Panel D: Difference in returns: voluntary versus forced resignation				
0	0.002	0.214	0.202	0.833
−1 to 0	−0.001	−0.060	0.055	0.690
−2 to 2	0.069	0.503	0.477	0.620
−5 to 5	0.016	0.500	0.449	0.622
−10 to 10	0.035	2.191	2.031	0.039**
−60 to −1	0.111	1.536	1.437	0.142
−60 to 30	0.14	1.580	1.580	0.134

This table shows the Cumulative Average Abnormal Returns (CAARs) of specific time windows around the announcement of non-conflictual resignations (panel A), of forced dismissals (panel B), and of age related retirements (panel C). Panel D shows the difference in returns of non-conflictual versus forced turnover. Day 0 is the announcement date of the resignation; −5 to 5 stands for an event window of 11 days from five days (−5) prior to the announcement day to five days subsequent to day 0.

Source: Own calculations.

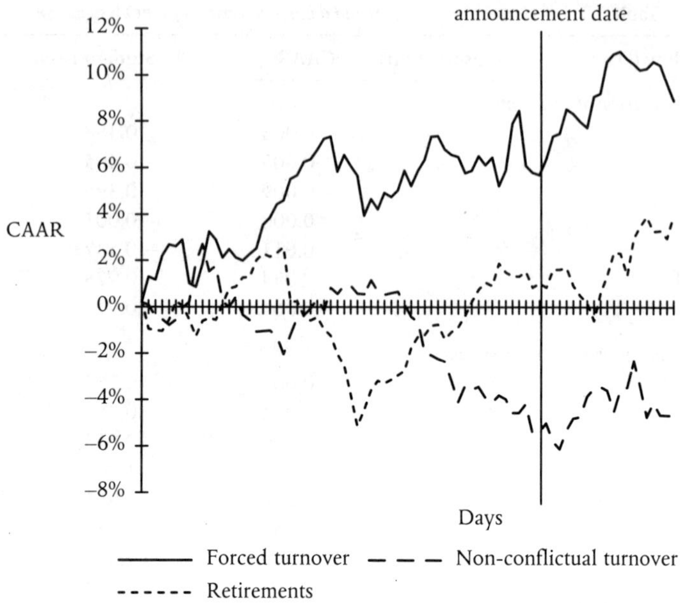

Figure 13.1. *Wealth effects subsequent to announcement of forced and voluntary resignations*

death and illness of CEOs), creates negative price pressure. In contrast, proposition 1, which states that forced turnover increases shareholder wealth, is sustained. Panel B shows that, for the event window of twenty days around the announcement day, share prices increase by almost 0.5 per cent within the 2 per cent level of statistical significance. Panel D investigates whether there is a difference in price reaction between announcements of non-conflictual and forced turnover: the market reacts significantly and positively to forced turnover in comparison with the announcement of non-conflictual departure. Surprisingly, the announcement of an age-related retirement triggers a negative price reaction (panel C), which contradicts proposal 3. In Table 13.3, the market price reaction takes place not on the announcement date itself but over a period of twenty days around day 0. This may result from the fact that in the case of conflicts or poor performance, the market may have anticipated a resignation, which can also be observed in Fig. 13.1 where the cumulative average abnormal returns (CAARs) drift upwards in the period prior to the announcement.

4.1.2. *Share Price Movements at Announcement of CEO Succession: Event Study Results*

Market reactions to changes in CEO and to internal or external promotions are expected to depend on past corporate performance. External CEO succession triggers stronger positive price reactions than internal succession if the renouncing management's performance, reflected in past corporate performance, was unsatisfactory (proposition 5a). If, on the contrary, past corporate performance was sound, internal promotion may create a less negative price reaction as the loss of company-specific human capital at the departure of the

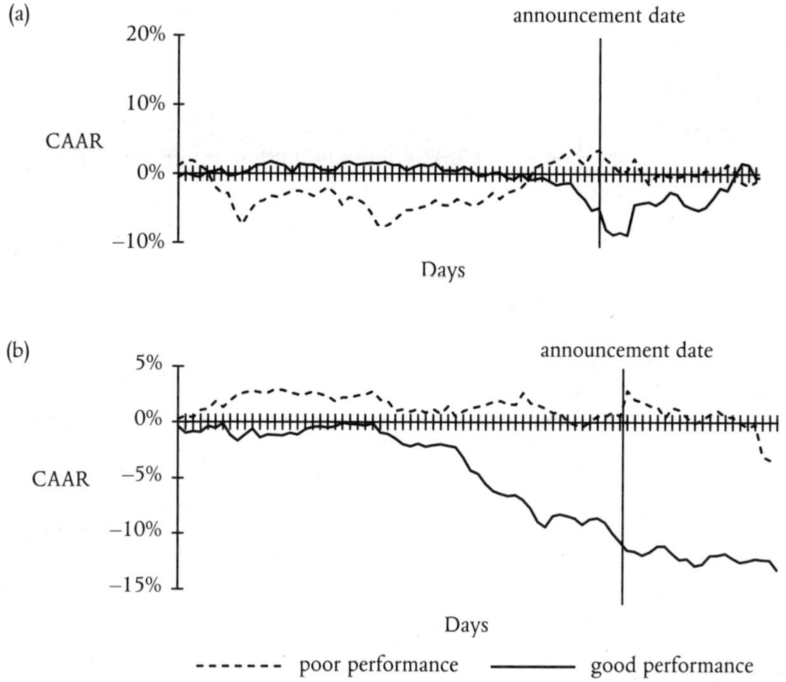

Figure 13.2. *Wealth effects subsequent to (a) internal and (b) external CEO succession in poorly and well-performing companies*

CEO is less (proposition 5b). In Fig. 13.2(a), the wealth effect of the nomination of an external CEO is depicted for poorly performing companies[7]: while none of the abnormal returns prior to the announcement dates are statistically significant, the CAAR increases at the announcement by more than 2 to 2.86 per cent. Figure 13.2(b) shows that in poorly performing companies with internal CEO succession, the CAAR is negative up to ten days prior to the announcement, then becomes positive, but drops by almost 1 per cent on the day of the announcement. All abnormal returns are not statistically significant apart from the price decline on the announcement day. These findings corroborate proposition 5a: in poorly performing companies, the nomination of an external CEO is greeted by the markets with a price increase. However, in poorly performing companies with an internal CEO promotion, the CAAR rises prior to the announcement presumably in anticipation of the removal of the incumbent CEO who is held responsible for the corporate performance. The market reacts negatively when an internal manager is promoted as this manager may be held partially responsible for past poor performance.

In companies with good past performance and with internal succession, there is a price decline from day -5 to $+4$, but this is not statistically significant (Fig. 13.2(b)). In the case of external succession in companies with a good performance track record, share prices decline significantly from day -12 and, after the announcement, the cumulative abnormal

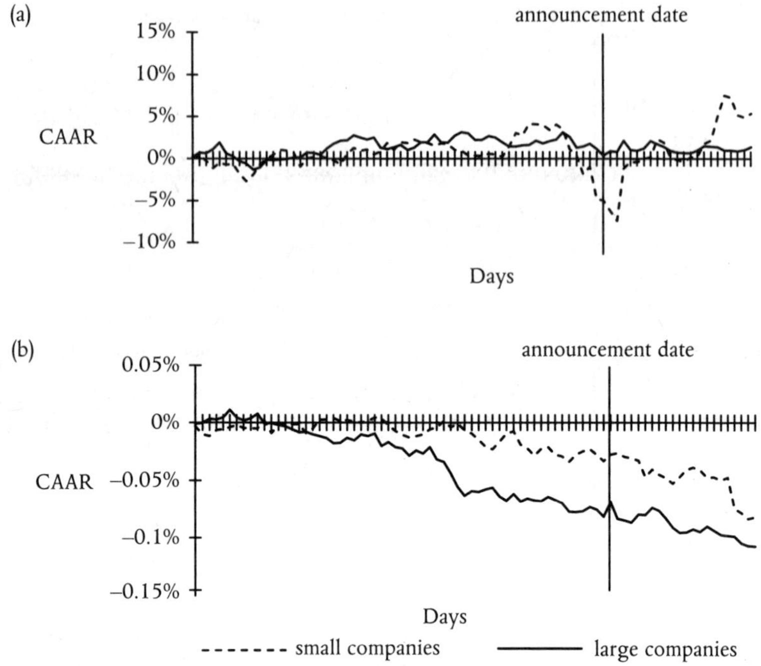

Figure 13.3. *Wealth effects subsequent to (a) internal and (b) external CEO succession in small and large companies*

returns levels off (Fig. 13.2(a)). It should be noted that the number of events is small, but that these findings are not incongruent with proposal 5b which states that turnover in well-performing companies induces a loss of human capital which is stronger when the new CEO is external to the company.

Figures 13.3(a) and (b) show the abnormal returns of an 80-day event window around the announcement of the promotion of an internal and external CEO respectively, in small and large companies. Internal succession coinciding with non-conflictual turnover may cause weaker (negative) reactions in larger companies than in smaller ones because the former usually have a pool of potential successors. Figure 13.3(a) corroborates proposal 6a: in small firms a significant negative market reaction of −7.34 per cent takes place over the period day −2 to +3. If past poor performance has led to CEO removal, the nomination of a new external CEO may cause larger positive market reactions in smaller companies as it is easier to turn around or redirect the strategy of such firms. Figure 13.3(b) does not support proposition 6b as abnormal returns decline prior to the event data and continue to decline in the three weeks subsequent to the event.

If the company is diversified and operates in several unrelated industries, the value of the human capital of a new top manager can be assessed with less precision than in undiversified companies. Hence, external succession may trigger a higher positive price reaction[8] in a diversified company as the value added by an external manager may be higher than in non-diversified firms. Proposal 7 is not supported by our evidence.

4.2. *Share Price Reaction Model*

Table 13.4 shows the relation between the cumulative annual average abnormal return in a 20-day event window at the announcement of CEO departure, and corporate size, past performance (industry corrected Return on Equity), degree of corporate diversification, type of CEO resignation (forced or voluntary), and origin of the CEO successor (internal or external). The explanatory variables in this cross-sectional regression explain a large proportion (48.6 per cent) of the total variation in share price reactions. Past performance, forced departure and the interaction terms of performance and background of the new CEO (internal or external nomination) are statistically significant (within the 5 per cent level).

In the case of a forced resignation by the incumbent CEO (resignation dummy = 1) and of poor past performance (e.g. industry-corrected ROE of −10 per cent), a positive price reaction of 2.9 per cent is expected since the negative performance effect of −1.4 per cent (β_{i2}) is more than compensated by the positive effect of the forced turnover with 4.3 per cent (β_{i5}). Hence, this evidence supports proposition 1, which states that a positive price reaction is expected when the CEO is forced to leave as a result of poor performance. The positive price reaction increases by a further 1 per cent[9] (β_{i8}) at the announcement of an external successor (succession dummy = 1), which supports proposition 5a. When the CEO resigns voluntarily (resignation dummy = 0), when he is succeeded by an internal manager (succession dummy = 0) and when industry-corrected past return on equity is positive (e.g. 10 per cent), a positive price reaction of 13.7 per cent is obtained. This does not corroborate proposition 2. However, this positive price reaction is sharply adjusted downwards to 3.7 per cent if the voluntarily departing CEO (after past good performance) is succeeded by an external manager. This may reflect the loss of human capital, as stated by proposition 4.

Propositions 6 and 7, which predict a relation between share price reactions, corporate size, and the degree of corporate diversification, are not sustained. Substituting industry-corrected ROE in the regression of Table 13.4 by the Treynor ratio and Tobin's Q only yielded significant results similar to the ones presented in Table 13.4 for the Treynor ratio. Substituting market capitalization by total assets, number of employees, total sales did not have an impact on the results.

4.3. *A CEO Disciplining Model*

Panel A of Table 13.5 exhibits the ownership structure and concentration for the sample of 325 listed companies. Panel A shows that industrial and commercial companies are the largest category of owners with an average of 22.2 per cent. The combined direct ownership concentration of institutions—banks, investment and pension funds and insurance companies—amounts to 20.2 per cent whereas holding companies own an average of 16.9 per cent. Similar to Germany (Boehmer chapter 11 this volume) and Belgium (Renneboog 2000), ownership structure is typically complex with stakes held through multiple tiers of ownership.

Table 13.4. *Results of the share price reaction model*

Independ. variable	Const. α_i	SIZE β_{i1}	PERF β_{i2}	HOM β_{i3}	ORIGIN β_{i4}	RESIGN β_{i5}	RESIGN* PERF β_{i6}	ORIGIN* SIZE β_{i7}	ORIGIN* PERF β_{i8}	ORIGIN* HOM β_{i9}
Coefficients	−0.029	−0.009	0.137**	−0.359	−0.088	0.043**	−0.049	0.007	−0.100**	0.764
t-stat.	−0.468	−1.100	2.474	−0.845	−1.189	2.355	−0.991	0.815	−2.256	1.480
p-value	0.645	0.285	0.023	0.408	0.249	0.029	0.334	0.425	0.036	0.155

R^2 adjusted: 0.486; *F*-test: 3.947 ***; Autocor. residuals (Durban Watson): 1.730, 0.075 with *p*-value (0.075); Sample size: 92.

This table shows the results of the share price reaction model presented in Table 13.3. The dependent variable is the Cumulative Average Abnormal Return over day −10 and +10 (0 is announcement of CEO turnover). RESIGN stands for resignation: equals 1 in case of forced resignation and 0 in case of voluntary resignation. Age-related retirements are excluded from the sample. ORIGIN stands for the origin of the successor: equals 1 if the new CEO is external (was not previously employed by the firm or was employed for maximally 1 year) or 0 if the CEO is internal. SIZE stands for corporate size measured by the logarithm of the market capitalization. PERFORM stands for performance measured by the change in ROE corrected for industry ROE in the year prior to the CEO substitution. HOM stands for the sector homogeneity of the firm measured by the correlation between the share price return of the firm and the return of the industrial sector. ***, **, and * stand for the significance at respectively 1, 5, and 10 per cent. The Kolmogorov–Smirnov test in both regressions indicates that the normality hypothesis of the residuals cannot be rejected: the significance tests are valid.

Table 13.5. *Ownership concentration by category of owner*

Sample: 325 firms	Mean (%)	Std. (%)	Skew.	Kurt.	Median (%)	75% (%)	Max. (%)
Panel A : Concentration of direct shareholdings by category of owner							
Holding companies	16.9	28.4	1.63	1.41	0.0	20.0	99.9
Banks	9.0	22.8	2.84	7.09	0.0	3.4	100.0
Insurance companies	6.7	20.0	3.25	9.56	0.0	0.0	95.1
Investment/pension funds	4.5	15.1	4.38	20.52	0.0	0.0	99.5
Industrial companies	22.2	32.5	1.21	−0.01	0.0	44.7	99.4
Individuals and families	0.2	1.3	6.09	38.42	0.0	0.0	10.0
Government stakes	2.1	10.9	5.73	32.39	0.0	0.0	79.4
Real estate firms	1.1	7.3	7.69	62.75	0.0	0.0	74.3
Executive directors	1.8	7.9	5.04	26.20	0.0	0.0	57.9
Non-executive directors	1.0	5.1	7.41	62.51	0.0	0.0	52.1
Personnel	0.1	0.5	10.18	110.61	0.0	0.0	5.6
Panel B : Concentration of direct and indirect shareholdings by category of owner							
Holding companies	14.9	28.4	1.82	1.99	0.0	10.2	99.9
Banks	7.5	20.8	3.23	9.75	0.0	0.0	100.0
Insurance companies	2.4	12.1	6.26	40.43	0.0	0.0	97.1
Investment/pension funds	3.6	13.1	4.84	26.07	0.0	0.0	98.9
Industrial companies	14.8	28.6	1.85	2.02	0.0	11.3	99.4
Individuals and families	2.9	13.1	5.41	30.55	0.0	0.0	99.3
Government stakes	13.1	26.3	1.99	2.63	0.0	10.0	99.4
Real estate firms	0.7	6.2	9.95	105.82	0.0	0.0	74.3
Executive directors	3.9	13.9	3.87	15.26	0.0	0.0	92.0
Non-executive directors	1.3	6.5	6.65	47.70	0.0	0.0	59.7
Personnel	0.4	4.8	12.60	161.94	0.0	0.0	66.7
Panel C: Largest direct shareholdings							
Largest	52.3	28.9	−0.04	−0.87	51.3	72.3	100.0
2nd largest	8.2	9.9	1.38	1.69	5.5	12.4	48.8
3rd largest	3.0	4.6	1.56	1.96	0.0	5.4	21.0
4th largest	1.3	2.8	2.41	5.65	0.0	0.0	15.6
5th largest	0.7	2.6	9.15	118.05	0.0	0.0	36.8
6th largest	0.2	0.9	4.87	24.05	0.0	0.0	6.7
7th largest	0.0	0.3	15.33	246.66	0.0	0.0	5.0
Panel D: Largest shareholdings (direct and indirect stakes combined)							
Largest	53.9	29.0	−0.15	−0.86	53.4	75.2	100.0
2nd largest	7.4	9.7	1.57	2.36	4.7	11.0	48.8
3rd largest	2.4	4.1	1.82	3.03	0.0	4.7	19.3
4th largest	1.1	2.7	2.76	7.98	0.0	0.0	15.6
5th largest	0.6	2.5	9.71	127.80	0.0	0.0	36.8
6th largest	0.2	0.8	5.50	31.37	0.0	0.0	6.7
7th largest	0.0	0.3	15.33	246.66	0.0	0.0	5.0

This table shows the descriptive statistics of ownership concentration for eleven categories of owner. Panel A classifies the direct shareholdings whereas in panel B the direct shareholdings are (re)classified based on the category of shareholder who ultimately controls (directly or indirectly by means of a cascade of intermediary shareholdings) the voting rights. The average size of the largest shareholdings is presented in panels C and D which respectively focus on direct and on direct and indirect voting right concentration. Std. is the standard deviation. Skew stands for skewness, Kurt stands for kurtosis, 75 % is the 75 per cent quartile, Max is the sample maximum.

Source: Own calculations.

Hence, control is with ultimate shareholders who control either directly or indirectly via affiliated companies, a large percentage of the voting rights. We define a relation between an ultimate shareholder and a target company as a control relation if: (i) there is a series of uninterrupted majority shareholdings on every ownership tier throughout the pyramid, or (ii) if there is a large shareholding of at least 25 per cent on every ownership level in the absence of other shareholders with stakes of blocking minority size or larger. Panel B shows the ownership concentration based on direct and indirect control relations: the ownership percentages are reclassified based on the shareholder category of the ultimate owner who directly or indirectly controls these direct share stakes. Comparing panels A and B, the most remarkable change is that the government directly and indirectly controls 13.1 per cent of the direct equity stakes of our sample companies. Panel B also shows that families and directors often use intermediate investment vehicles to own share stakes. In the average company, the largest shareholder holds a majority stake of 52.3 per cent (median of 51.3 per cent), or of 53.9 per cent (median of 53.4 per cent) if those direct shareholdings directly and indirectly controlled by the same ultimate shareholder are summed (panels C and D). This stands in stark contrast with the UK where a coalition of the five largest shareholders typically owns only 40 per cent of the shares (or voting rights). The second and third largest shareholder has typically no influence on how the company is run. In the highest ownership concentration quartile, the largest shareholder even has a supermajority of 75 per cent.

In Table 13.6, we investigate whether conflictual CEO removal resulting from poor corporate performance is caused by large shareholder activism or is facilitated by an efficient board structure. Past performance is measured both by lagged market corrected share price performance, Tobin's Q, levels and changes of return on equity (earnings after tax) and levels and changes of return on assets (operating earnings). Although there is strong evidence of performance-related top management disciplining in the USA (Hermalin and Weisbach 1991), UK (Franks *et al.* 2001), Japan (Kaplan and Minton 1994), and Belgium (Renneboog 2000), there seems to be no consistent relation for the sample of French companies between past performance and forced CEO departures. Neither the performance terms shown in Table 13.6 nor the interaction terms between performance and the disciplinary mechanisms (not shown) are statistically significant.

As ownership is strongly concentrated in France with the largest shareholder controlling a majority in the average company, board restructuring is expected to be initiated by this shareholder (such as holding companies, industrial companies). However, executive directors owning major share stakes may impede board restructuring. Institutional investors (banks, pension/investment funds, and insurance companies) are not expected to monitor if they intend to safeguard portfolio liquidity and to avoid transgressing the insider trading regulation. Proposition 8 is upheld by the findings of Table 13.6. The presence of a holding company in the ownership structure is positively correlated with the probability of a forced CEO resignation. However, it is questionable whether the large holding companies do discipline poorly performing CEOs because the interaction terms of performance and ownership by holding companies is not statistically significant. Thus, in the wake of poor performance, holding companies do not seem to be instrumental in removing the incumbent CEO. Banerjee *et al.* (1997) and Renneboog (2000) respectively, found no evidence of wealth creation for French and Belgian holding companies.

Table 13.6. *Conflictual CEO turnover, performance, ownership concentration and board composition*

	1988		1989		1990		1991		1992	
Sample size	373		297		374		374		369	
CEO turnover	314		253		315		315		312	
No turnover	59		44		59		59		57	
	Tobin's Q		**Share return**		**Δ ROE**		**ROA**		**Δ ROA**	
	Coef.	*p*	Coef.	*p*	Coef.	*p*	Coef.	*p*	Coef.	*p*
Intercept	6.56**	0.02	9.58**	0.03	6.63**	0.02	6.63**	0.02	7.86***	0.01
Performance *t*-1	−0.32	0.40	−0.19	0.75	−0.57	0.17	−1.23	0.43	−0.86	0.66
Performance *t*-2			−0.15	0.81	0.17	0.53			2.19	0.19
Ownership stake of the largest shareholder by class of ownership										
Holding co's	2.11**	0.04	3.94***	0.00	2.46**	0.02	2.17**	0.04	2.21**	0.04
Banks	−2.57	0.55	−2.62	0.59	−3.08	0.51	−2.88	0.50	−2.99	0.49
Institutions	0.70	0.66	1.53	0.37	1.54	0.30	0.76	0.62	0.58	0.73
Industrial co's	1.97**	0.04	1.17	0.34	2.26**	0.02	2.06**	0.03	1.86*	0.06
Families/indiv.	−0.56	0.81	0.25	0.93	0.18	0.94	−0.51	0.83	0.06	0.98
Government	1.07	0.37	2.75*	0.06	1.65	0.17	1.11	0.35	1.15	0.34
Executives	1.42	0.49	−3.30	0.38	1.19	0.56	1.48	0.48	2.14	0.30
Non-executives	3.48	0.14	4.10*	0.10	3.65	0.11	3.71	0.11	4.33*	0.09
Employees	0.84	0.71	−20.88	0.99	1.37	0.55	0.86	0.70	0.39	0.86
Board characteristics										
Shareh. Repres.	0.05**	0.03	0.06**	0.02	0.05**	0.02	0.05**	0.02	0.04*	0.06
Debth. Repres.	0.04***	0.00	0.04***	0.01	0.04***	0.00	0.04***	0.00	0.04***	0.00
Founder Repres.	−0.05*	0.08	−0.03	0.25	−0.04*	0.10	−0.05*	0.06	−0.05*	0.07
% Non-execs.	0.07**	0.02	0.11**	0.02	0.06**	0.02	0.07**	0.02	0.08***	0.01
CEO = Chair.	−0.22	0.86	−1.54	0.25	−0.19	0.88	−0.24	0.84	−0.37	0.76
Corporate characteristics										
Leverage	−0.09	0.94	0.66	0.69	0.29	0.82	0.10	0.94	0.41	0.76
Log of sales	−0.16***	0.01	−0.22***	0.01	−0.17***	0.01	−0.16***	0.01	−0.14**	0.03
Legal form	−0.76	0.56	−2.60*	0.09	−0.74	0.57	−0.91	0.49	−1.04	0.44
Exchange	−0.15	0.70	0.24	0.59	−0.18	0.63	−0.20	0.59	−0.25	0.55
Indus. fixed eff.	Yes		Yes		Yes		Yes		Yes	
Time fixed eff.	Yes		Yes		Yes		Yes		Yes	
−2 LogLikelih.	0.003		0.000		0.003		0.003		0.001	

This table shows a logit model estimating the probability of CEO turnover (dummy = 1) and its relation with past performance, as measured by Tobin's Q (averaged over *t*-1 and *t*-2), market corrected share price returns, changes in return on earnings (ROE), changes in return on assets (ROA) and ROA (averaged over *t*-1 and *t*-2). Shareh. Repres., Debth. Repres., and Founder Repres. stand for the % of the total board which represents, respectively, the shareholders, debtholders, and founders. % Non-execs. stands for the percentage of non-executive directors on the board. CEO = Chair is a dummy variable which equals 1 if the CEO combines his function with that of the Chairman. Exchange stands for the type of exchange (first or second market) which is a proxy for trading liquidity and the degree of corporate information disclosure. Indus. fixed eff. and Time fixed eff. stand for industry and time fixed effects, respectively. −2LogLikelih. is a Loglikelihoodtest.

Source: Own calculations.

Table 13.6 also shows that the probability of forced CEO turnover increases when industrial companies own substantial shareholdings. The fact that the interactive terms of industrial ownership with performance is statistically significant (10 per cent level) suggests that industrial companies assume a corporate governance role. It should be noted that the relation between CEO disciplining and ownership was only found after classifying the share stakes on the basis of the identity of the ultimate shareholders who control tier 1 directly or indirectly. Including only the direct shareholdings (by category of owner at the direct ownership level) did not yield any results. This supports proposition 9, which states that corporate governance actions are undertaken by ultimate shareholders rather than by the owners at the direct level. Table 13.6 also shows that banks or institutions do not partake in managerial disciplining. Furthermore, although many companies are (indirectly) controlled by the government, there is no evidence of performance-related corporate governance actions in these companies.

The relation between ownership concentration and disciplining is, at best, weak. The reason may be that much of shareholder monitoring and corporate governance actions is undertaken by shareholder representatives on the board of directors. To capture the board characteristics, the percentage of non-executive directors on the board is included as well as the percentage of directors representing the large shareholders, creditors and founding family. In line with USA and Belgian findings (Weisbach 1988; Renneboog 2000) but in contrast to UK findings (Faccio and Lasfer, Chapter 25, this volume; Franks *et al.* 2001), Table 13.6 shows that the higher the percentage of independent directors, the higher the probability of forced CEO turnover. There is also strong evidence that in companies with a high percentage of the non-executive directors representing the shareholders a higher probability forced CEO turnover is to be expected. Still, less forced CEO turnover is taking place when the board also comprises directors representing the founding family. This may result from the fact that these founding families are trying to defend the private benefits they derive from their (executive) positions on the board.[10] No relation was discovered between capital gearing and forced turnover, although a creditor's influence may be captured by the percentage of directors representing shareholders which is strongly correlated with forced CEO departure. Finally, there is evidence that forced CEO turnover occurs more frequently in smaller companies.

5. CONCLUSION

This study has analysed the share price reactions to changes in top management. A distinction was made among different types of CEO turnover: forced resignation, voluntary departures, and age-related retirements. The announcement of a forced CEO resignation is hailed favourably by the market with a small but significantly positive abnormal return of 0.5 per cent. The market may have anticipated the forced turnover since the abnormal return over a one-month period prior to the turnover amounts to 6 per cent. Whereas voluntary resignations do not cause price reactions, age-related turnover triggers a small negative price reaction. Subsequently, a more detailed classification of the change of top management was made based on the background of the successor (an internal versus external candidate), on the size of the corporation and the degree of corporate diversification. Expectedly, the nomination of an external manager following the performance-related forced resignation of a CEO causes a strong increase in abnormal returns of more than 2 per cent. The cumulative abnormal return of an internal CEO promotion in a poorly performing firm drops by almost 1 per cent on the day of the announcement. Presumably, this is because the internal manager is held (partially) responsible for past poor performance. In companies with good past performance and with internal succession, there is a price decline, but this is not statistically significant.

The chapter also analysed which corporate governance mechanisms are responsible for forced CEO turnover. A logit regression, did not reveal a relation between performance and CEO turnover. Furthermore, institutional investors, banks, and the government do not seem to provoke CEO departures even if they own large blocks of equity. The institutions may not be interested in influencing corporate policy or taking corporate control actions—such as the disciplining of top management—as they may constitute market sensitive private information. This might immobilize their share participations as they must avoid violating insider-trading regulation. The monitoring inactivity of banks may be explained by conflicts of interest between their position as creditor and equity holder. The problems with Credit Lyonnais suggest a laissez-faire mentality on the government's part, as the intervention was late by many years. We did not find evidence that the government exerts control in the companies in which it holds majority shareholdings. In contrast, when industrial companies are major owners, there is evidence that forced turnover is facilitated. It seems that it is easier to remove management in smaller companies than in larger ones. On the part of holding companies, there is only some evidence that they take a monitoring role in the case of other listed holding companies. No correlation was discovered between the degree of leverage and forced CEO departures, although CEO turnover is facilitated if creditors have their own representatives on the board. Likewise, a high proportion of shareholder representatives on the board leads to a higher probability of forced CEO resignations. However, this probability decreases when the founding family is represented by one or more (executive) directors.

Notes

1. They find a 2.3 per cent price increase (significant at the 1%-level) over the period (+1 day; +30 days) if the announcement of the CEO departure (day 0) coincides with that of the nomination of a new CEO. The share price only increases by 2 per cent (significance within the 10%-level) over the period (+1 day; +30 days) if the departure and nomination announcements do not coincide. The fact that a resignation was expected by the market can be deduced from a price increase of 11 per cent (significance of 5 per cent) over a 30-day period prior to the CEO's resignation.
2. Price reactions will be less strongly negative after non-conflictual turnover and less strongly positive after conflictual turnover.
3. In '*sociétés à directoire*', separation between the functions of CEO and chairman of the board is obligatory.
4. The Viénot report states that '*le comité est favourable à l'introduction en droit français d'une option ouvrant au Conseil d'administration le choix entre le cumul ou la dissociation des fonctions de président et de directeur général*'.
5. The First Market or the Official Market consists of two markets: (1) monthly settlement market (RM, *réglement mensuel*) with 190 French stocks and 90 foreign ones, and (2) cash market with 260 French stocks and 110 foreign ones (with a transaction volume 25 times lower than that of the RM).

6. In the regressions, the logarithm of the consolidated data is included.
7. A promotion is defined as being external if the new CEO neither serves on the firm's board of directors, nor is employed by the firm for at least one year prior to promotion. Good and poor performance is defined as, respectively, above and below the median of the return on equity (ROE) corrected for the average industry ROE and taken over the year prior to the turnover. The findings are robust to the other definitions of performance described in Section 2.
8. Price reactions will be less strongly negative after non-conflictual turnover and less strongly positive after conflictual turnover.
9. A β of -0.1 multiplied a negative performance of -10 per cent and the succession dummy of 1.
10. Whereas the shareholder and creditor representatives are non-executive directors, our data do not show whether a founder representative is executive or non-executive director.

References

Aghion, P., and Bolton, P. (1992). An 'incomplete contracts' approach to financial contracting. *Review of Economic Studies* 59: 473.

Banerjee, S., Leleux, B., and Vermaelen, T. (1997). Large shareholdings and corporate control: An analysis of stake purchases by French holding companies. *European Financial Management* 3: 23.

Becht, M., and Mayer, C. (2001). The control of corporate Europe. In F. Barca and M. Becht (ed.), *The Control of Corporate Europe*. Oxford: Oxford University Press.

Boehmer, E. (2002). Who controls German corporations? this volume, Chapter 11.

Bolton, P., and von Thadden, E. L. (1998). Blocks, liquidity and corporate control. *Journal of Finance* 53: 1.

Brown, S., and Warner, J. (1980). Measuring security price performance. *Journal of Financial Economics* 8: 205.

Burkart, M., Gromb, D., and Panunzi, F. (1997). Large shareholders, monitoring and the value of the firm. *Quarterly Journal of Economics* 112: 693.

Denis, D. J., and Denis, D. K. (1993). Managerial discretion, managerial structure, and corporate performance: A study of leveraged recapitalisations. *Journal of Accounting and Economics* 16: 209.

——— (1995). Performance changes following management dismissals. *Journal of Finance* 50: 1029.

Dherment, I. (1998), 'Changements de dirigeant et richesse des actionnaires: l'incidence de la nature du départ', University of Aix-en-Provence I.A.E., Working Paper No. 523.

Etebari, A., Horrigan, J., and Landwehr, J. (1987). To be or not to be—reaction of stock returns to sudden deaths of corporate chief executive officers. *Journal of Business, Finance and Accounting* 14: 255.

Faccio, M. and Lasfez, A. M. (2002). Institutional share holders and corporate governance. the case of U.K. pension funds. This volume, chapter 25.

Franks, J., Mayer, C., and Renneboog, L. (2001). Who disciplines the management of poorly performing companies? *Journal of Financial Intermediation* 10: 209.

Furtado, E., and Rozeff, M. (1987). The wealth effects of company initiated management changes. *Journal of Financial Economics* 18: 147.

Goergen, M., and Renneboog, L. (2000). Insider control by large investor groups and managerial disciplining in Belgian listed companies. *Managerial Finance* 26: 22.

——— (2001). Corporate governance and economic performance in the UK. In K. Gugler (ed.), *Corporate Governance and Economic Performance*. Oxford: Oxford University Press.

Grossman, S. J., and Hart, O. (1980). Take-over bids, the free-rider problem, and the theory of the corporation. *Bell Journal of Economics* 11: 42.

Hermalin, B. E., and Weisbach, M. S. (1991). The effects of board composition and direct incentives on firm performance. *Financial Management* 20: 101.

Hubler, J., and Schmidt, G. (1996). 'L'effet des annonces de décisions de GRH sur les cours boursiers des entreprises françaises. Application d'une méthodologie d'études d'événements', XIIIes Journées Nationales des I.A.E., Tome 1, Toulouse, 16 and 17 April, 448.

Jensen, M. C., and Meckling, W. H. (1976). Theory of the firm: Managerial behaviour, agency costs and ownership structure. *Journal of Financial Economics* 3: 305.

Johnson, S., La Porta, R., Lopez-de-Silanes, F., and Shleifer, A. (2000). Tunnelling. American Economic Review 90: 22.

Johnson, W., Magee, R., Nagarajan, N., and Newman, H. (1985). An analysis of the stock price reaction to sudden executive deaths. *Journal of Accounting and Economics* 7: 151.

Kaplan, S. N., and Minton, B. A. (1994). Appointments of outsiders to Japanese boards: Determinants and implications for managers. *Journal of Financial Economics* 36: 225.

Knoeber, C. (1986). Golden parachutes, shark repellents and hostile tender offers. *American Economic Review* 76: 155.

Mahajan, A., and Lummer, S. (1993). Shareholder wealth effects of management changes. *Journal of Business Finance and Accounting* 20: 393.

Parrino, R. (1997). Turnover and outside succession: A cross-sectional analysis. *Journal of Financial Economics* 46: 165.

Pige, B. (1994). Le marché boursier réagit-il à l'annonce des changement de dirigeants? Paper presented at the Journées Internationales de l'AFFI, 23–25 June, Tunis.

Renneboog, L. (2000). Ownership, managerial control and the governance of companies listed on the Brussels Stock Exchange. *Journal of Banking and Finance* 24: 1959.

Ritter, J. (1991). The long-run performance of initial public offerings. *Journal of Finance* 46: 3.

Teoh, S., Welch, I., and Wong, T. (1998). Earnings management and the underperformance of seasoned equity offering. *Journal of Financial Economics* 50: 63.

Walsh, J., and Seward, J. (1990). On the efficiency of internal and external corporate control mechanisms. *Academy of Management Review* 15: 421.

Warner, J., Watts, R., and Wruck, K. (1988). Stock prices and top management changes. *Journal of Financial Economics* 20: 461.

Weisbach, M. (1988). Outside directors and CEO turnover. *Journal of Financial Economics* 20: 431.

Worrell, D., Davidson, W., and Glascock, J. (1993). Stockholder reactions to departures and appointments of key executives attributable to firings. *Academy of Management Journal* 36: 387.

Wymeersch, E. (1994). Aspects of corporate governance. *Journal of Corporate Governance* 2: 138.

PART IV

ECONOMIC PERFORMANCE AND GOVERNANCE STRUCTURES

14

How do Financial Systems Affect Economic Performance?

WENDY CARLIN AND COLIN MAYER

1. INTRODUCTION

There have been debates about the role of financial systems in corporate activity for the best part of a century. A consensus view is yet to emerge as to whether cross-country differences in the structure of financial, corporate and legal systems have any causal influence on cross-country economic performance. But interest in this question has stimulated attempts to assemble data banks on financial and corporate systems that allow international comparisons to be performed. The objective of this chapter is to review these debates, to present additional empirical evidence and to put forward some new interpretations of this evidence.

We begin Section 2 with the debates about the comparative merits of different financial, corporate, and legal systems for economic performance. These debates have a long history. Until recently, they primarily took the form of bilateral country comparisons on, for example, the role of banks in comparative British and German industrial performance since the late nineteenth century. The positive role of the German banking system in promoting German industrialization through the provision of external finance frequently acquired the status of a 'stylized fact' in the discussion of comparative performance. The influence of 'bank' versus 'market'-based financial systems was revisited in the examination of the post-war 'Golden Age' growth of the West European and Japanese economies. But more detailed empirical work, using individual firm and institution data, has frequently failed to identify the source of advantage of the German and Japanese systems. Scepticism has been heightened by the comparative performance of Anglo-American and Continental European/ Japanese systems during the 1990s.

The debate about the merits of different systems has been widened to include cross-country differences in ownership structures. Only recently has there been a systematic attempt to document differences in ownership structures across countries. The finding that the classic 'Berle–Means' corporation with widely dispersed ownership is not typical of large firms in most countries has encouraged studies of the impact of ownership concentration on

This chapter was first published as Carlin, C., and Mayer, C. 'How do Financial Systems Affect Economic Performance?' in X. Vives (ed.) (2000) *Corporate governance: Theoreticial and Empirical Perspectives*: 137–168.

performance. As in the 'bank versus market' debates, analysis has been conducted at the level of countries and individual firms and institutions. In the former, the question is whether concentrated ownership contributes to or detracts from country performance. In the latter, the variation in ownership concentration across firms within a country is exploited to identify the mechanisms through which ownership structure affects performance. The final aspect of comparative structures that is examined in Section 2 is that of legal codes. The significance of legal codes for corporate performance derives from the observation that investor and creditor protection varies appreciably across countries depending on the nature and origin of legal codes, and in particular whether they derive from common law (essentially English speaking) or civil law (Continental European) systems.

The evaluation of the debates on comparative financial, corporate, and legal systems in Section 2 indicates that while there are clear differences in structures, the impact of these differences on performance is much harder to establish. In particular, the mechanisms that are often hypothesized to provide the link from structural differences to performance are rarely present in firm-level data sets.

In Section 3, we move from the comparative systems to the growth literature where there is a well-developed body of analysis focusing on the role of financial development in comparative growth. The aim is to disentangle the question of whether economic growth leads to the development of a more mature financial system or whether the maturity of the financial system promotes economic growth. Such studies use large samples of countries at widely differing levels of per capita GDP. They invariably record that financial development measured by the size and depth of banking sectors and securities markets promotes economic growth.

While there is therefore considerable evidence that financial development—bank or market-based—is good for economic growth, there is no clear evidence from studies of advanced countries that one kind of financial or corporate system is better for growth than another. Institutional differences between advanced countries appear to have been very persistent over the last century during which performance measured by GDP per capita first diverged and then converged. This opens up the question of whether institutional differences in financial systems, ownership structure and legal systems may create a form of comparative rather than absolute advantage, for instance, whether they influence the type of activity in which a country specializes, rather than its aggregate performance.

This possibility is explored from a theoretical perspective in Section 4 and empirically in Section 5. Why might financial or ownership structure be related to the type of economic activity? The reason is that different forms of economic activity may have quite different characteristics associated with them that make the provision of particular forms of finance or certain types of governance arrangements desirable. For example, activities may differ in their degree of uncertainty or in the extent to which cooperation from stakeholders in the firm (employees, suppliers, and purchasers) is required for successful performance. Section 4 will describe theoretical models in which stock markets support activities where there is a high degree of uncertainty in production. By contrast, banks may be beneficial for activities in which uncertainty is low (because, for example, technology is relatively stable and well understood) but gestation periods are long. In addition, only concentrated owners may be able to offer the commitments required for stakeholders to invest in training or dedicated plant and machinery.

The models discussed in Section 4 suggest that there is a matching of institutional structure with the characteristics of different economic activities. In Section 5, we provide empirical support for this from an empirical study of fourteen OECD countries: we record a strong interrelation between type of financial and corporate system, the characteristics of different industries and their growth rates in different countries. In addition, we report that the channel through which this effect occurs is expenditures on research and development rather than fixed capital formation. We also report that the interaction between country structures and industrial activity is sensitive to stages of economic development.

In the conclusion, we discuss the implications for economic policy of the view that there may be an interrelation between institutional structure and type of activity.

2. FINANCIAL AND CORPORATE SYSTEMS AND ECONOMIC PERFORMANCE

In 1912, Joseph Schumpeter described how the granting of credit was central to entrepreneurship and innovation: 'while granting credit is not essential in the normal circular flow... it is certain that there is such a gap to bridge in the carrying out of new combinations. To bridge it is the function of the lender, and he fulfils it by placing purchasing power created ad hoc at the disposal of the entrepreneur.' Thorstein Veblen saw the process of judging firms as being a matter of 'standardised bureaucratic routine' undertaken by the intermediaries which he dubbed 'the lieutenants of finance' while 'the captaincy has been taken over by the syndicated bankers' (Veblen 1919: 81). However, others, most notably Robert Lucas, argue that economists 'badly over-stress' the significance of financial considerations in economic performance (Lucas 1988: 6).

While the role of financial systems is debated, the performance of different types of financial systems is even more heavily disputed. Clapham (1936) approvingly quoted a principal officer of one of the German Great Banks when he said: 'In Germany our banks are largely responsible for the development of the Empire, having fostered and built up its industries. ... To them, more than any other agency may be credited the splendid results thus far realised.' 'If his historical summary was not literally accurate,' Clapham said, 'it was accurate in substance' (Clapham 1936: 118). Kennedy (1987) talks in somewhat more measured but still supportive tones about the role of German banks: 'With all their documented imperfections, [capital markets in Germany], by making resources available to a large group of technologically progressive industries on a scale unequalled in Britain, account for much of the difference in the economic growth performance between [Germany] and Britain in the half century after 1865' (Kennedy 1987: 120). The withdrawal of British banks in the second half of the nineteenth century was prompted by a series of bank failures: 'the banks were by the 'eighties no longer showing such a readiness to act as partners in industrial concerns. They were moving further and further away from the concept of long term loans and were concentrating on an efficient national short term credit system' (Jefferys 1938: 119).

But others question this interpretation of German banking. Edwards and Fischer (1994) find that 'the commonly-held view of the merits of the German system of finance for investment, in terms of the supply of external finance to firms and corporate control, receives no support from the analysis of the available evidence' (Edwards and Fischer 1994: 240).

Edwards and Ogilvie (1996) go on to argue that, not only is the current role of German universal banking overstated, it probably never was as significant as suggested, even at its zenith at the turn of the century. 'The picture which emerges is not consistent with the claim that German universal banks exerted substantial control over industrial companies and provided significant amounts of finance. Although there were some cases of this, these were the exceptions to the general rule, which was for companies to finance themselves internally to a very great extent' (Edwards and Ogilvie 1996: 441).

There have been similar debates about Japanese banks. Hoshi *et al.* (1990) find that 'firms with financial structures in which free-rider and information problems are small perform better than other firms after the onset of distress. In particular, we show that firms in industrial groups—those with close financial relationships to their banks, suppliers, and customers—invest more and sell more after the onset of distress than non-group firms.' But this view has been challenged. Weinstein and Yafeh (1998) find that, even prior to the liberalization of financial markets in Japan, main bank clients did not exhibit higher profitability or growth than their industry peers. Moreover, banks could use their monopoly power to squeeze their clients' profits and inhibit their growth through conservative investment policies.[1]

The negative impression of banking systems has been reinforced by the recent experience of financial distress in the Far East. Instead of performing the active monitoring and governance function that financial intermediation theory ascribes to them, banks are perceived to have been at the centre of corrupt, crony systems. General perceptions have swung markedly from admiration for systems that have been associated with sustained high levels of investment and growth rates to severe criticism for their lack of openness and transparency.

In the last decade, the debate in the comparative systems and finance literature has widened to include other cross-country differences. Franks and Mayer (1998*a*) reported marked differences across countries in concentration of ownership. 'The United Kingdom and the United States of America have large quoted sectors, with share ownership dispersed across a large number of investors. In the case of the United Kingdom, the dominant shareholding group is institutional investors; in the United States, it is individual investors. In contrast, France and Germany have small quoted sectors. More significantly, even the largest quoted companies in general have at least one shareholder owning more than 25 per cent of the equity and frequently a majority shareholding. These large shareholdings are in particular associated with family and other corporate investors' (Franks and Mayer 1998*a*: 730).

These differences have recently been confirmed in two sets of studies that investigate concentration of both share ownership and voting power. The first, a large international comparison of ownership in twenty-seven countries, 'finds that the Berle and Means corporation is far from universal, and is quite rare on some definitions of control. Similarly, the so-called German model of bank control through equity is uncommon. Instead, controlling shareholders—usually the State or families—are present in most large companies. These shareholders have control rights in firms in excess of their cash flow rights, largely through the use of pyramids, but they also participate in management' (La Porta *et al.* 1998: 5 also, La Porta *et al.* 1999). The second is a more detailed study of nine European countries, which concludes, 'the most striking fact about blockholdings in Europe is that they are so much higher than in the U.S.A. . . . Within Europe, the level of concentration of voting power is by no means uniform; and these differences are rooted in differences in customs and the legal environment.... In the UK, the largest 250 listed companies report a very modest median value (of size of share blocks) of 9.9%; while at the other extreme, Germany, Austria, and Italy all exceed 50%' (Becht and Roell 1999).

Ownership may affect corporate performance in several ways. First, principal–agent models emphasize the significance of equity ownership for incentives. Higher-powered incentive arrangements for managerial remuneration might be expected in the dispersed stock market economies of the UK and USA because of the weak incentive for any individual shareholder to incur the costs of monitoring management. Large owners in Continental Europe may have more incentive and capacity to monitor corporate performance directly instead of using schemes relating pay to stock market performance to align managers' incentives with those of owners. However, to the extent that there is evidence on executive pay in different countries, it fails to reveal pronounced differences. In a comparison of the response of executive remuneration to performance (share price, earnings, changes in earnings and sales growth) in Japan and the USA, Kaplan (1994) concludes that Japanese 'compensation responds to all four performance measures, and the responses are generally similar to those in the United States.... Cash compensation is positively related to earnings, stock and sales performance. In most cases, the sensitivities in the two countries are not statistically different' (Kaplan 1994: 512).

Concentrations of ownership are likely to affect corporate control. The separation of ownership and control in the UK and USA has created free rider problems of corporate control and passive (in particular, institutional) investors. Concentrations of ownership may overcome free rider problems (Shleifer and Vishny 1986) but may worsen incentives and create conflicts between majority and minority investors (Burkhart *et al.* 1996; Shleifer and Vishny 1997). Conflicts between majority and minority shareholders would arise, for example, in the case in which the majority owner derived benefits from their control of the firm other than those associated with value maximization.

It is therefore an empirical matter whether concentrations improve corporate control and performance. In a comparison of relations between executive board turnover and performance in Japanese and USA firms, Kaplan (1994) concludes that: 'To a large extent, the turnover–performance relations are economically and statistically similar in Japan and the United States. The results are not consistent with Japanese managers being more highly penalized for poor sales growth. At the level of the top several executives, the results are also not consistent with Japanese managers being less highly penalized for poor stock performance than are US managers. Because boards of directors (or the entities that control them) are responsible for hiring and firing top executives, these results suggest that boards in both countries focus on similar performance objectives' (Kaplan 1994: 528).

In a similar vein, in a study of ownership and control in Germany, Franks and Mayer (1998*b*) conclude that there is 'little relation between concentration of ownership and the disciplining of management of poorly performing firms and little relation between the type of concentrated owner and board turnover. The pronounced influence which might have been expected from the very high levels of concentration of ownership in Germany and the distinctive forms in which shares are held through banks and pyramids is not in evidence' (Franks and Mayer 1998*b*: 28).

Whatever is the significance of the pronounced international differences in concentrated ownership, it does not appear to be associated with managerial incentives and disciplining. In fact, a common theme of many of the papers in this volume (see Bratton and McCahery, Chapter 2, this volume; Roe, Chapter 5, this volume) is that the standard principal–agent view of the firm is not applicable to most countries' financial and corporate systems. The standard view sees the central problem of firm organization as aligning the interests of managers with those of the investors supplying external finance. Hellwig (2000) disputes the notion that outside financiers control firms and instead argues that concern about retaining control is a dominant influence on the way in which managers structure financial and ownership policies. Alliances between bankers, lawyers, managers, and politicians help to cement insider systems of corporate control and, far from providing external investor monitoring and control, banks in Germany reinforce managerial autonomy. Allen and Gale (2000) note that the question of how managers can be best motivated to act in shareholder interests simply does not apply in many countries' corporate systems and, even in the UK and USA, is not relevant to many legal forms, including not-for-profit organizations and mutuals.

Recently, a third factor has been introduced into international comparisons of finance and control: the variation in legal systems across countries. La Porta *et al.* (1997) argue that the nature and operation of financial systems are related to differences in the degree of investor protection across countries, that is, the extent of protection of minorities. Legal rules vary systematically across countries depending on whether they are of English, French, German, or Scandinavian origin. Common law countries of the English tradition protect both shareholders and creditors the most, French civil law countries the least, and German and Scandinavian civil law countries somewhere in the middle. They find that 'civil law, and particularly French civil law, countries, have both the weakest investor protections and the least developed capital markets, especially as compared to common law countries' (La Porta *et al.* 1997: 1149). They argue that greater legal protection of minority owners implies less need for ownership concentration, which increases access of companies to external finance and reduces capital costs.

The studies referred to above from the comparative governance and finance literature have documented substantial and persistent differences in the extent of bank involvement in the corporate sector, in the extent of ownership concentration, and in the legal protection of investors. Yet, attempts to pin down the mechanisms linking differences in structure to performance outcomes have been less successful.

3. FINANCIAL DEVELOPMENT AND ECONOMIC GROWTH

Over the last few years, a literature has begun to emerge that attempts to use data from a large number of countries to establish the relevance of financial and legal systems for economic growth. The work has its origins in Goldsmith (1969) who correlated the relation between the size of financial systems, as measured by the ratio of the value of intermediary assets to GNP, and economic growth in thirty-five countries over the period 1860–1963. He reports a positive association but there are several obvious problems with Goldsmith's analysis. First, while the period of study is long, the sample size is small; second, the direction of causation is unclear; and, third, there is no control for other factors that might influence growth. In a series of studies, King and Levine have attempted to address these problems.

King and Levine (1993*a–c*) examine the growth of eighty countries over the period 1960–89. They use four measures of financial development: The first is the ratio of liquid liabilities to GDP, which measures the scale of financial intermediation in different countries. The second is the proportion of domestic credit outside of the central bank, which captures the development of a financial system beyond a central banking function. The third and fourth variables measure the allocation of credit to the private rather than the public sector (the ratio of claims on the non-financial private sector to domestic credit control and the ratio of gross claims on the private sector to GDP). In separate equations, three measures of growth (real per capita GDP growth, growth in capital stock per person, and total factor productivity growth) are regressed on the average values of these variables over the period 1960–89. The equations control for a range of other influences on growth, including initial income, education, government expenditure, inflation, and trade propensities.

King and Levine report a strong positive relation between the three measures of growth and the four measures of financial development. They also examine the extent to which financial development at the start of the period in 1960 predicts growth in the subsequent thirty years. They conclude, 'the initial level of financial development is a good predictor of subsequent rates of economic growth, physical capital accumulation and economic efficiency improvements over the next thirty years' (Levine 1997: 707).

There have been two studies that have looked at the significance of securities markets as well as bank development on economic growth. Levine and Zervos (1998) report the influence of stock markets as measured by their size (ratio of market capitalization to GDP) and value traded (as a proportion of GDP) as well as bank credit on economic growth across more than forty countries over the period 1976–93. They find that value traded is positively and significantly related to growth even when market capitalization is included in the equation. They conclude that 'stock market liquidity and banking development are both positively and robustly correlated with contemporaneous and future rates of economic growth... and since measures of stock market liquidity and banking development both enter the growth regressions significantly, the findings suggest that banks provide different financial services from those provided by stock markets' (Levine and Zervos 1998: 554).

Rajan and Zingales (1998) argue that despite the inclusion of other variables, there may be a problem of controlling for omitted variables, such as saving rates, in the above regressions. Instead, they focus on one way in which financial development may affect economic growth: via external finance. They argue that financial development should be most relevant to industries that are dependent on external finance and that these industries should grow fastest in countries with well-developed financial systems. They therefore look at thirty-six individual industries in forty-one different countries and examine the influence of the interaction between the external financial dependence of those industries and the financial development of the countries on the growth rates of those industries in the different countries over the period 1980–90. Rajan and Zingales use three measures of financial development of a country: the ratio of market capitalization to GDP, domestic credit to the private sector over GDP, and accounting standards. They measure financial dependence of an industry by the amount of external finance raised by firms in different industries in the

USA. They use the USA on the grounds that it has the best-developed capital markets in the world and that its firms face the least friction in raising finance. The USA therefore provides the purest measure of the true financing needs of industries.

Controlling for other influences on economic growth by including dummy variables for industries and countries, Rajan and Zingales report a strong relation between economic growth in different industries and countries and the interaction of financial development of countries and the financial dependence of industries. There is a particularly strong relation when accounting standards are used as the measure of financial development of countries. They conclude that their results 'suggest that financial development has a substantial supportive influence on the rate of economic growth and this works, at least partly, by reducing the cost of external finance to financially dependent firms' (Rajan and Zingales 1998: 584).

Demirgüç-Kunt and Maksimovic (1998) use firm level data to evaluate the influence of financial systems on growth. They estimate the excess growth of a firm over and above that which can be internally financed (with a zero dividend distribution) and from short-term finance (assuming that the firm maintains its current short-term borrowing to asset ratio). They examine the influence of market capitalization to GDP ratios, stock market turnover and bank deposits to GDP in thirty countries over the period 1980–95 on the excess growth of firms in those countries over the period 1986–91. They find that both stock market turnover and the size of the banking system are positively related to excess growth. They also include a measure of law and order (the extent to which the legal system of a country allows disputes to be mediated and contracts to be enforced) and find that this variable is also positively associated with excess growth. They conclude, 'an active stock market and a well-developed legal system are important in facilitating firm growth. Firms in countries that have active stock markets and high ratings for compliance with legal norms are able to obtain external funds and grow faster' (Demirgüç-Kunt and Maksimovic 1998: 2134).

More generally, Demirgüç-Kunt and Maksimovic (1999) provide support for Rajan and Zingales' (1998) argument that financial development may influence economic growth through external financing. They examine the amount and maturity of debt of firms in thirty countries over the period 1980–91 and relate these to turnover on stock markets, bank assets to GDP ratios, the same law and order variable described in the previous paragraph and measures of shareholder and creditor rights. They find that stock market turnover is associated with more long-term debt amongst large but not small firms and larger banking sectors are associated with more long-term debt of small but not large firms. Banks, therefore, appear to be particularly important in the financing of small firms and stock markets in the financing of large firms.

La Porta *et al.* (1998) report that the better investor protection in common law countries is reflected in higher dividend payouts than in civil law countries and lower dividend payouts by high than low growth companies in common but not civil law countries. Better investor protection therefore makes dividends more responsive to the investment needs of companies.

In sum, large sample, cross-country analyses that include developing as well as developed countries record a strong relation between financial development and economic growth. The Demirgüç-Kunt and Maksimovic (1999) and La Porta *et al.* (1998) studies suggest that financial and legal systems may affect different types of firms in different ways—an issue that we will address in the next section.

4. FINANCIAL SYSTEMS, CORPORATE SYSTEMS, AND TYPES OF ECONOMIC ACTIVITY: THEORY

4.1. *Financial Systems*

As noted in Section 2, a distinction is commonly drawn between bank and market oriented financial systems. Economic theory attributes a particular function to banks in monitoring corporate activities. Economies of scale in monitoring make banks more efficient monitors than individual market participants. On the other hand, as Allen (1993) notes, securities markets have the advantage of aggregating diverse views of a large number of market participants. Securities markets are therefore superior at promoting investment where there are legitimate grounds for differences in views. However, they are inefficient where good investment decisions require the costly accumulation of available information on, for example, the quality and performance of borrowers. This is an example of the way in which a bank-based system would be expected to benefit different kinds of activity from those promoted by a stock market oriented system.

Dewatripont and Maskin (1995) develop a model in which the structure of financial systems affects the degree of financial discipline imposed on firms. The structural difference that they have in mind is between a decentralized banking system with many small banks and a centralized system with one or a small number of banks. We will refer to the first as a multibank system and to the second as a single bank one. There are 'good' and 'bad' entrepreneurs and the former can choose either a fast project which is completed in one period or a slow project which takes two. The bad entrepreneur's project takes two periods to complete and is assumed to be poor. The type of project is only revealed in the period in which it is completed. In a decentralized banking system, an individual bank lacks the funds to refinance the project in the second period. In this case, Dewatripont and Maskin show that there is a credible mechanism through which banks can commit not to refinance poor projects even though refinancing would be worthwhile once the fixed costs of the project have been incurred. If a second bank is required to provide refinancing, and if costly monitoring of borrowers is necessary, then the first bank will anticipate that the returns to monitoring will have to be shared with the second bank and, hence, will have little incentive to monitor in the first place. This undermines the viability of a project requiring refinance and creates an incentive for entrepreneurs to choose only fast projects. Thus, a multibank system will impose hard budget constraints and exclude poor projects—but at the cost of also excluding efficient projects that are slow to generate revenues and require refinancing.

Multibank systems are therefore superior in imposing tough budget constraints on inefficient projects but are too short-termist in failing to sustain efficient long-term projects. It is plausible that industries differ in terms of the balance between short and long-term projects. If so, then the Dewatripont–Maskin model suggests that an economy with many small banks will be one in which industries with more short-term projects will be fostered whereas industries characterized by longer-term investment projects will fare better in an economy with a few large banks.

Huang and Xu (1999) describe a similar model but in this case activities differ not in the gestation of investment projects (all of which are 'slow' in the Dewatripont–Maskin sense) but in the extent of uncertainty attached to the success of projects. In their model, there are good and bad projects, the quality of which can only be ascertained by investors *ex post*. Projects can be financed by one or more banks. Huang and Xu assume that there is a choice of reorganization strategies available following a poor outcome for the project after the first period. As in the Dewatripont–Maskin model, the type of activity favoured by a multibank system hinges on the commitment not to refinance projects that turn out to be poor after the first period but which, ignoring the sunk cost, would be worth continuing. This occurs in the Huang and Xu model because each bank has access to private information that on its own is inadequate to come to a correct decision about how to reorganize a firm and where there are conflicts that discourage banks from sharing information with each other. As a consequence, multi-banks prefer to liquidate projects seeking refinancing. Since information sharing and conflicts of interest are eliminated by a single bank system, there will be no such commitment to liquidate projects that need refinance.

Where there is considerable uncertainty about returns from projects (i.e. there is a high proportion of bad projects) then the commitment to terminate projects is valuable and multi-bank systems invest more than do those with single lenders. Where uncertainty is low then single banks have more information with which to make *ex ante* investment decisions and they invest more. Multi-bank systems are therefore associated with R&D intensive industries, particularly when companies are young and uncertainty is high, and single bank systems with lower uncertainty, imitative investments.

In all of the above models, financial systems are associated with different types of corporate activities and investments. In Allen (1993), new technologies, where there are legitimate grounds for diverse expectations, benefit from securities markets or require information pooling through venture capitalists. More traditional investments, where uncertainty primarily relates to the borrower and the quality of management benefit from the economies of monitoring that banks can provide. In Dewatripont and Maskin (1995), fragmented banking systems are associated with short-term investments and single bank systems with long-term investments. In Huang and Xu (1999), multi-bank systems promote high-risk R&D investments and single banks lower risk, imitative investments.

4.2. *Corporate Ownership and Control*

The structure of corporate sectors, in particular the ownership and control of corporations, as well as the structure of financial systems may influence patterns of corporate activities. Using a model with many similarities to that discussed above for the financial system, Huang and Xu (1998) present a theory in which they argue that multi-investor financing dominates single investor financing of R&D when there is high uncertainty. Conversely, when investment is directed to more routine, incremental innovation, their model predicts the superiority of single investor or internal financing. The central idea in the model is the trade-off between the costs and benefits of finance from multiple external independent investors as compared with a single external investor or internal financing.

Huang and Xu focus on the benefits that come from having multiple independent investors financing the project because of their ability to commit not to refinance a project that is revealed *ex post* to be poor. It is assumed that conflicts of interest between the external investors prevent sharing of information that would make reorganization of a project revealed to be poor preferable to its liquidation. They assume that the entrepreneur learns the outcome of the R&D project earlier than those supplying the finance and will terminate the project if he knows that refinancing will not occur. The hard budget constraint that comes from multiple investors may therefore produce superior project selection because entrepreneurs terminate poor projects in a timely fashion. Just as in the single bank case described above, where there is no conflict of interest between investors (which is true if there is a single investor or the project is internally financed), information about the optimal reorganization strategy in the event of project failure will be shared, implying that entrepreneurs face a soft budget constraint. If there is little riskiness associated with the R&D project, this source of inefficiency may be outweighed by the lower costs of internal or single investor finance.

It is clear that the model closely parallels the one described above for multi- and single banks. Multiple investors will assist in the financing of high-risk projects where there is considerable uncertainty about quality and a significant fraction of projects will need to be terminated. Where risks are small then single investors can offer lower cost sources of finance. Huang and Xu therefore predict that single-investor financing will be observed during catch-up stages of development when R&D primarily takes the form of imitation but that multi-investor finance will dominate in economies at advanced stages of development that are undertaking higher risk R&D.

Concentration of ownership and of voting rights also affects the balance between preserving and transferring control rights. Large blockholders can preserve their control over firms, while markets in control are possible when ownership is dispersed. Incentives for owners to monitor and control are greater where ownership is concentrated and concentrated owners can display a greater degree of commitment to other stakeholders than dispersed shareholders. Unlike dispersed shareholders, large blockholders cannot anonymously withdraw from past commitments (see Franks and Mayer 1998). Activities that require a high level of irreversible investment by other stakeholders, in, for example, human skill formation and knowledge about customer markets, therefore benefit from having large committed rather than dispersed anonymous shareholders.

Rajan and Zingales (1998) argue that the 'new corporations' which rely heavily on high level human capital skills require different governance and control structures from traditional corporations that primarily employ physical assets. For example, restrictions on control by outside shareholders may be required to encourage investments by managers that shareholders would reject in favour of other options. But they also provide other examples in which the holders of human capital in the firm are so powerful that ownership by outsiders with no specific investments in the company is required for efficiency.

Flexibility in the implementation of new technologies without commitments to those associated with past production processes can be more easily implemented by dispersed anonymous shareholders than identifiable large shareholders. Stock markets will therefore be well suited to activities for which changes in control are warranted because, for instance, the qualities required for good management of established activities are quite different from those of an entrepreneurial company. The scientific knowledge required to start up a high

Table 14.1. *The association of different financial and corporate systems with corporate activities*

Financial and corporate systems	Benefit activities that require
Market systems	Diverse assessments and hard budget constraints
Banking systems	Monitoring by single party
Dispersed ownership	Hard budget constraints, flexibility in control
Concentrated ownership	Active governance and commitment

tech firm may, for example, be quite different from the management skill needed to run the same firm at a later date.

The arguments presented in this section suggest that there will be an association between financial systems, corporate systems, and corporate activities (Table 14.1). Where active involvement and high levels of commitment of owners in corporate governance are required then private benefits of control can be preserved through concentrated ownership or single bank systems. Where activities benefit from the diverse assessments of many investors, the imposition of hard budget constraints and flexibility in changing control then market finance, a fragmented multi-bank system and dispersed ownership will be observed. The former is particularly associated with long-term investments in relatively low risk, well-established activities and with R&D focused on incremental innovation. It is therefore best suited to more traditional manufacturing activities. The latter is better suited to shorter-term investments and to high-risk activities where R&D is directed towards more radical innovation.

Legal systems reinforce these effects. Those with the greatest degree of investor protection promote activities that are funded and controlled through the market; those with lesser investor protection encourage activities that require active corporate governance and bank finance.

5. FINANCIAL SYSTEMS, CORPORATE SYSTEMS, AND TYPES OF ECONOMIC ACTIVITY: EMPIRICAL EVIDENCE

Carlin and Mayer (1999) perform the first empirical analysis of the relation between the composition of economic activity and financial, corporate, and legal systems. To pursue the hypothesis that different systems might favour industries with different kinds of characteristics, they examine the interrelation between types of systems, the nature of different industries and the levels of activity in those industries in different countries.

Building on the theories described in Section 4, Carlin and Mayer evaluate whether there is a relationship between the growth rates of industries in different countries and the interaction between country structures (e.g. the degree of market and bank orientation of their financial systems) and industry characteristics (the dependence of industries on external equity or bank debt sources of finance and inputs of skilled labour). For example, it was suggested earlier that firms that are dependent on high levels of skilled labour would benefit from the commitment provided by concentrated ownership. In a cross-country context, Carlin and Mayer therefore ask whether industries identified as skill-intensive flourish in countries where ownership structures are concentrated, relative to the same industries in countries with dispersed ownership structures and relative to other industries that do not depend on high level skills.

Specifically they define:

$Y = k \times i$ matrix of i industrial growth rates in k countries
$X = s \times k$ matrix of s country structural features in k countries
$Z = c \times i$ matrix of c industry characteristics in i industries

They estimate B, the $s \times c$ matrix, which relates country structural characteristics and industry financing variables to industry growth rates in particular countries in the equation

$$Y = XBZ + \varepsilon$$

where ε is the error term in the regression. The basic sample comprises fourteen OECD countries and twenty-seven 3-digit industries over the period 1970–95.

The structure of different countries' financial systems (matrix X) is measured by the size of their stock markets, accounting standards, the ratio of bank credit to GDP and the degree of bank ownership of corporate equity. The structure of corporate systems is captured by the degree of concentration of ownership and by the extent of pyramid ownership. The characteristics of legal systems are measured in two ways: first, by indicators of legal protection of investors or creditors and second, by the common or civil law origin of the legal system as indicated by its source in English, German, Scandinavian, or French law.

There are positive correlations between the market capitalization/GDP ratio and a measure of accounting standards (0.29), between bank–firm ties (as measured by bank ownership of non-financial firms) and the ratio of credit to GDP (0.68), and between ownership concentration and a measure of the presence of pyramidal ownership structures (0.52). By contrast, there are negative correlations between accounting standards and the credit/GDP ratio (−0.46) and between accounting standards and ownership concentration (−0.20). There is a very low correlation between ownership concentration and the size of the banking sector (−0.04). These correlations are broadly consistent with the view that some clusters of institutional characteristics are found together in some countries and other clusters in other countries.

The characteristics of industries (matrix Z) are captured by the amount of external equity and bank finance and investment in skills in different industries. In line with the ideas discussed in Section 4, industries may differ in their underlying characteristics such as the uncertainty associated with R&D or the tendency for investment projects to be short- or long-lived or their reliance on human capital. Carlin and Mayer use as proxies for the different characteristics of industries the role of equity finance and bank loans as sources of investment finance and the use of skills (measured by the proportion of employees with off and on-the-job training) where these characteristics are measured in countries where institutional structures are thought to be most conducive to their elastic supply. In principle, one wants to establish the extent to which industries that face no institutional constraints use external sources of finance and invest in skills. In practice, one cannot observe these. Instead, Carlin and Mayer measure these variables in those countries in which institutional constraints are likely to be least binding: firms are thought to have easiest access to market sources of external finance in the USA, to bank loans in Japan and to skilled labour in Germany. The scale of external finance and skills in different industries is therefore measured in these three countries. For the twenty-seven industries, the correlation between equity dependent and bank-financed industries is 0.07, between equity dependent and skill-intensive industries is 0.17 and between bank-financed and skill-intensive industries is −0.46.

By creating interactive variables between the country structures and industry characteristics, the paper examines whether there is any interrelation between these variables and performance, as measured by the growth rates of industries in different countries over the period 1970–95. Growth rates in twenty-seven industries in fourteen OECD countries are regressed on the product of interactive variables between country structures and industry characteristics. The initial shares of industries in different countries are included in the growth regressions to account for catch-up and regression to the mean effects. Controls are provided for other variables by taking the difference of all of the variables from their respective means across the entire samples.

The paper reports strong evidence of a relation between industry growth rates in different countries and the interaction of country structures with industry characteristics. There is a particularly strong interactive effect of the country variables accounting standards and concentration of ownership with two industry characteristics—equity finance and skills. This means that industries that are dependent on equity finance and are skill-intensive grow particularly rapidly in countries with a large number of accounting standards and high levels of concentration of ownership. Information disclosure and ownership concentrations are associated with high growth rates of industries that are dependent on market finance and skill-intensive labour forces. These results are consistent with the thesis that market based financial systems are suited to activities in which there is a need for forms of finance that involve diverse assessments by a large number of participants. It is also consistent with concentrations of ownership benefiting activities that require investments to be made by other stakeholders, in this case employees.

The paper then performs similar analyses of the determinants of fixed investment shares and R&D shares (as a proportion of value added) in the twenty-seven different industries (fifteen for R&D) and fourteen OECD countries. The interactions between country structure and industry characteristic variables account for a far higher proportion of the variation in R&D than in fixed investment across industries and countries. The influence of country structures on industry growth rates therefore appears to come via R&D rather than FCF expenditures. This is further reflected in a similar relation of accounting standards to R&D as was reported above for growth. As in the growth equation, industries with high levels of external equity finance and that use skilled labour intensively have high R&D shares in countries with a large number of accounting standards. The relation with skills is particularly pronounced when the skills measure is restricted to the proportion of the workforce with the highest levels of qualifications. This suggests that information disclosure assists in the financing of the advanced skill training that is required in R&D. Unlike growth, there is no relation of concentration of ownership to R&D suggesting that concentrations of ownership provide the commitment that is required to encourage investment by the labour force and firms in basic but not the more mobile advanced skills training.

Consistent with the theories of Dewatripont and Maskin (1995), and Huang and Xu (1998), market systems that impose tight budget constraints are associated with higher growth in industries that are dependent on market sources of finance and investments in skills training. One interpretation of the finding that R&D levels are high relative to industry and country means in countries with high accounting standards in equity dependent and skill-intensive industries is the superiority of hard budget constraints for promoting R&D when there is high technological uncertainty, as suggested by Huang and Xu. It is plausible that equity dependent and high-skill intensive industries are those in which technological development is characterized by high uncertainty. Concentrations of ownership are associated with growth in industries requiring investments in less advanced skills training.

The paper repeats the analysis of the relation of growth to interactive country and industry variables on a set of four countries that were at an earlier stage of development as measured by GDP per capita in 1970 than the fourteen used in the above analysis. It records that the influence of concentration of ownership and banking structures is quite different from that found in developed countries. High levels of concentration of ownership are associated with lower rates of growth of industries that are dependent on external equity finance and skills in low GDP countries. Consistent with Huang and Xu (1998), the potential soft budget constraints associated with high concentrations of owners therefore act to the disadvantage of these industries in countries in their early stages of development. In addition, consistent with Gerschenkron's (1962) and Huang and Xu's (1999) theses on the role of banks in initial stages of development, there is evidence of higher rates of growth of bank dependent industries in the bank oriented developing but not developed countries.

Finally, the paper examines the influence of legal structures on industry growth rates and investment. A positive influence of investor protection is found in both the growth and R&D regressions. In the case of growth, it is associated with skill-intensive industries and in the case of R&D with equity financed industries. This supports the view that investor protection reinforces the effects of financial and corporate structures by promoting growth in external financed and skill-intensive industries through R&D expenditures. There is also some evidence that creditor protection promotes capital expenditure in skill-intensive industries.

Consistent with the theories of Section 4, support has therefore been found for an influence of the structure of financial, corporate, and legal systems on the composition of industrial activity. Market oriented financial systems are associated with high growth of external equity financed and skill-intensive industries. The effect comes through investment in R&D rather than fixed capital expenditures. High concentrations of ownership are also associated with high growth of these industries in developed countries but low growth of these industries in developing countries. Furthermore, their influence does not come via R&D even in developed countries. This suggests that, as predicted by Huang and Xu (1998), concentrations of ownership are associated with the growth of relatively low risk activities.

6. CONCLUSION

This chapter has provided an overview of the emerging literature on the influence of financial, corporate, and legal systems on economic performance in different countries. There has been considerable discussion over a long period of time of the influence of financial systems on economic performance. Nevertheless, as noted in Section 2, international comparisons of financial and corporate systems in developed countries fail to reveal clear effects of financial or corporate structures on economic performance. On the basis of this, one might conclude, as Allen and Gale (2000) do, that no financial or governance system performs particularly well in controlling agency problems and that solutions have to be sought elsewhere, in, for example, product market competition.

But the studies reported in Section 3 paint a rather different picture. There, empirical analyses pointed consistently to an important role for financial development in economic performance. There is a clear relation between economic growth across countries and the development of both banking systems and securities markets.

In Section 4, we described the emerging theoretical literature on the relation between financial and corporate systems and types of economic activity. Market oriented financial systems and those with dispersed ownership are expected to be associated with high risk R&D type activities where the imposition of tight budget constraints are important. Bank oriented systems and those with concentrated ownership should be associated with longer-term investment of a more imitative nature, where commitments to other stakeholders are required.

Section 5 reported the first empirical evidence in support of these theoretical propositions. There is clear evidence of an association between different financial and corporate systems and types of economic activity. Market oriented systems are associated with high growth of external equity dependent and high skill industries and this effect is associated with R&D effort. High concentrations of ownership are also associated with high growth of these industries in developed but not developing countries and the effect is not associated with R&D.

While empirical analyses of the relation between financial and corporate systems and types of economic activity are at a preliminary stage, if they are supported by further evidence then they have important policy implications. In particular, they imply that there is not necessarily a dominant financial and corporate system that is appropriate to all economies or all industries within an economy. What is right for a developed economy may be quite inappropriate for a developing one. What is suited to an innovative R&D intensive economy may be ill-suited to a more imitative one. There may be important trade-offs in matching systems with the industrial bases of countries and their stages of economic development and regulatory and legal policies towards financial and corporate systems need to be sensitive to these potential impacts on corporate activities.

Note

1. See also Caves and Uekusa (1976) and Nakatani (1984).

ACKNOWLEDGEMENTS

The research for this project was funded from a donation from the Peter Moores Foundation to the Said Business School. We are very grateful to Esra Erdem for excellent research assistance on this and related projects and to Marco Becht, Vicenc Salas, and Xavier Vives for comments on a previous version of this chapter.

References

Allen, F. (1993). Stock markets and resource allocation. In C. Mayer and X. Vives (ed.), *Capital Markets and Financial Intermediation.* Cambridge: Cambridge University Press.

Allen, F., and Gale, D. (2000). Corporate governance and competition. In X. Vives (ed.), *Corporate Governance: Theoritical Emprical Perspectives.* Cambridge: Cambridge University Press.

Becht, M., and Roell, A. (1999). Blockholdings in Europe: An international comparison. *European Economic Review* 43: 1049.

Burkhart, M., Gromb, D., and Panunzi, F. (1996). Large shareholder monitoring and the value of the firm. *Quarterly Journal of Economics* 112: 693.

Carlin, W., and Mayer, C. (1999). Finance, investment and growth. Mimeo.

Caves, R., and Uekusa, M. (1976). *Industrial Organisation in Japan.* Washington, D.C.: Brookings.

Clapham, J. H. (1936). *The Economic Development of France and Germany, 1815–1914.* Cambridge: Cambridge University Press.

Demirgüç-Kunt, A., and Maksimovic, V. (1999). Law, finance and firm growth. *Journal of Finance* 53: 2107.

——— (1999). Institutions, financial markets and firm debt maturity. *Journal of Financial Economics* 54: 295.

Dewatripont, M., and Maskin, E. (1995). Credit efficiency in centralised and decentralised economies. *Review of Economic Studies* 62: 541.

Edwards, J., and Fischer, K. (1994). *Banks, Finance and Investment in Germany.* Cambridge: Cambridge University Press.

—— and Ogilvie, S. (1996). Universal banks and German industrialization: A reappraisal. *Economic History Review* 49: 427.

Franks, J., and Mayer, C. (1998*a*). Ownership and control in Europe. In P. Newman (ed.), *The New Palgrave Dictionary of Economics and the Law.* Macmillan: London.

——— (1998*b*). Ownership and control of German corporations. Mimeo.

Gerschenkron, A. (1962). *Economic Backwardness in Historical Perspective.* Cambridge, MA: Harvard University Press.

Goldsmith, R. (1969). *Financial Structure and Development.* New Haven, CT: Yale University Press.

Hellwig, M. (2000). On the economics and politics of corporate finance and corporate control. In X. Vives (ed.), *Corporate Governance: Theoretical and Emprical Perspectives.* Cambridge: Cambridge University Press.

Hoshi, T., Kashyap, A., and Scharfstein, D. (1990). The role of banks in reducing the costs of financial distress in Japan. *Journal of Financial Economics* 27: 67.

Huang, H., and Xu, C. (1998). Financing mechanisms and R&D investment. London School of Economics, Mimeo.

——— (1999). Institutions, innovations and growth. *American Economic Review* 89: 438.

Jefferys, J. (1938). Trends in business organisation in Great Britain since 1856. University of London, Ph.D. Dissertation.

Kaplan, S. (1994). Top executive rewards and firm performance: A comparison of Japan and the United States. *Journal of Political Economy* 102: 510.

Kennedy, W. (1987). *Industrial Structure, Capital Markets and the Origins of British Economic Decline.* Cambridge: Cambridge University Press.

King, R., and Levine, R. (1993*a*). Financial intermediation and economic development. In C. Mayer and X. Vives (ed.), *Capital Markets and Financial Intermediation.* Cambridge: Cambridge University Press.

———(1993*b*). Finance and growth: Schumpeter might be right. *Quarterly Journal of Economics* 108: 717.

———(1993*c*). Finance, entrepreneurship and growth: Theory and evidence. *Journal of Monetary Economics* 32: 513.

La Porta, R., Lopez-de-Silanes, F., and Shleifer, A. (1999). Corporate ownership around the world. *Journal of Finance* 54: 471.

——and Vishny, R. (1997). Legal determinants of external finance. *Journal of Finance* 52: 1131.

——(1998). Agency problems and dividend policies around the world. Harvard University, Mimeo.

Levine, R. (1997). Financial development and economic growth: Views and agenda. *Journal of Economic Literature* 35: 688.

——and Zervos, S. (1998). Stock markets, banks, and economic growth. *American Economic Review* 88: 537.

Lucas, R. (1988). On the mechanics of economic development. *Journal of Monetary Economics* 22: 3.

Nakatani, I. (1984). The role of financial corporate groupings. In M. Aoki (ed.), *Economic Analysis of the Japanese Firm.* New York: North Holland.

Rajan, R., and Zingales, L. (1998). Financial dependence and growth. *American Economic Review* 88: 559.

Schumpeter, J. (1912, 1931). *Theory of Economic Development.* Cambridge, MA: Harvard University Press.

Shleifer, A., and Vishny, R. (1986). Large shareholders and corporate control. *Journal of Political Economy* 94: 461.

———(1997). A survey of corporate governance. *Journal of Finance* 52: 1131.

Veblen, T. (1919). Captains of finance and the engineers. *Dial* (June).

Weinstein, D., and Yafeh, Y. (1998). On the costs of a bank centred financial system: Evidence from the changing main bank relationships in Japan. *Journal of Finance* 53: 635.

15

Law and Equity Markets: A Simple Model

DAVIDE LOMBARDO AND MARCO PAGANO

1. INTRODUCTION

Recent research in corporate finance has highlighted the importance of legal institutions and judicial enforcement for the performance of capital markets. Equity markets are generally thought to be the most sensitive to the legal provisions in favour of financiers and to the effectiveness of judicial enforcement of these provisions.

By definition, shareholders are residual claimants to the income stream generated by companies: their income rights are less tightly specified than those of debt holders. Therefore, they are more exposed to the danger of opportunistic behaviour by managers, be it diversion of corporate resources or non-value-maximizing decisions (such as nepotistic appointments, pursuit of unprofitable 'pet' projects, low managerial effort, etc.). The main limit to such opportunistic behaviour is the set of legal rules protecting shareholders (often referred to as corporate governance legal standards), the effectiveness of courts in enforcing such rules, and the ability of shareholders to verify if their rights have been violated. The latter in turn depends on the transparency of corporate accounts and on the quality and timeliness of the information that companies disseminate.

It is generally believed that improving corporate governance rules, their enforcement and the quality of accounting standards should result in greater reliance on equity financing by companies. This could occur either because such institutional changes directly limit the amount of corporate resources diverted by managers or because they allow shareholders to monitor managers more cheaply and effectively. The hypothesis that stronger protection of shareholder rights leads to a broader market for external equity is central to the recent work by La Porta, Lopez de Silanes, Shleifer and Vishny (henceforth LLSV, 1997). It is present also in Modigliani and Perotti (1997), Carlin and Mayer (1999), Demirgüç-Kunt and Maksimovic (1998), Rajan and Zingales (1998), and Tadesse (1999).[1]

The presumption that better corporate governance rules and stricter judicial enforcement should lead to a larger amount of equity funding appears reasonable, being borne out by a host of microeconomic models of agency costs in corporate finance, starting with the seminal paper by Jensen and Meckling (1976). However, the literature has been silent on the effect that such improvements in the institutional framework should have on the equilibrium rate of return on equity and on the cost of capital faced by companies. This is not surprising, considering that microeconomic models of corporate finance take the opportunity cost of funds as exogenously given. For instance, Jensen and Meckling (1976) portray financiers as competing risk-neutral individuals who require companies to pay an expected rate of return (net of agency costs) equal to the interest rate, and the latter is assumed to be fixed. Perhaps this has induced many to presume that the rate of return on equity is unaffected by changes in the legal environment.

However, this need not be true if one shifts focus from a single company to the equity market as a whole. In this chapter, we show that the effect of the legal environment on the return on equity depends on the specific mechanism through which this change impacts the equity market. For instance, consider two different experiments. The first is a reduction of the private benefits that managers can extract from the company, for instance by introducing legal limits to transactions with other companies that may dilute the income rights of minority shareholders (mergers, asset sales, etc.). The second experiment is a reduction of the legal and auditing costs that shareholders must bear to prevent managerial opportunism. Such cost reduction may for example result from the introduction of class action suits or voting by mail. These two types of institutional changes can have opposite effects on the observed equilibrium rate of return on equity, controlling for undiversifiable risk, even though they both reduce agency costs and boost the size of the equity market.

We also show that the size of these effects on the equilibrium rate of return is increasing in the degree of international segmentation of equity markets. In fact, a by-product of our analysis is the conclusion that the magnitude of these effects provides new evidence on the degree of international segmentation of stock markets.

The degree of international integration also determines who gains and who loses from legal reforms, and therefore who will support or resist them. For instance, if legal rules are unexpectedly changed so as to reduce managerial diversion of corporate resources, in a fully integrated economy the gains are entirely reflected in an increase of stock prices (with no change in the rate of return) and therefore are reaped only by existing shareholders. In contrast, in an internationally segmented stock market, only a fraction of the benefits materializes in a stock price increase: the remainder translates into an increase of the expected rate of return, which accrues to future shareholders as well.

Apart from the intrinsic interest for the explanation of the international cross-section of stock returns, these issues are clearly relevant for the investing community. For instance, in a companion paper (Lombardo and Pagano, 2000), we find evidence that respect for the law and judicial efficiency are positively associated with the risk-adjusted return on equity. This suggests that fund managers and individual investors should stay away from countries with a poor legal environment and low corporate governance standards. To put it differently, there is an equity premium to good legal institutions. To the extent that investors are aware of such empirical regularity, international net equity flows should be directed to countries that are in the process of improving their legal and judicial systems. If so, the payoffs to such improvements include not only a broader local stock market, but also one that is more closely integrated in world capital markets.

The chapter is organized as follows. In Section 2, we present a simple model that allows us to analyse the effects of changes in the legal environment on equity market equilibrium. In Section 3, we study the relevant comparative statics in the benchmark case of a stock market fully integrated within world markets. In Section 4, we turn to the case of an internationally segmented equity market. In Section 5 we describe the effects of an increase in international integration. In Section 6 we show how this analytical framework can be used to interpret the empirical findings of LLSV (1997) and those of Lombardo and Pagano (2000). Section 7 concludes.

2. THE MODEL

Consider a simple environment with two countries: a small country, populated by N_h domestic investors, and the rest of the world, populated by N_w investors. A fraction λ of these N_w investors is able to invest also in the home market. We call these investors 'global' and subscript their asset demands by g. The remaining $(1-\lambda)N_w$ foreign investors only invest on the world market, because transaction or information costs prevent them from accessing the home market. We subscript their asset demands by f. Therefore, λ is an index of international integration (with $\lambda = 0$ there is no international presence in the home market; with $\lambda = 1$, the two markets are fully integrated). Throughout, asset demands have two subscripts: the first refers to the country where the asset is traded and the second to the investor's type. For instance, x_{hg} denotes the global investors' holdings of the home stock and x_{hf} the amount of the same asset held by foreign 'non-global' investors.

The rate of return on home equity $\widetilde{R}_h$ is a random variable with mean $1+\mu_h$ and standard deviation σ_h. Symmetrically, the rate of return on the world portfolio $\widetilde{R}_w$ is a random variable with mean $1+\mu_w$ and standard deviation σ_w. The covariance between the two rates of return is denoted by σ_{hw}.

The rate of return $\widetilde{R}_h$ is the cash flow that investors receive per dollar of their initial investment in home equity, net of any private benefits taken by the company's management. We assume that this cash flow can be entirely appropriated by managers as private benefits, unless shareholders pay legal and auditing costs c per dollar invested in home market equities.[2] One can think of these costs as lawyers' and accountants' fees needed to verify the truthfulness of the company's accounts.[3] However, payment of these fees does not fully eliminate the agency problem. Managers can still divert a fraction d of the investments' proceeds to their benefit. Therefore, the cost c merely ensures that no less than a fraction $1-d$ of the total returns is paid to shareholders.

Since the focus of the analysis is on the home equity market, we assume that in the foreign market there are neither agency problems (foreign managers do not steal) nor legal and auditing costs to secure payment from managers (foreign lawyers and accountants are free). Both assumptions are irrelevant to our results and just simplify the notation.

2.1. *Portfolio Choice*

To make the model as simple as possible, we assume that investors have mean–variance utility.[4] The problem of the representative j-type investor ($j = \{h, g, f\}$) is then

$$\underset{x_{hj}, x_{wj}}{\text{Max}}\ \text{E}(\widetilde{W}_{1j}) - \frac{b}{2}\text{Var}(\widetilde{W}_{1j}) - cx_{hj}, \tag{15.1}$$

where $\widetilde{W}_{1j}$ is the value of investor j's terminal wealth, b is an index for the investors' degree of risk aversion, x_{hj} and x_{wj} are the amounts she invests in the home and the world market respectively. The expected value of terminal wealth is

$$E(\widetilde{W}_{1j}) = (W_{0j} - x_{hj} - x_{wj})(1+r) + x_{hj}(1+\mu_h) + x_{wj}(1+\mu_w) \tag{15.2}$$

and its variance is

$$\mathrm{Var}(\widetilde{W}_{1j}) = \sigma_h^2 x_{hj}^2 + \sigma_w^2 x_{wj}^2 + 2\sigma_{hw} x_{hj} x_{wj}. \tag{15.3}$$

The foreign investor with no access to the domestic market, that is, investor f, has the additional constraint that her holdings of the domestic assets are zero: $x_{hf} = 0$.

By combining the first order conditions of the different types of investors, we can express the home market expected return as a function of the supply of equity funding to domestic companies (X_h^S) and of their 'beta' with the world stock market (see the Appendix for derivations):

$$\mu_h = r + c + b\left(\sigma_h^2 - \frac{\sigma_{hw}^2}{\sigma_w^2}\right)\frac{X_h^S}{N_h + \lambda N_w} + \beta_h(\mu_w - r), \tag{15.4}$$

where $\beta_h \equiv \sigma_{hw}/\sigma_w^2$, and the term in parenthesis is positive if the home market is less than perfectly correlated with the world market.

Equation (15.4) has the interpretation of an equity supply schedule: the required return on equity is an increasing function of the per capita funding supplied to domestic corporations by domestic and global investors. As the international integration parameter λ increases, this supply curve flattens out. With more foreign investors, the domestic equity risk borne by each of them decreases. In the limit it becomes negligible if their number N_w is very large compared to the funds supplied to domestic companies, that is, $X_h^S/(N_h + N_w) \approx 0$. Thus, with complete international integration the supply of equity funding becomes perfectly elastic.

2.2. *Demand for Equity Finance by Companies*

We model the other side of the stock market in the domestic economy in the simplest possible fashion. There is a continuum of entrepreneurs in the home market, each endowed with an investment opportunity requiring 100 per cent outside financing (the continuum assumption ensures price taking behaviour). The profit per unit of physical capital invested in project j (for $j \in [1, 2, \ldots, J]$) is a random variable, with expectation $1 + \pi_j$, and variance σ^2. The cost of a unit of physical capital is standardized at 1. Each investment project j has a maximum size s. Projects are ranked according to their profitability, so that, for $j \geqslant j'$, $\pi_j \leqslant \pi_j'$. For each j, there are $n(j)$ entrepreneurs with projects yielding π_j and therefore $N(j) = \int_0^j n(s)ds$ entrepreneurs with projects yielding at most π_j. All projects are perfectly correlated, so that in the eyes of the investors they are perfect substitutes, and therefore in equilibrium pay the same expected rate of return to investors.

The projects' profitability is increasing in the efficiency of the legal and judiciary institutions, measured by an index L. The idea is that a reduction in the resources needed to enforce breached contracts expands the production opportunity set of companies, and thereby their profitability. For instance, if default on leasing contracts is promptly sanctioned by courts, companies can rent their machinery rather than own it, which may be more efficient in some settings. Formally, we assume that $\pi_j = \pi_j(L)$, where π_j is increasing in L.

Recall that managers divert at most a fraction d of the company's cash flow to their own benefit, provided shareholders pay the auditing cost c per dollar invested. Investors rationally anticipate this diversion of resources, and therefore expect the company to distribute a liquidating dividend equal to $(1+\pi_j)(1-d)$ per share. Since investors are perfectly competitive, entrepreneurs can sell their shares at a price such that they all yield the same expected rate of return,[5] to be denoted by r^e. Thus, the market price of a share in project j is:

$$p_j = \frac{(1+\pi_j)(1-d)}{1+r^e}, \tag{15.5}$$

so that shares in firms with higher profitability command a proportionately higher price. Entrepreneurs with such projects capture the present value (PV) of the associated rents when they sell their shares.

The marginal project j^* that obtains financing has a market value per share equal to the replacement cost of capital (which is 1 by assumption), and thus generates no rents for the relevant entrepreneur:

$$p_j^* = 1 \Leftrightarrow 1+r^e = (1+\pi_j^*)(1-d), \tag{15.6}$$

which just says that profit-maximizing investment decisions require Tobin's q to be equal to 1. This decision rule implies a downward sloping demand for equity funding by the corporate sector as function of the expected required return on equity r^e:

$$X_h^D = \int_0^{j*} s \cdot p_j \cdot dN(j). \tag{15.7}$$

The aggregate demand for equity, X_h^D, is decreasing in r^e for two reasons. First, the price of each share is decreasing in the required rate of return r^e, from eqn (15.5). Second, the upper integration limit j^* in eqn (15.7) is itself decreasing in r^e, from eqn (15.6): as the required rate of return increases, the profitability of the marginal project must increase, so that fewer projects can be financed. Consider an example where $n(j)$ is a constant n and $\pi(j)$ is linear in j, according to the function $\pi(j) = \overline{\pi} - j$. Then the total demand for equity in (15.7) is:

$$X_h^D = \frac{sn}{2}\left(\frac{(1-d)(1+\overline{\pi})^2}{1+r^e} - \frac{1+r^e}{1-d}\right),$$

where the two effects of r^e just described are captured in the two terms inside the parenthesis.

Rewriting eqn (15.6) in terms of expected return, we obtain

$$r^e = \pi_j^* - d(1+\pi_j^*). \tag{15.8}$$

The private benefit d drives a wedge between the expected profitability of capital and the rate of return that can be credibly pledged to outside investors, just as a tax would do.

Graphically, this implies that the profitability of physical capital lies uniformly above the demand schedule expressed by the entrepreneurs as shown in Figs 15.1–15.6 (to be discussed below). The bottom line (the demand schedule) indicates the rate of return that investors expect to make on their investment. The top line (the expected profitability schedule) indicates the rate of return on companies' investment, gross of the diversion effected by managers. The distance between the two curves depends on the magnitude of *d*: they collapse to a single locus if $d=0$, that is, when managers can extract no private benefits. As *d* increases, therefore, the required profitability of the marginal project $\pi_j{}^*$ must increase, for given r^e: since the marginal expected profitability is a decreasing function of *j*, it is immediate that the marginal *j* is negatively related to *d*, that is, agency costs reduce investment.

The equilibrium rate of return and quantity are determined by the intersection of the demand schedule in eqn (15.8) and the supply schedule in eqn (15.4), that is, imposing the condition that $X_h^D = X_h^S$. This is equivalent to setting the required rate of return r^e anticipated by entrepreneurs equal to the expected rate of return required by investors, μ_h. In the figures this intersection (initially) occurs at point A. The equilibrium rate of return expected by investors can be read off their supply curve at point A (μ_{h0}). But this is only one component of the hurdle rate that the marginal project must pay in equilibrium. This hurdle rate must also include the expected amount diverted by managers. Graphically, the equilibrium hurdle rate is read off the expected profitability schedule, at point B (η_{h0}). It is the 'shadow' cost of capital to domestic companies, in that it determines the marginal project that they carry out. The tax-like wedge between the shadow cost of capital and the expected return paid to investors measures the severity of the agency problem in the equity market.[6]

2.3. *Effects of the Legal System on the Equity Market*

The legal system of the home market can affect the equity market in three different ways. First, it may affect the fraction of corporate profits that managers are able to divert. For instance, legal limits to managerial discretion concerning asset sales or merger agreements may curtail the scope for dilution of minority shareholders' income rights. Our model can capture an improvement of the legal system along this dimension—a reduction in managerial private benefits—by a reduction of the parameter *d*.

Second, the legal environment determines the legal and auditing costs that shareholders must incur in order to secure any payment from managers. For example, better accounting standards lower the cost of monitoring the company's performance, by reducing the need to rely on expensive expert advice by accountants, lawyers, and financial analysts. Similarly, the availability of class action suits and the possibility of voting by mail reduce the cost of shareholder activism. In our model, a reduction in auditing and legal costs is reflected in a lower value for the parameter *c*.

Finally, quite apart from its effects on the agency problem between managers and shareholders, better law enforcement may benefit companies by expanding the set of contracts with suppliers and customers that can be enforced in court. Equivalently, it can reduce the cost of enforcing these contracts. *Ex ante*, this makes a wider menu of transactions available to each company, which in general will increase its profitability. We capture this by an increase in the index of legal and judicial efficiency *L*, which raises the marginal productivity of physical capital and therefore the demand for equity funding by domestic firms.

In the next two sections, we use the model to study the effects of these three different factors of the equilibrium on the domestic equity market. We do so first under the assumption of perfect international integration of the equity market and then under the assumption of internationally segmented equity market.

3. AN INTERNATIONALLY INTEGRATED EQUITY MARKET

As explained in commenting on eqn (15.4) above, the equity supply schedule is flat when $\lambda = 1$ (the case of complete international integration), assuming that the number of foreign investors is large relative to the size of the domestic stock market. This case is depicted in Figs 15.1–15.3. In all three figures, the expected profitability of capital exceeds the demand for equity finance by companies. Of course, it is along the latter curve that one reads the rate of return that investors expect to receive from companies.

Figure 15.1 shows how the equilibrium of the equity market is affected by the ability of the legal system to constrain managerial diversion, as reflected in different levels of the parameter *d*. Countries with a lower level of managerial diversion (lower *d*) feature a demand curve closer to the expected profitability schedule. The associated equilibrium point is C instead of A. The rate of return earned by investors is the same irrespective of

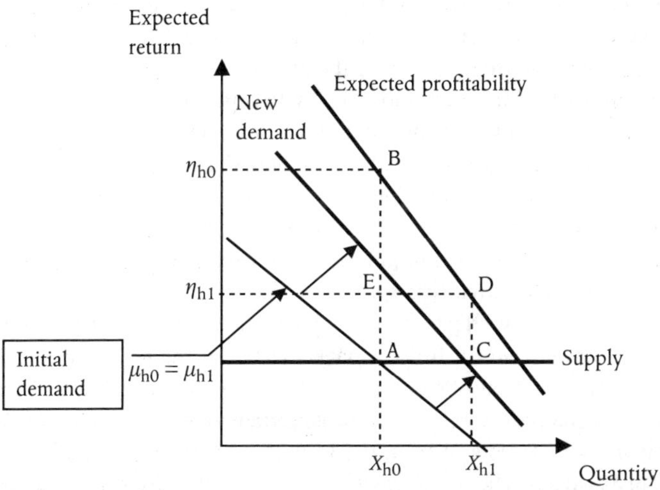

Figure 15.1. *Reduction of private benefits under international integration.*
This figure depicts the effects of an improvement in the legal and judicial system that reduces the fraction d of the company's profits that the manager can divert. After this improvement, managers can credibly commit to return more resources to outside investors: the demand for funds schedule shifts outward. The reduction in d shifts the equilibrium point from A to C. The rate of return stays constant at μ_{h0}, but the cost of equity capital decreases from η_{h0} (corresponding to point B) to η_{h1} (point D). The equilibrium amount of equity finance increases from X_{h0} to X_{h1}.

managerial diversion, due to the perfectly elastic supply of funds. Investors are willing to supply any amount of equity at the going expected rate of return. Therefore, a lower d results only in a higher equilibrium amount of equity: X_{h1} instead of X_{h0}.

Moreover, in countries where managers can extract less private benefits, a higher number of projects get financed, because the cost of capital (which equals the expected profitability of the marginal project, namely $\pi_j{}^*$) is lower: η_{h1} (point D) instead of η_{h0} (point B).[7] Projects that are not a fair investment opportunity in a jurisdiction where managers extract large private benefits are competitive when managerial discretion is curtailed. In terms of eqn (15.8), j^* and $N(j^*)$ are larger in countries where d is lower.

A lower level of d is also associated with a higher welfare for society as a whole. The gain stems from the projects that are funded in the low-d country but not in the high-d one. In the figure it is represented by the trapezoid ABDC, which is the integral of the expected profits net of the rate of return paid to shareholders (the social opportunity cost of capital). This welfare gain is entirely appropriated by the owner-managers of the additional projects, either in the form of additional private benefits or in the form of higher sale prices of equities. The owner-managers of infra-marginal projects are equally well-off in the two countries: what they fail to receive as private benefits in the low-d country, they gain in the form of a higher initial price of equities to the investing public. As a result, the low-d equilibrium is Pareto-superior relative to the high-d equilibrium.

This does not mean, however, that if a country starts with a legal system that allows high diversion, there will be no losers from a transition to a low-diversion regime. Consider, in fact, an unanticipated reduction in d. In this case, the initial entrepreneurs with infra-marginal projects have already sold their shares at a price that discounted extraction of high private benefits. Therefore, they fail to reap the benefit of the regime change, which accrues instead to the investors who bought those shares. In contrast, entrepreneurs who could not get funding before the regime change and obtain it under the new regime will gain. As a result, the change in legislation will be supported by the investing public and by entrepreneurs who currently cannot get funding, but will be fought by currently active entrepreneurs. Bebchuk (1999) and LLSV (1999) also stress that controlling groups have the incentive to oppose legal reform in order to protect their private benefits of control, especially when these are currently large.

Figure 15.2 illustrates the effects of a reduction in the auditing and legal costs that shareholders face to secure payment from managers (a fall in the parameter c). This change reduces the expected total rate of return required by investors, since they will need to spend fewer resources to enforce their claims. The equilibrium moves from point A to point C: the rate of return on equity is reduced (from μ_{h0} to μ_{h1}), while the quantity of equity financing increases from X_{h0} to X_{h1}. The cost of equity capital to firms is also reduced, from η_{h0} (point B) to η_{h1} (point D).

The distribution of welfare gains and losses is quite different relative to the previous case. Entrepreneurs of already active companies do not lose their private benefits, while their shareholders earn a capital gain (as before) and newly active entrepreneurs gain (as before). As a result, everyone is better off, except for lawyers and accountants!

Figure 15.3 shows the effect of a change in the legal regime that increases the profitability of investment, without affecting the agency problem between managers and shareholders.

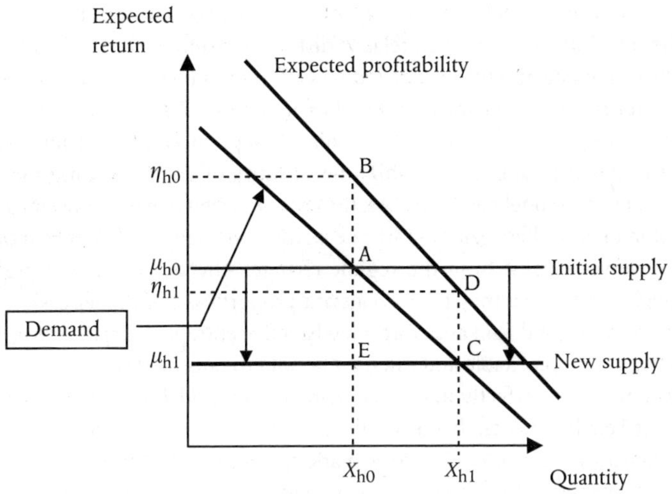

Figure 15.2. *Reduction of legal and auditing costs under international integration.*
This figure depicts the effects of a reduction in the legal and auditing costs needed to monitor managerial conduct. The investors' supply of funds schedule shifts downward. The (expected) rate of return decreases (it goes from μ_{h0} to μ_{h1}, as the equilibrium point moves from point A to point C). The cost of equity capital to firms decreases, from η_{h0} (corresponding to point B) to η_{h1} (point D). The equilibrium amount of equity finance increases from X_{h0} to X_{h1}.

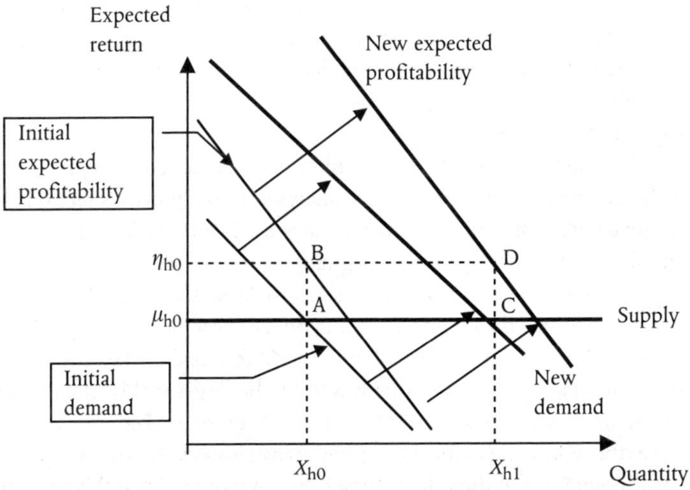

Figure 15.3. *Increase in expected profitability under international integration.*
This figure depicts the effects of an improvement of the legal system that increases the marginal productivity of capital. This is captured by an outward shift of the expected profitability of capital schedule. The associated increase in the demand for equity capital shifts the equilibrium point from A to C. The (expected) rate of return does not change (stays at μ_{h0}). Also, the cost of capital remains at the initial level. The equilibrium amount of equity finance increases from X_{h0} to X_{h1}.

In this case both the schedule for the expected profitability of physical capital and the demand schedule shift outward. Their relative distance remains unchanged, in the sense that the net-of-diversion rate of return generated by each project (which is read off the demand-for-funds curve) is a constant fraction $1-d$ of its expected profitability. Following this regime change, the equilibrium shifts from point A to point C. Once again, the investors' rate of return stays constant at μ_{h0}, while the quantity of equity funding increases from X_{h0} to X_{h1}. Under the model's assumptions, the cost of capital remains constant at η_{h0}.[8]

The distribution of welfare gains in this case is still more even-handed than in the previous experiment: everyone gains from the regime change. Already active entrepreneurs earn larger private benefits since they take a constant proportion d of bigger cash flows. Their shareholders reap a capital gain as before. Newly active entrepreneurs also gain, since their projects become more profitable and can now be sold to outside investors.

In conclusion, under perfectly integrated markets, our model predicts that any improvement in the legal environment either leaves the expected rate of return unchanged, or reduces it, while it increases the size of the stock market. It also increases the amount of capital invested by companies, while lowering their shadow cost of equity capital or leaving it unchanged.

4. AN INTERNATIONALLY SEGMENTED EQUITY MARKET

In this section, we consider a country that is not fully integrated in the world equity markets. Due to information asymmetries or other prohibitive transaction costs, only a small fraction λ of the world investors can access the domestic equity market. Under this scenario, the supply of equity funds to domestic companies is upward sloping, as can be seen from eqn (15.4). The restricted pool of investors that buys domestic shares requires a higher rate of return, the higher is the total amount of funding provided, because that translates into a higher per capita risk to be borne.

Figure 15.4 illustrates that the effect on equilibrium of a reduction in private benefits is now quite different from the benchmark case analysed in the previous section. The equilibrium return on equity is now inversely related to the private benefits d that managers can extract: in the figure, it increases from μ_{h0} (point A) to μ_{h1} (point C). The equilibrium amount of equity finance also increases (from X_{h0} to X_{h1}). The breakdown of the effect between the rate of return and amount of funding depends on the slope of the supply function, and therefore on the size of the pool of investors in the local market: the less integrated is the country in international markets (the lower λ), the larger will be the increase of the rate of return and the lower that of the size of the local equity market.

While it raises the return on equity, the regime change lowers the cost of capital from η_{h0} (point B) to η_{h1} (point D), and thereby increases the amount of physical investment taking place in the economy. The latter effect on the cost of equity capital has the same sign as in the corresponding experiment of Fig. 15.1.

The welfare and distributional consequences of a reduction in managerial diversion also differ relative to the case of perfect international integration, illustrated in Fig. 15.1. Consider two countries that have a different level of d but are otherwise identical. The low-d country as a whole is better off: in Fig. 15.4, a measure of the extra surplus enjoyed relative

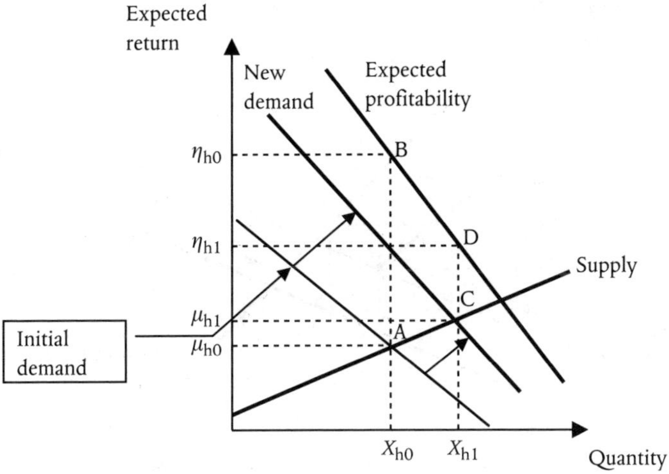

Figure 15.4. *Reduction of private benefits under international segmentation.*
This figure depicts the effects of an improvement in the legal and judicial system that reduces the fraction d of the company's profits that the manager can divert. After this improvement, managers can credibly commit to return more resources to outside investors: the demand for funds schedule shifts outward. The reduction in d shifts the observed equilibrium point from A to C. The rate of return increases from μ_{h0} to μ_{h1} but the cost of equity capital decreases from η_{h0} (corresponding to point B) to η_{h1} (point D). The equilibrium amount of equity finance increases from X_{h0} to X_{h1}.

to the high-*d* country is the area of the trapezoid ABDC. However, entrepreneurs who can get funding in both countries are worse off in the low-*d* country: not only do they consume a lower amount of perks, but also face a higher discount rate when selling their shares, and therefore get a lower price for them. Entrepreneurs who are active only in the low-*d* country are clearly better off than their counterparts in the high-*d* country. Similarly, investors are unambiguously better off in the low-*d* country, since they earn a higher expected rate of return (they bear more risk, but gain a surplus corresponding to the area of the trapezoid $\mu_{h0}\mu_{h1}CA$). The presence of winners and losers contrasts with the result obtained for the same comparison in the previous section, where we found that the low-*d* economy Pareto-dominated the high-*d* economy. However, the distributional effects of an unexpected transition from a high-*d* to a low-*d* regime are qualitatively similar to those of the internationally integrated economy. Already active entrepreneurs will stand to lose from the reform, while investors and newly active entrepreneurs will gain.

In Fig. 15.5 we analyse the effect of a reduction of the legal and auditing costs faced by shareholders. As in the internationally integrated economy, the equilibrium rate of return on equity falls from μ_{h0} (point A) to μ_{h1} (point C), while the quantity of equity financing increases from X_{h0} to X_{h1}. The cost of equity capital to firms is also reduced, from η_{h0} (point B) to η_{h1} (point D).

Finally, Fig. 15.6 illustrates the effects of an improvement in the legal and judicial system that increases the profitability of investment, without affecting the agency problem between

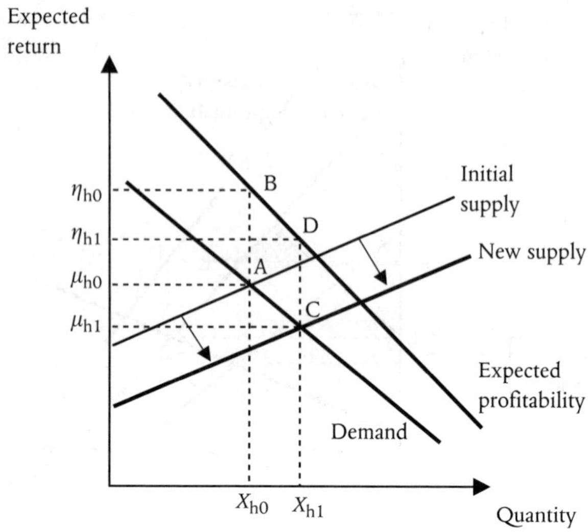

Figure 15.5. *Reduction of legal and auditing costs under international segmentation.*
This figure depicts the effects of a reduction in the legal and auditing costs needed to monitor managerial conduct. The investors' supply of funds schedule shifts downward and to the right. The (expected) rate of return decreases (it goes from μ_{h0} to μ_{h1}, as the equilibrium point moves from point A to point C). The cost of equity capital to firms decreases, from η_{h0} (corresponding to point B) to η_{h1} (point D). The equilibrium amount of equity finance increases from X_{h0} to X_{h1}.

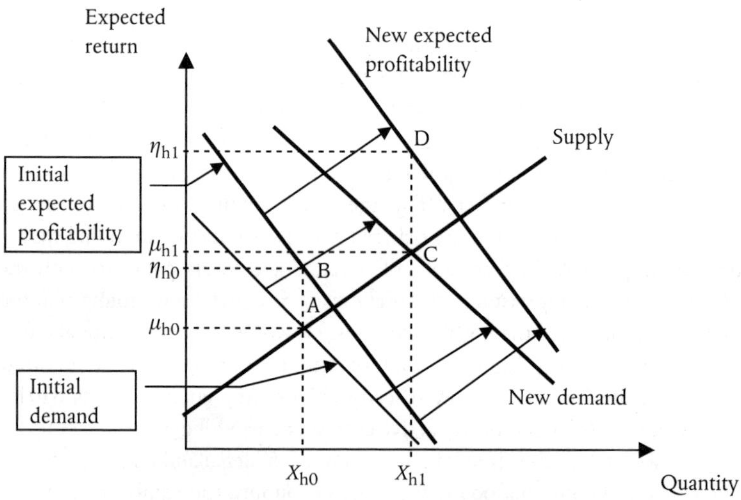

Figure 15.6. *Increase in expected profitability under international segmentation.*
This figure depicts the effects of an improvement of the legal system that increases the marginal productivity of capital. This is captured by an outward shift of the expected profitability schedule. The associated increase in the demand for equity capital shifts the equilibrium point from A to C. The (expected) rate of return increases (from μ_{h0} to μ_{h1}). The cost of capital increases, from η_{h0} (point B) to η_{h1} (point D). The equilibrium amount of equity finance increases from X_{h0} to X_{h1}.

the managers and their shareholders. As in Fig. 15.3, the regime change is represented by an outward shift of the expected profitability and the demand-for-funds schedules. In contrast with the case of Fig. 15.3, however, both the equilibrium rate of return paid to shareholders and the cost of equity capital relevant for firms' investment decisions increase. The rate of return moves from point A to point C, while the cost of capital moves from point B to point D. While the positive implications of the regime change are different from those in Fig. 15.3, the welfare implications are similar: everyone gains from it.

Summarizing, the novel prediction of the model with international segmentation is that improvements in the legal regime can bring about increases in the expected rate of return on equity. This happens when the scope for diversion by managers is reduced or when the legal regime change increases the expected profitability of investment.

5. EFFECTS OF INTERNATIONAL INTEGRATION

Our model can also be used to analyse the impact of increased international integration on the domestic equity market equilibrium, for a given legal environment. Lately, this issue has received increasing attention in research. Stulz (1999) highlights that globalization can raise domestic share prices via two channels. First, increased diversification opportunities reduce the required rate of return by lowering the risk premium (if the idiosyncratic variance of the liberalizing market exceeds its covariance with the world equity market). This increases equity prices by lowering the discount factor applied to a given stream of future cash flows. Second, exposure to international markets raises the pressure on managers to maximize shareholder value, because foreign investors have superior monitoring ability as well as resources to take over inefficiently managed companies. This second channel impacts stock prices by increasing the stream of cash flows that domestic companies will pay out to shareholders.

Our model easily captures the two mechanisms described by Stulz (1999). The increased diversification amounts to an increase in the fraction λ of foreign investors who access the domestic market. In Fig. 15.7, this flattens the supply of equity schedule (assuming that λ rises to its maximal value 1) and moves the equilibrium point from A to E, reducing both the expected return on equity (from μ_{h0} to μ_{h1}) and the cost of equity capital (from η_{h0} to η_{h1}). The reduction in the rate of return on equity is precisely the fall in the discount rate mentioned by Stulz, and leads to a jump of share prices, even though the future cash flow paid to shareholders remains constant. Martin and Rey (2000) derive the same effect of integration in the context of a simple general equilibrium model. They also show that financial integration expands the sets of projects that can obtain funding in equilibrium, as we do in Fig. 15.7.

To the extent that financial integration also increases the scrutiny of managers by investors, it should reduce the fraction d of private benefits, as suggested by Stulz. In Fig. 15.7, this is shown as an outward shift of the demand-for-funds schedule. This additional effect does not modify the rate of return received by investors but it further increases the stock price and the equilibrium amount of equity finance (from X_{h1} to X_{h2}). It also contributes to the reduction in the cost of equity capital (from η_{h1} to η_{h2}).

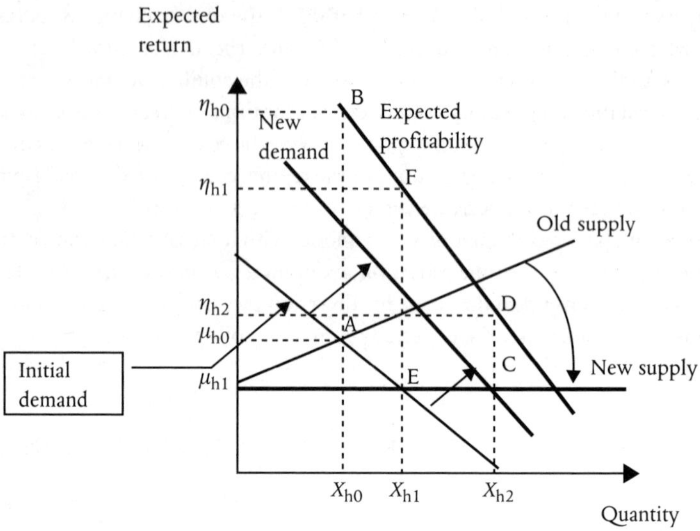

Figure 15.7. *Increase in international integration.*

This figure shows the effects of an increase in the degree of international integration. We consider two possible scenarios. In the first scenario, international integration only flattens the supply of equity finance, due to improved risk diversification. The equilibrium point moves from A to E, reducing both the equilibrium expected return on equity (from μ_{h0} to μ_{h1}) and the cost of equity capital (from η_{h0}, corresponding to point B, to η_{h1}, corresponding to point F). In the second scenario, international integration also reduces the fraction d of the company's profits that the manager can divert, so that the demand for funds schedule shifts outward. The equilibrium point moves to point C. This additional effect does not further modify the rate of return received by investors. However, it further expands the equilibrium amount of equity finance (from X_{h1} to X_{h2}) and it further reduces the cost of equity capital to companies (from η_{h1}, corresponding to point F, to η_{h2}, corresponding to point D).

6. INTERPRETING THE EVIDENCE

The model presented so far can be used to interpret the findings of cross-country empirical studies which analyse how equity markets are affected by differences in the legal system, especially in the protection of shareholders' rights, and in the degree of international integration.

First and foremost among these studies is the study by LLSV (1997), who document a positive correlation between the amount of external equity funding and indicators of the general quality of the legal environment (respect for the law and judicial efficiency) as well as specific measures of the protection of shareholder rights vis-à-vis company directors. LLSV interpret this positive correlation as resulting from the effect that better legal and judicial institutions have on the severity of agency problems between managers and external shareholders. This specific interpretation is indeed consistent with our model, as can be seen in Figs 15.1 and 15.4: a reduction in the scope for managerial diversion *d* increases the equilibrium amount of external equity. The same effect on quantities could also be caused by a reduction in the legal and auditing cost *c* that shareholders must bear to limit managerial private benefits, as shown in Figs 15.2 and 15.5. However, in our model the same relationship would also be observed even if the legal cross-country differences had no impact on the agency problems between managers and shareholders, but affected the profitability of companies via their effect on contractual relationships with downstream customers and input suppliers. This is illustrated in Figs 15.3 and 15.6.

Our model shows that, while better institutions invariably increase the equilibrium amount of external equity, they may affect the equilibrium rate of return quite differently. Their effect depends both on the degree of international integration of the domestic equity market and on whether they increase primarily the demand for equity by companies or its supply by investors. As seen above, in a perfectly integrated equity market, the effect can be either null (if the legal regime change impacts mainly the demand for equity by companies) or negative (if it translates into a reduction of the rate of return required by investors). When instead the domestic stock market is not integrated into world capital markets, an improvement in the legal environment can result either in an increased rate of return (if it affects demand for equity finance by companies) or in a decreased rate of return (if it increases the availability of equity funds supplied by investors).

So far the only empirical study investigating the cross-country relationship between the quality of institutions and the rate of return on equity is Lombardo and Pagano (2000). Their data set includes almost all the countries of the study by LLSV (1997). They find that indicators of the general quality of the legal environment have a consistently positive correlation with the risk-adjusted rate of return, whereas measures of the protection of shareholder rights have either no or negative impact on the return on equity.

Lombardo and Pagano employ two different measures of the rate of return on equity: the percentage return on each market stock index and accounting measures such as the dividend/yield ratio and the earnings/price ratio.

In regressions that use the first type of dependent variables, general measures of the quality of the legal environment appear as important explanatory factors besides betas and idiosyncratic risk. Variables measuring the protection of shareholder rights do not appear to have additional explanatory power. The correlation between respect for the law or judicial efficiency and the risk-adjusted rate of return on equity is positive and statistically significant. The implied effects are economically large. Increases in the respect for the law have a comparable impact on secondary market returns.

A second set of regressions is based on aggregate accounting measures of equity returns for developed markets alone. Despite the noise potentially present in these variables, they can still shed some light on the issue at hand. In particular, they are exempt from a bias that may plague secondary market returns in the presence of regime shifts. Suppose, for example, that some unanticipated institutional change permanently increases stock prices, leaving the required rate of return on equity unaffected. An econometrician who relies on stock return data will record a very high positive return in conjunction with the improvement in institutions. This may introduce an upward bias in the estimated relationship between a certain feature of institutions and the rate of return on equity. A positive coefficient may be found even if the true coefficient is zero.

Lombardo and Pagano find that when the rate of return on equity is measured by accounting variables, the effects of general measures of institutional quality are still positive, statistically significant and, if anything, even larger. So, for these variables, the concern just raised is not relevant. Also in this case, the LLSV index of anti-direction rights does not enter with a significant coefficient.

How can these results be interpreted in the light of the model developed in the previous sections? The positive impact of judicial efficiency and rule of law on the return on equity requires an upward sloping supply of equity by investors, that is, a substantial degree of segmentation between national stock markets. In this sense, the estimates agree with those by Bekaert and Harvey (1995), who find that the international CAPM has low explanatory power and attribute its failure to the segmentation of national markets. Harvey (1995) and Lombardo and Pagano (2000) further support the segmentation hypothesis by documenting that country-specific risk is priced in stock return regressions that include emerging markets.

The model also reveals that the positive cross-country correlation between risk-adjusted secondary market returns and quality of legal institutions can have two different (though possibly complementary) interpretations. The first one is that good laws and efficient courts curtail the private benefits of managers and controlling shareholders. The second explanation is that they improve the expected profitability of companies, and therefore the rate of return that they pay to their shareholders. This is because better laws and more effective courts expand the menu of contracts that companies can use in dealing with customers and suppliers, and reduce the cost of enforcing these contracts. One cannot tell which of these two effects dominates in the data, but there is no reason to attribute the observed correlation entirely to the effect of legal institutions on the agency problem between managers and shareholders. This note of caution applies also to the positive correlation between the breadth of equity markets and the quality of legal enforcement documented by LLSV (1997).

From a practical point of view, the presence of an equity premium to good legal institutions implies that fund managers and individual investors can earn a higher risk-adjusted rate of return by investing in countries with a sound legal environment and high corporate governance standards. Rather than compensating shareholders for a less investor-friendly environment, markets with poor legal standards pay them lower rates of return, once the implied risk is taken into account. To the extent that investors are aware of this, they should overweight companies incorporated in countries with superior legal and judicial systems. By the same token, international net equity flows should be directed to countries that are improving their legal and judicial systems, even if this process is perfectly anticipated.

These empirical findings also help to uncover the welfare consequences of a change in legal standards and judicial effectiveness. It is often thought that the costs of corporate insiders' opportunism are ultimately borne by the controlling shareholders themselves, in the form of a lower valuation for their shares, while the rate of return obtained by outside shareholders is unaffected. In contrast, these results, together with the model presented in the previous sections, suggest that the agency costs associated with legal laxity and judicial ineffectiveness fall upon outside shareholders, at least partly. By the same token, the investing community is bound to reap some of the advantages stemming from improvements in legal and judicial infrastructure. This may explain the investors' heightened interest for corporate governance rules and practices around the world.

7. CONCLUSIONS

We have presented a simple model to analyse the impact that the law and its enforcement have on equilibrium quantities and rates of returns in equity markets. Improvements in the legal system, while invariably associated with broader equity markets, have different effects on equity returns depending on the institutional change being considered and on the degree of international stock market segmentation.

The model is useful to interpret the results of recent empirical work, such as La Porta *et al.* (2000) and Lombardo and Pagano (2000). In particular, it can rationalize the observed cross-country pattern, whereby better institutions are associated both with broader equity markets and higher risk-adjusted returns on equity. This result is shown to be consistent with market equilibrium only if national equity markets are imperfectly integrated in the world market. In this case, the supply of equity finance to companies is described by an upward-sloping function, so that a larger demand for equity finance by companies is associated with a higher required return.

Our analysis identifies two distinct reasons why better legal institutions may be associated with a higher demand for equity finance by companies. First, good laws and efficient courts curtail the private benefits of managers, and this in turn increases both the return that companies pay to external shareholders and the availability of external equity finance. Second, better laws and more effective courts expand the menu of contracts that companies can use in dealing with customers and suppliers, and reduce the cost of enforcing these contracts. This makes companies more profitable, and hence raises their rate of return and the amount of financing they attract. One cannot tell which of these two effects dominates in the data, but there is no reason to attribute the observed correlation solely to the effect of legal institutions on companies' financial relationships.

Appendix

In this appendix, we spell out the derivations involved in obtaining eqn (15.4) in the text. The problems of the representative home investor and of the representative global investor are:

$$\underset{x_{hj},x_{wj}}{\text{Max}}\ \text{E}(\widetilde{W}_{1j}) - \frac{b}{2}\text{Var}(\widetilde{W}_{1j}) - cx_{hj}, \quad j=\{\text{h},\text{g}\}, \tag{15.a1}$$

where $(\widetilde{W}_{1j})$ is the value of investor j's terminal wealth, x_{hj} and x_{wj} are the amounts she invests in the home and the world market respectively. The expected value of terminal wealth is:

$$\text{E}(\widetilde{W}_{1j}) = (W_{0j} - x_{hj} - x_{wj})(1+r) + x_{hj}(1+\mu_h) + x_{wj}(1+\mu_w), \tag{15.a2}$$

and its variance is

$$\mathrm{Var}(\widetilde{W}_{1j}) = \sigma_{\mathrm{h}}^2 x_{\mathrm{h}\,j}^2 + \sigma_{\mathrm{w}}^2 x_{\mathrm{w}j}^2 + 2\sigma_{\mathrm{hw}} x_{\mathrm{h}\,j} x_{\mathrm{w}j}. \tag{15.a3}$$

Rearranging the first-order conditions of the above maximization problem, one obtains:

$$\mu_{\mathrm{h}} - r = c + b\sigma_{\mathrm{h}}^2 x_{\mathrm{h}j} + \mathrm{b}\sigma_{\mathrm{hw}} x_{\mathrm{w}j}, \tag{15.a4}$$

$$\mu_{\mathrm{w}} - r = b\sigma_{\mathrm{w}}^2 x_{\mathrm{w}j} + b\sigma_{\mathrm{hw}} x_{\mathrm{h}j}. \tag{15.a5}$$

Finally, the portfolio choice problem of the foreign investors who cannot diversify is:

$$\underset{x_{\mathrm{ww}}}{\mathrm{Max}}\ \mathrm{E}(\widetilde{W}_{1\mathrm{f}}) - \frac{b}{2}\mathrm{Var}(\widetilde{W}_{1\mathrm{f}}) \tag{15.a6}$$

subject to

$$\mathrm{E}(\widetilde{W}_{1\mathrm{f}}) = (W_{0\mathrm{f}} - x_{\mathrm{wf}})(1+r) + x_{\mathrm{wf}}(1+\mu_{\mathrm{w}}) \tag{15.a7}$$

and

$$\mathrm{Var}(\widetilde{W}_{1\mathrm{f}}) = \sigma_{\mathrm{w}}^2 x_{\mathrm{wf}}^2. \tag{15.a8}$$

Her first-order condition yields:

$$\mu_{\mathrm{w}} - r = b\sigma_{\mathrm{w}}^2 x_{\mathrm{wf}}. \tag{15.a9}$$

We define the total investment in the two stocks h and w respectively as:

$$N_{\mathrm{h}} x_{\mathrm{hh}} + \lambda N_{\mathrm{w}} x_{\mathrm{hg}} = X_{\mathrm{h}}, \tag{15.a10}$$

$$N_{\mathrm{h}} x_{\mathrm{wh}} + \lambda N_{\mathrm{w}} x_{\mathrm{wg}} + (1-\lambda) N_{\mathrm{w}} x_{\mathrm{wf}} = X_{\mathrm{w}}. \tag{15.a11}$$

Multiplying eqn (15.a4) first by N_{h} (setting $j=\mathrm{h}$) and then by λN_{w}(setting $j=\mathrm{g}$), substituting from eqns (15.a10) and (15.a11), and adding up, one obtains:

$$(N_{\mathrm{h}} + \lambda N_{\mathrm{w}})(\mu_{\mathrm{h}} - r) = (N_{\mathrm{h}} + \lambda N_{\mathrm{w}})c + b\sigma_{\mathrm{h}}^2 X_{\mathrm{h}} + b\sigma_{\mathrm{hw}}(X_{\mathrm{w}} - (1-\lambda)N_{\mathrm{w}} x_{\mathrm{wf}}). \tag{15.a12}$$

Similarly, multiplying eqn (15.a5) by N_{h} (with $j=\mathrm{h}$), (15.a5) by λN_{w} (with $j=\mathrm{g}$) and (15.a9) by $(1-\lambda)N_{\mathrm{w}}$, substituting again from eqns (15.a10) and (15.a11), and adding up, one obtains

$$(N_{\mathrm{h}} + N_{\mathrm{w}})(\mu_{\mathrm{w}} - r) = b\sigma_{\mathrm{w}}^2 X_{\mathrm{w}} + b\sigma_{\mathrm{hw}} X_{\mathrm{h}}. \tag{15.a13}$$

Replacing x_{wf} from eqn (15.a9) and X_{w} from eqn (15.a13) into eqn (15.a12) and rearranging, we obtain the home market expected return as a function of the supply of equity funding to domestic companies ($X_{\mathrm{h}}^{\mathrm{S}}$) and of its 'beta' with the world stock market:

$$\mu_{\mathrm{h}} = r + c + b\left(\sigma_{\mathrm{h}}^2 - \frac{\sigma_{\mathrm{hw}}^2}{\sigma_{\mathrm{w}}^2}\right)\frac{X_{\mathrm{h}}^{\mathrm{S}}}{N_{\mathrm{h}} + \lambda N_{\mathrm{w}}} + \beta_{\mathrm{h}}(\mu_{\mathrm{w}} - r), \tag{15.a14}$$

where $\beta_{\mathrm{h}} \equiv \sigma_{\mathrm{hw}}/\sigma_{\mathrm{w}}^2$. This is eqn (15.4) in the text.

Notes

1. For a cursory review of this literature, see Lombardo and Pagano (2000).
2. We envision a situation in which the financial resources contributed by managers and controlling shareholders are insufficient to operate companies, so that the marginal investor is an outside shareholder.
3. We sidestep the possible free-riding problem involved in monitoring management by assuming that only the shareholders who pay this cost can claim in court (or threaten to claim) the verifiable fraction $1 - d$ of the company's cash flow to which they are entitled.
4. As is well known, an utility index as the one in eqn (15.1) can either result directly from quadratic utility or from negative exponential utility and normal returns.
5. While treated parametrically by investors, the expected rate of return r^e is a variable to be determined in equilibrium.
6. Notice that the equilibrium amount of equity that investors provide to domestic companies, X_h, exceeds the value of corporate physical investment. The latter equals $N(j^*)s$, that is, the number of projects undertaken in equilibrium multiplied by their size. This does not arise from the agency problem, but from the fact that the value of outstanding equity also includes the PV of entrepreneurial rents on inframarginal companies, $X_h - N(j^*)s$.
7. As explained in the last section, with agency costs of external finance, the cost of equity capital exceeds the return that must be promised to outside investors. On top of this rate, the hurdle rate used in capital budgeting decisions will have to factor in the expected amount of private benefits taken by managers.
8. From eqn (15.6), the expected profitability of the marginal project (i.e. the cost of capital) exceeds by a fixed proportion $1 - d$ the expected rate of return paid to shareholders. Since the latter is constant in the presence of perfect international integration, the cost of capital cannot change.

References

Bebchuk, L. A. (1999). A rent-protection theory of corporate ownership and control. Harvard Law School, Center for Law, Economics and Business, Discussion Paper No. 260.

Bekaert, G., and Harvey, C. R. (1995). Time-varying world market integration. *Journal of Finance* 50: 403.

Carlin, W., and Mayer, C. (1999). Finance, investment and growth. CEPR, Discussion Paper No. 2233.

Demirgüç-Kunt, A., and Maksimovic, V. (1998). Law, finance, and firm growth. *Journal of Finance* 53: 2107.

Jensen, M., and Meckling, W. (1976). Theory of the firm: Managerial behavior, agency costs, and ownership structure. *Journal of Financial Economics* 3: 305.

Harvey, C. R. (1995). Predictable risk and return in emerging markets. *Review of Financial Studies* 8: 773.

La Porta, R., Lopez-de-Silanes, F., Shleifer, A., and Vishny, R. W. (1997). Legal determinants of external finance. *Journal of Finance* 52: 1131.

——(2000). Investor protection and corporate governance. *Journal of Financial Economics* 58: 3.

Lombardo, D., and Pagano, M. (2000). Legal determinants of the return on equity. CSEF Working Paper No. 24, http://www.dise.unisa.it/WP/wp24.pdf.

Martin, P., and Rey, H. (2000). Financial integration and asset returns. *European Economic Review* 44: 1327.

Modigliani, F., and Perotti, E. (1997). Protection of minority interests and development of security markets. *Managerial and Decision Economics* 18: 519.

Rajan, R. G., and Zingales, L. (1998). Financial dependence and growth. *American Economic Review* 88: 559.

Stulz, R. M. (1999). Globalization of equity markets and the cost of capital. *Journal of Applied Corporate Finance,* Fall, 8–25.

Tadesse, S. (1999). The information and monitoring role of capital markets. Paper presented at the 1999 WFA Meetings, Santa Monica, CA.

16

Investor Dominance and Strategic Transparency: On the Role of Corporate Governance for Product and Capital Market Competition

ENRICO PEROTTI AND ERNST-LUDWIG VON THADDEN

1. INTRODUCTION

The recent literature on the comparative advantages of different corporate governance models is an exciting area for competing ideas. Much attention has been dedicated to the comparison between the effectiveness of shareholder control over delegated monitoring by lenders. The debate over the comparative information efficiency of the two governance structures is particularly interesting. On the one hand, Diamond (1984) has argued that information gathering may be best delegated to intermediaries to avoid duplicating efforts.[1] On the other hand, the market microstructure literature has emphasized the importance of decentralized market trading to support information collection (see e.g. Holmström and Tirole 1993).

This chapter does not take a view on the quality of information gathering by banks versus markets; rather it focuses on their comparative effect on the diffusion of information. Our starting point is the widely accepted perception that bank-dominated firms are more opaque. As in Bhattacharya and Chiesa (1995), we argue that bank-dominated financing relationships are less transparent to external observers, while market financing results in more corporate information becoming known to both investors and competitors. There are many intuitive reasons for this argument. A main bank may be able to fund or arrange directly the entire investment requirement by its creditor firm, thus limiting information leakage to the market. Bank monitoring may further reduce the need for tight public transparency, and reduces the need to maintain dispersed investors constantly updated on the firm performance. Bank financing may lead to a low level of trading liquidity and this in turn may discourage information gathering by investors. For recent evidence of greater opaqueness of banks' assets, see Flannery *et al.* (1997).

This chapter adds to this list a new explanation, recognizing that, when information may be disclosed to more than one audience, it will have strategic effects in a context of imperfect competition (Bhattacharya and Ritter 1982; Gertner *et al.* 1988). Most of this literature has focused on the incentive to disclose once a firm has acquired some private information. Firms with good news prefer more or less disclosure depending on the nature of their private information. In general, firms like to signal when private information is positive, better firms may want to enhance visibility (e.g. by an initial public offering as a mean to commit to more disclosure, as in Stoughton *et al.* 1996). A counter-example is when the firm wishes to keep secret the profitability of its market to avoid entry (Gertner *et al.* 1988).

In our model we do not consider any *ex ante* information asymmetry; but we focus on the preference of the dominant investors on the *ex post* dissemination of information. In other words, companies become transparent not via direct disclosure (which may be unreliable) but indirectly via market prices. Product market competition takes place under endogenous information revelation via a simple market microstructure model, which allows us to study the interplay between market trading and strategic behaviour, and their dependence on corporate transparency policy. The model builds on the general result that under imperfect competition more opaque firms will exhibit less variability in profits and output relative to more transparent competitors (for an excellent survey, see Kühn and Vives 1994).

The economic intuition for the impact of transparency on profits is as follows. Less transparent firms reveal less to competitors on their competitive strength, which creates strategic advantages and disadvantages. When firms act on the basis of less information, their expectation over competitors' output is either too high or too low. This hurts firms which are strong, as it leads competitors to be more aggressive, forcing the firm to restrain its output; but it protects weak firms, which face less aggressive competition and can better protect their market share and profitability. As a result, under lack of transparency expected profits are lower, but the volatility of profits and output are lower as well. These results are quite robust and hold for the case of Cournot as well as Bertrand competition.

A reduced volatility (and in particular the higher profitability in the lower states) has the effect of increasing the return to all claimholders with a fixed claim on the firm. This implies that there is a natural preference by lenders for less *ex post* information dissemination, as they do not gain from higher profits but suffer from higher risk (Jensen and Meckling 1976). We are able to show that lender-dominated firms will not encourage transparency via informative prices, as this would endogenously undermine the value of lenders' claims. In contrast, firms dominated by shareholders prefer greater informativeness of prices, as information dissemination on average increases profitability as well as risk.

The well-known listing of Daimler-Benz on the NYSE, which shed light on a traditionally opaque company, is a possible example. While Deutsche Bank was the dominant investor in Daimler-Benz, it held at the time more than a quarter of the firm's equity and was thus more a shareholder than a lender.

Our main result is that competition among firms dominated by the same type of investors tends to produce symmetric equilibria in corporate transparency. Competition among equity-dominated firms generates more dissemination of information, while competition among lender-dominated firms tends to result in uninformative prices. Competition among firms with different types of dominant investors does not alter their transparency choice, although a lender's claim enjoys less protection from less public information if its firm faces a transparent competitor. Interestingly, lack of transparency relative to one's competitor does not necessarily constitute a strategic advantage. Finally, there may be interactive effects of information acquisition, leading to multiple equilibria. There are cases of strategic information complementarity where investors have an incentive to acquire information on one firm only if other investors choose to acquire information on its competitors; vice versa there are cases of strategic information substitutability when in equilibrium only one price is informative.

There are several empirical implications arising from our modelling. The main prediction is that lender-dominated firms (and firms in bank-dominated financial systems) are less transparent than equity-dominated firms (and firms in shareholder-oriented financial systems). Moreover, corporate profitability should be lower on average in bank-dominated firms, but less volatile than those in equity-dominated firms. As further equilibria exist if the level of debt is low, these predictions should be stronger, the higher the level of debt in the system.[2]

There is evidence that Japanese companies with influential main banks tend to be less profitable than more independent companies (Weinstein and Yafeh 1998) and they also tend to be less liquidity constrained (Hoshi *et al.* 1991). This is consistent with the model's suggestion that production is more supported in less profitable states under bank funding. Overall, these firms appear to have less variability in profitability and grow comparatively less than independent companies (Nakatani 1984). All these facts are consistent with our results that less transparent firms competing with more transparent rivals ought to have lower average output and profits and less volatility of economic results.

The remainder of this chapter is organized as follows. Section 2 sets out the model. In Sections 3–5 we analyse, in turn, product market competition, financial market activity, and investor choices to solve the model in the standard recursive fashion. Section 6 offers some interpretations, comparative statics, and concludes. We leave out the technical calculations needed to derive some formula in the text. They can be found in Perotti and von Thadden (2000).

2. THE MODEL

2.1. *Timing and Product Market Interaction*

The model is a dynamic game with five stages. In stage 1, the dominant investors in each firm determine the degree of *ex ante* transparency of the firm. In stage 2, firms receive some private information about their own quality (which we often refer to as its type). In stage 3, some agents in the stock market can choose to become informed about firm quality at some cost. In stage 4, there is trading in the firms' stocks, which may or may not reveal information. Finally, in stage 5, the two firms, after observing stock market prices, compete in the product market. Then, customers make their purchase, profits are realized and distributed to investors.

We consider two firms who compete on the product market. The firms produce differentiated products and act as Cournot competitors. Firms have either a high quality or a lower quality product, which has an effect on the relative attractiveness of their own product vis-à-vis their competitor's. Quality (or 'type') is described by a parameter θ_i which can take two values. When the product is of high quality, $\theta_i = \theta_H$, while $\theta_i = \theta_L$ otherwise, with $\theta_H > \theta_L$. Product quality is uncertain; *ex ante* either firm has a prior probability q of having a high quality product. The probability of high quality is common to both firms and commonly known.[3] Once output is realized, customers base their purchase on actual quality.

The inverse demand function faced by firm i is given by

$$P_i = \theta_i - Q_i - \gamma Q_j, \tag{16.1}$$

where $i = 1, 2, j \neq i$, and $-1 \leqslant \gamma \leqslant 1$. γ can be interpreted as the degree of substitutability between the firms' products, and describes the intensity of competition in the market. If $\gamma > 0$ the two goods are strategic substitutes under Cournot competition; if $\gamma < 0$, the goods are strategic complements. By inverting the demand system (eqn (16.1)) one sees that Bertrand competition has the same structure, with strategic complements becoming strategic substitutes and vice versa. Hence, although our discussion is in terms of quantity choices, the above specification covers the Bertrand case as well.[4] To simplify the exposition we will concentrate here on the case $\gamma \geqslant 0$; all our main results hold, with minor changes to some formulas, for arbitrary γ.

In order to focus on the impact of transparency on competition, we assume that productivity is constant across firms and that marginal costs for each firm are constant and normalized to zero. Finally, we assume throughout that the production decision of the firm is taken by managers who maximize profits, $\pi_i = P_i Q_i$, that is, that investors do not influence Q_i directly. This is in contrast to an important strand of the literature inspired by Brander and Lewis (1986), that analyses product market competition under the impact of capital structure. In particular, in Brander and Lewis (1986), if the firm has risky debt equity investors have an incentive to distort Q_i away from the profit-maximizing level in order to take advantage of limited liability. Since this effect is empirically not well documented and theoretically ambiguous, we choose to work with the simple assumption of profit maximization.[5]

2.2. *Capital Structure, Influence, and Information Dissemination*

Each firm has a capital structure consisting of debt and equity. The level of debt financing, given by D_i, and the allocation of governance rights (or influence) are taken to be exogenous.[6] We assume that either shareholders or lenders have a dominant influence. Thus, we interpret the dominant form of finance in terms of its governance role, or capacity to influence, rather than in terms of its explicit ownership rights or the quantity of financial capital supplied. While investor influence certainly has several different implications, we define influence here as the capacity to determine the *ex ante* transparency policy of a firm. This is a long-term choice which takes place before firms receive private information, and affects the cost and incentive for *ex post* information acquisition by market investors. A firm may choose a policy of transparency either by maintaining a broad *ex ante* disclosure policy, facilitating access to management and company resources for analysts and researchers, encouraging secondary trading in the firm's stock, list on stock exchanges with stringent disclosure requirements, etc.[7]

We assume that the governance rights enjoyed by the dominant investor are neither contractible nor transferable. This is realistic whenever, because of other contractual or legal provisions, the dominant investor always retains some discretion over long-term decisions, so that there cannot be reliable re-contracting. Thus, financial claims cannot be rearranged contingent on the information cost decision.[8]

The degree of *ex ante* transparency affects the cost of becoming informed about the firm *ex post*. For simplicity, we assume that a firm can be either transparent (T) or opaque (O) with no differential cost. As a result, the fixed cost for market investors of learning the firm's type is either K (for an opaque firm) or 0 (for a transparent firm). The revelation mechanism cannot be changed after private information is obtained.[9]

In the third period the stock market opens. We assume that both firms have traded equity. In order to simplify the information aggregation in the market, we assume that each firm has one (representative) potentially informed investor, who compares the cost of information acquisition with the expected gain from informed trading. If this investor chooses to become informed, she becomes perfectly informed about the firm's θ_i.

For the stock market interaction in stage 4, we employ the simplest possible market microstructure model in which gains on informed trading are possible.[10] We assume that in each market, in addition to the informed investor, there is a set of liquidity traders who, as an aggregate, trade a random amount $+\lambda$ or $-\lambda$ with equal probability $\frac{1}{2}$. Prices are set by a competitive market-maker at the expected future realization of the stock value, which equals final period equity return, conditional on the total order flow. When setting the price in one market, the market-maker observes the price realized in the other market.[11]

2.3. *Summary: the Game*

To wrap up the description of the model, we summarize here the five stages of the game, together with the relevant decision variables.

Stage 1: in each firm, the dominant investors choose the degree of transparency, T or O.
Stage 2: θ_1, θ_2 realized, private information of the firm.
Stage 3: in each stock, one investor chooses to become informed (I) or to remained not informed (N).
Stage 4: in each stock, a market price is realized based on liquidity trading and informed trading.
Stage 5: firms observe stock prices and compete by choosing quantities Q_i.

After the last stage, demand is realized and each individual firm's gross profits, π_i, are distributed among lenders, who hold a fixed claim D_i, and equityholders, who receive the residual.

3. PRODUCT MARKET COMPETITION

We analyse the game by solving for subgame perfect equilibria using backwards induction. Therefore, in order to understand the incentives to choose different degrees of transparency under any form of governance and to acquire and use information in the capital market, we first, in this section, examine the impact of more or less public information on product market interaction. Throughout this paper we will assume that the production decisions of the firm are taken by managers who maximize profits, $\pi_i = P_i Q_i$.[12]

From the way we have modelled capital market trading there can be only two outcomes concerning the public availability of information about a firm's θ: either an informed investor is present and her trading reveals θ completely, or there is no informed investor, in which case no information about θ is revealed. Equivalently, there is an informed investor who hides her trading motives perfectly behind liquidity trading, in which case again no information at all about θ is revealed to the market.[13] Therefore, we have two possible informational states for each firm, R (if its type θ has been revealed) or P (if its θ is still private information). In total, this yields four informational structures for market interaction, which we shall now discuss in turn.

3.1. *Competition under Symmetric Information*

We first consider competition under symmetric information, defined as a situation in which the information on each firm's θ is public, because it has been revealed through financial market activity. In order to keep the notation as simple as possible, we shall assume throughout the paper that firms produce a positive level of output whatever the constellation of (θ_1, θ_2), that is, that there is no exit. This requires assuming that demand even for a low quality product is sufficiently strong. The following assumption, which will be maintained throughout the paper, is sufficient to guarantee this in the different settings we consider later on:

$$\theta_L \geqslant \theta_H - \theta_L. \tag{16.2}$$

Both firms simultaneously choose their quantities Q_i to maximize profits, taking the other's choice as given. Hence, firm i chooses Q as to $\max_Q (\theta_i - Q - \gamma Q_j)Q$.

Firm i's behaviour will depend on its own θ and that of its competitor. We therefore have four different possible states, ij = HH, HL, LH, LL, for the interaction. It is straightforward to verify that the firm's actions in Nash equilibrium are given by

$$Q_{HL}^{RR} = \frac{1}{2+\gamma}\left(\theta_H + \frac{\gamma}{2-\gamma}(\theta_H - \theta_L)\right),$$

$$Q_{HH}^{RR} = \frac{\theta_H}{2+\gamma},$$

$$Q_{LL}^{RR} = \frac{\theta_L}{2+\gamma},$$

$$Q_{LH}^{RR} = \frac{1}{2+\gamma}\left(\theta_L - \frac{\gamma}{2-\gamma}(\theta_H - \theta_L)\right),$$

where the superscript RR denotes the fact that both firms' θ have been revealed. Q_{ij}^{RR} denotes a firm's equilibrium action if itself is of type i and its competitor of type j. The ordering of the four different output levels is intuitive. In fact, we have

$$Q_{HL}^{RR} > Q_{HH}^{RR} > Q_{LL}^{RR} > Q_{LH}^{RR},$$

where LH is the worst possible state for firm *i*, and the firm produces less than in state LL, the second worst state, etc.[14] The corresponding profits are

$$\pi_{ij}^{RR} = (Q_{ij}^{RR})^2, \tag{16.3}$$

and the ordering of equilibrium profits is the same as for equilibrium outputs.

The analysis of this standard form of market interaction is quite simple. The effect of complete information is in general to produce some implicit coordination in output decisions, as each firm conditions its production on the actual strength of its competitor's demand and thus on the competitor's ability to expand beyond its own market.

3.2. *Competition under Symmetrically Incomplete Information*

We now consider the case of competition when there is no public information about any firm's quality available. We shall index all variables by PP, as all the θ's are private information. Now, each firm makes its output decision at a time when there is imperfect information about the level of its competitor's product-specific demand θ_j. In this case each firm will choose output as a function only of its own θ_i, maximizes expected profits, and therefore produce as to $\max_Q (\theta_i - Q - \gamma E Q_j(\theta_j))Q$.

It is readily verified that the game again has a unique (Bayesian) Nash equilibrium,

$$Q_H^{PP} = \frac{1}{2+\gamma}\left(\theta_H + \frac{\gamma}{2}(1-q)(\theta_H - \theta_L)\right),$$

$$Q_L^{PP} = \frac{1}{2+\gamma}\left(\theta_L - \frac{\gamma}{2}q(\theta_H - \theta_L)\right),$$

where Q_i^{PP} denotes a firm's equilibrium action when it has quality θ_i. The corresponding profit levels in the four possible states, π_{HL}^{PP}, π_{HH}^{PP}, π_{LL}^{PP}, π_{LH}^{PP}, are obtained by straightforward computations reported in Perotti and von Thadden (1998).

As in the case of symmetric information, it is straightforward to show that these state-contingent profits are ordered as intuition suggests:

$$\pi_{HL}^{PP} > \pi_{HH}^{PP} > \pi_{LL}^{PP} > \pi_{LH}^{PP}.$$

Using the equilibrium quantities and profits derived above, it is easy to confirm the following general result from the industrial organization literature (see Kühn and Vives 1994).

Remark 1 Average output is the same in the symmetrically informed and uninformed case, while profits are both higher on average and more variable in the first case.

In brief, the main differences in strategic interaction vis-à-vis the symmetrically informed case is less aggressive output choice by the stronger firm in the most favourable state HL: thus the weaker firm is 'protected' by the lack of accurate information. In contrast, there is more output in the HH state, as both firms, attaching some probability in the event of the competitor being weak, produce more aggressively than in a transparent system. This can be interpreted as a result of 'poor coordination' due to less information, and leads to lower profitability. Thus, output in LL is lower, as both firms are too cautious due to the perceived risk of a strong competitor. Similarly, firms under uninformed competition tend to be more protected when in their weakest competitive position LH.

While profits are higher on average for weaker firms, the lack of common information leads to less coordination on output and, in the case of a very low γ, to lower profitability in state LH. In this case the competitive advantage is less than the coordination loss. From an *ex ante* perspective, however, the reduced profitability due to poor coordination in high quality states, when marginal profitability is highest, is greater than the profit gain in low quality states.

3.3. *Competition under Asymmetric Information*

The last case to consider is the asymmetric case, in which the type of one firm, say firm 1, is unknown to the market,[15] whereas the other's type is has been revealed. Now firm 1, when making its output decision, knows the state of firm 2, but firm 2 does not know θ_1. In this case, firm 1 will choose output as a function of θ_1 and θ_2 and therefore produce as to $\max_Q (\theta_1 - Q - \gamma Q_2(\theta_2))Q$, where Q depends on θ_1 and θ_2. Firm 2, on the other hand, seeks to $\max_Q (\theta_2 - Q - \gamma E_{\theta_1} Q_1(\theta_1, \theta_2))Q$, where Q depends on θ_2 only. It is straightforward (if lengthy) to show that the game has a unique (Bayesian) Nash equilibrium $(Q_H^{RP}, Q_L^{RP}, Q_{HL}^{PR}, Q_{HH}^{PR}, Q_{LL}^{PR}, Q_{LH}^{PR})$, which we spell out in Perotti and von Thadden (1998). Here, Q_i^{RP} is the equilibrium quantity produced by the firm whose θ has been revealed, if it has type $i \in \{L, H\}$, and Q_{ij}^{RP} the quantity produced by the firm with private information about its type (who faces a transparent competitor) when its own quality is i and that of its competitor j. The corresponding eight profit levels (for each state and each firm) can be found in Perotti and von Thadden (1998).

Again, it can easily be verified that equilibrium quantities and profits are ordered as in the two equilibria under symmetric information. For example, the profits of a transparent firm facing a non-transparent firm are highest when the firm has high quality and the competitor low quality, second highest when both have high quality, third highest when both have low quality, and lowest when the firm has low and its competitor high quality.

In order to understand the costs and benefits of disclosure in this context, it is useful to compare the profit levels of firm i in the case where both firms are transparent (π^{RR}) with those where firm j is transparent but firm i not (π^{PR}). It turns out that profits are more variable under fully transparent competition than under competition with asymmetric information. The reason is that by disclosing more, the firm allows its competitor to react more precisely to the situation on the product market, which makes the intercept of its residual demand more volatile (see Fried 1984; Li 1985).

What is more, one can show that profits are ordered state by state. Profits under full transparency, π^{PR}, are a 'median-preserving spread' of profits under unilateral non-transparency, π^{PR}, in the sense that π^{PR} is statewise lower than π^{PR} in the two unfavourable states (LL, LH) and statewise higher in the two favourable states (HH, HL). Thus expected profitability is always higher for the R firm than for the P firm in the strong quality state, and vice versa in the weaker quality state. The economic intuition can be expressed as follows. When in the state of high demand, a firm whose quality is revealed (R) can produce more aggressively than if it were opaque: the firm knows that its competitor is aware of its strength, and will thus restrain its output. In addition, in this case the R firm does not restrain its output when its competitor is strong, since it does not know it. On average its output turns out to be higher than under complete information. The opposite is true when the firm is weak.

In contrast, a P firm loses some market share when strong, but as in the symmetrically uninformed case, it has a higher average output when weak relative to the output of a visibly weak firm.[16] On average, competition under asymmetric information provides less protection of downside profits for an opaque firm than the symmetrically uninformed case.

4. INFORMATION AND TRADING IN THE STOCK MARKET

4.1. *Trading*

In the last but one stage of the game, one investor is either informed or uninformed about a firm's θ_i, depending on her choice to acquire information made beforehand, and interacts with uninformed liquidity traders through competitive market-makers. As mentioned earlier, we assume that the agents on the market for the stock of firm *i* observe the equilibrium stock price of firm *j* and vice versa. Suppose first that there is an informed investor in the market of, say, firm 1's stock. Given that liquidity trading is either $+\lambda$ or $-\lambda$, any trading by the informed investor which is different from $\pm\lambda$ leads to her information being revealed and her trading profits being zero. Hence, if she trades, she trades $+\lambda$ or $-\lambda$ units. It is easy to see that she maximizes trading profits by trading $-\lambda$ (shortselling) if $\theta_1 = \theta_L$ and $+\lambda$ (buying) if $\theta_1 = \theta_H$.

Whatever information is publicly available about firm 2, there are three possible trading outcomes for firm 1's stock. The first is that liquidity traders buy and that $\theta_1 = \theta_H$, which occurs with probability $\frac{1}{2}q$. In this case the aggregate order flow is $+2\lambda$ and θ_1 is fully revealed. We will denote the outcome that firm quality is fully revealed through trading by P. The second outcome, which happens with probability $\frac{1}{2}(1-q)$, is that liquidity traders and the informed investor sell, so that aggregate order flow is -2λ and θ_1 again is fully revealed. In the last case, informed trading just offsets liquidity trading and the aggregate order flow is 0. This case happens with probability $\frac{1}{2}$, and here no information about θ_1 is revealed (denoted by P: quality remains private information).

In each case, competitive market-makers set prices such that they make expected zero profits. In doing so, they take into account the available information about each firm's quality (θ_i) and the competitive structure on the product market generated by this information. Define the value of equity in the different contingencies as

$$e_{ij}^{xy} = \max(\pi_{ij}^{xy} - D, 0), \quad x, y \in \{P, R\}, \;\; i, j \in \{L, H\}, \tag{16.4}$$

where D is the firm's debt level and π_{ij}^{xy} are the firm's profits before debt, as derived in the last section, if the firm is of quality θ_i, its competitor of quality θ_j, and the availability of information about both firms' quality at the competition stage is described by $x \in \{P, R\}$ for the firm and by $y \in \{P, R\}$ for its competitor. Using this notation, the valuation of equity is straightforward.

Suppose first that the competitor's stock price is noninformative. Then the market value of the firm under consideration is equal to

$$\nu(2\lambda) = qe^{\text{RP}}_{\text{HH}} + (1-q)e^{\text{RP}}_{\text{HL}}$$

if the aggregate order flow received by the market-maker is 2λ, and, therefore, reveals the firm's quality to be θ_{H}. For an aggregate order flow of -2λ, the market value is

$$\nu(-2\lambda) = qe^{\text{RP}}_{\text{LH}} + (1-q)e^{\text{RP}}_{\text{LL}},$$

and if the aggregate order flow is 0, hence uninformative, the value is

$$\nu(0) = q^2 e^{\text{PP}}_{\text{HH}} + q(1-q)e^{\text{PP}}_{\text{HL}} + q(1-q)e^{\text{PP}}_{\text{LH}} + (1-q)^2 e^{\text{PP}}_{\text{LL}}.$$

In the first two cases, the informed investor makes zero profits on her trades, because her information is revealed fully in the aggregate order flow. In the last case, she makes positive profits at the expense of the liquidity traders.

Remark 2 An informed trader makes positive profits only in states in which the true type of the firm she trades in is not revealed.

If she has good information, her profits are

$$\begin{aligned} G_{\text{H}}(0) &= (qe^{\text{PP}}_{\text{HH}} + (1-q)e^{\text{PP}}_{\text{HL}} - \nu(0))\lambda \\ &= (1-q)(q(e^{\text{PP}}_{\text{HH}} - e^{\text{PP}}_{\text{LH}}) + (1-q)(e^{\text{PP}}_{\text{HL}} - e^{\text{PP}}_{\text{LL}}))\lambda, \end{aligned} \quad (16.5)$$

and

$$G_{\text{L}}(0) = q(q(e^{\text{PP}}_{\text{HH}} - e^{\text{PP}}_{\text{LH}}) + (1-q)(e^{\text{PP}}_{\text{HL}} - e^{\text{PP}}_{\text{LL}}))\lambda \quad (16.6)$$

if her information is negative.

The reasoning is analogous in the case where the competitor's stock price is informative. If aggregate order flows are 2λ or -2λ, the price is fully informative and an informed trader makes no profits, whereas she makes

$$G_{\text{H}j}(0) = (1-q)(e^{\text{PR}}_{\text{H}j} - e^{\text{PR}}_{\text{L}j})\lambda \quad (16.7)$$

if the aggregate order flow is uninformative, her information is good, and the competitor is revealed to be of type θ_j, $j \in \{\text{L}, \text{H}\}$. Correspondingly, if her information is bad, she makes profits of

$$G_{\text{L}j}(0) = q(e^{\text{PR}}_{\text{H}j} - e^{\text{PR}}_{\text{L}j})\lambda. \quad (16.8)$$

Remark 3 The return from informed trading is highest when the true state is the least likely state, as this produces a larger price correction; if $q = \frac{1}{2}$, the investor is indifferent between receiving good or bad news.

We can now compute the investor's expected profit from information acquisition. Consider first the case where there is no informed investor in the other market, so that the other firm's stock price will not be revealing. With probability $\frac{1}{2}$ the investor in firm 1's stock will be able to profit from her information, and expected profits are, by using eqns (16.5) and (16.6)

$$G^{N} = \tfrac{1}{2}(qG_{H}^{P}(0) + (1-q)G_{L}^{P}(0))$$

$$= q(1-q)(q(e_{HH}^{PP} - e_{LH}^{PP}) + (1-q)(e_{HL}^{PP} - e_{LL}^{PP}))\lambda, \qquad (16.9)$$

where the superscript N ('no informed investor') denotes the fact that there are no informed investors in the other market.

If there is an informed investor in the other market, the other firm's stock price will be informative with probability $\frac{1}{2}$, so expected profits for the informed investor in the first market are obtained by averaging over eqns (16.5)–(16.8).

$$G^{I} = \tfrac{1}{2}q(1-q)(q(e_{HH}^{PP} - e_{LH}^{PP}) + (1-q)(e_{HL}^{PP} - e_{LL}^{PP})$$

$$+ q(e_{HH}^{PR} - e_{LH}^{PR}) + (1-q)(e_{HL}^{PR} - e_{LL}^{PR}))\lambda, \qquad (16.10)$$

where the superscript I ('informed investor') denotes the fact that there is an informed investor in the other market.

Remark 4 The expected return from informed trading is increasing in the volume of liquidity trading λ.

This is a standard result from the literature on market microstructure. However, it acquires some interesting meaning in the context of the model, in which dominant investors may have differential preferences about the informativeness of prices. We return to this issue in the final discussion.

Remark 5 G^{I} and G^{N} are decreasing functions of γ.

The result again follows by direct computations using the explicit formulae in the appendix. Its basic intuition is simple: If competition becomes fiercer (i.e. if γ increases), corporate profits, and therefore the gains from exploiting information about these profits,decrease. What is less obvious and what the above remark brings out, is whether this basic intuition is still valid in our model of interrelated profit opportunities from information acquisition.

Clearly, the value of information about one stock depends on the trading activity in the other stock, as information on the competitor's strength affects the value of the stock. It turns out that G^{I} and G^{N} cannot be ordered in general; thus the incentives to acquire information are not quite straightforward to analyse.

4.2. *Information Collection*

Solving backwards, we now determine the outcomes of the information acquisition subgame on the stock market as a function of the firms' *ex ante* transparency policy. As described earlier, we denote the choices by the dominant investors in stage 1 by T ('transparent') and O ('opaque'). Remember that information acquisition in a T firm is costless, and in a O firm

$K > 0$. As before, we denote the decision to acquire information about a firm by I ('become informed') or N ('no information acquisition').

Proposition 1 *If $K < G^I$, G^N, then(I, I) is the only equilibrium in the information collection subgame for all possible T–O combinations.*

This case is somewhat trivial: the transparency decision has no economic effect, because information collection is cheap in any case. In the sequel, we shall not elaborate further on this case.

Proposition 2 *If G^I, $G^N < K$, then, for all possible* T–O *combinations, the unique equilibrium of the information collection subgame has* I *if the firm is* T *and* N *if* O.

This is an economically more interesting case. A firm which chooses T can be sure that there will be an informed investor, and a firm choosing O can be sure that there will be no informed investor.

A third possibility is that the cost of information gathering falls in the intermediate range. In this case each firm's share price will reflect any information revealed on the competitor's share price, so there is strategic interaction between the information gathering decisions of investors in the two stocks. This gives rise to multiple equilibria.

Proposition 3 *(a) If $G^N < K < G^I$, then (I, I) is an equilibrium of the information collection subgame for all possible* T–O *combinations. In addition, if both firms are opaque* (O, O)*, then* (N, N) *is also an equilibrium. As a result, in this case there is also an equilibrium in mixed strategies, where the probability of choosing* I *equals $x = (K - G^N)/(G^I - G^N)$.*

(b) If $G^I < K < G^N$, then (I, I) is the unique equilibrium of the information collection subgame if both firms are transparent (T, T)*.* (I, N) *is the unique equilibrium in the asymmetric case* (T, O)*, and* (I, N) *and* (N, I) *are the equilibria for* (O, O)*. In the case* (O, O) *there is also an equilibrium in mixed strategies, in which both investors choose to become informed with mixing probability $x = (G^N - K)/(G^N - G^I)$.*

The proofs of all the above three propositions follow immediately from elementary comparisons of costs and benefits in the four possible transparency combinations at stage 3.

While in the case of Proposition 2 the transparency decision in stage 1 determines the incentives for information acquisition unambiguously, Proposition 3 reflects the interesting intermediate case where the transparency decision by the dominant investor has some impact on information acquisition but is not completely decisive.

In general, I is a dominant strategy if the firm is transparent (T), whatever the information structure realized in the other market. The intuition is simply that transparency makes information acquisition inexpensive, and liquidity traders ensure that it is profitable. What is noteworthy is the possibility of multiple equilibria in information gathering when the firm is opaque. The nature of these equilibria depends on the ordering of G^I and G^N, and thus on the complementary or exclusionary nature of information acquisition in the two markets.

In case (a) ($G^N < G^I$), information acquisition is complementary across markets: investing in information about an opaque firm is profitable if and only if information is also acquired in the other market. In this case, investors may coordinate on information gathering, leading potentially to complete revelation, even when firms attempted to remain opaque. In case (b) ($G^{N} > G^{I}$), information acquisition in the two markets is exclusionary: investing in information about an opaque firm is profitable if and only if no information is acquired in the other market.

Comparing eqns (16.9) and (16.10) we see that $G^{I} > G^{N}$ if and only if

$$q(e_{HH}^{PR} - e_{LH}^{PR}) + (1-q)(e_{HL}^{PR} - e_{LL}^{PR}) > q(e_{HH}^{PP} - e_{LH}^{PP}) + (1-q)(e_{HL}^{PP} - e_{LL}^{PP}). \quad (16.11)$$

The left-hand side of eqn (16.11) reflects the value of information acquisition if an informed investor trades in the other market, and the right-hand side value of information if there is no such investor in the other market.[17]

The difference in the attractiveness of information gathering can be reinterpreted as the expected difference in the variation of the stock price under PR competition relative to PP competition. Intuitively, informed trading profits depend on the expected price 'surprise'. The relative attractivess of information gathering in the two cases depends more generally on the level of debt. We consider first the extreme case, when debt is riskless.

Remark 6 If debt is completely riskless in all contingencies, that is, if $e_{ij}^{Py} = \pi_{ij}^{Py} - \mathrm{D}$ for all $y \in \{\mathrm{P}, \mathrm{R}\}$ and $i, j \in \{\mathrm{L}, \mathrm{H}\}$, then $G^{I} = G^{N}$, that is, the value of information in one market is completely independent of information in the other.

The proof follows from straightforward computations using the formulae for π_{ij}^{Py} in the Appendix. Its intuition is simple: in the case of riskless debt, the average price change is the same whether the information structure in the product market is PP or PR.

Remark 7 When the debt level is such that it can be repaid whenever the firm has high quality, but never when it has low quality, then $G^{I} > G^{N}$.

Proof In this case $e_{Hj}^{Py} = \pi_{Hj}^{Py} - \mathrm{D}$ and $e_{Lj}^{Py} = 0$ for all $y \in \{\mathrm{P}, \mathrm{R}\}$ and $j \in \{\mathrm{L}, \mathrm{H}\}$. In this case explicit calculation yields that

$$q(\pi_{HH}^{PR} - \pi_{HH}^{PP}) + (1-q)(\pi_{HL}^{PR} - \pi_{HL}^{PP}) > 0 \quad (16.12)$$

from which the result immediately follows.

For intermediate debt levels, however, the ordering of G^{I} and G^{N} is ambiguous. For most parameter values, $G^{I} > G^{N}$. But the difference can be negative at moderate levels of debt, when the degree of competition, as expressed by the value of γ, is large and when quality is of little importance, that is when $\theta_H - \theta_L$ is small. In that case the variability of the stock price around its uninformative (i.e. expected) value is greater under PR competition, as a weak firm suffers much more from facing an opponent which is known to be stronger than what it gains from better coordination.

Remark 8 When the debt level is such that it can be always repaid except in the worst state LH, then $G^{I} > G^{N}$ as long as γ is small enough and $\theta_H - \theta_L$ large enough.

Proof In this case $e_{ij}^{Py} = \pi_{ij}^{Py} - D$ for all $y \in \{P, R\}$ and $ij \neq LH$, while $e_{LH}^{Py} = 0$ for all $y \in \{P, R\}$. We therefore have

$$G^I - G^N = \frac{q(1-q)}{2}\left[\frac{q(1-q)\gamma^2(\theta_H - \theta_L)^2}{(2-\gamma)^2}\right.$$

$$\left. -(1-q)\frac{q\gamma^2(\theta_H - \theta_L)}{4(2+\gamma)^2(2-\gamma)^2}\left[2\gamma(2-\gamma)\theta_L + q(4 - 2\gamma^2 + \gamma^3)(\theta_H - \theta_L)\right]\right].$$

This term is positive, unless $\theta_H - \theta_L$ is very small and γ is large. □

The interpretation is as follows. Payoffs to informed trading depend on the difference in firm profits when the firm quality is not revealed; thus the relative payoff $G^I - G^N$ compares the price surprise under a PR versus a PP outcome. An opaque firm facing a strong opponent usually has lower profits when its competitor is revealed, which implies a much lower profit in the lower state under PR. This decrease in profitability due to more aggressive competition is increasing in γ, as well as in the difference $\theta_H - \theta_L$. In other words, under a large γ the expected price change increases under PR relative to PP in the range π_{LH}^{PP}, π_{LH}^{PR}. As debt rises further, the net gain $G^I - G^N$ increases monotonically and it becomes unambiguously positive in the interval $(e_{LL}^{PP}, e_{LL}^{PR})$. On the other hand, when γ is small, the reduced profits due to this competitive effect are small relative to the reduced profits due to coordination loss: this results in less variability of price changes in the low states under PR. In this case the difference $G^I - G^N$ is always positive. Note that when the debt level D is above π_{HH}, the difference $G^I - G^N$ is always positive. To see this recall that the difference is positive for debt between π_{LL}^{PR} and the minimum π_{HH}; it may then decrease or increase, but it is always decreasing (π_{HL} are unambiguously higher under PR) until zero in the range π_{HL}^{PP} and π_{HL}^{PR}.

5. TRANSPARENCY CHOICE

In this section we investigate the choice of transparency at the first stage of the game. The two dominant investors choose simultaneously, with the objective of maximizing the expected future value of their financial claim. We consider here the case G^I, $G^N < K$ presented in Proposition 2, which offers the key insights also for the case of intermediate information costs.

For the analysis we have to distinguish between three different possible allocations of power in the two firms: the case where both firms are controlled by equity interests, where they are both controlled by debt interests, and the mixed case. It is clear that any theory in which debt and equity have different incentives can only apply to debt levels which are not excessive. Otherwise debt would become the residual claimant in all states and act like equity. We shall, therefore, assume from now on that in product market equilibrium equity always receives a positive payoff if the firm is of high quality, that is, in the states HH and HL.

Assumption A *$D_1, D_2 \leqslant \pi_{HH}^{ij}$ for all four possible information structures $ij = \{RR, RP, PR, PP\}$.*

This assumption is (much) stronger than needed for any of our results, but it shortens and unifies the presentation and, last but not least, is plausible in a wide range of situations.

5.1. *All Equity Control*

We begin by considering the case in which equity holders exert the dominant influence in both firms. Hence, in both firms, the choice of transparency is made such as to maximize

$$\mathrm{E}\max(\pi_i^*(\theta_1, \theta_2) - D_i, 0), \tag{16.13}$$

where E denotes the expectation over (θ_1, θ_2) and the revelation of information in the financial market (which is, of course, influenced by the choice of transparency), and $\pi_i^*(\theta_1,\theta_2)$ are equilibrium profits in the product market, given product quality and the information available after financial market activity. In order to understand the costs and benefits of transparency in this context, it is useful to compare the profit levels before debt payments of firm i in the case where both firms' types are revealed (π^{RR}, given by eqn (16.3)) with those where firm j's type is revealed but firm i's not (π^{PR}). As discussed in Section 3, the comparison shows that profits are more variable under fully revealed competition than under competition with asymmetric information, with π^{RR} being a 'median-preserving spread' of π^{PR}, in the sense that π^{RR} is statewise lower than π^{PR} in the two unfavourable states (LL, LH) and statewise higher in the two favourable states (HH, HL). Figure 16.1 summarizes the discussion given in Section 3.

This observation leads to the following proposition.

Proposition 4 *If both firms are controlled by equity interests and if* $G^{\mathrm{I}}, G^{\mathrm{N}} < K$*, then for all levels of debt* D_1, D_2 *satisfying Assumption A, in the unique subgame perfect equilibrium of the game, both firms are transparent.*

Proof Given the reasoning in the last section, a transparent firm will have its quality revealed in the financial markets with probability $\frac{1}{2}$, whereas an opaque firm will keep its quality secret with probability 1. Therefore, if firm j is transparent, an equity controlled firm i prefers to be transparent if

$$\delta(D_i) := \mathrm{E}\max(\pi_i^{\mathrm{RR}}(\theta_1, \theta_2) - D_i, 0) - \mathrm{E}\max(\pi_i^{\mathrm{PR}}(\theta_1,\theta_2) - D_i, 0) \geqslant 0. \tag{16.14}$$

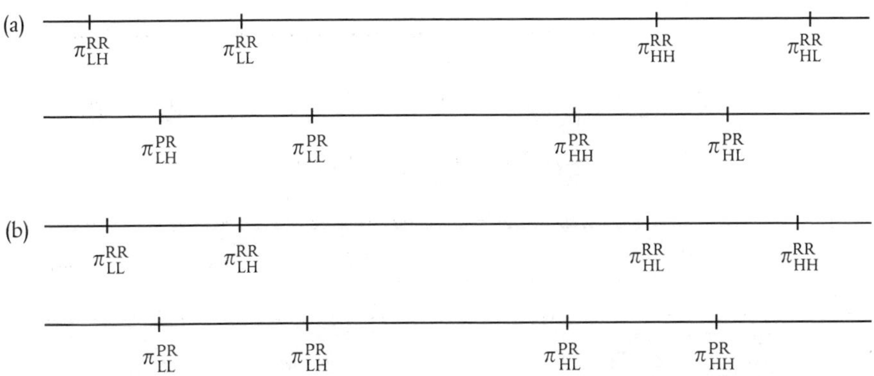

Figure 16.1. *(a) Comparing* RR *and* PR *($\gamma > 0$); (b) Comparing* RR *and* PR *($\gamma < 0$)*

The state-by-state comparison of profit levels given in Fig. 16.1 implies that $\delta(D_i) > 0$ for all D_i if $\delta(0) > 0$. This is because the graph of δ is (weakly) single-peaked, which becomes clear when walking backwards from π_{HL}^{RR} (where $\delta = 0$) in Fig. 16.2.

In other words, δ is positive for all D_i if only $E\pi_i^{RR} > E\pi_i^{PR}$. A lengthy calculation indeed establishes that

$$\delta(0) = q(1-q)\frac{\gamma^2}{(2-\gamma)^2}(\theta_H - \theta_L)^2\left(2 - \frac{\gamma^2}{4}\right) > 0 \tag{16.15}$$

for all γ. This also proves that OT and TO cannot be equilibrium transparency structures.

To prove uniqueness we have to compare the transparency structure OO with TO. As in the case of Fig. 16.1, it is straightforward to compare π^{PP} and π^{RP} state by state. Again, profits under transparency are a spread of profits under non-disclosure, as shown in Fig. 16.3.

An equity controlled firm wants to deviate from OO to TO if

$$\beta(D_i) := E\max(\pi_i^{RP}(\theta_1, \theta_2) - D_i, 0) - E\max(\pi_i^{PP}(\theta_1, \theta_2) - D_i, 0) > 0. \tag{16.16}$$

By the same argument as above, eqn (16.14) holds for all D_i if it holds for $D_i = 0$. Another calculation establishes that

$$\begin{aligned}\beta(0) &= E\pi_i^{TN} - E\pi_i^{NN} \\ &= q(1-q)\frac{\gamma^2}{(2+\gamma)^2(2-\gamma)^2}(\theta_H - \theta_L)^2\left(3 - \frac{\gamma^2}{4}\right) > 0 \end{aligned}\tag{16.17}$$

which concludes the proof. □

As the proof shows, transparency is, in fact, a dominant strategy in the game between equity holders at the first stage. The effect of complete information is in general to produce some implicit coordination in output decisions, as each firm conditions its production on

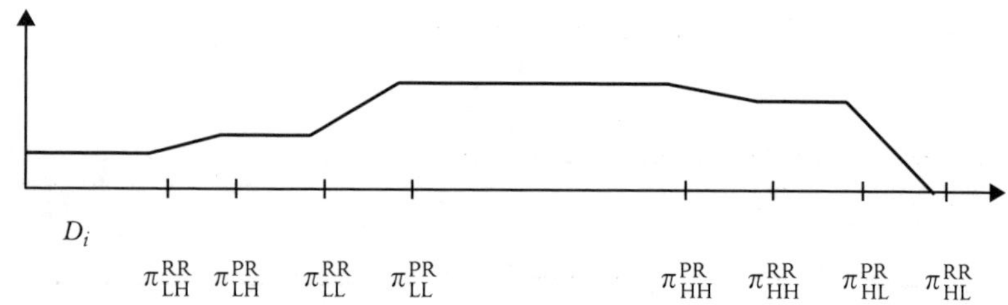

Figure 16.2. *The graph of* δ *(*$\gamma > 0$*)*

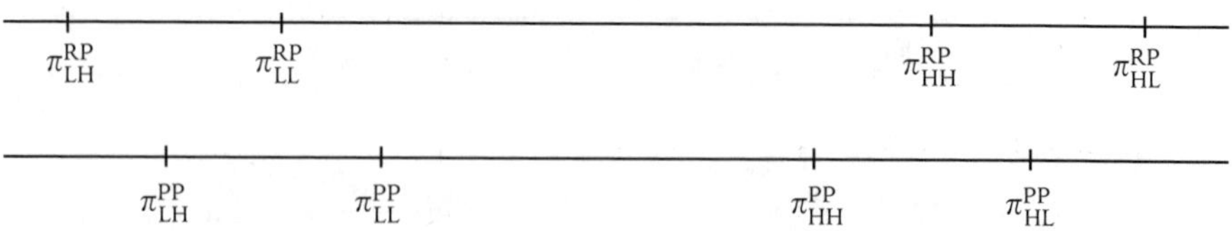

Figure 16.3. *Comparing* RP *and* PP *(*$\gamma > 0$*)*

the actual strength of its competitor's demand and thus on the competitor's ability to expand beyond its own market. This implicit coordination is so valuable that an equity-controlled firm unilaterally prefers to become transparent. Hence, the case of all equity control is a direct generalization of the results on endogenous information sharing cited in Section 3 to the case of a capital structure with debt and equity.

5.2. *All Debt Control*

We now turn to the case in which lenders exert the dominant influence in both firms. Hence, in both firms, the choice of transparency is made such as to maximize

$$E \min(\pi_i^*(\theta_1, \theta_2), D_i). \tag{16.18}$$

Figures 16.1 and 16.3 also provide the intuition about costs and benefits of information revelation in this case. Take the situation described in Fig. 16.3. A lender controlled firm which faces a non-transparent competitor has the choice between the random profits π^{PP} and $\frac{1}{2}(\pi^{PP} + \pi^{RP})$. Since the dominant interest now is to protect the downside of profits, lenders will prefer π^{PP} (if debt levels are not much higher than π^{RP}_{HH}, that is, if equity gets the upside of profits, which has been assumed in Assumption A). If their debt is above the smallest possible profit level under information structure RP, which is π^{RP}_{LH}, they will even strictly prefer π^{PP}.

This argument shows that the lowest possible profit level, π_{LH}, is an important threshold for the debt levels D_i, above which best responses are unique and below which best responses are arbitrary. Using this threshold, we can determine the best responses of dominant lenders:

Lemma 5. Suppose that $G^I, G^N < K$ and Assumption A holds.

1. If $D_i > \pi^{RR}_{LH}$, then O is the lenders' unique best response to T.
2. If $D_i \leqslant \pi^{RR}_{LH}$, then O and T are the lenders' best responses to T.
3. If $D_i > \pi^{RP}_{LH}$, then O is the lenders' unique best response to O.
4. If $D_i \leqslant \pi^{RP}_{LH}$, then O and T are the lenders' best responses to O.

Proof. If the competitor is transparent, firm i (strictly) prefers to be opaque if and only if

$$\eta(D_i) := E \min(D_i, \pi_i^{PR}(\theta_1, \theta_2)) - E \min(D_i, \pi_i^{RR}(\theta_1, \theta_2)) > 0.$$

As in the proof of Proposition 4, it is straightforward to draw the graph of η. Noting that $\eta(\pi^{RR}_{LH}) = 0, \eta(\pi^{RR}_{HL}) = -\delta(0)$, and $\delta(0) > 0$ by eqn (16.15), this graph has the form as in Fig. 16.4.

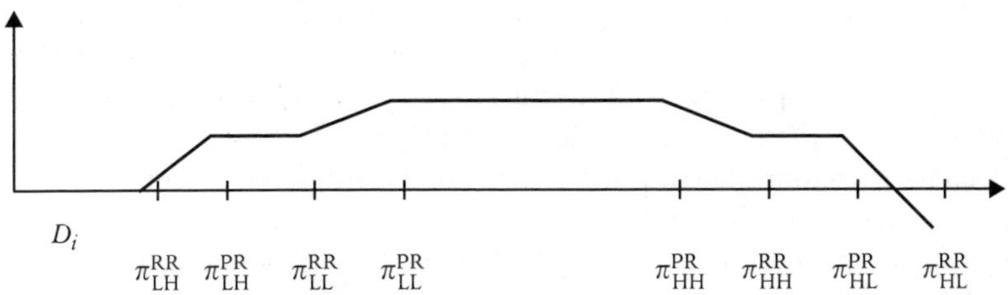

Figure 16.4. *The graph of η ($\gamma > 0$)*

An inspection of Fig. 16.4 proves 1 and 2. A similar argument for the case of the competitor's being opaque, establishes 3 and 4. □

Lemma 5 states that dominant lenders are indifferent with respect to the choice of transparency if and only if their debt is riskless under both information structures; otherwise, they strictly prefer opaqueness. Therefore, there can exist multiple equilibria caused by indifference. The Lemma also shows that the multiplicity of equilibria at the stage of transparency choice will depend on the relative sizes of π_{LH}^{RR} and π_{LH}^{RP}. However, these two values cannot be ranked in general.

Lemma 6 We have

$$\pi_{LH}^{RP} > \pi_{LH}^{RR} \Leftrightarrow \gamma(2-\gamma)\theta_L > (2-q(2-\gamma^2))(\theta_H - \theta_L).$$

Ceteris paribus, this inequality tends to hold for γ close to 1 (strong interaction in the product market), and does not hold for γ close to 0 and θ_L large relative to $(\theta_H - \theta_L)$. In this case the loss to a weak firm due to the stronger competition induced by disclosure is less then the resulting coordination gain. Hence, both possibilities can arise.

Lemmas 5 and 6 show that the game of transparency choice between two dominant lenders has different equilibria for different parameter constellations. To simplify the presentation, we focus on the case of symmetric debt levels, in which the number of different parameter constellations to consider reduces to four.

Proposition 7 *Suppose both firms are lender controlled, that $G^I, G^N < K$, that $D_1 = D_2 = D$, and that D satisfies Assumption A.*

If $D > \max(\pi_{LH}^{RP}, \pi_{LH}^{RR})$, the game has a unique subgame-perfect Nash equilibrium; in this equilibrium, both firms are opaque.

If $\pi_{LH}^{RR} \geqslant D > \pi_{LH}^{RP}$, there is a second subgame-perfect equilibrium, in which both firms are transparent.

If $\pi_{LH}^{RP} \geqslant D > \pi_{LH}^{RR}$, the game has three subgame-perfect equilibria; in the first, both firms are non-transparent, in the second and third, one firm is transparent and the other is not.

If $D \leqslant \min(\pi_{LH}^{RP}, \pi_{LH}^{RR})$, all four possible transparency combinations can arise in subgame-perfect equilibrium.

Proposition 7 follows immediately from Lemma 5. It states, most importantly, that general opaqueness is a subgame-perfect equilibrium outcome under lender control in all possible circumstances. If debt levels are so low that the dominant lenders become indifferent about their choice, additional equilibria will arise. In other words, opaqueness is unique unless debt is riskless under transparency. If debt levels are such that $\pi_{LH}^{RR} \geqslant D > \pi_{LH}^{RP}$ (the second case of Proposition 7), then the best response to opaqueness is still opaqueness, but the best response to transparency is indeterminate. Hence, (T, T) is an equilibrium choice. The situation for $\pi_{LH}^{RP} \geqslant D > \pi_{LH}^{RR}$ is analogous. Finally, if debt levels are so low that debt is riskless under any information structure, lenders are completely indifferent.[18] All equilibria but (O, O) are the result of indifference.

Proposition 7 provides a converse to Proposition 4: whereas in the case of all equity control firms in equilibrium will be transparent, dominant lenders when competing with each other necessarily choose to be opaque, if debt is risky.

5.3. *The Mixed Case*

To complete the analysis for the case G^I, $G^N < K$, we consider the case of competition between two different modes of control. For this, assume that firm 1, say, is dominated by equity interests, whereas firm 2 by lender interests. Hence, when determining its degree of transparency, firm 1's objectives are given by eqn (16.13) and firm 2's objectives by eqn (16.18). Given the results of the last two sections, the analysis is straightforward. By Proposition 4 firm 1's dominant strategy is T, to be transparent. By Lemma 5 the only threshold to consider for the choice of firm 2 therefore is π_{LH}^{RR}.

Proposition 8 *Suppose that firm 1 is equity controlled and firm 2 lender controlled, that* $G^I, G^N < K$, *and that debt levels satisfy Assumption A. If* $D_2 > \pi_{LH}^{RR}$, *the unique subgame-perfect equilibrium has firm 1 being transparent and firm 2 opaque. If* $D_2 \leqslant \pi_{LH}^{RR}$, *firm 1 in subgame-perfect equilibrium is transparent, and firm 2 is either transparent or opaque.*

The situation in Proposition 8 is a combination of those in the preceding two sections. Due to the increase in expected profits, equity will always prefer transparency, while the lenders' best response is opaqueness as long as debt is risky.[19] Hence, competition across firms under two different regimes of corporate control will tend to not change their chosen degree of transparency, as long as the dominant investors do not change.

6. CONCLUSIONS

In this chapter we have highlighted the impact of the dominant investors on the diffusion of information. We provide an incentive-based explanation for the casual observation that lender-dominated firms are more opaque, and suggest that besides the lower degree of transparency accompanying debt financing, the informativeness of traded security prices may be deliberately discouraged. An interesting side result is that the informational advantage of an opaque firm facing a transparent competitor does not translate in an outright competitive advantage. While lack of transparency ensures that it is shielded when in a weak competitive position, when the firm is in a strong position it cannot take full advantage of common knowledge of its strength to restrain output by competitors, losing market share precisely when its product is relatively profitable. Hence, the value of transparency depends on whether investors are interested in the upside or the downside of profits.

Our notion of debtor control captures a limited, but probably important part in some institutional settings of the corporate governance problem. One qualification, however, is that in order to exert control, debt holders must act in a concerted manner, which is usually impossible if debt is widely held, and that equity must be relatively weak. This is due to the fact that out of bankruptcy, equity has the formal control rights and can, therefore, impose its preferences on debt holders (unless explicitly restricted by covenants). As a consequence, we have the following rough taxonomy to anchor the classification of our theory institutionally. 'Equity control' is present whenever equity is strong (in particular, there is a large, active owner). 'Debt control' prevails if equity is weak and there are influential debt holders, in particular banks. Finally, if equity and debt are both relatively weak (e.g. widely held), we expect neither of our two modes to prevail, but rather management to be in control. In this latter case, our theory does not apply, but in the light of the literature on corporate governance and managerial discretion (see e.g. Shleifer and Vishny 1997) we suspect that management has a preference towards opaqueness.

In an international context, our notion of debt control is presumably more relevant to Japanese or European than to USA companies, where equity or management control seems to be the norm (out of Chapter 7 bankruptcy). Thus, on average, our model predicts higher corporate transparency in the USA (and perhaps the UK) relative to Japan and Europe. On the corporate level, we predict that the following attributes of publicly traded companies be clustered: equity dominance (in particular, concentrated, non-institutional ownership), corporate transparency, (relatively) informative stock prices, and volatile earnings. On the other side, we expect to observe jointly: dispersed equity with strong bank debt, less corporate transparency, less informative stock prices, and less volatile earnings.

Our model allows for several interesting comparative statics exercises which may shed light on some recent trends in European capital markets. For example, if market depth (in our model approximated by the amount of noise trading, λ) increases, trading profits G^{I} and G^{N} increase. Suppose that the economy is initially in a situation in which these profits are smaller than information costs K, so that banks can successfully prevent information from getting into the market. If λ increases until one or both of these profits exceed K, a policy of opaqueness no longer achieves this, and corporations tend to become more transparent even though this is not in the interest of debtholders. We would therefore argue that the large influx of international capital into the (continental) European financial market since the mid-1990s and the recent shift to more transparency of many European companies are related phenomena.

Similarly, we can identify economy-wide consequences of the recent push for 'shareholder value' in Europe, a fashion observed for some years now on the Continent. Suppose that information costs are in the intermediate range, $G^{N} < K < G^{I}$, a case not formally analyzed in the previous sections, and that the system is bank controlled with little information revelation. If now only a part of the population of firms (one of the two firms in our model) is pushed strongly and lastingly towards shareholder values (i.e. switches to 'equity control' in our model), this has a sweeping impact on the whole system. Because of the complementarity in information production, not only the first type of firm becomes transparent, but also for the still bank controlled firms informed trading becomes profitable. Hence, an exogenous policy change of one group of firms affects the transparency of all firms in equilibrium.

In related work we analyse in greater detail the allocation of nontransferable control rights as politically determined. We show there that bank dominance may emerge as a result of political support for a less competitive marketplace, which results in lower average asset values but also reduces the risks associated with employed individuals' stakeholder rents, which are in general undiversifiable.

In future work the model can also be extended to analysing some indirect cost of lack of transparency. It is possible that limited price informativeness may result, for instance, in reduced innovation or as a discouragement of entry by new firms. A particularly challenging question which we have begun to address is the question of the evolution of disclosure in financial systems historically dominated by banks. It is possible that the increasing pressure for shareholder value in countries such as Japan and Germany reflects changing conditions on the riskiness of loans and the impact of foreign competition. Moreover, opaqueness may be increasingly hard to sustain as trading liquidity rises due to rising global investment flows. This would lead to greater informativeness of prices, thus stronger competition and a greater average profitability and riskiness. We intend to return to these themes in the future.

Notes

1. A considerable literature has explored the long-term corporate performance in countries with active capital markets and those economies such as Japan and Germany where markets have less influence and strong direct ties exist between companies and financial intermediaries. See Carlin and Mayer (1999) for an interesting descriptive approach, and, for example, Rajan (1992) and von Thadden (1995) for theoretical work.
2. In an ongoing research project we look at the question of what determines the overall degree of bank influence versus a regulatory regime favourable to equity investment and shareholder dominance.
3. Given our linear demand specification, the difference in product quality can as well be interpreted as a difference in marginal costs. The two formulations are equivalent.
4. This specification of demand is standard and can be derived from quadratic preferences of a representative consumer (see e.g. Singh and Vives 1984).
5. We have investigated such incentives in an earlier version. The treatment is much more complex and does not add much to our results. For theoretical work on the general problem see, for example, Maksimovic (1988), Bolton and Scharfstein (1990) and Showalter (1995); for contrary empirical evidence see Chevalier (1995).
6. While a higher level of debt may be more typical for a creditor dominated firm (and may justify the creditor's influence), for the sake of generality we do not make such an assumption.
7. This applies, for example, to European firms deciding to list on the NYSE. Another example is the decision to switch from the British Unlisted Securities Market to the Official List of the LSE.
8. Transparency may require disclosing 'proprietary information', such as product specifications which increase competitors' technological or market information and thus reduce potential profits. Such costs may eliminate any shareholder incentive in buying out control over transparency from lenders.
9. There will be in general an *ex post* incentive to reveal more if the information is good, or less if the information is bad. We assume that there is no credible way to selectively communicate this information *ex post*, unless a reliable market-based mechanism has been established in advance to allow information to be easily observable to investors.
10. See, for example, Biais, Foucault, and Hillion (1997, ch. 3) for a discussion of this type of model.
11. This seems to be the more realistic assumption. One can also assume that stock prices do not reflect new information from the competing firm's stock, with no impact on our results.

12. In particular, we are not interested here in the issue of managerial self-interest (see e.g. Hart 1995). If one wants to, one can interpret profits as net of private managerial benefits.
13. This last feature is due to the assumption that liquidity traders buy and sell with the same probability. If those probabilities differed, information would be revealed partially in the case of a zero aggregate order flow.
14. If $\gamma<0$, that is, if the goods are strategic complements, we have $Q_{HH}^{TT}>Q_{HL}^{TT}>Q_{LH}^{TT}>Q_{LL}^{TT}$: in LL, the worst possible state for firm *i*, it produces less than in state LH, the second worst state, etc.
15. In equilibrium, this will occur either because no investor has been informed or because trading has not revealed any private information.
16. More specifically, the P firm's output in the lowest state LH is higher, and lower in the LL state, than under full disclosure.
17. Remember that information acquisition is *ex post* profitable only when the firm type is not revealed, that is, if the superscript of e_{ij}^{xy} has $x=P$.
18. Note that the cases ignored by assuming $D_1=D_2$, are straightforward extensions of those described in Proposition 7. If, for example, the debt level of firm 1 is high and that of firm 2 very low, non-transparency is the dominant choice for firm 1, while firm 2 is indifferent. In such cases (O, O) and (O, T) are both possible equilibrium outcomes.
19. If $D_2\leqslant\pi_{LH}^{RR}$ so that debt is riskless, we have again the possibility of an indeterminate response: firm 1 in subgame-perfect equilibrium is transparent, and firm 2 is either transparent or opaque.

References

Bhattacharya, S., and Chiesa, G. (1995). Proprietary information, financial intermediation, and research incentives. *Journal of Financial Intermediation* 4: 328.

—— and Ritter, J. (1982). Innovation and communication signalling with partial disclosure. *Review of Economic Studies* 50: 331.

Biais, B., Foucault, T., and Hillion, P. (1997). *Microstructure des marchés financiers.* Paris: Presses Universitaires de France.

Bolton, P., and Scharfstein, D. (1990). A theory of predation based on agency problems in financial contracting. *American Economic Review* 80: 93.

Brander, J., and Lewis, T. (1986). Oligopoly and financial structure. *American Economic Review* 76: 956.

Carlin, W., and Mayer, C. (1999). Finance, investment and growth. CEPR, Discussion Paper No. 2233.

Chevalier, J. (1995). Capital structure and product market competition: Empirical evidence from the supermarket industry. *American Economic Review* 85: 415.

Diamond, D. (1984). Financial intermediation and delegated monitoring. *Review of Economic Studies* 51: 393.

Flannery, M., Kwan, S., and Nimalendran, M. (1997). Market evidence on the opaqueness of banking firms' assets. University of Florida, Mimeo.

Fried, D. (1984). Incentives for information production and disclosure in a duopolistic environment. *Quarterly Journal of Economics* 99: 367.

Gertner, R., Gibbons, R., and Scharfstein, D. (1988). Simultaneous signalling to the capital and product markets. *RAND Journal of Economics* 19: 173.

Hart, O. (1995). *Firms, Contracts and Financial Structure.* Oxford: Oxford University Press.

Holmström, B., and Tirole, J. (1993). Market liquidity and performance monitoring. *Journal of Political Economy* 101: 678.

Hoshi, T., Kashyap, A., and Scharfstein, D. (1991). Corporate structure, liquidity, and investment: Evidence from Japanese industrial groups. *Quarterly Journal of Economics* 106: 33.

Jensen, M. C., and Meckling, W. H. (1976). Theory of the firm: Managerial behaviour, agency costs and ownership structure. *Journal of Financial Economics* 3: 305.

Kühn, K.-U., and Vives, X. (1994). Information exchanges among firms and their impact on competition. University Pompeu Fabra, Institut d'Analisi Economica, Barcelona, Mimeo.

Li, L. (1985). Cournot oligopoly with information sharing. *RAND Journal of Economics* 16: 521.

Maksimovic, V. (1988). Capital structure in repeated oligopolies. *RAND Journal of Economics* 19: 389.

Nakatani, I. (1984). The role of financial corporate grouping. In M. Aoki (ed.), *Economics Analysis of the Japanese Firm,* New York: North Holland.

Perotti, E., and von Thadden, E.-L. (2000). Dominant investors and strategic transparency. University of Lausanne, Mimeo.

Rajan, R. (1992). Insiders and outsiders: The choice between informed and arm's length debt. *Journal of Finance* 47: 1367.

Shleifer, A., and Vishny, R. (1997). A survey of corporate governance. *Journal of Finance* 52: 737.

Showalter, D. M. (1995). Oligopoly and financial structure: comment. *American Economic Review* 85: 647.

Singh, N., and Vives, X. (1984). Price and quantity competition in a differentiated duopoly. *RAND Journal of Economics* 16: 546.

Stoughton, N., Wong, K. P., and Zechner J. (1996). IPOs and product quality. University of Vienna, Mimeo.

von Thadden, E.-L. (1995). Long-term contracts, short-term investment and monitoring. *Review of Economic Studies* 62: 557.

Weinstein, D., and Yafeh, Y. (1998). On the costs of a bank-centered financial system: Evidence from changing main bank relations in Japan. *Journal of Finance* 53: 635.

17

Corporate Governance: Effects on Firm Performance and Economic Growth

MARIA MAHER AND THOMAS ANDERSSON

1. INTRODUCTION

The relationship between corporate governance and economic performance has become one of the most controversial issues faced by policymakers today. Each country has through time developed a wide variety of mechanisms to overcome the agency problems that arise from the separation of ownership and control. While some systems are characterized by wide dispersed ownership (outsider systems), others tend to be characterized by concentrated ownership or control (insider systems). In outsider systems of corporate governance (notably the USA and UK) the basic conflict of interest is between strong managers and widely dispersed weak shareholders. In insider systems (notably Continental Europe and Japan), on the other hand, the basic conflict is between controlling shareholders (or blockholders) and weak minority shareholders. Therefore, one of the most striking differences between countries' corporate governance systems is in the ownership and control of firms, and the identity of controlling shareholders.

Up until the early 1990s, it was thought that both the German and Japanese systems of corporate governance could deliver superior economic performance. Serious defects in the governance structures of the UK and the USA were thought to exist regarding the monitoring and control of publicly quoted companies. However, following the more recent weak performances of the Japanese and German economies, and the 1997 financial crisis in Asia, these previously highly regarded models have come under severe criticism. But if the Japanese and German systems of corporate governance are so fundamentally flawed, why did they work so well for so long? Furthermore, while the governance structures of the USA and UK are now being seen as the models to emulate, recent unease regarding issues such as accountability, transparency, and the level of executive pay has also bought these systems in for a reassessment.

This chapter looks at the various mechanisms employed in different systems (e.g. concentrated ownership, executive remuneration schemes, the market for takeovers, and cross-shareholdings amongst firms) and examines the evidence on whether or not they are conducive to firm performance and economic growth. While evidence on the overall economic implications of different corporate governance systems is often ambiguous, a number of potential channels of influence can be demonstrated. We show how the corporate governance framework can impinge upon the development of equity markets, R&D and innovative activity, entrepreneurship, and the development of an active SME sector, and thus impinge upon economic growth. We address some of the underlying factors that promote efficient corporate governance, and examine some of the strengths, weaknesses, and economic implications associated with various corporate governance systems.

Section 2 provides an analytical framework for understanding how corporate governance can affect corporate performance and economic growth. Section 3 discusses the critical differences in corporate governance systems in OECD countries. It then goes on to provide a qualitative assessment of the strengths, weaknesses, and economic implications associated with the different systems. Section 4 provides a review of the empirical evidence of the effect of corporate governance on corporate performance and economic performance, and Section 5 concludes. Wherever possible, we also identify those areas where policy implications emerge.

2. ANALYTICAL FRAMEWORK: SHAREHOLDER AND STAKEHOLDERS' MODELS OF GOVERNANCE

Before discussing the relationship between corporate governance, firm performance, and economic growth, it is useful to have a framework with which to understand how corporate governance can affect firm behaviour and economic performance. Corporate governance has traditionally been associated with the 'principal–agent' or 'agency' problem. A 'principal–agent' relationship arises when the person who owns a firm is not the same as the person who manages or controls it, in other words, there is a separation between ownership and control (Berle and Means 1932). However, since product market competition should provide incentives for firms to adopt the most efficient corporate governance mechanisms, some argue that we need not worry about corporate governance. Firms that do not adopt cost-minimizing governance mechanisms would presumably be less efficient and in the long run would be replaced. Rather than justifying public intervention, this line of argument says that the resolution of governance problems should be left to market participants. Thus, recent development in the managerial labour market, such as executive stock options and the market for corporate control, for example, leveraged and management buy-outs, are seen as market responses to institutional deficiencies.

On the other hand, competition alone cannot solve the market failures arising from the asymmetric information and hold-up problems that lie at the heart of corporate governance. Market failures resulting in socially inefficient outcomes are one of the strongest arguments in favour of policy intervention. However, we should keep in mind that the effectiveness and form of different corporate governance systems may be influenced by a number of factors, including product market competition, the structure of capital and labour markets, and the regulatory and legal environments.

In the economics debate on the subject there are basically two different models of the corporation, the shareholder model and the stakeholder model. In its narrowest sense (shareholder model), corporate governance describes the formal system of accountability of senior management to shareholders. In its widest sense (stakeholder model), corporate governance can be used to describe the network of formal and informal relations involving the corporation. In the following, we briefly discuss these two models and consider their differences and similarities.

2.1. *The Shareholder Model of the Firm*

According to the shareholder model the objective of the firm is to maximize shareholder wealth through allocative, productive, and dynamic efficiency. In other words, the objective of the firm is to maximize profits. The criterion by which performance is judged in this model can simply be taken as the market value of the firm. Managers and directors have an implicit obligation to ensure that firms are run in the interests of shareholders. However, the objectives of the principal (the shareholders) and the agent (the managers) differ when there is a separation of ownership and control. Managers do not bear the full costs or reap the full benefits of their actions. Therefore, although investors are interested in maximizing shareholder value, managers may have other objectives such as maximizing their salaries, growth in market share, or an attachment to particular investment projects.

The principal–agent problem is an essential element of the 'incomplete contracts' view of the firm first developed by Coase (1937). If it were possible to write a 'complete contract', owners could use a contract to perfectly align the interests and objectives of managers with their own. However, complete contracts are often unfeasible and it is impossible to foresee or describe all future contingencies. This incompleteness of contracts means that investors and managers will have to allocate 'residual control rights' in some way, where residual control rights are the rights to make decisions in unforeseen circumstances or in circumstances not covered by the contract.

Furthermore, investors cannot just write a contract that gives them all the residual control rights in the firm, since the reason why owners hire managers in the first place is that they needed managers' specialized human capital to run the firm and to generate returns. The 'agency' problem, therefore, is also an asymmetric information problem, that is, managers are better informed regarding what are the best alternative uses for the investors' funds. As a result, the manager ends up with substantial residual control rights and discretion to allocate funds as he chooses. There may be limits on this discretion specified in the contract, but the fact is that managers do have most of the residual control rights (Shleifer and Vishny 1997). This can lead to problems of management entrenchment and rent extraction by managers. One of the economic consequences of the possibility of *ex post* expropriation of rents (or opportunistic behaviour) by managers is that it reduces the amount of resources that investors are willing to put up *ex ante* to finance the firm (Grossman and Hart 1986). The resulting hold-up problem leads to socially inefficient levels of investment.

There are broadly three types of mechanisms that can be used to overcome the problems associated with the separation of ownership and control: (i) direct alignment of managers' interests with those of shareholders through, for example, executive compensation plans, stock options, and/or direct monitoring by boards; (ii) legal protection from expropriation by managers, through, for example, protection and enforcement of shareholder rights, and prohibitions against insider-dealing, and (iii) indirect means of corporate control such as those provided by capital markets, managerial labour markets, and markets for corporate control.

One of the critiques of the shareholder model is the implicit presumption that the conflicts are between strong entrenched managers and weak dispersed shareholders. This has led to an almost exclusive focus, in both the analytical work and in reform efforts, of resolving the monitoring and management entrenchment problems which are the main corporate governance problems in the principal–agent context with dispersed ownership. For example, most of this work has addressed concerns related to the role of the board of directors, stock options and executive remuneration, shareholder protection, the role of institutional investors and the effectiveness of the market for takeovers. However, the widely held firm, presumed in Berle and Means' (1932) seminal work, is not the rule but is rather the exception.[1] Instead, the dominant organizational form for the firm is one characterized by concentrated ownership.

One of the reasons why we observe ownership concentration may be due to the lack of investor protection. Another reason is that ownership concentration represents one way of resolving the monitoring problem. The difficulty with dispersed ownership is that the incentives to monitor management are weak. Shareholders have an incentive to 'free-ride' in the hope that other shareholders will do the monitoring, since the benefits from monitoring are shared with all shareholders whereas the full costs of monitoring are incurred by those who monitor. For the closely held corporation, the problem of corporate governance is more one of cross-shareholdings, holding companies and pyramids, or other mechanisms that dominant shareholders use to exercise control, often at the expense of minority investors. In this case, the protection of minority shareholders is critical.

Another critique of the shareholder approach is that the analytical focus on how to solve the corporate governance problem is too narrow. The shareholder approach to corporate governance is primarily concerned with aligning the interests of managers and shareholders and with ensuring the flow of external capital to firms. However, shareholders are not the only ones who make investments in the corporation. Therefore, any assessment of the strengths, weaknesses, and economic implications of different corporate governance frameworks needs a broader analytical framework which includes the incentives and disincentives faced by all stakeholders in the firm.

2.2. *The Stakeholder Model of the Firm*

The stakeholder model takes a broader view of the firm. According to the traditional stakeholder model, the corporation is responsible to a wider constituency of stakeholders other than shareholders. Other stakeholders may include contractual partners such as employees, suppliers, customers, creditors, and social constituents such as members of the community in which the firm is located, environmental interests, local and national governments, and society at large. The problem with the traditional stakeholder model of the firm is that it is difficult, if not impossible, to ensure that corporations fulfil such wider objectives.

However, given the potential consequences of corporate governance for economic performance, the notion that corporations have responsibilities to parties other than shareholders merits consideration. What matters is the impact that various stakeholders can have on the behaviour and performance of the firm and on economic growth. With this in mind, the stakeholder model has recently been redefined, where the emphasis has been to more narrowly define what constitutes a stakeholder. Therefore, the 'new' stakeholder model specifically defines stakeholders to be those actors who have contributed firm-specific assets, see Blair (1995). This redefinition is consistent with both the transaction costs and incomplete contract theories of the firm in which the firm can be viewed as a 'nexus of contracts', see Coase (1937), Williamson (1975, 1985), Jensen and Meckling (1976), Aoki *et al.* (1990), and Aghion and Bolton (1992).

The new stakeholder approach is a natural extension of the shareholder model. The 'best' firms according to this model are ones with committed suppliers, customers, and employees. However, opportunistic behaviour and hold-up problems arise whenever contracts are incomplete and firm specific investments need to be made. The principal–agent relationship discussed in the shareholder model is only one of the many areas in which this occurs. Under-investment in the stakeholder model would include investments by employees and suppliers, for example. Therefore, it is in the interest of the shareholders to take account other stakeholders, and to promote the development of long-term relations, trust, and commitment amongst various stakeholders (Mayer 1996). Corporate governance in this context becomes a problem of finding mechanisms that elicit firm specific investments on the part of various stakeholders, and that encourage active co-operation amongst stakeholders in creating wealth, jobs, and the sustainability of financially sound enterprises (OECD 1999).[2]

The benefit of the shareholder model is that it provides clear guidance in helping managers set priorities and establishes a mechanism for measuring the efficiency of the firms' management team as indicated by firm profitability. One of the critiques of the stakeholder model, or fears of participants in the reform process, is that managers or directors may use 'stakeholder' reasons to justify poor company performance. On the other hand, the benefit of the stakeholder model is its emphasis on overcoming problems of under-investment associated with opportunistic behaviour and in encouraging active co-operation amongst stakeholders to ensure the long-term profitability of the corporation. One of the most challenging tasks on the reform agenda, therefore, is how to develop corporate governance frameworks and mechanisms that encourage the socially efficient levels of investment by all major stakeholders. The difficulty, however, is to identify those frameworks and mechanisms which promote efficient levels of investment, while at the same time maintaining the performance accountability aspects provided by the shareholder model. At a minimum, this implies that mechanisms that promote stakeholder investment and co-operation should be adopted in conjunction with mechanisms aimed at ensuring accountability and preventing management entrenchment.

3. CORPORATE GOVERNANCE IN OECD COUNTRIES: STRENGTHS, WEAKNESSES, AND ECONOMIC IMPLICATIONS

Corporate governance systems can be distinguished according to the degree of ownership concentration and the identity of controlling shareholders. While some systems are characterized by wide dispersed ownership, others tend to be characterized by concentrated ownership where the controlling shareholder may be an individual, family holding, bloc alliance, financial institution, or other corporations acting through a holding company or via cross-shareholdings. Table 17.1 gives some international comparisons of ownership concentrations across OECD countries.[3] As can be seen from the table the average equity holding of the largest shareholder[4] varies from 40 to 80 per cent in most continental European countries whereas ownership concentration is substantially lower in the UK, USA, Japan, and the Netherlands.

However, in the absence of one share/one vote, data on direct ownership concentration can either under- or over-estimate actual control that shareholders exercise over the corporation. This is because countries have a variety of legal devices that can be used to separate ownership from control rights, see Box 17.1. Dispersed ownership and dispersed voting power is associated with many small shareholders, the absence of any large shareholders, and with one share/one vote. In this case, managers end up with substantial residual control rights but takeovers are possible. However, it is also possible to have dispersed ownership but concentrate voting power through the use of dual class shares, golden shares, proxy votes and voting trusts, the issue of stock with contingent voting rights triggered by control disputes,

Table 17.1. *International comparison of ownership concentration*[5]

	Year	Number of companies	Average largest stake (% of equity)
Austria	1996	600 largest listed and unlisted non-financial companies	82.2
		62 largest listed companies	52.4
Belgium	1995	135 listed companies	44.8
France	1996	282,322 listed and unlisted companies	66.2
		680 listed companies only	57.9
Germany	1996	402 listed companies	55.9
Italy	1996	4,173 listed and unlisted manufacturing companies	61.1
		214 listed companies only	48.0
The Netherlands	1996	137 listed companies	26.9
			45.3[a]
Spain	1995	394 listed companies	38.2
			47.1[b]
United Kingdom	1992	189 listed companies	14.4
United States of America	1980	457 listed non-financial companies	25.4[a]
Japan	1984	143 mining and manufacturing companies	33.1[a]
Korea	1996	30 largest chaebols	44.1[c]

[a]Percentage of outstanding shares owned by the largest five shareholders.
[b]Percentage of outstanding shares owned by the largest three shareholders.
[c]Share of ownership held by the founding family and relatives plus those of other companies in the group.

Sources: Austria: Gugler *et al.* (1999); Belgium: Becht *et al.* (1999); France: Bloch and Kremp (1999); Germany: Becht and Bohmer (1999); Italy: Bianchi *et al.* (1999); The Netherlands: de Jong *et al.* (1999); Spain: Crespi-Cladera and Garcia-Cestona (1999); UK: Goergen and Renneboog (1999); USA and Japan: Prowse (1994); Korea: OECD (1998*a*).

Box 17.1. *Taxonomy of ownership and voting power*

	Dispersed voting power	Concentrated voting power
Dispersed ownership		
Many small shareholders	One share/one vote	Voting power concentrated in the hands of blockholders via dual class shares, golden shares, proxy votes, voting trusts, etc.
Implications	'Strong managers, weak owners' takeovers are possible	'Strong Voting Blockholders, Weak Minority owners' takeovers are difficult
Concentrated ownership		
Large shareholders	Voting power of ownership diluted via capped voting	Voting rights aligned with ownership rights via one share/one vote, or concentrated via separation devices
Implications	'Strong Managers, Weak Owners' takeovers are difficult	'Weak Managers, Weak Minority owners, Strong Majority owners' takeovers are possible

and pyramiding. This gives rise to a situation of strong controlling blockholders and weak minority owners. Takeovers may be impossible in this case. When ownership is concentrated and voting rights are aligned with ownership rights, minority owners are again in a very weak position. Managers, however, are also weak and the majority owners retain residual control over the corporation. Takeovers are possible in this case since cash flow rights and voting rights are aligned. Systems of corporate governance found in OECD countries usually fall into one of these three categories.

Concentrated ownership but dispersed voting power can be accomplished through the use of voting caps that restrict voting rights of large share positions, and which can prevent large shareholders from monitoring or exercising control. Although this system affords some protection to minority shareholders from voting rights restrictions it has mainly disadvantages from a corporate governance perspective. This system has all the consequential problems of monitoring found in outsider systems but none of its advantages. This method results in low liquidity, low diversification possibilities for investors, and a high cost of capital. While an individual firm might choose this ownership structure, this governance structure is the exception rather than the rule. For these reasons, as a system of corporate governance, this structure is not really observed in practice.

Table 17.2 provides a comparison of voting power concentration in a number of OECD countries. As can be seen from the table, blockholdings in Continental Europe are considerably higher than in the USA and UK.[6] The median largest voting stake in listed companies in most European countries is over 50 per cent. This suggests that voting control by a large blockholder is the rule rather than the exception in Europe. Furthermore, in no European country is the median largest shareholder small enough to fall below the 5 per cent disclosure

Table 17.2. *Voting power concentration in listed industrial companies: Size of largest ultimate voting block (per cent)*

	Number of companies	Median largest voting block	Mean largest voting block
Austria	50	52.0	54.1
Belgium	121	50.6	41.2
	BEL20	45.1	38.3
France	CAC40	20.0	29.4
Germany	374	52.1	49.1
	DAX30	11.0	17.3
Italy	216	54.5	48.0
The Netherlands	137	43.5	42.3
Spain	193	34.2	40.1
UK[a]	250	9.9	14.4
USA			
NYSE	1,309	0[b]	3.6
NASDAQ	2,831	0[b]	3.4

[a]Random sample of 250 listed companies.
[b]Below the 5 per cent disclosure threshold.

Source: Becht and Röell (1999) and data from the European Corporate Governance Network.

threshold. Whereas in the USA over 50 per cent of companies have a largest shareholder who holds less than 5 per cent of the shares, there are virtually no such companies in Austria and Germany.

Not only do patterns of ownership concentration and control differ dramatically across countries, but the identity of owners does too. Some comparisons of the distribution of share ownership for a number of OECD countries can be found below in Table 17.3. In outsider systems of corporate governance, typical of the USA and UK, ownership is primarily associated with institutional investors, however, individual ownership is more prevalent in the USA than in the UK. This is not true of insider systems, where ownership is in the hands of either other corporations or controlling investors. For example, in the rest of Europe, Japan, and Korea, cross-shareholdings amongst firms are commonplace, relationships with banks are strong, and large family holdings often dominate institutional investors (Mayer 1996).

In addition to differences in ownership concentration and the identity of owners across OECD countries, significant regulatory differences also exist. Corporate governance is affected by the legal and regulatory framework in which firms operate (La Porta *et al.* 1997; Shleifer and Vishny 1997). At the same time, the legal and regulatory environments are partly the outcome of different corporate governance systems. Differences in countries' systems of corporate governance, and their interactions with the regulatory and legislative framework, and with the degree of competition in product and factor markets, have important implications for both firm performance and economic performance. These interactions

Table 17.3. *Ownership of common stock in selected OECD countries (per cent at year end)*

	USA (1996)	Japan (1994)	Germany (1996)	France (1994)	UK (1994)	Italy (1994)	Sweden (1996)	Australia[b] (1996)	Korea (1996)
Financial sector	46	44	30	8	68	8	30	37	26
Of which									
Banks and other financial institutions	7	28[a]	10	4	10	5	1	4	12
Insurance companies and pension funds	28	16[a]	12	2	50	3	14	25	6
Investment funds	12	—	8	2	8	—	15	8	8
Non-financial sector	54	56	70	92	32	92	70	63	74
Of which									
Non-financial enterprises	—	24	42	58	1	25	11	11	21
Individuals	49	24	15	19	21	50	19	20	34
Public authorities	—	1	4	4	1	8	8	—	7
Foreign	5	7	9	11	9	9	32	32	12
Total	100	100	100	100	100	100	100	100	100

[a]Pension funds in Japan are managed by trust banks and insurance companies. Division between banks and insurance companies are estimated. No data are available on the extent to which mutual funds own shares. Securities houses do manage such funds. These companies are included under other financial institutions.
[b]Australian figures are for the end of September 1996.

Note: Due to rounding, the figures may not add up to the total.

Sources: Japan: OECD (1996), Economic Surveys; France and Italy: OECD (1997), Economic Surveys, France; Korea: OECD (1998*a*), Economic Surveys; Australia: OECD (1998*b*), Economic Surveys; USA, UK, German, and Sweden: OECD (1998*c*), Financial Market Trends, no. 69.

lead to a systems approach to governance (Aoki 1994). The drawback is that it is often difficult to formulate in any precise way the interactions between the different constituents. The remainder of this section examines some of these potential channels of influence and looks at the various strengths and weaknesses of outsider and insider systems of corporate governance. Section 4, on the other hand, examines the available empirical evidence on the link between corporate governance and performance.

3.1. *Outsider Systems of Corporate Governance*

'Outsider' systems, typical of the USA and the UK, are characterized by relatively widely dispersed share ownership and high turnover. These systems emphasize the need for reliable and adequate information so that investors are able to make informed investment decisions. For example, regulation has traditionally been structured to provide information to, and create relative equality among, investors regarding access to information. For this purpose, disclosure requirements are fairly stringent and there is a strong emphasis on the protection of shareholder rights, and in particular those of minority investors. Elaborate rules prevent groups of shareholders from communicating and sharing information among themselves without making the information available to all shareholders. In addition, the legal framework supports the rights of shareholders to control the company and in many cases the board and management are explicitly accountable to shareholders.

Since strong minority shareholder protection is also associated with an active stock market, the corporate governance frameworks in the USA and UK promote stock market activity. Thus, long-term financing through equities and corporate bonds is an important feature of outsider systems. Debt financing by banks tends to be short term and banks tend to maintain arm's length relationships with the corporate sector, accounting for low debt–equity ratios. The monitoring and disciplining of management relies largely on capital markets. For example, share prices are likely to fall whenever management fails to maximize shareholder value, thus exposing the company to the threat of a takeover bid and the removal of inefficient management. In fact, liquid stock markets, strict trading rules, and adequate disclosure of information (all characteristics associated with outsider systems) are necessary in order for the market for corporate control to act as effective disciplining device. Some of the advantages of dispersed ownership, therefore, include enhanced liquidity of stocks and, consequently, better risk diversification possibilities for investors.

Another important aspect of an active equity market is that this also encourages innovative activity, entrepreneurship, and the development of a dynamic small and medium-sized enterprise (SME) sector. Venture capital and business angels are vital in supporting innovative activity and entrepreneurial talent. On the downside, however, the incentives to monitor management are particularly weak when ownership is dispersed due to 'free-rider' problems. With dispersed ownership, 'exit' instead of 'voice' is the consequence,[7] and managers end up with considerable discretion and the possibility to extract private benefits. Managers may use their discretion to maximize firm size rather than profits; to hoard cash flow rather than pay it out in the form of dividends; to pay themselves excessive salaries; or to entrench and protect themselves from indirect means of corporate control. Because of this, outsider systems are often associated with a lack of managerial accountability.

The corporate governance, legal, and regulatory frameworks in outsider systems have developed in response to the particular problems arising not only from the separation of ownership and control, but also from the diffuse nature of share ownership. Many of the reforms or practices aim at addressing weaknesses in monitoring; at strengthening managerial accountability; and at aligning the objectives of managers more closely with those of shareholders. In addition to a strong disclosure regime and an emphasis on shareholder rights, examples include monitoring by institutional investors or pension funds, well-functioning markets for corporate control, and executive remuneration and compensation packages aimed at encouraging managers to maximize shareholder value.

3.1.1 *The Role of Financial Institutions*

Commercial institutions in the USA have long been restricted by tougher legal and regulatory constraints, resulting in a more fragmented financial sector. For example, due to share ownership restrictions, equity holdings by commercial banks are especially low. Legislation in the USA also hinders banks in their client advisory capacity. For instance, where a client of a bank becomes insolvent, the legal doctrine of 'equitable subordination' downgrades the bank's claim on the firm's assets if it can be shown that they exerted a significant influence on the activities of the firm. While these constraints have encouraged dispersed ownership in the USA, they also discourage long-term relationships between financial institutions and the corporate sector. As a result, in comparison to other countries, commercial banks only play a passive role in the monitoring of listed companies.

However, share ownership in the UK, and increasingly in the USA, is characterized by the domination of institutional investors (see Table 17.3). In the last forty years, both the USA and the UK have seen a sharp rise in the proportion of equity held by financial institutions, coupled with the declining role of individuals in direct ownership. Rising from less than 10 per cent of all equities in the 1950s to over 40 per cent today, institutional investors have become the largest owners of equity in both countries. Over the same period, the proportion of shares directly held by individuals has fallen from about 90 per cent to around 50 per cent in the USA, and from about 50 per cent to around 20 per cent in the UK. The reasons for this trend can be attributed to the tax incentives extended by governments to collective schemes and the wide growth of mutual funds and unit trusts as a result of the advantages of wider diversification, professional management, and lower execution costs relative to direct share ownership. A further factor explaining this phenomenon has been the increasing tendency for companies to issue shares directly to institutional investors in the primary market, as their funding requirements have risen in recent years.

The high degree of share ownership held by institutional investors and pension funds is a major factor in the way corporate governance is being exercised in the UK and USA. While the increased monitoring by institutional investors is seen as an improvement in the way corporate governance is exercised in the USA and UK, there are still concerns as to who monitors the fund managers. The high level of concentration amongst institutional investors in the UK may only serve to exacerbate this problem. For example, the top twenty-five institutional investors in the UK control more than 40 per cent of the value of shares held by all institutional investors. Furthermore, the largest shareholders of listed companies are often the institutional investors and, as a consequence, many of the major companies have broadly similar ownership profiles.

3.1.2 *The Role of the Board of Directors*

In addition to the control exercised by institutional investors, another relatively low-cost monitoring device can be found in the board of directors. The board plays a major role in the corporate governance framework and is responsible for monitoring managerial performance and achieving an adequate return for shareholders, while preventing conflicts of interests and balancing competing demands on the corporation. When necessary, the board also has the authority to replace the management of the corporation. The board is also responsible for reviewing key executive and board remuneration.

However, in order for boards to effectively fulfil their monitoring role they must have some degree of independence from management. While the emphasis in outsider systems is on independence, in reality there is the very serious problem that, like management, the board too can become entrenched. This is particularly the case when board members are compensated for their activities, and are themselves responsible for overseeing executive and board remuneration. While compensation attracts high quality individuals as non-executive board members it also provides incentives to serve on a large number of boards. This in turn can interfere with performance, since service on too many boards reduces the monitoring ability of board members. Even if regulations were to limit the number of board positions that can be held, when you have dispersed ownership, agency problems arising from the separation and ownership and control still exist. Although the board in theory should represent the interests of shareholders and the company, in practice they often become part of the management of the corporation. Because of these problems, there is still a widely held perception of the board as a relatively weak monitoring device.

3.1.3 *The Role of Market Mechanisms*

Takeover threats can act as an effective disciplining mechanism and diminish the motivation for managerial opportunism. The USA in particular has an active market for corporate control as witnessed by the frequency of mergers and acquisitions, including a significant number of hostile takeovers. For example, in the mid-1980s alone, the value of USA mergers totalled approximately one trillion dollars, representing 40 per cent of average annual market capitalization. In the UK, there has been an average of over 200 mergers and acquisitions per year over the last decade, compared with an average of about fifty in Germany. While up until now the market for corporate control has not been a key feature of insider systems of corporate governance, this is gradually beginning to change, as mergers and acquisition activity is increasing and hostile takeovers are becoming more common.

At the same time, the intensity of the mergers and acquisitions market is not in and of itself evidence of a powerful disciplinary device at work. Takeovers can be prompted by rent-seeking behaviour, empire building, and tax minimization, as much as from a desire to boost efficiency levels. Therefore, it is not always correct to assume that a buoyant market for corporate control reflects the true extent of corporate monitoring. With legal, advisory, and financing costs constituting on average 4 per cent of the purchase price, this is also a particularly expensive way of aligning the interests of management with those of shareholders. Nevertheless, given the weakness of other disciplining mechanisms in outsider systems the market for corporate control plays a critical role in the governance process.

Product market competition can also to some extent act to reduce the scope for managerial inefficiency and opportunism. This is because there are fewer rents to be expropriated when markets are competitive. Competition provides a benchmark by which the performance of the firm can be judged when compared with the performance of other firms in a similar sector. However, the effects of product market competition are slow to act, forcing inefficient companies into bankruptcy only after a long period of time has elapsed, by which point most shareholder value has been eradicated. Bankruptcy legislation, by influencing the claims and control of different investors in the event of insolvency, also plays an important role in corporate governance.

3.1.4 *Short-Term Behaviour*

Although an active market for corporate control can act as a disciplining device on managerial behaviour, in an economy characterized by frequent takeovers, long-term commitments between stakeholders may be more difficult to sustain. Not only may this reduce overall investment by providing weak incentives for stakeholders to provide firm-specific investments, but it may also create biases in the type of investment projects undertaken. In fact, heavy reliance on financial markets may encourage managers to focus excessively on projects with short-term pay-offs even when this is to the detriment of long-term corporate performance. On the other hand, more competitive markets for finance and corporate control can lead to tighter monitoring of research activities by company managers, with a more careful selection of projects and strengthened cost control. This in turn can lead to increased efficiency in applied research. Special financial devices have also developed in outsider systems (e.g. NASDAQ in specialized capital markets) which may be more effective forms of risk financing for long-term R&D projects than traditional intermediaries in many insider banking systems of corporate governance.

However, projects with longer-term pay-offs, such as basic research, may still be undervalued as a result of stock market myopia. This impacts upon innovation, technological development and long-term economic growth since the purpose and contribution of basic research is to increase the pool of knowledge required for applied research, which may be hurt in the long run as a consequence (OECD 1998*d*). While a shift in R&D expenditures towards short-term, high-pay-off projects may have the effect of spurring higher productivity growth in the short to medium turn, any expansion thus triggered should be of a transitory nature. Policy makers in systems of corporate governance which tend to be more short term in nature, should pay particular attention to the potential consequences of reducing government funding for basic research.

By rejecting projects in which returns fail to satisfy investor demand for more rapid pay-offs, it does not necessarily follow that managers are inefficient or guilty of shortsightedness. However, executive compensation plans geared to align the interest of managers with those of shareholders may serve to exacerbate short-term behaviour. For instance, when managerial remuneration is due largely to stocks or stock options, managers have an incentive to maximize short-term results in order to increase their own compensation. Managers can maximize the total benefit to themselves by engaging in projects that maximize short-term shareholder value and then cash in on their stocks while moving to an executive position with another corporation. At the same time they benefit from the reputation effects of having increased shareholder value in their previous firm of employment. Therefore, while executive remuneration consisting largely of shares or stock-options would seem to align the interests of managers with those of shareholders, they may also distort incentives. This would also seem to concur with the view that executive pay packages in the UK and USA are becoming excessive. This, in turn, has coincided with a move by shareholders in these systems to limit executive remuneration, or at least to have it more closely linked to corporate performance.

3.2. *Insider Systems of Corporate Governance*

'Insider' systems typical of non-UK Europe, Japan, and Korea are characterized by concentrated ownership or voting power and a multiplicity of inter-firm relationships and corporate holdings. Institutional investors such as pension funds, mutual funds, and insurance companies play a much smaller role in corporate governance than is the case in outsider systems. Familial control, close relationships with banks, cross-shareholdings (both horizontal and vertical), and pyramidal structures of corporate holdings are dominant features of insider systems. The significance of these features is that they allow shareholders to extend their control at relatively low cost. Majority shareholders or controlling blockholders now have both the incentive to monitor management and the necessary power to influence the decision-making process. The basic conflict that arises in this system is between controlling owners and outside minority shareholders, that is, 'strong voting blockholders, weak minority owners' or 'weak managers, weak minority owners, strong majority owners'.

When voting power is concentrated but ownership is dispersed, management entrenchment is still a possibility, especially if the blockholders are managers themselves. This possibility is one of the arguments often used in support of the one-share/one-vote principle. The weak monitoring incentives associated with outsider systems also lead to management entrenchment, but at least with one-share/one-vote takeovers are possible. With dispersed ownership and concentrated voting power takeovers become virtually impossible. Furthermore, when there is a difference between cash flow rights and voting rights, the incentives for extracting private benefits are much stronger and collusion between managers and blockholders is more likely. In Continental Europe managers are often forced to maximize 'blockholder value' and this does not necessarily maximize minority shareholders' returns. For example, in pyramidal structures minority owners can be expropriated though intra-group transfers by blockholders that control the group. Blockholders could also agree to vote favourably on management sponsored proposals and be compensated by side payments. These incentives arise because blockholders only bear a fraction of the costs of these payments by forgoing the dividend payments associated with their cash flow rights, but receive the full benefits associated with any side payment.

One of the consequences of rent extraction by controlling shareholders is that it raises the cost of equity capital as minority shareholders demand a premium on shares issued. This problem may become particularly acute when small investors do not have enough legal rights to secure a return on their investment. This leads to a lack of liquidity in secondary markets as investors withhold funds, and a lack of opportunities for risk diversification as a consequence of illiquid markets. Capital markets in insider systems therefore tend to be much less well developed than those found in outsider systems. On the other hand, concentrated ownership encourages more long-term relationships and commitment amongst stakeholders. This, in turn, can lead to greater investment in firm-specific assets with possible positive implications for profitability in the long run.

3.2.1. *The Role of Banks in Corporate Governance*

Differences in corporate governance systems are thought to influence the cost of capital, the availability, and type of financing available to firms. For example, stock market capitalization

Table 17.4. *Market capitalization of listed domestic equity issues (as per cent of GDP at year end)*

	1975	1980	1985	1990	1993	1994	1995	1996
Australia (Assoc. of SE)	22	40	37	37	71	67	70	80
Austria	3	3	7	17	16	16	14	15
Belgium	15	8	26	33	37	36	37	44
Canada (Toronto and Vancouver)	30	45	45	43	61	59	66	86
Denmark	11	8	26	30	31	34	33	41
Finland	—	—	—	17	28	39	35	49
France	10	8	15	26	36	34	32	38
Germany (Assoc. of SE)	12	9	29	22	24	24	24	28
Greece	—	—	—	—	—	—	14	19
Ireland	—	—	—	—	—	—	40	49
Italy[a]	5	6	14	14	15	18	19	21
Japan	28	36	71	99	68	77	69	66
Korea	—	—	—	43	42	50	40	29
Mexico	—	—	—	16	50	31	32	32
The Netherlands	21	17	47	42	58	67	72	95
New Zealand	—	—	39	20	56	53	53	56
Norway	—	—	16	23	24	30	30	36
Spain	32	8	12	23	25	25	27	33
Sweden	3	10	37	40	58	66	75	95
Switzerland[b]	30	42	91	69	114	109	129	136
Turkey	—	—	—	—	20	17	12	17
United Kingdom	37	38	77	87	122	114	122	142
United States of America (NYSE, Amex and NASDAQ)[c]	48	50	57	56	81	75	98	114

[a]Italy—All Italy on a net basis since 1985.
[b]Switzerland—only Zurich through 1990.
[c]United States of America—including foreign shares in 1975.
Source: OECD (1998*c*), Financial Market Trends, February.

as a percentage of GDP in insider systems is normally lower than that found in outsider systems, as shown in Table 17.4. If the development of financial markets is linked with economic development then this can impinge upon economic growth. However, this may not matter if there are other sources of financing available to the corporate sector. For this reason, in insider systems there is a much greater emphasis on banks as providers of external finance and debt/equity ratios are typically higher.

Unlike the arm's length relationships between banks and corporate clients found in outsider systems, banks in insider systems tend to maintain more complex and longer-term relationships with the corporate sector. In Japan, Korea, and many of the Continental European countries, commercial banks play a leading role in the governance of the corporate sector. For example, banks often name representatives to the board and exercise considerable leadership and control in the company with which they have a relationship. The benefits of a 'bank-based' system are that banks perform important monitoring and screening functions, thereby reducing asymmetric information problems. The close relationships between banks and client firms in insider systems provides greater access to firm-specific information, and is thought to be a factor contributing to lower risk premiums, thus lowering the overall cost of capital faced by firms. However, the provision of information in bank-based systems relies on confidentiality, which runs counter to the requirements of strong public disclosure associated with outsider systems.

Asymmetric information problems become particularly important in the refinancing of failing firms. The failure of creditors to be able to distinguish between firms with good or bad prospects during periods of financial difficulty can result in premature liquidations. Insider systems, with their closer relationships between banks and the corporate sector, can mitigate some of these information problems and may result in a more efficient allocation of resources. Banks in insider systems also play a much more important role in the restructuring of poorly performing firms and it is often the case that financial institutions in the USA and UK intervene too late in corporate restructuring (Mayer 1996). Competition in financial markets in outsider systems may undermine the development of long-term relations between firms and financial institutions. For example, there is little incentive for banks to provide rescue funds to the corporate sector when there is competition in financial markets and firms are free to shift to the lowest cost supplier of finance once they are out of financial distress.

Insider systems, characterized by small and illiquid public capital markets, the absence of venture capital markets, and a reliance on debt financing, can hamper the development of a vibrant and thriving SME sector. New firms may find it very difficult to obtain financing since they have no established track record or long-term relationship with the financial sector. Banks, in this case, tend to be conservative in their lending policies. This is because banks face an asymmetric risk when assessing new start-ups. For example, in the worst case scenario the bank can lose all the credit it has extended to a new firm, but should the venture succeed the best the bank can hope for is to be fully repaid, including accrued interest. In this way, the bank is excessively exposed to downside risk.

While banks in general may have a lower tolerance to risk than shareholders, the close nature of the relationship tends to reduce asymmetric information and risks associated with uncertainty. Long-term relationships with banks, therefore, can also reduce biases that might favour investments that generate short-term improvements in performance (von Thadden 1995). For example, a lower cost of capital encourages more long-term investment.[8] Therefore, investments characterized by large 'sunk' costs are more likely to be undertaken in corporate governance systems that are based on long-term relationships with financial institutions. However, the overall effect of these opposing influences makes it difficult to predict which system of corporate governance is more likely to promote innovative activity.

3.2.2. *Long-Term Relationships: Intra-Group Holdings and Commitment*

Outsider systems of widely dispersed ownership, where shareholders can walk away from relations with other stakeholders without suffering any costs can, discourage firm-specific investment. The focus in insider systems is more on building long-term relationships with many of the contractual partners of the firm. It is thought that the continuous nature of relations between these groups, including banks, the workforce, contractors and clients, promotes a greater investment in firm-specific assets. However, the importance of long-term relationships and commitment for firm performance varies by industry sector or type of productive activity (Williamson 1985; Mayer 1996; Maher 1997). For example, Mayer (1996: 24) states that they are 'particularly important where productive activity depends on the involvement of and investment by a large number of stakeholders. Complex manufacturing processes, which require several different supplier and purchaser arrangements, may be particularly dependent on ownership patterns that promote commitment and trust. Ownership patterns are also relevant to activities that may require firm specific investments by employees in training and acquisition of skills. Incentives to undertake such investments may require commitments by employers to long-term employment and promotion policies within the firm.' Long-term relations and commitment are therefore important in high technology industries or activities with high asset specificity. In these industries it is the firm-specific investments made by various stakeholders, rather than the flow of external funds, that impinges upon the performance of the firm.[9]

The identity of owners can also have major economic implications. Ownership by one corporation in another effectively reduces transaction costs and 'hold-up' problems associated with incentives to engage in opportunistic behaviour. In this case, stakeholders have a greater incentive to invest in relationship-specific investment. On the other hand, complex patterns of ownership and large shareholdings can also impede the restructuring of firms and industries, and diminish the adaptability of firms to respond to changing circumstances and globalization. One of the problems with complex patterns of ownership and cross-shareholdings is that insiders need not always own an outright majority of a company in order to maintain control. For example, in Italy widespread equity linkages via pyramidal structures have made it possible for around 150 core groups to exert control over almost 6,500 firms.[10] Pyramidal groups, by providing a wide access to capital, have some of the benefits associated with dispersed ownership while minimizing the agency costs associated with the monitoring of management. However, this type of group structure is particularly prone to expropriation and a lack of transparency. Equity linkages via cross-shareholdings on the other hand facilitate strategic alliances and can be used to create a significant core of insiders. In Japan, for example, these cross holdings are concentrated among the keiretsu, which are made up of large corporations across a wide range of industries with banks at their centre. Through these linkages the strategic and operational decisions of the firm are overseen by the holding company.

Complex patterns of ownership serve to protect both the group and lower level holdings from hostile takeovers. For example, long-term relationships between firms, cemented by cross-shareholdings, may restrict the possibilities for a transfer of share ownership.[11] As a result, the market for corporate control in insider systems is less developed than in outsider systems. The absence of an effective market for corporate control may impede the development of an international production base and can prevent firms from entering through domestic acquisitions. In Germany, the limited importance of listed joint-stock companies, the role of cross-shareholdings between partner firms, and the important role of employee representation on company boards, all make it very difficult for outsiders to buy German firms. However, this is gradually changing and takeover activity, both in Japan and in Continental Europe, is on the increase. While long-term relationships between firms and suppliers can help promote efficiency gains, the subsequent increase in industry concentration can result in collusive behaviour and may weaken the overall level of competition in product markets. This suggests that insider systems of corporate governance may need to pay particular attention to strengthening competition policy and entry conditions for newcomers, including conditions for start-up of new firms.

3.3. *A Convergence in Systems?*

The agency problems that arise from the separation of ownership and control raise the need for a corporate governance framework which strengthens managerial accountability and encourages managers to maximize profits rather than pursue their own objectives. In addition, a good corporate governance framework needs to protect minority shareholders from rent extraction by either managers or controlling shareholders while at the same time encouraging efficient investment by stakeholders. The means by which this is attained varies widely across countries and, even within a single country, across industrial sectors. This is exemplified by the current divergence in corporate governance structures found in OECD countries. However, the increasing globalization of capital markets and liberalizing of international trade seem to have created an environment in which differences in corporate governance are becoming less severe. For example, while family companies often predominate in Australia, Canada, and New Zealand, this pattern of concentrated ownership coexists with a strong recognition of shareholders rights, as well as the importance of greater transparency in the corporate sector. In outsider systems, there has been a growing appreciation of the powerful monitoring incentives associated with concentrated ownership. Increasingly, institutional investors and pension funds in the UK and USA are becoming active participants in the corporate governance of firms in which they hold substantial holdings. Venture capital markets and second tier markets such as NASDAQ have also developed to accommodate outside financing towards closely held firms.

Convergence forces at work in both types of system are primarily a result of globalization of financial markets. Firms, and in particular large multinational firms, are increasingly adopting the best practices of existing systems in an effort to improve corporate efficiency and to attract external capital funds. For example, the capital requirements of major firms expanding abroad has led to a number of firms seeking a listing on foreign stock exchanges. Raising capital through foreign stock exchanges, where shareholders are more concerned about firm risks, is very different from a bank-based system, where the banks are more interested in the risk of default. This change in the method of financing is having a major impact on corporate governance. For example, in many insider systems the increasing importance of foreign investors as a source of capital for listed companies is raising the demand for more transparency and minority shareholder protection. The full implications of recent developments are hard to predict, but there appears to be an overall trend towards a degree of convergence in governance and financing patterns, with outsider systems adopting some of the features of insider systems, and vice versa. However, the extent of the remaining divergences between systems, which are historically contingent and rooted in cultural, historical and legal differences, suggests that complete convergence is unlikely.

4. CORPORATE GOVERNANCE AND PERFORMANCE: THE EMPIRICAL EVIDENCE

In this section, we examine some of the empirical evidence on (i) the effects of different types of ownership structure on firm performance; (ii) the conflicts that arise between different types of shareholders and the possible detrimental effects of dominant shareholders; (iii) entrenchment or rent extraction on the part of management and whether the existence of an active takeover market is an effective mechanism to correct managerial inefficiencies; and (iv) whether or not executive compensation packages are effective in aligning the interest of managers with those of shareholders.

4.1. *Ownership Concentration and Firm Performance*

One of the questions that arises when considering if corporate governance affects performance is whether or not owner-controlled firms are more profitable than manager-controlled firms. This question is central, particularly since concentrated holdings are the primary means of control in so many countries around the world. A priori it is not clear whether concentrated ownership and control will improve performance. Concentrated ownership by reducing agency problems and providing better monitoring incentives should lead to better performance. On the other hand, it might also lead to the extraction of private benefits by controlling blockholders at the expense of minority shareholders. If owner-controlled firms indeed are more profitable than manager-controlled firms this would suggest that insider systems have an advantage in that they provide better monitoring which leads to better performance.

Based on a comprehensive survey primarily of studies from the USA and UK, Gugler (1999) concludes that owner-controlled firms tend to significantly outperform manager-controlled firms.[12] This supports the hypothesis that large shareholders are active monitors in companies, and that direct shareholder monitoring helps boost the overall profitability of firms. The picture is less clear for other countries. For a sample of listed German manufacturing firms, Thonet and Poensgen (1979) found manager-controlled firms to significantly outperform owner-controlled firms in terms of profitability, but that owner-controlled firms had higher growth rates. Jacquemin and Ghellinck (1980), using French firm data, found no differences between familial and non-familial controlled firms. Prowse (1992) found no relationship between ownership concentration and profitability in Japanese companies. Although these few studies are not conclusive evidence, they do suggest that the policy conclusions of the results based on USA and UK data may not be transferable to other countries. Furthermore, levels of ownership concentration in the USA and UK are low relative to other countries. Once concentration reaches very high levels then it is not clear that more monitoring will continue to improve things and may actually work in the opposite direction.[13]

Whether or not owner-controlled firms outperform manager-controlled firms may also depend on the industry in question. Zeckhauser and Pound (1990) find that the superior performance of owner-controlled firms holds in industries with relatively low asset specificity (e.g. machinery and paper products), but there was no difference in industries with high asset specificity (e.g. computers). This suggests that the nature of the firm's investment and production decisions influences the asymmetry of information between principal and agent. For example, in industries where outside monitoring is particularly difficult, such as is the case in high asset specificity industries, large shareholders are less effective in overcoming agency problems and additional control mechanisms may be required.

Transferring the 'separation of ownership and control' view of monitoring as suggested by the large body of primarily USA and UK economic studies to Continental Europe, Korea, and Japan can also be misleading because the economic decision agents are very different. For example, holding companies, the state, banks, other non-financial corporations, and familial control are dominant features of insider systems. Different owners will have different objectives, and it is likely that the identity of owners will matter for firm performance. For example, managers of corporations under governmental or quasi-governmental control may have different incentives and will behave differently to managers of corporations in the private sector. For this reason, ownership concentration and the identity of owners should be viewed as variables that exert a simultaneous, but different, influence on firm performance.

Roe (1994) states that the low ownership concentration in the USA compared to other countries may be the result of policies initiated by controlling managers that discourage large holdings, for example, anti-takeover devices. This suggests that management entrenchment is a serious problem in the USA, and that policy makers in outsider systems should pay particular attention to the negative effects of mechanisms that are often employed by management to inhibit the market for corporate control. Where direct shareholder monitoring is weak, policy makers need to pay particular attention to the incentive effects created by other control mechanisms such as takeovers or managerial remuneration schemes. However, corporate governance structures are dynamic in nature. Recent changes in corporate governance in the USA and UK, such as the increased importance of institutional investors, can lead to reduced scope for management discretion and may act as a substitute for large shareholder monitoring.

Finally, several studies also stressed the importance of the effects of product market competition on managerial behaviour. For example, significant differences in the performance of owner-controlled versus manager-controlled firms are more likely in markets where the scope for managerial entrenchment is much higher, that is, in monopolistic or oligopolistic market structures. This is because in competitive markets there are fewer rents for management to expropriate and ownership structure is less likely to affect firm performance. Weaknesses in corporate governance are, therefore, more likely when firms are both management-controlled and when firms exert a high degree of market power. One of the policy implications arising from these results is that developments in corporate governance legislation should be developed in conjunction with regulatory reform and competition policy.

4.2. *Dominant Shareholders and the Expropriation of Minority Shareholders*

The presence of large shareholders tends to improve the supervision of management. At the same time, controlling blockholders or majority shareholders may use the firm for their own private benefit, expropriating rents at the expense of minority shareholders and other stakeholders. Given the detrimental consequences of expropriation, it is important to know whether or not expropriation is a problem. However, direct evidence on measuring the extent of expropriation of rents, by either large shareholders or controlling blockholders, which may include management, is difficult to obtain. Therefore, empirical studies have attempted to measure this in an indirect way. If control is associated with the ability to expropriate private benefits, then the market should 'value' control. For example, if shares with superior voting rights trade at a premium which is not accounted for by other factors, then this is taken as evidence for significant private benefits of control that may come at the expense of minority shareholders.[14]

Empirical evidence suggests that control is valued. For example, Barclay and Holderness (1989; 1992) find that in the USA, large blocks of equity trade at a substantial premium to the post-trade price of minority shares and that on average these blocks trade at a 20 per cent premium. Other studies also support this hypothesis by comparing the price of shares that have identical dividend rights but differential voting rights. For the USA, DeAngelo and DeAngelo (1985), Jarrell and Poulsen (1988), and Zingales (1995) find shares with superior voting rights trade at a premium, but that this premium is small. However, Zingales (1995) finds that the premium rises sharply in situations where control is contested, implying that controlling blockholders receive private benefits at the expense of minority shareholders. On the other hand, Holderness and Sheehan (1988) and Asquith and Wizman (1990) find only small, if any, transfers between stakeholders. Their results would imply a rejection of the hypothesis that expropriation of minority shareholders is the primary reason for majority ownership. However, evidence from countries where concentrated ownership is the norm suggests that expropriation of private benefits by controlling blockholders at the expense of other stakeholders is a major problem. While Bergstrom and Rydqvist (1990) find a relatively low premium for Sweden, studies on Israel, Italy, and Switzerland find substantial premiums. For example, Levy (1982) finds a 45.5 per cent voting premium in Israel, Horner (1988) finds a 20 per cent premium for Switzerland, and Zingales (1994) finds an 82 per cent premium on the Milan Stock Exchange.

The empirical evidence on Israel and Italy suggests that agency costs can be very large in some countries. Zingales (1994) conjectures that these private benefits of control are so large in Italy (around 30 per cent of firm value) because the legal system is ineffective in preventing exploitation by controlling blockholders. Therefore, the development (or strengthening) of policies aimed at protection of minority shareholders may be particularly needed in countries with relatively weak corporate governance systems that enable such expropriation to take place. This problem is particularly acute in systems characterized by pyramidal groups. However, even if one instituted corporate governance policies with strong protection of minority shareholders, it is likely the policies will be ineffective if legal systems remain weak. It may be the case that strong protection of minority investors in the USA prevents controlling shareholders from expropriating other stakeholders. What is needed, therefore, is a systemic approach that requires that problems in the legal and regulatory structure be addressed simultaneously with changes in corporate governance policies.

Since expropriation by controlling shareholders can deter minority investors, the result is often a small and illiquid public equity market. This would explain why in countries where expropriation is a major problem, capital markets remain relatively underdeveloped. La Porta *et al.* (1997) ranked investor protection according to a number of dimensions of shareholder and creditor protection. The authors find that investors are best protected in English common law countries, are somewhat protected by German and Scandinavian codes, and are most vulnerable in countries of French origin. They also find that good shareholder protection is one determinant of liquid equity markets. Small and illiquid equity markets need not be a concern if other sources of finance, either internal or external, still lead to an optimal level and mix of investment. However, it is not clear whether debt finance is an adequate substitute for equity finance for all types of investment. The empirical evidence suggests that R&D investment might be adversely affected when the main source of outside finance is debt. Gugler (1999) finds a positive relationship between stock market capitalization and R&D spending for fourteen OECD countries.[15] This result is also confirmed in studies by Long and Malitz (1985) and Bradley *et al.* (1984), who find a negative correlation between leverage and R&D activity. Countries with liquid equity markets, therefore, tend to invest more in R&D activity and high-tech firm start-ups. This finding has implications for both productivity and growth.

Overall, the empirical evidence supports the view that there are potential conflicts of interest between dominant shareholders and other stakeholders in the firm, and that there are detrimental effects associated with expropriation. The source of this conflict is not just the structure of ownership but is also due, in part, to the legislative framework which protects investor rights. For example, while non-voting stock is a low-cost instrument for remaining in control and raising outside equity capital, it is also a separation device that implies diluted incentives and facilitates shareholder expropriation. Therefore, the best policy response seems to be to allow (but restrict) the issuance of non-voting stock, while at the same time provide minority shareholders with the means and power to claim due compensation if expropriation arises. Barclay and Holderness (1992) argue against legal provisions that may inhibit or postpone the exercise of control by acquirers of large blocks. However, such prescriptions seem inappropriate in a continental European context where the protection of minority shareholders is much weaker. Recent legislative changes in some European countries are indeed aimed at correcting the expropriation of rents by controlling shareholders and at moving in the direction of enhanced minority shareholder protection. These legislative moves include preventing acquirers of large blocks from voting their shares until approved by other shareholders, or preventing blockholders from purchasing the remaining shares for a specified price.[16] High standards of disclosure and transparency can also help ensure the type of environment in which small shareholders feel comfortable investing in equity markets.[17]

4.3. *The Market for Corporate Control and Firm Performance*

It is often asserted that takeovers are a mechanism for removing the management of poorly performing firms. Takeovers act as a powerful disciplining tool since they enable anyone who identifies an under-performing company to buy a controlling interest and to reap any gains associated with transferring control from an inefficient management to an efficient one. The efficiency of takeovers as a disciplining mechanism, however, is a controversial and somewhat unresolved issue. Few hostile takeovers appear to be value improving and some result in outright reductions in value.

There are two approaches to analysing the effects of takeovers. One is to examine the share prices of the target and acquiring firms around the announcement date of the takeover. The empirical studies in this area find that target shareholders, on average, gain from tender offers. Higson and Elliot (1998) find that, in the UK during the 1975–90 period, target shareholders' average returns were 37 per cent and were positive in 88 per cent of the cases. Many other studies confirm these results (Jensen and Ruback 1983; DeAngelo *et al.* 1984; Jarrell *et al.* 1988; Franks and Mayer 1996). On the other hand, for bidder shareholders the returns, on average, are close to zero (Bradley *et al.* 1984; Franks and Harris 1989). Overall, the empirical evidence indicates that target shareholders are the prime winners of takeover contests.

Another approach is to look at the post-takeover performance of the merged group. If takeovers are a means of resolving problems associated with inefficient management, or with other efficiency gains, the *ex post* performance of the merger group should be better than the weighted average of the *ex ante* performance of the acquiring and target firm prior to the takeover. The vast majority of studies find no significant improvement in firm performance following a merger. In fact, most find a negative impact on performance, particularly in the case of unrelated or conglomerate mergers. While the evidence on hostile takeovers is somewhat more positive, many express doubt that the takeover process is an effective means for disciplining management (Ravenscraft and Scherer 1987; Franks and Mayer 1996). In this case, an active market for corporate control in the USA and UK does not necessarily reflect the extent to which managerial inefficiencies are being corrected.

There are several reasons why not all takeovers will serve to enhance firm value. First, the main objective of the bidder need not necessarily be profit maximization. For example, managerialist theories of the firm emphasize the size and growth objectives of managers, and one of the fastest ways to increase firm growth is to acquire another firm. Second, although there may be improvements in productive efficiency, takeovers may adversely affect dynamic efficiency by reducing firm-specific investment by various stakeholders.[18] Third, an active takeover market may only aggravate excessively short-term behaviour that can impinge on innovative activity and dynamic efficiency.[19]

Since the efficiency gains of takeovers are, at best, quite low and target shareholders are receiving an average premium of around 30–40 per cent, takeovers seem to be primarily motivated by other objectives rather than with the disciplining of management. Franks and Mayer (1996) found that there was little evidence that takeovers in the USA and UK were motivated by poor performance prior to the takeover bid and are primarily motivated by objectives, such as changes in corporate strategy or rent-seeking behaviour. Tax motives, in particular, have long been suspected as a contributor to merger and acquisition activity, and the available evidence seems to support this (Auerbach and Reishus 1988; Lehn and Poulsen 1987). The vast majority of studies find that target shareholder's gains come primarily at the expense of other stakeholders, labour in particular. While most of these studies find that employees losses mainly come in the form of lay-offs, reduced wages, or lower employment and wage growth, Pontiff *et al.* (1990) found that over 10 per cent of takeovers involve pension fund reversions, accounting for 10–13 per cent of takeover premia. Takeovers can also have negative externalities. For example, Shliefer and Summers (1988) point out that the acquisition of

Youngstown Sheet and Tube in 1970 resulted in more that a doubling of bankruptcies in Youngstown and a plummeting of house prices.

Even if there is no evidence that takeovers actually improve firm performance, this does not necessarily imply that the market for corporate control does not work as a disciplining device. Defensive or anti-takeover mechanisms, particularly those that do not require shareholder approval, inhibit the market for corporate control. These measures include poison-pills, greenmail, and state anti-takeover amendments. The late 1980s witnessed a sharp increase in the number of states in the USA adopting anti-takeover legislation and firms adopting poison-pills.[20] Nearly all of the studies that look at the welfare effects of anti-takeover measures find they reduce shareholder value. For example, Jarrell and Poulsen (1987) report significant negative stock-price effects associated with supermajority amendments; the SEC (1984) finds negative stock price effects associated with greenmail; and Malatesta and Walkling (1988), and Ryngaert (1988) each find that poison-pills harm target shareholders by reducing the probability of takeovers. More recently, Bertrand and Mullainathan (1999) examined the effects of state anti-takeover legislation and find that these laws raised annual wages by 1–2 per cent.[21] Their results imply that takeovers do act to discipline management since they reduce the scope for managerial discretion. The authors conclude that legislation imposing a moratorium on specified transactions, such as the sale of assets, mergers, and business combinations, unless the board votes otherwise, effectively gives the board the power to block hostile takeovers and help to entrench management. Jensen (1988) also points out that defensive measures effectively transfer critical control decisions from owners to managers.

In summary, although the evidence taken from actual takeovers does not seem to support the hypothesis that takeovers are an effective mechanism for disciplining poor management, evidence based on the use of anti-takeover amendments suggests otherwise. Mechanisms that inhibit the market for corporate control should therefore be viewed with apprehension. However, with legal, advisory, and financing costs totalling, on average, 4 per cent of the purchase price, this is a particularly expensive way of aligning the interests of management with those of shareholders (Franks and Mayer 1996). Takeovers, therefore, should be viewed in conjunction with other control devices. For example, if substitutive relationships exist one could strengthen these alternative mechanisms while not constraining hostile takeovers by regulation. Brickley and James (1987), Schranz (1993), and Kini *et al.* (1995) find that the number of outside directors and ownership concentration are effective substitutive mechanisms for takeovers. The evidence seems to suggest, therefore, that the market for corporate control should be allowed to function without restriction, but to rely on hostile takeovers as the only, or even the main, disciplinary device may not be optimal.

4.4. *Managerial Compensation and Firm Performance*

When other mechanisms do not function very well there may be a need for special incentives to induce managers to act in the interests of shareholders. This is often undertaken through the design of executive remuneration packages, typically consisting of salaries, bonuses, and stock options, which tie managerial compensation to the performance of the firm. In this way, managerial wealth is subjected to at least some of the same risks to which shareholders and the firm are exposed. However, the emphasis on executive remuneration packages varies from one country to another and the optimality of contingent performance based compensation depends on whether or not other direct monitoring alternatives are available. The empirical evidence confirms the substitutive effects between direct monitoring by owners and compensation incentives. For example, Kole (1997) finds that if there is a family representative either in management or on the board of directors, the probability of adopting an equity-based compensation plan is significantly reduced. Conyon and Leech (1993) also find that the level of director pay is lower in companies that have a higher share ownership or are defined as owner-controlled. Therefore, it is not surprising that managerial compensation tends to be lower in insider systems, since there are fewer informational asymmetries and less scope for managerial discretion.

Monitoring by the board or by institutional investors may also substitute for compensation incentives. In theory at least, the use of these other mechanisms should also reduce the level of pay-incentives needed to align managers' incentives with those of shareholders. Mehran (1995) finds that the presence of outside directors, rather than decreasing the level of executive remuneration, actually increases the percentage of equity-based compensation. This may reflect the fact that, in practice, board members also become entrenched. Separating the roles of chairman and CEO is often proposed as a way of increasing accountability. However, Conyon and Leech (1993) found no evidence that separating these roles had any effect on executive compensation levels. Cosh and Hughes (1997) also find no evidence that institutional holdings in the UK alter the level of executive remuneration or the pay–performance relationship. Therefore, the evidence suggests that the board and institutional investors, unlike direct shareholder monitoring, are relatively weak monitoring devices.

If the use of incentive devices is effective, then this should manifest itself in a positive relationship between managerial compensation and firm performance. Excluding stock options, current evidence indicates that sensitivities of pay to performance are quite small. For example, Murphy (1985), Coughlin and Schmidt (1985), and Barro and Barro (1990) all find pay–performance elasticities in the range 0.10–0.17. However, Hall and Liebman (1997) show that the driving force behind the pay–performance relationship is the use of both stock and stock options. When they include stock and stock options, they find a mean elasticity of 4.5, suggesting that a 10 per cent rise in performance leads to a 45 per cent increase in CEO remuneration. However, Murphy (1998) finds that most of this increase is attributable to a general increase in the stock market and that there is little evidence that higher pay–performance sensitivities lead to higher stock performance. A number of studies also find that company size, and changes in size, are much more significant determinants of executive pay than measures of shareholder value (Conyon and Leech 1993; Gregg *et al.* 1993; Main *et al.* 1994). This suggests that managers in this case may have an incentive to engage in mergers and acquisitions as a way of increasing their remuneration.

According to agency theory, it does not make sense for owners to compensate managers for events that are beyond their control. Nor do owners want to penalize managers due to negative outcomes that are not the fault of the manager. However, it is harder for an executive manager to claim that the company has performed poorly due to general market conditions if other benchmark companies are performing well. This says that contracts, in order to be efficient, should relate compensation to rises in relative performance. However,

Murphy (1985), Barro and Barro (1990), and Hall and Liebman (1997) find that, in general, managerial compensation does not depend upon the relative performance of the firm.[22] Ezzamel and Watson (1997) also find there are asymmetric adjustments in executive pay levels, for example, executives that were relatively underpaid in the previous period receive pay increases, whereas executives who were overpaid were not subjected to downward adjustments. This is consistent with the complaint of many shareholder groups that remuneration committees, rather than strengthening the pay–performance relationship, have the effect of bidding up executive pay. Executive compensation plans may also serve to exacerbate short-term behaviour. There are serious concerns regarding the current practice of management to issue debt and use the proceeds to buy back equity, thereby increasing the firm's share price. While in theory how a firm is financed should make no difference to its value, very high levels of corporate debt make a firm more vulnerable to bankruptcy in the event of a downturn.

These empirical findings raise serious concerns regarding not only the efficiency of executive remuneration contracts, but also the motives behind them. Because boards of directors set compensation contracts, there is a risk that boards align themselves more with management than with weak dispersed shareholders. Yermack (1997) finds that the timing of stock option awards coincides with favourable movements in company stock prices. Furthermore, the practice of re-pricing stock options when share prices fall makes a mockery out of the notion that options are designed to align the interest of managers with those of shareholders.[23] The empirical evidence seems to indicate that these contracts, rather than aligning the interests of managers and shareholders, are enabling managers to expropriate some of the rents from shareholders. These abuses are particularly likely when share ownership is fragmented and alternative control mechanisms are weak. All of this does not suggest that the use of share and share options should be restricted,[24] but rather that they should be more closely linked to performance. Given the inherent conflict of interest involved, a question arises as to whether the board of directors should set key elements of managerial contracts at all.[25] The empirical evidence indicates that it is shareholders that should ultimately decide on the level and shape of executive remuneration packages.[26]

5. CONCLUSIONS

Corporate governance affects the development and functioning of capital markets and exerts a strong influence on resource allocation. In an era of increasing capital mobility and globalization, it has also become an important framework condition affecting the industrial competitiveness and economies of OECD countries. This paper sets out to further develop our understanding of corporate governance and its effects on corporate and economic performance. In doing so, it addresses some of the underlying factors that promote efficient corporate governance, and examines some of the economic implications associated with various corporate governance systems.

Both insider and outsider systems of corporate governance have their strengths, weaknesses, and different economic implications. Corporate governance mechanisms also vary depending on industry sectors and type of productive activity. For example, in industries characterized by high asset specificity, such as many high-tech industries, monitoring is more difficult and different mechanisms may be required in order to improve firm performance. Identifying what constitutes good corporate governance practice, and under what circumstances, is a difficult task. This is partly because the effectiveness of corporate governance systems is influenced by differences in countries' legal and regulatory frameworks, and historical and cultural factors, in addition to the structure of product and factor markets. The challenge, therefore, is not only to identify the strengths and weaknesses in each individual system or group of systems, but also to identify what are the underlying conditions upon which these strengths and weaknesses depend.

Dispersed ownership brings higher liquidity, which can be vital for the development of innovative activity. On the other hand, it does not encourage commitment and long-term relationships that might be required for certain types of investments. For example, when corporations are owned and controlled by each other, this can reduce transaction costs and incentives to engage in opportunistic behaviour. Stakeholders, therefore, have a greater incentive to invest in relationship specific investment. On the other hand, this can also reduce the level of product market competition. The benefits of concentrated ownership are that it brings more effective monitoring of management and helps to overcome agency problems. However, the costs associated with concentrated ownership are low liquidity, reduced possibilities for risk diversification and impediments to entry by newcomers.

One of the main challenges facing policy makers is how to develop a good corporate governance framework which can secure the benefits associated with controlling shareholders acting as direct monitors, while at the same time ensuring that they do not expropriate excessive rents at the expense of other stakeholders. The empirical evidence to date seems to suggest that this is indeed a problem and that protection of minority shareholders is critical to the development of equity markets. Therefore, policy makers in insider systems need to pay particular attention to developing corporate governance frameworks that will not hinder the development of active equity markets. The search for good corporate governance practices should be based on an identification of what works in defined countries, to discern what broad principles can be derived from these experiences, and to examine the conditions for transferability of these practices to other countries. There is a need, therefore, for continued research that identifies what are the crucial improvements needed in different systems and in different situations.

Notes

1. See, for example, Shleifer and Vishny (1997), and Berglof (1997).
2. Blair (1995) also defines corporate governance in this broader context and argues that corporate governance should be regarded as the set of institutional arrangements for governing the relationships among all the stakeholders that contribute firm-specific assets. Zingales (1997) defines corporate governance as a 'complex set of constraints that shape the *ex post* bargaining over the quasi-rents generated in the course of the relationship'.
3. Until recently, lack of hard data has been a major impediment to research in this area. For the European countries, it was possible to get the most up-to-date information available based on the

recent work in this area by the European Corporate Governance Network (ECGN). Data for the USA and Japan, on the other hand, has had to rely on older studies.

4. Largest shareholder could be the holdings of an institutional investor or pension fund, a bank, other corporations, or individual and familial holdings.
5. Data on ownership concentration should be viewed with caution since disclosure requirements in most OECD countries relate not to ownership but to control.
6. Figures for the German DAX 30 and French CAC40 are atypical. For example, there is a minimum turnover requirement for membership of the DAX30, leading companies to widen their shareholder base in order to remain in the index. Similarly, the CAC40 is an unrepresentative group of the largest and most liquid companies on the exchange.
7. With dispersed ownership, if shareholders are unhappy, they will just sell their shares (exit) since they do not have the incentive, or the means available to them (voice), to engage in direct shareholder monitoring.
8. The low cost of funds is thought to have contributed to the relatively high level of domestic investment that has been a strong feature of the Japanese economy in the past.
9. Microsoft Corporation is a good example of this where it is the promotion and ability to retain human capital within the firm, rather than external funds, that impacts upon the firm's performance.
10. See OECD (1995), Economic Survey of Italy.
11. Often shares will not be sold without the understanding of the issuer.
12. Firms are usually classified as owner-controlled if there is a single block of equity exceeding 5 or 10 per cent. The dependent variable used in the studies surveyed were all proxies for the performance of the firms as measured by net income/net worth, Tobin's Q, or the riskiness of returns.
13. Empirical studies for both the USA and UK suggest that at low levels of concentration, performance increases as concentration increases, but then declines as concentration levels keep increasing, see Morck *et al.* (1988), McConnell and Servaes (1990), and Wruck (1989).
14. In some cases, non-voting stock has a preferred dividend. Therefore, the observed premium must be what is left over after having accounted for other differences in classes of shares, and which is then attributable to the superior voting rights, that is, the premium associated with control.
15. A regression of the effect of the ratio of stock market capitalization to GDP on the R&D/GDP ratio shows that a 10 per cent point 'deepening' of a country's stock market increases the R&D/GDP ratio by about 0.12 percentage points.
16. Italy, Belgium, Denmark, and France have passed laws requiring that every acquisition of more than 30 per cent of the equity of the firm be followed by a tender offer to all voting shares at the same price.
17. For example, the OECD Principles of Corporate Governance recommend mandatory and strict enforcement of disclosure requirements for pyramidal groups, the structure of ownership and voting rights, and for legal separation devices.
18. For example, if stakeholders anticipate that takeovers increase the probability that they will be expropriated *ex post* they may provide sub-optimal levels of firm-specific investment *ex ante* (Shleifer and Summers 1988).
19. However, Jarrell *et al.* (1988) state that no empirical evidence has been found to support this theory.
20. For example, the percentage of listed firms that were protected by such legislation increased from 38 per cent in 1987 to 77 per cent in 1988, see Comment and Schwert (1995).

21. Ryngaert and Netter (1988), and Schumann (1988) also present evidence on the negative effects of state anti-takeover amendments.
22. One of the reasons why this may be the case is that, under current accounting rules, stock options with a performance target have to be counted as a cost against profits, while options with a fixed exercise price do not reduce current earnings. Harmonization of accounting rules concerning stock options with a variable and a fixed exercise price would remove this distortion.
23. When share prices fell in the late summer of 1998, many firms re-priced their options so that executives enjoyed massive gains when the market rebounded (*The Economist*, 7 August 1999).
24. The use of stock options can reduce the costs of starting a company since new firms can hire employees with the promise of future benefits through the use of share options.
25. A study undertaken by the accountancy firm PricewaterhouseCoopers found that for a sample of 270 quoted companies in the UK, only seven firms put their remuneration report to a shareholder vote and only 5 per cent of companies disclosed, even in broad terms, how performance measures relate to long-term company objectives (*Financial Times*, 20 July 1999).
26. This is also in line with recent recommendations by the UK government. For example, this could be done by either requiring companies to put their remuneration report to an annual shareholder vote, or by allowing shareholders to put forward resolutions on remuneration to annual general meetings.

References

Aghion, P., and Bolton, P. (1992). An incomplete contracts approach to financial contracting. *Review of Economic Studies* 59: 473.

Aoki, M. (1994). The Japanese firm as a system of attributes: A survey and research agenda. In M. Aoki and R. Dore (ed.), *The Japanese Firm: Sources of Competitive Strength*. Oxford: Oxford University Press.

—— Dore, R., Gustaffson, B., and Williamson, O. (eds.) (1990). *The Firm as a Nexus of Treaties*. London: Sage Publications.

Asquith, P., and Wizman, T. (1990). Event risk, covenants, and bondholders' returns in leveraged buyouts. *Journal of Financial Economics* 27: 195.

Auerbach, A., and Reishus, D. (1988). Taxes and merger decision. In J. Coffee, L. Lowenstein, and S. Rose-Ackerman (ed.), *Knights, Raiders, and Targets: The Impact of the Hostile Takeover*. New York: Oxford University Press.

Barclay, M., and Holderness, C. (1989). Private benefits from control of public corporations. *Journal of Financial Economics* 25: 371.

—— —— (1992). The law and large block-trades. *The Journal of Law and Economics* 35: 265.

Barro, J. R., and Barro, R. J. (1990). Pay, performance and turnover of bank CEOs. *Journal of Labor Economics* 8: 448.

Becht, M., and Bohmer, E. (1999). Ownership and voting power in Germany. In F. Barca and M. Becht (ed.), *Ownership and Control: The European Perspective*. Oxford: Oxford University Press.

—— and Röell, A. (1999). Blockholdings in Europe: An international comparison. *European Economic Review* 43: 1049.

Becht, M., Chapelle, A., and Renneboog, L. (1999). Shareholding cascades: The separation of ownership and control in Belgium. In F. Barca and M. Becht (ed.), *Ownership and Control: The European Perspective*. Oxford: Oxford University Press.

Berglof, E. (1997). Reforming corporate governance: Redirecting the European agenda. *Economic Policy* 93.

Bergstrom, C., and Rydqvist, K. (1990). Ownership of equity in dual-class firms. *Journal of Banking and Finance* 14: 237.

Berle, A., and Means, G. (1932). *The Modern Corporation and Private Property*. New York: MacMillan.

Bertrand, M., and Mullainathan, S. (1999). Is there discretion in wage setting? A test using takeover legislation. *The RAND Journal of Economics* 30: 535.

Bianchi, M., Bianco, M., and Enriques, L. (1999). Pyramidal groups and the separation between ownership and control in Italy. In F. Barca and M. Becht (ed.), *Ownership and Control: The European Perspective*. Oxford: Oxford University Press.

Blair, M. (1995). *Ownership and Control: Rethinking Corporate Governance for the Twenty-First Century*. Washington, DC: Brookings Institute Press.

Bloch, L., and Kremp, E. (1999). Ownership and Voting Power in France. In F. Barca and M. Becht (ed.), *Ownership and Control: The European Perspective*. Oxford: Oxford University Press.

Bradley, M., Jarrell, G., and Kim, E. H. (1984). On the existence of an optimal capital structure: Theory and evidence. *Journal of Finance* 39: 857.

Brickley, J. A., and James, C. (1987). The takeover market, corporate board composition, and ownership structure: the case of banking. *Journal of Law and Economics* 30: 161.

Coase, R. H. (1937). The nature of the firm. *Economica* 4: 386.

Comment, R., and Schwert, G. W. (1995). Poison or placebo? Evidence on the deterrence and wealth effects of modern antitakeover measures. *Journal of Financial Economics* 39: 3.

Conyon, M. J., and Leech, D. (1993). Top pay, company performance and corporate governance. Warwick University, Economic Research Paper No. 410.

Cosh, A., and Hughes, A. (1997). Executive remuneration, executive dismissal and institutional shareholdings. *International Journal of Industrial Organization* 15: 469.

Coughlin, A. T., and Schmidt R. (1985). Executive compensation, management turnover, and firm performance: An empirical investigation. *Journal of Accounting and Economics* 7: 43.

Crespi-Cladera, R., and Garcia-Cestona, M. (1999). Ownership and control: a Spanish survey. In F. Barca and M. Becht (ed.), *Ownership and Control: The European Perspective*. Oxford: Oxford University Press.

DeAngelo, H., and DeAngelo, L. (1985). Managerial ownership of voting rights: A study of public corporations with dual classes of common stock. *Journal of Financial Economics* 14: 33.

—— and Rice, E. (1984). Going private: Minority freeze-outs and stockholder wealth. *Journal of Law and Economics* 27: 367.

de Jong, A., Kabir, R., Marra, T., and Röell, A. (1999). Ownership and control in The Netherlands. In F. Barca and M. Becht (ed.), *Ownership and Control: The European Perspective*. Oxford: Oxford University Press.

Ezzamel, M., and Watson, R. (1997). Wearing two hats: The conflicting control and management roles of non-executive directors. In K. Keasey, S. Thompson, and M. Wright (ed.), *Corporate Governance: Economic Management and Financial Issues*. Oxford: Oxford University Press.

Franks, J., and Harris, R. (1989). Shareholder wealth effects of corporate takeovers: The UK experience 1955–85. *Journal of Financial Economics* 23: 225.

—— and Mayer, C. (1996). Hostile takeovers and the correction of managerial failure. *Journal of Financial Economics* 40: 163.

Goergen, M., and Renneboog, L. (1999). Strong managers and passive institutional investors in the UK. In F. Barca and M. Becht (ed.), *Ownership and Control: The European Perspective*. Oxford: Oxford University Press.

Gregg, P., Machin, S., and Szymanski, S. (1993). The disappearing relationship between director's pay and corporate performance. *British Journal of Industrial Relations* 31: 1.

Grossman, S., and Hart, O. (1986). The costs and benefits of ownership: A theory of vertical and lateral integration. *Journal of Political Economy* 94: 691.

Gugler, K. (1999). Corporate governance and economic performance: A survey. University of Vienna, Working Paper.

Gugler, K., Kalss, S., Stomper, A., and Zechner, J. (1999). The separation of ownership and control: An Austrian perspective. In F. Barca and M. Becht (ed.), *Ownership and Control: The European Perspective.* Oxford: Oxford University Press.

Hall, B., and Liebman, J. (1997). Are CEOs really paid like bureaucrats? NBER, Working Paper No. 6213.

Higson, C., and Elliott, J. (1998). Post-takeover returns: The UK evidence. *Journal of Empirical Finance* 5: 27.

Holderness, C., and Sheehan, D. P. (1988). The role of majority shareholders in publicly held corporations: An exploratory analysis. *Journal of Financial Economics* 20: 317.

Horner, M. R. (1988). The value of the corporate voting right: Evidence from Switzerland. *Journal of Banking and Finance* 12: 69.

Jacquemin, A., and de Ghellinck, E. (1980). Familial control, size and performance in the largest French firms. *European Economic Review* 13: 81.

Jarrell, G. A., and Poulsen, A. B. (1987). Shark repellents and stock prices: The effects of antitakeover amendments since 1980. *Journal of Financial Economics* 19: 127.

——(1988). Dual-class recapitalizations as anti-takeover mechanisms: The recent evidence. *Journal of Financial Economics* 20: 129.

——Brickley, J., and Netter, J. (1988). The market for corporate control: The empirical evidence since 1980. *Journal of Economic Perspectives* 2: 49.

Jensen, M. (1988). The takeover controversy: Analysis and evidence. In J. Coffee, L. Lowenstein, and S. Rose-Ackerman (ed.), *Knights, Raiders, and Targets: The Impact of the Hostile Takeover.* New York: Oxford University Press.

——and Meckling, W. (1976). Theory of the firm: Managerial behaviour, agency costs and ownership structure. *Journal of Financial Economics* 3: 305.

——and Ruback, R. (1983). The market for corporate control: The scientific evidence. *Journal of Financial Economics* 11: 5.

Kini, O., Kracaw, W., and Mian, S. (1995). Corporate takeovers, firm performance, and board composition. *Journal of Corporate Finance* 1: 383.

Kole, S. R. (1997). The complexity of compensation contracts. *Journal of Financial Economics* 43: 79.

La Porta, R., Lopez-de-Silanes, F., Shleifer, A., and Vishny, R. (1997). Legal determinants of external finance. *Journal of Finance* 52: 1131.

Lehn, K., and Poulsen, A. B. (1987). Sources of value in leveraged buyouts. In *Public Policy Towards Corporate Takeovers.* New Brunswick, NJ: Transaction Publishers.

Levy, H. (1982). Economic evaluation of voting power of common stock. *Journal of Finance* 38: 79.

Long, M., and Malitz, I. (1985). The investment-financing nexus: Some empirical evidence. *Midland Corporate Finance Journal* 3: 53.

McConnel, J. J., and Servaes, H. (1990). Additional evidence on equity ownership and corporate value. *Journal of Financial Economics* 27: 595.

Maher, M. E. (1997). Transaction cost economics and contractual relations. *Cambridge Journal of Economics* 21: 147.

Main, B., Bruce, A., and Buck, T. (1994). Total board remuneration. *Managerial and Decision Economics* 12: 219.

Malatesta, P., and Walkling, R. (1988). Poison pill securities: Stockholder wealth, profitability, and ownership structure. *Journal of Financial Economics* 20: 347.

Mayer, C. (1996). Corporate governance, competition and performance. *OECD Economic Studies* 27: 7.

Mehran, H. (1995). Executive compensation structure, ownership, and firm performance. *Journal of Financial Economics* 38: 163.

Morck, R., Shleifer, A., and Vishny, R. (1988). Management ownership and market valuation: An empirical analysis. *Journal of Financial Economics* 20: 293.

Murphy, K. J. (1985). Corporate performance and managerial remuneration. *Journal of Accounting and Economics* 7: 11.

——(1998). Executive compensation. In Ashenfelter and Card (ed.), *A Handbook of Labour Economics*. Amsterdam: North-Holland.

OECD (1995). *Economic Surveys: Italy*. Paris: OECD.

——(1996). *Economic Surveys: Japan*. Paris OECD.

——(1997). *Economic Surveys: France*. Paris: OECD.

——(1998*a*). *Economic Surveys: Korea*. Paris: OECD.

——(1998*b*). *Economic Surveys: Australia*. Paris: OECD.

——(1998*c*). *Financial Market Trends*, No. 69, February, Paris: OECD.

——(1998*d*). *The OECD Jobs Strategy: Technology, Productivity and Job Creation*. Paris: OECD.

——(1999). *OECD Principles of Corporate Governance*. Paris: OECD.

Pontiff, J., Shleifer, A., and Weisbach, M. (1990). Reversion of excess pension assets after takeovers. *RAND Journal of Economics* 21: 600.

Prowse, S. D. (1992). The structure of corporate ownership in Japan. *Journal of Finance* 47: 1121.

——(1994). Corporate governance in international perspective: A survey of corporate control mechanisms among large firms in the United States, the United Kingdom, Japan and Germany. Bank of International Settlements, Economic Papers No. 41.

Ravenscraft, D., and Scherer, F. (1987). Life after takeover. *Journal of Financial Economics* 36: 147.

Roe, M. (1994). *Strong Managers, Weak Owners: The Political Roots of American Corporate Finance*. Princeton: Princeton University Press.

Ryngaert, M. (1988). The effect of poison pill securities on shareholder wealth. *Journal of Financial Economics* 20: 377.

——and Netter, J. (1988). Shareholder wealth effects of the Ohio antitakeover law. *Journal of Law, Economics and Organization* 4: 373.

Schranz, M. (1993). Takeovers improve firm performance: Evidence from the banking industry. *Journal of Political Economy* 101: 299.

Schumann, L. (1988). State regulation of takeovers and shareholder wealth: The case of New York's 1985 takeover statutes. *RAND Journal of Economics* 19: 557.

SEC (1984). *The Impact of Targeted Share Repurchases (Greenmail) on Share Prices*. Washington, DC: Office of the Chief Economist.

Shleifer, A., and Summers, L. (1988). Breach of trust in hostile takeovers. In A. Auerbach (ed.), *Corporate Takeovers: Causes and Consequences*. Chicago: University of Chicago Press.

——and Vishny, R. (1997). A survey of corporate governance. *Journal of Finance* 52: 737.

Thonet, P. J., and Poensgen, O. H. (1979). Managerial control of economic performance in West Germany. *Journal of Industrial Economics* 28: 23.

von Thadden, E. (1995). Long-term contracts, short-term investment and monitoring. *Review of Economic Studies* 62: 557.

Williamson, O. E. (1975). *Markets and Hierarchies*. New York: MacMillan.

——(1985). *The Economic Institutions of Capitalism*. New York: The Free Press.

Wruck, K. (1989). Equity ownership concentration and firm value. *Journal of Financial Economics* 23: 3.

Yermack, D. (1997). Good timing: CEO stock option awards and company news announcements. *Journal of Finance* 52: 449.

Zeckhauser, R., and Pound, J. (1990). Are large shareholders effective monitors? An investigation of share ownership and corporate performance. In R. Hubbard (ed.), *Asymmetric Information, Corporate Finance and Investment.* Chicago: University of Chicago Press.

Zingales, L. (1994). The value of the voting right: A study of the Milan stock exchange. *Review of Financial Studies* 7: 125.

——(1995). What determines the value of corporate votes? *Quarterly Journal of Economics* 110: 1075.

——(1997). Corporate governance. In P. Newman (ed.), *The New Palgrave Dictionary of Economics and Law.* London: MacMillan.

PART V

THE VALUE OF CORPORATE CONTROL AND REORGANIZATION OF THE FIRM

18

The Value of a Vote in the Market for Corporate Control: Canadian Evidence

CHRIS ROBINSON, JOHN RUMSEY, AND ALAN WHITE

1. INTRODUCTION

In this chapter, we investigate the value of a vote in the market for corporate control. The value of a vote is difficult to measure because it is impounded in the share price, which also reflects the value of claims on future cash flows that are available to all shareholders, controlling or otherwise. However, by examining companies with two classes of residual equity which differ in the share of control they offer, we can estimate the value of a vote.

Earlier research from nine countries has shown that superior voting (*A* henceforth) shares are worth more than restricted or non-voting (*B* henceforth) shares. Ang and Megginson (1989) (UK), Chung and Kim (1999) (Korea), Horner (1988) (Switzerland), Jog *et al.* (1985) (Canada), Lease *et al.* (1983; 1984) (US), Kunz and Angel (1996) (Switzerland), Levy (1983) (Israel), Muus (1998) (France), Robinson and White (1990) (Canada), Rydqvist (1988) (Sweden), and Zingales (1994) (Italy) all find that voting shares are worth more than otherwise identical non-voting shares, although there is considerable cross-sectional variation in the premiums paid for *A* shares relative to *B* shares. Lease *et al.* (1983) report premiums ranging from less than 1 per cent to 42 per cent for companies that did not have voting preferred stock, and small negative premiums for the *A* shares of four companies with voting preferred outstanding. Zingales (1994) reports that the average premium was 81.5 per cent for firms listed on the Milan Stock Exchange.

Bebchuk *et al.* (2000) analyse the agency costs of ownership structures that allow concentration of control with less than 50 per cent of the equity: dual class equity, pyramid shareholdings and interlocking holdings. They argue that these agency costs can be much higher than those imposed by controlling shareholders that also hold a majority of the cash flow rights. In the context of dual class equity, however, this does not explain why the price for *A* and *B* shares should differ in observed trades on the stock market. These trades occur between small shareholders that do not have controlling interests and cannot receive any part of the agency costs, or at least not directly in the form of differential cash flows.

The basis for the observed price difference has been explained in two ways. First, Levy (1983) suggests that the non-controlling voting shareholders may share in any premium paid in a takeover while the *B* shareholders are unlikely to do so. Thus, the two classes of equity will differ in price by the present value of the expected takeover premium.

Second, Lease *et al.* (1984) hypothesize that a controlling group is able to direct the firm's activities to benefit itself by means not available to other shareholders. Under this hypothesis, the control group benefits either from perquisite consumption or from the ability to control corporate decisions. The value of a vote is then related to the chance that the holder of the vote will participate in this perquisite consumption. This was later formalized by Rydqvist (1988) and Zingales (1994) who use a model of voting values under a fixed ownership structure developed by Milnor and Shapley (1978) to attempt to estimate the portion of the observed share price that can be attributed to voting. Using this model Zingales estimates that about 30 per cent of the observed share price is a result of voting value.

We estimate the value of a vote using similar explanatory variables to Levy, Rydqvist, and Zingales. We use a sample of companies with two classes of residual equity listed on the Toronto Stock Exchange (TSE) and find that the average value of a vote ranges from 3.5 per cent to 13 per cent of the average value of a company's equity.

A unique contractual characteristic of the Canadian data makes this estimation procedure more revealing. About half of the companies in our sample have takeover protection for the *B* shareholders, spelt out in the articles of incorporation. This protection, called a 'coattail', has not been reported for any country other than Canada. It is triggered by a takeover offer to the *A* shareholders which is not made identically to the *B* shareholders. The two basic mechanisms used are: (1) the *B* shares acquire the same voting rights as the *A* shares; or, (2) the *B* shares become convertible into the *A* shares for the purpose of tendering to the bid. Since the *B* shares outnumber the *A* shares in all cases, the *B* shareholders can defeat any takeover proposal, or make its acceptance very unlikely. Since August 1987 all new issues of dual class equity in Canada must include a coattail agreement for the *B* shares, so that the proportion of firms with two classes of shares without coattails is diminishing.

In other countries, investors with small holdings of *B* shares can participate indirectly in the benefits of control by selling their shares to someone buying control. For Canadian firms with a coattail provision this does not seem to be a viable explanation unless we assume that the coattail can be breached. Nonetheless, the average premium for *A* shares in companies with coattails is still significant, though smaller than the average premium observed for companies with no coattails. We propose a model of voting power and coalition formation that can explain this result even in the absence of a differential takeover premium.

Another valuable quality of the data is the large number of dual class shares traded on the TSE. Smith and Amoako-Adu (1991) report that at the end of 1987 a little over 15 per cent of all listed companies on the TSE had restricted shares and that they comprised about 11.5 per cent of the TSE 300 Composite Index. Over 140 *B* shares were listed on the TSE in 1984, the middle of our sample period. About half of these companies also had their *A* shares listed. The market capitalization of the companies with both classes listed ranged from \$6 million to \$2.1 billion in 1984 (only four companies had a capitalization less than \$20 million). The firms also differ widely in the size of block share holdings. In most cases both classes trade in reasonable volumes and with reasonable frequency.

Canada is between Europe and the USA, in terms of corporate governance and ownership concentration. Canadian law developed from the English common law, and the present securities and corporate law and regulations provide an environment for shareholders that is very similar to that in the USA. Accounting standards are much more developed than they are in Continental Europe in general.

Ownership is much more concentrated in Canada than in the USA, however. We can speak of three groups of enterprises in a control context. A significant group of Canadian businesses, particularly manufacturers, is controlled by foreign companies, more so than in any other developed nation in the world. Most of the controlling companies are American. Some of the subsidiaries have a minority float of shares listed on the stock markets, but most do not. A second group is companies that are widely held, as is more common in the USA. This group includes many of the largest Canadian companies whose market capitalization and trading volume dominates the Canadian stock markets. Banks, various resource-based companies from very large to very small companies, utilities, and Nortel Networks are notable in this group. The third group is companies controlled by individuals and families, directly or indirectly.[1] This third group is still very significant economically, comprises the largest number of exchange-listed companies and includes many very large enterprises. All the dual class equity firms are in this third group, but the majority of these family-controlled firms have single equity class structures. The ownership structure of this third group of companies looks much more like the situation found in Sweden, France, Switzerland, or Italy. Canadian banks cannot hold equity, unlike the situation in Japan and Germany. Institutional holders like pension funds and mutual funds have grown rapidly in recent years, but they have little influence in this third group because of the existing control positions.

The rest of the chapter is organized as follows. In Section 2, we show how the value of voting is reflected in the share prices and introduce two alternative variables to explain the observed cross-sectional variation. In Section 3, we describe the data sample that was used for testing purposes and discuss some of the legal and regulatory events that took place during our sample period. In Section 4, we examine the effectiveness of our models in explaining observed cross-sectional variation in voting premia. This leads to a discussion of how the value of control becomes reflected in the prices of small shareholdings and to alternative interpretations of the results. Finally, we draw some conclusions from our results.

2. THE VALUE OF A VOTE

The total value of the equity of the firm, S, can be decomposed into two components

$$S = E + V.$$

The first of these, E, is an economic component that is spontaneously available to all shareholders. It is convenient to think of it as the present value of cash distributions that will be made to all shareholders. The second component, V, is what we call a voting value. This is a value that derives from the ability of shareholders to exert control over the firm. We make no claims as to the source of V. It may be from the perquisite consumption proposed by Lease *et al.* (1984) or it may have other roots. We do assume in the empirical estimation that it is proportional to the total equity value, S.

The share prices for the two classes of equity P_A, P_B can similarly be decomposed into an economic value and a voting value

$$P_A = E_A + V_A,$$

$$P_B = E_B + \gamma V_B,$$

where subscripted values of V refer to the value per vote and $\gamma < 1$ is the number of votes each B share has (Each A share has one vote). Usually γ is zero. The proportionate observed price difference can then be related to the difference in voting value and the difference in economic value:

$$(P_A - P_B)/P_S = (V_A - \gamma V_B)/P_S + (E_A - E_B)/P_S, \qquad (18.1)$$

where P_S is the average stock price. Let N_A and N_B be the number of shares of each class outstanding, and then

$$P_S = (N_A P_A + N_B P_B)/(N_A + N_B).$$

We will refer to this proportionate price difference as the price premium. Many previous empirical studies have measured this value in many countries and found substantial cross-sectional variation across firms. The cross-sectional variation may be due to variations in economic values or to differences in voting values across firms.

The economic values, E_A and E_B, are not observable but the difference can be estimated as the present value of any difference in the dividends available to the two classes of shares. In most previous studies, these are reported to be small or zero. This suggests that the major cause of cross-sectional variation must be due to differences in voting value.

Previous attempts to explain the cross-sectional variation of the value of a vote have relied on two explanatory variables. For example, Levy (1983) and Zingales (1994) have related the value of the vote to the degree of concentration of control in the A shares. The motivation for this is that typically only A shares need be purchased to gain control so that in a takeover only A shareholders participate in any premium. If the total premium in the event of a takeover offer is some proportion k of the total value of the equity, S, the premium per share is then

$$k\,S/N_A = k[(N_A + N_B)/N_A]P_S = k(1/\alpha)P_S,$$

where α is the fraction of all shares that are A shares. As a result the observed price difference in (eqn 18.1) that cannot be attributed to economic differences is

$$(V_A - \gamma V_B)/P_S = k(1/\alpha). \qquad (18.2)$$

This assumes that the offer will be made soon. Since it is uncertain that an offer will be made and the offer will probably not be made until some future time the constant of proportionality, k, is really the expected present value of the proportion of the total equity value that will be received by the A shareholders.

The second explanatory variable that has been used to explain the observed cross-sectional variation in the premia is a measure of voting power proposed by Milnor and Shapley (1978). Milnor and Shapley investigate the voting power of atomistic voters (whom they refer to as 'an ocean') in a setting in which some voters have blocks of votes. This is similar to the case of the corporate share holdings. These typically can be characterized by one or more shareholders who hold blocks of votes that represents an appreciable fraction of all the votes. The remaining votes are widely distributed in small holdings we call portfolio investments. In this case, the portfolio investors play the role of oceanic voters and the blockholders have blocks of votes.

Milnor and Shapley postulate that the probability that a voter can exert control is the probability the voter is *pivotal*. A voter is pivotal when his votes determine the outcome. If he casts his votes in favour, the proposal will pass, but if he does not, then it will fail. Their measure of the voting power of the oceanic voters is the probability that one of them will be pivotal divided by the fraction of all votes that are held by the ocean. Defining ϕ_0 as the probability that one of the oceanic voters is pivotal and θ as the fraction of all votes that are in the ocean, the measure of oceanic voting power is ϕ_0 / θ.[2]

This measure of voting power has many intuitively appealing properties. It captures the extent to which voting power seems to be concentrated on the basis of the ownership structure. For example, when θ is large (close to one) and few shares are held in blocks, the measure is close to one. When there are two or more potential coalitions of blockholders, each of which has almost 50 per cent of the votes, the measure is very large. Finally, if one block contains more than half the votes the value of the measure is zero. Rydqvist (1988) uses this measure in testing hypotheses of voting value for Swedish dual class equity. Zingales (1994) uses it as an explanatory variable in exploring the benefits of control for Italian firms with multiple classes of equity.[3]

Within the class of voting shares ϕ_0/θ reflects voting power. Within all shares the voting power will then be $(1/\alpha)(\phi_0/\theta)$. The second alternative explanatory variable for the observed value of a vote is

$$(V_A - \gamma V_B)/P_S \propto (1/\alpha)\,(\phi_0 / \theta). \tag{18.3}$$

We use the explanatory variables in eqns (18.2) and (18.3) to explore the cross-sectional variation of the observed price difference for voting and restricted voting shares. In particular, we will examine the role of a coattail provision which prohibits takeover offers for only the *A* shares to see how it affects the cross-sectional variation of price premiums. Later, we will also provide an alternative interpretation of the meaning of these explanatory variables. In Section 3, the characteristics of our data set are described.

3. THE DATA AND THE REGULATORY ENVIRONMENT

The sample of data that we used to explore the value of a vote consisted of all the firms with two classes of voting shares listed on the TSE at any time between 1981 and 1990 for which both classes of shares traded, and ownership data could be obtained.

The total number of different firms in the sample was 93. The number of firms in the sample at any one time varied from a low of 47 in 1981 to a high of 77 in 1986. The sample was roughly evenly split between those firms with coattail provisions and those without.

For each company, price pairs were gathered for all days on which both classes of shares traded. For each firm, the average value of $(P_A - P_B)/P_S$ was calculated for each year. The ownership structure and characteristics of the shares (dividends, liquidation preference, takeover protection, conversion rights and number of shares outstanding) were determined from information circulars, prospectuses and correspondence with the companies. When a change in ownership structure took place (an infrequent event) the time-weighted average value of the ownership variables was used for the year in which the change took place. A number of alternative procedures for aggregating information over each year were tried.

We also carried out the tests on a month by month basis. The results were not sensitive to the aggregation scheme used. The annual results that are reported are representative of all the results. All the recorded holdings of more than 5 per cent of the votes were assumed to operate separately regardless of family affiliation unless a voting trust was in operation.

Table 18.1 provides summary data on the sample. The average price premium for voting shares rises through the sample period from about 2 per cent initially to about 15 or 20 per cent in 1990. The average value of ϕ_0, the Shapley number, is about 0.2. The largest block of votes for about half the companies is an absolute majority and hence $\phi_0=0$. The average value of α, the fraction of all shares that are unrestricted shares, is about 35 per cent. The average value of θ, the fraction of all votes that are found in the ocean, is about 43 per cent.

The sampling period was chosen to span a period in which regulatory policy on restricted voting shares was evolving in Canada. Prior to 1981, there was little explicit regulation for

Table 18.1. *Summary statistics*

Year	Firms	ϕ_0	α	$(P_A-P_B)/P_S$	θ	$\phi_0>0$	$\theta>0.5$
Panel A: The no coattail sample							
1981	32	0.17 (0.24)	0.40 (0.18)	0.032 (0.087)	0.44 (0.16)	14	9
1982	31	0.15 (0.22)	0.39 (0.18)	0.052 (0.12)	0.44 (0.15)	13	7
1983	31	0.18 (0.25)	0.38 (0.18)	0.012 (0.084)	0.44(0.17)	13	7
1984	31	0.17 (0.23)	0.36 (0.19)	0.053 (0.13)	0.44 (0.16)	12	7
1985	31	0.16 (0.23)	0.36 (0.20)	0.076 (0.17)	0.44 (0.14)	11	7
1986	28	0.14 (0.22)	0.33 (0.19)	0.14 (0.41)	0.43 (0.14)	9	5
1987	26	0.14 (0.23)	0.31 (0.19)	0.16 (0.27)	0.42 (0.14)	9	5
1988	24	0.15 (0.23)	0.29 (0.19)	0.16 (0.26)	0.41 (0.16)	10	5
1989	22	0.11 (0.19)	0.30 (0.20)	0.15 (0.29)	0.39 (0.14)	8	3
1990	21	0.13 (0.21)	0.29 (0.20)	0.20 (0.38)	0.38 (0.15)	8	3
Panel B: The coattail sample							
1981	14	0.13 (0.19)	0.47 (0.095)	0.011 (0.037)	0.38 (0.10)	6	2
1982	17	0.21 (0.23)	0.46 (0.15)	0.055 (0.075)	0.42 (0.12)	9	5
1983	27	0.24 (0.23)	0.43 (0.16)	0.029 (0.065)	0.46 (0.14)	16	11
1984	35	0.20 (0.23)	0.42 (0.16)	0.038 (0.053)	0.46 (0.14)	18	14
1985	36	0.22 (0.26)	0.43 (0.18)	0.051 (0.087)	0.47 (0.15)	19	13
1986	48	0.24 (0.28)	0.42 (0.18)	0.090 (0.18)	0.47 (0.17)	26	15
1987	50	0.23 (0.29)	0.40 (0.19)	0.13 (0.24)	0.45 (0.19)	28	14
1988	48	0.21 (0.28)	0.37 (0.19)	0.16 (0.45)	0.43 (0.18)	26	11
1989	47	0.17 (0.24)	0.37 (0.18)	0.12 (0.35)	0.40 (0.16)	24	7
1990	45	0.16 (0.22)	0.36 (0.17)	0.15 (0.28)	0.39 (0.14)	20	6

Means and standard deviations, by coattail and year. Standard deviations are in parentheses. The Shapley index ϕ_0 measures voting power of non-block shareholders. The ratio of the number of superior to subordinate voting shares is given by α. The normalized price difference of superior shares over subordinate share is given by $(P_A-P_B)/P_S$ (where P_S is an average price). The fraction of votes not held in blocks is given by θ.

restricted shares and few shares with coattail provisions. In 1981, the Ontario Securities Commission (OSC), the main regulatory body, carried out hearings on the regulation of restricted shares. It was initially proposed that the restricted shares be delisted but this recommendation was dropped from the final report (Maynes 1991). In 1984, the OSC modified the regulations to improve the protection available to holders of restricted voting shares. A regulation was introduced to require the approval of the holders of restricted voting shares for any changes in the capital structure that might affect them. This regulation also required the public disclosure of the differences in the voting rights of restricted and non-restricted shares. The OSC research for the hearings had found that the lack of disclosure left many investors unaware of the differences between the two classes. No controversial transactions had occurred to stimulate awareness of the significance of the differences. In 1987, the TSE introduced a regulation that required a coattail provision for all new restricted shares that were listed on the exchange. After this the number of firms without a coattail provision declined steadily due to natural attrition of takeovers, share reorganizations and dissolution. The total number of firms with dual class equity also declined for a time, but started to increase in the 1990s during an extended bull market when there were more initial public offerings by family-controlled firms.

At the same time as the regulatory changes were being put into place, a legal controversy affected one of the firms in the sample, Canadian Tire Corporation (CTC). CTC had had restricted shares outstanding since 1926. In 1983, there was a restructuring in which each voting share was split into one voting share and four non-voting shares and each non-voting share was split into five non-voting shares. This greatly increased the voting leverage of the voting shares. Voting control was held by less than 5 per cent of the total equity and 60.9 per cent of the voting shares were held in equal blocks by three children of one of the founders. At the same time a coattail provision was put into place. In late 1986, the three children tried to sell control to a group that already had about 15 per cent of the voting shares, without triggering the coattail provision. This attempt to evade the coattail was prohibited by the OSC in early 1987, a decision that was subsequently upheld in the courts.

This event was publicized widely. It led to increasing scrutiny of restricted voting shares and it is likely that the TSE rule change that occurred in 1987 was a result of this event. It also led to increasing pressure from fund managers to abolish restricted voting shares. Because of the extreme behaviour of CTC share prices, CTC was omitted from our sample for testing purposes, although it conformed well to our models.

The evidence on the average price difference between unrestricted and restricted share prices shown in Table 18.1 is consistent with the events just described. Prior to the reporting requirements that were put in place in 1984 the observed price difference is small. After 1984 and particularly after 1986, the observed price differences increased sharply. This presumably reflected increasing investor awareness of the difference between the two classes of equity. Although the price difference appears more pronounced for firms that do not have a coattail provision in place, the difference between the two samples is not statistically significant. The surprising result, however, is that the average premium is significantly positive for the coattail sample, even though a differential takeover offer is explicitly disallowed.

4. EMPIRICAL RESULTS

The economic value of the share is denoted by E_A or E_B. For many of the firms in the sample E_A and E_B will be different because of differences in dividends, liquidation rights, conversion rights, and liquidity.[4] In our sample liquidation rights and conversion rights do not have any material value. We attempted to control for the value of the relative liquidity of the two classes of shares by including the relative frequency of trading as a proxy for liquidity. It did not affect the results significantly and none of these results are reported.

For our sample the dividends on the *B* shares were always at least as large as the dividends on the *A* shares. The relationship between the dividends can be written $D_B = RD_A + \delta$, where the value of R and the maximum value of δ are specified in the share prospectus or the corporate charter. In our sample only three combinations of R and Δ were observed, $\delta > 0$ and $R = 1$, $\delta = 0$ and $R > 1$, and $\delta = 0$ and $R = 1$. In most of the sample (about 75 per cent of the firms) there were no dividend differences, $R = 1$ and $\delta = 0$. For eight out of the ninety-three firms in the sample the dividend on the restricted share was a multiple of the dividend on the unrestricted share, $R > 1$ and $\delta = 0$. For these firms R never exceeded 1.20. For thirteen out of the ninety-three firms in the sample $\delta > 0$. These were firms in which the restricted share received an extra or preferential dividend. For these firms δ was our best estimate of the expected payment. This was always very small. If $\delta = 0$, it can be shown that

$$E_A - E_B = \Delta_{AB}[P_S - (\alpha V_A + (1-\alpha)\gamma V_B)],$$

where

$$\Delta_{AB} = (1-R)/[\alpha + (1-\alpha)R].$$

If $\delta > 0$ then $\Delta_{AB} = 0$ and the expected extra dividend can be valued as a perpetuity

$$E_A - E_B = -\delta/k,$$

where k is an appropriate discount rate. Combining these two relationships gives

$$\begin{aligned} E_A - E_B &= \Delta_{AB}[P_S - (\alpha V_A + (1-\alpha)\gamma V_B)] - \delta/k \\ &= \Delta_{AB}[P_S - \alpha(V_A - \gamma V_B) - \gamma V_B] - \delta/k, \end{aligned}$$

where at most only one of δ or Δ_{AB} is non-zero.

Noting that γ is always very small (usually zero) and V_B is also likely to be small this can be approximated as

$$E_A - E_B = \Delta_{AB}[P_S - \alpha(V_A - \gamma V_B)] - \delta/k. \tag{18.4}$$

Combining (eqn 18.4) with eqns (18.1)–(18.3) provides two modified relationships

$$Y = \nu X_T - (\delta/k\,P_S), \tag{18.5}$$

and

$$Y = \nu X_S - (\delta/k\,P_S), \tag{18.6}$$

where ν is the constant of proportionality (assumed to be the same across firms) and

$$Y = [(P_A - P_B)/P_S] - \Delta_{AB}],$$
$$X_T = (1/\alpha) - \Delta_{AB},$$
$$X_S = (\phi_0/\theta)\,[(1/\alpha) - \Delta_{AB}].$$

Equations (18.5) and (18.6) are the basis for the empirical examination of the causes of cross-sectional variation in price premia. The regression equation that is used is

$$Y = \beta_0 + \beta_1 X_S + \beta_2 X_T + \beta_3 d + \varepsilon, \tag{18.7}$$

where Y is the relative price difference, X_S, the modified Shapley measure, X_T, the modified takeover measure, and $d = \delta/P_S$, the adjustment for differential dividends.

The mean and standard deviation of each of the variables in the regression model for each year are shown in Table 18.2. The contents of this table show that $X_T > X_S$. They also

Table 18.2. *Summary statistics of regression variables*

Year	Y	X_S	X_T	d	$D_A = D_B$
Panel A: The no coattail sample					
1981	0.037 (0.089)	1.14 (2.11)	3.29 (2.12)	0.0013 (0.0028)	24/32
1982	0.057 (0.12)	0.97 (2.07)	3.30 (2.12)	0.0014 (0.0032)	24/31
1983	0.016 (0.087)	1.02 (1.98)	3.43 (2.10)	0.0012 (0.0026)	23/31
1984	0.058 (0.13)	1.06 (1.89)	3.92 (2.71)	0.0013 (0.0035)	24/31
1985	0.080 (0.17)	1.11 (1.97)	4.15 (3.19)	0.0017 (0.0042)	23/31
1986	0.15 (0.40)	1.17 (2.12)	4.71 (3.83)	0.0012 (0.0035)	21/28
1987	0.17 (0.27)	1.03 (1.73)	4.87 (3.96)	0.00097 (0.0030)	21/26
1988	0.16 (0.26)	1.34 (2.34)	5.10 (3.85)	0.00054 (0.0017)	20/24
1989	0.15 (0.28)	1.11 (2.27)	5.17 (4.23)	0.00054 (0.0015)	18/22
1990	0.20 (0.38)	1.24 (2.37)	5.55 (4.58)	0.00071 (0.0023)	18/21
Panel B: The coattail sample					
1981	0.018 (0.045)	0.74 (1.12)	2.19 (0.45)	0.0017 (0.0045)	11/14
1982	0.060 (0.076)	1.10 (1.32)	2.37 (0.77)	0.0018 (0.0046)	13/17
1983	0.045 (0.075)	1.36 (1.60)	2.77 (1.34)	0.0017 (0.0039)	18/27
1984	0.050 (0.063)	1.17 (1.71)	2.93 (1.59)	0.0014 (0.0033)	25/35
1985	0.062 (0.092)	1.17 (1.76)	2.92 (1.67)	0.0012 (0.0029)	26/36
1986	0.11 (0.19)	1.23 (1.64)	3.05 (1.96)	0.00069 (0.0021)	33/48
1987	0.15 (0.24)	1.33 (1.87)	3.34 (2.10)	0.00036 (0.0011)	36/50
1988	0.17 (0.45)	1.25 (1.87)	3.77 (2.79)	0.00037 (0.0013)	36/48
1989	0.14 (0.35)	1.23 (1.88)	3.79 (2.89)	0.00032 (0.0011)	36/47
1990	0.17 (0.28)	1.30 (2.06)	4.04 (3.20)	0.00029 (0.0011)	35/45

Means and standard deviations, by coattail and year of the variables used in the regressions. Standard deviations are in parentheses. The dependent variable $y = (P_A - P_B)/P_S - \Delta_{AB}$, where $\Delta_{AB} = (D_A - D_B)/(\alpha D_A + (1-\alpha) D_B)$ when $D_A/D_B = E_A/E_B$ and zero otherwise. The independent variable $X_S = \phi_0/\theta\,[(1/\alpha) - \Delta_{AB}]$ is the modified Shapley measure and the independent variable $X_T = 1/\alpha - \Delta_{AB}$ is for the takeover measure of voting power. The dividend adjustment measure d is the amount of the extra or preferential dividend divided by the average share price P_S. The fraction of firms with equal dividends is labelled $D_A = D_B$.

indicate the very small magnitude of any preferential dividend differences which average less than 0.2 per cent of the average share price. The mean and standard deviation of the relative price difference adjusted for proportional dividend differences, Y, is almost the same as the mean and standard deviation of the unadjusted relative price difference, $(P_A - P_B)/P_S$, reported in Table 18.1.

Results for the regression equation (18.7) when regressed separately on the coattail and no coattail samples, are shown in Table 18.3. The results show that prior to 1986 neither model had any explanatory power in either sample. In only three out of twenty sample years was the intercept significantly different from zero.[5] After 1986, X_S seems to be the more significant explanatory variable for the coattail sample and X_T seems to be the more significant variable for the no coattail sample.

Table 18.3. *Impact of voting measures on price differences*

Year	$\hat{\beta}_0$	$\hat{\beta}_1$	$\hat{\beta}_2$	$\hat{\beta}_3$	Adj. R^2	Firms
Panel A: No coattail sample $Y = \beta_0 + \beta_1 \frac{\phi_0}{\theta}\left(\frac{1}{\alpha} - \Delta_{AB}\right) + \beta_2\left(\frac{1}{\alpha} - \Delta_{AB}\right) + \beta_3 d + \varepsilon$						
1981	0.0079 (0.031)	−0.011 (0.010)	0.0099 (0.0093)	3.8 (6.4)	−0.047	32
1982	0.052 (0.044)	0.010 (0.015)	0.00034 (0.013)	−7.8 (7.6)	−0.058	31
1983	−0.011 (0.033)	0.0024 (0.0099)	0.0042 (0.0091)	4.7 (6.6)	−0.059	31
1984	−0.019 (0.046)	−0.0044 (0.013)	0.016 (0.0093)	13* (6.8)	0.082	31
1985	0.046 (0.056)	0.0094 (0.017)	0.0023 (0.011)	5.6 (7.9)	−0.068	31
1986	0.18 (0.14)	−0.013 (0.040)	−0.0038 (0.023)	−4.9 (24)	−0.115	28
1987	−0.0081 (0.085)	−0.020 (0.026)	0.035* (0.013)	22 (17)	0.18	26
1988**	−0.10 (0.059)	−0.032* (0.014)	0.051** (0.0093)	87** (21)	0.62	24
1989**	−0.14* (0.064)	−0.051* (0.018)	0.056** (0.010)	103** (26)	0.62	22
1990**	−0.083 (0.11)	−0.076* (0.028)	0.060** (0.016)	69* (30)	0.43	21
Panel B: Coattail sample $Y = \beta_0 + \beta_1 \frac{\phi_0}{\theta}\left(\frac{1}{\alpha} - \Delta_{AB}\right) + \beta_2\left(\frac{1}{\alpha} - \Delta_{AB}\right) + \beta_3 d + \varepsilon$						
1981	0.00059 (0.051)	0.0079 (0.0094)	0.0046 (0.023)	−3.1 (2.3)	0.045	14
1982	0.027 (0.058)	0.029 (0.015)	−0.00002 (0.026)	−2.9 (3.8)	0.21	17
1983	0.089** (0.029)	0.010 (0.011)	−0.026 (0.013)	−0.93 (3.3)	0.072	27
1984	0.062** (0.20)	0.0074 (0.0073)	−0.011 (0.0078)	−1.5 (2.8)	−0.015	35
1985	0.061 (0.032)	0.017 (0.011)	−0.010 (0.011)	−0.68 (5.3)	−0.013	36
1986**	−0.0034 (0.044)	0.054** (0.014)	0.0038 (0.012)	18 (11)	0.26	48
1987**	−0.012 (0.053)	0.066** (0.016)	0.018 (0.015)	−20 (26)	0.34	50
1988**	−0.079 (0.098)	0.11** (0.030)	0.023 (0.021)	−22 (45)	0.27	48
1989**	−0.076 (0.079)	0.065* (0.025)	0.031 (0.017)	−16 (42)	0.19	47
1990**	0.0024 (0.061)	0.046* (0.018)	0.023 (0.012)	−36 (33)	0.21	45

Regression of the normalized price difference Y between A and B shares against Shapley and takeover measures of the value of votes. Results are shown for the coattail and no coattail sample for different years. The coefficients β_1 and β_2 measure respectively the impact of the Shapley measure and of the takeover measure on the observed price difference. The normalized preferential and constant amount greater dividend is also used as an explanatory variable d. Standard errors are given in parentheses.** and * stand for significance at 5 and 10 per cent, respectively.

The estimated value of β_3 ($\approx 1/k$) was usually not significantly different from zero. When β_3 was significantly different from zero it implied a discount rate of less than 1 per cent per year. This is difficult to explain except to note that the variable d may be acting as a proxy for some other source of value. The results may also arise from a spurious correlation caused by a common divisor, P_S, in both the dependent and independent variables. The variable Δ_{AB} when not zero also enters into both dependent and independent variables.

To explore the effects of spurious correlation the regressions were redone with Δ_{AB} set to zero. The results were not perceptibly different from those reported in Tables 18.3–18.5. To test the sensitivity of the results to our estimates of d, and to again minimize spurious correlation the regression were redone omitting the firms for which $d > 0$. The other parameter estimates and the other significance levels did not change materially as a result of this change.

Table 18.4. *Impact of Shapley voting measure on price differences*

Year	$\hat{\beta}_0$	$\hat{\beta}_1$	$\hat{\beta}_2$	Adj. R^2	Firms
Panel A: The no coattail sample $Y = \beta_0 + \beta_1 \frac{\phi_0}{\theta}\left(\frac{1}{\alpha} - \Delta_{AB}\right) + \beta_2 d + \varepsilon$					
1981	0.040* (0.019)	−0.0062 (0.0083)	2.3 (6.4)	−0.049	32
1982	0.059* (0.024)	0.0095 (0.011)	−8.3 (7.4)	0.014	31
1983	0.0076 (0.019)	0.0040 (0.0084)	3.5 (6.5)	−0.044	31
1984	0.041 (0.028)	0.0035 (0.012)	9.7 (6.8)	0.012	31
1985	0.061 (0.039)	0.0096 (0.015)	4.8 (7.6)	−0.038	31
1986	0.18 (0.095)	−0.016 (0.037)	−4.7 (23)	−0.070	28
1987	0.17* (0.067)	−0.013 (0.029)	12 (18)	−0.058	26
1988	0.15** (0.061)	−0.011 (0.021)	62 (31)	0.083	24
1989	0.13 (0.069)	−0.013 (0.026)	64 (40)	0.028	22
1990	0.22* (0.098)	−0.034 (0.034)	40 (38)	−0.0084	21
Panel B: The coattail sample $Y = \beta_0 + \beta_1 \frac{\phi_0}{\theta}\left(\frac{1}{\alpha} - \Delta_{AB}\right) + \beta_2 d + \varepsilon$					
1981	0.0096 (0.014)	0.018 (0.0099)	−3.0 (2.5)	0.26	14
1982	0.027 (0.022)	0.034* (0.012)	−3.0 (3.4)	0.37	17
1983	0.055* (0.021)	−0.0019 (0.0093)	−4.4 (3.9)	−0.028	27
1984	0.050** (0.014)	0.0034 (0.0064)	−3.4 (3.3)	−0.014	35
1985	0.050* (0.020)	0.012 (0.0089)	−2.1 (5.5)	0.012	36
1986	0.031 (0.031)	0.053** (0.014)	15 (12)	0.23	48
1987	0.061 (0.038)	0.072** (0.015)	−24 (27)	0.30	50
1988	0.018 (0.071)	0.12** (0.029)	−24 (45)	0.25	48
1989	0.048 (0.059)	0.075** (0.025)	−21 (44)	0.14	47
1990	0.10* (0.046)	0.054** (0.018)	−35 (34)	0.15	45

Regression of the normalized price difference Y between A and B shares against the Shapley measure of the value of votes. Results are shown for the no coattail (panel A) and coattail sample (panel B) for different years. The coefficient β_1 measures the impact on the share price of the measure of voting power. The adjustment Δ_{AB} to the independent variable, is a proportional dividend adjustment. The normalized preferential and constant amount greater dividend is also used as an explanatory variable, d. Standard errors are in parentheses.** and * stand for significance at 5 and 10 per cent, respectively.

Table 18.5. *Impact of the takeover measure on price differences*

Year	$\hat{\beta}_0$	$\hat{\beta}_1$	$\hat{\beta}_2$	Adj. R^2	Firms
Panel A: The no coattail sample $Y = \beta_0 + \beta_1\left(\frac{1}{\alpha} - \Delta_{AB}\right) + \beta_2 d + \varepsilon$					
1981	0.027 (0.031)	0.0028 (0.0078)	0.25 (6.0)	−0.064	32
1982	0.049 (0.040)	0.0049 (0.010)	−6.2 (6.8)	−0.036	31
1983	−0.0056 (0.032)	0.0047 (0.0077)	4.6 (6.2)	−0.039	31
1984	−0.0093 (0.042)	0.013 (0.0084)	11 (6.5)	0.090	31
1985	0.054 (0.056)	0.0039 (0.010)	5.8 (7.7)	−0.048	31
1986	0.18 (0.14)	−0.0065 (0.021)	−6.0 (23)	−0.074	28
1987	−0.017 (0.081)	0.034* (0.012)	21 (16)	0.19	26
1988	−0.11 (0.064)	0.045** (0.0098)	79** (22)	0.53	24
1989	−0.12 (0.075)	0.044** (0.011)	84* (30)	0.48	22
1990	−0.070 (0.12)	0.043* (0.017)	51 (34)	0.22	21
Panel B: Coattail sample $Y = \beta_0 + \beta_1\left(\frac{1}{\alpha} - \Delta_{AB}\right) + \beta_2 d + \varepsilon$					
1981	−0.061 (0.055)	0.039 (0.025)	−4.3 (2.4)	0.22	14
1982	−0.0015 (0.061)	0.030 (0.024)	−5.0 (4.0)	0.11	17
1983	0.10** (0.032)	−0.019 (0.011)	−3.5 (3.7)	0.099	27
1984	0.077** (0.023)	−0.0075 (0.0068)	−3.5 (3.2)	0.014	35
1985	0.072* (0.033)	−0.0016 (0.0095)	−3.8 (5.5)	−0.046	36
1986	0.024 (0.050)	0.024 (0.014)	16 (13)	0.05	48
1987	0.014 (0.061)	0.046** (0.015)	−39 (30)	0.15	50
1988	0.016 (0.11)	0.045 (0.023)	−34 (51)	0.045	48
1989	−0.017 (0.083)	0.043* (0.017)	−25 (45)	0.092	47
1990	0.048 (0.063)	0.032* (0.012)	−42 (34)	0.12	45

Regression of the normalized price difference Y between A and B shares against the takeover measure of the value of votes. Results are shown for the no coattail (panel A) and coattail sample (panel B) for different years. The coefficient β_1 measures the impact on the share price of the measure of voting power. The adjustment Δ_{AB} to the independent variable, is a proportional dividend adjustment. The normalized preferential and constant amount greater dividend is also used as an explanatory variable, d. Standard errors are in parentheses.** and * stand for significance at 5 and 10 per cent, respectively.

Since the two explanatory variables are not dissimilar (both are proportional to $1/\alpha$) separate regressions were carried out using only one of the explanatory variables at a time. These results are shown in Tables 18.4 and 18.5. They are similar to those shown in Table 18.3. After 1986, the takeover model (Table 18.4) is a significant explanatory variable in the no coattail sample and the Shapley model (Table 18.5) is a significant explanatory variable in the coattail sample. The takeover model is also a significant explanatory variable in the coattail sample.

To interpret these results it is necessary to consider how voting value becomes reflected in observed share prices. The value from voting arises from the ability to control the actions of the firm. However not all shareholders will have the same ability to exert this control. For example, if one individual has more than 50 per cent of the votes it is unlikely that any other shareholder will have much opportunity to influence the firm. As a result, it appears that all of the value of voting will be captured by the majority shareholder and none by anyone else.

In general the observed value of the vote based on observed share prices will depend on whose shares are being traded. In practice the prices that are observed are usually the prices for trades between portfolio investors that do not own an appreciable number of shares in the corporation. Most of these shareholders do not attend annual meetings and probably do not vote or vote only by proxy. They are certainly not in any position to either influence the activities of the corporation or to receive benefits from the corporation that are not available to all other shareholders. As a result the votes do not have any direct value to these shareholders.

The most obvious reason for the observed price premium for the *A* shares is that they will participate in any premium that may be offered in the event of a takeover bid while the *B* shareholders are unlikely to receive a similar offer. This means that the observed price difference equals the expected present value of any future takeover premium. It is this anticipated premium on a potential takeover that is reflected in the *A* share price, a form of indirect value to voting.

For the firms in our data set that have a coattail provision, any offer to buy control must be extended equally to both classes of shares. In this case, the observed price premium for *A* shares should be zero. The average observed price premiums for the firms in our sample in Table 18.1 reveals that there is not a great deal of difference between the average premiums for coattail and no coattail firms. Further, the results in Tables 18.4 and 18.5 show that X_T is a significant explanatory variable for the observed premium. One possible reason for this might be that shareholders do not believe that the coattail provision will be effective. However, the fact that the Shapley measure, X_S, is significant for this group of firms suggests that something else may be going on.

4.1. *The Coalition Formation Model*

The takeover model bases the value of a vote on its value to someone acquiring majority control of the firm in a takeover. In this section, we provide a somewhat different explanation for the premium based on a model of coalition formation. In each firm in our sample there are one or more investors who own substantial fractions of the outstanding voting shares. If it is possible for one or more of these blockholders to form a coalition that gives them almost 50 per cent of the votes there may be an incentive for the coalition members to buy up *A* shares from the portfolio investors. By doing this, the coalition may be able to achieve absolute control. This inclination to buy up shares from portfolio investors will be strongly accentuated if there is another competing coalition that has close to 50 per cent of the vote. In this case, both coalitions may be trying to purchase shares in the open market.

This behaviour is similar to a creeping takeover in which a controlling position is acquired by buying up small holdings sequentially.[6] It differs from a creeping takeover in that the coalitions need not exist for the incentive to purchase shares to exist. It is only necessary that the potential to form the coalitions exists to make buying up free shares attract-ive. These extra votes will enhance the blockholder's negotiating position in forming the coalition should it come to pass. The purchase of these shares will also forestall other blockholders who may have similar intentions.

Table 18.6. *Canadian Tire*

	December 1983	May 1985	May 1986	August 1986
Sibling 1	20.3%	20.3%	20.3%	20.3%
Sibling 2	20.3%	20.3%	20.3%	20.3%
Sibling 3	20.3%	20.3%	20.3%	20.3%
Pension plan	12.2%	12.2%	12.2%	12.2%
Dealers	0.0%	13.4%	16.5%	17.4%
Widely held	26.9%	13.5%	10.4%	9.5%
A share price	$15.00	$12.25	$21.00	$25.00
B share price	$13.00	$9.00	$15.50	$13.75

This inclination of blockholders to buy voting shares from portfolio investors should provide buying pressure that will drive up the price of the *A* shares in some circumstances. There is some anecdotal evidence of this sort of behaviour in the previously mentioned case of Canadian Tire. Canadian Tire is Canada's largest hardware chain. Independent dealers own and operate the retail stores, while CTC owns the wholesale distribution network and the credit card facility. CTC charges no franchise fees or royalties, collecting its revenue as the exclusive wholesaler to the retail stores. In CTC the *A* shares represented only 4.4 per cent of the total number of shares outstanding. Three siblings and the employees' pension fund held most of the *A* shares (Table 18.6). From 1984 to 1986, the price of the *A* shares rose steadily relative to the price of the *B* shares. Also during this period, a cooperative organization of all the dealers (Dealers, henceforth) started buying *A* shares. The distribution of the *A* shares and prices of *A* and *B* shares at some dates in this period were as shown in the table.

The increase in premium seen here is consistent with the price pressure story. This is a situation in which several different coalitions have almost half the votes.[7] As the Dealer's holding increased the competing coalitions came closer to 50 per cent of the votes and the apparent demand for the free *A* shares rose. Since CTC acted as the sole wholesaler supplying the Dealers it is clear that there may be substantial value to control for any coalition involving the Dealers.[8]

The voting model proposed by Milnor and Shapley (1978) captures many of the properties of this proposed inclination by blockholders to buy up shares from portfolio investors. The measure of voting power is largest when there are potential competing coalitions that have almost half the votes. It is small when no one has any significant degree of control and zero when someone has absolute control. It may be that this is the reason that it becomes an explanatory variable when takeovers are perceived to be unlikely.

4.2. *Two Alternative Interpretations*

If the premium paid for *A* shares in the no coattail sample is based on anticipated participation in a takeover premium then the coefficient of X_T in Table 18.5 should reflect the expected present value of the proportion of the total equity value that will be received by the *A* shareholders. The observed value of the coefficient on the takeover variable in Table 18.5

is about 4.5 per cent. To interpret the magnitude of this coefficient it is helpful to provide a simple model that formalizes the arguments that led to eqn (18.2). We refer to this model as the windfall takeover process. In this framework, the premium offered in the event of a takeover arises from an opportunity to improve the operation of the company. This opportunity arises only occasionally. It is not likely that a takeover will take place but if it does there may be substantial gains available.

Suppose that takeover offers arrive according to a Poisson process. The probability that an offer arrives in some time interval dt is $\lambda\, dt$. Also suppose that the expected premium that the A shareholders will receive conditional on an offer being made is proportional to the total equity value at the time the offer is made. At the time of the offer, t, the premium on A shares is then $k\, P_S(t)/\alpha$. Finally, let us assume that this average share (which is a portfolio of A and B shares) pays a continuous proportional dividend at rate q. This assumption is an approximation to reality that greatly simplifies subsequent calculations.

The present value of the expected takeover premium is

$$P_A - P_B = \int_0^{\infty} PV[KP_S(t)/\alpha e^{-\lambda t}\lambda]\, dt,$$

where PV represents a present value operator. Assuming that k and α are constant, and that the Poisson process does not affect the appropriate discount rate, this can be written as:

$$\begin{aligned} P_A - P_B &= k/\alpha \int_0^{\infty} PV[P_S(t)]\, e^{-\lambda t}\,\lambda\, dt, \\ &= kP_S(0)/\alpha \int_0^{\infty} e^{-qt} e^{-\lambda t}\,\lambda\, dt, \\ &= kP_S(0)/\alpha\,[\lambda/(q+\lambda)]. \end{aligned}$$

Comparing this to eqns (18.5 and 18.7) reveals that the coefficient on the takeover variable in Table 18.5 of about 0.045 corresponds to $k/(q+\lambda)$ in this model. This means that under the assumptions of this model the fraction of the total equity value that will be paid as a takeover premium is

$$k \approx 0.045[1 + (q/\lambda)]. \tag{18.8}$$

If λ is very large the probability of an immediate takeover offer arriving approaches 1 and k approaches the observed premium, 4.5 per cent. If λ is small it is unlikely that there will be a takeover offer soon and k must be large in order to justify the current observed premium.

The probability that a takeover offer will be made, λ, can be estimated from the observed frequency of such offers. Megginson (1990) reports that 43 of 152 British firms with dual class shares were acquired during the period 1955–82. This corresponds to $\lambda \approx 0.01$.[9] Smith and Amoako-Adu (1995) report that forty-three of ninety-eight Canadian firms with dual class shares were acquired during the period 1981–92. This corresponds to $\lambda \approx 0.0366$. A plausible value for the dividend rate, q, is about 3 per cent, close to the average dividend yield on listed Canadian stocks. Using these values in (eqn 18.8) suggests that 8 per cent $\leqslant k \leqslant$ 18 per cent.

Under the admittedly simple assumptions of the windfall takeover model, the expected takeover premium in firms with dual class shares is estimated to be between 8 and 18 per cent of the total equity value. This is roughly consistent with the *ex post* results reported by Jensen and Ruback (1983). In firms with only a single class of equity, the price premium (defined as the takeover premium divided by the stock price) offered in a takeover is the fraction of the total equity value that is paid as a premium. A proxy for this is the abnormal returns to selling shareholders in a takeover. Jensen and Ruback report that these abnormal returns were between 20 and 30 per cent. The expected takeover premium implied by the windfall takeover model would be higher if the dividend rate were higher than 3 per cent or the intensity of the Poisson process were less than 1 per cent.

An alternative explanation of the takeover model casts a different interpretation on the coefficient of X_T. Consider why a purchaser would be willing to offer a premium in order to gain control of a company. One reason is that it will be possible for this purchaser to implement some change or improvement in the company that will increase its value. It is this idea that underlies the windfall model that was just discussed.

A second reason that a purchaser would be willing to offer a premium to gain control of a company is merely to capture the benefits of control. The size of the premium that could be offered in this case depends on the value of these captured benefits of control. This is a source of benefit that is available to anyone who can attain control, including current shareholders. This can be viewed as a sort of steady-state takeover model in that it is always possible. If the value of a vote that is reflected in the market price for *A* share is less than the value that a vote has to some potential investor, that investor will have an incentive to accumulate votes by buying in the market. This will lead to an evolving ownership structure. The evolution may be a gradual accumulation of votes in one or more blocks, or it may be an offer for control of the firm that entails buying all the shares of one class. To the extent that neither of these events occurs, we assume that the value of a vote that is reflected in the market price is at least as high as the value of this best alternative use of the vote.

This second view of the of the takeover premium can be formalized by considering the value of a vote to a bidder who plans to buy a block of shares that will command 50 per cent or more of the votes. We assume that the bidder will buy only *A* shares and that he will be forced to make a follow up offer for all the *A* shares. This is consistent with prevailing Ontario securities law that requires that any offer that is made to more than five shareholders, or any offer at a price more than 15 per cent above the market price requires follow up offers to be made to all shareholders of the same class.

This buyer will have total control and so will capture all the value of voting. The value of this control per *A* share purchased is

$$V_A = V/N_A = V/(\alpha N_S),$$

where N_A is the number of *A* shares outstanding, N_S is the total number of shares outstanding, and α is the fraction of all shares that are class *A* shares. Because the value of control is completely captured by the *A* shares, $V_B = 0$. If the value of V_A reflected in current market prices is less than this there is incentive for a buyer to buy *A* shares. In this case

$$(V_A - \gamma V_B)/P_S = V/(\alpha N_S P_S) = (V/S)(1/\alpha).$$

Comparing this with (eqn 18.2) reveals that the coefficient on X_T can be interpreted as V/S, the fraction of total equity value that can be attributed to voting control.

Similarly, if we take the Milnor–Shapley model at its face value and assume that when they are pivotal the oceanic shareholders actually capture the value of control it can be shown that

$$(V_A - \gamma V_B)/P_S \approx (V/S)(1/\alpha)(\phi_0/\theta).$$

This relationship is exactly true when $\gamma = 0$ and is approximately true for small γ. Comparing this with (eqn 18.3) reveals that the coefficient on X_S can again be interpreted as V/S, the fraction of total equity value that can be attributed to voting control.

Under these interpretations, the regression results in Tables 18.3–18.5 for both the takeover and Shapley models indicate that the fraction of the total equity value that can be attributed to voting control is on the order of 4–12 per cent. This is much smaller than the values estimated by Zingales (1994) and Muus (1998) but it is in rough accordance with the results of Barclay and Holderness (1989) and Chung and Kim (1999).

5. CONCLUSIONS

Observed price differences between *A* and *B* shares must ultimately be ascribed to benefits that are available only to the holders of *A* shares. The obvious reason is that *A* shareholders may receive higher prices than *B* shareholders in a takeover, because only the *A* shares give voting control. However, in Canada there exists an unique contractual situation where some firms with dual class equity disallow differential takeover prices, and yet the *A* shares held by small shareholders still command a statistically significant premium.

In this chapter, we have examined two models that explain how these benefits may come to be reflected in the prices of shares held by individuals who will never directly enjoy them. Both models are based on the assumption that the observed value of the price premium arises from the ability of the *A* shareholders to capitalize on abnormally high prices for *A* shares. These premium prices may be offered by someone attempting to buy outright control or from someone who already has a substantial block of votes who is trying to augment his position.

In the early part of the test period, the average price difference was small and neither explanatory variable was successful in explaining the observed cross-sectional differences. This may be due to the fact that investors were not fully informed about the differences between the two classes of shares. In the latter half of the sample when public events attracted investors' attention to the differences between different classes of shares the average price differences became larger. A takeover model became a significant explanatory variable for firms that had no coattail. A voting power model was a significant explanatory variable for firms that had a coattail provision.

The empirical results suggest that if the observed premium is a result of an expected windfall takeover (a relatively rare event in which substantial gains may be reaped by the buyer), the expected gain to the *A* shareholders in the event of the takeover is between 8 and 18 per cent of the total equity value. Under an alternative steady-state takeover model the premium merely reflects the value that anyone can capture by buying control. In this case, the empirical results suggest that about 3.5–4.5 per cent of the total equity value can be attributed to voting control. A literal interpretation of the Shapley–Milnor model gives a similar estimate of the value of control in cases in which a coattail provision prohibits a takeover offer.

This estimated value of control based on the takeover model was remarkably consistent over the last four years of the sample. It was about the same in each year, and it was about the same for firms with and without a coattail provision (although not statistically significant for the set of firms with a coattail provision). The estimated value is roughly consistent with the results of Barclay and Holderness (1989) who on the basis of observed takeover premiums estimated the value of control to be about 4 per cent in the USA. The estimated value of control based on the Shapley–Milnor measure of voting power was also fairly stable across the last five years and of the same order of magnitude as that based on the takeover model.

Our findings are also consistent with investor belief that the coattail provisions are at least partially effective. The takeover model had explanatory power in the sample of firms without a coattail provision. The Shapley–Milnor model had explanatory power only in the sample of firms with a coattail provision. Tests of the difference between the two samples showed that the two models behaved significantly differently in the two samples. These results appeared only after regulatory and legal decisions supporting the legitimacy of a coattail provision were made.

Two related issues arise in comparing our results with those of other researchers. Different countries have quite different contractual forms of dual class equity and regulations governing dual class equity and minority shareholder rights. For example, the coattail provision appears to exist only in Canada. The value of a vote is also quite different in different countries, with the highest values in Italy (over 80 per cent) and France (over 50 per cent) and the lowest values in Canada, the USA, and Sweden. Muus (1998) summarizes these differences and briefly explores three possible causes that are related to the different environments—shareholder rights, enforceability of shareholder rights, and accounting standards. He does not investigate the specific differences between contractual provisions like coattails, differential dividends, and liquidity preferences, nor does he analyse the environmental differences in much detail. A more complete investigation of corporate governance related to dual class equity in different countries and regulatory regimes is an interesting subject for future research.

ACKNOWLEDGEMENTS

The authors would like to thank Sanjai Bhagat, Michael Brennan, Sris Chatterjee, Myron Gordon, Elizabeth Maynes, Kristian Rydqvist, Chester Spatt, Rex Thompson, and an anonymous referee for helpful comments. The financial support of the Financial Research Foundation of Canada is also appreciated.

Notes

1. By control we mean significant voting blocks, not necessarily a majority.
2. The value of ϕ_0 can be calculated using an algorithm developed by Milnor and Shapley. The algorithm computes ϕ_0 on the basis of the number of large blocks of votes, the number of votes in each block, and the number of votes in the ocean.

3. Eckbo and Verma (1994) use the Milnor–Shapely value as one way of measuring ownership concentration for empirical tests of a model of corporate dividend decisions.
4. Some of these differences are similar to those reported by Partch (1986) for US corporations with multiple classes of equity. The restricted shares usually traded less frequently than the unrestricted shares. The average value of the ratio of the number of days on which the restricted shares traded to the number of days on which the unrestricted shares traded was about 0.8.
5. All references to significance refer to statistical significance at the 5 per cent level.
6. Under prevailing Ontario securities law attempts to carry out a creeping takeover usually will lead to a court mandated follow up offer. However, a coalition that already owned almost 50 per cent of the votes could probably do this successfully.
7. Some contextual information suggested that it was unlikely that the pension fund would join any coalition and disagreements among the siblings meant that a coalition of the three family members was unlikely.
8. As mentioned in Section 3, the dealers attempted to circumvent the coattail provision at the end of 1986 and made an offer to buy enough *A* shares to achieve control. This offer was disallowed and the takeover was abandoned.
9. If n events are observed in N trials each of length T then an estimate for λ is $n/(NT)$.

References

Ang, J., and Megginson, W. (1989). Restricted voting shares, ownership structure and the market value of dual class firms. *Journal of Financial Research* 12: 301.

Barclay, M. J., and Holderness, C. G. (1989). Private benefits from control of public corporations. *Journal of Financial Economics* 25: 371.

Bebchuk, L., Kraakman, R., and Triantis, G. (2000). Stock pyramids, cross-ownership and dual class equity. In R. Morck (ed.), *Concentrated Corporate Ownership*. Chicago: University of Chicago Press, p. 295.

Chung, K., and Kim, J.-K. (1999). Corporate ownership and the value of a vote in an emerging market. *Journal of Corporate Finance* 5: 35.

Eckbo, E., and Verma, S. (1994). Managerial share ownership, voting power and cash dividend policy. *Journal of Corporate Finance* 1: 33.

Horner, M. (1988). The value of the corporate voting right. *Journal of Banking and Finance* 12: 69.

Jensen, M. C., and Ruback, R. S. (1983). The market for corporate control: The scientific evidence. *Journal of Financial Economics* 11: 5.

Jog, V., Riding, A., and Seguin, P. (1985). Shareholders' reactions to issuances of restricted voting common stock. In W. Rentz (ed.), *Administrative Sciences Association of Canada 1985 Proceedings*, 10.

Kunz, R. M., and Angel, J. J. (1996). Factors affecting the value of the stock voting right: Evidence from the Swiss equity market. *Financial Management* 25: 7.

Lease, R., McConnell, J., and Mikkelson, W. (1983). The market value of control in publicly-traded corporations. *Journal of Financial Economics* 11: 439.

—— (1984). The market value of differential voting rights in closely held corporations. *Journal of Business* 57: 443.

Levy, H. (1983). Economic evaluation of voting power of common stock. *Journal of Finance* 38: 80.

Maynes, E. (1991). Evidence on the value of a stock exchange listing. *Canadian Journal of Administrative Science* 8: 179.

Megginson, W. L. (1990). Restricted voting stock acquisition premiums and the market value of corporate control. *Financial Review* 25: 175.

Milnor, J. W., and Shapley, L. S. (1978). Values of large games II: Oceanic games. *Mathematics of Operations Research* 3: 290.

Muus, C. (1998). Non-voting shares in France: An empirical analysis of the voting premium. Johann Wolfgang Goethe-Universität (Frankfurt am Main), Finance and Accounting Working Paper No. 22.

Partch, M. M. (1986). The creation of a class of limited voting common stock and shareholder wealth. *Journal of Financial Economics* 18: 313.

Robinson, C. M., and White, A. D. (1990). Empirical evidence on the relative valuation of voting and restricted shares. *Canadian Journal of Administrative Science* 7: 9.

Rydqvist, K. (1988). Empirical investigation of the voting premium. Northwestern University, Working Paper No. 35.

Smith, B., and Amoako-Adu, B. (1991). Financing Canadian corporations with restricted shares. National Centre for Management Research and Development, Monograph Series.

—— (1995). Relative prices of dual class shares. *Journal of Financial and Quantitative Analysis* 30: 223.

Zingales, L. (1994). The value of the voting right: A study of the Milan Stock Exchange experience. *Review of Financial Studies* 7: 125.

19

Managerial Disciplining and the Market for (Partial) Corporate Control in the UK

JULIAN FRANKS, COLIN MAYER, AND LUC RENNEBOOG

1. HOSTILE TAKEOVERS AND THE CORRECTION OF MANAGERIAL FAILURE

In the USA, hostile takeovers or the mere threat of a hostile takeover are believed to be an effective check on managerial autonomy. A firm is continually auctioned and if the company is worth more to a potential acquirer than it is currently worth, a raid may occur which will subsequently lead to board and asset restructuring and potentially to performance increases. Confirmation of this monitoring role of the USA takeover market is provided by Martin and McConnell (1991). Apart from the USA, the UK is one of the few countries with an active market for corporate control. Whereas Germany has experienced only four hostile takeover attempts in the post-Second World War period, there were eighty hostile takeover bids in the UK in the period 1985–6 alone. Drawing on Franks and Mayer (1996), this section examines the role of the hostile takeover market in the UK in the period 1985–6, at the height of the mergers and acquisitions-wave of the 1980s.

Out of the eighty hostile bids, thirty-five were successful, twenty-three remained independent and twenty-two were subsequently acquired. If hostile takeovers perform a disciplinary role, increased managerial turnover is expected as well as large-scale restructuring. Panel A of Table 19.1 reports total board and executive director turnover for subsamples of accepted bids, successful hostile bids (the revised offer was accepted after initial resistance) and unsuccessful hostile bids (the raider was successfully warded off). A successful hostile bid results, in most cases, in the resignation of the complete board. Even when a hostile attempt was successfully fended off, substantial board restructuring takes place with 39 per cent of the directors leaving the board.

In 53 per cent of the successful hostile takeovers, considerable asset restructuring takes place; more than 10 per cent of the total value of fixed assets of the merged firms are sold off. Asset sales of this scale only occur in 26 per cent of the accepted bids. In contrast to the other categories of bids, companies with unsuccessful hostile bids continue to exist as independent companies such that post-bid asset restructuring can be studied in detail. Panel B of Table 19.1 shows that 60 per cent of the companies sold off more than 10 per cent of fixed assets, two years after an unsuccessful bid. Thus, a failed takeover attempt may still

Table 19.1. *Director turnover and asset disposal subsequent to hostile bids*

Panel A: Resignations

Turnover	Accepted bid (AB)	Successful hostile (SH)	Unsuccessful hostile (UH)	*T*-stat.	
				(SH)–(AB)	(UH)–(SH)
Total board	50% (34)	90% (31)	39% (31)	3.52***	−4.01***
Executive directors	50% (26)	88% (26)	36% (22)	3.00***	−3.76***

Panel B: Asset disposal as % of tangible assets for unsuccessful bids around year of the bid (B)

B−1	*B*	*B*+1	*B*+2	*B*+3	Average
8.5% (0)	9.2% (25)	13.3% (42)	17.2% (53)	19.4% **(60)	11.0% (42)

Panel A reports the proportion of directors who resign in the two years subsequent to the accepted, successful hostile and unsuccessful hostile bids. Sample size is given in parenthesis. Panel B gives the asset disposal as a percentage of tangible assets for unsuccessful bids around the year of the bid (*B*). The proportion of subsample companies with asset disposal as a percentage of tangible assets of more than 10 per cent is given in parenthesis. ***, **, * stand for significance at the 1, 5, and 10 per cent level, respectively.

Source: Franks and Mayer (1996).

contain an important warning signal to the incumbent management. These results demonstrate that successful hostile takeover bids generally lead to substantial board and assets sales. However, even for companies that were able to ward off a hostile takeover, there is evidence of a large proportion of managerial resignations and of asset restructuring.

Table 19.2 summarizes pre-bid performance for the bid-subsamples and for samples of non-merging firms that were matched with accepted and successful hostile bids. Panel A displays the abnormal returns calculated over one, two, and five years prior to the bid. Parametric and non-parametric statistical tests do not detect any statistically significant difference in mean returns among the subsamples. Therefore, the null hypothesis that average performance among accepted, successful hostile and unsuccessful hostile bids do not differ cannot be rejected. Surprisingly, the average pre-bid abnormal returns between accepted bids and the matched non-merging companies are not statistically significant, nor are the differences between successful hostile bids and the matched sample. Similar conclusions are reached for dividend changes (panel B) and cash flow to assets ratios (not shown). There is, however, one performance variable which captures differences in performance: the Tobin's Q (the ratio of market to replacement cost valuation) of successful hostile bids is significantly lower than the one of a matched non-merged sample and of the unsuccessful hostile bids. This suggests that hostile bids are successful in companies with undervalued growth opportunities.

Franks and Mayer (1996) conclude that hostile takeover bids bring about substantial board and asset restructuring but do not find any evidence—apart from for the Tobin's Q measure—that weak performance drives the market for corporate control. In fact, companies subject to a hostile bid do not perform worse than the average listed firm on the London Stock Exchange (LSE). This raises the question as to whether underperformance

Table 19.2. *Performance prior to takeover bids*

	Accepted bids (%)	Matched non-merging co's (%)	Successful hostile bids (%)	Matched non-merging co's (%)	Unsuccessful hostile bids (%)
Panel A: Abnormal returns prior to hostile take-over bid					
Mean 5 years prior	4.53	0.83	−0.14	0.14	2.71
2 years prior	7.75	−7.84	−6.09	2.26	5.07
1 year prior	7.77	1.99	−7.68	7.90	−2.84
Panel B: Dividend changes 1 year prior to hostile take-over bid					
Omitted	5.6		5.9		2.8
Decrease	14.3		2.9		5.7
No change	22.9		14.7		17.1
Increase	51.4		73.5		71.4
N/A	2.9		2.9		2.8
Panel C: Tobin's Q					
1980	0.72	0.92	0.82	1.12	0.80
1985–6	1.13	1.25	1.04	1.11	1.22

This table shows the performance prior to the takeover bids. Performance is defined as abnormal returns (panel A), dividend changes (panel B), and Tobin's Q (panel C). The subsamples of accepted bids and successful hostile bids are matched by size and industry with companies listed on the London Stock Exchange.

Source: Franks and Mayer (1996).

triggers other corporate governance mechanisms, like the disciplinary role of large shareholders, which is the focus of the remainder of this chapter. Furthermore, we investigate whether an alternative market for corporate control arises, namely a market in substantial share stakes or a market in partial corporate control.

2. OWNERSHIP CONCENTRATION AND CHANGES IN CONTROL STRUCTURES

Whereas diffuse ownership encourages shirking of monitoring and control responsibilities by owners (Demsetz 1983), Shleifer and Vishny (1986) show that concentrated shareholdings can mitigate these free rider problems of corporate control. As a result, we would predict more active corporate governance in the presence of concentrated ownership. Burkart *et al.* (1997) show that optimal ownership structure depends on the performance of a company: when it is performing well a diffuse ownership structure increases managerial discretion and enhances managerial effort, while poor performance necessitates closer monitoring through concentrated ownership.

Empirical evidence by Weisbach (1988), Warner *et al.* (1988) and Coughlan and Schmidt (1985) shows that top management in USA corporations is replaced rapidly after poor share price performance. The evidence of McConnell and Servaes (1990) shows that corporate performance, as measured by Tobin's Q, initially rises with low levels of ownership and then falls with high ownership. In the wake of corporate underperformance, the exercise of control by separate classes of large shareholders may be based on different monitoring abilities, superior information, or different valuation of control (Demsetz and Lehn 1985; Barclay and Holderness 1989; 1991). Control by insiders, in particular directors and families, may be more heavily influenced by private benefits which may come at the cost for outside shareholders. Hermalin and Weisbach (1991) find that at low levels of ownership concentration, corporate performance increases with managerial ownership up to a level of 1 per cent as managers' and shareholders' interests are more closely aligned. However, if it decreases beyond this level, management is able to insulate itself from disciplinary sanctions. *Therefore, we expect that higher board turnover is associated with poor performance and concentrated outside shareholdings, but that large inside holdings impede board changes.*

In light of the predicted relation between ownership and control, we would expect to observe changing patterns of ownership over time. During periods of good performance, the advantages of managerial discretion may argue for dispersed share ownership. However, greater concentrations of share ownership might be expected to emerge during periods of financial difficulty. *In particular, we would expect to observe increased concentrations in the hands of those who are best placed to exercise control.*

Most recent codes of good corporate governance, for example, the Cadbury Report of 1992 and the Hampel Report of 1998, point to the importance of non-executive directors. As agents of investors, non-executive directors should assist in the monitoring and disciplining of management. In the USA, Weisbach (1988) reports a closer relation of CEO turnover to performance in firms in which non-executive directors dominate the board. Non-executive directors are subject to the external labour market disciplining of non-executive directors (Fama and Jensen 1983). For instance, Kaplan and Reishus (1990) find that directors of poorly performing companies are likely to lose directorships in their own companies and are unlikely to be offered new directorships in other companies. Similarly, Gilson (1990) finds that directors who left the boards of distressed companies held approximately one-third fewer directorships after their departure. *Hence, we expect a higher level of executive board and CEO turnover in poorly performing companies as the proportion of non-executive directors increases. However, the replacement of the CEO might be impeded by the lack of separation of the role of chairman and chief executive officer and by the CEO's tenure.*

3. DATA SOURCES AND DESCRIPTION

3.1. *Sample Description*

A comparative performance analysis of a sample of poorly performing and average performing companies was carried out. In order to relate this analysis to the hostile takeover study reported in Section 1, two sets of eighty companies were chosen from the population of industrial and commercial companies listed on the LSE in 1985. The selection process of firms was carried out as follows: all listed industrial companies were ranked according to annual abnormal returns over the period June 1984–July 1985 and one sample was randomly selected from the lowest quintile of annual abnormal returns while a second one was randomly drawn from average performing firms represented by the third quintile. Abnormal returns were calculated from the London Share Price Database (LSPD) with correction for thin trading (Dimson betas) and with Bayesian updating.

For the poor performers, abnormal returns were −61.4 versus −0.7 per cent for the average performers; the raw returns were −39.4 and 19.9 per cent for the two respective samples. As complete data for nine companies were unavailable, they were subsequently deleted. As a result, the worst performing sample consists of seventy-four companies. Included in this sample were nineteen firms that were taken over during the period 1985–9 and three of which went into insolvency. Of the seventy-seven average performing firms, twenty-one were acquired over the same period and one went bankrupt. In line with Section 1, it is striking that the incidence of takeovers in the worst performing sample is similar to the average performing sample.

The average size ('assets employed' or total assets minus short time liabilities) of all non-financial companies on the LSE is £160.9 million in 1985. Of the lowest performance sample, average size is £97.9 million, whereas average size of the average performers is £130.2 million. The size of the latter is evenly distributed across four size quartiles, but 38 per cent of companies of the lowest abnormal return sample are in the lowest size quartile and only 16.3 per cent are in the highest size quartile. Differences in size reflect, in part, the fact that poor performance shrinks companies' assets and the fact that there are more recent IPOs in the sample with worst performance. Of the seventy-four worst performer firms, thirty-four were recent IPOs (floated in the period 1980–4), while only thirteen average performing companies went public in the same period.[1] Within the lowest abnormal return sample, the market capitalization of half the recent IPOs is lower than the sample median. The worst performing sample has higher betas and variances than the other sample. The *P*/*E* ratio of the poor performers is only 8.1 compared with 16.4 for the average performers. This is consistent with poor performers being more risky and lower growth stocks than average. Most industry sectors are represented in both samples.

3.2. *Boards*

3.2.1. *Board Composition*

For each sample, data on the composition of the board of directors were compiled from annual reports, Datastream, the *Financial Times*, and Nexus databases for each year from 1984 to 1991. The proportion of the executive and non-executive board members was collected, including data on the CEO and the Chairman. It was not possible to identify executive and non-executive directors separately in annual reports or other public sources of information for slightly less than half of the poor performers and about one-third of the average performers.

Board size of average and worst performing companies is similar in 1985, with a mean of 7.5 and a median of 7 which rises slightly to 8 in 1988. Executive directors form a majority of board members of both samples: non-executives on average represent 40 per cent of the board. There is no difference in board composition of the two samples and the average number of executives and non-executive directors remains relatively stable over time at 4.5 and 3.5 respectively, with a median of 4 and 3 over the period 1985 through 1988.

3.2.2. *Board Turnover*

Board turnover as well as reasons for resignations using the annual reports from 1984 to 1991, press releases on new listings on the LSE, the *Financial Times*, and Nexus databases were examined. A distinction between natural and enforced turnover was made. A resignation was classified as 'natural' if the director was described as having left the board for reasons of retirement, death, or illness. Otherwise the resignation was classified as being enforced.[2] In addition, we recorded whether the managing director and the chairman of the board resigned or whether they relinquished their functions but remained on the board. Since the focus of this paper is on forms of corporate restructuring other than takeovers or bankruptcies, turnover in the year of and subsequent to takeovers or receivership are excluded.

Panel A of Table 19.3 states that the cumulative total board turnover over a four-year period—for reasons other than retirement, illness, and death—in the poorly and average performing sample amounts to respectively 46 and 27 per cent. This difference is statistically significant at the 1 per cent level and results from executive directors' removals rather than non-executives' resignations. Separating the samples into recent IPOs and mature firms yields similar results. Panel B reports that the incidence of resignations of CEOs is significantly higher in the worse performing companies than average performers: in one-third of the worst performing firms the CEO is fired whereas this is only the case in 17 per cent of average performing firms. There are no cases in average performers of multiple resignations/discharges of CEOs but there are a significant number of cases in the worst performing sample for the period 1985–9. With regard to chairmen turnover, a similar picture is sketched (panel C). There is therefore prima facie evidence of a disciplining function of both CEOs and chairmen of boards when performance is bad.

3.2.3. *Ownership*

Data on the size of shareholdings, including stakes of 5 per cent or more of market capitalization, were collected.[3] These large shareholdings were classified into seven categories: (i) investment trusts, unit trusts, and pension funds; (ii) insurance companies; (iii) banks—these three categories are combined into an institutional investor category; (iv) executive and non-executive directors and their families and trusts; (v) venture capital companies; (vi) industrial and commercial companies; and (vii) other major shareholders, mainly individuals. We will refer to directors and their families as 'insiders' and to industrial and commercial companies and individuals and families as 'outsiders'. As some companies had nominee companies as major shareholders, we contacted company secretaries or financial directors of all firms and in almost all cases were able to identify the beneficial shareholder behind the nominees. The beneficiary of the nominee company is usually an institutional investor who amalgamates a number of holdings to reduce administrative costs. Some directors' total shareholdings consist of beneficial and non-beneficial share stakes, which were both collected. With regard to the non-beneficial share stakes, the directors are usually acting as trustees for a family, charity or trust and those directors do not own the cash flow rights.

Table 19.3. *Board, chairman, and CEO turnover*

	Worst performance			Average performance			Difference in means	
	N	Mean (%)	St. dev.	*N*	Mean (%)	St. dev.	*T*-stat.	WMW: *p*
Panel A: Cumulative turnover of total board and (non)-executive directors over 1985–8								
Total board	55	45.7	32.9	57	26.6	26.7	3.16***	0.002***
Total board	23	33.3	29.5	45	25.0	23.8	1.25	0.279
Exec. directors	23	35.8	31.1	45	23.1	27.3	1.73*	0.077*
Non-executive dir.	23	27.2	37.8	45	26.9	33.1	0.03	0.974
Panel B: Percentage of sample companies with at least 1, 2 or 3 CEOs leaving								
1 CEO leaves								
1985–8	55	33.3	47.6	57	16.9	37.8	2.06**	0.043**
2 CEOs leave								
1985–9	51	9.8	30.0	56	0.0	0.0	2.50**	0.017**
3 CEOs leave								
1985–9	51	5.9	23.8	56	0.0	0.0	1.86*	0.069*
Panel C: Percentage of sample companies with at least 1, 2 or 3 Chairmen leaving								
1 Chairman leaves								
1985–8	55	38.6	49.1	57	22.0	41.8	1.96*	0.053*
2 Chairmen leave								
1985–9	51	8.8	28.5	55	3.4	18.3	1.21	0.228
3 Chairmen leave								
1985–9	51	3.9	19.6	55	1.8	13.4	0.66	0.513

For both samples with worst and average performing companies, the turnover of the board, (non)-executive directors, chairmen and CEOs are shown for the period 1985–8. Director turnover is proportional to total number of directors. Executive and non-executive turnover is proportional to the total number of executive and non-executive directors, respectively. The worst performing companies are randomly drawn from all listed companies on the LSE within the lowest abnormal return quintile in July 1984 to June 1985. The average performing companies are randomly selected from the middle quintile of abnormal performance. Sample means comparison is performed via *T*-statistic and the Wilcoxon–Mann–Whitney test. *N* stands for the number of companies in the sample, St. dev. for the standard deviation and WMW: *p* for the *p*-value of the Wilcoxon–Mann–Whitney test. ***, ** and * stand for statistical significance at 1, 5 and 10 per cent, respecitvely.

Source: Own calculations based on annual reports.

Still, as they can usually utilize the voting rights of both beneficial and non-beneficial shares, the combined holdings were included in the regressions.[4]

Table 19.4 reports the incidence of concentrated shareholdings of 5 per cent or more. There is no significant difference in overall levels of concentration in the two samples: aggregate ownership stakes of 5 per cent and more amount to 35–42 per cent in each sample (Panel A). Concentrations of shareholdings in Continental European countries are typically much higher. For instance, 84 per cent of Italian companies with more than 1,000 employees have a single shareholder owning a majority of the shares (Bianco *et al.* 1995). Renneboog (2000) shows that in 93 per cent of Belgian industrial companies listed on the Brussels Stock Exchange a single shareholder owns a block of at least 25 per cent of voting

Table 19.4. *Aggregate large share stakes of 5 per cent and more by category of owner*

	Worst performance			Average performance			Difference in means	
	N	Mean (%)	St. dev.	*N*	Mean (%)	St. dev.	*T*-stat.	WMW: *p*
Panel A: Ownership concentration of all large shareholders (owning 5% or more)								
1985	70	39.0	25.0	75	34.8	25.6	0.994	0.305
1985	56	39.9	25.4	59	35.7	25.7	0.878	0.364
1988	56	42.3	22.9	59	38.4	27.2	0.847	0.358
Panel B: Ownership of directors and their families (owning 5% or more)								
1985	70	24.2	25.7	75	21.2	23.8	0.740	0.486
1985	56	25.6	26.5	59	20.7	22.7	0.878	0.365
1988	56	20.2	21.6	59	23.2	26.2	−0.659	0.689
Panel C: Ownership of all industrial and commercial co's (owning 5% or more)								
1985	70	8.1	16.4	75	3.0	9.3	2.261**	0.013**
1985	56	8.4	17.1	59	3.9	10.3	1.720*	0.085*
1988	56	10.6	21.1	59	3.9	9.9	2.204**	0.050**
Panel D: Ownership concentration of all institutional investors (owning 5% or more)								
1985	70	5.0	8.8	75	8.5	13.8	−1.815*	0.041**
1985	56	4.0	7.5	59	8.9	14.9	−2.166**	0.028**
1988	59	9.9	12.9	59	9.0	13.0	0.365	0.715

This table summarizes the aggregated large shareholdings for the years 1985 and 1988 for both the poorly and average performing sample companies. The class of total institutional investors consists of unit trusts, investment trusts, pension funds, insurance companies and banks. *N*, Mean, and St. dev. stand for respectively, the number of sample companies, the mean of aggregate concentrated ownership and the standard deviation. WMW: *p* stands for the *p*-value of the Wilcoxon–Mann–Whitney test. Data are collected from the annual reports. ***, **, and * stand for statistical significance at 1, 5, and 10 per cent.

Source: Own calculations based on annual reports.

rights. Franks and Mayer (2001) report that more than 25 per cent of shares are held by a single shareholder in 85 per cent of the largest German quoted companies. Subsequent panels record concentrated ownership of the most important shareholding categories. Insiders (managers, directors, and their families) own the largest combined ownership stake (panel B): in both samples they own 20–25 per cent of market capitalization. There is no statistical difference in director ownership between worst and average performing sample. However, there is a statistically significantly higher level of ownership held by industrial companies in the worst performers than in average ones (panel C). Stakes in average companies are between 3 and 4 per cent while they amount to around 10 per cent in poorly performing companies. In contrast, panel D records that institutional ownership is lower in poorly performing companies.[5] Nowhere are holdings by banks found to be significant; on average, banks own less than 1 per cent of reported share stakes.

The distribution of ownership stakes by investor class in 1985 is presented in Table 19.5. Within both samples of poorly and average performing firms, directors hold the vast majority of large shareholdings (above blocking minorities of 25 per cent). About 60 per cent of

Table 19.5. *Distribution of the size of the share stakes by investor class*

1985	[5, 10%[	[10, 15%[	[15, 25%[	[25, 50%[	[50, 100%]
Panel A: Sample of poorly performing companies					
Institutions					
All co's	29.7	5.4	4.1	4.1	0.0
IPOs	13.5	1.4	1.4	0.0	0.0
Industrial co's					
All co's	5.4	2.7	8.1	9.5	2.7
IPOs	2.7	0.0	5.4	5.4	0.0
Individuals					
All co's	1.4	2.7	1.4	1.4	0.0
IPOs	0.0	1.4	1.4	1.4	0.0
Directors					
All co's	8.1	5.4	9.5	18.9	20.3
IPOs	2.7	0.0	4.1	12.2	13.5
Panel B: Sample of average performing companies					
Institutions					
All co's	37.7	10.4	9.1	3.9	2.6
IPOs	3.9	3.9	1.3	0.0	0.0
Industrial co's					
All co's	3.9	1.3	0.0	7.8	0.0
IPOs	0.0	1.3	0.0	0.0	0.0
Individuals					
All co's	6.5	3.9	3.9	0.0	0.0
IPOs	1.3	0.0	1.3	0.0	0.0
Directors					
All co's	5.2	10.4	6.5	19.5	16.9
IPOs	2.6	1.3	1.3	5.2	5.2

This table records the percentage of sample companies in which particular investor classes hold shareholdings of a specific size in 1985. The class of total institutional investors consists of unit trusts, investment trusts, pension funds, insurance companies, and banks. The percentage of recent IPOs (introduced on the London Stock Exchange over the period 1980–4) with share stakes of a specific size is shown in parentheses. Total number of companies is 74 for the lowest abnormal return sample (panel *A*) and 77 in the zero abnormal return sample (panel *B*). There is a total of 34 IPOs in panel *A* and of 13 in panel *B*.

Source: Own calculations from annual reports.

the presence of such large share blocks in the worst performance sample can be explained by the fact that these blocks are held in recent IPOs (by founding families or original owners).[6] The second most important category of owners are industrial companies which control blocking minorities (blocks of 25 per cent or more) in respectively 12 and 8 per cent of the worst and average samples. Over time, the relative importance of shareholder classes remains intact, although the average cumulative shareholding of the directors decreases as directors (in recent IPOs) gradually reduce their investments (Goergen and Renneboog, Chapter 10, this volume).

3.4. *Sales of share stakes*

Although the traditional market for corporate control appears to be unrelated to performance, there is evidence of a market in share stakes in poorly performing companies. For each shareholder category, the shareholders were divided into 'old' and 'new' shareholders. The new owners are those acquiring stakes of at least 5 per cent in the current year; old shareholders held share stakes of 5 per cent or more in previous year. Three directions of change in ownership patterns are investigated: decreases and increases by 'old' (incumbent) investors and the emergence of 'new' shareholders. As about half of the changes in ownership take place in poor performing firms, two markets for share stakes can be distinguished: (i) a corporate control market which is triggered by poor performance and is followed by increased disciplinary actions against weak management (see next section), and (ii) a market for share stakes due to liquidity trading or strategic trading; for example, trading following disputes among major shareholders regarding the strategic path of the company.

Over the period 1985 to 1987, 'old' directors decreased their shareholdings in thirty-nine poorly performing companies by more than 5 per cent while there were six and sixteen increases of more than 5 per cent respectively by old and new directors. Outside investors' sales of shareholdings were balanced by purchases by industrial and commercial companies. The fact that the number of increases in shareholdings is reasonably close to the number of decreases indicates that share blocks do not tend to be dissipated. The reason is that voting rights that form part of a shareholding block are more valuable than individual voting rights due to the value of control reflected in a control premium. The pattern of share stake sales in worst performing companies is similar to that for average performers. In recent IPOs a larger number of sales by directors occur. This is particularly pronounced in average performing companies: in 1985 the average size of director holdings was 34 per cent—by 1988 this had fallen to 22 per cent. These share stakes are purchased by industrial companies and institutional investors.

4. MANAGERIAL DISCIPLINING BY OLD AND NEW SHAREHOLDERS

Relating executive board turnover to performance, total ownership concentration and the interaction between performance and ownership for the merged samples, yields a significant (negative) interaction term and thus evidence of a higher executive turnover in poorly performing companies in the presence of concentrated shareholdings. This suggests that disciplining of management is facilitated when free riding on corporate control is limited due to strong ownership concentration. For the sample of average performing companies, there is evidence of a negative relation between board turnover and concentration of ownership. Table 19.6 sheds some light on this relation as it examines the influence of particular categories of large shareholders on board turnover. Ownership is disaggregated into three classes: institutional investors (banks, insurance companies, and pension funds), outsiders (industrial and commercial companies, individual, and family investors) and insiders (directors). Panel A reports that there is evidence of significantly higher turnover of

Table 19.6. *Disciplinary actions against executive directors by old and new shareholders*

	Independent variables (1985–8)							Obs.	R^2 adj.
	Constant	Performance	Institutions	Outsiders	Insiders	Size	Industry		
Panel A: All sample companies									
All	82.2***	−0.67***	−0.40	1.89***	−1.60***	Yes	Yes	109	15.9***
	(0.000)	(0.003)	(0.544)	(0.010)	(0.005)				
IPOs	117.6**	−0.27	−0.72	1.80	−2.54**	Yes	Yes	35	5.5
	(0.011)	(0.575)	(0.753)	(0.181)	(0.040)				
Non-IPOs	85.2***	−0.74**	−0.01	0.60	−1.50**	Yes	Yes	74	13.6***
	(0.000)	(0.023)	(0.992)	(0.305)	(0.023)				
Panel B: Worst performing companies									
All	87.4***		0.56	1.70**	−1.62**	Yes	Yes	52	6.6***
	(0.002)		(0.691)	(0.023)	(0.022)				
IPOs	145.0***		−2.16	1.98	−2.73**	Yes	Yes	27	11.9*
	(0.001)		(0.377)	(0.112)	(0.018)				
Non-IPOs	52.7		2.03	2.24**	−1.71	Yes	Yes	25	5.4
	(0.238)		(0.346)	(0.050)	(0.182)				
Panel C: Average performing companies									
All	98.9***		−0.06	−0.43	−1.81**	Yes	Yes	57	12.1**
	(0.000)		(0.927)	(0.564)	(0.025)				
Non-IPOs	104.1***		−0.37	0.54	−1.77*	Yes	Yes	48	7.7*
	(0.000)		(0.607)	(0.547)	(0.075)				
	Constant	Performance	Increase institutions	Increase outsiders	Increase insiders	Size	Industry	Obs.	R^2 adj.
Panel D: All sample companies									
All	55.5***	−0.45**	3.93	5.36***	4.10**	Yes	Yes	109	21.6***
	(0.000)	(0.045)	(0.124)	(0.001)	(0.036)				
All	51.6***	−0.25	6.44**	6.50**	4.63*	Yes	Yes	70	24.5***
	(0.000)	(0.351)	(0.048)	(0.012)	(0.079)				
Panel E: Worst performing companies									
All	40.0	−0.60	−1.06	7.01***	9.60***	Yes	Yes	52	33.6***
	(0.240)	(0.228)	(0.725)	(0.000)	(0.001)				
All	11.4	−0.61	2.73	7.99***	17.67***	Yes	Yes	24	64.7***
	(0.738)	(0.266)	(0.462)	(0.008)	(0.000)				
Panel F: Average performing companies									
All	56.4***	0.75	12.84***	1.41	1.03	Yes	Yes	57	7.2*
	(0.000)	(0.632)	(0.007)	(0.714)	(0.706)				
All	68.0***	0.87	5.88	5.08	−3.06	Yes	Yes	45	3.2
	(0.000)	(0.545)	(0.223)	(0.208)	(0.336)				

This table reports whether executive board turnover is associated with concentrated shareholdings of specific shareholder categories: institutional, outsider, and insider shareholders. The independent and dependent variables (apart from performance) are averaged over 1985–8. Performance, institutions, outsiders, and insiders respectively stand for the performance (abnormal returns over 1984–5), ownership concentration of institutional investors, of outsiders (industrial and commercial companies, and individuals and families) and insider shareholders (directors and their families). Size is the logarithm of assets employed. Industry stands for the industry dummies. Increases stand for the gross increases by category of owner. IPOs are the companies introduced on the London Stock Exchange in the period 1980–4. Non-IPOs are all sample companies floated before 1980. Turnover and shareholdings are collected from the annual reports. Performance data are from the London Share Price Database (LSPD). All parameter estimates are in 000s, *p*-values are given between parentheses. ***, **, and * stand for statistical significance at the 1, 5, and 10 per cent level. The *s in the R^2 adj. represent statistical significance of the *F*-test.

boards of poorly performing companies in the presence of concentrated share stakes held by outsiders.[7] In contrast, if directors hold large equity stakes executive board turnover is substantially reduced in both average and poorly performing companies (panels A, B, and C). This negative relation is consistent with directors owning substantial shareholdings impeding board changes to protect the private benefits they derive from control. This is most pronounced in recent IPOs where, as noted above, holdings by directors are particularly large (panel B). In the case of non-IPOs, directors appear to be unable to inhibit board turnover in poorly performing companies, but outside shareholders seem to discipline management (panel B). There is no significant relation between shareholdings of institutional investors and board turnover in either average or poorly performing companies (panels A, B, and C).

Concisely, we find support for our claim that executive board turnover is higher in poorly performing companies in the presence of outsider (non-institutional) shareholders and lower in the presence of insider shareholdings. The influence of insiders is most pronounced in recent IPOs where their holdings are particularly large. Consistent with Lai and Sudarsanam (1997), institutions do not appear to be involved in disciplining poorly performing management.

We also investigated, for the merged samples, the interrelation between performance and ownership concentration of the three main shareholder categories by including interaction variables of performance with ownership by category of investor (now shown). Only the interactive term with outside ownership concentration was statistically negatively significant, confirming that board turnover is high in the presence of poor performance and large outside ownership.[8] The interactive term with director ownership was not significant, consistent with the observation that directors with strong voting power impede board turnover regardless of share price performance.

In order to investigate whether share price performance over 1984–5 triggers changes in substantial shareholdings in 1985 and subsequent periods, we regress abnormal returns on the following dependent variables: (i) decreases, (ii) increases by existing shareholders, and (iii) increases by new shareholders, each by category of owner.[9] While industrial companies owning large share stakes decrease their holdings when performance is low, poor performance also leads industrial companies purchasing a large share block. The latter effect statistically dominates the former. The fact that performance triggers both significant selling and purchasing of share stakes suggests that within this category of owner, there are shareholders with strong and weak monitoring abilities. Poor performance causes incumbent directors to decrease their holdings (significance level of 1 per cent) and is also correlated with increased holdings of new directors (at a significance level of 10 per cent). Neither incumbent directors nor industrial companies owning large blocks consistently increase their equity stakes in the wake of poor performance. All this suggests that there is a market in share stakes in poorly performing companies with old industrial investors and directors selling out to other companies and new directors rather than exercising control themselves. Furthermore, the sale of share stakes by old directors is part of a change in corporate control in the face of deteriorating corporate performance rather than simply portfolio diversification. Institutional investors neither reduce nor increase their holdings in poorly performing companies.

In sum, we observe a market in share stakes in poorly performing companies. Active shareholders—corporate investors and directors—trade shares in poorly performing companies: old corporations and directors sell out to new.[10]

Table 19.6 (panels D, E, and F) examines whether shareholders use increased control power resulting from larger ownership stakes in poorly performing companies to remove executive directors. The independent ownership variables relate to the combined holdings of old and new shareholdings in the relevant category.[11] Panels D and E demonstrate that the relation between board turnover and share ownership changes is particularly pronounced for outside investors and (new) directors: a significantly higher level of board turnover in poorly performing companies occurs where there are increases in large share stakes held by industrial and commercial companies and by (new) directors. This suggests that where disciplining of management is required, concentration emerges in the hands of those best placed to exert it. There is little relation between board turnover and increases in institutional investor stakes. Instead, Table 19.6 reveals that the relation between increased institutional holdings and board turnover is most pronounced in the average performing companies. These findings are valid for both recent IPOs and companies that have been listed for longer periods of time. We therefore find a relation between the exercise of corporate control and increased share ownership by active investors, in particular corporate shareholders and new directors. We can therefore conclude that there is partial market in share blocks in the UK.

Finally, the impact of board composition on managerial disciplining is analysed. In poorly performing companies, the higher the proportion of non-executive directors, the higher the executive director turnover. This relation is statistically significant and is significant for the whole period and for three out of the five years from 1985 to 1989 at the 5 per cent level. However, the relation is absent for average performing sample and for poorly performing recent IPOs (where directors can insulate themselves from monitoring activities). This finding is consistent with the emphasis placed by the Cadbury committee on the presence of non-executive directors on the boards of companies. Likewise, separating the functions of CEO and chairman increases the probability of management removal in poorly performing companies (but not in average performers or recent IPOs).

In order to investigate whether one of the above corporate governance forces dominate the other, the ownership structure, changes in large shareholdings and board composition are integrated into one single turnover-model. We still find strong evidence of managerial entrenchment in all companies independent of performance. Contrary to institutions, outside shareholders owning large share stakes discipline underperforming management (in worst performing companies), as reflected by a level of statistical significance of 5 per cent. A large proportion of non-executive directors and the separation of the functions of CEO and chairman, which were significant (at respectively 6 and 4 per cent levels) are now only marginally significant (10 per cent level). Faccio and Lasfer (Chapter 25, this volume) also cast doubt on the effectiveness of the internal corporate governance mechanisms in the UK as they find a generally weak relationship between firm value and managerial ownership, board structure and the combination of managerial ownership and board structure (see also Cosh and Hughes 1996). Previous evidence that (mainly new) outside shareholders and directors who increase their share stakes or obtain new equity stakes do so in order to discipline management in the worst performing companies is confirmed.

5. CONCLUSION

This chapter compares ownership and control in two samples of UK quoted firms with markedly different performance; the first sample is drawn from the lowest quintile of performance, the second comes from the middle quintile. As takeovers do not perform an explicit corporate disciplining task in the UK (as shown by Franks and Mayer 1996), the disciplinary role of large shareholders and of new shareholders who increase voting power is analysed.

This study reports a strong relation between the exercise of corporate control in the UK in the form of executive board turnover and corporate performance. Consistent with the literature on free rider problems and large share stakes, concentrated ownership is associated with more active corporate governance than dispersed share ownership. However, the paper also finds that the nature of the owner is of critical importance: corporate investors exercise more control than institutional investors and those with private benefits of control, such as directors, may impede the exercise of good governance. Managerial entrenchment is present most in recent IPOs where director shareholdings are particularly high.

But perhaps the most interesting observation in this chapter relates to the dynamic relation between ownership, control, and performance. Where poor performance is observed, sales of share stakes occur between different investors. Our findings suggest that substantial changes in these share stakes occur in the absence of tender offers or mergers, and without a violation of the UK Takeover Code's mandatory offer rule. In particular, there is a market in shares between new and old non-institutional shareholders and directors. These trades in shares are associated with significant changes in boards of poorly performing companies.

There is not much evidence that the presence of non-executive directors and the separation of the role of chairman and chief executive exert a significant impact on corporate governance. There are some interesting parallels between the UK and Germany. While levels of concentration of ownership are much greater in Germany than in the UK, there is more evidence of an influence of concentration of ownership on the disciplining of management in the UK than in Germany. This may result from the private benefits of control of large shareholders in Germany impeding the exercise of corporate control in an analogous fashion to the negative influence of directors' holdings on board turnover in the UK. Takeovers are not the method by which managerial discipline is imposed in either country; instead, partial sales of share stakes are more closely associated with the exercise of corporate governance in both countries.

An important issue concerns the ability of coalition formations in the UK to overcome impediments to changes in control from regulatory rules. The Takeover Code, for example, imposes mandatory bid requirements once share stakes of more than 30 per cent have been accumulated. The ability to circumvent such rules through the formation of coalitions may come at the expense of the minority shareholders whom regulatory rules are designed to protect. On the other hand, the ability of large shareholders to exercise control at low cost may be an important contribution to good corporate governance.

Notes

1. Of the 34 poorly performing companies introduced in the period 1980–4, 10 were introduced in 1984, 14 in 1982–3, and 10 in 1980–1. Four of the average performing IPOs were floated in 1984, 6 in 1982–3, and 3 in 1980–1.
2. A director was classified as 'retiring' when his retirement was age related. Sixty-three was chosen as the minimum retirement age and an earlier retirement was viewed as enforced. Public announcements of a director or manager being fired are rare. In the annual reports a variety of euphemisms for enforced turnover are used, such as 'leaves by mutual consent', 'parts the company to spend more time with his family' or 'desires to pursue an alternative career'. Weisbach (1988) confirms that 'companies do not announce the true reason behind their CEO's resignation'; he too only adjusts his statistics on resignations for deaths, illness, and retirements at an age over sixty-three.
3. Listed companies have been required to record shareholders with 5 per cent or more of equity capital since 1985. In 1989 the reporting level was reduced to 3 per cent.
4. The relations among directors' ownership, turnover and performance do not change significantly by ignoring the non-beneficial shareholdings.
5. It should be noted that institutional investors are de facto the largest investor group. This does not show up in Table 19.4 because the vast majority of institutional holdings are below 5 per cent and are, therefore, not liable to be disclosed in this period of this study.
6. The fact that the lowest quintile of performance counts a disproportionately large number of recent IPOs may be due to the well-documented long-term IPO underperformance (see e.g. Goergen 1999).
7. All regressions are corrected for size (log of assets employed) as well as for industry.
8. The interactive term is statistically significant in most of the individual years as well as across the period as a whole.
9. Tables are available upon request.
10. The results remain valid when recent IPOs are excluded from the sample. Moreover, there is no significant size effect.
11. The data on increases in holdings of 'new' investors contain an unavoidable bias, due to disclosure regulation. Suppose a shareholder increases its stake from 4.9 to 5.1 per cent. This will be recorded as an increased holding of 5.1 per cent because stakes less than 5 per cent do not have to be disclosed.

References

Barclay, M. J., and Holderness, C. G. (1989). Private benefits from control of public corporations. *Journal of Financial Economics* 25: 371.

——(1991). Negotiated block trades and corporate control. *Journal of Finance* 46: 861.

Bianco, M., Gola, C., and Signorini, L. F. (1995). Dealing with separation between ownership and control: State, family, coalitions and pyramidal groups in Italian corporate governance. Banca d'Italia, Working Paper.

Burkart, M., Gromb, D., and Panunzi, F. (1997). Large shareholders, monitoring and the value of the firm. *Quarterly Journal of Economics* 112: 693.

Cosh, A., and Hughes, A. (1996). The changing anatomy of corporate control and the market for executives in the UK. Cambridge ESRC Centre for Business Research, Working Paper.

Coughlan, A. T., and Schmidt, R. M. (1985). Executive compensation, managerial turnover and firm performance: An empirical investigation. *Journal of Accounting and Economics* 7: 42.

Demsetz, H. (1983). The structure of ownership and the theory of the firm. *Journal of Law and Economics* 26: 375.

—— and Lehn, K. (1985). The structure of corporate ownership: Causes and consequences. *Journal of Political Economy* 93: 1155.

Faccio, M., and Lasfer, A. (2002). Institutional share holders and corporate governance: the case of UK pension funds, this volume, chapter 25.

Fama, E., and Jensen, M. (1983). Separation of ownership and control. *Journal of Law and Economics* 26: 301.

Franks, J., and Mayer, C. (1996). Hostile take-overs in the UK and the correction of managerial failure. *Journal of Financial Economics* 40: 163.

—— (2001). The ownership and control in German corporations. London Business School, Working Review of Financial Studies. 14: 209.

Gilson, S. C. (1990). Bankruptcy, boards, banks and blockholders. *Journal of Financial Economics* 27: 355.

Goergen, M. (1999). Insider retention and long-run performance in German and UK IPOs. UMIST School of Management, Working Paper.

—— and Renneboog, L. (2002). Prediction of control concentration in German and UK initial public offerings, this volume, chapter 10.

Hermalin, B. E., and Weisbach, M. S. (1991). The effects of board composition and direct incentives on firm performance. *Financial Management* 20: 101.

Kaplan, S., and Reishus, D. (1990). Outside directorships and corporate performance. *Journal of Financial Economics* 27: 389.

Lai, J., and Sudarsanam, S. (1997). Corporate restructuring in response to performance decline: Impact of ownership, governance and lenders. *European Finance Review* 1: 197.

Martin, J., and McConnell, J. J. (1991). Corporate performance, corporate take-overs and management turnover. *Journal of Finance* 46: 671.

McConnell, J. J., and Servaes, H. (1990). Additional evidence on equity ownership and corporate value. *Journal of Financial Economics* 27: 595.

Renneboog, L. (2000). Ownership, managerial control and the governance of large shareholder listed on the Brussels Stock Exchange. *Journal of Banking and Finance* 24: 1959.

Shleifer, A., and Vishny, R. W. (1986). Large shareholder and corporate control. *Journal of Political Economy* 94: 461.

Warner, J. B., Watts, R. L., and Wruck, K. H. (1988). Stock prices and top management changes. *Journal of Financial Economics* 20: 431.

Weisbach, M. S. (1988). Outside directors and CEO turnover. *Journal of Financial Economics* 20: 413.

20

A Comparison of English and American Bankruptcy Procedures

JULIAN R. FRANKS AND WALTER N. TOROUS

1. INTRODUCTION

It has become fashionable for countries to change their insolvency procedures. As a result, there exists a great variety of insolvency codes and procedures for dealing with insolvent and distressed companies. One way of distinguishing between them is on the basis of a debtor or creditor orientation. A second distinction can be made according to the origins of the procedures: the extent to which procedures are based on commercial contracts between lenders and borrowers and the extent to which they are governed by statute. USA insolvency procedures are governed largely by statute, for example, the 1978 Bankruptcy Act. In contrast, England's insolvency procedures are largely based on commercial contracts between lenders and borrowers.

Given their different origins, it is unsurprising that the two countries' procedures vary considerably. The main objective of Chapter 11 of the US Bankruptcy Act is to maintain the business as a going concern. As a result, the code has been deliberately designed to be debtor-oriented. Substantial rights are given to the borrowing company, called the debtor-in-possession (DIP), to continue running the business while a reorganization plan is being worked out. Advocates of Chapter 11 argue that such procedures result in a higher incidence of going concerns for the debtor company as well as for its suppliers and customers. The sceptics argue that costs are higher and returns to creditors lower as a result of the bankruptcy process, and that far too many uneconomic enterprises are allowed to stay in business, in some cases dragging down other companies.

England's main procedure, called 'administrative receivership', provides for a creditor-controlled procedure with little if any court involvement. Under this procedure, the main (senior) creditor, with a special mortgage called a floating charge, may appoint a representative to administer the insolvent company and if necessary sell it as a going concern or liquidate it. The lack of court involvement and the dominant role of one creditor, means the procedure is frequently quick and presumably less costly. Critics argue, however, that the senior creditor may have little interest in the company's upside potential and therefore have less interest in keeping the company alive, especially if it requires some additional financing.

We might expect that differences in legal rules in distinct countries might give rise to very different interest rates on loans for loans of similar risk. More debtor friendly procedures might be expected to have higher interest rates on debt than creditor friendly procedures. We might also expect that in the event of distress or insolvency, costs of financial distress and recovery rates to creditors would vary across countries. These differences can create incentives for lenders and borrowers as well as governments to change insolvency procedures and codes. Harmonization of capital markets creates powerful incentives to harmonize regulation and legal rules. For example, the European Union (EU) is trying to harmonize legal rules across countries in the EU to foster trade and capital markets.

2. WHAT SHOULD THE BANKRUPTCY PROCESS AIM TO ACCOMPLISH?

We judge the comparative efficiency of a bankruptcy code according to three criteria.

2.1. *Does it Encourage Adherence to the Terms of the Debt Contract?*

The first criterion for evaluating the efficiency of an insolvency code is the extent to which it minimizes renegotiating problems. Efficiency in this sense may be interpreted as a speedy, low-cost process that maintains the priority of claims. For example, an insolvency process that provides creditors with strong incentives to surrender some of their claims to shareholders would violate the original agreement between lender and borrower. Such violations may affect not only the outcome of reorganizations, but also the pricing of debt when issued and, in the extreme, the availability of credit.

2.2. *Does it Preserve Promising Enterprises While Dissolving Uneconomic Ones?*

Consistent with standard economic valuation criteria, all companies with a reasonable expectation of earning their cost of capital after a reorganization ought to be preserved, while all others should be liquidated. Moreover, the system should encourage any additional new investment necessary to maintain an insolvent, but economically viable firm as an operating concern, provided there is an adequate incremental return to all the firm's claimants from that new investment. If the additional investment is not forthcoming under these conditions and the firm's assets are broken up, then we describe the liquidation as premature. But, if the investment is undertaken when the firm would be worth more broken up than whole, then liquidation has been unjustifiably postponed (we refer to this as 'deferred' liquidation). The optimal bankruptcy code in this respect is one that minimizes the probability of both premature as well as deferred liquidations.

Premature liquidation could happen for a number of reasons. The system could allow too little time to collect information about the relative values of liquidation versus continuation of the enterprise. Or the system could discourage new financing, in part because of potential 'leakage' of value from proposed investments to existing creditors (Gertner and Scharfstein 1991).

2.3. *Does it Minimize the Direct Costs of Insolvency?*

The third criterion is the size of the direct ('deadweight') costs of the insolvency process, including legal and accounting fees. This might also be taken to include the costs borne by other stakeholders in the firm, for example, employees, suppliers, and customers—groups that do not have sufficient financial claims against the company to compensate them for the losses in the event of default. They are also often excluded from the decision to liquidate or to maintain the firm as a going concern (Shleifer and Summers 1988).

3. ENGLISH INSOLVENCY PROCEDURES

In examining English procedures it is useful to distinguish the period prior to the 1986 Insolvency Act from that subsequent to it. Prior to the Act there were two principal routes to formal reorganization: (1) liquidation, and (2) receivership or administrative receivership. After 1986 two collective procedures were introduced, both requiring court involvement. As we shall see, they are quite different from receivership.

3.1. *Liquidation*

Any creditor with a debt in excess of £75 or the company itself may apply for the appointment of a liquidator. In compulsory liquidations, however, the appointment requires the permission of the commercial court, the Court in Chancery. The petition may be opposed by the company or by any other creditor. The role of the liquidator is to sell enough of the firm's assets, either in whole or piecemeal, to satisfy all creditors' claims. The liquidator must also supervise the distribution of funds to creditors and ensure an orderly winding up of the business. Although there is no legal stay of creditors' claims in a voluntary liquidation, there is a de facto stay since the company can apply for a compulsory liquidation under the supervision of the court. In that event, there would be a legally imposed stay of claims until the liquidation is complete.

3.2. *Receivership*

A receiver is appointed by a creditor that is designated the appointor. The appointor must have a particular security or mortgage (in the USA called a 'lien') on the firm's assets, referred to as a fixed or a floating charge. A fixed charge is a claim on the immovable assets of a company—for example, land and buildings; a floating charge may be taken on the assets as a whole, including stocks and work-in-progress. In the absence of a secured creditor with a fixed or floating charge, a receiver cannot be appointed. In such cases, the only alternative prior to 1986 was the appointment of a liquidator.

A receiver is appointed over a particular asset and an administrative receiver is appointed over the entire company's assets (or substantially the whole). The administrative receiver has two options. He might continue to run the business prior to sale or he might sell the business almost immediately. In the latter case the sale might be as a going concern or as a piecemeal sale. The objective of the receiver is to repay the loans of the creditor appointing him—that is, the appointor. If the receiver has any surplus he will repay other creditors such as trade creditors. If there is anything remaining after repaying all the creditors, the receiver will pass the surplus back to the company's owners. The decision by the receiver as to whether the business is liquidated or sold as a going concern depends upon the circumstances, for example, whether the business is generating positive net cash flow and whether other companies are interested in purchasing the company.

During receivership, if new funds are required prior to sale, then those funds will usually come from the senior creditor who appointed the receiver. As a result, the decision to keep the firm as a going concern, or to liquidate it, is often in the hands of the receiver and his appointor. If the appointor should contribute new funds, other creditors may benefit from that infusion without bearing any of the costs.[1] When an insolvent business is sold as a going concern, it is often sold to existing management. The latter is often the highest bidder because it has superior information about the enterprise's potential value.

The receiver's appointment cannot in principle be challenged, except on technical grounds. However, other creditors whose payments are in default may apply for repayment or, failing repayment, may apply for the appointment of a liquidator. In a study by Franks and Sussman (2000) of small to medium-sized insolvent companies, they found that the large majority of creditors appointing the administrative receiver were commercial banks. They also found that other (unsecured) creditors rarely tried to appoint a liquidator in the event a receiver was appointed. We shall see below that the main reason for the passivity of these other creditors was because of their very low recovery rates in the event of insolvency.

Whereas the liquidator is responsible to all creditors, the responsibility of the receiver is to repay the creditor who appointed him—that is, the creditor with the fixed charge. In the case of the administrative receiver, the first duty is to his appointor, although he is responsible for repaying other creditors with fixed charges and preferential creditors.[2] As the receiver is selected and appointed by only one creditor, the interests of the unsecured creditors will be of much lower priority.

To prevent the receiver from acting in a way that disadvantages other creditors, the law imposes various restrictions. For example, the receiver has a duty to sell the assets for their full price. For example, in the case of *American Express* v. *Hurley* (1983), the receiver was successfully sued for failing to advertise properly the sale of an asset. This duty of care is an important constraint on a receiver's ability to favour his appointor at the expense of other creditors.

In deciding whether to continue operating an insolvent company, the receiver must consider the following: (1) the costs of the process, especially if the company is small; (2) the willingness of customers to continue dealing with an insolvent company; and (3) the need to provide guarantees if the business must be kept running. Moreover, he will be concerned about the effect of his actions on his reputation as a professional receiver. If he is perceived to have managed the receivership badly, he may not be appointed again. There is also a risk to his reputation if he sells assets too quickly. Nevertheless, the strong impression taken from insolvency practitioners is that there is less risk for the receiver from a too rapid sale of assets than from raising new funds to maintain an uneconomic business as a going concern. The receiver's reputation is made all the more important because a small group of commercial banks usually hold the floating charge in many companies and therefore appoint the administrative receiver.

To illustrate the potential dilemma faced by a receiver, consider the following actual case of reorganization. A creditor had a charge on a company with two hotels. He appointed an administrative receiver who determined their realizable value as bricks and mortar to be £1.2 million. If kept as a going concern, however, the assets would have a higher value of £1.8 million. The appointor held a floating charge and was owed £1.8 million plus interest. The hotels were only breaking even, and although the resale market in hotels was volatile, it was also rising. As a result, the receiver decided to run the hotels as a going concern. Subsequently, the roof of one hotel collapsed and the repair cost of £100,000 had to be paid by the appointor. The other creditors refused to contribute since they believed little would be left over to repay their claims. The roof repair illustrates an important risk to the appointor from running the business as a going concern. That is, if new monies have to be invested, creditors other than the appointor may refuse to contribute even though they would likely benefit from the new investment.

A second, more serious conflict could have arisen if the amount owed to the appointor had been £1.2 million, instead of £1.8 million. At £1.2 million, the amount owed would have exactly equalled the realizable value. As a result, the receiver would have had little incentive to maintain the business as a going concern prior to a sale; it would expose him to the risk of loss without increasing the value of the potential proceeds to the appointor. In contrast, other creditors would benefit if the proceeds should exceed £1.2 million, but would not share in the losses if the proceeds fell short of that.

The receiver in this case was asked the following question: If the hotels' realizable value had been equal to the amount owed to the appointor, would he have continued to maintain the business as a going concern? The receiver responded yes since he considered that he had some duty to other creditors and that selling the business for more than its liquidation value would enhance his reputation. At the same time, however, he felt that other creditors would not have been able to sue him if the hotels had been liquidated. As things turned out, the hotels were eventually sold at a price of £3.1 million, sufficient to meet not only the appointor's claim but also part of other creditors' claims.

To summarize, we evaluate the choice between liquidation and receivership. Whereas any creditor may apply for the appointment of a liquidator, a receiver may be appointed only if there is a secured creditor. When liquidation is the only possibility for the company, the two forms of insolvency differ very little. The differences emerge only when there is a possibility of maintaining the firm as a going concern. The powers of the receiver to maintain the firm as a going concern are greater than those of the liquidator. For example, certain contracts entered into by the company prior to insolvency can be terminated by the receiver, even if the business is maintained as a going concern.

3.3. *Collective Procedures: Administration*

The 1986 Insolvency Act created a new procedure known as the administration. In the latter case the Companies Court appoint an administrator. The company or any creditor may apply for the appointment. Like the receiver, the administrator must be an insolvency practitioner.

Unlike the receiver, the administrator represents all creditors' claims. As any one creditor does not appoint the administrator, some of the potential conflicts that arise in receivership are diminished. The administrator has strong powers to delay repaying creditors' claims, at least for a limited period. This power to delay is often referred to as a 'stay'. For example, interest and repayment on loans are stayed while the administration order is outstanding. Also, the owner of a leased asset may be prevented from repossessing the asset during administration if it is deemed necessary for the running of the company. Also, the administrator has greater powers to raise funds than the receiver does.

When there are creditors with floating charges, however, such creditors can and do typically prevent the initial appointment of an administrator by appointing an administrative receiver instead. In such cases, the courts cannot impose an administrator on creditors, even if they determine the company and its creditors would be better served in doing so. Creditors also have the power to oppose the plan of an administrator and to vote to end its administration. Also, any reorganization plan proposed by the administrator must be approved by a majority of creditors.

Prominent examples in which administrators have been appointed are Polly Peck, Maxwell Communications, and Olympia and York. In the Maxwell case, the administrator was permitted by the USA Bankruptcy Court to take control and manage some of the USA companies.

The Report of Sir Kenneth Cork's Review Committee, which was presented to Parliament in 1982, recommended changes to the insolvency legislation that would have moved England significantly towards a Chapter 11-type of code. The creation of the administrator is considered by some observers to have met that objective. They correctly note that the administrator is appointed by the court not creditors, serves the interests of all creditors, and has greater powers to postpone or stay creditors' claims.

Some insolvency practitioners maintain, however, that the primary accomplishment of the 1986 Act has been simply to extend the old system of administrative receivership to a broader range of cases. As mentioned earlier, receivers could previously only be appointed in cases where creditors had a fixed or floating charges. Any benefits of such an extension, however, have been limited by an important obstacle: under the 1986 Act, the appointment of an administrator can normally be blocked by other creditors through the appointment of a receiver. For example, a secured creditor is likely to exercise the right to appoint a receiver if he perceives a conflict of interest with other creditors. Such conflicts can make the appointment of the administrator potentially valuable, since those conflicts can result in premature liquidation.[3] Administration can allow a better coordination of creditors and resolve those conflicts.

There have been relatively few administrator appointments since the 1986 Act—hundreds compared with the many thousands of receiverships. However, administrator appointments are frequently made for large companies where the value of coordinating creditors is greatest.

3.4. *Company Voluntary Arrangements*

A Company Voluntary Arrangement (CVA) is a second collective procedure introduced by the 1986 Act. It is the only procedure specifically allowing the borrower to remain in control of the company pending the preparation of a reorganization plan. The court participates in the CVA and appoints an insolvency practitioner to advise it on the desirability of reorganization. Like Administration, a CVA can in practice only be implemented if the main secured creditors are in favour, and this usually means the bank lender.

4. USA BANKRUPTCY PROCEDURES

The Bankruptcy Reform Act of 1978 governs corporate bankruptcy in the USA. In particular, Chapter 11 of the Code allows a firm to remain in operation while a plan of reorganization is worked out with its creditors. Since the borrower or debtor remains in possession during Chapter 11, the company is called 'the debtor-in-possession'. The motivation for introducing Chapter 11 and its related procedures was to increase the possibility that financially distressed firms would emerge from reorganization as going concerns. To facilitate this outcome, management of the debtor firm typically remains in office and substantial rights are conferred upon the DIP. The rationale for Chapter 11 is that a more debtor-oriented code improves the likelihood of a firm remaining a going concern.

4.1. *Liquidation*

An alternative to Chapter 11 is Chapter 7. Chapter 7 is the liquidation section of the 1978 Act. Under this provision a trustee is appointed to sell the insolvent business, usually piecemeal, that is, it is closed prior to sale. Management of insolvent concerns prefers Chapter 11 since they often remain in control, whereas in Chapter 7 they are replaced automatically.

4.2. *Chapter 11 Procedure*

Once in Chapter 11, the debtor retains control of the business, although on some occasions the bankruptcy court appoints a trustee to oversee the firm's operations. For example, a trustee was appointed in the Eastern Airlines bankruptcy. Nevertheless, there is detailed court oversight of the reorganization process. For example, decisions requiring the approval of the court include major investment and divestiture decisions or sales of assets to raise cash.

Interest payments to unsecured creditors are suspended during Chapter 11 proceedings. Furthermore, the filing of a bankruptcy petition automatically restrains creditors—which can number in the thousands for large publicly held corporations—from taking actions against the debtor to collect their debts or enforce their security by repossessing assets. As a result, the debtor firm continues to receive cash flows from the firm's underlying operations, while payments on some or all of the firm's debt is suspended or stayed. These Chapter 11 provisions thus effect a dramatic improvement in the firm's cash flows while increasing the pressure on creditors to agree to a debt restructuring.

The debtor has the exclusive right to propose a plan of reorganization during the first 120 days after filing with the court for Chapter 11. Exclusivity is often extended by the court, although creditors have the right to object. For example, in the Manville bankruptcy, exclusivity was extended ten times. If the debtor's exclusivity is terminated, any interested party, such as a creditor, may propose its own plan of reorganization. A total of sixteen plans of reorganization were submitted in the bankruptcy of Allegheny International, the first seven by management and the remaining nine by creditors and investors.

A plan of reorganization divides creditors into classes, usually based on the seniority of their claims. Approval requires a majority of each class in number and two-thirds in amount voting to accept a plan. If a particular class rejects a plan, the plan can still be confirmed by forcing the non-assenting class to accept proceeds, in accordance with absolute priority, from a hypothetical liquidation. For example, a plan of reorganization was 'crammed down' on the preferred shareholders of Beker Industries: they received nothing instead of the $300,000 allotted to them in the original plan they rejected.

Creditors are also afforded certain protection as well. For example, if a firm files for Chapter 11, creditors may petition for the immediate liquidation of the firm, or for the bankruptcy petition to be denied. Creditors also have the right to file an involuntary bankruptcy petition against a firm.

4.3. *Workouts versus Chapter 11*

Most firms enter Chapter 11 only after attempting an informal reorganization or workout outside of bankruptcy. A workout can take the form of an exchange offer for outstanding debt, a renegotiation of bond covenants, or a negotiated reduction of interest payments or extension of loan maturities. Workouts generally involve lower direct costs than Chapter 11 cases because the time spent in informal reorganization is generally much shorter.

Nevertheless, there are several reasons why workouts may fail and firms enter Chapter 11. First, by the Trust Indenture Act of 1939, changing the principal amount, interest rate, or maturity date of a publicly held bond requires approval of 100 per cent of the bondholders, in contrast to the non-unanimity provisions of Chapter 11. Second, Chapter 11's automatic stay provision prevents a 'run' on the firm's assets by creditors, thereby providing an orderly means of settling claims. Third, workouts can have adverse tax effects. For example, if a firm experiences a change in control as a result of a workout, its use of net operating tax loss carry forwards may be severely restricted. Other advantages of Chapter 11 include the ability to avoid actual or potential legal judgments, as in the cases of Smith International and Texaco.

Some firms, such as Crystal Oil, have attempted to combine the low administrative costs of a workout with the non-unanimity requirements and tax benefits of Chapter 11 by filing a 'pre-packaged' bankruptcy petition. In a pre-packaged bankruptcy, a firm files for Chapter 11 with a plan of reorganization that has already been accepted by the required number of claim holders.

The bankruptcy of Eastern Airlines provides an extreme example of how the debtor-oriented nature of the USA bankruptcy code may result in firms being maintained as going concerns when it is in creditors' best interest to have the firm liquidated. At the time of bankruptcy filing, Eastern Airlines publicly stated it had sufficient funds ($3.7 billion) to repay its liabilities ($3.4 billion) in full. One year later, Eastern proposed to repay its creditors ($1.6 billion). The company's final plan of reorganization, which was rejected by creditors, proposed a repayment of only $850 million. When the firm was eventually liquidated, the creditors received only about $340 million.

Throughout the attempts to reorganize Eastern formally, the bankruptcy court and court-appointed trustee strove to maintain the firm as a going concern. An important part of this reorganization process was the approval by the court of DIP financing allowing the firm to continue operations. Equally essential to this unfortunate outcome was the court's granting management numerous extensions of exclusivity to formulate plans of reorganization. Unfortunately for Eastern's creditors, these efforts cost them over $3 billion.

5. DIFFERENCES BETWEEN AMERICAN AND ENGLISH PROCEDURES

Table 20.1 provides a comparison of the insolvency procedures in the two countries. In England we describe both administrative receivership and administration, and in the USA we describe Chapter 11.

Table 20.1. *Comparison of English and American insolvency procedures*

Characteristics	England: Receivership/Administration	United States: Chapter 11
Managerial Control	Insolvency practitioner: previous managers must relinquish control	Debtor-in-possession: previous managers retain control or new managers appointed
Requirements for entry into procedure	Firm cannot meet payments to creditors	Firm need not be insolvent
Automatic stay against creditor claims	None in receivership. Three months initial stay in administration but can be extended by vote of creditors	Most of creditor claims are included in the stay and the stay lasts for the period of reorganization
Management of liabilities	Little scope to renegotiate debts in receivership and limited scope in administration	Great discretion to renegotiate firm's debts
Constraints on firm as a going concern	Receiver will liquidate firm if it is greater than going concern value	No compulsion to liquidate providing positive operating cash flow
Bankruptcy financing	Little scope for new financing in bankruptcy to have priority over pre-bankruptcy claims in receivership; more scope in administration	Significant scope for new financing to have priority over pre-bankruptcy debts (called 'debtor in possession financing')
Preservation of residual claim of equityholders	Little negotiation between creditors, absolute priority prevails and rarely does equity receive anything in receivership; more scope for renegotiation in administration	In majority of cases deviations of absolute priority in favour of equity
Direct costs	Lower because (i) short period, (ii) creditors minimally involved in process	Higher because (i) long periods, (ii) court is extensively involved in process

5.1. *Management Control*

In England the board of directors relinquishes control of the company when a receiver, liquidator, or administrator is appointed. These professionals are licensed insolvency practitioners, usually qualified accountants. In the USA, by contrast, existing management often remains in control of the business throughout the entire reorganization process, although the company is subject to detailed supervision by the court. For example, the salaries of the directors of Texaco, which sought protection in Chapter 11, were reduced by the court. In contrast to England, the USA insolvency process is administered by lawyers including workout specialists.

One often-cited study by Gilson (1989) reported that only 30 per cent of the top management of financially distressed firms remain in place by the end of the formal reorganization process. Even when it is replaced, and then only with the agreement of the court, the new management typically represents the debtor and is usually composed of professional managers with a working knowledge of the industry.

5.2. *Liquidation versus Going-Concern Value*

In Chapter 11 there is no duty on management (or the court) to liquidate even if the liquidation value is thought to be greater than the going-concern value. Determining these values is in itself a lengthy and costly process. The implication is that the business could be kept running even when it would be worth more to creditors to liquidate. Eastern Airlines is an example where a business was maintained as a going concern when it was clear that creditors would have received a larger repayment from the immediate realization of the firm's assets.

5.3. *Direct Costs of Each System*

The direct costs of Chapter 11 can be expected to be greater than those of receivership because the receiver (and to a lesser extent the administrator) can act without having to report back to creditors or the court on a day-to-day basis. In the UK there is little ongoing discussion of individual decisions with creditors requiring their approval, especially in receivership. This lack of need for ongoing consultation makes the receivership process relatively quick and therefore of short duration, perhaps months or only weeks. However, Franks and Sussman (2000) found that in their sample of small receiverships, the costs of the process averaged about 24 per cent of the realized proceeds of receivership (before costs).

By contrast, the Chapter 11 process in the USA can be unduly protracted. For example, in the case of Wickes, which was reorganized in 1985, the period spent in Chapter 11 was almost three years. The expenses of the reorganization totalled $250 million, of which between $75 and $120 million have been attributed to inefficiencies in the Chapter 11 process. These costs represent as much as 25 per cent of the value of the reorganized firm. However, comparable figures for small Chapter 11 firms are not available.

5.4. *The Relative Efficiency of English and American Procedures*

At the beginning of this chapter, we set forth three criteria to judge the efficiency of insolvency procedures. One was the extent to which the code is likely to minimize both premature and needlessly protracted liquidations. The USA code appears to have strong incentives to maintain the firm as a going concern even when it is worth more in liquidation. In contrast English procedures emphasize the rights of creditors—and in some cases giving priority to only one creditor—and this may lead to too many premature liquidations.

The DIP financing provisions of the USA process allow the debtor to raise new funds that have priority over most pre-insolvency claims. In England the receiver and administrator frequently raises funds from the secured creditors to keep the business going prior to a sale. However, maintaining a business as a going concern may require substantial funds for investment that the secured creditors are not willing to supply. In addition, other classes of creditors may not be willing to give up priority in order to accommodate new capital. In principle at least, the debtor financing provisions of the USA code allow the court to give new capital supra priority. This feature of the USA Code is justified by the fact that there are large stakeholders, such as employees and suppliers, who are not usually party to the liquidation decision. However, the USA code achieves this objective somewhat indirectly by giving power and value to the DIP rather than directly to those other stakeholders.

A second criterion of efficiency is the consistency of the insolvency procedures with the terms of the debt contract. Chapter 11 provides strong protection to the DIP and thus may upset the priority of claims. The code effectively grants shareholders an option on the value of the company—one that rises in value if the value of the firm rises, without the possibility of loss if the value falls. The value of the option is increased to the extent these parties can extend (or threaten to extend) the period in Chapter 11, since a longer period increases the probability the firm value will rise and shareholders will receive some payment. Also, as the case of Eastern Airlines bears out, the longer period increases the costs of insolvency, a burden that falls primarily on creditors.

A number of studies have found that the majority of Chapter 11 reorganizations provide for deviations from absolute priority in favour of shareholders and, in some cases, junior or unsecured creditors (Franks and Torous 1989; 1994). If the courts strictly enforced the principle of absolute priority, shareholders would receive some consideration in a reorganization plan only after creditors' claims had been satisfied in full. One of our own studies found that deviations from absolute priority occurred in voluntary reorganizations or workouts, and were substantially larger than in Chapter 11. The size of these deviations is one reason why the code has recently come in for such a sustained attack.

In contrast to USA practice, receivership results in a speedy settlement of claims and strict adherence to the priority of claims. This is achieved because creditors obtain control of the company when it enters the formal insolvency process. Unsecured creditors, however, may be unduly disadvantaged by receivership. Franks and Sussman (2000) found that their median recovery rate was about 1 per cent of the face value of their claims. Although it is probably too early to evaluate the position of administrator, the small number of cases using the new appointment suggests that it has not produced radical changes in insolvency provisions. Certainly, the experience to date does not suggest that it is functioning as the

UK equivalent to Chapter 11 (though some would say this was never the intent of the legislation).

The third criterion is the size of the dead-weight costs of bankruptcy, which include all the direct costs associated with the bankruptcy process. The Chapter 11 process can be expected to incur higher costs than that of receivership because it is much lengthier and involves more day-to-day reporting to the court and to creditors. The costs of each code have an important effect upon the incentives to complete workouts. In the USA, because of both the direct and indirect costs of the bankruptcy process, there are strong incentives for the insolvent company to come to an informal agreement with creditors. Also, creditors are more likely to come to a voluntary agreement with the company, which can then enter Chapter 11 to obtain ratification of the plan. Such 'pre-packaging' has two advantages. Court approval will reduce the possibility of subsequent litigation and force small creditors, or even individual large ones, to accept the agreement because of the strong voting provisions that favour majority approval.

There are also incentives in England to reorganize privately. Franks and Sussman (2000) reported that about 75 per cent of their sample of distressed firms successfully recovered outside the formal insolvency procedures. The bulk of the remaining 25 per cent went into administrative receivership or liquidation. Nonetheless, there are serious concerns in the UK that current legislation does not provide sufficient incentives to reorganize voluntarily. Also, the high level of workouts in the USA reflects, in part, the high costs of the Chapter 11 process and its deterrent effect.

Both the direct and indirect costs will affect how debt contracts are written and the interest rate paid on particular types of debt. For example, it is possible that two identical firms with the same capital structure in the two countries will pay different interest rates on their debt when the bankruptcy codes differ as they do in the USA and the UK. Also, it might be expected that where deviations from absolute priority occur in favour of shareholders, the margin paid to the lenders will be higher. Margins will also be higher where the company can be maintained as a going concern when it is worth more in liquidation.

It is likely that pronounced differences between insolvency codes could lead also to differences in the prevalence of different types of debt. For example, in Chapter 11 payments on financial leases must continue to be paid in reorganization even though interest and repayments on other debts are stayed. As a result, financial leases may be more attractive to lenders in the USA than other types of debt.

One criterion includes the interests of corporate stakeholders not represented in the bankruptcy process. The USA system indirectly gives considerable weight to these interests by means of incentives to keep the firm running and the discretion allowed by bankruptcy judges. For example, lawsuits brought by individuals who may have been harmed by a company's products have been admitted as a legitimate claim against the firm in bankruptcy.

However, the benefits to the stakeholders of a company in Chapter 11 may be offset by costs imposed on stakeholders in other companies. There is serious concern in the USA that the Chapter 11 process is being used by some firms to acquire a competitive advantage. For example, if firms in an industry are generally in financial difficulties, then those firms entering Chapter 11 may find access to new financing less costly than those firms that are in distress but have not entered bankruptcy. Managers of solvent USA airlines have been particularly vigorous in their complaints that airlines in Chapter 11 have enjoyed an unfair competitive advantage.

6. CONCLUSION

It should be clear that both American and English procedures have potentially significant defects. The USA code encourages lengthy, expensive, and contentious bargaining that can lead to a change in the priority of claims and thus violation of the original terms of the debt contract. Its length and expense can provide the debtor and individual creditors with the threat to waste the assets of other creditors unless they agree to write down their claims.

The UK process of receivership, by contrast, is usually expeditious and adheres strictly to the provisions of the debt contract. Creditors obtain control of the firm and, as a consequence, there is strict adherence to the debt contract. This may be achieved, however, at the cost of too many premature liquidations. Moreover, there must also be some concern that the receivership process disadvantages unsecured creditors.

Nor does it appear that the appointment of an administrator allowed by the Insolvency Act of 1986 has significantly corrected these faults. For one thing, the number of such appointments has been relatively small, perhaps in large part because secured creditors can block the appointment. Secondly, although funds can often be raised from existing lenders to keep a business going, it is not clear whether this substitutes for the DIP financing that characterizes Chapter 11 reorganizations.

Notes

1. As a result, there could be an under-investment problem (see Gertner and Scharfstein 1991).
2. Preferential creditors are mostly the tax authorities.
3. There is evidence that creditors on some occasions allow an administration even when they hold a floating charge and could appoint a receiver. This suggests that collective procedures can add value over receivership.

References

Franks, J., and W. Torous (1989). An empirical investigation of US firms in reorganization. *Journal of Finance* 44: 747.

——(1994). How shareholders and creditors fare in workouts and Chapter 11 Reorganizations. *Journal of Financial Economics* 35: 349.

——and Sussman, O. (2000). The cycle of corporate distress, rescue and dissolution: A study of small and medium size UK companies. London Business School, Working Paper.

Gertner, R., and Scharfstein, D. (1991). A theory of workouts and the effects of reorganization law. *Journal of Finance* 46: 1189.

Gilson, S. (1989). Management turnover and financial distress. *Journal of Financial Economics* 25: 241.

Shleifer, A., and Summers, L. (1988). Breach of trust in hostile takeovers. In A. Auerbach (ed.) (1991), *Corporate Takeovers: Causes and Consequences.* Chicago: Chicago University Press, p. 33.

21

Reorganization Law and Dilution Threats in Different Financial Systems

ULRICH HEGE AND PIERRE MELLA-BARRAL

1. INTRODUCTION

In many European countries, there is an ongoing process and debate about bankruptcy law reform, stimulated by what is perceived as the success of Chapter 11 of the US Bankruptcy Code of 1978. The French bankruptcy laws of 1985 and 1995 and the new German insolvency code enacted in 1999 have accordingly weakened creditor rights and facilitated court-supervised reorganization (Kaiser 1996; White 1996). In Britain, where the Insolvency Code gives a clear advantage to senior creditors, there is an active debate about reforming the bankruptcy legislation (Franks and Nyborg 1996), as for example in the Netherlands and Italy. The discussion is not confined to Western Europe: Transition economies in East and Central Europe have faced the need for a massive and parallel financial restructuring of firms, and recent financial crises in debt-laden emerging markets have underscored the potentially high cost of insufficient bankruptcy laws and lacking reorganization procedures. In a historical perspective, there is a striking coincidence between major reforms of bankruptcy laws and of banking laws in the USA and in Germany (Hauswald 1996).

The economic debate on the optimal reorganization law[1] has long recognized that the efficiency of such a law should be gauged in light of the presumed performance of the market solutions taking hold in the absence of a law, respectively the market for distressed asset sales and out-of-court debt restructurings or workouts.[2] There is substantial empirical evidence that the credit structure of a distressed firm matters for the performance of the market solutions, by showing that workouts are likely to fail when the firm's creditor base is dispersed.[3] This suggests that the optimal structure of a bankruptcy code depends on the financial system as the determinant of the typical degree of creditor dispersion.

If holdout problems among multiple creditors, together with imperfect markets for distressed assets, are the principal reasons why market solutions may fail, then the analysis should naturally investigate the mechanisms that could overcome the resistance of dispersed creditors to make concessions. To have concessions decided upon by court order or majority vote, typical features of reorganization laws, is one obvious alternative. Another is to give the debtor the means to force concessions by diluting the value of the claims of holdouts. Vehicles to engineer such dilution threats are, for example, exit consents, cash tender offers and asset spin-offs, and these devices are frequently adopted in distressed out-of-court debt reschedulings (Hege and Mella-Barral 2002).

The purpose of the chapter is to analyse the interdependence of bankruptcy law and financial system while explicitly (i) addressing the choice between court-supervised reorganization and workouts, and (ii) taking into account that a distressed debtor can resort to dilution threats like exit consents, potentially a powerful alternative to court-supervised reorganization.

In the chapter, workouts are analysed in a situation of asymmetric information about the true value of the firm. In the first step of the analysis, only pari passu exchange offers are considered in workouts, that is, offers where creditors are proposed new debt claims of equal seniority. A dispersed creditor structure will then lead to a renegotiation breakdown, while debt renegotiation with a single lender is (second best) efficient. The chapter proposes a simple signalling explanation of the choice between private and public debt: managers of riskier firms will use bank loans because flexible renegotiation of loans is more important to them, but bank credit has higher interest rates. High-quality firms will issue public debt as a credible signal of their quality, and get access to more attractive borrowing rates.

In this model, introducing a reorganization law is not necessarily efficient and the efficiency varies across financial systems. A reorganization law is more likely to be beneficial in a market-based system. It will tend to speed up disintermediation, and increase the number of bankruptcy filings—both of these predictions were observed in the USA after 1978 (reform of the Bankruptcy Code). Frequently cited shortcomings of the Chapter 11 procedures are less harmful than commonly perceived, and they will typically even improve the efficiency of the reorganization procedure, as they increase the incentives to choose bank debt and to renegotiate out of court. This is true for delays in the procedure, violations of the absolute priority rule and management bias in the procedure.

In the second step, the assumption of pari passu renegotiation offers is abandoned and renegotiation offers for more senior claims (dilution threats) are taken into account. The question is then how these dilution threats affect the relationship between bankruptcy code and financial system. Dilution threats will always significantly improve the chances for a successful workout with diffusely held debt. Should dilution threats therefore be welcomed, as often suggested in the Law and Economics literature? And if so, should they be viewed as a substitute or rather a complement of court-supervised reorganization? The analysis reveals the following. Suppose dilution threats are possible, and the introduction of a reorganization law is considered. The renegotiation efficiency of public debt firms will actually go down in this case, making the introduction of a reorganization law in most cases an undesirable move. Conversely, suppose the question is whether the planned introduction of a reorganization law should be accompanied by supporting financial securities legislation permitting dilution threats. The answer is affirmative in a market-based system, where such a coordinated legislative is a welfare improvement. By contrast, in a bank-based system, it would reduce welfare. Overall, the case for a reorganization law is weakened if dilution threats are taken into account, but the optimal law design will again depend on the financial system.

The present chapter is a companion paper to Hege (2002), where an extensive and more general account of the analysis with pari passu exchange offers is given. Hege (2002), however, does not address dilution threats. A few other papers combine a choice between workouts and court-supervised reorganization but they omit the debt structure choice and are of more limited scope. Hold-out effects if there are many creditors are demonstrated in a few other papers, notably Bolton and Scharfstein (1996). White (1994) conceives of Chapter 11 as a filtering device which makes the emergence of inefficient pooling equilibria less likely. Two earlier papers, Berkovitch and Israël (1999) and Detragiache (1994), discuss how the optimal bankruptcy design may depend on the dominant debt source of firms, or on the financial system. Both papers, however, ignore the decision between workout and court-supervised reorganization, and the alternative of dilution threats, and they do not consider that the design of the reorganization procedure interacts with the composition of the financial system.

Concerning dilution threats, Roe (1987) argues that they may be desirable by increasing the chances that out-of-court restructurings succeed. By contrast, Gertner and Scharfstein (1991), and similarly Kahan and Tuckman (1993) argue that debtors can abuse them to obtain excessive debt concessions, which may lead to additional sources of inefficiencies like overinvestment. Hege and Mella-Barral (2002) show that this problem all but goes away if subsequent rounds of dilution threats are taken into account as well as the willingness of the debtor to commit, via the design of the debt contract, to an *ex post* efficient renegotiation strategy.

The chapter is organized as follows: the model is set up in Section 2. The following two sections summarize results which have been developed and proved in Hege (2002): Section 3 reviews debt renegotiation and the market equilibrium, and Section 4, the impact of a court-supervised reorganization procedure and of presumed deficiencies in the USA Bankruptcy Code. Section 5 analyses the model if the issue of more senior claims (dilution threats) is taken into account. Section 6 concludes.

2. THE MODEL

The model portrays a levered firm run by a risk-neutral owner-manager. In t_0, the owner-manager of the firm chooses between public debt (bonds) or bank debt, and in t_1, the owner-manager has access to an uncertain investment opportunity. All financial variables are expressed in t_0 present values. The investment opportunity in t_1 necessitates costs of I which are unknown in t_0. The common prior belief is that I is uniformly distributed over a unit interval, $I \sim U[\underline{I}, \bar{I}]$, where $\bar{I} = \underline{I} + 1$. In t_1, the owner-manager learns privately the realization of I, but investors remain uninformed about I. The project yields a sure incremental cash flow of R. It is assumed that $R - \bar{I} > 1$, that is, even the most costly project is profitable and yields an expected surplus, $R - \bar{I}$, in excess of the interval of uncertainty about the investment costs.[4]

From the assets already in place in t_0, the firm derives an uncertain cash flow Y in t_2. Y determines whether the firm will have abundant or little internal funds available. As of t_0, Y is projected to be low, $Y = \underline{Y}$, with probability θ and high, $Y = \bar{Y}$, with probability $1 - \theta$. Y is publicly observable in t_1, and it determines the state at the time the investment decision is made: In the good state $\bar{Y}$ the firm is rich in internal funds Y, while in the bad state $\underline{Y}$ the firm is poor in internally generated cash and is likely to need outside funds to invest. The

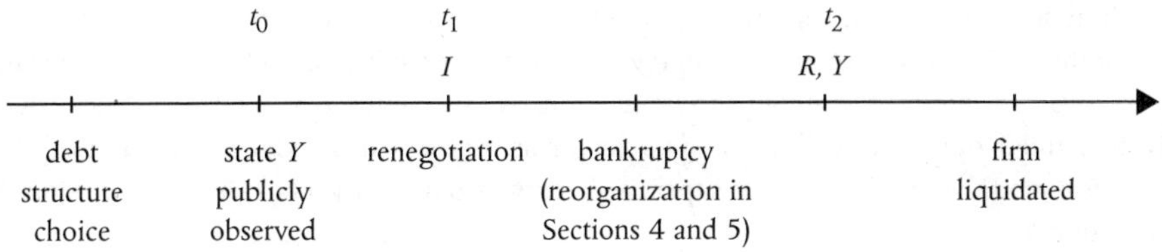

Figure 21.1. *Time line*

probability θ can be directly interpreted as the business risk of the firm, as will be seen. In t_0, the value θ is private information of the firm's owner. For simplicity, it is assumed that θ is uniformly distributed with a minimum of $\underline{\theta}$ and a maximum of $\bar{\theta}$, $\theta \sim U[\underline{\theta}, \bar{\theta}]$. The timing of the model is summarized in Fig. 21.1.

As of t_0, the firm has debt outstanding with a face value D, maturing in t_2. We assume that the owner-manager does not consider reducing the leverage D by adding equity or another form of financial security. The capital strcture choice of the owner-manager is only whether to finance this debt with private debt, that is bank debt, or with publicly traded debt. D is exogenously fixed in spite of the cost of financial distress which is analysed. This assumption should be interpreted as follows: There are advantages to debt financing which outweigh the financial distress costs as of t_0, though this dominance may be reversed in t_1 when the bad state $\underline{Y}$ is realized.[5]

Moreover, we assume that the debt level D is so high that:

$$\bar{Y}+R-\bar{I}>D>\underline{Y}+R-\underline{I}. \qquad (21.1)$$

We briefly discuss the implication of this assumption on the investment decision in t_1, when the state Y is known. We start with the first inequality, $\bar{Y}+R-\bar{I}>D$, which addresses the good state $\bar{Y}$. In the good state, the owner-manager can pledge a total deterministic revenue of $\bar{Y}+R$ towards financiers, of which D is already pledged away. Thus, the owner-manager can raise in t_1 incremental financing of at most $\bar{Y}+R-D$. She needs to finance I. The first inequality assures that the incremental financing constraint $\bar{Y}+R-D$ is always larger than $\bar{I}$, the highest possible investment need, so investment is always possible.

The second inequality, $D>\underline{Y}+R-\underline{I}$ addresses the bad state $\underline{Y}$. The owner-manager can then only raise $\underline{Y}+R-D$ in incremental financing. The second inequality assures that this is always lower than $\underline{I}$, the minimal investment need. Thus, condition (eqn (21.1)) implies that the investment project can always be financed in the good state, but never in the bad state.

Therefore, since undertaking the project would be desirable in all circumstances, a classic debt overhang problem[6] arises if and only if the bad state is realized. This overhang problem creates a rationale for a state-contingent debt claim, that is, the possibility to adjust D to a low level enough so that the project can be financed even in the bad state $\underline{Y}$. State-contingent debt can be obtained through debt renegotiation.

The timing in t_1 is as follows. After Y is publicly revealed, debt can be renegotiated. Renegotiation is modelled as a one stage take-it-or-leave-it offer. In case of public debt, the owner-manager is making the offer. In case of bank debt, the bank makes the offer.[7] There is no cost associated with debt renegotiation.

The renegotiation game captures debt renegotiation out-of-court. After debt renegotiation, any of the creditors can file for bankruptcy if the firm is not able to meet the payments due in t_1 or t_2. Bankruptcy is tantamount to liquidation, as in Chapter 7 of the USA Code. Then the investment opportunity I is lost and remaining assets are distributed respecting priority. In the basic model, there is no court-supervised reorganization procedure. This is introduced in Section 4.

In principle, neither the equityholder nor the owner-manager should retain any value when the firm is in financial distress. However, only the manager knows the true value of I and how much debt reduction is precisely needed in order to realize the project value $R-I$. He tries to solicit excessive debt reductions from the creditors so as to retain a positive value when the firm emerges from debt renegotiation. The owner-manager may raise as much fresh money as investors are willing to lend to him. Unless the firm is declared bankrupt, he can keep, and ultimately consume, any amount raised in excess of I.

The workout is successful if and only if the debt level after renegotiation D does not exceed $R-I$. If this condition is satisfied, $D \leqslant R-I$, then the owner-manager could obtain funds from any of the following three sources: (i) The initial lender(s) who hold debt claims worth D; (ii) the owner of the firm, provided she has a sufficiently deep pocket; (iii) new investors. The reason that all three would make the same financing decision, is that any earlier investment is sunk and makes no difference. Also, competition on the capital markets ensures that the financier of the project receives a zero profit on the funds I. Therefore, whether old or new investors provide the funds in t_1, makes no difference in the old investors' renegotiation behaviour. The equilibrium concept applied throughout is Perfect Bayesian Equilibrium.

3. NO REORGANIZATION LAW

3.1. *Renegotiating Private and Public Debt*

We will solve the model backwards in the usual fashion, starting with the decisions after the state is known. Renegotiation will only be undertaken if the bad state $\underline{Y}$ has been realized. Only pari passu offers, offering debt claims of equal or lower priority, are considered in this and the next section. In the case of private debt, the bank's take-it-or-leave-it offer will start renegotiation, and the owner-manager will accept any offer that gives him more than zero. The bank has all the bargaining power. Like a monopolist who takes demand effects into account when fixing prices, the bank solves for its optimal debt forgiveness by taking into account that more concessions will increase the success probability of the workout. The success probability of this offer will depend on the distribution of I which the bank has to guess. The analysis is straightforward. Recall that the value of the good project $R-I$, is always larger than 1, the interval of uncertainty about the true costs I. Therefore, the bank finds it optimal to make a relatively large concession such that the remaining debt is just $\underline{Y}+R-\bar{I}$: The good project will always be possible, regardless of the true value of I. Making a less generous concession reduces the success probability and gives the bank a smaller revenue.

Turning to the case of public debt, we assume that exchange offers are not made conditional on unanimous consent.[8] It is useful to sketch some elements of the analysis since we will use them again in Section 5; a full account can be found in Hege (2002). Suppose $n-1$ investors do exchange, and consider the problem of the nth investor. The optimal exchange offer, which is conditional on success, will offer to exchange each debt contract with face value D/n for a new contract with lower face value of $(\underline{Y}+\underline{V}+x)/n$, where x denotes the aggregate debt level that is offered to the bondholders in excess of the face value that a bank would keep. $x\in[0, 1]$ is chosen from the range of uncertainty about I, and captures at the same time the bankruptcy probability. We can then analyse the nth bondholder's incentives:

1. If the nth bondholder approves the exchange, then the success probability is $1-x$. The nth investor would then earn a profit of π^{e}:

$$\pi^{\mathrm{e}}=(1-x)\frac{\underline{Y}+R-\bar{I}+x}{n}+x\frac{\underline{Y}}{n}.$$

2. If the nth bondholder holds out, then this decision reduces the success probability for the exchange offer overall by an amount of $\mu^{n}(x)$, n's probability of being pivotal for the success. The nth bondholder's expected payoff π^{h} in this case is:

$$\pi^{\mathrm{h}}=x\frac{\underline{Y}}{n}+(1-x)\begin{cases} D/n & \text{with probability } 1-\mu^{n}(x) \\ \underline{Y}/n & \text{with probability } \mu^{n}(x). \end{cases}$$

The nth bondholder will accept the exchange offer if $\pi^{\mathrm{h}}\leqslant\pi^{\mathrm{e}}$, or if (after simplifications):

$$(1-\mu^{n}(x))D+\mu^{n}(x)\underline{Y}\leqslant x+\underline{Y}+R-\bar{I}. \tag{21.2}$$

Under the 'best' exchange offer from the owner-manager's point of view, this incentive constraint is just binding. For inequality (21.2) to be satisfied, $\mu^{n}(x)$ must be strictly larger than zero, since $D>x+\underline{Y}+R-\bar{I}>\underline{Y}$. But then $x\to 1$ is necessary for $\mu^{n}(x)$ to be bounded away from zero. As the share of a single investor in the total debt gets smaller and smaller, the probability of her being pivotal for the success of reorganization out of court must vanish. This in turn implies that the *ex ante* probability of successful renegotiation goes to zero as the number of bondholders increases. We can summarize our insights as follows.[9]

Observation 1

(i) If the firm uses private debt, then renegotiation is successful with probability one;

(ii) if the firm issues public debt, then the probability of renegotiation being successful goes to zero as n, the number of investors, goes to infinity.

Incomplete information is a necessary ingredient for this result. If there was perfect information about I then the owner-manager would submit an offer that is just sufficient to achieve efficiency, but needs every single investor's approval. This is tantamount to conditioning on unanimous approval.

3.2. *The Market Equilibrium*

Since θ is private information of the owner-manager, the market equilibrium is a signalling equilibrium where owner-managers self-select in their choice of debt instrument that will truthfully disclose according to their θ-type. The costly signal is the expected costs of financial distress which vary according to the type θ and the debt instrument: The higher the failure risk, the more beneficial is it to have renegotiable private debt. Private debt is efficient in the bad state, and moreover it offers a direct benefit to the owner-manager in the form of a fraction of the renegotiation surplus. Owners who attach a low probability to financial distress prefer inefficient renegotiation. In turn, they will receive a more favourable interest rate.

We conjecture that all types θ higher than some cut-off type θ^C choose private debt, and all types below θ^C use public debt. When issuing private debt, debt with a face value of D will be priced at an initial value of $B_0 < D$, which discounts for the bankruptcy risk such that a bank who does not know the type θ excepts just a zero profit. Similarly, if the owner-manager issues public debt with face value D, the issue value will be $D_0 < D$.[10] In addition, the owner-manager of a bank-financed expects to keep some surplus in the event of successful renegotiation, which is equal to $\frac{1}{2}$.[11]

Comparison of the respective pay-offs characterizes the cutoff type θ^C, the type just indifferent between bank debt and public debt, via the condition $B_0 - D_0 + \theta^C \frac{1}{2} = 0$. This condition can be written as:

$$\theta^C(1 + R - \bar{I}) = (\bar{\theta} - \underline{\theta})(D - \underline{Y}) - \bar{\theta}(R - \bar{I}). \tag{21.3}$$

Equation (21.3) characterizes the separating market equilibrium, which expresses the following trade-off: Since there is a continuum of types θ, but only a single discrete signal (the choice between bank or public debt), firms self-select into two pools: Firms at the good end of the quality interval, $\theta \in [\underline{\theta}, \theta^C)$, will signal their high quality by using public debt. This is cheaper, but implies higher costs in the event of financial distress. Firms at the poor end of the quality interval, $\theta \in (\theta^C, \bar{\theta}]$, find giving up debt renegotiation too costly. They prefer to be pooled with all the firms at the risky end and to pay a higher risk premium. Either such a separating equilibrium exists, or all firm types issue bank debt.[12]

4. INTRODUCING A REORGANIZATION LAW

In this section, court-supervised reorganization is introduced. In the extensive-form game, court-supervised reorganization will be introduced as an alternative to straight bankruptcy: after the workout, if the firm is still insolvent (i.e. cannot meet its obligations at t_1 or t_2) there is now a choice between filing for straight liquidation as before or filing for court-supervised reorganization. Creditors and the owner-manager have a right to file for court-supervised reorganization if out-of-court renegotiation fails, as under Chapter 11 of the USA Bankruptcy Code of 1978.

The reorganization procedure modelled here is inspired by Chapter 11 of the USA Bankruptcy Code of 1978. We begin by analysing a 'perfect' procedure, where we assume efficient decision-making about continuation and liquidation, no delay, and respect for the priority of claims. We will first revisit the model under such a perfect procedure, and then briefly discuss how the outcome changes if imperfections in the Bankruptcy Code are taken into account.

4.1. *Perfect Court-Supervised Reorganization*

The reorganization procedure here is 'perfect' or frictionless: The court decides without any delay, and the court always takes the efficient decision concerning the continuation of the firm, by imposing the minimum debt reduction needed to get the profitable project going. This implies that the court collects and publicly reveals the private information about the investment cost I.[13] Finally, the old creditors are given all the transferable surplus. Court-supervised reorganization procedure, however, is costly. There is a flat bankruptcy cost of $b < R - \bar{I}$ having priority over creditors.[14]

With perfect court-supervised reorganization as an option, if renegotiation is not successful, then creditors will file for court-supervised reorganization since bankruptcy costs are below the expected value of the profitable project, $b < R - EI$. The interesting part of the results (Observation 2) refers to the case where $b < 1$, that is, where b is smaller than the range of values of I. Then even for a private debt firm, the workout will fail if investment costs I are high, and the firm will end up in court-supervised reorganization with a positive probability. The reason is that the owner-manager will only truthfully reveal that $I < \underline{I} + b$ if renegotiation were to fail otherwise. By contrast, the prospects of working out public debt (in the limit where the number of creditors n approaches infinity) remain as slim as before. The impact of introducing Chapter 11-style reorganization procedures can be summarized as follows.

Observation 2

(i) With private debt, renegotiation will be successful with probability $\min\{1, b\}$;

(ii) with public debt, the probability of successful renegotiation goes to zero as the number of creditors goes to infinity;

(iii) the proportion of public debt firms and the number of bankruptcy filings (including court-supervised reorganization) will increase after court-supervised reorganization is introduced.

To see the intuition, consider part (iii) first. In the separating market equilibrium, the decision of the marginal firm using public debt is important, and it depends on two effects: First, court-supervised reorganization mitigates the cost of financial distress of this firm, since only the bankruptcy cost b, but not the investment opportunity is lost if a workout fails. The distress cost for high-quality firms is in fact reduced from $R - I$ to b. Therefore, since distress costs are lower, the marginal credit risk quality of a firm finding public debt attractive will also be lower. Second, banks take court-supervised reorganization into account and make less generous offers in the renegotiation stage. This will reduce the probability of avoiding bankruptcy to b from 1. In other words, deadweight losses now also arise for firms using bank debt, even though they are smaller ones than under public debt. Both effects make private debt look less attractive than before. As for the increase in the number of bankruptcy filings, there are two reasons: First, less firms will have bank debt which can be renegotiated out-of-court. Second, of those, a greater proportion will not succeed in a workout.

Importantly, court-supervised reorganization exerts countervailing effects on the debt restructuring capacity of private and of public debt firms: It improves efficiency for public debt firms, but it affects private debt firms adversely. Moreover, there will be a third effect: The proportion of public debt firms will grow due to the introduction of a reorganization. But overall efficiency is smaller for public debt firms than for private debt firms, implying a negative welfare impact of the third effect.

The overall efficiency impact of introducing a reorganization law is therefore ambiguous, and it depends on the financial system. Since the debt structure, which represents different financial systems, is endogenous in this model, the comparative statics of the underlying financial system requires to vary the exogenous parameter which drives the debt structure. The adequate efficiency criterion in the present model is comparing the total expected deadweight loss under financial distress incurred under any of the bankruptcy law regimes. The following result obtains:

Observation 3 The financial system determines whether a perfect reorganization law is efficient or not:

(i) In a bank-based system (in a system where the proportion of public debt firms is small), introducing a perfect reorganization law is inefficient;
(ii) in a market-based system (in a system where the proportion of public debt firms is large), introducing a perfect reorganization law is efficient.

A good intuition for Observation 3 is gained by first considering only those firms that do not change their creditor structure. Among these, firms with public debt gain, firms with bank debt lose from introducing a perfect reorganization law. The efficiency effect of court-supervised reorganization must clearly be positive if a vast majority of firms have dispersed public debt, and vice versa. It remains to consider the third effect, the shift in the creditor structure leading to, on average, more public debt. This effect is dominated by the direct effect if either private or public debt dominates over the range of firm types. In intermediate cases where both public and private debt are well-represented across the range of firm types, this shift effect could be responsible for turning the total welfare impact negative. Finally, if b is small, then the loss of using public debt instead of bank debt is small, and a reorganization law is always efficient.

To summarize, the efficiency of a reorganization law depends crucially on the dominant source of borrowing, banks or bond markets. The more firms rely on market-based debt instruments, the more likely will there be a benefit from introducing a reorganization law. Moreover, consider an economy with a massive bankruptcy problem, that is, a country where a large number of financial distress cases occur concomitantly, as happened recently in an emerging market hit by financial crises or in transition economies. The massive bankruptcy problem is not in itself a sufficient reason to recommend the introduction of a court-based reorganization procedure: This inevitably lowers the incentives to successfully manage debt renegotiation out-of-court, an effect which is likely to dominate in a bank-oriented financial system.

Therefore, the model has clear implications concerning the relationship between bankruptcy costs and financial system. The fact that a lean and fast reorganization procedure (where b is small) is always efficient is by itself not surprising. Less expected, however, is the opposite case: A bank-based financial system may be better off having an 'expensive' reorganization procedure rather than a 'cheap' one. An intuition can be gained from rehearsing the implication of 'perfect' court-supervised reorganization: Less costly bankruptcy procedures weaken at the same time the *ex post* incentives for banks to renegotiate out-of-court and the *ex ante* incentives for managers to choose private debt, and both effects have a negative impact on the efficiency of the law.

4.2. *Imperfections in the Reorganization Procedure*

The way Chapter 11 works in practice has attracted a great deal of criticism in recent years.[15] Attention has primarily focused on concerns that Chapter 11 (i) involves a long and extremely costly procedure; that (ii) it leads to violations of the Absolute Priority Rule; and that (iii) outcomes are inefficient, with typically a management bias leading systematically to inefficient continuation of firms that should be liquidated. We will briefly review how these concerns would impact the performance and desirability of Chapter 11 in the present model.

4.2.1. *Cost and Delays in the Court-Supervised Reorganization Procedure*

We investigate the comparative statics of a change in b, by assuming for simplicity that $b<1$. A workout for a bank-financed firm will then fail with probability $1-b$, causing a loss of b. For a public debt firm, the workout will always fail, meaning that the bankruptcy cost b accrues always. Therefore, the expected deadweight loss due to bankruptcy is $(1-F(b))b+F(b)\underline{b}(1-b)$, where $F(b)$ is the proportion of bank-financed firms, $F(b)=(\underline{\theta}-\theta^{C})(\underline{\theta}-\overline{\theta})$.

We find that the expected deadweight loss due to bankruptcy may be increasing or decreasing as a function of bankruptcy costs b. The reason for this ambiguity lies in the interaction between court-supervised and out-of-court debt restructuring. Only if bankruptcy costs are already low is a reduction b unambiguously a good thing. Otherwise, it may make things worse. This is more likely to be the case if bankruptcy costs are relatively high (close to or larger than 1). Moreover, the higher the proportion of public debt firms, the larger the benefit from a reduction in b.

This observation has a clear implication for a market-oriented financial system like the USA. The critiques that bankruptcy costs are excessive may well have a point since USA firms rely predominantly on the bond market for their debt financing. However, making the Chapter 11 procedure leaner and faster—this was the intention of the 1994 reform, and could be the result if the incentives for reaching pre-packaged bankruptcy agreements are further improved—could still have a negative effect overall. In the model, this is precisely the case if b is high! This can be interpreted as implying that a veritable trap for bankruptcy reform may arise in a system where (i) public debt markets dominate and (ii) the costs of legal procedures are high.

4.2.2. *Violations of the Absolute Priority Rule*

In practice, the Absolute Priority Rule (APR), the principle that junior claimants should not receive anything before all senior claims have been served in full, is routinely violated.[16] Chapter 11 is often blamed for this, in particular since incumbent management retains substantial control rights under Chapter 11: Management has the exclusive initial right to submit a reorganization plan within 120 days, and this deadline is frequently extended. After the reorganization plan has been submitted, a vote will be held requiring the consent of at least two-third of the claims and the claimants in each class of claims (where classes are organized according to seniority). This implies that the consent of the shareholders is needed.[17] The requirement to win approval of the shareholders is seen as a likely source for violations of APR. To incorporate these ideas, we assume that the manager retains a positive benefit $f > 0$ when the firm emerges from the court procedure. The owner-manager's retention f is a convenient measure of the severity of the violation of the absolute priority rule (equity deviations).

Intuitively, one would expect that equity deviations should make public debt more attractive—after all, the owner-manager receives a positive payoff if the firm emerges from bankruptcy, and this happens more frequently with public debt. This is, however, only one side of the effects. The other side is that the bank will adjust its renegotiation strategies endogenously to allow for equity deviations. The bank knows that its offer will not be accepted unless the owner-manager can retain at least f, and the bank offers accordingly. It turns out that the two effects are exactly offsetting: The increment in the owner-manager's expected payoff in the financial distress case, if using public debt relative to bank debt, does not depend on f, and neither does the market equilibrium, that is, the fractions of firms financed by private or by public debt. The present model, by strictly focusing on the incentive structure of debt renegotiation, offers the following explanation why equity deviations are so systematic in practice: Equity deviations in court may be a good thing, or at least be neutral, because they make it less attractive to opt for court-supervised procedures instead of a workout.

4.2.3. *Management Bias of Court-Supervised Reorganization*

In the discussion surrounding Chapter 11, the 'management bias' of the procedure is frequently cited, which may be taken as an indication that inefficient decision-making is more likely to suffer from a distortion in the opposite direction: In this view, courts tend to rule in favour of too much continuation when liquidation would be efficient. The following is a typical story told in order to understand how inefficient outcomes may come about: A coalition of manager and bankruptcy judge can play a dominant role during reorganization. Managers have a straightforward interest in the continuation of the firm, and they might find support from a judge who is afraid of liquidating an ailing enterprise prematurely. Together, they can easily keep the firm afloat for a very long time, at the expense of creditors who see a drop in the liquidation value in the meantime.

To introduce management bias in a certainly sketchy, and rather informal, manner, suppose there is uncertainty about the quality of the project (i.e. about R), and suppose the owner-manager has private information about the quality of the project. The private information arrives after debt contracts are signed, but prior to the debt renegotiation stage at the end of period 1. Suppose the owner-manager is willing to undertake the project even if it is bad, because he draws a private benefit from continuation. In our model, such a private benefit emerges endogenously, since the firm keeps some revenues whenever a successful workout is engineered. We can then consider a comparison between two bankruptcy procedures: In the perfect procedure, the court always gets informed about the project and decides efficiently. In the procedure with management bias, there are systematic errors in the court's decision-making, frequently allowing firms to continue with bad projects even though they should not. Following the by now familiar logic, the effective bankruptcy costs are higher in the second case. Therefore, we find that having a management bias in the court-supervised reorganization procedure will, as compared to the perfect procedure, always increase the share of bank debt, but have ambiguous welfare effects.

5. EXCHANGE OFFERS WITH HIGHER SENIORITY

5.1. *Dilution Threats and Exit Consents*

In this section, we drop the assumption that only pari passu exchange offers, exchange offers proposing new claims of lower or equal seniority, are possible. In the practice of corporate bond workouts in the USA, exchange offers proposing debt of higher seniority or tender offer offering cash in exchange for surrendering the bonds are very common.[18] Popular tools are so-called exit consents: In an exit consent, the bondholders' approval of more senior debt issues is tied to the opportunity to participate in the exchange offer, creating a powerful tool to force dispersed creditors into accepting unfavourable exchange terms. More specifically, an exit consent is used if the corporate bond contains a seniority covenant, that is, a covenant prohibiting the issue of higher seniority debt without the consent of the bondholders. The seniority covenant, which is not a core item protected by the unanimity clause of the Trust Indenture Act, can be waived by the approval of a majority or super-majority of bondholders. An exit consent ties the two provisions: Only those bondholders agreeing to the waiver of the seniority covenant may participate in the exchange for new bonds of higher seniority.

Hege and Mella-Barral (2002) argue that debtors have other instruments at their disposal besides exit consents, that yield a similar effect of exploiting the non-cohesiveness of dispersed creditors. In fact, any vehicle which asks dispersed creditors for concessions in their income rights (coupons and repayments of principal) by offering more or privileged liquidation rights uses the same economic mechanism of dilution which is behind an exit consent: The improvement in liquidation rights must come at the expense of other creditors, since in the case of bankruptcy, the remaining firm value belongs to the creditors (APR). Hege and Mella-Barral (2002) call all vehicles relying on this mechanism dilution threats; popular examples are cash offers, asset sales, and asset spin-offs.

In the legal literature, exit consents are typically seen in a favourable light, in spite of the potential abuse of creditors' right which they may entail. The argument, elaborated, for example, by Roe (1987), is that by forcing debtholders to make concessions, they are an effective means of keeping hold-out problems among many dispersed debtholders in check. Hege and Mella-Barral (2002) find similarly that it is in the shareholders' interest to design the debt contract in a way which commits them to use exit consents in an efficient way. They may then be the only means of introducing a renegotiation option into widely dispersed debt.

Shareholders, however, may not limit the use of exit consents to such efficient purposes, they may also deploy them in a purely opportunistic fashion to increase equity value at the expense of debt values. This aspect is highlighted in the analysis of Gertner and Scharfstein (1991): they show that shareholders may abuse exit consents to obtain inefficient debt concessions, causing firms to overinvest and thus destroy value. The authors call this the 'hold-in' effect. For similar reasons, Coffee and Klein (1991) argue in favour of abolishing exit consent. Kahan and Tuckman (1993), however, find in their empirical analysis no indication that hold-ins are a concern in reality. This is the backdrop of our analysis here, which investigates the following question: How does the interdependence of financial system and reorganization law change if dilution threats are possible?

5.2. *No Reorganization Law*

In analogy to Section 2, we assume first that there is no reorganization law. We analyse again the *n*th bondholder's incentives:

(a) If the bondholder approves the exchange, then she is offered senior debt claims with face value $(\underline{Y}+R-\bar{I}+x^S)/n$ in exchange for surrendering each bond with a face value of D/n, so she is asked for a concession of $\hat{D}/n = D/n-(\underline{Y}+R-\bar{I}+x)/n$. As before, $x^S \in [0, 1]$ is chosen from the range of values of I for which information is incomplete, and x^S is at the same time the probability that the workout fails whereas the success probability is $1-x^S$. When accepting, the *n*th investor would then earn a profit of π^e:

$$\pi^e = x^S\frac{\underline{Y}}{n} + (1-x^S)\frac{\underline{Y}+R-\bar{I}+x^S}{n}.$$

(b) If the *n*th bondholder holds out, then this decision reduces the success probability for the exchange offer overall by an amount of $\mu^S(x)$, *n*'s probability of being pivotal for the success, where $\mu^S(x^S)=\hat{D}/(1-x^S)n$. The optimal strategy for the owner-manager in this case is to make an unconditional offer, guaranteeing that tendering bondholders are senior to all holdouts if the offer fails (not enough capital can be raised to finance I).[19] A holdout bondholder will then anticipate that she will be junior to all bondholders who accept the exchange offer. We anticipate that in equilibrium, all bondholders will have the right incentives to accept the offer, so when calculating her profits as a holdout, the bondholder needs to take into account that all $n-1$ other bondholders accept and become senior to her. Therefore, the *n*th bondholder's expected payoff π^h in this case is:

$$\pi^h = \begin{cases} D/n & \text{with probability } (1-x^S)(1-\mu^S(x^S)) \\ \max\left(0, \underline{Y} - \frac{n-1}{n}\left(\underline{Y}+R-\bar{I}+x^S\right)\right) & \text{with probability } x^S + (1-x^S)\mu^S(x^S). \end{cases}$$

When the number of shareholders *n* becomes larger and larger, obviously $\max(0, \underline{Y}-(n-1)/n\,(\underline{Y}+R-\bar{I}+x^S))=0$ at some point. Assuming that the incentive condition for the *n*th bondholder accepting the exchange offer (if all other bondholders tendering), $\pi^h \leqslant \pi^e$, holds with equality, it can be written as:

$$(1-x^S)(1-\mu^S(x))D = \underline{Y} + (R-\bar{I}+x^S)(1-x^S). \tag{21.4}$$

This is a quadratic equation in x^S:

$$x^{S^2} - x^S(D - R + \bar{I} + 1) + D - \underline{Y} - R + \bar{I} = 0. \tag{21.5}$$

But the latter equation can be true even if $1 - \mu^S(x^S) \to 1$, as long as x^S, that is, the chance of a failure of the exchange offer, is large enough. Investigation of the properties of this quadratic expression gives us the following result:

Proposition 1 *Suppose there is no court-supervised reorganization procedure and exchange offers attaching dilution threats are possible. Suppose the number of investors n goes to infinity.*

(i) Out-of-court renegotiation of public debt fails with a probability x^S which is positive but strictly less than one.

(ii) The smaller the return R and the larger the creditors' minimum concession $D - \underline{Y} - (R - \bar{I})$, the larger is the probability x^S of renegotiation failure.

Proof See the Appendix. □

In the proof, we also show that no other equilibrium exists. Part (i) of Proposition 1 needs to be contrasted with Observation 1. There, it was shown that exchange offers will always fail when senior offers were excluded. Now, there is always a positive probability for an exchange offer to succeed, even if debt is maximally dispersed. The reason for this difference is the effect of the dilution threat: The essential mechanism of offering senior debt is to dilute the value of bondholders attempting to hold out. That means that if the number of tendering bondholders is large enough, not only will the minimum acceptance rate of the exchange offer be met, but all of the remaining asset values will be distributed among those debtholders that have tendered, leaving nothing to the holdouts. As a consequence, the position of a potential holdout is weakened, explaining the result.

Part (ii) of Proposition 1 discusses the comparative statics which are easy to understand: the more bondholders collectively stand to lose by accepting the offer compared to their nominal claim, captured by the minimum concession $D - (R - \bar{I}) - \underline{Y}$, the higher must be the stakes for a bondholder attempting to hold out in order to guarantee the incentive condition $\pi^e \geqslant \pi^h$, that is, the larger must be the probability that the workout attempt fails and that consequently, the holdouts receive nothing.

5.3. *Perfect Reorganization Law*

Next, we turn to the case where a perfect reorganization law is introduced. We consider two questions: (i) If the existing financial securities laws give debt issuers a wide margin of exercising dilution threats against debtholders, for example, via exit consents, how would this affect our analysis concerning the effects of introducing a reorganization law? (ii) When introducing a reorganization law, should it be accompanied by an amendment of the financial securities legislation facilitating the use of dilution threats?

(i) Redoing the analysis to answer the first question, we find that π^h, the pay-off of a holdout bondholder, is unchanged, at least as long n is large (i.e. so large that under an unconditional offer, holdouts receive nothing in case the exchange offer fails). However, the pay-off of tendering bondholders is different: if the exchange offer fails, the firm will then go into court-supervised reorganization, implying an aggregate loss of only b to the investors. The payoff π^{e} can be rewritten as:

$$\pi^{e} = \begin{cases} \underline{Y} + R - \bar{I} + x^{R} & \text{with probability } (1 - x^{R}) \\ \underline{Y} + R - \bar{I} + \frac{1}{2}x^{R} + b & \text{with probability } x^{R}. \end{cases}$$

Now if the incentive constraint $\pi^{h} \leqslant \pi^{e}$ is just binding, we get the quadratic equation:

$$\tfrac{1}{2}x^{R^2} - x^{R}(D + 1 - b) + (D - \underline{Y} - R + \bar{I}) = 0. \tag{21.6}$$

The comparison of the two quadratic expressions allows us to analyse the effects of introducing a reorganization law, under the assumption that exchange offers for more senior claims are possible. We find:

Proposition 2 *Suppose exchange offers offering more senior debt are possible. Consider public debt as n goes to infinity.*

(i) The failure probability of out-of-court renegotiation with public debt is strictly larger than in the absence of a reorganization law;
(ii) the welfare effect of introducing a perfect reorganization law is always negative in a bank-based financial system, and more often negative in a market-based financial system than it was with pari passu offers.

Proof See the Appendix. □

Thus, the answer to the first question is markedly different from what was the case without dilution threats (Observation 3): If they have access to the use of dilution threats, public debt firms work out more efficiently without a reorganization law.

Proposition 2 demonstrates that if the possibility to attach dilution threats is already established, the welfare analysis of a reorganization law is dramatically different. Since it will increase the financial distress cost for public debt firms and leave them unchanged for bank debt firms, the average financial distress costs in most cases will go up. Only the third and indirect effect making firms migrate from public to bank debt is now positive, but this effect is likely to be dominated by the direct effects.

(ii) What does this then imply for the welfare impact of introducing a joint regime of a perfect reorganization law together with legislation facilitating the use of dilution threats like exit consents? Recall that public debt firms will work out more efficiently with dilution threats than without (Proposition 1), but less efficiently in the joint regime than if dilution threats stand alone without a reorganization law (Proposition 2). This is the backdrop for this analysis, for which we posit the following effects.

In a market-based financial system, if a joint regime (reorganization law plus possibility to attach dilution threats) is introduced, the welfare impact is positive.

Proposition 3 *(i) In a market-based financial system, if a joint regime (reorganization law plus possibility to attach dilution threats) is introduced, the welfare impact is positive.*
(ii) In a bank-based system, if a joint regime is introduced, the welfare impact is negative.

Proof See the Appendix. □

The intuition for this finding is not far away from the reason behind Observation 3: Public debt firms benefit, bank debt firms suffer from the introduction of the joint regime, and finally there is an indirect third effect making marginal bank debt firms switch to public debt. The overall welfare effect depends on which of the segments was dominating prior to the introduction of the joint regime.

5.4. *Comparative Statics of Bankruptcy Costs*

Finally, we explore the question of how the cost efficiency of the reorganization procedure impacts the design of the reorganization law. Here, we take up the first step of our analysis of imperfections in the reorganization law, the comparative statics with respect to the bankruptcy costs b. Recall that we found in Section 3 that an increase in b has an ambiguous effect: It makes reorganization more costly, but improves the incentives to use bank debt, and to work out more efficiently.

How is this analysis changed if we allow for exchange offers proposing more senior claims, and does a decrease in bankruptcy costs b change the efficiency of public debt firms? We find the following, rather surprising, answer:

Proposition 4 *Consider a change in bankruptcy costs b.*

(i) The failure probability of out-of-court renegotiation is strictly increasing in b for public debt, but strictly decreasing in b for bank debt;
(ii) for bankruptcy costs b being low enough, public debt firms have a higher probability of successful out-of-court renegotiation than bank-financed firms.

Proof See the Appendix. □

Proposition 4 shows that the lower the total bankruptcy costs b are, the more effective is a reorganization law in giving incentives for successful debt renegotiation out-of-court. The reason is that the smaller the b is, the less the tendering bondholders stand to lose from a failure of reorganization, therefore the less often is breakdown needed to deter holdouts. This is in remarkable contrast to the effect which a reorganization law has on bank-financed firms: The smaller is b, the less likely is a bank-financed firm to successfully work out. As a result, for rather low values of b, it is actually possible that the efficiency properties of both types of firms cross over, that is, public debt firms are becoming the more efficient ones, as far as the financial distress costs are concerned.

What is the effect on the market equilibrium? With public debt suddenly the more efficient debt form for firms in financial distress, it is clear that issuing public debt cannot work any longer as a signal for a low expected risk of getting into financial distress. This role will now be taken over by bank debt, since it carries the higher bankruptcy costs; issuing bank debt can therefore credibly convey the signal that the owner-manager anticipates a low risk of distress. The separating equilibrium flips over: High risk firms will issue public debt, and low risk firms will use the less renegotiation-friendly bank debt, but get a more favourable lending rate in return.[20]

6. CONCLUSION

This chapter discusses how the introduction of a reorganization law depends on the financial system. In a bank-based system, debtors tend to have credit from a single or a few lenders, while in a market-based system, tradeable debt instruents are preferred and creditors of a company tend to be more dispersed. A reorganization law like the USA Bankruptcy Code of 1978 will only be beneficial if the typical creditor structure is sufficiently dispersed so as to create serious hold-out problems; otherwise it will do more harm than good, since it diminishes incentives to find privately negotiated solutions. The policy debate on the bankruptcy law needs to take these general equilibrium effects into account.

This chapter specifically addresses the role of a reorganization law if the debtor can take recourse to dilution threats as an alternative tool to overcome holdout problems. Dilution threats are the possibility to offer senior claims to creditors willing to exchange, while eroding the value of potential holdouts. The chapter confirms that dilution threats can go a long way to establish the efficiency of out-of-court renegotiation even with a dispersed creditor base. They substantially diminish the benefits from a reorganization law even in a market-based system, while leaving the negative judgement about reorganization laws in bank-based systems unchanged. Thus, on balance, dilution threats further weaken the case for a reorganization law.

Starting from a situation where neither dilution threats nor a reorganization law are available, passing legislation which at the same time introduces a reorganization law and makes dilution threats feasible has a positive welfare impact in a market-based system, but a negative impact in a bank-based system. In a wider perspective, this analysis shows that legislation regulating how debtors can use dilution threats is an essential complement to the optimal bankruptcy legislation. This important link, which has not been emphasized previously, is certainly worthy of further analysis.

Appendix

Proof of Proposition 1. First, one can verify that there is no separating equilibrium in mixed strategies. This is for the same reason as in the absence of senior offers: For a mixed strategy equilibrium, $\pi^h = \pi^e$ would have to hold. But x under the condition $\pi^h = \pi^e$ is independent of $R - I$. So the exchange offer cannot release information about the true value of the firm when it has simultaneously to satisfy the equilibrium constraint. Hence, there is only a pooling equilibrium where all types of I will make the same common offer (implying that this pooling offer will lead to unsuccessful renegotiation for some types even if accepted).

We are left with the proof of the properties of x^S. They are implicitly defined by (21.5). First, setting $x^S = 0$ in (21.5) yields:

$$D - \underline{Y} - R + \bar{I} > 0. \tag{21.7}$$

Second, setting $x^S = 1$ in (21.5) yields:

$$-\underline{Y} < 0. \tag{21.8}$$

Differentiating (21.5) yields:

$$2x^{S} - D - \underline{Y} - R + \bar{I}. \tag{21.9}$$

Note that expression (21.9) shows (*i*) that the slope of x^S is negative $\forall x^S < 1/2$ since $D - \underline{Y} - R - \bar{I} > 1$ from the parameter assumption (21.1), and (*ii*) that x^S is strictly convex, continuous and continuously differentiable $\forall x^S \in (0, 1)$. This proves the claim that there is a unique solution of (21.5) $x^S \in (0, 1)$. Next, note that $\sqrt{(D-R+\bar{I}+1)^2 - 4(D-R+\bar{I}-\underline{Y})} = \sqrt{(D-R+\bar{I}-1)^2 + 4\underline{Y}}$. The solution to the quadratic expression (21.5) can therefore be written as:

$$x^S = \tfrac{1}{2}(D-R+\bar{I}+1) - \tfrac{1}{2}\sqrt{(D-R+\bar{I}-1)^2 + 4\underline{Y}}. \tag{21.10}$$

Differentiating (21.5) with respect to D gives:

$$\frac{\partial x^S}{\partial D} = \tfrac{1}{2}(1 - (D-R+\bar{I}-1)((D-R+\bar{I}-1)^2 + 4\underline{Y})^{-1/2}) > 0. \tag{21.11}$$

Moreover, $\partial x^S/\partial D = -\partial x^S/\partial \bar{I}$. Finally, $\partial x^S/\partial R < 0$ follows directly from differentiating (21.11).

Proof of Proposition 2. π^h can be written analogously to Proposition 1, π^e and the quadratic expression (21.6) for x^R guaranteeing the incentive condition $\pi^e \geqslant \pi^h$ are stated in the text.

We need to show that $x^R > x^S$. Equating (21.5) and (21.6) shows that x^S and x^R will satisfy:

$$x^{S^2} - x^S(D-R+\bar{I}+1) = \tfrac{1}{2}x^{R^2} - x^R(D-b+1). \tag{21.12}$$

Moreover, both sides in (21.12) are equal to $-(D-\underline{Y}-R+\bar{I}) < 0$. Draw the curve of $x^{S^2} - x^S(D-R-\bar{I}+1)$ and of $\frac{1}{2}x^{R^2} - x^R(D-b+1)$. Since $R - \bar{I} > b$ and both brackets in (21.12) are positive, $x^{S^2} - x^S(D-R-\bar{I}+1)$ will always have a higher value than $\frac{1}{2}x^{R^2} - x^R(D-b+1)$, for all $x^S = x^R \in [0, 1]$. It follows that to satisfy equality at a negative value, $-(D-\underline{Y}-R+\bar{I})$, $x^R > x^S$. □

Proof of Proposition 3. Recall that there are three effects to be taken into account: the welfare effect on public debt firms (positive), on bank debt firms (negative if $b < 1$) and on firms switching from private to public debt (negative).

Suppose almost all firms are financed by public debt. Then the effect on public debt firms will be dominant, since the mass of bank-debt firms and the mass of bank debt firms switching to public debt are negligible. The overall effect must be positive.

Suppose almost all firms are bank financed and $b < 1$. Then the effect on bank firms is negative and the effect on firms switching from bank debt to public debt is also negative, while the positive effect on public debt firms is negligible. □

Proof of Proposition 4. To show (i), differentiate (21.6) implicitly with respect to b:

$$\frac{\partial x^{\mathrm{R}}}{\partial b}(x^{\mathrm{R}}-(D-b+1))+x^{\mathrm{R}}=0.$$

Since $x^{\mathrm{R}} \leqslant 1$ and $D > b$, the expression in brackets is negative, showing that $\partial x^{\mathrm{R}}/\partial b > 0$. The claim concerning private debt firms is proven in Hege (2002). (ii) Notice first that the probabilities for both types of firms are continuous in b. Consider then the case of $b \to 0$. Following Observation 2 (i), this implies that renegotiation with bank debt will always fail. (See Hege (2002) for a proof.) On the other hand, with public debt we know that this probability $x^{\mathrm{R}} \in (0, 1)$. Notably, for $b \to 0$, the probability x^{R} is given by (21.6),

$$\tfrac{1}{2}x^{\mathrm{R}^2} - x^{\mathrm{R}}(D+1) + (D\underline{Y} - R + \bar{I}) = 0. \tag{21.13}$$

Now suppose that $x^{\mathrm{R}} \to 1$. Consider (21.14) for $x^{\mathrm{R}} = 1$:

$$\tfrac{1}{2} - (D+1) + (D - \underline{Y} - R + \bar{I}) < 0. \tag{21.14}$$

which gives a contradiction, showing the claim.

Notes

1. Recent contributions include Bebchuk (1988), Aghion *et al.* (1992), Berkovitch *et al.* (1998), and Cornelli and Felli (1997).
2. The pre-eminent objection against a reorganization law, raised by Haugen and Senbet (1978) and others, argues that workouts (out-of-court renegotiation) should be a perfect substitute for court-supervised reorganization. The opposing view, dominant in the Law and Economics literature (see e.g. Jackson (1986)), argues that court-supervised reorganization is needed to overcome inefficiencies in out-of-court debt renegotiation, which would be due to free-rider or hold-out problems.
3. For USA evidence, see for instance Gilson *et al.* (1990), Gilson (1997), Franks and Torous (1989, 1994), Asquith *et al.* (1994), James (1996), and Brown *et al.* (1995).
4. This assumption is not essential for the results, but simplifies the algebra. Also, we would obtain the same result if we assumed that R is uncertain and I is known.
5. Hege (2002) rigorously derives the optimal capital structure in the same framework.
6. See Myers (1977) for the origin of this concept.
7. This bargaining model was chosen to capture two real world features: (i) Exchange offers are almost always initiated by managers and decided upon by investors. (ii) Banks wield considerable bargaining power in debt restructurings. The results are robust with respect to the renegotiation procedure.
8. Empirically, exchange offers are frequently made conditional on a certain threshold of approval, but never on everyone's approval. A manager, when making an exchange offer simultaneously to many dispersed bondholders, will not rely on all bondholders actually responding, let alone all bondholders responding rationally. The assumption does not exclude that exchange offers are made conditional on success.
9. Formal proofs for this and the three following Observations in Section 4 are contained in Hege (2002).

10. Straightforward calculations yield:

$$B_0 = \left(1 - \frac{\bar{\theta} + \theta^C}{2}\right)D + \left(\frac{\bar{\theta} + \theta^C}{2}\right)(\underline{Y} + R - \bar{I}),$$

and

$$D_0 = \left(1 - \frac{\underline{\theta} + \theta^C}{2}\right)\mathrm{D} + \left(\frac{\underline{\theta} + \theta^C}{2}\right)\underline{Y}.$$

11. Renegotiation succeeds with probability 1, the bank reduces its claim to $D = R - \bar{I}$, and the owner keeps the remainder, which is $R - EI - D = \frac{1}{2}$.
12. The separating equilibrium will only exist if the cutoff θ^C is strictly interior in the interval $(\underline{\theta}, \bar{\theta})$. Hege (2000) discusses the necessary and sufficient conditions.
13. The latter assumption is probably quite realistic: Under Chapter 11, the manager is required to reveal under oath all relevant information about the present financial standing of the firm. Reorganization plans are usually quite detailed and contain information not readily available to outside investors.
14. The restriction $b < R - \bar{I}$ is obvious. Otherwise there is no gain from using court-supervised reorganization.
15. See, for example, White (1989), Bradley and Rosenzweig (1992), Franks and Torous (1989, 1994), Aghion *et al.* (1992), and Bebchuk and Chang (1992).
16. See, for example, Eberhart *et al.* (1990), Franks and Torous (1989, 1994), and White (1989).
17. If the reorganization plan fails to win approval, the court can move on to a 'cram-down': roughly, a cram-down amounts to setting up and enacting a reorganization plan without the claimholders' consent. As the court is bound by rules, a cram-down is generally a time-consuming and very costly procedure; it is hardly used at all.
18. Gertner and Scharfstein (1991), Brown *et al.* (1993), Chatterjee *et al.* (1995) all document this in their distressed firms samples.
19. Moreover, the owner-manager will set the minimum acceptance rate sufficiently low to guarantee that all bondholders expect the offer to be accepted.
20. This is true if the parameter constellation supports a separating equilibrium; the conditions for this to be the case are analogous to those in n. 10. If this is not the case, then all firms issue public debt.

References

Aghion, P., Hart, O., and Moore, J. (1992). The economics of bankruptcy reform. *Journal of Law, Economics and Organization* 8: 523.

Asquith, P., Gertner, R., and Scharfstein, D. (1994). Anatomy of financial distress: An examination of junk-bond issuers. *Quarterly Journal of Economics* 109: 625.

Bebchuk, L. A. (1988). A new approach to corporate reorganization. *Harvard Law Review* 101: 775.

—— and Chang, H. (1992). Bargaining and the division of value in corporate reorganization. *Journal of Law, Economics and Organization* 8: 253.

Berkovitch, E., Israel, R., and Zender, J. (1998). The design of bankruptcy law: A case for management bias in bankruptcy reorganization. *Journal of Financial and Quantitative Analysis* 33: 441.

—— —— —— (1999). Optimal bankruptcy laws across financial systems. *Review of Financial Studies* 12: 347.

Bolton, P., and Scharfstein, D. (1996). Optimal debt structure and the number of creditors. *Journal of Political Economy* 104: 1.

Bradley, M., and Rosenzweig, M. (1992). The untenable case for Chapter 11. *Yale Law Journal* 101: 1043.

Brown, D. T., James, C. M., and Mooradian, R. M. (1993). The information content of distressed restructurings involving public and private debt claims. *Journal of Financial Economics* 33: 93.

Chatterjee, S., Dhillon, U. S., and Ramirez, G. G. (1995). Coercive tender and exchange offers in distressed high-yield debt restructurings: An empirical analysis. *Journal of Financial Economics* 38: 333.

Coffee, J., and Klein, W. (1991). Bondholder coercion: The problem of constrained choice in debt tender offers and recapitalizations. *University of Chicago Law Review* 58: 1207.

Cornelli, F., and Felli, L. (1997). Ex ante efficiency of bankruptcy procedures. *European Economic Review* 41: 475.

Detragiache, E. (1994). Public versus private borrowing: A theory with implications for bankruptcy reform. *Journal of Financial Intermediation* 3: 327.

Eberhart, A. C., Moore, W. T., and Roenfeldt, R. L. (1990). Security pricing and deviations from the absolute priority rule in bankruptcy proceedings. *Journal of Finance* 45: 1457.

Franks, J. R., and Torous, W. N. (1989). An empirical investigation of US firms in reorganization. *Journal of Finance* 44: 747.

——— (1994). A comparison of financial recontracting in distressed exchanges and in Chapter 11 reorganizations. *Journal of Financial Economics* 35: 349.

—— and Nyborg, K. G. (1996). Control rights, debt structure, and the loss of private benefits: The case of the UK insolvency code. *Review of Financial Studies* 9: 1165.

Gertner, R., and Scharfstein, D. (1991). A theory of workouts and the effects of reorganization law. *Journal of Finance* 45: 1189.

Gilson, S. C. (1997). Transactions costs and capital structure choice: Evidence from financially distressed firms. *Journal of Finance* 52: 161.

—— Kose, J., and Lang, W. W. (1990). Troubled debt restructurings: An empirical study of private reorganization of firms in default. *Journal of Financial Economics* 27: 315.

Haugen, R. A., and Senbet, L. W. (1978). The insignificance of bankruptcy costs and the theory of optimal capital structure. *Journal of Finance* 33: 383.

Hauswald, R. B. H. (1996). Banking systems, bankruptcy arrangements and institutional complementarity. Indiana University, Mimeo.

Hege, U. (2002). Workouts, court-supervised reorganization and the choice between private and public debt. *Journal of Corporate Finance* (forthcoming).

—— and Mella-Barral P. (2002). Repeated dilution of diffusely held debt. mimeo, London Business School and HEC School of Management.

Jackson, T. H. (1986). *The Logic and Limits of Bankruptcy Law*. Cambridge MA: Harvard University Press.

James, C. (1996). Bank debt restructurings and the composition of exchange offers in financial distress. *Journal of Finance* 51: 711.

Kaiser, K. M. (1996). Prospects for reorganisation within European bankruptcy laws. *Financial Management* 25: 67.

Kahan, M., and Tuckman, B. (1993). Do bondholders lose from junk bond covenant changes? *Journal of Business* 66: 499.

Myers, S. C. (1977). Determinants of corporate borrowing. *Journal of Financial Economics* 5: 147.

Roe, M. J. (1987). The voting prohibition in bond workouts. *Yale Law Journal* 97: 232.

White, M. C. (1989). The corporate bankruptcy decision. *Journal of Economic Perspectives* 3: 129.

—— (1994). Corporate bankruptcy as a filtering device: Chapter 11 reorganizations and out-of-court debt restructurings. *Journal of Law, Economics and Organization* 10: 268.

—— (1996). The costs of corporate bankruptcy: A US–European comparison. In J. Bhandari and L. Weiss (ed.), *Bankruptcy: Economic and Legal Perspectives*. Cambridge: Cambridge University Press.

22

Using Options to Divide Value in Corporate Bankruptcy

LUCIAN ARYE BEBCHUK

1. INTRODUCTION

Reorganization is one of the two routes that a corporation in bankruptcy may take. When a corporation becomes insolvent and bankruptcy proceedings are commenced, the corporation will be either liquidated or reorganized. In liquidation, the assets of the corporation are sold, either piecemeal or as a going concern. The proceeds from this sale are then divided among all the participants—all those that hold claims against or interests in the corporation. In contrast, in a reorganization, there is no actual sale of the company's assets. Instead, there is a 'hypothetical' sale of the company to the existing participants—they 'pay' for the company with their existing claims and interests, which are cancelled, and they receive in exchange 'tickets' in the reorganized company (i.e. claims against or interests in this new entity). In the USA when large publicly-traded companies become insolvent, they usually pursue the reorganization route.

In an earlier work (Bebchuk 1988), I have put forward a new bankruptcy procedure for corporate reorganization based on the use of options. The options scheme can, despite the fact that the value of a reorganized company is likely to be nonverifiable by courts, implement quickly the contractually prescribed distribution of the reorganization pie. The proposed procedure has received some significant support in subsequent literature; for example, it was adapted as the basis for bankruptcy reform in the well-known proposals by Aghion *et al.* (1992) (and subsequently by Hart 1995; Hart *et al.* 1997). The procedure has also received its share of critical or sceptical reactions. In this chapter I revisit the options proposal. The chapter offers a refined version of the procedure, incorporating some of the suggestions that have been made, restates the case for it, and responds to some questions and objections that have been raised over the years.[1]

The chapter begins by discussing in Section 1 the two goals—of *ex post* and *ex ante* efficiency—that should guide the design of efficient bankruptcy procedures. Section 2 explains why a bargaining-based procedure, such as the one provided by Chapter 11 of

This chapter, which was part of the materials delivered in the course of my Anton Phillips lectures in Tilburg University, is largely based on *European Economic Review*, 44, Bebchuk, L., 'Using Options to Divide Value in Corporate Bankruptcy', 829–843, (2000), used here by kind permission of Elsevier Science.

USA law, cannot serve well these two goals. Section 3 describes how the refined version of the option procedure would operate. Section 4 demonstrates and discusses the effectiveness of the proposed procedure. In the course of their analysis, Sections 3 and 4 address some of the questions that have been raised concerning the execution and desirability of the procedure. Finally, Section 5 explains, also responding to questions that have been often raised, the relationship between the options approach to corporate reorganization and the Black–Scholes characterization of all corporate securities as options.[2]

2. TWO GOALS FOR BANKRUPTCY PROCEDURES

From an efficiency perspective, there are two objectives that bankruptcy rules—and the rules governing corporate reorganization in particular—should serve.[3]

(i) *Ex post* efficiency—Maximization of the value of the reorganized company. *Ex post,* given that the company has entered insolvency proceedings, it is desirable, other things equal that the total value of the assets—the total value that will be distributed among the participants—will be maximized. There are two elements to this objective. First, as little value as possible should be dissipated during the reorganization process; to this end, it is desirable to minimize the time that the process will take and the direct and indirect costs incurred during this process. Second, when the reorganization process ends, the company's assets will be allocated to their highest-valued use.

(ii) *Ex ante* efficiency—Optimal division of total value. From an efficiency perspective, what matters is not only that the total bankruptcy value will be as large as possible but also how this value will be divided among the participants. This *ex post* division has important *ex ante* consequences. In particular, to induce participants to provide finance to the company *ex ante,* it is desirable that, in the event of *ex post* insolvency, the value will be divided according to the distribution or ranking of priorities that were agreed upon contractually.

3. THE PROBLEMS OF THE BARGAINING-BASED APPROACH

3.1. *The Valuation Problem*

A major problem that reorganization rules face concerns valuation—the difficulty inherent in estimating the value of the reorganized company. Note that a problem of valuation does not exist in liquidation when an actual sale to an outsider takes place. The liquidation results in an exchange of the company's assets for cash (or cash equivalents). Whether or not this cash represents the true value of the assets sold, there is no question as to what is the total value that is available for distribution. The receiver running the liquidation thus can proceed by paying creditors according to the ranking of their claims until all the money runs out.

In contrast, the sale of the company's assets in a reorganization is fictional. Consequently, no verifiable, objective figure is available for the total value to be distributed and, as a result, also for the value of the various tickets in the reorganized company. The non-verifiability of the reorganization value is likely to lead participants to advance different estimates even if their true estimates are the same or differ little. Senior creditors have a strategic incentive to advance a low valuation, because a low valuation would entitle them to a larger fraction of the tickets in the reorganized company. For a similar reason, equityholders have a strategic incentive to advance a high valuation.

The way in which the law of the USA, and most other countries that have a reorganization process, has dealt with this problem of valuation is by leaving the division of value to a process of bargaining among the classes of the participants. The law has sought only to provide a set-up for this bargaining process and to establish constraints within which the division must take place. Under the rules governing USA reorganizations (usually referred to as 'Chapter 11'), a plan of reorganization will generally be confirmed if all the classes of participants approve it. As the objection of any class of participants makes confirmation of a reorganization plan more difficult, the designers of reorganization plans commonly seek to get the approval of all classes. As explained in the following sections, this bargaining-based procedure does not perform well in terms of either *ex post* or *ex ante* efficiency.

3.2. *How Bargaining Leads to* Ex Post *Inefficiency*

(i) The dissipation of value during the reorganization process: The reorganization process under the existing bargaining-based rules takes substantial time (see e.g. Weiss 1990). During this time, substantial value might be dissipated. To begin with, the Chapter 11 process involves substantial administrative costs (see Cutler and Summers 1988). Second, and more importantly, the company under reorganization might incur substantial 'indirect' costs from functioning inefficiently during the lengthy reorganization process. Since the managers might not face good incentives and market discipline, management decisions during the process are likely to be distorted. And potential business partners may be reluctant to deal with the company, or may demand especially favourable terms, as long as the insolvency cloud hovers above the company. The indirect costs are large because of the substantial delay produced by the bargaining process.

(ii) Potential inefficiencies in the structure emerging out of the process: There are reasons to suspect that inefficiency costs might be incurred even after the bargaining process ends, because the structure emerging out of the process might not be optimal. For example, White (1994) suggests that the existing process is biased in favour of continuation—that is, the company is likely to continue as a going concern even if the most efficient route would be liquidation. This argument is consistent with the empirical evidence that companies emerging out of reorganization often go through another financial restructuring within the subsequent few years (Hotchkiss 1995).

3.3. *How Bargaining Leads to* Ex Ante *Inefficiency*

The existing bargaining-based approach leads to a division of value that often deviates from the division that is prescribed by the participants' contractual rights. What each class gets under the existing process depends not only on the value to which it is contractually entitled but also on the various factors that affect the strength of its bargaining position under the existing rules.

In particular, because the equityholders can often block or at least delay the approval of a plan, they will have some bargaining power even when the value of debt exceeds the total reorganization value. Bebchuk and Chang (1992) develop a model of the bargaining under the existing rules that identifies three reasons as to why equityholders might be able to extract value even when creditors are not paid in full. The deviations in favour of equityholders that the bargaining process produces are well documented by empirical work—work indicating that, even when creditors are not paid in full, equityholders are often able to extract significant value (see e.g. Eberhart *et al.* 1990; Franks and Torous 1989; Weiss 1990).

4. THE OPTIONS PROCEDURE FOR CORPORATE BANKRUPTCY

Let us now turn to describing how the options procedure will operate.[4] Consider a company C that entered into corporate reorganization proceedings. While the options approach can in principle be applied to any company, it is especially fitting for publicly traded companies, and it will be assumed that C is such a company. According to the options approach, the procedure should proceed in accordance with the following stages:

Stage 1: Determination of the various classes of participants.
Stage 2: Distribution of appropriately designed options.
Stage 3: Exercise of the options—which would allocate all the securities of the reorganized company.
Stage 4: Decision by the shareholders of the reorganized company about the future course of the company.

4.1. *Stage 1: The Participants*

Suppose that the participants in the reorganization are grouped into n classes. Each class i has m_i equal units of participation (two or more units of participation might be of course owned by one agent). It will be assumed that each unit of a given class provides the unit's owner with the same entitlement in bankruptcy.

The reorganized company, which will be called RC, is going to have a given capital structure. One version of the option procedure would have the reorganized company start initially with an all-equity structure. Such a restriction should not be regarded as problematic; if another capital structure is superior to an all-equity structure, it can be expected that at Stage 4, when the new shareholders will be able to make efficient choices for RC, they will move to the optimal structure. Another version of the option procedure would have the capital structure of RC set by an expert (say, an investment banker) chosen by the supervising court. If this expert does not choose the optimal capital structure, then again the shareholders would likely replace it once the securities of RC are distributed. Whatever is going to be the capital structure of RC, it will be possible to divide the securities of RC available for division into equal units. Let us denote by s the number of units of RC's securities that will be available for division among the participants.

The total value of the (s units of) securities of RC to be distributed among the participants is V. The question for the reorganization process, and for the options procedure, will be how to divide V among the participants. The desirable division of value (assuming that V is known) is given by the *ex ante* contractual terms agreed upon by the participants.

(If some of the creditors are involuntary (such as tort creditors), the desirable division would be the one prescribed by law for these creditors.) We shall assume that the contractually specified distribution is sequential. In a sequential distribution, classes are ranked, and any given class is entitled to get some value only after higher-ordered classes have been paid in full. Bebchuk (1998*b*) shows how the options procedure can be adjusted to implement contractually prescribed distributions that are not sequential—for example, distributions under which the equityholders are supposed to get some value even if the debtholders are not paid in full.

Specifically, let us suppose that any given class i should get value only after classes $j<i$ have been paid in full. The full payment needed to satisfy the claims of each class i is D_i. The last class, n, is a class of equityholders. For this class n, the residual claimant, we can define $D_n = \infty$. For each class i, let us also denote by $\overline{D}_i$ the total value of the claims of the classes above it; that is,

$$\overline{D}_i = \sum_{j=1}^{i-1} D_j.$$

Thus, under the desired distribution, each class i is entitled to get value only if $V > \overline{D}_i$. Also, no class i should get a value exceeding D_i nor (given limited liability) a value below 0. Thus, the value to which a class i is entitled is $E_i = \min[D_i, \max(O, V - \overline{D}_i)]$. As to members of class i, for each one of the m_i units of class i, the owner of the unit is entitled to a value of $(1/m_i)\, E_i$.

In describing the operation of the procedure, it will be helpful to use at times a simple example. In the example to be used, RC has three classes of participants: a class of 100 senior claims, each owed 1; a class of junior creditors, each owed 1; and a class of 100 equityholders, each holding one unit of equity. And suppose that the reorganized company RC is going to have 100 units of securities with a total value of V. In this case, if $V < 100$, then each senior creditor is entitled to $V/100$ and junior creditors and equityholders should get 0. If $200 > V > 100$, then senior creditors are entitled to 1 each, junior creditors are entitled to $V - 1$ each, and equityholders should get 0. Finally, if $V > 200$, senior and junior creditors should get 1 each, and equityholders should get $V - 2$ each.

4.2. *Stage 2: The Options to be Distributed*

If V were verifiable by courts, then we would have no problem in deciding how to divide the securities of RC among the participants to accomplish the contractual distribution of V. However, V is not verifiable by courts, and the question is how to implement the desired distribution given that V is not verifiable. The idea behind the option procedure is to divide the securities through the distribution to participants of options that are so designed that no participant would have a basis for complaining about receiving less than the value to which he is entitled.

At Stage 2, the options are to be distributed. Under the proposed method, the units of RC's securities will not be distributed to the participants right away but instead they will be held by a 'clearing agent' (CA). The participants will get certain rights (options) with respect to RC's securities held by the CA, and the participants' decisions concerning the exercise of their rights will determine the ultimate distribution of RC's units. As will be explained below, CA will not have any discretion—it will follow mechanically a prescribed procedure in responding to participants' exercise decisions. Accordingly, the function of serving as a CA can be assigned to an office of the company RC (as was assumed in the 1988 proposal), to a clerk of the supervising bankruptcy court, or to some hired outside party.

The critical aspect of the method, to which we will now turn, is the setting of the terms of the options. In the simple three-class example introduced above, the options would be set as follows. There will be three types of options. Each senior creditor will receive one type-1 right. Under certain circumstances described below, a type-1 right will be redeemed by the CA at Stage 3 for a value of 1. If the right is not redeemed, however, its holder would be entitled to receive at Stage 3 one unit of RC.

As to the junior creditor, each will receive one type-2 right. Under certain circumstances, type-2 rights will be redeemed by the CA at Stage 3 for 1. If the right is not redeemed, its holder would have the option to purchase one unit of RC for 1. If the holder of the right would like to exercise this option in the event that the right is not redeemed, the holder would have to submit such a request to the CS by the time of Stage 3.

Finally, each equityholder will receive one type-3 right. A type-3 right may not be redeemed by the CA. The holder of such a right will have at Stage 3 the option to purchase one unit of RC for 2. Again, to exercise this option, the holder would have to submit an exercise request to the CA by Stage 3.

In the more general case of n classes, there will be n types of rights. The members of class i will get all the type-i rights. Each class of rights will include s (divisible) units to be divided among the members of the class, (s/m_i) type-i rights for each unit of class i. Under certain circumstances to be described below, type-i rights will be redeemed by the CA for a certain price—a price equal to D_i/s, the per right prorata amount 'owed' to class i. If the right is not redeemed, its holder will have the option to purchase one unit of RC for a price equal to $\overline{D}_i s$, the per right amount 'owed' to classes above i. A holder of a type-1 right who will wish to exercise the option to purchase one unit of RC in the event that the right will not be redeemed will have to submit their rights to the CA by Stage 3 (accompanied by an appropriate commitment to pay the exercise price).

Stage 3 should in principle come as soon as practicable after Stage 2. Since participants might need a little bit of time to understand the terms of the options given to them and to decide whether to exercise the options included in them, it might be desirable to provide them with such time—say, a month. In this interim period between Stages 2 and 3, rights will be transferable and trading in the rights is thus likely to take place.

4.3. *Stage 3: Exercising the Options*

The exercise decisions that the holders of rights will make by Stage 3 will determine how CA will distribute all the units of RC among the holders of rights. Given how the terms of the distributed rights are set, the CA will always distribute all the units of RC in a way that will fully respect the terms of the distributed rights. The reason for this is that the terms of the options will be set so that the net obligation of the CA towards all those that will submit options will always add up to the *s* units of RC that the CA will have available for distribution.

To illustrate this point, consider the three-class example used above, and consider the three main possible scenarios. Suppose first that all of the holders of type-3 rights wish to exercise their options. In this case, CA will provide them with all the 100 units of RC (one unit for each right submitted) and will use the 200 received from them to redeem all of the type-1 and type-2 rights. Suppose next that no type-3 rights are submitted for exercise, but that all holders of type-2 rights wish to exercise them. In such a case, CA will give all of the RC units to these holders of type-2 rights, and it will use the 100 received from them to redeem all of the type-1 rights. Finally, suppose that no type-3 or type-2 rights are submitted for exercise: in this case, all of the units of RC will be distributed to the holders of type-1 rights.[5]

4.4. *Stage 4: The Post-Exercise Course of Action*

Once the options are exercised, the company will be out of the insolvency process and will have a body of shareholders. During the insolvency process, efficient decision-making about what to do with *R*'s assets cannot take place because it is not clear who owns the assets, but once the assets are removed from insolvency to a 'normal' corporate structure, their allocation will no longer be subject to the distortions arising from insolvency. As is the case with any new company, shareholders will choose directors among whatever rival teams (offering alternative plans and qualifications) will compete. The shareholders—and the directors chosen by them—will have an incentive to take that course of action—continuation, strategic reorientation, partial or full liquidation, etc.—which would maximize company value.

The contribution of Aghion *et al.* (1992) to the options procedure was in their suggestion to add a formal process of choosing among 'bids' at Stage 4. They proposed that shareholders will be offered cash or non-cash bids (the latter might be just offers to run the company with the shareholders retaining their shares) and will vote to choose one among them. The value of this addition does not lie in having the shareholders vote to choose among alternatives. Even without this special procedure, the shareholders would be essentially making such a choice when electing the first directors; the vote on the first directors would represent a choice among the alternative plans put forward in the proxy materials of the managers seeking to be elected (including possibly plans to sell to a given potential buyer for a given price). Rather, the Aghion–Hart–Moore suggestion adds a valuable element because of their suggestion that bids for what to do at Stage 4 (or, on an alternative formulation, plans offered by those seeking to be elected as directors at Stage 4) be submitted already at Stage 2 before options need to be exercised. As will be explained below, having this information already at Stage 2 would help participants make their exercise decisions.

Let us conclude the description of how the procedure would operate by observing that it would streamline the insolvency process considerably. Compared with the existing bargaining-based process, the options procedure would get the company faster out of insolvency (with its associated financial distress costs) and into efficient decision-making.

The proposed procedure would thus improve *ex post* efficiency. As we now turn to show, the procedure would also improve *ex ante* efficiency by implementing the contractually prescribed distribution.

5. THE IMPLEMENTATION OF THE DESIRED DISTRIBUTION

5.1. *Consistency with Participants' Entitlements*

Let us first show in the context of the simple example used above why no participant would have any basis for complaining about the outcome of the options procedure. Consider first the senior creditors. If they retain their type-1 rights until Stage 3, they will end up in one of two positions. First, their rights might be redeemed for 1 each, in which case they will be paid in full. Alternatively, their rights might not be redeemed, in which case they will end up with all the units of RC and thus would have no basis for complaining, as they would be getting the whole reorganization pie.

Consider now the junior creditors. If they retain their rights until Stage 3, they again will end up in one of two situations. First, their rights might be redeemed, in which case their claims will be paid in full. Alternatively, each junior creditor will have an option to purchase one unit of RC for 1. And since the holder of each unit is never entitled to more than $V/100-1$, this option will make the value of $V/100-1$ accessible to the holder.

Finally, if the equityholders will retain their rights, they will have an option to purchase one unit of RC for 2, and since each equityholder is never entitled to a positive value exceeding $V/100-2$, having the option would make this value accessible to the equityholder.

Turning to the more general case, let us consider a participant with an estimate V_p of V that, without loss of generality, holds one unit of participation in class i. Using V_p for V, observe that the participant is entitled, according to his own estimate of V, to a value of

$$E_p=(1/m_i)\min[D_i, \max(O, V_p-\overline{D}_i)].$$

Let us now show that the participant will never have any basis for complaining about getting less than this value. If $V_p \leqslant \overline{D}_i$, then the participant is entitled to 0. Of course, the participant will always get no less than 0 under the proposed method. Now if $V_p > \overline{D}_i$, then the participant is entitled to get $E_p=(1/m_i)\min[D_i, \max(O, V_p-\overline{D}_i)]$. However, by submitting the participant's option for exercise, and assuming $V=V_p$, the participant will be able to get at least the following.

Proposition *For any estimate V_p that any given participant has of V, the options procedure will provide the participant with a value that does not fall below the value to which the participant is entitled, using the participant's own estimate V_p of V, according to the contractually specified distribution.*

Note that, while the participant will never get less than E_p—the value to which the participant is entitled given the participant's own estimate of V—the participant might end up with more than E_p. This might happen in the event that other participants have higher estimates of V than V_p. In such a case, the participant might end up with his right redeemed or purchased in the market for a value exceeding that to which the participant is entitled assuming that V is equal to V_p.

Note also that a potentially attractive feature of the options procedure is its decentralized nature. Participants will not be acting as classes with all the coordination and collective action problems involved in action by class. Rather, each participant will make his own decision as to what to do with his options and will be able to act on his own estimate of V. To be sure, participants will be allowed to coordinate and acquire information collectively, and they would be able to rely on the estimates provided by the market trading in the options, but they would not have to do so and would be free to act on the basis of whatever estimate of V they have.

5.2. *Problems of Liquidity and Information*

(i) Liquidity constraints. One objection that has been raised to the options procedure is that, to exercise the options, participants other than the most senior creditors might need to invest additional capital. And to the extent that such participants are liquidity constrained, they might be denied their contractual entitlement. This problem indeed might cause the procedure to implement the desired distribution imperfectly. But in assessing the significance of this problem, the following qualifications need to be taken into account. First, in the case of reorganization of publicly-traded companies, most of the participants might hold only a small fraction of their portfolio in claims or shares of the reorganized company, and the problem of liquidity constraints thus might not be widespread. Second, even a liquidity-constrained participant might be able to get sufficient funds for exercising his options by pledging the purchased units of RC as a collateral. For example, suppose that in the used example, a junior creditor estimates V to be 170, but the market estimates V to be 150 and type-2 options thus trade at 0.5; in such a case, the junior creditor will be able to borrow the 1 needed to exercise his option by pledging the bought unit of RC as a collateral. Finally, observe that in the worst-case scenario a liquidity-constrained participant still would be able to sell his options in the market. This implies that even in the worst-case scenario the participant would not fare worse than how the participant would fare if the assets were sold in an auction.

(ii) Another objection that has been raised is that, to work, the options procedure requires that participants have a lot of information about V on which to base their exercise decisions. In evaluating this objection, note first that the procedure does not increase the participants' need for information about V; under the existing bargaining-based process, classes would also have to bargain on the basis of whatever estimate of V they have. It has been suggested that the bargaining process generates information about V because the committee representing each class can acquire information about V. But if there are some efficiencies to acquiring information as a class rather than individually, the proposed procedure would not prevent the formation for each class of a committee that (perhaps with the help of an investment banker) will acquire information about V and disseminate it to class members. Indeed, under the options procedure, participants would have an important additional source of information about V—the market trading in the options. Furthermore, as noted earlier, additional information might be provided by requiring that managerial teams seeking to be elected to run the company at Stage 4 or buyers seeking to acquire it at Stage 4 submit their proposals already at Stage 2. Finally, note that a participant that would be still uninformed would always be able to sell his options in the market and thus still would never fare worse than in an auction of the company.

6. RELATIONSHIP TO THE BLACK–SCHOLES CHARACTERIZATION OF SECURITIES AS OPTIONS

It would be worthwhile to relate the options approach to corporate bankruptcy to the approach put forward by the seminal paper of Black and Scholes (1972) (B–S). B–S pointed out that any corporate security can be viewed as equivalent to a certain option (or a set of options) with respect to the company's assets—and can be accordingly valued using the B–S option pricing formula.

Consider a company that is formed at $T=0$ with two classes: there are 100 equityholders each holding one share; and there are 100 debtholders each owed 1 which is due at $T=1$. Let us denote by V the total value of the company's assets at $T=1$. B–S implicitly assumed that, when time $T=1$ arrives, the shareholders will get the value of $V-100$ if $V>100$ and zero otherwise (with the remainder in both cases going to the debtholders). Given this assumption, the shareholders will have at $T=1$ an option to get V for an immediate exercise price of 100. The value of this option at $T=1$, B–S assumed, is straightforward: max $(V-100, 0)$ for the shareholders as a whole or max $(V/100-1, 0)$ per share. While B–S assumed that valuing this option at $T=1$ is straightforward, they focused on the question of placing a value on this option (i.e. the share of the company) prior to $T=1$, when the asset value V is following a random process and its ultimate value V at $T=1$ is not yet known. This feature is the one that made difficult the valuation problem—which B–S sought to solve with their pricing formula.

In the B–S analysis, then, it was assumed that, at $T=1$, value will be partitioned in accordance with the contract between debt and equity—the equityholders will get $\max[V/100-1, 0]$ each and the debtholders will get $\min(1, V/100)$ each. The problem on which B–S focused was limited to valuing these claims prior to $T=1$. Essentially, B–S assumed that the 'legal technology' is perfect enough so that the contract between the equity and debt will be enforced at $T=1$ in a way that would split V according to the 'contractual partition'. This would indeed be the case if V were verifiable; with verifiable V, courts would have no problem in implementing the contractual partition at $T=1$.

But the legal technology under the existing legal rules is not perfect in this way. As Section 2 highlighted, V is not verifiable and, if the company files for Chapter 11, V will be partitioned by bargaining that might produce a division that differs from the contractual partition. Thus, under the existing rules, when $T=1$ arrives, the shareholders might end up with a value different than max $(V/100-1, 0)$ each and the debtholders might get a value different than min $(1, V/100)$ each. For example, equityholders might be able to extract some value even if V is less than 100.

Note that the above observation implies that, under the existing rules, it would not be accurate to value shares prior to $T=1$ by using the B–S formula and assuming that at $T=1$ each share will have a value of max $[(V/100-1), 0]$. Rather, it is necessary to figure out what amount the shareholders will be able to extract at the bargaining at $T=1$ bargaining, and then to plug this $T=1$ amount into the option pricing formula.

The proposed options procedure seeks to ensure that the value at $T=1$ will be divided according to the contractual partition, as B–S assumed that will happen but as might often not happen under the existing rules. That is, the options approach seeks to improve the legal technology that would be used for implementing the contractual partition. To do so, the options approach starts, as did B–S, from the observation that the value that the equity-holders should get at $T=1$ is equal to the value of an option to get V for an immediate exercise price of 100. But rather than making use of this observation to value the equity at times prior to $T=1$, the option procedure uses this observation to provide the equity-holders with the value to which they are entitled at $T=1$. While in the B–S analysis the equivalence of securities to options was just a tool for calculation, the option procedure under consideration suggests that bankruptcy be done by actually writing out the options to which the value of the shares is equivalent, replacing the shares with such options written with respect to a clearing agent in the way described above, and letting the share-holders make their own decisions with respect to the options. In such a way, we have seen, it is possible to overcome the problem arising from the non-verifiability of V by courts and to implement the contractual partition at $T=1$.

In essence, the recognition that the value to which any security holders are entitled at $T=1$ can be characterized as an option that enables us to implement the contractual division of value at $T=1$ even when V is not verifiable and courts could not divide value according to the contractual partition. As the analysis above has shown, this division could be implemented by actually writing out the options and distributing them to participants. In other words, the recognition that all corporate securities can be viewed as options on the company's assets can be used to make the contractual partition of value self-enforcing and one that does not require that the value of the assets be ever verifiable by courts. The recognition that securities can be viewed as options, then, can be used not only as a tool for calculating the worth of securities prior to the date in which the value of the assets must be partitioned, but also as a tool for improving the technology by which the value of the assets will be divided.

7. CONCLUSION

The options approach offers an attractive alternative to the bargaining-based approach of existing rules. By moving the company quickly out of insolvency proceedings and into efficient decision-making about the assets, the options procedure would improve *ex post* efficiency. And by overcoming the valuation problem and implementing the distribution of value prescribed by participants' contractual entitlements, the procedure would improve *ex ante* efficiency.

Notes

1. Bebchuk (1999) seeks to address all the questions that have been raised about the proposal. This short chapter attempts to deal only with a few of them.
2. One subject that is beyond the scope of this short chapter is a full comparison between the options procedure and auctions. Supporters of auctions (Baird 1986; Jensen 1991) propose that the assets

of an insolvent firm be always auctioned. Critics of auctions worry that they might not generally enable capturing the full value of the assets. For example, Shleifer and Vishny (1992) argue that, when a firm becomes insolvent, other firms in the industry, which are natural potential buyers, are likely to face liquidity problems. While a full comparison is beyond the scope of this paper, it will be observed that under the option procedure each participant would fare at least as well as (and possibly better) than under an auction if the auction were to take place at the same time as the exercise of the auctions.

3. See Bebchuk (1998*a*). While the division of the bankruptcy pie might be also guided by fairness considerations and the options scheme might be also helpful in this regard, the current chapter focuses only on efficiency considerations.
4. This section offers a refined version of the main elements of the procedure. See Bebchuk (1988) for discussion of some needed additional elements, including the treatment of security interests, outstanding contracts with favourable terms, and concentration of claims in one hand.
5. Such scenarios are ones in which at Stage 3 holders of all rights of a certain type act in the same way. Given that the rights are going to be traded, this is indeed likely to be the case: if some holders of rights do not wish to exercise them while others do wish to do so, the former should be willing to sell their rights and the latter should be willing to buy them. But it should be emphasized that the CA would have no problem respecting all the rights and distributing all the units of RC in scenarios of partial submission of rights of certain type (Bebchuk 1988: 787–8).

References

Aghion, P., Hart, O., and Moore, J. (1992). The economics of bankruptcy reform. *Journal of Law, Economics, and Organization* 8: 523.

Baird, D. (1986). The uneasy case for corporate reorganizations. *Journal of Legal Studies* 15: 127.

Bebchuk, L. (1988). A new approach to corporate reorganizations. *Harvard Law Review* 101: 775.

——(1998*a*). 'Chapter 11'. In *The New Palgrave Dictionary for Law and Economics.*

——(1998*b*). A generalization of the options approach to corporate reorganization. Paper presented at the American Law and Economics Association 1998 meeting.

——(2002). The options approach to corporate bankruptcy. Harvard Law School, Manuscript (in preparation).

——and Chang, H. (1992). Bargaining and the division of value in corporate reorganization. *Journal of Law, Economics, and Organization* 8: 253.

Black, F., and Scholes, M. (1972). The pricing of options and corporate liabilities. *Journal of Political Economy* 81: 637.

Cutler, D. M., and Summers, L. H. (1988). The costs of conflict resolution and financial distress: Evidence from the Texaco–Pennzoil litigation. *RAND Journal of Economics* 19: 157.

Eberhart, A. C., Moore, W. T., and Roenfeldt, R. L. (1990). Security pricing and deviations from the absolute priority rule in bankruptcy proceedings. *Journal of Finance* 45: 1457.

Franks, J. R., and Torous, W. N. (1989). An empirical investigation of U.S. firms in reorganization. *Journal of Finance* 44: 747.

Hart, O. (1995). *Firms, Contracts, and Financial Structure.* Oxford: Oxford University Press.

——, LaPorta, R., Lopez-de-Silanes, F., and Moore, J. (1997). A new bankruptcy procedure that uses multiple auctions. *European Economic Review* 41: 461.

Hotchkiss, E. (1995). Postbankruptcy performance and management turnover. *Journal of Finance* 50: 3.

Jensen, M. (1991). Corporate control and the politics of finance. *Journal of Applied Corporate Finance* 4: 13.

Shleifer, A., and Vishny, R. (1992). Liquidation value and debt capacity: A market equilibrium approach. *Journal of Finance* 47: 1343.

Weiss, L. A. (1990). Bankruptcy resolution: Direct costs and violation of priority of claims. *Journal of Financial Economics* 27: 285.

PART VI

THE ROLE OF INSTITUTIONAL SHAREHOLDERS IN CORPORATE GOVERNANCE

23

Less is More: Making Institutional Investor Activism a Valuable Mechanism of Corporate Governance

ROBERTA ROMANO

1. INTRODUCTION

Institutional investors have in the past decade increasingly engaged in corporate governance activities, introducing proposals under Rule 14a-8, the Securities and Exchange Commission's (SEC) proxy proposal rule,[1] and privately negotiating with management of targeted firms with the stated goal of improving corporate performance. For example, since the mid-1980s, institutions have submitted shareholder proposals on corporate governance, consisting principally of proposals to eliminate defensive tactics to takeovers, to adopt confidential proxy voting, to enhance board independence, and to restrict executive compensation, to hundreds of firms. Before 1986 only a small set of individual investors engaged in such activism: from 1979 to 1983, religious groups and between six or seven individuals, depending on the year, submitted more than half of all proposals, which ranged in the hundreds every year (e.g. Liebeler 1984: 438 and n. 86). From 1986 until the early 1990s, five institutions (four public pension funds and TIAA-CREF, a pension fund primarily for university teachers and administrators) accounted for almost 20 per cent of all proposals (e.g. Del Guercio and Hawkins 1999: 297; Sander 1991: 3). Since 1994, unions have overtaken public pension funds as the most active corporate governance proposal sponsors (Thomas and Martin 1998: 51–2). Over a dozen unions and union pension funds, including both national and local level organizations, have used the proxy mechanism to sponsor such proposals (ibid.: 52).

Commentators (e.g. Black 1992; Roe 1994: 233–53) have in general commended institutional shareholder activism, at least in part from a belief that it would replicate the blockholding-based governance systems of Germany and Japan and thereby fill the void in managerial monitoring which occurred at the end of the 1980s with the decline in hostile takeovers in the United States of America (although the bloom now is off Germany and Japan's corporate governance systems given far superior USA economic performance for over a decade and the increase in hostile takeover activity in recent years). In this view, more active engagement in corporate governance by institutional investors can substitute for the discipline imposed on managers from the threat of a hostile takeover.

As shareholder activism on corporate governance matters has become more pervasive, financial economists have attempted to measure the effect of activism on targeted firms' performance. Although the finance literature focuses, among institutional investors, on proposals by public pension funds—given the relatively recent appearance of union activism—because most union proposals are not substantively different from those sponsored by public pension funds, it is unlikely that the findings would differ markedly for union proposals. This contention is supported by the fact that the voting levels, which are an excellent proxy for the value of a proposal, for union proposals involving corporate governance do not significantly differ from those obtained for public pension fund proposals on the same subjects (Thomas and Martin 1998: 68).

This chapter reviews the corporate finance literature on corporate governance activism involving shareholder proposals and uses it to inform normative recommendations concerning the proposal process. The finance literature presents an apparent paradox: notwithstanding commentators' generally positive assessment of the development of shareholder activism, the empirical studies suggest that it has an insignificant effect on targeted firms' performance. Very few find evidence of a positive impact, and some even find a significant negative stock price effect from activism.

There have been two literature reviews, by Karpoff (1998) and Black (1998), that reach the same negative assessment of shareholder activism's impact, but they have not focused on the gulf between the empirical and normative literature.[2] Karpoff seeks to reconcile the disparate conclusions in finance studies, which he emphasizes are due to different definitions of what counts as a success and thus are more apparent than real; his objective is not to explain the gulf between the finance literature and the legal commentary. Black, who in light of the empirical finance literature shifted from an optimistic assessment of institutional investor activism to that of a 'pessimist', offers a set of possible explanations for the overall insignificance of activism: that most proposals are precatory and are ignored by management; that institutional investors are unable to organize effectively to influence management or uninformed about what issues to propose; and that the overall level of activism—a small number of institutions spending a trivial amount of money—is low (Black 1998: 463).

The precatory content of shareholder proposals is not sufficient to explain the insignificant price effects. Management often responds to precatory proposals, even those receiving less than a majority of the shares. For instance, of 130 firms adopting confidential voting for the proxy process, a proposal for confidential voting was offered at only one-third of the firms and in only four cases did the proposal receive a majority of votes (Romano 2002). It is possible that the market does not react to shareholder proposals because most proposals do not obtain sufficient support to evoke a management response, rather than because the proposal must be couched in precatory language. The reasoning would be that because shareholder proposals do not obtain a majority of votes, there is little reason to assume that the management action sought by the proponent will be adopted, and hence nothing to price. However, the support for proposals has been increasing over time, it is considerable for specific categories of proposals and, as noted, management may respond to a proposal that does not obtain majority support. This suggests that studies should find significant price effects for proposals offered in the later years of samples in which voting support increased, or at least for the subsamples of proposals that can be expected to obtain relatively high voting support and to induce a management response. The lack of significant price effects for even subsamples of proposals implies that something other than the explanation that the market assumes proposals will be ignored by management is at work.

Black's explanation of proposals' insignificant price effects as due to institutions' inability to organize effectively is also unpersuasive, as the institutional investors who sponsor proposals hold non-trivial blocks in many firms and have networking organizations on corporate governance activities that largely mitigate collective action concerns. His alternative contention that these shareholders have limited information concerning what proposals are efficacious is consistent with this chapter's explanation that the apparent paradox is related to the substance of submitted proposals, but it is not the sole explanation of the data—fund managers might well be informed about which proposals are useful and still champion fruitless proposals, if managers obtain personal benefits from submitting such a proposal, given the absence of strong incentives of boards of public funds to monitor their staff. The fact that in contrast to public pension funds, private pension and mutual funds do not engage in activism has been explained by the competitive nature of the industry, or more pejoratively, as cost-conscious private funds' free-riding on the expenditures of activist public funds (Pozen 1994; Black 1998). I would emphasize a further, complementary explanation: that such institutions' managers are less likely to obtain personal (private) benefits from engaging in shareholder activism than public and union fund managers.[3] Both explanations are supported by survey data indicating that private fund managers perceive the costs and benefits of shareholder activism differently from public pension fund managers (Downes *et al.* 1999: 32–4).

Finally, Black's explanation that proposals' insignificant price impact is due to the overall low level of shareholder activism is an incomplete explanation: it is not institutions' low expenditure level, but rather the specific objectives of their activism, that have resulted in the absence of a price effect.[4] Even if institutions were to spend more resources on their proposals in order to ensure voting success, unless the subject of their proposals was also significantly altered, there would be no change in the stock price reaction. It is the thesis of this chapter that the problem with shareholder activism is that the governance reforms that institutions are proposing have no significant cash flow effects.

This chapter then provides an alternative explanation of the apparent paradox in the literature that I believe is preferable to Black's conjectures, because it can rationalize the disparate findings of insignificance and significance in the empirical studies as well as the finding that management is often responsive to shareholder activism despite its precatory form. Namely, financial economists have not been able to identify a positive performance effect of shareholder activism because much of that activism is, in fact, misdirected. I reach this conclusion by relating the studies of shareholder activism to the studies of the underlying corporate governance devices that are the object of that activity. A review of that literature makes evident that for a very large proportion of the governance structures that are the focus of shareholder activism, such as independent boards of directors, limits on executive compensation, and confidential proxy voting, there is a paucity or utter absence of data that demonstrate that such devices improve performance. Hence, it should not be surprising that shareholder activism directed at reforming those governance structures does not produce positive results, and that this result would persist regardless of proposals' expected voting support.

Negotiated agreements between institutional investors and management, after which a proposal is withdrawn, on occasion produce positive price effects. The chapter provides an explanation, based on updating of information on firm quality, of this distinctive result compared to that for submitted proposals: given that the substantive distribution of withdrawn and submitted proposals is indistinguishable, the withdrawn proposal induces a positive price effect because it provides information about management quality otherwise obscured by the firm's poor performance (that the managers desire to be responsive to investor concerns and will not seek to entrench themselves and prevent shareholders from taking actions, such as accepting a takeover bid, that improve firm value). A negative price effect is analogously understood as the response to a negotiation indicating to the market that management's quality is lower than previously believed. The information updating explanation is preferable to a more straightforward value-maximizing explanation of the empirical results, that when management negotiates with a shareholder and the proposal is withdrawn it is because it is a value-maximizing proposal, and when it does not negotiate, it is because the proposal is not value-maximizing. The value-maximizing explanation is inconsistent with the studies that find negative price effects from negotiations. It is also unsatisfactory because there is not sufficient heterogeneity among proposal targets to explain why the same type of proposal would be value-maximizing for some firms (where it is withdrawn) and not others, which would be required by this explanation given that the empirical results are indistinguishable by proposal type.

The wide gulf between the priors of commentators and pension fund managers and the reality conveyed by the data presents a perplexing picture: why are time and effort being devoted to fruitless or marginal activities? This chapter does not answer this question directly, although there is a plausible explanation relating to pursuit of personal benefits (such as political ambitions, or collective bargaining goals) rather than portfolio firm value-maximization by proposal proponents, who are not private sector fund managers. There are also data substantiating this conjecture: the New York City public pension fund manager emphasized her activism in seeking election to higher office (Romano 1993*a*: 822); and union funds have targeted firms where there were ongoing contract negotiations (Thomas and Martin 1998: 61–2). This chapter takes as a given problematic motivational issues and seeks instead to recommend devices that will provide fund boards in charge of oversight, as well as fund managers, with more information and incentives that will minimize the effect of agency problems on portfolio performance and activist reform efforts.

The chapter takes a two-pronged approach to the problem of ineffective shareholder activism. First, the chapter recommends adoption of a mechanism of internal control, something akin to a good management practice, whereby funds would engage in periodic comprehensive review of their shareholder-activism programmes to identify the most fruitful governance objectives. Such evaluations would increase information and thereby improve the quality of decision-making and aid in ensuring that the funds' proxy activities are directed at maximizing portfolio firms' value. This should increase the benefit from activism to the beneficiaries of the funds, and is accordingly an appropriate policy from the perspective of the fiduciary obligations of fund managers. To provide an impetus for individual compliance, the chapter recommends that industry associations should adopt good practice standards for activism programmes that will furnish guidelines for individual funds. It also suggests the use of independent third parties, such as public accounting firms, to certify that funds' activism programmes have been thoroughly reviewed.

The chapter further advocates changing the SEC proxy proposal rules, to reduce the current subsidy of proposal sponsorship unless a proposal achieves substantial voting success, or to permit firms to opt out, in whole or in part, of the current subsidized proposal regime. This second reform proposal will provide incentives for funds to undertake comprehensive internal revaluations of their shareholder proposal programmes because unsuccessful policies (those that do not garner substantial support) will become more expensive to pursue. For example, the estimated present value of the cost of the current regime, compared to one of the proposed reforms, subsidization of only shareholder proposals obtaining 40 per cent of the votes cast, ranges between $293 million and $1.9 billion. It would also better track the state law approach to the reimbursement of expenses of proxy fights, which are not covered by the SEC shareholder proposal rule, in which successful challengers can recover their costs.[5] In contrast to shareholder proposals, proxy fights are not typically waged over marginal matters and the empirical literature has consistently identified significant positive wealth effects from this activity.[6] No doubt the difference in the wealth effect of proxy fights and shareholder proposals is a function of the different incentives created by the cost reimbursement rules: in contrast to sponsors of shareholder proposals who bear no financial risk, proxy fight contestants will incur the substantial expense of a contest only where they expect a victory to produce a significant improvement in corporate performance.

2. EXPLAINING THE NEGLIGIBLE IMPACT OF SHAREHOLDER ACTIVISM ON PERFORMANCE

This section reconciles the seeming disparity between the goals of pension fund activism—shareholder proposals and private negotiations with management—with the empirical literature that finds that such activism has, at best, minimal impact on corporate performance. It does so by relating the empirical research on the effect of pension fund corporate governance activism on firm performance to the empirical research on the performance effects of the underlying governance objectives of shareholder activists. It begins, however, by sketching which firms are targeted, in order to establish that shareholder proposals should, in fact, be evaluated by their impact on corporate performance.

2.1. *What Firms do Institutional Investors Target?*

To ensure that it is appropriate to evaluate the efficacy of institutional investors' activism by whether there is an impact on corporate performance, it is necessary to identify which firms activist pension funds target. Namely, are they targeting poorly performing firms? For if pension funds' efforts at improving corporate governance were not related to concerns over corporate performance, then using improvement in performance as a benchmark for evaluating funds' behaviour would be inappropriate. In particular, we would not expect to find significant performance effects from shareholder proposals if targeted firms were among the top-tier performers, for such firms would be less able to improve their performance significantly. As there may be a number of firms in a fund's portfolio with subpar performance, in considering the impact of activism on performance it is also necessary to ascertain whether funds follow target selection strategies that can be considered rational: namely, do they select firms for which they have a higher probability of success, on the assumption that a successful campaign is essential for performance improvements.

2.1.1. *Targets of Shareholder Activism are Poor Performers*

Several studies find that firms that are the targets of shareholder activism are, indeed, poor performers (compared to the market or industry-peers) on a variety of stock and accounting measures: abnormal stock returns, growth in operating income, return on assets, operating return on sales, sales growth, and market-to-book ratio.[7] However, not all studies find significant differences on all measures.[8] In part, differences among studies are a function of the selection criteria of the activist institutions. Since 1988, for instance, the California Public Employees' Retirement System (CalPERS) has explicitly chosen its targets from among the poor performers in its portfolio (Smith 1996: 232), whereas the Teachers Insurance Annuity Association-College Retirement Equities Fund (TIAA-CREF), the pension fund for university educators at private institutions and some state systems, uses firms' corporate governance characteristics rather than a performance criterion (Carleton *et al.* 1998: 1338–40). Not surprisingly, the one study focusing solely on TIAA-CREF's initiatives did not find the targets to have been poor performers (ibid.: 1356). But even TIAA-CREF's objectives are explicitly couched in the ideal of improving performance.[9] The finding of target firms' subpar performance across a variety of samples of institutional investor activism supports the notion that the appropriate benchmark for measuring the value of corporate governance shareholder proposals is their impact upon corporate performance.

2.1.2. *Targets have High Institutional and Low Insider Shareholdings*

There are also considerable data that institutional investors select their targets strategically to increase the probability of success—that is, they consider the composition of the firm's shareholder voting pool, and not simply performance, in choosing proposal targets. Several studies find a negative relation between the receipt of shareholder proposals and insider ownership, and a positive relation between proposal receipt and institutional ownership.[10] In fact, TIAA-CREF expressly uses institutional ownership as a criterion for target selection (Carleton *et al.* 1998: 1339). This strategic behaviour is consistent with the selection of targets for which the probability of success is high. Insiders, of course, are not expected to vote for proposals restricting their discretion or otherwise requiring them to establish governance structures that they have not voluntarily adopted. Institutional shareholders, who have far greater incentives to engage in informed voting compared to individual shareholders because of the size and extent of their holdings, are hypothesized to vote for proposals enhancing shareholders' ability to monitor management with greater frequency than other outside investors. And indeed, that is precisely the way such investors vote: the percentage of votes cast for shareholder proposals is negatively related to insider ownership and positively related to institutional ownership (Gordon and Pound 1993: 713; Gillan and Starks 2000: 295).

It is reassuring that studies find a positive correlation between proposal submission and institutional shareholdings, as it suggests that pension funds that are corporate governance activists are, in fact, concerned with the success of their undertakings. But it should be noted that the studies all involved the targets of public pension fund activism, so it is not known whether union funds follow a similar strategy.

We can, accordingly, conclude that public pension funds sponsoring corporate governance proposals are not engaged in symbolic politics, as is true of sponsors of social responsibility proposals (proposals addressing social issues and corporate social policy, such as doing business in Northern Ireland or animal testing), which receive far more limited support than corporate governance proposals. For example, in 1994, social responsibility proposals rarely received more than 20 per cent of the vote while corporate governance proposals at times received 40 per cent (Cary and Eisenberg 1995: 374), and in 1991–2, 51 of 169 corporate governance proposals received more than 33 per cent of the vote compared to only 1 of 165 social responsibility proposals.[11] In addition, although no social responsibility proposal has ever passed, from 1986 to 1990, 25 corporate governance proposals received a majority of the votes (Sander 1991: 86), and the number of corporate governance proposals obtaining a majority has continued to increase dramatically in the 1990s, with 30 passing in 1999 alone (IRRC 1999*a*: 4).

Of course, a proposal that passes does not mean that it will be adopted—to be submissible under the SEC rules, proposals involving ordinary business decisions must be precatory because corporate law delegates such decision-making to the board.[12] Although many boards respond even to unsuccessful proposals, boards can and, on occasion do, disregard majority votes, particularly on takeover defence rescissions (Hamermesh 1998: 421–2).

Recent shareholder proposals have sought to prevent the possibility of such an outcome by phrasing the proposal as a bylaw amendment (which, if passed, would mandate board action). Whether such a strategy is permissible has not yet been adjudicated in Delaware, but an Oklahoma court upheld the inclusion of this type of proposal under the SEC proposal rules as a proper subject for shareholder action, under a state statute similar to Delaware's.[13] The issue has also been the subject of extensive commentary, most of which advocates permitting such bylaw proposals, or some subset of them (e.g. Coffee 1997; Gordon 1997; Hamermesh 1998; Macey 1998), as has the further open question whether boards can subsequently repeal shareholder-passed bylaws (e.g. Coffee 1997; Hamermesh 1998). Notwithstanding the still open question whether an intransigent management can be required to adopt the policies that are the subject of a successful (majority-supported) shareholder proposal, given the data on firm targeting we can conclude that institutional sponsors of corporate governance proposals are attempting to use their resources effectively in their choice of targets.

2.2. *What is the Relation Between Activism and Performance?*

Shareholder proposals have no significant effect on firm performance, but private negotiations over proposals in advance of the shareholders' meeting often have a short-term positive impact and, on occasion, even a negative impact. This section reviews and reconciles these seemingly inconsistent data.

2.2.1. *Studies of Proxy Proposals*

Despite the apparent rationality of public pension funds' targeting—targeted firms tend to be poor performers with a shareholder pool that is predisposed to vote for corporate governance proposals—there is an absence of evidence that such activism has any discernible positive impact on corporate performance. Across the most comprehensive studies of shareholder proposals, there is a uniform finding of no significant relation between proposal submissions and target firm performance.[14] The studies are summarized in panel A of Table 23.1. Although the overall conclusion is that proposals do not affect performance, in the comprehensive studies of shareholder proposals there are subsamples that have significant effects: the significant positive returns are not related to proposal submission activity, but the significant negative returns are.[15]

Wahal (1996), for example, finds no significant improvement in the long-term stock or accounting performance in the targets of public pension fund activism, both for submitted proxy proposals and nonproxy contact (sending a letter to management expressing concern about performance without subsequently introducing a proxy proposal). But Wahal does find a significant short-term stock price effect for the nonproxy contacts around the announcement of their targeting, in contrast to the proxy proposals. Karpoff *et al.* (1996) also find no significant stock price reaction to proxy proposals and no operating performance improvements over one to three years following the shareholder proposal (for all firms and for the subset of firms where the proposal was offered by CalPERS). But for a subset of proposals—those involving executive compensation—the stock price reaction to the proposal was significantly negative. However, multivariate regression did not confirm a significant difference between compensation-related and other proposals.[16]

Gillan and Starks (2000) similarly find no significant stock price reaction to proxy proposals offered by institutional investors, but a significant negative stock price reaction to the subset of proposals seeking rescission of poison pills that are sponsored by institutional investors.[17] Del Guercio and Hawkins (1999) also find no significant stock price effect from proxy proposals around the announcement date or in the long term (measured over three years after the proposal) and no significant improvements in long-term operating performance. In addition, in contrast to Wahal (1996), they do not find any difference in announcement date returns when their sample is divided into proxy proposals and nonproxy (negotiated outcome) firms. But they do find a significant positive stock price effect for proposals offered by the State of Wisconsin Investment Board (SWIB) around the outcome date (the annual meeting date or the news date of a withdrawn proposal), and marginally significant (10 per cent level) negative returns on the announcement date for proposals relating to antitakeover defences and board composition or structure.[18]

Finally, Forjan (1999), whose sample of proposals is not limited to institutional investor activism, finds a significantly negative stock price reaction on the proxy mailing date for firms subject to a shareholder proposal in the 1978–91 proxy seasons; the abnormal return is not significant when cumulated over one and two day intervals before and after the mailing date. Whether the finding would persist were the sample restricted to proposals by

Table 23.1. *Studies of shareholder activism*

Panel A: Performance effects of shareholder proposals

Study	No. of proposals	No. of firms	Sponsors	Years	Performance effect
Del Guercio and Hawkins (1999)	224	125	5 activist funds	1987–93	Insignificant
Forjan (1999)	798	467	Individuals and institutions	1978–91	Negative
Gillan and Starks (2000)	2,042 (463)	452 (n.a.)	Individuals and institutions (8 funds and unions)	1987–94	Insignificant
Karpoff *et al.* (1996)	522	269	Individuals and institutions	1986–90	Insignificant
Smith (1996)	78	51 (39 and 20 for some statistical tests)	California Public Employees Retirement System (CalPERS)	1987–93	Insignificant
Strickland *et al.* (1996)	163	85	United Shareholders Assn (USA)	1992–3	Insignificant
Wahal (1996)	306	146	9 activist funds	1987–93	Insignificant

Panel B: Performance effects of shareholder negotiations (nonproxy targeting)

Study	No. of non-proxy targeting	No. of firms	Sponsors	Years	Performance effect
Carleton *et al.* (1998)	62	45	TIAA-CREF	1992–6	Mixed
Chidambaran and Woidtke (1999)	224	168	Individuals and institutions	1985–95	Insignificant; negative for public and union funds after 1992
Crutchley *et al.* (1998)	n.a.	47	CalPERS' target list	1992–7	Insignificant; pre-1994 targets positive; post-1994 targets negative
Del Guercio and Hawkins (1999)	16	n.a.	5 activist funds	1987–93	Insignificant
Forjan (1999)	27	27	Individuals and institutions	1978–91	Positive
Opler and Sokobin (1995)	n.a.	96	Council of Institutional Investors' list	1991–3	Positive
Smith (1996)	n.a.	19	CalPERS	1987–93	Positive
Strickland *et al.* (1996)	53	34	USA	1992–3	Positive
Wahal (1996)	50	n.a.	9 activist funds	1987–93	Positive

Note: n.a. = information not available.

institutional sponsors as in the previously discussed studies of Wahal (1996), Karpoff *et al.* (1996), and Del Guercio and Hawkins (1999), is not known.

Disaggregated by proposal type, the significant negative returns occur solely for proposals to repeal staggered boards and to ban greenmail or golden parachutes. Forjan further finds that for a subset of twenty-seven firms where management reached an early agreement with the proposal sponsor or where the proposal passed with a majority vote, the announcement effect is significantly positive, but he does not provide a breakdown of the twenty-seven cases into negotiated and passing proposals, nor does he provide information concerning the subject matter of these proposals, to permit further analysis of his data for this chapter's purposes.

A more narrowly-gauged study by Smith (1996), focused solely on proposals sponsored by CalPERS, the largest activist public pension fund, reports similar results to those of the broader-based studies. Smith finds no significant stock price effect and no long-term effect on the firms' operating performance from CalPERS's activism, but a positive stock price effect for the subset of CalPERS's proposals that succeeded.[19] However, what Smith classifies as successful proposals partially overlap with Wahal's nonproxy category, as they are described as instances where the targeted firm either adopted the shareholder resolution or reached a settlement with CalPERS which resulted in the proposal's withdrawal. In addition, he finds a negative stock price effect upon the targeting event for the subsample of proposals offered in 1987–8, the sample years when CalPERS was selecting targets by the presence of antitakeover defences rather than financial performance, and during which none of its efforts succeeded, in contrast to the later years' corporate governance proposals.

Similarly, a study of the proposals submitted by the United Shareholders' Association (USA), a non-profit shareholder advocacy organization which was founded by T. Boone Pickens, a prominent hostile takeover bidder during the 1980s, and whose members were primarily small shareholders, also found no significant stock price effect (Strickland *et al.* 1996). Announcement of a successful negotiation agreement that resulted in a potential proposal's withdrawal, however, produced a positive stock price effect.

2.2.2. *Why do Proposals have Insignificant Performance Effects?*

The consistent findings of statistical insignificance for shareholder proposals are most plausibly a function of the value of the corporate governance mechanism that is the object of the proposals. The governance mechanisms of greatest interest to shareholder activists—board reforms, takeover defences, executive compensation, and confidential voting—have been the subject of extensive research. In brief, the types of board and compensation reforms advocated by proposal sponsors have not been found to be value-enhancing corporate governance devices, and the results of the empirical research on antitakeover devices are mixed, with only some findings of a negative impact from some of the tactics that shareholder proposals seek to rescind. The implementation of confidential voting has no impact on voting outcomes or on firm performance.

(i) *Boards of directors*

A focus of shareholder proposals that is typically commended by commentators (e.g. Millstein and MacAvoy 1998) entails altering board composition and structure to enhance its independence from management. Proposals of such board reforms range from 9 to 16 per cent of the total corporate governance proposals in the shareholder activism studies. However, firms whose boards have a majority of independent directors do not perform significantly better than those whose boards are controlled by insiders,[20] nor do firms which split the function of board chairmen and chief executive officer (CEO) compared to firms that do not split these positions,[21] the board structure on which shareholder proposals focus.

Although independent boards do not affect performance, and hence cannot be said to perform an ongoing monitoring function, they may provide an episodic monitoring function, by benefiting shareholders in extraordinary or crisis situations. For example, Weisbach (1988) found that there is a higher probability of CEO turnover after significant poor performance when outsiders control the board compared to insider-controlled boards, although Mikkelson and Partch (1997) find no correlation between board composition, CEO turnover and performance. Consistent with a crisis-management view, an event study of the appointment of an outside director reports a significant positive price effect even when a majority is already independent (Rosenstein and Wyatt 1990). Appointing an independent director could signal that a company plans to address business problems even if board composition does not affect the firm's long-run profitability.

The research on the effect of outside boards for takeover targets is also ambiguous: one study found that board composition does not affect the likelihood of a takeover or the size of the premium (Shivdasani 1993), while another found that shareholder premiums were higher for targets with outsider-dominated boards, particularly when the firm resisted the bid, but board composition did not affect the success of a bid and the mean total takeover gain was not significantly different for outsider board firms (i.e. the greater gains to target shareholders with independent boards came from lower bidder returns) (Cotter *et al.* 1997). Finally, management-led buyouts of firms with outsider boards have higher abnormal returns than those with insider boards (Lee *et al.* 1992) and takeover bidders with outsider boards experience less negative abnormal returns on the announcement of their bids than those with insider boards (Byrd and Hickman 1992), while the data on the impact of independent boards on the value obtained from divestitures is ambiguous (Hanson and Song 2000).

Because the vast majority of firms will not be involved in hostile takeovers or management-buyouts, the expected benefit from increasing board independence for the average firm is quite low, particularly as there are no data indicating that the frequency of these acquisitive events is higher for firms with independent boards. Moreover, the probability of CEO turnover after poor performance, although it may well be higher for independent boards, is still extremely low and, of course, the board's independent composition did not avert the poor performance. It would therefore be fair to conclude that the benefit to shareholders from an independent board's performance in certain extraordinary situations is sufficiently limited to render more decisive, for assessing the significance of board composition reform, the overwhelming evidence that independent boards do not produce significant performance improvements. This point has even more force because the finding of a positive impact on decision-making of independent boards in extraordinary circumstances is itself in controversy as it is not uniformly identified in the literature.

One explanation for the failure to find performance improvements with independent boards is that the optimal board structure may well vary across firms. As the choice of board structure is endogenous to management, if firms with different requirements select differing proportions of outside directors, then we would not expect to find significant performance effects in a cross-sectional study of boards. Shareholder proposals to change board structure, accordingly, will not enhance firm value where management has already optimized on the board's independence dimension; they will enhance value only if management has made a mistake. The failure to document positive price effects from shareholder proposals on board composition thus suggests that pension funds do not possess superior information regarding optimal board structure and, correlatively, that activism is not functioning to improve a suboptimal board composition decision. Supporting this inference is the fact that firms that are targeted for shareholder proposals typically already have a majority of outside directors (John and Klein 1995) and they may well have a higher proportion of outsiders than non-targeted firms (Smith 1996: 240).

A study by Agrawal and Knoeber (1996), that attempts to control statistically for the problem of the endogeneity of corporate governance devices provides further data that is at odds with the belief of proponents of independent boards. They find a negative impact on performance from board independence after controlling for other governance devices, and thus contend that firms are currently suboptimizing board composition by nominating too many outside directors.

In a subsequent paper, Agrawal and Knoeber (2001) examined board composition more closely and identified a subset of 'political' outside directors, whose career experience is conjectured to aid firms' governmental interactions, that is, directors with political experience or law degrees (such as former high-level government and military officials serving on aerospace and defence firms' boards). They suggest that the negative correlation between performance and board composition identified in their earlier article may be spurious, in that, firms subject to political interference are poor performers and also have more outside directors, particularly of the political variety. Consequently, board composition choices may not be suboptimal, as they initially concluded. Regardless of which of Agrawal and Knoeber's contentions is correct, whether corporate boards have the optimal amount of outside directors or too many, their research implies that the market will not positively value shareholder proposals seeking to move boards any further along the independence dimension.

(ii) *Takeover defences*

The most popular type of proposal sponsored by institutional investors (between 36 and 48 per cent of institutional proposals) involves elimination of takeover defences, and the overwhelming majority of these proposals concern rescission of poison pills. The empirical literature on the price effects of the adoption of poison pills is, however, inconclusive. Initial studies reported a significant negative price effect on the adoption of a poison pill,[22] but the results of subsequent research are mixed, with one study still finding a negative effect while several studies reported insignificant price effects for pills adopted after 1984.[23] Moreover, one study found a positive price effect for pill adoptions where the board of directors consists of a majority of outsiders, and a negative effect for firms with insider boards (Brickley *et al.* 1994).

The finding by one study of a positive impact of board composition on market reactions to pills suggests that investors view independent boards as having a higher probability of using a pill to run an auction and raise the premium received rather than to deter a control transfer, and that, under such circumstances, they prefer to trade off a decreased probability of a bid for an increased probability of an auction (should a bid occur). Indeed, Brickley *et al.* (1994) found that bids for firms with pills and independent boards resulted in significantly more auctions than firms with pills but without independent boards. This is consistent with the finding that independent boards generate higher target shareholder gains but not a higher rate of successful bids—a higher frequency of auctions provides an explanation for these data. This finding also suggests another difficulty in interpreting the empirical literature which may explain the disparate empirical results: a pill adoption may provide new information to investors concerning a firm's probability of a takeover, or management's level of resistance to a bid, and hence price effects may be a function of the market's assessment of that information (that is, a signalling effect) rather than the value attributed to the pill itself.

Further complicating the interpretation of the impact of poison pill adoptions, the efficacy of a pill's defensive effect, and hence the market reaction, may be related to other defences already in place. While this contention is theoretically plausible, the few studies examining the price effect of pill adoptions in conjunction with antitakeover charter amendments have disparate results: they find either no difference or a more positive return for firms with a prior antitakeover amendment.[24] It must be noted, however, that the results of studies of the adoption of antitakeover charter amendments are also mixed, with the most frequent result, statistically insignificant price effects.[25] This is not of itself surprising since shareholders must approve the amendments, and we would not expect them to vote for provisions that are contrary to their interest. Indeed, Agrawal and Mandelkar (1990) find a positive relation between the wealth effect of an antitakeover charter amendment proposal and the firm's institutional ownership (presumably the firm's most informed voters). Moreover, in contrast to the poison pill studies, there is a more negative stock price reaction to charter amendments when the board is outsider-dominated (Sundaramurthy *et al.* 1997). Thus, the benefits to shareholders from independent board composition with regard to defensive tactics are, in fact, ambiguous.

The studies of the interaction of poison pills and charter amendments may not be the best test of the thesis that the efficacy of a poison pill depends on firms' other defences, however, because the most prevalent amendment in the study samples, a fair price provision, has little impact on a pill's defensive potency. A more informative test would be to examine the most effective defence in conjunction with a pill, a staggered board, rather than aggregated data on antitakeover charter amendments. Although even here, the impact may be largely theoretical for it is unlikely that a management which lost a proxy fight would continue to retain a pill and resist the bid. The limited impact of a staggered board in practice is, without doubt, a reason why pills were re-crafted to include deadhand provisions that sought to lock in which directors could redeem a pill, albeit unsuccessfully, as these tactics were struck down by the courts.[26]

The ambiguous results concerning the wealth effects of poison pills parallel the disagreement among commentators over the efficacy of takeover auctions (e.g. Easterbrook and Fischel 1982; Gilson 1982), as a pill's principal impact, providing management with time to find a preferred bidder, is to foster an auction rather than to end a bid preclusively.[27] It is therefore not surprising that shareholder proposals to rescind poison pills have not produced positive stock price effects. Rescission would be expected to improve performance only if pill adoption were more unequivocally a value-decreasing event.

The discussion of the corporate finance literature on takeover defences has focused on poison pills not only because they are the subject of the most prevalent shareholder proposal on defensive tactics' repeal, but also because some studies have found significant performance effects for subsets of proposals containing poison pill rescissions. Before discussing those results in relation to the finance literature, it must be noted that the defences besides poison pills that are the most common subject of shareholder proposals, cumulative voting, staggered boards and golden parachutes, have not been as intensively empirically investigated as poison pills.

The wealth effects reported in the small number of studies examining such defences are not uniformly negative but are also positive or insignificant, calling into question the efficacy of proposals to rescind them, similar to the inference drawn from the research on poison pills. For example, although the one study of board-sponsored amendments to eliminate cumulative voting found a negative price effect (Bhagat and Brickley 1984),[28] the one study of the adoption of golden parachutes found positive price effects (Lambert and Larckner 1985), and the two charter amendment studies that separated out proposals to classify the board found no significant effect (Mahoney *et al.* 1996; Jarrell and Poulsen 1987). These findings suggest that only proposals to restore cumulative voting might produce a beneficial wealth effect for shareholders, but the only shareholder activism study that separately reported the impact of this type of proposal found no significant effect (Forjan 1999: 67). It should further be noted that the same study found a negative price effect for proposals to rescind golden parachutes and staggered boards, defences which have been found to have positive or insignificant price effects, a combination of findings consistent with the conclusion that such proposals are misguided from the perspective of shareholder wealth-maximization.

Smith's finding of a significant negative price effect for the CalPERS' proposals in 1987–8 which focused on takeover defences and were largely poison pill proposals, Gillan and Starks's (2000) similar finding for institutional investors' poison pill proposals, and Del Guercio and Hawkins's (1999) finding of a marginally significant negative price effect for antitakeover and board proposals (the bulk of the proposals in the group are antitakeover proposals, and poison pill rescissions predominate among these proposals),[29] are consistent with the studies that find that poison pills do not decrease shareholder wealth and may, on occasion, increase it. This interpretation of the literature is supported by a study of poison pill shareholder proposals that found that targeted firms more frequently revise their poison pills than nontargeted firms (Bizjak and Marquette 1998). If such revisions, undertaken by management's being responsive to shareholder actions, weaken a pill's effectiveness, a negative market response anticipating such an effect explains the shareholder proposal data.

(iii) *Executive compensation*

Proposals concerning executive compensation, which typically seek reductions in the level of pay, are a much smaller proportion of corporate governance proposals than the antitakeover proposals. In the Karpoff *et al.* (1996) study, they were approximately 10 per cent

(42 of 408 identified proposals), and none were sponsored by pension funds. Although there are also no compensation proposals in Del Guercio and Hawkins's (1999) study of pension fund activism, public pension funds do sponsor this type of proposal, while at a far lower rate than proposals on defensive tactics (less than 10 per cent of their proposals) (e.g. Wahal 1996: 9; Smith 1996: 234).

This category of proposals was the subset producing negative price effects in the Karpoff *et al.* (1996) study. The substance of the proposals may explain this fact: proposals calling for limits on executive compensation are at odds with the empirical literature that finds that compensation and performance are positively correlated (e.g. Murphy 1985; Mehran 1995). A majority of the compensation-related shareholder proposals in the Karpoff *et al.* (1996) study called for limits on executive pay or requirements that directors own stock. While directors' compensation in stock might function as an incentive-aligning device that improves performance, in fact, studies investigating the relation between performance and directors' stock ownership have not consistently documented a significant positive relation.[30] It should also be noted that all five of the CalPERS-sponsored executive compensation proposals in Smith's (1996) study were proposals to reduce top management's compensation. It is also important to add that, despite the small number, these proposals were 15 per cent of the proposals Smith identified as successful, the same success rate achieved by the takeover defence proposals in his sample.

Two studies have focused solely on the impact upon actual pay levels of executive compensation proposals. The initial study of the effect on firm compensation policy of shareholder proposals involving executive compensation, by Johnson *et al.* (1997), found that both compensation levels and sensitivity of pay to performance decreased for firms targeted by CalPERS, but there was no significant effect on compensation from the submission of a shareholder proposal in general. Although their study does not indicate whether CalPERS' activism was directed at compensation issues for all of the targeted sample firms, it does provide anecdotal instances of management agreeing to reduce executive pay after meetings with CalPERS. Their anecdotes are consistent with Smith's (1996) reported high success rate of CalPERS' executive compensation proposals (80 per cent). Given the literature detailing the positive impact of total compensation, as well as incentive (equity) compensation, on performance, to the extent CalPERS' activism results in lower compensation that is less sensitive to performance, it is not beneficial to targeted firms' shareholders.

The second study, by Thomas and Martin (1999), found that the compensation of targeted firms' CEOs did not increase as rapidly as that of non-targeted firms' CEOs after targeting, but the decrease was not statistically significant. This corroborates the results of Johnson *et al.*'s (1997) study concerning the absence of an impact of compensation proposals. Prior to targeting, Thomas and Martin find that the targeted firms' managers had higher compensation than the average compensation of managers in similarly-sized firms in their industry, and received more of their compensation in the form of incentive pay (stock options) than non-targeted firm managers, but only the cash salary component is statistically different. The higher than industry-average compensation level persisted after the proposal, despite the lower rate of increase in pay.[31]

After targeting, the targeted firms' CEOs' compensation packages shifted more toward cash than to long-term incentive compensation (that is, stock options, not cash salaries were reduced).[32] Although this difference was also not statistically significant, it is a result, similar to that of Johnson *et al.*'s (1997) study, that suggests that executive compensation proposals do not benefit shareholders because they reduce, rather than promote, the use of the compensation form that better aligns shareholder and manager interests than fixed cash payments, incentive stock options (e.g. Holmstrom 1979). In fact, adoptions of incentive compensation plans have positive price effects (Brickley *et al.* 1985).

The conclusion that shareholder activism involving compensation issues is non-value-maximizing is further supported by the finding of Prevost and Wagster (1999) that firms on CalPERS' 1990 and 1991 'hit list'—the firms CalPERS was publicly targeting under its shareholder activism programme in those years—experienced a negative stock price effect to two events in 1992: Congressional hearings on a bill to permit shareholder resolutions on executive compensation and increase proxy disclosure on compensation; and an SEC proposal thereafter to increase the shareholder votes required on executive compensation issues and to adopt a new method of valuing stock options in proxy statements.

Prevost and Wagster (1999) interpret these data as indicating that facilitating corporate governance directed at executive compensation by increased disclosure rules does not benefit shareholders because the disclosure, equally available to stakeholders with interests other than value-maximization, such as unions, political activists and the press, as it is to investors, will encourage stakeholder pressure on boards to weaken the 'pay-for-performance' sensitivity of management compensation. Their explanation of the data is corroborated by the studies of executive compensation proposals: a negative stock price reaction to the SEC disclosure rule indicates an expectation that firms will be pressured to diminish incentive compensation plans, and this expectation is borne out, as the performance sensitivity of the pay of executives at CalPERS-targeted firms decreased significantly, and at union-targeted firms decreased, albeit insignificantly, after being targeted subsequent to the SEC rule change.

Given the content of many compensation proposals—to limit pay and restrict incentive compensation practices—it is not a surprise that shareholder activism, when compensation is the object, has not been found to improve performance. The perverse effects that would accompany the adoption of such proposals—decreased incentives for managers to increase share value—in all likelihood explains the negative stock price reaction to CalPERS' activism in connection with such proposals, as there is a higher probability that boards will respond to CalPERS' compensation demands (and indeed they have done so), than to the individual shareholders who more typically sponsor compensation proposals. It must also be noted that other shareholders appear to be aware of the problematic value of the proposals. Compensation proposals receive far less voting support than other corporate governance proposals, typically not much more than 10 per cent compared to over 30 per cent for proposals involving defensive tactics.[33]

One recent form of executive compensation proposal involves preventing the resetting of executive stock option contracts (or subjecting resetting to shareholder approval). If options are not repriced after stock price declines, the executive receiving them will be unable to profit from that form of incentive compensation (the option exercise price will be above the stock price at expiration). Shareholders opposed to repricing contend that it simply rewards poor performance, in contrast to repricing firms' contentions that it is necessary to retain valuable employees whose compensation has otherwise declined (Bryant 1998). This category of proposal has, unfortunately, not been empirically studied, as it is a relatively new object of activism. Owing to recent accounting changes for the treatment of repriced options, the number of firms reporting option repricing has declined (IRRC 2000*a*). Consequently, shareholder proposals to prohibit repricing may not prove to be prevalent enough to become a subject worthy of empirical research.

Although there has been no empirical research on shareholder proposals to prevent repricing, there has been some investigation on the efficacy of option resetting, and this research does not support a conclusion that it should be banned as activist investors have proposed: studies have found that the impact of option repricing on shareholders is insignificant, although the impact on the executives whose options are repriced is great (Brenner *et al.* 2000; Chance *et al.* 2000; Chidambaran and Prabhala 2000). In addition, a study examining the characteristics of firms that reprice options found that it does not entrench management because the top management turnover of firms repricing options is significantly higher the year after the repricing than the CEO turnover for non-repricers (Chidambaran and Prabhala 2000). As we do not know whether these are voluntary or involuntary departures, this finding may also undercut the contention in favour of repricing that it is necessary to retain top managers. However, among repricing firms, the CEO turnover rate was significantly higher when the CEO's option was not repriced (40 per cent of the repricing firms) compared to when it was, and thus the authors conclude that the relation between repricing and turnover shows up in higher turnover in the absence of repricing rather than lower turnover in its presence, which supports the rationale offered for repricing by its proponents (ibid.: 24–5).

(iv) *Confidential voting*

Proposals to adopt confidential voting equal proposals to eliminate defensive tactics in frequency of institutional sponsorship, ranging from 18 to 44 per cent of the proposals in studies of institutional investor activism. In contrast to the other categories of shareholder proposals, which are substantively directed, proposals for confidential voting seek to alter shareholder voting patterns and thereby recalibrate the internal dynamics of the firm with the expectation that this will improve performance. The rationale for this expectation is that conflicts of interest prevent some shareholders from voting against management where to do so would maximize share value (e.g. Pound 1988).

In particular, proponents of confidential voting contend that money managers aspire to do business with the firm whose shares they hold, such as to manage the firm's pension fund, and that such business prospects would be jeopardized by voting against management (Pound 1988; Black 1992; LTV Corp. 1995). They correspondingly expect that money managers will not feel constrained to vote with management when it is against their interest as shareholders, were management to be unable to ascertain how they voted (that is, they believe that confidential voting will eliminate institutional investors' conflicts of interest in proxy voting).

It is intuitively plausible to expect voting institutions to affect outcomes: in the USA election context, for instance, the adoption of 'Australian' ballots—state-prepared and administered ballots that are secret, in contrast to the party ballot system—was associated with an increase in ticket-splitting, although the change in ballot form (organized by office rather than party) appears to have had a more significant effect than the confidentiality of the ballot (Rusk 1970). However, it is also quite possible that the main effect of the Australian ballot was not to alter voting outcomes but rather, to reduce party expenditures on election campaigns, as it eliminated the bribes parties were paying voters under the open ballot system because they no longer could be assured of the bribes' desired outcome (Gerber 1993).[34] Under this alternative hypothesis, the procedural reform was adopted because it was in the interest of the major political parties, and not simply due to effective reformist agitation. The analogous argument in the proxy context is that managers adopt confidential voting because they do not expect it to produce voting outcomes that are adverse to their interest.

I conducted a study of the effect of confidential shareholder voting and concluded that it does not matter (Romano 2002). I examined voting outcomes on shareholder, as well as management, proposals before and after firms' adoption of confidential voting. Paralleling the findings concerning shareholder proposals substantively directed at improving corporate governance by reforming board composition, repealing takeover defences and altering executive compensation, confidential voting has no significant impact on voting outcomes. In particular, there is no significant impact on voting support for shareholder proposals from the adoption of confidential voting. Controlling for past performance and insider, block, and institutional ownership, as well as firm and time specific effects, only the type of proposal affects voting outcomes: shareholder proposals to repeal or modify defensive tactics or to adopt confidential voting are positively related to outcomes. The support for management proposals is positively related to the adoption of confidential voting, but not when the firms ever experiencing a proxy fight, whose proposals have higher support in all years, are excluded from the sample, an effect contrary to confidential voting proponents' expectation that the support of management would decline upon its adoption.[35]

The change in voting procedure also had no impact on performance: there was no stock price effect upon the announcement of the procedural change, nor did long run stock performance improve over one to three years after its implementation (ibid.). Of course, if, as this chapter contends, the object of the overwhelming majority of shareholder proposals does not improve performance, than changing the voting procedure to enhance the probability of such proposals' adoption will not improve performance either.

The insignificant impact of confidential voting on voting outcomes plausibly explains why many firms voluntarily adopt the procedure: it does not matter. The conclusion to draw from the data on confidential voting is consistent with the overall conclusion drawn from the more extensive empirical literature studying the three other principal categories of shareholder proposals: the benefit of promoting such proposals is marginal because the procedure has no discernible behavioural effect.

2.3. *Private Negotiations and Information Updating Regarding Managerial Quality*

In contrast to submitted proposals, institutional investors' private negotiation governance strategies on occasion produce significant positive stock price effects. These results are consistent with, as previously discussed, Wahal's finding distinguishing between submitted proxy proposals and successful private negotiations that obviated the need for a proposal,

Smith's finding of a positive effect for successful targeting (assuming this subsample is dominated by instances of nonproxy rather than proxy activism), and Forjan's finding of a positive announcement effect for successful negotiations (assuming that the cases of negotiations dominate those of the proposals that passed in his 27-firm sample combining the two cases). Two more recent studies, however, find that negotiation activity in the mid-1990s is associated with a negative effect on performance. The studies of negotiated agreements are summarized in panel B of Table 23.1.

Carleton *et al.* (1998) examined the impact of the corporate governance activities of TIAA-CREF, which seeks to negotiate privately with firms it has targeted and typically reaches an agreement with management that results in its not having to submit a proposal. They found no significant changes in accounting measures of long-term performance from TIAA-CREF's activism, but the stock price effect of the initial targeting was significant, depending on the substantive content of the negotiations. It was significantly positive for targeting with the goal of restricting poison pills, significantly negative for targeting seeking to increase the diversity of the composition of the board of directors, and insignificant for targeting to institute confidential voting.[36]

Another positive finding concerning 'behind the scenes' activism involves a study by Strickland *et al.* (1996) of the firms targeted by USA. When management agreed to USA's requested changes prior to the proxy proposal submission deadline, the targeted firms experienced positive stock price effects in contrast to the insignificant effect when USA presented a proxy proposal. The negotiated agreements involved takeover defences (subdivided into poison pill and golden parachute removal proposals), board composition and confidential voting; contrary to the TIAA-CREF study, there was no difference in the sign and significance of the price effects across USA's three types of proposals. To identify the source of the wealth gain for the subset of agreements to remove takeover defences, Strickland *et al.* calculated the firms' abnormal returns on the announcement of the defences' adoptions: they were insignificantly negative for poison pills and insignificantly positive for golden parachutes. There was also no relation between the abnormal returns upon the announcement of the defences and the abnormal returns upon the announcement of their negotiated removal, which makes it difficult to identify the source of the wealth gain from the negotiations.

Opler and Sokobin (1995) examined the returns of firms on the Council of Institutional Investors' (CII) 'focus-list' of poor performers. The CII is an organization of public and private pension funds that serves as a clearing-house for the funds' corporate governance activities. Opler and Sokobin find that the targeted firms experience better market and operating performance than the market as a whole and other benchmark portfolios in the year subsequent to their inclusion on the CII list. They infer from this result that co-ordinated investor action that takes place behind the scenes ('quiet activism') is effective in improving firm performance, in contrast to the proxy proposal route, which often involves campaigns by one investor, and for which studies do not find positive effects. This is only an inference because we do not know whether the firms on the focus-list were indeed the targets of institutional investor activism. But it is consistent with the findings of Carleton *et al.* (1998), Weisbach (1988), Smith (1996), Strickland *et al.* (1996), and Wahal (1996) concerning privately negotiated (nonproposal) activism by institutional investors.

Crutchley *et al.* (1998) investigate targeting activities of CalPERS by examining the stock price reaction to a firm's initial placement on the fund's publicly announced list of targets. They find a short-run positive price effect that disappears over a year after the announcement and conclude that for the full sample there is no lasting impact on performance. They then divide their sample into two, the early years, 1992–4, when CalPERS' activist corporate governance campaign was quite visible, and the later years, 1995–7, when it played a 'quieter', that is, a less visible, behind-the-scene role. They find that over the years after targeting, the early years' subsample has a significantly positive cumulative return, whereas the later years' subsample's cumulative return is negative. After finding that restructuring actions taken by the targeted firms after targeting do not affect the size of the abnormal return, their conclusion, in contrast to that of Opler and Sokobin, is that visible or aggressive public activism, and not quiet activism, increases shareholder wealth.

Finally, Chidambaran and Woidtke (1999) studied the shareholder proposals that were withdrawn from 1985 to 1995. They find that the characteristics of firms where proposals are withdrawn have changed over time, particularly after the adoption in 1992 by the SEC of changes in the proxy process to facilitate shareholder communication. In contrast to the other four studies evaluating negotiations over proposals, their measure of firm value is the change over the proposal year in Tobin's Q, the ratio of the firm's market to book value. A Tobin's Q that is greater than 1 indicates that the market values the firm's assets above their book value (that is, the firm has significant intangible asset value). This is interpreted as an indicia of good performance. Although for the full sample of withdrawn proposals there is no significant performance effect, for the set of proposals withdrawn post-1992 whose sponsors were public or union funds, there is a negative valuation effect (a statistically significant decrease in Tobin's Q), in contrast to proposals withdrawn before 1992, where the valuation effect (change in Tobin's Q) was positive albeit insignificant. Chidambaran and Woidtke (1999) interpret the data as indicating that the 1992 proxy reforms provided institutional investors with excessive bargaining power such that they became able to pressure managers to accept non-value-maximizing proposals. This is because the firms whose proposals were withdrawn after 1992 also had lower levels of management stock ownership than the firms whose proposals were withdrawn before 1992, and they reason that institutional pressure to adopt non-value-maximizing proposals will be more effective where management does not have significant voting power.[37] Hence, Chidambaran and Woidtke also reach a diametrically opposite conclusion from Opler and Sokobin (1995) concerning behind-the-scenes activism by institutional investors, that it is not a shareholder wealth-enhancing activity.

The conventional explanation of the findings of positive performance effects from successful negotiations and insignificant effects from proposal submissions is that managers negotiate only when proposals are value-maximizing, and shareholders bid the price up in anticipation of the proposal's implementation. Proposals that are submitted, in this view, are those that management recognizes as non-value-maximizing, and therefore not worthy of negotiation. There is no market reaction to submissions because although the proposal is negatively assessed, it is not expected to pass (or not expected to be implemented by management if passed). To reconcile the finding of a negative reaction to a proposal sponsored by institutional investors in Gillan and Starks (2000), the value-maximization explanation needs to contend that the market believes a non-value-maximizing proposal might be adopted if sponsored by an institutional investor. The finding of negative performance effects from negotiations in the studies of Crutchley *et al.* (1998), and Chidambaran and Woidtke (1999), however, cannot be rationalized by this explanation, since their findings suggest that, to the contrary, management negotiates over non-value-maximizing proposals.

A more helpful explanation in that it better reconciles the paradoxical findings of both positive and negative performance effects from negotiated agreements (private activism) and insignificant effects from shareholder proposals on the same issues, is a screening explanation of management behaviour. In a context in which investors are not informed about management quality while managers are informed,[38] shareholder proposal negotiations can provide investors with a means to screen the high from the low quality managers. From this perspective, the positive (negative) price effects from private activism are not indicia of a positive (negative) assessment of the subject matter of the activism (i.e. whether it is value-maximizing), but rather, indicate investors' assessment of management's quality, that it will be (will not be) responsive to shareholders' concerns over the need to improve firm value.

The difference in stock price reaction to the two events (proposals and negotiations) in this explanation is a function of learning—information updating concerning management quality by the market from the occurrence of shareholder activism—rather than the market's assessment of the value of the underlying activism's objectives. The market views nonproxy (negotiated settlement) activism as a screen for determining that management quality is high: because management was sufficiently responsive to the institutional investor's concern that it was willing to withdraw its proposal, investors update their evaluation of management quality as less prone to self-entrenchment and more apt to improve performance. If an institutional investor's proposal is submitted instead of withdrawn, it could provide negative information regarding management's quality, as it would indicate management's non-responsiveness to shareholder concerns, or low quality. But failure to negotiate, in this scenario, need not provide new information, because the market will have already perceived the management of targeted firms to be of low quality given prior poor performance. Hence, we would intuitively not expect studies to consistently observe a negative stock price effect upon proposal submissions.

The information-revealing story of the stock price effects of negotiations raises several questions. First, why would the reaction to a proposal enable investors to screen management's quality? The information concerning management's response to shareholder activism is informative in this scenario because it enables investors to screen, from among poorly performing firms, those with lower quality management because it would be more expensive for low, rather than high, quality managers to be responsive. This is an equilibrium story only if it is costly for lower quality managers to mimic higher quality managers by negotiating proposal withdrawals. The effectiveness of the screen provided by a successful negotiation will clearly be a more costly strategy for lower-quality managers to undertake compared to higher-quality managers when the subject is a proposal to eliminate a defensive tactic: the former type of managers are more likely to be the target of a hostile bid and replaced. This factor makes the high quality managers' action not easily mimicked by poor quality management even for proposal categories where the impact will not be as clearly disparate across managerial quality: since most firms do not experience only one type of proposal,[39] lower-quality managers cannot negotiate over only one type of proposal while refusing to negotiate over proposals on takeover defences.

A second question raised by the information updating explanation of the stock price effects of negotiated agreements is why don't managers signal quality on their own, instead of waiting to react to action by uniformed investors (shareholder proposals)? The response is that the explanation is not offered as the sole means by which adverse selection problems in equity markets are resolved. Management may signal an investment's quality by other means, for instance, through the choice of capital structure (Ross 1977), auditor selection (Titman and Trueman 1986), stock ownership (Leland and Pyle 1977), and underpricing of initial public offerings (Welch 1989).[40] Rather, shareholder proposals can induce further (and possibly more precise) sorting of managerial quality to the extent that poor performance diminishes the credibility of other signals managers provide regarding their quality. Managers might not expect shareholders to reassess their quality negatively upon poor performance, especially if this was an industry-wide phenomenon, and therefore they might not believe that further signalling was necessary. Such perceptions by managers would be consistent with the fact that not all poorly performing firms are targeted by institutional investors. In this scenario, a shareholder proposal reveals information to managers regarding the market's updated perception of their quality, and thereby evokes further sorting in response.

It should be noted that all of the studies finding uniform positive price effects associated with private negotiations had sample periods ending in 1993. The negative reaction to private activism in the mid-1990s suggests that the self-selection induced by such activity now indicates low rather than high management quality. The change in the identity of proposal sponsors—from public pension funds to union funds—in conjunction with some change in the type of proposal—an increase in proposals on executive compensation—could explain the changed market perception of the negotiation process.[41] In addition, the cumulating of experience indicating that past negotiations did not improve performance might lead investors to reassess the significance of proposals as a screen: private negotiated activism, in this information updating scenario, is viewed as redirecting management's time and energy away from improving performance to less useful activities, and hence makes it more likely that low, rather than high, quality managers respond to investor initiatives. In these changed circumstances, the costly screen provided by high quality managers that low quality managers cannot duplicate is the *absence* of a response. This is plausible if a failure to respond to activism provides information to takeover bidders that the firm has a set of dissatisfied institutional investors who would be receptive to a bid, for low quality managers have more at risk from being the subjects of a hostile bid than high quality ones.

Alternatively, if the subsample firms experiencing negative valuation effects in the post-1992 samples had been targets of proposal negotiations previously, then the negative effect could be explained as a downward revision of prior beliefs regarding managerial quality because shareholders had to come back with additional proposals. The downward revision hypothesis is provided support by a study of proxy proposals by Prevost and Rao (2000), which subdivided firms between those receiving proposals sponsored by institutional investors known to engage in pre-submission negotiations, such as CalPERS, and other public fund investors, and then subdivided the activist investor targets between those receiving proposals over more than one year and those receiving proposals only once. Not only do Prevost and Rao find a significant negative price effect for the thirty-two proposals submitted by the activist funds and no significant effect for the overall sample, but they also find that the negative wealth effects last for much wider event intervals for the ten multiple year proposal firms than for the twenty-two single proposal firms.

Admittedly, the Prevost and Rao (2000) study's sample size is small. But the findings are consistent with the information updating explanation. The returns are significant only for proposals submitted by institutions whose pre-proposal activism is highly visible. These are situations in which the proposal's appearance on the proxy indicates to the market that management was not responsive to the investor, and the information effect is magnified for firms receiving multiple proposals.

Prevost and Rao's data suggest that in instances of multiple submissions, investors update their beliefs concerning management quality. Investors conclude that a persistently unresponsive management will be unwilling or unable to undertake necessary steps to improve firm value. That is, investors learn that the targets are firms with low quality management as the managers have not learned from their 'first exposure' to institutions' proposals on how to avert future submissions. Thus, they lower their expected valuation of the firm's future cash flows.

All of Prevost and Rao's findings of negative significance are independent of proposal category, further corroborating the information updating hypothesis compared to the value-maximizing explanation. Moreover, the expectation of poor performance due to low management quality offered as the interpretation of the more negative statistical results for multiple proposal firms is a rational expectation: that is, it is in fact borne out by subsequent data. Prevost and Rao report that both long-run stock returns and accounting measures of long-term performance decline significantly for the multiple proposal firms, but not for the single proposal firms. In short, managers who do not respond to institutional investors' concerns—managers of firms where proposals are actually submitted for a vote—are conjectured by investors to be managers of low quality, and that assessment is confirmed when a second proposal is submitted. And the screen is accurate: the longer-term subsequent performance of firms with such managers is worse.

Finally, where Carleton *et al.*'s (1998) study's results of significance differ from those of the shareholder proposal studies,[42] a signalling explanation seems especially apt at reconciling the differences, rather than a value-maximizing explanation of institutional activism. Carleton *et al.* found that private negotiations involving restrictions on poison pills had a positive impact, compared to the negative impact of antitakeover proposals (which were primarily poison pill rescission proposals) in the Smith (1996), and Gillan and Starks (2000) studies, and the marginally significant negative result in the Del Guercio and Hawkins (1999) study. Although Carleton *et al.*'s result is consistent with the initial empirical studies that found a negative wealth effect of poison pills, it is also consistent with a management quality updating explanation: Smith (1996), Gillan and Starks (2000), and

Del Guercio and Hawkins (1999), who do not find positive price effects, are examining submitted proposals whereas Carleton *et al.*, who find positive effects, are not. Thus, the management of the firms in Carleton *et al.*'s study could have been perceived as more responsive to investor concerns and thus less prone to entrenchment in the use of a poison pill defence, than those in the other three studies. In addition, CalPERS' activity in early years concentrated on defensive tactics, which is the period when Crutchley *et al.* (1998) found its activism had a positive price effect. It is, however, inconsistent with Smith's finding of a negative effect from defensive tactic activism by CalPERS, although this result was for an earlier time period than that covered by Carleton *et al.*'s study.

The value maximizing explanation could also explain the difference between the results on defensive tactic activism in Carleton *et al.* and the shareholder proposal studies on the rationale that, in contrast to other institutions, TIAA-CREF accurately targeted firms that would not be benefited by takeover defences, and all institutional targeting is aggregated in studies finding no price effect. It is more difficult for it to explain satisfactorily the finding that not all of TIAA-CREF's negotiations produce positive effects.

If, as the value-maximizing explanation maintains, management only negotiates over proposals that will improve performance, then either all of TIAA-CREF's negotiations should be positively assessed and not only poison pill negotiations, or management should not have entered into negotiations over the proposals that were not-value-maximizing (those for which the price effects were not positive). The mixed results in Carleton *et al.*'s study can be reconciled with the value-maximizing explanation of negotiations by maintaining that two of the three foci of TIAA-CREF's activism have very little impact on performance. This is consistent with this chapter's analysis of institutional activism and bolsters this chapter's conclusion that such activity needs to be reassessed.

I have elaborated and emphasized the information updating explanation over the value-maximization explanation of the findings in studies of nonproxy (negotiated) activism because it has far greater explanatory power, particularly with regard to the finding that private activism in recent years has had a negative effect. It reconciles more of the disparities across the entire set of shareholder activism studies than the value-maximizing explanation. Interpreting the price effect as information on management quality explains why a particular type of proposal may have a price effect when privately raised with management but not when appearing in a proxy, and why that effect might differ when management negotiates with a different type of institution. The positive price effect relates to management's quality, not any specific action that is being undertaken to improve performance. At the same time, the information updating explanation is consistent with the finding that targeted firms' long-term performance does not significantly improve, whatever the form of activism. Even a high quality management will not improve performance if it must direct its time and effort on implementing shareholders' proposals that have no effect on performance.

2.4. *Structural Changes Following Shareholder Activism*

In addition to examining the impact of activism on performance, some studies investigate whether firms engage in corporate restructuring or other governance reforms after they have been targeted by institutional investors. The rationale is that the undertaking of significant structural change by firms after a proxy targeting is an alternative means by which to gauge the success of shareholder activism. The assumption is that such changes will eventually improve performance. This scenario would provide a concrete basis for the signalling explanation of the positive returns to nonproxy activism: the market expects a more responsive management to adopt policies that will increase shareholder wealth, and the anticipation of such action explains the positive returns. It would, at best, provide only tangential support for the value-maximizing explanation of positive returns to nonproxy activism, because the price effect is supposed to be measuring the subject of the negotiations, which are not the restructuring transactions. The link for that explanation would be that the outcome of the negotiated agreements, such as a board composition change or a takeover defence rescission, produced the subsequent restructuring.

There is considerable divergence across studies concerning whether targeted firms make significant structural changes, such as fire the CEO or sell substantial assets. The differences would appear to be related to the studies' variation in findings concerning stock price performance. Karpoff *et al.* (1996), who found no stock price effects, find little evidence of policy changes in direct response to the proxy vote, and, in particular, that CEO turnover is not related to receipt of a shareholder proposal. The studies finding subsample positive stock price effects, however, tend to find an increase in the level of asset divestitures of the targeted firms. For instance, Smith (1996) finds no significant difference in CEO turnover in targeted firms compared to industry and performance control groups, but significantly higher sales of assets by the targeted firms. And Opler and Sokobin (1995) find a decrease in CEO turnover but an increase in asset sales after CII targeting. The fit is less exact with the results in Del Guercio and Hawkins (1999): they find significantly more newspaper reports of restructuring activity and increased employee, but not increased CEO, turnover in targeted firms compared to an industry and performance control group as well as for various subsamples, and increased CEO and employee turnover for the board proposal subsample, but neither the full sample nor the subsamples experiencing significant restructuring activity, had significant positive returns. Huson (1997) also finds that CalPERS targets engage in more asset divestitures than a set of control firms over three years subsequent to the targeting, although the control group is quite imprecise (the control firms are either smaller or better performers than the CalPERS targets); he does not, however, investigate the price effects of the targeting.

Finally it should be noted that while TIAA-CREF's activism was successful—Carleton *et al.* (1998) find that virtually all of the firms targeted by TIAA-CREF adapted their governance structures to accommodate the fund's objective—the changes in TIAA-CREF-targeted firms reported by Carleton *et al.* are less substantial than the structural changes examined in other studies, such as CEO turnover and asset dispositions. The responses to TIAA-CREF's activism consist of refinements to poison pill plans, establishment of confidential voting, and commitments to increase minority and female representation on boards. It is improbable that such modest adjustments to corporate policy affect performance by leading to the more substantive responses found in the other studies, a conclusion supported by the absence of positive significance for most of the TIAA-CREF negotiated settlements. The sole positive price effects subsample, the poison pill negotiations, raise the prospect of potential premiums, or future CEO change or asset sales if no bid is forthcoming, after a pill's relaxation.

Unfortunately, this hypothesis cannot be tested because Carleton *et al.* do not investigate whether the TIAA-CREF-targeted firms subsequently experienced any restructurings.

The suggestion of a three-way association among positive price effects, shareholder activism, and subsequent structural changes, is consistent with the research examining the impact on performance of the most substantial form of investor activism: proxy fights for control. Studies of proxy contests consistently find more favourable effects from this form of investor activism than do studies of shareholder proposals. The stock price reactions to proxy fights are significantly positive (whether or not the dissidents actually win).[43] Moreover, the contests have significant firm-level consequences: firms that are the subject of proxy fights for control typically experience top management turnover regardless of outcome and they are often sold or liquidated shortly thereafter (DeAngelo and DeAngelo 1989). This result—the high frequency of subsequent acquisition, restructuring or CEO change—in all likelihood accounts for the increase in value created by the initiation of a proxy fight compared to a proxy proposal. In fact, the most recent and most comprehensive study of proxy fights finds that most of the positive price effects of proxy contests are driven by firms that are acquired soon after the contest; when there is no acquisition, the gains in shareholder wealth from the proxy fight are sustained only by firms whose CEO is replaced (Mulherin and Poulsen 1998). And, of course, the literature is replete with the positive effect on target shareholder wealth from acquisitions (for a summary see Romano 1992).

From a cost-benefit perspective, it is not surprising that more restructuring occurs after proxy fights than after shareholder proposals, and that, accordingly, the performance effect of proxy fights is greater than that of proxy proposals. Proxy fights are a far more expensive form of shareholder activism than shareholder proposals and restructuring is typically the contestants' objective. The insignificant effect on performance of shareholder proposals may relate to the low-level efforts of investors engaging in such activism (e.g. Black 1998) compared to proxy fights. But while it is true that proxy proposal activism is inexpensive compared to proxy contests, the insignificant performance results of shareholder activism are, in my judgement, due to its objectives: independent boards, compensation limits, confidential voting and, albeit more ambiguously, poison pill rescissions, are not only inexpensive actions to undertake compared to the goals of a proxy fight or corporate takeover (division sales and top management change) but they are also corporate governance devices that do not have any measurable effect on share value.

3. IMPROVING THE IMPACT OF CORPORATE GOVERNANCE ACTIVISM

The striking absence of evidence that shareholder activism improves targeted firms' performance raises the core question whether institutions should reassess their shareholder proposal agenda, in order to manage their resources more effectively. This chapter takes a two-pronged approach to the issue. First, it suggests a mechanism of internal control, whereby fund boards would engage in periodic review of their staff's shareholder-activism programmes to identify the most fruitful governance objectives. Second, it advocates increasing the incentive to undertake internal evaluations by proposing elimination or substantial reduction of the subsidy of proxy proposal sponsorship unless a proposal achieves substantial voting support.

3.1. *Internal Controls: Refocusing Activist Programmes*

One means of reducing the likelihood that shareholder activism is non-value-maximizing activity is to improve the quality of decision-making by institutional investors by encouraging implementation of comprehensive, formal internal reviews of corporate governance programmes. Such reviews should include an evaluation of the empirical research relating to the objective of contemplated proposals or private negotiations, as well as the voting outcome of previously submitted proposals. The review should be forwarded to the fund board and not simply the officers or employees supervising activism programmes. This would enable a fund board to identify better what activity is worthwhile, facilitating the fulfilment of their fiduciary obligations to fund beneficiaries. A formal mechanism of reporting on a fund's activities and their effectiveness would put fund trustees and fund managers on a more equal footing and thus lessen the possibility that better-informed managers could rationalize an agenda to a board in terms of good corporate governance practices that consists, in fact, of non-value-enhancing proposals.

The formal review of corporate governance activities should also be incorporated in the fund's annual report or statement sent to beneficiaries or holders of fund shares. As a publicly available document, it will be of use to fund participants willing to expend the effort to monitor fund managers' efforts at enhancing the value of their portfolio. In addition, legislators and taxpayers who finance public pensions will also be better able to identify inappropriate expenditures that could affect the funding of plan assets for which they are legally liable.

What should be a fund's response to the proposed review? At minimum, proxy proposals that have a negative impact upon performance given the literature on corporate governance devices, such as those involving executive compensation limits, ought to be scrapped, in favour of those whose effect is at least arguably ambiguous, such as, proposals to relax takeover defences. Such a policy will also require the fund's staff to develop firm-specific knowledge to engage in activism: just as the empirical literature finds that the stock price effect of takeover defences varies with firm characteristics, such as board composition (Brickley *et al.* 1994) and firm size (Fields and Todd 1995), proposals to eliminate those defences would, accordingly, be more beneficial for some firms than others. If a fund does not possess adequate firm-specific knowledge, proposals whose impact is highly firm-dependent, such as takeover defence rescissions, ought to be discouraged. In fact, some institutional investors are aware of this problem and have adapted their governance activities accordingly. Del Guercio and Hawkins (1999: 305–6) note that the heavily-indexed New York City pension fund does not sponsor poison pill proposals because they 'require too much company-specific knowledge'.

Similarly, proxy proposals that receive little support from other investors (which not surprisingly and invariably are those whose substantive objectives produce the least positive impact on firm value) should be re-evaluated, with an eye to their elimination. The reasoning for such a criterion is that support levels are an excellent proxy for the judgement of other informed investors that the proposal is in their interest. Hence, proposals that obtain a higher level of voting support have a higher probability of being those that maximize share value. Only if shareholders' beliefs were biased concerning the value of a specific type of proposal, would the level of voting support not be an accurate proxy for the proposal's impact on performance. Given the large number and diversity of institutional investors and their information sources, systematic errors across investors over proposal valuation effects is, however, simply not a plausible scenario. The more plausible assumption is that shareholder mistakes on the value of a particular governance device are randomly distributed. In such a scenario, with a large number of voting shareholders, investor errors will cancel out and the proportion of yes votes is the best estimate of the proposal's value.

A case in point involves proposals on defensive tactics. Aboumeri (1997), for instance, notes that it is surprising that shareholders vote in large numbers to rescind poison pills despite his research showing substantial benefits from those defences. The literature on the impact of poison pills on takeovers is, however, ambiguous and, in particular, the effect appears to vary considerably with firm characteristics (e.g. Brickley *et al.* 1994). It is therefore altogether reasonable for investors to believe that the removal of a pill will be beneficial for some firms, and to support such proposals, notwithstanding Aboumeri's claim. There is, however, a possible non-random error in this context which would affect the significance attributable to voting results. If uninformed shareholders believe that the institutional sponsors of proposals on defensive tactics are informed about the relevant firm-level characteristics, and the sponsors are not so informed, then the proposals might attract more votes than justified at specific firms. The comprehensive review procedure would mitigate such a problem, for as institutions conscientiously engage in activist programme revaluations, they will thereafter undertake such proposals only when they have the requisite firm-specific knowledge.

Periodic programme review is also important because shareholder activism in the proxy process is not costless, even though it is certainly inexpensive compared to activism involving control changes. For example, CalPERS estimates the annual cost of its activism programme at $500,000, which is 0.002 per cent of the fund's domestic holdings (Smith 1996: 245). Del Guercio and Hawkins (1999: 328) indicate that the activist pension funds in their study similarly spent less than half of a basis point per year on their corporate governance programmes, with an expenditure range from $50,000 to $1 million. They also state that TIAA-CREF spends annually $1 million or 0.002 per cent of assets on its corporate governance programme. Other corporate governance strategies, such as voting against management proposals and board nominees of poorly-performing firms, are far cheaper to implement than an activist agenda; for instance, one estimate of the annual cost of a 'just vote no' programme is $100,000 (Grundfest 1993: 911).

Given the cost differential between active and passive mechanisms of monitoring management and the ineffectiveness of shareholder activism at improving corporate performance, from a fiduciary standpoint, fund managers ought to have to justify programme expenditures to their boards. Identifying which specific corporate structures or processes enhance share value by reference to readily available data, rather than wishful thinking concerning their probable effects, will improve the quality of decision-making and should produce corporate governance programmes which are consonant with the funds' fiduciary obligations. Although it could be contended that the expected decline in proposals due to adoption of such a thorough review process would reduce the information obtained regarding management quality from a proposal submission indicating failed negotiation, in fact, the effect would in all likelihood be heightened. Funds will shift to proposals that are more likely to obtain higher voting support, such as defensive tactic rescissions, and hence ones more costly for low quality managers to negotiate over.

The details of an appropriately enhanced system of internal control for a shareholder activism programme cannot be minutely specified. The reasons are two-fold: first, because the benefit of some corporate governance mechanisms varies with firm-specific characteristics, too minutely specified criteria would freeze a fund's ability to respond differentially to varying situations. Second, given the dynamic evolution of the corporate form and governance devices, it would not be prudent to advocate the termination of all corporate governance activism. Instead, a filter mechanism regarding the proposals the fund submits ought to be implemented, which takes account of the literature but which is sufficiently fluid to be able to adapt to new findings and circumstances.

Pension fund boards should find implementation of the proposed review process sufficiently desirable to do so voluntarily as a good management practice. But it might well be difficult for boards to evaluate their programmes' efficacy, as they are not likely to possess the requisite expertise. Inability to evaluate an activism programme effectively, in turn, might lead to hesitancy in adopting the proposed formal review process or implementing it effectively.

A potentially more important problem for implementation is a fund board that is subject to political pressure itself: board members are often political appointees or elected officials, who may support an activist agenda favoured by constituents, and be led to place less weight on concerns over portfolio value than other fiduciaries (Romano 1993*a*). Politicization of a fund board would greatly attenuate the incentive to undertake the proposed review. In such cases, implementing the review procedure may well be in the interest of the fund managers, for it could provide political cover for a manager focused on maximizing the value of portfolio firms from a politicized board whose members are instead interested in implementing political and social investment objectives. This has been a problem, for instance, for the CalPERS staff. Politicians on the fund's board recently advanced an investment policy opposed by the staff for financial reasons, tobacco stock divestment, and the staff recommended amending proposed divestiture legislation supported by the State Treasurer, a fund board member, to include indemnification for 'board members, money managers and others connected with the fund from potential liabilities' from implementing the policy if the bill were enacted (Chernoff 2000*a*). Indeed, the political composition of the CalPERS board is considered to affect 'every single activity' of the fund, 'from the benefits side to investment policy to corporate governance' (Chernoff 2000*b*). To the extent that the source of non-value-maximizing activism is fund boards and not fund managers, it would be in the managers' self-interest to implement the proposed review procedure that provides external evaluations to the fund board, as it would be a shield against potential fiduciary liability.

There are a number of possible avenues for achieving widespread adoption of adequate internal control practices despite deficiencies in expertise or incentives within a fund's administration, the most promising being the promulgation of good practice standards by industry associations. If the Government Finance Officers Association (GFOA) or the Investment Company Institute (ICI), the trade groups for public pension fund officials and private mutual funds, respectively, for example, were to adopt good practice guidelines that included comprehensive evaluations of shareholder activism programmes, this would have a salutary impact on individual fund practices. External pressure generated by reputable organizations' recommendation of a serious review process could mitigate political pressures on board members to not conform to the practice. It would surely be a source of support to fund managers seeking to fulfil their fiduciary obligations against a politicized board.

The CII and national union organizations such as the AFL-CIO, which have been active promoters and co-ordinators of the corporate governance movement, could also perform such a guidance function. In addition, private organizations, including business trade organizations such as the Business Roundtable, the National Association of Corporate Directors, and the Conference Board, the corporate bar, stock exchanges and public accounting firms, could be recruited to formulate standards for shareholder activism programmes. All of these private business organizations have already been involved in varying degrees in devising recommendations for corporate governance standards for boards of directors and audit committees.[44]

The involvement of private sector organizations in the establishment of good practices is important because government entities are rarely as knowledgeable as private organizations regarding the best institutional procedures. The gap in expertise between regulators and the regulated is well illustrated by what has occurred in the establishment of international capital standards for banks. In the most recent international capital standard adopted for market risk, banking regulators have acknowledged that they lag significantly behind the banking industry in risk measurement expertise: they adopted an internal model approach to the calculation of market risk, in which the bank's, rather than the regulator's, model estimates the value at risk in the bank's portfolio and therefore establishes the amount of capital required (Federal Reserve System 1996).

An alternative route for attaining widespread formal review of fund activism is to mandate the review through a certification requirement: funds could be required to obtain a letter from an independent third party, such as the firm's auditor, on a periodic basis, certifying that the institution has undertaken a comprehensive review of its activism programme.[45] Certification of such a process is altogether reasonable, and in accord with current trends in auditing, in particular, the movement to certify processes rather than transactions or outputs (items that are verifiable quantitatively and hence the substance of traditional audits) (e.g. Dennis 1997; KPMG 1999*b*). Moreover, accounting firms in recent years have been required to review a variety of qualitative information concerning firms' internal controls, including issues such as year 2K compliance, and they have increasingly been marketing their auditing services as 'assurance services', through which they express a willingness to certify matters beyond financial accounting data during an audit.[46]

In addition, a special committee of the American Institute of Certified Public Accountants (AICPA) created in 1994 to report on the 'current state and future' of audit and assurance services, defined 'assurance services' as 'independent professional services that improve the quality of information, or its content, for decision makers' (AICPA 1997). It proposed examples of assurance services that comport with certification of activism programme reviews: the examples of assurance regarding compliance with company policies and assurance regarding investment managers' conformity with performance presentation standards. Quite clearly, evaluation of the effectiveness of a review of corporate governance programmes is no less certifiable by an auditor than the other nonfinancial matters that auditing firms have undertaken in recent years. Indeed, auditors' experience in such areas makes them better suited to undertake a certifying function than other professionals with expertise in the proxy process, such as lawyers and consulting firms. To the extent that standards of good practices for activist programmes are developed, the accountants could certify whether the fund was in compliance with such standards, and not simply that it has engaged in a comprehensive review.

If fund regulators required certification of reviews of activism programmes,[47] then institutional investors plainly would have to undertake the necessary evaluative reviews, but the varied identity of proposal sponsors and potential sponsors renders implementation of a uniform certification requirement problematic. Not only are public pension funds regulated by state legislatures, but also, union pension funds are regulated by the Department of Labor (DoL)[48] while mutual funds, which have not been involved in corporate governance activism but have been encouraged to do so,[49] are regulated by the SEC.[50] Moreover, in the absence of a promulgated standard of good practices, the certification requirement will not provide very effective protection for fund beneficiaries, for the independent third party verifies only the undertaking of a comprehensive review, and not the outcome—the efficacy of the fund's programme. These concerns suggest the need to craft an additional mechanism to ensure that fund managers' incentives are aligned with engaging in an investor activism programme that maximizes the value of the fund's portfolio.

3.2. *External Controls: Shifting the Financial Burden of Shareholder Proposals*

Beyond the difficulty of implementing a certification requirement to ensure compliance with the proposed comprehensive review of activism programmes, there is a further problem with relying solely on internal controls to resolve fund beneficiaries' problem that fund activist programmes are not cost-effective. Because the most active funds are public pension funds that are defined benefit plans, the beneficiaries' payouts are independent of the funds' endowment. Hence, fund managers will not have powerful incentives to adopt comprehensive evaluations even if some funds would for fear of adverse signalling, since their beneficiaries are not as actively monitoring fund performance as are shareholders of mutual funds. Politicians are also not likely to target fund activism out of concern about taxpayer expense as the expenditures on such activities are relatively small and some non-value-maximizing forms of activism may actually provide political benefits: limiting executive compensation has, for instance, been a perennial focus of Congressional attention.[51] Consequently, another mechanism is necessary to provide incentives to public pension fund managers and boards.

One means of providing an incentive to fund managers to engage in more cost-effective forms of activism is to eliminate the subsidy of losing proposals under the SEC's proxy proposal rules. If funds incur the cost of a losing proposal, then the fund managers will have to scrutinize, on a continuing basis, the fund's corporate governance programme, to determine which proposals are most likely to attract voting support, because their cash position will be affected if they do not. Admittedly, the incentive created by this proposal is low-powered, as fund beneficiaries are not likely to be able to monitor fund outflows or budget reallocations due to a poorly performing corporate governance programme. But over time the expenses from losing proposal reimbursements will affect fund performance, and the fund board will have increased incentives to intervene. Such board action is in the fund manager's interest to avoid, as it could have adverse employment repercussions beyond the immediate curtailment of discretion upon the intervention, and managers anticipating the possibility of such action will adjust their behaviour regarding shareholder proposals from the outset.

3.2.1. *Should Proxy Proposals be Subsidized?*

It is textbook economics that parties bearing the full cost of their actions make better decisions than those that do not. When a person does not bear the full cost of his or her activity, they will engage in more of the activity, for in equating the marginal benefits and costs of the enterprise, a lower level of benefit from the activity suffices to meet the reduced cost. But under the shareholder proposal regime, this analysis is generally thought to be overridden by collective action concerns. Namely, if the cost of action by an individual shareholder is greater than the shareholder's pro rata benefit albeit less than the aggregate gain to all shareholders, the activity will be under-, rather than over-supplied. The proxy proposal regime assumes that this is the proper calculation of the costs and benefits of shareholder proposals.

Where there are private benefits from the shareholder's action, that is, benefits that accrue solely to the proposal sponsor and that are not proportionately shared by all shareholders as is the case with an increase in firm value, then matching pro-rated costs and benefits will not produce the optimal level of activity. This is because when costs are allocated across all shareholders, small private benefits will induce individual action that does not benefit shareholders in the aggregate.[52]

It is quite probable that private benefits accrue to some investors from sponsoring at least some shareholder proposals. The disparity in identity of sponsors—the predominance of public and union funds, which, in contrast to private sector funds, are not in competition for investor dollars—is strongly suggestive of their presence. Examples of potential benefits which would be disproportionately of interest to proposal sponsors are progress on labour rights desired by union fund managers, and enhanced political reputations for public pension fund managers,[53] as well as advancements in personal employment, the 'revolving door' issue for government employees, whose salaries are considerably lower than the private sector. It is possible that engaging in activism will enhance an individual's subsequent job opportunities, analogous to suggestions that prosecutors bring high profile criminal cases either to further political careers or partnerships in top criminal defence firms, a charge directed at the white collar crime prosecutions brought by Rudolph Guliani, a US attorney who later became Mayor of New York, and others in his office who went on to prominent law firms (Fischel 1995: 98–102, 302–3). For example, a top official involved in CalPERS' corporate governance programme, Richard Koppes, joined a law firm that advises management on takeover defences after leaving the fund. As such career concerns—enhancement of political reputations or subsequent employment opportunities—do not provide a commensurate benefit to private fund managers, we do not find them engaging in investor activism.

The private benefits implicated in career concerns also have a higher likelihood of being present in certain classes of proposals than others. For example, proposals to limit executive compensation and increase board diversity, appealing to populist sentiment or the political preferences of some constituents, are more likely to enhance political reputations for fund managers than confidential voting or takeover defence rescission proposals. There is far greater media publicity surrounding executive compensation and minority representation issues, and these proposals implicate the kinds of social issues on which political reputations can be advanced, in contrast to more mundane corporate governance devices.[54] This conjecture has plausibility given the far lower level of voting support for executive compensation and board proposals compared to confidential voting and defensive tactic proposals by those who have a financial stake in firms.

A broader set of proposals—all those making managers' life more uncomfortable—may provide private benefits to union fund managers seeking a more accommodating management; these include proposals rescinding takeover tactics as well as proposals to limit executive pay and enhance board independence. But the takeover defence proposals may also be offered strategically, to gain support and goodwill from other investors that is hoped will carry over to future issues of greater importance to labour. Although such a carryover is a 'private' benefit to the union, it is not a 'private' benefit in the strict sense because any gain from the specific proposal, such as an increase in stock value from rescission of a poison pill, is a pro rata gain.

Although it may have had relevance historically, the rationale advanced for the shareholder proposal rule's subsidization of sponsors' costs, a collective action problem, has little relevance for contemporary capital markets, in which a majority of shares is held by institutional investors (Brancato 1997: 19–20). Institutional investors own large blocks of stock and often cannot sell shares in a poorly managed firm because their fund is indexed to a portfolio including that firm. Consequently, they experience far less of a free rider problem than the individual shareholder whose hypothesized dilemma motivated adoption of a cost-subsidization regime.

In addition, there are a number of organizations, such as the CII, the IRRC, and the Institutional Shareholders Service (ISS), which is a private consulting firm that provides advice on proxy voting and other voting services to institutional investors, that collect and disseminate information to institutional investors concerning corporate governance issues, which further reduces the need for a regulatory solution to a hypothesized collective action problem. The AFL-CIO has also published a detailed set of voting guidelines for union funds (IRRC 1998*a*) and the possibilities of inexpensive and widespread dissemination of information through the Internet are already present and potentially enormous. Besides the websites of the AFL-CIO, CalPERS, CII, and other organizations that detail their corporate governance activities, some small activist funds are posting on their websites how they have voted their proxies and are encouraging use of their sites to facilitate individual shareholder participation in an activist agenda (IRRC 1999*b*).

3.2.2. *Proposed Reform of the Proposal Process*

Subsidization is not necessary for active use of the proxy process by investors and, in fact, it has created perverse incentives for institutional investors, as the best available data suggest that fund managers are not using the proposal process in the furtherance of the best interest of their beneficiaries.[55] This chapter accordingly advocates revising the present proxy proposal regime to reduce such incentives. It presents three alternative approaches that would all have the salutary effect of changing funds' incentives by reducing the subsidy: (i) adoption of a vote cut-off below which the sponsor must fully reimburse the firm for the cost of submitting the proposal; (ii) use of a sliding scale of reimbursement depending on the level of votes obtained; and (iii) shareholder selection of the extent of subsidization of proposals. The third option is my preferred approach, but in contrast to the other two proposals, it is at odds with the mandatory approach of the SEC rules.

The proposition that shareholders should finance their proposals is not a novel idea. Commentators writing in the 1980s critiqued the shareholder proposal subsidy, contending that the mismatched incentives for individual shareholders arising from the subsidy were greater than the benefits from reducing free rider problems (e.g. Fischel 1982; Leibeler 1984; Dent 1985). In particular, these commentators emphasized the extremely low voting support for the proposals and the small number of 'professional gadfly' individual sponsors. Although the critique of the regime necessarily differed in the 1980s' context of individual sponsors and low support levels, the policy position is equally apt today in the quite different landscape of institutions' higher-support-generating proposals.

In particular, the essential incentive mismatch of the rule identified by earlier critiques is as relevant for institutional as it is for individual investors, given the opportunity for fund managers to obtain private benefits from proposal sponsorship. If institutional sponsors obtain private benefits, then not only is there even less cause for other shareholders to subsidize such activity, but also, special cause for concern: such benefits accrue to the fund manager and not the fund beneficiaries, who are in a similar position to that of the other shareholders, as they benefit solely from proposals producing performance improvements. Moreover, the free rider problem justifying subsidization of individual investor action is mitigated for institutions given their larger ownership positions and their participation in trade organizations that assemble detailed information on governance issues. Finally, the corporate finance literature, which was not available to the 1980s commentators, strongly bolsters the case for altering the policy of subsidized access to the proxy machinery because it indicates persuasively that proposal sponsors are frequently not pursuing a value-maximizing agenda.

Critics of the shareholder proposal regime have advocated repeal of the entire SEC rule governing proxy proposals (e.g. Leibeler 1984; Dent 1985). Complete repeal may well be a worthy ideal, as voting rules are more properly issues of state corporate law than federal securities law,[56] and securities regulation would be better served by a competitive state regime rather than the current federal regulatory monopoly.[57] But such a reform goes well beyond the immediate problem identified in this chapter, which is the absence of incentives for proposal sponsors, and more specifically, public fund managers, to increase the efficacy of their corporate governance activities within the contours of the existing shareholder proposal regime. This chapter focuses on the one piece of the proxy proposal regime that, if altered, would have the greatest impact on institutional activism because it will have the greatest incentive effect, the subsidization of shareholder proposals.

The first proposal is elimination of the subsidy, unless the proposal gains substantial support. Such an approach is consistent with the state law approach to the collective action problem: proxy contestants must pay their own expenses, although shareholders may approve successful challengers' expenditures *ex post.*[58] The strongest source of support for such a reform is the fact that the state law approach to cost recovery has been far more successful than the federal proxy regime in aligning individual shareholders' incentives with the aggregate interest. In contrast to the shareholder proposal regime, proxy fights are not devoted to social issues tangentially related to corporate governance or to inconsequential structural reforms that have no relation to the profitability of corporate operations. More importantly, they result in significant improvements in firm performance while shareholder proposals do not. The superior outcome from the operation of state law should not be surprising: the competition across states for corporate charters produces laws that tend to enhance shareholder welfare, and the absence of competition in the federal securities regime renders it considerably less responsive to investors' concerns, and therefore less likely to produce wealth-maximizing rules (e.g. Romano 1993*b*; Easterbrook and Fischel 1991: 81–4).

Absolute success (50 per cent), the state law proxy expense reimbursements standard, need not be the standard for retention of full subsidization of the proposal. Rather, an appropriate benchmark for success could be 40 per cent, by analogy to success in the takeover process. Hostile takeovers which offer shareholders a substantial premium for tendering, for example, rarely obtain 100 per cent of outstanding shares but rather, more typically obtain 75 per cent, as there are inevitably shareholders who cannot or do not tender their shares in time; the number of tendered shares rises to over 85 per cent when the bidder's pre-offer shareholdings are included (see Comment and Jarrell 1987: 301). A 40 per cent success rate for proxy proposal reimbursement is therefore roughly equivalent to the tendering rate in the average successful takeover (that is, it is 80 per cent of 50 per cent).

A 40 per cent support cut-off level for reimbursement is advanced as a reference point for discussion, with the caveat that too low a reimbursement threshold will discourage institutions' scrutiny of the efficacy of their activism, leaving too much room for the sponsorship of proposals whose private benefits outweigh aggregate gains.[59] An alternative approach that could work as well is a sliding scale of proportional reimbursement: the successful proponent is fully reimbursed, and thereafter, the reimbursement rate is proportionate to the votes received in relation to the votes necessary for success. Thus, the sponsor whose proposal obtains a 40 per cent vote share does not have free access but rather, pays 20 per cent of the proposal's costs (that is, the reimbursement is the ratio of 40 per cent of 50 per cent). However, the sliding scale approach could also incorporate the 40 per cent level of the first (cut-off) approach as the measure of 'success' for free access, and proportionately reduce the subsidy for vote levels below 40 per cent. Under this second approach, a proposal sponsor always receives some cost subsidization (the subsidy is reduced, but never eliminated completely).

A relaxed standard of success for proposal reimbursement (less than 40 per cent or the sliding scale approach) would be appropriate despite the significantly higher threshold at state law for proxy fight expenditure reimbursement, if the potential private benefits to proponents of shareholder proposals are far lower than the private benefits realizable to proxy fight contestants. In such a scenario, the adverse incentive effect of subsidization due to a divergence in private and social benefits would be reduced. For example, if private benefits are non-existent, the proposals offered would uniformly be expected to increase share value (but we would also expect such proposals to receive high levels of support). There is, however, no compelling reason to expect private benefits to be close to zero in the shareholder proposal context, particularly given institutions' continued pursuit of specific proposals despite an absence of any performance effects, the glaring disparity across the types of institutions—public rather than private funds—that engage in such activity, and the failure of the vast majority of proposals to receive even close to a majority of the votes. Accordingly, setting a meaningful threshold for proposal subsidization is highly desirable.

In addition, to the extent that the social benefits of the proposal are significant compared to private benefits, more shareholders can be expected to vote for the proposal. In this regard, establishing a sufficiently high voting threshold is a means of ensuring the proper private–social benefit calculation by the proposal sponsor. While the private costs of a corporate governance proposal are not likely to vary with the substance of the proposal, the private benefits may well do so.

The first two approaches to reduce the shareholder proposal subsidy (whether achieved by a specified cut-off, such as 40 per cent, for obtaining any reimbursement or through a sliding scale reduction in reimbursement amount) have the all-or-nothing approach of all SEC rules: they are mandatory regulations applicable to all issuers. But a third approach, which I find more attractive, is to permit firms, by shareholder vote, to choose their proxy proposal regime, opting from among full, partial, or no subsidy regimes, for all or some proposals or proposal sponsors. Such an optional approach would, in fact, mesh with the enabling feature of state corporate law, and in this respect is a more fitting approach for proxy procedures than a mandatory rule, because the proxy process (voting) is integrally related to a corporation's internal affairs, the subject matter of state law, which recognizes the necessity for firms to tailor governance devices to their particular needs.

It is not at all self-evident that elimination of the subsidy for shareholder proposals will emerge as the most prevalent choice of issuers under an optional proposal regime.[60] Institutional investors who engage in corporate activism will not be predisposed to opt for a regime that eliminates the current subsidy of their activity. However, as activist shareholders hold only a small proportion of any corporation's stock, they will need the support of other shareholders to maintain a full subsidization regime. Hence, the benefit of an optional approach to the proxy process is that the decision to subsidize proposals will be voluntarily rendered by the firm's stockholders as a group, rather than imposed upon them by SEC fiat. Of course, the pension fund beneficiaries who bear the cost of institutional activism that is non-value-maximizing will not benefit from this approach if the majority of a firm's investors do not wish to withdraw the subsidy.

None of the alternative reimbursement proposals explicitly requires management to reimburse the corporation for shareholder proposals it opposes that are adopted, or for management proposals that are defeated. It might be desirable to have symmetrical treatment, as there is no reason for shareholders to incur expenditures by management opposing proposals that they support, or proposing matters that they do not wish to be implemented. The potential loss of the screening value of a proposal's submission compared to private negotiations that could result from a reduction in proposal activity when proposal sponsors are at risk of loss of the subsidy will not, however, be offset by symmetrical reimbursement treatment for managers. This is because if managers bear a personal cost upon their position's defeat they should be more willing to negotiate over a proposal's withdrawal (that is, requiring managerial reimbursement enhances the shareholder–sponsor's bargaining position), regardless of the manager's quality.

There are two principal reasons not to mandate a symmetrical requirement of management reimbursement. First, it is impossible to implement and police such a requirement because such reimbursements can be easily covered by increased compensation to the managers without detection. Second, the rationale for permitting managers to respond to a shareholder proposal, as well as to submit proposals, provision of information to shareholders from those better-situated to identify benefits and costs of specific proposals, cuts against charging management for losing proposals. The financial risk imposed by a reimbursement requirement may result in a reduction of the information management provides shareholders regarding proposals. The reasons for not mandating a managerial reimbursement requirement are further arguments in favour of the optional approach to proposal subsidization: given the trade-off entailed by a policy of managerial reimbursement, the appropriate choice may well vary across firms, making it preferable to permit each firm's investors to choose whether to treat managers and shareholders symmetrically with regard to the cost of proposals.

Finally, because the determination of a proposal sponsor's required reimbursement occurs after the firm has incurred the proposal's submission costs, there is a problem regarding enforcement. Namely, there must be a method of ensuring that a sponsor of a losing proposal pays the firm the requisite reimbursement amount.

There are, at least, two possible solutions to this problem. One approach is to require that proposal sponsors post a bond, analogous to securities-for-expenses statutes in state corporation codes, which require the plaintiff in a shareholder suit to post a bond to cover defence costs should the plaintiff lose.[61] The size of the bond would vary according to which of the three reimbursement schemes were adopted and could vary based on the substance of the proposal, using as a benchmark the expected vote given historical voting data across firms by proposal types. A second approach is to precondition the right to submit a proposal upon the stockholder's not having any outstanding reimbursement due to a firm from a losing proposal. This condition would be added to the other eligibility criteria in Rule 14a-8, the continuous ownership of a specified amount of stock.[62]

The first approach, posting a bond, has a higher likelihood of restricting the use of the proposal process by small-resource organizations and individual investors, compared to the second approach, as they need to have cash on hand in advance of a proposal's submission. It is thus probable that it will be subject to greater criticism than the reimbursement proposal itself for chilling proposals. But it is the preferable approach, because the second approach creates additional enforcement problems.

In particular, a ban on subsequent proposals would have to apply to all proposals to be offered at any firm in the future and not simply proposals at the firm that was not reimbursed. Otherwise, a shareholder could repeatedly put up losing proposals by choosing a new target, without ever having to make a reimbursement payment. While the specific firm that has not been reimbursed by a particular sponsor would be able to enforce the approach because it knows who has not paid a bill, it would be no simple task for other firms to determine whether a shareholder proposal proponent was in default to another firm. The SEC would have to create and maintain an elaborate national registry for issuers to report delinquent proposal proponents, and make it accessible to all registrants to track potential proposal sponsors (or have agency staff enforce the reimbursement requirement, a costly arrangement).

In addition, the subsequent proposal ban approach may be subject to abuse due to a sponsor identification problem. Some organizations, most typically union funds whose members hold shares in their individual capacity, use individual shareholders to sponsor their proposals. These organizations would then not be subject to the subsequent prohibition, even though they had supported losing proposals that were not reimbursed, because they could continue to engage in activism by finding new individual sponsors. It would be exceedingly difficult, however, to apply the subsequent proposal ban to an entity other than the official sponsor of a losing proposal (the individual in these instances), as it could result in unwieldy litigation over whether or not a shareholder was acting independently, and the point of the reform is to rationalize and render more effective the shareholder proposal regime. Indeed, the precondition of payment before another proposal can be proffered could generate additional subjects of litigation, such as, disputes over the assessed cost of a losing proposal, as payment of the assessed amount determines the right of the shareholder to engage in subsequent activism. All of these concerns render the posting of a bond a more cost-effective mechanism than subsequent proposal prohibition for ensuring that the reform to end the subsidy has bite—that the sponsors of losing proposals bear their cost.

3.2.3. *Would Reducing the Shareholder Proposal Subsidy be Effective?*

Would a shift in the cost of the shareholder proposal regime in fact create an incentive for institutional investors to engage in a comprehensive evaluation of their activism programmes? The data on corporate expenditures on shareholder proposals are sketchy and imprecise, but the best and only available estimate suggests that eliminating the subsidy would have a salutary incentive effect. The data source of the estimate is the SEC. In a 1998 release regarding proposed reforms of the proxy proposal rule, the SEC indicated that respondents to a 1997 agency-administered questionnaire reported an average (median) expenditure of approximately $50,000 ($10,000) on printing, distribution and tabulation costs for including a shareholder proposal, and $37,000 ($10,000) on the determination whether to include a proposal.[63]

The mean estimates submitted to the SEC imply that eliminating the subsidization of shareholder proposals would add almost 20 per cent to CalPERS' current expenditures on its activist programme with just one proposal failure. Such an effect should provide an impetus to the CalPERS staff to fine-tune its programme. Using the lower median cost estimate of $20,000 instead of the average estimate of $87,000, incentives for the staff to be more selective regarding proposal sponsorship would be more attenuated, as it would require CalPERS to incur at least four defeats under a full subsidy elimination regime to approach the 20 per cent mark.

In actual practice, the impact of the reform on a fund like CalPERS would be quite variable because its record of success varies considerably: in 1998, for instance, CalPERS sponsored four proposals, only one of which obtained more than 40 per cent of the votes (IRRC 1998*b*), whereas in 1995 it sponsored only two proposals, both of which met the 40 per cent test (IRRC 1995). Thus, under the first approach with a 40 per cent cut-off for reimbursement, CalPERS' 1998 activism would have cost between 12 per cent to 52 per cent of its activism budget, depending on whether the median or mean SEC estimate is used as the reimbursement benchmark, while its 1995 agenda would have had no cost impact. Under the partial reimbursement of the second proposed approach, the cost of CalPERS' activism would obviously be less, and hence the incentive to review that activity seriously would be that much weaker.

Clearly the incentive provided by the proposed reform will depend on the cost that a losing proposal sponsor must pay, as well as the extent of the investor's activism programme. But unless the investor's demand for activism is inelastic, a dubious proposition given conventional economic assumptions, the reform will result in its sponsoring fewer proposals, or retaining the same number but being more selective concerning which proposals are submitted, as either approach (full or partial reimbursement) will raise the cost of activism that does not have broad support across shareholders. Either adjustment in fund behaviour will have a similar outcome: there will be fewer instances of low-vote-attracting proposals.

For a more comprehensive perspective on the costs of the shareholder proposal process of the proposed reforms, the effect of the proposed subsidy reduction was estimated for shareholder proposals submitted in 1997 and 1998. The IRRC (1999*c*; 1998*c*) reported the voting results for 254 of 255 shareholder proposals on corporate governance submitted to 175 firms in 1998, and for 283 proposals submitted to 179 firms in 1997. The absolute number of proposals receiving over 50 per cent of the votes cast is about the same in the two years, 32 and 31, respectively, and an additional 26 (28) proposals in 1998 (1997) received at least 40 per cent of the votes, the proposed cut-off for sponsors' full reimbursement. Thus, a 40 per cent cut-off would result in reimbursement of 23 per cent of the 1998 submitted proposals (21 per cent of 1997 proposals).

The average level of support was 26 per cent in 1998 and 24 per cent in 1997, an increase of 2 per cent, similar to the annual increase in support for shareholder proposals on defensive tactics reported by organizations collecting voting data, such as the IRRC (1998*d*) and the proxy solicitation firm, Georgeson and Company (1998). The medians reveal a similar increase, 20.3 per cent in 1997 compared to 23 per cent in 1998. Thus, a 20 per cent vote cut-off for subsidization would cover half of the proposals submitted in these two years. The bottom quartile of the distribution of votes on shareholder proposals in 1998 (1997) consists of proposals with less than 10 per cent (9 per cent) of the votes cast.

The cost of the shareholder proposal regime, using the SEC estimates for the 1998 data, is indicated in Table 23.2 in the 0 per cent cut-off row in the table (the current regime subsidizes all proposals), as is the cost of a reformed regime under a variety of vote cut-off levels.[64] As the table indicates, the cost is non-trivial from the point of view of individual proposal sponsors who would otherwise be paying these amounts, but not when compared to the aggregate market value of publicly traded firms. To determine the subsidy for proposals not attracting a majority, the 50 per cent cut-off row estimates are subtracted from

Table 23.2. *Estimated cost of shareholder proposal regime 1997–8*

Vote cut-off for subsidy (%)	No. of proposals in 1997	No. of proposals in 1998	Subsidy extent ($mill.) 1997	Subsidy extent ($mill.) 1998
Panel A: Corporate governance proposals				
50	31	32	$2.7 ($.6)	$2.8 ($.6)
40	59	58	$5 ($1.2)	$5 ($1.2)
30	94	91	$8.2 ($1.9)	$7.9 ($1.8)
20	142	141	$12.4 ($2.8)	$12.3 ($2.8)
10	196	188	$17.1 ($3.9)	$16.4 ($3.8)
0	283	254	$24.6 ($5.7)	$22.1 ($5.1)
Panel B: Social responsibility proposals				
50	0	0	0	0
40	0	0	0	0
30	0	1	0	$.09 ($.02)
20	0	2	0	$.2 ($.04)
10	14	16	$1.2 ($0.3)	$1.4 ($0.3)
0	95	104	$8.3 ($1.9)	$9.1 ($2.1)

Data Sources: IRRC Corporate Governance Service, Voting Results 1997 (1998); IRRC Corporate Governance Service, Voting Results 1998 (1999); IRRC Social Policy Shareholder Resolutions in 1997: Issues, Votes and Views of Institutional Investors (Jan. 1998); and IRRC Social Policy Shareholder Resolutions in 1998: Issues, Votes and Views of Institutional Investors (Jan. 1999). Proposals covered by both IRRC services are included in panel A, corporate governance proposals. Average cost estimates per proposal of $87,000 (median cost estimate per proposal of $20,000) were obtained from a survey of issuers by the Securities and Exchange Commission, reported in Amendments to Rules on Shareholder Proposals, Release No. 34-40,018, 63 Fed. Reg. 29,106, 29,114 (28 May 1998).

those in the 0 per cent cut-off row; this provides an estimate of $22 million in 1997 and $19 million in 1998, using the SEC's mean estimate of $87,000 in corporate expenditures per proposal, for an average over the two years of nearly $21 million. Averaging over the two years, the subsidy ranges from approximately $18 million to $7 million, for a vote cut-off of 40 per cent and 10 per cent respectively, which approximate the top and lower quartiles of the distribution of votes cast.[65] Another way to express this result is that elimination of the subsidy for proposals that fail to obtain 40 per cent of the votes would save targeted firms an estimated $18 million annually.

The estimate of the cost of the shareholder proposal regime is greater when social responsibility proposals are included in the calculation: although fewer in number than corporate governance proposals, these proposals receive far lower levels of support. The second panel in Table 23.2 contains a parallel calculation of the cost of the subsidy for social responsibility proposals submitted in 1997 and 1998.[66] As no such proposal received a majority of the votes, the subsidy for proposals not attracting a majority is simply the estimate in the 0 per cent cut-off row, $9.1 million in 1998 and $8.3 million in 1997, respectively, using, as before, the SEC's mean proposal expenditure estimate of $87,000. Combining the estimated cost of these proposals with that of the corporate governance proposals, using a voting cut-off of either 40 per cent or 10 per cent and averaging the cost over the two years, results in an estimated cost savings that ranges from $27 million to $14 million.

As this calculation, shown in Table 23.2, indicates, the proposed elimination or reduction of the subsidy of shareholder proposals should have a much greater impact on social responsibility proposals than corporate governance proposals because such proposals receive much lower levels of support. But this would be a felicitous outcome from the viewpoint of corporate law as social responsibility proposals are not directed at improving corporate performance, which is the aim of corporate law. Indeed, the SEC's approach to such shareholder proposals perversely stands corporate law on its head, because it permits a minority of shareholders to dictate the expenditure of corporate funds for non-profit-maximizing uses when core principles of corporate law require unanimity for waste of assets, and prohibit reimbursement of proxy expenses for contests undertaken for personal reasons.[67] That is one reason why these proposals one included in this chapter's recommended reform, despite the focus only on corporate governance proposals. The other reason for their inclusion is to mitigate shareholder efforts to avoid the subsidy reduction by rephrasing corporate governance proposals as social responsibility proposals. An additional attractive benefit of the third reform option, shareholder selection of the proposal regime, is that it returns the proxy process to the corporate law decision-making norm, whereby the minority is bound by the majority,[68] as a majority of the shareholders would choose the extent of the subsidization of shareholder proposals. In short, it, as well as the alternative proposed reforms, would put an end to what has been an egregious abuse of the proxy process.

The average cost per firm in 1998 of corporate governance proposals is approximately $126,000, and in 1997, it is $140,000. The 1998 average cost falls to $110,000 and $97,000 if proposals obtaining 50 per cent and 40 per cent of the votes, respectively, are excluded. The comparable figures for 1997 are $123,000 and $109,000 respectively. But as two-thirds of the firms received only one corporate governance proposal in each year, their estimated expenditure is $87,000. To understand the robustness of these figures, we need to consider the distribution of proposals obtaining a majority of the votes, as these proposals should be subsidized by the regime. The distribution of corporate governance proposals across firms by year and voting support is reported in Table 23.3.[69] Of the firms receiving only one corporate governance proposal, in both years, 13 firms' proposals obtained a majority of the votes cast. Of the firms experiencing multiple corporate governance proposals, over the two years, the proposals of only three firms all obtained over 50 per cent of the votes (8 proposals). For most of the firms receiving more than one proposal, no proposal obtained 50 per cent of the votes (55 of 67 such firms in 1997 and 39 of 55 in 1998). This means that the cost of the regime to multiple proposal firms is much higher than the estimated average, reaching as high as $435,000 for the 2 firms in 1998 with 5 proposals, and $348,000 for 2 firms with 4 proposals in 1997, none of which obtained 50 per cent of the votes.

The distribution pattern is similar if the vote cut-off is 40 per cent: while 9 (14) more single proposal and 13 (11) more multiple proposal firms meet this criterion in 1998 (1997), again, most of the additional multiple proposal firms had only one proposal that obtained over 40 per cent of the votes (10 in 1998 and 9 in 1997). Of course, the cost estimates are conservative because none of the estimates, whether by firm or in the aggregate, include the

Table 23.3. *Distribution of corporate governance proposals by firm and voting support 1997–8*

No. of proposals	No. of firms, 1997	No. of firms with 50% (40%) proposals, 1997	No. of firms, 1998	No. of firms with 50% (40%) proposals, 1998
1	112	13 (14)	120	13 (9)
2	40	4 (7)	38	14 (8)*
3	21	6 (1)*	11	1 (5)
4	2	1 (3)	4	1 (1)
5	4	1 (0)	2	0 (0)

Notes: The columns 'No. of firms with 50% (40%)' indicate the number of firms where a proposal obtained at least 50% (between 40 and 49%) of the votes cast, of the firms receiving the number of proposals indicated in the cell's row in the year indicated in the cell's column.

*Indicates a cell in which one firm has been counted more than once (in both the 50% and 40% entries) because it received one proposal that obtained 50% and one that obtained between 40% and 49% of the votes cast.

Data Sources: IRRC, Corporate Governance Service, Voting Results 1997 (1998); IRRC, Corporate Governance Service, Voting Results 1998 (1999).

resources expended by firms on omitted proposals (proposals excluded for failing to meet the SEC's criteria for submission).[70] Yet, the resources spent on omitted proposals—the expenditure on determining whether to include a proposal—are approximately equal to the additional expenditure on those that are included—the mailing and distribution costs (mean SEC estimates of $37,000 compared to $50,000; identical medians). From this perspective, all of the cost figures presented considerably underestimate the cost of the regime.

The cost estimates in Table 23.2, even if refined to reflect the actual distribution of proposals across firms, do not impose a heavy burden on shareholders who are subsidizing proposal sponsors and voting against the proposals. But even seemingly low annual expenditures add up: the present value of the cost of the regime is, at a minimum, $315 million, using the historical market risk premium of 9.2 per cent as the capitalization rate (Ross *et al.* 1999: 227–8).[71] This is a minimum because there is considerable debate over whether this is an accurate estimate of the equity risk premium: it was significantly lower in the nineteenth century and beginning of the twentieth century,[72] and many financial economists predict a lower premium in the future.[73] Using as the capitalization rate, for example, the average risk premium from either 1802–70 or 1871–1925, 1.4 and 4.4 per cent respectively, or the overall average premium of 5.1 per cent from 1802–1997 (Ross *et al.* 1999: 228), the subsidy of shareholder proposals under the current regime is $2.1 billion, $659 million, or $569 million. The savings to firms from eliminating the subsidy for shareholder proposals that fail to receive at least 40 per cent of the votes range, across the differing historical capitalization rates, from $1.9 billion to $293 million. These sums are not trivial. Moreover, the estimates are conservatively biased because they assume there will be no growth in the number of proposals presented, although the number has increased over time.

Some might contend that because the cost estimates are quite modest compared to the market value of publicly-traded firms, it is unnecessary to rein in the subsidy as the problem is self-correcting: informed funds can be expected to revise their activist strategies in the face of the new learning of the finance literature. In this view, it is better for shareholders to bear the relatively low cost of the subsidy during an adjustment period in which institutions reassess their activist programmes, than for them to operate under a reformed regime that reduced the subsidy. There are two rationales that could be advanced in support of this position. First, a reduction in the subsidy could undermine whatever deterrent effect is provided by shareholder proposals, and second, it could decrease the extent of governance innovations that arise from institutional investors' experimentation with governance reforms through proposal sponsorship, as they would no longer be able to offer, at no cost to themselves, proposals that take several years of submission before they achieve substantial support.

These objections to the need for reform are not, however, persuasive. A significant deterrent effect is improbable because of the lack of any performance effect from, and the infrequency of top management turnover after, proposal submissions. In addition, the experimentation aspect of shareholder proposals is attenuated: the governance proposals offered by institutional investors have not been directed at novel devices for which there have been no empirical research on performance effects. For example, the drive to propose independent directors in the 1990s occurred after most firms' boards had a majority of outside directors and substantial research had been undertaken regarding their impact, and the defensive tactics that were the object of the initiation of shareholder proposals had been the subject of prior empirical study, although the performance effect of defences has been found to differ over time, which has changed the calculus concerning the efficacy of shareholder targeting of them. But experimentation over governance reforms will not be eliminated by a reduction in the subsidy—it will instead require a higher threshold for action.

Most important, the premise of the contention, that activist institutions will significantly alter their governance programmes as the results of the finance literature are publicized, is dubious. The disparity in proposal sponsorship across public and private fund managers strongly suggests that there is an agency problem, so that the regime will not, in fact, be subject to self-correction. The current regime provides no incentive to mitigate an agency problem in institutional proposal sponsorship. Instead, it encourages the submission of proposals that have private benefits and hence may not be value-maximizing, by allocating proposal costs across all shareholders. Accordingly, the more compelling response to the current regime's relatively low annual cost compared to market capitalization is to recognize that the relatively low cost is a contributing factor to the tolerance of a wasteful regime.

Although the case is exceedingly strong for reducing, if not eliminating, the subsidization of shareholder proposals, in all likelihood, such a reform of the proxy proposal process will be politically difficult to implement. It is improbable that politically well-connected institutions (public pension funds and unions) which have been obtaining access to the proxy process for free will voluntarily agree to begin paying for it. Indeed, institutional investors have opposed even minor changes that could limit their free access to the proxy process, such as an increase in the minimum threshold of votes required for a proposal's re-submission in a subsequent year. It is, however, hoped that this chapter's marshalling of the evidence and analysis of the dismal ineffectiveness of the institutional investor activism agenda will alter the view of those investors (or at least of nonactivist institutional investors) of the proposal process such that they will acknowledge, and support, the need for meaningful reform.

4. CONCLUSION

Shareholder proposals, although an increasingly prominent feature of institutional investor corporate governance activism since the mid-1980s, have not had a significant impact on firm performance. The most plausible explanation for the absence of a discernible positive effect has been large scale misdirection in the form that such activism has taken: many proposals have focused on reforming board composition and structure and limiting executive compensation, yet empirical studies of such reforms consistently indicate that they do not improve performance. In addition, proposals to implement confidential voting also provide no benefit because the procedural change does not significantly alter voting outcomes. Finally, proposals to remove takeover defences need to be directed at firms where they will do the most good, such as those with insider-controlled boards, yet proposal sponsors often lack the knowledge of specific firm characteristics to engage in precision targeting, diminishing the likelihood that the proposal will improve performance.

Although submitting a proposal is not as expensive as other forms of shareholder activism, such as waging a proxy fight, the lacklustre results of such activity suggest that institutional investors should implement greater internal controls to monitor their corporate governance programmes, redirecting the resources expended on activism to their highest valued use. Adoption of industry-wide good practice standards for corporate governance programmes and third-party certification of the internal review process would spur individual funds to undertake careful and comprehensive reviews of their activism programmes.

Funds' incentives to engage in ongoing scrutiny of their governance programmes would further be enhanced were the federal rules for shareholder proposals revised to require proposal sponsors either to incur the full cost of a losing proposal or a substantial part of the cost, or, better still, to permit firms by a shareholder vote to select their proposal subsidization regime. By increasing the probability that institutional efforts at corporate governance activism will improve targeted firms' share values, these recommendations will not only benefit all targeted firm shareholders but will also encourage fund boards to perform more attentively their fiduciary obligations to fund beneficiaries.

ACKNOWLEDGEMENT

I would like to thank Ian Ayres, Robert Daines, Jill Fisch, Zohar Goshen, Henry Hansmann, D. Bruce Johnsen, Marcel Kahan, Jonathan Karpoff, Alvin Klevorick, Jonathan Macey, Alan Palmiter, Robert Pozen, Ed Rock, Randall Thomas, Michael Weisbach, and participants at the Tilburg Conference on Convergence and Diversity in Corporate Governance Regimes and Capital Markets, Yale Law School and Ohio State University College of Law faculty workshops, Columbia University School of Law Legal Theory workshop, New York University Center for Law and Business Law and Finance Series Mini-Conference on Shareholder Proposals, CEPR/CeRP/ESF/FEEM/Fondazione Courmayeur–CNPDC Conference on the Firm and its Shareholders: The Evolving Role of Corporate Finance and the Yale Law School Center for the Study of Corporate Law Nov. 2000 Roundtable for helpful comments. A version of this chapter was published the *Yale Journal on Regulation* 18: 174 (2001).

Notes

1. 17 C.F.R. § 240.14a-8 (2000).
2. In addition, Gillan and Starks (1998) survey all forms of institutional investor activism and not solely shareholder proposals; they conclude that there is no empirical evidence that such activity improves performance, although in theory it is beneficial for large shareholders to become active monitors of management.
3. See text and accompanying notes 53-4 *infra* (discussing possible private benefits).
4. While the number of institutions engaging in activism is very small (not much more than a dozen), the number of entities that have engaged in hostile takeovers is not that much greater when compared to the differential magnitude of the price effects. For example, in 1986, only 40 out of 3,300 takeovers were hostile offers, and that was an all time high (Jensen 1988), and the premiums in hostile takeovers, averaging 30 or 50 per cent depending on the time period, are incorporated in the stock price immediately upon the announcement of the bid, often with significant run-up (averaging 40 per cent of the eventual premium) prior to the announcement (Jarrell and Poulsen 1989: 226–7, 244).
5. See, for example, *Rosenfeld* v. *Fairchild Engine & Airplane Corp.*, 309 N.Y. 168, 128 N.E.2d 291 (1955). To obtain reimbursement, the proxy fight must be over policy and not personal issues, but it is not terribly difficult to characterize personal disputes as policy disagreements.
6. See, for example, Mulherin and Poulsen (1998); Ikenberry and Lakonishok (1993); Borstadt and Zwirlein (1992); DeAngelo and DeAngelo (1989); Dodd and Warner (1983).
7. See Forjan (1999) (stock returns $4\frac{1}{2}$ month period preceding proposal); Karpoff *et al.* (1996) (market-to-book ratio, operating return on sales, sales growth; stock returns only in univariate tests); Strickland *et al.* (1996) (stock returns); Wahal (1996) (stock returns, return on assets); Bizjak and Marquette (1998) (market-to-book ratio, growth in operating income); Johnson and Shackell (1997) (sales growth); John and Klein (1995) (stock returns, income); Opler and Sokobin (1995) (stock returns, return on assets).
8. For a comparison across studies see Karpoff (1998: 20–1).
9. TIAA-CREF selects targets by their failure to follow corporate governance procedures that it has endorsed (Carleton *et al.* 1998: 1339). It believes those procedures improve performance or otherwise enhance firm value. TIAA-CREF's chairman and chief executive officer, in explaining its corporate governance activities, asserted that 'sound practices of corporate governance will make a difference in the future performance of companies' (Biggs 1995). CalPERS is even more explicit concerning its motivation: 'At CalPERS, corporate governance is about making money...' (Karpoff 1998: 7, n. 2, quoting CalPERS' 1998 Global Corporate Governance Principles).
10. See Bizjak and Marquette (1998) (low insider ownership); Carleton *et al.* (1998) (same); Bizjak and Marquette (1998) (institutional ownership high); Carleton *et al.* (1998) (same); Karpoff *et al.* (1996) (same); Smith (1996) (same). A few studies do not find such significant relations. See Karpoff *et al.* (1996) (difference in inside ownership insignificant); Smith (1996) (same); Johnson and Shackell (1997) (institutional ownership low). Of these studies, it should be noted, however, that the Johnson and Shackell study, the only one finding targets have fewer institutional investors than non-targeted firms, examines solely executive compensation proposals, which, in contrast to the governance proposals examined in the other studies, tend more commonly to be offered by individual investors than pension funds (Heard 1995: 760).
11. John and Klein (1995: 16). In the 1980s, social responsibility proposals gained less than 3 per cent of the votes (Leibeler 1984: 450–2). Average support for corporate governance

proposals increased throughout the 1980s and for the five highest support categories ranged from 25.8 to 42.1 per cent by 1990 (Sander 1991: 5). While social responsibility proposals' support has also increased, the averages for the two highest support categories were 12.4 and 9.75 per cent in 1990 (ibid. C-2 to C-8 (my calculation)). Social responsibility proposals are not the focus of this chapter because they are not advanced in order to improve corporate performance and are consequently not compatible with the objective of USA corporate law, which is to maximize share value.

12. See 17 C.F.R. § 240.14a-8(i) (2000). Proposals involving matters that are subject to shareholder action are submissible in non-precatory form.
13. See *International Bhd. of Teamsters Gen. Fund* v. *Fleming Companies, Inc.*, No. CIV-96-1650-A, 1997 U.S. Dist. LEXIS 2980 (W.D. Okla. 24 Jan 1997). The issue is whether poison pills are a proper subject for shareholder action (i.e. bylaw amendments) or ordinary business matters that are within the authority of the board.
14. Daily *et al.* (1996); Wahal (1996); Karpoff, Malatesta, and Walkling (1996); Del Guercio and Hawkins (1999); Gillan and Starks (2000). As the Daily *et al.* study does not provide information on proposals' content, which is the focus of this chapter's analysis, it is not discussed. When the performance measure is the short-term stock price (abnormal return) reaction to a particular 'event', such as the announcement of submission of a shareholder proposal or the initiation of negotiation over a proposal, the econometric methodology used to determine the performance effect is called an event study. Event studies investigate the impact of new information upon expected stock returns, which are estimated by an asset pricing model that most commonly depends on the return on the market; the residual of the linear regression of the stock return of event firms on the market return during the event interval is the abnormal return or performance measure due to the event, as it represents the change in stock return beyond the model's predicted return in the absence of the event (Brown and Warner 1985).
15. One study by Akhigbe *et al.* (1997: 570) has found a significant long-term positive valuation effect of shareholder activism (144 firms, average abnormal stock returns of 23 per cent within three years after activism). This study is not included in the table because it combined shareholder proposals with proxy fights. The study's performance results are driven by the proxy fights in the sample. Although the authors did not classify their sample by activism form (i.e. individuals seeking a block of board seats are not differentiated from proposals to add independent directors to the board), they did classify it by activist type: institutional investor, individual, and groups of large shareholders, with the latter two categories consisting of individuals known for engaging in proxy fights. They find the individual and shareholder group variables are positively related to the size of the abnormal return (ibid.: 572), which indicates that the significance of their results depends on the proxy fights in the sample.
16. The sample in Karpoff *et al.* (1996) includes proposals by both public pension funds and other investors; the stock price effects are insignificant whether the proposals are separately grouped by type of proponent (such as by a pension fund or an individual investor) or aggregated. Although the returns were significantly negative for the full sample on the day after the proxy mailing date (ibid.: 381), they do not explicitly report this result and instead report the insignificance of the negative cumulative returns (ibid.: 382). As discussed in part II.B.2.c. infra, and as evident in their data, executive compensation proposals are a small fraction of the proposals offered by institutional investors, and this undoubtedly contributes to the difference between their result and the absence of negative price effects in the other studies, which do not separately examine this proposal category.
17. In contrast to the results in Karpoff *et al.* (1996), Gillan and Starks (2000: 299) further find a small positive stock price reaction (0.2 per cent) to the full set of individually-sponsored proposals.

18. Two other findings of significant positive returns in Del Guercio and Hawkins' (1999) study are, in my judgement, problematic and are therefore not relied upon in this chapter's analysis. They find significant positive returns on the outcome dates for the sample of proposals sponsored by CalPERS but the significance of this subsample is driven by one firm with a confounding event—at the same time as the outcome date for CalPERS' proposal to rescind Avon Products' poison pill, newspapers reported that a noted corporate raider had acquired a 10 per cent block of Avon stock and intended to make a hostile takeover bid. When the Avon observation is eliminated from the CalPERS subsample, the returns are no longer significant (Del Guercio and Hawkins 1999: 325). They also find marginally positive significant returns (10 per cent level) for board-related proposals cumulated over one month before the announcement date through one month after the outcome date. The length of the period—several months—and the absence of significant returns over the shorter intervals around either event date counsels against attributing the statistical finding to the funds' activism.
19. An additional study which focused on CalPERS, by Nesbitt (1994), is not discussed in the text because it uses an idiosyncratic and unreliable calculation of the performance measure. Nesbitt finds that half of the firms CalPERS targeted with proxy proposals experienced positive returns above the S&P 500 index over a five-year period after the date of CalPERS' first letter to the firm. He does not, however, provide statistical tests of his data. Moreover, in contrast to the other studies of CalPERS' activism, Nesbitt does not adjust for the firms' market risk in evaluating performance, which renders his results less reliable (if the targeted firms were riskier than the market, higher than market returns would be expected). Compounding the problem with interpreting his results, the number of firms in his sample declines dramatically over time, which increases the likelihood that there is selection bias in the data. Finally, he is examining stock prices over several years, which introduces considerable noise, making it difficult to attribute with confidence any price effect to CalPERS' targeting. In fact, Del Guercio and Hawkins (1999) find that the higher returns of targeted firms over the S&P 500 index is not statistically significant, and a control sample of non-targeted firms, comparable in performance, size, and industry to the targeted firms, has a similar increase in returns compared to the market. They thus conclude that the improved performance Nesbitt attributes to CalPERS is due to some other factor, such as mean reversion (ibid.: 326). Consequently, in my judgement, Nesbitt's results are not reliable, compared to all of the other studies that do not identify long-term positive performance effects from activism.
20. The extensive literature is reviewed in Romano (1996) and Bhagat and Black (1999). The overwhelming majority of studies find no significant correlation between performance and independence. Only one study finds a positive relation (Millstein and MacAvoy 1998), while a few, including Bhagat and Black (1999) find a negative relation. Both of these studies use time series performance data but have only one observation of independence, which makes it difficult to attribute the measured performance to the board's independence as we do not know whether the independence measure is constant over the period; in particular, Millstein and MacAvoy's independence measure is from 1994 while performance is averaged over 1991–5, and Bhagat and Black's independence measure is from 1991 while performance is tracked from 1985 to 1995.
21. Of six studies of the split in office, four find no difference or, in fact, an improvement in performance in the firms where the positions are not split (Berg and Smith 1978; Chaganti *et al.* 1985; Baliga *et al.* 1996; Brickley *et al.* 1997) whereas two find improved performance in firms where the positions are split (Rechner and Dalton 1991; Pi and Timme 1993). I adopt the results of the majority of the studies, that splitting the positions does not improve performance, particularly because that is also the finding of the most comprehensive and sophisticated study, which is also the most recent one, that by Brickley *et al.* (1997).

22. Office of Chief Economist of the Securities and Exchange Commission (1986) (firms subject to takeover speculation without confounding effects had negative returns); Jarrell and Poulsen (1986) (firms without confounding events and firms subject to takeover speculation had negative returns); Malatesta and Walkling (1988) (full sample had negative returns as well as firms without confounding effects); Ryngaert (1988) (firms subject to takeover speculation as well as firms without confounding events had negative returns). Even these studies had either full or subsamples of firms with insignificant price effects.
23. Comment and Schwert (1995) (no significant effect); Datta and Iskandar-Datta (1996) (insignificant for full sample but significantly negative for a small subset of firms (nine) that were subject to a takeover); Johnson and Meade (1996) (insignificant effect); Mahoney *et al.* (1996) (negative price effect for pills adopted 1984–8). It should be noted that there is an interpretation of the insignificant effects of pills in later year event studies that is consistent with their having a negative impact on shareholder wealth: the adoption of poison pills after the tactic was upheld by the Delaware Supreme Court in 1985 could have been anticipated by shareholders and thus the negative impact was already impounded in the stock price at the pill announcement date.
24. Ryngaert (1988) finds no significant differences in abnormal returns for firms with or without classified board amendments and fair price or supermajority amendments. In contrast, Johnson and Meade (1996: 15–16) report that firms that do not have antitakeover charter amendments had insignificant negative abnormal returns whereas firms with fair price or supermajority amendments had insignificant positive abnormal returns, and the difference in mean abnormal return for the two groups is significant at 10 per cent. When the antitakeover amendment firms are subdivided by type, the returns to the firms with fair price provisions in place are significantly positive, and significantly different from the firms with no amendments, but not from the firms with supermajority amendments. The Johnson and Meade (1996) data would thus appear to indicate that shareholder wealth effects from pills are lower for firms with no prior defences.
25. For example, DeAngelo and Rice (1983) (insignificant effect); Linn and McConnell (1983) (positive or insignificant effect); Jarrell and Poulsen (1987) (insignificant effect for fair price amendments, the majority of sample); Brickley *et al.* (1988) (insignificant effect). But as in the poison pill case, there are studies that find significant negative price effects. For example, Mahoney *et al.* (1996) (negative effect for full sample and some but not all subsamples); Jarrell and Poulsen (1987) (negative effect for full sample and for supermajority amendment subsample); McWilliams and Sen (1997) (insignificant effect for firms with independent boards and negative effect for firms with insider boards). Moreover, one study correcting for anticipation effects for the adoption of charter amendments, finds a significant negative return (Bhagat and Jefferis 1991).
26. For example, *Quickturn Design Sys., Inc.* v. *Mentor Graphics Corp.*, 721 A.2d 1281 (Del. 1998).
27. Studies showing that firms with poison pills are not subject to fewer successful takeover bids than firms without such defences include Comment and Schwert (1995) and Aboumeri (1997).
28. The one study of charter amendments that separated out cumulative voting reductions from the other amendments also found a significant negative effect, but the sample size (twenty-one proposals) is small (Mahoney *et al.* 1996: 537).
29. Del Guercio and Hawkins (1999) also found that virtually all of the SWIB proposals that had a positive price effect at the time of the outcome date (the annual meeting date or the news date of a withdrawn proposal) were proposals to rescind poison pills (ibid.: 298). One explanation for this contrary result might be market anticipation of a subsequent acquisition given knowledge of the level of shareholder support for pill rescission, as the date is after the vote. But Del Guercio

and Hawkins report that SWIB's targets were not significantly more likely to be subject to a takeover attempt than other sample firms, although targets receiving antitakeover proposals were (ibid.: 318–19). An alternative explanation is that the result is spurious (i.e. due to some other factor) because the event date is the shareholder meeting date, in contrast to the event date in the studies that identified negative effects, proxy mailing date: random samples using annual meeting dates produce positive returns, in contrast to those using proxy mailing dates (Brickley 1986). Finally, SWIB, as an active stock-picking fund, is well-informed concerning its specified targets and focuses on antitakeover issues, in contrast to other activist institutions that are more heavily indexed and hence less informed about the particulars of their portfolio firms. SWIB might therefore be better able to identify firms where pill rescissions do maximize share value than other proponents of such measures, whose proposals, along with SWIB's, are included in the studies finding negative price effects. Accordingly, firm-specific information (such as board composition), which appears in the finance literature to affect significantly the impact of poison pills on firms, may also affect the efficacy of shareholder proposals to repeal such defences, and explain the contrary finding regarding SWIB's proposals.

30. Mehran (1995: 180) (no relation); Morck *et al.* (1988) (non-linear relation); Bhagat *et al.* (1999) (positive relation between past performance and directors stock ownership).
31. These authors use a different year than Johnson *et al.* (1997) for post-proposal compensation, which, besides the difference in sample composition, may explain the slight difference in results. When they examine compensation two years after the proposal, they find the decrease in incentive pay is significant, as well as the increase in salary (ibid.: 1067).
32. One of the study's results that Thomas and Martin (1999: 1069) state that they cannot explain, the finding that CEO's industry-adjusted compensation level post-proposal is higher for individual rather than union sponsors, can be explained when considered in conjunction with Johnson *et al.*'s (1997) finding that, regarding CalPERS, institutional investors exercise more influence on compensation committees than individuals.
33. Thomas and Martin (1999) report 11.3 per cent as the average support for compensation proposals while Del Guercio and Hawkins (1999) report an average support of 34 per cent for corporate governance proposals which did not include any compensation proposals. This difference in relative voting support is consistent across samples (e.g. Sander 1991; Gordon and Pound 1993; Romano 2002).
34. Gerber (1993) provides a model for when political parties would prefer a secret to open ballot in order to reduce bribery. The conditions under which USA states switched to the Australian ballot in the late nineteenth century—increasingly competitive elections—are consistent with the model predictions. In support of this hypothesis, in a history of the ballot reform, Fredman (1968: 85) states that over time, several observers pointed out that the Australian ballot checked obvious bribery abuses but did not seriously weaken the power of political machines. In addition, Heckelman (2000: 205) examines voting turnout in the presence of secret ballots and finds that there is a positive income effect, which suggests that the poor were more likely to vote prior to the enactment of secret ballots (i.e. when they could sell their votes).
35. A possible explanation is that managers introduce proposals shareholders prefer after the procedural change compared to pre-adoption proposals, for the proxy fight firms. As the voting change followed the proxy fight, attribution of such an effect is difficult. But because the effect disappears when proxy firms, which have higher support levels in all years, are excluded, it cannot be concluded that confidential voting induces behavioral changes in management regarding proposals for the majority of firms.
36. The stock price effects around the time in which the firms publicly announced their action to comply with TIAA-CREF's demands were generally not statistically significant, but these were

not robust tests because very few firms publicly announced these actions (number of observations ranged from one to 11 firms, depending on the subsample).

37. These data suggest that before 1992 negotiated compromises were more likely to occur when proposals were value-maximizing propositions than post-1992. Chidambaran and Woidtke (1999) buttress this contention with an examination of the subset of proposals for which they can classify whether management adopted the withdrawn proposal as is or whether the parties reached a compromise on the proposal's substance; they find that post-1992, proposals accepted as is had a significant negative impact on firm value, and before 1992, compromises had a significant positive effect, but they do not indicate how representative, or what percentage, of the full sample, this subsample is. Their conclusions are consistent with those of Choi (2000). Choi finds that after the 1992 proxy reforms, unions and religious groups increased their sponsorship of proposals and proposal targets had higher levels of insider ownership, and he concludes that post-1992 proposal sponsors are more interested in using the proxy process as a bargaining tool than for maximizing shareholder welfare.
38. There is a large economics literature on adverse selection (markets with products of varying quality which cannot be observed prior to purchase); for a good textbook introduction to screening (also termed self-selection) and signalling models in which markets overcome adverse selection—the difference in model depends on which party, the uninformed or informed, acts first—see Kreps (1990: 625–52). The argument in the text draws from this literature but it is not a rigorous application because it is not an exact fit with a screening model. Although the uninformed act first—investors target management with proposals—they do not offer different discrete contracts, as in a screening model, and managements instead sort themselves by their different responses to the uniformly offered 'contract', a more active role associated with signalling models in which the informed move first. I believe the analogy is apt despite the imprecision because under plausible conditions both screening and signalling models produce outcomes in which high and low quality managers are identified (i.e. a 'separating equilibrium' is produced).
39. For example, for firms that have adopted confidential voting, two-thirds of the firms receiving a proposal to eliminate a defensive tactic received another type of proposal at the same meeting (Romano 2002).
40. There are numerous signalling models directed at explaining underpricing of initial public offerings, and the empirical support is mixed. See, for example, Jegadeesh *et al.* (1993). The signalling literature typically considers the need for management to signal the quality of the firm's projects rather than the quality of the managers themselves, but in practice it is often difficult to distinguish between these—replacement of managers does not always resolve a firm's difficulties—and thus the text does not attempt to do so either.
41. There could be different information provided to investors from union activism if management, in exchange for termination of a corporate governance campaign by a union, capitulates to employment-related demands that it would otherwise reject. Then, while a failed negotiation would indicate to the market that management had opted not to engage in compromising tactics, a withdrawn proposal would indicate that management had entered into a disadvantageous labour deal, and successful negotiations should produce a negative, not positive price effect when the activist is a union as opposed to a pension fund. There is some anecdotal evidence that prolonged union campaigns are on occasion successful in obtaining management accommodation. For example, the Amalgamated Clothing and Textile Workers Union's corporate campaign against J. P. Stevens, which was part of its efforts to organize the company's workforce, succeeded in getting management to bargain with the union, as evidenced by a settlement term in which the union promised not to engage in further corporate campaign tactics (Schwab and Thomas 1998). But most union proposals are not sponsored in the context of labour disputes. In addition,

initially managements did not enter into negotiations with union proposal sponsors, which explains, at least in part, the increase in the share of proposals sponsored by unions after 1992 reported by Choi (2000). In recent years they have begun to negotiate with unions (e.g. IRRC 2000*b*). To the extent that unions make up a larger percentage of the sponsors of the withdrawn proposals in the post-1992 subsample in the Chidambaran and Woidtke (1999) study, the difference in information content is a possible explanation of their finding of a negative valuation effect from proposal withdrawals. This interpretation would enable the information updating explanation to reconcile all of the activism studies' disparate performance effects.

42. Carleton *et al.*'s (1998) varying findings of statistical significance based on the content of TIAA-CREF's activism can be reconciled with the empirical literature on the underlying governance devices. The finding that TIAA-CREF's efforts to increase board diversity has a negative impact on performance is consistent with one study (Gertner and Kaplan 1996) that identified value-maximizing boards (boards chosen by leveraged buyout firms going public) as having fewer female directors than the average board. The studies relating board composition to performance do not examine directors' personal attributes of gender and race, the object of TIAA-CREF's proposal, but the failure to find a positive effect on performance in the more general board studies of director independence is consistent with the finding that TIAA-CREF's board proposals do not increase target firm value, because increasing director diversity typically would be achieved by the addition of independent directors under TIAA-CREF's policy. The finding of insignificance for confidential voting adoptions is consistent with the finding in Romano (2002) that the practice does not significantly affect voting outcomes. The finding of a positive impact for negotiations on poison pills is consistent with the results of the earliest empirical studies of negative price reactions to pill adoptions, as well as with a signalling explanation, which is discussed in the text.
43. See note 6, *supra* (collecting references).
44. Millstein and MacAvoy (1998: 1288–9) list the business and bar organizations that have produced corporate governance standards for boards. The New York Stock Exchange and National Association for Securities Dealers, in response to SEC concerns, created the Blue Ribbon Committee on Improving the Effectiveness of Corporate Audit Committees, which issued a report in February 1999 with recommendations for improving audit committees, and accounting firms have followed up with statements of audit committee standards (e.g. PricewaterhouseCoopers 1999; KPMG 1999*a*).
45. To the extent that there is concern that such work could compromise the independence of the auditor, use of a different public accounting firm could be required. But this work would not appear to create a significant independence issue as it does not constitute self-review of the auditing function as do other appraisal and valuation services.
46. The websites of several accounting firms refer to their provision of 'assurance services' in conjunction with traditional auditing services. For example, PricewaterhouseCoopers Health Care Practice, Assurance, and Business Advisory Service, at http://www.pwchealth.com/services/business.html (visited 15 October 1999); KPMG International Services, Assurance at http://www.kpmg.com/services/Default.asp (visited 15 October 1999).
47. Accounting regulatory bodies, such as the Government Accounting Standards Board (GASB) and Financial Accounting Standards Board (FASB), are not the appropriate loci of authority for such certification, as their mandates are directed at disclosures of the costs and revenues of firm output.
48. The DoL's authority over union funds comes from its administration of ERISA, the Employee Retirement Income Security Act of 1974, 29 U.S.C. § 1000 *et seq.* (2000), and the Taft-Hartley Act, 29 U.S.C. § 186(c)(5) (2000) (multiemployer plans).

49. For example, John Bogle, founder of the Vanguard Group, one of the largest fund families that offers low-cost indexed funds, called on mutual funds to 'live up to their responsibility of corporate citizenship' and promote better corporate governance and wield their voting power to oppose management on issues harmful to shareholders, such as excessive stock options (McGough and Tam 1999).
50. The SEC's regulatory authority over mutual funds is derived from the Investment Company Act of 1940, 15 U.S.C. §§ 80a-1 *et seq.* (2000).
51. For example, I.R.C. § 162(m) (2000) (eliminating tax deductibility of executive compensation over $1 million unless performance-based and performance goals set by compensation committee with two independent directors and approved by shareholders).
52. For a discussion of the divergence between private and social gains and the allocation of costs in proxy contests see Bebchuk and Kahan (1990: 1092–5).
53. The following articles discuss examples of this behaviour: Jarley and Maranto (1990); Rock (1991: 479–81); Romano (1993*a*: 801–19, 822); and Schwab and Thomas (1998: 1032–4).
54. For example, the New York City controller and trustee for the New York City Employees' Retirement Funds, when running for the Democratic party nomination for the USA Senate, highlighted her fund's sponsorship of proposals for independent directors, in order to obtain 'more accountable management', including elimination of 'fat executive compensation plans' (Holtzman 1992).
55. Individual investors may, of course, also misuse the process if they obtain consumption, rather than investment, benefits from offering proposals that are not in the interest of the other shareholders.
56. See, for example, *Business Roundtable* v. *SEC*, 905 F.2d 406 (D.C. Cir. 1990) (concluding that the SEC regulation of corporate voting rules is beyond its authority because it is a subject matter of state law).
57. See Romano (1998) (advocating comprehensive reform of the federal securities law by permitting issuers to choose their securities regime, analogous to the choice of corporate charter, from among the fifty states as well as the SEC or other nations). The present chapter underscores the merit of such an approach: the SEC has not formulated proxy proposal rules that ensure institutional investors have appropriate incentives in using the process to improve the value of the targeted firm.
58. See *Rosenfeld* v. *Fairchild Engine*, 309 N.Y. 168, 128 N.E.2d 291 (1955). The shareholder proposal rule is not applicable to proxy fights. See Rule 14(a)-8(c)(8) and (9), 17 C.F.R. § 240.14a-8(c)(8) and (9) (2000) (stating that proposals relating to an election to office and proposals counter to a management proposal are excludable).
59. Other commentators have considered different benchmarks. For instance, George Dent, who modified his position favouring repeal of the shareholder proposal rule in the 1990s when institutions became active on takeover issues, advocates requiring the posting of a bond to cover corporate costs if a proposal does not garner a respectable level of support, and while he does not specify a numerical criterion for the proposal, he suggests 20 per cent as one possible minimum (Dent 1989: 823). In addition, Bebchuk and Kahan (1990: 1122, 1128) would retain the actual success (50 per cent) rule for proxy fights, although they suggest, without specifying a concrete number, that a lower threshold may be appropriate for proxy fights over issues as opposed to board seats. They are not, of course, discussing shareholder proposals, where the costs of the action are much lower and the private benefits, given the parties involved, qualitatively different.
60. As an alternative to her proposal to repeal the shareholder proposal regime, Liebeler (1984: 462, 464) also proposed that corporations should adopt bylaws imposing minimum ownership requirements in order to bring proposals before the annual meeting that were greater than the

SEC's minimal threshold requirement, as well as bylaws requiring reimbursement of the cost of proposals. She considered these second-best measures to protect corporate interests while the SEC rule remained on the books. By choosing a bylaw for the reimbursement rule, in contrast to this chapter's proposal, Liebeler's proposal would permit management to eliminate the subsidy without shareholder approval, as managers typically can amend bylaws on their own. See, for example, Del. Code Ann. tit. 8, § 109 (1998) (corporate charter may confer power to adopt, amend or repeal bylaws on directors). The difference in decision-maker is the reason why, in contrast to the discussion in the text, Leibeler expects firm-level choice to result in elimination of the subsidy.

61. For example, Cal. Corp. Code § 800 (1999) (at motion of defendant, court may require plaintiff to post a bond for reasonable expenses, not to exceed $50,000). Dent (1989: 823) advanced such a proposal.
62. 17 C.F.R. 240.14a-8(b) (2000) (to be eligible to submit a proposal under rule, proponent must have held continuously at least $2,000 in market value or 1 per cent of stock entitled to vote on proposal, for at least one year by the date of the proposal's submission).
63. See Amendments to Rules on Shareholder Proposals, Release No. 34-40,018, 17 C.F.R. § 240, 63 Fed. Reg. 29,106, 29,114 (28 May 1998) (eighty firms reporting on proposal inclusion determination costs and 67 reporting on printing and other direct costs). The SEC noted that it was unclear whether the responses it received accounted for more than one proposal. This estimate was one of only three estimates that I could find. The second estimate was in response to a request for information on the cost of compliance with the shareholder proposal rules in 1976: the SEC received one estimate, from a firm which reported it spent $22,450 per included proposal, and $3,740 per excluded proposal, for a total expenditure of over $150,000 on sixteen proposals. See Proposed Amendments to Rule 14(a)-8 Under the Securities Exchange Act of 1934 Relating to Proposals by Security Holders, Securities Exchange Act Release No. 34-19,135, 47 Fed. Reg. 47,420, 47,424 n. 17 (14 October 1982). Given the absence of a basis to judge the representativeness of this firm, this estimate is useless. The third estimate I found is in Susan Liebeler's article proposing repeal of the rule, from an informal survey conducted by the American Society of Corporate Secretaries (ASCS) in response to proposed changes in the shareholder proposal rule in 1982: the ASCS reported an average cost of $94,775 per company or $10,275 per proposal (Liebeler 1984: 454 n. 157). Even adjusting for inflation, the 1997 SEC survey cost estimate is much higher (five times) than the 1982 ASCS estimate.
64. Table 23.2 uses votes as a percentage of votes cast to classify proposals. For less than 10 per cent of the corporate governance proposals reported by the IRRC (1998*c*; 1999*c*), the company specified a different voting requirement in its proxy statement. As a result, the cut-off assigned in Table 23.2 to 21 corporate governance proposals in 1997 and 22 in 1998 would be lower, using the firms' vote tally. The figures in the text therefore underestimate the cost of the regime if one were to use as the cut-off percentage, the vote necessary for a proposal's passage, rather than the percentage of votes cast.
65. The subsidy for a 40 per cent cut-off is determined by subtracting the amount in the 40 per cent row from the amount in the 0 per cent row; similarly, the subsidy for a 10 per cent cut-off is determined by subtracting the amount in the 10 per cent row from the amount in the 0 per cent row.
66. Voting results on social responsibility proposals were obtained from the IRRC (1998*e*; 1999*d*). Where a proposal is an overlap—that is, where it is tracked by both IRRC services—it is counted as a corporate governance proposal (there were 20 overlaps in 1997, and 17 in 1998). The withdrawal and omission rate for the social responsibility proposals is high: including overlapping proposals, by my count, of 299 initial social responsibility proposals in 1997, 115 came to a vote, and in 1998, 121 of 293 tracked proposals came to a vote.

67. See, for example, *Schreiber* v. *Bryan*, 396 A.2d 512, 518 (Del. Ch. 1978) (majority cannot ratify waste of assets); *Rosenfeld* v. *Fairchild Engine*, 309 N.Y. 168, 128 N.E.2d 291 (1955) (limitation of proxy fight expenditure reimbursement). Although managers can spend corporate assets on charitable contributions without shareholder approval, *A.P. Smith Mfg. Co.* v. *Barlow*, 13 N.J. 145, 98 A.2d 581, appeal dismissed, 346 U.S. 861 (1953), consistent with corporate law's centralization in management of decision-making that does not involve fundamental corporate changes, this non-majoritarian context is not a relevant benchmark because management is not the source of the decision to subsidize shareholder proposals. The SEC's proxy regime is one of the only instances in which an allocation of corporate assets is determined by individual shareholders without a need to obtain the support of at least a majority of the owners. The only other instance is derivative lawsuits, but in that context, the minority shareholder's ability to expend corporate resources on the litigation is greatly restricted by state courts.
68. For example, fundamental changes to the corporate form require the vote of at least a majority of the shareholders. For example, Del. Code Ann. tit. §§ 242, 251, 271 (1998) (majority stockholder vote required for charter amendment, merger, and sale of assets).
69. This chapter does not undertake a similar calculation for social responsibility proposals because they are not the focus of concern of this chapter and they appear to be slightly less clustered across target firms than corporate governance proposals. For example, in 1997, of 74 firms voting on such proposals, 55 (74 per cent) voted on only one proposal, and only two (3 per cent) voted on more than two proposals (IRRC 1998*e*: 77–84).
70. Nor are expenditures on withdrawn proposals (proposals for which the firm and sponsor negotiated an agreement resulting in the proposal's withdrawal) included. How many of these proposals would have received a substantial proportion of votes is unknown. While we might expect management to reach a negotiated settlement only on proposals that it deems likely to obtain a high level of support, the negative performance associated with such compromises in recent years reported by Chidambaran and Woidtke (1999) cautions that this may not be the case.
71. The present value of a perpetuity is the annual cash flow divided by the capitalization rate. The numerator used for this calculation is the average over 1997 and 1998 of the cost of corporate governance and social responsibility proposals that did not obtain a majority of votes (the estimates in the 50 per cent cut-off row subtracted from those in the 0 per cent cut-off row in Table 23.2), or $29 million. If the proposed 40 per cent cut-off for full reimbursement were adopted, the numerator would be $27 million.
72. The risk premium averaged 1.4 per cent from 1802 to 1870 and 4.4 per cent from 1871 to 1925, compared to 9.2 per cent from 1926 to 1997 (Ross *et al.* 1999: 228).
73. Cornell (1999: 200), for example, predicts a reasonable forward-looking range for the risk premium of 5–7 per cent. The capitalized cost using this rate range is from $580 million to $414 million.

References

Aboumeri, J. (1997). Poison pills and shareholder value/1992–96. *Aspen Law and Business Corporation* 68: 1.

Agrawal, A., and Knoeber, C. R. (2001). Do some outside directors play a political role? *Journal of Law and Economics* 44: 179.

—— —— (1996). Firm performance and mechanisms to control agency problems between managers and shareholders. *Journal of Financial and Quantitative Analysis* 31: 377.

—— and Mandelker, G. N. (1990). Large shareholders and the monitoring of managers: The case of antitakeover charter amendments. *Journal of Financial and Quantitative Analysis* 25: 143.

AICPA (1997). Report of the Special Committee on Assurance Services (available at the website of the AICPA: http//www.aicpa.org).

Akhigbe, A., Madura, J., and Tucker, A. L. (1997). Long-term valuation effects of shareholder activism. *Applied Financial Economics* 7: 567.

Baliga, B. R., Moyer, R. C., and Rao, R. S. (1996). CEO duality and firm performance: What's the fuss? *Strategic Management Journal* 17: 41.

Bebchuk, L. A., and Kahan, M. (1990). A framework for analyzing legal policy towards proxy contests. *California Law Review* 78: 1073.

Berg, S. V., and Smith, S. K. (1978). CEO and board chairman: A quantitative study of dual vs. unitary board leadership. *Directors and Boards* 3: 34.

Bhagat, S., and Black, B. (1999). The uncertain relationship between board composition and firm performance. *Business Lawyer* 54: 921.

—— and Brickley, J. A. (1984). Cumulative voting: The value of minority shareholder voting rights. *Journal of Law and Economics* 27: 339.

—— Carey, D. C., and Elson, C. M. (1999). Director ownership, corporate performance and management turnover. *Business Lawyer* 54: 885.

—— and Jefferis, R. (1991). Voting power in the proxy process: The case of antitakeover charter amendments. *Journal of Financial Economics* 30: 193.

Biggs, J. (1995). Why TIAA-CREF is active in corporate governance. Participant 2. (Nov.)

Bizjak, J. M., and Marquette, C. J. (1998). Are shareholder proposals all bark and no bite? Evidence from shareholder resolutions to rescind poison pills. *Journal of Financial and Quantitative Analysis* 33: 499.

Black, B. S. (1992). Agents watching agents; The promise of institutional investor voice. *UCLA Law Review* 39: 811.

—— (1998). Shareholder activism and corporate governance in the United States. In P. Newman (ed.), *The New Palgrave Dictionary of Economics and the Law*, Volume 3, London: MacMillan Reference Limited.

Borstadt, L., and Zwirlein, T. (1992). The efficient monitoring role of proxy contests: An empirical analysis of post-contest control changes and firm performance. *Financial Management* 22.

Brancato, C. K. (1997). *Institutional Investors and Corporate Governance.* Chicago: Irwin Professional Pub.

Brenner, M., Sundaram, R. K., and Yermack, D. (2000). Altering the terms of executive stock options. *Journal of Financial Economics* 57: 103.

Brickley, J. A. (1986). Interpreting common stock returns around proxy statement disclosures and annual shareholder meetings. *Journal of Financial and Quantitative Analysis* 21: 343.

——, Bhagat, S., and Lease, R. C. (1985). The impact of long-range managerial compensation plans on shareholder wealth. *Journal of Accounting and Economics* 7: 115.

—— Coles, J. L., and Jarrell, G. (1997). Leadership structure: Separating the CEO and chairman of the board. *Journal of Corporate Finance* 3: 189.

—— —— and Terry, R. L. (1994). Outside directors and the adoption of poison pills. *Journal of Financial Economics* 35: 371.

—— Lease, R. C., and Smith, Jr., C. W. (1988). Ownership structure and voting on antitakeover amendments. *Journal of Financial Economics* 20: 267.

Brown, S., and Warner, J. B. (1985). Using daily stock returns: The case of event studies. *Journal of Financial Economics* 14: 205.

Bryant, A. (1998). Stock options that raise investors' ire. *New York Times*, 27 March, D1.

Byrd, J. W., and Hickman, K. A. (1992). Do outside directors monitor managers? Evidence from tender offer bids. *Journal of Financial Economics* 32: 195.

Carleton, W. T., Nelson, J. M., and Weisbach, M. S. (1998). The influence of institutions on corporate governance through private negotiations: Evidence from TIAA-CREF. *Journal of Finance* 53: 1335.

Cary, W. L., and Eisenberg, M. A. (1995). *Corporations: Cases and Materials.* New York: Foundation Press.

Chaganti, R. S., Mahajan, V., and Sharma, S. (1985). Corporate board size, composition and corporate failures in retailing industry. *Journal of Management Studies* 22: 400.

Chance, D. M., Kumar, R., and Todd, R. B. (2000). The 'repricing' of executive stock options. *Journal of Financial Economics* 57: 129.

Chernoff, J. (2000*a*). CalPERS mulls political issues. *Pensions and Investments* 21, (May 1).

——(2000*b*). CalPERS Tilts toward Labor. *Pensions and Investments* 3, (May 1).

Chidambaran, N. K., and Prabhala, N. (2000). Executive stock option repricing, internal governance mechanisms, and management turnover (unpublished manuscript).

——and Woidtke, T. (1999). The role of negotiations in corporate governance: Evidence from withdrawn shareholder-initiated proposals (unpublished manuscript).

Choi, S. (2000). Proxy issue proposals: Impact of the 1992 SEC proxy reforms. *Journal of Law, Economics, and Organization* 16: 233.

Coffee, Jr., J. C. (1997). The bylaw battlefield: Can institutions change the outcome of corporate control contests. *University of Miami Law Review* 51: 605.

Comment, R., and Jarrell, G. A. (1987). Two-tier and negotiated tender offers, the imprisonment of the free-riding shareholder. *Journal of Financial Economics* 19: 283.

——and Schwert, G. W. (1995). Poison or placebo? Evidence on the deterrence and wealth effects of modern antitakeover measures. *Journal of Financial Economics* 39: 3.

Cornell, B. (1999). *The Equity Risk Premium.* New York: John Wiley & Sons.

Cotter, J. F., Shivdasani, A., and Zenner, M. (1997). Do independent directors enhance target shareholder wealth during tender offers. *Journal of Financial Economics* 43: 195.

Crutchley, C. E., Hudson, C. D., and Jensen, M. R. H. (1998). Shareholder wealth effects of CalPERS' Activism. *Financial Services Review* 7: 1.

Daily, C. M., Johnson, J. L., Ellstrand, A. E., and Dalton, D. R. (1996). Institutional investor activism; follow the leaders? (unpublished manuscript).

Datta, S., and Iskandar-Datta, M. (1996). Takeover defenses and wealth effects on securityholders: The case of poison pill adoptions. *Journal of Banking and Finance* 20: 1231.

DeAngelo, H., and DeAngelo, L. (1989). Proxy contests and the governance of publicly held corporations. *Journal of Financial Economics* 23: 29.

——and Rice, E. M. (1983). Antitakeover charter amendments and shareholder wealth. *Journal of Financial Economics* 11: 329.

Del Guercio, D., and Hawkins, J. (1999). The motivation and impact of pension fund activism. *Journal of Financial Economics* 52: 293.

Dennis, A. (1997). Becoming a business partner: Involvement of internal audit departments in business management. *Journal of Accountancy* 183: 72.

Dent, Jr., G. W. (1985). SEC Rule 14a-8: A study in regulatory failure. *New York Law School Law Review* 30: 1.

——(1989). Response: Proxy regulation in search of a propose: A reply to Professor Ryan. *Georgia Law Review* 23: 815.

Dodd, P., and Warner, J. B. (1983). On corporate governance: A study of proxy contests. *Journal of Financial Economics* 11: 401.

Downes, Jr., G., Houminer, R. E., and Hubbard, R. G. (1999). *Institutional Investors and Corporate Behavior.* Washington, D.C.: AEI Press.

Easterbrook, F. H., and Fischel, D. R. (1982). Auctions and sunk costs in tender offers. *Stanford Law Review* 35: 1.

——(1991). *The Economic Structure of Corporate Law.* Cambridge, MA: Harvard University Press.

Federal Reserve System (1996). Risk-Based Capital Standards: Market Risk, 12 C.F.R pts. 208 and 225.

Fields, A., and Todd, J. M. (1995). Firm size, antitakeover charter amendments, and the effect of state antitakeover legislation. *Managerial Finance* 21: 35.

Fischel, D. R. (1982). The corporate governance movement. *Vanderbilt Law Review* 35: 1259.

——(1995). *Payback.* New York: HarperCollins Publishers.

Forjan, J. M. (1999). The wealth effects of shareholder-sponsored proposals. *Review of Financial Economics* 8: 61.

Fredman, L. E. (1968). *The Australian Ballot: The Story of an American Reform.* East Lansing: Michigan State University Press.

Georgeson and Company, Inc. (1998). 1998 Annual Meeting Season Wrap-Up Corporate Governance. (available at their website: www.georgeson.com).

Gerber, A. (1993). The adoption of the secret ballot (unpublished manuscript).

Gertner, R., and Kaplan, S. N. (1996). The value maximizing board (unpublished manuscript).

Gillan, S. L., and Starks, L. T. (1998). A survey of shareholder activism: Motivation and empirical evidence. *Contemporary Finance Digest* 2: 10.

——(2000). Corporate governance proposals and shareholder activism: The role of institutional investors. *Journal of Financial Economics* 57: 275.

Gilson, R. J. (1982). Seeking competitive bids versus pure passivity in tender offer defense. *Stanford Law Review* 35: 51.

Gordon, J. N. (1997). 'Just Say Never?' poison pills, deadhand pills, and shareholder-adopted bylaws: An essay for Warren Buffett. *Cardozo Law Review* 19: 511.

Gordon L. A., and Pound, J. (1993). Information, ownership structure, and shareholder voting: Evidence from shareholder-sponsored corporate governance proposals. *Journal of Finance* 48: 697.

Grundfest, J. (1993). Just vote no: A minimalist strategy for dealing with barbarians inside the gates. *Stanford Law Review* 45: 857.

Hamermesh, L. A. (1998). Corporate democracy and stockholder-adopted by-laws: Taking back the street? *Tulane Law Review* 73: 409.

Hanson, R. C., and Song, M. H. (2000). Managerial ownership, board structure, and the division of gains in divestitures. *Journal of Corporate Finance* 6: 55.

Heard, J. E. (1995). Executive compensation: Perspective of the institutional investor. *University of Cincinnati Law Review* 63: 749.

Heckelman, J. C. (2000). Revisiting the relationship between secret ballots and turnout. *American Politics Quarterly* 28: 194.

Holmstrom, B. (1979). Moral hazard and observability. *Bell Journal of Economics* 13: 324.

Holtzman, E. (1992). When management falls down on the job; pension funds can put independent directors on the board. *Washington Post,* 26 May, A17.

Huson, M. (1997). Does governance matter? Evidence from CalPERS interventions. Institute for Financial Research, Faculty of Business, University of Alberta, Working Paper No. 3-97.

Ikenberry, D., and Lakonishok, J. (1993). Corporate governance through the proxy contest: Evidence and implications. *Journal of Business* 66: 405.

IRRC (1995). Checklist of 1995 shareholder proposals. *Corporate Governance Bulletin* 24 (July–Sept.). Washington, D.C.: IRRC.

——(1998*a*). AFL-CIO proxy voting guidelines could form unions into formidable voting bloc. XVI *Corporate Governance Bulletin* 21 (July–Oct.). Washington, D.C.: IRRC.

——(1998*b*). Checklist of 1998 U.S. Corporate Governance Shareholder Proposals. *Corporate Governance Bulletin* 27 (April–June). Washington, D.C.: IRRC.

IRRC (1998*c*). Corporate Governance Service, Voting Results 1997. Washington, D.C.: IRRC.

——(1998*d*). Voting on U.S. governance shareholder resolutions. *Corporate Governance Bulletin* 3 (April–June). Washington, D.C.: IRRC.

——(1998*e*). Social policy shareholder resolutions in 1997: Issues, votes and views of institutional investors. Washington, D.C.: IRRC.

——(1999*a*). *Corporate Governance Bulletin* (April–June). Washington, D.C.: IRRC.

——(1999*b*). New websites post proxy voting activity. *Corporate Governance Highlights* 10: 65 (16 April). Washington, D.C.: IRRC.

——(1999*c*). Corporate Governance Service, Voting Results 1998. Washington, D.C.: IRRC.

——(1999*d*). Social Policy Shareholder Resolutions in 1998: Issues, Votes and Views of Institutional Investors. Washington, D.C.: IRRC.

——(2000*a*). Number of companies repricing options has plummeted, IRRC finds. *Corporate Governance Highlights* 105 (7 July). Washington, D.C.: IRRC.

——(2000*b*). Update on Union Funds. *Corporate Governance Highlights* 11: 17 (4 Feb.). Washington, D.C.: IRRC.

Jarley, P., and Maranto, C. L. (1990). Union corporate campaigns: An assessment. *Industrial and Labor Relations Review* 43: 505.

Jarrell, G. A., and Poulsen, A. B. (1986). Shark repellents and poison pills: Stockholder protection—from the good guys or the bad guys? *Midland Corporate Finance Journal* 4: 39.

——(1987). Shark repellents and stock prices: The effects of antitakeover amendments since 1980. *Journal of Financial Economics* 19: 127.

——(1989). Stock trading before the announcement of tender offers: Insider trading or market anticipation? *Journal of Law, Economics, and Organization* 5: 225.

Jegadeesh, N., Weinstein, M., and Welch, I. (1993). An empirical investigation of IPO returns and subsequent equity offerings. *Journal of Financial Economics* 34: 153.

Jensen, M. C. (1988). Takeovers: Their causes and consequences. *Journal of Economic Perspectives* 2: 21 (winter).

John, K., and Klein, A. (1995). Shareholder proposals and corporate governance (unpublished manuscript).

Johnson, D. J., and Meade, N. L. (1996). Shareholder wealth effects of poison pills in the presence of anti-takeover amendments. *Journal of Applied Business Research* 12: 10.

Johnson, M. F., Porter, S., and Shackell, M. B. (1997). Stakeholder pressure and the structure of executive compensation (unpublished manuscript).

——and Shackell, M. B. (1997). Shareholder proposals on executive compensation (unpublished manuscript).

Karpoff, J. M. (1998). Does shareholder activism work? A survey of empirical findings (unpublished manuscript).

——Malatesta, P. and Walkling, R. (1996). Corporate governance and shareholder initiatives: Empirical evidence. *Journal of Financial Economics* 42: 365.

KPMG (1999*a*). *Shaping the Audit Committee Agenda* USA: KPMG LLP.

——(1999*b*). *The Financial Statement Audit* USA: KPMG LLP.

Kreps, D. (1990). *A Course in Microeconomic Theory.* Princeton, NJ: Princeton University Press.

Lambert, R., and Larckner, D. (1985). Golden parachutes, executive decision-making and shareholder wealth. *Journal of Accounting and Economics* 7: 179.

Lee, C., Rosenstein, S., Rangan, N., and Davidson, W. N. (1992). Board composition and shareholder wealth: The case of management buyouts. *Financial Management* 21: 58.

Leland, H. E., and Pyle, D. H. (1977). Information asymmetries, financial structure, and financial intermediation. *Journal of Finance* 32: 371.

Liebeler, S. W. (1984). A proposal to rescind the shareholder proposal rule. *Georgia Law Review* 18: 425.

Linn, S. C. and McConnell, J. (1983). An empirical investigation of the impact of 'Antitakeover' amendments on common stock prices. *Journal of Financial Economics* 11: 361.

LTV Corp. (1995). Proxy Statement (March 3) (available in Lexis COMPNY library, Proxy file).

Macey, J. R. (1998). The legality and utility of the shareholder rights bylaw. *Hofstra Law Review* 26: 835.

Mahoney, J. M., Sundaramurthy, C., and Mahoney, J. T. (1996). The differential impact on shareholder wealth of various antitakeover provisions. *Managerial and Decision Economics* 17: 531.

Malatesta, P. H., and Walkling, R. A. (1988). Poison pill securities: Stockholder wealth, profitability and ownership structure. *Journal of Financial Economics* 20: 347.

McGough, R., and Tam, P.-W. (1999). Bogle urges role in corporate governance. *Wall Street Journal*, 21 Oct., C23.

McWilliams, V. B., and Sen, N. (1997). Board monitoring and antitakeover amendments. *Journal of Financial and Quantitative Analysis* 32: 491.

Mehran, H. (1995). Executive compensation structure, ownership, and firm performance. *Journal of Financial Economics* 38: 163.

Mikkelson, W. H., and Partch, M. M. (1997). The decline of takeovers and disciplinary managerial turnover. *Journal of Financial Economics* 44: 205.

Millstein, I. M., and MacAvoy, P. W. (1998). Essay: The active board of directors and performance of the large publicly traded corporation. *Columbia Law Review* 98: 1283.

Morck, R., Shleifer, A., and Vishny, R. W. (1988). Management ownership and corporate performance: An empirical analysis. *Journal of Financial Economics* 20: 293.

Mulherin, J. H., and Poulsen, A. B. (1998). Proxy contests and corporate change: Implications for shareholder wealth. *Journal of Financial Economics* 47: 279.

Murphy, K. (1985). Corporate performance and managerial remuneration: An empirical analysis. *Journal of Accounting and Economics* 7: 11.

Nesbitt, S. L. (1994). Long-term rewards from shareholder activism: A study of the CalPERS effect. *Journal of Applied Corporate Finance* 75 (Winter).

Office of Chief Economist of the Securities and Exchange Commission (1986). *The Effects of Poison Pills on the Wealth of Target Shareholders.* Washington D.C.: United States Government Printing Office.

Opler, T., and Sokobin, J. (1995). Does coordinated institutional activism work? An analysis of the activities of the council of institutional investors. Charles A. Dice Center for Research in Financial Economics, Fischer College of Business, Ohio State University, Working Paper No. 95-5.

Pi, L., and Timme, S. G. (1993). Corporate control and bank efficiency. *Journal of Banking and Finance* 17: 515.

Pound, J. (1988). Proxy contests and the efficiency of shareholder oversight. *Journal of Financial Economics* 20: 237.

Pozen, R. C. (1994). Institutional investors: The reluctant activists. *Harvard Business Review* (Jan./Feb.), 140.

Prevost, A. K., and Rao, R. P. (2000). Of what value are shareholder proposals sponsored by public pension funds? *Journal of Business* 73: 177.

—— and Wagster, J. D. (1999). Impact of the 1992 Changes in the SEC Proxy Rules and Executive Compensation Reporting Requirements (unpublished manuscript).

PricewaterhouseCoopers (1999). *Audit Committees: Best Practices for Protecting Shareholder Interests.* USA: PricewaterhouseCoopers LLP.

Rechner, P. L., and Dalton, D. R. (1991). CEO duality and organizational performance: A longitudinal analysis. *Strategic Management Journal* 12: 155.

Rock, E. B. (1991). The logic and (uncertain) significance of institutional shareholder activism. *Georgetown Law Journal* 79: 445.

Roe, M. J. (1994). *Strong Managers, Weak Owners.* Princeton, N.J.: Princeton University Press.

Romano, R. (1992). A guide to takeovers: Theory, evidence, and regulation. *Yale Journal on Regulation* 9: 119.

——(1993*a*). Public pension fund activism in corporate governance reconsidered. *Columbia Law Review* 93: 795.

——(1993*b*). *The Genius of American Corporate Law.* Washington, D.C.: AEI Press.

——(1996). Corporate law and corporate governance. *Industrial and Corporate Change* 5: 277.

——(1998). Empowering investors: A market approach to securities regulation. *Yale Law Journal* 107: 2359.

——(2002). Does confidential proxy voting matter? (unpublished manuscript).

Rosenstein, S., and Wyatt, J. G. (1990). Outside directors, board independence, and shareholder wealth. *Journal of Financial Economics* 26: 175.

Ross, S. A. (1977). The determinants of financial structure: The incentive signalling approach. *Bell Journal of Economics* 8: 23.

—— Westerfield, R. W., and Jaffe, J. F. (1999). *Corporate Finance,* 5th edn. Boston: Irwin/McGraw-Hill.

Rusk, J. G. (1970). The effect of the Australian ballot reform on split ticket voting: 1876–1908. *American Political Science Review* 64: 1220.

Ryngaert, M. (1988). The effect of poison pill securities on shareholder wealth. *Journal of Financial Economics* 20: 377.

Sander, W. (1991). *Shareholder Voting Almanac.* Washington, D.C.: IRRC.

Schwab, S. J., and Thomas, R. S. (1998). Realigning corporate governance: Shareholder activism by labor unions. *Michigan Law Review* 96: 1018.

Shivdasani, A. (1993). Board composition, ownership structure, and hostile takeovers. *Journal of Accounting and Economics* 16: 167.

Smith, M. (1996). Shareholder activism by institutional investors: Evidence from CalPERS. *Journal of Finance* 51: 227.

Strickland, D., Wiles, K., and Zenner, M. (1996). A requiem for the USA: Is small shareholder monitoring effective. *Journal of Financial Economics* 40: 319.

Sundaramurthy, C., Mahoney, J. M., and Mahoney, J. T. (1997). Board structure, antitakeover provisions, and stockholder wealth. *Strategic Management Journal* 18: 231.

Thomas, R. S., and Martin, K. J. (1998). Should labor be allowed to make shareholder proposals? *Washington Law Review* 73: 41.

——(1999). The effect of shareholder proposals on executive compensation. *University of Cincinnati Law Review* 67: 1021.

Titman, S., and Trueman, B. (1986). Information quality and the value of new issues. *Journal of Accounting and Economics* 8: 159.

Wahal, S. (1996). Pension fund activism and firm performance. *Journal of Financial and Quantitative Analysis* 31: 1.

Weisbach, M. (1988). Outside directors and CEO turnover. *Journal of Financial Economics* 20: 431.

Welch, I. (1989). Seasoned offerings, imitation costs, and the underpricing of initial public offerings. *Journal of Finance* 44: 421.

24

Reducing the Costs of Proxy Voting

GEOF P. STAPLEDON AND JONATHAN J. BATES

1. INTRODUCTION

In recent years, there have been several regulatory changes in the UK directed at removing the need for share certificates and decreasing the settlement period for share transactions. Further reforms have been proposed (HM Treasury 1999). These changes have been justified on efficiency grounds.

At the same time, there has been growing concern about the low level of voting by institutional investors in listed UK companies. Although the latest figure is 50 per cent, during the 1990s it was common for only 30–40 per cent of a company's equity to be voted at a shareholder meeting (PIRC 1998; 1999). Unlike in the USA, where private-sector pension plans (the largest category of institutional investor) are effectively obliged to vote due to regulations made under the ERISA legislation,[1] the most relevant legal obligation on UK institutional investors is merely to consider whether to vote (Stapledon 2000). But voting by institutional investors is increasingly seen as an important element of corporate governance (OECD 1999: section I; Financial Services Authority 2000: Combined Code, Part E.1). And empirical studies have demonstrated that the voting right has economic value, although that value can change depending on the circumstances (Lease *et al.* 1983; Grossman and Hart 1988; Barclay and Holderness 1989; Zingales 1994; 1995; Nicodano 1998).

In the light of this, in 1998 and again in 1999 the British government warned that if the level of voting by institutions did not increase, regulations to mandate voting may be imposed (Martinson 1998; 1999*a*). This led to the formation of the Committee of Inquiry into UK Vote Execution (Newbold Committee), which spent nine months investigating why the voting record of institutional investors (pension funds, in particular) has, overall, been so poor. The Newbold Committee (1999: para. 1.7) found that, among other things, 'the voting cycle represents a tortuous process'.

This chapter explains why voting is currently a tortuous process for many institutional investors (domestic and foreign) holding shares in UK companies, and then details a reform

The key ideas in this chapter are based on those in a paper prepared by the authors for the Department of Trade and Industry in September 1999. The authors thank Judith Hanratty of BP Amoco plc, and Dan Prentice for helpful comments on that earlier paper prepared for the DTI. The usual disclaimer applies.

proposal aimed at reducing the costs involved in the voting process, and potentially providing further benefits. The chapter's focus is institutional share ownership because institutions account for about 70 per cent of listed UK equities.[2] While the chapter focuses on the UK corporate sector and UK regulations, its themes apply more broadly—for two reasons: first, the existing regulatory scheme that gives rise to the voting difficulties in the UK (outlined in the next paragraph) is closely mirrored in many other countries. Most common law countries whose corporate law grew out of the English companies legislation of the mid-nineteenth century have retained the central concept under which the registered holder of shares (called the 'member' in the current UK statute) has the right to receive meeting documents and to vote.[3] Second, the institutional investor sectors in countries like Canada, Australia, and New Zealand closely resemble that in the UK, in relation to the use of investment management firms and custodians. So, although this chapter refers throughout to UK regulations and UK ownership structures, it is likely that the chapter's central themes and the reform suggestion developed in relation to the UK statute are of some relevance in other jurisdictions.

The reform proposal advocated in this chapter would be effected via a change from a mandatory rule to an enabling rule. Examining the nature of the current 'mandatory' rule is essential in understanding the significance of the proposed change. In short, a key impediment to institutional investor voting stems from a combination of these three factors:

1. Section 22 of the Companies Act 1985 (UK), under which a company's 'members' are defined as those persons entered in the company's register of members, commonly called the share register in the case of companies limited by shares. Where institutional investors invest in equities, they commonly engage custodians. It is the custodian whose name is entered in the company's register of members.
2. Those sections of the Companies Act[4] and companies' articles that require general meeting documents to be sent to members which also confer the right to vote on these members (i.e. the persons entered in the share register e.g., custodians); and
3. The fact that, in practice, the power to determine how to vote shares held in a custodian's name normally rests not with the custodian (the member) but elsewhere, often with a fund manager.[5]

The combination of these three factors means that meeting documents and votes must pass through custodians who serve as nothing more than conduits in these processes. This in itself is costly. But there is an additional shortcoming with the existing rule: it is a factor in unsuccessful attempts to vote. The Newbold Committee (1999: 3) received evidence of 'mismatches' where institutional investors' voting instructions given to custodians were not registered in the final result. As flagged in a moment, whether this impact on the level of institutional investor voting is a costly feature of the current rule depends on whether institutional investor voting is an efficiency-enhancing activity from society's viewpoint. In any event, the proposal detailed later in the chapter would enable a member, acting on the instructions of the beneficial owner, where the member is not the beneficial owner, to designate a person to whom general meeting documents[6] must be sent, and from whom a completed proxy form must be accepted. It is expected that the designated person would often be the fund manager engaged by the beneficial owner of the shares. In essence, the proposed reform would enable custodians to be by-passed in the voting process.

The proposed provision described below involves a clear distinction between the 'operational' and 'property' incidents of shareholding. The provision would not compromise the property aspects of share ownership, namely security of title and security of transfer. It would affect only one operational aspect of shareholding: exercise of the voting right. But once activated, the provision would alter fundamentally the traditional notion of share ownership by separating its operational and property aspects.[7]

Two key benefits appear certain to flow from the proposed reform: first, the reform should go some way to reducing the complexity inherent in the existing system and thereby reducing the costs currently involved in exercising voting rights. This reveals the main premise of this chapter: that there is evidence to suggest that there are costs which arise in the transfer of meeting documentation to, and the transmission of voting instructions from, the person who has the interest in the potential benefit of holding voting rights (e.g. a pension fund trustee representing the fund beneficiaries; or a fund manager who, under contractual obligations and performance incentives, stands to gain from the outcome of voting right exercise).

Second, there should be a spin-off benefit for listed companies. This indirect benefit to companies should flow from the identification of voting-right holders that would occur under the proposed provision. Companies currently pay external firms to analyse the share register to determine the identity of the largest voting-right holders (Stapledon 1996: 322). There would be less demand for this service in its current form—and cost savings for companies (an indirect benefit for all shareholders)—if there were to be a reasonably significant take-up of the designation power by members. It is not possible, in the absence of empirical data, to do more than speculate about the magnitude of these two benefits.

A third benefit may also flow from the reform proposal. On the assumption that institutional investor activism increases efficiency in certain cases, any measure that makes it easier for institutional investors to exercise their voting rights, and leads to a higher level of successful attempts to vote by institutional investors, would enhance the gains from institutional investor activism. The assumption just stated is important. This article does not contribute to the central issue in the debate about the efficiency potential of institutional investor activism. The only contribution made to that debate is that, assuming institutional investor activism increases efficiency in certain cases, the potential gains will be partially dependent on a low-cost system for the operational incidents of a share.

It is acknowledged that certain costs would accompany the introduction of a provision like the one proposed. However, it is argued below that the benefits of the proposal are likely to outweigh the costs. Also, importantly, the proposal respects the importance to financial market participants of secure title and secure transfers, and of anonymity for those investors who seek it.

The remainder of the chapter is structured as follows. Section 2 identifies the three main 'interest-holders' in a parcel of shares: the member or registered shareholder; the beneficial owner; and the holder of the control rights. In some cases, one person will hold all three interests, but in the case of institutional share ownership this is rare. This is followed by two sections which provide data on the proportion of the UK equity market owned beneficially by institutions, and controlled by institutions, respectively. This helps illustrate the practical importance of the reform proposal made later in the chapter. Section 5 unpacks institutional share ownership. That is, it identifies, by legal analysis, the three interest-holders for each of the main categories of institutional investor: insurance companies; pension funds; unit trusts; investment trusts; and open-ended investment companies. Section 5 explains in more detail how the structure of institutional share ownership is problematic for voting. Section 9 considers whether market rather than regulatory mechanisms may provide a solution to the voting problem. It is considered unlikely that the main market mechanism currently available—the power of attorney—will be utilized widely. The reform proposal is then explained and justified through what is essentially a preliminary cost–benefit analysis. Section 10 raises the possibility of the proposed bypassing procedure being extended to other incidents of shareholding, for instance, payment of dividends.

2. THE INTEREST-HOLDERS IN SHARES

Assessing the shareholding population of listed UK companies involves identifying three main interest-holders in any parcel of shares:

1. *The member.* That is, the person/entity entered on the company's register of members. The member is also known as the registered shareholder or the legal owner of the shares. For example, where a custodian holds shares on behalf of a client, the custodian is the member. It is common to refer to shares held by custodians as being held by 'nominees'. This reflects a structure under which a custodian holds shares on a bare trust for its client.
2. *The beneficial owner of the shares.* For example, where the member is a trustee, it holds the shares on trust for the beneficiaries of the trust, who are (collectively) the beneficial owners of the shares. Even where the member is a custodian appointed by the trustee, the shares are still, ultimately, held on trust for the beneficiaries of the trust.[8]
3. *The holder of the control rights.* In this chapter, the term 'control rights' means the right to receive information from a listed public company, and the right to exercise votes attached to shares.[9] For example, where the trustee of a pension scheme engages a fund management firm to manage the scheme's equity investments, the fund management contract typically provides the fund manager with the power to give voting instructions to the custodian (the registered shareholder/member), subject to any overriding instruction from the trustee (Stapledon 1996: 89).[10] Here, the fund manager holds the voting control right attaching to the shares.[11]

Sometimes all three interests are held by the one person/entity, but, as shown later in the chapter, in the case of institutional share ownership it is more common for at least two different parties to be involved.

3. BENEFICIAL OWNERSHIP OF LISTED UK EQUITIES

Table 24.1 provides the most current aggregate statistics on the beneficial ownership of listed UK equities.

Table 24.1. *Beneficial ownership of UK equities, 1998*

Sector of beneficial owner	Beneficial ownership of total listed UK equities (% of market)
Insurance companies	23.5
Pension funds	22.1
Unit trusts, investment trusts and other institutions	10.6
Overseas	24.0
Individuals	16.5
Charities	1.9
Industrial and commercial companies	1.2
Banks	0.1
Public sector	0.1
Total	100

Source: Office for National Statistics (1999). Figures as at 31 December 1997.

The classes of beneficial owner listed in Table 24.1 that fall within the definition of institutional investor are life insurance companies, pension funds, unit trusts, investment trusts, and other financial institutions. The shareholdings of banks identified in Table 24.1 should not be classified as institutional shareholdings. Most large UK banks have fund management arms which manage equities on behalf of pension funds and other beneficial owners, but the shares owned beneficially by banks are mostly either corporate holdings or the result of debt-for-equity swaps. They are not portfolio investments.

As at 1998, domestic institutional investors owned 56 per cent of the UK share market. However, overseas-based institutional investors are a growing force in the UK share market. They probably accounted for at least half the overseas holding of 24 per cent.[12] Taking one-half as an estimate, the figure for total (domestic and overseas) institutional ownership of listed UK equities would be almost 70 per cent.

The proportion of shares held by local institutions increased markedly in the UK between the early 1960s and the early 1990s. The total holding of locally based institutions was: 29 per cent in 1963; 34 per cent in 1969; 47 per cent in 1975; 58 per cent in 1981; and 60 per cent in 1992 (Office for National Statistics 1999).

As Table 24.1 shows, the total for domestic institutions had slipped back a bit (to 56 per cent) by 1998. This seems to be attributable to pension schemes re-allocating some of their holdings into bonds (Office for National Statistics 1999: para. 3.12). This, in turn, is presumably at least partly a result of the minimum funding requirement imposed by the Pensions Act 1995 (UK).

The total 'overseas' holding of UK equities increased from 7 per cent in 1963 to 13 per cent in 1992. It then accelerated to 24 per cent by 1998. As a significant proportion of the total overseas holding would be the shareholdings of overseas-based institutional investors, the slight decline in the proportionate holding of local institutions between 1992 and 1998 has almost certainly been offset by an increase in the holding of overseas institutions.

Another clear trend in the UK is the decline in the proportionate holding of individuals: from 54 per cent in 1963 to 16.5 per cent in 1998. This is explained partly by the growing proportionate holding of the institutions, and partly by individuals swapping their money from directly held shares to indirect investment in equities via investments in unit trusts, investment trusts and pension funds.[13]

The two primary causes of the increased proportion of listed UK equities held by local institutions now, compared to the early 1960s, appear to be: (1) the growth in long-term saving since the Second World War, and the resultant massive increase in funds available to the institutions for investment (Davies 1993: 70–3); and (2) the disposition of insurance companies and pension funds towards equities, since the 1960s. There are several factors behind each of (1) and (2). In relation to (1), demographic trends, inadequate state pensions and income growth have all contributed (Davis 1991). In relation to (2), the concern of institutions to protect their capital bases during periods of inflation, and the relative performance of equities compared to gilts and cash since the end of the First World War, appear to be the central factors. Over any rolling 20-year period from 1918 to 1990, UK equities produced better returns than gilts and Treasury Bills (WM Company 1990: 4–6).[14]

4. CONTROL OF LISTED UK EQUITIES

An important thing to note about Table 24.1 is that equities owned beneficially by institutional investors (insurance companies, pension funds, unit trusts, investment trusts, and other financial institutions) are managed by fund management firms. Some fund management firms are 'in-house' at the institutions, such as Prudential Portfolio Managers Ltd., which is a wholly owned subsidiary of Prudential Corporation plc (the large UK life insurance and financial services group).[15] Other fund management firms might be termed 'external' investment managers. In the case of firms such as Mercury Asset Management plc and Schroder Investment Management Ltd., for example, the vast majority of assets under management are those of external clients such as pension fund trustees.

Fund management firms manage not only the funds of the institutional investors just mentioned, but also the funds of individuals, charities, and other bodies. The proportion of the UK equity market managed by locally based fund management firms would, therefore, have been higher than the proportion of total equities owned by domestic institutions as detailed in Table 24.1. This distinction is significant because (as mentioned above) it is common for fund managers to have the power to exercise the voting rights attached to their clients' equity investments. Possession of the power to exercise the voting right attached to a share, places one in the position of, effectively, 'controller' of that share. Thus, the proportion of the equity market managed by fund managers is a close approximation of the proportion of the equity market controlled by them. However, the way in which the control rights attached to shares are allocated is not static. Although it is still common for the voting right to be delegated to the fund manager under the fund management agreement, there is evidence that some large UK pension scheme trustees have recently varied the typical arrangement by shifting the voting right from the fund manager to another firm, also in the business of fund management, but marketing itself as an 'active investor' from a corporate governance perspective. The recipient of the voting right charges a fee for exercising that right on behalf of the pension scheme. This fee provides some evidence of the economic value of the voting right in the UK (cf. Zingales 1995).[16]

Nevertheless, at present the proportion of the UK equity market managed by fund managers is still a close approximation of the proportion of the equity market controlled by them. On that basis, Table 24.2 shows the fund management firms that controlled significant stakes in the listed UK equity market at the beginning of 1998. The investment management arms of financial conglomerates and insurance companies dominate. There were nine of each category in the top twenty UK-based fund managers, at the date of Table 24.2.

A striking point that emerges when comparing Tables 24.1 and 24.2 is that pension schemes are significant beneficial owners of equities, but relatively insignificant controllers of equities. The explanation lies in the widespread use by pension schemes of external fund managers. Indeed, only one in-house pension fund manager ranked in the top twenty equities managers at the date of Table 24.2. This was Hermes Investment Management Ltd.,

Table 24.2. *Twenty largest managers of listed UK equities, 1998*

Fund manager	Market share[a]	Running total
Prudential (Ins.)	3.87	3.87
Mercury (FC)	3.52	7.39
Schroder (FC)	3.42	10.81
Barclays (FC)	2.21	13.02
Legal & General (Ins.)	2.11	15.13
Phillips & Drew (FC)	2.08	17.21
Morgan Grenfell (FC)	2.03	19.24
Standard Life (Ins.)	2.03	21.27
Gartmore (FC)	1.92	23.19
Royal (Ins.)	1.91	25.10
CGU (Ins.)	1.77	26.87
Hill Samuel (FC)	1.47	28.34
Norwich Union (Ins.)	1.36	29.70
Threadneedle (Ins.)	1.27	30.97
Hermes (Pens.)	1.17	32.14
HSBC (FC)	1.03	33.17
Scottish Widows (Ins.)	1.01	34.18
Fleming (FC)	0.98	35.16
M&G (Indep.)	0.96	36.12
AMP (UK) (Ins.)	0.94	37.06

[a]'Market share' equals value of local equities under management ÷ total domestic market capitalization.

Sources: Our own calculations based on information in Hymans Robertson (1998) and London Stock Exchange (1998); information supplied by Michelle Edkins (Corporate Governance Executive, Hermes Investment Management Ltd.); and company annual reports. Figures as at 31December 1997.

Abbreviations: See Appendix.

which is owned by the trustee of the BT Pension Scheme, and manages the bulk of the assets of that scheme and the Post Office's pension schemes.[17] As at 31 December 1998, 80 per cent of directly invested UK pension schemes[18] used solely external fund managers, while only 12 per cent managed their assets wholly in-house, and 8 per cent used both external and in-house fund managers.[19] Minns (1980: 41) conducted a study using 1975 data, and found that: pension funds owned beneficially 16.8 per cent of listed UK equities, but controlled only 5.6 per cent; whereas banks, stockbroking firms and merchant banks owned beneficially only 1.1 per cent of listed UK equities, but controlled (through their investment management arms) 23.9 per cent.

It appears beyond doubt that a similar contrast exists today, given: (i) the large beneficial holding of pension funds but virtual absence of in-house pension fund managers among the largest equities managers; and (ii) the tiny beneficial holding of banks but prevalence of financial conglomerates among the largest equities managers. This contrast is very significant for present purposes. Where the trustee of a pension scheme engages an external fund manager, the trustee usually also engages an external custodian in whose name the scheme's equity investments are registered. The use of external custodians is, in general, accompanied by logistical difficulties in the exercise of voting rights. Where a pension scheme's trustee employs in-house fund managers, the scheme's assets are often registered in the name of the trustee[20] or another internal entity. Here, voting is a less complicated issue. But, as highlighted above, pension scheme trustees use external fund managers more commonly than in-house fund managers, which explains the extent of the voting difficulties reported by the Newbold Committee, which in turn provided the impetus for this chapter's reform proposal.

5. THE STRUCTURE OF INSTITUTIONAL SHARE OWNERSHIP AND CONTROL

5.1. *Insurance Companies*

Major insurance companies operating in the UK fall into three groups: (1) Mutually owned companies. Mutuals are 'owned' by their policyholders (or certain types of policyholders). That is, the policyholders are the members of a mutual insurance company;[21] (2) companies limited by shares and listed on the London Stock Exchange. As with other companies limited by shares, it is the registered shareholders who are the members of a share-capital insurance company; and (3) companies limited by shares and which are subsidiaries of other companies, including overseas-based insurance groups and UK and overseas banks.

Most of the equity investments of insurance companies are in their life funds as opposed to their general funds, such as household, vehicle, and/or health.

Registered ownership. Although practices vary among the insurers, it is common for equity investments to be registered in the insurance company's own name. Less commonly, a custodian may be engaged to be the registered owner of the shares (in which case the custodian is the member of the investee company concerned; but it holds the shares on a bare trust for the insurance company, which is the beneficial owner).

Beneficial ownership. The insurance company is the beneficial owner of the equity investments and other assets which make up its insurance funds, and back the policies issued by it.

Policyholders have no collective rights of ownership (legal or beneficial) in respect of the assets backing their insurance policies. Instead, they are creditors of the insurance company. This is the case regardless of whether the insurer is a mutual or a share-capital company.

In addition, the members (i.e. the shareholders in the case of a share-capital insurance company; and the policyholders, in their capacity as members, in the case of a mutual) have no ownership interest, legal or beneficial, in the equity investments or other assets of an insurance company. The insurance company is treated by the law as a legal entity separate from its members.[22] The insurance company is the owner of the assets backing the policies that it issues; the company's members have a membership interest and membership rights, but no ownership interest in the company's assets.[23]

Control rights. Virtually every well-known UK company authorized to write life insurance has a fund management subsidiary (or division) which manages the investment of most, if not all, of the group's insurance funds. Where an insurer's equity investments are managed in-house in this way, the voting control rights attaching to the shares would normally rest with the insurer's fund management staff. Some small insurers, which do not have the resources to conduct investment management, use external fund managers.[24] In these cases, the control rights would normally be delegated to the external fund management firm.

5.2. *Pension Funds*

Nearly all funded occupational pension schemes are constituted as trusts, separate from their sponsoring entities.[25] They may have individual trustees, but most large schemes have a corporate trustee, which is usually a wholly owned subsidiary of the sponsoring employer. The directors of a corporate trustee are usually senior executives of the sponsor, plus member representatives.[26]

There are three ways in which the cashflows of funded pension schemes may be invested: in insurance policies; in pooled funds; or directly invested.

5.2.1. *Insured Schemes*

Small pension schemes often just take out insurance policies. The policy is usually a with-profits endowment policy or a deposit-administration contract (which operates similarly to a bank account) (Goode Committee 1993: paras 2.4.23–2.4.26). The policy of an insured pension scheme is treated like most other insurance policies: the premiums are pooled together with those of other policies into a large fund which is invested in the name of the insurance company. The insurance company is the beneficial owner of any equity investments, and (as detailed above) normally also the registered owner and the holder of the control rights. The pension scheme trustee is simply the owner of one or more insurance policies.

5.2.2. *Pooled Funds*

A pooled pension fund is one in which the moneys of a number of different pension schemes are aggregated and invested, as one fund, by an external fund manager. Most pooled funds are either unit-linked insurance funds (known as life company 'managed funds') or authorized unit trusts.[27] In relation to managed funds, a unit-linked insurance fund is not a separate legal entity: the life company merely keeps separate accounts recording the assets representing the fund, the present value of those assets, and transfers of cash into and out of the fund (Linklaters and Paines 1989: para. A2.0310). The fund forms part of the insurer's life fund, and is notionally divided into units. Trustees of pension schemes effectively buy 'units' in the fund, which are then liquidated as necessary to meet the schemes' obligations as they fall due (Goode Committee 1993: para. 2.4.27). In law, however, the beneficial owner of the assets comprising a managed fund is the insurance company. The insurance company is (as detailed above) normally also the registered owner and the holder of the control rights. The investing pension scheme trustees own just their insurance policies.

5.2.3. *Directly Invested Pension Schemes*

Most large pension schemes are directly invested. Here, the scheme trustee invests directly in assets such as equities, bonds, and/or real property.

Registered ownership. In the case of a directly invested pension scheme, the registered owner of equity investments may be the trustee of the scheme, or a custodian engaged by the trustee. The latter is very common.

Some custodians use a 'pooled nominee system' under which the shareholdings of all clients are registered in just one nominee name (with reliance on internal records to differentiate the different underlying holdings). The single nominee holding is sometimes called an 'omnibus account'. Other custodians use a 'designated nominee system' under which each client's holding is registered in a unique name (for example, ABC Nominees Ltd., A/C 001, ABC Nominees Ltd., A/C 002, etc.) (Securities and Investments Board 1993: ch. 6).

Beneficial ownership. The beneficiaries of a directly invested pension scheme are, collectively, the ultimate beneficial owners of the scheme's equity investments. This is the case regardless of whether the registered owner is the scheme trustee or a custodian.

Where the scheme trustee is the registered owner, it—like the trustee of any trust—holds the shares on trust for the scheme beneficiaries. It does not matter whether the pension scheme has individual trustees or a corporate trustee.[28] Even a corporate trustee, under trust law principles, has no beneficial interest in the scheme assets. The assets are held by the corporate trustee on trust for the scheme beneficiaries.[29]

Where a custodian is the registered owner, that custodian holds the shares on a bare trust for its client, in this case the trustee of the pension scheme. But the trustee itself holds scheme assets on trust for the scheme beneficiaries.[30] The scheme beneficiaries are, therefore, collectively the ultimate beneficial owners of a directly invested pension scheme's equity investments, regardless of who is on the share register.

Control rights. Where the scheme trustee is the registered owner of a directly invested pension scheme's equity investments, the law of trusts dictates that the exercise of voting rights is a matter for the trustee.[31] It would be open to the trustee to 'retain' those voting rights or to delegate them, for example, to an external fund manager hired to manage the scheme's assets.[32]

Where a custodian is the registered shareholder, it is the member and therefore receives general meeting notices and proxy voting material. It, as a matter of company law, has the right to exercise voting rights or to appoint a proxy to do so on its behalf.[33] However, the custodian holds the shares as a bare trustee, and as such it is required under equitable principles—and usually also by an express contractual provision—to exercise the voting rights as directed by the pension scheme's trustee, or somebody specified by the trustee. Thus, a modern fund management agreement (the contract between the scheme trustee and the external fund manager) will often provide that the fund manager may, at its discretion, give voting instructions to the custodian, subject always to any specific instructions from the trustee (Stapledon 1996: 89).

5.3. *Unit Trusts*

Unit trusts are open-ended investment funds operated under a trust structure. They may be authorized or unauthorized; only authorized unit trusts may be marketed to the public.[34] Authorized unit trust schemes must have a trustee independent of a manager.[35] The trustee is responsible for the custody or control of the scheme's assets.[36]

Registered ownership. The registered owner of a unit trust scheme's equity investments may be the trustee of the scheme, or a custodian engaged by the trustee.

Beneficial ownership. Beneficial ownership of a unit trust's assets rests with the collective body of unit-holders.[37] Where a custodian is the registered owner, the unit-holders' collective beneficial interest arises in the same indirect way that the beneficiaries of a directly invested pension scheme enjoy beneficial ownership of assets registered in a custodian's name.[38]

Control rights. Ordinarily, the manager of an authorized unit trust scheme possesses the control rights attached to the scheme's equity investments. Under the Regulations, the voting rights attached to the property of an authorized unit trust scheme must be exercised or not exercised as directed by the manager.[39]

5.4. *Investment Trusts*

Investment trusts are closed-end investment funds. Despite their name, they are not trusts; they are public companies. As companies, they are legal entities separate from the persons who invest in them (i.e. their shareholders).[40]

Most investment trust companies engage a fund management firm to manage their assets. In fact, many existing investment trusts were promoted, and effectively established, by fund management firms. The choice of, and contractual engagement of, the fund management firm to manage the assets of a newly established investment trust might therefore seem a foregone conclusion. However, the Listing Rules of the Financial Services Authority (2000: paras 21.9(d), 21.10, 21.20) include a requirement that the board of directors of a listed investment trust 'must be able to demonstrate that it will act independently of any investment managers of the investment [trust] and a majority must not be employees of or professional advisers to the investment managers or any other company in the same group as the investment managers'.

Registered ownership. The registered owner of an investment trust's equity investments may be the investment trust company itself, or a custodian engaged by it. Where a custodian is the registered owner, it holds the shares on a bare trust for the investment trust company.

Beneficial ownership. The beneficial ownership of an investment trust's equity investments rests with the investment trust company. The investment trust's own shareholders have no ownership interest, legal or equitable, in the assets of the investment trust.[41]

Control rights. The control rights attached to an investment trust's equity investments are commonly delegated by the board of directors of the investment trust to the fund manager of the trust's assets.

5.5. *Open-Ended Investment Companies*

An open-ended investment company (OEIC) is a pooled investment vehicle that, as its name suggests, is open-ended like a unit trust. However, OEICs differ from unit trusts because OEICs are companies. Investors receive shares rather than units.[42]

OEICs must have: (1) one or more directors. One director must be a body corporate authorized under the Financial Services Act 1986 to carry out investment business; this director, called the Authorized Corporate Director (ACD), is responsible for the day-to-day management of the scheme; and (2) a 'depositary' to whom the scheme property is 'entrusted' for 'safekeeping' under the Regulations. The depositary must be independent of the OEIC and its directors.

Registered ownership. The registered owner of an OEIC's equity investments may be the depositary of the OEIC, or a custodian engaged by the depositary.[43] In either case, the shares are held on a bare trust for the OEIC (Morse 1976: para. 5A.006).

Beneficial ownership. The beneficial ownership of an OEIC's equity investments rests with the OEIC. The OEIC's own shareholders have no ownership interest—legal or beneficial—in the assets of the OEIC.[44]

Control rights. The control rights attached to an OEIC's equity investments are the responsibility of the ACD. The depositary (or other registered holder) must exercise the voting rights attached to equity investments as directed by the ACD.[45]

6. THE CASE FOR REFORM

As highlighted earlier, there are three interest-holders in any parcel of shares in a listed company: the member (or 'registered shareholder' or 'legal owner'); the beneficial owner; and the holder of the control rights. Sometimes all three interests will be held by the one person. But, where institutional investors are concerned, the analysis above shows that there will commonly be two or three different parties involved.

Figure 24.1 shows a typical arrangement for a 'directly invested' pension scheme.[46] It is, despite its appearance, actually a simplified illustration of the typical arrangement. In reality, the picture is often more complicated due to two factors. First, custodians sometimes amalgamate several clients' shareholdings. That is, they register the shareholdings of several different clients in a single nominee name (e.g. ABC Nominees Ltd.) rather than registering each client's holding in a unique (or 'designated') nominee name (e.g. ABC Nominees Ltd. A/C 001, ABC Nominees Ltd. A/C 002, ABC Nominees Ltd. A/C 003, etc.). As mentioned earlier, the use of a single nominee is known as a 'pooled nominee system' of registration or an 'omnibus account'.[47] Here, the custodian relies on internal records to differentiate the different underlying holdings.

Second, large pension schemes will often engage more than one fund manager, and there may as a result be more than one custodian holding shares on the scheme's behalf in a particular listed company.

The example of a directly invested pension scheme has been given because, in terms of UK equity holdings, directly invested pension schemes account for a very significant proportion of total holdings of institutional investors: approximately 30 per cent, which translates to about 21 per cent of the entire listed UK equities market as at 1998.[48] However,

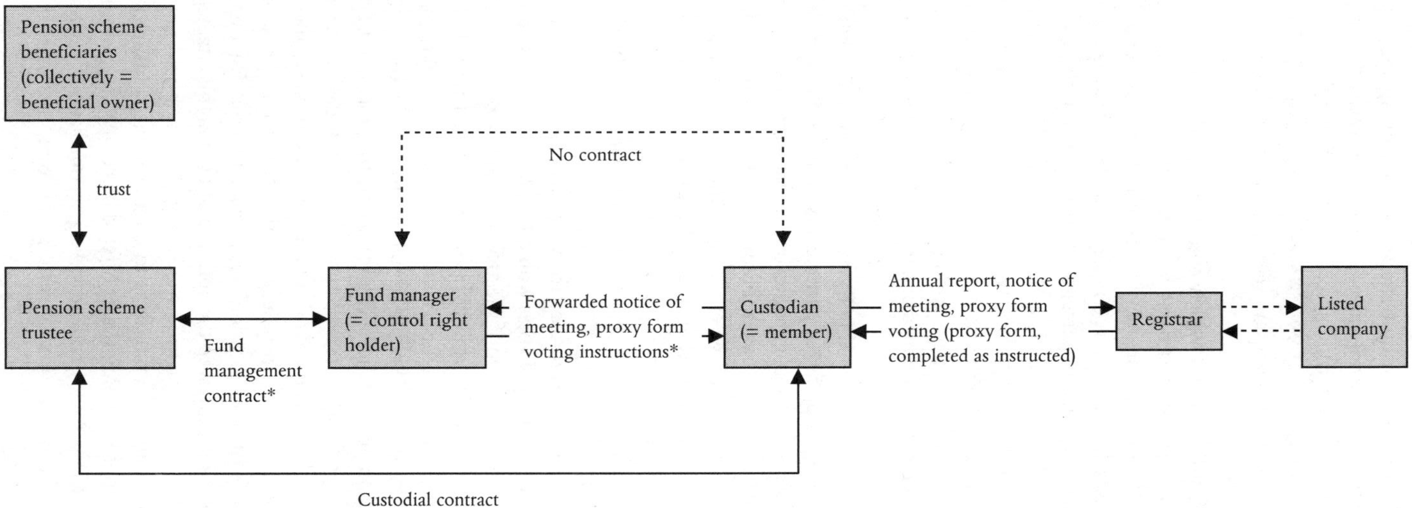

Figure 24.1. *Typical directly invested pension scheme*

**Commonly the fund management contract gives the fund manager power to give voting instructions to the custodian. The fund management contract usually says that these voting instructions are subject to any instructions that the trustee(s) of the scheme may give from time to time. See Stapledon (1996).*

it was demonstrated earlier that other institutional investment arrangements also commonly entail two or more interest-holders. And, indeed, where directly invested private investors hold their equity investments through nominee accounts, there will also be at least two interest-holders (DTI 1996; Davies 1999: 345–6). Similar issues to those considered below in relation to directly invested pension schemes will, therefore, sometimes apply to these other types of investors.

The sections of the Companies Act which confer information and voting rights on the registered holder were perfectly justifiable when they were introduced in nineteenth-century predecessor legislation and for many years afterwards. Shareholding structures would, in a majority of cases, have been very simple in the sense that there would have been only one interest-holder in a particular parcel of shares. However, there have been major changes in the structure of share ownership and control in the UK and elsewhere in recent decades. These changes have come about largely due to the massive increase in institutional share ownership.[49] These changes in the marketplace mean that the rule that was efficient in earlier years is now a source of costs in the voting process. This is because, even where the registered holder is now merely an intermediary, under the current rule that party must be involved in the voting process.

As well as the additional costs involved in the voting process, the Newbold Committee (1999: 2) reported that the 'multiplicity of participants in the voting cycle and the lack of modern technological means to allow communication of votes by those participants has led to a system where opportunities for mistakes abound'. The Committee (ibid., see also para. 1.8) received evidence of 'mismatches' where institutional investors' instructions to vote were not registered in the final result. That is, an attempt was made to vote, but due to a breakdown somewhere along the line the proxy form was never actually received by the listed company's registrar. The evidence suggests that breakdowns will often involve the custodian (ibid. para. 2.13).

The Newbold Committee (ibid.: 3) formed the view that the introduction of electronic means of transmission and recording of votes would not, by itself, lead to a higher level of voting. As Fig. 24.1 demonstrates, even if electronic voting were introduced overnight, there would still be a situation where, typically, a custodian is interposed between the fund manager (holder of control rights) and the company's registrar. And in terms of the added costs involved in the voting process flowing from the current rule, the evidence suggests that electronic voting will not remove these. This is because the process must still take place. If the interface between fund managers and custodians required to generate and lodge a proxy appointment and voting instruction is not internally resourced, then a third party service is used. To the extent that costs are reduced by the economies of mass processing and electronic communication, costs savings would be expected to result. But this does not alter the structure of the process: in contrast to the option proposed in this chapter.

Any analysis of the role of custodians in the voting process should not overlook the benefits of the services provided by custodians to their customers. Institutional investors are likely to value cost savings in trading shares offered by competing custodians, administrative convenience in settling trades and providing reconciliation, a sense of security, and in some cases secrecy both from other investors and companies over their investment choices.

7. COULD THE PROBLEM BE OVERCOME WITHOUT REGULATORY REFORM?

Decreasing the costs involved in the process of voting and decreasing the incidence of unsuccessful attempts to vote need not involve regulatory change. There are likely to be some developments through market processes. The most likely development is the use of powers of attorney.

The Newbold Committee (ibid.: 9) forecast an increased use of powers of attorney once electronic voting becomes more common. This would involve the custodian (the 'member') providing a power of attorney in favour of the fund manager (the holder of the control rights) after being instructed to do so by the pension scheme trustee. The company (or its registrar) would be given a copy of the power of attorney. This would enable the company's registrar validly to recognize a proxy form transmitted directly by the fund manager to the registrar.[50]

However, there are several disadvantages that suggest that the costs in the current system will not be significantly reduced through market forces alone. First, the custodian may not be able to direct the company's registrar to send the notice of meeting and proxy form straight to the fund manager. The power of attorney may work only in one direction, that is, when the completed proxy form is returned to the company's registrar. Second, even if the power of attorney did work in both directions, it is a paper-dependent process with verification requirements. Third, from an international perspective, use of a UK-specific power of attorney is unlikely to be the most attractive option for foreign control right holders.

The issue of the appropriate response to the problems presented by the 'member' concept has current policy significance.[51] Government has shown increased willingness to find regulatory means to boost the level of voting in UK public companies.[52] The choices available to it include primary legislation (such as reform of the Companies Act as advocated in this chapter), reform of securities regulation, and promotion of self-regulatory practices. The option of using securities regulation might be considered an attractive alternative to primary legislation. If USA precedent were followed, intermediaries would be obliged under securities market regulations to distribute information to beneficial owners of shares, and voting procedures would have been made available to those persons. Costs would be levied directly on issuing companies.[53] There are, it seems, reasons peculiar to the USA for the evolution of this form of 'voting regulation'. In particular, federal securities law overlays state corporate law. And, since general corporate law is within the constitutional jurisdiction of the states, a primary legislation solution would be beyond the constitutional limits of the federal government's power.[54] The UK does not face this difficulty.

8. A REGULATORY SOLUTION

8.1. *Outline of Proposed Reform*

Regulatory change could facilitate the exercise of the control right and decrease the incidence of unsuccessful attempts to vote. The proposal outlined below would involve changes to the UK Companies Act and could be bolstered by associated changes to the financial services regulatory regime. The proposal involves a clear distinction between the 'operational' and 'property' incidents of shareholding. The proposal would not compromise the property aspects of share ownership, for example, security of title and security of transfer. It would affect only one operational aspect of shareholding: the exercise of the voting right.

The proposal would effectively enable a bypassing of the custodian, or other intermediary, in both directions. A provision of the Companies Act would enable a company to opt into a regime. The provision would say that, once a company has opted into the regime, a member has the right to notify the company of a 'designated person' in respect of a 'designated shareholding' on the company's share register: (1) to whom 'meeting documents' must be sent; (2) who is entitled—to the exclusion of the member—to exercise the voting rights attached to the designated shares; and (3) from whom the company must accept proxy instructions.

'Meeting documents' could be defined as the annual report, notice of meeting, proxy form, and any other documents which the company is required to send,[55] or chooses to send, to members in respect of a general meeting.

The provision should state that, once a company has been notified of a designated person, the only person to whom the company is required to send meeting documents is the designated person.[56] The company should not be required to send the documents to the member as well. If the provision required the documents to be sent to the designated person and the member: transaction costs would increase; and there would be no obvious benefit given that the member (the custodian in the pension scheme example) has waived their power over voting by making the notification.

It would be a matter of contract between the member and the designated person as to whether the meeting documents received by the designated person must be copied to the member. Similarly, it would be a matter of contract between the beneficial owner and the designated person as to whether the meeting documents received by the designated person must be copied to the beneficial owner. This contracting process would allocate cost and risk. In the pension scheme example, the pension scheme trustee would be the contracting party on behalf of the beneficial owners—the collective body of beneficiaries.

In the pension scheme example, the pension scheme trustee would direct the custodian (the member) to notify some or all listed companies in which shares are held that the designated person in respect of those shares is the fund manager. The actual processes would very likely be automated. It should be possible for custodians to provide the listed company's registrar with the details of the designated person by way of an electronic file transfer on the meeting record date.

A provision of this nature would probably lead to an extra element in competition between custodians. In all likelihood, not all custodians would offer the designation service as part of their package of services. A client, for example, a pension scheme trustee, who wanted its equity investments to be designated, could shop around for a new custodian if the incumbent did not offer the service. It would be a matter of contract between the client (beneficial owner) and the custodian as to whether the client could direct the custodian to make a designation.

In terms of comparable existing provisions, the closest is probably the USA 'recognition procedure'. For example, the Indiana Business Corporation Law permits a company to adopt a recognition procedure under which a beneficial owner of shares that are registered in the name of a nominee may be recognized by the company as the shareholder. The extent of that recognition is at the discretion of the company.[57] This procedure is drawn from section 7.23 of the Model Business Corporation Act 1997 Supplement.[58] There are two major limitations on this USA model. First, it has not been adopted by Delaware (home to a very large proportion of major USA companies), New York or California (among other states). Second, as the extent of recognition is a matter for each company that chooses to adopt the recognition procedure, the regime established by a particular company may be limited to distribution of shareholder meeting documents and proxy forms by the company. That is, the actual voting procedure may still involve the registered holder with the proxy votes having to pass through the registered holder on their way to the company. This type of single-direction regime is, in any event, effectively applicable to all major USA companies—even those whose state of incorporation has not legislated to apply the Model Business Corporation Act procedure—due to federal securities law.

Rules promulgated by the Securities and Exchange Commission (SEC) pursuant to the Securities Exchange Act of 1934 impose certain obligations on companies and financial intermediaries (registered brokers and dealers; and banks) with the objective of beneficial owners of shares receiving company reports and proxy solicitation material. Under Rule 14a-13(a), if a listed company knows that shares are held 'of record' in nominee name, and the company intends to solicit proxies, the company must: (1) inquire of record holders (registered holders) as to the number of copies necessary to supply material to beneficial owners; (2) supply that material to the record holders who respond to the inquiries; and (3) pay the record holder's reasonable expenses for completing the mailing of the material to beneficial owners.[59]

This is a single-direction regime. Unlike the provision that this chapter proposes, the SEC rules do not address the costs problems related to the involvement of custodians in the voting process.

8.2. *Should the Provision be an Enabling Provision, a Default Rule or a Mandatory Rule?*

It was noted earlier that the rules of the Companies Act 1985 which, in our view, contribute to the problem do not fit neatly into the traditional categorization of 'mandatory', 'enabling', and 'default' rules. Rather, they are 'boundary-setting' rules which in combination have the effect of determining who is included within, and conversely who is excluded from, the company law framework. The solution proposed can be defined within the traditional framework, and this is set out below.

The provision could be:

(1) an enabling provision, applying only to those companies that opt in (via a clause in their articles);
(2) a default rule, applying to all companies except those whose shareholders have elected to waive the rule;
(3) or a mandatory rule, applying to all companies regardless of what their articles say.[60]

The provision should not be a mandatory rule, because for some companies and their shareholders, the regime would be very unlikely to confer net benefits. For example, a listed company in which a majority of the shares are controlled by one investor—possibly the company's founder—and which has only a handful of institutional shareholders. Here, the costs to the company of facilitating designations may very well outweigh any benefits. The majority shareholder will control the general meeting—at least in normal circumstances (cf. Davies 1997: 707–17, discussing the equitable constraint on the power of majority shareholders to bind the minority). But as time goes by and ownership disperses, and the number of institutional shareholders increases, the cost–benefit equation may change and thereby encourage shareholders and the board to adopt the regime. This may be seen as a useful step in promoting institutional investor interest in the company, particularly among USA institutional investors.

The choice is therefore between a default rule and an enabling provision. If it were to be a default rule, there would be transaction costs for those companies that choose to opt out. They would have to insert a clause into their articles of incorporation to waive the rule. On the other hand, if it were to be an enabling provision, there would be transaction costs (associated with inserting a clause into the articles) for those companies that choose to opt in.

In general, whether any regulatory provision should be a default rule or an enabling provision depends on whether the provision corresponds with the preferences of most companies, and their shareholders (Cheffins 1997: 262). If so, it should be a default rule, in order to minimize transaction costs. If not, then it should be an enabling provision—again, in order to minimize transaction costs.[61]

It seems likely that a provision of this nature would correspond with the preferences of a majority of listed companies, but of only a small minority of unlisted companies. The above example of a listed company for which the provision may entail more costs than benefits was a company controlled by its founder, and with few institutional shareholders. However, a very large proportion of companies listed on the London Stock Exchange are widely held, with no controlling non-institutional shareholder (Franks and Mayer 1996; Stapledon 1996: 188). For listed companies, therefore, a default rule appears preferable to an enabling provision. On the other hand, compared to the average listed company, many unlisted public companies, and virtually all private companies, would have: (a) far fewer shareholders; (b) very few or no 'arm's length' institutional shareholders;[62] and (c) few or no beneficial shareholders using an external custodian to hold legal title to the shares, or a fund manager to 'manage' their investment in the company. For these reasons, the cost–benefit equation for unlisted companies would normally see the costs of the provision outweighing the benefits. For unlisted companies, therefore, an enabling provision appears preferable to a default rule.

A solution may lie in the multi-tiered regulatory approach that has become common in the corporate and financial sectors in the UK. The provision in the Companies Act would be an enabling provision available to all companies, and it would effectively become a default rule for listed companies via the Financial Services Authority Listing Rules. It should be remembered, however, that this would not be tantamount to a mandatory rule because a company would merely be making the regime available to those investors in co-operation with legal owners who contract to take up the designated person status.

The question of the appropriate boundaries of company law is an interesting topic for the current UK Company Law Review. The proposal in this chapter has particular relevance to that topic because it suggests redefining the existing boundaries. It implies a policy choice that company law should not be excluded as a regulatory tool for defining and enforcing certain of the legal incidents of the relationships between investors and the enterprises in which they invest; in other words, the legal process of voting.[63]

8.3. *The Shares Subject to a Designation must be Specified*

A designation would relate to a particular registered shareholding. Assume a fund manager is a designated person in respect of shares in XYZ plc registered in the name of custodian ABC on behalf of a pension scheme (the beneficial owner). The same fund manager makes a further investment in XYZ plc shares, using custodian ABC again, but on behalf of a different client (beneficial owner). The original designation would not apply in relation to the newly-acquired shares. This would clearly be the case where the custodian uses a designated nominee system because the newly-acquired shares would be registered in a name different to the name in which the original shares were registered.

But what if the custodian uses a pooled nominee system?[64] The provision would have to allow for a custodian whose registered holding is held on behalf of, say, thirty different clients (beneficial owners). The custodian (member) in this example might be required to notify the listed company of a designated person in relation to only one client's underlying holding which might be 3,000,000 shares out of the 65,000,000 total shares in that company registered in the name of that custodian.

It should be pointed out that if, as recommended below, only meeting-specific designations were allowed, further purchases and sales of shares would not be problematic. A designation would take effect only on the record date[65] for a particular general meeting, and the relevant number of shares could be precisely identified as those held at the record date.

8.4. *Should only Meeting-Specific Designations be Allowed?*

An issue for consideration is whether the provision should allow only meeting-specific designations or also standing designations. A 'standing designation' is one that is valid for all future general meetings of the company concerned until revoked. It may be desirable for the provision to give a member the option of making a standing designation. Where, as in the pension scheme example, the member is not the beneficial owner, it will be the beneficial owner who will be driving the decision as to whether or not the member makes a designation. And the beneficial owner may wish to take the low transaction cost option of having the member make a standing designation, rather than having the member make a new meeting-specific designation each time a general meeting is convened. This may be the case, for example, where a pension scheme 'indexes' most or all of its UK equity holdings.[66] A key reason why some institutional investors choose to index their equity holdings is because the fund management fees to manage a portfolio passively are considerably lower than those charged for managing a portfolio using active management techniques.[67]

On the other hand, allowing standing designations would introduce extra risk because a listed company's registrar would need to reconcile on an ongoing basis the registered shareholdings that have been made subject to designations. When a complete shareholding is sold, the member ceases to be a member. In the pension scheme example, when the pension scheme's entire holding in a listed company is sold, then: (1) if the custodian uses a designated nominee system,[68] the unique name used by the custodian to register that holding is removed from the listed company's share register; or (2) if the custodian uses a pooled nominee system,[69] the custodian's name will remain on the listed company's share register but its registered shareholding will be smaller.

In either case the nomination of the designated person is no longer of any relevance. But if only meeting-specific designations were to be allowed, and not also standing designations, a sale of shares would not be problematic. Legal relations between a listed company and a designated person, in relation to the operational incidents of shareholding, would arise only at the record date for the particular meeting. The number of shares subject to a particular designation could be precisely identified as those held at the record date. Legal relations between listed company and designated person would end once the general meeting had been held.[70]

On balance, it seems preferable to allow only meeting-specific designations. Certainly, meeting-specific designations should at least be an optional, if not the exclusive, form of designation. A meeting-specific designation would be advantageous for a control-right holder seeking anonymity. In the pension scheme example, the fund manager may see strategic benefit in not having its identity revealed in respect of a particular registered shareholding for a particular period of time. Provided its client, here, the pension scheme trustee, was comfortable with this, no designation would be made for that shareholding even if the trustee's general policy was that designations should be made. It would be a matter of contract. A meeting-specific designation could always be made in respect of a later general meeting if circumstances changed.

If confidential voting is a concern to investors, directors and company secretaries of public companies could be expected to put in place procedures to ensure that voting instructions are attributed to designations only for the purposes of recording and tabulating the vote. This expectation seems in line with the representative nature of the non-executive directors' role; they could be expected to provide the necessary assurance to investor-shareholders on this point.[71]

8.5. *Should the Proposal be Limited to Institutional Investors?*

A case could be made for the provision to be limited, at least initially, to institutional investors. The Newbold Committee's inquiry has revealed problems with the existing system as far as institutional investors are concerned. In contrast, when the Department of Trade and Industry (DTI) consulted on private (individual) shareholders' corporate governance rights in 1996/7, it found little evidence that private shareholders either found the existing system inadequate or supported reforms (DTI 1996).

The shortening of settlement periods and the introduction of the CREST electronic settlement system has led to an increasing proportion of private investors holding their equity investments through custodians (DTI 1996: para. 2.3; Davies 1999). Here, just as with institutional investors, the custodian is the registered shareholder (member) and is therefore the recipient of general meeting documents and the party who sends the completed proxy form to the company. However, private investors currently have the option of 'CREST sponsored membership' as an alternative to using a custodian or holding their shares in paper form. Private investors who take up CREST sponsored membership gain the benefits of holding and transferring shares in electronic form through CREST, but at the same time keep their name on the company's register of members, thus receiving general meeting documents directly from the company, and voting directly (DTI 1996: para. 2.5). As mentioned above, the DTI's consultation revealed a lack of significant support for legislative change to give private investors further mechanisms for gaining direct corporate governance rights.

On the other hand, it may be politically difficult to 'sell' a reform of this nature if private shareholders were to be excluded. It may be expedient to make the provision available in respect of any shareholding, regardless of whether the beneficial holder is an institutional or private investor, or otherwise. In terms of additional costs, these may prove to be minimal if the take-up of the provision by private investors reflects the low level of private investor interest in the issue when the DTI consulted on it in 1996–7.

8.6. *Stock Lending*

Where stock lending takes place,[72] this new system could achieve the recommendation of the Newbold Committee (1999: para. 2.23) that stock lending agreements should include a condition that the borrower undertakes to vote the shares in accordance with the directions of the lender. The condition could specify the designated person as the party in accordance with whose instructions the borrower must exercise voting rights.

8.7. *Property in the Information Supplied*

Consideration should be given to the question of the 'property' in the information (the details about the designated person) held by the custodian and passed to the listed company, or the listed company's external registrar. Although not the subject matter of this chapter, the exercise of construing the legal issues surrounding the holding and disclosure of information should not provide either a conceptual or practical problem. Part VI of the Companies Act currently (1) requires anyone with an 'interest' in 3 per cent or more of a public company's share capital to disclose details of the interest to the company; the legislation then requires the company to make this information available in a publicly accessible register,[73] and (2) empowers public companies to 'trace' interests—that is, to require anyone with an interest in the company's shares (no matter how small or large the interest) to provide information about their identity as well as the nature of the interest; the legislation then requires that this information be made available by the company in a publicly accessible register.[74]

The definition of 'interest' is extremely broad and covers voting-right holders.[75] The process under which this information is actually procured for listed companies is well established. In fact, for companies that currently operate a shareholder identification programme using the tracing power, the introduction and widespread take-up of the designation provision recommended in this article would probably not reveal much new information to the company.

While companies legislation has an established system for identification of those with voting power to the company in this way, the wider issue of protection of that data once lawfully obtained under the legislation is an issue for a separate analysis.

8.8. *Supportive Financial Services Regulations*

The regime could be bolstered by regulations under the Financial Services Act 1986 (UK) to require custodians and other intermediaries holding shares as nominees for beneficial owners to bring to each client's attention that they or their fund manager (or other appointed agent) could be a 'designated person'. The supervision of this conduct of business by authorized firms should also ensure specific and not general disclosure; ensure that clients' details, given to a custodian to be relayed to listed companies under the designation provision, are used by the custodian only for this purpose; and ensure intermediaries' terms of trade do not unfairly establish obstacles to the designation.[76]

9. BENEFITS AND COSTS OF THE REFORM PROPOSAL

9.1. *Categorizing Benefits and Costs*

The issue for regulatory reform is whether existing law, which allocates control rights only to those persons who are 'members' on the register, is optimal. To determine whether or not the existing legal regime is optimal requires analysis of the benefits and costs of it, and of alternative regimes. The description, below, of the benefits and costs of the reform proposal also contains analysis of the benefits and costs of the current legal regime.

It is difficult to categorize and quantify the costs and benefits of a system which plainly allocates the rights of control to those who in reality do not hold them. It is acknowledged, therefore, that this is an area where input is needed from users of the existing system to identify and quantify the benefits and costs of the current system, and to comment on anticipated benefits and costs of the reform proposal. The main (and simple) contention made here is that, if the law permits the voting right to be exercised as a matter of legal process without interposing the custodian whose name is entered on the register of members, then costs will reduce.

9.2. *Sources of Benefits*

9.2.1. *Cost Savings from Reduction in Complexity*

This chapter argues that there is a prima facie case for regulatory reform based on the complexity inherent in the existing legal regime (as analysed earlier in the chapter), and the dissatisfaction about this among institutional investors, as reported by the Newbold Committee (1999: paras 1.7–1.8):

> For all institutions the voting cycle represents a tortuous process which must be conducted against a background of set deadlines imposed by the Companies Act 1985, by companies themselves and, in relation to the Annual General Meeting (AGM), by The Combined Code. The greater the number of links, the greater the complexity...

The costs flowing from the current complex system stem largely from the custodian (member) having to be involved in the voting process. To recap: the manner in which the control rights are defined in company law, focusing on the 'member' or registered holder, does not reflect how they are distributed in practice. The distribution of material to the actual holder of the voting control right, and the process by which votes are cast, is complex. Complex processes cost, and the cost is ultimately borne by investors (whether pension fund beneficiaries, insurance companies, or private investors (direct or indirect)). That is, the costs are shared over the investors in any given company: they are passed through the financial system. They are part of the cost of ownership; not the cost of capital to the entrepreneurs who establish and run public companies, but a cost to those who contribute their capital to the enterprise.

9.2.2. *Possible Efficiency Gains from Greater Level of Institutional Investor Voting*

The following passage from the report of the Newbold Committee (ibid. para. 1.8) highlights a second potential source of benefit from our reform proposal:

> [V]oting outcomes on issues which concern the strategic or financial direction of a company are clearly crucial. Indeed, in matters of corporate governance, key opportunities to convey institutional [investor] sentiment to companies may be lost or not fully exploited [due to the complexity of the voting system].

The benefit here is that, assuming institutional investor activism increases efficiency in certain cases, any measure that makes it easier for institutional investors to exercise their voting rights, and leads to a higher level of successful attempts to vote by institutional investors, would enhance the gains from institutional investor activism. The assumption is important, because this chapter does not contribute to the central issue in the debate about the efficiency potential of institutional investor activism. The only contribution made to that debate is that, assuming institutional investor activism increases efficiency in certain cases, the potential gains will be partially dependent on a low-cost system for the operational incidents of a share.

Does institutional investor voting and other forms of involvement in corporate governance enhance efficiency? Empirical studies have produced mixed results.[77] Recent work by Romano (Chapter 23, this volume) suggests that the mixed results may be a factor of which specific corporate governance feature was being targeted in the institutional investor voting or other action. Romano demonstrates that institutional activism aimed at board structure and composition, for example, does not generally produce a statistically significant effect on company performance. This, according to Romano, is explicable by the fact that board structure and composition itself does not have a statistically significant impact on corporate performance. This fact is discernible from a review of the broad range of empirical studies in this area.[78] On the other hand, institutional investor activism aimed at dismantling certain kinds of takeover defences, by voting against them, is often associated with positive share-price performance. Romano attributes this to the fact that these types of takeover defences have themselves been shown, empirically, to be shareholder-wealth destroying.

The upshot of the USA empirical studies, in particular, appears to be that the growth in institutional shareholdings over recent decades has had an impact on corporate performance, but not in an across-the-board sense. Exercise of voting rights by USA institutional investors does appear to be value enhancing in some areas, such as removal of certain types of takeover defences. So, to the extent that voting by institutional investors is an efficiency-enhancing activity, barriers to the exercise of voting rights by these types of investors are a cost for the company as a whole—ultimately spread over the entire shareholder body—and therefore for society. A low-cost system for exercising voting rights where there are multiple interest-holders in a parcel of shares should enhance any long run gains that flow from institutional investor activism.

9.2.3. *Cost Savings from Identification of Control-Right Holders*

Companies currently pay external firms to analyse the share register to determine the identity of the largest control-right holders (Stapledon 1996: 322). Firms providing this type of service include information service providers and also stockbroking firms. The service provider gleans from the share register every registered holding above a threshold level (which in some cases is as low as 10,000 shares, but is usually either 20,000, 25,000, or 30,000 shares).[79] Databases showing the fund managers (control-right holders) and beneficial owners sitting behind nominee holdings are matched against the collected registered holdings to construct a list of the largest control-right holders.[80] Companies use this information for, among other things, determining which fund managers to invite to management presentations, and road-shows. The information is therefore an integral element of corporate governance in the listed sector.[81]

There would be less demand for this service in its current form and cost savings for companies (ultimately a benefit spread across the entire body of shareholders) if there were to be a reasonably significant take-up of the designation power by members. The designation would reveal the identity of, in most cases, the fund manager controlling the shares in question.

9.2.4. *Preservation of Security of Title and Security of Transfer*

One obvious benefit of the current system is that section 22(2) of the Companies Act 1985 (UK) provides a solid foundation for two aspects of an equity securities market trading system: security of title and security of transfer. Section 22(2) provides that every person who agrees to become a member, and whose name is entered in the register of members, is a member of the company. By security of title, a person or their agent is assured that they own the share because they can point to an entry in a register.[82] By security of transfer, a person or their agent can, in a clear, transparent, and simple manner, transfer shares and receive consideration in exchange, or equally receive shares and transfer consideration in exchange. Settlement of transactions is therefore effected by reference to the register.[83] Participants in the UK equity market value security of title and security of transfer. Liquidity and efficiency is enhanced by these aspects of the existing UK system.[84]

For two reasons, equity market participants should have confidence that a reform like the one proposed in this chapter need not sacrifice the 'property' aspects of trading and holding shares—that is, security of title and transfer: first, the proposal goes only to certain 'operational' aspects of shares (voting and receiving general meeting information). It would not interfere with the 'property' aspects, although it would be necessary to reconcile the entry in the register with the designation(s) for that holding. Second, developments in the trading and settlement procedures for equity securities, and in the clearing and custodial functions, arguably imply that the role of a company's register of members in providing security of title and transfer is in any event disappearing, at least for the majority of investors who hold shares in uncertificated form. The remainder of this section explains this point.

HM Treasury (1999) has recently consulted on amendments to the Uncertificated Securities Regulations 1995 (UK). These regulations enable electronic trading and settlement in shares: they specify the property rights arising in uncertificated securities and their transfer. The consultation paper seeks responses on certain suggested amendments that are proposed in the name of 'efficiency and security of national and international settlement systems' (HM Treasury 1999: Introduction). Specifically, the proposal is to eliminate the gap between settlement and registration, with the effect of reducing 'the risk and perception of risk in the settlement system' (ibid. para. 8). The 'gap' is the time between settlement of a trade in the CREST system, and the confirmation from the company's registrar of change to the register. Paradoxically, this approach indicates that, rather than being a foundation of security of transfer, current section 22(2) is perceived as a source of risk to future UK competitiveness because it involves the company's registrar having a role in title and transfer of uncertificated securities.

The UK government proposes that section 22 should be amended to provide that, in relation to uncertificated securities, membership of a company arises when stock accounts within an operator system are updated (ibid. para. 9). 'Stock accounts' are the records of holdings of securities of CREST members, typically financial intermediaries, and custodians. Under the existing regulations, a 'participating issuer' (company) is required to enter on the register of members the number of shares each member holds in uncertificated form, and certificated form, respectively.[85] Such an entry provides security of title.[86] A participating issuer is required to register a transfer of title to uncertificated units in accordance with an operator instruction, thus providing security of transfer.[87] In addition to the change to section 22(2), the proposal would require company issuers to arrange for CREST to keep the register for uncertificated securities, and for CREST to accept this obligation.

Another relevant development is the change in structure of nominee accounts maintained by custodians. There has been a marked increase in the use of pooled nominee systems under which the investments of many clients are registered in just one nominee name.[88] Custodians rely on their internal records to differentiate underlying entitlements. One reason for this trend is consolidation in the custodial services sector. USA global custodians, in particular, have acquired UK custodians and in the integration process have persuaded clients to switch from designated accounts into pooled accounts. This could imply that investors accept the security of title and transfer associated with a move to pooled holding.[89] It also reinforces the idea that security of title and transfer is provided for investors not by company issuers, but through the electronic record-keeping systems of the custodian and other financial intermediaries participating in systems such as CREST.

In summary, then, the role a company's register of members plays in providing security of title and transfer appears to be diminishing because of developments in the financial services sector.

9.3. *Costs*

9.3.1. *Transitional Costs*

Introduction of the reform proposal would entail transitional costs for company registrars and custodians where the power to designate was taken up. These would centre on the development or adoption of systems. However, some custodians' systems already contain data on control-right holders linked to registered shareholdings in particular companies.[90] In these cases, the transitional systems costs would be minimal.

9.3.2. *Ongoing Costs*

It could be argued that the proposal would see companies spending more on general meeting documents, in that: currently, where a custodian operates a pooled nominee system, a listed company is obliged to send only one annual report and notice of meeting, etc., because there is only one 'member'; whereas, if the proposal were to be implemented and then taken up enthusiastically, meeting documents would have to be sent to many different fund managers, acting as the designated persons in respect of a single pooled custodial holding.

This argument overlooks the fact that, under current practice, listed companies commonly send multiple copies of the annual report and notice of meeting to any custodian running a pooled account, and the custodian then distributes these to control-right holders.

Companies' registrars would face some ongoing costs. For example, costs incurred when processing designations. Even where, as is very commonly the case, the registrar is an external firm engaged by the listed company, and not an in-house operation, the registrar's costs would ultimately find their way back to client listed companies, and thus all shareholders. Custodians, too, would face ongoing costs associated with processing designations. However, where a designation is made, the custodian is no longer involved in the processing of votes so there is an offsetting cost saving.

Also, this chapter has advocated that the provision should operate as an enabling provision for unlisted companies and, by operation of the Financial Services Authority Listing Rules, as a default rule for listed companies—not a mandatory rule.[91] Any unlisted company for which the designation power would probably be more costly than beneficial would not opt into the regime. And any listed company for which the designation power would probably be more costly than beneficial could ask its shareholders to amend its articles and waive the provision.

Finally, bearing in mind that any system will involve costs, the proposal has the advantage of making the costs more transparent. Under the optional system proposed in this chapter, companies and investors who choose designation will have made a conscious decision on the basis of mutual benefit. This is consistent with the principle set out in the Combined Code that companies should be ready, where practicable, to enter into a dialogue with institutional shareholders based on a mutual understanding of objectives (Financial Services Authority 2000: Combined Code, Principle C1).[92]

9.4. *Conclusion*

This section of the chapter has categorized the sources of benefits and costs likely to be associated with a reform of the nature proposed earlier. At this stage, the authors are not in a position to discuss the magnitude of the various benefits and costs due to the lack of empirical data. Nevertheless, the authors believe that, on balance, the benefits of the proposed reform are likely to outweigh the costs, in the listed company sector overall. This view is subject to industry participants identifying any further benefits or costs not identified thus far. It is also based on the assumption that the provision would not be a mandatory rule, but rather an enabling provision, with secondary regulation making it a default rule able to be waived under the Articles of Association for all listed companies. Further, the rule would allow listed companies to make meeting-specific designations.

10. POSSIBLE EXTENSIONS OF THE PROPOSAL

The proposal discussed in this chapter is confined to delivery of general meeting documents, and voting. The importance of these matters to corporate governance suggests that they are the most pressing incidents of shareholding to be considered in a reform of this nature.

If the proposal were to be implemented successfully, then at a later stage it may be appropriate to consider whether other incidents of shareholding should be added to the items able to be designated. For example: payment of dividends (inherently a property incident of shareholding); and other powers given to members by the Companies Act, for example, to requisition general meetings[93] and to requisition the serving of a tracing notice under Part VI.[94]

11. CONCLUSION

If reform along the lines advocated in this chapter were to take place, it would not be the first time company law had recognized the interests of persons other than members on the register. Part VI of the Companies Act 1985 (UK) deals with 'Disclosure of Interests in Shares'. As discussed earlier in this chapter, the Part VI provisions are designed to enable companies to discover the identity of those who exercise control over the shares in the company. The provisions both require holders of interests above a threshold level, generally three per cent, to disclose them, and enable companies to 'trace' the identity of holders of interests in their shares. Section 209 is interesting in this regard. The section exempts certain financial services providers who could acquire otherwise notifiable interests in the course of their business. As the exemption covers only 'technical' interests, the exemption saves these firms the cost that would flow from having to disclose, but without undermining the goal of Part VI. In sum, company law has in this respect been responsive to change by imposing duties on investors, and granting powers to companies, while at the same time taking account of developments in financial market products. This chapter has considered whether it is desirable, in respect of control rights, to provide a mechanism which instead grants rights to investors and imposes duties on companies in certain circumstances.

Appendix. **Abbreviations used in Table 24.2**

FC	fund management arm of a financial conglomerate
Indep.	independent fund manager
Ins.	fund management arm of insurance company
Pens.	in-house manager of pension fund assets
AMP (UK)	AMP Asset Management plc (now Henderson Investors)
Barclays	Barclays Global Investors Ltd.
CGU	CGU Asset Management
Fleming	Fleming Investment Management Ltd.

Gartmore	Gartmore Investment Management plc
Hermes	Hermes Investment Management Ltd.
Hill Samuel	Hill Samuel Asset Management Ltd.
HSBC	HSBC Asset Management
Legal & General	Legal & General Investment Management Ltd.
M&G	M&G Investment Management Ltd. (now owned by Prudential)
Mercury	Mercury Asset Management plc
Morgan Grenfell	Morgan Grenfell Investment Management Ltd.
Norwich Union	Norwich Union Investment Management Ltd.
Phillips & Drew	Phillips & Drew Fund Management Ltd.
Prudential	Prudential Portfolio Managers Ltd.
Royal	Royal & SunAlliance plc
Schroder	Schroder Investment Management Ltd.
Scottish Widows	Scottish Widows Investment Management
Standard Life	Standard Life Investments Ltd.
Threadneedle	Threadneedle Investments

Notes

1. Employee Retirement Income Security Act.
2. See [p. 571]. From the mid-1960s to 1998, the proportion of listed UK equities held directly by individuals reduced sharply from 54 per cent to 16.5 per cent (Office for National Statistics 1999). Over the same period, indirect investment in equities by individuals—through collective investment vehicles (e.g. unit and investment trusts)—has increased considerably, in part offsetting the reduction in the proportion of the stock market held directly by individuals (Committee on Private Share Ownership 1996: 2). The term 'listed UK equities' means issued ordinary shares of UK-registered companies listed on the London Stock Exchange.
3. For example, Canada (Canada Business Corporations Act 1985, § 51(1): '(1) A corporation... may... treat the registered owner of a security as the person exclusively entitled to vote, to receive notices, to receive any interest, dividend or other payments in respect of the security, and otherwise to exercise all the rights and powers of an owner of the security'; § 51(4): 'A corporation is not required to inquire into the existence of, or see to the performance or observance of, any duty owed to a third person by a registered holder of any of its securities or by anyone whom it treats, as permitted or required by this section, as the owner or registered holder thereof'); Australia (Corporations Law, §§ 231, 249J, 250E); New Zealand (Companies Act 1993, §§ 89(2), 96); Singapore (Companies Act 1967, §§ 148, 158); Malaysia (Companies Act 1965, §§ 148, 158). In the case of Canada, note that the various Securities Commissions have adopted a USA-style 'recognition' procedure: Canadian Securities Administrators (1987, 1998). The USA recognition procedure is outlined [on p. 582–3].
4. See Companies Act 1985 (UK), §§ 370, 372.
5. The nature of the current rule which allocates the rights of control to a member (contained principally in §§ 22 and 360 but bolstered by other provisions) is a categorization rule. It is mandatory in the sense that it defines the persons who are subject to the rights and duties of the statutory framework. The effect of this so-called mandatory rule is to exclude those outside the category from having direct access to those rights. In [section 8.2], which sets out the proposed solution, the rules necessary to carry out the proposed reform are defined in the traditional 'mandatory', 'default', and 'enabling' manner.

6. Including, in the case of an AGM, the annual report and accounts, the notice of meeting and the proxy form.
7. The ideas in this chapter continue a line of analysis to which Manne (1964) contributed several decades ago. Professor Manne characterized the share as a package composed of two parts: 'an underlying investment interest and a vote' (ibid.: 1430). He argued that the system of corporate law should permit the transfer of the vote without the transfer of the investment interest, in effect the delegation of voting power by investors to financial market participants. At the time Professor Manne wrote this article, he argued that rules on disclosure of information in proxy contests lowered the cost of securing information for shareholders and thereby opened the voting option for them (ibid.: 1443). Equally, he argued that collective action by brokers and investment advisers on behalf of shareholders was made more feasible by the lower-cost means of securing information (ibid.: 1443). This chapter follows the spirit of Manne's conceptual clarity in separating the components of a share. But 36 years later, and in a different jurisdiction, this chapter addresses whether it is not time to reassess whether the ownership structures that have grown up in the shadow of a company law framework have frustrated the objective of a freely transferable vote component of a share which Professor Manne argued is central to the health of the system of corporate law.
8. See [p. 576].
9. The former 'information right' includes information required by statute as well as, for example, the Financial Services Authority Listing Rules. The 'voting right' includes any matter on which shareholder approval is required or sought voluntarily—for example, election of directors, takeovers, or changes in capital structure. As discussed towards the end of the chapter, another issue for consideration is whether additional rights could be added to the reform model, for instance, rights to receive declared dividends and to requisition general meetings.
10. The fund manager will normally also have an unrestricted power to sell the shares. See Pensions Act 1995 (UK), § 34, in relation to the power of pension scheme trustees to delegate their powers. Whether in practice the fund manager has an unrestricted 'ability' to sell the shares will be influenced by economic considerations. It may not be possible to sell certain shares at a particular time due to a lack of willing buyers at an acceptable price. Note also that the allocation of the voting control right is by no means a static area. As discussed below, there is some evidence that some large UK institutional investors have varied the typical arrangements just described.
11. The terms on which different fund managers hold those rights will differ according to specific contractual arrangements with beneficial owners.
12. USA institutions held 8 per cent of listed UK equities at early 1999 (Riley 1999).
13. See note 2 above.
14. A lesser factor behind (b) was the statutory recognition given to equities as acceptable trust investments by the Trustee Investments Act 1961 (UK); equity investments were previously possible only if there was an express power in the trust deed.
15. These internal fund management subsidiaries normally also offer their services to external clients (such as pension fund trustees). For example, as at 31 December 1997, Prudential Portfolio Managers Ltd. managed £9,634 million on behalf of external pension funds—about 10 per cent of its total funds under management from the UK (£93,197 million). The amount of external pension fund assets managed by Legal & General Investment Management Ltd. at the same time was even greater: £25,789 million (45 per cent of its total funds under management from the UK (£57,264 million)) (Hymans Robertson 1998).
16. Voting services operated by firms outside the fund management industry are also appearing. See, for example (http://www.manifest.co.uk).
17. Hermes now also manages some external funds, but it is classified as an in-house fund manager here because a very large proportion of its funds under management are internal funds.

18. The difference between 'directly invested', 'pooled' (or 'managed'), and 'insured' pension schemes is explained at [p. 575–577].
19. Own calculations based on figures in National Association of Pension Funds (1999: 57).
20. As mentioned at note [28] below, most large pension schemes have a corporate trustee rather than individual trusteess.
21. Many mutuals are companies limited by guarantee.
22. *Salomon* v. *A Salomon & Co. Ltd.* (1897) AC 22.
23. *Salomon* v. *A Salomon & Co. Ltd.* (1897) AC 22; *Macaura* v. *Northern Assurance Co. Ltd.* (1925) AC 619.
24. For example, in 1993 Crown Financial Services Ltd., the UK life insurance, pensions and unit trust subsidiary of Crown Life of Canada, ceased to manage its funds in-house. Its funds under management, some £700 million, did not amount to the 'critical mass' necessary for high-quality fund management. Therefore, fund management was contracted out to an external fund management firm: 'Lazard to Manage Crown Funds' (*Financial Times*, 19 January 1993: 21).
25. Local authority schemes are not formally constituted as trusts. They are constituted under the Superannuation Act 1972 (UK), and regulated under various sets of regulations made under that Act. The local authority ('administering authority') is nevertheless in a position analogous to that of a trustee (Quarrell 1990: ch. 4).
26. See Pensions Act 1995 (UK), §§ 16–21, in relation to member representatives.
27. For unit trusts, see [section 5.3.].
28. The more common of the two options is a corporate trustee. Here, a company is appointed as the trustee of the scheme. The directors of that company are sometimes loosely referred to as the scheme's trustees. In law, though, the company is the trustee.
29. The beneficial interest of the scheme's beneficiaries is reflected in the wording of Companies Act 1985 (UK), § 209(1)(a).
30. In similar circumstances, an Australian court was prepared to 'look through' the two trusts and find that the registered owner of the assets owed fiduciary duties to the ultimate beneficiaries: *Australian Sec. Comm.* v. *AS Nominees Ltd.*, 18 ACSR 459, 472 (1995).
31. There is a debate about whether institutional investors should be required to exercise their voting rights in the interests of good corporate governance. Importantly, however, existing UK law imposes no obligation to vote. As far as pension fund trustees are concerned, the principal duty is to give real and genuine consideration to whether, and if so how, votes should be cast (Stapledon 2000).
32. See Pensions Act 1995 (UK), § 34.
33. Companies Act 1985 (UK), § 370(1), (2); Table A, Art. 38.
34. Financial Services Act 1986 (UK), § 76.
35. Financial Services Act 1986 (UK), § 78(2).
36. Financial Services (Regulated Schemes) Regulations 1991 (UK), reg. 7.10.2.
37. *Charles* v. *Federal Commissioner of Taxation* (1954) 90 CLR 598, at 609; Linklaters and Paines (1989: para. A2.0420).
38. See [section 5.2.3.].
39. Financial Services (Regulated Schemes) Regulations 1991 (UK), reg. 7.11.1. There is an exception where the scheme property is shares or units in collective investment schemes managed or otherwise operated by the manager or its associates.
40. *Salomon* v. *A Salomon & Co. Ltd.* (1897) AC 22.
41. *Salomon* v. *A Salomon & Co. Ltd.* (1897) AC 22; *Macaura* v. *Northern Assurance Co. Ltd.* (1925) AC 619.
42. OEICs are regulated under the Open-Ended Investment Companies (Investment Companies with Variable Capital) Regulations 1996 (UK), and the Financial Services (Open-Ended Investment Companies) Regulations 1997 (UK).

43. The depositary is permitted to entrust some or all of the scheme's property to a third party (e.g. a custodian): Open-Ended Investment Companies (Investment Companies with Variable Capital) Regulations 1996 (UK), reg. 5(2)(b).
44. Open-Ended Investment Companies (Investment Companies with Variable Capital) Regulations 1996 (UK), reg. 39(2).
45. Financial Services (Open-Ended Investment Companies) Regulations 1997 (UK), reg. 6.02, para. 3b.
46. See [section 5.2.3.], for discussion of directly invested pension schemes.
47. See [section 5.2.3.].
48. Own calculations based on figures in National Association of Pension Funds (1999) and Office for National Statistics (1999).
49. There have been other factors. For example, measures taken to speed up the settlement process have led to an increasing number of private investors holding shares through nominees.
50. There have been somewhat similar developments in the USA. The clearing agency Depository Trust Corporation of New York uses a nominee called Cede and Co. Ltd. Cede and Co. executes an 'omnibus proxy' to all persons on its book on the record date with the power of substitution. This enables the 'street names' (i.e. banks and brokers) to be proxy with a power of substitution. However, it is not clear that the power of substitution is a power to appoint multiple substitutes. Also, due largely to investors' concerns over disclosure of identities, and contact details, a private-sector provider (not the listed company) sends the voting material and receives back voting instructions.
51. Indeed the Company Law Review Steering Group (2000: paras 4.6–4.18) has raised the issue discussed in this chapter for consultation in its March 2000 consultation document.
52. Under a 1999 reform, pension scheme trustees must now declare in their statement of investment principles 'their policy (if any) in relation to the exercise of the rights (including voting rights) attaching to investments': Occupational Pension Schemes (Investment) Regulations 1996 (SI 1996/3127), reg. 11A (inserted by the Occupational Pension Schemes (Investment, and Assignment, Forfeiture, Bankruptcy, etc) Amendment Regulations 1999 (SI 1999/1849)). The statement of investment principles is a requirement of the Pensions Act 1995 (UK). The scheme trustee, or any investment manager hired by the trustee, must exercise powers of investment 'with a view to giving effect to [these] principles . . . so far as reasonably practicable': § 36(5).
53. See [p. 583] below.
54. As discussed in [section 8.1.] below, some USA states have adopted a primary legislation solution: the 'recognition procedure'.
55. Whether by the Companies Act (UK), the company's articles, the Financial Services Authority Listing Rules or any other regulation.
56. Therefore, it would only be once a designation is made that a legal relationship between the company and a non-member control-right holder would arise. Equally, the provision would relieve the company from duties and liabilities to the member in respect of control rights attached to shares that have been designated.
57. Indiana Business Corporation Law, § 23-1-30-4(a).
58. The Official Comment explains § 7.23 in this way: 'Traditionally, a corporation recognizes only the registered owner as the owner of shares. Indeed, § 1.40 defines "shareholder" basically as the registered owner of shares. But it has become a common practice for persons purchasing shares to have them registered in the "street name" of a broker–dealer or other financial institution, principally to facilitate transfer by eliminating the need for the beneficial owner's signature and delivery. In addition, in order to avoid the burdens of processing securities transfers, which caused a crisis in the securities industry in the late 1960s, a system of securities depositories (defined as "clearing corporations" in § 8-102(3) of the Uniform Commercial Code) has been developed.

In this system, financial institutions deposit securities with the depository, which becomes the registered owner of the shares. Transfers between depositories are then accomplished by book entry of the depository. As a result, there may be two entities interposed between the corporation and the beneficial owner with the depository being the registered owner for the account of the brokerage firm that in turn holds the shares for the account of the beneficial owner.

The purpose of § 7.23 is to facilitate direct communication between the corporation and the beneficial owner by authorizing the corporation to create a procedure for bypassing both the registered owner and intermediate brokerage firms. The adoption of this procedure is discretionary with each corporation and affirmative action by the corporation is necessary to accomplish it. The procedure is also discretionary with the shareholder, who must elect to follow the applicable procedure prescribed by the corporation. The shareholder retains all of his rights except those granted to the beneficial owner' (Statutory comparison Model Business Corporation Act, Annotated 1997: S7-130).

59. Where the list of record holders indicates a clearing agency, the company is required to make the same enquiries of the agency and the participants whose names are disclosed to the company as a matter of course by that agency. Rules 14(b)-1 and 14(b)-2 set out the obligations of registered brokers and dealers and banks in relation to prompt forwarding of company documents to beneficial owners. Similar provisions apply where proxies are not solicited but the same material is distributed: Rule 14(c)-7. In certain circumstances, the company may itself distribute materials (such as the annual report) to beneficial holders, in which case the company must in its enquiry of holders of record indicate that it will do so. This relieves the holders of record of their duties in respect of mailing those persons: Rules 14(a)-13(c), 14(b)-1(c)(2)(ii), and 14(b)-2(c)(2)(ii).
60. For an analysis of enabling, default and mandatory rules in company law, generally, see Cheffins (1997: 216–63).
61. This is probably an oversimplification of the relevant considerations. Klausner (1995) argues that network externalities may be associated with default rules in corporate law, in much the same way as network externalities arguably exist in 'network' industries like the personal computer industry. That is, just as the value to a particular person of an IBM-compatible PC depends on how many other people own PCs and thereby create markets for compatible software, hardware, and repair services, default rules in company law may eventually become entrenched after a body of legal interpretation and understanding builds up around them. This may be a good thing or a bad thing: 'The right default term can enhance social wealth by facilitating coordination and thereby creating network values that individual firms may be unable to create themselves. . . . On the other hand, the wrong default rule can promote the formation of suboptimal contracts': Klausner (1995: 829). See also Ayres and Gertner (1989).
62. An arm's length institutional shareholder is one holding a relatively small proportion of the total issued shares in a company as part of a diversified portfolio of equity investments. In contrast, the venture-capital arm of an institutional investor may hold a significant proportion of the issued shares in an unlisted public company.
63. Note that under the existing Financial Services Act regulatory framework the role of the intermediary (e.g. custodial service provider) is set out: Before a firm provides safe custody services to a customer, it must notify the customer in writing of the obligations which the firm will have to the customer in relation to: exercising voting rights (Rule 4.109(1)(e) of the Client Money and Custody Rules within the Securities and Futures Authority Rules).
64. See [section 5.2.3.].
65. The term 'record date' refers to a definitive point in time at which eligibility to vote or appoint a proxy for a particular general meeting is determined. Under the current system in the UK, this 'record date' is effectively 48 hours before the meeting because of the combination of § 372(5) of

the Companies Act (UK)—which has the effect of prohibiting a company from refusing to receive a proxy appointment more than 48 hours before the meeting—and reg. 34(1) of the Uncertificated Securities Regulations 1995 (UK)—which allows a company to determine who has the right to vote in relation to uncertifcated securities at a time not more than 48 hours before a meeting. In a paper based system where proxy forms along with the notice of meeting are sent out to those persons on the register weeks before the date of the meeting, there is a requirement to reconcile the persons and holdings of those to whom notices were sent at that earlier time, with the record of the persons and number of votes received up to the 48 hour cut-off. This presents logistical challenges for those involved in collating the vote. There may be some merit in the UK Company Law Review considering the benefits and costs of other approaches, such as that in the USA where there is a 'voting record date' set well in advance of the meeting. The data effective at that point in time determines who is entitled to receive documentation and to exercise a vote.

66. 'Indexing' or 'passive' fund management involves the purchase of a portfolio of shares that matches the shares included in a particular stock market index, such as the FT All Share Index (which consists of the largest 700 or so companies listed on the London Stock Exchange).
67. Fees for indexed management of a wholesale (institutional) segregated fund are as low as five basis points (0.05 of 1 per cent of the value of funds under management) per annum, compared to about fifty basis points (0.5 of 1 per cent of the value of funds under management) for an actively managed UK equities wholesale segregated fund. It is estimated that about 20 per cent of listed UK equities are currently under indexed management (Martinson 1999*b*). It may be that a pension scheme's trustee would want a standing designation made in relation to the scheme's 'core' holding in a particular company, but a meeting-specific designation (or no designation at all) in respect of a 'satellite' holding in the same company. The trustee would be guided by the fund manager responsible for the satellite holding. The fund manager might, for instance, see strategic benefit in not becoming a designated person in relation to the satellite holding.
68. See [section 5.2.3.].
69. See [section 5.2.3.].
70. On the other hand, if the provision were to allow standing designations, there would be an ongoing legal relationship between a listed company and a designated person, in relation to the operational incidents of shareholding.
71. The Listing Rules suggest that voting instructions should be known to companies. See Financial Services Authority (2000: Combined Code, provision E.1.3): 'Institutional shareholders should take steps to ensure that their voting intentions are being translated into practice.' In practice, there is a range of approaches to vote communication from institutional investors to company representatives (often investor relations or company secretarial functions). Some investors personally inform companies of their voting intentions in advance. Others maintain a strictly confidential, and last minute approach.
72. Stock lending is a common practice in the UK equity market. It involves a shareholder (normally an institutional investor) 'lending' some of its shares in a particular listed company to another entity (often a stockbroker) to enable the other entity to cover a short position temporarily. A fee is paid to the institutional investor for this service.
73. Companies Act 1985, §§ 198–211, 219. In some circumstances, the disclosure threshold for investment managers and other financial institutions is 10 per cent rather than 3 per cent: § 199.
74. Companies Act 1985, §§ 212–219.
75. Companies Act 1985, § 208.
76. Other general legislation on contractual terms may apply.
77. There is a review of most of the USA studies in Black (1998). For UK studies, see Faccio and Lasfer (2000); Franks *et al.* (2001). See also Stapledon (1999).

78. For a review of studies of the impact of board composition on corporate performance, see Stapledon and Lawrence (1997).
79. It is common for registered holdings of 10,000 and above (for small and medium-sized listed UK companies) and of 30,000 and above (for large listed UK companies) to account for over 90 per cent of the issued ordinary share capital.
80. In some instances, the listed company—or the service provider as agent of the company—supplements or confirms this information by regularly serving notices under Companies Act 1985 (UK), § 212, on the largest registered shareholders. As discussed above, § 212 gives a public company power to require a person whom the company knows or reasonably believes to have, or to have had, an interest in its shares, to provide details about that interest.
81. For a description of this interaction between company managements and fund managers, see Stapledon (1996: 100–6, 117–21).
82. This is a simplification. An entry in the register is evidence of ownership. Of course, ownership will be absolute when the interest in the shares is absolute and the title indefeasible.
83. Transactions in most listed UK equities are cleared and settled in uncertificated form through the CREST system.
84. The benefits of security of title and transfer extend to the company or issuer of securities as well. Section 360 of the Companies Act 1985 (UK) provides that 'No notice of any trust, express, implied, or constructive, shall be entered on the register, or be receivable by the registrar, in the case of companies registered in England and Wales'.
85. Uncertificated Securities Regulations 1995 (UK), reg. 19(1).
86. Uncertificated Securities Regulations 1995 (UK), reg. 20(1) provides that an entry on a register mentioned in reg. 19(1) shall be evidence of such a title to the units as would be evidenced if the entry on the register related to units of that security held in certificated form.
87. Uncertificated Securities Regulations 1995 (UK), reg. 23(1).
88. See [section 5.2.3.].
89. According to anecdotal evidence gathered from meetings with fund management firms, clients are comfortable with their investments being held in pooled accounts because they do not consider there to be any material risk. The main benefit is the saving in transaction costs when large trades are made on behalf of a number of clients. These savings arise because, instead of being reconciled to designated accounts in CREST, a single entry is made in the CREST system, and the custodian's system provides a record of designation to a particular client. A cost of adopting a pooled system arises from the added work involved in processing corporate actions (e.g. voting) and dividend entitlements, because clients' entitlements must be reconciled back to the pool. This 'cost' prompted one manager to persuade clients to switch back to designated accounts.
90. Anecdotal evidence provided to the authors.
91. See [section 8.2.].
92. Listing Rule 12.43A requires a company to describe in its annual report how it has applied this and the other principles in the Combined Code.
93. Companies Act 1985 (UK), § 368.
94. Companies Act 1985 (UK), § 214.

References

Ayres, I., and Gertner, R. (1989). Filling gaps in incomplete contracts: An economic theory of default rules. *Yale Law Journal* 99: 87.

Barclay, M. J., and Holderness, C. G. (1989). Private benefits from control of public corporations. *Journal of Financial Economics* 25: 371.

Black, B. S. (1998). Shareholder activism and corporate governance in the United States. In P. Newman (ed.), *The New Palgrave Dictionary of Economics and the Law*. New York: Stockton Press.

Canadian Securities Administrators (1987). *National Policy Instrument No. 41: Communication with Beneficial Owners of Securities of a Reporting Issuer*. Toronto: Canadian Securities Administrators.

——(1998). *Proposed National Instrument 54–101: Communication with Beneficial Owners of Securities of a Reporting Issuer*. Toronto: Canadian Securities Administrators.

Cheffins, B. R. (1997). *Company Law: Theory, Structure and Operation*. Oxford: Clarendon Press.

Committee on Private Share Ownership (1996). (Weinberg, chair), Report. London: London Stock Exchange.

Company Law Review Steering Group (2000). *Modern Company Law for a Competitive Economy: Developing the Framework*. London: DTI.

Davies, P. L. (1993). Institutional Investors in the United Kingdom. In D. D. Prentice and P. R. J. Holland (ed.), *Contemporary Issues in Corporate Governance*. Oxford: Clarendon Press.

——(1997). *Gower's Principles of Modern Company Law*. London: Sweet & Maxwell.

——(1999). The United Kingdom. In T. Baums and E. Wymeersch (ed.), *Shareholder Voting Rights and Practices in Europe and the United States*. London: Kluwer.

Davis, E. P. (1991). International diversification of institutional investors. Bank of England Discussion Papers, Technical Series, No. 44.

DTI (1996). Department of Trade and Industry. *Private Shareholders: Corporate Governance Rights: A Consultative Document*. London: DTI.

Faccio, M., and Lasfer, M. A. (2000). Do occupational pension funds monitor companies in which they hold large stakes? *Journal of Corporate Finance* 6: 71.

Financial Services Authority (2000). *The Listing Rules*. London: Financial Services Authority.

Franks, J. R., and Mayer, C. P. (1996). Corporate control: A synthesis of the international evidence. London Business School, Working Paper.

——and Renneboog, L. (2001). Who disciplines management in poorly performing companies? *Journal of Financial Intermediation* 10, 209–248.

Goode Committee (1993). Pension Law Review Committee, Report, Cm. 2342. London: HMSO.

Grossman, S. J., and Hart, O. D. (1988). One share–one vote and the market for corporate control. *Journal of Financial Economics* 20: 175.

HM Treasury (1999). The Uncertificated Securities Regulations 1995: A Proposal for Consultation by HM Treasury. London: HM Treasury (available at http://www.hm-treasury.gov.uk/docs/1999/uncertsec.html)

Hymans Robertson (1998). *1998 Pension Fund Investment Manager Survey*. Glasgow: Hymans Robertson.

Klausner, M. (1995). Corporations, corporate law, and networks of contracts. *Virginia Law Review* 81: 757.

Lease, R., McConnell, J., and Mikkelson, W. (1983). 'The market value of control in publicly traded corporations. *Journal of Financial Economics* 11: 439.

Linklaters and Paines (1989). *Unit Trusts: The Law and Practice*. London: Longman.

London Stock Exchange (1998). *Primary Market Fact Sheet*. London: London Stock Exchange.

Manne, H. (1964). Some theoretical aspects of share voting—an essay in honor of Adolf A. Berle. *Columbia Law Review* 64: 1427.

Martinson, J. (1998). Beckett retains option of law to enforce corporate best practice. *Financial Times*, 5 March.

——(1999*a*). Fighting fit. *Financial Times*, 29 January, p. 17.

——(1999*b*). Index-tracking inevitable, says insurers' head. *Financial Times*, 19 February, p. 12.

Minns, R. (1980). *Pension Funds and British Capitalism*. London: Heinemann.

Morse, G. (ed.) (1976). *Palmer's Company Law*. London: Sweet & Maxwell.

Nicodano, G. (1998). Corporate groups, dual-class shares and the value of voting rights. *Journal of Banking and Finance* 22: 1117.

National Association of Pension Funds (1999). *Annual Survey of Occupational Pension Schemes.* London: NAPF.

Newbold Committee (1999). Committee of Inquiry into UK Vote Execution (Y. Newbold, chair), Report. London: NAPF.

Office for National Statistics (1999). *Share Ownership: A Report on the Ownership of Shares at 31st of December 1997.* London: The Stationery Office.

OECD (1999). *Organisation for Economic Co-operation and Development, OECD Principles of Corporate Governance.* Paris: OECD.

PIRC (1998). *Pensions and Investments Research Consultants, Proxy Voting Trends at UK Companies 1993–1998.* London: PIRC.

——(1999). *Pensions and Investments Research Consultants, Proxy Voting Trends 1999.* London: PIRC.

Quarrell, J. J. (1990). *The Law of Pension Fund Investment.* London: Butterworths.

Riley, B. (1999). Now for tracker cats. *Financial Times,* 6 March, FT Money, p.16.

Securities and Investments Board (1993). *Custody Review Discussion Paper.* London: Securities and Investments Board.

Stapledon, G. P. (1996). *Institutional Shareholders and Corporate Governance.* Oxford: Clarendon Press.

——(1999). Share ownership and control in listed Australian companies. University of Melbourne, Working Paper (available on SSRN at ID=164129).

——(2000). Institutional investors: What are their responsibilities as shareholders? In J. Parkinson, A. Gamble, and G. Kelly (ed.), *The Political Economy of the Company.* Oxford: Hart Publishing.

——and Lawrence, J. J. (1997). Board composition, structure and independence in Australia's largest listed companies. *Melbourne University Law Review.* 21: 150.

WM Company (1990). *UK Pension Fund Service Annual Review.* London: WM Company.

Zingales, L. (1994). The value of the voting right: A study of the Milan Stock Exchange experience. *Review of Financial Studies* 7: 125.

——(1995). What determines the value of corporate votes? *Quarterly Journal of Economics* 110: 1047.

25

Institutional Shareholders and Corporate Governance: The Case of UK Pension Funds

MARA FACCIO AND M. AMEZIANE LASFER

1. INTRODUCTION

Large blockholding is considered to be one of the mechanisms for controlling the agency problems which arise whenever managers have incentives to pursue their own interests at the expense of those of shareholders. However the primarily USA empirical evidence provided to date on the role and effectiveness of blockholders is mixed (Shleifer and Vishny 1997). The purpose of this chapter is to analyse the monitoring role of occupational pension funds, the largest category of shareholders in the UK. We focus specifically on these funds because of the large dimension of their overall stakes in the UK market, the particular structure of their portfolios, and their investment objectives. We consider these funds to be pressure-resistant institutions as opposed to other institutions, such as banks, investment and unit trusts and insurance companies (Brickley *et al.* 1994). By comparing companies in which occupational pension funds hold large stakes against a control group of companies listed on the London Stock Exchange (LSE), we test the hypotheses that monitoring increases with ownership concentration and, as a result, occupational pension funds reduce agency conflicts and lead companies to increase their performance.

Over the last few years, the issue of involvement of pension funds in the running of companies has been subject to an extensive debate. On the one hand, pension funds are perceived by the public to be short-termists and to impose their views on companies in which they invest by, for example, making them pay dividends and not invest in the long term (Hutton 1995).[1] On the other hand, academic studies show that pension funds do not get involved in corporate monitoring because they find it easier and cheaper to sell their holdings, and that they do not want to sit on the board for fear of getting price sensitive information or because of the agency problems within the funds themselves.[2] In addition, the UK pension funds, despite the size of their holdings, are not known for their monitoring

This chapter draws partly on M. Faccio and M. A. Lasfer (2000), 'Do Occupational Pension Funds Monitor Companies in which they Hold Large Stakes?', *Journal of Corporate Finance*. 6, 71–110.

and hardly vote at the annual general meetings (NAPF 1996*b*; *Financial Times* 1997).[3] At the same time, policymakers tend to rely on these institutions to promote corporate governance (Cadbury 1992; Greenbury 1995).[4] Therefore, the testing of the empirical hypotheses in a pension fund dominated market such as the UK where companies suffer from the same free cash flow problems as their USA counterparts, will contribute to the current corporate governance debate and will strengthen the evidence provided to date.[5]

We analyse the shareholding section in the financial statements of all UK quoted non-financial companies and construct a test sample of companies in which pension funds hold more than 3 per cent of the issued share capital. Our test sample includes 289 companies (18 per cent of the total population). A control sample is constructed by matching each test firm by industry and size.[6] We find that companies in which pension funds hold large stakes do not adopt the Code of Best Practice, that is, split the roles of chairman and CEO, have more non-executive directors and/or narrow the size of their board. These results are not consistent with the recommendations of Cadbury (1992) and Greenbury (1995). These companies are also not more profitable than the control firms. We report weak and even negative relationship between occupational pension funds blockholdings and firm value. Our overall results are consistent with previous USA evidence (e.g. Romano 1994; Wahal 1996) and cast doubt on the effectiveness of UK occupational pension funds' monitoring role.

The rest of the chapter is structured as follows. Section 2 presents the theoretical background and in Section 3 the hypotheses are formulated. Section 4 describes the data and Section 5 presents the results. Section 6 concludes this chapter.

2. THEORETICAL FRAMEWORK

In this section, we review the literature on the role of large shareholders, present the structure of the pension fund industry and corporate governance system in the UK, and set up the hypotheses.

2.1. *Review of the Literature*

Unlike the relationship-based corporate governance system of Japan and Germany, where ownership is concentrated and markets are relatively illiquid, the UK is a market-based system characterized by liquid markets and unconcentrated company ownership.[7] The issue, although not trivial, has been considered in the literature only recently when agency theorists argue that public corporations suffer from excessive costs as managers pursue their own interests rather than the interests of shareholders (Jensen 1986). As a result, there is a need for establishing mechanisms to make managers maximize shareholder wealth. These mechanisms include shareholding of managers, intermediaries and large blockholders (McConnell and Servaes 1990; Morck *et al.* 1988), outside directors (Cotter *et al.* 1997), debt policy (Lasfer 1995; McConnell and Servaes 1995), the market for corporate control and incentive contracts (Hart 1995), large intermediaries (Diamond 1984; Admati *et al.* 1994), and long-term relationships (Ayres and Cramton 1994).

In theory, Diamond (1984) suggests that a large intermediary can represent a better solution to agency conflicts because of economies of scale and diversification. Admati *et al.*

(1994) argue that when monitoring is costly, the intermediary will monitor only if this will result in a modification in a firm's pay-off structure and lead to net gains. Similarly, Shleifer and Vishny (1997) and Agrawal and Knoeber (1996) suggest that large investors, because of the relevance of the resources invested, have all the interest and the power to monitor and promote better governance of companies. However, Maug (1998) argues that while liquid markets make corporate governance more effective as it is cheaper and easier to acquire and hold large stakes, they also reduce large shareholders' incentive to monitor because they can sell their holdings easily. Kahn and Winton (1998) show that intervention is a function of the size of the institution's stake, firm-specific factors and institution's trading profit.

The primarily USA-based empirical evidence provided to date on the effectiveness of shareholder activism is mixed.[8] For example, Wahal (1996) and Karpoff *et al.* (1996) find little evidence that operating performance of companies that are the target of pension funds proposals improves. These results are consistent, among other things, with the arguments of Murphy and Van Nuys (1994) and Romano (1994) that pension funds are not effective monitors because of the agency problems within the funds themselves. In contrast, Smith (1996) and Nesbitt (1994) find that companies targeted by large pension funds, such as CalPERS, increase significantly their performance. More recently, Del Guercio and Hawkins (1999) show that the monitoring effectiveness depends on the investment strategies of pension funds and find that, unlike proposals sponsored by externally-managed funds, those made by internally-managed funds are not associated with general increases in governance-related events at target firms. Other studies find a weak relationship between large institutional holdings and firm value or rates of return (Agrawal and Knoeber 1996; Demsetz and Lehn 1985).

2.2. *The UK Pension Funds Industry*

In addition to the state-sponsored pension scheme, we find in the UK occupational pension schemes that are organized and sponsored by employers and individual pension schemes offered by financial institutions. Occupational pension schemes dominate the UK pension fund industry. For example, in 1997 the overall value of occupational pension funds' assets (including insured schemes) reached £635 billion compared to individual pension schemes assets of £190 billion (ABI 1998).[9] Occupational pension funds also invest most of their funds in equities and they are the largest equity investors in the OECD countries (Davis 1995). For example, in 1993, 78 per cent of assets were invested in equities, 12 per cent in fixed income securities and the remaining in cash and property (Business Monitor 1997). This is partly due to the fact that they run defined benefit plans where individuals do not bear the investment risk (NAPF 1996*b*). Another reason for the preference of equities over fixed income securities relates to the tax-exempt status of pension funds who, like charities, are not subject to capital gains tax and claim back a tax credit when they receive dividends (Lasfer 1996). The predominance of pension funds in the UK market has only been recent. For example, In 1963 they held 7 per cent of all UK equities and individuals were the main shareholders with 58.7 per cent. By 1993, pension funds stakes increased to 34.7 per cent (London Stock Exchange 1995). In contrast, in the USA individuals held 50 per cent in 1990 followed by pension funds with 20.1 per cent, increasing to 25.4 per cent in 1995 (Prowse 1994; Brancato 1997). The USA pension funds also invest a lower proportion of their assets in equities. For example, in 1990, out of the total assets of $2,491 billion, 38.6 per cent are invested in equities but these investments are concentrated in large firms and this proportion has not changed over the 1970–90 period (Charkham 1995; Davis 1995; Stapledon 1996; Brancato 1997).

In managing these assets, the funds are subject to trust law and implicitly follow the prudent-man concept that implies that the money is invested for the sole benefit of the beneficiaries. However, there is no explicit prudent-man rule and the pension trust law is very flexible making the legal barriers against institutional activism weaker in the UK compared to the USA where active shareholders that hold a 'block of shares' are subject to filing requirements, such as section 13(d) of the Williams Act, and they can be sued for breaching disclosure duties of their plans or proposals.

The UK pension fund industry is also highly concentrated. For example, in 1994, the largest five in-house managed occupational pension funds managed assets worth £65.8 billion, 14.8 per cent of all occupational pension funds assets (NAPF 1996*a*) and British Telecommunications by itself accounted for £17.2 billion. The largest sixty-eight schemes, whose assets value exceeds £1 billion in 1995, accounted for 57.3 per cent of all occupational pension funds assets (PFA 1996). The same concentration is observed in the industry of fund managers where, at the end of 1996, the top twenty segregated fund managers managed assets worth £285.7 billion on behalf of occupational pension funds and, as a whole, managed assets of some £1,029.2 billion (*Financial Times* 1997).

2.3. *The UK Corporate Governance System*

Following the recent concerns about the way in which remuneration packages for senior executives have been determined, the spectacular collapse of a number of large companies and the fraudulent use of the pension fund monies to finance an illegal scheme for supporting the share price of Maxwell Communications Corporation, the Committee on the Financial Aspects of Corporate Governance (referred to as the Cadbury Committee after its chairman) was set up to look at the changes needed in corporate governance in the UK and published a report in December 1992 (Cadbury 1992). At the heart of the report is the Code of Best Practice which details the role and composition of the board of directors, the appointment of non-executive directors, the disclosure of the remuneration of executive directors and the renewal of their contracts, and the way companies should report and audit their accounts. The main recommendation is that the offices of the chairman and the chief executive officer should be separated to prevent excessive concentration of power in boardrooms and that companies should appoint independent non-executive directors of high calibre so that their views will carry weight in board discussions.[10] The code defines the various roles non-executive directors should play. For example, they are to be in a majority on the nominating committee which is responsible for making recommendations for board membership, they should be the sole or majority members of the remuneration committee which makes recommendations to the board on the pay of executive directors, and of the audit committee whose function is to advise on the appointment of auditors, to ensure the integrity of the company's financial statements and to discuss with the auditors any problems arising during the course of the audit.[11]

3. HYPOTHESES

The Cadbury report relied on large institutional shareholders, such as pension funds, for the application of its recommendations. In particular, these funds are expected to monitor boards where there is a concentration of power in the hands of the chief executive, seek to promote the influence of non-executive directors and they are expected to bring about changes in underperforming companies rather than dispose of their shares. However, Del Guercio and Hawkins (1999) show that the level of monitoring by pension funds depends significantly on the way their assets are managed. In the UK pension funds assets can be managed in three different ways: self-managed, externally managed, and insured. Within self-managed schemes, the trustees of the scheme define asset allocation, portfolio selection policies and directly invest pension fund assets. Within externally-managed schemes, the investment power is wholly or in part delegated to one or few external managers. In the case of insured schemes, the funds are invested in insurance policies or managed through fund contracts taken out with an insurance company.

Following the arguments of Admati *et al.* (1994) and Diamond (1984), we would expect large funds and those that hold large stakes, to be more active in corporate monitoring. For such funds the monitoring costs are minimized because they are likely to understand when activism is necessary, they are large enough to make monitoring effective, and their large holdings are expected to alleviate the free-rider problem that makes atomistic shareholders' action non-rational and inefficient. In this case, we expect internally-managed occupational pension funds to have a stronger incentive to monitor for the following reasons: (i) these funds are larger than externally-managed and insured schemes (Minns 1980; Blake 1995; NAPF 1996*a*); (ii) they control directly or indirectly the investment and the voting decisions; (iii) many large companies managed their pension schemes internally (Stapledon 1996); and (iv) their objective is likely to maximize the value of funds in order to minimize the company's contributions and, possibly, use any pension fund surplus to inflate company's profits (Short and Keasey 1997). In contrast, funds that delegate their investment functions to external managers effectively disconnect their activism efforts from their investment actions (Del Guercio and Hawkins 1999). Furthermore, since such funds will not be able to trade profitably on any private information that results from their activism, they are not likely to monitor or to publicize their activism efforts. The level of monitoring role of externally-managed pension funds will depend on the content of the contract with the trustees and the level of competition among fund managers. Since we do not have data on these contracts and on the investments made on behalf of pension funds, we cannot expect all externally-managed funds to monitor.

However, internally-managed occupational pension funds may not monitor individual companies if they find it easier to sell, if they do not want to gain access to price sensitive information or if they themselves are subject to agency problems. In addition, given that these funds are defined benefits schemes, they are likely to be indexed and passive to minimize their management risk and transaction costs, and to fit the needs of long-term pension investors (Tomlinson 1998). Del Guercio and Hawkins (1999) argue that such passive management style will lead pension funds to monitor by promoting spill-over effects that boost the performance of the stock market overall rather than specific stocks.

The monitoring role of pension funds can however, take different forms. First, they can monitor the size of the board (Cadbury 1992).[12] Jensen (1993) argues that as the size of the board increases, its ability to control management decreases and the communication and co-ordination problems increase. Consistent with this proposition, Yermack (1996) and Eisenberg *et al.* (1998) find a negative correlation between board size and firm performance. Thus, our first hypothesis can be constructed as follows: H_{01}: Internally-managed pension funds do not lead companies in which they hold large stakes to restrict the size of their board.

Second, pension funds are expected to monitor the board composition so that it becomes more accountable to the shareholders. In this case, they are expected to lead companies to adopt the Code of Best Practice defined by Cadbury (1992), that is, to split the roles of chairman and chief executive officer, to have a high proportion of non-executive directors and to restrain executive pay.[13] Thus, our second hypothesis is: H_{02}: Internally-managed pension funds do not lead companies in which they hold large stakes to adopt the Code of Best Practice.

Third, pension funds are expected to monitor the performance of firms in which they hold large stakes. This implies that such companies have a higher value than widely held companies and/or companies held by other blockholders. However, the level of performance is likely to be affected by other factors such as industry in which the company is operating. Thus, our third hypothesis is: H_{03}: Companies in which occupational pension funds hold large stakes have a lower value than other companies.

4. SAMPLE CONSTRUCTION AND DEFINITION OF PROXY VARIABLES

To test the aforementioned hypotheses, we construct a test sample by searching the financial statements of all the 1,640 non-financial companies quoted in the LSE in 1995–6 for those where occupational pension funds hold large stakes. To avoid survivorship bias, our sample includes all companies for which the relevant data is available even if they are currently extinct. We exclude financial companies because of the specificity of some of their ratios, such as leverage, which cannot be related to the level of risk and/or resolution of their agency conflicts.[14]

We rely on any disclosed holding above 3 per cent threshold in the accounts and reported in Extel Financial[15] and define these as occupational pension funds holdings or blockholders. All the holdings of directors are disclosed even if they are zero (the Company Act of 1985).

Although this cut-off point of 3 per cent is constraining, it is the only data available. We, nevertheless, posit that the holding of 3 per cent or above is significant to warrant monitoring and to allow us to test directly the Admati *et al.* (1994) and Diamond (1984) propositions. We find 289 individual companies (18 per cent of our total sample) with at least one occupational pension fund holding above 3 per cent, and 356 large stakes held by ninty-nine individual occupational pension funds. We split the other major disclosed holdings (other than managerial holdings) into institutional and non-institutional blockholding depending on the identity of the shareholders. We compare the performance of our test firms against a control group of companies with similar size and industry characteristics. We collect all the relevant accounting and financial data from Extel Financial and from each company's accounts.

We use five definitions of pension fund holdings: LPF; the first largest stake held by pension funds, and TPF, the sum of all pension fund holding to analyse pension fund individual and collective monitoring roles; IPF, the ratio of pension fund investment in our test sample over their total assets to assess the magnitude of such investment in their portfolio;[16] NPF, the number of occupational pension funds in our test firms, and LNPFA, the logged value of the largest pension fund's assets. To control for the managerial entrenchment hypothesis we use Dir, the proportion of shares held by the directors.[17] Any other large stake, Block, is used to control for the monitoring role of blockholders.

We use accounting rates of return and a one-year share price return ($R_{i,t-12 \text{ to } t}$) to proxy for firm performance, and Tobin's *Q* (the ratio of market value of equity plus book value of debt over total assets) (Agrawal and Knoeber 1996), market-to-book (M/B), and market-to-sales (M/S) (Lins and Servaes 1999) to measure firm value. These variables are, however, ambiguous measures of value-added by pension funds investments, since they can also capture the value of future investment opportunities. As in Yermack (1996), we control for growth opportunities by using the P/E ratio. We use market value of equity (ME), or total assets (TA), to control for size and Mlev, defined as long-term debt over market value of equity plus long-term debt, and Blev, defined as long-term debt over shareholders' funds plus long-term debt, to test for the monitoring role of debtholders. Finally, we use the following variables to measures the size and composition of the board: split, a dummy variable equal to 1 if the role of chairman and CEO are differentiated, nechair, a dummy equal to 1 if the position of chairman is covered by a non-executive director, #DIR, number of directors, and %NED, the proportion of non-executive directors in the board.

5. EMPIRICAL RESULTS

5.1. *Univariate Analysis*

Table 25.1 reports the descriptive statistics of financial attributes of the test and control firms. We compute the *t*-statistics to test for differences in means and the Mann–Whitney *p*-value to test for differences in medians.[18] The results show that comparing the industry and size-adjusted control group, the block and managerial holdings in our test firms are not statistically different. Blockholders hold an average of 34 per cent in our test firms and 36.5 per cent in our control sample. Insiders hold an average of 14.5 per cent in our test firms and 14 per cent in our control sample. The test statistics for differences in means and medians are not statistically significant at any confidence level. The results imply that block or managerial ownership does not affect our analysis. However, insiders and blockholders hold significantly larger stakes in our test firms than occupational pension funds, suggesting that these funds do not invest a large proportion of their assets in our test companies.

Table 25.1 also shows that the value of our test firms is significantly lower than that of our control group. The average Tobin's *Q* of our test firms is 1.16 while that of the control group is 1.62. The same conclusion is reached when we use M/B and M/S as alternative

Table 25.1. *Descriptive statistics on means of selected data on the test and control firms*

Variables	Test sample		Control sample		*t*-statistics: difference in means	Mann–Whitney; *p*-value
	Mean	Median	Mean	Median		
Block	34.00	32.48	36.54	34.82	−1.29	0.135
Dir	14.53	6.02	14.01	7.38	0.32	0.875
ME (£m)	96.7	28.1	121.1	31.1	−1.26	0.875
TA (£m)	125	33.4	122	32.0	0.12	0.519
Q	1.16***	0.87***	1.61***	0.94***	−2.21	0.005
M/S	1.33*	0.60*	2.65*	0.65*	−1.68	0.051
M/B	2.78*	1.68***	3.44*	1.87***	−1.68	0.004
ROA %	6.13	8.90	4.10	8.70	1.03	0.550
ROE %	−1.10	11.30	11.95	12.00	−1.16	0.113
ROS %	5.49	6.80	−0.00	6.50	1.11	0.758
$R_{i,t-12 \text{ to } t}$%	23.57	15.40	20.04	5.75	0.74	0.133
P/E	9.68	8.25	9.33	8.36	0.48	0.101
Mlev %	11.34***	5.80**	17.90***	12.75**	−3.21	0.012
Blev %	14.58***	9.90	21.01***	13.30	−3.08	0.458
Split	0.84	1.00	0.88	1.00	−1.61	0.121
#DIR	5.92	6.00	5.80	6.00	0.85	0.382
%NED	0.40	0.40	0.38	0.40	1.31	0.334

The descriptive statistics of the proxy variables are provided here. The test sample includes all companies that reported pension fund holdings above 3 per cent in 1995–6, a total of 586 observations. The control sample includes industry- and size-matched firms. Block is the proportion of outstanding equity owned by blockholders other than directors and occupational pension funds; Dir is the proportion of outstanding equity capital owned by directors; ME is market value of equity at balance sheet date; TA is total assets; *Q* is the ratio of market value of equity plus book value of debt over total assets; *M/S* is the market value of equity plus book value of debt over sales; *M/B* is the market value of equity over book value of equity; $R_{i,t-12 \text{ to } t}$ is a one-year stock return; *P/E* is the price-earnings ratio at the balance sheet date; Blev is the ratio of long-term debt over long-term debt plus shareholders' funds; Mlev is the ratio of long-term debt over long-term debt plus market value of equity; Split is a dummy variable equals to 1 if the roles of chairman and CEO are split; #DIR is the number of directors in the board; %NED is the proportion of non-executive directors.***, **, *: Significance at 0.01, 0.05 and 0.10 levels respectively.

measures of firm value. At the same time, our test companies have lower leverage than our control firms do. However, in terms of accounting and market rates of return and PE ratio, our test companies are not different from the control firms. These results do not reject H_{03} and suggest that our test companies do not outperform other firms.

The test and control companies have also exactly the same average number of directors (about 6), ranging between 2 and 15, and the same proportion of non-executive directors (about 40 per cent). The proportion of our control companies that split the roles of chairman and CEO (namely 88 per cent) is higher than that of our test firms (84 per cent). These results are striking. They do not reject H_{01}–H_{03} and suggest that pension funds investments do not lead companies to better performance nor do they increase the likelihood of compliance with the Cadbury (1992) recommendations.

5.2. *Multivariate Analysis*

Table 25.2 reports the results of the Logit regressions where the various agency variables are considered simultaneously. The dependent variable is equal to 1 if company *i* is in the test sample and 0 if it is part of the control sample. The results are consistent with those reported in Table 25.1 and show that our test companies have significantly lower value that that of the control firms while they are not more profitable or not more likely to split the roles of chairman and chief executive officer, have less directors or more non-executive directors

Table 25.2. *Logit regressions with probability that pension fund holding exceeds 3 per cent of shares in 1995–6*

	(1)	(2)	(3)	(4)	(5)	(6)
Constant	0.71***	0.61***	0.52***	0.52***	0.47*	0.79***
	(6.64)	(6.69)	(31.91)	(32.16)	(1.84)	(6.93)
Split	−0.014	−0.017				−0.005
	(−0.27)	(−0.31)				(−0.09)
#DIR	0.011	0.016				0.008
	(1.18)	(1.58)				(0.70)
%NED	0.04	0.042				−0.02
	(0.37)	(0.36)				(−0.19)
Dir	−0.003	0.005				−0.00
	(−0.28)	(0.53)				(−0.00)
Block	−0.002				0.001	−0.002*
	(−1.55)				(0.10)	(−1.85)
Q			−0.01***		−0.108*	−0.015***
			(−2.14)		(−1.72)	(−2.20)
M/*S*				−0.01***		
				(−2.51)		
ROA			0.04			
			(0.92)			
ROS				0.013		0.05
				(0.75)		(0.64)
$R_{i,\,t-12\text{ to }t}$					0.006	
					(0.03)	
Blev					−1.65***	−0.025
					(−3.48)	(−0.95)
X^2	1.05	0.66	2.33*	2.81*	16.53***	1.42

The dependent variable is equal to 1 for companies that reported pension fund holding above 3 per cent in 1995–6 and to 0 for industry- and size-matched control firms. *M*/*S* is market value of equity plus book value of debt over sales; *Q* is the ratio of market value of equity plus book value of debt over total assets; Blev is the ratio of long-term debt over long-term debt plus shareholders' funds; $R_{i,\,t-12\text{ to }t}$ is a one-year share price return; Split is a dummy variable equals to 1 if the roles of chairman and CEO are split; #DIR is the number of directors on the board; %NED is the proportion of non-executive directors in the board; Dir is the proportion of outstanding equity held by directors; Block is the proportion of outstanding equity capital held by blockholders other than directors and occupational pension funds; X^2, the chi-squared, is used to test that all slopes of the Logit regression are zero by comparing the restricted and the unrestricted log likelihoods. *t*-values are in parentheses. ***, **, *: significance at the 0.01, 0.05 and 0.10 level, respectively.

than our control group. These latter issues were the main focus of the recommendations of Cadbury (1992) which relied on pension funds for their implementation.

Equation 6, Table 25.2, controls for differences in other monitoring mechanisms to account for the fact that the various mechanisms may be substitutes. The results show that the main difference between our test and control firms is the measure of firm value (Q), suggesting that our test firms have lower value than the control firms.[19] The coefficient of blockholding is also negative and significant at the 10 per cent confidence level, suggesting that, after controlling for all other differences between our test and control firms, the test companies have lower blockholdings than our control firms. No single pension fund-monitoring variable is significant at any confidence level. These results do not reject H_{01}–H_{03} and cast doubt on the monitoring role of pension funds in the UK.

In Table 25.3 we analyse the causal relationship between board structure and pension funds holdings by running a set of regressions with the dependent variables which proxy for board structure measured in 1996–7 and the explanatory variables such as pension funds holdings in 1995–6. We hypothesize that pension funds require companies in which they hold large stakes in 1995–6 to adopt the Cadbury's (1992) board structure in 1996–7. We follow McConnell and Servaes (1995) and focus separately on low and high growth firms using E/P ratio as a proxy for growth opportunities. Firms with E/P ratio above (equal or below) the median are classified as low (high) growth. For low growth firms pension funds holdings is expected to be positively related to the adoption of the Cadbury (1992) recommendations because they are more likely to suffer from the free cash flow problem.

The first three columns of Table 25.3 report the results of the Logit regression where the dependent variable is equal to 1 if the roles of CEO and Chairman are split and zero otherwise. The results show that the coefficients of the pension fund variables are positive but not significant. When we split our sample into high and low growth companies, still, none of the pension funds variables is significant. We tested for possible multicollinearity problem by running the regressions with each single variable. We find (but do not report) that the holdings of directors (Dir) is negative and significant. In addition, the coefficient of block shareholders (Block) is negative but insignificant. None of the occupational pension funds variables is significant.

Columns 4–6 provide the results of the Logit regressions where the dependent variable is equal to 1 if the company has appointed a non-executive director as chairman and zero otherwise. We find that, for the whole sample, the coefficients of pension fund incidence (IPF), and pension fund size (LNPFA), are positive and significant (though only at the 10 per cent level). These coefficients become insignificant when regressions are run separately for high and low growth firms. Also, the coefficient of directors' ownership is negative and significant for the whole sample. In addition, when we run the regressions with a single independent variable, we find that the IPF is still positive and significant (1.36 with $t=1.71$) for the whole sample. For the low-Q companies, we find that the coefficient of total pension funds (TPF) is positive and significant (0.06 and $t=1.93$). The coefficient of directors' ownership (Dir) is negative and significant while that of blockholders is positive and significant.

The last three columns present the results of the OLS regressions where the dependent variable is the proportion of non-executive directors in the board. The results show that

Table 25.3. *Determinants of board structure for low and high growth firms*

	Split			Nechair			%NED		
	All	Low growth	High growth	All	Low growth	High growth	All	Low growth	High growth
Constant	−8.322*	−7.691	−10.648	−4.915	−6.596	−3.103	0.193	0.047	0.326
	(−2.12)	(−1.38)	(−1.32)	(−1.15)	(−0.92)	(−0.53)	(0.72)	(0.13)	(0.79)
Dir	−0.007	−0.003	−0.008	−0.026**	−0.023	−0.025	−0.00003	−0.00004	0.00004
	(−0.80)	(−0.22)	(−0.52)	(−2.25)	(−1.23)	(−1.51)	(−0.04)	(−0.05)	(0.04)
Block	0.002	−0.003	0.023	0.003	0.011	0.003	0.0003	−0.0002	0.001
	(0.14)	(−0.21)	(0.98)	(0.31)	(0.58)	(0.22)	(0.44)	(−0.21)	(0.76)
TPF	0.077	0.009	0.205	0.051	0.034	0.063	0.002	0.003	−0.001
	(1.11)	(0.19)	(1.22)	(1.50)	(0.76)	(1.22)	(0.88)	(1.34)	(−0.28)
LNPFA	0.263	0.402	0.148	0.376*	0.586	0.220	−0.008	−0.001	−0.010
	(1.47)	(1.50)	(0.62)	(1.92)	(0.69)	(0.80)	(−0.69)	(−0.06)	(−0.60)
IPF	0.917	1.655	0.085	3.509*	6.124	2.209	0.001	0.062	−0.001
	(0.81)	(0.75)	(0.11)	(1.91)	(1.53)	(1.28)	(0.08)	(1.08)	(−0.09)
Blev	−0.528	0.269	−1.567	0.489	0.724	0.312	0.092	0.165	0.064
	(−0.63)	(0.13)	(−1.13)	(0.52)	(0.46)	(0.24)	(1.51)	(1.52)	(0.79)
$R_{i,t-12 \text{ to } t}$	0.230	0.028	0.421	−0.480	−0.491	−0.456	0.014	−0.002	0.029
	(0.75)	(0.07)	(0.84)	(−1.24)	(−0.69)	(−0.94)	(0.73)	(−0.09)	(1.07)
LN(TA)	0.217	0.013	0.459	−0.217	−0.418	−0.112	0.019**	0.019	0.016
	(1.19)	(0.04)	(1.36)	(−1.25)	(−1.31)	(−0.51)	(2.12)	(1.19)	(1.25)
Pseudo R^2 or R^2	5.31%	4.13%	10.81%	13.70%	18.85%	9.21%	1.10%	3.28%	0.00%

In each regression, the dependent variable is computed for the period 1996–7, while all independent variables are one-year lagged (i.e. 1995–6). The regressions are run separately for all 250 companies (All), low-growth companies (119), and high-growth companies (131). Growth opportunities are measured using the median *E/P* ratio. The first six columns are Logit regressions where Split or Nechair are equal to 1 if the company has split the roles of its chairman and chief executive officer or has a non-executive director as a chairman, and zero otherwise. In these regressions the Pseudo-R^2 measures the goodness of fit. In the last three columns, we run OLS regression with the proportion of non-executive on the board %NED as the dependent variable. TPF is the proportion of outstanding equity owned by all identified pension funds; IPF is the ratio of occupational pension funds holdings over their total assets; LNPFA is the log of the asset value of the pens ion fund; Dir is the proportion of outstanding equity owned by the directors; Block is the proportion of outstanding equity capital held by blockholders other than directors and occupational pension funds; $R_{i,t-12 \text{ to } t}$ is a one-year stock return. ***, **, *: significance at the 0.01, 0.05 and 0.10 level, respectively.

none of the pension fund variables is significant. When the regressions are run separately, we find that only size (Ln(TA)) and leverage (Blev) are positive and significant.

The overall results do not provide strong support for the occupational pension fund monitoring of the board structure. At the same time, board structure is unrelated to market performance, suggesting that the recent trend towards the adoption of the Cadbury's prescriptions was not related to the presence of agency conflicts, but rather dictated by some 'need of visibility' by companies. We do, however, report some evidence consistent with monitoring role of other than pension funds institutional shareholders and of debtholders, at least with regard to the appointment of non-executive directors within low growth firms. There is also some evidence that managerial ownership is used to entrench the position of incumbent managers as the coefficient of directors' ownership is, in most cases, negative and significant. Franks and Mayer (2001) also report a similar relationship. We simulated our results using growth in profits, market returns and *Q* as proxies for growth opportunities and/or presence of agency conflicts. The results are qualitatively similar to those reported in Table 25.3.

5.3. *Pension Funds Investments and Firm Value*

In this section, we focus only on our test-companies and test for the relationship between firm value and ownership structure. A simple correlation matrix, not reported, shows a weak relationship between the various measures of occupational pension fund holdings and firm value. The split dummy variable is positively related to leverage, block ownership, size, and proportion of non-executive directors in the board, but negatively related to directors' holdings. This suggests that the larger the company and the higher the debt–equity ratio, blockholding and the proportion of non-executive directors in the board, the higher its propensity to split the roles of chairman and CEO. However, none of the occupational pension fund measure is statistically related to the split dummy, implying that pension funds, individually or collectively, do not push companies to split the roles of chairman and chief executive officer. Finally, directors' holdings are negatively related to the proportion of non-executive directors in the board, suggesting that such holdings exacerbate the potential agency conflicts between the board and the management.

In Table 25.4, columns (1)–(3), we report the results of the regressions of firm value, as measured by Tobin's *Q* in 1996–7, against various measures of occupational pension funds holdings measures in the previous financial year. Equations (1)–(3) indicate that, with the exception of TPF stakes none of the various measures of pension funds holdings explain firm value. The TPF stakes variable is, actually, negative and significant, suggesting that pension funds collectively destroy value. Even after controlling for other monitoring mechanisms documented in the previous literature (Agrawal and Knoeber 1996; Yermack 1996), such as size and *P*/*E*, firm value is still negatively related to total pension funds holdings (eqn (3)). Although the IPF and the LNPFA are positively related to firm value, they are not significant.

In contrast to previous studies (Yermack 1996; Eisenberg *et al.* 1998), we report a positive relationship between firm value and the number of directors. The difference in the results could be due to the fact that our companies are relatively middle-sized compared to

Table 25.4. *Relationship between firm value and pension fund holdings*

Variables	*Q*			*M/S*	
	(1)	(2)	(3)	(4)	(5)
Intercept	−0.972	2.139**	1.027	0.878	1.092***
	(−0.64)	(2.45)	(0.65)	(0.43)	(3.23)
TPF	−0.031**	−0.041***	−0.052***	0.006	
	(−2.48)	(−3.09)	(−2.73)	(0.25)	
NPF			0.096	−0.309	−0.275*
			(0.61)	(−1.53)	(−1.96)
LNPFA	0.109		0.094	0.005	
	(1.60)		(1.49)	(0.07)	
IPF	0.035		0.094	0.378***	0.376***
	(0.48)		(1.52)	(4.73)	(5.43)
Dir		0.004	0.002	0.005	
		(1.48)	(0.23)	(0.41)	
Dir^2			0.00002	−0.0001	
			(0.17)	(−0.55)	
Block			−0.003	0.001	
			(−0.70)	(0.22)	
Blev			−0.045	−0.842	−0.788
			(−0.10)	(−1.48)	(−1.53)
Ln(TA)		−0.094*	−0.147**	−0.005	
		(−1.88)	(−2.32)	(−0.06)	
Split		−0.202	−0.215	−0.549***	−0.518***
		(−1.39)	(−1.44)	(−2.86)	(−2.85)
No. Dir		0.073**	0.076**	0.063	0.067*
		(2.20)	(2.26)	(1.46)	(1.70)
%NED		0.664*	0.702*	0.464	
		(1.78)	(1.82)	(0.94)	
P/E		0.036***	0.034***	0.032***	0.032***
		(5.98)	(5.55)	(4.04)	(4.13)
Adj. R^2 %	1.98%	19.67%	18.91%	18.13%	20.18%
F	2.80**	8.83***	5.02***	4.80***	10.40***

The sample includes all companies that reported occupational pension fund holding above 3 per cent. In columns (1)–(3) we use *Q*, the ratio of market value of equity plus book value of debt over total assets, as the dependent variable. In columns (4) and (5), the results are simulated using the market value of equity to sales as dependent variable. The dependent variables are measured in 1996–7 while the independent variables are measured in 1995–6. TPF is the proportion of outstanding equity owned by all identified pension funds; IPF is the ratio of occupational pension funds holdings over their total assets; LNPFA is the log of the market value of the largest pension fund's asset; NPF is the number of occupational pension funds; Dir is the proportion of outstanding equity owned by the directors; Dir^2 is its squared value; Block is the proportion of outstanding equity capital held by blockholders other than directors and occupational pension funds; #DIR is the number of directors; Split is a dummy variable equals to 1 if the roles of chairman and CEO are split; %NED is the proportion of non-executive directors; *P/E* is the price–earnings ratio at the balance sheet date. *t*-values are in parentheses. *, **, ***: significance at 10, 5 and 1 per cent level respectively.

the sample of small companies of Eisenberg *et al.* (1998) and that of large companies of Yermack (1996). Finally, the coefficients of the holdings of directors' variable and its squared value are not significant suggesting that there is neither a linear nor a non-linear relationship between value and managerial ownership. These results are not consistent with the findings of McConnell and Servaes (1990, 1995).

We simulate these results using market value of the firm over sales as a proxy for firm value (Lins and Servaes 1999). The results, reported in eqns (4) and (5), show a positive relationship between value and pension fund incidence, but a negative relationship with the number of pension funds. The coefficient of block ownership is not significant in any regression. We also simulate our results by using sales as a measure of size and capital expenditure over total assets as a proxy for growth opportunities. The results (not reported) are qualitatively similar to these reported in Table 25.4. Overall, our results suggest that pension funds do not add value to companies in which they hold large stakes.

5.4. *Pension Fund Holdings on Firms' Long-Term Performance*

We analyse the long-term performance of our test firms by comparing the changes in firm value and stock price performance over the sample periods 1994–5 and 1996–7. As in Karpoff *et al.* (1996) and Del Guercio and Hawkins (1999), we investigate whether companies in which pension funds hold large stakes rebound more quickly from poor performance or maintain their good performance over a longer time period.

We evaluate the abnormal performance by computing the arithmetic change over the two sample periods in Q less industry-median Q, and by stock market returns. We compute the Share Price Return from a buy-and-hold strategy over the sub-periods 1994–5 and 1996–7 as follows:

$$\text{Returns}_{i,t,T} = \prod_{n=t}^{T}\left\{1 + r_{i,n}\right\} - \prod_{n=t}^{T}\left\{1 + r_{s,n}\right\},$$

where

$$r_{i,n} = \frac{P_{i,n}}{P_{i,n-1}} - 1 \quad \text{and} \quad r_{s,n} = \frac{\text{Industry index}_n}{\text{Industry index}_{n-1}} - 1.$$

This measure of performance accounts for the fact that occupational pension funds are long-term investors and does not suffer from cumulating biases observed in arithmetic mean returns (Conrad and Kaul 1993; Wahal 1996). We eliminate survivorship bias by including dead companies in our sample. Out of the 289 test companies, thirty-four (11.76 per cent) are excluded because they went public after 1995 and we could not compute the market performance for the first period.

The results reported in Table 25.5 show that, for the full sample, the industry-adjusted Q has decreased from 0.163 to 0.072. The decrease in both the average and median firm value is statistically significant. The results suggest that, over time, the value of companies in which occupational pension funds hold large stakes decrease. As in Wahal (1996), we split the sample into overperformers and underperformers. Overperforming (underperforming) companies are companies with Tobin's Q higher (lower) than the median. The overperforming companies have done worst over the two sample periods. Their average

Table 25.5. *Pension funds holdings and long-term stock price performance*

	1994–5			1996–7		*t*-statistics: difference in means	Mann–Whitney *p*-value
	N	Mean	Median	Mean	Median		
Panel A: Industry-adjusted firm value Q							
Full sample	255	0.16***	−0.08***	0.07***	−0.10***	2.72	0.009
Overperform.	128	0.67***	0.35***	0.48***	0.15***	3.22	0.000
Underperform.	127	−0.35	−0.32	−0.34	−0.31	−0.58	0.237
Panel B: Industry-adjusted share price return %							
Full sample	255	11.65	−3.44	14.4	0.00	−0.41	0.233
Overperform.	128	62.66***	30.75***	18.59***	0.00***	−4.51	0.000
Underperform.	127	−38.96***	−33.35***	10.25***	−0.42***	6.94	0.000

The sample includes all companies that displayed (at least) one relevant pension fund holding. The abnormal returns are buy-and-hold returns adjusted for the industry index. The sample is divided into a sample of underperformers (underperform.) and overperformers (overperform.) based on the median performance of the firm in 1994–5. For example, if the industry-adjusted Q (Share Price Return) for a firm is lower (higher) than the median, the firm is classified as an underperformer (overperformer). *, **, ***: significance at 10, 5 and 1 per cent, respectively.

value has decreased from 0.67 to 0.48. The decrease in the mean median is statistically significant. In contrast, the average and the median Tobin's Q of the underperforming companies did not change significantly. These companies have underperformed in the 1994–5 period and carried on underperforming in 1996–7. These results are striking as they imply that companies, in which occupational pension funds hold large stakes, decrease in value through time, and those that are already underperforming do not improve. In sum, it appears that pension funds are passive investors: they do not make companies in which they hold large stakes improve their performance and they do not sell their holdings in companies that are underperforming.

Panel B reports the results based on the industry-adjusted share price returns. For the full sample, companies have increased their performance from 11.65 to 14.4 per cent. However, the difference in means (and medians) is not statistically significant. The stock price performance of the sub-sample of the overperforming firms declined significantly from 62.66 to 18.59 per cent (*t*-statistic of the difference in means = −4.51), while under-performing companies increased their performance from −38.96 to 10.25 per cent (*t*-statistic of the difference in means = 6.94). As in Wahal (1996), our results indicate that both the overperforming and under-performing companies experience return reversals. As such our results are consistent with the mean reversion hypothesis and cannot be attributed to pension funds investments.[20]

6. DISCUSSION AND CONCLUSION

In this chapter, we analysed the performance of companies in which occupational pension funds hold large stakes and tested the hypotheses that, because of their size, structure, and objectives, these funds should be effective monitors of UK companies. We showed that our test firms are small and have low value. These companies are also not likely to be more efficient than the control group. We report that pension funds do not add value to the companies in which they hold large stakes. Our results cast doubt on the monitoring role of pension funds that are considered, in theory, to be the main promoters of corporate governance in the UK. At the same time, we showed that, despite the relatively poor performance of the companies in which they invest, occupational pension funds do not opt for an 'exit' strategy.

Our results suggest that, once 'locked in' pension funds find it difficult and costly to monitor because their holdings tend to represent relatively small fractions of the total values of the funds' assets (0.15 per cent). Thus, our results are consistent with Admati *et al.*'s. (1994) proposition that, given that monitoring is costly, these funds will not monitor as this is not likely to result in a modification in the firm's pay-off structure and will not lead to net gains. They cannot also sell their holdings for fear of selling at a discount or conveying information to the market. They may also refrain from intervening publicly for fear of drawing to public attention the difficulties the company is facing and/or trading on insider information. However, our results could also imply that pension funds are passive investors, investing most of their funds in the index. The results could also imply that the investments we analysed in this chapter are peripheral, and that pension funds choose to invest in low *Q* firms to benefit from return reversals on these securities.

Notes

1. Hutton (1995) argues that 'pension funds... have become classic absentee landlords, exerting power without responsibility and making exacting demands upon companies without recognizing their reciprocal obligations as owners' (ibid.: 304).
2. For example, Drucker (1976: 82) stipulates that 'pension funds are not "owners", they are investors. They do not want control... If they do not like a company or its management, their duty is to sell the stock.' More recently, Porter (1997) argues that institutional investors, despite their substantial aggregate holdings, do not sit on corporate boards and have virtually no real influence on management's behaviour because they invest nearly all their assets in index funds rather than directly in companies. Short and Keasey (1997) suggest that once pension funds are locked in, it is costly to get involved in monitoring and they cannot exit in case they are considered to trade on insider information. Murphy and Van Nuys (1994) argue that pension funds are run by individuals who do not have the proper incentives to maximize fund value.
3. In contrast, in the USA, investments and activism programmes of pension funds are developed and implemented by fund staff then overseen and approved by trustees (Del Guercio and Hawkins 1999).
4. Cadbury (1992: 6.16) notes that 'Because of their collective stake, we look to the institutions in particular, with the backing on Institutional Shareholders' Committee, to use their influence as owners to ensure that the companies in which they have invested comply with the Code'. The National Association of Pension Funds also endorses such recommendations (NAPF 1996*b*).
5. A number of studies document the free cash flow problem in the UK. For example, Franks and Mayer (2001) find that UK companies pay high dividends relative to German companies; Lasfer (1995) shows that debt mitigates the free cash flow problem; Lasfer (1997) provides evidence that firms with free cash flow problems pay scrip, rather than cash, dividends. The reports of Cadbury (1992) and Greenbury (1995) are a manifestation of the previous wider debate on the various corporate governance issues detailed in Charkham (1995), Stapledon (1996), and Keasey *et al.* (1997).

6. Companies Act 1995, §§ 198 and 199 requires UK companies to disclose in their accounts the name of any investor who holds 3 per cent or more of the issued share capital.
7. See Chew (1997) for a collection of papers dealing with these two corporate governance systems.
8. See Black (1998) and Karpoff (1998) for a survey.
9. Similarly, in the USA, the value of DC plans in 1993 was $1,068 billion compared to $1,248 billion for DB plans. However, DC schemes are growing at much faster rates of 19 per cent per year, compared to 14 per cent for DB plans, Jepson (1998).
10. The report states that 'no one individual has unfettered powers of decision. Where the chairman is also chief executive, it is essential that there should be a strong and independent element on the board, with a recognized senior member.'
11. The Code of Best Practice recommended an audit committee of at least three non-executive directors with written terms of reference (No. 4.3) and the institution of a nomination committee as an internal committee within the board (No. 4.30). This committee should be composed of a majority of on-executive directors and chaired by the chairman of the board.
12. The report summarizes the functions of the board as follows: 'The responsibilities of the board include setting up the company's strategic aims, providing the leadership to put them into effect, supervising the management of the business and reporting to shareholders on their stewardship.' As to the financial aspects of corporate governance, the report mentions: 'the way in which boards set financial policy and oversee its implementation, including the use of financial controls, and the process whereby they report on the activities and progress of the company to the shareholders'.
13. See John and Senbet (1998) for an extensive survey of the monitoring role of corporate board of directors and Stapledon (1996: 138–53) for the monitoring role of non-executive directors.
14. The choice of the 1995–6 sample period is driven by data availability. The data on shareholding is inserted manually because Extel Financial provides only the latest data on shareholding in text format and this data is not available in machine-readable form. Other similar studies also use short time period, see Karpoff (1998) for a review. Our results are sample-period dependent because we find, but did not report, that the vast majority of companies (83 per cent of our test firms) had large pension funds holdings in both 1992 and 1996 periods and the magnitude of those holdings has not changed significantly.
15. Extel Financial is a financial database micro-system that provides accounting as well as financial and reference data for all UK companies and many international companies.
16. The ideal would be to exclude from the denominator of this ratio other assets such as property, cash and fixed income securities, but the desegregated data on equity investment is not available.
17. This variable includes director's holdings but excludes those of officers. UK quoted companies are required to disclose in their financial statements the proportion of shares held directly and indirectly by executive and non-executive directors (Companies Act 1985). However, no similar disclosure applies to officers. This legal disclosure requirement means that we had to define managerial ownership as ownership by members of the board of directors. Although this definition is consistent with that of Morck *et al.* (1988), it differs from that of McConnell and Servaes (1990) and Denis and Sarin (1999) as we do not include shares owned by corporate officers not members of the board.
18. We exclude fifty-eight companies with negative book value of equity due to goodwill write-offs when we use the *M/B* ratio, book leverage and return on equity. The inclusion of these companies did not, however, alter our reported results.
19. The negative relationship between pension fund investments and Q has been widely documented in the investment literature. For example, Lakonishok *et al.* (1994) show that pension funds invest in glamour stocks (low book-to-market firms), because the previous success of the glamour

stocks helps institutions justify their portfolio selection to their investors but these stocks generally underperform value stocks (high book-to-market firms).

20. We obtained similar results by using the industry median return and market index as a benchmark and by matching our test firms by prior performance or *M/B* and size. Similar results are obtained when we concentrate on survived companies, and exclude IPO firms.

References

Admati, A. R., Pfleiderer, P., and Zechner, J. (1994). Large shareholder activism, risk sharing, and financial market equilibrium. *Journal of Political Economy* 102: 1097.

Agrawal, A., and Knoeber, C. R. (1996). Firm performance and mechanisms to control agency problems between managers and shareholders. *Journal of Financial and Quantitative Analysis* 31: 377.

Ayres, I., and Cramton, P. (1994). Relational investing and agency theory. *Cardozo Law Review* 15: 1033.

Black, B. S. (1998). Shareholder activism and corporate governance in the united states. In Newman (ed.), *The Palgrave Dictionary of Economics and the Law*. London: Macmillan.

Blake, D. (1995). *Pension Schemes and Pension Funds in the United Kingdom*. Oxford: Clarendon Press.

Brancato, C. K. (1997). *Institutional Investors and Corporate Governance: Best Practice for Increasing Corporate Value*. Chicago: McGraw Hill.

Brickley, J. A., Lease, R. C., and Smith, C. W. Jr. (1994). Corporate voting: Evidence from charter amendment proposals. *Journal of Corporate Finance* 1: 5.

Business Monitor (1997). London: Central Statistical Office.

Cadbury, A. (1992). *Report of the Committee on the Financial Aspects of Corporate Governance*. London: Gee.

Charkham, J. (1995). *Keeping Good Company: A Study of Corporate Governance in Five Countries*. Oxford: Oxford University Press.

Chew, D. H. (ed.) (1997). *Studies in International Corporate Finance and Governance Systems: A Comparison of the US, Japan and Europe*. New York: Oxford University Press.

Conrad, J., and Kaul, G. (1993). Long-term market overreaction or biases in computed returns? *Journal of Finance* 48: 39.

Cotter, J. F., Shivdasani, A., and Zenner, M. (1997). Do independent directors enhance target shareholder wealth during tender offers? *Journal of Financial Economics* 43: 195.

Davis, E. P. (1995). *Pension Funds. Retirement-Income, Security and Capital Markets. An International Perspective*. Oxford: Clarendon Press.

Del Guercio, D., and Hawkins, J. (1999). The Motivation and Impact of Pension Fund Activism. *Journal of Financial Economics* 52: 293.

Demsetz, H., and Lehn, K. (1985). The structure of corporate ownership: Causes and consequences. *Journal of Political Economy* 93: 1155.

Denis, D. J., and Sarin, A. (1999). Ownership and board structures in publicly traded corporations. *Journal of Financial Economics* 52: 187.

Diamond, D. W. (1984). Financial intermediation and delegated monitoring. *Review of Economic Studies* 51: 393.

Drucker, P. F. (1976). *The Unseen Revolution: How Pension Fund Socialism Came to America*. London: Heinemann.

Eisenberg, T., Sundgren, S., and Wells, M. T. (1998). Large board size and decreasing firm value in small firms. *Journal of Financial Economics* 48: 35.

Financial Times (1997). FT survey on pension fund investment. *Financial Times*, 9 May.

Franks, J. R., and Mayer, C. (2001). The ownership and control of German corporations. Review of Financial Studies. 14, 943.

Greenbury, R. (1995). *Directors' Remuneration: Report of a Study Group Chaired by Sir Richard Greenbury.* London: Gee.

Hart, O. (1995). *Firms, Contracts, and Financial Structure.* Oxford: Oxford University Press.

Hutton, W. (1995). *The State We Are In.* London: Vintage Press.

Jensen, M. C. (1986). Agency costs of free cash flow, corporate finance, and takeovers. *American Economic Review* 76: 323.

—— The modern industrial revolution, exit, and the failure of internal control systems. *Journal of Finance* 48: 831.

Jepson, J. (1998). US defined benefits and defined contribution: Comparison and implications. Paper presented at the 1998 NAPF Conference, Eastbourne, UK.

John, K., and Senbet, L. W. (1998). Corporate governance and board effectiveness. *Journal of Banking and Finance* 22: 371.

Kahn, C., and Winton, A. (1998). Ownership structure, speculation and shareholder intervention. *Journal of Finance* 53: 99.

Karpoff, J. M. (1998). Does shareholder activism work? A survey of empirical findings. Unpublished manuscript, University of Washington.

—— Malatesta, P. H., and Walkling, R. A. (1996). Corporate governance and shareholder initiatives: Empirical evidence. *Journal of Financial Economics* 42: 365.

Keasey, K. S., Thompson, S., and Wright, M. (eds.) (1997). *Corporate Governance: Economic, Management, and Financial Issues.* Oxford: Oxford University Press.

Lakonishok, J., Shleifer, A., and Vishny, R. W. (1994). Contrarian investment, extrapolation, and risk. *Journal of Finance* 49: 1541.

Lasfer, M. A. (1995). Agency costs, taxes and debt: The UK evidence. *European Financial Management* 1: 265.

—— (1996). Taxes and dividends: The UK evidence. *Journal of Banking and Finance* 20: 455.

—— (1997). On the motivation for paying script dividends. *Financial Management* 26: 62.

Lins, K., and Servaes, H. (1999). International evidence on the value of diversification. *Journal of Finance* 54: 2215.

London Stock Exchange (1995). *Survey on Share Ownership.* London: London Stock Exchange.

Maug, E. (1998). Large shareholders as monitors: Is there a trade-off between liquidity and control? *Journal of Finance* 53: 65.

McConnell, J. J., and Servaes, H. (1990). Additional evidence on equity ownership and corporate value. *Journal of Financial Economics* 27: 595.

—— (1995). Equity ownership and the two faces of debt. *Journal of Financial Economics* 39: 131.

Minns, R. (1980). *Pension Funds and British Capitalism: The Ownership and Control of Shareholders.* London: Heinemann.

Morck, R., Shleifer, A., and Vishny, R. W. (1988). Management ownership and market valuation: An empirical analysis. *Journal of Financial Economics* 20: 293.

Murphy, K., and Van Nuys, K. (1994). State pension fund shareholder activism. Harvard Business School, Working Paper.

NAPF (1996*a*). *Year Book.* London: National Association of Pension Funds.

—— (1996*b*). *Good Corporate Governance.* London: National Association of Pension Funds.

Nesbitt, S. L. (1994). Long-term rewards from shareholder activism: A study of the CalPERS effect. *Journal of Applied Corporate Finance* 6: 75.

PFA (1996). *Pension Funds and their Advisers.* London: PFA.

Porter, M. E. (1997). Capital choices: Changing the way America invests in industry. In D. H. Chew (ed.), *Studies in International Corporate Finance and Governance Systems: A Comparison of the US, Japan and Europe.* New York: Oxford University Press.

Prowse, S. (1994). Corporate governance in an international perspective: A survey of corporate control mechanisms amongst large firms in the United States, the United Kingdom, Japan and Germany. BIS, Economic Papers No. 41.

Romano, R. (1994). Public pension fund activism in corporate governance reconsidered. *Columbia Law Review* 93: 795.

Shleifer, A., and Vishny, R. W. (1997). A survey of corporate governance. *Journal of Finance* 52: 737.

Short, H., and Keasey, K. (1997). Institutional shareholders and corporate governance in the United Kingdom. In K. S. Keasey, S. Thompson, and M. Wright (ed.), *Corporate Governance: Economic, Management, and Financial Issues.* Oxford: Oxford University Press.

Smith, M. P. (1996). Shareholder activism by institutional investors: Evidence from CalPERS. *Journal of Finance* 51: 227.

Stapledon, G. P. (1996). *Institutional Shareholders and Corporate Governance.* Oxford: Clarendon Press.

Tomlinson, L. (1998). Should the future be all passive? Paper presented at the 1998 NAPF Conference, Eastbourne, UK.

Wahal, S. (1996). Pension fund activism and firm performance. *Journal of Financial and Quantitative Analysis* 31: 1.

Yermack, D. (1996). Higher market valuation of companies with a small board of directors. *Journal of Financial Economics* 40: 185.

PART VII

EXECUTIVE COMPENSATION

26

Stock-Based Executive Compensation

MARTIN J. CONYON AND KEVIN J. MURPHY

1. INTRODUCTION

This chapter focuses on the importance of stock-based compensation for top corporate executives. Throughout Europe and USA, there have been repeated calls to align the interests of executives with those of shareholders by linking executive compensation more closely to company performance. Stock-based pay, including stock options as well as performance and employment-contingent equity grants, provides a direct link between pay and performance and plays a key role in mitigating 'agency problems' between managers and shareholders. In this chapter, we analyse the various forms of stock-based pay and discuss how to value and measure the incentives from the various schemes. In addition, we document the prevalence of stock-based pay in Europe, and contrast these results to the USA experience.

In Section 2 we discuss the composition of executive pay packages, and analyse and critique the standard approaches in valuing stock-based pay. In addition, we document the relative importance of stock-based compensation in the USA and Europe. Due to the difficulties in assembling comparable time-series and cross-sectional data on option and equity holdings for most countries (Conyon and Murphy 2000) a significant focus of our analysis in this chapter is on the USA and the UK. We show that, while stock options have emerged as the single largest component of compensation for USA executives, the use of stock options among UK and other European companies is still relatively modest.

Section 3 explores the importance of stock-based compensation in providing financial incentives for top executives. Chief Executive Officer (CEO) wealth is linked directly to company share-price performance through their share holdings, their option holdings, and through shares awarded through long-term incentive plans. Following our approach in Conyon and Murphy (2000), we show that these various holdings can be aggregated to form an 'effective' ownership percentage or 'pay–performance sensitivity'. We document that for a large sample of companies (about 1,500 in USA and 500 in UK) the pay–performance sensitivity among USA executives far exceeds the comparable sensitivity for UK executives. Unfortunately, because of data-availability limitations, we are unable to contrast USA and UK sensitivities with those in other European economies.

The two main stylized facts emerging from Sections 2 and 3 are: (i) that the USA uses stock-based compensation more intensively than Europe, and (ii) that the financial incentives from stock rewards are also greater in the USA. Section 4 explores a partial explanation for the relative popularity of stock-based pay (especially stock options) in the USA compared to the UK and the rest of Europe: differences in the tax and accounting regimes. We show that, while personal income tax rates and rules in the USA and UK are generally quite similar, at least some of the observed differences in compensation and incentives can be explained by differences in the extent to which options payouts are deductible as business expenses to the option-granting companies. Section 5 concludes with some unanswered questions and directions for future research.

2. PREVALENCE AND VALUATION OF STOCK-BASED PAY

2.1. *Forms of Stock-Based Compensation*

The primary forms of stock-based compensation are stock options, restricted stock, and performance shares. Stock options are contracts that give the recipient the right (but not the obligation) to buy a share of stock at a pre-specified price (called the 'exercise' or 'strike' price) for a pre-specified term. Conceptually, the exercise price can be set above, below, or at the grant-date share price, or can vary over time with inflation or movements in broad stock indices; the standard practice in both the USA and the UK is to fix exercise prices at the grant-date share price. Options in the USA typically are granted with terms of ten years; in the UK option maturity terms range between seven and ten years. Stock options are usually not exercisable immediately at grant, but rather only become exercisable with the passage of time and/or the attainment of performance thresholds. The standard practice in the USA is for options to 'vest' and become exercisable over time independent of performance,[1] while options in the UK often include performance criteria. Employees leaving the firm are typically allowed to exercise vested options upon their termination, while unvested options are forfeited.

Restricted stock grants are 'restricted' in the sense that the recipients cannot sell or transfer the shares for a period of time, and will forfeit the shares if they leave the firm prior to vesting. Performance shares are essentially a promise for future delivery of shares, conditional on continued employment (like restricted stock) and on meeting various performance thresholds. Both restricted stock and performance share plans are common in the USA, although their prevalence is much lower than stock option plans. The standard practice in the UK is to grant performance shares (often called 'Long-Term Incentive Plans' or LTIPs) and not restricted stock; indeed, in recent years, LTIPs have replaced options as the predominant form of stock-based pay among UK CEOs.

Closely related to stock-based plans are cash plans that replicate the payouts from stock plans. For example, 'stock appreciation rights' give recipients the right to the spread between the market price of the stock and the exercise price, and thus replicate the payouts from stock options. Phantom stock plans give recipients the value of shares at some future date, subject to continued employment and/or performance criteria, and thus replicate the payouts from restricted stock and performance share plans. These cash plans are particularly popular in non-public and closely held corporations, where traditional stock-based plans are impossible or unattractive.

In addition to stock-based compensation, top executives receive a variety of other forms of fixed and performance-contingent compensation, including salaries, bonuses, and benefits. Base salaries are set annually and are typically determined by industry surveys and other market factors affecting the supply and demand for high quality labour. Annual bonuses are typically paid based on current accounting performance. In addition to annual bonuses, many firms adopt multi-year bonus plans with payouts based on accounting performance measured over several years. Finally, executives receive a myriad of other forms of pay, including pension benefits, deferred pay opportunities, life insurance, and other benefits available broadly in the organization.

2.2. *The Global Importance of Stock-Based Compensation*

Stock-based pay has increased dramatically in the USA over the past decade, especially in the largest corporations. Figure 26.1 depicts the relative importance of stock-based pay for CEOs in S&P 500 Industrials (i.e. the S&P 500 companies excluding utilities and finance firms).

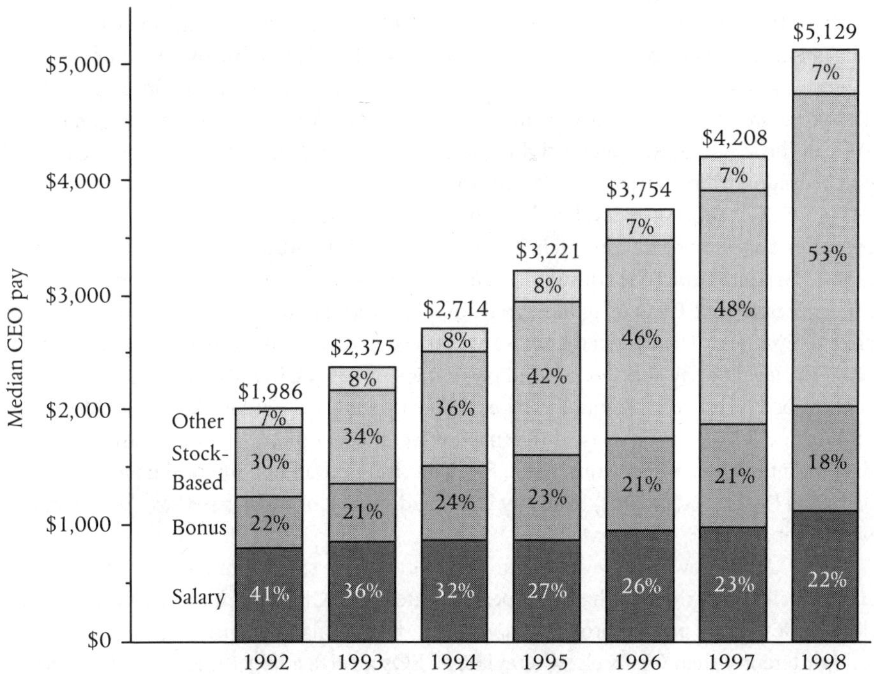

Figure 26.1. *CEO compensation in USA S&P 500 industrials. The statistics (in 1998-constant dollars) give the median CEO's compensation in thousands of USD and are derived from Compustat's ExecuComp database, and exclude utilities and financials. Stock-based pay includes stock options (valued at Black–Scholes), restricted stock grants (valued at face value), and performance shares (valued at the target grant). Pay component percentages are derived by computing the percentages for each CEO, and averaging across CEOs; the bar height depicts median compensation.*

The bar height depicts median total compensation, including salaries, realized bonuses, stock-based compensation, and other pay. Stock-based pay includes the grant-date stock options (valued using the Black–Scholes formula; see the discussion in Section 2.3), restricted stock grants (valued at year-end stock prices), and performance shares (valued as the target grant multiplied by the year-end stock price). Pay component percentages are derived from ExecuComp data by computing the percentages for each CEO, and averaging across CEOs.

Figure 26.1 shows that the total level of executive pay in USA has increased substantially between 1992 and 1998: median CEO pay levels in S&P 500 Industrials has more than doubled from under $2.0 million in 1992 to over $5 million in 1998. The increase primarily reflects a dramatic growth in stock-based compensation, which swelled from 30 to 53 per cent of total compensation, representing a five-fold increase in dollar terms. Most of the increase in stock-based compensation, in turn, reflects the growth in stock option grants, which grew from 23 per cent of compensation in 1992 to 44 per cent of compensation in 1998. (Over the same time period, the value of restricted stock and performance shares tripled in dollar value, but increased only slightly, 7 to 9 per cent, as a percentage of total compensation.)

The data underlying Fig. 26.1 are available through USA disclosure requirements, which became effective for fiscal years beginning in 1992. Unfortunately, comparable time-series data are not available for European companies; only the UK has disclosure requirements as extensive as those in the USA, and the UK requirements were not introduced until 1997. Therefore, we cannot replicate the time-series analysis in Fig. 26.1 for European companies. We can, however, draw some insights on European trends and practices in stock-based compensation from a variety of different sources.

Figure 26.2 shows the level and composition of CEO pay in USA and nine European countries, based on data reported in Towers Perrin's 1999 Worldwide Total Remuneration report. The data depict the consulting company's estimates of 'typical' or 'competitive' pay for a representative CEO in an industrial company with approximately US$250 million in annual revenues.[2] The data in the figure are ranked in descending order of total compensation. The level of pay and stock-based percentage for USA CEOs ($1,351,000 and 32 per cent, respectively), is substantially lower than that suggested in Fig. 26.1 for 1998 ($5.1 million and 53 per cent). These differences reflect the fact that Fig. 26.1 is based on actual data from the largest USA firms, while Fig. 26.2 is based on hypothetical data from a typical small (by USA standards) firm: pay levels and the use of stock-based pay both increase with company size.[3]

Figure 26.2 shows that, even when conditioning on small firms, American firms pay substantially more than do their European counterparts: CEO pay in the USA is more than double the average pay in Europe.[4] Importantly, the data also show that USA executives are paid differently than CEOs elsewhere: USA CEOs receive a larger fraction of their pay in the form of stock-based pay (32 per cent) than any of their global counterparts. Stock-based pay accounts for only between 7 and 17 per cent of pay in the UK, France, Germany, Italy, the Netherlands, Spain, and Sweden. In Belgium and Switzerland the fraction of pay is even lower at 3 per cent. It is worth stressing that the 1999 Towers Perrin data indicate that all of these European economies now use at least some form of stock-based compensation—even though the fraction is low compared with the USA.

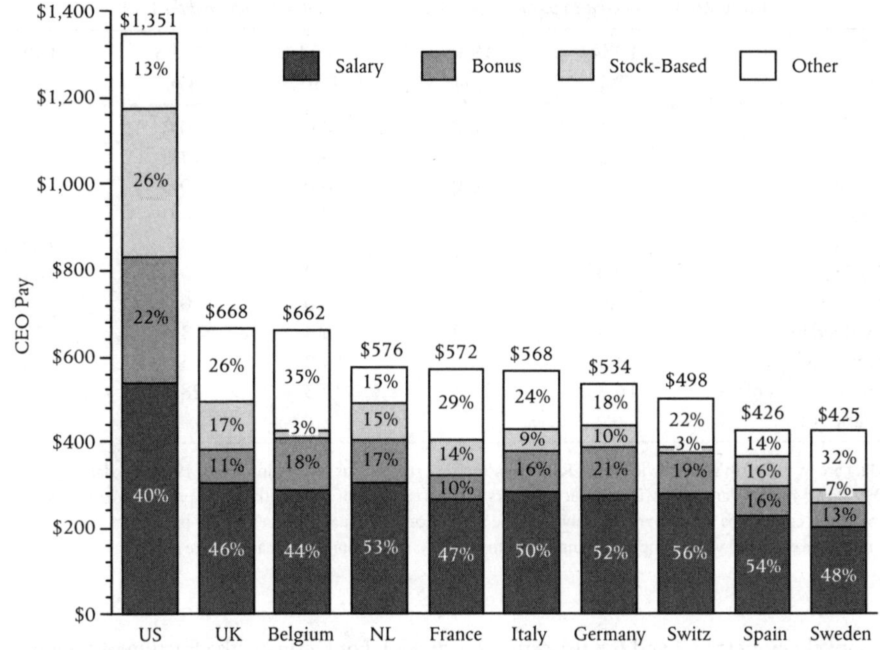

Figure 26.2. *USA versus European CEO pay levels and structures. The data from Towers Perrin's 1999 Worldwide Total Remuneration report are used with permission. Data reflects Towers Perrin's estimate of competitive CEO pay as of April 1999 for industrial companies with approximately USA $250 million in annual revenues. CEO pay is shown for the following countries: US, UK, France, the Netherlands, Italy, Switzerland, Belgium, Germany, Spain, and Sweden. Local currency amounts are converted into USA dollars using April 1999 exchange rates. Salaries are defined as base salary plus other regular payments (such as vacation pay, 13th-month pay, and regular bonuses unrelated to performance); bonuses include target performance-based cash awards. Stock-based pay includes the grant-date expected value of option grants and annualized targets from performance share plans. Other compensation includes both voluntary and compulsory company contributions and the value of perquisites.*

Table 26.1 shows how the importance of stock-based pay has changed over time in the USA and in nine European countries using Towers Perrin's Worldwide Total Remuneration (WWTR) surveys for the selected years 1984, 1988, 1992, 1996, and 1999. The data for the years 1992 to 1996 are based on Abowd and Kaplan's (1999) analysis of the WWTR surveys. We collected the data for 1999. The data for the USA indicate a marked increase in stock-based pay from 1984 to 1996, but (in contrast to the results in Fig. 26.1) no discernible positive trend in the 1990s. Stock-based pay (as a percentage of total pay) has increased steadily over time in France, Italy, and Switzerland, while remaining fairly constant in the UK.

By 1999 all countries are using at least some fraction of stock-based compensation to reward CEOs. This includes those countries which Towers Perrin report did not use stock-based pay in 1996. Of these, the use of stock-based pay by Belgium and Sweden is

Table 26.1. *Stock-based pay (as a percentage of total pay) in Europe and the USA*

	1984 (%)	1988 (%)	1992 (%)	1996 (%)	1999 (%)
Belgium	0.0	0.0	0.0	0.0	3.2
France	12.3	13.3	15.6	14.6	14.3
Germany	0.0	0.0	0.0	0.0	9.7
Italy	0.0	0.0	0.5	4.0	9.1
Netherlands	0.0	0.0	0.0	0.0	14.6
Spain	0.0	0.0	0.0	0.0	16.0
Sweden	0.0	0.0	0.0	0.0	6.8
Switzerland	1.9	1.9	3.4	3.6	3.1
United Kingdom	14.5	14.6	15.7	15.0	16.6
United States of America	16.9	28.3	32.3	28.7	32.1

Data are from Perrin's Worldwide Total Remuneration reports (various issues), including 1984–92 data reported by Abowd and Kaplan (1999). Data reflects Towers Perrin's estimate of competitive CEO pay as of April 1997 for industrial companies with approximately USA $250 million in annual revenues. Stock-based pay includes the grant-date expected value of option grants and annualized targets from performance share plans.

relatively modest (3.2 and 6.8 per cent respectively). For Germany the fraction of total pay that is stock based is about 10 per cent, but for the Netherlands and Spain the figure is even higher at about 15 per cent.

Time-series data on stock-option plans (as opposed to all stock-based plans) are unavailable for most European countries. However, Fig. 26.3 shows the time-series trend in the prevalence of stock option plans in the UK and the USA, reproduced from Conyon and Murphy (2000). The UK data are constructed from Main (1999), who, in turn, uses data provided by a large compensation-consulting firm. The USA data are constructed primarily from the Conference Board 'Top Executive Compensation' reports, which cover predominately S&P 500 companies.[5] The data for 'USA Small and MidCap' firms are extracted from ExecuComp, and defined as the fraction of MidCap and SmallCap companies in which the top five executives hold any options during the year.

As reported by Main (1999) and depicted in Fig. 26.3, the prevalence of option schemes in the UK grew dramatically from the mid-1980s to the early 1990s. In particular, in 1978 only 10 per cent of UK companies offered options to their top executives, by 1983 over 30 per cent of companies had established option schemes, and by 1986 this figure had increased to almost 100 per cent. However, the use of stock options in the UK fell substantially in the mid-1990s; by 1997 only 68 per cent of companies were in a position to offer options to their top executives. In contrast to the UK, Fig. 26.2 shows that the prevalence of option plans in the USA has increased rather than decreased in recent years. In particular, the percentage of large firms with option plans grew from 82 per cent in 1992 to 97 per cent in 1997. The growth in prevalence is more pronounced in smaller firms: in 1992 only 55 per cent of all small and mid-cap firms offered options to their top executives whereas 96 per cent of the companies had plans in place by 1997.

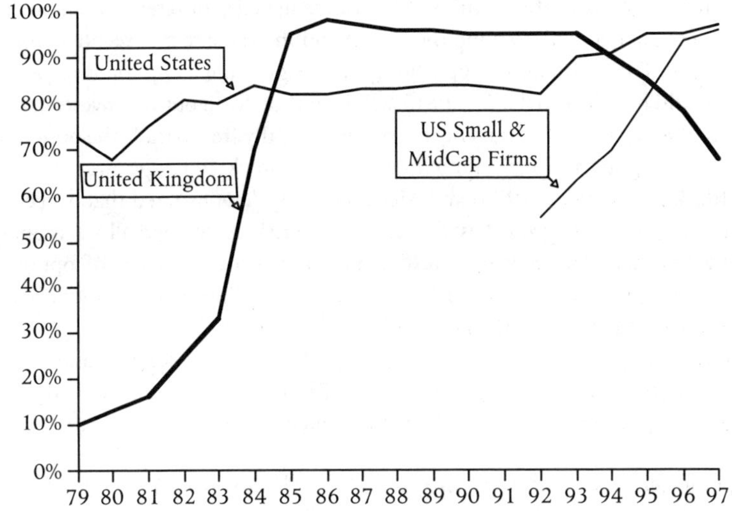

Figure 26.3. *Prevalence of stock option plans (1979–97). Data are from Conyon and Murphy (2000), who base their UK results on Main (1999). USA data 1979–96 from the Conference Board 'Top Executive Compensation' reports (various issues). USA data for 1997 include percentage of S&P 500 companies that have executives holding options (these data closely track the Conference Board data from 1992 to 1996). USA Small and MidCap data include percentage of companies in the S&P MidCap 400 and SmallCap 600 that have executives holding options.*

Figure 26.3 shows the percentage of companies that have option plans, but does not provide information on the magnitude of the grants to executives. However, using British data from Hemmington Scott and the PricewaterhouseCoopers Corporate Register, Conyon and Murphy (2000) estimate the total number of options held by the CEO in 1991 and 1997. Based on about 400 UK companies CEO, option holdings (measured as a percentage of common equity) fell from 0.26 in 1991 to 0.22 per cent in 1997; median holdings over the same time period increased slightly from 0.09 to 0.11 per cent. In contrast, the average option holdings by American CEOs in over 1000 ExecuComp firms grew from 0.87 per cent in 1992 (the first year such shares were publicly disclosed) to 1.1 per cent in 1997; median holdings grew from 0.16 to 0.64 per cent over the same time period.

Several stylized facts emerge from our prevalence results. First, pay levels and the use of stock-based compensation is much higher for American executives than for their European counterparts. Second, the use of stock-based pay in the USA has increased dramatically over the past decade. In contrast, the trend in stock-based pay among European companies is positive but modest, and the use of stock options (as opposed to other forms of stock-based pay) has actually declined in recent years in the UK.

2.3. *Executive Stock Options: Valuation Issues*

Most applications of executive stock options in both research and practice require placing a 'value' on the options as of the grant date. In constructing such a value, it is important to distinguish between two often-confused but fundamentally different valuation concepts: the cost to the company of granting the option and the value to an executive from receiving the option. The economic or opportunity cost of granting an option is the amount the company could have received if it were to sell the option to an outside investor rather than giving it to the executive. The outside investor is generally free to trade the option, and can also take actions (such as short-selling the underlying stock) to hedge away the risk of the option. Black and Scholes (1973) and Merton (1973) demonstrated that, since investors can hedge, options can be valued as if investors were risk neutral and all assets appreciated at the risk-free rate. This risk-neutrality assumption forms the basis of option-pricing theory and is central to all option pricing models, including binomial models, arbitrage pricing models, and Monte Carlo methodologies.[6]

The most widely used valuation methodology in the executive compensation literature is the Black–Scholes (1973) pricing formula. The Black–Scholes option valuation formula, modified to incorporate continuous dividend payments, is given by

$$\text{Option value} = n\{P_e^{-\ln(1+d)T}N(z) - Xe^{-\ln(1+r)T}N(z-\sigma\sqrt{T})\} \tag{26.1}$$

where

n = Number of options granted
P = Grant-date stock price
X = Exercise price
T = Expiration term (years)
d = Annualized dividend yield
σ = Annual stock-price volatility
r = Risk-free interest rate

$$z = \frac{\ln(P/X) + (\ln(1+r) - \ln(1+d) + \sigma^2/2)T}{\sigma\sqrt{T}}$$

$N()$ = Cumulative normal distribution function.

In our calculations, and in practice, the risk-free interest rate is usually estimated as the yield on same-currency default-free government securities maturing at the end of the option term. Volatilities are estimated as $\sqrt{12}$ times the standard deviation of continuously compounded monthly returns over the prior forty-eight months, while dividend yields are estimated over the prior three years. In cases where the executive receives more than a single grant during the year, each grant is valued separately.

Ignoring complications related to early exercise, potential forfeiture, and executive inside information, option valuation formulas such as the Black–Scholes formula are appropriate for measuring the amount outside investors would pay for an option. However, as emphasized by Lambert *et al.* (1991) and Hall and Murphy (2000, 2002), Black–Scholes values do not measure the value of the non-tradeable option to a risk-averse executive. In contrast to outside investors, company executives cannot trade or sell their options, and are also forbidden from hedging the risks by short-selling company stock. In addition, while outside investors tend to be well-diversified (holding small amounts of stock in a large number of companies), company executives are inherently undiversified, with their physical as well as human capital invested disproportionately in their company. For these reasons, company executives will generally place a much lower value on company stock options than would outside investors.

Figure 26.4, replicated from Hall and Murphy (2000), shows how executive values differ from Black–Scholes values. The figure is based on a ten-year stock option with an exercise price of $X = \$30$, and shows how the value of the option varies with changes in the stock price. The 'realized payout' line is simply current value of the option if exercised today, MAX(0, Price-X), and the 'Black–Scholes Cost' shows the Black–Scholes value, which we interpret as the company's cost of granting the option. The executive values are based on 'certainty equivalents' assuming that executives have constant relative risk aversion with coefficient 2. 'Executive value' lines (which plot the certainty-equivalent values as a function of stock prices) are drawn for a CEO with 33, 50, and 66 per cent of his wealth invested in company stock. The executive value lines are generally below the Black–Scholes line, $V(P) < C(P)$, indicating that risk-averse executives value non-tradaeble

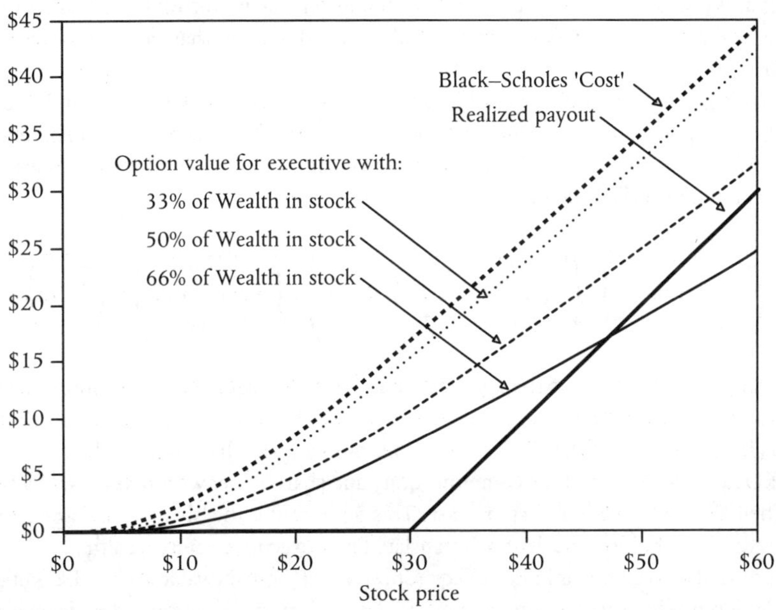

Figure 26.4. *Executive value lines: option values for undiversified executives. Figure is from Hall and Murphy (2000a). Executive values are estimated using the 'certainty equivalence' approach, and are defined as the amount of riskless cash compensation the executive would exchange for the option. Certainty equivalents are estimated numerically assuming that the executive has constant relative risk aversion 2, and assuming (using the Capital Asset Pricing Model, CAPM) that the distribution of stock prices in $T = 10$ years is lognormal with volatility $\sigma = 0.30$ and expected value $(r_f + \beta(r_m - r_f) - \sigma^2/2)T$, where $\beta = 1$ is the firm's systematic risk, $r_f = 6$ per cent is the risk-free rate, and $r_m - r_f = 6.5$ per cent is the equity premium.*

options at significantly less than their cost to the company.[7] Moreover, executives with large holdings of company stock (relative to their wealth) place lower values on options.

3. STOCK-BASED COMPENSATION AND FINANCIAL INCENTIVES

3.1. *Financial Incentives and Shareholder Wealth: Pay for Performance*

Having identified the relative importance of stock-based compensation in the USA, the UK, and other European countries, we now address the relationship between stock-based compensation and financial incentives. Stock-based compensation provides a direct link between shareholder wealth and CEO wealth, because each dollar increase in the stock price increases the value of stock options, restricted stock, and performance shares. In addition, changes in the stock price also directly affects the value of the CEO's stock holdings and his holdings of previously granted options, restricted stock, and performance shares. Taken together, stock-based compensation, coupled with holdings of stock and prior grants of stock-based compensation, provide financial incentives for managers to take actions to increase shareholder wealth, and to avoid actions that decrease shareholder wealth.

Following Jensen and Murphy (1990*a*), Murphy (1999), and Conyon and Murphy (2000), an appropriate way to measure the financial link between CEO and shareholder wealth is the CEO's 'effective' ownership percentage or 'Pay–Performance Sensitivity' (PPS), computed as the following delta-weighted average.[8]

$$\text{PPS} = \begin{pmatrix}\text{Shares Held as}\\ \text{\% of Firm}\\ \text{Shares}\end{pmatrix} + \begin{pmatrix}\text{Options Held}\\ \text{as \% of Firm}\\ \text{Shares}\end{pmatrix} \times \begin{pmatrix}\text{Option}\\ \text{Delta}\end{pmatrix} + \begin{pmatrix}\text{LTIP Shares}\\ \text{as \% of Firm}\\ \text{Shares}\end{pmatrix} \times \begin{pmatrix}\text{LTIP}\\ \text{Delta}\end{pmatrix}. \quad (26.2)$$

Equation (26.2) decomposes the aggregate pay for performance term into three elements (see Conyon and Murphy 2000). The first term on the right-hand side of the equation reflects how the value of the CEO's stock holdings varies with changes in the stock price. If a CEO holds 5 per cent of the common equity and shareholder wealth increases by \$100, then the CEO receives \$5 of that increase. This 5 per cent is the 'sharing rate' arising from a change in shareholder wealth that is translated into executive equity wealth.

The second term on the right side of eqn (26.2) reflects how the value of the CEO's unexercised option holdings varies with changes in the stock price. An option provides the same incentives as a share of stock only if the option is deep 'in the money' (i.e. the share price is far in excess of the exercise price). In general, each stock option should count somewhat less than one share of stock when adding the holdings to form an aggregate measure of effective ownership. In constructing our aggregate measure of CEO incentives, we weight each option by the 'Option Delta', which is the slope of the Black–Scholes valuation line depicted in Fig. 26.4.[9] The option delta, δ, is calculated as the derivative of the option value (eqn (26.1)) with respect to the stock price, $\delta = (1+d)^T N(z)$, where d, T, and $N(z)$ are defined in eqn (26.1). The option delta ranges from near zero (for deep out-of-the-money options) to near one (for deep in-the-money options on non-dividend paying stock).

Since executives typically hold a portfolio of stock options issued at various dates and at various exercise prices, the second term in eqn (26.2) should be calculated separately for each current and prior grant, summing to arrive at the total pay–performance sensitivity from options. Under UK reporting requirements, many companies report details on every outstanding unexercised option, and calculating the delta for each prior grant is straightforward. However, details on prior grants are seldom available; in the USA, for example, companies are required to report only aggregate data (total number and year-end 'spread') for previously granted but unexercised options. Fortunately, for a sample of UK firms where full information on prior grants is available, Conyon and Sadler (2001) have demonstrated that calculations of deltas based on the 'average' prior grant is quantitatively similar to the full information share-weighted option delta. Therefore, treating all prior grants as a single grant at an average exercise price provides a good approximation of the effective ownership from stock options.

The final term in eqn (26.2) is the incentives from LTIP grants, including both restricted stock and performance shares. LTIP shares are not equivalent to unrestricted shares since potentially they are subject to forfeiture if certain employment and performance objectives are not achieved. In eqn (26.2) we can potentially weight each LTIP share by an 'LTIP Delta', which is a measure of the change in value of each LTIP share for an incremental change in the share price. Calculating analytical LTIP deltas for performance-contingent grants is potentially complicated and as a simplification we assume an LTIP delta of unity independent of performance-vesting contingencies. Clearly, future research would want to probe the validity of this assumption.

3.2. *Stock-Based Financial Incentives in the USA and the UK*

Table 26.2, constructed from Conyon and Murphy (2000), shows the stock ownership and effective ownership of CEOs in the UK and the USA, for companies grouped by country, size, and industry group. The table shows that British CEOs hold an average of \$11.4 million in shares of their companies stock, substantially lower than the near \$100 million average holdings among American CEOs. The ownership distribution is significantly skewed: the median holdings for UK and USA executives are \$700,000 and \$5.3 million, respectively. Interestingly, the value of shares held by the CEO declines with company size in the UK, but increases with company size in the USA. In the largest firms, USA CEOs hold on average shares worth \$237 million (median \$8.1 million), while UK CEOs hold shares worth only \$5.5 million (median \$500,000).

Since agency costs arise when agents receive less than 100 per cent of the value of output, the CEO's share of ownership is a natural measure of the severity of the agency problem. As reported in Table 26.2, the average and median shareholdings for UK CEOs (expressed as a percentage of outstanding shares) are 2.13 and 0.05 per cent, respectively, significantly smaller than the average and median holdings among USA CEOs of 3.10 and 0.29 per cent, respectively. In the largest firms, USA CEOs hold on average 1.61 per cent of their company's shares (median 0.09 per cent), while UK CEOs hold only 0.21 per cent

Table 26.2. *Summary statistics for stock-based CEO incentives, by company size and industry*

Group	Share holdings ($ millions)		Share holdings (% of common)		Option holdings (% of common)		Pay-performance sensitivity (%)	
	Mean	Median	Mean	Median	Mean	Median	Mean	Median
UK								
All companies	11.4	0.7	2.13	0.05	0.24	0.11	2.33	0.25
By firm sales (millions)								
Less than $125	16.1	2.3	4.38	0.63	0.38	0.21	4.72	1.09
$125 to $300	15.5	1.1	2.55	0.14	0.24	0.14	2.75	0.42
$300 to $920	7.4	0.2	0.76	0.02	0.19	0.12	0.91	0.16
Above $920	5.5	0.5	0.21	0.01	0.10	0.04	0.31	0.05
By industry								
Mining/manufacturing	9.8	0.4	1.91	0.04	0.24	0.14	2.11	0.23
Financial services	9.7	1.4	1.98	0.07	0.19	0.05	2.14	0.31
Utilities	0.3	0.2	0.01	0.00	0.03	0.02	0.05	0.02
Other	15.2	1.2	2.64	0.10	0.28	0.11	2.89	0.37
USA								
All companies	98.4	5.3	3.10	0.29	1.18	0.72	4.18	1.48
By firm sales (millions)								
Less than $125	27.1	3.4	5.32	0.96	1.84	1.37	6.98	3.65
$125 to $300	38.9	4.8	3.94	0.58	1.39	0.94	5.20	2.05
$300 to $920	52.6	4.3	2.36	0.25	1.12	0.70	3.43	1.26
Above $920	236.8	8.1	1.61	0.09	0.62	0.40	2.17	0.56
By industry								
Mining/manufacturing	55.0	5.1	2.78	0.31	1.22	0.76	3.87	1.53
Financial services	207.8	12.4	2.25	0.31	0.98	0.52	3.17	1.01
Utilities	10.1	0.9	0.25	0.05	0.35	0.12	0.53	0.16
Other	148.9	6.9	4.63	0.38	1.40	0.95	5.96	2.01

This table is derived from Conyon and Murphy (2000), table 5. UK data from the largest companies in fiscal 1997, ranked by market capitalization. USA data include firms in the S&P 500, the S&P MidCap 400, the S&P SmallCap 600, and companies in S&P supplemental indices. Revenues for financial firms defined as net interest income (banks) and total income (insurance companies). UK pounds are converted to USA dollars using the average 1997 exchange rate, 1.63£/$. The Pay–Performance Sensitivity is defined as:

$$\begin{pmatrix}\text{Shares Held as}\\ \text{\% of Firm}\\ \text{Shares}\end{pmatrix} + \begin{pmatrix}\text{Options Held}\\ \text{as \% of Firm}\\ \text{Shares}\end{pmatrix} \times \begin{pmatrix}\text{Option}\\ \text{Delta}\end{pmatrix} + \begin{pmatrix}\text{LTIP Shares}\\ \text{as \% of Firm}\\ \text{Shares}\end{pmatrix} \times \begin{pmatrix}\text{LTIP}\\ \text{Delta}\end{pmatrix},$$

where $0 < \text{Option Delta} < 1$ is the share-weighted-average slope of the Black–Scholes function at the year-end stock price, for options outstanding at the fiscal year end, and $(\text{LTIP Delta}) = 1$.

(median 0.01 per cent). In fact, whether measured in dollars or percentages, or at averages or medians, share ownership among USA CEOs is substantially higher than ownership among UK CEOs for each size and industry group in Table 26.2. Consequently, share ownership mitigates more of the agency problem in the USA than in the UK.

Holdings of unexercised stock options also provide a direct link between CEO and shareholder wealth, because the value of the options held increases with increases in the share price. Table 26.2 shows that the average USA executive holds options to purchase 1.18 per cent of the company's outstanding shares (median 0.72 per cent), while the average UK executive holds options to purchase only 0.24 per cent (median 0.11 per cent) of his company's shares. Again, pair-wise comparisons from the top and bottom panels of Table 26.2 reveal that holdings of previously granted but unexercised stock options are substantially higher in the USA than in the UK for every size and industry group.

Finally, holdings of unvested LTIP shares provide an additional direct link between CEO and shareholder wealth. First, the value of the underlying shares naturally increases 'dollar-for-dollar' with increases in the share price. Second, there is an additional link to the extent that the shares vest only upon meeting share-based performance criteria. The average USA executive holds LTIP shares (primarily restricted stock) on 0.09 per cent of the company's outstanding shares, while the average UK executive holds LTIP shares on 0.03 per cent; the median LTIP shareholdings is zero in both countries.

The final two columns of Table 26.2 show the average and median pay–performance sensitivity (eqn (26.2)) for CEOs grouped by country, company size, and industry. The average and median pay–performance sensitivities for USA CEOs are 4.18 per cent and 1.48 per cent, respectively, significantly higher than the average (2.33 per cent) and median (0.25 per cent) sensitivities for UK CEOs. In the largest firms, the median USA CEO has a sensitivity, or effective ownership, of 0.56 per cent, more than ten times the effective ownership of their British counterparts.

3.3. *Stock Options and Performance Shares in the UK*

Options in the UK became controversial in 1995, after executives in several recently privatized electric utilities exercised options worth millions of pounds. The influential Greenbury Report (1995) encouraged companies to replace their option plans with LTIP performance share plans which 'may be as effective, or more so, than improved share option schemes in linking rewards to performance' (Greenbury 1995: para. 6.32). In addition, the Greenbury code recommended that all long-term incentive schemes, including executive stock option plans, should be subject to 'challenging performance criteria' (ibid. para. 6.38). In response to the Greenbury Report and the ongoing controversy, many British companies have switched towards granting performance shares instead of options, or have added performance criteria to their existing option plans.

Table 26.3 describes stock-based pay practices in the 200 largest companies in the UK in fiscal year 1997. The first two rows show that nearly all (98.5 per cent) of the top companies have option plans, but only about two-thirds (67 per cent) of the chief executives actually participate in the plan. On the other hand, companies are making more use of grants under LTIPs: row 3 indicates that 49.5 per cent of companies have now introduced an LTIP scheme. Among companies with LTIP plans in place, 36 per cent award top executives options in addition to LTIP grants, while 64 per cent substitute LTIP grants for options.

Table 26.3. *CEO stock options and performance criteria in the UK*

	Number	%
Panel A: Structure of CEO compensation		
Percentage of companies with stock option plans	199	98.5
Percentage of CEOs who now participate in current executive option plan	134	67.0
Percentage of companies that introduced a long-term incentive plan (LTIP)	99	49.5
Percentage of companies that have introduced LTIPs and in which the CEO does participate in the executive option plan (complement)	36	36.4
Percentage of companies that have introduced LTIPs and in which the CEO does not participate in the executive option plan (substitute)	63	63.6
Percentage of current company executive option schemes that attach a performance criteria	123	61.5
Panel B: Performance measure attached to CEO stock options		
Earnings per share	82	71.9
Share price, or total shareholder return	25	21.9
Net asset value	3	2.6
Profits	2	1.8
Net Assets Per Share	1	0.9
Return on net assets	1	0.9
Total	114	100

This table is derived from Conyon *et al.* (2000), based on CEO compensation contracts at 200 large UK listed companies in fiscal year 1997. The upper part of the table uses data on 200 companies. The lower part of the table is constructed for the 114 companies who have performance criteria attached to the stock of options and also where the performance criteria could be identified. Sample selection required that companies be in existence since 1990, that the CEO held options (either current or prior grants), and that the company supplied complete information about CEO option portfolios to value using the Black–Scholes method.

Well over half (123 firms, or 61.5 per cent) of the 200 largest UK corporations have attached performance criteria to their stock option plans. We were able to identify the criteria for 114 of these 123 firms. The lower half of Table 26.3 summarizes the prevalence of specific criteria among these 114 firms. In the overwhelming majority of companies (72 per cent), options become exercisable only if the company meets specific earnings-per-share targets. In twenty-five companies (22 per cent), options become exercisable only if the company achieves a threshold stock-price appreciation or total shareholder return.

Although the specific details of the performance criteria vary across firms, the typical plans allows options to be exercised only if EPS growth exceeds approximately 2 per cent per year. Conyon *et al.* (2000) show that performance criteria are very rarely binding (based on historical EPS data) and consequently are likely to have little impact on the valuation of the stock of options held by the CEO or the related PPS. In addition, while the fact that 61.5 per cent of the top 200 UK firms attach performance criteria to their option grants is impressive, it is also misleading because only a small fraction of the grants to any particular executive are covered by the criteria.

4. STOCK-BASED COMPENSATION: TAX AND ACCOUNTING CONSIDERATIONS

As documented in the preceding section, stock-based compensation coupled with stock ownership mitigates agency problems by aligning the interests of managers and shareholders. However, although the incentive rationale for stock-based compensation is undeniably compelling, the prevalence of forms of stock-based compensation are driven, at least in the USA, by tax and accounting considerations.[10] In this section, we will explore whether differences in tax and accounting regimes in the USA and Europe can help explain the relative popularity of stock-based pay in the USA compared to Europe. As in much of our preceding analysis, we focus primarily on Anglo-American comparisons, but also provide some details on tax regimes on the Continent.

4.1. *The United States of America*

4.1.1. *Individual Taxes*

Cash compensation received by USA executives is taxed as personal income in the year paid, as is the value of performance shares when they are earned, and restricted stock when restrictions lapse. Executives in the USA are typically taxed at the highest marginal tax rate, which is currently about 40 per cent (the top USA bracket indexed for inflation is currently about $285,000 for married taxpayers). The full tax rate in the USA is somewhat higher, due to state and local taxes ranging from 0 to about 10 per cent, depending on jurisdiction.

As long as the exercise price is not 'too far' below the grant-date market price, the granting of stock options does not constitute a taxable event in the USA. The personal tax consequences upon exercise depend on whether the options are 'qualified' or 'non-qualified' for favourable tax treatment. For non-qualified options, the exercise-date spread between the market and exercise price constitutes taxable personal income to the executive. For qualified options, the executive pays nothing upon exercise (provided that he continues to hold the stock), and pays capital gains taxes (currently 20 per cent) when he eventually sells the stock.[11]

4.1.2. *Corporate Taxes*

American corporations are allowed to deduct 'reasonable' compensation expenses from corporate earnings. In general (subject to the caveat in the next paragraph), corporations deduct the value of cash compensation, performance shares, and restricted stock at the same time from the individual's taxable income. For non-qualified options, the exercise-date spread between the market and exercise price constitutes deductible compensation expense to the company. However, for qualified options, the company receives no deduction.

A unique feature of the USA tax code is the existence of limits on the deductibility of 'non-performance-based' compensation. Under rules passed by the Clinton administration in 1993, compensation is divided into two categories—performance-based and non-performance-based—and the amount of non-performance-based pay in excess of $1 million is not deductible from corporate profits as a business expense. Salaries and fringe benefits fall into the non-performance-based category, as do restricted stock awards (unless there are meaningful formula-based performance targets that must be met prior to vesting). Bonuses fall into the performance-based category only if the amount each executive receives is determined by an explicit formula based on an explicit (and disclosed) performance measure (bonuses with discretionary components fall into the non-performance-based category). This USA deductibility limitation applies only to the top five executives in publicly traded corporations, and does not apply to lower-level (but highly paid) employees, or to executives in privately held companies. Research on the effects of the deductibility limitation has concluded that the rule has played, at most, a small role in determining the level and structure of USA compensation plans (Perry and Zenner 2000; Rose and Wolfram 2002). Therefore, this rule alone cannot explain the stark differences between USA and European pay practices.

4.1.3. *Accounting Considerations for Stock Options*

As long as stock options have a pre-specified exercise price and expiration date, companies incur an accounting charge equal to the grant-date 'spread' between the market price and the exercise price (amortized over the life of the option).[12] This 'quirk' in the USA financial accounting rules—which implies no accounting charge for fair-market-value and premium options—creates a gap between the economic and accounting costs of options. The fact that stock option compensation is essentially 'free' from an accounting perspective helps explain the popularity of 'broad-based' company-wide option programmes that are difficult to rationalize from an incentive standpoint. In addition, the accounting rules apply only to options with fixed exercise prices and expiration terms, and not to indexed options, performance-triggered options, or options with variable terms.

4.2. *United Kingdom*

4.2.1. *Individual Taxes*

As in the USA, cash compensation received by UK executives is taxed as personal income in the year paid. Executives are typically taxed at the highest marginal tax rate which (again, as in the USA) is currently about 40 per cent. The top UK income rate affects incomes above approximately £28,000, or about $50,000. Shares earned through LTIP plans are generally taxed as ordinary income upon the lapsing of any employment or performance restrictions.[13]

The personal tax consequences of options in the UK are similar to those in the USA, and depend on whether the options are qualified ('approved' in UK jargon) or non-qualified ('unapproved') for favourable tax treatment. For non-qualified options, the exercise-date spread between the market and exercise price constitutes taxable personal income to the executive. For qualified options, the executive pays nothing upon exercise (provided that he continues to hold the stock), and pays capital gains taxes when he eventually sells the stock. An interesting difference in the USA and UK situations is that, in recent years, the capital gains tax rate in the UK has increased from 30 to 40 per cent in contrast to the USA where capital gains tax rates have fallen from 28 to 20 per cent. Since the primary benefit of qualified options reflects the spread between the tax rates on ordinary income and capital gains, we would expect that qualified options would be relatively more popular in the USA.[14]

4.2.2. *Corporate Taxes*

When an executive exercises an option to purchase stock, or 'earns' performance shares, the company can satisfy their commitment by either purchasing shares on the open market, or by issuing new shares. This choice determines whether the company can deduct the value of performance shares or the 'spread' on options as a compensation expense: shares purchased in the market create a deductible expense, while issuing new shares does not. In practice, exe-cut-ives receiving options typically receive newly issued shares, while executives earning LTIP shares receive shares that had been previously purchased and held in an appropriate employee trust. Therefore, in practice, options in the UK do not typically generate deductible compensation expense, while LTIP shares do generate deductible expense.

A recent innovation in the treatment of options in the UK is the tax payable by companies and employees under the guise of National Insurance Contributions (NIC). This is a social tax payable by employees and employers. The NIC rules were extended to the exercise of non-qualified (unapproved) options granted after early 1999. This change will have little impact on UK executives since most will have already hit the NIC contribution ceiling. However, it will represent a significant additional charge to employers who will now face an additional payroll tax of approximately 12 per cent of the gain made by UK executives on stock options.

4.2.3. *Accounting Considerations for Stock Options*

The accounting treatment of executive stock options in the UK is also similar to the USA: firms do not generally have to report options issued at the money as a compensation expense.[15] In particular, the accounting charge is the grant-date spread between the market value and the exercise price, which is zero for options granted at the money. LTIP shares, which are effectively options with a zero exercise price, generate an accounting charge equal to the current share price.

4.3. *Stock-Based Compensation in other European Countries*

4.3.1. *Individual Taxes*

From the employee's point of view, the tax treatment of options is broadly similar across most of Europe (and the USA). In general a tax charge only arises at exercise and the taxable amount is calculated as the difference between the market value of the underlying shares at the exercise date and exercise price. The granting of options thus rarely gives rise to an immediate tax liability, provided the options are not issued at a discount to the market share price at the time of the grant. This is not the case, however, in the Netherlands, Denmark, or Belgium.

In the Netherlands, the granting of options that are deemed unconditional (i.e. are not subject to the performance criteria) gives rise to an immediate tax liability. Tax is charged on the expected future increase in the value of the option. The precise charge is obviously open to negotiation, but in certain circumstances the expected increase can be taken to be 7.5 per cent of the fair market value of the underlying shares at the taxable date. If performance restrictions are attached, the options are regarded as conditional grants and in this case, the tax liability is deferred until the date the grant becomes unconditional.

The situation in Denmark is very similar to that in the Netherlands, although here the tax treatment also depends on whether the option is to be settled through the issuance of new shares, or through the purchase of shares already in issue. Where new shares are to be issued, tax is due at the grant date if the award has no performance conditions attached. If such conditions do exist, then as in the Netherlands, the tax liability is deferred until the performance criteria have been met and the award vests unconditionally. Again, as in the Netherlands, the amount on which tax is charged reflects the expected future growth in the option value. In contrast, where the option is to be satisfied through existing shares, the tax liability is usually deferred until exercise.

Recent changes to tax law in Belgium have resulted in options no longer being taxed at exercise, but instead only at the grant date (or specifically sixty days thereafter), with no further tax being due either at the exercise of the option or the subsequent sale of the shares. As in the two countries above, the amount on which tax is due at the grant date is set to reflect the expected growth in the value of the option and is not limited to the spread (if any exists) between the exercise price and underlying share price.

4.3.2. *Corporate Taxes*

In most countries, employers can treat as a deductible expense, costs that are incurred through satisfying options through the purchase of shares already in issue. However, where options are satisfied through the issuing of new shares (as is the case in the UK), it is unlikely that a taxable deduction can be made. However, even in these cases there are often mechanisms to achieve some form of deductibility for option costs. For example, in France, Lusty (1997: 61) claims that from the employer's perspective 'the costs to the company are tax deductible if the appropriate conditions are met'. It is rarely clear however exactly what all the conditions are and even within countries the deductibility of option expenses is frequently decided on a case by case negotiation between the company and the local tax authority.

4.3.3. *Accounting Considerations for Stock Options*

The accounting implications of options among European countries is difficult to summarize with great confidence. As with the USA and UK, within each country there may be different types of plans. France, for example, has traditional stock option plans, and also collective stock purchase plans available to those companies that have a head office within the European Union and shares quoted on the Paris Stock Exchange (Lusty 1997). French law requires that shareholders decide upon key provisions of the plans, while the directors are responsible for the smaller details. When granting options, the exercise price cannot be set at less than 80 per cent of the average of the quoted prices over the previous twenty days. Furthermore, the board is able to restrict the resale of the subscribed or purchased shares for up to three years following the grant (ibid.).

In the Netherlands there is a difference between unconditional stock option grants and conditional stock option grants, while in Denmark there is a distinct difference in the treatment of options depending on whether the option provides a right to subscribe to new shares or acquire shares that are already in issue. In Ireland the distinction is between approved and unapproved schemes (classified on the basis of whether the Irish Revenue/Tax authority criteria are met).

Given these diverse and complex plans, it is difficult to get precise information on the accounting treatment of options in continental Europe. In general, and in contrast to the USA situation where options generate tax benefits but no accounting charge, Europeans tend to treat consistently the tax and accounting treatments of options. That is, no charge is usually made to the profit and loss accounts in regard to options unless a real expense has been incurred. However, there does appear to be a movement within Europe not only towards greater disclosure of all forms of option information within company accounts, but also a recognition that even options granted at the money have an immediate value.

4.4. *Discussion*

The popularity of stock-based compensation plans (especially stock option plans) in the USA is consistent with the importance of tax and accounting considerations. In particular, under USA rules, the primary form of stock-based compensation (non-qualified options issued with an exercise price equal to the grant-date market price) is essentially free from an accounting standpoint (because there is no charge to accounting earnings) and beneficial from a tax standpoint (because companies are allowed to deduct the spread upon exercise as a compensation expense). This apparent 'win–win' situation reflects the peculiar decoupling in the USA of financial reporting for tax purposes and accounting purposes; items that generate income or expenses for tax purposes do not necessarily generate income or expenses for accounting purposes.

In Europe, the tax and accounting regimes tend to be more consistent than in the USA. If options are invisible in accounting statements they are likely invisible for tax purposes as well. Similarly, if companies deduct as compensation expense amounts paid in stock-based compensation, they are likely required to take a charge against accounting earnings as well. Overall, the combined tax and accounting benefit of granting options in European firms is clearly muted relative to the USA, and we believe this difference plays at least a partial role in explaining the differences in international pay practices.

5. CONCLUSION

Stock options have emerged as the largest component of compensation among CEOs in the USA and, along with stock ownership, are instrumental in linking CEO and shareholder wealth. The popularity of stock options in the USA stands in stark contrast to the relative paucity of options, and stock-based compensation in general, among European top executives. Similarly, the high stockholdings of American executives relative to their European counterparts (measured in both dollars and as a fraction of company shares) also is a striking difference. In this chapter we have argued that the USA accounting and tax regimes may help explain these important international differences in stock-based pay. However, accounting and tax considerations provide at best a partial explanation for the relative popularity, and do not explain cross-country differences among European countries. Clearly, analysing and better understanding these international pay differences is an important direction for future research.

Perhaps more important than understanding the causes of international pay differences is asking whether or not the differences matter: does increased reliance on stock-based compensation and higher levels of executive ownership translate into higher shareholder returns? It is tempting to argue that the stellar performance of the USA stock markets over the past decade reflect, at least in part, increases in stock-based pay and ownership among USA executives. However, it is equally tempting to argue that the sustained 'bull market' in the USA has lowered executive resistance to holding stock and receiving more of their pay in stock-based components.

Unfortunately, in spite of two decades of active research in executive compensation, there is surprisingly little direct evidence that higher pay–performance sensitivities lead to higher stock-price performance. We know that stock prices tend to increase when companies grant stock options or announce new stock-based pay programmes (Brickley *et al.* 1985; Yermack 1997). We also know that Tobin's Q-Ratios increase with management ownership, at least over some ranges (Morck *et al.* 1988; McConnell and Servaes 1990). In addition, there is an accumulation of anecdotal studies of leveraged buyouts, restructurings, and changes in company compensation policies and strategy that suggest managerial incentives play a key role (see Murphy 1999, for a partial summary of the evidence).

Overall, the evidence is consistent with the hypothesis that stock-based incentives are important drivers of managerial actions and corporate performance.[16] There remains little direct evidence, however, on the returns a company can expect from introducing aggressive performance-based compensation plans. The existing evidence is, at best, suggestive, and we believe that fully analysing and documenting the effect of executive incentives on subsequent performance is a fruitful, if not critical, direction for future research in executive compensation.

Notes

1. Some USA plans accelerate vesting for superior performance, but the options will vest independent of performance as long as the recipient remains employed by the firm throughout the option term.
2. In conducting this survey, Towers Perrin asked executive pay consultants in each of the 11 countries represented in Fig. 26.2 to use local-market conditions to formulate competitive pay recommendations for a hypothetical CEO in a $250 million industrial company, as of April 1999. Survey responses in local currencies are converted into USA dollars using April 1999 exchange rates.
3. We derived a version of Fig. 26.1 based on S&P 'Small Cap' firms instead of S&P 500 Industrials. The fiscal 1996 data from the Small Cap firms matches closely the hypothetical data in the Towers Perrin survey.
4. Conyon and Murphy (2000) provide a detailed comparison of pay practices in the USA and the UK, which is the European country with the most extensive use of stock-based compensation, and is among the highest-paying European countries. We find that, after controlling for size, industry, growth opportunities, CEO human capital, and other observable characteristics, USA CEOs earn 45 per cent more in cash pay and 190 per cent more in total pay than do UK CEOs.
5. The Conference Board discontinued their plan-prevalence data series in 1997. For this year, we use ExecuComp data on the fraction of S&P 500 companies in which the top five executives hold any share options. This definition of prevalence closely tracks the Conference Board's survey responses for the 1992–6 period where both sources of prevalence data are available.

6. See Hull (1993) for a comprehensive discussion of the various pricing models.
7. The executive-value line can actually lie above the Black–Scholes line when executives are sufficiently diversified and have sufficiently low risk aversion.
8. In their original formulation, Jensen and Murphy (1990*b*) measured the change in CEO wealth per $1,000 change in shareholder wealth, which equals the effective ownership percentage multiplied by ten.
9. Our approach measures the change in the Black–Scholes value of the CEO's option holdings, but does not measure the change in the CEO's personal valuation. Conceptually, a better measure of CEO incentives would use the slope of the Executive Value line in Fig. 26.4 rather than the slope of the Black–Scholes line.
10. See, for example, Miller and Scholes (1982), Abowd and Bognanno (1995), and Scholes and Wolfson (1992).
11. The gain upon exercise of a qualified option is often subject to the 'alternative minimum tax' at a rate between the capital gains rate and the ordinary income tax rate.
12. The current accounting rules for stock and options issued to employees are defined by APB Opinion No. 25, issued in October 1972. In the early 1990s, the Financial Accounting Standard Board (FASB) considered explicit accounting charges for options, but adopted instead enhanced footnote disclosure.
13. In both the USA and the UK, executives receiving shares with employment or performance restrictions have some discretion on when the shares constitute taxable income. In particular, executives can elect to pay taxes upon grant of restricted shares, or defer payment until the restrictions lapse.
14. In both countries, there are limitations and restrictions imposed on granting qualified options. In addition, as discussed earlier, non-qualified options in the USA generate a tax savings to the company not available with qualified options. For these reasons, most option grants to top executives in both countries are non-qualified.
15. The accounting treatment of long-term pay (including stock options) in the UK is outlined in UITF Abstract 17 (1998), relating to Employee Share Schemes. Although the UITF (in an earlier Abstract 10, 1994) recognized that share options do give rise to a compensation benefit for the recipient, it notes that: 'given the practical difficulties of attributing a meaningful estimated money value to an option at the date of grant, and differing views on whether, and if so how, to apportion any benefit over time, the UITF has concluded that it is not presently practicable for it to specify an appropriate valuation method for options as a benefit in kind.'
16. See, for example, Masson (1971) and Abowd (1990), who offer evidence suggesting that stock-based incentives improve subsequent stock-price performance.

References

Abowd, J. (1990). Does performance-based managerial compensation affect corporate performance? *Industrial and Labor Relations Review* 43: 52.

——and Bognanno, M. (1995). International differences in executive and managerial compensation. In R. Freeman and L. Katz (ed.), *Differences and Changes in Wage Structure.* Chicago: University of Chicago Press.

——and Kaplan, D. S. (1999). Executive compensation: Six questions that need answering. *Journal of Economic Perspectives* (forthcoming).

Black, F., and Scholes, M. (1973). The pricing of options and corporate liabilities. *Journal of Political Economy* 81: 637.

Brickley, J., Bhagat, S., and Lease, R. (1985). The impact of long-range managerial compensation plans on shareholder wealth. *Journal of Accounting and Economics* 7: 115.

Conyon, M. J., and Sadler, G. V. (2001). CEO compensation, option incentives and information disclosure. Review of Financial Economics, forthcoming.

——and Murphy, K. J. (2000). The prince and the pauper? CEO pay in the US and UK. *Economic Journal* 110: 640.

——Peck, S., Sadler, G., and Read, L., (2000). Executive compensation contracts: UK Evidence, Long Range Planning, 33: 478.

Greenbury, R. (1995). *Directors' Remuneration: Report of a Study Group Chaired by Sir Richard Greenbury.* London: Gee Publishing.

Hall, B. J., and Murphy, K. J. (2000). Optimal exercise prices for executive stock options. *American Economic Review* 90: 209.

———(2002). Stock options for undiversified executives. *Journal of Accounting and Economics*, 33: forthcoming.

Hull, J. (1993). *Options, Futures, and other Derivative Securities*, 2nd edn. New Jersey: Prentice Hall.

Jensen, M., and Murphy, K. J. (1990*a*). Performance pay and top-management incentives. *Journal of Political Economy* 98: 225.

———(1990*b*). CEO incentives: It's not how much you pay, but how. *Harvard Business Review* 68: 138.

Lambert, R., Larcker, D., and Verrecchia, D. (1991). Portfolio consideration in valuing executive compensation. *Journal of Accounting Research* 29: 129.

Lusty, S. A. M. (1997). *Equity Derivative Applications to Own Share Schemes, in Equity Derivatives: Applications in Risk Management and Investment.* New York: Lehman Brothers RISK Publications.

Main, B. G. (1999). The rise and fall of executive share options in Britain. In J. Carpenter and D. Yermack (1998) (ed.), *Executive Compensation and Shareholder Value: Theory and Evidence.* Dordrecht: Kluwer Academic Press.

Masson, R. (1971). Executive motivations, earnings, and consequent equity performance. *Journal of Political Economy* 79: 1278.

McConnell, J., and Servaes, H. (1990). Additional evidence on equity ownership and corporate value. *Journal of Financial Economics* 27: 595.

Merton, R. (1973). Theory of rational option pricing. *Bell Journal of Economics and Management Science* 4: 141.

Miller, M., and Scholes, M. (1982). Executive compensation, taxes and incentives. In W. Sharpe and C. Cootner (ed.), *Financial Economics: Essays in Honor of Paul Cootner.* Englewood Cliffs, NJ: Prentice Hall.

Morck, R., Shleifer, A., and Vishny, R. (1988). Management ownership and market valuation: An empirical analysis. *Journal of Financial Economics* 20: 293.

Murphy, K. J. (1999). Executive compensation. In O. Ashenfelter and D. Card (ed.), *Handbook of Labor Economics*, vol. 3: Amsterdam: North Holland.

Perry, T., and Zenner, M. (2000). CEO compensation in the 1990s: Shareholder alignment or shareholder expropriation? *Wake Forest Law Review* 35: 123.

Rose, N., and Wolfram, C. (2002). *Regulating CEO pay: Assessing the Impact of the Tax-deductibility Cap on Executive Compensation.* Journal of Labor Economics, forthcoming.

Scholes, M. S., and Wolfson, M. A. (1992). *Taxes and Business Strategy: A Planning Approach.* New Jersey: Prentice Hall.

Yermack, D. (1997). Good timing: CEO stock option Awards and company news announcements *Journal of Finance*, 52: 449.

27

Cash-Based Executive Compensation in Spain and the UK

RAFEL CRESPÍ, CARLES GISPERT, AND LUC RENNEBOOG

1. INTRODUCTION

For the largest tier of US firms, the degree to which the chief executive officers' (CEOs) compensation is related to corporate performance has been thoroughly investigated over the last two decades (Murphy 1999). A tight positive relation between managerial remuneration and corporate performance is important to reduce the tension between shareholders and managers resulting from differing objectives. Such agency costs are particularly prominent in the case of a high degree of separation of ownership and control. For example, in more than 85 per cent of listed UK firms, there is no large shareholder owning a share stake of 25 per cent or more (Franks *et al.* 2001). Hence, it is not surprising that within Europe, it was the UK that first adopted a code of conduct regarding the disclosure and the strengthening of the pay-for-performance relation. In contrast to the UK ownership structures, 85 per cent of listed Continental European firms have one shareholder (group) owning at least a blocking minority (of 25 per cent). In more than half the companies one investor (group) wields absolute voting control (50 per cent or more of the voting rights) (Barca and Becht 2001). Only recently, codes of good corporate governance in the Netherlands, Belgium, and Germany suggest more disclosure of top executive pay. The information provided in most Continental Europe is sparse: usually only superficial information is provided on managerial compensation with no or incomplete data on remuneration in the form of stock options. Spanish corporations for instance only provide data on cash based compensation (fixed salary and bonus) of all directors combined. However limited the information for Spain, data on board compensation have at last been available since 1989.

In this chapter, we contrast the relation between top executive cash compensation and corporate performance for the UK and for Spain, as each country represents very different corporate governance systems. The empirical findings enable us to make a direct comparison as similar data, time periods and samples are used. Some of the questions we try to answer are: Is cash-based compensation influenced by accounting or share price returns or merely determined by corporate size? Is executive remuneration related to different performance measures in both countries? Is the pay-for-performance elasticity influenced by industry peer group performance? To what extent is the difference between governance structures a relevant determinant of the performance/compensation relationship? While the underlying basic concept of corporate governance, as inscribed UK corporate law, is the maximization of shareholder value, Spanish firms (as in many other Continental European countries) are adhering more to a stakeholder approach. Thus, one might expect a stronger relation between pay and corporate performance in the UK than in Spain. This is however not the case as our results show that UK CEOs' cash-based compensation hinges more on corporate sales growth. Our findings show that Spanish executive directors' compensation is also sensitive to changes in sales, but depends to a large extent on share price and accounting performance. Executive directors of Spanish firms controlled by strong investor groups are rewarded by increases in cash remuneration if their companies generate increases in shareholder value. However, this positive relation is only valid in as far as share returns exceed those of the industry peers. In Spanish companies with low ownership concentration, managerial compensation is more sensitive to accounting returns (changes in return on assets). High capital leverage also gears management's attention to accounting returns.

The remainder of this chapter is organized as follows. Section 2 provides a concise overview of the literature and formulates the propositions. Section 3 justifies the sample selection, details differences in control concentration and supplies the data sources. Section 4 interprets the results from the pay-for-performance models while Section 5 offers a conclusion.

2. OVERVIEW OF THE LITERATURE AND PROPOSITIONS

2.1. *The Structure of CEO Remuneration and Size and Industry Effects*

Numerous papers have analysed the determinants of US top executive remuneration and have documented the strong correlation with corporate size (usually measured by sales). Murphy (1999), for example, shows that the pay–sales elasticities were in the range [0.25, 0.35] in the 1970s, declined to [0.15, 0.28] in the mid-1980s and rose again in the 1990s. A pay–sales elasticity of 0.3 signifies that the CEO of a firm that generates 20 per cent more sales than the average firm, will earn 6 per cent more. This may result from the fact that larger firms require higher managerial qualifications and skill levels to cope with higher job complexity. Hence, we propose that UK and Spanish executives of larger companies receive higher compensation (proposition 1). Top executive pay levels do not only vary by corporate size but differ substantially by industrial sector. The pay–sales sensitivities are much higher in manufacturing industries than in financial services and utilities, a phenomenon similar across countries.

Murphy (1999) observes increasing convergence of top executive pay levels and of remuneration structures resulting from the emergence of an international market for top managers, the abolition of legal prohibitions on executive stock options (e.g. Japan in 1997) and the use of peer groups to determine competitive levels of compensation. Still, comparative remuneration research for twelve OECD countries has shown that the total CEO pay in the USA is roughly double that in any other country even after controlling for differences in purchasing power and taxation of direct pay and perquisites (Abowd and Bognanno 1995).

This substantial discrepancy between the USA and all other countries is only observed at the level of the CEO and does not extend to lower-level management. The structure of the total remuneration in the USA is also different from other countries. In the USA, top managers receive a higher proportion of their total income in stock options and a smaller fraction in the form of fixed salary, bonus (usually as a percentage of base salary), long-term incentive plans, pension benefits, and severance arrangements.

2.2. *Incentive Effects of Corporate Performance*

In order to stimulate managerial effort in such a way that the interests of self-interested risk-averse managers are aligned with those of shareholders, part of top management remuneration should be tied to corporate performance. Although accounting performance measures are practical as the relation between management's day-to-day activities are directly translated into year-end profitability, accounting measures have two inherent problems. Firstly, management is responsible for the annual report and can hence (temporarily) manipulate accounting earnings (Healy 1985). For example, accelerating or delaying expenses and revenues can influence the reported year-end results (Oyer 1998) and the choice of accounting methods (like inventory accounting methods) may inflate or deflate annual earnings (Holthausen *et al.* 1995). Hence, management may adjust its actions to maximize bonuses based on annual accounting performance. Secondly, accounting results reflect past performance rather than future opportunities. Dechow and Sloan (1991) and Gibbons and Murphy (1992) show that accounting yardsticks may cause management to increase short-term profitability at the expense of future income, for example by cutting advertising and R&D expenditures. From a shareholders' perspective, incentive contracts based on accounting performance should only be used if actions affecting accounting returns are closely related to actions that similarly influence share price returns. The use of share return incentive contracts that are linear and constant across periods will reduce managers' incentive to adjust effort from year to year and to shift costs and revenues across fiscal years (Holmstrom and Milgrom 1987).

Stock option plans have gained in popularity over the last two decades in the USA and over the last five years in Continental Europe. Still, it should be noted that the use of stock options may lead to managerial decisions aiming at share price increases not supported by value-increasing investment projects. For example, executives may be tempted to avoid dividends and favour share repurchases (Lambert *et al.* 1989). Furthermore, as stock options increase in value along with the share price volatility, management may take on riskier investment projects (DeFusco *et al.* 1990).

A manager can benefit explicitly from increases in shareholder wealth if he owns shares or has been granted stock options, but managerial wealth is also tied implicitly to stock price performance through (yearly) salary adjustments and accounting linked bonuses. For US CEOs, the (implicit) pay–performance elasticities based in salary plus bonus have tripled from 0.4 cents per $1,000 in the 1970s to 1.4 cents in the 1990s (Murphy 1999). In addition, the variance in these elasticities has increased in the 1990s. Although Jensen and Murphy (1990) conclude that CEO pay-for-performance sensitivities are low with a sharing rate of 0.325 per cent, a 10 per cent increase in value in a corporation of $5 billion yields the CEO a wealth increase of $1.6 million in a one-year period. Investigating the sensitivity of total CEO wealth (fixed salary, bonus, ownership, and stock options) reveals that the larger part of this sensitivity is driven by stock options and share ownership (Hall and Liebman 1998). In Section 4, we investigate the implicit wealth change of the UK and Spanish CEO following changes in shareholder value and accounting returns. In other words, we measure the pay-for-performance elasticity whereby remuneration is gauged by total cash-based income (salary and bonus). A high pay-for-share price performance suggests that management's actions are focused on value creation (proposition 2). Including relative corporate performance provides incremental information about the management's actions. By splitting the stochastic component of corporate performance into an industry component and an idiosyncratic return, we can proxy management's relative performance (Gibbons and Murphy 1990, Conyon and Murphy 2000). Thus, a positive pay-for-corporate performance and a negative pay-for-industry performance suggest that management is rewarded for outperforming its industry (proposition 3).

2.3. *Corporate Governance Systems*

Low concentration of control (defined as voting power), can be found in Anglo-American countries, where on average, a single shareholder does not hold more than 15 per cent. Furthermore, multiple class voting shares or voting restrictions are not common (Becht and Mayer 2001). When voting power is dispersed, free riding on monitoring might occur as a single shareholder bears all the costs of control but only benefits in direct proportion to his share stake.

Whilst low ownership concentration and the market for corporate control are characteristic of market-oriented governance systems, a majority of companies in Continental Europe and Japan have high concentrations of ownership and control, which enables investors to monitor the performance of the firm better. Much of the recent commentary on the impact of concentrated ownership on shareholder behaviour suggests that increases in ownership tend to limit free-rider problems. Still, from an efficiency perspective, there are costly drawbacks to this approach of controlling management. On the shareholders' part, it requires giving up liquidity and investing a large proportion of wealth implying a longer-term commitment to the firm. As a consequence, large shareholders may incur greater costs due to their willingness to make an investment that requires them to forgo liquidity and to invest in corporate monitoring. In effect, the major shareholders' investment is to some extent 'locked up' in the company. The costs of reduced liquidity for the large shareholder can be more than compensated by the value of private benefits of control as control can allow a large shareholder to extract rents from the company. The private benefits of control are non-transferable benefits beyond the financial return on investment. For example, if a car producer attracts a subcontractor to supply car seats, a large shareholding in the subcontracting company can yield an important strategic advantage. A large shareholder will obtain a seat on the board of directors as well confidential information on the firm's cost structure or on contracts to supply competitors. For example, such a large shareholder could, after obtaining such strategic information, renew negotiations about the subcontractor's prices. Consequently, such transactions can lead to the creation of another kind of agency conflict, namely infringement of minority shareholders' rights. In reality, the liquidity-private benefit trade-off is not as severe as described here since in most European countries the liquidity constraints of large shareholders are relaxed by the design of pyramidal structures of shareholdings. Using such pyramids (of shareholding cascades), liquidity is maintained while at the same time voting power is preserved (Crespí-Cladera and Gispert-Pellicer 1999*a*; 1999*b*). Another solution (which also applies in Spain) to cope with reduced shareholding liquidity is issuing dual class voting shares to separate ownership and control.

For the UK and Spain, the relevant differences in corporate governance characteristics can be summarized as follows: (i) shareholding concentration is much higher in Spain than in the UK; (ii) pyramidal and complex ownership structures have been created in most Spanish corporations, via intermediate holding companies; (iii) the Spanish corporate sector (industrial holding companies) owns a large stake in itself; (iv) bank holdings are generally small in both countries (unless—for Spain—if the company is part of a financial group); (v) institutions are the largest category of shareholders in the UK where institutional shareholder activism is rising, but institutions, in voting control terms, are largely unimportant in Spain; and (vi) director ownership is high in the UK and leads to managerial entrenchment.

The pay-for-share price performance elasticity is expected to be stronger in market-based corporate governance systems (proposition 4a) because: (i) agency costs between shareholders and management are higher than in a blockholder dominated system; (ii) its capital markets are better developed; and (iii) the corporate goal (as reflected in corporate law) is the creation of shareholder value (La Porta *et al.* 1998). It should be noted that the period we investigate is prior to the publication of the UK Greenbury Report in 1995 and of the Spanish Olivencia Report of 1998, both of which intended to strengthen the pay-for-performance relation. The alternative hypothesis states that a stronger pay-for-share price performance relation of a blockholder dominated governance system may result from the fact that blockholders are able to impose value enhancing remuneration policies upon management. Furthermore, in a system of weak owners and strong managers (a market-based system as in Roe 1994), the managers may be able to set a compensation policy (with accounting benchmarks) that matches their own utility function.

Even within the market-based and the blockholder-oriented systems, we expect that remuneration schemes depend on varying degrees of corporate control: the pay-for-shareholder elasticities are higher in companies with high control concentration than in widely held firms (proposition 4b). If a company is highly levered, management should generate sufficient cash flow in order to service its debt. A lack of sufficient cash flow increases the probability of bankruptcy. Therefore, we expect management of highly levered companies to have short-term accounting aims and to have a higher pay-for-accounting performance (proposition 5).

3. DATA DESCRIPTION

3.1. *Sample Selection and Data Sources*

For the UK, data on remuneration, ownership (voting rights), performance, capital structure, and board structure are collected for the period 1988–1993. A sample of 250 companies was randomly selected from all the companies quoted on the London Stock Exchange in

1988, excluding financial institutions, real estate companies and insurance companies. We only retained companies with at least three years of data in the first four years of the sample period to allow panel data analyses to be undertaken. Companies delisted through takeovers or insolvencies for the first three years, between 1988 and 1990, were therefore excluded from the data set. In addition, seven of the original 250 companies were dropped through lack of performance data. For the period up to 1993, 6 per cent of the 243 were acquired, and none went into receivership.[1] If those same companies are tracked to 1997, the rate of acquisition increases to 13 per cent, and none entered into formal bankruptcy procedures. Remuneration and ownership (control) data are collected from the notes in the annual reports. Share price and accounting data are gathered from the London Share Price Database (LSPD) and Datastream, respectively.

A sample was constructed consisting of all Spanish companies, both industrial companies and financial institutions, listed on the Madrid Stock Exchange for at least four years within the period 1989–1994. The requirement of at least four years of data to be included in our database enables us to investigate the dynamics of the pay-for-performance relationship but eliminates companies introduced to the stock exchange since 1992. Missing data in the official files of the Spanish regulatory and supervisory agency of the Spanish stock markets (Comisión Nacional del Mercado de Valores (CNMV))—in spite of mandatory disclosure rules—reduces the number of companies with full information to 113. These companies are active in nine industrial sectors. The sample can be split into eighty-eight listed non-financial companies and twenty-five banks. The results for the sub-sample of industrial companies will be discussed separately. At the end of our period of analysis, the total sample represents nearly 80 per cent of the market capitalization of the Spanish Stock Exchanges. The sub-sample of industrial companies accounts for a 30 per cent of listed companies but represents 76 per cent of market capitalization, whereas the twenty-five Spanish banks represent 52 per cent of all listed banks and 85 per cent of the banks' market capitalization. The fact that larger companies generally comply better to the disclosure of information requirements may induce a size bias. Ownership data for all directors and the substantial shareholders (owning at least 5 per cent of equity) as well as accounting data are collected from the files of the CNMV. Given the importance of ownership pyramid structures, both direct and indirect share stakes have been collected for all the large shareholders. When more than one shareholder at higher ownership tiers own substantial share stake in a company which controls the direct share stakes in a listed Spanish firm, we have taken care to avoid double counting of voting rights. Share price, dividend and stock split data are collected from the databases of the Madrid Stock Exchange. The annual reports were consulted for the board remuneration data.

3.2. *Remuneration and Performance Data*

For the UK sample period, only the remuneration of the highest paid director is reported in the annual reports. It was only after the publication of the report of the Remuneration Committee (the Greenbury Report) in 1995 that the disclosure of remuneration was expanded.[2] Our UK remuneration data comprise the fixed salary and (if applicable) a bonus for the highest paid director. Usually, the highest paid director is the CEO but if another executive director earns more, the remuneration of both the highest paid director and the

CEO are reported. If the chairman fulfils an executive position, his salary is usually also disclosed. We believe that the error we make by not including stock options is limited because management options were not frequently granted over the period 1988–93. If data on management options are reported, the notes of the annual reports merely mention that the management has participated in a management options scheme. Thus, the annual reports do not allow us to measure the potential wealth impact of options grants because we cannot identify how many options management received, under which conditions the options could be exercised (exercise price, time to maturity, etc.).

In spite of repeated calls in Continental Europe for more disclosure about top management remuneration, embedded in the recent debates related to the creation of codes of good corporate governance practice, little progress has been made. At best, some generic data on the board of directors as a whole have recently been disclosed. Whereas Continental European managers regard disclosure as a breach of privacy, publication of the level and performance sensitivity of top management pay—consisting of fixed salary, short- and long-term cash incentives like bonuses, stock options and pension benefits—is important as it enables the shareholders to fine-tune managerial incentives. For listed Spanish companies, the combined cash remuneration of the total board of directors of listed Spanish companies is mentioned in the annual reports. We extrapolate the information of a few remuneration examples and approximate the Spanish CEO's cash compensation by taking fifteen times the average yearly compensation of the non-executive director serving on the CEO's board and we also assume that the CEO's compensation is 25 per cent higher than the average executive director compensation.[3] Management options have only been introduced recently and do not play an important role in top management remuneration during the sample period for Spain.

The descriptive statistics of Tables 27.1 and 27.2 show that the average remuneration of the CEO in the UK amounts to £188,361 yearly (with a median of £142,000), whereas the approximate compensation for the Spanish executive director in an industrial listed company averages £143,234 (with a median of £106,565).[4] All Spanish data presented in pesetas are converted into Pounds Sterling at the exchange rate at 31 December of the year the data refers. In spite of the fact that the UK firms are smaller than the Spanish ones in terms of total assets (respectively, £476 million versus £624 million; see Tables 27.1 and 27.2), UK CEO salaries are higher than in Spain. Furthermore, over the sample period, a minority of UK CEOs may even derive additional income from management options that are not included in the compensation figures of this study. It should be noted that, in the remainder of this study, we do not focus on the levels of CEO compensation but rather on whether or not performance triggers a change in top management remuneration. Higher changes in cash-based compensation for the UK (with 11 per cent a year) can be observed with only 1 per cent for Spanish industrial companies (or 1.7 per cent for all sample firms).

The dividend corrected share price returns of Spanish and UK companies are significantly different with averages amounting to -5 and $+5$ per cent, respectively. Tables 27.1 and 27.2 reveal that the bottom quintile of Spanish industrial firms has performed substantially worse (-37.5 per cent) than that of the UK (-12.6 per cent). Still the Spanish total sample firms have a share price return over the period 1991–5 of 7 per cent, which indicates that the financial firms performed well over the sample period (Table 27.2 and Table 27.A.1 of Appendix). In terms of accounting returns, UK firms also outperformed the

Table 27.1. *Descriptive statistics for the UK*

Variables	Description	Mean (std.)	Median	Q25%	Q75%
REM	Remuneration of highest paid director	GBP 188,361 (164 003)	142,000	94,000	225,000
Δln REM	Change in logarithm of remuneration of CEO	0.110 (0.34)	0.088	0.000	0.197
SHR	Share price return (logarithm)	0.057 (0.41)	0.088	−0.126	0.228
AISHR	Average industry shareholder return	0.092 (0.18)	0.115	−0.022	0.196
ROA	Return on assets	0.095 (0.115)	0.105	0.061	0.152
AIROA	Average industry ROA	−0.002 (0.0487)	0.0013	−0.036	0.011
Δln(St)	Changes in logarithm of total sales turnover	0.094 (0.19)	0.079	−0.006	0.178
Total assets	Total assets. Value in books	GBP 476,393 M	83,000	26,012	246,209
Total sales	Total sales turnover	GBP 925,192 M	183,360	83,680	552,016
C^1	% of direct and indirect shares of largest shareholder	15.42 (12.95)	11.66	6.75	21.3
C^n	Sum of all large share blocks (> 5%)	36.76 (23.26)	35.63	18.11	53.04
LEV	Capital gearing	33.61 (39.22)	29.44	16.97	41.65

The descriptive statistics for the UK sample, which consists of listed industrial companies, are shown here. The data are averaged over 1989–93. Std. stands for standard deviation. Numbers are in Pounds Sterling.

Sources: Own calculations, data from annual reports, LSPD, Datastream.

Spanish sample with a return on assets 9.5 per cent versus 2.8 per cent. As expected (La Porta *et al.* 1997), Spanish corporations depend more on debt finance than UK ones: leverage in Spain is 47 per cent versus 34 per cent in the UK.

3.3. *Ownership and Control Concentration*

Annual reports and the files of the CNMV were consulted to collect data for respectively UK and Spanish firms. All shareholdings of directors have to be disclosed as well as all substantial share stakes (3 per cent or more in the UK and 5 per cent or more for Spain) for other categories of owner. The data include all beneficial shareholdings. The shareholder using a nominee construction in the UK was identified in all cases after contacting the Company Secretary or Controller. In almost all cases, such a shareholder is an institution that uses the nominee structure to reduce the administrative burden of holding nominal shares for clients.

Table 27.2. *Descriptive statistics for Spain*

Variables	Description	Mean (std.)	Median	Q25%	Q75%
CEO	CEO remuneration	GBP 143,234 (134, 273)	106,565	58,550	180,557
Δln REM	Changes in log. of total board remuneration/ exec. directors	0.009 (0.48)	0.047	−0.045	0.173
SHR	Share price return (logarithm)	$-0.054^{\dagger}$ (0.55)	0.007	−0.375	0.233
AISHR	Average industry shareholder return	$0.040^{\dagger}$ (0.33)	0.037	−0.178	0.25
ROA	Return on assets	0.028 (0.144)	0.036	0.011	0.076
AIROA	Average industry ROA	0.032 (0.039)	0.035	0.018	0.057
Δln(St)	Changes in logarithm of total sales turnover	0.037 (0.348)	0.047	−0.041	0.120
Total assets	Total assets. Value in books	GBP 624,074 M	162,356	60,583	520,828
Total sales	Total sales turnover	GBP 355,063 M	100,364	27,267	250,951
C^1	% of direct and indirect shares of largest shareholder	46.80 (27.26)	42.86	25.15	66.48
C^n	Sum of all large share blocks (> 5%)	61.75 (25.26)	62.61	45.91	83.33
LEV	Capital gearing (%)	46.50 (22.60)	46.50	29.00	61.50

The descriptive statistics for the Spanish sample, which consists of listed industrial companies, are shown here. Std. stands for standard deviation. The data are averaged over 1991–5 († means that average is taken over 1990–4). Data are in Pounds Sterling.

Sources: Own calculations, data from Datastream, CNMV, Madrid Stock Exchange.

That the control concentration and structure of Spanish and UK companies is entirely different is confirmed by Tables 27.1 and 27.2. Summing all major shareholdings in Spanish and UK firms, the accumulated voting rights amounts to 61 per cent for Spain and to 37 per cent in the UK.[5] Whereas the largest shareholder in the average listed UK company owns a share stake of 15 per cent, the largest investor (group) in the average listed Spanish firm controls more than 46 per cent, almost absolute majority control. As in all listed UK companies, the one-share–one-vote principle is upheld (Goergen and Renneboog 2001, this volume, Chapter 10) such that the percentage of voting right concentration is equivalent to the percentage of the total voting rights. In contrast, in Spanish corporations, ownership pyramiding is often used as a way of amassing voting rights with limited cash flow rights (Bratton and McCahery 1999; Crespí-Cladera and García-Cestona 2001). In order to capture the true voting control for Spanish firms, we have collected data about the ownership structure of the first-tier corporate shareholder. Subsequently, we have reconstructed the ownership pyramid for each corporate shareholder as long as the control chain was not broken and until the (ultimate) shareholder was either an individual or family, the government or a widely held corporation. We have summed the first-tier ownership stakes controlled directly or indirectly (via intermediate investment vehicles) by the same ultimate investor (group) and classified these first-tier shareholdings according to the identity of the ultimate shareholder.[6]

Table 27.3 (panel A) shows that, on average, at least three shareholders are needed to form a blocking minority (25 per cent stake) in the UK whereas in the average Spanish firm

Table 27.3. *Control concentration by category of owner*

Panel A: Direct and indirect ownership concentration held by the largest blockholders

	UK	Spain (total sample)
C^1: Top blocks (%)	15.42	48.23
C^3: 3 largest blocks (%)	26.84	56.59
C^5: 5 largest blocks (%)	32.99	60.38
C^{all}: all voting blocks (%)	36.76	61.28

Panel B: Direct and indirect ownership concentration by category held by the largest blockholders

Categories of shareholder (%):	UK	Spain		
	Total sample (non-financial co's)	Non-financial sample	Financial sample	Total sample
Banks	5.1	5.2	7.5	6.4
Insurance firms	4.0	—	—	—
Investment/pension funds	7.0	—	—	—
Financial other than banking	—	6.0	10.7	8.4
Executive directors	4.5	—	—	—
Non-executive directors	5.0	—	—	—
Total directors	9.5	6.5	4.3	6.0
Domestic companies	—	16.3	14.3	15.3
Foreign companies	—	11.9	4.7	8.3
Total industrial companies	10.6	28.2	19.0	23.5
Families and individuals	5.2	9.3	12.5	11.0
Government	6.7	4.9	0.4	2.6
Real estate	0.1	0.0	0.0	0.0

The percentage of voting rights of the largest shareholder, of the three and five largest shareholders and of all shareholders (panel A) for UK and Spain are shown here. Panel B reports the average percentage of equity held by the largest shareholder and subsequently classified into one of the shareholder categories. The averages in panel B are calculated for companies with a large shareholder (holding 3 per cent or more in the UK, or 5 per cent or more in Spain). Classification of large shareholdings in Spanish companies depends on both direct and indirect ownership relations. For every first-tier Spanish corporate shareholder, the ownership pyramid was constructed. Higher ownership tiers were investigated for as long as the control chain was not broken and for as long as the (ultimate) shareholder was either an individual or family, the government or a widely held corporation. Subsequently, the first tier-ownership stakes controlled directly or indirectly (via intermediate investment vehicles) by the same ultimate investor (group) were aggregated. Note that the averages in panel A are calculated across all companies (including those without known large shareholders); the averages in panel B are calculated across those companies in which a large shareholder of a specific category was present.

three shareholders hold absolute majority control. The Spanish and UK corporate landscapes do not only differ in terms of concentration of control but also in terms of the nature of ownership. Institutional shareholders are the most important ownership category in the UK (panel B of Table 27.3). It should be noted that the average percentage of 16 per cent held by investment and pension funds, banks and insurance firms in UK industrial companies only reflects the average of the ownership stakes of 3 per cent and more. Taking into account also the small institutional shareholdings (smaller than 3 per cent) would yield a total institutional ownership percentage of more than 60 per cent. In Spanish industrial companies, the substantial institutional shareholdings (of more than 5 per cent) average to about 11 per cent. In Spanish banks, large ownership stakes held by other banks and insurance companies sum to more than 18 per cent on average.

The accumulated large shareholdings of directors is almost 10 per cent in the UK while the directors of the sample of Spanish companies do not own a substantial equity stake. There are several reasons why directors own higher share stakes in Anglo-American firms than in Continental Europe. Goergen and Renneboog (2001, this volume, Chapter 10) show that UK firms that are brought to the stock exchange are much younger (on average they are fourteen years old since incorporation) and that founding families usually retain substantial shareholdings.[7] The Spanish data may suffer from lack of disclosure of director's shareholdings: directors are obliged to disclose the size of their personal shareholdings but the use of pyramiding with intermediate investment vehicles may make the director ownership data somewhat opaque.[8] In both the UK and Spain, industrial companies are an important shareholder category: their substantial shareholdings average to 11 per cent of the total equity for the UK and even to 28.2 per cent in Spanish industrial firms. The UK government has avoided share ownership in the UK since the privatization wave of the second half of the 1980s: regional investment companies only own a share stake in two listed firms. In contrast, the government owned a substantial share in the Spanish economy (mainly in oil, tobacco, energy, and telecommunications) via holding companies and state owned banks. Subsequent to our sample period, after the 1995 Spanish privatization process, government participation has almost disappeared and the state has been replaced by a large number of Spanish retail investors, some large Spanish institutional investors (banks, for the most part) and some international institutional investors (Crespí-Cladera and García-Cestona 2001).

4. METHODOLOGY

Two panels of data are formed for the five-year period[9] 1989–93 (UK) and 1990–5 (Spain) with each firm-year representing a separate observation. The firm-years in which a change in CEO took place, are excluded: 147 UK firm-years (or 11 per cent of a total of 1,338) are eliminated versus 108 Spanish firm-years (or 22 per cent of a total of 489). The relation between CEO remuneration, performance, corporate size and other variables (like voting right structure, leverage, and board structure) is given by the following model:

$$\ln(\text{REM})_{i,t} = \Psi_t + v_i + \beta_{i,1} \ln(\text{sh.val.})_{i,t-1} + \beta_{i,2} \ln(\text{ind.sh.val.})_{i,t-1} + \beta_{i,3} \ln(\text{SIZE})_{i,t-1} + \beta_{i,4} (\text{OTH})_{i,t-1} + \varepsilon_{i,t},$$

where ln is the natural logarithm, REM, the Remuneration, sh.val., the Share value (price), ind.sh.val., the share value of industry, SIZE, the Sales, OTH, the corporate governance variables like voting right structure, leverage, board structure, etc., i, the company i, t, the year, ψ, the time trend, and υ the firm-specific effect that varies across CEOs (or executive directors) but not over time.

In order to estimate the sensitivity of CEO remuneration to performance, we take the first differences such that the model is modified as follows:

$$\Delta \ln(\text{REM})_{i,t} = \beta_1\, \Delta \ln(\text{sh.val.})_{i,t-1} + \beta_2\, \Delta \ln(\text{ind.sh.val.})_{i,t-1} + \beta_3\, \Delta \ln(\text{SIZE})_{i,t-1} + \beta_4\, \Delta(\text{OTH})_{i,t-1} + \text{YR}_t + \xi_{i,t},$$

where Δ is the first differences operator $\Delta X_{i,t} = X_{i,t} - X_{i,t-1}$, YR stands for the dummy variables capturing time trends and ξ, the error term. If we assume that pay-for-performance relations are constant across executives over time, the subscripts i should not be shown. Note that taking first differences has eliminated the firm-specific effects (υ).

Measuring remuneration and performance as changes in logarithms gives coefficients that can be interpreted as pay-for-performance elasticities, measuring these variables as changes in dollar amounts gives pay-for-performance sensitivities. There is no a priori advantage to the use of elasticities (Coughlan and Schmidt 1985) over sensitivities (Jensen and Murphy 1990). Murphy (1999) mentions that in the elasticity approach, rates of return explain more of the cross-sectional variation of Δln(CEO pay) than changes in shareholder value explain of Δ(CEO pay) in the sensitivity approach. Boschen and Smith (1995) note that employing a first-differenced specification of the compensation variable implies that changes in compensation persist over time. The estimated explanatory parameters of changes in compensation capture rent transfers across periods.

We include both lagged share price returns and accounting returns (i) because there may be time lags between corporate performance and the remuneration committee's decision to increase salary and/or bonus, and (ii) because including contemporaneous accounting returns along with lagged share price returns may induce multicollinearity into the model as the accounting effect may already have been captured by past share price returns due to their forward-looking nature. The regression estimations are performed with a heteroscedasticity consistent covariance matrix estimator (White 1980). Time effects are accounted for by including time dummies and the innovations remove firm-specific fixed effects. In order to address the endogeneity problems, data on voting rights, debt policy and size were also lagged for one and two years.

5. RESULTS

Even though corporate performance may be improving, the board may not consider this to be a sufficient reason to increase top management's compensation if corporate performance lags the industry peers. Hence, along with corporate share price performance, the performance of the industry is included in the models of Tables 27.4–27.6. Panel A of Table 27.4 reveals that there is no statistically significant relation between changes in CEO cash-based compensation and share price returns in UK companies, but the model shows a strong relation

Table 27.4. *The relation between top management compensation and performance*

	UK		Spain	
	(1)	(2)	(3)	(4)
Panel A: Dependent variable: $\Delta ln\ REM_{it}$				
$SHR_{i,t-1}$	0.038 (0.033)		−0.170** (0.069)	
$AISHR_{i,t-1}$	−0.004 (0.162)		0.086 (0.164)	
$SHR_{i,t-2}$		−0.049 (0.038)		0.181*** (0.066)
$AISHR_{i,t-2}$		−0.257 (0.190)		−0.012 (0.152)
$\Delta\ln(S_t)$	0.160*** (0.059)	0.120* (0.064)	0.187* (0.101)	0.165* (0.100)
Year dummies	Yes	Yes	Yes	Yes
Observations	748	591	275	282
F-test	3.808***	1.717	1.766*	2.096**
R^2	0.035	0.017	0.044	0.051
Panel B: Dependent variable: $\Delta ln\ REM_{it}$				
$SHR_{i,t-1}$	0.051 (0.036)		−0.217*** (0.079)	
$AISHR_{i,t-1}$	0.004 (0.173)		−0.005 (0.192)	
$SHR_{i,t-2}$		−0.023 (0.037)		0.285*** (0.077)
$AISHR_{i,t-2}$		−0.162 (0.204)		−0.185 (0.178)
$\Delta\ln(1+ROA_{i,t-1})$	−0.022 (0.063)	0.019 (0.063)	1.625*** (0.460)	1.423*** (0.446)
$\Delta\ln(1+AIROA_{i,t-1})$	0.511 (0.313)	0.550 (0.350)	−0.621 (1.044)	−1.529 (1.029)
$\Delta\ln(S_t)$	0.169*** (0.063)	0.180*** (0.068)	0.203* (0.110)	0.201* (0.107)
C^1	0.0002 (0.001)	0.0005 (0.001)	−0.039 (0.054)	−0.033 (0.053)
Year dummies	Yes	Yes	Yes	Yes
Observations	721	571	244	250
F	2.824***	1.870*	2.567***	2.934***
R^2	0.038	0.029	0.099	0.109

The results of a first differenced OLS regression with a heteroscedasticity consistent covariance matrix estimator (White 1980) are given here. Δ stands for the first difference operator, ln is the natural logarithm, REM stands for total CEO remuneration (excluding income for management options), SHR is the share price return, AISHR is the average industry share price return, ROA is the return on assets, AIROA is the average return on assets by industry, SIZE stands for total sales, C^1 is the shareholding of the largest shareholder, SIZE stands for total sales. Standard error is between parentheses. ***, **, * stand for statistical significance at respectively 1, 5, and 10 per cent.

Source: Own calculations.

between increases in corporate size (measured by sales) and remuneration. CEO remuneration is augmented when corporate sales grow. As a result, we reject proposition 2 that states that the average UK remuneration policy was focused on value creation in the pre-Greenbury period. We do not reject proposition 1 as corporate size seems to be the main determinant of CEO remuneration. It may well be that managing large corporations requires unique managerial skills that require additional compensation. Most other studies on UK remuneration largely confirm these findings: they either do not find any pay-for-performance relation

Table 27.5. *The influence of control concentration on the pay-for-performance relation*

	Dependent variable: $\Delta\ln \text{REM}_{it}$			
	UK		Spain	
	(1)	(2)	(3)	(4)
$\text{SHR}_{i,t-1}$	0.054 (0.048)		−0.029 (0.112)	
$\text{AISHR}_{i,t-1}$	−0.036 (0.183)		0.002 (0.210)	
$\text{SHR}_{i,t-2}$		−0.096* (0.051)		0.025 (0.102)
$\text{AISHR}_{i,t-2}$		−0.211 (0.214)		0.017 (0.191)
$\Delta\ln(1+\text{ROA}_{i,t-1})$	−0.047 (0.077)	−0.004 (0.068)	1.847*** (0.530)	1.928*** (0.510)
$\Delta\ln(1+\text{AIROA}_{i,t-1})$	0.233 (0.407)	−0.055 (0.452)	−1.741 (1.241)	−2.678** (1.286)
$\Delta\ln(S_t)$	0.168*** (0.064)	0.176*** (0.068)	0.226** (0.108)	0.224** (0.103)
$\text{DC}^*\ \text{SHR}_{i,t-1}$	−0.0007 (0.072)		−0.320** (0.152)	
$\text{DC}^*\ \text{AISHR}_{i,t-1}$	−0.010 (0.147)		−0.099 (0.212)	
$\text{DC}^*\ \text{SHR}_{i,t-2}$		0.140* (0.073)		0.565*** (0.143)
$\text{DC}^*\ \text{AISHR}_{i,t-2}$		−0.044 (0.149)		−0.607*** (0.226)
$\text{DC}^*\ \Delta\ln(1+\text{ROA}_{i,t-1})$	0.060 (0.134)	0.147 (0.178)	−1.063 (0.979)	−1.718* (0.908)
$\text{DC}^*\ \Delta\ln(1+\text{AIROA}_{i,t-1})$	0.558 (0.554)	1.184** (0.575)	3.346** (1.661)	4.125** (1.848)
Year dummies	Yes	Yes	Yes	Yes
Observations	721	571	244	250
F	2.262***	2.065**	3.209***	4.515***
R^2	0.040	0.043	0.153	0.199

The results of a first differenced OLS regression with a heteroscedasticity consistent covariance matrix estimator (White 1980) are given here. Δ stands for the first difference operator, ln is the natural logarithm, REM stands for total CEO (UK) or executive director (Spain) remuneration (excluding income for management options), SHR is share price return, AISHR is the average industry share price return, ROA is the return on assets, AIROA is the average return on assets by industry, SIZE stands for total sales, DC stands for a dummy variable which equals 1 if the share concentration of the largest shareholder is above the sample average, and 0 otherwise. Standard error is between parentheses. ***, **, * stand for statistical significance at respectively 1, 5, and 10 per cent.

Source: Own calculations.

(Greg *et al.* 1993; Conyon 1997) or find that size is the main determinant of executive director compensation (Conyon and Leech 1994; Cosh and Hughes 1997; Conyon 1998).

For listed Spanish companies, the parameter estimates of CEO compensation with corporate sales are similar in size, but less statistically significant (within 10 per cent level). In contrast to the UK, there is a significant positive pay-for-share price performance elasticity in Spanish listed companies. When the share return increases in regression (4), the CEO's remuneration is adjusted but only after a time lag of more than one year. For the shareholders, a strong link between managerial remuneration and corporate performance measured by share price returns is preferable as it shows that the managers are geared towards the creation of shareholder value. The findings for Spain in Table 27.4 corroborate propositions 1 and 2.

Table 27.6. *The influence of leverage on the pay-for-performance relation*

	Dependent variable: $\Delta\ln \text{REM}_{it}$			
	UK		Spain	
	(1)	(2)	(3)	(4)
$\text{SHR}_{i,t-1}$	−0.005 (0.53)		−0.084 (0.185)	
$\text{AISHR}_{i,t-1}$	−0.092 (0.190)		0.063 (0.274)	
$\text{SHR}_{i,t-2}$		−0.073 (0.049)		0.352** (0.141)
$\text{AISHR}_{i,t-2}$		−0.046 (0.215)		−0.244 (0.269)
$\Delta\ln(1+\text{ROA}_{i,t-1})$	0.157 (0.174)	0.068 (0.154)	−0.850 (1.132)	−0.910 (1.026)
$\Delta\ln(1+\text{AIROA}_{i,t-1})$	1.075** (0.446)	1.207** (0.512)	−2.144 (1.763)	−1.999 (1.810)
$\Delta\ln(S_t)$	0.181*** (0.063)	0.179*** (0.068)	0.154 (0.164)	0.181 (0.152)
$\text{DL}^* \text{SHR}_{i,t-1}$	0.093 (0.073)		−0.089 (0.239)	
$\text{DL}^* \text{AISHR}_{i,t-1}$	0.158 (0.138)		−0.034 (0.299)	
$\text{DL}^* \text{SHR}_{i,t-2}$		0.099 (0.072)		−0.188 (0.186)
$\text{DL}^* \text{AISHR}_{i,t-2}$				
$\text{DL}^* \Delta\ln$		−0.133 (0.137)		0.465 (0.312)
$(1+\text{ROA}_{i,t-1})$	−0.194 (0.186)	−0.066 (0.169)	3.082** (1.285)	2.885** (1.181)
$\text{DL}^* \Delta\ln(1+\text{AIROA}_{i,t-1})$	−0.968* (0.533)	−1.000* (0.573)	−2.072 (2.908)	−4.706 (3.104)
Year dummies	Yes	Yes	Yes	Yes
Observations	725	575	137	140
F	2.824***	1.762**	2.204**	2.899***
R^2	0.049	0.036	0.173	0.212

The results of a first differenced OLS regression with a heteroscedasticity consistent covariance matrix estimator (White 1980) are given here. Δ stands for the first difference operator, ln is the natural logarithm, REM stands for total CEO (UK) or executive director (Spain) remuneration (excluding income for management options), SHR is the share price return, AISHR is the average industry share price return, ROA is the return on assets, AIROA is the average return on assets by industry, SIZE stands for total sales, DL stands for a dummy variable which equals 1 if the leverage (debt/total assets) is above the sample average, and 0 otherwise. Standard error is between parentheses. ***, **, * stand for statistical significance at respectively 1, 5, and 10 per cent.

Source: Own calculations.

When management experiences little corporate monitoring, they may prefer to relate remuneration to accounting performance, which they can to a certain extent control. Panel B of Table 27.3 shows the relation between CEO remuneration and share price and accounting performance. In the average listed UK company in the pre-Greenbury period, there is no relation between accounting performance and managerial remuneration. Managers are only rewarded for growth of total sales. In contrast, model (4) shows that managerial compensation in Spain is sensitive to performance improvement as the executive directors' income increases along with increases in shareholders' return and in accounting performance (measured by return on assets). Interestingly, the variables reflecting industry performance (both in terms of share price and return on assets) are negatively correlated (although not statistically significant) with changes in CEO remuneration. This finding combined with the fact that the parameter coefficients of corporate and industry returns in model (4) are of similar size suggests that corporate performance is evaluated relative to the industry. The positive effect of high share returns on CEO remuneration is cancelled when the industry's share prices are augmenting as well. Similarly, the effect of a large increase in return on assets on executive director remuneration is undone by rising industry ROAs. These results support proposition 3.

Although the agency conflicts between management and shareholder are expected to be larger in a market-oriented governance system (the UK), we do not find evidence of a remuneration policy targeted at resolving those agency conflicts. It is rather in the blockholder-oriented system where we discover the strongest positive pay-for-share price performance elasticity. This may result from the fact that monitoring shareholders with voting power are needed to impose a compensation policy geared towards value maximization. Hence, our findings do not support proposition 4a.

Although the control distributions between the UK and Spain are substantially different, there are companies within each governance regime with and without high concentration of control. The pay-for-share price performance elasticity is expected to be larger in companies with strong control concentration. In these firms, blockholders may ensure that managerial compensation depends on the creation of corporate value. The management of companies without blockholders may have more discretion and hence relate the remuneration policy to those performance yardsticks under their control. In Table 27.5, the impact of control concentration on compensation is investigated by interacting the model with a dummy variable equalling 1 if the largest shareholder's control stake is above the sample average. The non-interactive parameter estimates depict the relation between remuneration, performance, and size for firms with higher ownership dispersion while the sum of the non-interactive and the respective interactive coefficients give the remuneration sensitivity for companies with above median concentration of voting control. Table 27.5 reports a strong elasticity of CEO remuneration to sales growth for UK firms. Neither share price performance nor accounting returns, lagged by one year, has an impact on UK companies with strong or low control concentration (regression (1)). Including two year lags, yields a negative relation of share returns with remuneration changes (at low levels of statistical significance) for firms with low control concentration. Such a relation is non-existent for companies in strong control firms (the parameter estimates of the lagged share returns in regression (2) approximately cancel out: −0.096 and 0.140). When the accounting performance of the industry is performing well, the UK CEO seems to benefit financially. All in all, it seems that UK CEOs' cash-based salaries are strongly depending on corporate size instead of corporate performance, such that proposition 1 cannot be rejected whereas proposition 4b is rejected.

Like for the UK, the average Spanish executive director's remuneration is sensitive to corporate growth. While there is no relation between share price performance and executive director remuneration in widely held firms, model (4) shows that increases of corporate value in companies with high concentration of voting rights lead to an increased cash-based reward for the CEO. Still, share returns only trigger CEO remuneration increases more than one year after the increase in corporate value and only when the share price increase is higher than that of the industrial sector. Coefficients 0.565 and −0.607 in model (4) point out that a CEO is not rewarded if his company (with high ownership concentration) performs equally well as the industry peers. In Spanish firms with more diffuse ownership, executive directors' cash compensation depends on the accounting performance: if the company's return on assets outperforms its industry peers, the CEO's compensation is augmented in the subsequent year. The pay-for-accounting performance relation is not present in companies with high control concentration (the ROA and industry ROA coefficients, 1.9 versus −1.7, and −2.7 and 4.1 largely neutralize one another). In companies with blockholders, managerial compensation seems to depend on the creation of shareholder value, which supports proposition 4b.

One may argue that pay-for-share price performance schemes and the presence of large shareholders are substitute mechanisms that ensure that managerial actions remain geared towards value maximization. In firms with strong blockholder monitoring there may be less need to resort to incentive-based executive compensation schemes. However, the findings of Table 27.5 show that a strong pay-for-share price performance relation is only imposed in companies with large blockholders and are thus complementary mechanisms in Spain. The lack of any performance-linked remuneration in the pre-Greenbury period has pointed out the cutting need for the development of a code strengthening managerial remuneration and corporate performance.

In highly leveraged firms, a higher dependence of management remuneration on accounting returns is expected because decreases in earnings and, certainly, negative earnings may lead to an undermining of the solvency of the firm and could easily trigger bankruptcy. Hence, the CEO of a highly levered company may be financially rewarded if he can generate sufficiently high accounting returns. Table 27.6 confirms that changes in the CEO remuneration of the average UK firm are predominantly influenced by growth in corporate size. For the UK, proposition 5 is not sustained: in a company with less reliance on debt finance, the CEO's salary is augmented when this firm's industrial sector performs well. In highly levered firms, there is no relation with the corporate performance of industry peers (in models (1) and (2), the coefficients of the firm's and industry's ROA cancel out). For highly levered Spanish firms, we cannot reject hypothesis 5: when the company's ROA augments, the CEO's remuneration is adjusted upwards.

6. CONCLUSION

In the UK, where the main agency costs may result from differing interests between shareholders and managers, we expect a strong relation between share performance and CEO remuneration. However, the remuneration policy is not geared towards value creation, but changes in corporate size, measured by sales growth, drive compensation revisions. This suggests that managing larger firms requires special (and hence more scarce) managerial skills. Even in those UK sample companies with high control concentration, no significant pay-for-performance relation was uncovered.

In Spain, CEOs of larger listed firms are also better compensated than those of small companies. We also find that increases in corporate value are followed by increases in (cash-based) CEO remuneration. However, this positive pay-for-share price performance elasticity is not present in all Spanish corporations: a remuneration policy aiming at corporate value maximization is only exerted in companies with a high degree of shareholder control. From this, we conclude that large shareholder monitoring is not a substitute for a share price performance-based remuneration policy as only strong blockholders seem to be able to impose this compensation scheme upon management. It should be noted that share prices trigger increases in CEO remuneration (at least one year subsequently) only if the share price returns are higher than those of the industry peers.

In Spanish firms without high control concentration, modifications in managerial remuneration depend upon changes in accounting returns in prior years: if the change in the firm's return on assets outperforms (or is less negative than) the industry ROA, the executive directors' cash compensation increases in the subsequent period. In these companies, the lack of blockholders gives management more discretion to have the remuneration policy depend upon accounting returns that can to some extent be influenced by management. Finally, we also investigated performance sensitivity of managerial remuneration in firms with high leverage and expect a positive relation between capital gearing and accounting information because sufficiently high accounting performance enables a highly levered firm to service its debt. This is confirmed by the evidence: whereas CEO remuneration in low leverage companies does not depend upon changes in return on assets, there is a strong pay-for-accounting performance in companies with a high capital gearing.

Appendix

Table 27.A.1. *Descriptive statistics for Spain (1991–5)*

Model variable	Description	Mean (std.)	Median	Q25%	Q75%
CEO	CEO remuneration	GBP 167,059 (188,278)	111,524	58,420	197,011
Δln REM	Changes in log. of total board remuneration/ exec. directors	0.017 (0.51)	0.043	−0.035	0.182
SHR	Share price return (logarithm)	0.070† (0.50)	0.025	−0.322	0.197
AISHR	Average industry shareholder return	0.023† (0.32)	0.024	−0.174	0.207
ROA	Return on assets	0.018 (0.129)	0.026	0.009	0.052
AIROA	Average industry ROA	0.015 (0.028)	0.023	0.007	0.035
Δln(St)	Changes in logarithm of total sales turnover	0.042 (0.227)	0.0469	−0.042	0.126
Total assets	Total assets. Value in books	GBP 1,818,788 M	327,289	81,301	949,914
Total sales	Total sales turnover	GBP 386,533M	116,769	39,743	327,829
C^1	% of direct and indirect shares of largest shareholder	48.23% (29.7)	45.28	24.60	74.56

Table 27.A.1. *Continued*

Model variable	Description	Mean (std.)	Median	Q25%	Q75%
C^n	Sum of all large share blocks (> 5%)	61.28% (27.26)	64.46	41.48	86.52
LEV	Capital gearing	$0.465^{\dagger\dagger}$ (0.226)	0.465	0.290	0.615

The descriptive statistics for the Spanish sample, which consists of both industrial and financial firms, are given here. Std. stands for standard deviation. The data are averaged over 1991–5 († means that average is taken over 1990–4, †† banks are not included). Data are in Pounds Sterling.

Sources: Own calculations, data from Datastream, CNMV, Madrid Stock Exchange.

Notes

1. Three had their respective quotations suspended or cancelled; one company was taken private; and the equity of three other firms was converted into a different security.
2. The annual reports after 1995 disclose for the executive directors: the base salary, the bonus (annual and long-term incentives), share options, retirement benefits.
3. The Spanish CEO's cash-based compensation if proxied as follows: (cash-based remuneration of the whole board × 15)/[number of non-executive directors + (number of executive directors excluding CEO × 12) + 15]. It should be noted that the pay-for-performance relation is not very sensitive to variations in this definition as we need to calculate the pay-for-performance elasticity for which pay and performance are measured as changes of the natural logarithm. In fact, calculating the pay-for-performance relation with pay defined as changes in logarithm of total board compensation does not significantly change our conclusions in Section 4.
4. The CEOs of the large listed banks earn substantially more than their counterparts working for industrial firms. The average Spanish CEO's cash-based compensation amounts to £167,059 for the whole sample (industrial and financial firms combined): see Appendix.
5. The accumulated ownership numbers in Tables 27.1 and 27.2 are not directly comparable for Spain and UK as the Spanish ownership disclosure threshold is 5 per cent while that of the UK is 3 per cent. Adding only those equity stakes of 5 per cent for the UK and more yields average ownership percentage of 30 per cent, which is less than half of that in Spain. Detailed discussion of ownership disclosure rules and other corporate governance regulation is given in Goergen and Renneboog (this volume, Chapter 10) for the UK and in Crespí-Cladera and García-Cestona (2001) for Spain.
6. As documented by the European Corporate Governance Network (Becht and Röell 1998), the European directive on ownership disclosure of 1989 has been interpreted by most European regulators as regarding the disclosure of voting rights or control concentration rather than of control concentration and has translated accordingly in national regulation. We use the terms ownership concentration and voting rights or control concentration interchangeably for both UK and Spanish companies throughout the paper.
7. Fifteen per cent of the UK sample is composed of recent IPOs, introduced maximally five years prior to the start of the sample period. Goergen and Renneboog (2001) describe how ownership concentration held by founding families evolves subsequent to floatation.
8. Directors can spread this ownership stake across several family members such that each of such ownership stakes remains below the disclosure threshold: this way, a de facto substantial blockholding can be hidden from the public eye. It should also be noted that we did not assign the voting rights of non-beneficial shareholdings, for which directors are trustees, to these directors.
9. Due to first differencing of the dependent variable the six year periods were reduced by one year.

References

Abowd, J., and Bognanno, M. (1995). International differences in executive and managerial compensation. In R. Freeman and L. Katz (ed.), Differences and Changes in Wage Structures, Chicago NBER.

Barca, F., and Becht, M. (ed.). (2001). *The Control of Corporate Europe.* Oxford: Oxford University Press.

Becht, M., and Mayer, C. (2001). The Control of Corporate Europe, In F. Barca and M. Becht (ed.), *The Control of Corporate Europe.* Oxford: Oxford University Press.

—— and Röell, A. (1998). European corporate governance: Trading off liquidity against control. *European Economic Review* 43: 1071.

Boschen, J. F., and Smith, K. J. (1995). You can pay me now and you can pay me later: The dynamic response of executive compensation to firm performance. *Journal of Business* 68: 577.

Bratton, W., and McCahery, J. (1999). Comparative corporate governance and the theory of the firm: The case against global cross-reference. *Columbia Journal of Transnational Law* 38: 213.

Conyon, M. (1997). Corporate governance and executive compensation. *International Journal of Industrial Organization* 15: 493.

—— (1998). Directors' pay and turnover: An application to a sample of large UK firms. *Oxford Bulletin of Economics and Statistics* 60: 485.

—— and Leech, D. (1994). Top pay, company performance and corporate governance. *Oxford Bulletin of Economics and Statistics* 56: 229.

—— and Murphy, K. J. (2000). The prince and the pauper? CEO pay in the US and UK. *Economic Journal* 110: 640.

Cosh, A., and Hughes, A. (1997). Executive remuneration, executive dismissals and institutional shareholders. *International Journal of Industrial Organization* 15: 469.

Coughlan, A., and Schmidt, R. (1985). Executive compensation, management turnover and firm performance: An empirical investigation. *Journal of Accounting and Economics* 7: 43.

Crespí-Cladera, R., and García-Cestona, M. (2001). Ownership and control of the Spanish listed firms. In F. Barca and M. Becht (ed.), *The Control of Corporate Europe.* Oxford: Oxford University Press.

—— and Gispert-Pellicer, C. (1999*a*). Block transfers: Implications for the governance of Spanish corporations. University Autonoma of Barcelona Working Paper.

—— (1999*b*). Board remuneration, performance, and governance of large Spanish companies. Social Science Research Network. Working Paper Series.

Dechow, P., and Sloan, R. (1991). Executive incentives and the horizon problem. *Journal of Accounting and Economics* 14: 51.

DeFusco, R., Johnson, R., and Zorn, T. (1990). The effect of executive stock option plans on stockholders and bondholders. *Journal of Finance* 45: 617.

Franks, J., Mayer, C., and Renneboog, L. (2001). Who disciplines the management of poorly performing companies? *Journal of Financial Intermediation,* 10: 209.

Gibbons, R., and Murphy, K. (1990). Relative performance evaluations for Chief Executive Officers. *Industrial and Labor Relations Review* 43: 30.

—— (1992). Does executive compensation affect investment? *Journal of Political Economy* 100: 468.

Goergen, M., and Renneboog, L. (2002). Strong managers and passive institutional investors in the UK. In F. Barca and M. Becht (ed.), *The Control of Corporate Europe.* Oxford: Oxford University Press.

—— —— (2001). Prediction of control concentration in German and UK initial public offerings, this volume, Chapter 10.

Greg, P., Machin, S., and Szymanski, S. (1993). The disappearing relations between directors' pay and corporate performance. *British Journal of Industrial Relations* 31: 1.

Hall, B., and Liebman, J. (1998). Are CEOs really paid like bureaucrats? *Quarterly Journal of Economics* 113: 653.

Healy, P. (1985). The effect of bonus schemes on accounting decisions. *Journal of Accounting and Economics* 102: 258.

Holmstrom, B., and Milgrom, P. (1987). Aggregation and linearity in the provision of intertemporal incentives. *Econometrica* 55: 303.

Holthausen, R., Larcker, D., and Sloan, R. (1995). Annual bonus schemes and the manipulation of earnings. *Journal of Accounting and Economics* 19: 29.

Jensen, M. C., and Murphy, K. (1990). Performance pay and top-management incentives. *Journal of Political Economy* 98: 225.

Lambert, R., Lanen, W., and Larcker, D. (1989). Executive stock option plans and corporate dividend policy. *Journal of Financial and Quantitative Analysis* 24: 409.

La Porta, R., Lopez-de-Silanes, F., Shleifer, A., and Vishny, R. (1997). Legal determinants of external finance. *Journal of Finance* 52: 1131.

—— (1998). Law and Finance. *Journal of Political Economy* 106: 1113.

Murphy, K. (1999). Executive compensation. In O. Ashenfelter and D. Card (ed.), *Handbook of Labor Economics*. Amsterdam: North-Holland.

Oyer, P. (1998). Fiscal year ends and non-linear incentive contracts: The effect on business seasonality. *Quarterly Journal of Economics* 113: 149.

Roe, M. (1994). *Strong Managers, Weak Owners: The Political Roots of American Corporate Finance*. Princeton: Princeton University Press.

White, H. (1980). A heteroscedasticity-consistent covariance matrix estimator and a direct test for heteroscedasticity. *Econometrica* 48: 3.

28

Employee Stock Option Grants and Firm Performance in the Netherlands

PIET DUFFHUES, REZAUL KABIR, GERARD MERTENS, AND PETER ROOSENBOOM

1. INTRODUCTION

Although executive stock options—the right granted to management and/or employees to buy a company's stock at a pre-specified price during a specified length of time—have become a well-established part of management compensation in the USA (Hall and Liebman 1998; Murphy 1999), their use has permeated Continental Europe only recently. Listed companies in the Netherlands started to use this form of compensation extensively as of the mid-1990s. The idea underlying the use of stock options is that they can turn paid managers into owners, thus aligning their interests with those of shareholders. As a result, company managers will be more motivated to strive towards firms' financial-markets-related performance. Moreover, these stock-based compensation plans may not only strengthen the link between compensation and performance for existing recipients, but can also assist a firm in bringing talented new staff onboard. This appears especially relevant in high-tech sector firms.

Stock-based compensation has fuelled an avalanche of criticism from different sources. The Prime Minister of the Netherlands qualifies some option schemes as 'exhibitionistic enrichment'. The main Dutch trade union federation argues that, because of stock option awards, a typical Dutch manager now earns many times the wage of an average factory worker. This raises questions of justice and inequality of incomes and may, in turn, undermine harmonious labour relations within the country (*Het Financieele Dagblad*, 31 August 1999). Duffhues (2000) stresses the agency aspects of stock option plans referring to incentives to earnings management and/or distorted financial decision making. He proposes to introduce a new type of compensation option namely 'Delayed Average Rate Executive Call Options' (DARECOs). The pay-off of this option is based on the average realized market price during the employment contract of the option holder.

The controversy with stock options is also present in other European countries like Belgium, France, Germany, and Spain. The *Wall Street Journal Europe* in its 12 December 1999 issue reviews the situation in Europe and notes the following: 'stock options and the wealth that accompanies success in the new economy are widely regarded in Europe as immoral, unjust or just plain excessive'. *The Economist* (7 August 1999) also observes that the spread of stock options may be distorting the economy, contributing to a temporary overvaluation of equities, encouraging shortsighted managerial decisions, and storing up problems for companies in the future.

In the wake of this heated discussion, we sketch the main characteristics of employee stock option plans adopted by Dutch listed companies. A campaign for better governance and transparent disclosure regarding executive compensation has started in the Netherlands in 1997 following recommendations of the Peters Committee.[1] One of these recommendations was that stock options issued to board members and other employees should be reported in annual reports together with the most important conditions. Since no legal requirement exists, Dutch companies voluntarily disclose information on aggregate compensation. Other important details such as the level and the composition of each executive's compensation, stock option grant date, stock option terms, and managerial share ownership are usually not reported. Almost three-quarters of Dutch quoted firms award stock options as part of employee compensation schemes. In more than 70 per cent of cases, stock options are exclusively granted to directors and senior managers. The popularity of stock options as a form of executive compensation has increased considerably as can be observed from the fact that half of all outstanding management stock options was granted in 1997.

The results of this chapter suggest that granting stock options depends on corporate operating performance. While controlling for firm-specific characteristics such as firm-size, leverage and industry, and corporate governance characteristics such as ownership structure and anti-takeover devices, we also find that stock option grants influence future firm performance.

The outline of the remaining part of the chapter is as follows. Section 2 explores the contrasting merits, expounds the pros and cons of stock options and concisely reviews prior research. Section 3 describes the sample and Section 4 presents the features of employee stock option plans in the Netherlands. The relationship between corporate performance and employee stock option grants is investigated in Section 5. Finally, Section 6 summarizes the main findings.

2. THE PROS AND CONS OF EXECUTIVE STOCK OPTIONS

The first argument in favour of executive stock option schemes is that agency conflict between managers and shareholders are reduced. With an increased alignment of interests, managers have incentives to take those actions that increase shareholder wealth. Empirical evidence on the use of stock option schemes come primarily from the USA. Heath *et al.* (1999) find that the mean expected value of stock options constitutes 160 per cent of base yearly salary in the US (the median is 35 per cent). Conyon and Murphy (1999) compare the composition of chief executive officers' pay in the US with that of the UK. They find that stock option grants constitute one-third of total pay of US CEOs compared to only 10 per cent for UK CEOs. In addition, the median stock option compensation for US CEOs is more than ten times that of UK CEOs. Hall and Liebman (1998) find that, for a given change in firm value, the incentive effects of salary and bonus changes are fifty-three times smaller than those from stock options. With long-term compensation schemes, managers have, therefore, increased incentives to spend more effort to achieve higher earnings and/or market value.

A second argument is that executive stock options reduce the risk-averse behaviour of managers (Murphy 1999). When managers receive compensation in the form of fixed salary only, they do not have additional incentives in searching for new and value maximizing investments. This feature, along with their inability to diversify firm-specific human capital and their concern for job security, reinforces a tendency for managers towards avoiding risky investment projects. Empirical support of the risk-averse hypothesis in the US is found by DeFusco *et al.* (1990). For firms announcing the adoption of executive stock options plans, they find an increase in the variability of stock returns.

Thirdly, stock option plans can also bring about considerable tax advantages for employees and firms (Beatty 1995; Conyon and Murphy 1999). The tax impact of stock options in the Netherlands is analysed by Veld (1999). For personal income tax purposes, the value of employee stock options is determined by Dutch tax authorities as a percentage of the price of the underlying stock and is taxed as ordinary income at the moment these options are received by an employee. This rule can lead to a favourable tax treatment of employee stock options in a booming market.[2] Moreover, if an employee can demonstrate that the fiscal value of stock options is above the fair value (which is hardly the case), then the option is taxed according to the fair value.

Finally, stock option schemes are considered to be an attractive employment condition for both existing and new employees. Granting stock options has become a necessity in competitive and international labour markets, where retaining and attracting highly qualified personnel is an outright challenge. In this way, employee options schemes reduce a firm's asset risk, which results in a lower systematic risk of the stock (Duffhues 2000).

There exist several arguments against the use of employee stock options. Some authors do not find a strong link between executive stock options and performance (Jensen and Murphy 1990). Likewise, Conyon *et al.* (1995) report a very small pay–performance sensitivity in the UK. Stock options may make managers non-neutral with respect to risk-taking. Given that stock options become more valuable as the volatility of stock returns increases, managers may be inclined to raise company risk in an inadvertent way. Yermack (1997) confirms this potentially opportunistic behaviour by USA managers who receive stock options prior to the release of good news. Furthermore, executive stock options may allow managers to convert private information into hard cash through insider trading transactions.

Another important criticism of executive stock options is that these are poorly understood. Executive stock options are not transferable and the exercise decision is made by executives who can influence the stock price itself. Stock option plans easily get the nod of non-executive board members, without a deep understanding of the complex nature of stock options and the incentives they create (Hall and Liebman 1998). Additionally, the costs of stock options for the shareholders and the firm are not adequately reported in company's financial statements (Matsunaga 1995; Duffhues *et al.* 1999). Murray *et al.* (1998) find that USA companies granting management options overstated their profits by as much as 50 per cent in the financial year ending 1998. Stock options are often stumbling stones in mergers between US and foreign companies (*The Economist*, 8 May 1999).[3] Finally, stock options create puzzles for risk managers because of the short position in the stock after granting options. These positions create emphatic questions about the need for hedging (Duffhues 2000).

3. SAMPLE DESCRIPTION

Our investigation is based on all 168 industrial firms listed on the Amsterdam Exchanges at the end of 1998. Companies in the Netherlands are encouraged to voluntarily disclose information on top management compensation—including salary, bonus, and stock options—in the annual reports. No other strict requirements exist for full and timely disclosure. Information on the award of stock option plans is disclosed by 119 companies (71 per cent of all listed Dutch companies) in the annual reports. Six recent IPOs were excluded from the sample.

As there is no standardized reporting practice, Dutch companies disclose compensation-related information in annual reports in a variety of ways. It is common for companies to report the aggregate compensation of all board members. Thus, it is not possible to know managerial compensation on individual basis. Some companies report only the total number of outstanding employee stock options while some others report only the total number of options granted during the particular year. Many companies report information on stock options granted to all employees as a whole without providing separate figures on those granted to board members. Only a few Dutch companies report separately detailed information on stock options, salary and bonus for individual managers. It is also difficult to assess the reason of granting employee stock options. The most cited reason for using stock option schemes is the desire to strengthen the involvement of managers and employees in the firm (mentioned by 18 per cent of firms).

For all firms listed in 1998, which report employee stock options grants in the 1997 annual reports, we hand-collect all disclosed information: option-specific data such as price and number of options granted to management and other employees, price and number of options exercised, and the total number of stock options outstanding. Total assets, total sales, market capitalization, and/or its number of employees, firm-age, operating income, after-tax net income and industry type are collected from annual reports, and from the database REACH.

Prior studies show that compensation practices differ across industries (DeFusco *et al.* 1990; Conyon and Murphy 1999; Murphy 1999). Thirteen per cent of our sample belongs to the construction industry, 10 per cent to metals and machinery, and 9 per cent to each of these three industries: electronics, financials, and wholesale trade. Computer and technology-oriented firms constitute 6 per cent of the sample.

The descriptive statistics of sample firms as of 1997 are shown in Table 28.1: Panel A reports firm characteristics and Panel B presents performance measures. The company with the largest market value of common equity that has adopted a stock option plan is valued at Euro 108 billion (Royal Dutch), while the smallest firm has a market value equal to Euro 3.9 million (Porceleyne Fles). The median debt-to-equity ratio (D/E) is almost 2, but varies widely. For instance, the D/E ratio of the financial firm van der Hoop Effektenbank is almost 38, whereas that of Philips Electronics amounts to a mere 1.7. Philips Electronics has the largest number of employees (268, 000 employees) followed by Ahold (121, 000 employees),

Table 28.1. *Summary statistics of sample firms awarding employee stock options*

	TA (Euro '000)	TS (Euro '000)	MVE (Euro '000)	*D/E*	EMPL	Listing
Panel A: Firm characteristics						
Mean	9,239,983	3,206,061	3,567,355	3.29	13,461	23
Median	349,168	519,273	334,224	1.91	2,684	13
Minimum	1446	366	3,918	0.09	12	2
Maximum	379,560,378	71,135,040	108,284,212	37.99	268,431	118
Standard deviation	45,883,050	8,754,860	11,873,057	4.92	35,111	23
No. of firms	113	110	113	113	113	112

	EPS (Euro)	OPS (Euro)	ROA (%)	ROE (%)	PE	*M/B*
Panel B: Firm performance						
Mean	2.087	3.189	0.087	0.173	17.615	5.766
Median	1.507	2.268	0.097	0.176	14.561	2.655
Minimum	2.111	2.119	−1.784	−5.850	−19.423	0.340
Maximum	13.623	18.698	0.369	1.713	113.353	113.621
Standard deviation	2.192	3.146	0.201	0.636	16.446	12.341
No. of firms	113	113	113	113	113	113

The table shows summary statistics for the following variables: total assets (TA), total sales (TS), market value of equity (MVE), debt/equity ratio (*D/E*), average number of people employed (EMPL), number of years elapsed since the start of listing (Listing), earnings per share (EPS), operating earnings per share (OPS), return on total assets (ROA), return on common equity (ROE), price–earnings ratio (PE), market-to-book ratio of common equity (*M/B*).

but the median firm has 2,684 persons on the payroll. Data on the number of years a company has been listed on the Amsterdam Exchanges (Listing) are also collected. Internatio-Müller has a trading history of 118 years, but the median listing period is thirteen years.

The summary statistics of the performance of firms awarding employee stock options is reported in Panel B of Table 28.1. The median firm reports earnings-per-share (EPS) of Euro 1.5 and operating earnings-per-share (OPS) of Euro 2.27 for the book year 1997. Data on four stock price and accounting based firm performance measures are collected: return on book value of total assets (ROA), return on book value of common equity (ROE), price–earnings ratio (PE), and market-to-book ratio of common equity (*M/B*).[4]

4. THE AWARD OF EMPLOYEE STOCK OPTIONS

All but two sample companies disclosed data on the total number of options outstanding at fiscal year-end 1997. The first column of Table 28.2 (TOTOPT) shows that the average firm has 1.30 million employee stock options outstanding and that the number of options varies widely. For instance, Baan Company has 22.3 million outstanding stock options,

Table 28.2. *Summary statistics of employee stock options granted by Dutch firms*

	TOTOPT	MNGOPT	MGRNT97	MNGT/TOT	GRNT/MNGT	GRNT/TOT	OPT/NOS	EX/SHRP	EX/BVE	EX/MVE
Mean	1,305,262	582,752	349,255	0.732	0.500	0.377	0.026	0.875	0.117	0.023
Median	292,000	132,400	72,500	1	0.434	0.313	0.015	0.868	0.039	0.013
Minimum	4,000	4,000	2	0.037	0.034	0	0.001	0.189	0.002	0.001
Maximum	22,309,000	7,109,538	7,712,000	1	1	1.236	0.231	1.803	1.637	0.310
Standard Deviation	3,394,763	1,245,433	978,733	0.366	0.323	0.298	0.032	0.278	0.270	0.034
No. of firms	111	59	79	59	44	74	111	107	106	106

The table shows summary statistics for the following variables: total number of outstanding options (end of 1997) (TOTOPT); total number of outstanding options granted to management (MNGOPT); number of options granted to management in 1997 (MGRNT97); fraction of management options relative to total outstanding options (MNGT/TOT); fraction of management options granted in 1997 relative to outstanding management options (GRNT/MNGT); fraction of management options granted in 1997 relative to total outstanding options (GRNT/TOT); fraction of total options relative to total number of shares outstanding (OPT/NOS); fraction of average exercise price relative to end-of-year share price (EX/SHRP); fraction of total exercise value relative to end-of-year book value of equity (EX/BVE); fraction of total exercise value relative to end-of-year market value of equity (EX/MVE).

whereas Porceleyne Fles has only 4,000 stock options. The median number of total outstanding stock options amounts to 292,000. The second column of Table 28.2 provides information on the total number of management options outstanding (MNGOPT). Only fifty-nine firms (52 per cent) disclose this information. In light of the opaque disclosure on management options, we cannot ascertain whether these options belong to executive/non-executive board members and/or senior managers.[5] Management options are most widespread at Philips Electronics, with the maximum number of management options outstanding equal to 7.1 million, whereas Porceleyne Fles has only 4,000 options. It is interesting to note that in two firms, managers are kept out of stock option plans as these are targeted at other employees on an exclusive basis. Seventy-nine companies (70 per cent) disclose information on stock options awarded to senior managers during the fiscal year 1997 (MGRNT97). The average number of options granted during the year 1997 equals 349,255 while the median number amounts to 72,500. Many multinational enterprises such as Royal Dutch, Philips, Ahold, PolyGram, KNP-BT, and KLM are leading the way in granting management options.

The fraction of total outstanding management options relative to the total outstanding stock options (MNGT/TOT) is presented in the fifth column of Table 28.2: the lion's share of stock options (73 per cent) is granted to board members and senior managers. The next two columns of Table 28.2 show the fraction of management options granted in 1997 relative to the total number of outstanding management options (GRNT/MNGT) and relative to the total number of outstanding stock options (GRNT/TOT), respectively. Fifty per cent of total management options is granted in 1997. The number of stock options granted to senior managers in 1997 is equal to 38 per cent of the total number of outstanding stock options.

The fraction of total stock options relative to the total number of outstanding common stocks (OPT/NOS) averages 3 per cent, while the median is 1.5 per cent. In contrast, Aboody (1996) reports that the mean fraction of outstanding stock options relative to outstanding shares is 9.4 per cent in the US (median is 7.5 per cent). This low ratio for our sample firms indicates that Dutch firms are exposed to neither a huge risk of earnings-per-share dilution nor voting power dilution. But, the risk of dilution can be substantial for specific companies. For instance, the sample contains one firm which has granted stock options to its employees amounting to 23 per cent of total common shares outstanding.

Information on the exercise price of stock options is also collected from annual reports. Several firms disclose detailed information containing the exercise price of stock options with differing maturities. In the final three columns of Table 28.2, the fraction of the average exercise price relative to the share price (EX/SHRP) is disclosed. As companies do not usually report the prevailing market price of stocks at the time of granting stock options or announce the exact grant date, the end-of-fiscal year share price is used as a benchmark. The average exercise price of employee stock options is about 88 per cent of the end-of-year share price. Murphy (1999) reports that the exercise price equals the grant-date fair market value in 95 per cent of the regular option grants in the USA. The mean fraction of total exercise value relative to the book value of firm's equity (EX/BVE) equals 12 per cent (with a median of 4 per cent). Finally, the average fraction of total exercise value relative to the market value of common equity (EX/MVE) is 2.3 per cent.

5. EMPLOYEE STOCK OPTIONS AND FIRM PERFORMANCE

We now test the relationship between stock option grants and firm performance. The standard testing procedure followed in the compensation literature uses manager's compensation as the dependent variable and firm performance as the independent variable (Murphy 1999). As stock options are a form of incentive-based compensation, a non-contemporaneous form of relationship is estimated. Previous studies (Conyon and Murphy 1999; Murphy 1999) indicate that monitoring mechanisms used by shareholders usually depend on size, leverage, and industry. As other governance mechanisms may influence executive compensation, we control for these governance characteristics. For example, when ownership concentration of firms is high, shareholders have higher incentives to monitor managers more closely, which reduces the need to use incentive-based compensation. We also control for the presence of anti-takeover devices. Almost all Dutch firms have multiple takeover defence measures that reduce the disciplinary effect of the market for corporate control (Kabir *et al.* 1997). In the absence of takeover threats, shareholders may try to restore managerial discipline with increased incentive-based compensation. Managers of protected firms may also have a decisive say in setting their own compensation.

Regressions (1) and (2) of Table 28.3 are univariate, relating previous year's performance with current year's stock option grants. These results indicate that previous period's operating performance has a positive influence on stock option grants. The multivariate analysis (regressions (3) and (4)) include firm-specific and corporate governance characteristics. Including four control variables does not affect the positive relationship between firm performance and stock option grants. The ROA coefficient increases slightly, but the corresponding *t*-value declines somewhat. ROE is also positive and statistically significant. Firm size, as measured by the natural logarithm of total assets, is negatively related with stock option grants. Leverage, as measured by the debt–equity ratio, is significantly positive in regression (3), but insignificant in regression (4). Ownership concentration, as measured by the Herfindahl value of all blockholdings, is insignificant in both regressions. Similarly, the coefficient of the anti-takeover device, which is a dummy variable that equals 1 if a firm has issued non-voting shares and 0 otherwise, has no significant impact on stock option grants.[6] Since firm size and ownership concentration are correlated, a separate regression is estimated omitting firm size, but the results do not materially change. The results obtained from this study are qualitatively similar to those reported by de Jong *et al.* (2000). Likewise, they do not find a significant relationship between firm value as measured by Tobin's Q and different corporate governance characteristics like ownership structure and anti-takeover measures.

By granting stock options to managers and employees, subsequent performance of firms is expected to improve. Therefore, we estimate a model using ROA and ROE for the year 1998 as the dependent variable and stock option grants in 1997 as the explanatory variable. The regression results are presented in Panel B of Table 28.3. The univariate results of regressions (5) and (6) show that stock options granted in 1997 have a significant positive impact on the ROA and ROE in 1998. Of the four control variables, none is statistically significant in regression (7), and only leverage is significant in regression (8). The regression

Table 28.3. *Regression results for stock option grants and firm performance*

Panel A: Regression of stock option grants on prior firm performance

	(1)	(2)	(3)	(4)
Intercept	0.325*** (7.577)	0.334*** (9.187)	1.327*** (4.451)	1.473*** (5.597)
Return on assets	0.460** (1.946)		0.596 (1.539)	
Return on equity		0.101*** (2.799)		0.163** (2.105)
Firm-size			−0.076*** (−3.827)	−0.078*** (−4.139)
Leverage			0.235* (1.913)	−0.025 (−0.972)
Ownership concentration			0.141 (0.708)	0.078 (0.394)
Anti-takeover device			−0.006 (−0.095)	0.005 (0.071)
Adj. R^2	0.04	0.09	0.27	0.29
F-statistic	3.79**	7.84***	5.76***	6.35***

Panel B: Regression of future firm performance on stock option grants

	(5) ROA98	(6) ROE98	(7) ROA98	(8) ROE98
Intercept	0.067*** (5.220)	0.242*** (2.948)	0.197** (2.268)	0.682 (1.347)
Stock option grants	0.102*** (3.966)	0.463*** (2.818)	0.726** (2.206)	0.273 (1.433)
Firm-size			−0.009 (−1.620)	−0.038 (−1.125)
Leverage			0.004 (1.215)	0.082*** (4.192)
Ownership concentration			−0.036 (−0.620)	−0.396 (−1.174)
Anti-takeover device			0.012 (0.674)	0.020 (0.191)
Adj. R^2	0.19	0.10	0.16	0.26
F-statistic	15.68***	7.94***	3.21	5.16***

This table shows the results for the regression model where the dependent variable is the fraction of management options granted in 1997 relative to total outstanding options (panel A). The explanatory variables are the following: firm performance in 1996 measured by ROA and ROE; firm-size is the natural logarithm of book value of total assets; leverage is measured by the debt–equity ratio; ownership concentration is measured by the Herfindahl index of all blockholdings; anti-take-over device is measured by a dummy variable with a value of 1 if the firm has preferred defense share mechanism, 0 otherwise. Panel B shows the results for the regression model where firm performance of 1998 (measured by ROA and ROE) is used as the dependent variable. The explanatory variables include stock option grants defined as the fraction of management options granted in 1997 relative to total outstanding options. The *t*-statistic is reported within parentheses. ***, **, and * represent statistical significance at 1, 5, and 10 per cent level, respectively.

analysis is also performed with industry dummies, none of which is statistically significant. Overall, the results presented here indicate that employee stock option grants are closely related to firm's accounting performance. Well performing companies issue stock options and, once options are granted, there is an impact on firm performance.

6. CONCLUSION

Stock options are increasingly used as part of management and employee remuneration in the Netherlands. There exists no legal regulation mandating publicly traded companies to disclose information on executive compensation and employee stock options, though there are 'recommendations' of accounting organizations. Seventy-one per cent of Dutch listed companies disclose information about management and employee stock option schemes. Stock options are largely the prerogative of managers. On balance, 73 per cent of total employee stock options are held by executive board members and top managers. Half of all outstanding management stock options are granted in 1997 alone. We find a positive relationship between stock option grants and firm's operating performance. Firms with high returns grant relatively more employee stock options. Furthermore, stock option schemes lead to higher operating performance in the subsequent year.

ACKNOWLEDGEMENTS

We are grateful to the editors and to Jenke ter Hoist for helpful comments on an earlier draft. This research was financially supported by APB and PGGM pension funds.

Notes

1. The Committee on Corporate Governance, popularly known as the Peters Committee (named after its chairman), addressed corporate governance issues in the Netherlands. It has formulated forty recommendations on the disclosure of governance-related information and the working of management and supervisory boards. The Peters Committee is equivalent to the Cadbury Committee in the UK.
2. In the US, stock options generally do not result in taxable income until the year of exercise or later. In addition, this income is often taxed at a reduced capital gains rate.
3. Investors and executives of non-US firms appear to have difficulties in accepting the generous stock option compensation practice prevailing in US firms.
4. A meaningful analysis would involve comparing performance with that of a matched sample of firms without stock options. But, the small number of Dutch listed firms without stock options does not allow such analysis.
5. Many firms report options awarded to top ranking officials without making specific reference to management board. It is also not possible to determine whether managers of the remaining sample firms receive stock options or not. Hence, these and following descriptive statistics should be interpreted with some caution.
6. Additional analysis is performed including industry dummies in these regressions. The coefficients of industry dummies are mostly positive but not statistically significant. Also, other proxies for ownership concentration and anti-takeover devices are used as explanatory variables. There are no qualitative changes in the obtained findings. These regression results are, therefore, not presented.

References

Aboody, D. (1996). Market valuation of employee stock options. *Journal of Accounting and Economics* 22: 357.

Beatty, A. (1995). The cash flow and informational aspects of employee stock ownership plans. *Journal of Financial Economics* 38: 211.

Conyon, M., and Murphy, K. (1999). The prince and the pauper? CEO pay in the US and UK. *Economic Journal* 110: 640.

Conyon, M., Gregg, P., and Machin, S. (1995). Taking care of business: Executive compensation in the United Kingdom. *Economic Journal* 105: 704.

DeFusco, R., Johnson, R., and Zorn, T. (1990). The effect of executive stock option plans on stockholders and bondholders. *Journal of Finance* 45: 617.

de Jong, A., deJong, D., Mertens, G., and Wasley, C. (2000). The role of self-regulation in corporate governance: Evidence from the Netherlands. Tilburg University CentER, Discussion Paper.

Duffhues, P. (2000). *Ondernemingsfinanciering: oriëntatie op integratie.* Deventer: Kluwer.

—— Kabir, R. and Mertens, G. (1999). Personeelsopties, financieringstheorie en verslaggeving. *Economisch Statistische Berichten* 84: 504.

Economist (1999). A survey of pay. 8 May, 1.

Hall, B., and Liebman, J. (1998). Are CEOs really paid like bureaucrats? *Quarterly Journal of Economics* 113: 653.

Heath, C., Huddart, S., and Lang, M. (1999). Psychological factors and stock option exercise. *Quarterly Journal of Economics* 114: 601.

Jensen, M., and Murphy, K. (1990). Performance pay and top-management incentives. *Journal of Political Economy* 98: 225.

Kabir, R., Cantrijn, D., and Jeunink, A. (1997). Takeover defenses, ownership structure and stock returns in the Netherlands: An empirical analysis. *Strategic Management Journal* 18: 97.

Matsunaga, S. (1995). The effects of financial reporting costs on the use of employee stock options. *Accounting Review* 70: 1.

Murphy, K. (1999). Executive compensation. In O. Ashenfelter and D. Card (ed.), *Handbook of Labor Economics.* Amsterdam: North-Holland.

Murray, D., Smithers, A., and Emerson, J. (1998). USA: The impact of employee stock options. 'Smithers Report', Report No.117. London: Smithers & Co. Ltd., 1.

—— (1999). The trouble with stock options. 7 August, 11.

Veld, C. (1999). The taxonomy of employee stock options in the Netherlands. Tilburg University CentER, Discussion Paper.

Yermack, D. (1997). Good timing: CEO stock options awards and company news announcements. *Journal of Finance* 52: 449.

Index